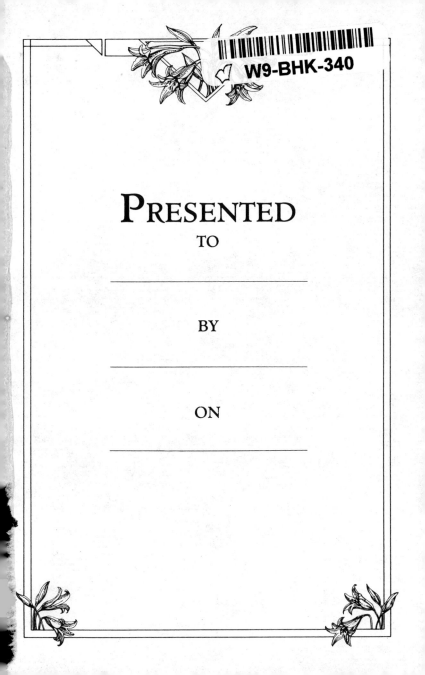

PRESENTED

TO

BY

ON

WOMEN'S
DEVOTIONAL
NEW TESTAMENT
WITH PSALMS & PROVERBS

WOMEN'S
DEVOTIONAL
NEW TESTAMENT
WITH PSALMS & PROVERBS

NEW INTERNATIONAL VERSION

Zondervan

Library of Congress Catalog Card Number 90-081694

Published by Zondervan Publishing House
Grand Rapids, Michigan 49530, U.S.A.
Printed in the United States of America

Acquisitions Editor: Martha Manikas-Foster
Project Editor: Jean E. Syswerda
Designed by: Sharon Wright
A special thanks to Michael and Dorene Briggs for their creative idea for this special edition.

06 07 08 09 10 14 13 12 11 10

CONTENTS

INTRODUCTION
NIV WOMEN'S DEVOTIONAL

Welcome to the NIV Women's Devotional New Testament! Are you ready to embark on an exciting journey through God's Word? You say you're too busy to take on any new adventures this year? This Bible is designed just for *you*—one of today's women who wants to step out into God's Word to discover encouragement and comfort, and yet who feels tugged in a hundred different directions.

Written for, by and about today's woman, the NIV Women's Devotional New Testament will reach you right where you are. But it won't leave you there! With God's Word and the sensitive and insightful reflections of many godly women, this Bible will transport you step by step on a journey to Christian maturity.

Several features make the NIV Women's Devotional New Testament an exceptional devotional guide:

The Bible

The NIV Women's Devotional New Testament features the text of the New International Version. This version's readability and accuracy make it the most popular modern translation available today. Included here are the books of the New Testament as well as the books of Psalms and Proverbs.

The Devotions

All of the daily and weekend devotions are written by women—women who have experienced both the joys and struggles of Christian living and who are willing to share those triumphs and trials with you. Each devotion is located within the text, in close proximity to the Scripture passage on which it is based.

The Introductions

The introduction to each Bible book succinctly highlights that book's practical themes. Each introduction gives you interesting facts and helpful background information to aid your understanding as you read that particular book and the accompanying devotional meditation.

Ease of Use

If you are like most women today, your life is full—you may even say sometimes that your life is too full. There are so many things to do, so many demands on your time. So we've designed the NIV Women's Devotional New Testament to give you a quick and easy Bible reading/devotional meditation plan to help you walk the road to maturity and growth.

The devotions in the NIV Women's Devotional New Testament take a distinctive pattern following the days of the week: Monday, Tuesday, Wednesday, Thursday, Friday. In recognition of your need for something different on the weekend, we've developed "Weekending"—combining one provocative devotional thought with short Scripture readings for both Saturday and Sunday.

No matter what day of the week you begin your reading, you simply turn to a devotion for that day. Then for the next day, look to the bottom of the devotion for the page number on which you'll find the next day's devotion. For example, if you start on a Monday, you could turn to the first devotion in the book of Matthew, page 5. Glance at

PREFACE

THE NEW INTERNATIONAL VERSION is a completely new translation of the Holy Bible made by over a hundred scholars working directly from the best available Hebrew, Aramaic and Greek texts. It had its beginning in 1965 when, after several years of exploratory study by committees from the Christian Reformed Church and the National Association of Evangelicals, a group of scholars met at Palos Heights, Illinois, and concurred in the need for a new translation of the Bible in contemporary English. This group, though not made up of official church representatives, was transdenominational. Its conclusion was endorsed by a large number of leaders from many denominations who met in Chicago in 1966.

Responsibility for the new version was delegated by the Palos Heights group to a self-governing body of fifteen, the Committee on Bible Translation, composed for the most part of biblical scholars from colleges, universities and seminaries. In 1967 the New York Bible Society (now the International Bible Society) generously undertook the financial sponsorship of the project—a sponsorship that made it possible to enlist the help of many distinguished scholars. The fact that participants from the United States, Great Britain, Canada, Australia and New Zealand worked together gave the project its international scope. That they were from many denominations—including Anglican, Assemblies of God, Baptist, Brethren, Christian Reformed, Church of Christ, Evangelical Free, Lutheran, Mennonite, Methodist, Nazarene, Presbyterian, Wesleyan and other churches—helped to safeguard the translation from sectarian bias.

How it was made helps to give the New International Version its distinctiveness. The translation of each book was assigned to a team of scholars. Next, one of the Intermediate Editorial Committees revised the initial translation, with constant reference to the Hebrew, Aramaic or Greek. Their work then went to one of the General Editorial Committees, which checked it in detail and made another thorough revision. This revision in turn was carefully reviewed by the Committee on Bible Translation, which made further changes and then released the final version for publication. In this way the entire Bible underwent three revisions, during each of which the translation was examined for its faithfulness to the original languages and for its English style.

All this involved many thousands of hours of research and discussion regarding the meaning of the texts and the precise way of putting them into English. It may well be that no other translation has been made by a more thorough process of review and revision from committee to committee than this one.

From the beginning of the project, the Committee on Bible Translation held to certain goals for the New International Version: that it would be an accurate translation and one that would have clarity and literary quality and so prove suitable for public and private reading, teaching, preaching, memorizing and liturgical use. The Committee also sought to preserve some measure of continuity with the long tradition of translating the Scriptures into English.

In working toward these goals, the translators were united in their commitment to the authority and infallibility of the Bible as God's Word in written form. They believe that it contains the divine answer to the deepest needs of humanity, that it sheds unique light on our path in a dark world, and that it sets forth the way to our eternal well-being.

The first concern of the translators has been the accuracy of the translation and its fidelity to the thought of the biblical writers. They have weighed the significance of the lexical and grammatical details of the Hebrew, Aramaic and Greek texts. At the same time, they have striven for more than a word-for-word translation. Because thought patterns and syntax differ from language to language, faithful communication of the meaning of the writers of the Bible demands frequent modifications in sentence structure and constant regard for the contextual meanings of words.

A sensitive feeling for style does not always accompany scholarship. Accordingly the Committee on Bible Translation submitted the developing version to a number of stylistic consultants. Two of them read every book of both Old and New Testaments twice—once before and once after the last major revision—and made invaluable suggestions. Samples of the translation were tested for clarity and ease of reading by various kinds of people—young and old, highly educated and less well educated, ministers and laymen.

Concern for clear and natural English—that the New International Version should be idiomatic but not idiosyncratic, contemporary but not dated—motivated the translators and consultants. At the same time, they tried to reflect the differing styles of the biblical writers. In view of the international use of English, the translators sought to avoid obvious Americanisms on the one hand and obvious Anglicisms on the other. A British edition reflects the comparatively few differences of significant idiom and of spelling.

As for the traditional pronouns "thou," "thee" and "thine" in reference to the Deity, the translators judged that to use these archaisms (along with the old verb forms such as "doest," "wouldest" and "hadst") would violate accuracy in translation. Neither Hebrew, Aramaic nor Greek uses special pronouns for the persons of the Godhead. A present-day translation is not enhanced by forms that in the time of the King James Version were used in everyday speech, whether referring to God or man.

For the Old Testament the standard Hebrew text, the Masoretic Text as published in the latest editions of *Biblia Hebraica,* was used throughout. The Dead Sea Scrolls contain material bearing on an earlier stage of the Hebrew text. They were consulted, as were the Samaritan Pentateuch and the ancient scribal traditions relating to textual changes. Sometimes a variant Hebrew reading in the margin of the Masoretic Text was followed instead of the text itself. Such instances, being variants within the Masoretic tradition, are not specified by footnotes. In rare cases, words in the consonantal text were divided differently from the way they appear in the Masoretic Text. Footnotes indicate this. The translators also consulted the more important early versions—the Septuagint; Aquila, Symmachus and Theodotion; the Vulgate; the Syriac Peshitta; the Targums; and for the Psalms the *Juxta Hebraica* of Jerome. Readings from these versions were occasionally followed where the Masoretic Text seemed doubtful and where accepted principles of textual criticism showed that one or more of these textual witnesses appeared to provide the correct reading. Such instances are footnoted. Sometimes vowel letters and vowel signs did not, in the judgment of the translators, represent the correct vowels for the original consonantal text. Accordingly some words were read with a different set of vowels. These instances are usually not indicated by footnotes.

The Greek text used in translating the New Testament was an eclectic one. No other piece of ancient literature has such an abundance of manuscript witnesses as does the New Testament. Where existing manuscripts differ, the translators made their choice of readings according to accepted principles of New Testament textual criticism. Footnotes call attention to places where there was uncertainty about what the original text was. The best current printed texts of the Greek New Testament were used.

There is a sense in which the work of translation is never wholly finished. This applies to all great literature and uniquely so to the Bible. In 1973 the New Testament in the New International Version was published. Since then, suggestions for corrections and revisions have been received from various sources. The Committee on Bible Translation carefully considered the suggestions and adopted a number of them. These were incorporated in the first printing of the entire Bible in 1978. Additional revisions were made by the Committee on Bible Translation in 1983 and appear in printings after that date.

As in other ancient documents, the precise meaning of the biblical texts is sometimes uncertain. This is more often the case with the Hebrew and Aramaic texts than with the Greek text. Although archaeological and linguistic discoveries in this century aid in understanding difficult passages, some uncertainties remain. The more significant of these have been called to the reader's attention in the footnotes.

In regard to the divine name *YHWH,* commonly referred to as the *Tetragrammaton,* the translators adopted the device used in most English versions of rendering that name as "LORD" in capital letters to distinguish it from *Adonai,* another Hebrew word rendered "Lord," for which small letters are used. Wherever the two names stand together in the Old Testament as a compound name of God, they are rendered "Sovereign LORD."

Because for most readers today the phrases "the LORD of hosts" and "God of hosts" have little meaning, this version renders them "the LORD Almighty" and "God Almighty." These renderings convey the sense of the Hebrew, namely, "he who is sovereign over all the 'hosts' (powers) in heaven and on earth, especially over the 'hosts' (armies) of Israel." For readers unacquainted with Hebrew this does not make clear the distinction between *Sabaoth* ("hosts" or "Almighty") and *Shaddai* (which can also be translated "Almighty"), but the latter occurs infrequently and is always footnoted. When *Adonai* and *YHWH Sabaoth* occur together, they are rendered "the Lord, the LORD Almighty."

As for other proper nouns, the familiar spellings of the King James Version are generally retained. Names traditionally spelled with "ch," except where it is final, are usually spelled in this translation with "k" or "c," since the biblical languages do not have the sound that "ch" frequently indicates in English—for example, in *chant.* For well-known names such as Zechariah, however, the traditional spelling has been retained. Variation in the spelling of names in the original languages has usually not been indicated. Where a person or place has two or more different names in the Hebrew, Aramaic or Greek texts, the more familiar one has generally been used, with footnotes where needed.

To achieve clarity the translators sometimes supplied words not in the original texts but required by the context. If there was uncertainty about such material, it is enclosed in brackets.

Also for the sake of clarity or style, nouns, including some proper nouns, are sometimes substituted for pronouns, and vice versa. And though the Hebrew writers often shifted back and forth between first, second and third personal pronouns without change of antecedent, this translation often makes them uniform, in accordance with English style and without the use of footnotes.

Poetical passages are printed as poetry, that is, with indentation of lines with separate stanzas. These are generally designed to reflect the structure of Hebrew poetry. This poetry is normally characterized by parallelism in balanced lines. Most of the poetry in the Bible is in the Old Testament, and scholars differ regarding the scansion of Hebrew lines. The translators determined the stanza divisions for the most part by analysis of the subject matter. The stanzas therefore serve as poetic paragraphs.

As an aid to the reader, italicized sectional headings are inserted in most of the books. They are not to be regarded as part of the NIV text, are not for oral reading, and are not intended to dictate the interpretation of the sections they head.

The footnotes in this version are of several kinds, most of which need no explanation. Those giving alternative translations begin with "Or" and generally introduce the alternative with the last word preceding it in the text, except when it is a single-word alternative; in poetry quoted in a footnote a slant mark indicates a line division. Footnotes introduced by "Or" do not have uniform significance. In some cases two possible translations were considered to have about equal validity. In other cases, though the translators were convinced that the translation in the text was correct, they judged that another interpretation was possible and of sufficient importance to be represented in a footnote.

In the New Testament, footnotes that refer to uncertainty regarding the original text are introduced by "Some manuscripts" or similar expressions. In the Old Testament, evidence for the reading chosen is given first and evidence for the alternative is added after a semicolon (for example: Septuagint; Hebrew *father*). In such notes the term "Hebrew" refers to the Masoretic Text.

It should be noted that minerals, flora and fauna, architectural details, articles of clothing and jewelry, musical instruments and other articles cannot always be identified with precision. Also measures of capacity in the biblical period are particularly uncertain (see the table of weights and measures following the text).

Like all translations of the Bible, made as they are by imperfect man, this one undoubtedly falls short of its goals. Yet we are grateful to God for the extent to which he has enabled us to realize these goals and for the strength he has given us and our colleagues to complete our task. We offer this version of the Bible to him in whose name and for whose glory it has been made. We pray that it will lead many into a better understanding of the Holy Scriptures and a fuller knowledge of Jesus Christ the incarnate Word, of whom the Scriptures so faithfully testify.

The Committee on Bible Translation

June 1978
(Revised August 1983)

Names of the translators and editors may be secured
from the International Bible Society,
translation sponsors of the New International Version,
P.O. Box 62970, Colorado Springs,
Colorado,
80962-2970 U.S.A.

NEW TESTAMENT

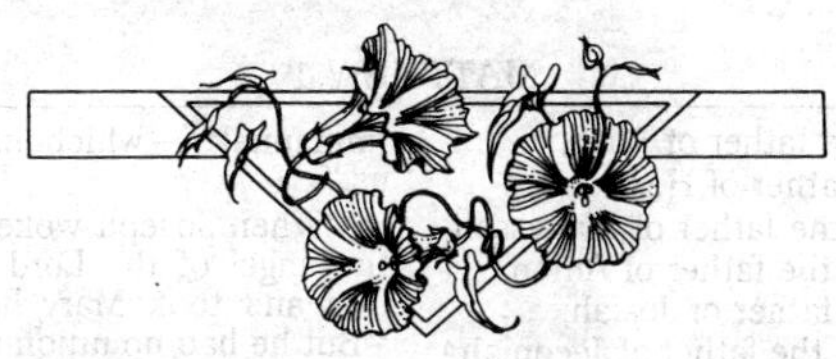

MATTHEW writes this gospel to emphasize how Jesus fulfills God's promises from the Old Testament. He includes numerous sayings of Jesus about living as one of his disciples and as a member of the church, concluding with the command of Jesus to make disciples of all nations. As you read this book, ask yourself whether you are living as a disciple of Jesus, as well as how you can tell others the story of Jesus.

MATTHEW

The Genealogy of Jesus

1 A record of the genealogy of Jesus Christ the son of David, the son of Abraham:

2Abraham was the father of Isaac,
Isaac the father of Jacob,
Jacob the father of Judah and his brothers,
3Judah the father of Perez and Zerah, whose mother was Tamar,
Perez the father of Hezron,
Hezron the father of Ram,
4Ram the father of Amminadab,
Amminadab the father of Nahshon,
Nahshon the father of Salmon,
5Salmon the father of Boaz, whose mother was Rahab,
Boaz the father of Obed, whose mother was Ruth,
Obed the father of Jesse,
6and Jesse the father of King David.

David was the father of Solomon, whose mother had been Uriah's wife,
7Solomon the father of Rehoboam,
Rehoboam the father of Abijah,
Abijah the father of Asa,
8Asa the father of Jehoshaphat,
Jehoshaphat the father of Jehoram,
Jehoram the father of Uzziah,
9Uzziah the father of Jotham,

Jotham the father of Ahaz,
Ahaz the father of Hezekiah,
10Hezekiah the father of Manasseh,
Manasseh the father of Amon,
Amon the father of Josiah,
11and Josiah the father of Jeconiah[a]
and his brothers at the time of
the exile to Babylon.

12After the exile to Babylon:
Jeconiah was the father of Sheal-
tiel,
Shealtiel the father of Zerubbabel,
13Zerubbabel the father of Abiud,
Abiud the father of Eliakim,
Eliakim the father of Azor,
14Azor the father of Zadok,
Zadok the father of Akim,
Akim the father of Eliud,
15Eliud the father of Eleazar,
Eleazar the father of Matthan,
Matthan the father of Jacob,
16and Jacob the father of Joseph,
the husband of Mary, of whom
was born Jesus, who is called
Christ.

17Thus there were fourteen generations
in all from Abraham to David, fourteen
from David to the exile to Babylon, and
fourteen from the exile to the Christ.[b]

The Birth of Jesus Christ

18This is how the birth of Jesus Christ
came about: His mother Mary was
pledged to be married to Joseph, but before they came together, she was found to
be with child through the Holy Spirit.
19Because Joseph her husband was a righteous man and did not want to expose her
to public disgrace, he had in mind to divorce her quietly.

20But after he had considered this, an
angel of the Lord appeared to him in a
dream and said, "Joseph son of David, do
not be afraid to take Mary home as your
wife, because what is conceived in her is
from the Holy Spirit. 21She will give birth
to a son, and you are to give him the name
Jesus,[c] because he will save his people
from their sins."

22All this took place to fulfill what the
Lord had said through the prophet:
23"The virgin will be with child and will
give birth to a son, and they will call him
Immanuel"[d]—which means, "God with
us."

24When Joseph woke up, he did what
the angel of the Lord had commanded
him and took Mary home as his wife.
25But he had no union with her until she
gave birth to a son. And he gave him the
name Jesus.

The Visit of the Magi

2 After Jesus was born in Bethlehem in
Judea, during the time of King Herod,
Magi[e] from the east came to Jerusalem
2and asked, "Where is the one who has
been born king of the Jews? We saw his
star in the east[f] and have come to worship him."

3When King Herod heard this he was
disturbed, and all Jerusalem with him.
4When he had called together all the people's chief priests and teachers of the law,
he asked them where the Christ[g] was to
be born. 5"In Bethlehem in Judea," they
replied, "for this is what the prophet has
written:

6" 'But you, Bethlehem, in the land of
Judah,
are by no means least among the
rulers of Judah;
for out of you will come a ruler
who will be the shepherd of my
people Israel.'[h]"

7Then Herod called the Magi secretly
and found out from them the exact time
the star had appeared. 8He sent them to
Bethlehem and said, "Go and make a
careful search for the child. As soon as
you find him, report to me, so that I too
may go and worship him."

9After they had heard the king, they
went on their way, and the star they had
seen in the east[i] went ahead of them until it stopped over the place where the
child was. 10When they saw the star, they
were overjoyed. 11On coming to the
house, they saw the child with his mother
Mary, and they bowed down and worshiped him. Then they opened their treasures and presented him with gifts of gold
and of incense and of myrrh. 12And having
been warned in a dream not to go back to
Herod, they returned to their country by
another route.

[a] *11* That is, Jehoiachin; also in verse 12 [b] *17* Or *Messiah.* "The Christ" (Greek) and "the Messiah" (Hebrew) both mean "the Anointed One." [c] *21* *Jesus* is the Greek form of *Joshua,* which means *the* *Lord saves.* [d] *23* Isaiah 7:14 [e] *1* Traditionally *Wise Men* [f] *2* Or *star when it rose* [g] *4* Or *Messiah* [h] *6* Micah 5:2 [i] *9* Or *seen when it rose*

The Escape to Egypt

13When they had gone, an angel of the
Lord appeared to Joseph in a dream. "Get
up," he said, "take the child and his
mother and escape to Egypt. Stay there
until I tell you, for Herod is going to
search for the child to kill him."

14So he got up, took the child and his
mother during the night and left for
Egypt, 15where he stayed until the death
of Herod. And so was fulfilled what the
Lord had said through the prophet: "Out
of Egypt I called my son."[a]

16When Herod realized that he had
been outwitted by the Magi, he was furious, and he gave orders to kill all the boys
in Bethlehem and its vicinity who were
two years old and under, in accordance
with the time he had learned from the
Magi. 17Then what was said through the
prophet Jeremiah was fulfilled:

18"A voice is heard in Ramah,
  weeping and great mourning,
Rachel weeping for her children
  and refusing to be comforted,
because they are no more."[b]

The Return to Nazareth

19After Herod died, an angel of the Lord
appeared in a dream to Joseph in Egypt
20and said, "Get up, take the child and his
mother and go to the land of Israel, for
those who were trying to take the child's
life are dead."

21So he got up, took the child and his
mother and went to the land of Israel.
22But when he heard that Archelaus was
reigning in Judea in place of his father
Herod, he was afraid to go there. Having
been warned in a dream, he withdrew to
the district of Galilee, 23and he went and
lived in a town called Nazareth. So was
fulfilled what was said through the prophets: "He will be called a Nazarene."

John the Baptist Prepares the Way

3 In those days John the Baptist came,
preaching in the Desert of Judea 2and
saying, "Repent, for the kingdom of heav-
en is near." 3This is he who was spoken of
through the prophet Isaiah:

"A voice of one calling in the desert,
'Prepare the way for the Lord,
  make straight paths for him.' "[c]

4John's clothes were made of camel's
hair, and he had a leather belt around his
waist. His food was locusts and wild honey. 5People went out to him from Jerusalem and all Judea and the whole region of
the Jordan. 6Confessing their sins, they
were baptized by him in the Jordan River.

7But when he saw many of the Pharisees and Sadducees coming to where he
was baptizing, he said to them: "You
brood of vipers! Who warned you to flee
from the coming wrath? 8Produce fruit in
keeping with repentance. 9And do not
think you can say to yourselves, 'We have
Abraham as our father.' I tell you that out
of these stones God can raise up children
for Abraham. 10The ax is already at the
root of the trees, and every tree that does
not produce good fruit will be cut down
and thrown into the fire.

11"I baptize you with[d] water for repentance. But after me will come one who is
more powerful than I, whose sandals I am
not fit to carry. He will baptize you with
the Holy Spirit and with fire. 12His winnowing fork is in his hand, and he will
clear his threshing floor, gathering his
wheat into the barn and burning up the
chaff with unquenchable fire."

The Baptism of Jesus

13Then Jesus came from Galilee to the
Jordan to be baptized by John. 14But John
tried to deter him, saying, "I need to be
baptized by you, and do you come to
me?"

15Jesus replied, "Let it be so now; it is
proper for us to do this to fulfill all righteousness." Then John consented.

16As soon as Jesus was baptized, he
went up out of the water. At that moment
heaven was opened, and he saw the Spirit
of God descending like a dove and lighting on him. 17And a voice from heaven
said, "This is my Son, whom I love; with
him I am well pleased."

The Temptation of Jesus

4 Then Jesus was led by the Spirit into
the desert to be tempted by the devil.
2After fasting forty days and forty nights,
he was hungry. 3The tempter came to him
and said, "If you are the Son of God, tell
these stones to become bread."

4Jesus answered, "It is written: 'Man
does not live on bread alone, but on every
word that comes from the mouth of
God.'[e]"

5Then the devil took him to the holy
city and had him stand on the highest

[a] *15* Hosea 11:1 [b] *18* Jer. 31:15 [c] *3* Isaiah 40:3 [d] *11* Or *in* [e] *4* Deut. 8:3

point of the temple. [6]"If you are the Son
of God," he said, "throw yourself down.
For it is written:

" 'He will command his angels
concerning you,
and they will lift you up in their
hands,
so that you will not strike your foot
against a stone.'[a]"

[7]Jesus answered him, "It is also written: 'Do not put the Lord your God to the
test.'[b]"
[8]Again, the devil took him to a very
high mountain and showed him all the
kingdoms of the world and their splendor.
[9]"All this I will give you," he said, "if you
will bow down and worship me."
[10]Jesus said to him, "Away from me,
Satan! For it is written: 'Worship the Lord
your God, and serve him only.'[c]"
[11]Then the devil left him, and angels
came and attended him.

Jesus Begins to Preach

[12]When Jesus heard that John had
been put in prison, he returned to Galilee. [13]Leaving Nazareth, he went and
lived in Capernaum, which was by the
lake in the area of Zebulun and Naphtali
— [14]to fulfill what was said through the
prophet Isaiah:

[15]"Land of Zebulun and land of
Naphtali,
the way to the sea, along the
Jordan,
Galilee of the Gentiles—
[16]the people living in darkness
have seen a great light;
on those living in the land of the
shadow of death
a light has dawned."[d]

[17]From that time on Jesus began to
preach, "Repent, for the kingdom of heav-
en is near."

The Calling of the First Disciples

[18]As Jesus was walking beside the Sea
of Galilee, he saw two brothers, Simon
called Peter and his brother Andrew.
They were casting a net into the lake, for
they were fishermen. [19]"Come, follow
me," Jesus said, "and I will make you
fishers of men." [20]At once they left their
nets and followed him.
[21]Going on from there, he saw two other brothers, James son of Zebedee and his
brother John. They were in a boat with
their father Zebedee, preparing their nets.
Jesus called them, [22]and immediately
they left the boat and their father and followed him.

Jesus Heals the Sick

[23]Jesus went throughout Galilee,
teaching in their synagogues, preaching
the good news of the kingdom, and healing every disease and sickness among the
people. [24]News about him spread all over
Syria, and people brought to him all who
were ill with various diseases, those suffering severe pain, the demon-possessed,
those having seizures, and the paralyzed,
and he healed them. [25]Large crowds from
Galilee, the Decapolis,[e] Jerusalem, Judea and the region across the Jordan followed him.

The Beatitudes

5 Now when he saw the crowds, he
went up on a mountainside and sat
down. His disciples came to him, [2]and he
began to teach them, saying:

[3]"Blessed are the poor in spirit,
for theirs is the kingdom of heaven.
[4]Blessed are those who mourn,
for they will be comforted.
[5]Blessed are the meek,
for they will inherit the earth.
[6]Blessed are those who hunger and
thirst for righteousness,
for they will be filled.
[7]Blessed are the merciful,
for they will be shown mercy.
[8]Blessed are the pure in heart,
for they will see God.
[9]Blessed are the peacemakers,
for they will be called sons of God.
[10]Blessed are those who are persecuted
because of righteousness,
for theirs is the kingdom of heaven.

[11]"Blessed are you when people insult
you, persecute you and falsely say all
kinds of evil against you because of me.
[12]Rejoice and be glad, because great is
your reward in heaven, for in the same
way they persecuted the prophets who
were before you.

Salt and Light

[13]"You are the salt of the earth. But if
the salt loses its saltiness, how can it be

[a]6 Psalm 91:11,12 [b]7 Deut. 6:16 [c]10 Deut. 6:13 [d]16 Isaiah 9:1,2 [e]25 That is, the Ten Cities

made salty again? It is no longer good for
anything, except to be thrown out and
trampled by men.
14"You are the light of the world. A city
on a hill cannot be hidden. 15Neither do
people light a lamp and put it under a
bowl. Instead they put it on its stand, and
it gives light to everyone in the house.
16In the same way, let your light shine before men, that they may see your good
deeds and praise your Father in heaven.

The Fulfillment of the Law

17"Do not think that I have come to
abolish the Law or the Prophets; I have
not come to abolish them but to fulfill
them. 18I tell you the truth, until heaven
and earth disappear, not the smallest letter, not the least stroke of a pen, will by
any means disappear from the Law until
everything is accomplished. 19Anyone
who breaks one of the least of these commandments and teaches others to do the
same will be called least in the kingdom
of heaven, but whoever practices and
teaches these commands will be called
great in the kingdom of heaven. 20For I
tell you that unless your righteousness
surpasses that of the Pharisees and the
teachers of the law, you will certainly not
enter the kingdom of heaven.

Murder

21"You have heard that it was said to

MONDAY

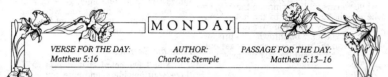

VERSE FOR THE DAY:	*AUTHOR:*	*PASSAGE FOR THE DAY:*
Matthew 5:16	*Charlotte Stemple*	*Matthew 5:13–16*

Keep Shining

THIS verse was dramatically illustrated when we were missionaries in Vietnam during the war. While our husbands were away from home, a missionary friend and I were invited by a Korean general to an important military ceremony. The only women amidst thousands of Korean, Vietnamese and American troops, we sat on the reviewing stand with the three-nation generals to watch the elaborate ceremonies and observe the presentation of medals to individuals and units. Later, after hors d'oeuvres, we were among the guests selected to receive lovely gifts.

Still thoroughly mystified as to why we had been invited, we were conducted to the general's mess where we ate a sumptuous meal on crested china and gold-plated flatware.

Finally, at the end of the meal, the Korean general called for his interpreter and, after polite opening conversation on both sides, said to me, "I am sure you are wondering why I invited you here today!" He continued with this remarkable comment: "When I was a small boy in Korea, an American lady missionary led me to Jesus Christ, and I never had an opportunity to thank her. So wherever I go, I look up the missionaries and honor them!"

There are no doubt many who have illuminated our paths through this life. As we are obedient to his command there will be those whose lives we may brighten. Let your light so shine!

Additional Scripture Readings:
Philippians 2:12–16; 1 Thessalonians 1:6–9

Go to page 8 for your next devotional reading.

the people long ago, 'Do not murder,[a] and anyone who murders will be subject to judgment.' 22But I tell you that anyone who is angry with his brother[b] will be subject to judgment. Again, anyone who says to his brother, 'Raca,[c]' is answerable to the Sanhedrin. But anyone who says, 'You fool!' will be in danger of the fire of hell.

23"Therefore, if you are offering your gift at the altar and there remember that your brother has something against you, 24leave your gift there in front of the altar. First go and be reconciled to your brother; then come and offer your gift.

25"Settle matters quickly with your adversary who is taking you to court. Do it while you are still with him on the way, or he may hand you over to the judge, and the judge may hand you over to the officer, and you may be thrown into prison. 26I tell you the truth, you will not get out until you have paid the last penny.[d]

Adultery

27"You have heard that it was said, 'Do not commit adultery.'[e] 28But I tell you that anyone who looks at a woman lustfully has already committed adultery with her in his heart. 29If your right eye causes you to sin, gouge it out and throw it away. It is better for you to lose one part of your body than for your whole body to be thrown into hell. 30And if your right hand causes you to sin, cut it off and throw it away. It is better for you to lose one part of your body than for your whole body to go into hell.

Divorce

31"It has been said, 'Anyone who divorces his wife must give her a certificate of divorce.'[f] 32But I tell you that anyone who divorces his wife, except for marital unfaithfulness, causes her to become an adulteress, and anyone who marries the divorced woman commits adultery.

Oaths

33"Again, you have heard that it was said to the people long ago, 'Do not break your oath, but keep the oaths you have made to the Lord.' 34But I tell you, Do not swear at all: either by heaven, for it is God's throne; 35or by the earth, for it is his footstool; or by Jerusalem, for it is the city of the Great King. 36And do not swear by your head, for you cannot make even one hair white or black. 37Simply let your 'Yes' be 'Yes,' and your 'No,' 'No'; anything beyond this comes from the evil one.

An Eye for an Eye

38"You have heard that it was said, 'Eye for eye, and tooth for tooth.'[g] 39But I tell you, Do not resist an evil person. If someone strikes you on the right cheek, turn to him the other also. 40And if someone wants to sue you and take your tunic, let him have your cloak as well. 41If someone forces you to go one mile, go with him two miles. 42Give to the one who asks you, and do not turn away from the one who wants to borrow from you.

Love for Enemies

43"You have heard that it was said, 'Love your neighbor[h] and hate your enemy.' 44But I tell you: Love your enemies[i] and pray for those who persecute you, 45that you may be sons of your Father in heaven. He causes his sun to rise on the evil and the good, and sends rain on the righteous and the unrighteous. 46If you love those who love you, what reward will you get? Are not even the tax collectors doing that? 47And if you greet only your brothers, what are you doing more than others? Do not even pagans do that? 48Be perfect, therefore, as your heavenly Father is perfect.

Giving to the Needy

6 "Be careful not to do your 'acts of righteousness' before men, to be seen by them. If you do, you will have no reward from your Father in heaven.

2"So when you give to the needy, do not announce it with trumpets, as the hypocrites do in the synagogues and on the streets, to be honored by men. I tell you the truth, they have received their reward in full. 3But when you give to the needy, do not let your left hand know what your right hand is doing, 4so that your giving may be in secret. Then your Father, who sees what is done in secret, will reward you.

[a]21 Exodus 20:13 [b]22 Some manuscripts *brother without cause* [c]22 An Aramaic term of contempt [d]26 Greek *kodrantes* [e]27 Exodus 20:14 [f]31 Deut. 24:1 [g]38 Exodus 21:24; Lev. 24:20; Deut. 19:21 [h]43 Lev. 19:18 [i]44 Some late manuscripts *enemies, bless those who curse you, do good to those who hate you*

Prayer

5"And when you pray, do not be like the
hypocrites, for they love to pray standing
in the synagogues and on the street corners to be seen by men. I tell you the
truth, they have received their reward in
full. 6But when you pray, go into your
room, close the door and pray to your Father, who is unseen. Then your Father,
who sees what is done in secret, will reward you. 7And when you pray, do not
keep on babbling like pagans, for they
think they will be heard because of their
many words. 8Do not be like them, for
your Father knows what you need before
you ask him.
9"This, then, is how you should pray:

" 'Our Father in heaven,
hallowed be your name,
10your kingdom come,
your will be done
on earth as it is in heaven.
11Give us today our daily bread.
12Forgive us our debts,
as we also have forgiven our
debtors.
13And lead us not into temptation,
but deliver us from the evil one.[a]'

14For if you forgive men when they sin
against you, your heavenly Father will
also forgive you. 15But if you do not forgive men their sins, your Father will not
forgive your sins.

Fasting

16"When you fast, do not look somber
as the hypocrites do, for they disfigure
their faces to show men they are fasting.
I tell you the truth, they have received
their reward in full. 17But when you fast,
put oil on your head and wash your face,
18so that it will not be obvious to men
that you are fasting, but only to your Father, who is unseen; and your Father, who
sees what is done in secret, will reward
you.

Treasures in Heaven

19"Do not store up for yourselves treasures on earth, where moth and rust destroy, and where thieves break in and
steal. 20But store up for yourselves treasures in heaven, where moth and rust do
not destroy, and where thieves do not
break in and steal. 21For where your treasure is, there your heart will be also.

22"The eye is the lamp of the body. If
your eyes are good, your whole body will
be full of light. 23But if your eyes are bad,
your whole body will be full of darkness.
If then the light within you is darkness,
how great is that darkness!
24"No one can serve two masters. Either he will hate the one and love the other, or he will be devoted to the one and
despise the other. You cannot serve both
God and Money.

Do Not Worry

25"Therefore I tell you, do not worry
about your life, what you will eat or drink;
or about your body, what you will wear. Is
not life more important than food, and
the body more important than clothes?
26Look at the birds of the air; they do not
sow or reap or store away in barns, and
yet your heavenly Father feeds them. Are
you not much more valuable than they?
27Who of you by worrying can add a single
hour to his life[b]?
28"And why do you worry about
clothes? See how the lilies of the field
grow. They do not labor or spin. 29Yet I
tell you that not even Solomon in all his
splendor was dressed like one of these.
30If that is how God clothes the grass of
the field, which is here today and tomorrow is thrown into the fire, will he not
much more clothe you, O you of little
faith? 31So do not worry, saying, 'What
shall we eat?' or 'What shall we drink?' or
'What shall we wear?' 32For the pagans
run after all these things, and your heavenly Father knows that you need them.
33But seek first his kingdom and his righteousness, and all these things will be giv-
en to you as well. 34Therefore do not worry about tomorrow, for tomorrow will worry about itself. Each day has enough
trouble of its own.

Judging Others

7 "Do not judge, or you too will be
judged. 2For in the same way you
judge others, you will be judged, and with
the measure you use, it will be measured
to you.
3"Why do you look at the speck of saw-
dust in your brother's eye and pay no attention to the plank in your own eye?
4How can you say to your brother, 'Let me
take the speck out of your eye,' when all
the time there is a plank in your own eye?

[a]13 Or *from evil*; some late manuscripts *one, / for yours is the kingdom and the power and the glory forever. Amen.* [b]27 Or *single cubit to his height*

5You hypocrite, first take the plank out of your own eye, and then you will see clearly to remove the speck from your brother's eye.

6"Do not give dogs what is sacred; do not throw your pearls to pigs. If you do, they may trample them under their feet, and then turn and tear you to pieces.

Ask, Seek, Knock

7"Ask and it will be given to you; seek and you will find; knock and the door will be opened to you. 8For everyone who asks receives; he who seeks finds; and to him who knocks, the door will be opened.

9"Which of you, if his son asks for bread, will give him a stone? 10Or if he asks for a fish, will give him a snake? 11If you, then, though you are evil, know how to give good gifts to your children, how much more will your Father in heaven give good gifts to those who ask him! 12So in everything, do to others what you

TUESDAY

VERSE FOR THE DAY: *Matthew 6:27* | *AUTHOR:* *Beth Donigan Seversen* | *PASSAGE FOR THE DAY:* *Matthew 6:25–34*

Those Baby Monitors!

WORRY and exhaustion were creeping up on me. My daughter Kate was ten days old and asleep in her crib on the second floor of our small Cape Cod home. I had neglected to ask my husband to instruct me in the use of our new baby monitor and was certain it was quite beyond me. "What did mothers do before the invention of baby monitors?" I asked myself as I ironed in the basement.

The doctor had given me strict instructions due to the trauma of Kate's birth: "One trip up and down the stairs a day, for two weeks!" Yet, there I was, running up two flights of stairs in between each garment I ironed, leaning breathlessly over the crib rail to assure myself that my helpless little babe was still breathing. On the trip back to the basement I would scold myself harshly for being this silly. But, once again, while I was bending over the ironing board, fearful thoughts relentlessly teased, "What if crib death steals my baby away or what if she chokes and I'm not there?" So, back up the stairs I tread.

After one of those completed round trips, the question I'd asked earlier interrupted my fretting. What did mothers do before baby monitors? The still small voice residing in my heart replied, "They trusted in the Lord far more, worried far less, and got a lot more accomplished!" My thoughts were drawn next to Matthew 6:25,27: "Therefore I tell you, do not worry about your life . . . . Who of you by worrying can add a single hour to his life?" I knew then it was time to pause and confess: "Thank you, Father, that little Kate is of great value to you and that she is under your constant watch. I am ashamed of my worries. Please forgive me and help me to trust her life to you. Amen."

Additional Scripture Readings:
Ezra 8:21–23; Psalm 94:17–19

Go to page 12 for your next devotional reading.

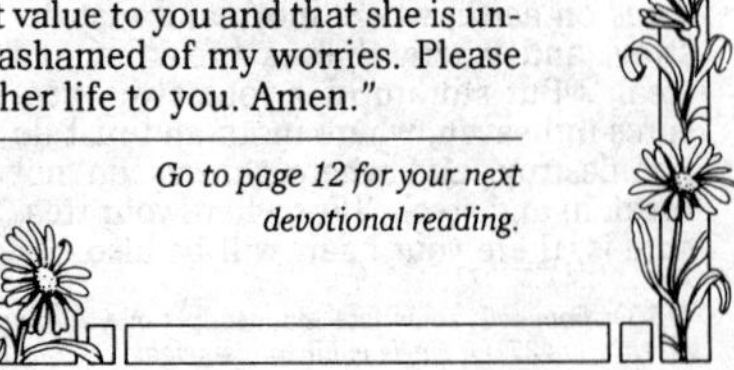

would have them do to you, for this sums up the Law and the Prophets.

The Narrow and Wide Gates

13"Enter through the narrow gate. For wide is the gate and broad is the road that leads to destruction, and many enter through it. 14But small is the gate and narrow the road that leads to life, and only a few find it.

A Tree and Its Fruit

15"Watch out for false prophets. They come to you in sheep's clothing, but inwardly they are ferocious wolves. 16By their fruit you will recognize them. Do people pick grapes from thornbushes, or figs from thistles? 17Likewise every good tree bears good fruit, but a bad tree bears bad fruit. 18A good tree cannot bear bad fruit, and a bad tree cannot bear good fruit. 19Every tree that does not bear good fruit is cut down and thrown into the fire. 20Thus, by their fruit you will recognize them.

21"Not everyone who says to me, 'Lord, Lord,' will enter the kingdom of heaven, but only he who does the will of my Father who is in heaven. 22Many will say to me on that day, 'Lord, Lord, did we not prophesy in your name, and in your name drive out demons and perform many miracles?' 23Then I will tell them plainly, 'I never knew you. Away from me, you evildoers!'

The Wise and Foolish Builders

24"Therefore everyone who hears these words of mine and puts them into practice is like a wise man who built his house on the rock. 25The rain came down, the streams rose, and the winds blew and beat against that house; yet it did not fall, because it had its foundation on the rock. 26But everyone who hears these words of mine and does not put them into practice is like a foolish man who built his house on sand. 27The rain came down, the streams rose, and the winds blew and beat against that house, and it fell with a great crash."

28When Jesus had finished saying these things, the crowds were amazed at his teaching, 29because he taught as one who had authority, and not as their teachers of the law.

The Man With Leprosy

8 When he came down from the mountainside, large crowds followed him. 2A man with leprosy[a] came and knelt before him and said, "Lord, if you are willing, you can make me clean."

3Jesus reached out his hand and touched the man. "I am willing," he said. "Be clean!" Immediately he was cured[b] of his leprosy. 4Then Jesus said to him, "See that you don't tell anyone. But go, show yourself to the priest and offer the gift Moses commanded, as a testimony to them."

The Faith of the Centurion

5When Jesus had entered Capernaum, a centurion came to him, asking for help. 6"Lord," he said, "my servant lies at home paralyzed and in terrible suffering."

7Jesus said to him, "I will go and heal him."

8The centurion replied, "Lord, I do not deserve to have you come under my roof. But just say the word, and my servant will be healed. 9For I myself am a man under authority, with soldiers under me. I tell this one, 'Go,' and he goes; and that one, 'Come,' and he comes. I say to my servant, 'Do this,' and he does it."

10When Jesus heard this, he was astonished and said to those following him, "I tell you the truth, I have not found anyone in Israel with such great faith. 11I say to you that many will come from the east and the west, and will take their places at the feast with Abraham, Isaac and Jacob in the kingdom of heaven. 12But the subjects of the kingdom will be thrown outside, into the darkness, where there will be weeping and gnashing of teeth."

13Then Jesus said to the centurion, "Go! It will be done just as you believed it would." And his servant was healed at that very hour.

Jesus Heals Many

14When Jesus came into Peter's house, he saw Peter's mother-in-law lying in bed with a fever. 15He touched her hand and the fever left her, and she got up and began to wait on him.

16When evening came, many who were demon-possessed were brought to him,

[a]*2* The Greek word was used for various diseases affecting the skin—not necessarily leprosy. [b]*3* Greek *made clean*

and he drove out the spirits with a word and healed all the sick. 17This was to fulfill what was spoken through the prophet Isaiah:

> "He took up our infirmities
> and carried our diseases."[a]

The Cost of Following Jesus

18When Jesus saw the crowd around him, he gave orders to cross to the other side of the lake. 19Then a teacher of the law came to him and said, "Teacher, I will follow you wherever you go."

20Jesus replied, "Foxes have holes and birds of the air have nests, but the Son of Man has no place to lay his head."

21Another disciple said to him, "Lord, first let me go and bury my father."

22But Jesus told him, "Follow me, and let the dead bury their own dead."

Jesus Calms the Storm

23Then he got into the boat and his disciples followed him. 24Without warning, a furious storm came up on the lake, so that the waves swept over the boat. But Jesus was sleeping. 25The disciples went and woke him, saying, "Lord, save us! We're going to drown!"

26He replied, "You of little faith, why are you so afraid?" Then he got up and rebuked the winds and the waves, and it was completely calm.

27The men were amazed and asked, "What kind of man is this? Even the winds and the waves obey him!"

The Healing of Two Demon-possessed Men

28When he arrived at the other side in the region of the Gadarenes,[b] two demon-possessed men coming from the tombs met him. They were so violent that no one could pass that way. 29"What do you want with us, Son of God?" they shouted. "Have you come here to torture us before the appointed time?"

30Some distance from them a large herd of pigs was feeding. 31The demons begged Jesus, "If you drive us out, send us into the herd of pigs."

32He said to them, "Go!" So they came out and went into the pigs, and the whole herd rushed down the steep bank into the lake and died in the water. 33Those tending the pigs ran off, went into the town and reported all this, including what had happened to the demon-possessed men. 34Then the whole town went out to meet Jesus. And when they saw him, they pleaded with him to leave their region.

Jesus Heals a Paralytic

9 Jesus stepped into a boat, crossed over and came to his own town. 2Some men brought to him a paralytic, lying on a mat. When Jesus saw their faith, he said to the paralytic, "Take heart, son; your sins are forgiven."

3At this, some of the teachers of the law said to themselves, "This fellow is blaspheming!"

4Knowing their thoughts, Jesus said, "Why do you entertain evil thoughts in your hearts? 5Which is easier: to say, 'Your sins are forgiven,' or to say, 'Get up and walk'? 6But so that you may know that the Son of Man has authority on earth to forgive sins. . . ." Then he said to the paralytic, "Get up, take your mat and go home." 7And the man got up and went home. 8When the crowd saw this, they were filled with awe; and they praised God, who had given such authority to men.

The Calling of Matthew

9As Jesus went on from there, he saw a man named Matthew sitting at the tax collector's booth. "Follow me," he told him, and Matthew got up and followed him.

10While Jesus was having dinner at Matthew's house, many tax collectors and "sinners" came and ate with him and his disciples. 11When the Pharisees saw this, they asked his disciples, "Why does your teacher eat with tax collectors and 'sinners'?"

12On hearing this, Jesus said, "It is not the healthy who need a doctor, but the sick. 13But go and learn what this means: 'I desire mercy, not sacrifice.'[c] For I have not come to call the righteous, but sinners."

Jesus Questioned About Fasting

14Then John's disciples came and asked him, "How is it that we and the Pharisees fast, but your disciples do not fast?"

15Jesus answered, "How can the guests of the bridegroom mourn while he is with them? The time will come when the

[a] *17* Isaiah 53:4 [b] *28* Some manuscripts *Gergesenes*; others *Gerasenes* [c] *13* Hosea 6:6

bridegroom will be taken from them; then
they will fast.
16"No one sews a patch of unshrunk
cloth on an old garment, for the patch
will pull away from the garment, making
the tear worse. 17Neither do men pour
new wine into old wineskins. If they do,
the skins will burst, the wine will run out
and the wineskins will be ruined. No,
they pour new wine into new wineskins,
and both are preserved."

A Dead Girl and a Sick Woman

18While he was saying this, a ruler came
and knelt before him and said, "My
daughter has just died. But come and put
your hand on her, and she will live."
19Jesus got up and went with him, and so
did his disciples.
20Just then a woman who had been
subject to bleeding for twelve years came
up behind him and touched the edge of
his cloak. 21She said to herself, "If I only
touch his cloak, I will be healed."
22Jesus turned and saw her. "Take
heart, daughter," he said, "your faith has
healed you." And the woman was healed
from that moment.
23When Jesus entered the ruler's house
and saw the flute players and the noisy
crowd, 24he said, "Go away. The girl is not
dead but asleep." But they laughed at
him. 25After the crowd had been put outside, he went in and took the girl by the
hand, and she got up. 26News of this
spread through all that region.

Jesus Heals the Blind and Mute

27As Jesus went on from there, two
blind men followed him, calling out,
"Have mercy on us, Son of David!"
28When he had gone indoors, the blind
men came to him, and he asked them,
"Do you believe that I am able to do
this?"
"Yes, Lord," they replied.
29Then he touched their eyes and said,
"According to your faith will it be done to
you"; 30and their sight was restored. Jesus
warned them sternly, "See that no one
knows about this." 31But they went out
and spread the news about him all over
that region.
32While they were going out, a man who
was demon-possessed and could not talk
was brought to Jesus. 33And when the demon was driven out, the man who had
been mute spoke. The crowd was amazed
and said, "Nothing like this has ever been
seen in Israel."
34But the Pharisees said, "It is by the
prince of demons that he drives out demons."

The Workers Are Few

35Jesus went through all the towns and
villages, teaching in their synagogues,
preaching the good news of the kingdom
and healing every disease and sickness.
36When he saw the crowds, he had compassion on them, because they were harassed and helpless, like sheep without a
shepherd. 37Then he said to his disciples,
"The harvest is plentiful but the workers
are few. 38Ask the Lord of the harvest,
therefore, to send out workers into his
harvest field."

Jesus Sends Out the Twelve

10 He called his twelve disciples to
him and gave them authority to
drive out evil[a] spirits and to heal every
disease and sickness.
2These are the names of the twelve
apostles: first, Simon (who is called Peter) and his brother Andrew; James son of
Zebedee, and his brother John; 3Philip
and Bartholomew; Thomas and Matthew
the tax collector; James son of Alphaeus,
and Thaddaeus; 4Simon the Zealot and
Judas Iscariot, who betrayed him.
5These twelve Jesus sent out with the
following instructions: "Do not go among
the Gentiles or enter any town of the Samaritans. 6Go rather to the lost sheep of
Israel. 7As you go, preach this message:
'The kingdom of heaven is near.' 8Heal
the sick, raise the dead, cleanse those
who have leprosy,[b] drive out demons.
Freely you have received, freely give. 9Do
not take along any gold or silver or copper
in your belts; 10take no bag for the journey, or extra tunic, or sandals or a staff;
for the worker is worth his keep.
11"Whatever town or village you enter,
search for some worthy person there and
stay at his house until you leave. 12As you
enter the home, give it your greeting. 13If
the home is deserving, let your peace rest
on it; if it is not, let your peace return to
you. 14If anyone will not welcome you or
listen to your words, shake the dust off
your feet when you leave that home or
town. 15I tell you the truth, it will be more

[a]1 Greek *unclean* [b]8 The Greek word was used for various diseases affecting the skin—not necessarily leprosy.

bearable for Sodom and Gomorrah on the
day of judgment than for that town. 16I
am sending you out like sheep among
wolves. Therefore be as shrewd as snakes
and as innocent as doves.
17"Be on your guard against men; they
will hand you over to the local councils
and flog you in their synagogues. 18On my
account you will be brought before governors and kings as witnesses to them and
to the Gentiles. 19But when they arrest
you, do not worry about what to say or
how to say it. At that time you will be
given what to say, 20for it will not be you
speaking, but the Spirit of your Father
speaking through you.
21"Brother will betray brother to death,
and a father his child; children will rebel
against their parents and have them put
to death. 22All men will hate you because
of me, but he who stands firm to the end
will be saved. 23When you are persecuted
in one place, flee to another. I tell you the
truth, you will not finish going through
the cities of Israel before the Son of Man
comes.
24"A student is not above his teacher,
nor a servant above his master. 25It is
enough for the student to be like his
teacher, and the servant like his master.
If the head of the house has been called
Beelzebub,[a] how much more the members of his household!
26"So do not be afraid of them. There is

[a]25 Greek *Beezeboul* or *Beelzeboul*

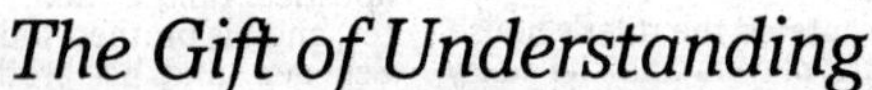

WEDNESDAY

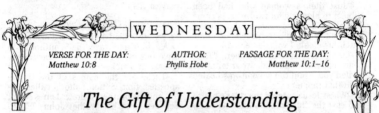

VERSE FOR THE DAY: *Matthew 10:8* | *AUTHOR:* *Phyllis Hobe* | *PASSAGE FOR THE DAY:* *Matthew 10:1–16*

The Gift of Understanding

SOMETIMES, when we love someone, we feel we just can't give them enough. We may even do without things we need ourselves. I think most parents feel that way about their children. Love makes us generous.

But generosity is more than giving.

If anyone could have showered gifts on those he loved, it was Jesus Christ. But he didn't. He provided for their basic needs; he saw to it that they had shelter and enough to eat. He watched them counting coins when he could have filled their laps with riches.

Jesus gave something more precious and more lasting than gifts. He gave understanding. He knew how hard it is to live in this world. He felt what others felt and couldn't put into words. And out of his understanding he gave what people truly need, such as forgiveness for Zacchaeus's guilt, hope for the cynical woman at the well, recovery for a dying child.

The next time you want to give a gift to someone you love, don't worry about how much you can afford to spend or how big the present ought to be. Consider, instead, what generosity really means: *understanding.* That's something each of us can afford to give—all the time.

Additional Scripture Readings:
Proverbs 20:5–6; John 4:10–14

Go to page 14 for your next devotional reading.

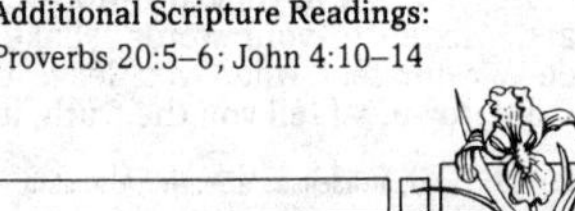

nothing concealed that will not be disclosed, or hidden that will not be made
known. 27What I tell you in the dark,
speak in the daylight; what is whispered
in your ear, proclaim from the roofs. 28Do
not be afraid of those who kill the body
but cannot kill the soul. Rather, be afraid
of the One who can destroy both soul and
body in hell. 29Are not two sparrows sold
for a penny[a]? Yet not one of them will fall
to the ground apart from the will of your
Father. 30And even the very hairs of your
head are all numbered. 31So don't be
afraid; you are worth more than many
sparrows.

32"Whoever acknowledges me before
men, I will also acknowledge him before
my Father in heaven. 33But whoever disowns me before men, I will disown him
before my Father in heaven.

34"Do not suppose that I have come to
bring peace to the earth. I did not come
to bring peace, but a sword. 35For I have
come to turn

" 'a man against his father,
a daughter against her mother,
a daughter-in-law against her
mother-in-law—
36 a man's enemies will be the
members of his own
household.'[b]

37"Anyone who loves his father or
mother more than me is not worthy of
me; anyone who loves his son or daughter
more than me is not worthy of me; 38and
anyone who does not take his cross and
follow me is not worthy of me. 39Whoever
finds his life will lose it, and whoever
loses his life for my sake will find it.

40"He who receives you receives me,
and he who receives me receives the one
who sent me. 41Anyone who receives a
prophet because he is a prophet will receive a prophet's reward, and anyone who
receives a righteous man because he is a
righteous man will receive a righteous
man's reward. 42And if anyone gives even
a cup of cold water to one of these little
ones because he is my disciple, I tell you
the truth, he will certainly not lose his
reward."

Jesus and John the Baptist

11 After Jesus had finished instruct-
ing his twelve disciples, he went
on from there to teach and preach in the
towns of Galilee.[c]

2When John heard in prison what
Christ was doing, he sent his disciples 3to
ask him, "Are you the one who was to
come, or should we expect someone
else?"

4Jesus replied, "Go back and report to
John what you hear and see: 5The blind
receive sight, the lame walk, those who
have leprosy[d] are cured, the deaf hear,
the dead are raised, and the good news is
preached to the poor. 6Blessed is the man
who does not fall away on account of
me."

7As John's disciples were leaving, Jesus
began to speak to the crowd about John:
"What did you go out into the desert to
see? A reed swayed by the wind? 8If not,
what did you go out to see? A man
dressed in fine clothes? No, those who
wear fine clothes are in kings' palaces.
9Then what did you go out to see? A
prophet? Yes, I tell you, and more than a
prophet. 10This is the one about whom it
is written:

" 'I will send my messenger ahead of
you,
who will prepare your way before
you.'[e]

11I tell you the truth: Among those born of
women there has not risen anyone greater
than John the Baptist; yet he who is least
in the kingdom of heaven is greater than
he. 12From the days of John the Baptist
until now, the kingdom of heaven has
been forcefully advancing, and forceful
men lay hold of it. 13For all the Prophets
and the Law prophesied until John. 14And
if you are willing to accept it, he is the
Elijah who was to come. 15He who has
ears, let him hear.

16"To what can I compare this generation? They are like children sitting
in the marketplaces and calling out to
others:

17" 'We played the flute for you,
and you did not dance;
we sang a dirge,
and you did not mourn.'

18For John came neither eating nor drinking, and they say, 'He has a demon.' 19The
Son of Man came eating and drinking,
and they say, 'Here is a glutton and a

[a]*29* Greek *an assarion* [b]*36* Micah 7:6 [c]*1* Greek *in their towns* [d]*5* The Greek word was used for various diseases affecting the skin—not necessarily leprosy. [e]*10* Mal. 3:1

drunkard, a friend of tax collectors and "sinners." ' But wisdom is proved right by her actions."

Woe on Unrepentant Cities

20Then Jesus began to denounce the cities in which most of his miracles had been performed, because they did not repent.
21"Woe to you, Korazin! Woe to you, Bethsaida! If the miracles that were performed in you had been performed in Tyre and Sidon, they would have repented long ago in sackcloth and ashes.
22But I tell you, it will be more bearable for Tyre and Sidon on the day of judgment than for you.
23And you, Capernaum, will you be lifted up to the skies? No, you will go down to the depths.[a] If the miracles that were performed in you had been performed in Sodom, it would have remained to this day.
24But I tell you that it will be more bearable for Sodom on the day of judgment than for you."

Rest for the Weary

25At that time Jesus said, "I praise you,

[a]23 Greek *Hades*

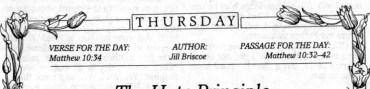

THURSDAY

VERSE FOR THE DAY: *Matthew 10:34*

AUTHOR: *Jill Briscoe*

PASSAGE FOR THE DAY: *Matthew 10:32–42*

The Hate Principle

JESUS cared about the family. But he knew that ministry would bring its own strains. One day he was talking to his people and he said, "If anyone comes to me and does not hate his father and mother, his wife and children, his brothers and sisters—yes, even his own life—he cannot be my disciple" (Luke 14:26). This has been called the "hate" principle. Jesus obviously did not mean we are to hate those people in our families who are closest to us. He had already told us to love God with all our hearts and our neighbors as ourselves.

Terms used to define the emotions and affections were frequently comparative. Jesus was saying that "natural affection is to be, as compared with the Christian's devotedness to Christ, as if it were hate" (*Oxford NIV Scofield Study Bible,* p. 1074). Christ illustrated this principle in his own person when talking of the new relationships of the kingdom: "Pointing to his disciples, he said, 'Here are my mother and my brothers. For whoever does the will of my Father in heaven is my brother and sister and mother'" (Matthew 12:49–50).

Jesus knew the coming of the gospel would bring division within families—it brought it in his own. But this did not mean that Jesus was not firmly in favor of "family." He cared for his mother from his cross, appeared to his oldest brother James after the resurrection, and united his family in ministry in Jerusalem. The gospel will bring reactions and responses—even from within our families. Disciples must be ready for them.

Additional Scripture Readings:
Mark 7:9–13; John 19:25–27

Go to page 16 for your next devotional reading.

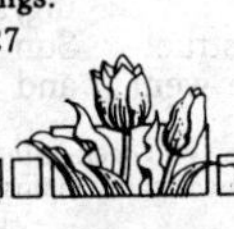

Father, Lord of heaven and earth, because you have hidden these things from
the wise and learned, and revealed them
to little children. 26Yes, Father, for this
was your good pleasure.
27"All things have been committed to
me by my Father. No one knows the Son
except the Father, and no one knows the
Father except the Son and those to whom
the Son chooses to reveal him.
28"Come to me, all you who are weary
and burdened, and I will give you rest.
29Take my yoke upon you and learn from
me, for I am gentle and humble in heart,
and you will find rest for your souls. 30For
my yoke is easy and my burden is light."

Lord of the Sabbath

12 At that time Jesus went through
the grainfields on the Sabbath. His
disciples were hungry and began to pick
some heads of grain and eat them. 2When
the Pharisees saw this, they said to him,
"Look! Your disciples are doing what is
unlawful on the Sabbath."
3He answered, "Haven't you read what
David did when he and his companions
were hungry? 4He entered the house of
God, and he and his companions ate the
consecrated bread—which was not lawful
for them to do, but only for the priests.
5Or haven't you read in the Law that on
the Sabbath the priests in the temple desecrate the day and yet are innocent? 6I
tell you that one[a] greater than the temple
is here. 7If you had known what these
words mean, 'I desire mercy, not sacrifice,'[b] you would not have condemned
the innocent. 8For the Son of Man is Lord
of the Sabbath."
9Going on from that place, he went into
their synagogue, 10and a man with a shriveled hand was there. Looking for a reason
to accuse Jesus, they asked him, "Is it
lawful to heal on the Sabbath?"
11He said to them, "If any of you has a
sheep and it falls into a pit on the Sabbath, will you not take hold of it and lift
it out? 12How much more valuable is a
man than a sheep! Therefore it is lawful
to do good on the Sabbath."
13Then he said to the man, "Stretch out
your hand." So he stretched it out and
it was completely restored, just as sound
as the other. 14But the Pharisees went
out and plotted how they might kill
Jesus.

God's Chosen Servant

15Aware of this, Jesus withdrew from
that place. Many followed him, and he
healed all their sick, 16warning them not
to tell who he was. 17This was to fulfill
what was spoken through the prophet Isaiah:

18"Here is my servant whom I have
chosen,
the one I love, in whom I delight;
I will put my Spirit on him,
and he will proclaim justice to the
nations.
19He will not quarrel or cry out;
no one will hear his voice in the
streets.
20A bruised reed he will not break,
and a smoldering wick he will not
snuff out,
till he leads justice to victory.
21 In his name the nations will put
their hope."[c]

Jesus and Beelzebub

22Then they brought him a demon-possessed man who was blind and mute, and
Jesus healed him, so that he could both
talk and see. 23All the people were astonished and said, "Could this be the Son of
David?"
24But when the Pharisees heard this,
they said, "It is only by Beelzebub,[d] the
prince of demons, that this fellow drives
out demons."
25Jesus knew their thoughts and said to
them, "Every kingdom divided against itself will be ruined, and every city or
household divided against itself will not
stand. 26If Satan drives out Satan, he is
divided against himself. How then can his
kingdom stand? 27And if I drive out demons by Beelzebub, by whom do your
people drive them out? So then, they will
be your judges. 28But if I drive out demons by the Spirit of God, then the kingdom of God has come upon you.
29"Or again, how can anyone enter a
strong man's house and carry off his possessions unless he first ties up the strong
man? Then he can rob his house.
30"He who is not with me is against me,
and he who does not gather with me scatters. 31And so I tell you, every sin and
blasphemy will be forgiven men, but the
blasphemy against the Spirit will not be
forgiven. 32Anyone who speaks a word

[a]6 Or *something*; also in verses 41 and 42 [b]7 Hosea 6:6 [c]21 Isaiah 42:1-4 [d]24 Greek *Beezeboul* or *Beelzeboul*; also in verse 27

FRIDAY

VERSE FOR THE DAY: *Matthew 11:28* | *AUTHOR:* *Diane Head* | *PASSAGE FOR THE DAY:* *Matthew 11:25–30*

His Rest

DO you ever feel as though you have nothing to give? That so many demands are made of you that you've become depleted . . . empty . . . exhausted?

Do you have an automatic signal when your posterior hits the bottom of a chair—immediately a voice from the farthest room in the house calls "MOTHER . . . " as if the house were on fire?

If you answered a hearty "amen" to the above, congratulations. You're a bonafide member of twentieth-century motherhood. One of the conditions of membership is that you exchange your calm and orderly life for upheaval, busyness and whirlwind activity.

We entered motherhood so eagerly—babes in our arms and stars in our eyes. So cuddly and cute, these wee ones took hold of our hearts and lives. We didn't know the gentle thump, thump, thump of their hearts was the ticking of a time bomb, ready to explode with the energy of an atomic bomb at any minute. As parents, we are the managers and harnessers of this energy, so we fill our days with clever schemes and fancy plans to keep our children occupied. Soon we find ourselves caught in the great car pool of life. We pick up and drop off mini-ballerinas, soccer players, piano virtuosos and future NFL champions until life is little more than a blur.

If ever anyone needed rest, it's today's mother. And I have great news. There is rest for us—a rest more rejuvenating than a long and leisurely nap, and more soothing to frayed nerves than a Brahms concert. This rest reaches into the depths of our souls and claims us from within.

This special promise of rest comes from Jesus' words in Matthew 11:29: "Take my yoke upon you and learn from me . . . and you will find rest." The yoke spoken of in this passage is fashioned of discipline and discipleship; its lining is love. Rather than bringing restriction, it brings refreshment. Through this yoke he calls us to learn of himself and find quietness and blessed rest.

Rest for the soul is the most desirable rest. It affects not only our spiritual health, but our emotional and physical health as well. The only way to receive this rest is to sit at Christ's feet and hear his word, to take the time to learn more about who he is and what he is like.

Additional Scripture Readings:
Exodus 33:12–14; Mark 6:30–31

Go to page 20 for your next devotional reading.

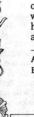

against the Son of Man will be forgiven,
but anyone who speaks against the Holy
Spirit will not be forgiven, either in this
age or in the age to come.

33"Make a tree good and its fruit will be
good, or make a tree bad and its fruit will
be bad, for a tree is recognized by its fruit.
34You brood of vipers, how can you who
are evil say anything good? For out of the
overflow of the heart the mouth speaks.
35The good man brings good things out of
the good stored up in him, and the evil
man brings evil things out of the evil
stored up in him. 36But I tell you that men
will have to give account on the day of
judgment for every careless word they
have spoken. 37For by your words you will
be acquitted, and by your words you will
be condemned."

The Sign of Jonah

38Then some of the Pharisees and
teachers of the law said to him, "Teacher,
we want to see a miraculous sign from
you."

39He answered, "A wicked and adulterous generation asks for a miraculous sign!
But none will be given it except the sign
of the prophet Jonah. 40For as Jonah was
three days and three nights in the belly of
a huge fish, so the Son of Man will be
three days and three nights in the heart of
the earth. 41The men of Nineveh will
stand up at the judgment with this generation and condemn it; for they repented
at the preaching of Jonah, and now one[a]
greater than Jonah is here. 42The Queen
of the South will rise at the judgment
with this generation and condemn it; for
she came from the ends of the earth to
listen to Solomon's wisdom, and now one
greater than Solomon is here.

43"When an evil[b] spirit comes out of a
man, it goes through arid places seeking
rest and does not find it. 44Then it says, 'I
will return to the house I left.' When it
arrives, it finds the house unoccupied,
swept clean and put in order. 45Then it
goes and takes with it seven other spirits
more wicked than itself, and they go in
and live there. And the final condition of
that man is worse than the first. That is
how it will be with this wicked generation."

Jesus' Mother and Brothers

46While Jesus was still talking to the
crowd, his mother and brothers stood
outside, wanting to speak to him.
47Someone told him, "Your mother and
brothers are standing outside, wanting to
speak to you."[c]

48He replied to him, "Who is my mother, and who are my brothers?" 49Pointing
to his disciples, he said, "Here are my
mother and my brothers. 50For whoever
does the will of my Father in heaven is my
brother and sister and mother."

The Parable of the Sower

13 That same day Jesus went out of
the house and sat by the lake.
2Such large crowds gathered around him
that he got into a boat and sat in it, while
all the people stood on the shore. 3Then
he told them many things in parables,
saying: "A farmer went out to sow his
seed. 4As he was scattering the seed,
some fell along the path, and the birds
came and ate it up. 5Some fell on rocky
places, where it did not have much soil. It
sprang up quickly, because the soil was
shallow. 6But when the sun came up, the
plants were scorched, and they withered
because they had no root. 7Other seed fell
among thorns, which grew up and choked
the plants. 8Still other seed fell on good
soil, where it produced a crop—a hundred, sixty or thirty times what was sown.
9He who has ears, let him hear."

10The disciples came to him and asked,
"Why do you speak to the people in parables?"

11He replied, "The knowledge of the secrets of the kingdom of heaven has been
given to you, but not to them. 12Whoever
has will be given more, and he will have
an abundance. Whoever does not have,
even what he has will be taken from him.
13This is why I speak to them in parables:

"Though seeing, they do not see;
though hearing, they do not hear or
understand.

14In them is fulfilled the prophecy of Isaiah:

" 'You will be ever hearing but never
understanding;
you will be ever seeing but never
perceiving.
15For this people's heart has become
calloused;
they hardly hear with their ears,

[a]41 Or *something*; also in verse 42 [b]43 Greek *unclean* [c]47 Some manuscripts do not have verse 47.

and they have closed their eyes.
Otherwise they might see with their
eyes,
hear with their ears,
understand with their hearts
and turn, and I would heal them.'[a]

16But blessed are your eyes because they
see, and your ears because they hear.
17For I tell you the truth, many prophets
and righteous men longed to see what
you see but did not see it, and to hear
what you hear but did not hear it.

18"Listen then to what the parable of
the sower means: 19When anyone hears
the message about the kingdom and does
not understand it, the evil one comes and
snatches away what was sown in his
heart. This is the seed sown along the
path. 20The one who received the seed
that fell on rocky places is the man who
hears the word and at once receives it
with joy. 21But since he has no root, he
lasts only a short time. When trouble or
persecution comes because of the word,
he quickly falls away. 22The one who received the seed that fell among the thorns
is the man who hears the word, but the
worries of this life and the deceitfulness
of wealth choke it, making it unfruitful.
23But the one who received the seed that
fell on good soil is the man who hears the
word and understands it. He produces a
crop, yielding a hundred, sixty or thirty
times what was sown."

The Parable of the Weeds

24Jesus told them another parable:
"The kingdom of heaven is like a man
who sowed good seed in his field. 25But
while everyone was sleeping, his enemy
came and sowed weeds among the wheat,
and went away. 26When the wheat sprout-
ed and formed heads, then the weeds also
appeared.

27"The owner's servants came to him
and said, 'Sir, didn't you sow good seed in
your field? Where then did the weeds
come from?'

28" 'An enemy did this,' he replied.

"The servants asked him, 'Do you want
us to go and pull them up?'

29" 'No,' he answered, 'because while
you are pulling the weeds, you may root
up the wheat with them. 30Let both grow
together until the harvest. At that time I
will tell the harvesters: First collect the
weeds and tie them in bundles to be
burned; then gather the wheat and bring
it into my barn.' "

The Parables of the Mustard Seed and the Yeast

31He told them another parable: "The
kingdom of heaven is like a mustard seed,
which a man took and planted in his
field. 32Though it is the smallest of all
your seeds, yet when it grows, it is the
largest of garden plants and becomes a
tree, so that the birds of the air come and
perch in its branches."

33He told them still another parable:
"The kingdom of heaven is like yeast that
a woman took and mixed into a large
amount[b] of flour until it worked all
through the dough."

34Jesus spoke all these things to the
crowd in parables; he did not say anything to them without using a parable.
35So was fulfilled what was spoken
through the prophet:

"I will open my mouth in parables,
I will utter things hidden since the
creation of the world."[c]

The Parable of the Weeds Explained

36Then he left the crowd and went into
the house. His disciples came to him and
said, "Explain to us the parable of the
weeds in the field."

37He answered, "The one who sowed
the good seed is the Son of Man. 38The
field is the world, and the good seed
stands for the sons of the kingdom. The
weeds are the sons of the evil one, 39and
the enemy who sows them is the devil.
The harvest is the end of the age, and the
harvesters are angels.

40"As the weeds are pulled up and
burned in the fire, so it will be at the end
of the age. 41The Son of Man will send out
his angels, and they will weed out of his
kingdom everything that causes sin and
all who do evil. 42They will throw them
into the fiery furnace, where there will be
weeping and gnashing of teeth. 43Then
the righteous will shine like the sun in
the kingdom of their Father. He who has
ears, let him hear.

The Parables of the Hidden Treasure and the Pearl

44"The kingdom of heaven is like treasure hidden in a field. When a man found
it, he hid it again, and then in his joy went

[a]*15* Isaiah 6:9,10 [b]*33* Greek *three satas* (probably about 1/2 bushel or 22 liters) [c]*35* Psalm 78:2

and sold all he had and bought that field.

45 “Again, the kingdom of heaven is like a merchant looking for fine pearls. 46 When he found one of great value, he went away and sold everything he had and bought it.

The Parable of the Net

47 “Once again, the kingdom of heaven is like a net that was let down into the lake and caught all kinds of fish. 48 When it was full, the fishermen pulled it up on the shore. Then they sat down and collected the good fish in baskets, but threw the bad away. 49 This is how it will be at the end of the age. The angels will come and separate the wicked from the righteous 50 and throw them into the fiery furnace, where there will be weeping and gnashing of teeth.

51 “Have you understood all these things?” Jesus asked.

“Yes,” they replied.

52 He said to them, “Therefore every teacher of the law who has been instructed about the kingdom of heaven is like the owner of a house who brings out of his storeroom new treasures as well as old.”

A Prophet Without Honor

53 When Jesus had finished these parables, he moved on from there. 54 Coming to his hometown, he began teaching the people in their synagogue, and they were amazed. “Where did this man get this wisdom and these miraculous powers?” they asked. 55 “Isn't this the carpenter's son? Isn't his mother's name Mary, and aren't his brothers James, Joseph, Simon and Judas? 56 Aren't all his sisters with us? Where then did this man get all these things?” 57 And they took offense at him.

But Jesus said to them, “Only in his hometown and in his own house is a prophet without honor.”

58 And he did not do many miracles there because of their lack of faith.

John the Baptist Beheaded

14 At that time Herod the tetrarch heard the reports about Jesus, 2 and he said to his attendants, “This is John the Baptist; he has risen from the dead! That is why miraculous powers are at work in him.”

3 Now Herod had arrested John and bound him and put him in prison because of Herodias, his brother Philip's wife, 4 for John had been saying to him: “It is not lawful for you to have her.” 5 Herod wanted to kill John, but he was afraid of the people, because they considered him a prophet.

6 On Herod's birthday the daughter of Herodias danced for them and pleased Herod so much 7 that he promised with an oath to give her whatever she asked. 8 Prompted by her mother, she said, “Give me here on a platter the head of John the Baptist.” 9 The king was distressed, but because of his oaths and his dinner guests, he ordered that her request be granted 10 and had John beheaded in the prison. 11 His head was brought in on a platter and given to the girl, who carried it to her mother. 12 John's disciples came and took his body and buried it. Then they went and told Jesus.

Jesus Feeds the Five Thousand

13 When Jesus heard what had happened, he withdrew by boat privately to a solitary place. Hearing of this, the crowds followed him on foot from the towns. 14 When Jesus landed and saw a large crowd, he had compassion on them and healed their sick.

15 As evening approached, the disciples came to him and said, “This is a remote place, and it's already getting late. Send the crowds away, so they can go to the villages and buy themselves some food.”

16 Jesus replied, “They do not need to go away. You give them something to eat.”

17 “We have here only five loaves of bread and two fish,” they answered.

18 “Bring them here to me,” he said. 19 And he directed the people to sit down on the grass. Taking the five loaves and the two fish and looking up to heaven, he gave thanks and broke the loaves. Then he gave them to the disciples, and the disciples gave them to the people. 20 They all ate and were satisfied, and the disciples picked up twelve basketfuls of broken pieces that were left over. 21 The number of those who ate was about five thousand men, besides women and children.

Jesus Walks on the Water

22 Immediately Jesus made the disciples get into the boat and go on ahead of him to the other side, while he dismissed the crowd. 23 After he had dismissed them, he went up on a mountainside by himself to pray. When evening came, he was there alone, 24 but the boat was

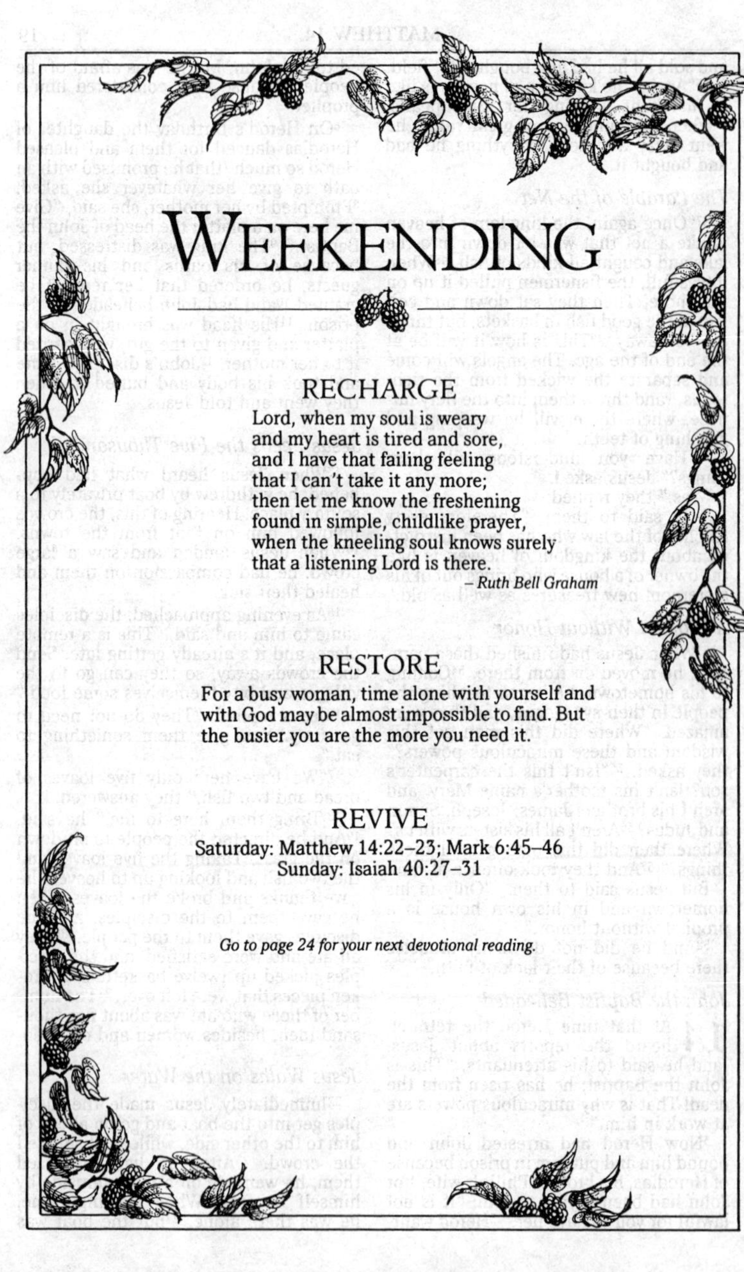

WEEKENDING

RECHARGE

Lord, when my soul is weary
and my heart is tired and sore,
and I have that failing feeling
that I can't take it any more;
then let me know the freshening
found in simple, childlike prayer,
when the kneeling soul knows surely
that a listening Lord is there.

— Ruth Bell Graham

RESTORE

For a busy woman, time alone with yourself and with God may be almost impossible to find. But the busier you are the more you need it.

REVIVE

Saturday: Matthew 14:22–23; Mark 6:45–46
Sunday: Isaiah 40:27–31

Go to page 24 for your next devotional reading.

already a considerable distance[a] from land, buffeted by the waves because the wind was against it.

25During the fourth watch of the night Jesus went out to them, walking on the lake. 26When the disciples saw him walking on the lake, they were terrified. "It's a ghost," they said, and cried out in fear.

27But Jesus immediately said to them: "Take courage! It is I. Don't be afraid."

28"Lord, if it's you," Peter replied, "tell me to come to you on the water."

29"Come," he said.

Then Peter got down out of the boat, walked on the water and came toward Jesus. 30But when he saw the wind, he was afraid and, beginning to sink, cried out, "Lord, save me!"

31Immediately Jesus reached out his hand and caught him. "You of little faith," he said, "why did you doubt?"

32And when they climbed into the boat, the wind died down. 33Then those who were in the boat worshiped him, saying, "Truly you are the Son of God."

34When they had crossed over, they landed at Gennesaret. 35And when the men of that place recognized Jesus, they sent word to all the surrounding country. People brought all their sick to him 36and begged him to let the sick just touch the edge of his cloak, and all who touched him were healed.

Clean and Unclean

15 Then some Pharisees and teachers of the law came to Jesus from Jerusalem and asked, 2"Why do your disciples break the tradition of the elders? They don't wash their hands before they eat!"

3Jesus replied, "And why do you break the command of God for the sake of your tradition? 4For God said, 'Honor your father and mother'[b] and 'Anyone who curses his father or mother must be put to death.'[c] 5But you say that if a man says to his father or mother, 'Whatever help you might otherwise have received from me is a gift devoted to God,' 6he is not to 'honor his father[d]' with it. Thus you nullify the word of God for the sake of your tradition. 7You hypocrites! Isaiah was right when he prophesied about you:

8" 'These people honor me with their
lips,
but their hearts are far from me.
9They worship me in vain;
their teachings are but rules taught
by men.'[e]"

10Jesus called the crowd to him and said, "Listen and understand. 11What goes into a man's mouth does not make him 'unclean,' but what comes out of his mouth, that is what makes him 'unclean.' "

12Then the disciples came to him and asked, "Do you know that the Pharisees were offended when they heard this?"

13He replied, "Every plant that my heavenly Father has not planted will be pulled up by the roots. 14Leave them; they are blind guides.[f] If a blind man leads a blind man, both will fall into a pit."

15Peter said, "Explain the parable to us."

16"Are you still so dull?" Jesus asked them. 17"Don't you see that whatever enters the mouth goes into the stomach and then out of the body? 18But the things that come out of the mouth come from the heart, and these make a man 'unclean.' 19For out of the heart come evil thoughts, murder, adultery, sexual immorality, theft, false testimony, slander. 20These are what make a man 'unclean'; but eating with unwashed hands does not make him 'unclean.' "

The Faith of the Canaanite Woman

21Leaving that place, Jesus withdrew to the region of Tyre and Sidon. 22A Canaanite woman from that vicinity came to him, crying out, "Lord, Son of David, have mercy on me! My daughter is suffering terribly from demon-possession."

23Jesus did not answer a word. So his disciples came to him and urged him, "Send her away, for she keeps crying out after us."

24He answered, "I was sent only to the lost sheep of Israel."

25The woman came and knelt before him. "Lord, help me!" she said.

26He replied, "It is not right to take the children's bread and toss it to their dogs."

27"Yes, Lord," she said, "but even the dogs eat the crumbs that fall from their masters' table."

28Then Jesus answered, "Woman, you have great faith! Your request is granted."

[a]24 Greek *many stadia* [b]4 Exodus 20:12; Deut. 5:16 [c]4 Exodus 21:17; Lev. 20:9 [d]6 Some manuscripts *father or his mother* [e]9 Isaiah 29:13 [f]14 Some manuscripts *guides of the blind*

And her daughter was healed from that
very hour.

Jesus Feeds the Four Thousand

29Jesus left there and went along the
Sea of Galilee. Then he went up on a
mountainside and sat down. 30Great
crowds came to him, bringing the lame,
the blind, the crippled, the mute and
many others, and laid them at his feet;
and he healed them. 31The people were
amazed when they saw the mute speaking, the crippled made well, the lame
walking and the blind seeing. And they
praised the God of Israel.
32Jesus called his disciples to him and
said, "I have compassion for these people; they have already been with me three
days and have nothing to eat. I do not
want to send them away hungry, or they
may collapse on the way."
33His disciples answered, "Where could
we get enough bread in this remote place
to feed such a crowd?"
34"How many loaves do you have?"
Jesus asked.
"Seven," they replied, "and a few small
fish."
35He told the crowd to sit down on the
ground. 36Then he took the seven loaves
and the fish, and when he had given
thanks, he broke them and gave them to
the disciples, and they in turn to the people. 37They all ate and were satisfied. Afterward the disciples picked up seven
basketfuls of broken pieces that were left
over. 38The number of those who ate was
four thousand, besides women and children. 39After Jesus had sent the crowd
away, he got into the boat and went to the
vicinity of Magadan.

The Demand for a Sign

16 The Pharisees and Sadducees
came to Jesus and tested him by
asking him to show them a sign from
heaven.
2He replied,[a] "When evening comes,
you say, 'It will be fair weather, for the sky
is red,' 3and in the morning, 'Today it will
be stormy, for the sky is red and overcast.'
You know how to interpret the appearance of the sky, but you cannot interpret
the signs of the times. 4A wicked and
adulterous generation looks for a miraculous sign, but none will be given it except
the sign of Jonah." Jesus then left them
and went away.

The Yeast of the Pharisees and Sadducees

5When they went across the lake, the
disciples forgot to take bread. 6"Be careful," Jesus said to them. "Be on your
guard against the yeast of the Pharisees
and Sadducees."
7They discussed this among themselves and said, "It is because we didn't
bring any bread."
8Aware of their discussion, Jesus
asked, "You of little faith, why are you
talking among yourselves about having
no bread? 9Do you still not understand?
Don't you remember the five loaves for
the five thousand, and how many basketfuls you gathered? 10Or the seven loaves
for the four thousand, and how many basketfuls you gathered? 11How is it you
don't understand that I was not talking to
you about bread? But be on your guard
against the yeast of the Pharisees and
Sadducees." 12Then they understood that
he was not telling them to guard against
the yeast used in bread, but against the
teaching of the Pharisees and Sadducees.

Peter's Confession of Christ

13When Jesus came to the region of
Caesarea Philippi, he asked his disciples,
"Who do people say the Son of Man is?"
14They replied, "Some say John the
Baptist; others say Elijah; and still others,
Jeremiah or one of the prophets."
15"But what about you?" he asked.
"Who do you say I am?"
16Simon Peter answered, "You are the
Christ,[b] the Son of the living God."
17Jesus replied, "Blessed are you, Simon son of Jonah, for this was not revealed to you by man, but by my Father in
heaven. 18And I tell you that you are Peter,[c] and on this rock I will build my
church, and the gates of Hades[d] will not
overcome it.[e] 19I will give you the keys of
the kingdom of heaven; whatever you
bind on earth will be[f] bound in heaven,
and whatever you loose on earth will be[f]
loosed in heaven." 20Then he warned his
disciples not to tell anyone that he was
the Christ.

[a] 2 Some early manuscripts do not have the rest of verse 2 and all of verse 3. [b] 16 Or *Messiah*; also in verse 20 [c] 18 *Peter* means *rock*. [d] 18 Or *hell* [e] 18 Or *not prove stronger than it* [f] 19 Or *have been*

Jesus Predicts His Death

21From that time on Jesus began to explain to his disciples that he must go to
Jerusalem and suffer many things at the
hands of the elders, chief priests and
teachers of the law, and that he must be
killed and on the third day be raised to
life.
22Peter took him aside and began to rebuke him. "Never, Lord!" he said. "This
shall never happen to you!"
23Jesus turned and said to Peter, "Get
behind me, Satan! You are a stumbling
block to me; you do not have in mind the
things of God, but the things of men."
24Then Jesus said to his disciples, "If
anyone would come after me, he must
deny himself and take up his cross and
follow me. 25For whoever wants to save
his life[a] will lose it, but whoever loses his
life for me will find it. 26What good will it
be for a man if he gains the whole world,
yet forfeits his soul? Or what can a man
give in exchange for his soul? 27For the
Son of Man is going to come in his Father's glory with his angels, and then he
will reward each person according to
what he has done. 28I tell you the truth,
some who are standing here will not taste
death before they see the Son of Man
coming in his kingdom."

The Transfiguration

17 After six days Jesus took with him
Peter, James and John the brother
of James, and led them up a high mountain by themselves. 2There he was transfigured before them. His face shone like
the sun, and his clothes became as white
as the light. 3Just then there appeared before them Moses and Elijah, talking with
Jesus.
4Peter said to Jesus, "Lord, it is good
for us to be here. If you wish, I will put up
three shelters—one for you, one for Moses and one for Elijah."
5While he was still speaking, a bright
cloud enveloped them, and a voice from
the cloud said, "This is my Son, whom I
love; with him I am well pleased. Listen
to him!"
6When the disciples heard this, they
fell facedown to the ground, terrified.
7But Jesus came and touched them. "Get
up," he said. "Don't be afraid." 8When
they looked up, they saw no one except
Jesus.
9As they were coming down the mountain, Jesus instructed them, "Don't tell
anyone what you have seen, until the Son
of Man has been raised from the dead."
10The disciples asked him, "Why then
do the teachers of the law say that Elijah
must come first?"
11Jesus replied, "To be sure, Elijah
comes and will restore all things. 12But I
tell you, Elijah has already come, and
they did not recognize him, but have done
to him everything they wished. In the
same way the Son of Man is going to suffer at their hands." 13Then the disciples
understood that he was talking to them
about John the Baptist.

The Healing of a Boy With a Demon

14When they came to the crowd, a man
approached Jesus and knelt before him.
15"Lord, have mercy on my son," he said.
"He has seizures and is suffering greatly.
He often falls into the fire or into the water. 16I brought him to your disciples, but
they could not heal him."
17"O unbelieving and perverse generation," Jesus replied, "how long shall I stay
with you? How long shall I put up with
you? Bring the boy here to me." 18Jesus
rebuked the demon, and it came out of
the boy, and he was healed from that moment.
19Then the disciples came to Jesus in
private and asked, "Why couldn't we
drive it out?"
20He replied, "Because you have so little faith. I tell you the truth, if you have
faith as small as a mustard seed, you can
say to this mountain, 'Move from here to
there' and it will move. Nothing will be
impossible for you.[b]"
22When they came together in Galilee,
he said to them, "The Son of Man is going
to be betrayed into the hands of men.
23They will kill him, and on the third day
he will be raised to life." And the disciples were filled with grief.

The Temple Tax

24After Jesus and his disciples arrived
in Capernaum, the collectors of the two-
drachma tax came to Peter and asked,
"Doesn't your teacher pay the temple
tax[c]?"
25"Yes, he does," he replied.
When Peter came into the house, Je-

[a]25 The Greek word means either *life* or *soul*; also in verse 26. [b]20 Some manuscripts *you. 21But this kind does not go out except by prayer and fasting.* [c]24 Greek *the two drachmas*

sus was the first to speak. "What do you think, Simon?" he asked. "From whom do the kings of the earth collect duty and taxes—from their own sons or from others?"

26"From others," Peter answered.

"Then the sons are exempt," Jesus said
to him. 27"But so that we may not offend
them, go to the lake and throw out your line. Take the first fish you catch; open its mouth and you will find a four-drachma coin. Take it and give it to them for my tax and yours."

The Greatest in the Kingdom of Heaven

18 At that time the disciples came to Jesus and asked, "Who is the greatest in the kingdom of heaven?"
2He called a little child and had him
stand among them. 3And he said: "I tell

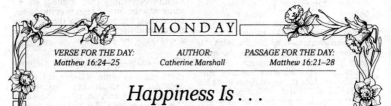

MONDAY

VERSE FOR THE DAY: *Matthew 16:24–25*

AUTHOR: *Catherine Marshall*

PASSAGE FOR THE DAY: *Matthew 16:21–28*

Happiness Is . . .

AS I've been pondering the subject of happiness this morning—an elusive and seemingly unattainable state for so many—I am led to these words of Jesus:

> If anyone would come after me, he must deny himself and take up his cross and follow me. For whoever wants to save his life will lose it, but whoever loses his life for me will find it (Matthew 16:24–25).

I believe the secret of happiness lies imbedded in those words, painful though they appear to be. How else explain radiant people like the young man who sat in our living room and described how his six-year-old boy had died in his arms from leukemia. Today this man finds fulfillment in giving himself totally to helping college students. Or the woman I visited recently whose husband had turned out to be a homosexual and demanded a divorce. Some years later, this woman also lost her eyesight. Yet she is a cheerful, loving person, fully self-supporting.

You might say that such people almost have a right to be unhappy. That they are not, lies in the way they spend themselves for others.

I have observed that when any of us embarks on the pursuit of happiness for ourselves, it eludes us. Often I've asked myself why. It must be because happiness comes to us only as a dividend. When we become absorbed in something demanding and worthwhile above and beyond ourselves, happiness seems to be there as a by-product of the self-giving.

Additional Scripture Readings:
Luke 10:30–37; Acts 2:42–47

Go to page 26 for your next devotional reading.

you the truth, unless you change and become like little children, you will never
enter the kingdom of heaven. 4Therefore,
whoever humbles himself like this child
is the greatest in the kingdom of heaven.
5"And whoever welcomes a little child
like this in my name welcomes me. 6But
if anyone causes one of these little ones
who believe in me to sin, it would be better for him to have a large millstone hung
around his neck and to be drowned in the
depths of the sea.
7"Woe to the world because of the
things that cause people to sin! Such
things must come, but woe to the man
through whom they come! 8If your hand
or your foot causes you to sin, cut it off
and throw it away. It is better for you to
enter life maimed or crippled than to
have two hands or two feet and be thrown
into eternal fire. 9And if your eye causes
you to sin, gouge it out and throw it away.
It is better for you to enter life with one
eye than to have two eyes and be thrown
into the fire of hell.

The Parable of the Lost Sheep

10"See that you do not look down on
one of these little ones. For I tell you that
their angels in heaven always see the face
of my Father in heaven.[a]
12"What do you think? If a man owns a
hundred sheep, and one of them wanders
away, will he not leave the ninety-nine on
the hills and go to look for the one that
wandered off? 13And if he finds it, I tell
you the truth, he is happier about that
one sheep than about the ninety-nine
that did not wander off. 14In the same way
your Father in heaven is not willing that
any of these little ones should be lost.

A Brother Who Sins Against You

15"If your brother sins against you,[b] go
and show him his fault, just between the
two of you. If he listens to you, you have
won your brother over. 16But if he will not
listen, take one or two others along, so
that 'every matter may be established by
the testimony of two or three witnesses.'[c]
17If he refuses to listen to them, tell it to
the church; and if he refuses to listen
even to the church, treat him as you
would a pagan or a tax collector.
18"I tell you the truth, whatever you
bind on earth will be[d] bound in heaven,
and whatever you loose on earth will be[d]
loosed in heaven.
19"Again, I tell you that if two of you on
earth agree about anything you ask for, it
will be done for you by my Father in heav-
en. 20For where two or three come together in my name, there am I with them."

The Parable of the Unmerciful Servant

21Then Peter came to Jesus and asked,
"Lord, how many times shall I forgive my
brother when he sins against me? Up to
seven times?"
22Jesus answered, "I tell you, not seven
times, but seventy-seven times.[e]
23"Therefore, the kingdom of heaven is
like a king who wanted to settle accounts
with his servants. 24As he began the settlement, a man who owed him ten thousand talents[f] was brought to him. 25Since
he was not able to pay, the master ordered that he and his wife and his children and all that he had be sold to repay
the debt.
26"The servant fell on his knees before
him. 'Be patient with me,' he begged,
'and I will pay back everything.' 27The servant's master took pity on him, canceled
the debt and let him go.
28"But when that servant went out, he
found one of his fellow servants who
owed him a hundred denarii.[g] He
grabbed him and began to choke him.
'Pay back what you owe me!' he
demanded.
29"His fellow servant fell to his knees
and begged him, 'Be patient with me, and
I will pay you back.'
30"But he refused. Instead, he went off
and had the man thrown into prison until
he could pay the debt. 31When the other
servants saw what had happened, they
were greatly distressed and went and told
their master everything that had happened.
32"Then the master called the servant
in. 'You wicked servant,' he said, 'I canceled all that debt of yours because you
begged me to. 33Shouldn't you have had
mercy on your fellow servant just as I had
on you?' 34In anger his master turned him
over to the jailers to be tortured, until he
should pay back all he owed.
35"This is how my heavenly Father will

[a] 10 Some manuscripts *heaven. 11The Son of Man came to save what was lost.* [b] 15 Some manuscripts do not have *against you.* [c] 16 Deut. 19:15 [d] 18 Or *have been* [e] 22 Or *seventy times seven* [f] 24 That is, millions of dollars [g] 28 That is, a few dollars

TUESDAY

VERSE FOR THE DAY:	*AUTHOR:*	*PASSAGE FOR THE DAY:*
Matthew 18:19	*Rosalind Rinker*	*Matthew 18:18–20*

The Secret of Power

JESUS teaches us to pray together in dialogue prayer in order to release God's power to bind evil and release good. Dialogue prayer is simply conversational prayer, two people praying back and forth. The audible words are necessary for agreement and for giving love. This prayer-power requires the presence of our risen Lord and our cooperation in audible prayer. This changes us and the situations for which we pray.

We abandon clichés and use short childlike sentences that are honest, specific and personal. In a nutshell: pray to Jesus, our risen Lord, from the child in your heart. This enables the child we each keep silent in our hearts to pray with others and together find love, freedom and joy.

Here are four subjects to guide you: 1. *Jesus is here* (worship). 2. *Thank you, Lord* (for gifts given: spiritual, physical, material, for people, and for the good earth). 3. *Forgive me, Lord* (confession, using "I" not "we"). 4. *Help my sister/brother* (intercession).

Experience has taught us that first worship, and then thanksgiving, open our hearts and mouths. Confession, the third point, is necessary because without it, we do not easily receive the Spirit's guidance for intercession.

Here's an example of confession: "Lord, help us to love others more than we do." But when urged to be personal, honest and specific, the woman's confession becomes: "Lord, help me to love that person I work with."

This then leads into the prayer partner's intercession, when she can pray, "Lord, you promised forgiveness when we confess (1 John 1:9). Now show her what next she should do in her life," or similar comforting words blended with thanksgiving.

In this way we share one another's joys and burdens and become living members of our risen Lord, who teaches us to love one another as he loves us.

Additional Scripture Readings:
Colossians 4:2–4; James 5:13–16

Go to page 35 for your next devotional reading.

treat each of you unless you forgive your
brother from your heart."

Divorce

19 When Jesus had finished saying
these things, he left Galilee and
went into the region of Judea to the other
side of the Jordan. 2Large crowds followed him, and he healed them there.
3Some Pharisees came to him to test
him. They asked, "Is it lawful for a man to
divorce his wife for any and every reason?"
4"Haven't you read," he replied, "that
at the beginning the Creator 'made them
male and female,'[a] 5and said, 'For this
reason a man will leave his father and
mother and be united to his wife, and the
two will become one flesh'[b]? 6So they are
no longer two, but one. Therefore what
God has joined together, let man not separate."
7"Why then," they asked, "did Moses
command that a man give his wife a certificate of divorce and send her away?"
8Jesus replied, "Moses permitted you
to divorce your wives because your hearts
were hard. But it was not this way from
the beginning. 9I tell you that anyone who
divorces his wife, except for marital unfaithfulness, and marries another woman
commits adultery."
10The disciples said to him, "If this is
the situation between a husband and
wife, it is better not to marry."
11Jesus replied, "Not everyone can accept this word, but only those to whom it
has been given. 12For some are eunuchs
because they were born that way; others
were made that way by men; and others
have renounced marriage[c] because of the
kingdom of heaven. The one who can accept this should accept it."

The Little Children and Jesus

13Then little children were brought to
Jesus for him to place his hands on them
and pray for them. But the disciples rebuked those who brought them.
14Jesus said, "Let the little children
come to me, and do not hinder them, for
the kingdom of heaven belongs to such as
these." 15When he had placed his hands
on them, he went on from there.

The Rich Young Man

16Now a man came up to Jesus and
asked, "Teacher, what good thing must I
do to get eternal life?"
17"Why do you ask me about what is
good?" Jesus replied. "There is only One
who is good. If you want to enter life,
obey the commandments."
18"Which ones?" the man inquired.
Jesus replied, " 'Do not murder, do not
commit adultery, do not steal, do not give
false testimony, 19honor your father and
mother,'[d] and 'love your neighbor as
yourself.'[e]"
20"All these I have kept," the young
man said. "What do I still lack?"
21Jesus answered, "If you want to be
perfect, go, sell your possessions and give
to the poor, and you will have treasure in
heaven. Then come, follow me."
22When the young man heard this, he
went away sad, because he had great
wealth.
23Then Jesus said to his disciples, "I
tell you the truth, it is hard for a rich man
to enter the kingdom of heaven. 24Again I
tell you, it is easier for a camel to go
through the eye of a needle than for a rich
man to enter the kingdom of God."
25When the disciples heard this, they
were greatly astonished and asked, "Who
then can be saved?"
26Jesus looked at them and said, "With
man this is impossible, but with God all
things are possible."
27Peter answered him, "We have left everything to follow you! What then will
there be for us?"
28Jesus said to them, "I tell you the
truth, at the renewal of all things, when
the Son of Man sits on his glorious
throne, you who have followed me will
also sit on twelve thrones, judging the
twelve tribes of Israel. 29And everyone
who has left houses or brothers or sisters
or father or mother[f] or children or fields
for my sake will receive a hundred times
as much and will inherit eternal life.
30But many who are first will be last, and
many who are last will be first.

The Parable of the Workers in the Vineyard

20 "For the kingdom of heaven is like
a landowner who went out early in
the morning to hire men to work in his
vineyard. 2He agreed to pay them a denarius for the day and sent them into his
vineyard.

a4 Gen. 1:27 b5 Gen. 2:24 c12 Or *have made themselves eunuchs* d19 Exodus 20:12-16; Deut. 5:16-20 e19 Lev. 19:18 f29 Some manuscripts *mother or wife*

3"About the third hour he went out and
saw others standing in the marketplace
doing nothing. 4He told them, 'You also
go and work in my vineyard, and I will pay
you whatever is right.' 5So they went.
"He went out again about the sixth
hour and the ninth hour and did the same
thing. 6About the eleventh hour he went
out and found still others standing
around. He asked them, 'Why have you
been standing here all day long doing
nothing?'
7" 'Because no one has hired us,' they
answered.
"He said to them, 'You also go and
work in my vineyard.'
8"When evening came, the owner of the
vineyard said to his foreman, 'Call the
workers and pay them their wages, beginning with the last ones hired and going on
to the first.'
9"The workers who were hired about
the eleventh hour came and each received a denarius. 10So when those came
who were hired first, they expected to receive more. But each one of them also
received a denarius. 11When they received
it, they began to grumble against the
landowner. 12'These men who were hired
last worked only one hour,' they said,
'and you have made them equal to us who
have borne the burden of the work and
the heat of the day.'
13"But he answered one of them,
'Friend, I am not being unfair to you.
Didn't you agree to work for a denarius?
14Take your pay and go. I want to give the
man who was hired last the same as I gave
you. 15Don't I have the right to do what I
want with my own money? Or are you envious because I am generous?'
16"So the last will be first, and the first
will be last."

Jesus Again Predicts His Death

17Now as Jesus was going up to Jerusalem, he took the twelve disciples aside
and said to them, 18"We are going up to
Jerusalem, and the Son of Man will be
betrayed to the chief priests and the
teachers of the law. They will condemn
him to death 19and will turn him over to
the Gentiles to be mocked and flogged
and crucified. On the third day he will be
raised to life!"

A Mother's Request

20Then the mother of Zebedee's sons
came to Jesus with her sons and, kneeling down, asked a favor of him.
21"What is it you want?" he asked.
She said, "Grant that one of these two
sons of mine may sit at your right and the
other at your left in your kingdom."
22"You don't know what you are asking," Jesus said to them. "Can you drink
the cup I am going to drink?"
"We can," they answered.
23Jesus said to them, "You will indeed
drink from my cup, but to sit at my right
or left is not for me to grant. These places
belong to those for whom they have been
prepared by my Father."
24When the ten heard about this, they
were indignant with the two brothers.
25Jesus called them together and said,
"You know that the rulers of the Gentiles
lord it over them, and their high officials
exercise authority over them. 26Not so
with you. Instead, whoever wants to become great among you must be your servant, 27and whoever wants to be first must
be your slave— 28just as the Son of Man
did not come to be served, but to serve,
and to give his life as a ransom for many."

Two Blind Men Receive Sight

29As Jesus and his disciples were leaving Jericho, a large crowd followed him.
30Two blind men were sitting by the roadside, and when they heard that Jesus was
going by, they shouted, "Lord, Son of David, have mercy on us!"
31The crowd rebuked them and told
them to be quiet, but they shouted all the
louder, "Lord, Son of David, have mercy
on us!"
32Jesus stopped and called them.
"What do you want me to do for you?" he
asked.
33"Lord," they answered, "we want our
sight."
34Jesus had compassion on them and
touched their eyes. Immediately they received their sight and followed him.

The Triumphal Entry

21 As they approached Jerusalem and
came to Bethphage on the Mount
of Olives, Jesus sent two disciples, 2say-
ing to them, "Go to the village ahead of
you, and at once you will find a donkey
tied there, with her colt by her. Untie
them and bring them to me. 3If anyone
says anything to you, tell him that the
Lord needs them, and he will send them
right away."
4This took place to fulfill what was spoken through the prophet:

5"Say to the Daughter of Zion,
'See, your king comes to you,
gentle and riding on a donkey,
on a colt, the foal of a donkey.' "[a]

6The disciples went and did as Jesus
had instructed them. 7They brought the
donkey and the colt, placed their cloaks
on them, and Jesus sat on them. 8A very
large crowd spread their cloaks on the
road, while others cut branches from the
trees and spread them on the road. 9The
crowds that went ahead of him and those
that followed shouted,

"Hosanna[b] to the Son of David!"

"Blessed is he who comes in the
name of the Lord!"[c]

"Hosanna[b] in the highest!"

10When Jesus entered Jerusalem, the
whole city was stirred and asked, "Who is
this?"
11The crowds answered, "This is Jesus,
the prophet from Nazareth in Galilee."

Jesus at the Temple

12Jesus entered the temple area and
drove out all who were buying and selling
there. He overturned the tables of the
money changers and the benches of those
selling doves. 13"It is written," he said to
them, " 'My house will be called a house
of prayer,'[d] but you are making it a 'den
of robbers.'[e]"
14The blind and the lame came to him
at the temple, and he healed them. 15But
when the chief priests and the teachers of
the law saw the wonderful things he did
and the children shouting in the temple
area, "Hosanna to the Son of David," they
were indignant.
16"Do you hear what these children are
saying?" they asked him.
"Yes," replied Jesus, "have you never
read,

" 'From the lips of children and
infants
you have ordained praise'[f]?"

17And he left them and went out of the
city to Bethany, where he spent the night.

The Fig Tree Withers

18Early in the morning, as he was on his
way back to the city, he was hungry.
19Seeing a fig tree by the road, he went up
to it but found nothing on it except
leaves. Then he said to it, "May you never
bear fruit again!" Immediately the tree
withered.
20When the disciples saw this, they
were amazed. "How did the fig tree wither
so quickly?" they asked.
21Jesus replied, "I tell you the truth, if
you have faith and do not doubt, not only
can you do what was done to the fig tree,
but also you can say to this mountain,
'Go, throw yourself into the sea,' and it
will be done. 22If you believe, you will receive whatever you ask for in prayer."

The Authority of Jesus Questioned

23Jesus entered the temple courts, and,
while he was teaching, the chief priests
and the elders of the people came to him.
"By what authority are you doing these
things?" they asked. "And who gave you
this authority?"
24Jesus replied, "I will also ask you one
question. If you answer me, I will tell you
by what authority I am doing these
things. 25John's baptism—where did it
come from? Was it from heaven, or from
men?"
They discussed it among themselves
and said, "If we say, 'From heaven,' he
will ask, 'Then why didn't you believe
him?' 26But if we say, 'From men'—we
are afraid of the people, for they all hold
that John was a prophet."
27So they answered Jesus, "We don't
know."
Then he said, "Neither will I tell you by
what authority I am doing these things.

The Parable of the Two Sons

28"What do you think? There was a man
who had two sons. He went to the first
and said, 'Son, go and work today in the
vineyard.'
29" 'I will not,' he answered, but later
he changed his mind and went.
30"Then the father went to the other
son and said the same thing. He answered, 'I will, sir,' but he did not go.
31"Which of the two did what his father
wanted?"
"The first," they answered.
Jesus said to them, "I tell you the truth,
the tax collectors and the prostitutes are
entering the kingdom of God ahead of
you. 32For John came to you to show you
the way of righteousness, and you did not

[a]5 Zech. 9:9 [b]9 A Hebrew expression meaning "Save!" which became an exclamation of praise; also in verse 15 [c]9 Psalm 118:26 [d]13 Isaiah 56:7 [e]13 Jer. 7:11 [f]16 Psalm 8:2

believe him, but the tax collectors and
the prostitutes did. And even after you
saw this, you did not repent and believe
him.

The Parable of the Tenants

33"Listen to another parable: There was
a landowner who planted a vineyard. He
put a wall around it, dug a winepress in it
and built a watchtower. Then he rented
the vineyard to some farmers and went
away on a journey. 34When the harvest
time approached, he sent his servants to
the tenants to collect his fruit.

35"The tenants seized his servants; they
beat one, killed another, and stoned a
third. 36Then he sent other servants to
them, more than the first time, and the
tenants treated them the same way.
37Last of all, he sent his son to them.
'They will respect my son,' he said.

38"But when the tenants saw the son,
they said to each other, 'This is the heir.
Come, let's kill him and take his inheritance.' 39So they took him and threw him
out of the vineyard and killed him.

40"Therefore, when the owner of the
vineyard comes, what will he do to those
tenants?"

41"He will bring those wretches to a
wretched end," they replied, "and he will
rent the vineyard to other tenants, who
will give him his share of the crop at harvest time."

42Jesus said to them, "Have you never
read in the Scriptures:

" 'The stone the builders rejected
has become the capstone[a];
the Lord has done this,
and it is marvelous in our eyes'[b]?

43"Therefore I tell you that the kingdom of God will be taken away from you
and given to a people who will produce its
fruit. 44He who falls on this stone will be
broken to pieces, but he on whom it falls
will be crushed."[c]

45When the chief priests and the Pharisees heard Jesus' parables, they knew he
was talking about them. 46They looked
for a way to arrest him, but they were
afraid of the crowd because the people
held that he was a prophet.

The Parable of the Wedding Banquet

22 Jesus spoke to them again in parables, saying: 2"The kingdom of
heaven is like a king who prepared a wedding banquet for his son. 3He sent his servants to those who had been invited to
the banquet to tell them to come, but
they refused to come.

4"Then he sent some more servants and
said, 'Tell those who have been invited
that I have prepared my dinner: My oxen
and fattened cattle have been butchered,
and everything is ready. Come to the wedding banquet.'

5"But they paid no attention and went
off—one to his field, another to his business. 6The rest seized his servants, mistreated them and killed them. 7The king
was enraged. He sent his army and destroyed those murderers and burned their
city.

8"Then he said to his servants, 'The
wedding banquet is ready, but those I invited did not deserve to come. 9Go to the
street corners and invite to the banquet
anyone you find.' 10So the servants went
out into the streets and gathered all the
people they could find, both good and
bad, and the wedding hall was filled with
guests.

11"But when the king came in to see
the guests, he noticed a man there who
was not wearing wedding clothes.
12'Friend,' he asked, 'how did you get in
here without wedding clothes?' The man
was speechless.

13"Then the king told the attendants,
'Tie him hand and foot, and throw him
outside, into the darkness, where there
will be weeping and gnashing of teeth.'

14"For many are invited, but few are
chosen."

Paying Taxes to Caesar

15Then the Pharisees went out and laid
plans to trap him in his words. 16They
sent their disciples to him along with the
Herodians. "Teacher," they said, "we
know you are a man of integrity and that
you teach the way of God in accordance
with the truth. You aren't swayed by men,
because you pay no attention to who they
are. 17Tell us then, what is your opinion?
Is it right to pay taxes to Caesar or not?"

18But Jesus, knowing their evil intent,
said, "You hypocrites, why are you trying
to trap me? 19Show me the coin used for
paying the tax." They brought him a denarius, 20and he asked them, "Whose portrait is this? And whose inscription?"

21"Caesar's," they replied.

Then he said to them, "Give to Caesar

[a]42 Or *cornerstone* [b]42 Psalm 118:22,23 [c]44 Some manuscripts do not have verse 44.

what is Caesar's, and to God what is God's."

22When they heard this, they were amazed. So they left him and went away.

Marriage at the Resurrection

23That same day the Sadducees, who say there is no resurrection, came to him with a question. 24"Teacher," they said, "Moses told us that if a man dies without having children, his brother must marry the widow and have children for him. 25Now there were seven brothers among us. The first one married and died, and since he had no children, he left his wife to his brother. 26The same thing happened to the second and third brother, right on down to the seventh. 27Finally, the woman died. 28Now then, at the resurrection, whose wife will she be of the seven, since all of them were married to her?"

29Jesus replied, "You are in error because you do not know the Scriptures or the power of God. 30At the resurrection people will neither marry nor be given in marriage; they will be like the angels in heaven. 31But about the resurrection of the dead—have you not read what God said to you, 32'I am the God of Abraham, the God of Isaac, and the God of Jacob'[a]? He is not the God of the dead but of the living."

33When the crowds heard this, they were astonished at his teaching.

The Greatest Commandment

34Hearing that Jesus had silenced the Sadducees, the Pharisees got together. 35One of them, an expert in the law, tested him with this question: 36"Teacher, which is the greatest commandment in the Law?"

37Jesus replied: " 'Love the Lord your God with all your heart and with all your soul and with all your mind.'[b] 38This is the first and greatest commandment. 39And the second is like it: 'Love your neighbor as yourself.'[c] 40All the Law and the Prophets hang on these two commandments."

Whose Son Is the Christ?

41While the Pharisees were gathered together, Jesus asked them, 42"What do you think about the Christ[d]? Whose son is he?"

"The son of David," they replied.

43He said to them, "How is it then that David, speaking by the Spirit, calls him 'Lord'? For he says,

44" 'The Lord said to my Lord:
"Sit at my right hand
until I put your enemies
under your feet." '[e]

45If then David calls him 'Lord,' how can he be his son?" 46No one could say a word in reply, and from that day on no one dared to ask him any more questions.

Seven Woes

23 Then Jesus said to the crowds and to his disciples: 2"The teachers of the law and the Pharisees sit in Moses' seat. 3So you must obey them and do everything they tell you. But do not do what they do, for they do not practice what they preach. 4They tie up heavy loads and put them on men's shoulders, but they themselves are not willing to lift a finger to move them.

5"Everything they do is done for men to see: They make their phylacteries[f] wide and the tassels on their garments long; 6they love the place of honor at banquets and the most important seats in the synagogues; 7they love to be greeted in the marketplaces and to have men call them 'Rabbi.'

8"But you are not to be called 'Rabbi,' for you have only one Master and you are all brothers. 9And do not call anyone on earth 'father,' for you have one Father, and he is in heaven. 10Nor are you to be called 'teacher,' for you have one Teacher, the Christ.[d] 11The greatest among you will be your servant. 12For whoever exalts himself will be humbled, and whoever humbles himself will be exalted.

13"Woe to you, teachers of the law and Pharisees, you hypocrites! You shut the kingdom of heaven in men's faces. You yourselves do not enter, nor will you let those enter who are trying to.[g]

15"Woe to you, teachers of the law and Pharisees, you hypocrites! You travel over land and sea to win a single convert, and when he becomes one, you make him twice as much a son of hell as you are.

[a]32 Exodus 3:6 [b]37 Deut. 6:5 [c]39 Lev. 19:18 [d]42,10 Or *Messiah* [e]44 Psalm 110:1
[f]5 That is, boxes containing Scripture verses, worn on forehead and arm [g]13 Some manuscripts *to.* *14Woe to you, teachers of the law and Pharisees, you hypocrites! You devour widows' houses and for a show make lengthy prayers. Therefore you will be punished more severely.*

16“Woe to you, blind guides! You say, ‘If anyone swears by the temple, it means nothing; but if anyone swears by the gold of the temple, he is bound by his oath.’ 17You blind fools! Which is greater: the gold, or the temple that makes the gold sacred? 18You also say, ‘If anyone swears by the altar, it means nothing; but if anyone swears by the gift on it, he is bound by his oath.’ 19You blind men! Which is greater: the gift, or the altar that makes the gift sacred? 20Therefore, he who swears by the altar swears by it and by everything on it. 21And he who swears by the temple swears by it and by the one who dwells in it. 22And he who swears by heaven swears by God’s throne and by the one who sits on it.

23“Woe to you, teachers of the law and Pharisees, you hypocrites! You give a tenth of your spices—mint, dill and cummin. But you have neglected the more important matters of the law—justice, mercy and faithfulness. You should have practiced the latter, without neglecting the former. 24You blind guides! You strain out a gnat but swallow a camel.

25“Woe to you, teachers of the law and Pharisees, you hypocrites! You clean the outside of the cup and dish, but inside they are full of greed and self-indulgence. 26Blind Pharisee! First clean the inside of the cup and dish, and then the outside also will be clean.

27“Woe to you, teachers of the law and Pharisees, you hypocrites! You are like whitewashed tombs, which look beautiful on the outside but on the inside are full of dead men’s bones and everything unclean. 28In the same way, on the outside you appear to people as righteous but on the inside you are full of hypocrisy and wickedness.

29“Woe to you, teachers of the law and Pharisees, you hypocrites! You build tombs for the prophets and decorate the graves of the righteous. 30And you say, ‘If we had lived in the days of our forefathers, we would not have taken part with them in shedding the blood of the prophets.’ 31So you testify against yourselves that you are the descendants of those who murdered the prophets. 32Fill up, then, the measure of the sin of your forefathers!

33“You snakes! You brood of vipers! How will you escape being condemned to hell? 34Therefore I am sending you prophets and wise men and teachers. Some of them you will kill and crucify; others you will flog in your synagogues and pursue from town to town. 35And so upon you will come all the righteous blood that has been shed on earth, from the blood of righteous Abel to the blood of Zechariah son of Berekiah, whom you murdered between the temple and the altar. 36I tell you the truth, all this will come upon this generation.

37“O Jerusalem, Jerusalem, you who kill the prophets and stone those sent to you, how often I have longed to gather your children together, as a hen gathers her chicks under her wings, but you were not willing. 38Look, your house is left to you desolate. 39For I tell you, you will not see me again until you say, ‘Blessed is he who comes in the name of the Lord.’[a]”

Signs of the End of the Age

24 Jesus left the temple and was walking away when his disciples came up to him to call his attention to its buildings. 2“Do you see all these things?” he asked. “I tell you the truth, not one stone here will be left on another; every one will be thrown down.”

3As Jesus was sitting on the Mount of Olives, the disciples came to him privately. “Tell us,” they said, “when will this happen, and what will be the sign of your coming and of the end of the age?”

4Jesus answered: “Watch out that no one deceives you. 5For many will come in my name, claiming, ‘I am the Christ,[b]’ and will deceive many. 6You will hear of wars and rumors of wars, but see to it that you are not alarmed. Such things must happen, but the end is still to come. 7Nation will rise against nation, and kingdom against kingdom. There will be famines and earthquakes in various places. 8All these are the beginning of birth pains.

9“Then you will be handed over to be persecuted and put to death, and you will be hated by all nations because of me. 10At that time many will turn away from the faith and will betray and hate each other, 11and many false prophets will appear and deceive many people. 12Because of the increase of wickedness, the love of most will grow cold, 13but he who stands firm to the end will be saved. 14And this gospel of the kingdom will be preached in the whole world as a testimony to all nations, and then the end will come.

[a]39 Psalm 118:26 [b]5 Or *Messiah*; also in verse 23

15"So when you see standing in the holy
place 'the abomination that causes desolation,'[a] spoken of through the prophet
Daniel—let the reader understand—
16then let those who are in Judea flee to
the mountains. 17Let no one on the roof
of his house go down to take anything out
of the house. 18Let no one in the field go
back to get his cloak. 19How dreadful it
will be in those days for pregnant women
and nursing mothers! 20Pray that your
flight will not take place in winter or on
the Sabbath. 21For then there will be
great distress, unequaled from the beginning of the world until now—and never to
be equaled again. 22If those days had not
been cut short, no one would survive, but
for the sake of the elect those days will be
shortened. 23At that time if anyone says
to you, 'Look, here is the Christ!' or,
'There he is!' do not believe it. 24For false
Christs and false prophets will appear and
perform great signs and miracles to deceive even the elect—if that were possible. 25See, I have told you ahead of time.

26"So if anyone tells you, 'There he is,
out in the desert,' do not go out; or, 'Here
he is, in the inner rooms,' do not believe
it. 27For as lightning that comes from the
east is visible even in the west, so will be
the coming of the Son of Man. 28Wherever
there is a carcass, there the vultures will
gather.

29"Immediately after the distress of
those days

" 'the sun will be darkened,
  and the moon will not give its light;
the stars will fall from the sky,
  and the heavenly bodies will be
    shaken.'[b]

30"At that time the sign of the Son of
Man will appear in the sky, and all the
nations of the earth will mourn. They will
see the Son of Man coming on the clouds
of the sky, with power and great glory.
31And he will send his angels with a loud
trumpet call, and they will gather his
elect from the four winds, from one end of
the heavens to the other.

32"Now learn this lesson from the fig
tree: As soon as its twigs get tender and
its leaves come out, you know that summer is near. 33Even so, when you see all
these things, you know that it[c] is near,
right at the door. 34I tell you the truth,
this generation[d] will certainly not pass
away until all these things have happened. 35Heaven and earth will pass
away, but my words will never pass away.

The Day and Hour Unknown

36"No one knows about that day or
hour, not even the angels in heaven, nor
the Son,[e] but only the Father. 37As it was
in the days of Noah, so it will be at the
coming of the Son of Man. 38For in the
days before the flood, people were eating
and drinking, marrying and giving in marriage, up to the day Noah entered the ark;
39and they knew nothing about what
would happen until the flood came and
took them all away. That is how it will be
at the coming of the Son of Man. 40Two
men will be in the field; one will be taken
and the other left. 41Two women will be
grinding with a hand mill; one will be tak-
en and the other left.

42"Therefore keep watch, because you
do not know on what day your Lord will
come. 43But understand this: If the owner
of the house had known at what time of
night the thief was coming, he would
have kept watch and would not have let
his house be broken into. 44So you also
must be ready, because the Son of Man
will come at an hour when you do not
expect him.

45"Who then is the faithful and wise
servant, whom the master has put in
charge of the servants in his household to
give them their food at the proper time?
46It will be good for that servant whose
master finds him doing so when he returns. 47I tell you the truth, he will put
him in charge of all his possessions. 48But
suppose that servant is wicked and says
to himself, 'My master is staying away a
long time,' 49and he then begins to beat
his fellow servants and to eat and drink
with drunkards. 50The master of that servant will come on a day when he does not
expect him and at an hour he is not aware
of. 51He will cut him to pieces and assign
him a place with the hypocrites, where
there will be weeping and gnashing of
teeth.

The Parable of the Ten Virgins

25 "At that time the kingdom of heav-
en will be like ten virgins who took
their lamps and went out to meet the
bridegroom. 2Five of them were foolish
and five were wise. 3The foolish ones took

[a] *15* Daniel 9:27; 11:31; 12:11 [b] *29* Isaiah 13:10; 34:4 [c] *33* Or *he* [d] *34* Or *race* [e] *36* Some manuscripts do not have *nor the Son.*

their lamps but did not take any oil with
them. 4The wise, however, took oil in jars
along with their lamps. 5The bridegroom
was a long time in coming, and they all
became drowsy and fell asleep.

6"At midnight the cry rang out: 'Here's
the bridegroom! Come out to meet him!'

7"Then all the virgins woke up and
trimmed their lamps. 8The foolish ones
said to the wise, 'Give us some of your oil;
our lamps are going out.'

9" 'No,' they replied, 'there may not be
enough for both us and you. Instead, go to
those who sell oil and buy some for yourselves.'

10"But while they were on their way to
buy the oil, the bridegroom arrived. The
virgins who were ready went in with him
to the wedding banquet. And the door
was shut.

11"Later the others also came. 'Sir! Sir!'
they said. 'Open the door for us!'

12"But he replied, 'I tell you the truth,
I don't know you.'

13"Therefore keep watch, because you
do not know the day or the hour.

The Parable of the Talents

14"Again, it will be like a man going on
a journey, who called his servants and entrusted his property to them. 15To one he
gave five talents[a] of money, to another
two talents, and to another one talent,
each according to his ability. Then he
went on his journey. 16The man who had
received the five talents went at once and
put his money to work and gained five
more. 17So also, the one with the two talents gained two more. 18But the man who
had received the one talent went off, dug
a hole in the ground and hid his master's
money.

19"After a long time the master of those
servants returned and settled accounts
with them. 20The man who had received
the five talents brought the other five.
'Master,' he said, 'you entrusted me with
five talents. See, I have gained five more.'

21"His master replied, 'Well done, good
and faithful servant! You have been faithful with a few things; I will put you in
charge of many things. Come and share
your master's happiness!'

22"The man with the two talents also
came. 'Master,' he said, 'you entrusted
me with two talents; see, I have gained
two more.'

23"His master replied, 'Well done, good
and faithful servant! You have been faithful with a few things; I will put you in
charge of many things. Come and share
your master's happiness!'

24"Then the man who had received the
one talent came. 'Master,' he said, 'I
knew that you are a hard man, harvesting
where you have not sown and gathering
where you have not scattered seed. 25So I
was afraid and went out and hid your talent in the ground. See, here is what belongs to you.'

26"His master replied, 'You wicked,
lazy servant! So you knew that I harvest
where I have not sown and gather where
I have not scattered seed? 27Well then,
you should have put my money on deposit with the bankers, so that when I returned I would have received it back with
interest.

28" 'Take the talent from him and give
it to the one who has the ten talents.
29For everyone who has will be given
more, and he will have an abundance.
Whoever does not have, even what he has
will be taken from him. 30And throw that
worthless servant outside, into the darkness, where there will be weeping and
gnashing of teeth.'

The Sheep and the Goats

31"When the Son of Man comes in his
glory, and all the angels with him, he will
sit on his throne in heavenly glory. 32All
the nations will be gathered before him,
and he will separate the people one from
another as a shepherd separates the
sheep from the goats. 33He will put the
sheep on his right and the goats on his
left.

34"Then the King will say to those on
his right, 'Come, you who are blessed by
my Father; take your inheritance, the
kingdom prepared for you since the creation of the world. 35For I was hungry and
you gave me something to eat, I was
thirsty and you gave me something to
drink, I was a stranger and you invited me
in, 36I needed clothes and you clothed
me, I was sick and you looked after me, I
was in prison and you came to visit me.'

37"Then the righteous will answer him,
'Lord, when did we see you hungry and
feed you, or thirsty and give you something to drink? 38When did we see you a
stranger and invite you in, or needing
clothes and clothe you? 39When did we

[a]15 A talent was worth more than a thousand dollars.

WEDNESDAY

VERSE FOR THE DAY:
Matthew 25:24–25

AUTHOR:
Hope MacDonald

PASSAGE FOR THE DAY:
Matthew 25:14–30

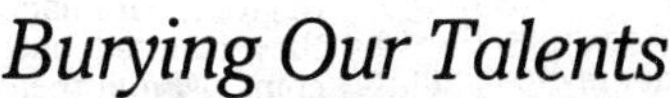

Burying Our Talents

THIS is a parable of God's call for faithfulness in the use of our talents. It is also a parable of warning and promise.

Not long ago, I was sitting in a small group. The discussion centered around evangelism. One of the members breathed a sigh of relief and said, "Well, that's just not my gift." With that statement he buried his God-given talent to share the love of Jesus with others. How many of us have buried our talents in search of that "special" gift?

Today we often expect our talents to come completely developed, neatly labeled, and tied with a shining red ribbon. If they don't, then we proclaim, they aren't "my gifts." The result is that we limit God—he is put in a box—and we restrict our potential for service. I wonder how many neglected opportunities slip by because of this kind of thinking? Gordon Fee refers to these self-imposed limitations as "hardening of the categories"!

We forget in this day of instant satisfaction that none of our talents come full-grown. It's only as we cultivate them that they begin to mature and multiply. The more we use them, the more others are blessed through them. Soon we discover that God has given us a multitude of gifts and equipped us with endless resources.

God is calling each of us to a life of adventure. Remember, an adventure is not an adventure unless there is some risk involved. Are we willing to take risks in our walk with Jesus? Are we willing to look a little foolish from time to time as we seek to develop new talents? If we are, God will continue to bring us new opportunities of service.

The warning of this parable is this: God holds us responsible for our lives and what we do with them.

The joyful reward is this: One day we will stand before our great God and hear him say, "Well done, good and faithful servant!" (Matthew 25:21).

Additional Scripture Readings:
Exodus 4:10–12; Ephesians 3:14–21

Go to page 37 for your next devotional reading.

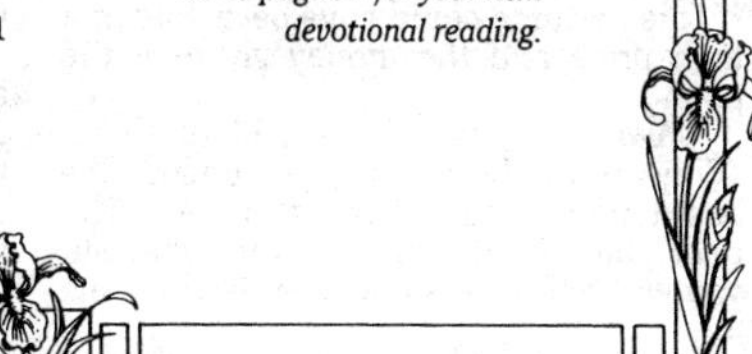

see you sick or in prison and go to visit
you?'

40"The King will reply, 'I tell you the
truth, whatever you did for one of the
least of these brothers of mine, you did
for me.'

41"Then he will say to those on his left,
'Depart from me, you who are cursed,
into the eternal fire prepared for the devil
and his angels. 42For I was hungry and
you gave me nothing to eat, I was thirsty
and you gave me nothing to drink, 43I was
a stranger and you did not invite me in, I
needed clothes and you did not clothe
me, I was sick and in prison and you did
not look after me.'

44"They also will answer, 'Lord, when
did we see you hungry or thirsty or a
stranger or needing clothes or sick or in
prison, and did not help you?'

45"He will reply, 'I tell you the truth,
whatever you did not do for one of the
least of these, you did not do for me.'

46"Then they will go away to eternal
punishment, but the righteous to eternal
life."

The Plot Against Jesus

26 When Jesus had finished saying all
these things, he said to his disciples, 2"As you know, the Passover is two
days away—and the Son of Man will be
handed over to be crucified."

3Then the chief priests and the elders
of the people assembled in the palace of
the high priest, whose name was Caiaphas, 4and they plotted to arrest Jesus in
some sly way and kill him. 5"But not during the Feast," they said, "or there may be
a riot among the people."

Jesus Anointed at Bethany

6While Jesus was in Bethany in the
home of a man known as Simon the Leper, 7a woman came to him with an alabaster jar of very expensive perfume, which
she poured on his head as he was reclining at the table.

8When the disciples saw this, they were
indignant. "Why this waste?" they asked.
9"This perfume could have been sold at a
high price and the money given to the
poor."

10Aware of this, Jesus said to them,
"Why are you bothering this woman? She
has done a beautiful thing to me. 11The
poor you will always have with you, but
you will not always have me. 12When she
poured this perfume on my body, she did
it to prepare me for burial. 13I tell you the
truth, wherever this gospel is preached
throughout the world, what she has done
will also be told, in memory of her."

Judas Agrees to Betray Jesus

14Then one of the Twelve—the one
called Judas Iscariot—went to the chief
priests 15and asked, "What are you willing
to give me if I hand him over to you?" So
they counted out for him thirty silver
coins. 16From then on Judas watched for
an opportunity to hand him over.

The Lord's Supper

17On the first day of the Feast of Unleavened Bread, the disciples came to
Jesus and asked, "Where do you want us
to make preparations for you to eat the
Passover?"

18He replied, "Go into the city to a certain man and tell him, 'The Teacher says:
My appointed time is near. I am going to
celebrate the Passover with my disciples
at your house.' " 19So the disciples did as
Jesus had directed them and prepared
the Passover.

20When evening came, Jesus was reclining at the table with the Twelve.
21And while they were eating, he said, "I
tell you the truth, one of you will betray
me."

22They were very sad and began to say
to him one after the other, "Surely not I,
Lord?"

23Jesus replied, "The one who has
dipped his hand into the bowl with me
will betray me. 24The Son of Man will go
just as it is written about him. But woe to
that man who betrays the Son of Man! It
would be better for him if he had not been
born."

25Then Judas, the one who would betray him, said, "Surely not I, Rabbi?"
Jesus answered, "Yes, it is you."[a]

26While they were eating, Jesus took
bread, gave thanks and broke it, and gave
it to his disciples, saying, "Take and eat;
this is my body."

27Then he took the cup, gave thanks
and offered it to them, saying, "Drink
from it, all of you. 28This is my blood of
the[b] covenant, which is poured out for
many for the forgiveness of sins. 29I tell
you, I will not drink of this fruit of the
vine from now on until that day when I

[a]25 Or *"You yourself have said it"* [b]28 Some manuscripts *the new*

drink it anew with you in my Father's kingdom."

30When they had sung a hymn, they went out to the Mount of Olives.

Jesus Predicts Peter's Denial

31Then Jesus told them, "This very night you will all fall away on account of me, for it is written:

" 'I will strike the shepherd,
and the sheep of the flock will be scattered.'[a]

32But after I have risen, I will go ahead of you into Galilee."

33Peter replied, "Even if all fall away on account of you, I never will."

34"I tell you the truth," Jesus answered,

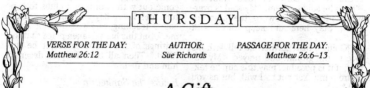

[a]31 Zech. 13:7

THURSDAY

VERSE FOR THE DAY: *Matthew 26:12*

AUTHOR: *Sue Richards*

PASSAGE FOR THE DAY: *Matthew 26:6–13*

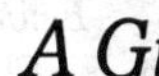

A Gift

SHE came bearing a gift of love, probably without invitation, and certainly without forewarning. We are told that while Christ was reclining at table at the home of Simon the Leper, she came and poured a very expensive perfume on his head. The disciples, Christ's specially chosen men, became indignant when they saw her anoint the Lord in this manner. " 'Why this waste?' they asked. 'This perfume could have been sold at a high price and the money given to the poor.' " But Christ said to them, "Why are you bothering this woman? She has done a beautiful thing to me . . . . When she poured this perfume on my body, she did it to prepare me for burial" (Matthew 26:8–9).

She was obviously a very sensitive woman, wanting to give something special to the Lord before he was taken away. She had a great deal of spiritual discernment as well. She had heard of Christ's coming execution, and believed it. Even so, her gift and her basis for giving it were not understood even by these special men, the leaders of the early church. But Jesus understood. He appreciated her outpouring of love and made a promise like no other in Scripture. Christ said, "Wherever this gospel is preached throughout the world, what she has done will also be told, in memory of her" (Matthew 26:13).

Just as this woman's gift was misunderstood by the leaders of the early church, many churches today criticize women for trying to share their special gifts. It's comforting to know that our gifts are acceptable, accepted and appreciated by the Lord when given in love. He understands our motivations; he accepts what we bring.

Father, help us to give cheerfully and to accept graciously.

Additional Scripture Readings:
Luke 21:1–4; Romans 14:6–8

Go to page 39 for your next devotional reading.

"this very night, before the rooster crows, you will disown me three times."

35But Peter declared, "Even if I have to die with you, I will never disown you." And all the other disciples said the same.

Gethsemane

36Then Jesus went with his disciples to a place called Gethsemane, and he said to them, "Sit here while I go over there and pray." 37He took Peter and the two sons of Zebedee along with him, and he began to be sorrowful and troubled. 38Then he said to them, "My soul is overwhelmed with sorrow to the point of death. Stay here and keep watch with me."

39Going a little farther, he fell with his face to the ground and prayed, "My Father, if it is possible, may this cup be taken from me. Yet not as I will, but as you will."

40Then he returned to his disciples and found them sleeping. "Could you men not keep watch with me for one hour?" he asked Peter. 41"Watch and pray so that you will not fall into temptation. The spirit is willing, but the body is weak."

42He went away a second time and prayed, "My Father, if it is not possible for this cup to be taken away unless I drink it, may your will be done."

43When he came back, he again found them sleeping, because their eyes were heavy. 44So he left them and went away once more and prayed the third time, saying the same thing.

45Then he returned to the disciples and said to them, "Are you still sleeping and resting? Look, the hour is near, and the Son of Man is betrayed into the hands of sinners. 46Rise, let us go! Here comes my betrayer!"

Jesus Arrested

47While he was still speaking, Judas, one of the Twelve, arrived. With him was a large crowd armed with swords and clubs, sent from the chief priests and the elders of the people. 48Now the betrayer had arranged a signal with them: "The one I kiss is the man; arrest him." 49Going at once to Jesus, Judas said, "Greetings, Rabbi!" and kissed him.

50Jesus replied, "Friend, do what you came for."[a]

Then the men stepped forward, seized Jesus and arrested him. 51With that, one of Jesus' companions reached for his sword, drew it out and struck the servant of the high priest, cutting off his ear.

52"Put your sword back in its place," Jesus said to him, "for all who draw the sword will die by the sword. 53Do you think I cannot call on my Father, and he will at once put at my disposal more than twelve legions of angels? 54But how then would the Scriptures be fulfilled that say it must happen in this way?"

55At that time Jesus said to the crowd, "Am I leading a rebellion, that you have come out with swords and clubs to capture me? Every day I sat in the temple courts teaching, and you did not arrest me. 56But this has all taken place that the writings of the prophets might be fulfilled." Then all the disciples deserted him and fled.

Before the Sanhedrin

57Those who had arrested Jesus took him to Caiaphas, the high priest, where the teachers of the law and the elders had assembled. 58But Peter followed him at a distance, right up to the courtyard of the high priest. He entered and sat down with the guards to see the outcome.

59The chief priests and the whole Sanhedrin were looking for false evidence against Jesus so that they could put him to death. 60But they did not find any, though many false witnesses came forward.

Finally two came forward 61and declared, "This fellow said, 'I am able to destroy the temple of God and rebuild it in three days.' "

62Then the high priest stood up and said to Jesus, "Are you not going to answer? What is this testimony that these men are bringing against you?" 63But Jesus remained silent.

The high priest said to him, "I charge you under oath by the living God: Tell us if you are the Christ,[b] the Son of God."

64"Yes, it is as you say," Jesus replied. "But I say to all of you: In the future you will see the Son of Man sitting at the right hand of the Mighty One and coming on the clouds of heaven."

65Then the high priest tore his clothes and said, "He has spoken blasphemy! Why do we need any more witnesses? Look, now you have heard the blasphemy. 66What do you think?"

"He is worthy of death," they answered.

[a]*50* Or *"Friend, why have you come?"* [b]*63* Or *Messiah*; also in verse 68

[67]Then they spit in his face and struck him with their fists. Others slapped him [68]and said, "Prophesy to us, Christ. Who hit you?"

Peter Disowns Jesus

[69]Now Peter was sitting out in the courtyard, and a servant girl came to him. "You also were with Jesus of Galilee," she said.

[70]But he denied it before them all. "I don't know what you're talking about," he said.

[71]Then he went out to the gateway, where another girl saw him and said to the people there, "This fellow was with Jesus of Nazareth."

[72]He denied it again, with an oath: "I don't know the man!"

[73]After a little while, those standing there went up to Peter and said, "Surely

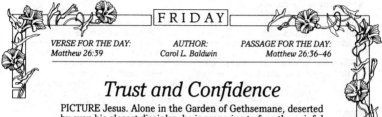

FRIDAY

VERSE FOR THE DAY: *Matthew 26:39*

AUTHOR: *Carol L. Baldwin*

PASSAGE FOR THE DAY: *Matthew 26:36–46*

Trust and Confidence

PICTURE Jesus. Alone in the Garden of Gethsemane, deserted by even his closest disciples, he is preparing to face the painful death of crucifixion. Not only will he die an innocent man; he will experience a bitter separation from his heavenly Father and the agony of bearing the punishment for the sins of his people.

How does our Lord respond at this moment of tremendous trial and testing?

His simple yet powerful response pricks our consciences as he speaks the ultimate prayer of trust and confidence: "My Father, if it is possible, may this cup be taken from me. Yet not as I will, but as you will" (Matthew 26:39). Can there be a more graphic demonstration of trust in God? Can there ever be a better example of submission to our heavenly Father's will?

Jesus' actions and attitude provide a model to all believers of how we are to face the difficult tasks, and the emotional, spiritual or physical struggles that God ordains for us.

Scripture reminds us that we are not to be surprised when suffering and trials come into our lives (1 Peter 1:6–7; 4:12–13); rather we are to rejoice that God is refining in us the precious jewel of faith, which is of far greater worth than gold.

Every problem with our children, each disagreement with our husbands, each stressful assignment at our jobs provides an opportunity to call on God to strengthen our faith, to develop our perseverance, to build our character and to ground our hope deeper in him (Romans 5:3–4).

May God grant us an increase in our trust in him, even as Jesus displayed. May he build in us precious Christian character, refined in the furnace of his discipline and love.

Additional Scripture Readings:
Daniel 3:13–19; James 1:2–4

Go to page 41 for your next devotional reading.

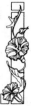

you are one of them, for your accent gives you away."

74 Then he began to call down curses on himself and he swore to them, "I don't know the man!"

Immediately a rooster crowed. 75 Then Peter remembered the word Jesus had spoken: "Before the rooster crows, you will disown me three times." And he went outside and wept bitterly.

Judas Hangs Himself

27 Early in the morning, all the chief priests and the elders of the people came to the decision to put Jesus to death. 2 They bound him, led him away and handed him over to Pilate, the governor.

3 When Judas, who had betrayed him, saw that Jesus was condemned, he was seized with remorse and returned the thirty silver coins to the chief priests and the elders. 4 "I have sinned," he said, "for I have betrayed innocent blood."

"What is that to us?" they replied. "That's your responsibility."

5 So Judas threw the money into the temple and left. Then he went away and hanged himself.

6 The chief priests picked up the coins and said, "It is against the law to put this into the treasury, since it is blood money." 7 So they decided to use the money to buy the potter's field as a burial place for foreigners. 8 That is why it has been called the Field of Blood to this day. 9 Then what was spoken by Jeremiah the prophet was fulfilled: "They took the thirty silver coins, the price set on him by the people of Israel, 10 and they used them to buy the potter's field, as the Lord commanded me."[a]

Jesus Before Pilate

11 Meanwhile Jesus stood before the governor, and the governor asked him, "Are you the king of the Jews?"

"Yes, it is as you say," Jesus replied.

12 When he was accused by the chief priests and the elders, he gave no answer. 13 Then Pilate asked him, "Don't you hear the testimony they are bringing against you?" 14 But Jesus made no reply, not even to a single charge—to the great amazement of the governor.

15 Now it was the governor's custom at the Feast to release a prisoner chosen by the crowd. 16 At that time they had a notorious prisoner, called Barabbas. 17 So when the crowd had gathered, Pilate asked them, "Which one do you want me to release to you: Barabbas, or Jesus who is called Christ?" 18 For he knew it was out of envy that they had handed Jesus over to him.

19 While Pilate was sitting on the judge's seat, his wife sent him this message: "Don't have anything to do with that innocent man, for I have suffered a great deal today in a dream because of him."

20 But the chief priests and the elders persuaded the crowd to ask for Barabbas and to have Jesus executed.

21 "Which of the two do you want me to release to you?" asked the governor.

"Barabbas," they answered.

22 "What shall I do, then, with Jesus who is called Christ?" Pilate asked.

They all answered, "Crucify him!"

23 "Why? What crime has he committed?" asked Pilate.

But they shouted all the louder, "Crucify him!"

24 When Pilate saw that he was getting nowhere, but that instead an uproar was starting, he took water and washed his hands in front of the crowd. "I am innocent of this man's blood," he said. "It is your responsibility!"

25 All the people answered, "Let his blood be on us and on our children!"

26 Then he released Barabbas to them. But he had Jesus flogged, and handed him over to be crucified.

The Soldiers Mock Jesus

27 Then the governor's soldiers took Jesus into the Praetorium and gathered the whole company of soldiers around him. 28 They stripped him and put a scarlet robe on him, 29 and then twisted together a crown of thorns and set it on his head. They put a staff in his right hand and knelt in front of him and mocked him. "Hail, king of the Jews!" they said. 30 They spit on him, and took the staff and struck him on the head again and again. 31 After they had mocked him, they took off the robe and put his own clothes on him. Then they led him away to crucify him.

The Crucifixion

32 As they were going out, they met a man from Cyrene, named Simon, and

[a] *10* See Zech. 11:12,13; Jer. 19:1-13; 32:6-9.

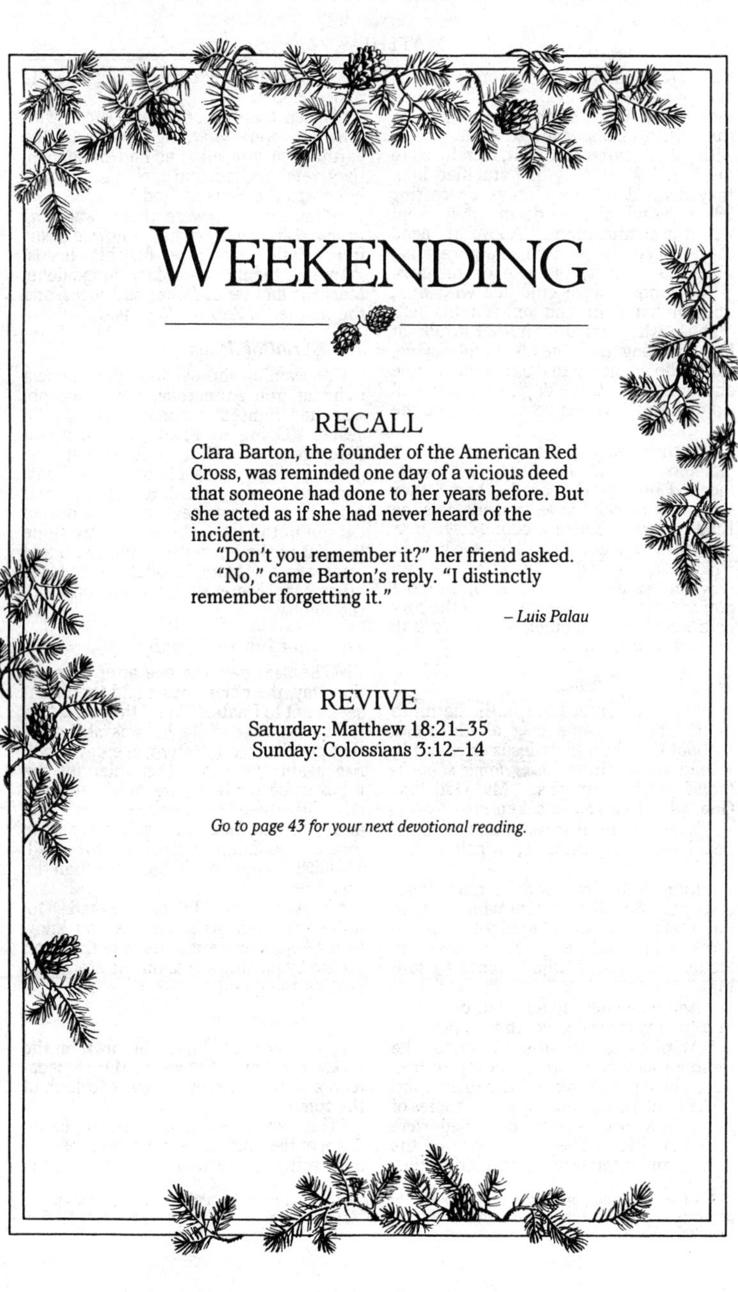

WEEKENDING

RECALL

Clara Barton, the founder of the American Red Cross, was reminded one day of a vicious deed that someone had done to her years before. But she acted as if she had never heard of the incident.

"Don't you remember it?" her friend asked.

"No," came Barton's reply. "I distinctly remember forgetting it."

– Luis Palau

REVIVE

Saturday: Matthew 18:21–35
Sunday: Colossians 3:12–14

Go to page 43 for your next devotional reading.

they forced him to carry the cross. 33They came to a place called Golgotha (which means The Place of the Skull). 34There they offered Jesus wine to drink, mixed with gall; but after tasting it, he refused to drink it. 35When they had crucified him, they divided up his clothes by casting lots.[a] 36And sitting down, they kept watch over him there. 37Above his head they placed the written charge against him: THIS IS JESUS, THE KING OF THE JEWS. 38Two robbers were crucified with him, one on his right and one on his left. 39Those who passed by hurled insults at him, shaking their heads 40and saying, "You who are going to destroy the temple and build it in three days, save yourself! Come down from the cross, if you are the Son of God!"

41In the same way the chief priests, the teachers of the law and the elders mocked him. 42"He saved others," they said, "but he can't save himself! He's the King of Israel! Let him come down now from the cross, and we will believe in him. 43He trusts in God. Let God rescue him now if he wants him, for he said, 'I am the Son of God.' " 44In the same way the robbers who were crucified with him also heaped insults on him.

The Death of Jesus

45From the sixth hour until the ninth hour darkness came over all the land. 46About the ninth hour Jesus cried out in a loud voice, *"Eloi, Eloi,*[b] *lama sabachthani?"*—which means, "My God, my God, why have you forsaken me?"[c]

47When some of those standing there heard this, they said, "He's calling Elijah."

48Immediately one of them ran and got a sponge. He filled it with wine vinegar, put it on a stick, and offered it to Jesus to drink. 49The rest said, "Now leave him alone. Let's see if Elijah comes to save him."

50And when Jesus had cried out again in a loud voice, he gave up his spirit.

51At that moment the curtain of the temple was torn in two from top to bottom. The earth shook and the rocks split. 52The tombs broke open and the bodies of many holy people who had died were raised to life. 53They came out of the tombs, and after Jesus' resurrection they went into the holy city and appeared to many people.

54When the centurion and those with him who were guarding Jesus saw the earthquake and all that had happened, they were terrified, and exclaimed, "Surely he was the Son[d] of God!"

55Many women were there, watching from a distance. They had followed Jesus from Galilee to care for his needs. 56Among them were Mary Magdalene, Mary the mother of James and Joses, and the mother of Zebedee's sons.

The Burial of Jesus

57As evening approached, there came a rich man from Arimathea, named Joseph, who had himself become a disciple of Jesus. 58Going to Pilate, he asked for Jesus' body, and Pilate ordered that it be given to him. 59Joseph took the body, wrapped it in a clean linen cloth, 60and placed it in his own new tomb that he had cut out of the rock. He rolled a big stone in front of the entrance to the tomb and went away. 61Mary Magdalene and the other Mary were sitting there opposite the tomb.

The Guard at the Tomb

62The next day, the one after Preparation Day, the chief priests and the Pharisees went to Pilate. 63"Sir," they said, "we remember that while he was still alive that deceiver said, 'After three days I will rise again.' 64So give the order for the tomb to be made secure until the third day. Otherwise, his disciples may come and steal the body and tell the people that he has been raised from the dead. This last deception will be worse than the first."

65"Take a guard," Pilate answered. "Go, make the tomb as secure as you know how." 66So they went and made the tomb secure by putting a seal on the stone and posting the guard.

The Resurrection

28 After the Sabbath, at dawn on the first day of the week, Mary Magdalene and the other Mary went to look at the tomb.

2There was a violent earthquake, for an angel of the Lord came down from heaven and, going to the tomb, rolled back the

[a]35 A few late manuscripts *lots that the word spoken by the prophet might be fulfilled: "They divided my garments among themselves and cast lots for my clothing"* (Psalm 22:18) [b]46 Some manuscripts *Eli, Eli* [c]46 Psalm 22:1 [d]54 Or *a son*

stone and sat on it. 3His appearance was
like lightning, and his clothes were white
as snow. 4The guards were so afraid of
him that they shook and became like
dead men.
5The angel said to the women, "Do not
be afraid, for I know that you are looking
for Jesus, who was crucified. 6He is not
here; he has risen, just as he said. Come
and see the place where he lay. 7Then go
quickly and tell his disciples: 'He has risen from the dead and is going ahead of
you into Galilee. There you will see him.'
Now I have told you."
8So the women hurried away from the
tomb, afraid yet filled with joy, and ran to
tell his disciples. 9Suddenly Jesus met
them. "Greetings," he said. They came to
him, clasped his feet and worshiped him.
10Then Jesus said to them, "Do not be

MONDAY

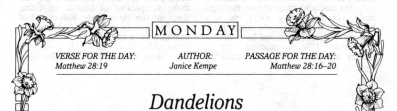

VERSE FOR THE DAY: Matthew 28:19 — *AUTHOR:* Janice Kempe — *PASSAGE FOR THE DAY:* Matthew 28:16–20

Dandelions

DANDELIONS! No matter how carefully I try to pull one up, I never get the whole thing. The root stays deep in the ground, threatening to grow up and blossom again.

But despite their bad reputation, dandelions are pretty little flowers with their yellow strands all tucked neatly into the center. And truly they are the most beautiful of all flowers when presented clutched in a child's dirty little hand. No one gets yelled at for picking them. Perhaps they grow only to be used and enjoyed by children.

Dandelions are ignored or attacked, never nurtured or cared for, and yet they always bloom profusely. They demand no pampering or special attention to yield their bright blossoms; they pop up in fields, in lawns, and between cracks in the sidewalk, even in the best neighborhoods. Can you imagine trying to grow them in a garden? They'd sneak through the boundaries and pop their sunny yellow faces up in the surrounding lawn. They would never stay put!

Christians should be more like dandelions. Our sunny yellow faces should be a reminder that simple faith has deep roots that are impossible to dislodge. Our vast number would show the world that even though we are not fancy or pampered we are evident everywhere, even in the best neighborhoods.

We should be as easily accessible as a dandelion. Jesus was. We need to get out of our gardens and jump across the boundaries that keep us where people expect to find us. We need to show our sunny yellow faces in all the spots that need a little brightening up—the crack in the sidewalk or the lawn of a country club.

Additional Scripture Readings:
Acts 8:1–4; Colossians 2:6–7

Go to page 47 for your next devotional reading.

afraid. Go and tell my brothers to go to Galilee; there they will see me."

The Guards' Report

11While the women were on their way, some of the guards went into the city and reported to the chief priests everything that had happened. 12When the chief priests had met with the elders and devised a plan, they gave the soldiers a large sum of money, 13telling them, "You are to say, 'His disciples came during the night and stole him away while we were asleep.' 14If this report gets to the governor, we will satisfy him and keep you out of trouble." 15So the soldiers took the money and did as they were instructed. And this story has been widely circulated among the Jews to this very day.

The Great Commission

16Then the eleven disciples went to Galilee, to the mountain where Jesus had told them to go. 17When they saw him, they worshiped him; but some doubted. 18Then Jesus came to them and said, "All authority in heaven and on earth has been given to me. 19Therefore go and make disciples of all nations, baptizing them in[a] the name of the Father and of the Son and of the Holy Spirit, 20and teaching them to obey everything I have commanded you. And surely I am with you always, to the very end of the age."

[a]*19* Or *into*; see Acts 8:16; 19:5; Romans 6:3; 1 Cor. 1:13; 10:2 and Gal. 3:27.

MARK writes this gospel to tell the basic story about Jesus. He recounts miracles, parables and other sayings of Jesus. Almost half of his book deals with the final week of Jesus' life, ending with his death on the cross and his resurrection from the dead. As you read this book, notice how full of life and emotion Jesus is and how caring he is. Note too why he came into the world—to give his life for you (Mark 10:45). God wants you to accept his Son Jesus as your own personal Savior and Lord.

MARK

John the Baptist Prepares the Way

1 The beginning of the gospel about Jesus Christ, the Son of God.[a]

2It is written in Isaiah the prophet:

"I will send my messenger ahead of
you,
who will prepare your way"[b]—
3"a voice of one calling in the desert,
'Prepare the way for the Lord,
make straight paths for him.' "[c]

4And so John came, baptizing in the
desert region and preaching a baptism of
repentance for the forgiveness of sins.
5The whole Judean countryside and all
the people of Jerusalem went out to him.
Confessing their sins, they were baptized
by him in the Jordan River. 6John wore
clothing made of camel's hair, with a
leather belt around his waist, and he ate
locusts and wild honey. 7And this was his
message: "After me will come one more
powerful than I, the thongs of whose sandals I am not worthy to stoop down and

[a]*1* Some manuscripts do not have *the Son of God.* [b]*2* Mal. 3:1 [c]*3* Isaiah 40:3

untie. 8I baptize you with[a] water, but he will baptize you with the Holy Spirit."

The Baptism and Temptation of Jesus

9At that time Jesus came from Nazareth in Galilee and was baptized by John in the Jordan. 10As Jesus was coming up out of the water, he saw heaven being torn open and the Spirit descending on him like a dove. 11And a voice came from heaven: "You are my Son, whom I love; with you I am well pleased."

12At once the Spirit sent him out into the desert, 13and he was in the desert forty days, being tempted by Satan. He was with the wild animals, and angels attended him.

The Calling of the First Disciples

14After John was put in prison, Jesus went into Galilee, proclaiming the good news of God. 15"The time has come," he said. "The kingdom of God is near. Repent and believe the good news!"

16As Jesus walked beside the Sea of Galilee, he saw Simon and his brother Andrew casting a net into the lake, for they were fishermen. 17"Come, follow me," Jesus said, "and I will make you fishers of men." 18At once they left their nets and followed him.

19When he had gone a little farther, he saw James son of Zebedee and his brother John in a boat, preparing their nets. 20Without delay he called them, and they left their father Zebedee in the boat with the hired men and followed him.

Jesus Drives Out an Evil Spirit

21They went to Capernaum, and when the Sabbath came, Jesus went into the synagogue and began to teach. 22The people were amazed at his teaching, because he taught them as one who had authority, not as the teachers of the law. 23Just then a man in their synagogue who was possessed by an evil[b] spirit cried out, 24"What do you want with us, Jesus of Nazareth? Have you come to destroy us? I know who you are—the Holy One of God!"

25"Be quiet!" said Jesus sternly. "Come out of him!" 26The evil spirit shook the man violently and came out of him with a shriek.

27The people were all so amazed that they asked each other, "What is this? A new teaching—and with authority! He even gives orders to evil spirits and they obey him." 28News about him spread quickly over the whole region of Galilee.

Jesus Heals Many

29As soon as they left the synagogue, they went with James and John to the home of Simon and Andrew. 30Simon's mother-in-law was in bed with a fever, and they told Jesus about her. 31So he went to her, took her hand and helped her up. The fever left her and she began to wait on them.

32That evening after sunset the people brought to Jesus all the sick and demon-possessed. 33The whole town gathered at the door, 34and Jesus healed many who had various diseases. He also drove out many demons, but he would not let the demons speak because they knew who he was.

Jesus Prays in a Solitary Place

35Very early in the morning, while it was still dark, Jesus got up, left the house and went off to a solitary place, where he prayed. 36Simon and his companions went to look for him, 37and when they found him, they exclaimed: "Everyone is looking for you!"

38Jesus replied, "Let us go somewhere else—to the nearby villages—so I can preach there also. That is why I have come." 39So he traveled throughout Galilee, preaching in their synagogues and driving out demons.

A Man With Leprosy

40A man with leprosy[c] came to him and begged him on his knees, "If you are willing, you can make me clean."

41Filled with compassion, Jesus reached out his hand and touched the man. "I am willing," he said. "Be clean!" 42Immediately the leprosy left him and he was cured.

43Jesus sent him away at once with a strong warning: 44"See that you don't tell this to anyone. But go, show yourself to the priest and offer the sacrifices that Moses commanded for your cleansing, as a testimony to them." 45Instead he went out and began to talk freely, spreading the news. As a result, Jesus could no

[a] *8* Or *in* [b] *23* Greek *unclean*; also in verses 26 and 27 [c] *40* The Greek word was used for various diseases affecting the skin—not necessarily leprosy.

longer enter a town openly but stayed outside in lonely places. Yet the people still came to him from everywhere.

Jesus Heals a Paralytic

2 A few days later, when Jesus again
entered Capernaum, the people
heard that he had come home. 2So many
gathered that there was no room left, not
even outside the door, and he preached
the word to them. 3Some men came,
bringing to him a paralytic, carried by
four of them. 4Since they could not get
him to Jesus because of the crowd, they
made an opening in the roof above Jesus
and, after digging through it, lowered the
mat the paralyzed man was lying on.
5When Jesus saw their faith, he said
to the paralytic, "Son, your sins are forgiven."
6Now some teachers of the law were
sitting there, thinking to themselves,
7"Why does this fellow talk like that? He's
blaspheming! Who can forgive sins but
God alone?"
8Immediately Jesus knew in his spirit
that this was what they were thinking in
their hearts, and he said to them, "Why
are you thinking these things? 9Which is
easier: to say to the paralytic, 'Your sins
are forgiven,' or to say, 'Get up, take your
mat and walk'? 10But that you may know
that the Son of Man has authority on
earth to forgive sins . . . ." He said to the

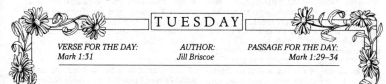

TUESDAY

VERSE FOR THE DAY:
Mark 1:31

AUTHOR:
Jill Briscoe

PASSAGE FOR THE DAY:
Mark 1:29–34

A Must, Not a Maybe

WHEN you have a heart for God you have a heart for ministry. The two go hand in hand. When Jesus captured a life, healed a sick body or soul or mind, the recipient of those blessings invariably began to minister. Only on two occasions did Jesus have to tell them to do so. When Jairus's daughter was brought back from the dead, Jesus told her parents to "give her something to eat" (Mark 5:43), and when the Lord appeared first to Mary Magdalene after his resurrection, he told her to go tell the disciples that she had seen the Lord (John 20:17–18).

When you meet the Master, ministry naturally follows. Jesus forgave a sinful woman "her many sins," and she began to love him much (Luke 7:47). Having been forgiven much you begin to love much, and ministry is the natural outcome.

Martha and Mary, greatly loved by Jesus, loved him back by serving him, each in her own way. The mother of the disciple James, along with others, served the Lord by preparing his body for burial (Luke 24:10), while Joanna supported Jesus out of her own means (Luke 8:3). Even the woman at the well, having met Jesus, began at once to share her discovery with the people in her town (John 4:28–29).

You do not need to twist arms once you have had a personal encounter with the Christ of Galilee. Ministry is not then a maybe—it's a must.

Additional Scripture Readings:
Mark 2:14–15; John 1:43–46

Go to page 52 for your next devotional reading.

paralytic, 11"I tell you, get up, take your mat and go home." 12He got up, took his mat and walked out in full view of them all. This amazed everyone and they praised God, saying, "We have never seen anything like this!"

The Calling of Levi

13Once again Jesus went out beside the lake. A large crowd came to him, and he began to teach them. 14As he walked along, he saw Levi son of Alphaeus sitting at the tax collector's booth. "Follow me," Jesus told him, and Levi got up and followed him.

15While Jesus was having dinner at Levi's house, many tax collectors and "sinners" were eating with him and his disciples, for there were many who followed him. 16When the teachers of the law who were Pharisees saw him eating with the "sinners" and tax collectors, they asked his disciples: "Why does he eat with tax collectors and 'sinners'?"

17On hearing this, Jesus said to them, "It is not the healthy who need a doctor, but the sick. I have not come to call the righteous, but sinners."

Jesus Questioned About Fasting

18Now John's disciples and the Pharisees were fasting. Some people came and asked Jesus, "How is it that John's disciples and the disciples of the Pharisees are fasting, but yours are not?"

19Jesus answered, "How can the guests of the bridegroom fast while he is with them? They cannot, so long as they have him with them. 20But the time will come when the bridegroom will be taken from them, and on that day they will fast.

21"No one sews a patch of unshrunk cloth on an old garment. If he does, the new piece will pull away from the old, making the tear worse. 22And no one pours new wine into old wineskins. If he does, the wine will burst the skins, and both the wine and the wineskins will be ruined. No, he pours new wine into new wineskins."

Lord of the Sabbath

23One Sabbath Jesus was going through the grainfields, and as his disciples walked along, they began to pick some heads of grain. 24The Pharisees said to him, "Look, why are they doing what is unlawful on the Sabbath?"

25He answered, "Have you never read what David did when he and his companions were hungry and in need? 26In the days of Abiathar the high priest, he entered the house of God and ate the consecrated bread, which is lawful only for priests to eat. And he also gave some to his companions."

27Then he said to them, "The Sabbath was made for man, not man for the Sabbath. 28So the Son of Man is Lord even of the Sabbath."

3 Another time he went into the synagogue, and a man with a shriveled hand was there. 2Some of them were looking for a reason to accuse Jesus, so they watched him closely to see if he would heal him on the Sabbath. 3Jesus said to the man with the shriveled hand, "Stand up in front of everyone."

4Then Jesus asked them, "Which is lawful on the Sabbath: to do good or to do evil, to save life or to kill?" But they remained silent.

5He looked around at them in anger and, deeply distressed at their stubborn hearts, said to the man, "Stretch out your hand." He stretched it out, and his hand was completely restored. 6Then the Pharisees went out and began to plot with the Herodians how they might kill Jesus.

Crowds Follow Jesus

7Jesus withdrew with his disciples to the lake, and a large crowd from Galilee followed. 8When they heard all he was doing, many people came to him from Judea, Jerusalem, Idumea, and the regions across the Jordan and around Tyre and Sidon. 9Because of the crowd he told his disciples to have a small boat ready for him, to keep the people from crowding him. 10For he had healed many, so that those with diseases were pushing forward to touch him. 11Whenever the evil[a] spirits saw him, they fell down before him and cried out, "You are the Son of God." 12But he gave them strict orders not to tell who he was.

The Appointing of the Twelve Apostles

13Jesus went up on a mountainside and called to him those he wanted, and they came to him. 14He appointed twelve—designating them apostles[b]—that they might be with him and that he might send them out to preach 15and to have authori-

[a]11 Greek *unclean*; also in verse 30 [b]14 Some manuscripts do not have *designating them apostles.*

ty to drive out demons. 16These are the twelve he appointed: Simon (to whom he gave the name Peter); 17James son of Zebedee and his brother John (to them he gave the name Boanerges, which means Sons of Thunder); 18Andrew, Philip, Bartholomew, Matthew, Thomas, James son of Alphaeus, Thaddaeus, Simon the Zealot 19and Judas Iscariot, who betrayed him.

Jesus and Beelzebub

20Then Jesus entered a house, and again a crowd gathered, so that he and his disciples were not even able to eat. 21When his family heard about this, they went to take charge of him, for they said, "He is out of his mind."

22And the teachers of the law who came down from Jerusalem said, "He is possessed by Beelzebub[a]! By the prince of demons he is driving out demons."

23So Jesus called them and spoke to them in parables: "How can Satan drive out Satan? 24If a kingdom is divided against itself, that kingdom cannot stand. 25If a house is divided against itself, that house cannot stand. 26And if Satan opposes himself and is divided, he cannot stand; his end has come. 27In fact, no one can enter a strong man's house and carry off his possessions unless he first ties up the strong man. Then he can rob his house. 28I tell you the truth, all the sins and blasphemies of men will be forgiven them. 29But whoever blasphemes against the Holy Spirit will never be forgiven; he is guilty of an eternal sin."

30He said this because they were saying, "He has an evil spirit."

Jesus' Mother and Brothers

31Then Jesus' mother and brothers arrived. Standing outside, they sent someone in to call him. 32A crowd was sitting around him, and they told him, "Your mother and brothers are outside looking for you."

33"Who are my mother and my brothers?" he asked.

34Then he looked at those seated in a circle around him and said, "Here are my mother and my brothers! 35Whoever does God's will is my brother and sister and mother."

The Parable of the Sower

4 Again Jesus began to teach by the lake. The crowd that gathered around him was so large that he got into a boat and sat in it out on the lake, while all the people were along the shore at the water's edge. 2He taught them many things by parables, and in his teaching said: 3"Listen! A farmer went out to sow his seed. 4As he was scattering the seed, some fell along the path, and the birds came and ate it up. 5Some fell on rocky places, where it did not have much soil. It sprang up quickly, because the soil was shallow. 6But when the sun came up, the plants were scorched, and they withered because they had no root. 7Other seed fell among thorns, which grew up and choked the plants, so that they did not bear grain. 8Still other seed fell on good soil. It came up, grew and produced a crop, multiplying thirty, sixty, or even a hundred times."

9Then Jesus said, "He who has ears to hear, let him hear."

10When he was alone, the Twelve and the others around him asked him about the parables. 11He told them, "The secret of the kingdom of God has been given to you. But to those on the outside everything is said in parables 12so that,

" 'they may be ever seeing but never
    perceiving,
  and ever hearing but never
    understanding;
otherwise they might turn and be
    forgiven!'[b]"

13Then Jesus said to them, "Don't you understand this parable? How then will you understand any parable? 14The farmer sows the word. 15Some people are like seed along the path, where the word is sown. As soon as they hear it, Satan comes and takes away the word that was sown in them. 16Others, like seed sown on rocky places, hear the word and at once receive it with joy. 17But since they have no root, they last only a short time. When trouble or persecution comes because of the word, they quickly fall away. 18Still others, like seed sown among thorns, hear the word; 19but the worries of this life, the deceitfulness of wealth and the desires for other things come in and choke the word, making it unfruitful. 20Others, like seed sown on good soil,

[a]22 Greek *Beezeboul* or *Beelzeboul* [b]12 Isaiah 6:9,10

hear the word, accept it, and produce a crop—thirty, sixty or even a hundred times what was sown."

A Lamp on a Stand

21He said to them, "Do you bring in a lamp to put it under a bowl or a bed? Instead, don't you put it on its stand? 22For whatever is hidden is meant to be disclosed, and whatever is concealed is meant to be brought out into the open. 23If anyone has ears to hear, let him hear."

24"Consider carefully what you hear," he continued. "With the measure you use, it will be measured to you—and even more. 25Whoever has will be given more; whoever does not have, even what he has will be taken from him."

The Parable of the Growing Seed

26He also said, "This is what the kingdom of God is like. A man scatters seed on the ground. 27Night and day, whether he sleeps or gets up, the seed sprouts and grows, though he does not know how. 28All by itself the soil produces grain—first the stalk, then the head, then the full kernel in the head. 29As soon as the grain is ripe, he puts the sickle to it, because the harvest has come."

The Parable of the Mustard Seed

30Again he said, "What shall we say the kingdom of God is like, or what parable shall we use to describe it? 31It is like a mustard seed, which is the smallest seed you plant in the ground. 32Yet when planted, it grows and becomes the largest of all garden plants, with such big branches that the birds of the air can perch in its shade."

33With many similar parables Jesus spoke the word to them, as much as they could understand. 34He did not say anything to them without using a parable. But when he was alone with his own disciples, he explained everything.

Jesus Calms the Storm

35That day when evening came, he said to his disciples, "Let us go over to the other side." 36Leaving the crowd behind, they took him along, just as he was, in the boat. There were also other boats with him. 37A furious squall came up, and the waves broke over the boat, so that it was nearly swamped. 38Jesus was in the stern, sleeping on a cushion. The disciples woke him and said to him, "Teacher, don't you care if we drown?"

39He got up, rebuked the wind and said to the waves, "Quiet! Be still!" Then the wind died down and it was completely calm.

40He said to his disciples, "Why are you so afraid? Do you still have no faith?"

41They were terrified and asked each other, "Who is this? Even the wind and the waves obey him!"

The Healing of a Demon-possessed Man

5 They went across the lake to the region of the Gerasenes.[a] 2When Jesus got out of the boat, a man with an evil[b] spirit came from the tombs to meet him. 3This man lived in the tombs, and no one could bind him any more, not even with a chain. 4For he had often been chained hand and foot, but he tore the chains apart and broke the irons on his feet. No one was strong enough to subdue him. 5Night and day among the tombs and in the hills he would cry out and cut himself with stones.

6When he saw Jesus from a distance, he ran and fell on his knees in front of him. 7He shouted at the top of his voice, "What do you want with me, Jesus, Son of the Most High God? Swear to God that you won't torture me!" 8For Jesus had said to him, "Come out of this man, you evil spirit!"

9Then Jesus asked him, "What is your name?"

"My name is Legion," he replied, "for we are many." 10And he begged Jesus again and again not to send them out of the area.

11A large herd of pigs was feeding on the nearby hillside. 12The demons begged Jesus, "Send us among the pigs; allow us to go into them." 13He gave them permission, and the evil spirits came out and went into the pigs. The herd, about two thousand in number, rushed down the steep bank into the lake and were drowned.

14Those tending the pigs ran off and reported this in the town and countryside, and the people went out to see what had happened. 15When they came to Jesus, they saw the man who had been pos-

[a]*1* Some manuscripts *Gadarenes*; other manuscripts *Gergesenes* [b]*2* Greek *unclean*; also in verses 8 and 13

sessed by the legion of demons, sitting
there, dressed and in his right mind; and
they were afraid. 16Those who had seen it
told the people what had happened to the
demon-possessed man—and told about
the pigs as well. 17Then the people began
to plead with Jesus to leave their region.
18As Jesus was getting into the boat,
the man who had been demon-possessed
begged to go with him. 19Jesus did not let
him, but said, "Go home to your family
and tell them how much the Lord has
done for you, and how he has had mercy
on you." 20So the man went away and began to tell in the Decapolis[a] how much
Jesus had done for him. And all the people were amazed.

A Dead Girl and a Sick Woman

21When Jesus had again crossed over by
boat to the other side of the lake, a large
crowd gathered around him while he was
by the lake. 22Then one of the synagogue
rulers, named Jairus, came there. Seeing
Jesus, he fell at his feet 23and pleaded
earnestly with him, "My little daughter is
dying. Please come and put your hands
on her so that she will be healed and
live." 24So Jesus went with him.

A large crowd followed and pressed
around him. 25And a woman was there
who had been subject to bleeding for
twelve years. 26She had suffered a great
deal under the care of many doctors and
had spent all she had, yet instead of getting better she grew worse. 27When she
heard about Jesus, she came up behind
him in the crowd and touched his cloak,
28because she thought, "If I just touch his
clothes, I will be healed." 29Immediately
her bleeding stopped and she felt in her
body that she was freed from her suffering.

30At once Jesus realized that power had
gone out from him. He turned around in
the crowd and asked, "Who touched my
clothes?"

31"You see the people crowding against
you," his disciples answered, "and yet
you can ask, 'Who touched me?' "

32But Jesus kept looking around to see
who had done it. 33Then the woman,
knowing what had happened to her, came
and fell at his feet and, trembling with
fear, told him the whole truth. 34He said
to her, "Daughter, your faith has healed
you. Go in peace and be freed from your
suffering."

35While Jesus was still speaking, some
men came from the house of Jairus, the
synagogue ruler. "Your daughter is dead,"
they said. "Why bother the teacher any
more?"

36Ignoring what they said, Jesus told
the synagogue ruler, "Don't be afraid; just
believe."

37He did not let anyone follow him except Peter, James and John the brother of
James. 38When they came to the home of
the synagogue ruler, Jesus saw a commotion, with people crying and wailing loudly. 39He went in and said to them, "Why
all this commotion and wailing? The
child is not dead but asleep." 40But they
laughed at him.

After he put them all out, he took the
child's father and mother and the disciples who were with him, and went in
where the child was. 41He took her by the
hand and said to her, *"Talitha koum!"*
(which means, "Little girl, I say to you,
get up!"). 42Immediately the girl stood up
and walked around (she was twelve years
old). At this they were completely astonished. 43He gave strict orders not to let
anyone know about this, and told them to
give her something to eat.

A Prophet Without Honor

6 Jesus left there and went to his
hometown, accompanied by his disciples. 2When the Sabbath came, he began
to teach in the synagogue, and many who
heard him were amazed.

"Where did this man get these things?"
they asked. "What's this wisdom that has
been given him, that he even does miracles! 3Isn't this the carpenter? Isn't this
Mary's son and the brother of James, Joseph,[b] Judas and Simon? Aren't his sisters here with us?" And they took offense
at him.

4Jesus said to them, "Only in his hometown, among his relatives and in his own
house is a prophet without honor." 5He
could not do any miracles there, except
lay his hands on a few sick people and
heal them. 6And he was amazed at their
lack of faith.

Jesus Sends Out the Twelve

Then Jesus went around teaching from
village to village. 7Calling the Twelve to
him, he sent them out two by two and
gave them authority over evil[c] spirits.

8These were his instructions: "Take

[a] *20* That is, the Ten Cities [b] *3* Greek *Joses*, a variant of *Joseph* [c] *7* Greek *unclean*

WEDNESDAY

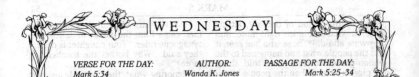

VERSE FOR THE DAY: *Mark 5:34* | *AUTHOR:* *Wanda K. Jones* | *PASSAGE FOR THE DAY:* *Mark 5:25–34*

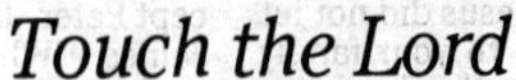

Touch the Lord

MARK 5:25–34 speaks of a woman who had been bleeding for twelve years. She had seen many doctors but none were able to make her well. And while she spent all her money seeking a cure, her condition only grew worse.

Then she heard about Jesus and believed that if she could get to him and just touch him she would be healed. What a testimony to her persistence!

Imagine the scene: "A large crowd followed and pressed around him" (Mark 5:24). Some were blind, some deaf, some were mothers carrying children. And no doubt the day was hot and the road dusty. But this particular woman determined that in spite of the crowd she was going to touch Jesus and be healed. And she was!

Jesus responded to faith's touch by asking, "Who touched my clothes?" (Mark 5:30). The woman fell at his feet and told him her problem. How characteristic of the Master to respond in a comforting voice when he said, "Daughter, your faith has healed you. Go in peace and be freed from your suffering" (Mark 5:34).

Jesus is just as interested in your need as he was in this woman's need many years ago. Whatever your situation, whatever your problem, he stands ready to help you.

About two years ago I had the opportunity to witness about my faith to a woman who was near death. At the same time I had the privilege to hear her reaffirm her faith in Jesus Christ. She sang many of the hymns she had loved as a young girl, including "Blessed Assurance" and "What a Friend We Have in Jesus." We prayed together, and the next day she went to heaven with a smile on her face. She had touched the Lord on earth, and now she would be with him in heaven.

You may be looking for answers because you're in a faltering marriage. Or you may be hurting because you have been abused or neglected. Remember the woman of Mark 5. She sought Jesus and was determined to find him. When she did, he met her needs. He will meet yours. Ask him.

Additional Scripture Readings:
John 20:24–29; Hebrews 4:14–16

Go to page 55 for your next devotional reading.

nothing for the journey except a staff—no bread, no bag, no money in your belts. 9Wear sandals but not an extra tunic. 10Whenever you enter a house, stay there until you leave that town. 11And if any place will not welcome you or listen to you, shake the dust off your feet when you leave, as a testimony against them."

12They went out and preached that people should repent. 13They drove out many demons and anointed many sick people with oil and healed them.

John the Baptist Beheaded

14King Herod heard about this, for Jesus' name had become well known. Some were saying,[a] "John the Baptist has been raised from the dead, and that is why miraculous powers are at work in him."

15Others said, "He is Elijah."

And still others claimed, "He is a prophet, like one of the prophets of long ago."

16But when Herod heard this, he said, "John, the man I beheaded, has been raised from the dead!"

17For Herod himself had given orders to have John arrested, and he had him bound and put in prison. He did this because of Herodias, his brother Philip's wife, whom he had married. 18For John had been saying to Herod, "It is not lawful for you to have your brother's wife." 19So Herodias nursed a grudge against John and wanted to kill him. But she was not able to, 20because Herod feared John and protected him, knowing him to be a righteous and holy man. When Herod heard John, he was greatly puzzled[b]; yet he liked to listen to him.

21Finally the opportune time came. On his birthday Herod gave a banquet for his high officials and military commanders and the leading men of Galilee. 22When the daughter of Herodias came in and danced, she pleased Herod and his dinner guests.

The king said to the girl, "Ask me for anything you want, and I'll give it to you." 23And he promised her with an oath, "Whatever you ask I will give you, up to half my kingdom."

24She went out and said to her mother, "What shall I ask for?"

"The head of John the Baptist," she answered.

25At once the girl hurried in to the king with the request: "I want you to give me right now the head of John the Baptist on a platter."

26The king was greatly distressed, but because of his oaths and his dinner guests, he did not want to refuse her. 27So he immediately sent an executioner with orders to bring John's head. The man went, beheaded John in the prison, 28and brought back his head on a platter. He presented it to the girl, and she gave it to her mother. 29On hearing of this, John's disciples came and took his body and laid it in a tomb.

Jesus Feeds the Five Thousand

30The apostles gathered around Jesus and reported to him all they had done and taught. 31Then, because so many people were coming and going that they did not even have a chance to eat, he said to them, "Come with me by yourselves to a quiet place and get some rest."

32So they went away by themselves in a boat to a solitary place. 33But many who saw them leaving recognized them and ran on foot from all the towns and got there ahead of them. 34When Jesus landed and saw a large crowd, he had compassion on them, because they were like sheep without a shepherd. So he began teaching them many things.

35By this time it was late in the day, so his disciples came to him. "This is a remote place," they said, "and it's already very late. 36Send the people away so they can go to the surrounding countryside and villages and buy themselves something to eat."

37But he answered, "You give them something to eat."

They said to him, "That would take eight months of a man's wages[c]! Are we to go and spend that much on bread and give it to them to eat?"

38"How many loaves do you have?" he asked. "Go and see."

When they found out, they said, "Five—and two fish."

39Then Jesus directed them to have all the people sit down in groups on the green grass. 40So they sat down in groups of hundreds and fifties. 41Taking the five loaves and the two fish and looking up to heaven, he gave thanks and broke the loaves. Then he gave them to his disciples

[a]*14* Some early manuscripts *He was saying* [b]*20* Some early manuscripts *he did many things*
[c]*37* Greek *take two hundred denarii*

to set before the people. He also divided
the two fish among them all. 42They all
ate and were satisfied, 43and the disciples
picked up twelve basketfuls of broken
pieces of bread and fish. 44The number of
the men who had eaten was five thousand.

Jesus Walks on the Water

45Immediately Jesus made his disciples
get into the boat and go on ahead of him
to Bethsaida, while he dismissed the
crowd. 46After leaving them, he went up
on a mountainside to pray.
47When evening came, the boat was in
the middle of the lake, and he was alone
on land. 48He saw the disciples straining
at the oars, because the wind was against
them. About the fourth watch of the night
he went out to them, walking on the lake.
He was about to pass by them, 49but when
they saw him walking on the lake, they
thought he was a ghost. They cried out,
50because they all saw him and were terrified.
Immediately he spoke to them and
said, "Take courage! It is I. Don't be
afraid." 51Then he climbed into the boat
with them, and the wind died down. They
were completely amazed, 52for they had
not understood about the loaves; their
hearts were hardened.
53When they had crossed over, they
landed at Gennesaret and anchored
there. 54As soon as they got out of the
boat, people recognized Jesus. 55They ran
throughout that whole region and carried
the sick on mats to wherever they heard
he was. 56And wherever he went—into
villages, towns or countryside—they
placed the sick in the marketplaces. They
begged him to let them touch even the
edge of his cloak, and all who touched
him were healed.

Clean and Unclean

7 The Pharisees and some of the teachers of the law who had come from Jerusalem gathered around Jesus and 2saw
some of his disciples eating food with
hands that were "unclean," that is, unwashed. 3(The Pharisees and all the Jews
do not eat unless they give their hands a
ceremonial washing, holding to the tradition of the elders. 4When they come from
the marketplace they do not eat unless
they wash. And they observe many other
traditions, such as the washing of cups,
pitchers and kettles.[a])
5So the Pharisees and teachers of the
law asked Jesus, "Why don't your disciples live according to the tradition of the
elders instead of eating their food with
'unclean' hands?"
6He replied, "Isaiah was right when he
prophesied about you hypocrites; as it is
written:

" 'These people honor me with their
lips,
but their hearts are far from me.
7They worship me in vain;
their teachings are but rules taught
by men.'[b]

8You have let go of the commands of God
and are holding on to the traditions of
men."
9And he said to them: "You have a fine
way of setting aside the commands of
God in order to observe[c] your own traditions! 10For Moses said, 'Honor your father and your mother,'[d] and, 'Anyone
who curses his father or mother must be
put to death.'[e] 11But you say that if a man
says to his father or mother: 'Whatever
help you might otherwise have received
from me is Corban' (that is, a gift devoted
to God), 12then you no longer let him do
anything for his father or mother. 13Thus
you nullify the word of God by your tradition that you have handed down. And you
do many things like that."
14Again Jesus called the crowd to him
and said, "Listen to me, everyone, and
understand this. 15Nothing outside a man
can make him 'unclean' by going into
him. Rather, it is what comes out of a
man that makes him 'unclean.'[f]"
17After he had left the crowd and entered the house, his disciples asked him
about this parable. 18"Are you so dull?"
he asked. "Don't you see that nothing
that enters a man from the outside can
make him 'unclean'? 19For it doesn't go
into his heart but into his stomach, and
then out of his body." (In saying this,
Jesus declared all foods "clean.")
20He went on: "What comes out of a
man is what makes him 'unclean.' 21For
from within, out of men's hearts, come

[a]4 Some early manuscripts *pitchers, kettles and dining couches* [b]6,7 Isaiah 29:13 [c]9 Some manuscripts *set up* [d]10 Exodus 20:12; Deut. 5:16 [e]10 Exodus 21:17; Lev. 20:9 [f]15 Some early manuscripts *'unclean.'* [16]*If anyone has ears to hear, let him hear.*

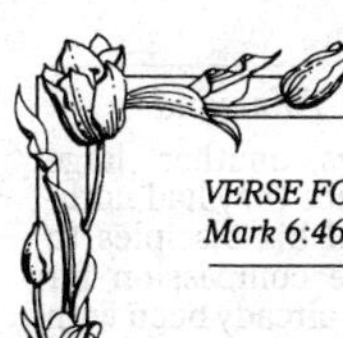

VERSE FOR THE DAY:
Mark 6:46

AUTHOR:
Elisabeth Elliot

PASSAGE FOR THE DAY:
Mark 6:45–52

Meeting God Alone

A VERY tall man, wrapped in a steamer rug, kneeling alone by a chair. When I think of my father, who died in 1963, this is often the first image that comes to mind. It was the habit of his life to rise early in the morning—usually between 4:30 and 5:00 A. M. to study his Bible and to pray. We did not often see him during that solitary hour (he purposed to make it solitary), but we were used to seeing him on his knees.

My father, an honest and humble disciple of the Lord Jesus, wanted to follow his example: "Very early in the morning . . . Jesus got up, left the house and went off to a solitary place, where he prayed" (Mark 1:35).

Christians may (and ought to) pray anytime and anywhere, but we cannot well do without a special time and place to be alone with God. Most of us find that early morning is not an easy time to pray. I wonder if there is an *easy* time.

The simple fact is that early morning is probably the *only* time when we can be fairly sure of not being interrupted. Where can we go? We may need to find a literal closet or a bathroom or a parked car. We may walk outdoors and pray. But we must *arrange* to pray, to be alone with God sometime every day.

The Bible is God's message to everybody. We deceive ourselves if we claim to want to hear his voice but neglect the primary channel through which it comes. We must read his Word. We must obey it.

When we have heard God speak, what then shall we say to God? In an emergency or when we suddenly need help, the words come easily: "Oh, God!" or "Lord, help me!" During our quiet time however, it is a good thing to remember that we are here not to pester God but to adore him.

All creation praises him all the time—the winds, the tides, the oceans, the rivers, move in obedience; the song sparrow, the molecules in their cells, the stars in their courses, and the burning seraphim do, without protest of slovenliness, exactly what their Maker intended, and thus praise him.

We read that our heavenly Father actually looks for people who will worship him in spirit and in reality. Imagine! God is looking for worshipers. Will he always have to go to a church to find them, or might there be one here and there in an ordinary house, kneeling alone by a chair?

Additional Scripture Readings:
Isaiah 55:6–11; John 4:23–24

Go to page 58 for your next devotional reading.

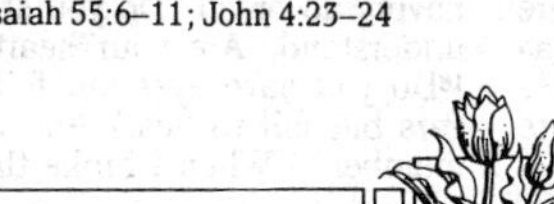

evil thoughts, sexual immorality, theft, murder, adultery, 22 greed, malice, deceit, lewdness, envy, slander, arrogance and folly. 23 All these evils come from inside and make a man 'unclean.' "

The Faith of a Syrophoenician Woman

24 Jesus left that place and went to the vicinity of Tyre.[a] He entered a house and did not want anyone to know it; yet he could not keep his presence secret. 25 In fact, as soon as she heard about him, a woman whose little daughter was possessed by an evil[b] spirit came and fell at his feet. 26 The woman was a Greek, born in Syrian Phoenicia. She begged Jesus to drive the demon out of her daughter.

27 "First let the children eat all they want," he told her, "for it is not right to take the children's bread and toss it to their dogs."

28 "Yes, Lord," she replied, "but even the dogs under the table eat the children's crumbs."

29 Then he told her, "For such a reply, you may go; the demon has left your daughter."

30 She went home and found her child lying on the bed, and the demon gone.

The Healing of a Deaf and Mute Man

31 Then Jesus left the vicinity of Tyre and went through Sidon, down to the Sea of Galilee and into the region of the Decapolis.[c] 32 There some people brought to him a man who was deaf and could hardly talk, and they begged him to place his hand on the man.

33 After he took him aside, away from the crowd, Jesus put his fingers into the man's ears. Then he spit and touched the man's tongue. 34 He looked up to heaven and with a deep sigh said to him, *"Ephphatha!"* (which means, "Be opened!"). 35 At this, the man's ears were opened, his tongue was loosened and he began to speak plainly.

36 Jesus commanded them not to tell anyone. But the more he did so, the more they kept talking about it. 37 People were overwhelmed with amazement. "He has done everything well," they said. "He even makes the deaf hear and the mute speak."

Jesus Feeds the Four Thousand

8 During those days another large crowd gathered. Since they had nothing to eat, Jesus called his disciples to him and said, 2 "I have compassion for these people; they have already been with me three days and have nothing to eat. 3 If I send them home hungry, they will collapse on the way, because some of them have come a long distance."

4 His disciples answered, "But where in this remote place can anyone get enough bread to feed them?"

5 "How many loaves do you have?" Jesus asked.

"Seven," they replied.

6 He told the crowd to sit down on the ground. When he had taken the seven loaves and given thanks, he broke them and gave them to his disciples to set before the people, and they did so. 7 They had a few small fish as well; he gave thanks for them also and told the disciples to distribute them. 8 The people ate and were satisfied. Afterward the disciples picked up seven basketfuls of broken pieces that were left over. 9 About four thousand men were present. And having sent them away, 10 he got into the boat with his disciples and went to the region of Dalmanutha.

11 The Pharisees came and began to question Jesus. To test him, they asked him for a sign from heaven. 12 He sighed deeply and said, "Why does this generation ask for a miraculous sign? I tell you the truth, no sign will be given to it." 13 Then he left them, got back into the boat and crossed to the other side.

The Yeast of the Pharisees and Herod

14 The disciples had forgotten to bring bread, except for one loaf they had with them in the boat. 15 "Be careful," Jesus warned them. "Watch out for the yeast of the Pharisees and that of Herod."

16 They discussed this with one another and said, "It is because we have no bread."

17 Aware of their discussion, Jesus asked them: "Why are you talking about having no bread? Do you still not see or understand? Are your hearts hardened? 18 Do you have eyes but fail to see, and ears but fail to hear? And don't you remember? 19 When I broke the five loaves

[a] *24* Many early manuscripts *Tyre and Sidon*　[b] *25* Greek *unclean*　[c] *31* That is, the Ten Cities

for the five thousand, how many basketfuls of pieces did you pick up?"
"Twelve," they replied.
20"And when I broke the seven loaves
for the four thousand, how many basketfuls of pieces did you pick up?"
They answered, "Seven."
21He said to them, "Do you still not understand?"

The Healing of a Blind Man at Bethsaida

22They came to Bethsaida, and some
people brought a blind man and begged
Jesus to touch him. 23He took the blind
man by the hand and led him outside the
village. When he had spit on the man's
eyes and put his hands on him, Jesus
asked, "Do you see anything?"
24He looked up and said, "I see people;
they look like trees walking around."
25Once more Jesus put his hands on
the man's eyes. Then his eyes were
opened, his sight was restored, and he
saw everything clearly. 26Jesus sent him
home, saying, "Don't go into the village.[a]"

Peter's Confession of Christ

27Jesus and his disciples went on to the
villages around Caesarea Philippi. On the
way he asked them, "Who do people say
I am?"
28They replied, "Some say John the
Baptist; others say Elijah; and still others,
one of the prophets."
29"But what about you?" he asked.
"Who do you say I am?"
Peter answered, "You are the Christ.[b]"
30Jesus warned them not to tell anyone
about him.

Jesus Predicts His Death

31He then began to teach them that the
Son of Man must suffer many things and
be rejected by the elders, chief priests
and teachers of the law, and that he must
be killed and after three days rise again.
32He spoke plainly about this, and Peter
took him aside and began to rebuke him.
33But when Jesus turned and looked at
his disciples, he rebuked Peter. "Get behind me, Satan!" he said. "You do not
have in mind the things of God, but the
things of men."
34Then he called the crowd to him
along with his disciples and said: "If anyone would come after me, he must deny
himself and take up his cross and follow
me. 35For whoever wants to save his life[c]
will lose it, but whoever loses his life for
me and for the gospel will save it. 36What
good is it for a man to gain the whole
world, yet forfeit his soul? 37Or what can
a man give in exchange for his soul? 38If
anyone is ashamed of me and my words in
this adulterous and sinful generation, the
Son of Man will be ashamed of him when
he comes in his Father's glory with the
holy angels."

9 And he said to them, "I tell you the
truth, some who are standing here
will not taste death before they see the
kingdom of God come with power."

The Transfiguration

2After six days Jesus took Peter, James
and John with him and led them up a
high mountain, where they were all
alone. There he was transfigured before
them. 3His clothes became dazzling
white, whiter than anyone in the world
could bleach them. 4And there appeared
before them Elijah and Moses, who were
talking with Jesus.
5Peter said to Jesus, "Rabbi, it is good
for us to be here. Let us put up three shelters—one for you, one for Moses and one
for Elijah." 6(He did not know what to
say, they were so frightened.)
7Then a cloud appeared and enveloped
them, and a voice came from the cloud:
"This is my Son, whom I love. Listen to
him!"
8Suddenly, when they looked around,
they no longer saw anyone with them except Jesus.
9As they were coming down the mountain, Jesus gave them orders not to tell
anyone what they had seen until the Son
of Man had risen from the dead. 10They
kept the matter to themselves, discussing
what "rising from the dead" meant.
11And they asked him, "Why do the
teachers of the law say that Elijah must
come first?"
12Jesus replied, "To be sure, Elijah
does come first, and restores all things.
Why then is it written that the Son of Man
must suffer much and be rejected? 13But
I tell you, Elijah has come, and they have

[a]26 Some manuscripts *Don't go and tell anyone in the village*
[b]29 Or *Messiah.* "The Christ" (Greek) and "the Messiah" (Hebrew) both mean "the Anointed One."
[c]35 The Greek word means either *life* or *soul*; also in verse 36.

FRIDAY

VERSE FOR THE DAY:
Mark 9:23

AUTHOR:
Mrs. Charles E. Cowman

PASSAGE FOR THE DAY:
Mark 9:14–32

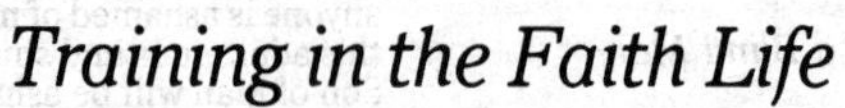

Training in the Faith Life

THE "everything" in this verse does not always come simply for the asking. God is ever seeking to teach us the way of faith, and in our training in the faith life there must be room for the trial of faith, the discipline of faith, the patience of faith, the courage of faith, and often many stages are passed before we really realize what is the end of faith, namely, the victory of faith.

Real moral fiber is developed through discipline of faith. You have made your request of God, but the answer does not come. What are you to do?

Keep on believing God's Word; never be moved away from it by what you see or feel, and thus as you stand steady, enlarged power and experience is being developed. The fact of looking at the apparent contradiction as to God's Word and being unmoved from your position of faith make you stronger on every other line.

Often God delays purposely, and the delay is just as much an answer to your prayer as is the fulfillment when it comes.

In the lives of all the great Bible characters, God worked thus. Abraham, Moses and Elijah were not great in the beginning, but were made great through the discipline of their faith, and only thus were they fitted for the positions to which God had called them.

For example, in the case of Joseph whom the Lord was training for the throne of Egypt, it was not the prison life with its hard beds or poor food that tried him, but it was the word God had spoken into his heart in the early years concerning elevation and honor which were greater than his brethren were to receive; it was this which was ever before him, when every step in his career made it seem more and more impossible of fulfillment. These were hours that tried his soul, but hours of spiritual growth and development.

No amount of persecution tries like such experiences as these. When God has spoken of his purpose to do, and yet the days go on and he does not do it, that is truly hard; but it is a discipline of faith that will bring us into a knowledge of God which would otherwise be impossible.

Additional Scripture Readings:
James 5:10–11; 1 Peter 5:8–10

Go to page 60 for your next devotional reading.

done to him everything they wished, just
as it is written about him."

The Healing of a Boy With an Evil Spirit

14When they came to the other disciples, they saw a large crowd around them
and the teachers of the law arguing with
them. 15As soon as all the people saw
Jesus, they were overwhelmed with wonder and ran to greet him.
16"What are you arguing with them
about?" he asked.
17A man in the crowd answered,
"Teacher, I brought you my son, who is
possessed by a spirit that has robbed him
of speech. 18Whenever it seizes him, it
throws him to the ground. He foams at
the mouth, gnashes his teeth and becomes rigid. I asked your disciples to
drive out the spirit, but they could not."
19"O unbelieving generation," Jesus replied, "how long shall I stay with you?
How long shall I put up with you? Bring
the boy to me."
20So they brought him. When the spirit
saw Jesus, it immediately threw the boy
into a convulsion. He fell to the ground
and rolled around, foaming at the mouth.
21Jesus asked the boy's father, "How
long has he been like this?"
"From childhood," he answered. 22"It
has often thrown him into fire or water to
kill him. But if you can do anything, take
pity on us and help us."
23" 'If you can'?" said Jesus. "Everything is possible for him who believes."
24Immediately the boy's father exclaimed, "I do believe; help me overcome
my unbelief!"
25When Jesus saw that a crowd was
running to the scene, he rebuked the
evil[a] spirit. "You deaf and mute spirit,"
he said, "I command you, come out of
him and never enter him again."
26The spirit shrieked, convulsed him violently and came out. The boy looked
so much like a corpse that many said,
"He's dead." 27But Jesus took him by the
hand and lifted him to his feet, and he
stood up.
28After Jesus had gone indoors, his disciples asked him privately, "Why couldn't
we drive it out?"
29He replied, "This kind can come out
only by prayer.[b]"
30They left that place and passed
through Galilee. Jesus did not want anyone to know where they were, 31because
he was teaching his disciples. He said
to them, "The Son of Man is going to be
betrayed into the hands of men. They
will kill him, and after three days he will
rise." 32But they did not understand
what he meant and were afraid to ask
him about it.

Who Is the Greatest?

33They came to Capernaum. When he
was in the house, he asked them, "What
were you arguing about on the road?"
34But they kept quiet because on the way
they had argued about who was the greatest.
35Sitting down, Jesus called the Twelve
and said, "If anyone wants to be first, he
must be the very last, and the servant of
all."
36He took a little child and had him
stand among them. Taking him in his
arms, he said to them, 37"Whoever welcomes one of these little children in my
name welcomes me; and whoever welcomes me does not welcome me but the
one who sent me."

Whoever Is Not Against Us Is for Us

38"Teacher," said John, "we saw a man
driving out demons in your name and we
told him to stop, because he was not one
of us."
39"Do not stop him," Jesus said. "No
one who does a miracle in my name can
in the next moment say anything bad
about me, 40for whoever is not against us
is for us. 41I tell you the truth, anyone who
gives you a cup of water in my name because you belong to Christ will certainly
not lose his reward.

Causing to Sin

42"And if anyone causes one of these
little ones who believe in me to sin, it
would be better for him to be thrown into
the sea with a large millstone tied around
his neck. 43If your hand causes you to sin,
cut it off. It is better for you to enter life
maimed than with two hands to go into
hell, where the fire never goes out.[c]
45And if your foot causes you to sin, cut it
off. It is better for you to enter life crippled than to have two feet and be thrown

[a]25 Greek *unclean* [b]29 Some manuscripts *prayer and fasting* [c]43 Some manuscripts *out,* 44*where / " 'their worm does not die, / and the fire is not quenched.'*

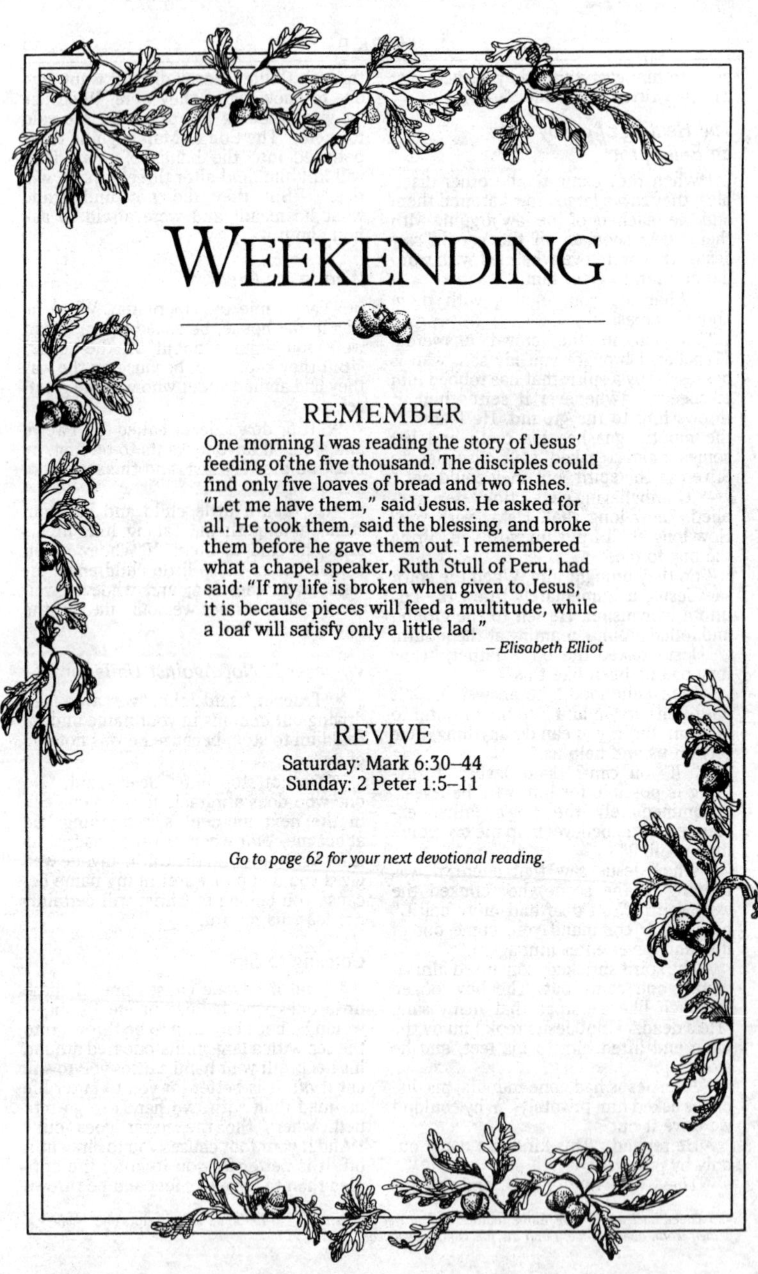

WEEKENDING

REMEMBER

One morning I was reading the story of Jesus' feeding of the five thousand. The disciples could find only five loaves of bread and two fishes. "Let me have them," said Jesus. He asked for all. He took them, said the blessing, and broke them before he gave them out. I remembered what a chapel speaker, Ruth Stull of Peru, had said: "If my life is broken when given to Jesus, it is because pieces will feed a multitude, while a loaf will satisfy only a little lad."

– Elisabeth Elliot

REVIVE

Saturday: Mark 6:30–44
Sunday: 2 Peter 1:5–11

Go to page 62 for your next devotional reading.

into hell.[a] 47And if your eye causes you to
sin, pluck it out. It is better for you to
enter the kingdom of God with one eye
than to have two eyes and be thrown into
hell, 48where

" 'their worm does not die,
and the fire is not quenched.'[b]

49Everyone will be salted with fire.

50"Salt is good, but if it loses its saltiness, how can you make it salty again?
Have salt in yourselves, and be at peace
with each other."

Divorce

10 Jesus then left that place and went
into the region of Judea and across
the Jordan. Again crowds of people came
to him, and as was his custom, he taught
them.

2Some Pharisees came and tested him
by asking, "Is it lawful for a man to divorce his wife?"

3"What did Moses command you?" he
replied.

4They said, "Moses permitted a man to
write a certificate of divorce and send her
away."

5"It was because your hearts were hard
that Moses wrote you this law," Jesus replied. 6"But at the beginning of creation
God 'made them male and female.'[c]
7'For this reason a man will leave his father and mother and be united to his
wife,[d] 8and the two will become one
flesh.'[e] So they are no longer two, but
one. 9Therefore what God has joined together, let man not separate."

10When they were in the house again,
the disciples asked Jesus about this. 11He
answered, "Anyone who divorces his wife
and marries another woman commits
adultery against her. 12And if she divorces
her husband and marries another man,
she commits adultery."

The Little Children and Jesus

13People were bringing little children
to Jesus to have him touch them, but the
disciples rebuked them. 14When Jesus
saw this, he was indignant. He said to
them, "Let the little children come to me,
and do not hinder them, for the kingdom
of God belongs to such as these. 15I tell
you the truth, anyone who will not receive
the kingdom of God like a little child will
never enter it." 16And he took the children in his arms, put his hands on them
and blessed them.

The Rich Young Man

17As Jesus started on his way, a man
ran up to him and fell on his knees before
him. "Good teacher," he asked, "what
must I do to inherit eternal life?"

18"Why do you call me good?" Jesus answered. "No one is good—except God
alone. 19You know the commandments:
'Do not murder, do not commit adultery,
do not steal, do not give false testimony,
do not defraud, honor your father and
mother.'[f]"

20"Teacher," he declared, "all these I
have kept since I was a boy."

21Jesus looked at him and loved him.
"One thing you lack," he said. "Go, sell
everything you have and give to the poor,
and you will have treasure in heaven.
Then come, follow me."

22At this the man's face fell. He went
away sad, because he had great wealth.

23Jesus looked around and said to his
disciples, "How hard it is for the rich to
enter the kingdom of God!"

24The disciples were amazed at his
words. But Jesus said again, "Children,
how hard it is[g] to enter the kingdom of
God! 25It is easier for a camel to go
through the eye of a needle than for a rich
man to enter the kingdom of God."

26The disciples were even more
amazed, and said to each other, "Who
then can be saved?"

27Jesus looked at them and said, "With
man this is impossible, but not with God;
all things are possible with God."

28Peter said to him, "We have left everything to follow you!"

29"I tell you the truth," Jesus replied,
"no one who has left home or brothers or
sisters or mother or father or children or
fields for me and the gospel 30will fail to
receive a hundred times as much in this
present age (homes, brothers, sisters,
mothers, children and fields—and with
them, persecutions) and in the age to
come, eternal life. 31But many who are
first will be last, and the last first."

[a]*45* Some manuscripts *hell, 46where / " 'their worm does not die, / and the fire is not quenched.'*
[b]*48* Isaiah 66:24 [c]*6* Gen. 1:27 [d]*7* Some early manuscripts do not have *and be united to his wife.*
[e]*8* Gen. 2:24 [f]*19* Exodus 20:12-16; Deut. 5:16-20 [g]*24* Some manuscripts *is for those who trust in riches*

MONDAY

VERSE FOR THE DAY:
Mark 10:14

AUTHOR:
Rosalind Rinker

PASSAGE FOR THE DAY:
Mark 10:13–16

Jesus and Little Children

AS you read Mark 10:13–16, picture yourself in the time of Christ, the sun warm on your hair and your sandals dusty as you watch Jesus surrounded by numerous people. In your imagination stand in one of the following roles:

As a parent bringing your children to Jesus,
As one of the crowd waiting to see Jesus,
As a child yourself, needing Jesus.

Hear the indignation in Jesus' voice when the disciples tried to shield him. Hear the loving care and concern in his voice as he held out his arms inviting the children to come.

As a parent: Picture yourself bringing your child (or children). Watch other parents push a shy child forward, or an ailing child. The children love Jesus, and they touch him; one little girl lays her head on his shoulder. Jesus takes time for each one . . . blessing, touching, loving, and sending each back to his or her parents with joy. Who can ever be the same after having been touched by Jesus!

Are your children grown? Yet in your mind they are still your little ones, so bring those grown men or women to Jesus as the children you know them to be. Jesus will touch them and bless them. Do it now and do it often.

As a single person: There are children you love among your neighbors or relatives, whom you can bring to Jesus in your prayers as, in your imagination, you watch Jesus hold and bless them.

You, yourself: Right now be a child in the arms of Jesus, whatever your age. Let him hold you. No matter what age, deep in our hearts we are all children who desire to rest in those strong arms. My dear mother, at age eighty-three, reflected some of that when she said, "I am still a little girl of twelve running around my father's farm in Minnesota."

Close your eyes and see yourself as a child in the arms of Jesus. In reassuring words he speaks to you:

"My child, I care about you. I love you unconditionally. Trust me. I love you."

Additional Scripture Readings:
Mark 9:36–37; Luke 7:11–15

Go to page 64 for your next devotional reading.

Jesus Again Predicts His Death

32They were on their way up to Jerusalem, with Jesus leading the way, and the
disciples were astonished, while those
who followed were afraid. Again he took
the Twelve aside and told them what was
going to happen to him. 33"We are going
up to Jerusalem," he said, "and the Son
of Man will be betrayed to the chief
priests and teachers of the law. They will
condemn him to death and will hand him
over to the Gentiles, 34who will mock him
and spit on him, flog him and kill him.
Three days later he will rise."

The Request of James and John

35Then James and John, the sons of
Zebedee, came to him. "Teacher," they
said, "we want you to do for us whatever
we ask."

36"What do you want me to do for you?"
he asked.

37They replied, "Let one of us sit at
your right and the other at your left in
your glory."

38"You don't know what you are asking," Jesus said. "Can you drink the cup
I drink or be baptized with the baptism I
am baptized with?"

39"We can," they answered.

Jesus said to them, "You will drink the
cup I drink and be baptized with the baptism I am baptized with, 40but to sit at my
right or left is not for me to grant. These
places belong to those for whom they
have been prepared."

41When the ten heard about this, they
became indignant with James and John.
42Jesus called them together and said,
"You know that those who are regarded as
rulers of the Gentiles lord it over them,
and their high officials exercise authority
over them. 43Not so with you. Instead,
whoever wants to become great among
you must be your servant, 44and whoever
wants to be first must be slave of all. 45For
even the Son of Man did not come to be
served, but to serve, and to give his life as
a ransom for many."

Blind Bartimaeus Receives His Sight

46Then they came to Jericho. As Jesus
and his disciples, together with a large
crowd, were leaving the city, a blind man,
Bartimaeus (that is, the Son of Timaeus),
was sitting by the roadside begging.
47When he heard that it was Jesus of Nazareth, he began to shout, "Jesus, Son of
David, have mercy on me!"

48Many rebuked him and told him to be
quiet, but he shouted all the more, "Son
of David, have mercy on me!"

49Jesus stopped and said, "Call him."

So they called to the blind man, "Cheer
up! On your feet! He's calling you."
50Throwing his cloak aside, he jumped to
his feet and came to Jesus.

51"What do you want me to do for you?"
Jesus asked him.

The blind man said, "Rabbi, I want to
see."

52"Go," said Jesus, "your faith has
healed you." Immediately he received his
sight and followed Jesus along the road.

The Triumphal Entry

11 As they approached Jerusalem and
came to Bethphage and Bethany
at the Mount of Olives, Jesus sent two of
his disciples, 2saying to them, "Go to the
village ahead of you, and just as you enter
it, you will find a colt tied there, which no
one has ever ridden. Untie it and bring it
here. 3If anyone asks you, 'Why are you
doing this?' tell him, 'The Lord needs it
and will send it back here shortly.' "

4They went and found a colt outside in
the street, tied at a doorway. As they untied it, 5some people standing there
asked, "What are you doing, untying that
colt?" 6They answered as Jesus had told
them to, and the people let them go.
7When they brought the colt to Jesus and
threw their cloaks over it, he sat on it.
8Many people spread their cloaks on the
road, while others spread branches they
had cut in the fields. 9Those who went
ahead and those who followed shouted,

"Hosanna![a]"

"Blessed is he who comes in the
name of the Lord!"[b]

10"Blessed is the coming kingdom of
our father David!"

"Hosanna in the highest!"

11Jesus entered Jerusalem and went to
the temple. He looked around at everything, but since it was already late, he
went out to Bethany with the Twelve.

Jesus Clears the Temple

12The next day as they were leaving

[a]9 A Hebrew expression meaning "Save!" which became an exclamation of praise; also in verse 10
[b]9 Psalm 118:25,26

Bethany, Jesus was hungry. [13]Seeing in the distance a fig tree in leaf, he went to find out if it had any fruit. When he reached it, he found nothing but leaves, because it was not the season for figs.
[14]Then he said to the tree, "May no one ever eat fruit from you again." And his disciples heard him say it.
[15]On reaching Jerusalem, Jesus entered the temple area and began driving out those who were buying and selling there. He overturned the tables of the money changers and the benches of those selling doves,
[16]and would not allow anyone to carry merchandise through the temple courts.
[17]And as he taught them, he said, "Is it not written:

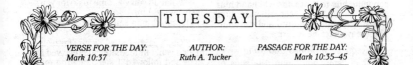

TUESDAY

VERSE FOR THE DAY: *Mark 10:37*

AUTHOR: *Ruth A. Tucker*

PASSAGE FOR THE DAY: *Mark 10:35–45*

The Sin of Self-Promotion

AS Americans, competition and rivalry seem to be in our blood. We are taught from early childhood that we must be better than others. We strive for recognition and prestige and tend to focus solely on ourselves. James and John would have fit well into our society. They sought the ultimate recognition—to sit at the right and left hand of Jesus in the kingdom.

Jesus had a pointed response for them that should give us all pause for reflection. While the rulers of the Gentiles lord it over those under them, such behavior is not befitting one who follows Christ. "Instead, whoever wants to become great among you must be your servant" (Mark 10:43).

That spirit of servanthood, which often is lacking in American culture, is much more visible among Africans—at least among African students at Moffat College of Bible in Kenya, where I have taught for several summers. Instead of the dog-eat-dog competition that is evident among my American students, I have noted a genuine concern for one another, especially in regard to grades at testing times. My African students appear most pleased, not when they alone perform well, but when the others perform well also. Indeed, if they were all to receive A's, there would be jubilation. Not so with my American students, whose real satisfaction comes only from being on top.

I have had to do some soul-searching myself on this issue. The competition for grades and the struggle for recognition in athletics that characterized my own student days have been subtly replaced by other forms of competition that are more befitting teachers and writers. But such a spirit is not becoming for a follower of Jesus. The Lord's words were direct, and he offered no excuses for those "handicapped" by their cultural heritage.

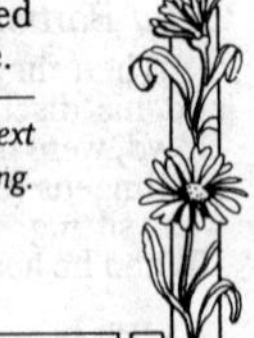

Additional Scripture Readings:
1 Samuel 24:1–13; Philippians 2:3–5

Go to page 66 for your next devotional reading.

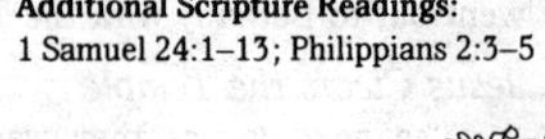

" 'My house will be called
a house of prayer for all nations'[a]?

But you have made it 'a den of robbers.'[b]"

18The chief priests and the teachers of the law heard this and began looking for a way to kill him, for they feared him, because the whole crowd was amazed at his teaching.

19When evening came, they[c] went out of the city.

The Withered Fig Tree

20In the morning, as they went along, they saw the fig tree withered from the roots. 21Peter remembered and said to Jesus, "Rabbi, look! The fig tree you cursed has withered!"

22"Have[d] faith in God," Jesus answered. 23"I tell you the truth, if anyone says to this mountain, 'Go, throw yourself into the sea,' and does not doubt in his heart but believes that what he says will happen, it will be done for him. 24Therefore I tell you, whatever you ask for in prayer, believe that you have received it, and it will be yours. 25And when you stand praying, if you hold anything against anyone, forgive him, so that your Father in heaven may forgive you your sins.[e]"

The Authority of Jesus Questioned

27They arrived again in Jerusalem, and while Jesus was walking in the temple courts, the chief priests, the teachers of the law and the elders came to him. 28"By what authority are you doing these things?" they asked. "And who gave you authority to do this?"

29Jesus replied, "I will ask you one question. Answer me, and I will tell you by what authority I am doing these things. 30John's baptism—was it from heaven, or from men? Tell me!"

31They discussed it among themselves and said, "If we say, 'From heaven,' he will ask, 'Then why didn't you believe him?' 32But if we say, 'From men' . . . ." (They feared the people, for everyone held that John really was a prophet.)

33So they answered Jesus, "We don't know."

Jesus said, "Neither will I tell you by what authority I am doing these things."

The Parable of the Tenants

12 He then began to speak to them in parables: "A man planted a vineyard. He put a wall around it, dug a pit for the winepress and built a watchtower. Then he rented the vineyard to some farmers and went away on a journey. 2At harvest time he sent a servant to the tenants to collect from them some of the fruit of the vineyard. 3But they seized him, beat him and sent him away empty-handed. 4Then he sent another servant to them; they struck this man on the head and treated him shamefully. 5He sent still another, and that one they killed. He sent many others; some of them they beat, others they killed.

6"He had one left to send, a son, whom he loved. He sent him last of all, saying, 'They will respect my son.'

7"But the tenants said to one another, 'This is the heir. Come, let's kill him, and the inheritance will be ours.' 8So they took him and killed him, and threw him out of the vineyard.

9"What then will the owner of the vineyard do? He will come and kill those tenants and give the vineyard to others. 10Haven't you read this scripture:

" 'The stone the builders rejected
has become the capstone[f];
11the Lord has done this,
and it is marvelous in our eyes'[g]?"

12Then they looked for a way to arrest him because they knew he had spoken the parable against them. But they were afraid of the crowd; so they left him and went away.

Paying Taxes to Caesar

13Later they sent some of the Pharisees and Herodians to Jesus to catch him in his words. 14They came to him and said, "Teacher, we know you are a man of integrity. You aren't swayed by men, because you pay no attention to who they are; but you teach the way of God in accordance with the truth. Is it right to pay taxes to Caesar or not? 15Should we pay or shouldn't we?"

But Jesus knew their hypocrisy. "Why are you trying to trap me?" he asked. "Bring me a denarius and let me look at it." 16They brought the coin, and he asked

[a]*17* Isaiah 56:7 [b]*17* Jer. 7:11 [c]*19* Some early manuscripts *he* [d]*22* Some early manuscripts *If you have* [e]*25* Some manuscripts *sins.* 26*But if you do not forgive, neither will your Father who is in heaven forgive your sins.* [f]*10* Or *cornerstone* [g]*11* Psalm 118:22,23

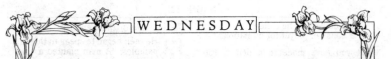

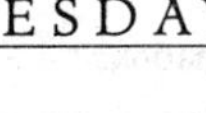

WEDNESDAY

VERSE FOR THE DAY:	*AUTHOR:*	*PASSAGE FOR THE DAY:*
Mark 11:24	*Hope MacDonald*	*Mark 11:22–25*

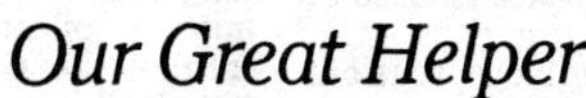

Our Great Helper

WHILE searching for a book I wanted to buy recently, I heard a pleasant voice ask, "May I help you?" Once I described the book, we soon found it. I left the store with my requested treasure happily tucked under my arm, and I thought, "I wonder how often God asks me this same question, but I'm too busy to hear?"

Maybe he's asking if there are any mountains in our lives that we need help in moving today—mountains of disappointment, heartache or fear. Sometimes these mountains can loom so large before us that we are no longer able to see Jesus. Yet it's here, while sitting in the shadow of our dark, cold mountain, that we can turn to Mark 11 and read what Jesus said. He gives us his pattern for prayer and sums up all we will ever need to know about it. The pattern is this: pray, ask, believe, forgive.

To pray is a supernatural way of getting to know a supernatural God. When we pray, God makes us his partners! He chooses us to become part of his ministry here on earth.

When Jesus inquires, "May I help you?" he wants us to respond in childlike trust. He wants us to ask. Sometimes he answers in a miraculous way, but most of the time he simply opens our spiritual eyes and shows us what *we* can do to bring about the answer. Then he gives us the ability to do it.

To believe is to give God the right to answer our prayer in the way he sees best. Remember, Jesus never gave a sermon on unanswered prayer because, from his viewpoint, all prayers are answered. When we learn to believe God, we find our attention is no longer on our mountain. It becomes focused instead on Jesus, who alone is worthy of our trust.

When we forgive, we open a channel to God. Jesus asks us to forgive others "so that your Father in heaven may forgive you your sins" (Mark 11:25).

God longs for us to live in the joy of walking by faith—praying, asking, believing, forgiving. When we do, we find we're no longer sitting alone in the shadow of the mountain.

Additional Scripture Readings:
Matthew 6:5–15; Philippians 4:6–7

Go to page 72 for your next devotional reading.

them, "Whose portrait is this? And whose
inscription?"
"Caesar's," they replied.
17 Then Jesus said to them, "Give to
Caesar what is Caesar's and to God what
is God's."
And they were amazed at him.

Marriage at the Resurrection

18 Then the Sadducees, who say there is
no resurrection, came to him with a question. 19 "Teacher," they said, "Moses
wrote for us that if a man's brother dies
and leaves a wife but no children, the
man must marry the widow and have children for his brother. 20 Now there were
seven brothers. The first one married
and died without leaving any children.
21 The second one married the widow,
but he also died, leaving no child. It
was the same with the third. 22 In fact,
none of the seven left any children. Last
of all, the woman died too. 23 At the
resurrection[a] whose wife will she be,
since the seven were married to her?"
24 Jesus replied, "Are you not in error
because you do not know the Scriptures
or the power of God? 25 When the dead
rise, they will neither marry nor be given
in marriage; they will be like the angels in
heaven. 26 Now about the dead rising—
have you not read in the book of Moses,
in the account of the bush, how God said
to him, 'I am the God of Abraham, the
God of Isaac, and the God of Jacob'[b]?
27 He is not the God of the dead, but of the
living. You are badly mistaken!"

The Greatest Commandment

28 One of the teachers of the law came
and heard them debating. Noticing that
Jesus had given them a good answer, he
asked him, "Of all the commandments,
which is the most important?"
29 "The most important one," answered
Jesus, "is this: 'Hear, O Israel, the Lord
our God, the Lord is one.[c] 30 Love the
Lord your God with all your heart and
with all your soul and with all your mind
and with all your strength.'[d] 31 The second is this: 'Love your neighbor as yourself.'[e] There is no commandment greater
than these."
32 "Well said, teacher," the man replied.
"You are right in saying that God is one
and there is no other but him. 33 To love
him with all your heart, with all your understanding and with all your strength,
and to love your neighbor as yourself is
more important than all burnt offerings
and sacrifices."
34 When Jesus saw that he had answered wisely, he said to him, "You are
not far from the kingdom of God." And
from then on no one dared ask him any
more questions.

Whose Son Is the Christ?

35 While Jesus was teaching in the temple courts, he asked, "How is it that the
teachers of the law say that the Christ[f] is
the son of David? 36 David himself, speaking by the Holy Spirit, declared:

" 'The Lord said to my Lord:
"Sit at my right hand
until I put your enemies
under your feet." '[g]

37 David himself calls him 'Lord.' How
then can he be his son?"
The large crowd listened to him with
delight.
38 As he taught, Jesus said, "Watch out
for the teachers of the law. They like to
walk around in flowing robes and be
greeted in the marketplaces, 39 and have
the most important seats in the synagogues and the places of honor at banquets. 40 They devour widows' houses and
for a show make lengthy prayers. Such
men will be punished most severely."

The Widow's Offering

41 Jesus sat down opposite the place
where the offerings were put and watched
the crowd putting their money into the
temple treasury. Many rich people threw
in large amounts. 42 But a poor widow
came and put in two very small copper
coins,[h] worth only a fraction of a penny.[i]
43 Calling his disciples to him, Jesus
said, "I tell you the truth, this poor widow
has put more into the treasury than all
the others. 44 They all gave out of their
wealth; but she, out of her poverty, put in
everything—all she had to live on."

Signs of the End of the Age

13 As he was leaving the temple, one
of his disciples said to him, "Look,
Teacher! What massive stones! What
magnificent buildings!"

[a]23 Some manuscripts *resurrection, when men rise from the dead,* [b]26 Exodus 3:6 [c]29 Or *the Lord our God is one Lord* [d]30 Deut. 6:4,5 [e]31 Lev. 19:18 [f]35 Or *Messiah* [g]36 Psalm 110:1 [h]42 Greek *two lepta* [i]42 Greek *kodrantes*

2"Do you see all these great buildings?"
replied Jesus. "Not one stone here will be
left on another; every one will be thrown
down."

3As Jesus was sitting on the Mount of
Olives opposite the temple, Peter, James,
John and Andrew asked him privately,
4"Tell us, when will these things happen?
And what will be the sign that they are all
about to be fulfilled?"

5Jesus said to them: "Watch out that no
one deceives you. 6Many will come in my
name, claiming, 'I am he,' and will deceive many. 7When you hear of wars and
rumors of wars, do not be alarmed. Such
things must happen, but the end is still to
come. 8Nation will rise against nation,
and kingdom against kingdom. There will
be earthquakes in various places, and
famines. These are the beginning of birth
pains.

9"You must be on your guard. You will
be handed over to the local councils and
flogged in the synagogues. On account of
me you will stand before governors and
kings as witnesses to them. 10And the
gospel must first be preached to all nations. 11Whenever you are arrested and
brought to trial, do not worry beforehand
about what to say. Just say whatever is
given you at the time, for it is not you
speaking, but the Holy Spirit.

12"Brother will betray brother to death,
and a father his child. Children will rebel
against their parents and have them put
to death. 13All men will hate you because
of me, but he who stands firm to the end
will be saved.

14"When you see 'the abomination that
causes desolation'[a] standing where it[b]
does not belong—let the reader understand—then let those who are in Judea
flee to the mountains. 15Let no one on the
roof of his house go down or enter the
house to take anything out. 16Let no one
in the field go back to get his cloak.
17How dreadful it will be in those days for
pregnant women and nursing mothers!
18Pray that this will not take place in winter, 19because those will be days of distress unequaled from the beginning,
when God created the world, until now—
and never to be equaled again. 20If the
Lord had not cut short those days, no one
would survive. But for the sake of the
elect, whom he has chosen, he has shortened them. 21At that time if anyone says
to you, 'Look, here is the Christ[c]!' or,
'Look, there he is!' do not believe it. 22For
false Christs and false prophets will appear and perform signs and miracles to
deceive the elect—if that were possible.
23So be on your guard; I have told you
everything ahead of time.

24"But in those days, following that distress,

" 'the sun will be darkened,
and the moon will not give its light;
25the stars will fall from the sky,
and the heavenly bodies will be
shaken.'[d]

26"At that time men will see the Son of
Man coming in clouds with great power
and glory. 27And he will send his angels
and gather his elect from the four winds,
from the ends of the earth to the ends of
the heavens.

28"Now learn this lesson from the fig
tree: As soon as its twigs get tender and
its leaves come out, you know that summer is near. 29Even so, when you see
these things happening, you know that it
is near, right at the door. 30I tell you the
truth, this generation[e] will certainly not
pass away until all these things have happened. 31Heaven and earth will pass
away, but my words will never pass away.

The Day and Hour Unknown

32"No one knows about that day or
hour, not even the angels in heaven, nor
the Son, but only the Father. 33Be on
guard! Be alert[f]! You do not know when
that time will come. 34It's like a man going away: He leaves his house and puts
his servants in charge, each with his assigned task, and tells the one at the door
to keep watch.

35"Therefore keep watch because you
do not know when the owner of the house
will come back—whether in the evening,
or at midnight, or when the rooster crows,
or at dawn. 36If he comes suddenly, do
not let him find you sleeping. 37What I say
to you, I say to everyone: 'Watch!' "

Jesus Anointed at Bethany

14 Now the Passover and the Feast of
Unleavened Bread were only two
days away, and the chief priests and the
teachers of the law were looking for some
sly way to arrest Jesus and kill him. 2"But

[a]14 Daniel 9:27; 11:31; 12:11 [b]14 Or *he*; also in verse 29 [c]21 Or *Messiah* [d]25 Isaiah 13:10; 34:4 [e]30 Or *race* [f]33 Some manuscripts *alert and pray*

not during the Feast," they said, "or the
people may riot."
3While he was in Bethany, reclining at
the table in the home of a man known as
Simon the Leper, a woman came with an
alabaster jar of very expensive perfume,
made of pure nard. She broke the jar and
poured the perfume on his head.
4Some of those present were saying in-
dignantly to one another, "Why this waste
of perfume? 5It could have been sold for
more than a year's wages[a] and the money
given to the poor." And they rebuked her
harshly.
6"Leave her alone," said Jesus. "Why
are you bothering her? She has done a
beautiful thing to me. 7The poor you will
always have with you, and you can help
them any time you want. But you will not
always have me. 8She did what she could.
She poured perfume on my body beforehand to prepare for my burial. 9I tell
you the truth, wherever the gospel is
preached throughout the world, what she
has done will also be told, in memory of
her."
10Then Judas Iscariot, one of the
Twelve, went to the chief priests to betray
Jesus to them. 11They were delighted to
hear this and promised to give him money. So he watched for an opportunity to
hand him over.

The Lord's Supper

12On the first day of the Feast of Unleavened Bread, when it was customary to
sacrifice the Passover lamb, Jesus' disciples asked him, "Where do you want us to
go and make preparations for you to eat
the Passover?"
13So he sent two of his disciples, telling
them, "Go into the city, and a man carrying a jar of water will meet you. Follow
him. 14Say to the owner of the house he
enters, 'The Teacher asks: Where is my
guest room, where I may eat the Passover
with my disciples?' 15He will show you a
large upper room, furnished and ready.
Make preparations for us there."
16The disciples left, went into the city
and found things just as Jesus had told
them. So they prepared the Passover.
17When evening came, Jesus arrived
with the Twelve. 18While they were reclining at the table eating, he said, "I tell you
the truth, one of you will betray me—one
who is eating with me."
19They were saddened, and one by one
they said to him, "Surely not I?"
20"It is one of the Twelve," he replied,
"one who dips bread into the bowl with
me. 21The Son of Man will go just as it is
written about him. But woe to that man
who betrays the Son of Man! It would be
better for him if he had not been born."
22While they were eating, Jesus took
bread, gave thanks and broke it, and gave
it to his disciples, saying, "Take it; this is
my body."
23Then he took the cup, gave thanks
and offered it to them, and they all drank
from it.
24"This is my blood of the[b] covenant,
which is poured out for many," he said to
them. 25"I tell you the truth, I will not
drink again of the fruit of the vine until
that day when I drink it anew in the kingdom of God."
26When they had sung a hymn, they
went out to the Mount of Olives.

Jesus Predicts Peter's Denial

27"You will all fall away," Jesus told
them, "for it is written:

" 'I will strike the shepherd,
and the sheep will be scattered.'[c]

28But after I have risen, I will go ahead of
you into Galilee."
29Peter declared, "Even if all fall away,
I will not."
30"I tell you the truth," Jesus answered,
"today—yes, tonight—before the rooster
crows twice[d] you yourself will disown me
three times."
31But Peter insisted emphatically,
"Even if I have to die with you, I will never
disown you." And all the others said the
same.

Gethsemane

32They went to a place called Gethsemane, and Jesus said to his disciples, "Sit
here while I pray." 33He took Peter, James
and John along with him, and he began to
be deeply distressed and troubled. 34"My
soul is overwhelmed with sorrow to the
point of death," he said to them. "Stay
here and keep watch."
35Going a little farther, he fell to the
ground and prayed that if possible the
hour might pass from him. 36"*Abba*,[e] Father," he said, "everything is possible for

[a]5 Greek *than three hundred denarii* [b]24 Some manuscripts *the new* [c]27 Zech. 13:7 [d]30 Some early manuscripts do not have *twice.* [e]36 Aramaic for *Father*

you. Take this cup from me. Yet not what
I will, but what you will."
37Then he returned to his disciples and
found them sleeping. "Simon," he said to
Peter, "are you asleep? Could you not
keep watch for one hour? 38Watch and
pray so that you will not fall into temptation. The spirit is willing, but the body is
weak."
39Once more he went away and prayed
the same thing. 40When he came back, he
again found them sleeping, because their
eyes were heavy. They did not know what
to say to him.
41Returning the third time, he said to
them, "Are you still sleeping and resting?
Enough! The hour has come. Look, the
Son of Man is betrayed into the hands of
sinners. 42Rise! Let us go! Here comes my
betrayer!"

Jesus Arrested

43Just as he was speaking, Judas, one
of the Twelve, appeared. With him was a
crowd armed with swords and clubs, sent
from the chief priests, the teachers of the
law, and the elders.
44Now the betrayer had arranged a signal with them: "The one I kiss is the man;
arrest him and lead him away under
guard." 45Going at once to Jesus, Judas
said, "Rabbi!" and kissed him. 46The men
seized Jesus and arrested him. 47Then
one of those standing near drew his sword
and struck the servant of the high priest,
cutting off his ear.
48"Am I leading a rebellion," said
Jesus, "that you have come out with
swords and clubs to capture me? 49Every
day I was with you, teaching in the temple
courts, and you did not arrest me. But the
Scriptures must be fulfilled." 50Then everyone deserted him and fled.
51A young man, wearing nothing but a
linen garment, was following Jesus. When
they seized him, 52he fled naked, leaving
his garment behind.

Before the Sanhedrin

53They took Jesus to the high priest,
and all the chief priests, elders and teachers of the law came together. 54Peter followed him at a distance, right into the
courtyard of the high priest. There he sat
with the guards and warmed himself at
the fire.
55The chief priests and the whole Sanhedrin were looking for evidence against
Jesus so that they could put him to death,
but they did not find any. 56Many testified
falsely against him, but their statements
did not agree.
57Then some stood up and gave this
false testimony against him: 58"We heard
him say, 'I will destroy this man-made
temple and in three days will build another, not made by man.' " 59Yet even then
their testimony did not agree.
60Then the high priest stood up before
them and asked Jesus, "Are you not going
to answer? What is this testimony that
these men are bringing against you?"
61But Jesus remained silent and gave no
answer.
Again the high priest asked him, "Are
you the Christ,[a] the Son of the Blessed
One?"
62"I am," said Jesus. "And you will see
the Son of Man sitting at the right hand
of the Mighty One and coming on the
clouds of heaven."
63The high priest tore his clothes. "Why
do we need any more witnesses?" he
asked. 64"You have heard the blasphemy.
What do you think?"
They all condemned him as worthy of
death. 65Then some began to spit at him;
they blindfolded him, struck him with
their fists, and said, "Prophesy!" And the
guards took him and beat him.

Peter Disowns Jesus

66While Peter was below in the courtyard, one of the servant girls of the high
priest came by. 67When she saw Peter
warming himself, she looked closely at
him.
"You also were with that Nazarene,
Jesus," she said.
68But he denied it. "I don't know or understand what you're talking about," he
said, and went out into the entryway.[b]
69When the servant girl saw him there,
she said again to those standing around,
"This fellow is one of them." 70Again he
denied it.
After a little while, those standing near
said to Peter, "Surely you are one of
them, for you are a Galilean."
71He began to call down curses on himself, and he swore to them, "I don't know
this man you're talking about."
72Immediately the rooster crowed the
second time.[c] Then Peter remembered

[a]61 Or *Messiah* [b]68 Some early manuscripts *entryway and the rooster crowed* [c]72 Some early manuscripts do not have *the second time.*

the word Jesus had spoken to him: "Before the rooster crows twice[a] you will disown me three times." And he broke down
and wept.

Jesus Before Pilate

15 Very early in the morning, the
chief priests, with the elders, the
teachers of the law and the whole Sanhedrin, reached a decision. They bound
Jesus, led him away and handed him over
to Pilate.
2"Are you the king of the Jews?" asked
Pilate.
"Yes, it is as you say," Jesus replied.
3The chief priests accused him of many
things. 4So again Pilate asked him,
"Aren't you going to answer? See how
many things they are accusing you of."
5But Jesus still made no reply, and Pilate was amazed.
6Now it was the custom at the Feast to
release a prisoner whom the people requested. 7A man called Barabbas was in
prison with the insurrectionists who had
committed murder in the uprising. 8The
crowd came up and asked Pilate to do for
them what he usually did.
9"Do you want me to release to you the
king of the Jews?" asked Pilate, 10know-
ing it was out of envy that the chief
priests had handed Jesus over to him.
11But the chief priests stirred up the
crowd to have Pilate release Barabbas instead.
12"What shall I do, then, with the one
you call the king of the Jews?" Pilate
asked them.
13"Crucify him!" they shouted.
14"Why? What crime has he committed?" asked Pilate.
But they shouted all the louder, "Crucify him!"
15Wanting to satisfy the crowd, Pilate
released Barabbas to them. He had Jesus
flogged, and handed him over to be crucified.

The Soldiers Mock Jesus

16The soldiers led Jesus away into the
palace (that is, the Praetorium) and
called together the whole company of soldiers. 17They put a purple robe on him,
then twisted together a crown of thorns
and set it on him. 18And they began to call
out to him, "Hail, king of the Jews!"
19Again and again they struck him on the
head with a staff and spit on him. Falling
on their knees, they paid homage to him.
20And when they had mocked him, they
took off the purple robe and put his own
clothes on him. Then they led him out to
crucify him.

The Crucifixion

21A certain man from Cyrene, Simon,
the father of Alexander and Rufus, was
passing by on his way in from the country,
and they forced him to carry the cross.
22They brought Jesus to the place called
Golgotha (which means The Place of the
Skull). 23Then they offered him wine
mixed with myrrh, but he did not take it.
24And they crucified him. Dividing up his
clothes, they cast lots to see what each
would get.
25It was the third hour when they crucified him. 26The written notice of the
charge against him read: THE KING OF THE
JEWS. 27They crucified two robbers with
him, one on his right and one on his left.[b]
29Those who passed by hurled insults at
him, shaking their heads and saying, "So!
You who are going to destroy the temple
and build it in three days, 30come down
from the cross and save yourself!"
31In the same way the chief priests and
the teachers of the law mocked him
among themselves. "He saved others,"
they said, "but he can't save himself!
32Let this Christ,[c] this King of Israel,
come down now from the cross, that we
may see and believe." Those crucified
with him also heaped insults on him.

The Death of Jesus

33At the sixth hour darkness came over
the whole land until the ninth hour.
34And at the ninth hour Jesus cried out in
a loud voice, *"Eloi, Eloi, lama sabachthani?"*—which means, "My God, my God,
why have you forsaken me?"[d]
35When some of those standing near
heard this, they said, "Listen, he's calling
Elijah."
36One man ran, filled a sponge with
wine vinegar, put it on a stick, and offered
it to Jesus to drink. "Now leave him
alone. Let's see if Elijah comes to take
him down," he said.
37With a loud cry, Jesus breathed his
last.

[a]72 Some early manuscripts do not have *twice*. [b]27 Some manuscripts *left,* [28]*and the scripture was fulfilled which says, "He was counted with the lawless ones"* (Isaiah 53:12) [c]32 Or *Messiah*
[d]34 Psalm 22:1

38The curtain of the temple was torn in
two from top to bottom. 39And when the
centurion, who stood there in front of
Jesus, heard his cry and[a] saw how he
died, he said, "Surely this man was the
Son[b] of God!"

40Some women were watching from a
distance. Among them were Mary Magdalene, Mary the mother of James the younger and of Joses, and Salome. 41In Galilee
these women had followed him and cared
for his needs. Many other women who
had come up with him to Jerusalem were
also there.

The Burial of Jesus

42It was Preparation Day (that is, the
day before the Sabbath). So as evening
approached, 43Joseph of Arimathea, a
prominent member of the Council, who
was himself waiting for the kingdom of
God, went boldly to Pilate and asked for
Jesus' body. 44Pilate was surprised to
hear that he was already dead. Summon-
ing the centurion, he asked him if Jesus
had already died. 45When he learned from
the centurion that it was so, he gave the
body to Joseph. 46So Joseph bought some
linen cloth, took down the body, wrapped
it in the linen, and placed it in a tomb cut
out of rock. Then he rolled a stone
against the entrance of the tomb. 47Mary
Magdalene and Mary the mother of Joses
saw where he was laid.

The Resurrection

16 When the Sabbath was over, Mary
Magdalene, Mary the mother of
James, and Salome bought spices so that
they might go to anoint Jesus' body. 2Very
early on the first day of the week, just
after sunrise, they were on their way to
the tomb 3and they asked each other,

[a]39 Some manuscripts do not have *heard his cry and* [b]39 Or *a son*

THURSDAY

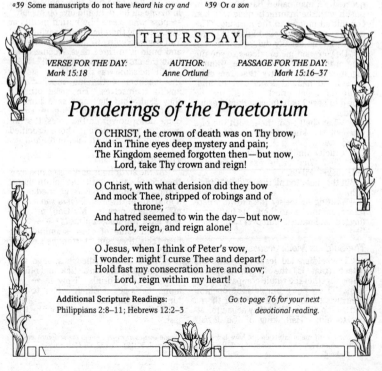

VERSE FOR THE DAY: *Mark 15:18* | *AUTHOR:* *Anne Ortlund* | *PASSAGE FOR THE DAY:* *Mark 15:16–37*

Ponderings of the Praetorium

O CHRIST, the crown of death was on Thy brow,
And in Thine eyes deep mystery and pain;
The Kingdom seemed forgotten then—but now,
Lord, take Thy crown and reign!

O Christ, with what derision did they bow
And mock Thee, stripped of robings and of throne;
And hatred seemed to win the day—but now,
Lord, reign, and reign alone!

O Jesus, when I think of Peter's vow,
I wonder: might I curse Thee and depart?
Hold fast my consecration here and now;
Lord, reign within my heart!

Additional Scripture Readings:
Philippians 2:8–11; Hebrews 12:2–3

Go to page 76 for your next devotional reading.

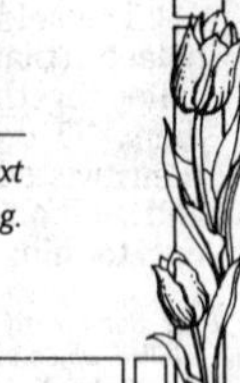

"Who will roll the stone away from the
entrance of the tomb?"
4But when they looked up, they saw
that the stone, which was very large, had
been rolled away. 5As they entered the
tomb, they saw a young man dressed in a
white robe sitting on the right side, and
they were alarmed.
6"Don't be alarmed," he said. "You are
looking for Jesus the Nazarene, who was
crucified. He has risen! He is not here.
See the place where they laid him. 7But
go, tell his disciples and Peter, 'He is going ahead of you into Galilee. There you
will see him, just as he told you.' "
8Trembling and bewildered, the wom-
en went out and fled from the tomb. They
said nothing to anyone, because they
were afraid.

[The earliest manuscripts and some other ancient witnesses do not have Mark 16:9–20.]

9When Jesus rose early on the first day
of the week, he appeared first to Mary
Magdalene, out of whom he had driven
seven demons. 10She went and told those
who had been with him and who were
mourning and weeping. 11When they
heard that Jesus was alive and that she
had seen him, they did not believe it.
12Afterward Jesus appeared in a different form to two of them while they were
walking in the country. 13These returned
and reported it to the rest; but they did
not believe them either.
14Later Jesus appeared to the Eleven as
they were eating; he rebuked them for
their lack of faith and their stubborn re-
fusal to believe those who had seen him
after he had risen.
15He said to them, "Go into all the
world and preach the good news to all
creation. 16Whoever believes and is baptized will be saved, but whoever does not
believe will be condemned. 17And these
signs will accompany those who believe:
In my name they will drive out demons;
they will speak in new tongues; 18they
will pick up snakes with their hands; and
when they drink deadly poison, it will not
hurt them at all; they will place their
hands on sick people, and they will get
well."
19After the Lord Jesus had spoken to
them, he was taken up into heaven and
he sat at the right hand of God. 20Then
the disciples went out and preached everywhere, and the Lord worked with them
and confirmed his word by the signs that
accompanied it.

LUKE writes this gospel to present Jesus as a Savior for the whole human race. The stories emphasize how kind and loving Jesus is to those despised by society (such as tax collectors, Samaritans, the poor, and women). He stresses the importance of prayer in Jesus' life. As you read this book, be sure that you have repented of your sins and have claimed Jesus as your own personal Savior. Ask yourself whether you show the same sort of compassion to others that Jesus showed.

LUKE

Introduction

1 Many have undertaken to draw up an
account of the things that have been
fulfilled[a] among us, 2just as they were
handed down to us by those who from the
first were eyewitnesses and servants of
the word. 3Therefore, since I myself have
carefully investigated everything from the
beginning, it seemed good also to me to
write an orderly account for you, most excellent Theophilus, 4so that you may
know the certainty of the things you have
been taught.

The Birth of John the Baptist Foretold

5In the time of Herod king of Judea
there was a priest named Zechariah, who
belonged to the priestly division of Abijah; his wife Elizabeth was also a descendant of Aaron. 6Both of them were upright
in the sight of God, observing all the
Lord's commandments and regulations
blamelessly. 7But they had no children,
because Elizabeth was barren; and they
were both well along in years.
8Once when Zechariah's division was

[a]1 Or *been surely believed*

on duty and he was serving as priest before God, 9he was chosen by lot, according to the custom of the priesthood, to go
into the temple of the Lord and burn incense. 10And when the time for the burning of incense came, all the assembled
worshipers were praying outside.

11Then an angel of the Lord appeared
to him, standing at the right side of the
altar of incense. 12When Zechariah saw
him, he was startled and was gripped with
fear. 13But the angel said to him: "Do not
be afraid, Zechariah; your prayer has been
heard. Your wife Elizabeth will bear you a
son, and you are to give him the name
John. 14He will be a joy and delight to
you, and many will rejoice because of his
birth, 15for he will be great in the sight of
the Lord. He is never to take wine or other
fermented drink, and he will be filled
with the Holy Spirit even from birth.[a]
16Many of the people of Israel will he
bring back to the Lord their God. 17And
he will go on before the Lord, in the spirit
and power of Elijah, to turn the hearts of
the fathers to their children and the disobedient to the wisdom of the righteous
—to make ready a people prepared for
the Lord."

18Zechariah asked the angel, "How can
I be sure of this? I am an old man and my
wife is well along in years."

19The angel answered, "I am Gabriel. I
stand in the presence of God, and I have
been sent to speak to you and to tell you
this good news. 20And now you will be
silent and not able to speak until the day
this happens, because you did not believe
my words, which will come true at their
proper time."

21Meanwhile, the people were waiting
for Zechariah and wondering why he
stayed so long in the temple. 22When he
came out, he could not speak to them.
They realized he had seen a vision in the
temple, for he kept making signs to them
but remained unable to speak.

23When his time of service was completed, he returned home. 24After this his
wife Elizabeth became pregnant and for
five months remained in seclusion.
25"The Lord has done this for me," she
said. "In these days he has shown his favor and taken away my disgrace among
the people."

The Birth of Jesus Foretold

26In the sixth month, God sent the angel Gabriel to Nazareth, a town in Galilee,
27to a virgin pledged to be married to a
man named Joseph, a descendant of David. The virgin's name was Mary. 28The
angel went to her and said, "Greetings,
you who are highly favored! The Lord is
with you."

29Mary was greatly troubled at his
words and wondered what kind of greeting this might be. 30But the angel said to
her, "Do not be afraid, Mary, you have
found favor with God. 31You will be with
child and give birth to a son, and you are
to give him the name Jesus. 32He will be
great and will be called the Son of the
Most High. The Lord God will give him
the throne of his father David, 33and he
will reign over the house of Jacob forever;
his kingdom will never end."

34"How will this be," Mary asked the
angel, "since I am a virgin?"

35The angel answered, "The Holy Spirit
will come upon you, and the power of the
Most High will overshadow you. So the
holy one to be born will be called[b] the
Son of God. 36Even Elizabeth your relative is going to have a child in her old age,
and she who was said to be barren is in
her sixth month. 37For nothing is impossible with God."

38"I am the Lord's servant," Mary answered. "May it be to me as you have
said." Then the angel left her.

Mary Visits Elizabeth

39At that time Mary got ready and hurried to a town in the hill country of Judea,
40where she entered Zechariah's home
and greeted Elizabeth. 41When Elizabeth
heard Mary's greeting, the baby leaped in
her womb, and Elizabeth was filled with
the Holy Spirit. 42In a loud voice she exclaimed: "Blessed are you among women,
and blessed is the child you will bear!
43But why am I so favored, that the mother of my Lord should come to me? 44As
soon as the sound of your greeting
reached my ears, the baby in my womb
leaped for joy. 45Blessed is she who has
believed that what the Lord has said to
her will be accomplished!"

Mary's Song

46And Mary said:

"My soul glorifies the Lord
47 and my spirit rejoices in God my
Savior,

[a]15 Or *from his mother's womb* [b]35 Or *So the child to be born will be called holy,*

FRIDAY

VERSE FOR THE DAY:
Luke 1:46–47

AUTHOR:
Anne Ortlund

PASSAGE FOR THE DAY:
Luke 1:26–38

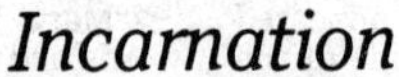

Incarnation

"THE Lord is in His holy house"—
Oh, grace beyond describing,
That Christ in me should please to dwell—
Immanuel residing!
"My soul doth magnify the Lord,"
I sing with lowly Mary,
That God should choose to enter in
This
humble sanctuary!

Not now in little Bethlehem,
As in the tender story;
Not now upon a mercy seat,
The bright *Shekinah* glory,
But in the body of His saint
He maketh His residing,
Both He in me and I in Him
In
fellowship abiding.

Within my heart a burning bush,
Within, a mountain smoking;
This flesh of mine a temple veil,
The wondrous Presence cloaking;
Within this broken earthenware
A high and holy treasure:
Oh, mystery of mysteries!
Oh, grace
beyond all measure!

"The Lord is in His Holy house"—
Mysterious habitation!
I feel His presence here within
And offer my oblation.
Keep burning, incense of my soul!
Keep cleansing me, O Laver!
I want to serve and praise my God
Forever
and forever!

Additional Scripture Readings:
John 14:23–27; 2 Corinthians 1:21–22

Go to page 78 for your next devotional reading.

[48]for he has been mindful
of the humble state of his servant.
From now on all generations will call
me blessed,
[49] for the Mighty One has done great
things for me—
holy is his name.
[50]His mercy extends to those who fear
him,
from generation to generation.
[51]He has performed mighty deeds with
his arm;
he has scattered those who are
proud in their inmost thoughts.
[52]He has brought down rulers from
their thrones
but has lifted up the humble.
[53]He has filled the hungry with good
things
but has sent the rich away empty.
[54]He has helped his servant Israel,
remembering to be merciful
[55]to Abraham and his descendants
forever,
even as he said to our fathers."

[56]Mary stayed with Elizabeth for about
three months and then returned home.

The Birth of John the Baptist

[57]When it was time for Elizabeth to
have her baby, she gave birth to a son.
[58]Her neighbors and relatives heard that
the Lord had shown her great mercy, and
they shared her joy.
[59]On the eighth day they came to circumcise the child, and they were going to
name him after his father Zechariah,
[60]but his mother spoke up and said, "No!
He is to be called John."
[61]They said to her, "There is no one
among your relatives who has that
name."
[62]Then they made signs to his father, to
find out what he would like to name the
child. [63]He asked for a writing tablet, and
to everyone's astonishment he wrote,
"His name is John." [64]Immediately his
mouth was opened and his tongue was
loosed, and he began to speak, praising
God. [65]The neighbors were all filled with
awe, and throughout the hill country of
Judea people were talking about all these
things. [66]Everyone who heard this wondered about it, asking, "What then is this
child going to be?" For the Lord's hand
was with him.

Zechariah's Song

[67]His father Zechariah was filled with
the Holy Spirit and prophesied:

[68]"Praise be to the Lord, the God of
Israel,
because he has come and has
redeemed his people.
[69]He has raised up a horn[a] of salvation
for us
in the house of his servant David
[70](as he said through his holy prophets
of long ago),
[71]salvation from our enemies
and from the hand of all who hate
us—
[72]to show mercy to our fathers
and to remember his holy covenant,
[73] the oath he swore to our father
Abraham:
[74]to rescue us from the hand of our
enemies,
and to enable us to serve him
without fear
[75] in holiness and righteousness
before him all our days.

[76]And you, my child, will be called a
prophet of the Most High;
for you will go on before the Lord
to prepare the way for him,
[77]to give his people the knowledge of
salvation
through the forgiveness of their
sins,
[78]because of the tender mercy of our
God,
by which the rising sun will come
to us from heaven
[79]to shine on those living in darkness
and in the shadow of death,
to guide our feet into the path of
peace."

[80]And the child grew and became
strong in spirit; and he lived in the desert
until he appeared publicly to Israel.

The Birth of Jesus

2 In those days Caesar Augustus issued
a decree that a census should be tak-
en of the entire Roman world. [2](This was
the first census that took place while Qui-
rinius was governor of Syria.) [3]And everyone went to his own town to register.
[4]So Joseph also went up from the town
of Nazareth in Galilee to Judea, to Bethlehem the town of David, because he be-

[a]69 *Horn* here symbolizes strength.

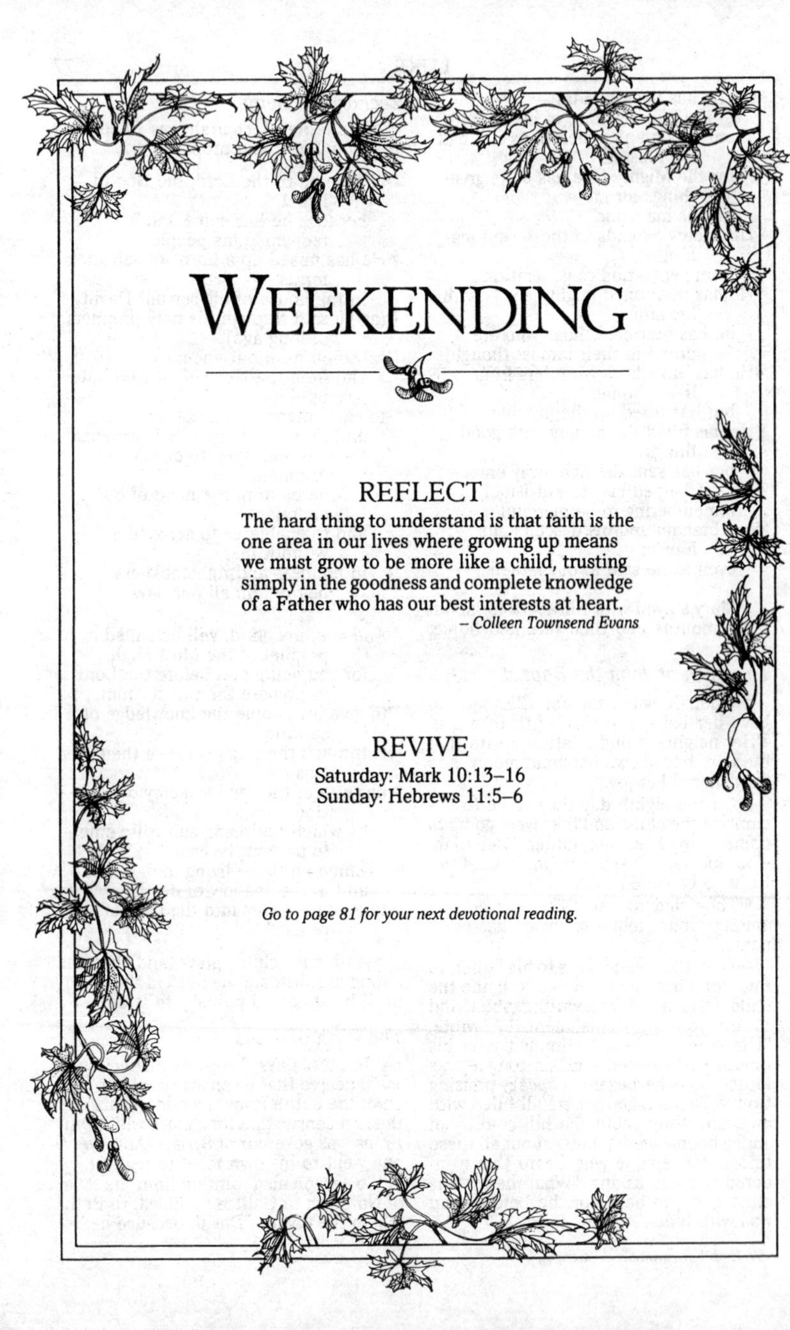

WEEKENDING

REFLECT

The hard thing to understand is that faith is the one area in our lives where growing up means we must grow to be more like a child, trusting simply in the goodness and complete knowledge of a Father who has our best interests at heart.

– Colleen Townsend Evans

REVIVE

Saturday: Mark 10:13–16
Sunday: Hebrews 11:5–6

Go to page 81 for your next devotional reading.

longed to the house and line of David.
5He went there to register with Mary, who
was pledged to be married to him and was
expecting a child. 6While they were there,
the time came for the baby to be born,
7and she gave birth to her firstborn, a son.
She wrapped him in cloths and placed
him in a manger, because there was no
room for them in the inn.

The Shepherds and the Angels

8And there were shepherds living out in
the fields nearby, keeping watch over
their flocks at night. 9An angel of the Lord
appeared to them, and the glory of the
Lord shone around them, and they were
terrified. 10But the angel said to them,
"Do not be afraid. I bring you good news
of great joy that will be for all the people.
11Today in the town of David a Savior has
been born to you; he is Christ[a] the Lord.
12This will be a sign to you: You will find
a baby wrapped in cloths and lying in a
manger."

13Suddenly a great company of the
heavenly host appeared with the angel,
praising God and saying,

14"Glory to God in the highest,
and on earth peace to men on
whom his favor rests."

15When the angels had left them and
gone into heaven, the shepherds said to
one another, "Let's go to Bethlehem and
see this thing that has happened, which
the Lord has told us about."

16So they hurried off and found Mary
and Joseph, and the baby, who was lying
in the manger. 17When they had seen
him, they spread the word concerning
what had been told them about this child,
18and all who heard it were amazed at
what the shepherds said to them. 19But
Mary treasured up all these things and
pondered them in her heart. 20The shepherds returned, glorifying and praising
God for all the things they had heard and
seen, which were just as they had been
told.

Jesus Presented in the Temple

21On the eighth day, when it was time
to circumcise him, he was named Jesus,
the name the angel had given him before
he had been conceived.

22When the time of their purification
according to the Law of Moses had been
completed, Joseph and Mary took him to
Jerusalem to present him to the Lord
23(as it is written in the Law of the Lord,
"Every firstborn male is to be consecrated
to the Lord"[b]), 24and to offer a sacrifice in
keeping with what is said in the Law of
the Lord: "a pair of doves or two young
pigeons."[c]

25Now there was a man in Jerusalem
called Simeon, who was righteous and devout. He was waiting for the consolation
of Israel, and the Holy Spirit was upon
him. 26It had been revealed to him by the
Holy Spirit that he would not die before
he had seen the Lord's Christ. 27Moved by
the Spirit, he went into the temple courts.
When the parents brought in the child
Jesus to do for him what the custom of
the Law required, 28Simeon took him in
his arms and praised God, saying:

29"Sovereign Lord, as you have
promised,
you now dismiss[d] your servant in
peace.
30For my eyes have seen your salvation,
31 which you have prepared in the
sight of all people,
32a light for revelation to the Gentiles
and for glory to your people Israel."

33The child's father and mother marveled at what was said about him. 34Then
Simeon blessed them and said to Mary,
his mother: "This child is destined to
cause the falling and rising of many in
Israel, and to be a sign that will be spoken
against, 35so that the thoughts of many
hearts will be revealed. And a sword will
pierce your own soul too."

36There was also a prophetess, Anna,
the daughter of Phanuel, of the tribe of
Asher. She was very old; she had lived
with her husband seven years after her
marriage, 37and then was a widow until
she was eighty-four.[e] She never left the
temple but worshiped night and day, fasting and praying. 38Coming up to them at
that very moment, she gave thanks to God
and spoke about the child to all who were
looking forward to the redemption of Jerusalem.

39When Joseph and Mary had done everything required by the Law of the Lord,
they returned to Galilee to their own
town of Nazareth. 40And the child grew

[a] *11* Or *Messiah.* "The Christ" (Greek) and "the Messiah" (Hebrew) both mean "the Anointed One"; also in verse 26. [b] *23* Exodus 13:2,12 [c] *24* Lev. 12:8 [d] *29* Or *promised, / now dismiss* [e] *37* Or *widow for eighty-four years*

and became strong; he was filled with
wisdom, and the grace of God was upon
him.

The Boy Jesus at the Temple

41Every year his parents went to Jerusalem for the Feast of the Passover. 42When
he was twelve years old, they went up to
the Feast, according to the custom. 43Af-
ter the Feast was over, while his parents
were returning home, the boy Jesus
stayed behind in Jerusalem, but they
were unaware of it. 44Thinking he was in
their company, they traveled on for a day.
Then they began looking for him among
their relatives and friends. 45When they
did not find him, they went back to Jerusalem to look for him. 46After three days
they found him in the temple courts, sitting among the teachers, listening to
them and asking them questions. 47Ev-
eryone who heard him was amazed at his
understanding and his answers. 48When
his parents saw him, they were astonished. His mother said to him, "Son, why
have you treated us like this? Your father
and I have been anxiously searching for
you."

49"Why were you searching for me?" he
asked. "Didn't you know I had to be in my
Father's house?" 50But they did not understand what he was saying to them.

51Then he went down to Nazareth with
them and was obedient to them. But his
mother treasured all these things in her
heart. 52And Jesus grew in wisdom and
stature, and in favor with God and men.

John the Baptist Prepares the Way

3 In the fifteenth year of the reign of
Tiberius Caesar—when Pontius Pilate was governor of Judea, Herod tetrarch of Galilee, his brother Philip tetrarch of Iturea and Traconitis, and Lysa-
nias tetrarch of Abilene— 2during the
high priesthood of Annas and Caiaphas,
the word of God came to John son of
Zechariah in the desert. 3He went into all
the country around the Jordan, preaching
a baptism of repentance for the forgiveness of sins. 4As is written in the book of
the words of Isaiah the prophet:

"A voice of one calling in the desert,
'Prepare the way for the Lord,
make straight paths for him.
5Every valley shall be filled in,
every mountain and hill made low.
The crooked roads shall become
straight,
the rough ways smooth.
6And all mankind will see God's
salvation.' "[a]

7John said to the crowds coming out to
be baptized by him, "You brood of vipers!
Who warned you to flee from the coming
wrath? 8Produce fruit in keeping with repentance. And do not begin to say to
yourselves, 'We have Abraham as our father.' For I tell you that out of these
stones God can raise up children for
Abraham. 9The ax is already at the root of
the trees, and every tree that does not
produce good fruit will be cut down and
thrown into the fire."

10"What should we do then?" the crowd
asked.

11John answered, "The man with two
tunics should share with him who has
none, and the one who has food should
do the same."

12Tax collectors also came to be baptized. "Teacher," they asked, "what
should we do?"

13"Don't collect any more than you are
required to," he told them.

14Then some soldiers asked him, "And
what should we do?"

He replied, "Don't extort money and
don't accuse people falsely—be content
with your pay."

15The people were waiting expectantly
and were all wondering in their hearts if
John might possibly be the Christ.[b]
16John answered them all, "I baptize you
with[c] water. But one more powerful than
I will come, the thongs of whose sandals
I am not worthy to untie. He will baptize
you with the Holy Spirit and with fire.
17His winnowing fork is in his hand to
clear his threshing floor and to gather the
wheat into his barn, but he will burn up
the chaff with unquenchable fire." 18And
with many other words John exhorted the
people and preached the good news to
them.

19But when John rebuked Herod the tetrarch because of Herodias, his brother's
wife, and all the other evil things he had
done, 20Herod added this to them all: He
locked John up in prison.

The Baptism and Genealogy of Jesus

21When all the people were being baptized, Jesus was baptized too. And as he

[a]6 Isaiah 40:3-5 [b]15 Or *Messiah* [c]16 Or *in*

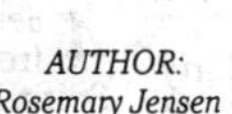

MONDAY

VERSE FOR THE DAY: *Luke 2:52*

AUTHOR: *Rosemary Jensen*

PASSAGE FOR THE DAY: *Luke 2:41–52*

Growing in Wisdom

IN Luke 2:52 we learn that "Jesus grew in wisdom and stature, and in favor with God and men." It is not difficult to understand how Jesus grew in stature—he just got taller! But how could the Son of God grow in wisdom? Did he not already have all wisdom? Did he lack anything? Was he not perfect? Yes, he was filled with wisdom—as much wisdom as a child without life experience can have.

It may help to remember that a few ounces of milk can fill an infant boy, but it would take a few quarts to fill a teenage boy. The difference is that the teenager has increased his capacity for milk. As Jesus grew physically, he also grew in his capacity for wisdom as he learned from his experiences. What is our individual capacity for wisdom? Could we increase that capacity?

Wisdom comes when we examine the experiences God gives us and discern what we have (or should have) learned from them. Nothing that has happened to us should be wasted (Romans 8:28). Because it is sometimes painful, often we do not take the time or effort to discover the reason for the "gift" of our personal experiences. When we do not learn as we should, we stop growing until we learn those same lessons through another experience tailor-made by God to make us mature (James 1:2–4). Most often we gain insight into our experiences only after earnest, persistent prayer. Psalm 43 is a wonderful model of persistent prayer; it opens up to us a person searching to know what God wants to reveal about a specific experience.

Perhaps we should try writing out what we have learned about God, ourselves and life during and then after an important experience. As we learn these lessons, I think we'll find that we will not need to learn them again in exactly the same way! This increases our individual capacity to learn greater lessons and gain deeper wisdom (Matthew 13:12).

Additional Scripture Readings:
1 Corinthians 13:11–12; James 1:22–25

Go to page 85 for your next devotional reading.

was praying, heaven was opened [22]and the Holy Spirit descended on him in bodily form like a dove. And a voice came from heaven: "You are my Son, whom I love; with you I am well pleased."

[23]Now Jesus himself was about thirty years old when he began his ministry. He was the son, so it was thought, of Joseph,

the son of Heli, [24]the son of Matthat,
the son of Levi, the son of Melki,
the son of Jannai, the son of Joseph,
[25]the son of Mattathias, the son of Amos,
the son of Nahum, the son of Esli,
the son of Naggai, [26]the son of Maath,
the son of Mattathias, the son of Semein,
the son of Josech, the son of Joda,
[27]the son of Joanan, the son of Rhesa,
the son of Zerubbabel, the son of Shealtiel,
the son of Neri, [28]the son of Melki,
the son of Addi, the son of Cosam,
the son of Elmadam, the son of Er,
[29]the son of Joshua, the son of Eliezer,
the son of Jorim, the son of Matthat,
the son of Levi, [30]the son of Simeon,
the son of Judah, the son of Joseph,
the son of Jonam, the son of Eliakim,
[31]the son of Melea, the son of Menna,
the son of Mattatha, the son of Nathan,
the son of David, [32]the son of Jesse,
the son of Obed, the son of Boaz,
the son of Salmon,[a] the son of Nahshon,
[33]the son of Amminadab, the son of Ram,[b]
the son of Hezron, the son of Perez,
the son of Judah, [34]the son of Jacob,
the son of Isaac, the son of Abraham,
the son of Terah, the son of Nahor,
[35]the son of Serug, the son of Reu,
the son of Peleg, the son of Eber,
the son of Shelah, [36]the son of Cainan,
the son of Arphaxad, the son of Shem,
the son of Noah, the son of Lamech,
[37]the son of Methuselah, the son of Enoch,
the son of Jared, the son of Mahalalel,
the son of Kenan, [38]the son of Enosh,
the son of Seth, the son of Adam,
the son of God.

The Temptation of Jesus

4 Jesus, full of the Holy Spirit, returned from the Jordan and was led by the Spirit in the desert, [2]where for forty days he was tempted by the devil. He ate nothing during those days, and at the end of them he was hungry.

[3]The devil said to him, "If you are the Son of God, tell this stone to become bread."

[4]Jesus answered, "It is written: 'Man does not live on bread alone.'[c]"

[5]The devil led him up to a high place and showed him in an instant all the kingdoms of the world. [6]And he said to him, "I will give you all their authority and splendor, for it has been given to me, and I can give it to anyone I want to. [7]So if you worship me, it will all be yours."

[8]Jesus answered, "It is written: 'Worship the Lord your God and serve him only.'[d]"

[9]The devil led him to Jerusalem and had him stand on the highest point of the temple. "If you are the Son of God," he said, "throw yourself down from here. [10]For it is written:

" 'He will command his angels
concerning you
to guard you carefully;
[11]they will lift you up in their hands,
so that you will not strike your foot
against a stone.'[e]"

[12]Jesus answered, "It says: 'Do not put the Lord your God to the test.'[f]"

[13]When the devil had finished all this tempting, he left him until an opportune time.

Jesus Rejected at Nazareth

[14]Jesus returned to Galilee in the power of the Spirit, and news about him spread through the whole countryside. [15]He taught in their synagogues, and everyone praised him.

[16]He went to Nazareth, where he had been brought up, and on the Sabbath day he went into the synagogue, as was his custom. And he stood up to read. [17]The scroll of the prophet Isaiah was handed to him. Unrolling it, he found the place where it is written:

[18]"The Spirit of the Lord is on me,

[a]32 Some early manuscripts *Sala* [b]33 Some manuscripts *Amminadab, the son of Admin, the son of Arni*; other manuscripts vary widely. [c]4 Deut. 8:3 [d]8 Deut. 6:13 [e]11 Psalm 91:11,12 [f]12 Deut. 6:16

because he has anointed me
to preach good news to the poor.
He has sent me to proclaim freedom
for the prisoners
and recovery of sight for the blind,
to release the oppressed,
19 to proclaim the year of the Lord's
favor."[a]

20Then he rolled up the scroll, gave it
back to the attendant and sat down. The
eyes of everyone in the synagogue were
fastened on him, 21and he began by saying to them, "Today this scripture is fulfilled in your hearing."
22All spoke well of him and were
amazed at the gracious words that came
from his lips. "Isn't this Joseph's son?"
they asked.
23Jesus said to them, "Surely you will
quote this proverb to me: 'Physician, heal
yourself! Do here in your hometown what
we have heard that you did in Capernaum.' "
24"I tell you the truth," he continued,
"no prophet is accepted in his hometown.
25I assure you that there were many widows in Israel in Elijah's time, when the
sky was shut for three and a half years and
there was a severe famine throughout the
land. 26Yet Elijah was not sent to any of
them, but to a widow in Zarephath in the
region of Sidon. 27And there were many in
Israel with leprosy[b] in the time of Elisha
the prophet, yet not one of them was
cleansed—only Naaman the Syrian."
28All the people in the synagogue were
furious when they heard this. 29They got
up, drove him out of the town, and took
him to the brow of the hill on which the
town was built, in order to throw him
down the cliff. 30But he walked right
through the crowd and went on his way.

Jesus Drives Out an Evil Spirit

31Then he went down to Capernaum, a
town in Galilee, and on the Sabbath began to teach the people. 32They were
amazed at his teaching, because his message had authority.
33In the synagogue there was a man
possessed by a demon, an evil[c] spirit. He
cried out at the top of his voice, 34"Ha!
What do you want with us, Jesus of Nazareth? Have you come to destroy us? I
know who you are—the Holy One of
God!"
35"Be quiet!" Jesus said sternly. "Come
out of him!" Then the demon threw the
man down before them all and came out
without injuring him.
36All the people were amazed and said
to each other, "What is this teaching?
With authority and power he gives orders
to evil spirits and they come out!" 37And
the news about him spread throughout
the surrounding area.

Jesus Heals Many

38Jesus left the synagogue and went to
the home of Simon. Now Simon's mother-in-law was suffering from a high fever,
and they asked Jesus to help her. 39So he
bent over her and rebuked the fever, and
it left her. She got up at once and began
to wait on them.
40When the sun was setting, the people
brought to Jesus all who had various
kinds of sickness, and laying his hands on
each one, he healed them. 41Moreover,
demons came out of many people, shouting, "You are the Son of God!" But he rebuked them and would not allow them to
speak, because they knew he was the
Christ.[d]
42At daybreak Jesus went out to a solitary place. The people were looking for
him and when they came to where he
was, they tried to keep him from leaving
them. 43But he said, "I must preach the
good news of the kingdom of God to the
other towns also, because that is why I
was sent." 44And he kept on preaching in
the synagogues of Judea.[e]

The Calling of the First Disciples

5 One day as Jesus was standing by the
Lake of Gennesaret,[f] with the people
crowding around him and listening to the
word of God, 2he saw at the water's edge
two boats, left there by the fishermen,
who were washing their nets. 3He got into
one of the boats, the one belonging to
Simon, and asked him to put out a little
from shore. Then he sat down and taught
the people from the boat.
4When he had finished speaking, he
said to Simon, "Put out into deep water,
and let down[g] the nets for a catch."
5Simon answered, "Master, we've
worked hard all night and haven't caught
anything. But because you say so, I will
let down the nets."

[a]*19* Isaiah 61:1,2 [b]*27* The Greek word was used for various diseases affecting the skin—not necessarily leprosy. [c]*33* Greek *unclean*; also in verse 36 [d]*41* Or *Messiah* [e]*44* Or *the land of the Jews*; some manuscripts *Galilee* [f]*1* That is, Sea of Galilee [g]*4* The Greek verb is plural.

6When they had done so, they caught
such a large number of fish that their nets
began to break. 7So they signaled their
partners in the other boat to come and
help them, and they came and filled both
boats so full that they began to sink.
8When Simon Peter saw this, he fell at
Jesus' knees and said, "Go away from me,
Lord; I am a sinful man!" 9For he and all
his companions were astonished at the
catch of fish they had taken, 10and so
were James and John, the sons of Zebedee, Simon's partners.

Then Jesus said to Simon, "Don't be
afraid; from now on you will catch men."
11So they pulled their boats up on shore,
left everything and followed him.

The Man With Leprosy

12While Jesus was in one of the towns,
a man came along who was covered with
leprosy.[a] When he saw Jesus, he fell with
his face to the ground and begged him,
"Lord, if you are willing, you can make
me clean."
13Jesus reached out his hand and
touched the man. "I am willing," he said.
"Be clean!" And immediately the leprosy
left him.
14Then Jesus ordered him, "Don't tell
anyone, but go, show yourself to the
priest and offer the sacrifices that Moses
commanded for your cleansing, as a testimony to them."
15Yet the news about him spread all the
more, so that crowds of people came to
hear him and to be healed of their sicknesses. 16But Jesus often withdrew to
lonely places and prayed.

Jesus Heals a Paralytic

17One day as he was teaching, Pharisees and teachers of the law, who had
come from every village of Galilee and
from Judea and Jerusalem, were sitting
there. And the power of the Lord was
present for him to heal the sick. 18Some
men came carrying a paralytic on a mat
and tried to take him into the house to lay
him before Jesus. 19When they could not
find a way to do this because of the
crowd, they went up on the roof and lowered him on his mat through the tiles into
the middle of the crowd, right in front of
Jesus.
20When Jesus saw their faith, he said,
"Friend, your sins are forgiven."
21The Pharisees and the teachers of the
law began thinking to themselves, "Who
is this fellow who speaks blasphemy?
Who can forgive sins but God alone?"
22Jesus knew what they were thinking
and asked, "Why are you thinking these
things in your hearts? 23Which is easier:
to say, 'Your sins are forgiven,' or to say,
'Get up and walk'? 24But that you may
know that the Son of Man has authority
on earth to forgive sins. . . ." He said to
the paralyzed man, "I tell you, get up,
take your mat and go home." 25Immedi-
ately he stood up in front of them, took
what he had been lying on and went
home praising God. 26Everyone was
amazed and gave praise to God. They
were filled with awe and said, "We have
seen remarkable things today."

The Calling of Levi

27After this, Jesus went out and saw a
tax collector by the name of Levi sitting
at his tax booth. "Follow me," Jesus said
to him, 28and Levi got up, left everything
and followed him.
29Then Levi held a great banquet for
Jesus at his house, and a large crowd of
tax collectors and others were eating with
them. 30But the Pharisees and the teachers of the law who belonged to their sect
complained to his disciples, "Why do you
eat and drink with tax collectors and 'sinners'?"
31Jesus answered them, "It is not the
healthy who need a doctor, but the sick.
32I have not come to call the righteous,
but sinners to repentance."

Jesus Questioned About Fasting

33They said to him, "John's disciples
often fast and pray, and so do the disciples of the Pharisees, but yours go on eating and drinking."
34Jesus answered, "Can you make the
guests of the bridegroom fast while he is
with them? 35But the time will come
when the bridegroom will be taken from
them; in those days they will fast."
36He told them this parable: "No one
tears a patch from a new garment and
sews it on an old one. If he does, he will
have torn the new garment, and the patch
from the new will not match the old.
37And no one pours new wine into old
wineskins. If he does, the new wine will
burst the skins, the wine will run out and
the wineskins will be ruined. 38No, new
wine must be poured into new wineskins.

[a]12 The Greek word was used for various diseases affecting the skin—not necessarily leprosy.

TUESDAY

VERSE FOR THE DAY:
Luke 5:16

AUTHOR:
Gini Andrews

PASSAGE FOR THE DAY:
Luke 5:12–16

Loneliness

LIKE fatigue, like hunger, loneliness is part of being human. Fatigue is cured by sleep and hunger by eating, but how do we handle loneliness? It's our very nature to seek an alter ego, a heart that responds to our human ache for understanding.

Our favorite women of the Bible were no strangers to periods of aloneness, which, interestingly, often presaged important events: Mary, during her pregnancy; Ruth, bereaved in Moab; Esther, in a pagan harem; Hannah, childless for years in a culture where barrenness was a disgrace.

In his crowded adult life, there were times when Jesus chose to be alone, deliberately making himself unavailable so that he might nourish his soul in communion with his Father. He experienced both isolation and alienation. His query to his disciples when the fawning crowds drifted off, "Will you also go away?" and his Gethsemane "Watch with me"—these are lonely words.

Yet even Jesus did not use his relationship with God as a substitute for human companionship. He found sustenance with his three closest disciples—Peter, James and John—and in the home of Mary, Martha and Lazarus.

But even the most congenial marriage, the closest friendship, the most satisfying child-parent relationship is both transient and unpredictable. Although some 1,500 years have passed since St. Augustine remarked that our hearts will never be at rest away from the One who made them, it's still true.

Just because he has created us as unique individuals, our Father knows the best way to fill each one's empty places. It is only God who can fill our deepest longings, who never has an appointment elsewhere, who never replaces us with someone he likes better, who promises never to leave us totally alone. He is the only one who wants to be and always can be the unfailing companion on our journey.

Additional Scripture Readings:
1 Kings 19:1–10; Psalm 27:7–10

Go to page 93 for your next devotional reading.

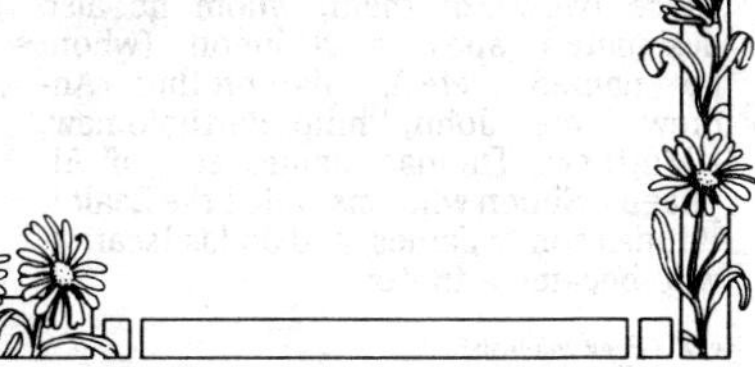

39And no one after drinking old wine
wants the new, for he says, 'The old is
better.' "

Lord of the Sabbath

6 One Sabbath Jesus was going
through the grainfields, and his disciples began to pick some heads of grain,
rub them in their hands and eat the ker-
nels. 2Some of the Pharisees asked, "Why
are you doing what is unlawful on the
Sabbath?"

3Jesus answered them, "Have you never read what David did when he and his
companions were hungry? 4He entered
the house of God, and taking the consecrated bread, he ate what is lawful only
for priests to eat. And he also gave some
to his companions." 5Then Jesus said to
them, "The Son of Man is Lord of the Sabbath."

6On another Sabbath he went into the
synagogue and was teaching, and a man
was there whose right hand was shriveled.
7The Pharisees and the teachers of the
law were looking for a reason to accuse
Jesus, so they watched him closely to see
if he would heal on the Sabbath. 8But
Jesus knew what they were thinking and
said to the man with the shriveled hand,
"Get up and stand in front of everyone."
So he got up and stood there.

9Then Jesus said to them, "I ask you,
which is lawful on the Sabbath: to do
good or to do evil, to save life or to destroy it?"

10He looked around at them all, and
then said to the man, "Stretch out your
hand." He did so, and his hand was completely restored. 11But they were furious
and began to discuss with one another
what they might do to Jesus.

The Twelve Apostles

12One of those days Jesus went out to
a mountainside to pray, and spent the
night praying to God. 13When morning
came, he called his disciples to him and
chose twelve of them, whom he also
designated apostles: 14Simon (whom
he named Peter), his brother Andrew, James, John, Philip, Bartholomew,
15Matthew, Thomas, James son of Alphaeus, Simon who was called the Zealot,
16Judas son of James, and Judas Iscariot,
who became a traitor.

Blessings and Woes

17He went down with them and stood
on a level place. A large crowd of his disciples was there and a great number of
people from all over Judea, from Jerusalem, and from the coast of Tyre and Sidon, 18who had come to hear him and to
be healed of their diseases. Those troubled by evil[a] spirits were cured, 19and the
people all tried to touch him, because
power was coming from him and healing
them all.

20Looking at his disciples, he said:

"Blessed are you who are poor,
for yours is the kingdom of God.
21Blessed are you who hunger now,
for you will be satisfied.
Blessed are you who weep now,
for you will laugh.
22Blessed are you when men hate you,
when they exclude you and insult
you
and reject your name as evil,
because of the Son of Man.

23"Rejoice in that day and leap for joy,
because great is your reward in heaven.
For that is how their fathers treated the
prophets.

24"But woe to you who are rich,
for you have already received your
comfort.
25Woe to you who are well fed now,
for you will go hungry.
Woe to you who laugh now,
for you will mourn and weep.
26Woe to you when all men speak well
of you,
for that is how their fathers treated
the false prophets.

Love for Enemies

27"But I tell you who hear me: Love
your enemies, do good to those who hate
you, 28bless those who curse you, pray for
those who mistreat you. 29If someone
strikes you on one cheek, turn to him the
other also. If someone takes your cloak,
do not stop him from taking your tunic.
30Give to everyone who asks you, and if
anyone takes what belongs to you, do not
demand it back. 31Do to others as you
would have them do to you.

32"If you love those who love you, what
credit is that to you? Even 'sinners' love
those who love them. 33And if you do
good to those who are good to you, what

[a]18 Greek *unclean*

credit is that to you? Even 'sinners' do
that. 34And if you lend to those from
whom you expect repayment, what credit
is that to you? Even 'sinners' lend to 'sinners,' expecting to be repaid in full. 35But
love your enemies, do good to them, and
lend to them without expecting to get
anything back. Then your reward will be
great, and you will be sons of the Most
High, because he is kind to the ungrateful
and wicked. 36Be merciful, just as your
Father is merciful.

Judging Others

37"Do not judge, and you will not be
judged. Do not condemn, and you will not
be condemned. Forgive, and you will be
forgiven. 38Give, and it will be given to
you. A good measure, pressed down,
shaken together and running over, will be
poured into your lap. For with the measure you use, it will be measured to you."

39He also told them this parable: "Can
a blind man lead a blind man? Will they
not both fall into a pit? 40A student is not
above his teacher, but everyone who is
fully trained will be like his teacher.

41"Why do you look at the speck of saw-
dust in your brother's eye and pay no attention to the plank in your own eye?
42How can you say to your brother,
'Brother, let me take the speck out of
your eye,' when you yourself fail to see
the plank in your own eye? You hypocrite,
first take the plank out of your eye, and
then you will see clearly to remove the
speck from your brother's eye.

A Tree and Its Fruit

43"No good tree bears bad fruit, nor
does a bad tree bear good fruit. 44Each
tree is recognized by its own fruit. People
do not pick figs from thornbushes, or
grapes from briers. 45The good man brings
good things out of the good stored up in
his heart, and the evil man brings evil
things out of the evil stored up in his
heart. For out of the overflow of his heart
his mouth speaks.

The Wise and Foolish Builders

46"Why do you call me, 'Lord, Lord,'
and do not do what I say? 47I will show
you what he is like who comes to me and
hears my words and puts them into practice. 48He is like a man building a house,
who dug down deep and laid the foundation on rock. When a flood came, the torrent struck that house but could not
shake it, because it was well built. 49But
the one who hears my words and does not
put them into practice is like a man who
built a house on the ground without a
foundation. The moment the torrent
struck that house, it collapsed and its destruction was complete."

The Faith of the Centurion

7 When Jesus had finished saying all
this in the hearing of the people, he
entered Capernaum. 2There a centurion's
servant, whom his master valued highly,
was sick and about to die. 3The centurion
heard of Jesus and sent some elders of
the Jews to him, asking him to come and
heal his servant. 4When they came to
Jesus, they pleaded earnestly with him,
"This man deserves to have you do this,
5because he loves our nation and has
built our synagogue." 6So Jesus went with
them.

He was not far from the house when
the centurion sent friends to say to him:
"Lord, don't trouble yourself, for I do not
deserve to have you come under my roof.
7That is why I did not even consider myself worthy to come to you. But say the
word, and my servant will be healed. 8For
I myself am a man under authority, with
soldiers under me. I tell this one, 'Go,'
and he goes; and that one, 'Come,' and he
comes. I say to my servant, 'Do this,' and
he does it."

9When Jesus heard this, he was amazed
at him, and turning to the crowd following him, he said, "I tell you, I have not
found such great faith even in Israel."
10Then the men who had been sent returned to the house and found the servant well.

Jesus Raises a Widow's Son

11Soon afterward, Jesus went to a town
called Nain, and his disciples and a large
crowd went along with him. 12As he approached the town gate, a dead person
was being carried out—the only son of his
mother, and she was a widow. And a large
crowd from the town was with her.
13When the Lord saw her, his heart went
out to her and he said, "Don't cry."

14Then he went up and touched the
coffin, and those carrying it stood still. He
said, "Young man, I say to you, get up!"
15The dead man sat up and began to talk,
and Jesus gave him back to his mother.

16They were all filled with awe and
praised God. "A great prophet has appeared among us," they said. "God has
come to help his people." 17This news

about Jesus spread throughout Judea[a]
and the surrounding country.

Jesus and John the Baptist

18John's disciples told him about all
these things. Calling two of them, 19he
sent them to the Lord to ask, "Are you the
one who was to come, or should we expect someone else?"
20When the men came to Jesus, they
said, "John the Baptist sent us to you to
ask, 'Are you the one who was to come, or
should we expect someone else?' "
21At that very time Jesus cured many
who had diseases, sicknesses and evil
spirits, and gave sight to many who were
blind. 22So he replied to the messengers,
"Go back and report to John what you
have seen and heard: The blind receive
sight, the lame walk, those who have leprosy[b] are cured, the deaf hear, the dead
are raised, and the good news is preached
to the poor. 23Blessed is the man who
does not fall away on account of me."
24After John's messengers left, Jesus
began to speak to the crowd about John:
"What did you go out into the desert to
see? A reed swayed by the wind? 25If not,
what did you go out to see? A man
dressed in fine clothes? No, those who
wear expensive clothes and indulge in
luxury are in palaces. 26But what did you
go out to see? A prophet? Yes, I tell you,
and more than a prophet. 27This is the
one about whom it is written:

" 'I will send my messenger ahead of
you,
who will prepare your way before
you.'[c]

28I tell you, among those born of women
there is no one greater than John; yet the
one who is least in the kingdom of God is
greater than he."
29(All the people, even the tax collectors, when they heard Jesus' words, acknowledged that God's way was right, because they had been baptized by John.
30But the Pharisees and experts in the law
rejected God's purpose for themselves,
because they had not been baptized by
John.)
31"To what, then, can I compare the
people of this generation? What are they
like? 32They are like children sitting in
the marketplace and calling out to each
other:

" 'We played the flute for you,
and you did not dance;
we sang a dirge,
and you did not cry.'

33For John the Baptist came neither eating bread nor drinking wine, and you say,
'He has a demon.' 34The Son of Man came
eating and drinking, and you say, 'Here is
a glutton and a drunkard, a friend of tax
collectors and "sinners." ' 35But wisdom
is proved right by all her children."

Jesus Anointed by a Sinful Woman

36Now one of the Pharisees invited
Jesus to have dinner with him, so he went
to the Pharisee's house and reclined at
the table. 37When a woman who had lived
a sinful life in that town learned that
Jesus was eating at the Pharisee's house,
she brought an alabaster jar of perfume,
38and as she stood behind him at his feet
weeping, she began to wet his feet with
her tears. Then she wiped them with her
hair, kissed them and poured perfume on
them.
39When the Pharisee who had invited
him saw this, he said to himself, "If this
man were a prophet, he would know who
is touching him and what kind of woman
she is—that she is a sinner."
40Jesus answered him, "Simon, I have
something to tell you."
"Tell me, teacher," he said.
41"Two men owed money to a certain
moneylender. One owed him five hundred denarii,[d] and the other fifty. 42Nei-
ther of them had the money to pay him
back, so he canceled the debts of both.
Now which of them will love him more?"
43Simon replied, "I suppose the one
who had the bigger debt canceled."
"You have judged correctly," Jesus
said.
44Then he turned toward the woman
and said to Simon, "Do you see this woman? I came into your house. You did not
give me any water for my feet, but she wet
my feet with her tears and wiped them
with her hair. 45You did not give me a
kiss, but this woman, from the time I entered, has not stopped kissing my feet.
46You did not put oil on my head, but she
has poured perfume on my feet. 47There-
fore, I tell you, her many sins have been
forgiven—for she loved much. But he
who has been forgiven little loves little."

[a]17 Or *the land of the Jews* [b]22 The Greek word was used for various diseases affecting the skin—not necessarily leprosy. [c]27 Mal. 3:1 [d]41 A denarius was a coin worth about a day's wages.

48Then Jesus said to her, "Your sins are forgiven."

49The other guests began to say among themselves, "Who is this who even forgives sins?"

50Jesus said to the woman, "Your faith has saved you; go in peace."

The Parable of the Sower

8 After this, Jesus traveled about from one town and village to another, proclaiming the good news of the kingdom of God. The Twelve were with him, 2and also some women who had been cured of evil spirits and diseases: Mary (called Magdalene) from whom seven demons had come out; 3Joanna the wife of Cuza, the manager of Herod's household; Susanna; and many others. These women were helping to support them out of their own means.

4While a large crowd was gathering and people were coming to Jesus from town after town, he told this parable: 5"A farmer went out to sow his seed. As he was scattering the seed, some fell along the path; it was trampled on, and the birds of the air ate it up. 6Some fell on rock, and when it came up, the plants withered because they had no moisture. 7Other seed fell among thorns, which grew up with it and choked the plants. 8Still other seed fell on good soil. It came up and yielded a crop, a hundred times more than was sown."

When he said this, he called out, "He who has ears to hear, let him hear."

9His disciples asked him what this parable meant. 10He said, "The knowledge of the secrets of the kingdom of God has been given to you, but to others I speak in parables, so that,

" 'though seeing, they may not see;
 though hearing, they may not
  understand.'[a]

11"This is the meaning of the parable: The seed is the word of God. 12Those along the path are the ones who hear, and then the devil comes and takes away the word from their hearts, so that they may not believe and be saved. 13Those on the rock are the ones who receive the word with joy when they hear it, but they have no root. They believe for a while, but in the time of testing they fall away. 14The seed that fell among thorns stands for those who hear, but as they go on their way they are choked by life's worries, riches and pleasures, and they do not mature. 15But the seed on good soil stands for those with a noble and good heart, who hear the word, retain it, and by persevering produce a crop.

A Lamp on a Stand

16"No one lights a lamp and hides it in a jar or puts it under a bed. Instead, he puts it on a stand, so that those who come in can see the light. 17For there is nothing hidden that will not be disclosed, and nothing concealed that will not be known or brought out into the open. 18Therefore consider carefully how you listen. Whoever has will be given more; whoever does not have, even what he thinks he has will be taken from him."

Jesus' Mother and Brothers

19Now Jesus' mother and brothers came to see him, but they were not able to get near him because of the crowd. 20Someone told him, "Your mother and brothers are standing outside, wanting to see you."

21He replied, "My mother and brothers are those who hear God's word and put it into practice."

Jesus Calms the Storm

22One day Jesus said to his disciples, "Let's go over to the other side of the lake." So they got into a boat and set out. 23As they sailed, he fell asleep. A squall came down on the lake, so that the boat was being swamped, and they were in great danger.

24The disciples went and woke him, saying, "Master, Master, we're going to drown!"

He got up and rebuked the wind and the raging waters; the storm subsided, and all was calm. 25"Where is your faith?" he asked his disciples.

In fear and amazement they asked one another, "Who is this? He commands even the winds and the water, and they obey him."

The Healing of a Demon-possessed Man

26They sailed to the region of the Gerasenes,[b] which is across the lake from Galilee. 27When Jesus stepped ashore, he was met by a demon-possessed man from the town. For a long time this man had

[a] *10* Isaiah 6:9 [b] *26* Some manuscripts *Gadarenes*; other manuscripts *Gergesenes*; also in verse 37

not worn clothes or lived in a house, but had lived in the tombs. 28When he saw Jesus, he cried out and fell at his feet, shouting at the top of his voice, "What do you want with me, Jesus, Son of the Most High God? I beg you, don't torture me!" 29For Jesus had commanded the evil[a] spirit to come out of the man. Many times it had seized him, and though he was chained hand and foot and kept under guard, he had broken his chains and had been driven by the demon into solitary places.

30Jesus asked him, "What is your name?"

"Legion," he replied, because many demons had gone into him. 31And they begged him repeatedly not to order them to go into the Abyss.

32A large herd of pigs was feeding there on the hillside. The demons begged Jesus to let them go into them, and he gave them permission. 33When the demons came out of the man, they went into the pigs, and the herd rushed down the steep bank into the lake and was drowned.

34When those tending the pigs saw what had happened, they ran off and reported this in the town and countryside, 35and the people went out to see what had happened. When they came to Jesus, they found the man from whom the demons had gone out, sitting at Jesus' feet, dressed and in his right mind; and they were afraid. 36Those who had seen it told the people how the demon-possessed man had been cured. 37Then all the people of the region of the Gerasenes asked Jesus to leave them, because they were overcome with fear. So he got into the boat and left.

38The man from whom the demons had gone out begged to go with him, but Jesus sent him away, saying, 39"Return home and tell how much God has done for you." So the man went away and told all over town how much Jesus had done for him.

A Dead Girl and a Sick Woman

40Now when Jesus returned, a crowd welcomed him, for they were all expecting him. 41Then a man named Jairus, a ruler of the synagogue, came and fell at Jesus' feet, pleading with him to come to his house 42because his only daughter, a girl of about twelve, was dying.

As Jesus was on his way, the crowds almost crushed him. 43And a woman was there who had been subject to bleeding for twelve years,[b] but no one could heal her. 44She came up behind him and touched the edge of his cloak, and immediately her bleeding stopped.

45"Who touched me?" Jesus asked.

When they all denied it, Peter said, "Master, the people are crowding and pressing against you."

46But Jesus said, "Someone touched me; I know that power has gone out from me."

47Then the woman, seeing that she could not go unnoticed, came trembling and fell at his feet. In the presence of all the people, she told why she had touched him and how she had been instantly healed. 48Then he said to her, "Daughter, your faith has healed you. Go in peace."

49While Jesus was still speaking, someone came from the house of Jairus, the synagogue ruler. "Your daughter is dead," he said. "Don't bother the teacher any more."

50Hearing this, Jesus said to Jairus, "Don't be afraid; just believe, and she will be healed."

51When he arrived at the house of Jairus, he did not let anyone go in with him except Peter, John and James, and the child's father and mother. 52Meanwhile, all the people were wailing and mourning for her. "Stop wailing," Jesus said. "She is not dead but asleep."

53They laughed at him, knowing that she was dead. 54But he took her by the hand and said, "My child, get up!" 55Her spirit returned, and at once she stood up. Then Jesus told them to give her something to eat. 56Her parents were astonished, but he ordered them not to tell anyone what had happened.

Jesus Sends Out the Twelve

9 When Jesus had called the Twelve together, he gave them power and authority to drive out all demons and to cure diseases, 2and he sent them out to preach the kingdom of God and to heal the sick. 3He told them: "Take nothing for the journey—no staff, no bag, no bread, no money, no extra tunic. 4Whatever house you enter, stay there until you leave that town. 5If people do not welcome you, shake the dust off your feet when you leave their town, as a testimony against them." 6So they set out and went

[a]29 Greek *unclean* [b]43 Many manuscripts *years, and she had spent all she had on doctors*

from village to village, preaching the gospel and healing people everywhere.

7Now Herod the tetrarch heard about all that was going on. And he was perplexed, because some were saying that John had been raised from the dead, 8others that Elijah had appeared, and still others that one of the prophets of long ago had come back to life. 9But Herod said, "I beheaded John. Who, then, is this I hear such things about?" And he tried to see him.

Jesus Feeds the Five Thousand

10When the apostles returned, they reported to Jesus what they had done. Then he took them with him and they withdrew by themselves to a town called Bethsaida, 11but the crowds learned about it and followed him. He welcomed them and spoke to them about the kingdom of God, and healed those who needed healing.

12Late in the afternoon the Twelve came to him and said, "Send the crowd away so they can go to the surrounding villages and countryside and find food and lodging, because we are in a remote place here."

13He replied, "You give them something to eat."

They answered, "We have only five loaves of bread and two fish—unless we go and buy food for all this crowd." 14(About five thousand men were there.)

But he said to his disciples, "Have them sit down in groups of about fifty each." 15The disciples did so, and everybody sat down. 16Taking the five loaves and the two fish and looking up to heaven, he gave thanks and broke them. Then he gave them to the disciples to set before the people. 17They all ate and were satisfied, and the disciples picked up twelve basketfuls of broken pieces that were left over.

Peter's Confession of Christ

18Once when Jesus was praying in private and his disciples were with him, he asked them, "Who do the crowds say I am?"

19They replied, "Some say John the Baptist; others say Elijah; and still others, that one of the prophets of long ago has come back to life."

20"But what about you?" he asked. "Who do you say I am?"

Peter answered, "The Christ[a] of God."

21Jesus strictly warned them not to tell this to anyone. 22And he said, "The Son of Man must suffer many things and be rejected by the elders, chief priests and teachers of the law, and he must be killed and on the third day be raised to life."

23Then he said to them all: "If anyone would come after me, he must deny himself and take up his cross daily and follow me. 24For whoever wants to save his life will lose it, but whoever loses his life for me will save it. 25What good is it for a man to gain the whole world, and yet lose or forfeit his very self? 26If anyone is ashamed of me and my words, the Son of Man will be ashamed of him when he comes in his glory and in the glory of the Father and of the holy angels. 27I tell you the truth, some who are standing here will not taste death before they see the kingdom of God."

The Transfiguration

28About eight days after Jesus said this, he took Peter, John and James with him and went up onto a mountain to pray. 29As he was praying, the appearance of his face changed, and his clothes became as bright as a flash of lightning. 30Two men, Moses and Elijah, 31appeared in glorious splendor, talking with Jesus. They spoke about his departure, which he was about to bring to fulfillment at Jerusalem. 32Peter and his companions were very sleepy, but when they became fully awake, they saw his glory and the two men standing with him. 33As the men were leaving Jesus, Peter said to him, "Master, it is good for us to be here. Let us put up three shelters—one for you, one for Moses and one for Elijah." (He did not know what he was saying.)

34While he was speaking, a cloud appeared and enveloped them, and they were afraid as they entered the cloud. 35A voice came from the cloud, saying, "This is my Son, whom I have chosen; listen to him." 36When the voice had spoken, they found that Jesus was alone. The disciples kept this to themselves, and told no one at that time what they had seen.

The Healing of a Boy With an Evil Spirit

37The next day, when they came down from the mountain, a large crowd met him. 38A man in the crowd called out, "Teacher, I beg you to look at my son, for

[a]20 Or *Messiah*

he is my only child. 39A spirit seizes him and he suddenly screams; it throws him into convulsions so that he foams at the mouth. It scarcely ever leaves him and is destroying him. 40I begged your disciples to drive it out, but they could not."

41"O unbelieving and perverse generation," Jesus replied, "how long shall I stay with you and put up with you? Bring your son here."

42Even while the boy was coming, the demon threw him to the ground in a convulsion. But Jesus rebuked the evil[a] spirit, healed the boy and gave him back to his father. 43And they were all amazed at the greatness of God.

While everyone was marveling at all that Jesus did, he said to his disciples, 44"Listen carefully to what I am about to tell you: The Son of Man is going to be betrayed into the hands of men." 45But they did not understand what this meant. It was hidden from them, so that they did not grasp it, and they were afraid to ask him about it.

Who Will Be the Greatest?

46An argument started among the disciples as to which of them would be the greatest. 47Jesus, knowing their thoughts, took a little child and had him stand beside him. 48Then he said to them, "Whoever welcomes this little child in my name welcomes me; and whoever welcomes me welcomes the one who sent me. For he who is least among you all—he is the greatest."

49"Master," said John, "we saw a man driving out demons in your name and we tried to stop him, because he is not one of us."

50"Do not stop him," Jesus said, "for whoever is not against you is for you."

Samaritan Opposition

51As the time approached for him to be taken up to heaven, Jesus resolutely set out for Jerusalem. 52And he sent messengers on ahead, who went into a Samaritan village to get things ready for him; 53but the people there did not welcome him, because he was heading for Jerusalem. 54When the disciples James and John saw this, they asked, "Lord, do you want us to call fire down from heaven to destroy them[b]?" 55But Jesus turned and rebuked them, 56and[c] they went to another village.

The Cost of Following Jesus

57As they were walking along the road, a man said to him, "I will follow you wherever you go."

58Jesus replied, "Foxes have holes and birds of the air have nests, but the Son of Man has no place to lay his head."

59He said to another man, "Follow me."

But the man replied, "Lord, first let me go and bury my father."

60Jesus said to him, "Let the dead bury their own dead, but you go and proclaim the kingdom of God."

61Still another said, "I will follow you, Lord; but first let me go back and say good-by to my family."

62Jesus replied, "No one who puts his hand to the plow and looks back is fit for service in the kingdom of God."

Jesus Sends Out the Seventy-two

10 After this the Lord appointed seventy-two[d] others and sent them two by two ahead of him to every town and place where he was about to go. 2He told them, "The harvest is plentiful, but the workers are few. Ask the Lord of the harvest, therefore, to send out workers into his harvest field. 3Go! I am sending you out like lambs among wolves. 4Do not take a purse or bag or sandals; and do not greet anyone on the road.

5"When you enter a house, first say, 'Peace to this house.' 6If a man of peace is there, your peace will rest on him; if not, it will return to you. 7Stay in that house, eating and drinking whatever they give you, for the worker deserves his wages. Do not move around from house to house.

8"When you enter a town and are welcomed, eat what is set before you. 9Heal the sick who are there and tell them, 'The kingdom of God is near you.' 10But when you enter a town and are not welcomed, go into its streets and say, 11'Even the dust of your town that sticks to our feet we wipe off against you. Yet be sure of this: The kingdom of God is near.' 12I tell you, it will be more bearable on that day for Sodom than for that town.

13"Woe to you, Korazin! Woe to you,

[a]42 Greek *unclean* [b]54 Some manuscripts *them, even as Elijah did* [c]55,56 Some manuscripts *them. And he said, "You do not know what kind of spirit you are of, for the Son of Man did not come to destroy men's lives, but to save them." 56And* [d]1 Some manuscripts *seventy;* also in verse 17

WEDNESDAY

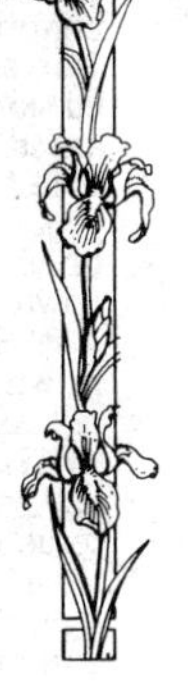

VERSE FOR THE DAY:	*AUTHOR:*	*PASSAGE FOR THE DAY:*
Luke 10:33	*Alma Barkman*	*Luke 10:25–37*

First Aid

ALTHOUGH not a registered professional, I do get my share of nursing experience, particularly while substituting for the school secretary. The minute I set foot inside the door, casualties start gravitating toward the office—scraped elbows, skinned knees, old wounds, fresh nosebleeds, raised toenails, broken blisters, upset stomachs.

I have learned that a school secretary opens a well-stocked first-aid kit long before sharpening any pencils. By midafternoon the office is apt to resemble a hospital ward.

Not only that, but old Florence Nightingale is not accorded any degree of privacy. The casualty victims from school are beginning to spill over into my house. Yesterday the doorbell rang, and a terrified young fellow hopping up and down on my doorstep tried to tell me that his pal was bleeding to death on the road—massive hemorrhage.

I ran to the site of the accident, where the victim was just untangling himself from the wreckage of his bicycle. Judging from his groans, I thought he had amputated his leg.

Somehow I managed to get him into my bathroom and wash off his wounds. An accurate diagnosis confirmed my suspicions: he had simply scraped the scab from a previous injury. I solemnly conjured up an impressive-looking bandage, and he was back on the road in no time at all, completely cured.

The therapeutic value of Band-Aids may well be disputed, but this is one "lady of the lamp" who keeps her medicine chest well stocked.

Whether it is a tiny sliver in a chubby finger, or cancer clawing at a ravaged frame, pain demands priority. Why then am I so hesitant in dispensing consolation? Do I wait until an emergency demands it before investing in a "first-aid" kit? Must I first suffer physically, mentally, emotionally, or spiritually before I learn the healing value of a soothing hand, a mutual tear, a sympathizing heart, an understanding word?

Surely I do well to keep my medicine chest well stocked with love and compassion as well as with bandages, for I never know when I will be called upon to deal with tragedy, or when tragedy may call to deal with me.

Additional Scripture Readings:
Acts 3:1–10; James 2:14–17

Go to page 95 for your next devotional reading.

Bethsaida! For if the miracles that were performed in you had been performed in Tyre and Sidon, they would have repented long ago, sitting in sackcloth and ashes. 14But it will be more bearable for Tyre and Sidon at the judgment than for you. 15And you, Capernaum, will you be lifted up to the skies? No, you will go down to the depths.[a]

16"He who listens to you listens to me; he who rejects you rejects me; but he who rejects me rejects him who sent me."

17The seventy-two returned with joy and said, "Lord, even the demons submit to us in your name."

18He replied, "I saw Satan fall like lightning from heaven. 19I have given you authority to trample on snakes and scorpions and to overcome all the power of the enemy; nothing will harm you. 20However, do not rejoice that the spirits submit to you, but rejoice that your names are written in heaven."

21At that time Jesus, full of joy through the Holy Spirit, said, "I praise you, Father, Lord of heaven and earth, because you have hidden these things from the wise and learned, and revealed them to little children. Yes, Father, for this was your good pleasure.

22"All things have been committed to me by my Father. No one knows who the Son is except the Father, and no one knows who the Father is except the Son and those to whom the Son chooses to reveal him."

23Then he turned to his disciples and said privately, "Blessed are the eyes that see what you see. 24For I tell you that many prophets and kings wanted to see what you see but did not see it, and to hear what you hear but did not hear it."

The Parable of the Good Samaritan

25On one occasion an expert in the law stood up to test Jesus. "Teacher," he asked, "what must I do to inherit eternal life?"

26"What is written in the Law?" he replied. "How do you read it?"

27He answered: " 'Love the Lord your God with all your heart and with all your soul and with all your strength and with all your mind'[b]; and, 'Love your neighbor as yourself.'[c]"

28"You have answered correctly," Jesus replied. "Do this and you will live."

29But he wanted to justify himself, so he asked Jesus, "And who is my neighbor?"

30In reply Jesus said: "A man was going down from Jerusalem to Jericho, when he fell into the hands of robbers. They stripped him of his clothes, beat him and went away, leaving him half dead. 31A priest happened to be going down the same road, and when he saw the man, he passed by on the other side. 32So too, a Levite, when he came to the place and saw him, passed by on the other side. 33But a Samaritan, as he traveled, came where the man was; and when he saw him, he took pity on him. 34He went to him and bandaged his wounds, pouring on oil and wine. Then he put the man on his own donkey, took him to an inn and took care of him. 35The next day he took out two silver coins[d] and gave them to the innkeeper. 'Look after him,' he said, 'and when I return, I will reimburse you for any extra expense you may have.'

36"Which of these three do you think was a neighbor to the man who fell into the hands of robbers?"

37The expert in the law replied, "The one who had mercy on him."

Jesus told him, "Go and do likewise."

At the Home of Martha and Mary

38As Jesus and his disciples were on their way, he came to a village where a woman named Martha opened her home to him. 39She had a sister called Mary, who sat at the Lord's feet listening to what he said. 40But Martha was distracted by all the preparations that had to be made. She came to him and asked, "Lord, don't you care that my sister has left me to do the work by myself? Tell her to help me!"

41"Martha, Martha," the Lord answered, "you are worried and upset about many things, 42but only one thing is needed.[e] Mary has chosen what is better, and it will not be taken away from her."

Jesus' Teaching on Prayer

11 One day Jesus was praying in a certain place. When he finished, one of his disciples said to him, "Lord, teach us to pray, just as John taught his disciples."

2He said to them, "When you pray, say:

[a] *15* Greek *Hades* [b] *27* Deut. 6:5 [c] *27* Lev. 19:18 [d] *35* Greek *two denarii* [e] *42* Some manuscripts *but few things are needed—or only one*

" 'Father,[a]
hallowed be your name,
your kingdom come.[b]
3Give us each day our daily bread.
4Forgive us our sins,
for we also forgive everyone who
sins against us.[c]
And lead us not into temptation.[d]' "

5Then he said to them, "Suppose one of
you has a friend, and he goes to him at midnight and says, 'Friend, lend me three loaves of bread,
6because a friend of mine on a journey has come to me, and I have nothing to set before him.'
7"Then the one inside answers, 'Don't bother me. The door is already locked, and my children are with me in bed. I can't get up and give you anything.'
8I tell you, though he will not get up and give him the bread because he is his friend,

[a]2 Some manuscripts *Our Father in heaven* [b]2 Some manuscripts *come. May your will be done on earth as it is in heaven.* [c]4 Greek *everyone who is indebted to us* [d]4 Some manuscripts *temptation but deliver us from the evil one*

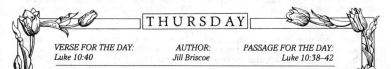

THURSDAY

VERSE FOR THE DAY:
Luke 10:40

AUTHOR:
Jill Briscoe

PASSAGE FOR THE DAY:
Luke 10:38–42

First Things First

I LOVE the way Jesus solved problems. He tackled them head on! He was a master at confronting people in such a way that it did not hinder his relationship with them afterward. Think of Martha, for instance. Jesus visited the home of Martha, Mary and Lazarus. Mary, Martha's sister, sat at Jesus' feet and listened to his words while Martha got mad about it! She got mad at Mary and she got mad at Jesus! There was a meal to prepare and nobody would help! I'm sure she got mad at Martha too, because you can't be happy with yourself when you're griping at other people!

It wasn't that Martha didn't know what it was to enjoy the Master's company, because we understand that Martha also sat at Jesus' feet. It was just a question of priorities. Martha was busy getting a banquet ready when soup and sandwiches would have been quite adequate. Jesus gently reminded her that she was worried and troubled about many "dishes" but Mary had chosen the best "dish"!

When Jesus saw women who were "distracted" by their serving—he did not fail to remind them that "man does not live on bread alone" (Matthew 4:4). First things need to come first! "First the Master, then the meat," he reminded Martha.

It isn't that the *doing* doesn't need doing, it's that the *being* must come first, and then we will find that the necessary part of the doing will get done! Later in Jesus' ministry we read that Martha served, and this time there was no complaining and no rebuke—first things *were* first (John 12:2).

Additional Scripture Readings:
Luke 9:57–62; John 12:1–3

Go to page 97 for your next devotional reading.

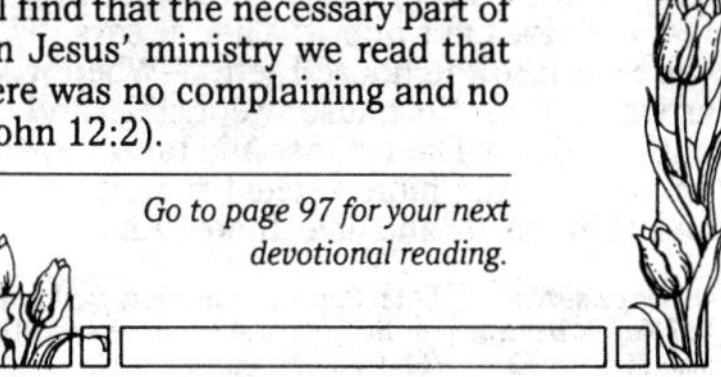

yet because of the man's boldness[a] he will get up and give him as much as he needs.

9"So I say to you: Ask and it will be given to you; seek and you will find; knock and the door will be opened to you. 10For everyone who asks receives; he who seeks finds; and to him who knocks, the door will be opened.

11"Which of you fathers, if your son asks for[b] a fish, will give him a snake instead? 12Or if he asks for an egg, will give him a scorpion? 13If you then, though you are evil, know how to give good gifts to your children, how much more will your Father in heaven give the Holy Spirit to those who ask him!"

Jesus and Beelzebub

14Jesus was driving out a demon that was mute. When the demon left, the man who had been mute spoke, and the crowd was amazed. 15But some of them said, "By Beelzebub,[c] the prince of demons, he is driving out demons." 16Others tested him by asking for a sign from heaven.

17Jesus knew their thoughts and said to them: "Any kingdom divided against itself will be ruined, and a house divided against itself will fall. 18If Satan is divided against himself, how can his kingdom stand? I say this because you claim that I drive out demons by Beelzebub. 19Now if I drive out demons by Beelzebub, by whom do your followers drive them out? So then, they will be your judges. 20But if I drive out demons by the finger of God, then the kingdom of God has come to you.

21"When a strong man, fully armed, guards his own house, his possessions are safe. 22But when someone stronger attacks and overpowers him, he takes away the armor in which the man trusted and divides up the spoils.

23"He who is not with me is against me, and he who does not gather with me, scatters.

24"When an evil[d] spirit comes out of a man, it goes through arid places seeking rest and does not find it. Then it says, 'I will return to the house I left.' 25When it arrives, it finds the house swept clean and put in order. 26Then it goes and takes seven other spirits more wicked than itself, and they go in and live there. And the final condition of that man is worse than the first."

27As Jesus was saying these things, a woman in the crowd called out, "Blessed is the mother who gave you birth and nursed you."

28He replied, "Blessed rather are those who hear the word of God and obey it."

The Sign of Jonah

29As the crowds increased, Jesus said, "This is a wicked generation. It asks for a miraculous sign, but none will be given it except the sign of Jonah. 30For as Jonah was a sign to the Ninevites, so also will the Son of Man be to this generation. 31The Queen of the South will rise at the judgment with the men of this generation and condemn them; for she came from the ends of the earth to listen to Solomon's wisdom, and now one[e] greater than Solomon is here. 32The men of Nineveh will stand up at the judgment with this generation and condemn it; for they repented at the preaching of Jonah, and now one greater than Jonah is here.

The Lamp of the Body

33"No one lights a lamp and puts it in a place where it will be hidden, or under a bowl. Instead he puts it on its stand, so that those who come in may see the light. 34Your eye is the lamp of your body. When your eyes are good, your whole body also is full of light. But when they are bad, your body also is full of darkness. 35See to it, then, that the light within you is not darkness. 36Therefore, if your whole body is full of light, and no part of it dark, it will be completely lighted, as when the light of a lamp shines on you."

Six Woes

37When Jesus had finished speaking, a Pharisee invited him to eat with him; so he went in and reclined at the table. 38But the Pharisee, noticing that Jesus did not first wash before the meal, was surprised.

39Then the Lord said to him, "Now then, you Pharisees clean the outside of the cup and dish, but inside you are full of greed and wickedness. 40You foolish people! Did not the one who made the outside make the inside also? 41But give what is inside ⌞the dish⌟[f] to the poor, and everything will be clean for you.

[a]8 Or *persistence* [b]11 Some manuscripts *for bread, will give him a stone; or if he asks for* [c]15 Greek *Beezeboul* or *Beelzeboul*; also in verses 18 and 19 [d]24 Greek *unclean* [e]31 Or *something*; also in verse 32 [f]41 Or *what you have*

FRIDAY

VERSE FOR THE DAY:
Luke 11:33

AUTHOR:
June Masters Bacher

PASSAGE FOR THE DAY:
Luke 11:33–36

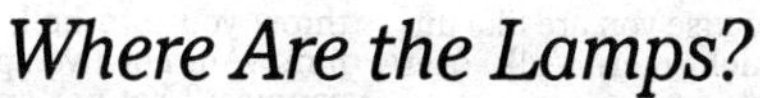

Where Are the Lamps?

IN a certain mountain village in Europe several centuries ago (so the story goes), a nobleman wondered what legacy to leave his townspeople. At last he decided to build them a church.

Nobody saw the complete plans until the church was finished. When the people gathered, they marveled at its beauty. But one noticed an incompleteness. "Where are the lamps?" he asked. "How will the church be lighted?"

The nobleman smiled. Then he gave each family a lamp. "Each time you are here, the area in which you sit will be lighted. But when you are not here, some part of God's house will be dark."

Today we live in a world of darkness, a darkness in which even our secular problem-solvers are beginning to stumble. In spite of our "social conscience," all around us is evidence of ignorance, illiteracy, and dark imaginings. Romans 2:19 tells us that we, as Christians, are "a light for those who are in the dark."

But the world is so big. And our lamp is so small. Yes, but we can light some small part each day. Look to the star-struck heavens. How small each star looks in the distance. Yet, put together, those tiny jewels can light the darkest night. Not one of those little lamps of heaven is ever missing—else the heavens would be less bright. Each of us is a star (or a lamp, if you will). And yes, we can make this world a brighter place. It all begins with the desire expressed in Michelangelo's prayer: "God, grant me the desire always to desire to be more that I can ever accomplish."

To think and pray about: Light your lamps. Let God send you in a new direction today. Meet someone at the crossroads of his or her life. Put on a bright face whether you feel like it or not. Gladness will come.

Additional Scripture Readings:
Matthew 5:14–16; 1 John 1:5–7

Go to page 100 for your next devotional reading.

42"Woe to you Pharisees, because you
give God a tenth of your mint, rue and all
other kinds of garden herbs, but you neglect justice and the love of God. You
should have practiced the latter without
leaving the former undone.
43"Woe to you Pharisees, because you
love the most important seats in the synagogues and greetings in the marketplaces.
44"Woe to you, because you are like un-
marked graves, which men walk over
without knowing it."
45One of the experts in the law answered him, "Teacher, when you say
these things, you insult us also."
46Jesus replied, "And you experts in the
law, woe to you, because you load people
down with burdens they can hardly carry,
and you yourselves will not lift one finger
to help them.
47"Woe to you, because you build
tombs for the prophets, and it was your
forefathers who killed them. 48So you testify that you approve of what your forefathers did; they killed the prophets, and
you build their tombs. 49Because of this,
God in his wisdom said, 'I will send them
prophets and apostles, some of whom
they will kill and others they will persecute.' 50Therefore this generation will be
held responsible for the blood of all the
prophets that has been shed since the beginning of the world, 51from the blood of
Abel to the blood of Zechariah, who was
killed between the altar and the sanctuary. Yes, I tell you, this generation will be
held responsible for it all.
52"Woe to you experts in the law, because you have taken away the key to
knowledge. You yourselves have not entered, and you have hindered those who
were entering."
53When Jesus left there, the Pharisees
and the teachers of the law began to oppose him fiercely and to besiege him with
questions, 54waiting to catch him in
something he might say.

Warnings and Encouragements

12 Meanwhile, when a crowd of many
thousands had gathered, so that
they were trampling on one another,
Jesus began to speak first to his disciples,
saying: "Be on your guard against the
yeast of the Pharisees, which is hypocrisy.
2There is nothing concealed that will not
be disclosed, or hidden that will not be
made known. 3What you have said in the
dark will be heard in the daylight, and
what you have whispered in the ear in the
inner rooms will be proclaimed from the
roofs.
4"I tell you, my friends, do not be afraid
of those who kill the body and after that
can do no more. 5But I will show you
whom you should fear: Fear him who, after the killing of the body, has power to
throw you into hell. Yes, I tell you, fear
him. 6Are not five sparrows sold for two
pennies[a]? Yet not one of them is forgotten by God. 7Indeed, the very hairs of your
head are all numbered. Don't be afraid;
you are worth more than many sparrows.
8"I tell you, whoever acknowledges me
before men, the Son of Man will also acknowledge him before the angels of God.
9But he who disowns me before men
will be disowned before the angels of
God. 10And everyone who speaks a word
against the Son of Man will be forgiven,
but anyone who blasphemes against the
Holy Spirit will not be forgiven.
11"When you are brought before synagogues, rulers and authorities, do not
worry about how you will defend yourselves or what you will say, 12for the Holy
Spirit will teach you at that time what you
should say."

The Parable of the Rich Fool

13Someone in the crowd said to him,
"Teacher, tell my brother to divide the inheritance with me."
14Jesus replied, "Man, who appointed
me a judge or an arbiter between you?"
15Then he said to them, "Watch out! Be
on your guard against all kinds of greed;
a man's life does not consist in the abundance of his possessions."
16And he told them this parable: "The
ground of a certain rich man produced a
good crop. 17He thought to himself, 'What
shall I do? I have no place to store my
crops.'
18"Then he said, 'This is what I'll do. I
will tear down my barns and build bigger
ones, and there I will store all my grain
and my goods. 19And I'll say to myself,
"You have plenty of good things laid up
for many years. Take life easy; eat, drink
and be merry." '
20"But God said to him, 'You fool! This
very night your life will be demanded
from you. Then who will get what you
have prepared for yourself?'

[a]6 Greek *two assaria*

21“This is how it will be with anyone who stores up things for himself but is not rich toward God.”

Do Not Worry

22Then Jesus said to his disciples: “Therefore I tell you, do not worry about your life, what you will eat; or about your body, what you will wear. 23Life is more than food, and the body more than clothes. 24Consider the ravens: They do not sow or reap, they have no storeroom or barn; yet God feeds them. And how much more valuable you are than birds! 25Who of you by worrying can add a single hour to his life[a]? 26Since you cannot do this very little thing, why do you worry about the rest?

27“Consider how the lilies grow. They do not labor or spin. Yet I tell you, not even Solomon in all his splendor was dressed like one of these. 28If that is how God clothes the grass of the field, which is here today, and tomorrow is thrown into the fire, how much more will he clothe you, O you of little faith! 29And do not set your heart on what you will eat or drink; do not worry about it. 30For the pagan world runs after all such things, and your Father knows that you need them. 31But seek his kingdom, and these things will be given to you as well.

32“Do not be afraid, little flock, for your Father has been pleased to give you the kingdom. 33Sell your possessions and give to the poor. Provide purses for yourselves that will not wear out, a treasure in heaven that will not be exhausted, where no thief comes near and no moth destroys. 34For where your treasure is, there your heart will be also.

Watchfulness

35“Be dressed ready for service and keep your lamps burning, 36like men waiting for their master to return from a wedding banquet, so that when he comes and knocks they can immediately open the door for him. 37It will be good for those servants whose master finds them watching when he comes. I tell you the truth, he will dress himself to serve, will have them recline at the table and will come and wait on them. 38It will be good for those servants whose master finds them ready, even if he comes in the second or third watch of the night. 39But understand this: If the owner of the house had known at what hour the thief was coming, he would not have let his house be broken into. 40You also must be ready, because the Son of Man will come at an hour when you do not expect him.”

41Peter asked, “Lord, are you telling this parable to us, or to everyone?”

42The Lord answered, “Who then is the faithful and wise manager, whom the master puts in charge of his servants to give them their food allowance at the proper time? 43It will be good for that servant whom the master finds doing so when he returns. 44I tell you the truth, he will put him in charge of all his possessions. 45But suppose the servant says to himself, ‘My master is taking a long time in coming,’ and he then begins to beat the menservants and maidservants and to eat and drink and get drunk. 46The master of that servant will come on a day when he does not expect him and at an hour he is not aware of. He will cut him to pieces and assign him a place with the unbelievers.

47“That servant who knows his master’s will and does not get ready or does not do what his master wants will be beaten with many blows. 48But the one who does not know and does things deserving punishment will be beaten with few blows. From everyone who has been given much, much will be demanded; and from the one who has been entrusted with much, much more will be asked.

Not Peace but Division

49“I have come to bring fire on the earth, and how I wish it were already kindled! 50But I have a baptism to undergo, and how distressed I am until it is completed! 51Do you think I came to bring peace on earth? No, I tell you, but division. 52From now on there will be five in one family divided against each other, three against two and two against three. 53They will be divided, father against son and son against father, mother against daughter and daughter against mother, mother-in-law against daughter-in-law and daughter-in-law against mother-in-law.”

Interpreting the Times

54He said to the crowd: “When you see a cloud rising in the west, immediately you say, ‘It’s going to rain,’ and it does. 55And when the south wind blows, you

[a]25 Or *single cubit to his height*

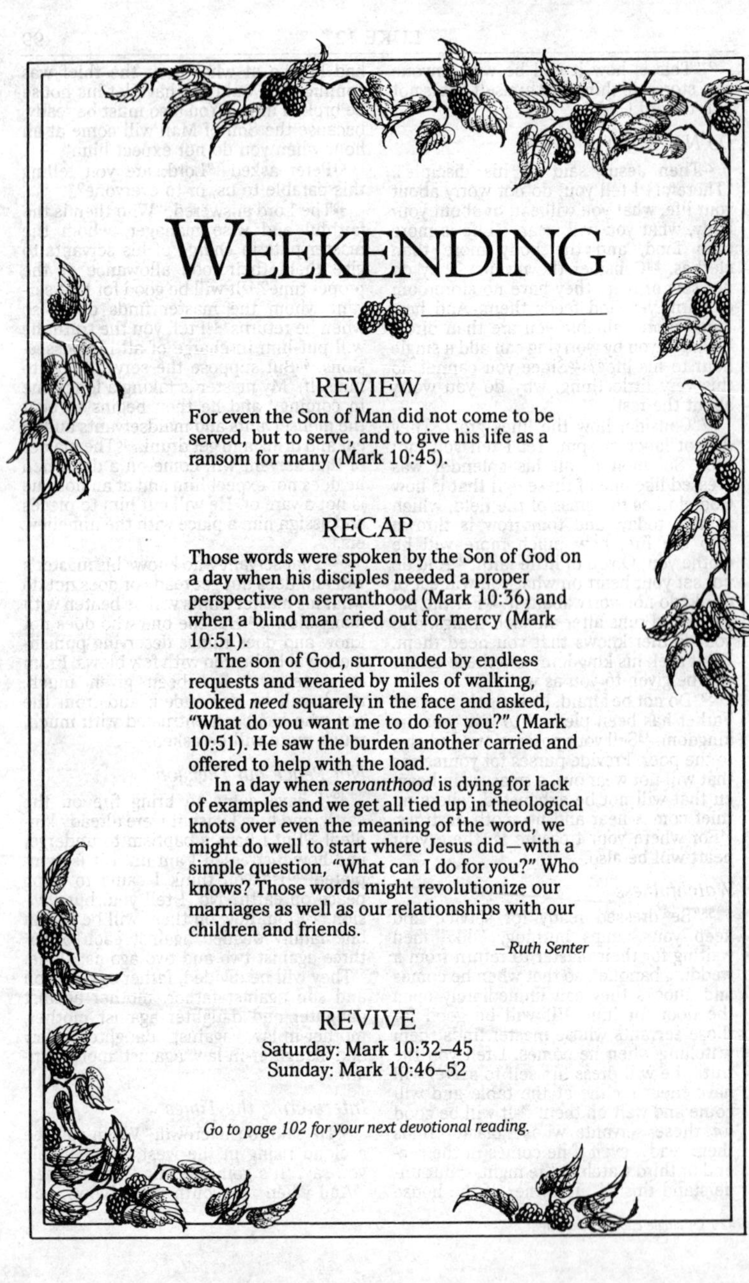

WEEKENDING

REVIEW

For even the Son of Man did not come to be served, but to serve, and to give his life as a ransom for many (Mark 10:45).

RECAP

Those words were spoken by the Son of God on a day when his disciples needed a proper perspective on servanthood (Mark 10:36) and when a blind man cried out for mercy (Mark 10:51).

The son of God, surrounded by endless requests and wearied by miles of walking, looked *need* squarely in the face and asked, "What do you want me to do for you?" (Mark 10:51). He saw the burden another carried and offered to help with the load.

In a day when *servanthood* is dying for lack of examples and we get all tied up in theological knots over even the meaning of the word, we might do well to start where Jesus did—with a simple question, "What can I do for you?" Who knows? Those words might revolutionize our marriages as well as our relationships with our children and friends.

– Ruth Senter

REVIVE

Saturday: Mark 10:32–45
Sunday: Mark 10:46–52

Go to page 102 for your next devotional reading.

say, 'It's going to be hot,' and it is. 56Hyp-
ocrites! You know how to interpret the
appearance of the earth and the sky. How
is it that you don't know how to interpret
this present time?
57"Why don't you judge for yourselves
what is right? 58As you are going with your
adversary to the magistrate, try hard to be
reconciled to him on the way, or he may
drag you off to the judge, and the judge
turn you over to the officer, and the officer throw you into prison. 59I tell you, you
will not get out until you have paid the
last penny.[a]"

Repent or Perish

13 Now there were some present at
that time who told Jesus about the
Galileans whose blood Pilate had mixed
with their sacrifices. 2Jesus answered,
"Do you think that these Galileans were
worse sinners than all the other Galileans
because they suffered this way? 3I tell
you, no! But unless you repent, you too
will all perish. 4Or those eighteen who
died when the tower in Siloam fell on
them—do you think they were more
guilty than all the others living in Jerusalem? 5I tell you, no! But unless you repent, you too will all perish."
6Then he told this parable: "A man had
a fig tree, planted in his vineyard, and he
went to look for fruit on it, but did not
find any. 7So he said to the man who took
care of the vineyard, 'For three years now
I've been coming to look for fruit on this
fig tree and haven't found any. Cut it
down! Why should it use up the soil?'
8" 'Sir,' the man replied, 'leave it alone
for one more year, and I'll dig around it
and fertilize it. 9If it bears fruit next year,
fine! If not, then cut it down.' "

A Crippled Woman Healed on the Sabbath

10On a Sabbath Jesus was teaching in
one of the synagogues, 11and a woman
was there who had been crippled by a
spirit for eighteen years. She was bent
over and could not straighten up at all.
12When Jesus saw her, he called her forward and said to her, "Woman, you are
set free from your infirmity." 13Then he
put his hands on her, and immediately
she straightened up and praised God.
14Indignant because Jesus had healed
on the Sabbath, the synagogue ruler said
to the people, "There are six days for
work. So come and be healed on those
days, not on the Sabbath."
15The Lord answered him, "You hypocrites! Doesn't each of you on the Sabbath untie his ox or donkey from the stall
and lead it out to give it water? 16Then
should not this woman, a daughter of
Abraham, whom Satan has kept bound
for eighteen long years, be set free on the
Sabbath day from what bound her?"
17When he said this, all his opponents
were humiliated, but the people were delighted with all the wonderful things he
was doing.

The Parables of the Mustard Seed and the Yeast

18Then Jesus asked, "What is the kingdom of God like? What shall I compare it
to? 19It is like a mustard seed, which a
man took and planted in his garden. It
grew and became a tree, and the birds of
the air perched in its branches."
20Again he asked, "What shall I compare the kingdom of God to? 21It is like
yeast that a woman took and mixed into
a large amount[b] of flour until it worked
all through the dough."

The Narrow Door

22Then Jesus went through the towns
and villages, teaching as he made his way
to Jerusalem. 23Someone asked him,
"Lord, are only a few people going to be
saved?"
He said to them, 24"Make every effort
to enter through the narrow door, because many, I tell you, will try to enter
and will not be able to. 25Once the owner
of the house gets up and closes the door,
you will stand outside knocking and
pleading, 'Sir, open the door for us.'
"But he will answer, 'I don't know you
or where you come from.'
26"Then you will say, 'We ate and drank
with you, and you taught in our streets.'
27"But he will reply, 'I don't know you
or where you come from. Away from me,
all you evildoers!'
28"There will be weeping there, and
gnashing of teeth, when you see Abraham, Isaac and Jacob and all the prophets in the kingdom of God, but you yourselves thrown out. 29People will come
from east and west and north and south,
and will take their places at the feast in

[a]59 Greek *lepton* [b]21 Greek *three satas* (probably about 1/2 bushel or 22 liters)

the kingdom of God. 30Indeed there are
those who are last who will be first, and
first who will be last."

Jesus' Sorrow for Jerusalem

31At that time some Pharisees came to
Jesus and said to him, "Leave this place
and go somewhere else. Herod wants to
kill you."

32He replied, "Go tell that fox, 'I will
drive out demons and heal people today
and tomorrow, and on the third day I will
reach my goal.' 33In any case, I must keep
going today and tomorrow and the next
day—for surely no prophet can die outside Jerusalem!

34"O Jerusalem, Jerusalem, you who
kill the prophets and stone those sent to
you, how often I have longed to gather
your children together, as a hen gathers
her chicks under her wings, but you were
not willing! 35Look, your house is left to
you desolate. I tell you, you will not see
me again until you say, 'Blessed is he who
comes in the name of the Lord.'[a]"

[a]35 Psalm 118:26

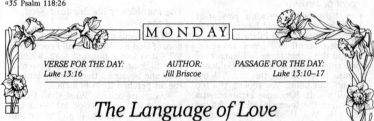

MONDAY

VERSE FOR THE DAY: *Luke 13:16*

AUTHOR: *Jill Briscoe*

PASSAGE FOR THE DAY: *Luke 13:10–17*

The Language of Love

JESUS understood us. Yes, he did! You can tell it by his language. It was the language of love. Paul says that love has good manners (1 Corinthians 13:5), and if you care to read the way the Lord Jesus addressed the women he met, you can actually hear love talking. He said "daughter," "little girl," and even "daughter of Abraham," as in this passage. What courtesy and comfort, for women in Jesus' day were treated like dirt. When the priggish Pharisees dragged a woman in front of him who was "caught in adultery," Jesus saved her from possible stoning and then dealt firmly with her (John 8:3–11). He was not rude or rough, but polite while firm.

It's awfully important how you talk to people. Jesus always seemed to say the right thing the right way! When I was a young youth worker I was given a lot of responsibility suddenly. It went to my head. Being a strong sort of character, it was not long before I was busy bossing everyone about. "Jill," my fellow worker sweetly said to me one day, "I would like to be asked—not told." I needed that! Jesus didn't boss women around. He understood us; he knew we liked to be asked, not told. He used the language of love, and so must we if we would follow in his steps and if we would see anything accomplished. Let's try a few good manners. It's amazing how many people will respond. Try saying "please" and "thank you" and "do you mind"—this is the language of love.

Additional Scripture Readings:
John 4:7–27; Colossians 4:6

Go to page 104 for your next devotional reading.

Jesus at a Pharisee's House

14 One Sabbath, when Jesus went to
eat in the house of a prominent
Pharisee, he was being carefully watched.
2There in front of him was a man suffering
from dropsy. 3Jesus asked the Pharisees
and experts in the law, "Is it lawful to
heal on the Sabbath or not?" 4But they
remained silent. So taking hold of the
man, he healed him and sent him away.

5Then he asked them, "If one of you
has a son[a] or an ox that falls into a well
on the Sabbath day, will you not immediately pull him out?" 6And they had nothing to say.

7When he noticed how the guests
picked the places of honor at the table, he
told them this parable: 8"When someone
invites you to a wedding feast, do not take
the place of honor, for a person more distinguished than you may have been invited. 9If so, the host who invited both of
you will come and say to you, 'Give this
man your seat.' Then, humiliated, you
will have to take the least important
place. 10But when you are invited, take
the lowest place, so that when your host
comes, he will say to you, 'Friend, move
up to a better place.' Then you will be
honored in the presence of all your fellow
guests. 11For everyone who exalts himself
will be humbled, and he who humbles
himself will be exalted."

12Then Jesus said to his host, "When
you give a luncheon or dinner, do not invite your friends, your brothers or relatives, or your rich neighbors; if you do,
they may invite you back and so you will
be repaid. 13But when you give a banquet,
invite the poor, the crippled, the lame,
the blind, 14and you will be blessed. Although they cannot repay you, you will be
repaid at the resurrection of the righteous."

The Parable of the Great Banquet

15When one of those at the table with
him heard this, he said to Jesus, "Blessed
is the man who will eat at the feast in the
kingdom of God."

16Jesus replied: "A certain man was
preparing a great banquet and invited
many guests. 17At the time of the banquet
he sent his servant to tell those who had
been invited, 'Come, for everything is
now ready.'

18"But they all alike began to make excuses. The first said, 'I have just bought a
field, and I must go and see it. Please excuse me.'

19"Another said, 'I have just bought five
yoke of oxen, and I'm on my way to try
them out. Please excuse me.'

20"Still another said, 'I just got married,
so I can't come.'

21"The servant came back and reported
this to his master. Then the owner of the
house became angry and ordered his servant, 'Go out quickly into the streets and
alleys of the town and bring in the poor,
the crippled, the blind and the lame.'

22" 'Sir,' the servant said, 'what you ordered has been done, but there is still
room.'

23"Then the master told his servant,
'Go out to the roads and country lanes
and make them come in, so that my
house will be full. 24I tell you, not one of
those men who were invited will get a
taste of my banquet.' "

The Cost of Being a Disciple

25Large crowds were traveling with
Jesus, and turning to them he said: 26"If
anyone comes to me and does not hate
his father and mother, his wife and children, his brothers and sisters—yes, even
his own life—he cannot be my disciple.
27And anyone who does not carry his
cross and follow me cannot be my disciple.

28"Suppose one of you wants to build a
tower. Will he not first sit down and esti-
mate the cost to see if he has enough
money to complete it? 29For if he lays the
foundation and is not able to finish it,
everyone who sees it will ridicule him,
30saying, 'This fellow began to build and
was not able to finish.'

31"Or suppose a king is about to go to
war against another king. Will he not first
sit down and consider whether he is able
with ten thousand men to oppose the one
coming against him with twenty thousand? 32If he is not able, he will send a
delegation while the other is still a long
way off and will ask for terms of peace.
33In the same way, any of you who does
not give up everything he has cannot be
my disciple.

34"Salt is good, but if it loses its saltiness, how can it be made salty again? 35It
is fit neither for the soil nor for the ma-
nure pile; it is thrown out.

[a]5 Some manuscripts *donkey*

TUESDAY

VERSE FOR THE DAY:
Luke 14:12

AUTHOR:
Joni Eareckson Tada

PASSAGE FOR THE DAY:
Luke 14:1–35

Changing the Subject

IMAGINE the scene in Luke 14:1–24. Jesus was invited to dinner at a Pharisee's home in the rich suburbs of Jerusalem. He noticed the wealthy people grabbing the best seats around the table. At that point, Jesus launched into a story about the sorts of dinner parties people ought to give—feasts for the forgotten, the homeless, the poor and the disabled.

The Lord added that although these poor people would not be able to repay them, the hosts would, nevertheless, be repaid at the resurrection (Luke 14:14).

You can imagine what happened next. Jesus probably sat down, put his napkin on his lap, and quietly picked up an hors d'oeuvre. Dead silence hung over the table as the wealthy people shot nervous glances at each other. Jesus had put a damper on the party spirit.

Finally, one of the dinner guests cleared his throat and spoke up. "Blessed is the man who will eat at the feast in the kingdom of God" (Luke 14:15). What an odd thing to say! It's as if he was thinking:

> *Jesus, I can't say that I follow your strange ideas about dining with cripples, but I do agree with what you said about heaven—it's so comforting to know that everything will turn out perfectly in the end.* *

The man, in other words, was trying his best to change the spiritual subject.

Sound familiar? I can't tell you how many times I have either consciously or unconsciously tried to change the spiritual subject with God when I sensed he was laying heavy, convicting things on my heart. But just as the Lord did not allow those dinner guests to change the subject (read Luke 14:15–24), we will find it just as difficult to divert God's attention from those issues that need to be addressed in our lives.

Additional Scripture Readings:
Luke 11:27–28; James 2:1–7

Go to page 106 for your next devotional reading.

*Robert Farrar Capon, *The Parables of Grace* (Grand Rapids: William B. Eerdmans Publishing Company. 1988), 130-131.

"He who has ears to hear, let him
hear."

The Parable of the Lost Sheep

15 Now the tax collectors and "sinners" were all gathering around to
hear him. 2But the Pharisees and the
teachers of the law muttered, "This man
welcomes sinners and eats with them."
3Then Jesus told them this parable:
4"Suppose one of you has a hundred
sheep and loses one of them. Does he not
leave the ninety-nine in the open country
and go after the lost sheep until he finds
it? 5And when he finds it, he joyfully puts
it on his shoulders 6and goes home. Then
he calls his friends and neighbors together and says, 'Rejoice with me; I have
found my lost sheep.' 7I tell you that in
the same way there will be more rejoicing
in heaven over one sinner who repents
than over ninety-nine righteous persons
who do not need to repent.

The Parable of the Lost Coin

8"Or suppose a woman has ten silver
coins[a] and loses one. Does she not light
a lamp, sweep the house and search carefully until she finds it? 9And when she
finds it, she calls her friends and neighbors together and says, 'Rejoice with me;
I have found my lost coin.' 10In the same
way, I tell you, there is rejoicing in the
presence of the angels of God over one
sinner who repents."

The Parable of the Lost Son

11Jesus continued: "There was a man
who had two sons. 12The younger one said
to his father, 'Father, give me my share of
the estate.' So he divided his property between them.
13"Not long after that, the younger son
got together all he had, set off for a distant country and there squandered his
wealth in wild living. 14After he had spent
everything, there was a severe famine in
that whole country, and he began to be in
need. 15So he went and hired himself out
to a citizen of that country, who sent him
to his fields to feed pigs. 16He longed to
fill his stomach with the pods that the
pigs were eating, but no one gave him
anything.
17"When he came to his senses, he said,
'How many of my father's hired men have
food to spare, and here I am starving to
death! 18I will set out and go back to my
father and say to him: Father, I have
sinned against heaven and against you.
19I am no longer worthy to be called your
son; make me like one of your hired men.'
20So he got up and went to his father.
"But while he was still a long way off,
his father saw him and was filled with
compassion for him; he ran to his son,
threw his arms around him and kissed
him.
21"The son said to him, 'Father, I have
sinned against heaven and against you. I
am no longer worthy to be called your
son.[b]'
22"But the father said to his servants,
'Quick! Bring the best robe and put it on
him. Put a ring on his finger and sandals
on his feet. 23Bring the fattened calf and
kill it. Let's have a feast and celebrate.
24For this son of mine was dead and is
alive again; he was lost and is found.' So
they began to celebrate.
25"Meanwhile, the older son was in the
field. When he came near the house, he
heard music and dancing. 26So he called
one of the servants and asked him what
was going on. 27'Your brother has come,'
he replied, 'and your father has killed the
fattened calf because he has him back
safe and sound.'
28"The older brother became angry and
refused to go in. So his father went out
and pleaded with him. 29But he answered
his father, 'Look! All these years I've been
slaving for you and never disobeyed your
orders. Yet you never gave me even a
young goat so I could celebrate with my
friends. 30But when this son of yours who
has squandered your property with prostitutes comes home, you kill the fattened
calf for him!'
31" 'My son,' the father said, 'you are
always with me, and everything I have is
yours. 32But we had to celebrate and be
glad, because this brother of yours was
dead and is alive again; he was lost and is
found.' "

The Parable of the Shrewd Manager

16 Jesus told his disciples: "There
was a rich man whose manager
was accused of wasting his possessions.
2So he called him in and asked him,
'What is this I hear about you? Give an
account of your management, because
you cannot be manager any longer.'

[a]8 Greek *ten drachmas,* each worth about a day's wages
[b]21 Some early manuscripts *son. Make me like one of your hired men.*

WEDNESDAY

VERSE FOR THE DAY: *Luke 15:6*

AUTHOR: *Rosalind Rinker*

PASSAGE FOR THE DAY: *Luke 15:1–7*

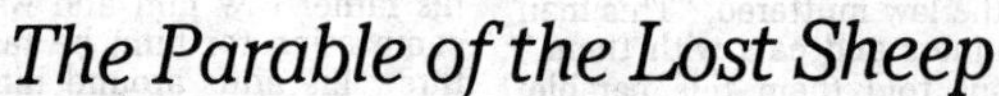

The Parable of the Lost Sheep

JESUS told the parable of the lost sheep to self-righteous leaders who criticized him because he welcomed sinners and even ate with them. His love and mercy are still reaching out to us today, for we are his sheep who have (with or without our consent) wandered into forbidden paths that seemed very innocent. We often shrink from calling anything "sin," but we do admit that sometimes we find ourselves alone, lost, and away from our Shepherd.

For a few moments, imagine you are that little lost one. How did you get lost?

* * * *

There you are, with the rest of the flock, on a hilltop chosen for its tender green grass. Suddenly something tastes better than grass. You don't know that it is tender young thistles but you do know you want more. Searching here and there, you are unaware that you are going downhill to find that delicious stuff. Then, your tummy full, you tuck your legs under your belly and fall right to sleep.

In the meantime, your Good Shepherd takes his flock back to the shelter. Only ninety-nine! Where is that missing little one? Leaving his faithful dog to guard the flock, he retraces his steps to the hilltop, searching, calling, praying.

And what about you? After a good nap you awaken, and . . . oh-oh . . . where are you? It is pitch-dark. Where are the other sheep? Where is your Shepherd? Strange noises frighten you and you say to yourself, "How did I ever get into this mess? How can I ever get out of it?"

With all your strength you cry out, "Maaa . . . maaa . . . Jesus, here I am!" The Good Shepherd hears that cry, and soon you are in his arms. His strong, tender hands are holding you. Feeling the beating of your little heart, he reassures you of his love, and your fears quiet down as you nestle in his arms.

> "My little one, you belong to me. I know what led you astray, but I found you. I'll always be there when you need me. My love is unconditional and eternal."

Additional Scripture Readings:
Psalm 23:1–4; John 10:11–16

Go to page 110 for your next devotional reading.

3"The manager said to himself, 'What
shall I do now? My master is taking away
my job. I'm not strong enough to dig, and
I'm ashamed to beg— 4I know what I'll do
so that, when I lose my job here, people
will welcome me into their houses.'

5"So he called in each one of his master's debtors. He asked the first, 'How much do you owe my master?'

6" 'Eight hundred gallons[a] of olive oil,' he replied.

"The manager told him, 'Take your bill, sit down quickly, and make it four hundred.'

7"Then he asked the second, 'And how much do you owe?'

" 'A thousand bushels[b] of wheat,' he replied.

"He told him, 'Take your bill and make it eight hundred.'

8"The master commended the dishonest manager because he had acted
shrewdly. For the people of this world are
more shrewd in dealing with their own
kind than are the people of the light. 9I
tell you, use worldly wealth to gain
friends for yourselves, so that when it is
gone, you will be welcomed into eternal
dwellings.

10"Whoever can be trusted with very little can also be trusted with much, and
whoever is dishonest with very little will
also be dishonest with much. 11So if you
have not been trustworthy in handling
worldly wealth, who will trust you with
true riches? 12And if you have not been
trustworthy with someone else's property, who will give you property of your
own?

13"No servant can serve two masters. Either he will hate the one and love the other, or he will be devoted to the one and despise the other. You cannot serve both God and Money."

14The Pharisees, who loved money,
heard all this and were sneering at Jesus.
15He said to them, "You are the ones who
justify yourselves in the eyes of men, but
God knows your hearts. What is highly
valued among men is detestable in God's
sight.

Additional Teachings

16"The Law and the Prophets were proclaimed until John. Since that time, the
good news of the kingdom of God is being
preached, and everyone is forcing his way
into it. 17It is easier for heaven and earth
to disappear than for the least stroke of a
pen to drop out of the Law.

18"Anyone who divorces his wife and marries another woman commits adultery, and the man who marries a divorced woman commits adultery.

The Rich Man and Lazarus

19"There was a rich man who was
dressed in purple and fine linen and lived
in luxury every day. 20At his gate was laid
a beggar named Lazarus, covered with
sores 21and longing to eat what fell from
the rich man's table. Even the dogs came
and licked his sores.

22"The time came when the beggar died
and the angels carried him to Abraham's
side. The rich man also died and was buried. 23In hell,[c] where he was in torment,
he looked up and saw Abraham far away,
with Lazarus by his side. 24So he called to
him, 'Father Abraham, have pity on me
and send Lazarus to dip the tip of his finger in water and cool my tongue, because
I am in agony in this fire.'

25"But Abraham replied, 'Son, remember that in your lifetime you received your
good things, while Lazarus received bad
things, but now he is comforted here and
you are in agony. 26And besides all this,
between us and you a great chasm has
been fixed, so that those who want to go
from here to you cannot, nor can anyone
cross over from there to us.'

27"He answered, 'Then I beg you, father, send Lazarus to my father's house,
28for I have five brothers. Let him warn
them, so that they will not also come to
this place of torment.'

29"Abraham replied, 'They have Moses and the Prophets; let them listen to them.'

30" 'No, father Abraham,' he said, 'but if someone from the dead goes to them, they will repent.'

31"He said to him, 'If they do not listen to Moses and the Prophets, they will not be convinced even if someone rises from the dead.' "

Sin, Faith, Duty

17 Jesus said to his disciples: "Things
that cause people to sin are bound
to come, but woe to that person through
whom they come. 2It would be better for
him to be thrown into the sea with a mill-

[a]6 Greek *one hundred batous* (probably about 3 kiloliters) [b]7 Greek *one hundred korous* (probably about 35 kiloliters) [c]23 Greek *Hades*

stone tied around his neck than for him to cause one of these little ones to sin. 3So watch yourselves.

"If your brother sins, rebuke him, and if he repents, forgive him. 4If he sins against you seven times in a day, and seven times comes back to you and says, 'I repent,' forgive him."

5The apostles said to the Lord, "Increase our faith!"

6He replied, "If you have faith as small as a mustard seed, you can say to this mulberry tree, 'Be uprooted and planted in the sea,' and it will obey you.

7"Suppose one of you had a servant plowing or looking after the sheep. Would he say to the servant when he comes in from the field, 'Come along now and sit down to eat'? 8Would he not rather say, 'Prepare my supper, get yourself ready and wait on me while I eat and drink; after that you may eat and drink'? 9Would he thank the servant because he did what he was told to do? 10So you also, when you have done everything you were told to do, should say, 'We are unworthy servants; we have only done our duty.' "

Ten Healed of Leprosy

11Now on his way to Jerusalem, Jesus traveled along the border between Samaria and Galilee. 12As he was going into a village, ten men who had leprosy[a] met him. They stood at a distance 13and called out in a loud voice, "Jesus, Master, have pity on us!"

14When he saw them, he said, "Go, show yourselves to the priests." And as they went, they were cleansed.

15One of them, when he saw he was healed, came back, praising God in a loud voice. 16He threw himself at Jesus' feet and thanked him—and he was a Samaritan.

17Jesus asked, "Were not all ten cleansed? Where are the other nine? 18Was no one found to return and give praise to God except this foreigner?" 19Then he said to him, "Rise and go; your faith has made you well."

The Coming of the Kingdom of God

20Once, having been asked by the Pharisees when the kingdom of God would come, Jesus replied, "The kingdom of God does not come with your careful observation, 21nor will people say, 'Here it is,' or 'There it is,' because the kingdom of God is within[b] you."

22Then he said to his disciples, "The time is coming when you will long to see one of the days of the Son of Man, but you will not see it. 23Men will tell you, 'There he is!' or 'Here he is!' Do not go running off after them. 24For the Son of Man in his day[c] will be like the lightning, which flashes and lights up the sky from one end to the other. 25But first he must suffer many things and be rejected by this generation.

26"Just as it was in the days of Noah, so also will it be in the days of the Son of Man. 27People were eating, drinking, marrying and being given in marriage up to the day Noah entered the ark. Then the flood came and destroyed them all.

28"It was the same in the days of Lot. People were eating and drinking, buying and selling, planting and building. 29But the day Lot left Sodom, fire and sulfur rained down from heaven and destroyed them all.

30"It will be just like this on the day the Son of Man is revealed. 31On that day no one who is on the roof of his house, with his goods inside, should go down to get them. Likewise, no one in the field should go back for anything. 32Remember Lot's wife! 33Whoever tries to keep his life will lose it, and whoever loses his life will preserve it. 34I tell you, on that night two people will be in one bed; one will be taken and the other left. 35Two women will be grinding grain together; one will be taken and the other left.[d]"

37"Where, Lord?" they asked.

He replied, "Where there is a dead body, there the vultures will gather."

The Parable of the Persistent Widow

18 Then Jesus told his disciples a parable to show them that they should always pray and not give up. 2He said: "In a certain town there was a judge who neither feared God nor cared about men. 3And there was a widow in that town who kept coming to him with the plea, 'Grant me justice against my adversary.'

4"For some time he refused. But finally he said to himself, 'Even though I don't fear God or care about men, 5yet because this widow keeps bothering me, I will see

[a]12 The Greek word was used for various diseases affecting the skin—not necessarily leprosy. [b]21 Or *among* [c]24 Some manuscripts do not have *in his day.* [d]35 Some manuscripts *left.* 36*Two men will be in the field; one will be taken and the other left.*

that she gets justice, so that she won't eventually wear me out with her coming!' "

[6]And the Lord said, "Listen to what the unjust judge says. [7]And will not God bring about justice for his chosen ones, who cry out to him day and night? Will he keep putting them off? [8]I tell you, he will see that they get justice, and quickly. However, when the Son of Man comes, will he find faith on the earth?"

The Parable of the Pharisee and the Tax Collector

[9]To some who were confident of their own righteousness and looked down on everybody else, Jesus told this parable: [10]"Two men went up to the temple to pray, one a Pharisee and the other a tax collector. [11]The Pharisee stood up and prayed about[a] himself: 'God, I thank you that I am not like other men—robbers, evildoers, adulterers—or even like this tax collector. [12]I fast twice a week and give a tenth of all I get.'

[13]"But the tax collector stood at a distance. He would not even look up to heaven, but beat his breast and said, 'God, have mercy on me, a sinner.'

[14]"I tell you that this man, rather than the other, went home justified before God. For everyone who exalts himself will be humbled, and he who humbles himself will be exalted."

The Little Children and Jesus

[15]People were also bringing babies to Jesus to have him touch them. When the disciples saw this, they rebuked them. [16]But Jesus called the children to him and said, "Let the little children come to me, and do not hinder them, for the kingdom of God belongs to such as these. [17]I tell you the truth, anyone who will not receive the kingdom of God like a little child will never enter it."

The Rich Ruler

[18]A certain ruler asked him, "Good teacher, what must I do to inherit eternal life?"

[19]"Why do you call me good?" Jesus answered. "No one is good—except God alone. [20]You know the commandments: 'Do not commit adultery, do not murder, do not steal, do not give false testimony, honor your father and mother.'[b] "

[21]"All these I have kept since I was a boy," he said.

[22]When Jesus heard this, he said to him, "You still lack one thing. Sell everything you have and give to the poor, and you will have treasure in heaven. Then come, follow me."

[23]When he heard this, he became very sad, because he was a man of great wealth. [24]Jesus looked at him and said, "How hard it is for the rich to enter the kingdom of God! [25]Indeed, it is easier for a camel to go through the eye of a needle than for a rich man to enter the kingdom of God."

[26]Those who heard this asked, "Who then can be saved?"

[27]Jesus replied, "What is impossible with men is possible with God."

[28]Peter said to him, "We have left all we had to follow you!"

[29]"I tell you the truth," Jesus said to them, "no one who has left home or wife or brothers or parents or children for the sake of the kingdom of God [30]will fail to receive many times as much in this age and, in the age to come, eternal life."

Jesus Again Predicts His Death

[31]Jesus took the Twelve aside and told them, "We are going up to Jerusalem, and everything that is written by the prophets about the Son of Man will be fulfilled. [32]He will be handed over to the Gentiles. They will mock him, insult him, spit on him, flog him and kill him. [33]On the third day he will rise again."

[34]The disciples did not understand any of this. Its meaning was hidden from them, and they did not know what he was talking about.

A Blind Beggar Receives His Sight

[35]As Jesus approached Jericho, a blind man was sitting by the roadside begging. [36]When he heard the crowd going by, he asked what was happening. [37]They told him, "Jesus of Nazareth is passing by."

[38]He called out, "Jesus, Son of David, have mercy on me!"

[39]Those who led the way rebuked him and told him to be quiet, but he shouted all the more, "Son of David, have mercy on me!"

[40]Jesus stopped and ordered the man to be brought to him. When he came near, Jesus asked him, [41]"What do you want me to do for you?"

[a]*11* Or *to* [b]*20* Exodus 20:12-16; Deut. 5:16-20

"Lord, I want to see," he replied.
42Jesus said to him, "Receive your
sight; your faith has healed you." 43Imme-
diately he received his sight and followed
Jesus, praising God. When all the people
saw it, they also praised God.

Zacchaeus the Tax Collector

19 Jesus entered Jericho and was
passing through. 2A man was there
by the name of Zacchaeus; he was a chief
tax collector and was wealthy. 3He wanted to see who Jesus was, but being a short
man he could not, because of the crowd.
4So he ran ahead and climbed a syca-
more-fig tree to see him, since Jesus was
coming that way.
5When Jesus reached the spot, he
looked up and said to him, "Zacchaeus,
come down immediately. I must stay at
your house today." 6So he came down at
once and welcomed him gladly.
7All the people saw this and began to
mutter, "He has gone to be the guest of a
'sinner.' "
8But Zacchaeus stood up and said to
the Lord, "Look, Lord! Here and now I
give half of my possessions to the poor,
and if I have cheated anybody out of anything, I will pay back four times the
amount."
9Jesus said to him, "Today salvation
has come to this house, because this
man, too, is a son of Abraham. 10For the
Son of Man came to seek and to save
what was lost."

The Parable of the Ten Minas

11While they were listening to this, he
went on to tell them a parable, because
he was near Jerusalem and the people

THURSDAY

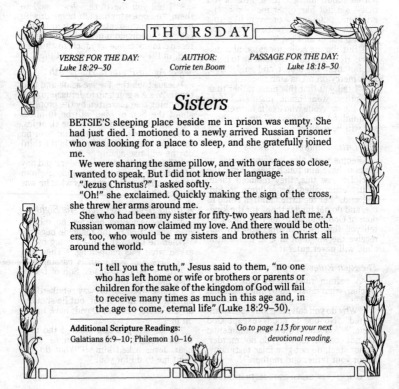

VERSE FOR THE DAY: Luke 18:29–30 | *AUTHOR:* Corrie ten Boom | *PASSAGE FOR THE DAY:* Luke 18:18–30

Sisters

BETSIE'S sleeping place beside me in prison was empty. She had just died. I motioned to a newly arrived Russian prisoner who was looking for a place to sleep, and she gratefully joined me.

We were sharing the same pillow, and with our faces so close, I wanted to speak. But I did not know her language.

"Jezus Christus?" I asked softly.

"Oh!" she exclaimed. Quickly making the sign of the cross, she threw her arms around me.

She who had been my sister for fifty-two years had left me. A Russian woman now claimed my love. And there would be others, too, who would be my sisters and brothers in Christ all around the world.

"I tell you the truth," Jesus said to them, "no one who has left home or wife or brothers or parents or children for the sake of the kingdom of God will fail to receive many times as much in this age and, in the age to come, eternal life" (Luke 18:29–30).

Additional Scripture Readings:
Galatians 6:9–10; Philemon 10–16

Go to page 113 for your next devotional reading.

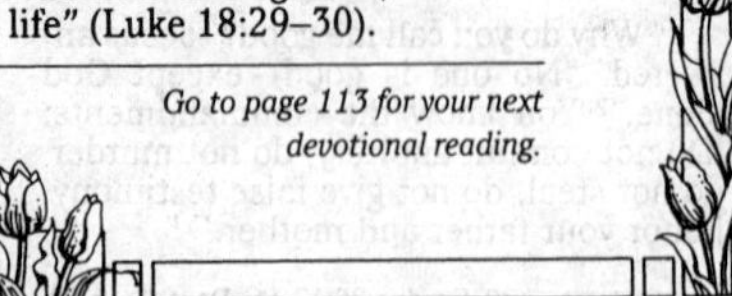

thought that the kingdom of God was going to appear at once. 12He said: "A man
of noble birth went to a distant country to
have himself appointed king and then to
return. 13So he called ten of his servants
and gave them ten minas.[a] 'Put this money to work,' he said, 'until I come back.'

14"But his subjects hated him and sent
a delegation after him to say, 'We don't
want this man to be our king.'

15"He was made king, however, and returned home. Then he sent for the servants to whom he had given the money, in
order to find out what they had gained
with it.

16"The first one came and said, 'Sir,
your mina has earned ten more.'

17" 'Well done, my good servant!' his
master replied. 'Because you have been
trustworthy in a very small matter, take
charge of ten cities.'

18"The second came and said, 'Sir, your
mina has earned five more.'

19"His master answered, 'You take
charge of five cities.'

20"Then another servant came and
said, 'Sir, here is your mina; I have kept it
laid away in a piece of cloth. 21I was afraid
of you, because you are a hard man. You
take out what you did not put in and reap
what you did not sow.'

22"His master replied, 'I will judge you
by your own words, you wicked servant!
You knew, did you, that I am a hard man,
taking out what I did not put in, and reap-
ing what I did not sow? 23Why then didn't
you put my money on deposit, so that
when I came back, I could have collected
it with interest?'

24"Then he said to those standing by,
'Take his mina away from him and give it
to the one who has ten minas.'

25" 'Sir,' they said, 'he already has ten!'

26"He replied, 'I tell you that to everyone who has, more will be given, but as
for the one who has nothing, even what
he has will be taken away. 27But those
enemies of mine who did not want me to
be king over them—bring them here and
kill them in front of me.' "

The Triumphal Entry

28After Jesus had said this, he went on
ahead, going up to Jerusalem. 29As he approached Bethphage and Bethany at the
hill called the Mount of Olives, he sent
two of his disciples, saying to them, 30"Go
to the village ahead of you, and as you
enter it, you will find a colt tied there,
which no one has ever ridden. Untie it
and bring it here. 31If anyone asks you,
'Why are you untying it?' tell him, 'The
Lord needs it.' "

32Those who were sent ahead went and
found it just as he had told them. 33As
they were untying the colt, its owners
asked them, "Why are you untying the
colt?"

34They replied, "The Lord needs it."

35They brought it to Jesus, threw their
cloaks on the colt and put Jesus on it.
36As he went along, people spread their
cloaks on the road.

37When he came near the place where
the road goes down the Mount of Olives,
the whole crowd of disciples began joyfully to praise God in loud voices for all the
miracles they had seen:

38"Blessed is the king who comes in the
name of the Lord!"[b]

"Peace in heaven and glory in the
highest!"

39Some of the Pharisees in the crowd
said to Jesus, "Teacher, rebuke your disciples!"

40"I tell you," he replied, "if they keep
quiet, the stones will cry out."

41As he approached Jerusalem and saw
the city, he wept over it 42and said, "If
you, even you, had only known on this
day what would bring you peace—but
now it is hidden from your eyes. 43The
days will come upon you when your enemies will build an embankment against
you and encircle you and hem you in on
every side. 44They will dash you to the
ground, you and the children within your
walls. They will not leave one stone on
another, because you did not recognize
the time of God's coming to you."

Jesus at the Temple

45Then he entered the temple area and
began driving out those who were selling.
46"It is written," he said to them, " 'My
house will be a house of prayer'[c]; but you
have made it 'a den of robbers.'[d]"

47Every day he was teaching at the temple. But the chief priests, the teachers of
the law and the leaders among the people
were trying to kill him. 48Yet they could
not find any way to do it, because all the
people hung on his words.

[a]13 A mina was about three months' wages. [b]38 Psalm 118:26 [c]46 Isaiah 56:7 [d]46 Jer. 7:11

The Authority of Jesus Questioned

20 One day as he was teaching the
people in the temple courts and
preaching the gospel, the chief priests
and the teachers of the law, together with
the elders, came up to him. 2"Tell us by
what authority you are doing these
things," they said. "Who gave you this authority?"

3He replied, "I will also ask you a question. Tell me, 4John's baptism—was it
from heaven, or from men?"

5They discussed it among themselves
and said, "If we say, 'From heaven,' he
will ask, 'Why didn't you believe him?'
6But if we say, 'From men,' all the people
will stone us, because they are persuaded
that John was a prophet."

7So they answered, "We don't know
where it was from."

8Jesus said, "Neither will I tell you by
what authority I am doing these things."

The Parable of the Tenants

9He went on to tell the people this parable: "A man planted a vineyard, rented it
to some farmers and went away for a long
time. 10At harvest time he sent a servant
to the tenants so they would give him
some of the fruit of the vineyard. But the
tenants beat him and sent him away empty-handed. 11He sent another servant, but
that one also they beat and treated
shamefully and sent away empty-handed.
12He sent still a third, and they wounded
him and threw him out.

13"Then the owner of the vineyard said,
'What shall I do? I will send my son,
whom I love; perhaps they will respect
him.'

14"But when the tenants saw him, they
talked the matter over. 'This is the heir,'
they said. 'Let's kill him, and the inheritance will be ours.' 15So they threw him
out of the vineyard and killed him.

"What then will the owner of the vineyard do to them? 16He will come and kill
those tenants and give the vineyard to
others."

When the people heard this, they said,
"May this never be!"

17Jesus looked directly at them and
asked, "Then what is the meaning of that
which is written:

> " 'The stone the builders rejected
> has become the capstone[a]'[b]?

18Everyone who falls on that stone will be
broken to pieces, but he on whom it falls
will be crushed."

19The teachers of the law and the chief
priests looked for a way to arrest him immediately, because they knew he had
spoken this parable against them. But
they were afraid of the people.

Paying Taxes to Caesar

20Keeping a close watch on him, they
sent spies, who pretended to be honest.
They hoped to catch Jesus in something
he said so that they might hand him over
to the power and authority of the governor. 21So the spies questioned him:
"Teacher, we know that you speak and
teach what is right, and that you do not
show partiality but teach the way of God
in accordance with the truth. 22Is it right
for us to pay taxes to Caesar or not?"

23He saw through their duplicity and
said to them, 24"Show me a denarius.
Whose portrait and inscription are on it?"

25"Caesar's," they replied.

He said to them, "Then give to Caesar
what is Caesar's, and to God what is
God's."

26They were unable to trap him in what
he had said there in public. And astonished by his answer, they became silent.

The Resurrection and Marriage

27Some of the Sadducees, who say
there is no resurrection, came to Jesus
with a question. 28"Teacher," they said,
"Moses wrote for us that if a man's brother dies and leaves a wife but no children,
the man must marry the widow and have
children for his brother. 29Now there were
seven brothers. The first one married a
woman and died childless. 30The second
31and then the third married her, and in
the same way the seven died, leaving no
children. 32Finally, the woman died too.
33Now then, at the resurrection whose
wife will she be, since the seven were
married to her?"

34Jesus replied, "The people of this age
marry and are given in marriage. 35But
those who are considered worthy of taking part in that age and in the resurrection from the dead will neither marry nor
be given in marriage, 36and they can no
longer die; for they are like the angels.
They are God's children, since they are
children of the resurrection. 37But in the
account of the bush, even Moses showed

[a]17 Or *cornerstone* [b]17 Psalm 118:22

that the dead rise, for he calls the Lord
'the God of Abraham, and the God of
Isaac, and the God of Jacob.'[a] 38He is not
the God of the dead, but of the living, for
to him all are alive."
39Some of the teachers of the law responded, "Well said, teacher!" 40And no
one dared to ask him any more questions.

Whose Son Is the Christ?

41Then Jesus said to them, "How is it
that they say the Christ[b] is the Son of
David? 42David himself declares in the
Book of Psalms:

"'The Lord said to my Lord:
"Sit at my right hand
43until I make your enemies
a footstool for your feet."'[c]

44David calls him 'Lord.' How then can he
be his son?"
45While all the people were listening,
Jesus said to his disciples, 46"Beware of
the teachers of the law. They like to walk
around in flowing robes and love to be
greeted in the marketplaces and have the
most important seats in the synagogues
and the places of honor at banquets.

[a]37 Exodus 3:6 [b]41 Or *Messiah* [c]43 Psalm 110:1

FRIDAY

VERSE FOR THE DAY: *Luke 21:2*
AUTHOR: *Jill Briscoe*
PASSAGE FOR THE DAY: *Luke 21:1–4*

When God Says Thank You

JESUS always notices women who throw everything they've got into the Lord's work! Sitting near the treasury at the temple, Jesus drew his disciples' attention to a poor widow. She was, I'm sure, unaware that Jesus was watching. She didn't have to be watched as she gave God everything she had. Her two small copper coins would have bought her a morsel of bread or five sparrows to eat (Luke 12:6–7), but she decided to go hungry and give her money to God instead. Two small coins weren't much. They weren't noticed, they weren't appreciated by other people until Jesus came along and saw what she did and made sure the twelve apostles saw it. He made sure that Luke and Mark recorded it and that the whole world read about it! Solomon's temple would stand without the help of the widow's coins, but Jesus knew that that sort of giving was the stuff of which the kingdom was made.

Jesus always notices the small offerings. Even if the widow herself didn't think her offering was worth the notice, Jesus disagreed and affirmed her in her service. Have you cast in all you can? Are you married to a man who will not allow you to serve God as you wish? Does financial strain limit you to giving little when you desire to give much? If you've indeed cast in all you possibly can of your money, time and service, God understands. He affirms you in it. He says thank you.

Additional Scripture Readings:
Acts 10:1–4; 2 Corinthians 9:6–7

Go to page 116 for your next devotional reading.

[47]They devour widows' houses and for a show make lengthy prayers. Such men will be punished most severely."

The Widow's Offering

21 As he looked up, Jesus saw the rich putting their gifts into the temple treasury. [2]He also saw a poor widow put in two very small copper coins.[a] [3]"I tell you the truth," he said, "this poor widow has put in more than all the others. [4]All these people gave their gifts out of their wealth; but she out of her poverty put in all she had to live on."

Signs of the End of the Age

[5]Some of his disciples were remarking about how the temple was adorned with beautiful stones and with gifts dedicated to God. But Jesus said, [6]"As for what you see here, the time will come when not one stone will be left on another; every one of them will be thrown down."

[7]"Teacher," they asked, "when will these things happen? And what will be the sign that they are about to take place?"

[8]He replied: "Watch out that you are not deceived. For many will come in my name, claiming, 'I am he,' and, 'The time is near.' Do not follow them. [9]When you hear of wars and revolutions, do not be frightened. These things must happen first, but the end will not come right away."

[10]Then he said to them: "Nation will rise against nation, and kingdom against kingdom. [11]There will be great earthquakes, famines and pestilences in various places, and fearful events and great signs from heaven.

[12]"But before all this, they will lay hands on you and persecute you. They will deliver you to synagogues and prisons, and you will be brought before kings and governors, and all on account of my name. [13]This will result in your being witnesses to them. [14]But make up your mind not to worry beforehand how you will defend yourselves. [15]For I will give you words and wisdom that none of your adversaries will be able to resist or contradict. [16]You will be betrayed even by parents, brothers, relatives and friends, and they will put some of you to death. [17]All men will hate you because of me. [18]But not a hair of your head will perish. [19]By standing firm you will gain life.

[20]"When you see Jerusalem being surrounded by armies, you will know that its desolation is near. [21]Then let those who are in Judea flee to the mountains, let those in the city get out, and let those in the country not enter the city. [22]For this is the time of punishment in fulfillment of all that has been written. [23]How dreadful it will be in those days for pregnant women and nursing mothers! There will be great distress in the land and wrath against this people. [24]They will fall by the sword and will be taken as prisoners to all the nations. Jerusalem will be trampled on by the Gentiles until the times of the Gentiles are fulfilled.

[25]"There will be signs in the sun, moon and stars. On the earth, nations will be in anguish and perplexity at the roaring and tossing of the sea. [26]Men will faint from terror, apprehensive of what is coming on the world, for the heavenly bodies will be shaken. [27]At that time they will see the Son of Man coming in a cloud with power and great glory. [28]When these things begin to take place, stand up and lift up your heads, because your redemption is drawing near."

[29]He told them this parable: "Look at the fig tree and all the trees. [30]When they sprout leaves, you can see for yourselves and know that summer is near. [31]Even so, when you see these things happening, you know that the kingdom of God is near.

[32]"I tell you the truth, this generation[b] will certainly not pass away until all these things have happened. [33]Heaven and earth will pass away, but my words will never pass away.

[34]"Be careful, or your hearts will be weighed down with dissipation, drunkenness and the anxieties of life, and that day will close on you unexpectedly like a trap. [35]For it will come upon all those who live on the face of the whole earth. [36]Be always on the watch, and pray that you may be able to escape all that is about to happen, and that you may be able to stand before the Son of Man."

[37]Each day Jesus was teaching at the temple, and each evening he went out to spend the night on the hill called the Mount of Olives, [38]and all the people came early in the morning to hear him at the temple.

[a]2 Greek *two lepta* [b]32 Or *race*

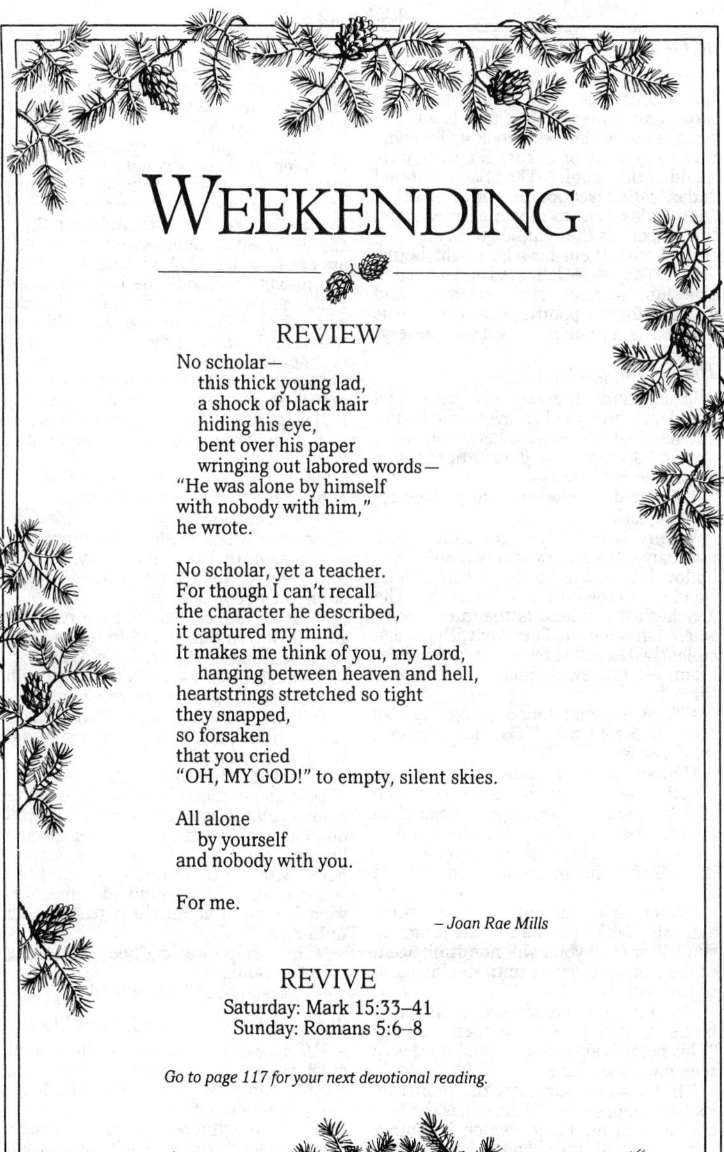

WEEKENDING

REVIEW

No scholar—
    this thick young lad,
    a shock of black hair
    hiding his eye,
    bent over his paper
    wringing out labored words—
"He was alone by himself
with nobody with him,"
he wrote.

No scholar, yet a teacher.
For though I can't recall
the character he described,
it captured my mind.
It makes me think of you, my Lord,
    hanging between heaven and hell,
heartstrings stretched so tight
they snapped,
so forsaken
that you cried
"OH, MY GOD!" to empty, silent skies.

All alone
    by yourself
and nobody with you.

For me.

– Joan Rae Mills

REVIVE

Saturday: Mark 15:33–41
Sunday: Romans 5:6–8

Go to page 117 for your next devotional reading.

Judas Agrees to Betray Jesus

22 Now the Feast of Unleavened
Bread, called the Passover, was approaching, 2and the chief priests and the
teachers of the law were looking for some
way to get rid of Jesus, for they were
afraid of the people. 3Then Satan entered
Judas, called Iscariot, one of the Twelve.
4And Judas went to the chief priests and
the officers of the temple guard and discussed with them how he might betray
Jesus. 5They were delighted and agreed to
give him money. 6He consented, and
watched for an opportunity to hand Jesus
over to them when no crowd was present.

The Last Supper

7Then came the day of Unleavened
Bread on which the Passover lamb had to
be sacrificed. 8Jesus sent Peter and John,
saying, "Go and make preparations for us
to eat the Passover."

9"Where do you want us to prepare for
it?" they asked.

10He replied, "As you enter the city, a
man carrying a jar of water will meet you.
Follow him to the house that he enters,
11and say to the owner of the house, 'The
Teacher asks: Where is the guest room,
where I may eat the Passover with my disciples?' 12He will show you a large upper
room, all furnished. Make preparations
there."

13They left and found things just as
Jesus had told them. So they prepared
the Passover.

14When the hour came, Jesus and his
apostles reclined at the table. 15And he
said to them, "I have eagerly desired to
eat this Passover with you before I suffer.
16For I tell you, I will not eat it again until
it finds fulfillment in the kingdom of
God."

17After taking the cup, he gave thanks
and said, "Take this and divide it among
you. 18For I tell you I will not drink again
of the fruit of the vine until the kingdom
of God comes."

19And he took bread, gave thanks and
broke it, and gave it to them, saying,
"This is my body given for you; do this in
remembrance of me."

20In the same way, after the supper he
took the cup, saying, "This cup is the new
covenant in my blood, which is poured
out for you. 21But the hand of him who is
going to betray me is with mine on the
table. 22The Son of Man will go as it has
been decreed, but woe to that man who
betrays him." 23They began to question
among themselves which of them it might
be who would do this.

24Also a dispute arose among them as
to which of them was considered to be
greatest. 25Jesus said to them, "The kings
of the Gentiles lord it over them; and
those who exercise authority over them
call themselves Benefactors. 26But you
are not to be like that. Instead, the greatest among you should be like the youn-
gest, and the one who rules like the one
who serves. 27For who is greater, the one
who is at the table or the one who serves?
Is it not the one who is at the table? But
I am among you as one who serves. 28You
are those who have stood by me in my
trials. 29And I confer on you a kingdom,
just as my Father conferred one on me,
30so that you may eat and drink at my
table in my kingdom and sit on thrones,
judging the twelve tribes of Israel.

31"Simon, Simon, Satan has asked to
sift you[a] as wheat. 32But I have prayed for
you, Simon, that your faith may not fail.
And when you have turned back,
strengthen your brothers."

33But he replied, "Lord, I am ready to
go with you to prison and to death."

34Jesus answered, "I tell you, Peter, before the rooster crows today, you will
deny three times that you know me."

35Then Jesus asked them, "When I sent
you without purse, bag or sandals, did
you lack anything?"

"Nothing," they answered.

36He said to them, "But now if you have
a purse, take it, and also a bag; and if you
don't have a sword, sell your cloak and
buy one. 37It is written: 'And he was numbered with the transgressors'[b]; and I tell
you that this must be fulfilled in me. Yes,
what is written about me is reaching its
fulfillment."

38The disciples said, "See, Lord, here
are two swords."

"That is enough," he replied.

Jesus Prays on the Mount of Olives

39Jesus went out as usual to the Mount
of Olives, and his disciples followed him.
40On reaching the place, he said to them,
"Pray that you will not fall into temptation." 41He withdrew about a stone's
throw beyond them, knelt down and
prayed, 42"Father, if you are willing, take

[a] *31* The Greek is plural. [b] *37* Isaiah 53:12

this cup from me; yet not my will, but
yours be done." 43An angel from heaven
appeared to him and strengthened him.
44And being in anguish, he prayed more
earnestly, and his sweat was like drops of
blood falling to the ground.[a]
45When he rose from prayer and went
back to the disciples, he found them
asleep, exhausted from sorrow. 46"Why
are you sleeping?" he asked them. "Get
up and pray so that you will not fall into
temptation."

Jesus Arrested

47While he was still speaking a crowd
came up, and the man who was called
Judas, one of the Twelve, was leading
them. He approached Jesus to kiss him,
48but Jesus asked him, "Judas, are you
betraying the Son of Man with a kiss?"
49When Jesus' followers saw what was
going to happen, they said, "Lord, should
we strike with our swords?" 50And one of
them struck the servant of the high priest,
cutting off his right ear.
51But Jesus answered, "No more of
this!" And he touched the man's ear and
healed him.
52Then Jesus said to the chief priests,
the officers of the temple guard, and the
elders, who had come for him, "Am I
leading a rebellion, that you have come
with swords and clubs? 53Every day I was
with you in the temple courts, and you
did not lay a hand on me. But this is your
hour—when darkness reigns."

Peter Disowns Jesus

54Then seizing him, they led him away
and took him into the house of the high

[a]44 Some early manuscripts do not have verses 43 and 44.

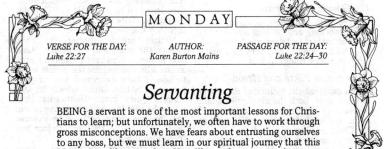

MONDAY

VERSE FOR THE DAY: *Luke 22:27*

AUTHOR: *Karen Burton Mains*

PASSAGE FOR THE DAY: *Luke 22:24–30*

Servanting

BEING a servant is one of the most important lessons for Christians to learn; but unfortunately, we often have to work through gross misconceptions. We have fears about entrusting ourselves to any boss, but we must learn in our spiritual journey that this Master is unlike any other. He will not abuse us or misuse us. He has our greatest interest at heart. He encourages us through our servanting to be all that we can be and then gives us his own Holy Spirit to empower us to become so. This Master is one who even laid down his life for those who were his servants.

He is a Master unlike any other. Not to be feared, he is worthy of our service.

Many of us think servanting means losing ourselves in such a way that we become people without personality, people without original thinking ability, people without giftedness. But when one serves this Master, the opposite is true: He makes us full, complete human beings filled with his own image, with his own amazing mentality. Paradoxically, while teaching us to be more like him, we become more of whom he created us to be.

Additional Scripture Readings:
John 13:12–17; 1 Peter 4:8–11

Go to page 119 for your next devotional reading.

priest. Peter followed at a distance. 55But when they had kindled a fire in the middle of the courtyard and had sat down together, Peter sat down with them. 56A servant girl saw him seated there in the firelight. She looked closely at him and said, "This man was with him."

57But he denied it. "Woman, I don't know him," he said.

58A little later someone else saw him and said, "You also are one of them."

"Man, I am not!" Peter replied.

59About an hour later another asserted, "Certainly this fellow was with him, for he is a Galilean."

60Peter replied, "Man, I don't know what you're talking about!" Just as he was speaking, the rooster crowed. 61The Lord turned and looked straight at Peter. Then Peter remembered the word the Lord had spoken to him: "Before the rooster crows today, you will disown me three times." 62And he went outside and wept bitterly.

The Guards Mock Jesus

63The men who were guarding Jesus began mocking and beating him. 64They blindfolded him and demanded, "Prophesy! Who hit you?" 65And they said many other insulting things to him.

Jesus Before Pilate and Herod

66At daybreak the council of the elders of the people, both the chief priests and teachers of the law, met together, and Jesus was led before them. 67"If you are the Christ,[a]" they said, "tell us."

Jesus answered, "If I tell you, you will not believe me, 68and if I asked you, you would not answer. 69But from now on, the Son of Man will be seated at the right hand of the mighty God."

70They all asked, "Are you then the Son of God?"

He replied, "You are right in saying I am."

71Then they said, "Why do we need any more testimony? We have heard it from his own lips."

23 Then the whole assembly rose and led him off to Pilate. 2And they began to accuse him, saying, "We have found this man subverting our nation. He opposes payment of taxes to Caesar and claims to be Christ,[b] a king."

3So Pilate asked Jesus, "Are you the king of the Jews?"

"Yes, it is as you say," Jesus replied.

4Then Pilate announced to the chief priests and the crowd, "I find no basis for a charge against this man."

5But they insisted, "He stirs up the people all over Judea[c] by his teaching. He started in Galilee and has come all the way here."

6On hearing this, Pilate asked if the man was a Galilean. 7When he learned that Jesus was under Herod's jurisdiction, he sent him to Herod, who was also in Jerusalem at that time.

8When Herod saw Jesus, he was greatly pleased, because for a long time he had been wanting to see him. From what he had heard about him, he hoped to see him perform some miracle. 9He plied him with many questions, but Jesus gave him no answer. 10The chief priests and the teachers of the law were standing there, vehemently accusing him. 11Then Herod and his soldiers ridiculed and mocked him. Dressing him in an elegant robe, they sent him back to Pilate. 12That day Herod and Pilate became friends—before this they had been enemies.

13Pilate called together the chief priests, the rulers and the people, 14and said to them, "You brought me this man as one who was inciting the people to rebellion. I have examined him in your presence and have found no basis for your charges against him. 15Neither has Herod, for he sent him back to us; as you can see, he has done nothing to deserve death. 16Therefore, I will punish him and then release him.[d]"

18With one voice they cried out, "Away with this man! Release Barabbas to us!" 19(Barabbas had been thrown into prison for an insurrection in the city, and for murder.)

20Wanting to release Jesus, Pilate appealed to them again. 21But they kept shouting, "Crucify him! Crucify him!"

22For the third time he spoke to them: "Why? What crime has this man committed? I have found in him no grounds for the death penalty. Therefore I will have him punished and then release him."

23But with loud shouts they insistently demanded that he be crucified, and their shouts prevailed. 24So Pilate decided to grant their demand. 25He released the man who had been thrown into prison for insurrection and murder,

[a]67 Or *Messiah* [b]2 Or *Messiah*; also in verses 35 and 39 [c]5 Or *over the land of the Jews*
[d]16 Some manuscripts *him."* 17*Now he was obliged to release one man to them at the Feast.*

the one they asked for, and surrendered
Jesus to their will.

The Crucifixion

26As they led him away, they seized Simon from Cyrene, who was on his way in
from the country, and put the cross on
him and made him carry it behind Jesus.
27A large number of people followed him,
including women who mourned and
wailed for him. 28Jesus turned and said to
them, "Daughters of Jerusalem, do not
weep for me; weep for yourselves and for
your children. 29For the time will come
when you will say, 'Blessed are the barren
women, the wombs that never bore and
the breasts that never nursed!' 30Then
" 'they will say to the mountains,
"Fall on us!"
and to the hills, "Cover us!" '[a]
31For if men do these things when the
tree is green, what will happen when it is
dry?"
32Two other men, both criminals, were
also led out with him to be executed.
33When they came to the place called the
Skull, there they crucified him, along
with the criminals—one on his right, the
other on his left. 34Jesus said, "Father,
forgive them, for they do not know what
they are doing."[b] And they divided up his
clothes by casting lots.
35The people stood watching, and the
rulers even sneered at him. They said,

[a]30 Hosea 10:8 [b]34 Some early manuscripts do not have this sentence.

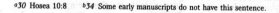

TUESDAY

VERSE FOR THE DAY: *Luke 23:34*
AUTHOR: *Eugenia Price*
PASSAGE FOR THE DAY: *Luke 23:26–43*

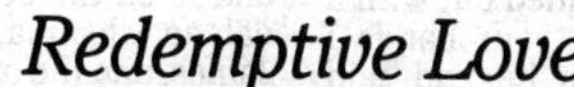

Redemptive Love

FOR three days they thought they had made it. His quiet, unbroken strength (almighty meekness) fanned their fury as they stood watching the heavy nails pierce his hands and feet, when the Roman soldiers secured him to his cross. He was taking into his heart the very sin that motivated this. Their hearts and minds were blinded by that sin. The same dark, inner drive which prodded the first man and woman toward the forbidden tree to satisfy their desire to know as much as God knew. In the heart of each man who plotted his death, there twisted the tormentor whom God hated. He did not hate these murderers, he hated the disease that had made them murderers. As the God-Man hung above them, praying for them, he loved them with the kind of love that could have healed them on the spot!

"Father, forgive them, for they do not know what they are doing" (Luke 23:34).

Down from his cross poured redemptive love in quantity enough for the whole human race. Enough for you. Enough for me. Far from decreasing because of our behavior against him, it seemed rather to increase. The same situation still exists today and will exist as long as the earth stands.

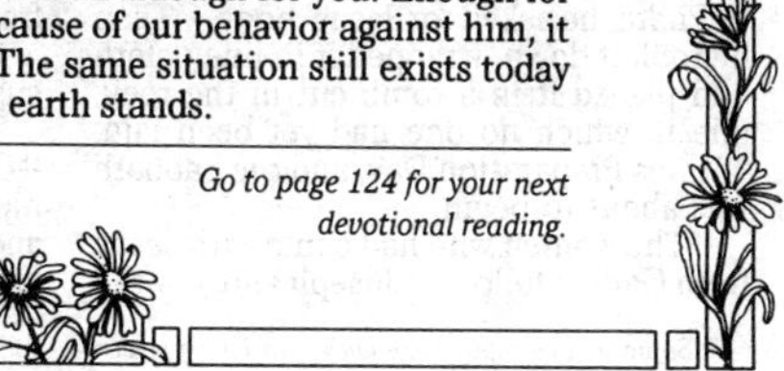

Additional Scripture Readings:
Matthew 23:37; Romans 5:8–11

Go to page 124 for your next devotional reading.

"He saved others; let him save himself if he is the Christ of God, the Chosen One."

36The soldiers also came up and mocked him. They offered him wine vinegar 37and said, "If you are the king of the Jews, save yourself."

38There was a written notice above him, which read: THIS IS THE KING OF THE JEWS.

39One of the criminals who hung there hurled insults at him: "Aren't you the Christ? Save yourself and us!"

40But the other criminal rebuked him. "Don't you fear God," he said, "since you are under the same sentence? 41We are punished justly, for we are getting what our deeds deserve. But this man has done nothing wrong."

42Then he said, "Jesus, remember me when you come into your kingdom.[a]"

43Jesus answered him, "I tell you the truth, today you will be with me in paradise."

Jesus' Death

44It was now about the sixth hour, and darkness came over the whole land until the ninth hour, 45for the sun stopped shining. And the curtain of the temple was torn in two. 46Jesus called out with a loud voice, "Father, into your hands I commit my spirit." When he had said this, he breathed his last.

47The centurion, seeing what had happened, praised God and said, "Surely this was a righteous man." 48When all the people who had gathered to witness this sight saw what took place, they beat their breasts and went away. 49But all those who knew him, including the women who had followed him from Galilee, stood at a distance, watching these things.

Jesus' Burial

50Now there was a man named Joseph, a member of the Council, a good and upright man, 51who had not consented to their decision and action. He came from the Judean town of Arimathea and he was waiting for the kingdom of God. 52Going to Pilate, he asked for Jesus' body. 53Then he took it down, wrapped it in linen cloth and placed it in a tomb cut in the rock, one in which no one had yet been laid. 54It was Preparation Day, and the Sabbath was about to begin.

55The women who had come with Jesus from Galilee followed Joseph and saw the tomb and how his body was laid in it. 56Then they went home and prepared spices and perfumes. But they rested on the Sabbath in obedience to the commandment.

The Resurrection

24 On the first day of the week, very early in the morning, the women took the spices they had prepared and went to the tomb. 2They found the stone rolled away from the tomb, 3but when they entered, they did not find the body of the Lord Jesus. 4While they were wondering about this, suddenly two men in clothes that gleamed like lightning stood beside them. 5In their fright the women bowed down with their faces to the ground, but the men said to them, "Why do you look for the living among the dead? 6He is not here; he has risen! Remember how he told you, while he was still with you in Galilee: 7'The Son of Man must be delivered into the hands of sinful men, be crucified and on the third day be raised again.' " 8Then they remembered his words.

9When they came back from the tomb, they told all these things to the Eleven and to all the others. 10It was Mary Magdalene, Joanna, Mary the mother of James, and the others with them who told this to the apostles. 11But they did not believe the women, because their words seemed to them like nonsense. 12Peter, however, got up and ran to the tomb. Bending over, he saw the strips of linen lying by themselves, and he went away, wondering to himself what had happened.

On the Road to Emmaus

13Now that same day two of them were going to a village called Emmaus, about seven miles[b] from Jerusalem. 14They were talking with each other about everything that had happened. 15As they talked and discussed these things with each other, Jesus himself came up and walked along with them; 16but they were kept from recognizing him.

17He asked them, "What are you discussing together as you walk along?"

They stood still, their faces downcast. 18One of them, named Cleopas, asked him, "Are you only a visitor to Jerusalem and do not know the things that have happened there in these days?"

[a]*42* Some manuscripts *come with your kingly power*

[b]*13* Greek *sixty stadia* (about 11 kilometers)

19“What things?” he asked.

“About Jesus of Nazareth,” they replied. “He was a prophet, powerful in word and deed before God and all the people. 20The chief priests and our rulers handed him over to be sentenced to death, and they crucified him; 21but we had hoped that he was the one who was going to redeem Israel. And what is more, it is the third day since all this took place. 22In addition, some of our women amazed us. They went to the tomb early this morning 23but didn’t find his body. They came and told us that they had seen a vision of angels, who said he was alive. 24Then some of our companions went to the tomb and found it just as the women had said, but him they did not see.”

25He said to them, “How foolish you are, and how slow of heart to believe all that the prophets have spoken! 26Did not the Christ[a] have to suffer these things and then enter his glory?” 27And beginning with Moses and all the Prophets, he explained to them what was said in all the Scriptures concerning himself.

28As they approached the village to which they were going, Jesus acted as if he were going farther. 29But they urged him strongly, “Stay with us, for it is nearly evening; the day is almost over.” So he went in to stay with them.

30When he was at the table with them, he took bread, gave thanks, broke it and began to give it to them. 31Then their eyes were opened and they recognized him, and he disappeared from their sight. 32They asked each other, “Were not our hearts burning within us while he talked with us on the road and opened the Scriptures to us?”

33They got up and returned at once to Jerusalem. There they found the Eleven and those with them, assembled together 34and saying, “It is true! The Lord has risen and has appeared to Simon.” 35Then the two told what had happened on the way, and how Jesus was recognized by them when he broke the bread.

Jesus Appears to the Disciples

36While they were still talking about this, Jesus himself stood among them and said to them, “Peace be with you.”

37They were startled and frightened, thinking they saw a ghost. 38He said to them, “Why are you troubled, and why do doubts rise in your minds? 39Look at my hands and my feet. It is I myself! Touch me and see; a ghost does not have flesh and bones, as you see I have.”

40When he had said this, he showed them his hands and feet. 41And while they still did not believe it because of joy and amazement, he asked them, “Do you have anything here to eat?” 42They gave him a piece of broiled fish, 43and he took it and ate it in their presence.

44He said to them, “This is what I told you while I was still with you: Everything must be fulfilled that is written about me in the Law of Moses, the Prophets and the Psalms.”

45Then he opened their minds so they could understand the Scriptures. 46He told them, “This is what is written: The Christ will suffer and rise from the dead on the third day, 47and repentance and forgiveness of sins will be preached in his name to all nations, beginning at Jerusalem. 48You are witnesses of these things. 49I am going to send you what my Father has promised; but stay in the city until you have been clothed with power from on high.”

The Ascension

50When he had led them out to the vicinity of Bethany, he lifted up his hands and blessed them. 51While he was blessing them, he left them and was taken up into heaven. 52Then they worshiped him and returned to Jerusalem with great joy. 53And they stayed continually at the temple, praising God.

[a]*26* Or *Messiah*; also in verse 46

JOHN writes this gospel to present Jesus, the powerful Son of God, who comes in human flesh, gives his life on the cross, and then returns to the Father—all with a view that we may believe in him and receive eternal life. His coming shows us how much the Father and the Son love us, and his parting command is that we should show the same sacrificial love to one another. As you read this book, be sure that you believe that Jesus is the Christ, the Son of God, and promise him that you will love others as he loves you.

JOHN

The Word Became Flesh

1 In the beginning was the Word, and
the Word was with God, and the Word
was God. 2He was with God in the beginning.
3Through him all things were made;
without him nothing was made that has
been made. 4In him was life, and that life
was the light of men. 5The light shines in
the darkness, but the darkness has not
understood[a] it.
6There came a man who was sent from
God; his name was John. 7He came as a
witness to testify concerning that light, so
that through him all men might believe.
8He himself was not the light; he came
only as a witness to the light. 9The true
light that gives light to every man was
coming into the world.[b]
10He was in the world, and though the
world was made through him, the world
did not recognize him. 11He came to that
which was his own, but his own did not

[a]5 Or *darkness, and the darkness has not overcome*

[b]9 Or *This was the true light that gives light to every man who comes into the world*

receive him. 12Yet to all who received
him, to those who believed in his name,
he gave the right to become children of
God— 13children born not of natural descent,[a] nor of human decision or a husband's will, but born of God.
14The Word became flesh and made his
dwelling among us. We have seen his glory, the glory of the One and Only,[b] who
came from the Father, full of grace and
truth.
15John testifies concerning him. He
cries out, saying, "This was he of whom I
said, 'He who comes after me has surpassed me because he was before me.' "
16From the fullness of his grace we have
all received one blessing after another.
17For the law was given through Moses;
grace and truth came through Jesus
Christ. 18No one has ever seen God, but
God the One and Only,[b,c] who is at the
Father's side, has made him known.

John the Baptist Denies Being the Christ

19Now this was John's testimony when
the Jews of Jerusalem sent priests and
Levites to ask him who he was. 20He did
not fail to confess, but confessed freely,
"I am not the Christ.[d]"
21They asked him, "Then who are you?
Are you Elijah?"
He said, "I am not."
"Are you the Prophet?"
He answered, "No."
22Finally they said, "Who are you? Give
us an answer to take back to those who
sent us. What do you say about yourself?"
23John replied in the words of Isaiah
the prophet, "I am the voice of one calling
in the desert, 'Make straight the way for
the Lord.' "[e]
24Now some Pharisees who had been
sent 25questioned him, "Why then do you
baptize if you are not the Christ, nor Elijah, nor the Prophet?"
26"I baptize with[f] water," John replied,
"but among you stands one you do not
know. 27He is the one who comes after
me, the thongs of whose sandals I am not
worthy to untie."
28This all happened at Bethany on the
other side of the Jordan, where John was
baptizing.

Jesus the Lamb of God

29The next day John saw Jesus coming
toward him and said, "Look, the Lamb of
God, who takes away the sin of the world!
30This is the one I meant when I said, 'A
man who comes after me has surpassed
me because he was before me.' 31I myself
did not know him, but the reason I came
baptizing with water was that he might be
revealed to Israel."
32Then John gave this testimony: "I saw
the Spirit come down from heaven as a
dove and remain on him. 33I would not
have known him, except that the one who
sent me to baptize with water told me,
'The man on whom you see the Spirit
come down and remain is he who will
baptize with the Holy Spirit.' 34I have
seen and I testify that this is the Son of
God."

Jesus' First Disciples

35The next day John was there again
with two of his disciples. 36When he saw
Jesus passing by, he said, "Look, the
Lamb of God!"
37When the two disciples heard him say
this, they followed Jesus. 38Turning
around, Jesus saw them following and
asked, "What do you want?"
They said, "Rabbi" (which means
Teacher), "where are you staying?"
39"Come," he replied, "and you will
see."
So they went and saw where he was
staying, and spent that day with him. It
was about the tenth hour.
40Andrew, Simon Peter's brother, was
one of the two who heard what John had
said and who had followed Jesus. 41The
first thing Andrew did was to find his
brother Simon and tell him, "We have
found the Messiah" (that is, the Christ).
42And he brought him to Jesus.
Jesus looked at him and said, "You are
Simon son of John. You will be called Cephas" (which, when translated, is Peter[g]).

Jesus Calls Philip and Nathanael

43The next day Jesus decided to leave
for Galilee. Finding Philip, he said to
him, "Follow me."
44Philip, like Andrew and Peter, was
from the town of Bethsaida. 45Philip

[a]*13* Greek *of bloods* [b]*14,18* Or *the Only Begotten* [c]*18* Some manuscripts *but the only* (or *only begotten*) *Son* [d]*20* Or *Messiah.* "The Christ" (Greek) and "the Messiah" (Hebrew) both mean "the Anointed One"; also in verse 25. [e]*23* Isaiah 40:3 [f]*26* Or *in*; also in verses 31 and 33 [g]*42* Both *Cephas* (Aramaic) and *Peter* (Greek) mean *rock*.

WEDNESDAY

VERSE FOR THE DAY:
John 1:14

AUTHOR:
Rosemary Jensen

PASSAGE FOR THE DAY:
John 1:1–18

The Word Became Flesh

THAT the Word, Jesus Christ, became a man is the wonder of wonders expressed simply in the phrase, "The Word became flesh" (John 1:14). Jesus had a human body just like you and I have. The *extraordinary* embraced the *ordinary* and produced a living person, fully God and fully human. The Holy Spirit extraordinarily impregnated an egg within the ordinary body of a woman. How could it happen? This is a mystery too profound to understand, but the written Word clearly says it is true.

And the Word "made his dwelling among us." He lived, breathed, ate, drank, slept, worked, laughed and spoke among us. He was real to the eye, real to the touch, real to the ear. He was here—in human flesh—living with men and women and little children.

You have probably wished that Jesus lived today in human flesh and that his house was in your neighborhood. Have you ever thought how wonderful it would be to knock on his door and say, "Jesus, would you show me what the Father is like?" Or, "Jesus, could you give me a hand building a desk for my child?" Or, "Jesus, I'm miserable, please tell me what I should do to patch it up with my husband."

As children of God we have the privilege of "fleshing out" Jesus Christ to others who also would like him as a neighbor. We, as Christians, have received the written Word into our hearts as a seed, miraculously affecting our whole person so that the very life of Christ is produced in us. We each live next door to people who can knock on our doors and say, "Will you please show me what God the Father is like?" And you and I can show them, because we have become somewhat like him as we have studied, worshiped and obeyed him. When someone says, "Could you please help me?" we can lend a helping hand because we have given our bodies over to be used in service to others. When a friend says, "Please help me with a broken relationship," we can give loving counsel because we have contemplated the Lord Jesus Christ in his Word and are able to tackle the problems that the people around us face.

As Christ became flesh and made his dwelling in us, will we become Christ in flesh to our neighbors?

Additional Scripture Readings:
John 14:11–14; Hebrews 2:14–18

Go to page 127 for your next devotional reading.

found Nathanael and told him, "We have
found the one Moses wrote about in the
Law, and about whom the prophets also
wrote—Jesus of Nazareth, the son of Joseph."
46"Nazareth! Can anything good come
from there?" Nathanael asked.
"Come and see," said Philip.
47When Jesus saw Nathanael approaching, he said of him, "Here is a true
Israelite, in whom there is nothing false."
48"How do you know me?" Nathanael
asked.
Jesus answered, "I saw you while you
were still under the fig tree before Philip
called you."
49Then Nathanael declared, "Rabbi,
you are the Son of God; you are the King
of Israel."
50Jesus said, "You believe[a] because I
told you I saw you under the fig tree. You
shall see greater things than that." 51He
then added, "I tell you[b] the truth, you[b]
shall see heaven open, and the angels of
God ascending and descending on the
Son of Man."

Jesus Changes Water to Wine

2 On the third day a wedding took
place at Cana in Galilee. Jesus' mother was there, 2and Jesus and his disciples
had also been invited to the wedding.
3When the wine was gone, Jesus' mother
said to him, "They have no more wine."
4"Dear woman, why do you involve
me?" Jesus replied. "My time has not yet
come."
5His mother said to the servants, "Do
whatever he tells you."
6Nearby stood six stone water jars, the
kind used by the Jews for ceremonial
washing, each holding from twenty to
thirty gallons.[c]
7Jesus said to the servants, "Fill the
jars with water"; so they filled them to the
brim.
8Then he told them, "Now draw some
out and take it to the master of the banquet."
They did so, 9and the master of the
banquet tasted the water that had been
turned into wine. He did not realize
where it had come from, though the servants who had drawn the water knew.
Then he called the bridegroom aside
10and said, "Everyone brings out the
choice wine first and then the cheaper
wine after the guests have had too much
to drink; but you have saved the best till
now."
11This, the first of his miraculous signs,
Jesus performed at Cana in Galilee. He
thus revealed his glory, and his disciples
put their faith in him.

Jesus Clears the Temple

12After this he went down to Capernaum with his mother and brothers and his
disciples. There they stayed for a few
days.
13When it was almost time for the Jewish Passover, Jesus went up to Jerusalem.
14In the temple courts he found men selling cattle, sheep and doves, and others
sitting at tables exchanging money. 15So
he made a whip out of cords, and drove all
from the temple area, both sheep and cattle; he scattered the coins of the money
changers and overturned their tables.
16To those who sold doves he said, "Get
these out of here! How dare you turn my
Father's house into a market!"
17His disciples remembered that it is
written: "Zeal for your house will consume me."[d]
18Then the Jews demanded of him,
"What miraculous sign can you show us
to prove your authority to do all this?"
19Jesus answered them, "Destroy this
temple, and I will raise it again in three
days."
20The Jews replied, "It has taken forty-
six years to build this temple, and you are
going to raise it in three days?" 21But the
temple he had spoken of was his body.
22After he was raised from the dead, his
disciples recalled what he had said. Then
they believed the Scripture and the words
that Jesus had spoken.
23Now while he was in Jerusalem at the
Passover Feast, many people saw the miraculous signs he was doing and believed
in his name.[e] 24But Jesus would not entrust himself to them, for he knew all
men. 25He did not need man's testimony
about man, for he knew what was in a
man.

Jesus Teaches Nicodemus

3 Now there was a man of the Pharisees
named Nicodemus, a member of the
Jewish ruling council. 2He came to Jesus
at night and said, "Rabbi, we know you
are a teacher who has come from God.

[a]*50* Or *Do you believe . . . ?* [b]*51* The Greek is plural. [c]*6* Greek *two to three metretes* (probably about 75 to 115 liters) [d]*17* Psalm 69:9 [e]*23* Or *and believed in him*

For no one could perform the miraculous
signs you are doing if God were not with
him."

3In reply Jesus declared, "I tell you the
truth, no one can see the kingdom of God
unless he is born again.[a]"

4"How can a man be born when he is
old?" Nicodemus asked. "Surely he cannot enter a second time into his mother's
womb to be born!"

5Jesus answered, "I tell you the truth,
no one can enter the kingdom of God unless he is born of water and the Spirit.
6Flesh gives birth to flesh, but the Spirit[b]
gives birth to spirit. 7You should not be
surprised at my saying, 'You[c] must be
born again.' 8The wind blows wherever it
pleases. You hear its sound, but you cannot tell where it comes from or where it
is going. So it is with everyone born of the
Spirit."

9"How can this be?" Nicodemus asked.

10"You are Israel's teacher," said Jesus,
"and do you not understand these things?
11I tell you the truth, we speak of what we
know, and we testify to what we have
seen, but still you people do not accept
our testimony. 12I have spoken to you of
earthly things and you do not believe;
how then will you believe if I speak of
heavenly things? 13No one has ever gone
into heaven except the one who came
from heaven—the Son of Man.[d] 14Just as
Moses lifted up the snake in the desert,
so the Son of Man must be lifted up,
15that everyone who believes in him may
have eternal life.[e]

16"For God so loved the world that he
gave his one and only Son,[f] that whoever
believes in him shall not perish but have
eternal life. 17For God did not send his
Son into the world to condemn the world,
but to save the world through him.
18Whoever believes in him is not condemned, but whoever does not believe
stands condemned already because he
has not believed in the name of God's one
and only Son.[g] 19This is the verdict: Light
has come into the world, but men loved
darkness instead of light because their
deeds were evil. 20Everyone who does evil
hates the light, and will not come into the
light for fear that his deeds will be exposed. 21But whoever lives by the truth
comes into the light, so that it may be
seen plainly that what he has done has
been done through God."[h]

John the Baptist's Testimony About Jesus

22After this, Jesus and his disciples
went out into the Judean countryside,
where he spent some time with them, and
baptized. 23Now John also was baptizing
at Aenon near Salim, because there was
plenty of water, and people were constantly coming to be baptized. 24(This was
before John was put in prison.) 25An argument developed between some of John's
disciples and a certain Jew[i] over the
matter of ceremonial washing. 26They
came to John and said to him, "Rabbi,
that man who was with you on the other
side of the Jordan—the one you testified
about—well, he is baptizing, and everyone is going to him."

27To this John replied, "A man can receive only what is given him from heaven.
28You yourselves can testify that I said, 'I
am not the Christ[j] but am sent ahead of
him.' 29The bride belongs to the bridegroom. The friend who attends the bridegroom waits and listens for him, and is
full of joy when he hears the bridegroom's
voice. That joy is mine, and it is now complete. 30He must become greater; I must
become less.

31"The one who comes from above is
above all; the one who is from the earth
belongs to the earth, and speaks as one
from the earth. The one who comes from
heaven is above all. 32He testifies to what
he has seen and heard, but no one accepts his testimony. 33The man who has
accepted it has certified that God is truthful. 34For the one whom God has sent
speaks the words of God, for God[k] gives
the Spirit without limit. 35The Father
loves the Son and has placed everything
in his hands. 36Whoever believes in the
Son has eternal life, but whoever rejects
the Son will not see life, for God's wrath
remains on him."[l]

Jesus Talks With a Samaritan Woman

4 The Pharisees heard that Jesus was
gaining and baptizing more disciples

[a]3 Or *born from above*; also in verse 7 [b]6 Or *but spirit* [c]7 The Greek is plural. [d]13 Some manuscripts *Man, who is in heaven* [e]15 Or *believes may have eternal life in him* [f]16 Or *his only begotten Son* [g]18 Or *God's only begotten Son* [h]21 Some interpreters end the quotation after verse 15. [i]25 Some manuscripts *and certain Jews* [j]28 Or *Messiah* [k]34 Greek *he* [l]36 Some interpreters end the quotation after verse 30.

than John, 2although in fact it was not
Jesus who baptized, but his disciples.
3When the Lord learned of this, he left
Judea and went back once more to Galilee.
4Now he had to go through Samaria.
5So he came to a town in Samaria called
Sychar, near the plot of ground Jacob had
given to his son Joseph. 6Jacob's well was
there, and Jesus, tired as he was from the
journey, sat down by the well. It was
about the sixth hour.
7When a Samaritan woman came to
draw water, Jesus said to her, "Will you
give me a drink?" 8(His disciples had gone
into the town to buy food.)
9The Samaritan woman said to him,
"You are a Jew and I am a Samaritan
woman. How can you ask me for a drink?"
(For Jews do not associate with Samaritans.[a])
10Jesus answered her, "If you knew the
gift of God and who it is that asks you for
a drink, you would have asked him and he
would have given you living water."
11"Sir," the woman said, "you have
nothing to draw with and the well is deep.
Where can you get this living water? 12Are
you greater than our father Jacob, who
gave us the well and drank from it himself, as did also his sons and his flocks
and herds?"
13Jesus answered, "Everyone who
drinks this water will be thirsty again,

[a]9 *Or do not use dishes Samaritans have used*

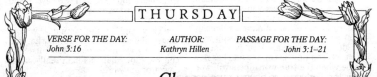

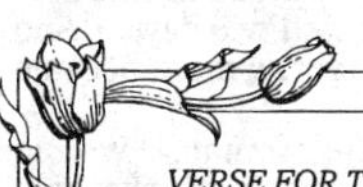

THURSDAY

VERSE FOR THE DAY: *John 3:16* | *AUTHOR:* *Kathryn Hillen* | *PASSAGE FOR THE DAY:* *John 3:1–21*

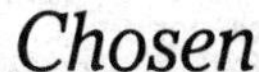

Chosen

IT was the day before Mother's Day, and our daughter Linda wanted to go shopping even though she was so little that her head was hardly visible over the store counter. Asking me to stay at the front, she headed for the back of Woolworth's, clutching her dollar bill. As I watched, she chose a relish dish and stood by the cash register, where she was overlooked by the busy clerks. She waited, dish in hand, jostled by other customers and ignored by the salespeople but firm in her resolve to buy a gift of her own choosing for her mother. She finally returned to me with her package and a smile of triumph.

That inexpensive dish is one of my most prized possessions, for it cost someone I love all that she had. It was bought with real sacrifice by one who went alone with no other aim than to please me. I cherish it, display it with my crystal and china, and use it proudly.

God's beloved Son, Jesus, came to the dime store of earth and chose to sacrifice his all for our redemption. As the Father watched, his love for his Son must have deepened. And how does God feel about those he purchased through death on the cross? Does God love us even more because of what his Son did for us? After all, that's what gives us worth.

Additional Scripture Readings:
2 Thessalonians 2:13–14; 1 Peter 2:9–10

Go to page 129 for your next devotional reading.

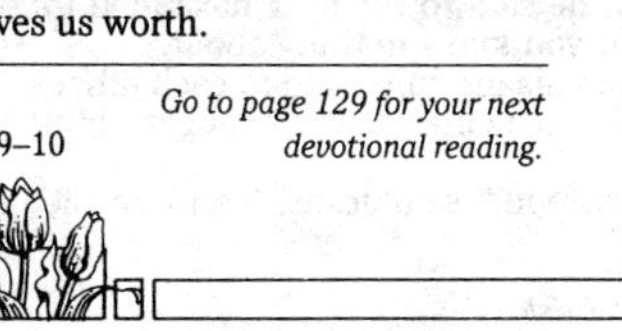

14but whoever drinks the water I give him will never thirst. Indeed, the water I give him will become in him a spring of water welling up to eternal life."

15The woman said to him, "Sir, give me this water so that I won't get thirsty and have to keep coming here to draw water."

16He told her, "Go, call your husband and come back."

17"I have no husband," she replied.

Jesus said to her, "You are right when you say you have no husband. 18The fact is, you have had five husbands, and the man you now have is not your husband. What you have just said is quite true."

19"Sir," the woman said, "I can see that you are a prophet. 20Our fathers worshiped on this mountain, but you Jews claim that the place where we must worship is in Jerusalem."

21Jesus declared, "Believe me, woman, a time is coming when you will worship the Father neither on this mountain nor in Jerusalem. 22You Samaritans worship what you do not know; we worship what we do know, for salvation is from the Jews. 23Yet a time is coming and has now come when the true worshipers will worship the Father in spirit and truth, for they are the kind of worshipers the Father seeks. 24God is spirit, and his worshipers must worship in spirit and in truth."

25The woman said, "I know that Messiah" (called Christ) "is coming. When he comes, he will explain everything to us."

26Then Jesus declared, "I who speak to you am he."

The Disciples Rejoin Jesus

27Just then his disciples returned and were surprised to find him talking with a woman. But no one asked, "What do you want?" or "Why are you talking with her?"

28Then, leaving her water jar, the woman went back to the town and said to the people, 29"Come, see a man who told me everything I ever did. Could this be the Christ[a]?" 30They came out of the town and made their way toward him.

31Meanwhile his disciples urged him, "Rabbi, eat something."

32But he said to them, "I have food to eat that you know nothing about."

33Then his disciples said to each other, "Could someone have brought him food?"

34"My food," said Jesus, "is to do the will of him who sent me and to finish his work. 35Do you not say, 'Four months more and then the harvest'? I tell you, open your eyes and look at the fields! They are ripe for harvest. 36Even now the reaper draws his wages, even now he harvests the crop for eternal life, so that the sower and the reaper may be glad together. 37Thus the saying 'One sows and another reaps' is true. 38I sent you to reap what you have not worked for. Others have done the hard work, and you have reaped the benefits of their labor."

Many Samaritans Believe

39Many of the Samaritans from that town believed in him because of the woman's testimony, "He told me everything I ever did." 40So when the Samaritans came to him, they urged him to stay with them, and he stayed two days. 41And because of his words many more became believers.

42They said to the woman, "We no longer believe just because of what you said; now we have heard for ourselves, and we know that this man really is the Savior of the world."

Jesus Heals the Official's Son

43After the two days he left for Galilee. 44(Now Jesus himself had pointed out that a prophet has no honor in his own country.) 45When he arrived in Galilee, the Galileans welcomed him. They had seen all that he had done in Jerusalem at the Passover Feast, for they also had been there.

46Once more he visited Cana in Galilee, where he had turned the water into wine. And there was a certain royal official whose son lay sick at Capernaum. 47When this man heard that Jesus had arrived in Galilee from Judea, he went to him and begged him to come and heal his son, who was close to death.

48"Unless you people see miraculous signs and wonders," Jesus told him, "you will never believe."

49The royal official said, "Sir, come down before my child dies."

50Jesus replied, "You may go. Your son will live."

The man took Jesus at his word and departed. 51While he was still on the way, his servants met him with the news that

[a]29 Or *Messiah*

his boy was living. 52When he inquired as
to the time when his son got better, they
said to him, "The fever left him yesterday
at the seventh hour."
53Then the father realized that this was
the exact time at which Jesus had said to
him, "Your son will live." So he and all his
household believed.
54This was the second miraculous sign
that Jesus performed, having come from
Judea to Galilee.

The Healing at the Pool

5 Some time later, Jesus went up to Jerusalem for a feast of the Jews. 2Now
there is in Jerusalem near the Sheep Gate
a pool, which in Aramaic is called Bethesda[a] and which is surrounded by five covered colonnades. 3Here a great number of
disabled people used to lie—the blind,
the lame, the paralyzed.[b] 5One who was
there had been an invalid for thirty-eight

[a]2 Some manuscripts *Bethzatha*; other manuscripts *Bethsaida* [b]3 Some less important manuscripts *paralyzed—and they waited for the moving of the waters. 4From time to time an angel of the Lord would come down and stir up the waters. The first one into the pool after each such disturbance would be cured of whatever disease he had.*

FRIDAY

VERSE FOR THE DAY: John 4:34

AUTHOR: Jill Briscoe

PASSAGE FOR THE DAY: John 4:27–38

More Important Than Lunch

JESUS had a heart for God. He had a sense of urgency that meant that some things were even more important than his lunch. I suspect some of us would rather die before we missed our lunch in order to do something for God! Jesus had a sense of purpose. He knew what he was supposed to be doing. He was on earth to talk to men and women about himself. That was why he took time out—even when he was tired and hungry—to explain the things of God to a rather disreputable lady. By the time the disciples came back after buying food, they found Jesus sitting by the well where they had left him; he was tired but triumphant. There is nothing that lifts the spirits as much as seeing someone respond to the gospel. As he watched the woman bringing back the men of her village to "see a man who told me everything I ever did," Jesus was satisfied!

There is nothing quite so fulfilling as completing an assignment for God. You said what was needed, you prayed with a child, you organized the study, you cooked for the homeless, and you finished it! You stuck to it till the job was done. The joy comes, of course, when you are doing *his* work. I will lose heart if I consider the work mine. Stuart caught me talking about "my women in my Bible study" one day, and he rightly rebuked me. They were not "my" women at all—they were Jesus' women! When I have a heart for God he will give me a heart for women, and ministry with them will always be more important than my lunch!

Additional Scripture Readings:
Mark 3:20; Hebrews 6:10–12

Go to page 131 for your next devotional reading.

years. 6When Jesus saw him lying there and learned that he had been in this condition for a long time, he asked him, "Do you want to get well?"

7"Sir," the invalid replied, "I have no one to help me into the pool when the water is stirred. While I am trying to get in, someone else goes down ahead of me."

8Then Jesus said to him, "Get up! Pick up your mat and walk." 9At once the man was cured; he picked up his mat and walked.

The day on which this took place was a Sabbath, 10and so the Jews said to the man who had been healed, "It is the Sabbath; the law forbids you to carry your mat."

11But he replied, "The man who made me well said to me, 'Pick up your mat and walk.' "

12So they asked him, "Who is this fellow who told you to pick it up and walk?"

13The man who was healed had no idea who it was, for Jesus had slipped away into the crowd that was there.

14Later Jesus found him at the temple and said to him, "See, you are well again. Stop sinning or something worse may happen to you." 15The man went away and told the Jews that it was Jesus who had made him well.

Life Through the Son

16So, because Jesus was doing these things on the Sabbath, the Jews persecuted him. 17Jesus said to them, "My Father is always at his work to this very day, and I, too, am working." 18For this reason the Jews tried all the harder to kill him; not only was he breaking the Sabbath, but he was even calling God his own Father, making himself equal with God.

19Jesus gave them this answer: "I tell you the truth, the Son can do nothing by himself; he can do only what he sees his Father doing, because whatever the Father does the Son also does. 20For the Father loves the Son and shows him all he does. Yes, to your amazement he will show him even greater things than these. 21For just as the Father raises the dead and gives them life, even so the Son gives life to whom he is pleased to give it. 22Moreover, the Father judges no one, but has entrusted all judgment to the Son, 23that all may honor the Son just as they honor the Father. He who does not honor the Son does not honor the Father, who sent him.

24"I tell you the truth, whoever hears my word and believes him who sent me has eternal life and will not be condemned; he has crossed over from death to life. 25I tell you the truth, a time is coming and has now come when the dead will hear the voice of the Son of God and those who hear will live. 26For as the Father has life in himself, so he has granted the Son to have life in himself. 27And he has given him authority to judge because he is the Son of Man.

28"Do not be amazed at this, for a time is coming when all who are in their graves will hear his voice 29and come out—those who have done good will rise to live, and those who have done evil will rise to be condemned. 30By myself I can do nothing; I judge only as I hear, and my judgment is just, for I seek not to please myself but him who sent me.

Testimonies About Jesus

31"If I testify about myself, my testimony is not valid. 32There is another who testifies in my favor, and I know that his testimony about me is valid.

33"You have sent to John and he has testified to the truth. 34Not that I accept human testimony; but I mention it that you may be saved. 35John was a lamp that burned and gave light, and you chose for a time to enjoy his light.

36"I have testimony weightier than that of John. For the very work that the Father has given me to finish, and which I am doing, testifies that the Father has sent me. 37And the Father who sent me has himself testified concerning me. You have never heard his voice nor seen his form, 38nor does his word dwell in you, for you do not believe the one he sent. 39You diligently study[a] the Scriptures because you think that by them you possess eternal life. These are the Scriptures that testify about me, 40yet you refuse to come to me to have life.

41"I do not accept praise from men, 42but I know you. I know that you do not have the love of God in your hearts. 43I have come in my Father's name, and you do not accept me; but if someone else comes in his own name, you will accept him. 44How can you believe if you accept praise from one another, yet make no ef-

[a]39 Or *Study diligently* (the imperative)

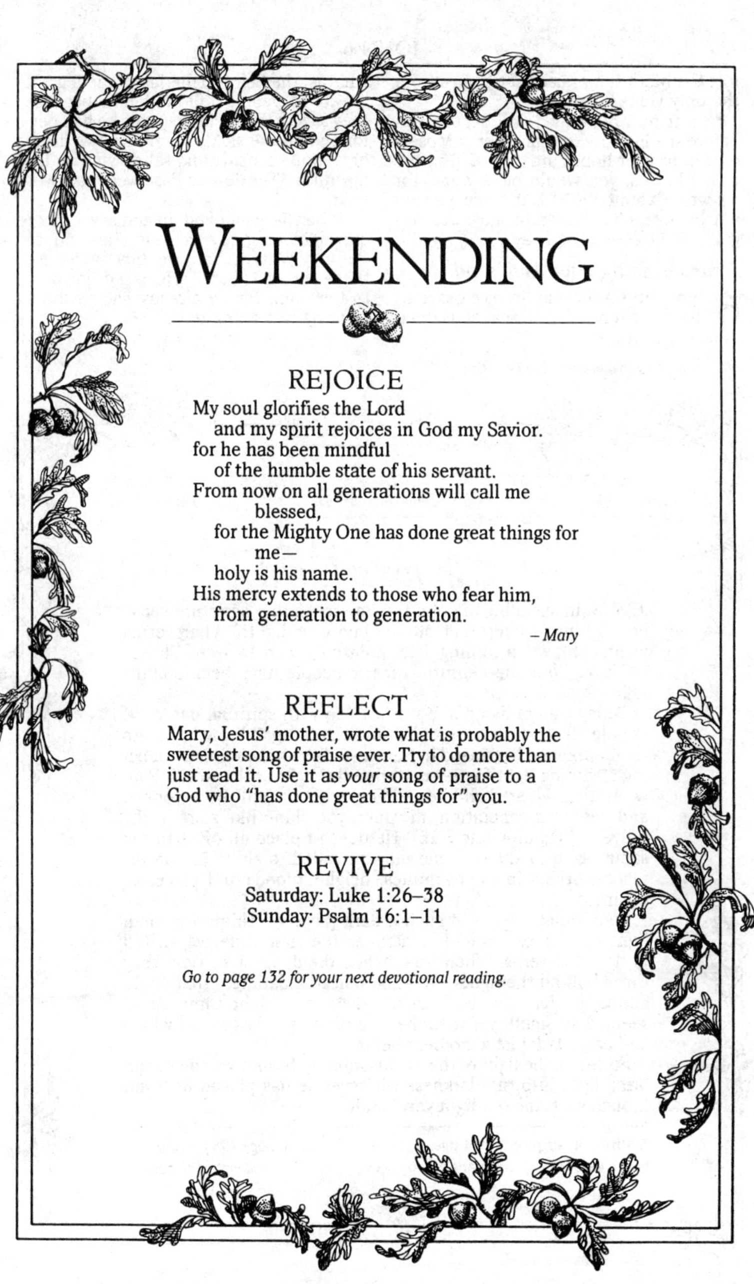

WEEKENDING

REJOICE

My soul glorifies the Lord
   and my spirit rejoices in God my Savior.
for he has been mindful
   of the humble state of his servant.
From now on all generations will call me
      blessed,
   for the Mighty One has done great things for
      me—
   holy is his name.
His mercy extends to those who fear him,
   from generation to generation.

– Mary

REFLECT

Mary, Jesus' mother, wrote what is probably the sweetest song of praise ever. Try to do more than just read it. Use it as *your* song of praise to a God who "has done great things for" you.

REVIVE

Saturday: Luke 1:26–38
Sunday: Psalm 16:1–11

Go to page 132 for your next devotional reading.

fort to obtain the praise that comes from
the only God[a]?
45"But do not think I will accuse you
before the Father. Your accuser is Moses,
on whom your hopes are set. 46If you believed Moses, you would believe me, for
he wrote about me. 47But since you do
not believe what he wrote, how are you
going to believe what I say?"

Jesus Feeds the Five Thousand

6 Some time after this, Jesus crossed to
the far shore of the Sea of Galilee
(that is, the Sea of Tiberias), 2and a great
crowd of people followed him because
they saw the miraculous signs he had performed on the sick. 3Then Jesus went up
on a mountainside and sat down with his
disciples. 4The Jewish Passover Feast was
near.
5When Jesus looked up and saw a great
crowd coming toward him, he said to
Philip, "Where shall we buy bread for
these people to eat?" 6He asked this only
to test him, for he already had in mind
what he was going to do.

[a]44 Some early manuscripts *the Only One*

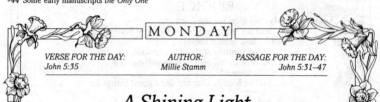

MONDAY

VERSE FOR THE DAY: *John 5:35*

AUTHOR: *Millie Stamm*

PASSAGE FOR THE DAY: *John 5:31–47*

A Shining Light

JESUS, in speaking of John the Baptist in this Scripture verse, called him "a lamp that burned and gave light." Wherever he went, John was a shining light, pointing others to Jesus Christ.

Throughout the centuries, many people have been shining lights for Jesus Christ.

Today we are living in a world filled with spiritual darkness. People all about us are groping for something to bring light into their darkened lives. God has entrusted to us the ministry of being a shining light for Jesus Christ, the light of the world. Paul wrote that we are "children of God without fault in a crooked and depraved generation, in which you shine like stars in the universe" (Philippians 2:15). He doesn't place all of us in the same place to shine. Some may be called to shine in faraway places; others in their families, neighborhoods and places of business.

Sometimes we are in such a dark place we think our small light cannot be seen. I remember the first time we visited Carlsbad Caverns. When we reached the deepest section, they turned off all the lights. We experienced a darkness that could almost be felt. Suddenly in the distance a light came on. It seemed so small, yet it shone brightly in the large area which had been dark just a moment before.

So Jesus, the light of the world, shining through our lives, can bring light into the darkness wherever he has placed us, even though we think our light very small.

Additional Scripture Readings:
Isaiah 49:5–6; 2 Corinthians 4:4–6

Go to page 135 for your next devotional reading.

7Philip answered him, "Eight months' wages[a] would not buy enough bread for each one to have a bite!"

8Another of his disciples, Andrew, Simon Peter's brother, spoke up, 9"Here is a boy with five small barley loaves and two small fish, but how far will they go among so many?"

10Jesus said, "Have the people sit down." There was plenty of grass in that place, and the men sat down, about five thousand of them. 11Jesus then took the loaves, gave thanks, and distributed to those who were seated as much as they wanted. He did the same with the fish.

12When they had all had enough to eat, he said to his disciples, "Gather the pieces that are left over. Let nothing be wasted." 13So they gathered them and filled twelve baskets with the pieces of the five barley loaves left over by those who had eaten.

14After the people saw the miraculous sign that Jesus did, they began to say, "Surely this is the Prophet who is to come into the world." 15Jesus, knowing that they intended to come and make him king by force, withdrew again to a mountain by himself.

Jesus Walks on the Water

16When evening came, his disciples went down to the lake, 17where they got into a boat and set off across the lake for Capernaum. By now it was dark, and Jesus had not yet joined them. 18A strong wind was blowing and the waters grew rough. 19When they had rowed three or three and a half miles,[b] they saw Jesus approaching the boat, walking on the water; and they were terrified. 20But he said to them, "It is I; don't be afraid." 21Then they were willing to take him into the boat, and immediately the boat reached the shore where they were heading.

22The next day the crowd that had stayed on the opposite shore of the lake realized that only one boat had been there, and that Jesus had not entered it with his disciples, but that they had gone away alone. 23Then some boats from Tiberias landed near the place where the people had eaten the bread after the Lord had given thanks. 24Once the crowd realized that neither Jesus nor his disciples were there, they got into the boats and went to Capernaum in search of Jesus.

Jesus the Bread of Life

25When they found him on the other side of the lake, they asked him, "Rabbi, when did you get here?"

26Jesus answered, "I tell you the truth, you are looking for me, not because you saw miraculous signs but because you ate the loaves and had your fill. 27Do not work for food that spoils, but for food that endures to eternal life, which the Son of Man will give you. On him God the Father has placed his seal of approval."

28Then they asked him, "What must we do to do the works God requires?"

29Jesus answered, "The work of God is this: to believe in the one he has sent."

30So they asked him, "What miraculous sign then will you give that we may see it and believe you? What will you do? 31Our forefathers ate the manna in the desert; as it is written: 'He gave them bread from heaven to eat.'[c]"

32Jesus said to them, "I tell you the truth, it is not Moses who has given you the bread from heaven, but it is my Father who gives you the true bread from heaven. 33For the bread of God is he who comes down from heaven and gives life to the world."

34"Sir," they said, "from now on give us this bread."

35Then Jesus declared, "I am the bread of life. He who comes to me will never go hungry, and he who believes in me will never be thirsty. 36But as I told you, you have seen me and still you do not believe. 37All that the Father gives me will come to me, and whoever comes to me I will never drive away. 38For I have come down from heaven not to do my will but to do the will of him who sent me. 39And this is the will of him who sent me, that I shall lose none of all that he has given me, but raise them up at the last day. 40For my Father's will is that everyone who looks to the Son and believes in him shall have eternal life, and I will raise him up at the last day."

41At this the Jews began to grumble about him because he said, "I am the bread that came down from heaven." 42They said, "Is this not Jesus, the son of Joseph, whose father and mother we know? How can he now say, 'I came down from heaven'?"

43"Stop grumbling among yourselves," Jesus answered. 44"No one can come to

a7 Greek *two hundred denarii* b19 Greek *rowed twenty-five or thirty stadia* (about 5 or 6 kilometers)
c31 Exodus 16:4; Neh. 9:15; Psalm 78:24,25

me unless the Father who sent me draws him, and I will raise him up at the last day. 45It is written in the Prophets: 'They will all be taught by God.'[a] Everyone who listens to the Father and learns from him comes to me. 46No one has seen the Father except the one who is from God; only he has seen the Father. 47I tell you the truth, he who believes has everlasting life. 48I am the bread of life. 49Your forefathers ate the manna in the desert, yet they died. 50But here is the bread that comes down from heaven, which a man may eat and not die. 51I am the living bread that came down from heaven. If anyone eats of this bread, he will live forever. This bread is my flesh, which I will give for the life of the world."

52Then the Jews began to argue sharply among themselves, "How can this man give us his flesh to eat?"

53Jesus said to them, "I tell you the truth, unless you eat the flesh of the Son of Man and drink his blood, you have no life in you. 54Whoever eats my flesh and drinks my blood has eternal life, and I will raise him up at the last day. 55For my flesh is real food and my blood is real drink. 56Whoever eats my flesh and drinks my blood remains in me, and I in him. 57Just as the living Father sent me and I live because of the Father, so the one who feeds on me will live because of me. 58This is the bread that came down from heaven. Your forefathers ate manna and died, but he who feeds on this bread will live forever." 59He said this while teaching in the synagogue in Capernaum.

Many Disciples Desert Jesus

60On hearing it, many of his disciples said, "This is a hard teaching. Who can accept it?"

61Aware that his disciples were grumbling about this, Jesus said to them, "Does this offend you? 62What if you see the Son of Man ascend to where he was before! 63The Spirit gives life; the flesh counts for nothing. The words I have spoken to you are spirit[b] and they are life. 64Yet there are some of you who do not believe." For Jesus had known from the beginning which of them did not believe and who would betray him. 65He went on to say, "This is why I told you that no one can come to me unless the Father has enabled him."

66From this time many of his disciples turned back and no longer followed him.

67"You do not want to leave too, do you?" Jesus asked the Twelve.

68Simon Peter answered him, "Lord, to whom shall we go? You have the words of eternal life. 69We believe and know that you are the Holy One of God."

70Then Jesus replied, "Have I not chosen you, the Twelve? Yet one of you is a devil!" 71(He meant Judas, the son of Simon Iscariot, who, though one of the Twelve, was later to betray him.)

Jesus Goes to the Feast of Tabernacles

7 After this, Jesus went around in Galilee, purposely staying away from Judea because the Jews there were waiting to take his life. 2But when the Jewish Feast of Tabernacles was near, 3Jesus' brothers said to him, "You ought to leave here and go to Judea, so that your disciples may see the miracles you do. 4No one who wants to become a public figure acts in secret. Since you are doing these things, show yourself to the world." 5For even his own brothers did not believe in him.

6Therefore Jesus told them, "The right time for me has not yet come; for you any time is right. 7The world cannot hate you, but it hates me because I testify that what it does is evil. 8You go to the Feast. I am not yet[c] going up to this Feast, because for me the right time has not yet come." 9Having said this, he stayed in Galilee.

10However, after his brothers had left for the Feast, he went also, not publicly, but in secret. 11Now at the Feast the Jews were watching for him and asking, "Where is that man?"

12Among the crowds there was widespread whispering about him. Some said, "He is a good man."

Others replied, "No, he deceives the people." 13But no one would say anything publicly about him for fear of the Jews.

Jesus Teaches at the Feast

14Not until halfway through the Feast did Jesus go up to the temple courts and begin to teach. 15The Jews were amazed and asked, "How did this man get such learning without having studied?"

16Jesus answered, "My teaching is not my own. It comes from him who sent me.

[a] *45* Isaiah 54:13 [b] *63* Or *Spirit* [c] *8* Some early manuscripts do not have *yet.*

TUESDAY

VERSE FOR THE DAY:
John 6:35

AUTHOR:
Rosalind Rinker

PASSAGE FOR THE DAY:
John 6:1–71

I Am the Living Bread

JOHN 6 is another miracle chapter. Here we see one more instance when Jesus taught spiritual truth through everyday things, as he had with water, seeds, a candle, a lamp, and a pearl.

This time, Jesus fed more than five thousand people when he broke five small barley loaves and distributed two small fish. Bread and water can sustain physical life indefinitely, yet Jesus said, "Man does not live on bread alone, but on every word that comes from the mouth of God" (Matthew 4:4).

Bread must be given, broken, and taken before it sustains life. The little boy gave his lunch, but Jesus gave his life. This relates directly to the central truth of the John 6 miracle because it concerns the person of our Lord. "I am the living bread that came down from heaven. If anyone eats of this bread, he will live forever. This bread is my flesh, which I will give for the life of the world" (John 6:51). Much as the barley loaves were broken, so too was Christ's *body* broken so that we could be takers of "living bread."

Jesus is capable of being the living bread because he is the Son of God. Just by observing Jesus in John 6 we can see how he deals with the crowd from an other-worldly perspective: 1. He knew what he was going to do (John 6:6). 2. He knew the superficial curiosity of the crowd (John 6:2). 3. He had compassion because of their physical and spiritual hunger (John 6:5,36–37). 4. He wanted cooperation (the boy, the disciples) before he would feed the crowd (John 6:8–9). 5. He had a sense of order and frugality (John 6:10,12–13). 6. He had a deep sense of mission, and the courage to tell of it in a language the crowd could understand and remember (John 6:35–40). 7. He predicted the Eucharist (Holy Communion) (John 6:56–57). 8. He was able to make a little count for a lot (John 6:10–11).

Dear ones, let us be takers and feed on the words of Jesus, the Son of God, our living bread. His words lead us directly back to him, the Redeemer and Savior of the world.

> I am the bread of life. He who comes to me will never go hungry, and he who believes in me will never be thirsty (John 6:35).

Additional Scripture Readings:
Psalm 119:103–104; Matthew 26:26

Go to page 145 for your next devotional reading.

17If anyone chooses to do God's will, he
will find out whether my teaching comes
from God or whether I speak on my own.
18He who speaks on his own does so to
gain honor for himself, but he who works
for the honor of the one who sent him is
a man of truth; there is nothing false
about him. 19Has not Moses given you the
law? Yet not one of you keeps the law.
Why are you trying to kill me?"

20"You are demon-possessed," the
crowd answered. "Who is trying to kill
you?"

21Jesus said to them, "I did one miracle, and you are all astonished. 22Yet, because Moses gave you circumcision
(though actually it did not come from
Moses, but from the patriarchs), you circumcise a child on the Sabbath. 23Now if
a child can be circumcised on the Sabbath so that the law of Moses may not be
broken, why are you angry with me for
healing the whole man on the Sabbath?
24Stop judging by mere appearances, and
make a right judgment."

Is Jesus the Christ?

25At that point some of the people of
Jerusalem began to ask, "Isn't this the
man they are trying to kill? 26Here he is,
speaking publicly, and they are not saying
a word to him. Have the authorities really
concluded that he is the Christ[a]? 27But
we know where this man is from; when
the Christ comes, no one will know where
he is from."

28Then Jesus, still teaching in the temple courts, cried out, "Yes, you know me,
and you know where I am from. I am not
here on my own, but he who sent me is
true. You do not know him, 29but I know
him because I am from him and he sent
me."

30At this they tried to seize him, but no
one laid a hand on him, because his time
had not yet come. 31Still, many in the
crowd put their faith in him. They said,
"When the Christ comes, will he do more
miraculous signs than this man?"

32The Pharisees heard the crowd whispering such things about him. Then the
chief priests and the Pharisees sent temple guards to arrest him.

33Jesus said, "I am with you for only a
short time, and then I go to the one who
sent me. 34You will look for me, but you
will not find me; and where I am, you cannot come."

35The Jews said to one another, "Where
does this man intend to go that we cannot
find him? Will he go where our people live
scattered among the Greeks, and teach
the Greeks? 36What did he mean when he
said, 'You will look for me, but you will
not find me,' and 'Where I am, you cannot
come'?"

37On the last and greatest day of the
Feast, Jesus stood and said in a loud
voice, "If anyone is thirsty, let him come
to me and drink. 38Whoever believes in
me, as[b] the Scripture has said, streams of
living water will flow from within him."
39By this he meant the Spirit, whom those
who believed in him were later to receive.
Up to that time the Spirit had not been
given, since Jesus had not yet been glorified.

40On hearing his words, some of the
people said, "Surely this man is the
Prophet."

41Others said, "He is the Christ."

Still others asked, "How can the Christ
come from Galilee? 42Does not the Scripture say that the Christ will come from
David's family[c] and from Bethlehem, the
town where David lived?" 43Thus the
people were divided because of Jesus.
44Some wanted to seize him, but no one
laid a hand on him.

Unbelief of the Jewish Leaders

45Finally the temple guards went back
to the chief priests and Pharisees, who
asked them, "Why didn't you bring him
in?"

46"No one ever spoke the way this man
does," the guards declared.

47"You mean he has deceived you
also?" the Pharisees retorted. 48"Has any
of the rulers or of the Pharisees believed
in him? 49No! But this mob that knows
nothing of the law—there is a curse on
them."

50Nicodemus, who had gone to Jesus
earlier and who was one of their own
number, asked, 51"Does our law condemn
anyone without first hearing him to find
out what he is doing?"

52They replied, "Are you from Galilee,
too? Look into it, and you will find that a
prophet[d] does not come out of Galilee."

[a]26 Or *Messiah*; also in verses 27, 31, 41 and 42 [b]37,38 Or / *If anyone is thirsty, let him come to me.* / *And let him drink,* 38*who believes in me.* / *As* [c]42 Greek *seed* [d]52 Two early manuscripts *the Prophet*

[The earliest manuscripts and many other ancient witnesses do not have John 7:53–8:11.]

53Then each went to his own home.

8 But Jesus went to the Mount of Olives. 2At dawn he appeared again in the temple courts, where all the people gathered around him, and he sat down to teach them. 3The teachers of the law and the Pharisees brought in a woman caught in adultery. They made her stand before the group 4and said to Jesus, "Teacher, this woman was caught in the act of adultery. 5In the Law Moses commanded us to stone such women. Now what do you say?" 6They were using this question as a trap, in order to have a basis for accusing him.

But Jesus bent down and started to write on the ground with his finger. 7When they kept on questioning him, he straightened up and said to them, "If any one of you is without sin, let him be the first to throw a stone at her." 8Again he stooped down and wrote on the ground.

9At this, those who heard began to go away one at a time, the older ones first, until only Jesus was left, with the woman still standing there. 10Jesus straightened up and asked her, "Woman, where are they? Has no one condemned you?"

11"No one, sir," she said.

"Then neither do I condemn you," Jesus declared. "Go now and leave your life of sin."

The Validity of Jesus' Testimony

12When Jesus spoke again to the people, he said, "I am the light of the world. Whoever follows me will never walk in darkness, but will have the light of life."

13The Pharisees challenged him, "Here you are, appearing as your own witness; your testimony is not valid."

14Jesus answered, "Even if I testify on my own behalf, my testimony is valid, for I know where I came from and where I am going. But you have no idea where I come from or where I am going. 15You judge by human standards; I pass judgment on no one. 16But if I do judge, my decisions are right, because I am not alone. I stand with the Father, who sent me. 17In your own Law it is written that the testimony of two men is valid. 18I am one who testifies for myself; my other witness is the Father, who sent me."

19Then they asked him, "Where is your father?"

"You do not know me or my Father," Jesus replied. "If you knew me, you would know my Father also." 20He spoke these words while teaching in the temple area near the place where the offerings were put. Yet no one seized him, because his time had not yet come.

21Once more Jesus said to them, "I am going away, and you will look for me, and you will die in your sin. Where I go, you cannot come."

22This made the Jews ask, "Will he kill himself? Is that why he says, 'Where I go, you cannot come'?"

23But he continued, "You are from below; I am from above. You are of this world; I am not of this world. 24I told you that you would die in your sins; if you do not believe that I am ⌞the one I claim to be⌟,[a] you will indeed die in your sins."

25"Who are you?" they asked.

"Just what I have been claiming all along," Jesus replied. 26"I have much to say in judgment of you. But he who sent me is reliable, and what I have heard from him I tell the world."

27They did not understand that he was telling them about his Father. 28So Jesus said, "When you have lifted up the Son of Man, then you will know that I am ⌞the one I claim to be⌟ and that I do nothing on my own but speak just what the Father has taught me. 29The one who sent me is with me; he has not left me alone, for I always do what pleases him." 30Even as he spoke, many put their faith in him.

The Children of Abraham

31To the Jews who had believed him, Jesus said, "If you hold to my teaching, you are really my disciples. 32Then you will know the truth, and the truth will set you free."

33They answered him, "We are Abraham's descendants[b] and have never been slaves of anyone. How can you say that we shall be set free?"

34Jesus replied, "I tell you the truth, everyone who sins is a slave to sin. 35Now a slave has no permanent place in the family, but a son belongs to it forever. 36So if the Son sets you free, you will be free indeed. 37I know you are Abraham's

[a]*24* Or *I am he*; also in verse 28 [b]*33* Greek *seed*; also in verse 37

descendants. Yet you are ready to kill me,
because you have no room for my word.
38I am telling you what I have seen in the
Father's presence, and you do what you
have heard from your father.[a]"

39"Abraham is our father," they answered.

"If you were Abraham's children," said
Jesus, "then you would[b] do the things
Abraham did. 40As it is, you are determined to kill me, a man who has told you
the truth that I heard from God. Abraham
did not do such things. 41You are doing
the things your own father does."

"We are not illegitimate children," they
protested. "The only Father we have is
God himself."

The Children of the Devil

42Jesus said to them, "If God were your
Father, you would love me, for I came
from God and now am here. I have not
come on my own; but he sent me. 43Why
is my language not clear to you? Because
you are unable to hear what I say. 44You
belong to your father, the devil, and you
want to carry out your father's desire. He
was a murderer from the beginning, not
holding to the truth, for there is no truth
in him. When he lies, he speaks his native
language, for he is a liar and the father of
lies. 45Yet because I tell the truth, you do
not believe me! 46Can any of you prove me
guilty of sin? If I am telling the truth, why
don't you believe me? 47He who belongs
to God hears what God says. The reason
you do not hear is that you do not belong
to God."

The Claims of Jesus About Himself

48The Jews answered him, "Aren't we
right in saying that you are a Samaritan
and demon-possessed?"

49"I am not possessed by a demon,"
said Jesus, "but I honor my Father and
you dishonor me. 50I am not seeking glory
for myself; but there is one who seeks it,
and he is the judge. 51I tell you the truth,
if anyone keeps my word, he will never
see death."

52At this the Jews exclaimed, "Now we
know that you are demon-possessed!
Abraham died and so did the prophets,
yet you say that if anyone keeps your
word, he will never taste death. 53Are you
greater than our father Abraham? He
died, and so did the prophets. Who do
you think you are?"

54Jesus replied, "If I glorify myself, my
glory means nothing. My Father, whom
you claim as your God, is the one who
glorifies me. 55Though you do not know
him, I know him. If I said I did not, I
would be a liar like you, but I do know
him and keep his word. 56Your father
Abraham rejoiced at the thought of seeing my day; he saw it and was glad."

57"You are not yet fifty years old," the
Jews said to him, "and you have seen
Abraham!"

58"I tell you the truth," Jesus answered,
"before Abraham was born, I am!" 59At
this, they picked up stones to stone him,
but Jesus hid himself, slipping away from
the temple grounds.

Jesus Heals a Man Born Blind

9 As he went along, he saw a man blind
from birth. 2His disciples asked him,
"Rabbi, who sinned, this man or his parents, that he was born blind?"

3"Neither this man nor his parents
sinned," said Jesus, "but this happened
so that the work of God might be displayed in his life. 4As long as it is day, we
must do the work of him who sent me.
Night is coming, when no one can work.
5While I am in the world, I am the light of
the world."

6Having said this, he spit on the
ground, made some mud with the saliva,
and put it on the man's eyes. 7"Go," he
told him, "wash in the Pool of Siloam"
(this word means Sent). So the man went
and washed, and came home seeing.

8His neighbors and those who had formerly seen him begging asked, "Isn't this
the same man who used to sit and beg?"
9Some claimed that he was.

Others said, "No, he only looks like
him."

But he himself insisted, "I am the
man."

10"How then were your eyes opened?"
they demanded.

11He replied, "The man they call Jesus
made some mud and put it on my eyes.
He told me to go to Siloam and wash. So
I went and washed, and then I could see."

12"Where is this man?" they asked him.

"I don't know," he said.

[a]38 Or *presence. Therefore do what you have heard from the Father.* [b]39 Some early manuscripts *"If you are Abraham's children," said Jesus, "then*

The Pharisees Investigate the Healing

13They brought to the Pharisees the man who had been blind. 14Now the day on which Jesus had made the mud and opened the man's eyes was a Sabbath. 15Therefore the Pharisees also asked him how he had received his sight. "He put mud on my eyes," the man replied, "and I washed, and now I see."

16Some of the Pharisees said, "This man is not from God, for he does not keep the Sabbath."

But others asked, "How can a sinner do such miraculous signs?" So they were divided.

17Finally they turned again to the blind man, "What have you to say about him? It was your eyes he opened."

The man replied, "He is a prophet."

18The Jews still did not believe that he had been blind and had received his sight until they sent for the man's parents. 19"Is this your son?" they asked. "Is this the one you say was born blind? How is it that now he can see?"

20"We know he is our son," the parents answered, "and we know he was born blind. 21But how he can see now, or who opened his eyes, we don't know. Ask him. He is of age; he will speak for himself." 22His parents said this because they were afraid of the Jews, for already the Jews had decided that anyone who acknowledged that Jesus was the Christ[a] would be put out of the synagogue. 23That was why his parents said, "He is of age; ask him."

24A second time they summoned the man who had been blind. "Give glory to God,[b]" they said. "We know this man is a sinner."

25He replied, "Whether he is a sinner or not, I don't know. One thing I do know. I was blind but now I see!"

26Then they asked him, "What did he do to you? How did he open your eyes?"

27He answered, "I have told you already and you did not listen. Why do you want to hear it again? Do you want to become his disciples, too?"

28Then they hurled insults at him and said, "You are this fellow's disciple! We are disciples of Moses! 29We know that God spoke to Moses, but as for this fellow, we don't even know where he comes from."

30The man answered, "Now that is remarkable! You don't know where he comes from, yet he opened my eyes. 31We know that God does not listen to sinners. He listens to the godly man who does his will. 32Nobody has ever heard of opening the eyes of a man born blind. 33If this man were not from God, he could do nothing."

34To this they replied, "You were steeped in sin at birth; how dare you lecture us!" And they threw him out.

Spiritual Blindness

35Jesus heard that they had thrown him out, and when he found him, he said, "Do you believe in the Son of Man?"

36"Who is he, sir?" the man asked. "Tell me so that I may believe in him."

37Jesus said, "You have now seen him; in fact, he is the one speaking with you."

38Then the man said, "Lord, I believe," and he worshiped him.

39Jesus said, "For judgment I have come into this world, so that the blind will see and those who see will become blind."

40Some Pharisees who were with him heard him say this and asked, "What? Are we blind too?"

41Jesus said, "If you were blind, you would not be guilty of sin; but now that you claim you can see, your guilt remains.

The Shepherd and His Flock

10 "I tell you the truth, the man who does not enter the sheep pen by the gate, but climbs in by some other way, is a thief and a robber. 2The man who enters by the gate is the shepherd of his sheep. 3The watchman opens the gate for him, and the sheep listen to his voice. He calls his own sheep by name and leads them out. 4When he has brought out all his own, he goes on ahead of them, and his sheep follow him because they know his voice. 5But they will never follow a stranger; in fact, they will run away from him because they do not recognize a stranger's voice." 6Jesus used this figure of speech, but they did not understand what he was telling them.

7Therefore Jesus said again, "I tell you the truth, I am the gate for the sheep. 8All who ever came before me were thieves and robbers, but the sheep did not listen to them. 9I am the gate; whoever enters through me will be saved.[c] He will come in and go out, and find pasture. 10The

[a] 22 Or *Messiah* [b] 24 A solemn charge to tell the truth (see Joshua 7:19) [c] 9 Or *kept safe*

thief comes only to steal and kill and destroy; I have come that they may have life,
and have it to the full.
11"I am the good shepherd. The good
shepherd lays down his life for the sheep.
12The hired hand is not the shepherd who
owns the sheep. So when he sees the wolf
coming, he abandons the sheep and runs
away. Then the wolf attacks the flock and
scatters it. 13The man runs away because
he is a hired hand and cares nothing for
the sheep.
14"I am the good shepherd; I know my
sheep and my sheep know me— 15just as
the Father knows me and I know the Father—and I lay down my life for the
sheep. 16I have other sheep that are not of
this sheep pen. I must bring them also.
They too will listen to my voice, and there
shall be one flock and one shepherd.
17The reason my Father loves me is that
I lay down my life—only to take it up
again. 18No one takes it from me, but I lay
it down of my own accord. I have authority to lay it down and authority to take it
up again. This command I received from
my Father."
19At these words the Jews were again
divided. 20Many of them said, "He is demon-possessed and raving mad. Why listen to him?"
21But others said, "These are not the
sayings of a man possessed by a demon.
Can a demon open the eyes of the blind?"

The Unbelief of the Jews

22Then came the Feast of Dedication[a]
at Jerusalem. It was winter, 23and Jesus
was in the temple area walking in Solomon's Colonnade. 24The Jews gathered
around him, saying, "How long will you
keep us in suspense? If you are the
Christ,[b] tell us plainly."
25Jesus answered, "I did tell you, but
you do not believe. The miracles I do in
my Father's name speak for me, 26but you
do not believe because you are not my
sheep. 27My sheep listen to my voice; I
know them, and they follow me. 28I give
them eternal life, and they shall never
perish; no one can snatch them out of my
hand. 29My Father, who has given them to
me, is greater than all[c]; no one can
snatch them out of my Father's hand. 30I
and the Father are one."
31Again the Jews picked up stones to
stone him, 32but Jesus said to them, "I
have shown you many great miracles from
the Father. For which of these do you
stone me?"
33"We are not stoning you for any of
these," replied the Jews, "but for blasphemy, because you, a mere man, claim
to be God."
34Jesus answered them, "Is it not written in your Law, 'I have said you are
gods'[d]? 35If he called them 'gods,' to
whom the word of God came—and the
Scripture cannot be broken— 36what
about the one whom the Father set apart
as his very own and sent into the world?
Why then do you accuse me of blasphemy
because I said, 'I am God's Son'? 37Do not
believe me unless I do what my Father
does. 38But if I do it, even though you do
not believe me, believe the miracles, that
you may know and understand that the
Father is in me, and I in the Father."
39Again they tried to seize him, but he
escaped their grasp.
40Then Jesus went back across the Jordan to the place where John had been
baptizing in the early days. Here he
stayed 41and many people came to him.
They said, "Though John never performed a miraculous sign, all that John
said about this man was true." 42And in
that place many believed in Jesus.

The Death of Lazarus

11 Now a man named Lazarus was
sick. He was from Bethany, the village of Mary and her sister Martha. 2This
Mary, whose brother Lazarus now lay
sick, was the same one who poured perfume on the Lord and wiped his feet with
her hair. 3So the sisters sent word to
Jesus, "Lord, the one you love is sick."
4When he heard this, Jesus said, "This
sickness will not end in death. No, it is for
God's glory so that God's Son may be glorified through it." 5Jesus loved Martha
and her sister and Lazarus. 6Yet when he
heard that Lazarus was sick, he stayed
where he was two more days.
7Then he said to his disciples, "Let us
go back to Judea."
8"But Rabbi," they said, "a short while
ago the Jews tried to stone you, and yet
you are going back there?"
9Jesus answered, "Are there not twelve
hours of daylight? A man who walks by
day will not stumble, for he sees by this
world's light. 10It is when he walks by

[a]22 That is, Hanukkah [b]24 Or *Messiah* [c]29 Many early manuscripts *What my Father has given me is greater than all* [d]34 Psalm 82:6

night that he stumbles, for he has no light."

11After he had said this, he went on to tell them, "Our friend Lazarus has fallen asleep; but I am going there to wake him up."

12His disciples replied, "Lord, if he sleeps, he will get better." 13Jesus had been speaking of his death, but his disciples thought he meant natural sleep.

14So then he told them plainly, "Lazarus is dead, 15and for your sake I am glad I was not there, so that you may believe. But let us go to him."

16Then Thomas (called Didymus) said to the rest of the disciples, "Let us also go, that we may die with him."

Jesus Comforts the Sisters

17On his arrival, Jesus found that Lazarus had already been in the tomb for four days. 18Bethany was less than two miles[a] from Jerusalem, 19and many Jews had come to Martha and Mary to comfort them in the loss of their brother. 20When Martha heard that Jesus was coming, she went out to meet him, but Mary stayed at home.

21"Lord," Martha said to Jesus, "if you had been here, my brother would not have died. 22But I know that even now God will give you whatever you ask."

23Jesus said to her, "Your brother will rise again."

24Martha answered, "I know he will rise again in the resurrection at the last day."

25Jesus said to her, "I am the resurrection and the life. He who believes in me will live, even though he dies; 26and whoever lives and believes in me will never die. Do you believe this?"

27"Yes, Lord," she told him, "I believe that you are the Christ,[b] the Son of God, who was to come into the world."

28And after she had said this, she went back and called her sister Mary aside. "The Teacher is here," she said, "and is asking for you." 29When Mary heard this, she got up quickly and went to him. 30Now Jesus had not yet entered the village, but was still at the place where Martha had met him. 31When the Jews who had been with Mary in the house, comforting her, noticed how quickly she got up and went out, they followed her, supposing she was going to the tomb to mourn there.

32When Mary reached the place where Jesus was and saw him, she fell at his feet and said, "Lord, if you had been here, my brother would not have died."

33When Jesus saw her weeping, and the Jews who had come along with her also weeping, he was deeply moved in spirit and troubled. 34"Where have you laid him?" he asked.

"Come and see, Lord," they replied.

35Jesus wept.

36Then the Jews said, "See how he loved him!"

37But some of them said, "Could not he who opened the eyes of the blind man have kept this man from dying?"

Jesus Raises Lazarus From the Dead

38Jesus, once more deeply moved, came to the tomb. It was a cave with a stone laid across the entrance. 39"Take away the stone," he said.

"But, Lord," said Martha, the sister of the dead man, "by this time there is a bad odor, for he has been there four days."

40Then Jesus said, "Did I not tell you that if you believed, you would see the glory of God?"

41So they took away the stone. Then Jesus looked up and said, "Father, I thank you that you have heard me. 42I knew that you always hear me, but I said this for the benefit of the people standing here, that they may believe that you sent me."

43When he had said this, Jesus called in a loud voice, "Lazarus, come out!" 44The dead man came out, his hands and feet wrapped with strips of linen, and a cloth around his face.

Jesus said to them, "Take off the grave clothes and let him go."

The Plot to Kill Jesus

45Therefore many of the Jews who had come to visit Mary, and had seen what Jesus did, put their faith in him. 46But some of them went to the Pharisees and told them what Jesus had done. 47Then the chief priests and the Pharisees called a meeting of the Sanhedrin.

"What are we accomplishing?" they asked. "Here is this man performing many miraculous signs. 48If we let him go on like this, everyone will believe in him, and then the Romans will come and take away both our place[c] and our nation."

49Then one of them, named Caiaphas, who was high priest that year, spoke up,

[a]*18* Greek *fifteen stadia* (about 3 kilometers) [b]*27* Or *Messiah* [c]*48* Or *temple*

"You know nothing at all! 50You do not realize that it is better for you that one man die for the people than that the whole nation perish."

51He did not say this on his own, but as high priest that year he prophesied that Jesus would die for the Jewish nation, 52and not only for that nation but also for the scattered children of God, to bring them together and make them one. 53So from that day on they plotted to take his life.

54Therefore Jesus no longer moved about publicly among the Jews. Instead he withdrew to a region near the desert, to a village called Ephraim, where he stayed with his disciples.

55When it was almost time for the Jewish Passover, many went up from the country to Jerusalem for their ceremonial cleansing before the Passover. 56They kept looking for Jesus, and as they stood in the temple area they asked one another, "What do you think? Isn't he coming to the Feast at all?" 57But the chief priests and Pharisees had given orders that if anyone found out where Jesus was, he should report it so that they might arrest him.

Jesus Anointed at Bethany

12 Six days before the Passover, Jesus arrived at Bethany, where Lazarus lived, whom Jesus had raised from the dead. 2Here a dinner was given in Jesus' honor. Martha served, while Lazarus was among those reclining at the table with him. 3Then Mary took about a pint[a] of pure nard, an expensive perfume; she poured it on Jesus' feet and wiped his feet with her hair. And the house was filled with the fragrance of the perfume.

4But one of his disciples, Judas Iscariot, who was later to betray him, objected, 5"Why wasn't this perfume sold and the money given to the poor? It was worth a year's wages.[b]" 6He did not say this because he cared about the poor but because he was a thief; as keeper of the money bag, he used to help himself to what was put into it.

7"Leave her alone," Jesus replied. "It was intended that she should save this perfume for the day of my burial. 8You will always have the poor among you, but you will not always have me."

9Meanwhile a large crowd of Jews found out that Jesus was there and came, not only because of him but also to see Lazarus, whom he had raised from the dead. 10So the chief priests made plans to kill Lazarus as well, 11for on account of him many of the Jews were going over to Jesus and putting their faith in him.

The Triumphal Entry

12The next day the great crowd that had come for the Feast heard that Jesus was on his way to Jerusalem. 13They took palm branches and went out to meet him, shouting,

"Hosanna![c]"

"Blessed is he who comes in the
name of the Lord!"[d]

"Blessed is the King of Israel!"

14Jesus found a young donkey and sat upon it, as it is written,

15"Do not be afraid, O Daughter of
Zion;
see, your king is coming,
seated on a donkey's colt."[e]

16At first his disciples did not understand all this. Only after Jesus was glorified did they realize that these things had been written about him and that they had done these things to him.

17Now the crowd that was with him when he called Lazarus from the tomb and raised him from the dead continued to spread the word. 18Many people, because they had heard that he had given this miraculous sign, went out to meet him. 19So the Pharisees said to one another, "See, this is getting us nowhere. Look how the whole world has gone after him!"

Jesus Predicts His Death

20Now there were some Greeks among those who went up to worship at the Feast. 21They came to Philip, who was from Bethsaida in Galilee, with a request. "Sir," they said, "we would like to see Jesus." 22Philip went to tell Andrew; Andrew and Philip in turn told Jesus.

23Jesus replied, "The hour has come for the Son of Man to be glorified. 24I tell you the truth, unless a kernel of wheat falls to the ground and dies, it remains only a single seed. But if it dies, it produces many

[a]*3* Greek *a litra* (probably about 0.5 liter) [b]*5* Greek *three hundred denarii* [c]*13* A Hebrew expression meaning "Save!" which became an exclamation of praise [d]*13* Psalm 118:25, 26 [e]*15* Zech. 9:9

seeds. 25The man who loves his life will lose it, while the man who hates his life in this world will keep it for eternal life. 26Whoever serves me must follow me; and where I am, my servant also will be. My Father will honor the one who serves me.

27"Now my heart is troubled, and what shall I say? 'Father, save me from this hour'? No, it was for this very reason I came to this hour. 28Father, glorify your name!"

Then a voice came from heaven, "I have glorified it, and will glorify it again." 29The crowd that was there and heard it said it had thundered; others said an angel had spoken to him.

30Jesus said, "This voice was for your benefit, not mine. 31Now is the time for judgment on this world; now the prince of this world will be driven out. 32But I, when I am lifted up from the earth, will draw all men to myself." 33He said this to show the kind of death he was going to die.

34The crowd spoke up, "We have heard from the Law that the Christ[a] will remain forever, so how can you say, 'The Son of Man must be lifted up'? Who is this 'Son of Man'?"

35Then Jesus told them, "You are going to have the light just a little while longer. Walk while you have the light, before darkness overtakes you. The man who walks in the dark does not know where he is going. 36Put your trust in the light while you have it, so that you may become sons of light." When he had finished speaking, Jesus left and hid himself from them.

The Jews Continue in Their Unbelief

37Even after Jesus had done all these miraculous signs in their presence, they still would not believe in him. 38This was to fulfill the word of Isaiah the prophet:

"Lord, who has believed our message
and to whom has the arm of the
Lord been revealed?"[b]

39For this reason they could not believe, because, as Isaiah says elsewhere:

40"He has blinded their eyes
and deadened their hearts,
so they can neither see with their
eyes,
nor understand with their hearts,
nor turn—and I would heal
them."[c]

41Isaiah said this because he saw Jesus' glory and spoke about him.

42Yet at the same time many even among the leaders believed in him. But because of the Pharisees they would not confess their faith for fear they would be put out of the synagogue; 43for they loved praise from men more than praise from God.

44Then Jesus cried out, "When a man believes in me, he does not believe in me only, but in the one who sent me. 45When he looks at me, he sees the one who sent me. 46I have come into the world as a light, so that no one who believes in me should stay in darkness.

47"As for the person who hears my words but does not keep them, I do not judge him. For I did not come to judge the world, but to save it. 48There is a judge for the one who rejects me and does not accept my words; that very word which I spoke will condemn him at the last day. 49For I did not speak of my own accord, but the Father who sent me commanded me what to say and how to say it. 50I know that his command leads to eternal life. So whatever I say is just what the Father has told me to say."

Jesus Washes His Disciples' Feet

13 It was just before the Passover Feast. Jesus knew that the time had come for him to leave this world and go to the Father. Having loved his own who were in the world, he now showed them the full extent of his love.[d]

2The evening meal was being served, and the devil had already prompted Judas Iscariot, son of Simon, to betray Jesus. 3Jesus knew that the Father had put all things under his power, and that he had come from God and was returning to God; 4so he got up from the meal, took off his outer clothing, and wrapped a towel around his waist. 5After that, he poured water into a basin and began to wash his disciples' feet, drying them with the towel that was wrapped around him.

6He came to Simon Peter, who said to him, "Lord, are you going to wash my feet?"

7Jesus replied, "You do not realize now what I am doing, but later you will understand."

8"No," said Peter, "you shall never wash my feet."

[a]34 Or *Messiah* [b]38 Isaiah 53:1 [c]40 Isaiah 6:10 [d]1 Or *he loved them to the last*

Jesus answered, "Unless I wash you,
you have no part with me."
9"Then, Lord," Simon Peter replied,
"not just my feet but my hands and my
head as well!"
10Jesus answered, "A person who has
had a bath needs only to wash his feet; his
whole body is clean. And you are clean,
though not every one of you." 11For he
knew who was going to betray him, and
that was why he said not every one was
clean.
12When he had finished washing their
feet, he put on his clothes and returned to
his place. "Do you understand what I
have done for you?" he asked them.
13"You call me 'Teacher' and 'Lord,' and
rightly so, for that is what I am. 14Now
that I, your Lord and Teacher, have
washed your feet, you also should wash
one another's feet. 15I have set you an example that you should do as I have done
for you. 16I tell you the truth, no servant
is greater than his master, nor is a messenger greater than the one who sent him.
17Now that you know these things, you
will be blessed if you do them.

Jesus Predicts His Betrayal

18"I am not referring to all of you; I
know those I have chosen. But this is to
fulfill the scripture: 'He who shares my
bread has lifted up his heel against me.'[a]
19"I am telling you now before it happens, so that when it does happen you
will believe that I am He. 20I tell you the
truth, whoever accepts anyone I send accepts me; and whoever accepts me accepts the one who sent me."
21After he had said this, Jesus was troubled in spirit and testified, "I tell you the
truth, one of you is going to betray me."
22His disciples stared at one another, at
a loss to know which of them he meant.
23One of them, the disciple whom Jesus
loved, was reclining next to him. 24Simon
Peter motioned to this disciple and said,
"Ask him which one he means."
25Leaning back against Jesus, he asked
him, "Lord, who is it?"
26Jesus answered, "It is the one to
whom I will give this piece of bread when
I have dipped it in the dish." Then, dip-
ping the piece of bread, he gave it to Judas Iscariot, son of Simon. 27As soon as
Judas took the bread, Satan entered into
him.
"What you are about to do, do quickly,"
Jesus told him, 28but no one at the meal
understood why Jesus said this to him.
29Since Judas had charge of the money,
some thought Jesus was telling him to
buy what was needed for the Feast, or to
give something to the poor. 30As soon as
Judas had taken the bread, he went out.
And it was night.

Jesus Predicts Peter's Denial

31When he was gone, Jesus said, "Now
is the Son of Man glorified and God is
glorified in him. 32If God is glorified in
him,[b] God will glorify the Son in himself,
and will glorify him at once.
33"My children, I will be with you only
a little longer. You will look for me, and
just as I told the Jews, so I tell you now:
Where I am going, you cannot come.
34"A new command I give you: Love one
another. As I have loved you, so you must
love one another. 35By this all men will
know that you are my disciples, if you
love one another."
36Simon Peter asked him, "Lord, where
are you going?"
Jesus replied, "Where I am going, you
cannot follow now, but you will follow
later."
37Peter asked, "Lord, why can't I follow
you now? I will lay down my life for you."
38Then Jesus answered, "Will you really
lay down your life for me? I tell you the
truth, before the rooster crows, you will
disown me three times!

Jesus Comforts His Disciples

14 "Do not let your hearts be troubled. Trust in God[c]; trust also in
me. 2In my Father's house are many
rooms; if it were not so, I would have told
you. I am going there to prepare a place
for you. 3And if I go and prepare a place
for you, I will come back and take you to
be with me that you also may be where I
am. 4You know the way to the place
where I am going."

Jesus the Way to the Father

5Thomas said to him, "Lord, we don't
know where you are going, so how can we
know the way?"
6Jesus answered, "I am the way and the
truth and the life. No one comes to the
Father except through me. 7If you really
knew me, you would know[d] my Father as

[a] 18 Psalm 41:9 [b] 32 Many early manuscripts do not have *If God is glorified in him.* [c] 1 Or *You trust in God* [d] 7 Some early manuscripts *If you really have known me, you will know*

WEDNESDAY

VERSE FOR THE DAY:	*AUTHOR:*	*PASSAGE FOR THE DAY:*
John 14:1	*Gloria Gaither*	*John 13:1–14:31*

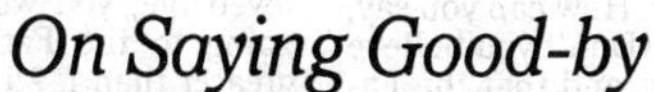

On Saying Good-by

TRAVELING has been a part of our lives from the very early days of our marriage. When our children were little, our singing took us away nearly every weekend and occasionally for longer periods of time. Although leaving was common, it was never easy. Suzanne said to us when she was three, "I know you have to go, but don't go without saying good-by." She knew that the leave-taking was very important to everyone's security and sense of purpose.

Even when the children were young, before we left they always insisted on knowing the answers to five very important questions: Where are you going? How long will you be gone? Can we come with you? Who will stay with us? When will you be back?

Over and over we would answer those questions with specific information. Then we would give advice like, "Don't argue. Take care of the dogs, and always love each other. Remember that whatever you do or wherever you go, you represent our family."

When Jesus was leaving his disciples to return to his Father, he, too, knew that leave-taking was very important. He didn't leave them without saying good-by. And the questions his children asked were the same ones our children used to ask. With specific clarity Jesus gave them answers, although they could not fully comprehend the dimensions of what he was telling them.

"I go to my Father," he said. "You can't come with me yet, but don't worry, I won't leave you alone. The Holy Spirit will be your constant companion, and I must go so that he can come. While I'm gone he will teach you everything you need to know. I will be gone, by my time, only a little while, though it may seem long to you. When I come again, it will be to take you where I have been all this time fixing up a special place for all of us to be together . . . forever. After that, we won't have to say good-by again."

Then Jesus gave some special parental instructions. "Love and take care of each other. The way you treat each other will tell the world about our family, so remember whose child you are. Some problems may come up, but whatever you need, you can ask for it using my name. All I have is at your disposal, and the Holy Spirit will see that you have it. When you feel lonely or afraid, rely on my promise that I have insulated you in prayer, and you belong to me."

Additional Scripture Readings:
Acts 1:6–11; 20:17–38

Go to page 147 for your next devotional reading.

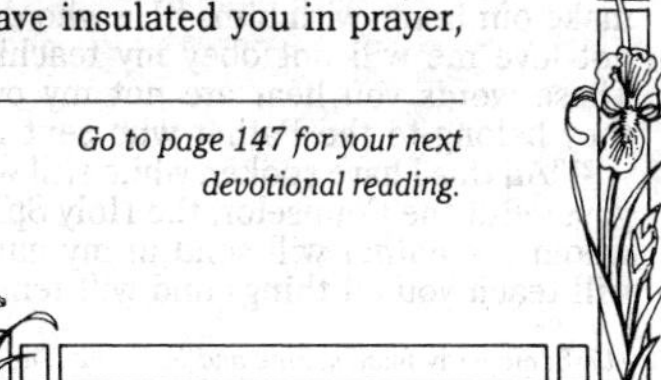

well. From now on, you do know him and have seen him."

[8]Philip said, "Lord, show us the Father and that will be enough for us."

[9]Jesus answered: "Don't you know me, Philip, even after I have been among you such a long time? Anyone who has seen me has seen the Father. How can you say, 'Show us the Father'? [10]Don't you believe that I am in the Father, and that the Father is in me? The words I say to you are not just my own. Rather, it is the Father, living in me, who is doing his work. [11]Believe me when I say that I am in the Father and the Father is in me; or at least believe on the evidence of the miracles themselves. [12]I tell you the truth, anyone who has faith in me will do what I have been doing. He will do even greater things than these, because I am going to the Father. [13]And I will do whatever you ask in my name, so that the Son may bring glory to the Father. [14]You may ask me for anything in my name, and I will do it.

Jesus Promises the Holy Spirit

[15]"If you love me, you will obey what I command. [16]And I will ask the Father, and he will give you another Counselor to be with you forever— [17]the Spirit of truth. The world cannot accept him, because it neither sees him nor knows him. But you know him, for he lives with you and will be[a] in you. [18]I will not leave you as orphans; I will come to you. [19]Before long, the world will not see me anymore, but you will see me. Because I live, you also will live. [20]On that day you will realize that I am in my Father, and you are in me, and I am in you. [21]Whoever has my commands and obeys them, he is the one who loves me. He who loves me will be loved by my Father, and I too will love him and show myself to him."

[22]Then Judas (not Judas Iscariot) said, "But, Lord, why do you intend to show yourself to us and not to the world?"

[23]Jesus replied, "If anyone loves me, he will obey my teaching. My Father will love him, and we will come to him and make our home with him. [24]He who does not love me will not obey my teaching. These words you hear are not my own; they belong to the Father who sent me.

[25]"All this I have spoken while still with you. [26]But the Counselor, the Holy Spirit, whom the Father will send in my name, will teach you all things and will remind you of everything I have said to you. [27]Peace I leave with you; my peace I give you. I do not give to you as the world gives. Do not let your hearts be troubled and do not be afraid.

[28]"You heard me say, 'I am going away and I am coming back to you.' If you loved me, you would be glad that I am going to the Father, for the Father is greater than I. [29]I have told you now before it happens, so that when it does happen you will believe. [30]I will not speak with you much longer, for the prince of this world is coming. He has no hold on me, [31]but the world must learn that I love the Father and that I do exactly what my Father has commanded me.

"Come now; let us leave.

The Vine and the Branches

15 "I am the true vine, and my Father is the gardener. [2]He cuts off every branch in me that bears no fruit, while every branch that does bear fruit he prunes[b] so that it will be even more fruitful. [3]You are already clean because of the word I have spoken to you. [4]Remain in me, and I will remain in you. No branch can bear fruit by itself; it must remain in the vine. Neither can you bear fruit unless you remain in me.

[5]"I am the vine; you are the branches. If a man remains in me and I in him, he will bear much fruit; apart from me you can do nothing. [6]If anyone does not remain in me, he is like a branch that is thrown away and withers; such branches are picked up, thrown into the fire and burned. [7]If you remain in me and my words remain in you, ask whatever you wish, and it will be given you. [8]This is to my Father's glory, that you bear much fruit, showing yourselves to be my disciples.

[9]"As the Father has loved me, so have I loved you. Now remain in my love. [10]If you obey my commands, you will remain in my love, just as I have obeyed my Father's commands and remain in his love. [11]I have told you this so that my joy may be in you and that your joy may be complete. [12]My command is this: Love each other as I have loved you. [13]Greater love has no one than this, that he lay down his life for his friends. [14]You are my friends if you do what I command. [15]I no longer call you servants, because a servant does not know his master's business. Instead, I

[a]*17* Some early manuscripts *and is* [b]*2* The Greek for *prunes* also means *cleans.*

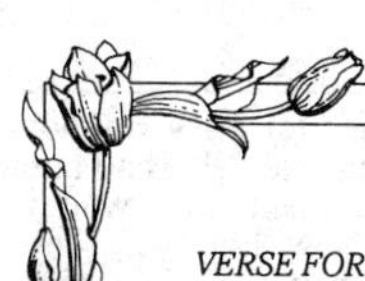

THURSDAY

VERSE FOR THE DAY:
John 15:2

AUTHOR:
Carol L. Baldwin

PASSAGE FOR THE DAY:
John 15:1–6

Divine Pruning

WHAT would you think if your best friend told you that she thought you needed to endure a long, intense and difficult trial so that God could prune away some of the sin in your life? You would probably think she was crazy! What if she persisted and said that you would perform your job as a mother, wife, teacher or saleswoman better after your trial was over? Which of us would willingly submit to those pruning shears, and which of us would turn, run and hide?

Jesus himself is the one who says that we need pruning:

> "I am the true vine, and my Father is the gardener. He cuts off every branch in me that bears no fruit, while every branch that does bear fruit he prunes so that it will be even more fruitful. . . . Neither can you bear fruit unless you remain in me" (John 15:1–2,4).

Here Jesus has issued warnings to all who profess to be believers. Unfruitful branches are those who confess Christ but never bear fruit because they don't genuinely remain in him—they will be cut away. Fruitful branches, those who truly remain in Christ, will be pruned in order to bear more fruit for his glory.

When was the last time you felt "pruned"? Perhaps it was when your invalid mother came to live with you and suddenly your responsibilities and work load at home increased dramatically. Or maybe it was when your employer passed you over for a promotion because he thought you weren't working hard enough.

Pruning is painful but profitable. James tells us that trials are occasions for joy because they will test our faith and develop in us perseverance and maturity (James 1:2–4).

We need God's help even to *desire* to yield ourselves to his pruning. May God bring people and events into our lives that will sanctify us so that we might bear true spiritual fruit for his glory and his kingdom's sake.

Additional Scripture Readings:
Matthew 7:16–20; Luke 13:6–9

Go to page 148 for your next devotional reading.

have called you friends, for everything
that I learned from my Father I have
made known to you. 16You did not choose
me, but I chose you and appointed you to
go and bear fruit—fruit that will last.
Then the Father will give you whatever
you ask in my name. 17This is my command: Love each other.

The World Hates the Disciples

18"If the world hates you, keep in mind
that it hated me first. 19If you belonged to
the world, it would love you as its own. As
it is, you do not belong to the world, but
I have chosen you out of the world. That
is why the world hates you. 20Remember
the words I spoke to you: 'No servant is
greater than his master.'[a] If they persecuted me, they will persecute you also. If
they obeyed my teaching, they will obey
yours also. 21They will treat you this way
because of my name, for they do not
know the One who sent me. 22If I had not
come and spoken to them, they would
not be guilty of sin. Now, however, they
have no excuse for their sin. 23He who
hates me hates my Father as well. 24If I
had not done among them what no one
else did, they would not be guilty of sin.
But now they have seen these miracles,
and yet they have hated both me and my
Father. 25But this is to fulfill what is written in their Law: 'They hated me without
reason.'[b]

26"When the Counselor comes, whom I
will send to you from the Father, the Spirit of truth who goes out from the Father,
he will testify about me. 27And you also
must testify, for you have been with me
from the beginning.

16 "All this I have told you so that you
will not go astray. 2They will put

[a]20 John 13:16 [b]25 Psalms 35:19; 69:4

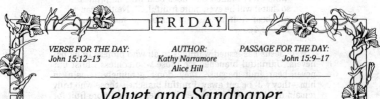

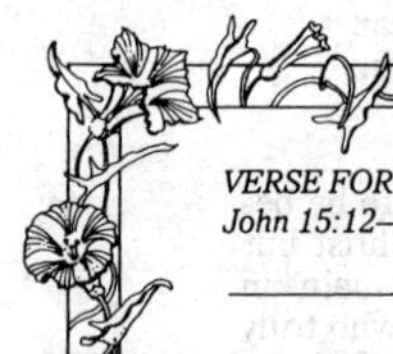

FRIDAY

VERSE FOR THE DAY:
John 15:12–13

AUTHOR:
Kathy Narramore
Alice Hill

PASSAGE FOR THE DAY:
John 15:9–17

Velvet and Sandpaper

WE all have known family or friends who bring out the worst in us instead of the best, rubbing us at just the wrong spots, uncovering our weaknesses rather than our strengths. They're like sandpaper. It is good to remember that Jesus encountered these sandpaper experiences at times even from within his inner circle. It is also good to remember that one of his close friends was one he knew would never understand him and would even betray him. He was a constant sandpaper to Jesus, yet Jesus loved him daily as he did the others. Even in this way he was laying down his life. Since we are also loved sacrificially we are to lay down our lives for each other (1 John 3:16).

But the Lord gives us others who are like velvet, whose words are comforting and supportive, and who really understand us. They are the soft cushions we need when we are scraped with the "sandpapers" and can listen to us as we explore the weaknesses and needs they bring out in us. They tangibly reveal God's perspective—just when we most need it.

Additional Scripture Readings:
John 13:18–30; Acts 9:23–28; 11:22–26

Go to page 149 for your next devotional reading.

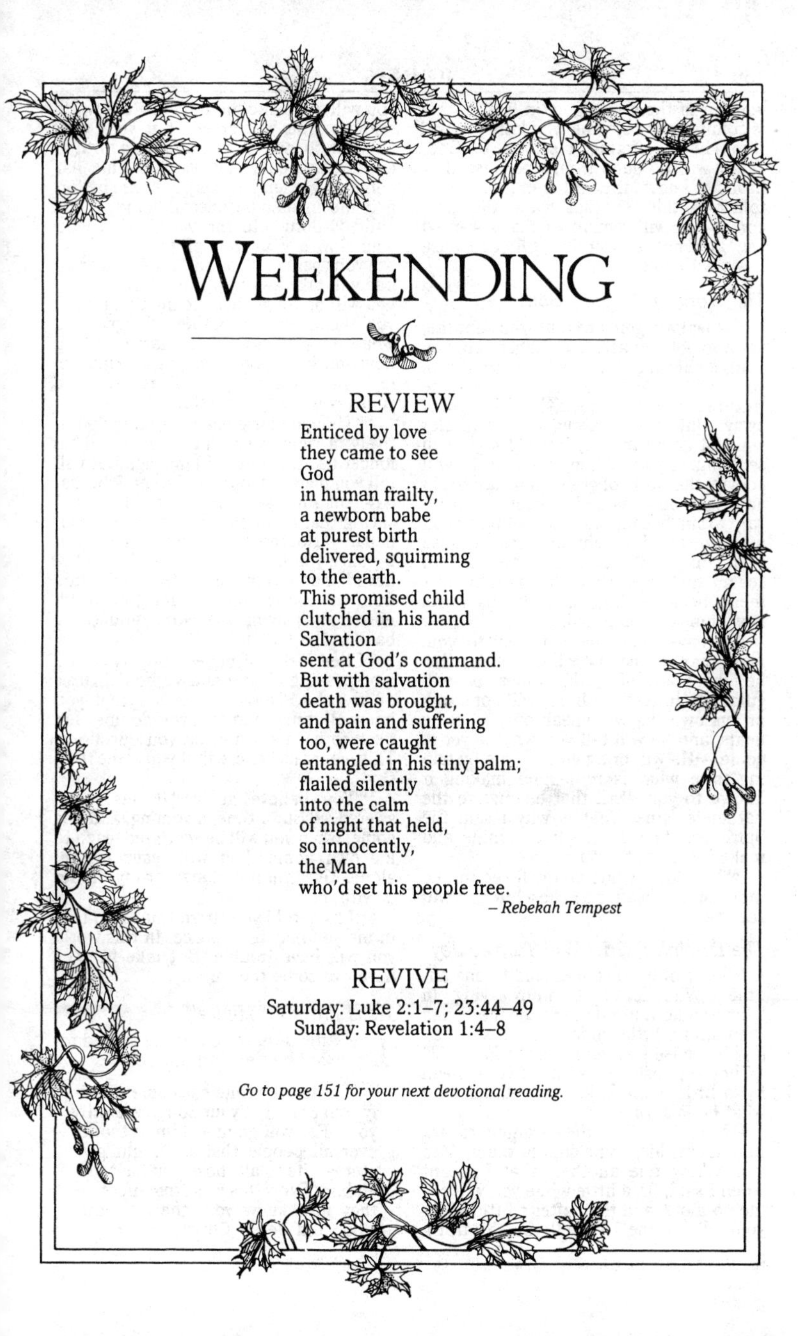

WEEKENDING

REVIEW

Enticed by love
they came to see
God
in human frailty,
a newborn babe
at purest birth
delivered, squirming
to the earth.
This promised child
clutched in his hand
Salvation
sent at God's command.
But with salvation
death was brought,
and pain and suffering
too, were caught
entangled in his tiny palm;
flailed silently
into the calm
of night that held,
so innocently,
the Man
who'd set his people free.

– Rebekah Tempest

REVIVE

Saturday: Luke 2:1–7; 23:44–49
Sunday: Revelation 1:4–8

Go to page 151 for your next devotional reading.

you out of the synagogue; in fact, a time is coming when anyone who kills you will think he is offering a service to God. 3They will do such things because they have not known the Father or me. 4I have told you this, so that when the time comes you will remember that I warned you. I did not tell you this at first because I was with you.

The Work of the Holy Spirit

5"Now I am going to him who sent me, yet none of you asks me, 'Where are you going?' 6Because I have said these things, you are filled with grief. 7But I tell you the truth: It is for your good that I am going away. Unless I go away, the Counselor will not come to you; but if I go, I will send him to you. 8When he comes, he will convict the world of guilt[a] in regard to sin and righteousness and judgment: 9in regard to sin, because men do not believe in me; 10in regard to righteousness, because I am going to the Father, where you can see me no longer; 11and in regard to judgment, because the prince of this world now stands condemned.

12"I have much more to say to you, more than you can now bear. 13But when he, the Spirit of truth, comes, he will guide you into all truth. He will not speak on his own; he will speak only what he hears, and he will tell you what is yet to come. 14He will bring glory to me by taking from what is mine and making it known to you. 15All that belongs to the Father is mine. That is why I said the Spirit will take from what is mine and make it known to you.

16"In a little while you will see me no more, and then after a little while you will see me."

The Disciples' Grief Will Turn to Joy

17Some of his disciples said to one another, "What does he mean by saying, 'In a little while you will see me no more, and then after a little while you will see me,' and 'Because I am going to the Father'?" 18They kept asking, "What does he mean by 'a little while'? We don't understand what he is saying."

19Jesus saw that they wanted to ask him about this, so he said to them, "Are you asking one another what I meant when I said, 'In a little while you will see me no more, and then after a little while you will see me'? 20I tell you the truth, you will weep and mourn while the world rejoices. You will grieve, but your grief will turn to joy. 21A woman giving birth to a child has pain because her time has come; but when her baby is born she forgets the anguish because of her joy that a child is born into the world. 22So with you: Now is your time of grief, but I will see you again and you will rejoice, and no one will take away your joy. 23In that day you will no longer ask me anything. I tell you the truth, my Father will give you whatever you ask in my name. 24Until now you have not asked for anything in my name. Ask and you will receive, and your joy will be complete.

25"Though I have been speaking figuratively, a time is coming when I will no longer use this kind of language but will tell you plainly about my Father. 26In that day you will ask in my name. I am not saying that I will ask the Father on your behalf. 27No, the Father himself loves you because you have loved me and have believed that I came from God. 28I came from the Father and entered the world; now I am leaving the world and going back to the Father."

29Then Jesus' disciples said, "Now you are speaking clearly and without figures of speech. 30Now we can see that you know all things and that you do not even need to have anyone ask you questions. This makes us believe that you came from God."

31"You believe at last!"[b] Jesus answered. 32"But a time is coming, and has come, when you will be scattered, each to his own home. You will leave me all alone. Yet I am not alone, for my Father is with me.

33"I have told you these things, so that in me you may have peace. In this world you will have trouble. But take heart! I have overcome the world."

Jesus Prays for Himself

17 After Jesus said this, he looked toward heaven and prayed:

"Father, the time has come. Glorify your Son, that your Son may glorify you. 2For you granted him authority over all people that he might give eternal life to all those you have given him. 3Now this is eternal life: that they may know you, the only true God, and Jesus Christ, whom you

[a]8 Or *will expose the guilt of the world* [b]31 Or *"Do you now believe?"*

MONDAY

VERSE FOR THE DAY:	*AUTHOR:*	*PASSAGE FOR THE DAY:*
John 16:20,22	*Sue Richards*	*John 16:17–24*

Coming Joy

AS much as two years after becoming single, I frequently found myself in tears at suppertime. My toddlers seemed to be tired by then, scrapping with each other, whining, hanging on me, and incessantly tattling on the crimes they committed against each other.

This is when Daddy is supposed to appear at the door, and both children run to their hero. Dad's arrival gives Mom a few minutes of peace while she prepares the evening meal, and later she has someone to share and commiserate with.

But no one comes while I'm preparing supper. And all I have to look forward to in the hours that lie ahead is refereeing my young wrecking crew, doing dishes, giving baths, reading stories, ending the nightly bedtime battle, and then my own lonely bed.

The thought that I'll always be a single parent is enough to start me sobbing at suppertime.

After a year of grieving for the loss of mate, companion, and father of my children, I knew I had to do something to survive the suppertime slump. I remembered some promises about joy that I'd cut out and stuck in a drawer years before. Though yellowed, wrinkled, and stained with an ancient cake batter, my promises were more precious than gold!

"Restore to me the joy of your salvation" (Psalm 51:12).

"You will grieve, but your grief will turn to joy . . . . and no one will take away your joy" (John 16:20,22).

"He who goes out weeping,
carrying seed to sow,
will return with songs of joy,
carrying sheaves with him" (Psalm 126:6).

Those words don't always start me dancing around the house. But they give me the courage to continue.

Thank you, Father, that joy will follow my sorrows.

Additional Scripture Readings:
Psalm 51:11–12; Isaiah 35:3–10

Go to page 153 for your next devotional reading.

have sent. 4 I have brought you glory on earth by completing the work you gave me to do. 5 And now, Father, glorify me in your presence with the glory I had with you before the world began.

Jesus Prays for His Disciples

6 "I have revealed you[a] to those whom you gave me out of the world. They were yours; you gave them to me and they have obeyed your word. 7 Now they know that everything you have given me comes from you. 8 For I gave them the words you gave me and they accepted them. They knew with certainty that I came from you, and they believed that you sent me. 9 I pray for them. I am not praying for the world, but for those you have given me, for they are yours. 10 All I have is yours, and all you have is mine. And glory has come to me through them. 11 I will remain in the world no longer, but they are still in the world, and I am coming to you. Holy Father, protect them by the power of your name—the name you gave me—so that they may be one as we are one. 12 While I was with them, I protected them and kept them safe by that name you gave me. None has been lost except the one doomed to destruction so that Scripture would be fulfilled.

13 "I am coming to you now, but I say these things while I am still in the world, so that they may have the full measure of my joy within them. 14 I have given them your word and the world has hated them, for they are not of the world any more than I am of the world. 15 My prayer is not that you take them out of the world but that you protect them from the evil one. 16 They are not of the world, even as I am not of it. 17 Sanctify[b] them by the truth; your word is truth. 18 As you sent me into the world, I have sent them into the world. 19 For them I sanctify myself, that they too may be truly sanctified.

Jesus Prays for All Believers

20 "My prayer is not for them alone. I pray also for those who will believe in me through their message, 21 that all of them may be one, Father, just as you are in me and I am in you. May they also be in us so that the world may believe that you have sent me. 22 I have given them the glory that you gave me, that they may be one as we are one: 23 I in them and you in me. May they be brought to complete unity to let the world know that you sent me and have loved them even as you have loved me.

24 "Father, I want those you have given me to be with me where I am, and to see my glory, the glory you have given me because you loved me before the creation of the world.

25 "Righteous Father, though the world does not know you, I know you, and they know that you have sent me. 26 I have made you known to them, and will continue to make you known in order that the love you have for me may be in them and that I myself may be in them."

Jesus Arrested

18 When he had finished praying, Jesus left with his disciples and crossed the Kidron Valley. On the other side there was an olive grove, and he and his disciples went into it.

2 Now Judas, who betrayed him, knew the place, because Jesus had often met there with his disciples. 3 So Judas came to the grove, guiding a detachment of soldiers and some officials from the chief priests and Pharisees. They were carrying torches, lanterns and weapons.

4 Jesus, knowing all that was going to happen to him, went out and asked them, "Who is it you want?"

5 "Jesus of Nazareth," they replied.

"I am he," Jesus said. (And Judas the traitor was standing there with them.) 6 When Jesus said, "I am he," they drew back and fell to the ground.

7 Again he asked them, "Who is it you want?"

And they said, "Jesus of Nazareth."

8 "I told you that I am he," Jesus answered. "If you are looking for me, then let these men go." 9 This happened so that the words he had spoken would be fulfilled: "I have not lost one of those you gave me."[c]

10 Then Simon Peter, who had a sword, drew it and struck the high priest's ser-

[a]6 Greek *your name*; also in verse 26 [b]17 Greek *hagiazo (set apart for sacred use* or *make holy)*; also in verse 19 [c]9 John 6:39

TUESDAY

VERSE FOR THE DAY: *John 17:26*

AUTHOR: *Anne Ortlund*

PASSAGE FOR THE DAY: *John 17:1–26*

Holy Ground

IT'S time to take off your shoes. You're about to move onto holy ground.

In all the literature written by human beings on this planet, John 17 is the only lengthy conversation ever recorded between God and God! You have quickies: "Let us make man in our image" (Genesis 1:26). "I praise you, Father . . . because you have hidden these things from the wise and learned, and revealed them to little children" (Matthew 11:25).

But here's a long discussion by God the Son with God the Father. (How self-revealing God is!) And when God talks with God, what are his godly, all-encompassing concerns? There are basically three:

1. John 17:1–5: the glory of the Father and the glory of the Son.

2. John 17:6–19: the well-being of believers—their protection, their unity, their joy, their sanctification . . . How he loves us!

3. John 17:20–26: the salvation of the world—that others will believe, that they will know. God yearns for them!

Do you want to move into the heart of God? Do you want to be "in sync" with him, sharing his own priorities? In John 15, just before Jesus went to the cross, he communicated these same three priorities among his final commands to his eleven disciples. And they're for you and me as well:

1. Make your chief concern the glory of the Father and the glory of the Son, through the power of the Spirit. Be zealous above all to put him first, first, first! Move away from all competition with his firstness; settle into him. As he said, "Remain in me" (John 15:1–11). That's your first priority.

2. Share his concern for the well-being of your fellow believers—their protection, their unity, their joy, their sanctification. Give your time, your gifts, yourself! As Jesus said, "Love each other" (John 15:12–17). That's your second priority.

3. Share his concern for this needy world; reach out! As he said, "You also must testify, for you have been with me from the beginning" (John 15:18–27). That's your third priority, your third area of concern.

So, here in John 17, take off your shoes. You're on holy ground. Sit at Jesus' feet. Learn his thinking. And give all you are to share his concerns, love his loves, accomplish his purposes.

Additional Scripture Readings:
Exodus 3:1–10; Mark 4:13–20

Go to page 157 for your next devotional reading.

vant, cutting off his right ear. (The servant's name was Malchus.)

[11]Jesus commanded Peter, "Put your sword away! Shall I not drink the cup the Father has given me?"

Jesus Taken to Annas

[12]Then the detachment of soldiers with its commander and the Jewish officials arrested Jesus. They bound him [13]and brought him first to Annas, who was the father-in-law of Caiaphas, the high priest that year. [14]Caiaphas was the one who had advised the Jews that it would be good if one man died for the people.

Peter's First Denial

[15]Simon Peter and another disciple were following Jesus. Because this disciple was known to the high priest, he went with Jesus into the high priest's courtyard, [16]but Peter had to wait outside at the door. The other disciple, who was known to the high priest, came back, spoke to the girl on duty there and brought Peter in.

[17]"You are not one of his disciples, are you?" the girl at the door asked Peter.

He replied, "I am not."

[18]It was cold, and the servants and officials stood around a fire they had made to keep warm. Peter also was standing with them, warming himself.

The High Priest Questions Jesus

[19]Meanwhile, the high priest questioned Jesus about his disciples and his teaching.

[20]"I have spoken openly to the world," Jesus replied. "I always taught in synagogues or at the temple, where all the Jews come together. I said nothing in secret. [21]Why question me? Ask those who heard me. Surely they know what I said."

[22]When Jesus said this, one of the officials nearby struck him in the face. "Is this the way you answer the high priest?" he demanded.

[23]"If I said something wrong," Jesus replied, "testify as to what is wrong. But if I spoke the truth, why did you strike me?" [24]Then Annas sent him, still bound, to Caiaphas the high priest.[a]

Peter's Second and Third Denials

[25]As Simon Peter stood warming himself, he was asked, "You are not one of his disciples, are you?"

He denied it, saying, "I am not."

[26]One of the high priest's servants, a relative of the man whose ear Peter had cut off, challenged him, "Didn't I see you with him in the olive grove?" [27]Again Peter denied it, and at that moment a rooster began to crow.

Jesus Before Pilate

[28]Then the Jews led Jesus from Caiaphas to the palace of the Roman governor. By now it was early morning, and to avoid ceremonial uncleanness the Jews did not enter the palace; they wanted to be able to eat the Passover. [29]So Pilate came out to them and asked, "What charges are you bringing against this man?"

[30]"If he were not a criminal," they replied, "we would not have handed him over to you."

[31]Pilate said, "Take him yourselves and judge him by your own law."

"But we have no right to execute anyone," the Jews objected. [32]This happened so that the words Jesus had spoken indicating the kind of death he was going to die would be fulfilled.

[33]Pilate then went back inside the palace, summoned Jesus and asked him, "Are you the king of the Jews?"

[34]"Is that your own idea," Jesus asked, "or did others talk to you about me?"

[35]"Am I a Jew?" Pilate replied. "It was your people and your chief priests who handed you over to me. What is it you have done?"

[36]Jesus said, "My kingdom is not of this world. If it were, my servants would fight to prevent my arrest by the Jews. But now my kingdom is from another place."

[37]"You are a king, then!" said Pilate.

Jesus answered, "You are right in saying I am a king. In fact, for this reason I was born, and for this I came into the world, to testify to the truth. Everyone on the side of truth listens to me."

[38]"What is truth?" Pilate asked. With this he went out again to the Jews and said, "I find no basis for a charge against him. [39]But it is your custom for me to release to you one prisoner at the time of the Passover. Do you want me to release 'the king of the Jews'?"

[40]They shouted back, "No, not him! Give us Barabbas!" Now Barabbas had taken part in a rebellion.

[a]24 Or *(Now Annas had sent him, still bound, to Caiaphas the high priest.)*

Jesus Sentenced to be Crucified

19 Then Pilate took Jesus and had
him flogged. 2The soldiers twisted
together a crown of thorns and put it on
his head. They clothed him in a purple
robe 3and went up to him again and
again, saying, "Hail, king of the Jews!"
And they struck him in the face.

4Once more Pilate came out and said to
the Jews, "Look, I am bringing him out to
you to let you know that I find no basis for
a charge against him." 5When Jesus came
out wearing the crown of thorns and the
purple robe, Pilate said to them, "Here is
the man!"

6As soon as the chief priests and their
officials saw him, they shouted, "Crucify!
Crucify!"

But Pilate answered, "You take him
and crucify him. As for me, I find no basis
for a charge against him."

7The Jews insisted, "We have a law,
and according to that law he must die,
because he claimed to be the Son of
God."

8When Pilate heard this, he was even
more afraid, 9and he went back inside the
palace. "Where do you come from?" he
asked Jesus, but Jesus gave him no answer. 10"Do you refuse to speak to me?"
Pilate said. "Don't you realize I have power either to free you or to crucify you?"

11Jesus answered, "You would have no
power over me if it were not given to you
from above. Therefore the one who handed me over to you is guilty of a greater
sin."

12From then on, Pilate tried to set
Jesus free, but the Jews kept shouting, "If
you let this man go, you are no friend of
Caesar. Anyone who claims to be a king
opposes Caesar."

13When Pilate heard this, he brought
Jesus out and sat down on the judge's
seat at a place known as the Stone Pavement (which in Aramaic is Gabbatha).
14It was the day of Preparation of Passover Week, about the sixth hour.

"Here is your king," Pilate said to the
Jews.

15But they shouted, "Take him away!
Take him away! Crucify him!"

"Shall I crucify your king?" Pilate
asked.

"We have no king but Caesar," the
chief priests answered.

16Finally Pilate handed him over to
them to be crucified.

The Crucifixion

So the soldiers took charge of Jesus.
17Carrying his own cross, he went out to
the place of the Skull (which in Aramaic
is called Golgotha). 18Here they crucified
him, and with him two others—one on
each side and Jesus in the middle.

19Pilate had a notice prepared and fastened to the cross. It read: JESUS OF NAZA-
RETH, THE KING OF THE JEWS. 20Many of the
Jews read this sign, for the place where
Jesus was crucified was near the city, and
the sign was written in Aramaic, Latin
and Greek. 21The chief priests of the Jews
protested to Pilate, "Do not write 'The
King of the Jews,' but that this man
claimed to be king of the Jews."

22Pilate answered, "What I have written, I have written."

23When the soldiers crucified Jesus,
they took his clothes, dividing them into
four shares, one for each of them, with
the undergarment remaining. This garment was seamless, woven in one piece
from top to bottom.

24"Let's not tear it," they said to one
another. "Let's decide by lot who will
get it."

This happened that the scripture might
be fulfilled which said,

"They divided my garments among
them
and cast lots for my clothing."[a]

So this is what the soldiers did.

25Near the cross of Jesus stood his
mother, his mother's sister, Mary the wife
of Clopas, and Mary Magdalene. 26When
Jesus saw his mother there, and the disciple whom he loved standing nearby, he
said to his mother, "Dear woman, here is
your son," 27and to the disciple, "Here is
your mother." From that time on, this
disciple took her into his home.

The Death of Jesus

28Later, knowing that all was now completed, and so that the Scripture would be
fulfilled, Jesus said, "I am thirsty." 29A jar
of wine vinegar was there, so they soaked
a sponge in it, put the sponge on a stalk
of the hyssop plant, and lifted it to Jesus'
lips. 30When he had received the drink,
Jesus said, "It is finished." With that, he
bowed his head and gave up his spirit.

[a]*24* Psalm 22:18

31Now it was the day of Preparation, and the next day was to be a special Sabbath. Because the Jews did not want the bodies left on the crosses during the Sabbath, they asked Pilate to have the legs broken and the bodies taken down. 32The soldiers therefore came and broke the legs of the first man who had been crucified with Jesus, and then those of the other. 33But when they came to Jesus and found that he was already dead, they did not break his legs. 34Instead, one of the soldiers pierced Jesus' side with a spear, bringing a sudden flow of blood and water. 35The man who saw it has given testimony, and his testimony is true. He knows that he tells the truth, and he testifies so that you also may believe. 36These things happened so that the scripture would be fulfilled: "Not one of his bones will be broken,"[a] 37and, as another scripture says, "They will look on the one they have pierced."[b]

The Burial of Jesus

38Later, Joseph of Arimathea asked Pilate for the body of Jesus. Now Joseph was a disciple of Jesus, but secretly because he feared the Jews. With Pilate's permission, he came and took the body away. 39He was accompanied by Nicodemus, the man who earlier had visited Jesus at night. Nicodemus brought a mixture of myrrh and aloes, about seventy-five pounds.[c] 40Taking Jesus' body, the two of them wrapped it, with the spices, in strips of linen. This was in accordance with Jewish burial customs. 41At the place where Jesus was crucified, there was a garden, and in the garden a new tomb, in which no one had ever been laid. 42Because it was the Jewish day of Preparation and since the tomb was nearby, they laid Jesus there.

The Empty Tomb

20 Early on the first day of the week, while it was still dark, Mary Magdalene went to the tomb and saw that the stone had been removed from the entrance. 2So she came running to Simon Peter and the other disciple, the one Jesus loved, and said, "They have taken the Lord out of the tomb, and we don't know where they have put him!"

3So Peter and the other disciple started for the tomb. 4Both were running, but the other disciple outran Peter and reached the tomb first. 5He bent over and looked in at the strips of linen lying there but did not go in. 6Then Simon Peter, who was behind him, arrived and went into the tomb. He saw the strips of linen lying there, 7as well as the burial cloth that had been around Jesus' head. The cloth was folded up by itself, separate from the linen. 8Finally the other disciple, who had reached the tomb first, also went inside. He saw and believed. 9(They still did not understand from Scripture that Jesus had to rise from the dead.)

Jesus Appears to Mary Magdalene

10Then the disciples went back to their homes, 11but Mary stood outside the tomb crying. As she wept, she bent over to look into the tomb 12and saw two angels in white, seated where Jesus' body had been, one at the head and the other at the foot.

13They asked her, "Woman, why are you crying?"

"They have taken my Lord away," she said, "and I don't know where they have put him." 14At this, she turned around and saw Jesus standing there, but she did not realize that it was Jesus.

15"Woman," he said, "why are you crying? Who is it you are looking for?"

Thinking he was the gardener, she said, "Sir, if you have carried him away, tell me where you have put him, and I will get him."

16Jesus said to her, "Mary."

She turned toward him and cried out in Aramaic, "Rabboni!" (which means Teacher).

17Jesus said, "Do not hold on to me, for I have not yet returned to the Father. Go instead to my brothers and tell them, 'I am returning to my Father and your Father, to my God and your God.' "

18Mary Magdalene went to the disciples with the news: "I have seen the Lord!" And she told them that he had said these things to her.

Jesus Appears to His Disciples

19On the evening of that first day of the week, when the disciples were together, with the doors locked for fear of the Jews, Jesus came and stood among them and said, "Peace be with you!" 20After he said this, he showed them his hands and side.

[a]36 Exodus 12:46; Num. 9:12; Psalm 34:20 [b]37 Zech. 12:10 [c]39 Greek *a hundred litrai* (about 34 kilograms)

WEDNESDAY

VERSE FOR THE DAY: *John 20:25*

AUTHOR: *Ruth A. Tucker*

PASSAGE FOR THE DAY: *John 20:24–31*

Doubting Believers

IT is not the faithful women (who told the doubting disciples of their risen Lord) with whom I identify most in the cast of characters who surround Jesus in the days before and after his death and resurrection. No, as I examine myself and my struggle with faith *and* doubt, I find that it is Thomas with whom I most identify.

Thomas was more than simply one doubting disciple who held out for proof of the resurrection—a skeptic who will be remembered forever for his lack of faith. No, Thomas stood in for all the rest of the followers of Jesus who, through the ages, have been afflicted with a disposition toward doubt. Like him, we are disciples, but disciples who are cynical at times, who often need more time to assimilate and test the facts.

Thomas merits no praise for his unbelieving mindset. But he and the other disciples, who initially doubted, offer skeptics through the ages assurance because they did not take for granted anything involving the Easter events. Indeed, the most powerful evidence for the resurrection of Jesus is the very fact that the disciples doubted. They were not like some people who are ready to latch on to any rumor or report that comes along—particularly if it bolsters their position. No, they demanded proof, and in doing so benefited the Christian church for all time.

For Jesus, however, the disciples' lack of faith was a deep disappointment, and I know that my own lack of faith at times surely must grieve the heart of my Lord. Yet, I know he understands my struggle, and I know he understands my prayer that reiterates the plea of another who struggled with unbelief when he cried out, "I do believe; help me overcome my unbelief!" (Mark 9:24).

Additional Scripture Readings:
Matthew 14:28–31; 1 John 1:1–3

Go to page 161 for your next devotional reading.

The disciples were overjoyed when they
saw the Lord.
21Again Jesus said, "Peace be with you!
As the Father has sent me, I am sending
you." 22And with that he breathed on
them and said, "Receive the Holy Spirit.
23If you forgive anyone his sins, they are
forgiven; if you do not forgive them, they
are not forgiven."

Jesus Appears to Thomas

24Now Thomas (called Didymus), one
of the Twelve, was not with the disciples
when Jesus came. 25So the other disciples
told him, "We have seen the Lord!"
But he said to them, "Unless I see the
nail marks in his hands and put my finger
where the nails were, and put my hand
into his side, I will not believe it."
26A week later his disciples were in the
house again, and Thomas was with them.
Though the doors were locked, Jesus
came and stood among them and said,
"Peace be with you!" 27Then he said to
Thomas, "Put your finger here; see my
hands. Reach out your hand and put it
into my side. Stop doubting and believe."
28Thomas said to him, "My Lord and
my God!"
29Then Jesus told him, "Because you
have seen me, you have believed; blessed
are those who have not seen and yet have
believed."
30Jesus did many other miraculous
signs in the presence of his disciples,
which are not recorded in this book. 31But
these are written that you may[a] believe
that Jesus is the Christ, the Son of God,
and that by believing you may have life in
his name.

Jesus and the Miraculous Catch of Fish

21 Afterward Jesus appeared again to
his disciples, by the Sea of Tiberias.[b] It happened this way: 2Simon Peter,
Thomas (called Didymus), Nathanael
from Cana in Galilee, the sons of Zebedee, and two other disciples were together. 3"I'm going out to fish," Simon Peter
told them, and they said, "We'll go with
you." So they went out and got into the
boat, but that night they caught nothing.
4Early in the morning, Jesus stood on
the shore, but the disciples did not realize
that it was Jesus.
5He called out to them, "Friends,
haven't you any fish?"
"No," they answered.
6He said, "Throw your net on the right
side of the boat and you will find some."
When they did, they were unable to haul
the net in because of the large number of
fish.
7Then the disciple whom Jesus loved
said to Peter, "It is the Lord!" As soon as
Simon Peter heard him say, "It is the
Lord," he wrapped his outer garment
around him (for he had taken it off) and
jumped into the water. 8The other disciples followed in the boat, towing the net
full of fish, for they were not far from
shore, about a hundred yards.[c] 9When
they landed, they saw a fire of burning
coals there with fish on it, and some
bread.
10Jesus said to them, "Bring some of
the fish you have just caught."
11Simon Peter climbed aboard and
dragged the net ashore. It was full of large
fish, 153, but even with so many the net
was not torn. 12Jesus said to them, "Come
and have breakfast." None of the disciples dared ask him, "Who are you?" They
knew it was the Lord. 13Jesus came, took
the bread and gave it to them, and did the
same with the fish. 14This was now the
third time Jesus appeared to his disciples
after he was raised from the dead.

Jesus Reinstates Peter

15When they had finished eating, Jesus
said to Simon Peter, "Simon son of John,
do you truly love me more than these?"
"Yes, Lord," he said, "you know that I
love you."
Jesus said, "Feed my lambs."
16Again Jesus said, "Simon son of John,
do you truly love me?"
He answered, "Yes, Lord, you know
that I love you."
Jesus said, "Take care of my sheep."
17The third time he said to him, "Simon
son of John, do you love me?"
Peter was hurt because Jesus asked
him the third time, "Do you love me?" He
said, "Lord, you know all things; you
know that I love you."
Jesus said, "Feed my sheep. 18I tell you
the truth, when you were younger you
dressed yourself and went where you
wanted; but when you are old you will
stretch out your hands, and someone else

[a]31 Some manuscripts *may continue to* [b]1 That is, Sea of Galilee [c]8 Greek *about two hundred cubits* (about 90 meters)

will dress you and lead you where you do
not want to go." 19Jesus said this to indicate the kind of death by which Peter
would glorify God. Then he said to him,
"Follow me!"
20Peter turned and saw that the disciple whom Jesus loved was following
them. (This was the one who had leaned
back against Jesus at the supper and had
said, "Lord, who is going to betray you?")
21When Peter saw him, he asked, "Lord,
what about him?"
22Jesus answered, "If I want him to remain alive until I return, what is that to
you? You must follow me." 23Because of
this, the rumor spread among the brothers that this disciple would not die. But
Jesus did not say that he would not die;
he only said, "If I want him to remain
alive until I return, what is that to you?"
24This is the disciple who testifies to
these things and who wrote them down.
We know that his testimony is true.
25Jesus did many other things as well.
If every one of them were written down, I
suppose that even the whole world would
not have room for the books that would
be written.

LUKE begins the second volume of his history of Christianity (Acts 1:1–3) by telling how Jesus pours out the Holy Spirit on the apostles. The Spirit in turn inspires them to spread the message of salvation from Jerusalem to Rome. In his story Luke stresses how unity and love prevail in the church and how God protects the missionaries from their enemies. As you read this book, think about how powerful the Holy Spirit still is in the church and in your own life and how God protects you against the forces of evil.

ACTS

Jesus Taken Up Into Heaven

1 In my former book, Theophilus, I
wrote about all that Jesus began to do
and to teach 2until the day he was taken
up to heaven, after giving instructions
through the Holy Spirit to the apostles
he had chosen. 3After his suffering, he
showed himself to these men and gave
many convincing proofs that he was alive.
He appeared to them over a period of
forty days and spoke about the kingdom
of God. 4On one occasion, while he was
eating with them, he gave them this command:
"Do not leave Jerusalem, but wait
for the gift my Father promised, which
you have heard me speak about. 5For
John baptized with[a] water, but in a few
days you will be baptized with the Holy
Spirit."

6So when they met together, they asked
him, "Lord, are you at this time going to
restore the kingdom to Israel?"

7He said to them: "It is not for you to
know the times or dates the Father has

[a]5 Or *in*

set by his own authority. 8But you will
receive power when the Holy Spirit comes
on you; and you will be my witnesses in
Jerusalem, and in all Judea and Samaria,
and to the ends of the earth."
9After he said this, he was taken up
before their very eyes, and a cloud hid
him from their sight.
10They were looking intently up into
the sky as he was going, when suddenly
two men dressed in white stood beside
them. 11"Men of Galilee," they said, "why
do you stand here looking into the sky?
This same Jesus, who has been taken
from you into heaven, will come back in
the same way you have seen him go into
heaven."

Matthias Chosen to Replace Judas

12Then they returned to Jerusalem
from the hill called the Mount of Olives,
a Sabbath day's walk[a] from the city.

[a]*12* That is, about 3/4 mile (about 1,100 meters)

THURSDAY

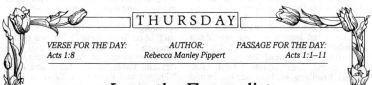

VERSE FOR THE DAY: *Acts 1:8*

AUTHOR: *Rebecca Manley Pippert*

PASSAGE FOR THE DAY: *Acts 1:1–11*

Jesus the Evangelist

JESUS told us that as the Father sent him into the world, so he is sending us (John 17:18; Acts 1:8). How then did the Father send him? Essentially he became one of us. "The Word became flesh" (John 1:14). God didn't send a telegram or shower evangelistic Bible study books from heaven or drop a million bumper stickers from the sky saying, "Smile, Jesus loves you." He sent a man, his Son, to communicate the message. His strategy hasn't changed. He still sends men and women—before he sends tracts and techniques—to change the world. You may think his strategy is risky, but that is God's problem, not yours.

In Jesus, then, we have our model for how to relate to the world, and it is a model of openness and identification. Jesus was a remarkably open man. He didn't think it was unspiritual for him (fully realizing he was the Son of God) to share his physical needs (John 4:7). He didn't fear losing his testimony by revealing to his disciples the depths of his emotional stress in the Garden of Gethsemane (Mark 14:32–52). Here is our model for genuine godliness. We see him asking for support and desiring others to minister to him. We must learn then to relate transparently and genuinely to others because that is God's style of relating to us. Jesus commands us to go and then preach, not to preach and then leave. We are not to shout the gospel from a safe and respectable distance, and remain detached. We must open our lives enough to let people see that we too laugh and hurt and cry. If Jesus left all of heaven and glory to become one of us, shouldn't we at least be willing to leave our dorm room or Bible study circle to reach out to a friend?

Additional Scripture Readings:
John 11:33–44; 1 Corinthians 2:1–5

Go to page 165 for your next devotional reading.

13When they arrived, they went upstairs
to the room where they were staying.
Those present were Peter, John, James
and Andrew; Philip and Thomas, Bartholomew and Matthew; James son of Alphaeus and Simon the Zealot, and Judas
son of James. 14They all joined together
constantly in prayer, along with the wom-
en and Mary the mother of Jesus, and
with his brothers.

15In those days Peter stood up among
the believers[a] (a group numbering about
a hundred and twenty) 16and said,
"Brothers, the Scripture had to be fulfilled which the Holy Spirit spoke long
ago through the mouth of David concerning Judas, who served as guide for those
who arrested Jesus— 17he was one of our
number and shared in this ministry."

18(With the reward he got for his
wickedness, Judas bought a field; there
he fell headlong, his body burst open and
all his intestines spilled out. 19Everyone
in Jerusalem heard about this, so they
called that field in their language Akel-
dama, that is, Field of Blood.)

20"For," said Peter, "it is written in the
book of Psalms,

" 'May his place be deserted;
  let there be no one to dwell in it,'[b]

and,

" 'May another take his place of
      leadership.'[c]

21Therefore it is necessary to choose one
of the men who have been with us the
whole time the Lord Jesus went in and
out among us, 22beginning from John's
baptism to the time when Jesus was tak-
en up from us. For one of these must
become a witness with us of his resurrection."

23So they proposed two men: Joseph
called Barsabbas (also known as Justus)
and Matthias. 24Then they prayed, "Lord,
you know everyone's heart. Show us
which of these two you have chosen 25to
take over this apostolic ministry, which
Judas left to go where he belongs."
26Then they cast lots, and the lot fell to
Matthias; so he was added to the eleven
apostles.

The Holy Spirit Comes at Pentecost

2 When the day of Pentecost came,
they were all together in one place.
2Suddenly a sound like the blowing of a
violent wind came from heaven and filled
the whole house where they were sitting.
3They saw what seemed to be tongues of
fire that separated and came to rest on
each of them. 4All of them were filled
with the Holy Spirit and began to speak
in other tongues[d] as the Spirit enabled
them.

5Now there were staying in Jerusalem
God-fearing Jews from every nation under
heaven. 6When they heard this sound, a
crowd came together in bewilderment,
because each one heard them speaking in
his own language. 7Utterly amazed, they
asked: "Are not all these men who are
speaking Galileans? 8Then how is it that
each of us hears them in his own native
language? 9Parthians, Medes and Ela-
mites; residents of Mesopotamia, Judea and Cappadocia, Pontus and Asia,
10Phrygia and Pamphylia, Egypt and the
parts of Libya near Cyrene; visitors from
Rome 11(both Jews and converts to Judaism); Cretans and Arabs—we hear them
declaring the wonders of God in our own
tongues!" 12Amazed and perplexed, they
asked one another, "What does this
mean?"

13Some, however, made fun of them
and said, "They have had too much
wine.[e]"

Peter Addresses the Crowd

14Then Peter stood up with the Eleven,
raised his voice and addressed the crowd:
"Fellow Jews and all of you who live in
Jerusalem, let me explain this to you; listen carefully to what I say. 15These men
are not drunk, as you suppose. It's only
nine in the morning! 16No, this is what
was spoken by the prophet Joel:

17" 'In the last days, God says,
  I will pour out my Spirit on all
      people.
Your sons and daughters will
      prophesy,
  your young men will see visions,
  your old men will dream dreams.
18Even on my servants, both men and
      women,
  I will pour out my Spirit in those
      days,
  and they will prophesy.
19I will show wonders in the heaven
      above

[a]15 Greek *brothers* [b]20 Psalm 69:25 [c]20 Psalm 109:8 [d]4 Or *languages*; also in verse 11
[e]13 Or *sweet wine*

and signs on the earth below,
blood and fire and billows of
smoke.
20The sun will be turned to darkness
and the moon to blood
before the coming of the great and
glorious day of the Lord.
21And everyone who calls
on the name of the Lord will be
saved.'[a]

22"Men of Israel, listen to this: Jesus of
Nazareth was a man accredited by God
to you by miracles, wonders and signs,
which God did among you through him,
as you yourselves know. 23This man was
handed over to you by God's set purpose
and foreknowledge; and you, with the
help of wicked men,[b] put him to death by
nailing him to the cross. 24But God raised
him from the dead, freeing him from the
agony of death, because it was impossible
for death to keep its hold on him. 25David
said about him:

" 'I saw the Lord always before me.
Because he is at my right hand,
I will not be shaken.
26Therefore my heart is glad and my
tongue rejoices;
my body also will live in hope,
27because you will not abandon me to
the grave,
nor will you let your Holy One see
decay.
28You have made known to me the
paths of life;
you will fill me with joy in your
presence.'[c]

29"Brothers, I can tell you confidently
that the patriarch David died and was buried, and his tomb is here to this day.
30But he was a prophet and knew that
God had promised him on oath that he
would place one of his descendants on
his throne. 31Seeing what was ahead, he
spoke of the resurrection of the Christ,[d]
that he was not abandoned to the grave,
nor did his body see decay. 32God has
raised this Jesus to life, and we are all
witnesses of the fact. 33Exalted to the
right hand of God, he has received from
the Father the promised Holy Spirit and
has poured out what you now see and
hear. 34For David did not ascend to heav-
en, and yet he said,

" 'The Lord said to my Lord:
"Sit at my right hand
35until I make your enemies
a footstool for your feet." '[e]

36"Therefore let all Israel be assured of
this: God has made this Jesus, whom you
crucified, both Lord and Christ."
37When the people heard this, they
were cut to the heart and said to Peter
and the other apostles, "Brothers, what
shall we do?"
38Peter replied, "Repent and be baptized, every one of you, in the name of
Jesus Christ for the forgiveness of your
sins. And you will receive the gift of the
Holy Spirit. 39The promise is for you and
your children and for all who are far off—
for all whom the Lord our God will call."
40With many other words he warned
them; and he pleaded with them, "Save
yourselves from this corrupt generation."
41Those who accepted his message were
baptized, and about three thousand were
added to their number that day.

The Fellowship of the Believers

42They devoted themselves to the apostles' teaching and to the fellowship, to
the breaking of bread and to prayer. 43Ev-
eryone was filled with awe, and many
wonders and miraculous signs were done
by the apostles. 44All the believers were
together and had everything in common.
45Selling their possessions and goods,
they gave to anyone as he had need. 46Ev-
ery day they continued to meet together
in the temple courts. They broke bread in
their homes and ate together with glad
and sincere hearts, 47praising God and
enjoying the favor of all the people. And
the Lord added to their number daily
those who were being saved.

Peter Heals the Crippled Beggar

3 One day Peter and John were going
up to the temple at the time of prayer
—at three in the afternoon. 2Now a man
crippled from birth was being carried to
the temple gate called Beautiful, where
he was put every day to beg from those
going into the temple courts. 3When he
saw Peter and John about to enter, he
asked them for money. 4Peter looked
straight at him, as did John. Then Peter
said, "Look at us!" 5So the man gave them

[a]*21* Joel 2:28-32 [b]*23* Or *of those not having the law* (that is, Gentiles) [c]*28* Psalm 16:8-11
[d]*31* Or *Messiah.* "The Christ" (Greek) and "the Messiah" (Hebrew) both mean "the Anointed One"; also in verse 36. [e]*35* Psalm 110:1

his attention, expecting to get something from them.

6Then Peter said, "Silver or gold I do not have, but what I have I give you. In the name of Jesus Christ of Nazareth, walk." 7Taking him by the right hand, he helped him up, and instantly the man's feet and ankles became strong. 8He jumped to his feet and began to walk. Then he went with them into the temple courts, walking and jumping, and praising God. 9When all the people saw him walking and praising God, 10they recognized him as the same man who used to sit begging at the temple gate called Beautiful, and they were filled with wonder and amazement at what had happened to him.

Peter Speaks to the Onlookers

11While the beggar held on to Peter and John, all the people were astonished and came running to them in the place called Solomon's Colonnade. 12When Peter saw this, he said to them: "Men of Israel, why does this surprise you? Why do you stare at us as if by our own power or godliness we had made this man walk? 13The God of Abraham, Isaac and Jacob, the God of our fathers, has glorified his servant Jesus. You handed him over to be killed, and you disowned him before Pilate, though he had decided to let him go. 14You disowned the Holy and Righteous One and asked that a murderer be released to you. 15You killed the author of life, but God raised him from the dead. We are witnesses of this. 16By faith in the name of Jesus, this man whom you see and know was made strong. It is Jesus' name and the faith that comes through him that has given this complete healing to him, as you can all see.

17"Now, brothers, I know that you acted in ignorance, as did your leaders. 18But this is how God fulfilled what he had foretold through all the prophets, saying that his Christ[a] would suffer. 19Repent, then, and turn to God, so that your sins may be wiped out, that times of refreshing may come from the Lord, 20and that he may send the Christ, who has been appointed for you—even Jesus. 21He must remain in heaven until the time comes for God to restore everything, as he promised long ago through his holy prophets. 22For Moses said, 'The Lord your God will raise up for you a prophet like me from among your own people; you must listen to everything he tells you. 23Anyone who does not listen to him will be completely cut off from among his people.'[b]

24"Indeed, all the prophets from Samuel on, as many as have spoken, have foretold these days. 25And you are heirs of the prophets and of the covenant God made with your fathers. He said to Abraham, 'Through your offspring all peoples on earth will be blessed.'[c] 26When God raised up his servant, he sent him first to you to bless you by turning each of you from your wicked ways."

Peter and John Before the Sanhedrin

4 The priests and the captain of the temple guard and the Sadducees came up to Peter and John while they were speaking to the people. 2They were greatly disturbed because the apostles were teaching the people and proclaiming in Jesus the resurrection of the dead. 3They seized Peter and John, and because it was evening, they put them in jail until the next day. 4But many who heard the message believed, and the number of men grew to about five thousand.

5The next day the rulers, elders and teachers of the law met in Jerusalem. 6Annas the high priest was there, and so were Caiaphas, John, Alexander and the other men of the high priest's family. 7They had Peter and John brought before them and began to question them: "By what power or what name did you do this?"

8Then Peter, filled with the Holy Spirit, said to them: "Rulers and elders of the people! 9If we are being called to account today for an act of kindness shown to a cripple and are asked how he was healed, 10then know this, you and all the people of Israel: It is by the name of Jesus Christ of Nazareth, whom you crucified but whom God raised from the dead, that this man stands before you healed. 11He is

" 'the stone you builders rejected,
which has become the capstone.'[d][e]

12Salvation is found in no one else, for there is no other name under heaven given to men by which we must be saved."

13When they saw the courage of Peter and John and realized that they were unschooled, ordinary men, they were astonished and they took note that these men

[a]18 Or *Messiah*; also in verse 20 [b]23 Deut. 18:15,18,19 [c]25 Gen. 22:18; 26:4 [d]11 Or *cornerstone* [e]11 Psalm 118:22

had been with Jesus. 14But since they
could see the man who had been healed
standing there with them, there was
nothing they could say. 15So they ordered
them to withdraw from the Sanhedrin
and then conferred together. 16"What are
we going to do with these men?" they
asked. "Everybody living in Jerusalem
knows they have done an outstanding
miracle, and we cannot deny it. 17But to
stop this thing from spreading any further
among the people, we must warn these
men to speak no longer to anyone in this
name."
18Then they called them in again and
commanded them not to speak or teach
at all in the name of Jesus. 19But Peter
and John replied, "Judge for yourselves
whether it is right in God's sight to obey
you rather than God. 20For we cannot
help speaking about what we have seen
and heard."
21After further threats they let them go.
They could not decide how to punish

FRIDAY

VERSE FOR THE DAY: Acts 4:32 | *AUTHOR:* Linda Ching Sledge | *PASSAGE FOR THE DAY:* Acts 4:23–35

No East or West

MY hometown church is on a winding street on the outskirts of old Honolulu. It was built in the 1880s by Boston missionaries who served the earliest Christian immigrants to Hawaii from Canton, China. After a century, the descendants of those first Cantonese Christians still worship there. It's a proud heritage. But for a youngster growing up in that church, it was sometimes confusing.

There were two sermons, one in English and one in Cantonese for the "old folks" who couldn't speak the language of their adopted homeland. As a child, I found the Chinese sermon long and boring. I could understand only a few words of Chinese so the words made no sense. Oh, how the long minutes dragged by!

Then one Sunday, at the closing hymn, I heard strange sounds from the pew behind me. It was an old Chinese grandfather singing at the top of his lungs . . . in Chinese!

It was so funny to hear two sets of words sung to the same tune at the same time. I couldn't resist peeking. The old man's head was thrown back, his eyes closed, and he was singing as if the words were pulled from his heart.

And suddenly, though I didn't know his words, I understood their meaning. And I began to sing too, straight from the heart:

In Christ there is no East or West,
In Him no South or North;
But one great fellowship of love
Throughout the whole wide earth.

Additional Scripture Readings:
Ephesians 2:12–20; Revelation 7:9–10

Go to page 167 for your next devotional reading.

them, because all the people were praising God for what had happened. 22For the man who was miraculously healed was over forty years old.

The Believers' Prayer

23On their release, Peter and John went back to their own people and reported all that the chief priests and elders had said to them. 24When they heard this, they raised their voices together in prayer to God. "Sovereign Lord," they said, "you made the heaven and the earth and the sea, and everything in them. 25You spoke by the Holy Spirit through the mouth of your servant, our father David:

" 'Why do the nations rage
  and the peoples plot in vain?
26The kings of the earth take their stand
  and the rulers gather together
against the Lord
  and against his Anointed One.[a] '[b]

27Indeed Herod and Pontius Pilate met together with the Gentiles and the people[c] of Israel in this city to conspire against your holy servant Jesus, whom you anointed. 28They did what your power and will had decided beforehand should happen. 29Now, Lord, consider their threats and enable your servants to speak your word with great boldness. 30Stretch out your hand to heal and perform miraculous signs and wonders through the name of your holy servant Jesus."

31After they prayed, the place where they were meeting was shaken. And they were all filled with the Holy Spirit and spoke the word of God boldly.

The Believers Share Their Possessions

32All the believers were one in heart and mind. No one claimed that any of his possessions was his own, but they shared everything they had. 33With great power the apostles continued to testify to the resurrection of the Lord Jesus, and much grace was upon them all. 34There were no needy persons among them. For from time to time those who owned lands or houses sold them, brought the money from the sales 35and put it at the apostles' feet, and it was distributed to anyone as he had need.

36Joseph, a Levite from Cyprus, whom the apostles called Barnabas (which means Son of Encouragement), 37sold a field he owned and brought the money and put it at the apostles' feet.

Ananias and Sapphira

5 Now a man named Ananias, together with his wife Sapphira, also sold a piece of property. 2With his wife's full knowledge he kept back part of the money for himself, but brought the rest and put it at the apostles' feet.

3Then Peter said, "Ananias, how is it that Satan has so filled your heart that you have lied to the Holy Spirit and have kept for yourself some of the money you received for the land? 4Didn't it belong to you before it was sold? And after it was sold, wasn't the money at your disposal? What made you think of doing such a thing? You have not lied to men but to God."

5When Ananias heard this, he fell down and died. And great fear seized all who heard what had happened. 6Then the young men came forward, wrapped up his body, and carried him out and buried him.

7About three hours later his wife came in, not knowing what had happened. 8Peter asked her, "Tell me, is this the price you and Ananias got for the land?"

"Yes," she said, "that is the price."

9Peter said to her, "How could you agree to test the Spirit of the Lord? Look! The feet of the men who buried your husband are at the door, and they will carry you out also."

10At that moment she fell down at his feet and died. Then the young men came in and, finding her dead, carried her out and buried her beside her husband. 11Great fear seized the whole church and all who heard about these events.

The Apostles Heal Many

12The apostles performed many miraculous signs and wonders among the people. And all the believers used to meet together in Solomon's Colonnade. 13No one else dared join them, even though they were highly regarded by the people. 14Nevertheless, more and more men and women believed in the Lord and were added to their number. 15As a result, people brought the sick into the streets and laid them on beds and mats so that at least Peter's shadow might fall on some of them as he passed by. 16Crowds gathered

[a]26 That is, Christ or Messiah [b]26 Psalm 2:1,2 [c]27 The Greek is plural.

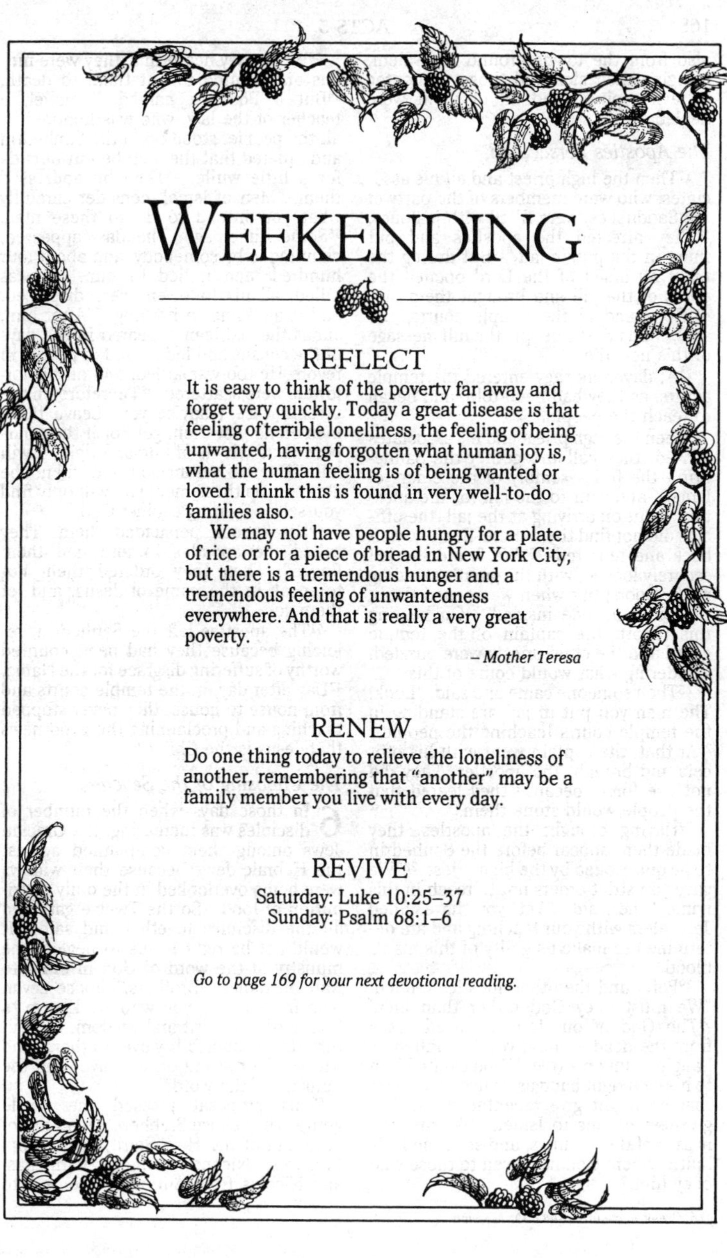

WEEKENDING

REFLECT

It is easy to think of the poverty far away and forget very quickly. Today a great disease is that feeling of terrible loneliness, the feeling of being unwanted, having forgotten what human joy is, what the human feeling is of being wanted or loved. I think this is found in very well-to-do families also.

We may not have people hungry for a plate of rice or for a piece of bread in New York City, but there is a tremendous hunger and a tremendous feeling of unwantedness everywhere. And that is really a very great poverty.

– Mother Teresa

RENEW

Do one thing today to relieve the loneliness of another, remembering that "another" may be a family member you live with every day.

REVIVE

Saturday: Luke 10:25–37
Sunday: Psalm 68:1–6

Go to page 169 for your next devotional reading.

also from the towns around Jerusalem, bringing their sick and those tormented by evil[a] spirits, and all of them were healed.

The Apostles Persecuted

17Then the high priest and all his associates, who were members of the party of the Sadducees, were filled with jealousy. 18They arrested the apostles and put them in the public jail. 19But during the night an angel of the Lord opened the doors of the jail and brought them out. 20"Go, stand in the temple courts," he said, "and tell the people the full message of this new life."

21At daybreak they entered the temple courts, as they had been told, and began to teach the people.

When the high priest and his associates arrived, they called together the Sanhedrin—the full assembly of the elders of Israel—and sent to the jail for the apostles. 22But on arriving at the jail, the officers did not find them there. So they went back and reported, 23"We found the jail securely locked, with the guards standing at the doors; but when we opened them, we found no one inside." 24On hearing this report, the captain of the temple guard and the chief priests were puzzled, wondering what would come of this.

25Then someone came and said, "Look! The men you put in jail are standing in the temple courts teaching the people." 26At that, the captain went with his officers and brought the apostles. They did not use force, because they feared that the people would stone them.

27Having brought the apostles, they made them appear before the Sanhedrin to be questioned by the high priest. 28"We gave you strict orders not to teach in this name," he said. "Yet you have filled Jerusalem with your teaching and are determined to make us guilty of this man's blood."

29Peter and the other apostles replied: "We must obey God rather than men! 30The God of our fathers raised Jesus from the dead—whom you had killed by hanging him on a tree. 31God exalted him to his own right hand as Prince and Savior that he might give repentance and forgiveness of sins to Israel. 32We are witnesses of these things, and so is the Holy Spirit, whom God has given to those who obey him."

33When they heard this, they were furious and wanted to put them to death. 34But a Pharisee named Gamaliel, a teacher of the law, who was honored by all the people, stood up in the Sanhedrin and ordered that the men be put outside for a little while. 35Then he addressed them: "Men of Israel, consider carefully what you intend to do to these men. 36Some time ago Theudas appeared, claiming to be somebody, and about four hundred men rallied to him. He was killed, all his followers were dispersed, and it all came to nothing. 37After him, Judas the Galilean appeared in the days of the census and led a band of people in revolt. He too was killed, and all his followers were scattered. 38Therefore, in the present case I advise you: Leave these men alone! Let them go! For if their purpose or activity is of human origin, it will fail. 39But if it is from God, you will not be able to stop these men; you will only find yourselves fighting against God."

40His speech persuaded them. They called the apostles in and had them flogged. Then they ordered them not to speak in the name of Jesus, and let them go.

41The apostles left the Sanhedrin, rejoicing because they had been counted worthy of suffering disgrace for the Name. 42Day after day, in the temple courts and from house to house, they never stopped teaching and proclaiming the good news that Jesus is the Christ.[b]

The Choosing of the Seven

6 In those days when the number of disciples was increasing, the Grecian Jews among them complained against the Hebraic Jews because their widows were being overlooked in the daily distribution of food. 2So the Twelve gathered all the disciples together and said, "It would not be right for us to neglect the ministry of the word of God in order to wait on tables. 3Brothers, choose seven men from among you who are known to be full of the Spirit and wisdom. We will turn this responsibility over to them 4and will give our attention to prayer and the ministry of the word."

5This proposal pleased the whole group. They chose Stephen, a man full of faith and of the Holy Spirit; also Philip, Procorus, Nicanor, Timon, Parmenas, and Nicolas from Antioch, a convert to

[a]16 Greek *unclean* [b]42 Or *Messiah*

MONDAY

VERSE FOR THE DAY: *Acts 5:9*

AUTHOR: *June Gunden*

PASSAGE FOR THE DAY: *Acts 5:1–11*

Giving to Receive Praise

GIVING generously to the needy is one sure way of impressing other Christians. If it becomes known that a certain family has given a lot of money or service to the church, other people respect and admire them for it.

This must have been especially true in a day when "from time to time those who owned lands or houses sold them, brought the money from the sales and put it at the apostles' feet, and it was distributed to anyone as he had need" (Acts 4:34–35). When someone sold property it would have been common knowledge what it was worth, and therefore other people would know how much had been given to the apostles.

In light of such widespread generosity, people of that day may have felt a little chagrined for it to be known that they had sold some property but had not shared the profits. Their "spiritual" reputation may have become tarnished, and they may never have been as highly thought of as those who were willing to give it all.

Accordingly, Ananias and Sapphira probably convinced themselves that by keeping some of the money for themselves they wouldn't be hurting anyone else (and they wouldn't be hurting their own reputation either). They opted to let others think they had given more than they really had. This hypocrisy, and the love of money and praise that motivated it, cost them their lives.

Jesus taught very clearly that giving to the needy must not be done for praise (Matthew 6:1–4). "When you give to the needy," he said, give "in secret" and "your Father . . . will reward you."

What if no one ever finds out that I've made a large contribution to the church? Does it matter? What if no one notices the hours I've spent helping someone else? Do I care? What if my efforts for the kingdom are largely unappreciated? Do I become discouraged?

If I am happy to serve when no one is there to give me credit, I am truly working for the Lord.

Additional Scripture Readings:
Matthew 23:5–12; Ephesians 6:7–8

Go to page 174 for your next devotional reading.

Judaism. 6They presented these men to the apostles, who prayed and laid their hands on them.

7So the word of God spread. The number of disciples in Jerusalem increased rapidly, and a large number of priests became obedient to the faith.

Stephen Seized

8Now Stephen, a man full of God's grace and power, did great wonders and miraculous signs among the people. 9Opposition arose, however, from members of the Synagogue of the Freedmen (as it was called)—Jews of Cyrene and Alexandria as well as the provinces of Cilicia and Asia. These men began to argue with Stephen, 10but they could not stand up against his wisdom or the Spirit by whom he spoke.

11Then they secretly persuaded some men to say, "We have heard Stephen speak words of blasphemy against Moses and against God."

12So they stirred up the people and the elders and the teachers of the law. They seized Stephen and brought him before the Sanhedrin. 13They produced false witnesses, who testified, "This fellow never stops speaking against this holy place and against the law. 14For we have heard him say that this Jesus of Nazareth will destroy this place and change the customs Moses handed down to us."

15All who were sitting in the Sanhedrin looked intently at Stephen, and they saw that his face was like the face of an angel.

Stephen's Speech to the Sanhedrin

7 Then the high priest asked him, "Are these charges true?"

2To this he replied: "Brothers and fathers, listen to me! The God of glory appeared to our father Abraham while he was still in Mesopotamia, before he lived in Haran. 3'Leave your country and your people,' God said, 'and go to the land I will show you.'[a]

4"So he left the land of the Chaldeans and settled in Haran. After the death of his father, God sent him to this land where you are now living. 5He gave him no inheritance here, not even a foot of ground. But God promised him that he and his descendants after him would possess the land, even though at that time Abraham had no child. 6God spoke to him in this way: 'Your descendants will be strangers in a country not their own, and they will be enslaved and mistreated four hundred years. 7But I will punish the nation they serve as slaves,' God said, 'and afterward they will come out of that country and worship me in this place.'[b] 8Then he gave Abraham the covenant of circumcision. And Abraham became the father of Isaac and circumcised him eight days after his birth. Later Isaac became the father of Jacob, and Jacob became the father of the twelve patriarchs.

9"Because the patriarchs were jealous of Joseph, they sold him as a slave into Egypt. But God was with him 10and rescued him from all his troubles. He gave Joseph wisdom and enabled him to gain the goodwill of Pharaoh king of Egypt; so he made him ruler over Egypt and all his palace.

11"Then a famine struck all Egypt and Canaan, bringing great suffering, and our fathers could not find food. 12When Jacob heard that there was grain in Egypt, he sent our fathers on their first visit. 13On their second visit, Joseph told his brothers who he was, and Pharaoh learned about Joseph's family. 14After this, Joseph sent for his father Jacob and his whole family, seventy-five in all. 15Then Jacob went down to Egypt, where he and our fathers died. 16Their bodies were brought back to Shechem and placed in the tomb that Abraham had bought from the sons of Hamor at Shechem for a certain sum of money.

17"As the time drew near for God to fulfill his promise to Abraham, the number of our people in Egypt greatly increased. 18Then another king, who knew nothing about Joseph, became ruler of Egypt. 19He dealt treacherously with our people and oppressed our forefathers by forcing them to throw out their newborn babies so that they would die.

20"At that time Moses was born, and he was no ordinary child.[c] For three months he was cared for in his father's house. 21When he was placed outside, Pharaoh's daughter took him and brought him up as her own son. 22Moses was educated in all the wisdom of the Egyptians and was powerful in speech and action.

23"When Moses was forty years old, he decided to visit his fellow Israelites. 24He saw one of them being mistreated by an Egyptian, so he went to his defense and avenged him by killing the Egyptian.

[a]3 Gen. 12:1 [b]7 Gen. 15:13,14 [c]20 Or *was fair in the sight of God*

25Moses thought that his own people
would realize that God was using him to
rescue them, but they did not. 26The next
day Moses came upon two Israelites who
were fighting. He tried to reconcile them
by saying, 'Men, you are brothers; why do
you want to hurt each other?'

27"But the man who was mistreating
the other pushed Moses aside and said,
'Who made you ruler and judge over us?
28Do you want to kill me as you killed the
Egyptian yesterday?'[a] 29When Moses
heard this, he fled to Midian, where he
settled as a foreigner and had two sons.

30"After forty years had passed, an angel appeared to Moses in the flames of a
burning bush in the desert near Mount
Sinai. 31When he saw this, he was amazed
at the sight. As he went over to look more
closely, he heard the Lord's voice: 32'I am
the God of your fathers, the God of
Abraham, Isaac and Jacob.'[b] Moses
trembled with fear and did not dare to
look.

33"Then the Lord said to him, 'Take off
your sandals; the place where you are
standing is holy ground. 34I have indeed
seen the oppression of my people in
Egypt. I have heard their groaning and
have come down to set them free. Now
come, I will send you back to Egypt.'[c]

35"This is the same Moses whom they
had rejected with the words, 'Who made
you ruler and judge?' He was sent to be
their ruler and deliverer by God himself,
through the angel who appeared to him in
the bush. 36He led them out of Egypt and
did wonders and miraculous signs in
Egypt, at the Red Sea[d] and for forty years
in the desert.

37"This is that Moses who told the Israelites, 'God will send you a prophet like
me from your own people.'[e] 38He was in
the assembly in the desert, with the angel
who spoke to him on Mount Sinai, and
with our fathers; and he received living
words to pass on to us.

39"But our fathers refused to obey him.
Instead, they rejected him and in their
hearts turned back to Egypt. 40They told
Aaron, 'Make us gods who will go before
us. As for this fellow Moses who led us
out of Egypt—we don't know what has
happened to him!'[f] 41That was the time
they made an idol in the form of a calf.
They brought sacrifices to it and held a
celebration in honor of what their hands
had made. 42But God turned away and
gave them over to the worship of the
heavenly bodies. This agrees with what is
written in the book of the prophets:

" 'Did you bring me sacrifices and
offerings
forty years in the desert, O house of
Israel?
43You have lifted up the shrine of
Molech
and the star of your god Rephan,
the idols you made to worship.
Therefore I will send you into exile'[g]
beyond Babylon.

44"Our forefathers had the tabernacle
of the Testimony with them in the desert.
It had been made as God directed Moses,
according to the pattern he had seen.
45Having received the tabernacle, our fathers under Joshua brought it with them
when they took the land from the nations
God drove out before them. It remained
in the land until the time of David, 46who
enjoyed God's favor and asked that he
might provide a dwelling place for the
God of Jacob.[h] 47But it was Solomon who
built the house for him.

48"However, the Most High does not
live in houses made by men. As the prophet says:

49" 'Heaven is my throne,
and the earth is my footstool.
What kind of house will you build for
me?
says the Lord.
Or where will my resting place be?
50Has not my hand made all these
things?'[i]

51"You stiff-necked people, with uncircumcised hearts and ears! You are just
like your fathers: You always resist the
Holy Spirit! 52Was there ever a prophet
your fathers did not persecute? They even
killed those who predicted the coming of
the Righteous One. And now you have betrayed and murdered him— 53you who
have received the law that was put into
effect through angels but have not obeyed
it."

The Stoning of Stephen

54When they heard this, they were furious and gnashed their teeth at him. 55But

[a]28 Exodus 2:14 [b]32 Exodus 3:6 [c]34 Exodus 3:5,7,8,10 [d]36 That is, Sea of Reeds [e]37 Deut. 18:15 [f]40 Exodus 32:1 [g]43 Amos 5:25-27 [h]46 Some early manuscripts *the house of Jacob* [i]50 Isaiah 66:1,2

Stephen, full of the Holy Spirit, looked up
to heaven and saw the glory of God, and
Jesus standing at the right hand of God.
56“Look,” he said, “I see heaven open and
the Son of Man standing at the right hand
of God.”

57At this they covered their ears and,
yelling at the top of their voices, they all
rushed at him, 58dragged him out of the
city and began to stone him. Meanwhile,
the witnesses laid their clothes at the feet
of a young man named Saul.

59While they were stoning him, Stephen prayed, “Lord Jesus, receive my
spirit.” 60Then he fell on his knees and
cried out, “Lord, do not hold this sin
against them.” When he had said this, he
fell asleep.

8 And Saul was there, giving approval
to his death.

The Church Persecuted and Scattered

On that day a great persecution broke
out against the church at Jerusalem, and
all except the apostles were scattered
throughout Judea and Samaria. 2Godly
men buried Stephen and mourned deeply
for him. 3But Saul began to destroy the
church. Going from house to house, he
dragged off men and women and put
them in prison.

Philip in Samaria

4Those who had been scattered
preached the word wherever they went.
5Philip went down to a city in Samaria
and proclaimed the Christ[a] there. 6When
the crowds heard Philip and saw the
miraculous signs he did, they all paid
close attention to what he said. 7With
shrieks, evil[b] spirits came out of many,
and many paralytics and cripples were
healed. 8So there was great joy in that
city.

Simon the Sorcerer

9Now for some time a man named Simon had practiced sorcery in the city and
amazed all the people of Samaria. He
boasted that he was someone great, 10and
all the people, both high and low, gave
him their attention and exclaimed, “This
man is the divine power known as the
Great Power.” 11They followed him because he had amazed them for a long
time with his magic. 12But when they believed Philip as he preached the good
news of the kingdom of God and the
name of Jesus Christ, they were baptized,
both men and women. 13Simon himself
believed and was baptized. And he followed Philip everywhere, astonished by
the great signs and miracles he saw.

14When the apostles in Jerusalem
heard that Samaria had accepted the
word of God, they sent Peter and John to
them. 15When they arrived, they prayed
for them that they might receive the Holy
Spirit, 16because the Holy Spirit had not
yet come upon any of them; they had simply been baptized into[c] the name of the
Lord Jesus. 17Then Peter and John placed
their hands on them, and they received
the Holy Spirit.

18When Simon saw that the Spirit was
given at the laying on of the apostles'
hands, he offered them money 19and said,
“Give me also this ability so that everyone
on whom I lay my hands may receive the
Holy Spirit.”

20Peter answered: “May your money
perish with you, because you thought you
could buy the gift of God with money!
21You have no part or share in this ministry, because your heart is not right before
God. 22Repent of this wickedness and
pray to the Lord. Perhaps he will forgive
you for having such a thought in your
heart. 23For I see that you are full of bitterness and captive to sin.”

24Then Simon answered, “Pray to the
Lord for me so that nothing you have said
may happen to me.”

25When they had testified and proclaimed the word of the Lord, Peter and
John returned to Jerusalem, preaching
the gospel in many Samaritan villages.

Philip and the Ethiopian

26Now an angel of the Lord said to Philip, “Go south to the road—the desert
road—that goes down from Jerusalem to
Gaza.” 27So he started out, and on his way
he met an Ethiopian[d] eunuch, an important official in charge of all the treasury of
Candace, queen of the Ethiopians. This
man had gone to Jerusalem to worship,
28and on his way home was sitting in his
chariot reading the book of Isaiah the
prophet. 29The Spirit told Philip, “Go to
that chariot and stay near it.”

30Then Philip ran up to the chariot and
heard the man reading Isaiah the pro-

[a]5 Or *Messiah* [b]7 Greek *unclean* [c]16 Or *in* [d]27 That is, from the upper Nile region

phet. “Do you understand what you are
reading?” Philip asked.

31“How can I,” he said, “unless someone explains it to me?” So he invited Philip to come up and sit with him.

32The eunuch was reading this passage
of Scripture:

“He was led like a sheep to the
slaughter,
and as a lamb before the shearer is
silent,
so he did not open his mouth.
33In his humiliation he was deprived of
justice.
Who can speak of his descendants?
For his life was taken from the
earth.”[a]

34The eunuch asked Philip, “Tell me,
please, who is the prophet talking about,
himself or someone else?” 35Then Philip
began with that very passage of Scripture
and told him the good news about Jesus.

36As they traveled along the road, they
came to some water and the eunuch said,
“Look, here is water. Why shouldn't I be
baptized?”[b] 38And he gave orders to stop
the chariot. Then both Philip and the eunuch went down into the water and Philip
baptized him. 39When they came up out
of the water, the Spirit of the Lord suddenly took Philip away, and the eunuch
did not see him again, but went on his
way rejoicing. 40Philip, however, appeared at Azotus and traveled about,
preaching the gospel in all the towns until he reached Caesarea.

Saul's Conversion

9 Meanwhile, Saul was still breathing
out murderous threats against the
Lord's disciples. He went to the high
priest 2and asked him for letters to the
synagogues in Damascus, so that if he
found any there who belonged to the
Way, whether men or women, he might
take them as prisoners to Jerusalem. 3As
he neared Damascus on his journey, suddenly a light from heaven flashed around
him. 4He fell to the ground and heard a
voice say to him, “Saul, Saul, why do you
persecute me?”

5“Who are you, Lord?” Saul asked.

“I am Jesus, whom you are persecuting,” he replied. 6“Now get up and go into
the city, and you will be told what you
must do.”

7The men traveling with Saul stood
there speechless; they heard the sound
but did not see anyone. 8Saul got up from
the ground, but when he opened his eyes
he could see nothing. So they led him by
the hand into Damascus. 9For three days
he was blind, and did not eat or drink
anything.

10In Damascus there was a disciple
named Ananias. The Lord called to him
in a vision, “Ananias!”

“Yes, Lord,” he answered.

11The Lord told him, “Go to the house
of Judas on Straight Street and ask for a
man from Tarsus named Saul, for he is
praying. 12In a vision he has seen a man
named Ananias come and place his hands
on him to restore his sight.”

13“Lord,” Ananias answered, “I have
heard many reports about this man and
all the harm he has done to your saints in
Jerusalem. 14And he has come here with
authority from the chief priests to arrest
all who call on your name.”

15But the Lord said to Ananias, “Go!
This man is my chosen instrument to carry my name before the Gentiles and their
kings and before the people of Israel. 16I
will show him how much he must suffer
for my name.”

17Then Ananias went to the house and
entered it. Placing his hands on Saul, he
said, “Brother Saul, the Lord—Jesus,
who appeared to you on the road as you
were coming here—has sent me so that
you may see again and be filled with the
Holy Spirit.” 18Immediately, something
like scales fell from Saul's eyes, and he
could see again. He got up and was baptized, 19and after taking some food, he re-
gained his strength.

Saul in Damascus and Jerusalem

Saul spent several days with the disciples in Damascus. 20At once he began to
preach in the synagogues that Jesus is the
Son of God. 21All those who heard him
were astonished and asked, “Isn't he the
man who raised havoc in Jerusalem
among those who call on this name? And
hasn't he come here to take them as prisoners to the chief priests?” 22Yet Saul
grew more and more powerful and baffled
the Jews living in Damascus by proving
that Jesus is the Christ.[c]

23After many days had gone by, the
Jews conspired to kill him, 24but Saul

[a]33 Isaiah 53:7,8 [b]36 Some late manuscripts *baptized?” 37Philip said, “If you believe with all your heart, you may.” The eunuch answered, “I believe that Jesus Christ is the Son of God.”* [c]22 Or *Messiah*

TUESDAY

VERSE FOR THE DAY: *Acts 9:3–4*

AUTHOR: *Jean Syswerda*

PASSAGE FOR THE DAY: *Acts 9:1–19*

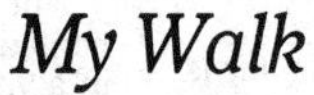

My Walk

SAUL was about as opposed to Christ and Christianity as one could get. He stood at Stephen's stoning, "giving approval to his death" (Acts 8:1). He was the one who was "breathing out murderous threats against the Lord's disciples" (Acts 9:1). Doesn't sound like someone I'd like to know on a personal basis.

Then, Christ appeared to Saul. A flashy conversion experience, with Christ speaking from the heaven to which he had returned. And Saul became Paul, the most effective Christian missionary the world has ever known.

It's hard for me to relate to that sort of experience. You see, I can't recall a time when I didn't love the Lord and want to serve him. I don't say that to sound pious or self-righteous . . . it's just the truth. I rebelled as a teenager against parental strictures and traditional structures, but I never rebelled against God.

There have been times when I thought I was lacking something because I had no dazzling experience to relate. But over the years I've come to realize the value of my quiet sort of experience.

And even though there haven't been blinding visions or bright lights, there have been times of definite comfort and guidance from God. Like when he spoke to me from Isaiah as a teenager, reassuring me that I wasn't a nobody:

> Fear not, for I have redeemed you;
> I have summoned you by name; you are mine
> (Isaiah 43:1).

Or when, as a young single adult, he promised to always stay with the project of making me all I should be in him: "Being confident of this, that he who began a good work in you will carry it on to completion until the day of Christ Jesus" (Philippians 1:6).

Your walk with God may not resemble Saul's (or Connie's or Mary's or Cheryl's), but it's *your* walk with a God who loves you and relates to you where you are.

Additional Scripture Readings:
Romans 8:30–39; 2 Peter 1:3–11

Go to page 177 for your next devotional reading.

learned of their plan. Day and night they
kept close watch on the city gates in order
to kill him. 25But his followers took him
by night and lowered him in a basket
through an opening in the wall.

26When he came to Jerusalem, he tried
to join the disciples, but they were all
afraid of him, not believing that he really
was a disciple. 27But Barnabas took him
and brought him to the apostles. He told
them how Saul on his journey had seen
the Lord and that the Lord had spoken to
him, and how in Damascus he had
preached fearlessly in the name of Jesus.
28So Saul stayed with them and moved
about freely in Jerusalem, speaking boldly in the name of the Lord. 29He talked
and debated with the Grecian Jews, but
they tried to kill him. 30When the brothers learned of this, they took him down to
Caesarea and sent him off to Tarsus.

31Then the church throughout Judea,
Galilee and Samaria enjoyed a time of
peace. It was strengthened; and encouraged by the Holy Spirit, it grew in
numbers, living in the fear of the Lord.

Aeneas and Dorcas

32As Peter traveled about the country,
he went to visit the saints in Lydda.
33There he found a man named Aeneas, a
paralytic who had been bedridden for
eight years. 34"Aeneas," Peter said to him,
"Jesus Christ heals you. Get up and take
care of your mat." Immediately Aeneas
got up. 35All those who lived in Lydda and
Sharon saw him and turned to the Lord.

36In Joppa there was a disciple named
Tabitha (which, when translated, is Dorcas[a]), who was always doing good and
helping the poor. 37About that time she
became sick and died, and her body was
washed and placed in an upstairs room.
38Lydda was near Joppa; so when the disciples heard that Peter was in Lydda, they
sent two men to him and urged him,
"Please come at once!"

39Peter went with them, and when he
arrived he was taken upstairs to the room.
All the widows stood around him, crying
and showing him the robes and other
clothing that Dorcas had made while she
was still with them.

40Peter sent them all out of the room;
then he got down on his knees and
prayed. Turning toward the dead woman,
he said, "Tabitha, get up." She opened
her eyes, and seeing Peter she sat up.
41He took her by the hand and helped her
to her feet. Then he called the believers
and the widows and presented her to
them alive. 42This became known all over
Joppa, and many people believed in the
Lord. 43Peter stayed in Joppa for some
time with a tanner named Simon.

Cornelius Calls for Peter

10 At Caesarea there was a man
named Cornelius, a centurion in
what was known as the Italian Regiment.
2He and all his family were devout and
God-fearing; he gave generously to those
in need and prayed to God regularly. 3One
day at about three in the afternoon he
had a vision. He distinctly saw an angel
of God, who came to him and said, "Cornelius!"

4Cornelius stared at him in fear. "What
is it, Lord?" he asked.

The angel answered, "Your prayers and
gifts to the poor have come up as a
memorial offering before God. 5Now send
men to Joppa to bring back a man named
Simon who is called Peter. 6He is staying
with Simon the tanner, whose house is by
the sea."

7When the angel who spoke to him had
gone, Cornelius called two of his servants
and a devout soldier who was one of his
attendants. 8He told them everything that
had happened and sent them to Joppa.

Peter's Vision

9About noon the following day as they
were on their journey and approaching
the city, Peter went up on the roof to pray.
10He became hungry and wanted something to eat, and while the meal was being prepared, he fell into a trance. 11He
saw heaven opened and something like a
large sheet being let down to earth by its
four corners. 12It contained all kinds of
four-footed animals, as well as reptiles of
the earth and birds of the air. 13Then a
voice told him, "Get up, Peter. Kill and
eat."

14"Surely not, Lord!" Peter replied. "I
have never eaten anything impure or unclean."

15The voice spoke to him a second
time, "Do not call anything impure that
God has made clean."

16This happened three times, and immediately the sheet was taken back to
heaven.

17While Peter was wondering about the

[a]36 Both *Tabitha* (Aramaic) and *Dorcas* (Greek) mean *gazelle*.

meaning of the vision, the men sent by
Cornelius found out where Simon's house
was and stopped at the gate. 18They
called out, asking if Simon who was
known as Peter was staying there.

19While Peter was still thinking about
the vision, the Spirit said to him, "Simon,
three[a] men are looking for you. 20So get
up and go downstairs. Do not hesitate to
go with them, for I have sent them."

21Peter went down and said to the men,
"I'm the one you're looking for. Why have
you come?"

22The men replied, "We have come
from Cornelius the centurion. He is a
righteous and God-fearing man, who is
respected by all the Jewish people. A holy
angel told him to have you come to his
house so that he could hear what you
have to say." 23Then Peter invited the
men into the house to be his guests.

Peter at Cornelius' House

The next day Peter started out with
them, and some of the brothers from Joppa went along. 24The following day he arrived in Caesarea. Cornelius was expecting them and had called together his relatives and close friends. 25As Peter entered
the house, Cornelius met him and fell at
his feet in reverence. 26But Peter made
him get up. "Stand up," he said, "I am
only a man myself."

27Talking with him, Peter went inside
and found a large gathering of people.
28He said to them: "You are well aware
that it is against our law for a Jew to associate with a Gentile or visit him. But
God has shown me that I should not call
any man impure or unclean. 29So when I
was sent for, I came without raising any
objection. May I ask why you sent for
me?"

30Cornelius answered: "Four days ago I
was in my house praying at this hour, at
three in the afternoon. Suddenly a man in
shining clothes stood before me 31and
said, 'Cornelius, God has heard your prayer and remembered your gifts to the poor.
32Send to Joppa for Simon who is called
Peter. He is a guest in the home of Simon
the tanner, who lives by the sea.' 33So I
sent for you immediately, and it was good
of you to come. Now we are all here in the
presence of God to listen to everything
the Lord has commanded you to tell us."

34Then Peter began to speak: "I now
realize how true it is that God does not
show favoritism 35but accepts men from
every nation who fear him and do what is
right. 36You know the message God sent
to the people of Israel, telling the good
news of peace through Jesus Christ, who
is Lord of all. 37You know what has happened throughout Judea, beginning in
Galilee after the baptism that John
preached— 38how God anointed Jesus of
Nazareth with the Holy Spirit and power,
and how he went around doing good and
healing all who were under the power of
the devil, because God was with him.

39"We are witnesses of everything he
did in the country of the Jews and in
Jerusalem. They killed him by hanging
him on a tree, 40but God raised him from
the dead on the third day and caused him
to be seen. 41He was not seen by all the
people, but by witnesses whom God had
already chosen—by us who ate and drank
with him after he rose from the dead.
42He commanded us to preach to the people and to testify that he is the one whom
God appointed as judge of the living and
the dead. 43All the prophets testify about
him that everyone who believes in him
receives forgiveness of sins through his
name."

44While Peter was still speaking these
words, the Holy Spirit came on all who
heard the message. 45The circumcised believers who had come with Peter were astonished that the gift of the Holy Spirit
had been poured out even on the Gentiles. 46For they heard them speaking in
tongues[b] and praising God.

Then Peter said, 47"Can anyone keep
these people from being baptized with
water? They have received the Holy Spirit
just as we have." 48So he ordered that
they be baptized in the name of Jesus
Christ. Then they asked Peter to stay with
them for a few days.

Peter Explains His Actions

11 The apostles and the brothers
throughout Judea heard that the
Gentiles also had received the word of
God. 2So when Peter went up to Jerusalem, the circumcised believers criticized
him 3and said, "You went into the house
of uncircumcised men and ate with
them."

4Peter began and explained everything
to them precisely as it had happened: 5"I
was in the city of Joppa praying, and in a
trance I saw a vision. I saw something like

[a]*19* One early manuscript *two*; other manuscripts do not have the number. [b]*46* Or *other languages*

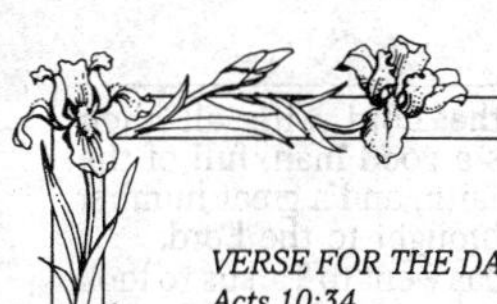

VERSE FOR THE DAY:
Acts 10:34

AUTHOR:
Mary Beckwith

PASSAGE FOR THE DAY:
Acts 10:34–38

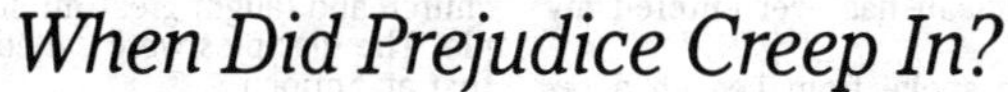

When Did Prejudice Creep In?

"IT must be a gentlemanbug," I thought I heard my little boy say.

"What did you say?" I asked him.

He said it again. "It must be a gentlemanbug."

Rob, then Robbie, gently pushed the ladybug onto his pudgy little hand. He had been playing with it for at least ten minutes. I was impressed that, at four years old, he knew the opposite for lady was gentleman and was able to label his new little friend accordingly.

But then I asked, "Why do you think it's a gentlemanbug?"

"Because he's smart!" was his ready reply.

Needless to say, I was in shock for a moment. Where had he gotten the idea that, in order to be smart, you had to be a man? And at the age of four, at that!

I quickly tried to recall if, in the last few days, I had said something that would have implied men were smarter than women. I couldn't remember anything. Maybe his father had made that implication somehow. I'd have to ask him.

I do recall at times when the kids asked me questions I didn't have the answers to I'd say, "We'll ask Daddy when he gets home." Maybe I'd done it enough to give the impression that dads are smarter than moms.

Anyway, this little episode made me question, How do prejudice and bias enter our lives? What causes us to judge others because of gender or color or whatever? It also taught me that when we show partiality and prejudice, we are setting examples for our children.

I am so thankful we have a heavenly Father who is no respecter of persons. He loves each one of us the same. And he desires that we in turn love one another with the same kind of love.

When I'm reminded of his unconditional, steadfast love, it helps me fight against the prejudice that tries to creep in, distort my conception of others, and tempts me to look at myself more highly than I should.

Additional Scripture Readings:
Romans 12:3–5; Galatians 3:26–28

Go to page 182 for your next devotional reading.

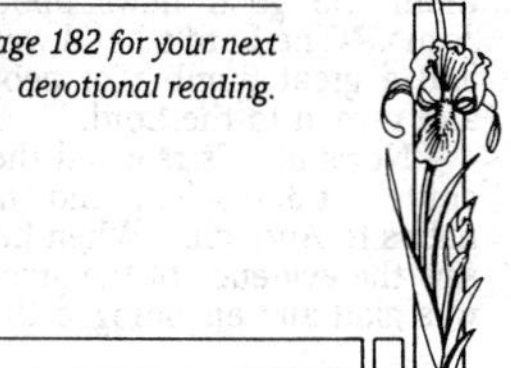

a large sheet being let down from heaven
by its four corners, and it came down to
where I was. 6I looked into it and saw
four-footed animals of the earth, wild
beasts, reptiles, and birds of the air.
7Then I heard a voice telling me, 'Get up,
Peter. Kill and eat.'

8"I replied, 'Surely not, Lord! Nothing
impure or unclean has ever entered my
mouth.'

9"The voice spoke from heaven a second time, 'Do not call anything impure
that God has made clean.' 10This happened three times, and then it was all
pulled up to heaven again.

11"Right then three men who had been
sent to me from Caesarea stopped at the
house where I was staying. 12The Spirit
told me to have no hesitation about going
with them. These six brothers also went
with me, and we entered the man's
house. 13He told us how he had seen an
angel appear in his house and say, 'Send
to Joppa for Simon who is called Peter.
14He will bring you a message through
which you and all your household will be
saved.'

15"As I began to speak, the Holy Spirit
came on them as he had come on us at
the beginning. 16Then I remembered
what the Lord had said: 'John baptized
with[a] water, but you will be baptized
with the Holy Spirit.' 17So if God gave
them the same gift as he gave us, who
believed in the Lord Jesus Christ, who
was I to think that I could oppose God?"

18When they heard this, they had no
further objections and praised God, saying, "So then, God has granted even the
Gentiles repentance unto life."

The Church in Antioch

19Now those who had been scattered by
the persecution in connection with Stephen traveled as far as Phoenicia, Cyprus
and Antioch, telling the message only to
Jews. 20Some of them, however, men
from Cyprus and Cyrene, went to Antioch
and began to speak to Greeks also, telling
them the good news about the Lord
Jesus. 21The Lord's hand was with them,
and a great number of people believed
and turned to the Lord.

22News of this reached the ears of the
church at Jerusalem, and they sent Barnabas to Antioch. 23When he arrived and
saw the evidence of the grace of God, he
was glad and encouraged them all to remain true to the Lord with all their
hearts. 24He was a good man, full of the
Holy Spirit and faith, and a great number
of people were brought to the Lord.

25Then Barnabas went to Tarsus to look
for Saul, 26and when he found him, he
brought him to Antioch. So for a whole
year Barnabas and Saul met with the
church and taught great numbers of people. The disciples were called Christians
first at Antioch.

27During this time some prophets came
down from Jerusalem to Antioch. 28One
of them, named Agabus, stood up and
through the Spirit predicted that a severe
famine would spread over the entire Roman world. (This happened during the
reign of Claudius.) 29The disciples, each
according to his ability, decided to provide help for the brothers living in Judea.
30This they did, sending their gift to the
elders by Barnabas and Saul.

Peter's Miraculous Escape From Prison

12 It was about this time that King
Herod arrested some who be-
longed to the church, intending to persecute them. 2He had James, the brother of
John, put to death with the sword. 3When
he saw that this pleased the Jews, he proceeded to seize Peter also. This happened
during the Feast of Unleavened Bread.
4After arresting him, he put him in prison,
handing him over to be guarded by four
squads of four soldiers each. Herod intended to bring him out for public trial
after the Passover.

5So Peter was kept in prison, but the
church was earnestly praying to God for
him.

6The night before Herod was to bring
him to trial, Peter was sleeping between
two soldiers, bound with two chains, and
sentries stood guard at the entrance.
7Suddenly an angel of the Lord appeared
and a light shone in the cell. He struck
Peter on the side and woke him up.
"Quick, get up!" he said, and the chains
fell off Peter's wrists.

8Then the angel said to him, "Put on
your clothes and sandals." And Peter did
so. "Wrap your cloak around you and follow me," the angel told him. 9Peter followed him out of the prison, but he had
no idea that what the angel was doing was
really happening; he thought he was seeing a vision. 10They passed the first and

[a]*16* Or *in*

second guards and came to the iron gate leading to the city. It opened for them by itself, and they went through it. When they had walked the length of one street, suddenly the angel left him.

11Then Peter came to himself and said, "Now I know without a doubt that the Lord sent his angel and rescued me from Herod's clutches and from everything the Jewish people were anticipating."

12When this had dawned on him, he went to the house of Mary the mother of John, also called Mark, where many people had gathered and were praying. 13Peter knocked at the outer entrance, and a servant girl named Rhoda came to answer the door. 14When she recognized Peter's voice, she was so overjoyed she ran back without opening it and exclaimed, "Peter is at the door!"

15"You're out of your mind," they told her. When she kept insisting that it was so, they said, "It must be his angel."

16But Peter kept on knocking, and when they opened the door and saw him, they were astonished. 17Peter motioned with his hand for them to be quiet and described how the Lord had brought him out of prison. "Tell James and the brothers about this," he said, and then he left for another place.

18In the morning, there was no small commotion among the soldiers as to what had become of Peter. 19After Herod had a thorough search made for him and did not find him, he cross-examined the guards and ordered that they be executed.

Herod's Death

Then Herod went from Judea to Caesarea and stayed there a while. 20He had been quarreling with the people of Tyre and Sidon; they now joined together and sought an audience with him. Having secured the support of Blastus, a trusted personal servant of the king, they asked for peace, because they depended on the king's country for their food supply.

21On the appointed day Herod, wearing his royal robes, sat on his throne and delivered a public address to the people. 22They shouted, "This is the voice of a god, not of a man." 23Immediately, because Herod did not give praise to God, an angel of the Lord struck him down, and he was eaten by worms and died.

24But the word of God continued to increase and spread.

25When Barnabas and Saul had finished their mission, they returned from[a] Jerusalem, taking with them John, also called Mark.

Barnabas and Saul Sent Off

13 In the church at Antioch there were prophets and teachers: Barnabas, Simeon called Niger, Lucius of Cyrene, Manaen (who had been brought up with Herod the tetrarch) and Saul. 2While they were worshiping the Lord and fasting, the Holy Spirit said, "Set apart for me Barnabas and Saul for the work to which I have called them." 3So after they had fasted and prayed, they placed their hands on them and sent them off.

On Cyprus

4The two of them, sent on their way by the Holy Spirit, went down to Seleucia and sailed from there to Cyprus. 5When they arrived at Salamis, they proclaimed the word of God in the Jewish synagogues. John was with them as their helper.

6They traveled through the whole island until they came to Paphos. There they met a Jewish sorcerer and false prophet named Bar-Jesus, 7who was an attendant of the proconsul, Sergius Paulus. The proconsul, an intelligent man, sent for Barnabas and Saul because he wanted to hear the word of God. 8But Elymas the sorcerer (for that is what his name means) opposed them and tried to turn the proconsul from the faith. 9Then Saul, who was also called Paul, filled with the Holy Spirit, looked straight at Elymas and said, 10"You are a child of the devil and an enemy of everything that is right! You are full of all kinds of deceit and trickery. Will you never stop perverting the right ways of the Lord? 11Now the hand of the Lord is against you. You are going to be blind, and for a time you will be unable to see the light of the sun."

Immediately mist and darkness came over him, and he groped about, seeking someone to lead him by the hand. 12When the proconsul saw what had happened, he believed, for he was amazed at the teaching about the Lord.

In Pisidian Antioch

13From Paphos, Paul and his compan-

a25 Some manuscripts *to*

ions sailed to Perga in Pamphylia, where
John left them to return to Jerusalem.
14From Perga they went on to Pisidian
Antioch. On the Sabbath they entered the
synagogue and sat down. 15After the reading from the Law and the Prophets, the
synagogue rulers sent word to them, saying, "Brothers, if you have a message of
encouragement for the people, please
speak."

16Standing up, Paul motioned with his
hand and said: "Men of Israel and you
Gentiles who worship God, listen to me!
17The God of the people of Israel chose
our fathers; he made the people prosper
during their stay in Egypt, with mighty
power he led them out of that country,
18he endured their conduct[a] for about
forty years in the desert, 19he overthrew
seven nations in Canaan and gave their
land to his people as their inheritance.
20All this took about 450 years.

"After this, God gave them judges until
the time of Samuel the prophet. 21Then
the people asked for a king, and he gave
them Saul son of Kish, of the tribe of Benjamin, who ruled forty years. 22After
removing Saul, he made David their king.
He testified concerning him: 'I have
found David son of Jesse a man after my
own heart; he will do everything I want
him to do.'

23"From this man's descendants God
has brought to Israel the Savior Jesus, as
he promised. 24Before the coming of
Jesus, John preached repentance and
baptism to all the people of Israel. 25As
John was completing his work, he said:
'Who do you think I am? I am not that
one. No, but he is coming after me, whose
sandals I am not worthy to untie.'

26"Brothers, children of Abraham, and
you God-fearing Gentiles, it is to us that
this message of salvation has been sent.
27The people of Jerusalem and their rulers did not recognize Jesus, yet in condemning him they fulfilled the words of
the prophets that are read every Sabbath.
28Though they found no proper ground for
a death sentence, they asked Pilate to
have him executed. 29When they had carried out all that was written about him,
they took him down from the tree and
laid him in a tomb. 30But God raised him
from the dead, 31and for many days he
was seen by those who had traveled with
him from Galilee to Jerusalem. They are
now his witnesses to our people.

32"We tell you the good news: What
God promised our fathers 33he has ful-
filled for us, their children, by raising up
Jesus. As it is written in the second
Psalm:

" 'You are my Son;
today I have become your
Father.'[b c]

34The fact that God raised him from the
dead, never to decay, is stated in these
words:

" 'I will give you the holy and sure
blessings promised to David.'[d]

35So it is stated elsewhere:

" 'You will not let your Holy One see
decay.'[e]

36"For when David had served God's
purpose in his own generation, he fell asleep; he was buried with his fathers and
his body decayed. 37But the one whom
God raised from the dead did not see
decay.

38"Therefore, my brothers, I want you
to know that through Jesus the forgiveness of sins is proclaimed to you.
39Through him everyone who believes is
justified from everything you could not be
justified from by the law of Moses. 40Take
care that what the prophets have said
does not happen to you:

41" 'Look, you scoffers,
wonder and perish,
for I am going to do something in
your days
that you would never believe,
even if someone told you.'[f]"

42As Paul and Barnabas were leaving
the synagogue, the people invited them
to speak further about these things on the
next Sabbath. 43When the congregation
was dismissed, many of the Jews and devout converts to Judaism followed Paul
and Barnabas, who talked with them and
urged them to continue in the grace of
God.

44On the next Sabbath almost the
whole city gathered to hear the word of
the Lord. 45When the Jews saw the
crowds, they were filled with jealousy and
talked abusively against what Paul was
saying.

[a]*18* Some manuscripts *and cared for them* [b]*33* Or *have begotten you* [c]*33* Psalm 2:7 [d]*34* Isaiah 55:3 [e]*35* Psalm 16:10 [f]*41* Hab. 1:5

46Then Paul and Barnabas answered
them boldly: "We had to speak the word
of God to you first. Since you reject it and
do not consider yourselves worthy of eternal life, we now turn to the Gentiles.
47For this is what the Lord has commanded us:

> " 'I have made you[a] a light for the
> Gentiles,
> that you[a] may bring salvation to
> the ends of the earth.'[b]"

48When the Gentiles heard this, they
were glad and honored the word of the
Lord; and all who were appointed for eternal life believed.
49The word of the Lord spread through
the whole region. 50But the Jews incited
the God-fearing women of high standing
and the leading men of the city. They
stirred up persecution against Paul and
Barnabas, and expelled them from their
region. 51So they shook the dust from
their feet in protest against them and
went to Iconium. 52And the disciples were
filled with joy and with the Holy Spirit.

In Iconium

14 At Iconium Paul and Barnabas
went as usual into the Jewish
synagogue. There they spoke so effectively that a great number of Jews and Gentiles believed. 2But the Jews who refused
to believe stirred up the Gentiles and poi-
soned their minds against the brothers.
3So Paul and Barnabas spent considerable time there, speaking boldly for the
Lord, who confirmed the message of his
grace by enabling them to do miraculous
signs and wonders. 4The people of the
city were divided; some sided with the
Jews, others with the apostles. 5There
was a plot afoot among the Gentiles and
Jews, together with their leaders, to mistreat them and stone them. 6But they
found out about it and fled to the
Lycaonian cities of Lystra and Derbe and
to the surrounding country, 7where they
continued to preach the good news.

In Lystra and Derbe

8In Lystra there sat a man crippled in
his feet, who was lame from birth and had
never walked. 9He listened to Paul as he
was speaking. Paul looked directly at
him, saw that he had faith to be healed
10and called out, "Stand up on your feet!"
At that, the man jumped up and began to
walk.
11When the crowd saw what Paul had
done, they shouted in the Lycaonian language, "The gods have come down to us
in human form!" 12Barnabas they called
Zeus, and Paul they called Hermes because he was the chief speaker. 13The
priest of Zeus, whose temple was just outside the city, brought bulls and wreaths to
the city gates because he and the crowd
wanted to offer sacrifices to them.
14But when the apostles Barnabas and
Paul heard of this, they tore their clothes
and rushed out into the crowd, shouting:
15"Men, why are you doing this? We too
are only men, human like you. We are
bringing you good news, telling you to
turn from these worthless things to the
living God, who made heaven and earth
and sea and everything in them. 16In the
past, he let all nations go their own way.
17Yet he has not left himself without testimony: He has shown kindness by giving
you rain from heaven and crops in their
seasons; he provides you with plenty of
food and fills your hearts with joy."
18Even with these words, they had difficulty keeping the crowd from sacrificing
to them.
19Then some Jews came from Antioch
and Iconium and won the crowd over.
They stoned Paul and dragged him outside the city, thinking he was dead. 20But
after the disciples had gathered around
him, he got up and went back into the
city. The next day he and Barnabas left
for Derbe.

The Return to Antioch in Syria

21They preached the good news in that
city and won a large number of disciples.
Then they returned to Lystra, Iconium
and Antioch, 22strengthening the disciples and encouraging them to remain true
to the faith. "We must go through many
hardships to enter the kingdom of God,"
they said. 23Paul and Barnabas appointed elders[c] for them in each church and,
with prayer and fasting, committed
them to the Lord, in whom they had
put their trust. 24After going through Pi-
sidia, they came into Pamphylia, 25and
when they had preached the word in
Perga, they went down to Attalia.
26From Attalia they sailed back to Antioch, where they had been committed to

[a]*47* The Greek is singular. [b]*47* Isaiah 49:6 [c]*23* Or *Barnabas ordained elders*; or *Barnabas had elders elected*

VERSE FOR THE DAY: *Acts 14:17*

AUTHOR: *June Masters Bacher*

PASSAGE FOR THE DAY: *Acts 14:14–18*

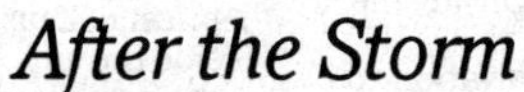

After the Storm

I WONDER how agnostics or atheists deal with mornings like this. But then, I (a believer!) had had trouble dealing with yesterday.

Following days of drenching rain, killer floods and general chaos, there came a freak downpour. Without warning, a black curtain of rain simply swallowed our city. I waded a lake that came to the hem of my skirt trying to find my car in the teachers' parking lot. Paperwork for the day was a total loss. My freshly done hair was soaked. I dripped in the front door to hear three children screaming like banshees (one mine, two somebody else's); a cold-nosed dog demanding dinner; and a husband who announced cheerfully that the roof was leaking in five places and the septic tank was overflowing.

"Let me in the door, *please!* " So began our evening. When my husband and I crept into bed, exhausted (at midnight), the boys were still giggling. The roof was still leaking (into pans and buckets). The rain was still raining. And the septic tank would have to be dealt with tomorrow.

I awoke with a start, wondering if once again the power had failed and our electric clock had stopped. It was full daylight, surely seven o'clock on a March day, and far too late to hope to get everybody off on a weekday morning. The clock appeared to be working, but how could it be so light at 4:30 A.M.?

I ran barefoot to the window and there hung the most breathtaking moon I've ever seen, suspended in a sky so clear that it appeared blue even in the pre-dawn. I watched in prayerful wonder until it was time to get the day on its feet. Only God could create such a day from yesterday's chaos—and put my heart back together!

To think and pray about: Do you think this kind of beauty follows chaos by accident? In what other ways does God, through nature, cleanse the world, the spirit? We walk through storms that strip us bare or cleanse us so we can grow again—according to our faith. God assures us that he's in charge. We can cope through prayer.

Additional Scripture Readings:
Genesis 9:12–16; Jonah 2:3—3:3

Go to page 185 for your next devotional reading.

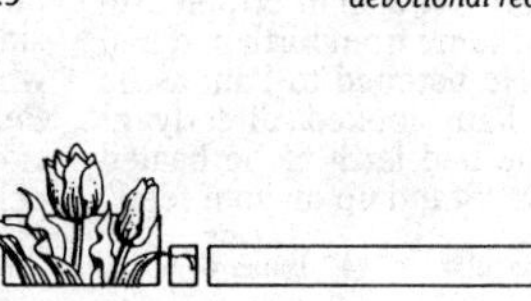

the grace of God for the work they had now completed. 27On arriving there, they gathered the church together and reported all that God had done through them and how he had opened the door of faith to the Gentiles. 28And they stayed there a long time with the disciples.

The Council at Jerusalem

15 Some men came down from Judea to Antioch and were teaching the brothers: "Unless you are circumcised, according to the custom taught by Moses, you cannot be saved." 2This brought Paul and Barnabas into sharp dispute and debate with them. So Paul and Barnabas were appointed, along with some other believers, to go up to Jerusalem to see the apostles and elders about this question. 3The church sent them on their way, and as they traveled through Phoenicia and Samaria, they told how the Gentiles had been converted. This news made all the brothers very glad. 4When they came to Jerusalem, they were welcomed by the church and the apostles and elders, to whom they reported everything God had done through them.

5Then some of the believers who belonged to the party of the Pharisees stood up and said, "The Gentiles must be circumcised and required to obey the law of Moses."

6The apostles and elders met to consider this question. 7After much discussion, Peter got up and addressed them: "Brothers, you know that some time ago God made a choice among you that the Gentiles might hear from my lips the message of the gospel and believe. 8God, who knows the heart, showed that he accepted them by giving the Holy Spirit to them, just as he did to us. 9He made no distinction between us and them, for he purified their hearts by faith. 10Now then, why do you try to test God by putting on the necks of the disciples a yoke that neither we nor our fathers have been able to bear? 11No! We believe it is through the grace of our Lord Jesus that we are saved, just as they are."

12The whole assembly became silent as they listened to Barnabas and Paul telling about the miraculous signs and wonders God had done among the Gentiles through them. 13When they finished, James spoke up: "Brothers, listen to me. 14Simon[a] has described to us how God at first showed his concern by taking from the Gentiles a people for himself. 15The words of the prophets are in agreement with this, as it is written:

16" 'After this I will return
  and rebuild David's fallen tent.
 Its ruins I will rebuild,
  and I will restore it,
17that the remnant of men may seek
   the Lord,
  and all the Gentiles who bear my
   name,
 says the Lord, who does these
   things'[b]
18 that have been known for ages.[c]

19"It is my judgment, therefore, that we should not make it difficult for the Gentiles who are turning to God. 20Instead we should write to them, telling them to abstain from food polluted by idols, from sexual immorality, from the meat of strangled animals and from blood. 21For Moses has been preached in every city from the earliest times and is read in the synagogues on every Sabbath."

The Council's Letter to Gentile Believers

22Then the apostles and elders, with the whole church, decided to choose some of their own men and send them to Antioch with Paul and Barnabas. They chose Judas (called Barsabbas) and Silas, two men who were leaders among the brothers. 23With them they sent the following letter:

The apostles and elders, your brothers,

To the Gentile believers in Antioch, Syria and Cilicia:

Greetings.

24We have heard that some went out from us without our authorization and disturbed you, troubling your minds by what they said. 25So we all agreed to choose some men and send them to you with our dear friends Barnabas and Paul— 26men who have risked their lives for the name of our Lord Jesus Christ. 27Therefore we are sending Judas and Silas to confirm by word of

[a]*14* Greek *Simeon*, a variant of *Simon*; that is, Peter

[b]*17* Amos 9:11,12

[c]*17,18* Some manuscripts *things'— / 18known to the Lord for ages is his work*

mouth what we are writing. 28It
seemed good to the Holy Spirit and
to us not to burden you with anything beyond the following requirements: 29You are to abstain from
food sacrificed to idols, from blood,
from the meat of strangled animals
and from sexual immorality. You will
do well to avoid these things.

Farewell.

30The men were sent off and went down
to Antioch, where they gathered the
church together and delivered the letter.
31The people read it and were glad for its
encouraging message. 32Judas and Silas,
who themselves were prophets, said
much to encourage and strengthen the
brothers. 33After spending some time
there, they were sent off by the brothers
with the blessing of peace to return to
those who had sent them.[a] 35But Paul
and Barnabas remained in Antioch,
where they and many others taught and
preached the word of the Lord.

Disagreement Between Paul and Barnabas

36Some time later Paul said to Barnabas, "Let us go back and visit the
brothers in all the towns where we
preached the word of the Lord and see
how they are doing." 37Barnabas wanted
to take John, also called Mark, with
them, 38but Paul did not think it wise to
take him, because he had deserted them
in Pamphylia and had not continued with
them in the work. 39They had such a
sharp disagreement that they parted company. Barnabas took Mark and sailed for
Cyprus, 40but Paul chose Silas and left,
commended by the brothers to the grace
of the Lord. 41He went through Syria and
Cilicia, strengthening the churches.

Timothy Joins Paul and Silas

16 He came to Derbe and then to Lystra, where a disciple named Timothy lived, whose mother was a Jewess
and a believer, but whose father was a
Greek. 2The brothers at Lystra and Iconium spoke well of him. 3Paul wanted to
take him along on the journey, so he circumcised him because of the Jews who
lived in that area, for they all knew that
his father was a Greek. 4As they traveled
from town to town, they delivered the decisions reached by the apostles and elders in Jerusalem for the people to obey.
5So the churches were strengthened in
the faith and grew daily in numbers.

Paul's Vision of the Man of Macedonia

6Paul and his companions traveled
throughout the region of Phrygia and
Galatia, having been kept by the Holy
Spirit from preaching the word in the
province of Asia. 7When they came to the
border of Mysia, they tried to enter Bithynia, but the Spirit of Jesus would not
allow them to. 8So they passed by Mysia
and went down to Troas. 9During the
night Paul had a vision of a man of Macedonia standing and begging him, "Come
over to Macedonia and help us." 10After
Paul had seen the vision, we got ready at
once to leave for Macedonia, concluding
that God had called us to preach the gospel to them.

Lydia's Conversion in Philippi

11From Troas we put out to sea and
sailed straight for Samothrace, and the
next day on to Neapolis. 12From there we
traveled to Philippi, a Roman colony and
the leading city of that district of Macedonia. And we stayed there several days.

13On the Sabbath we went outside the
city gate to the river, where we expected
to find a place of prayer. We sat down and
began to speak to the women who had
gathered there. 14One of those listening
was a woman named Lydia, a dealer in
purple cloth from the city of Thyatira,
who was a worshiper of God. The Lord
opened her heart to respond to Paul's
message. 15When she and the members of
her household were baptized, she invited
us to her home. "If you consider me a
believer in the Lord," she said, "come and
stay at my house." And she persuaded us.

Paul and Silas in Prison

16Once when we were going to the
place of prayer, we were met by a slave
girl who had a spirit by which she predicted the future. She earned a great deal of
money for her owners by fortune-telling.
17This girl followed Paul and the rest of
us, shouting, "These men are servants of
the Most High God, who are telling you
the way to be saved." 18She kept this up
for many days. Finally Paul became so
troubled that he turned around and said
to the spirit, "In the name of Jesus Christ

[a]33 Some manuscripts *them,* 34*but Silas decided to remain there*

I command you to come out of her!" At
that moment the spirit left her.
19When the owners of the slave girl realized that their hope of making money
was gone, they seized Paul and Silas and
dragged them into the marketplace to
face the authorities. 20They brought them
before the magistrates and said, "These
men are Jews, and are throwing our city
into an uproar 21by advocating customs
unlawful for us Romans to accept or practice."
22The crowd joined in the attack
against Paul and Silas, and the magistrates ordered them to be stripped and
beaten. 23After they had been severely
flogged, they were thrown into prison,
and the jailer was commanded to guard
them carefully. 24Upon receiving such orders, he put them in the inner cell and
fastened their feet in the stocks.
25About midnight Paul and Silas were
praying and singing hymns to God, and
the other prisoners were listening to
them. 26Suddenly there was such a violent earthquake that the foundations of
the prison were shaken. At once all the
prison doors flew open, and everybody's

FRIDAY

VERSE FOR THE DAY: *Act 16:30*

AUTHOR: *June Masters Bacher*

PASSAGE FOR THE DAY: *Acts 16:25–40*

What Can I Do?

"WHAT must I do to be saved?" asked the Philippian jailer. "Believe in the Lord Jesus " was the apostle Paul's answer. This single question and answer neatly summarize the teachings of the New Testament.

"What can I do?" ask our ministers and our doctors. "What can I do?" ask men caught in financial straits. Parents ask the question of teachers regarding their children's behavior or academic problems. A survey might show that this is one of the most common questions around. It became such a common rainy-day question in our home, I made a list of activities for our son to engage in so that he began looking forward to a storm! I made a list of stories, collected craft ideas, added suggestions for poems and Scripture passages to memorize and ended with "Look for a rainbow." The result was a happy day.

Jesus tells us that he came to earth that we might have life and have it more abundantly. How do we achieve an abundant Christian life? First, we believe with a faith so strong that the storms of life can threaten, but they cannot destroy. The abundant life begins for us here on earth and leads in natural transition into eternity. A wonderful thing, faith; a positive thing.

The positive attitude of Christian living communicates to those around us. "I am convinced," said my retiring principal after having spent over forty years in education (and an equal number of years teaching church school class), "that most folks are just about as happy as they set out to be!" He had the happiest faculty I have ever worked with.

Additional Scripture Readings:
John 10:9–10; Philippians 4:11–13

Go to page 186 for your next devotional reading.

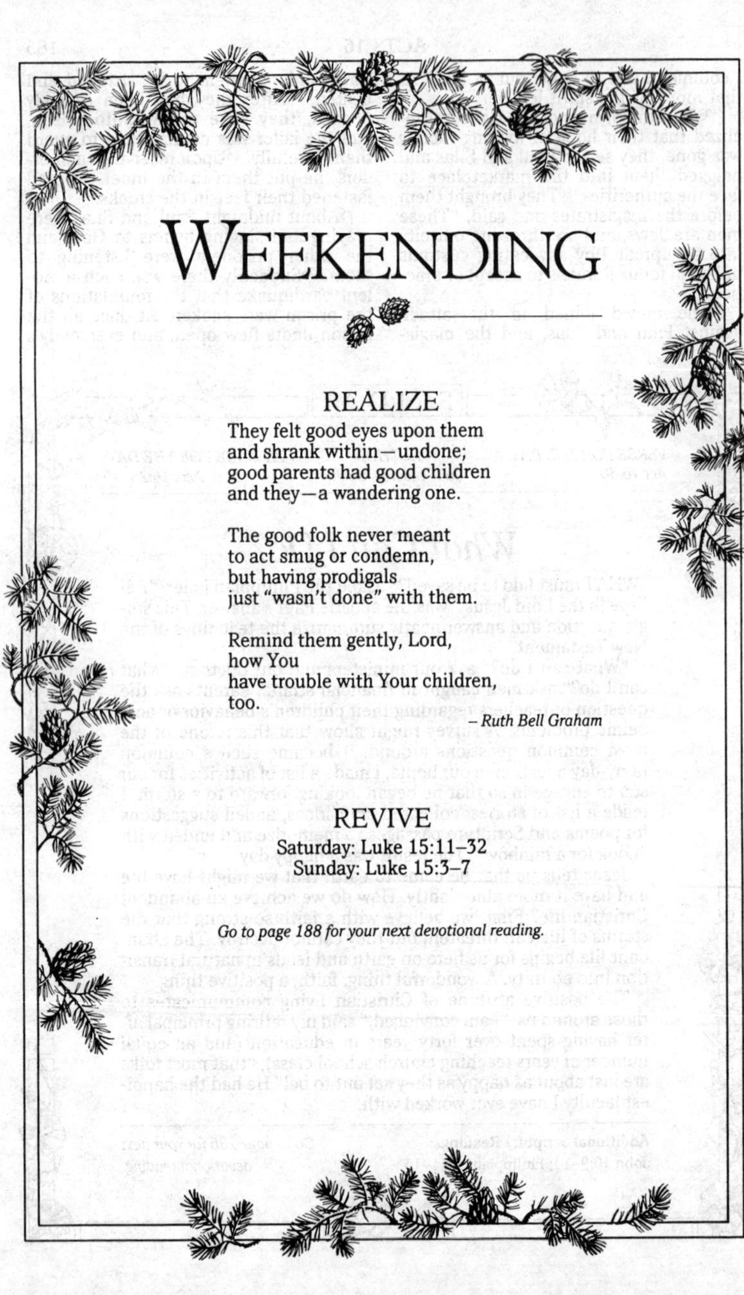

WEEKENDING

REALIZE

They felt good eyes upon them
and shrank within—undone;
good parents had good children
and they—a wandering one.

The good folk never meant
to act smug or condemn,
but having prodigals
just "wasn't done" with them.

Remind them gently, Lord,
how You
have trouble with Your children,
too.

– Ruth Bell Graham

REVIVE

Saturday: Luke 15:11–32
Sunday: Luke 15:3–7

Go to page 188 for your next devotional reading.

chains came loose. 27The jailer woke up, and when he saw the prison doors open, he drew his sword and was about to kill himself because he thought the prisoners had escaped. 28But Paul shouted, "Don't harm yourself! We are all here!"

29The jailer called for lights, rushed in and fell trembling before Paul and Silas. 30He then brought them out and asked, "Sirs, what must I do to be saved?"

31They replied, "Believe in the Lord Jesus, and you will be saved—you and your household." 32Then they spoke the word of the Lord to him and to all the others in his house. 33At that hour of the night the jailer took them and washed their wounds; then immediately he and all his family were baptized. 34The jailer brought them into his house and set a meal before them; he was filled with joy because he had come to believe in God—he and his whole family.

35When it was daylight, the magistrates sent their officers to the jailer with the order: "Release those men." 36The jailer told Paul, "The magistrates have ordered that you and Silas be released. Now you can leave. Go in peace."

37But Paul said to the officers: "They beat us publicly without a trial, even though we are Roman citizens, and threw us into prison. And now do they want to get rid of us quietly? No! Let them come themselves and escort us out."

38The officers reported this to the magistrates, and when they heard that Paul and Silas were Roman citizens, they were alarmed. 39They came to appease them and escorted them from the prison, requesting them to leave the city. 40After Paul and Silas came out of the prison, they went to Lydia's house, where they met with the brothers and encouraged them. Then they left.

In Thessalonica

17 When they had passed through Amphipolis and Apollonia, they came to Thessalonica, where there was a Jewish synagogue. 2As his custom was, Paul went into the synagogue, and on three Sabbath days he reasoned with them from the Scriptures, 3explaining and proving that the Christ[a] had to suffer and rise from the dead. "This Jesus I am proclaiming to you is the Christ,[a]" he said. 4Some of the Jews were persuaded and joined Paul and Silas, as did a large number of God-fearing Greeks and not a few prominent women.

5But the Jews were jealous; so they rounded up some bad characters from the marketplace, formed a mob and started a riot in the city. They rushed to Jason's house in search of Paul and Silas in order to bring them out to the crowd.[b] 6But when they did not find them, they dragged Jason and some other brothers before the city officials, shouting: "These men who have caused trouble all over the world have now come here, 7and Jason has welcomed them into his house. They are all defying Caesar's decrees, saying that there is another king, one called Jesus." 8When they heard this, the crowd and the city officials were thrown into turmoil. 9Then they made Jason and the others post bond and let them go.

In Berea

10As soon as it was night, the brothers sent Paul and Silas away to Berea. On arriving there, they went to the Jewish synagogue. 11Now the Bereans were of more noble character than the Thessalonians, for they received the message with great eagerness and examined the Scriptures every day to see if what Paul said was true. 12Many of the Jews believed, as did also a number of prominent Greek women and many Greek men.

13When the Jews in Thessalonica learned that Paul was preaching the word of God at Berea, they went there too, agitating the crowds and stirring them up. 14The brothers immediately sent Paul to the coast, but Silas and Timothy stayed at Berea. 15The men who escorted Paul brought him to Athens and then left with instructions for Silas and Timothy to join him as soon as possible.

In Athens

16While Paul was waiting for them in Athens, he was greatly distressed to see that the city was full of idols. 17So he reasoned in the synagogue with the Jews and the God-fearing Greeks, as well as in the marketplace day by day with those who happened to be there. 18A group of Epicurean and Stoic philosophers began to dispute with him. Some of them asked, "What is this babbler trying to say?" Others remarked, "He seems to be advocating foreign gods." They said this because

[a]3 Or *Messiah* [b]5 Or *the assembly of the people*

MONDAY

VERSE FOR THE DAY:
Acts 17:11

AUTHOR:
Elizabeth Larson

PASSAGE FOR THE DAY:
Acts 17:10–15

Counting the Cost

WE have many Bibles in our home, but one in particular is my sentimental favorite. It belonged to my husband before I adopted it, which makes it all the more dear to me. It has all his favorite passages underlined, his many little notes in the margins (I've read each one), and innumerable creases, smudges and torn spots, which are inevitable when a book is subjected to prolonged, loving abuse.

I must confess, I have added some features of my own: a few scribbles, various folds to mark my spot when I stop reading, the footprints of my preschooler who trampled the poor old book when I threw it behind the front seat of my car. But, worst of all, the cover is now threatening to fall off, due to the fact that I literally drop everything when my attention is caught by something else.

My favorite Bible. Its worth to me is great, but it wasn't until a few months ago that I realized the true cost of that book—a cost paid by others that I might freely possess my beloved book.

I was studying a history book when I came across a paragraph noting the words of a fifteenth-century bishop of England who wrote scornfully of certain women "which make themselves so wise by the Bible." It was the opinion of this bishop that women should have no right to study the Word of God. As I continued to read, I learned that some of the women so ridiculed by this bishop were wives and mothers who eventually died at the stake for refusing to accept any beliefs as God's truth "save what they can find expressly in the Bible."

I turned to my old favorite then, seeing it afresh. This book, which I handle with such careless, casual ease and freedom, would not be mine if it were not for those women (and men) who boldly claimed their right to have the Word of God—a right they paid for with their own blood.

Additional Scripture Readings:
Psalm 119:129–131; 2 Peter 1:15–21

Go to page 193 for your next devotional reading.

Paul was preaching the good news about
Jesus and the resurrection. 19Then they
took him and brought him to a meeting of
the Areopagus, where they said to him,
"May we know what this new teaching is
that you are presenting? 20You are bringing some strange ideas to our ears, and we
want to know what they mean." 21(All the
Athenians and the foreigners who lived
there spent their time doing nothing but
talking about and listening to the latest
ideas.)

22Paul then stood up in the meeting of
the Areopagus and said: "Men of Athens!
I see that in every way you are very religious. 23For as I walked around and
looked carefully at your objects of worship, I even found an altar with this inscription: TO AN UNKNOWN GOD. Now what
you worship as something unknown I am
going to proclaim to you.

24"The God who made the world and
everything in it is the Lord of heaven and
earth and does not live in temples built by
hands. 25And he is not served by human
hands, as if he needed anything, because
he himself gives all men life and breath
and everything else. 26From one man he
made every nation of men, that they
should inhabit the whole earth; and he
determined the times set for them and
the exact places where they should live.
27God did this so that men would seek
him and perhaps reach out for him and
find him, though he is not far from each
one of us. 28'For in him we live and move
and have our being.' As some of your own
poets have said, 'We are his offspring.'

29"Therefore since we are God's offspring, we should not think that the divine being is like gold or silver or stone—
an image made by man's design and skill.
30In the past God overlooked such ignorance, but now he commands all people
everywhere to repent. 31For he has set a
day when he will judge the world with justice by the man he has appointed. He has
given proof of this to all men by raising
him from the dead."

32When they heard about the resurrection of the dead, some of them sneered,
but others said, "We want to hear you
again on this subject." 33At that, Paul left
the Council. 34A few men became followers of Paul and believed. Among them
was Dionysius, a member of the Areopagus, also a woman named Damaris, and a
number of others.

In Corinth

18 After this, Paul left Athens and
went to Corinth. 2There he met a
Jew named Aquila, a native of Pontus,
who had recently come from Italy with his
wife Priscilla, because Claudius had ordered all the Jews to leave Rome. Paul
went to see them, 3and because he was a
tentmaker as they were, he stayed and
worked with them. 4Every Sabbath he
reasoned in the synagogue, trying to persuade Jews and Greeks.

5When Silas and Timothy came from
Macedonia, Paul devoted himself exclusively to preaching, testifying to the Jews
that Jesus was the Christ.[a] 6But when the
Jews opposed Paul and became abusive,
he shook out his clothes in protest and
said to them, "Your blood be on your own
heads! I am clear of my responsibility.
From now on I will go to the Gentiles."

7Then Paul left the synagogue and went
next door to the house of Titius Justus, a
worshiper of God. 8Crispus, the synagogue ruler, and his entire household believed in the Lord; and many of the Corinthians who heard him believed and were
baptized.

9One night the Lord spoke to Paul in a
vision: "Do not be afraid; keep on speaking, do not be silent. 10For I am with you,
and no one is going to attack and harm
you, because I have many people in this
city." 11So Paul stayed for a year and a
half, teaching them the word of God.

12While Gallio was proconsul of
Achaia, the Jews made a united attack on
Paul and brought him into court. 13"This
man," they charged, "is persuading the
people to worship God in ways contrary to
the law."

14Just as Paul was about to speak,
Gallio said to the Jews, "If you Jews were
making a complaint about some mis-
demeanor or serious crime, it would be
reasonable for me to listen to you. 15But
since it involves questions about words
and names and your own law—settle the
matter yourselves. I will not be a judge of
such things." 16So he had them ejected
from the court. 17Then they all turned on
Sosthenes the synagogue ruler and beat
him in front of the court. But Gallio
showed no concern whatever.

Priscilla, Aquila and Apollos

18Paul stayed on in Corinth for some

[a]5 Or *Messiah;* also in verse 28

time. Then he left the brothers and sailed
for Syria, accompanied by Priscilla and
Aquila. Before he sailed, he had his hair
cut off at Cenchrea because of a vow he
had taken. 19They arrived at Ephesus,
where Paul left Priscilla and Aquila. He
himself went into the synagogue and reasoned with the Jews. 20When they asked
him to spend more time with them, he
declined. 21But as he left, he promised, "I
will come back if it is God's will." Then
he set sail from Ephesus. 22When he landed at Caesarea, he went up and greeted
the church and then went down to Antioch.

23After spending some time in Antioch,
Paul set out from there and traveled from
place to place throughout the region of
Galatia and Phrygia, strengthening all the
disciples.

24Meanwhile a Jew named Apollos, a
native of Alexandria, came to Ephesus.
He was a learned man, with a thorough
knowledge of the Scriptures. 25He had
been instructed in the way of the Lord,
and he spoke with great fervor[a] and
taught about Jesus accurately, though he
knew only the baptism of John. 26He began to speak boldly in the synagogue.
When Priscilla and Aquila heard him,
they invited him to their home and explained to him the way of God more adequately.

27When Apollos wanted to go to
Achaia, the brothers encouraged him and
wrote to the disciples there to welcome
him. On arriving, he was a great help to
those who by grace had believed. 28For he
vigorously refuted the Jews in public debate, proving from the Scriptures that
Jesus was the Christ.

Paul in Ephesus

19 While Apollos was at Corinth, Paul
took the road through the interior
and arrived at Ephesus. There he found
some disciples 2and asked them, "Did
you receive the Holy Spirit when[b] you believed?"

They answered, "No, we have not even
heard that there is a Holy Spirit."

3So Paul asked, "Then what baptism
did you receive?"

"John's baptism," they replied.

4Paul said, "John's baptism was a baptism of repentance. He told the people to
believe in the one coming after him, that
is, in Jesus." 5On hearing this, they were
baptized into[c] the name of the Lord
Jesus. 6When Paul placed his hands on
them, the Holy Spirit came on them, and
they spoke in tongues[d] and prophesied.
7There were about twelve men in all.

8Paul entered the synagogue and spoke
boldly there for three months, arguing
persuasively about the kingdom of God.
9But some of them became obstinate;
they refused to believe and publicly ma-
ligned the Way. So Paul left them. He
took the disciples with him and had dis-
cussions daily in the lecture hall of Tyran-
nus. 10This went on for two years, so that
all the Jews and Greeks who lived in the
province of Asia heard the word of the
Lord.

11God did extraordinary miracles
through Paul, 12so that even handker-
chiefs and aprons that had touched him
were taken to the sick, and their illnesses
were cured and the evil spirits left them.

13Some Jews who went around driving
out evil spirits tried to invoke the name of
the Lord Jesus over those who were demon-possessed. They would say, "In the
name of Jesus, whom Paul preaches, I
command you to come out." 14Seven sons
of Sceva, a Jewish chief priest, were doing
this. 15⌞One day,⌟ the evil spirit answered
them, "Jesus I know, and I know about
Paul, but who are you?" 16Then the man
who had the evil spirit jumped on them
and overpowered them all. He gave them
such a beating that they ran out of the
house naked and bleeding.

17When this became known to the Jews
and Greeks living in Ephesus, they were
all seized with fear, and the name of the
Lord Jesus was held in high honor.
18Many of those who believed now came
and openly confessed their evil deeds.
19A number who had practiced sorcery
brought their scrolls together and burned
them publicly. When they calculated the
value of the scrolls, the total came to fifty
thousand drachmas.[e] 20In this way the
word of the Lord spread widely and grew
in power.

21After all this had happened, Paul decided to go to Jerusalem, passing through
Macedonia and Achaia. "After I have
been there," he said, "I must visit Rome
also." 22He sent two of his helpers, Timothy and Erastus, to Macedonia, while

[a]25 Or *with fervor in the Spirit* [b]2 Or *after* [c]5 Or *in* [d]6 Or *other languages* [e]19 A drachma was a silver coin worth about a day's wages.

he stayed in the province of Asia a little
longer.

The Riot in Ephesus

23About that time there arose a great
disturbance about the Way. 24A silversmith named Demetrius, who made silver
shrines of Artemis, brought in no little
business for the craftsmen. 25He called
them together, along with the workmen
in related trades, and said: "Men, you
know we receive a good income from this
business. 26And you see and hear how
this fellow Paul has convinced and led astray large numbers of people here in
Ephesus and in practically the whole
province of Asia. He says that man-made
gods are no gods at all. 27There is danger
not only that our trade will lose its good
name, but also that the temple of the
great goddess Artemis will be discredited,
and the goddess herself, who is worshiped throughout the province of Asia
and the world, will be robbed of her divine majesty."

28When they heard this, they were furious and began shouting: "Great is Artemis of the Ephesians!" 29Soon the whole
city was in an uproar. The people seized
Gaius and Aristarchus, Paul's traveling
companions from Macedonia, and rushed
as one man into the theater. 30Paul wanted to appear before the crowd, but the
disciples would not let him. 31Even some
of the officials of the province, friends of
Paul, sent him a message begging him not
to venture into the theater.

32The assembly was in confusion: Some
were shouting one thing, some another.
Most of the people did not even know
why they were there. 33The Jews pushed
Alexander to the front, and some of the
crowd shouted instructions to him. He
motioned for silence in order to make a
defense before the people. 34But when
they realized he was a Jew, they all shouted in unison for about two hours: "Great
is Artemis of the Ephesians!"

35The city clerk quieted the crowd and
said: "Men of Ephesus, doesn't all the
world know that the city of Ephesus is the
guardian of the temple of the great Artemis and of her image, which fell from
heaven? 36Therefore, since these facts are
undeniable, you ought to be quiet and
not do anything rash. 37You have brought
these men here, though they have neither
robbed temples nor blasphemed our goddess. 38If, then, Demetrius and his fellow
craftsmen have a grievance against anybody, the courts are open and there are
proconsuls. They can press charges. 39If
there is anything further you want to
bring up, it must be settled in a legal assembly. 40As it is, we are in danger of being charged with rioting because of today's events. In that case we would not be
able to account for this commotion, since
there is no reason for it." 41After he had
said this, he dismissed the assembly.

Through Macedonia and Greece

20 When the uproar had ended, Paul
sent for the disciples and, after encouraging them, said good-by and set out
for Macedonia. 2He traveled through that
area, speaking many words of encouragement to the people, and finally arrived in
Greece, 3where he stayed three months.
Because the Jews made a plot against
him just as he was about to sail for Syria,
he decided to go back through Macedonia. 4He was accompanied by Sopater
son of Pyrrhus from Berea, Aristarchus
and Secundus from Thessalonica, Gaius
from Derbe, Timothy also, and Tychicus
and Trophimus from the province of Asia.
5These men went on ahead and waited for
us at Troas. 6But we sailed from Philippi
after the Feast of Unleavened Bread, and
five days later joined the others at Troas,
where we stayed seven days.

Eutychus Raised From the Dead at Troas

7On the first day of the week we came
together to break bread. Paul spoke to the
people and, because he intended to leave
the next day, kept on talking until midnight. 8There were many lamps in the
upstairs room where we were meeting.
9Seated in a window was a young man
named Eutychus, who was sinking into a
deep sleep as Paul talked on and on.
When he was sound asleep, he fell to the
ground from the third story and was
picked up dead. 10Paul went down, threw
himself on the young man and put his
arms around him. "Don't be alarmed," he
said. "He's alive!" 11Then he went upstairs again and broke bread and ate. After talking until daylight, he left. 12The
people took the young man home alive
and were greatly comforted.

Paul's Farewell to the Ephesian Elders

13We went on ahead to the ship and
sailed for Assos, where we were going to

take Paul aboard. He had made this arrangement because he was going there on
foot. 14When he met us at Assos, we took
him aboard and went on to Mitylene.
15The next day we set sail from there and
arrived off Kios. The day after that we
crossed over to Samos, and on the following day arrived at Miletus. 16Paul had decided to sail past Ephesus to avoid spending time in the province of Asia, for he
was in a hurry to reach Jerusalem, if possible, by the day of Pentecost.

17From Miletus, Paul sent to Ephesus
for the elders of the church. 18When they
arrived, he said to them: "You know how
I lived the whole time I was with you,
from the first day I came into the province
of Asia. 19I served the Lord with great
humility and with tears, although I was
severely tested by the plots of the Jews.
20You know that I have not hesitated to
preach anything that would be helpful to
you but have taught you publicly and
from house to house. 21I have declared to
both Jews and Greeks that they must turn
to God in repentance and have faith in
our Lord Jesus.

22"And now, compelled by the Spirit, I
am going to Jerusalem, not knowing what
will happen to me there. 23I only know
that in every city the Holy Spirit warns me
that prison and hardships are facing me.
24However, I consider my life worth nothing to me, if only I may finish the race and
complete the task the Lord Jesus has giv-
en me—the task of testifying to the gospel of God's grace.

25"Now I know that none of you among
whom I have gone about preaching the
kingdom will ever see me again. 26There-
fore, I declare to you today that I am innocent of the blood of all men. 27For I have
not hesitated to proclaim to you the
whole will of God. 28Keep watch over
yourselves and all the flock of which the
Holy Spirit has made you overseers.[a] Be
shepherds of the church of God,[b] which
he bought with his own blood. 29I know
that after I leave, savage wolves will come
in among you and will not spare the flock.
30Even from your own number men will
arise and distort the truth in order to draw
away disciples after them. 31So be on your
guard! Remember that for three years I
never stopped warning each of you night
and day with tears.

32"Now I commit you to God and to the
word of his grace, which can build you up
and give you an inheritance among all
those who are sanctified. 33I have not coveted anyone's silver or gold or clothing.
34You yourselves know that these hands
of mine have supplied my own needs and
the needs of my companions. 35In everything I did, I showed you that by this kind
of hard work we must help the weak,
remembering the words the Lord Jesus
himself said: 'It is more blessed to give
than to receive.' "

36When he had said this, he knelt down
with all of them and prayed. 37They all
wept as they embraced him and kissed
him. 38What grieved them most was his
statement that they would never see his
face again. Then they accompanied him
to the ship.

On to Jerusalem

21 After we had torn ourselves away
from them, we put out to sea and
sailed straight to Cos. The next day we
went to Rhodes and from there to Patara.
2We found a ship crossing over to Phoenicia, went on board and set sail. 3After
sighting Cyprus and passing to the south
of it, we sailed on to Syria. We landed at
Tyre, where our ship was to unload its
cargo. 4Finding the disciples there, we
stayed with them seven days. Through
the Spirit they urged Paul not to go on to
Jerusalem. 5But when our time was up,
we left and continued on our way. All the
disciples and their wives and children accompanied us out of the city, and there
on the beach we knelt to pray. 6After saying good-by to each other, we went
aboard the ship, and they returned home.

7We continued our voyage from Tyre
and landed at Ptolemais, where we greeted the brothers and stayed with them for
a day. 8Leaving the next day, we reached
Caesarea and stayed at the house of Philip the evangelist, one of the Seven. 9He
had four unmarried daughters who prophesied.

10After we had been there a number of
days, a prophet named Agabus came
down from Judea. 11Coming over to us, he
took Paul's belt, tied his own hands and
feet with it and said, "The Holy Spirit
says, 'In this way the Jews of Jerusalem
will bind the owner of this belt and will
hand him over to the Gentiles.' "

12When we heard this, we and the people there pleaded with Paul not to go up
to Jerusalem. 13Then Paul answered,

[a]28 Traditionally *bishops* [b]28 Many manuscripts *of the Lord*

"Why are you weeping and breaking my
heart? I am ready not only to be bound,
but also to die in Jerusalem for the name
of the Lord Jesus." 14When he would not
be dissuaded, we gave up and said, "The
Lord's will be done."
15After this, we got ready and went up
to Jerusalem. 16Some of the disciples
from Caesarea accompanied us and
brought us to the home of Mnason, where
we were to stay. He was a man from Cyprus and one of the early disciples.

Paul's Arrival at Jerusalem

17When we arrived at Jerusalem, the
brothers received us warmly. 18The next
day Paul and the rest of us went to see
James, and all the elders were present.
19Paul greeted them and reported in detail what God had done among the Gentiles through his ministry.
20When they heard this, they praised
God. Then they said to Paul: "You see,
brother, how many thousands of Jews
have believed, and all of them are zealous
for the law. 21They have been informed
that you teach all the Jews who live
among the Gentiles to turn away from
Moses, telling them not to circumcise
their children or live according to our customs. 22What shall we do? They will certainly hear that you have come, 23so do

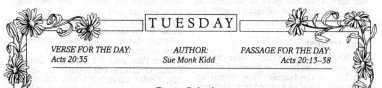

TUESDAY

VERSE FOR THE DAY: *Acts 20:35*

AUTHOR: *Sue Monk Kidd*

PASSAGE FOR THE DAY: *Acts 20:13–38*

On Giving

I have always been fascinated with Brother Roger of Taize, France, the founder of a Christian community where persons from twenty different countries and many Christian denominations live, work and pray together. One of the remarkable things about Taize is that so many young people have flocked there.

In an interview Brother Roger was asked why the young were so attracted to Taize. He responded by telling a story about his life. When he was young, children were made to keep their distance from their elders, he said. More that anything he longed for someone to give him an ear, to listen and understand what was in his heart of hearts. But it never happened. Finally Brother Roger made the resolution that became the motivation of his entire life. He determined to give to others the very thing he yearned for himself. He committed himself to listen to and understand every human being, especially the young. So at Taize he sat and listened to the young, asking himself: What are they suffering? What lies beneath their hearts? What are their gifts?

By attempting to give the very understanding he was seeking, Brother Roger found it in even greater measure. This principle never fails. If you seek to be understood, then dedicate your life to understanding others. If you seek to be comforted, then dedicate yourself to giving comfort. If you seek a greater faith, then commit yourself to planting it in others.

Additional Scripture Readings:
Luke 6:32–38; 1 John 4:10–12

Go to page 204 for your next devotional reading.

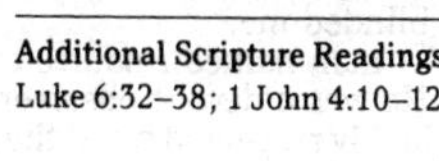

what we tell you. There are four men with
us who have made a vow. 24Take these
men, join in their purification rites and
pay their expenses, so that they can have
their heads shaved. Then everybody will
know there is no truth in these reports
about you, but that you yourself are living
in obedience to the law. 25As for the Gentile believers, we have written to them our
decision that they should abstain from
food sacrificed to idols, from blood, from
the meat of strangled animals and from
sexual immorality."

26The next day Paul took the men and
purified himself along with them. Then
he went to the temple to give notice of
the date when the days of purification
would end and the offering would be
made for each of them.

Paul Arrested

27When the seven days were nearly
over, some Jews from the province of Asia
saw Paul at the temple. They stirred up
the whole crowd and seized him, 28shout-
ing, "Men of Israel, help us! This is the
man who teaches all men everywhere
against our people and our law and this
place. And besides, he has brought
Greeks into the temple area and defiled
this holy place." 29(They had previously
seen Trophimus the Ephesian in the city
with Paul and assumed that Paul had
brought him into the temple area.)

30The whole city was aroused, and the
people came running from all directions.
Seizing Paul, they dragged him from the
temple, and immediately the gates were
shut. 31While they were trying to kill him,
news reached the commander of the Roman troops that the whole city of Jerusalem was in an uproar. 32He at once
took some officers and soldiers and ran
down to the crowd. When the rioters
saw the commander and his soldiers,
they stopped beating Paul.

33The commander came up and arrested him and ordered him to be bound with
two chains. Then he asked who he was
and what he had done. 34Some in the
crowd shouted one thing and some
another, and since the commander could
not get at the truth because of the uproar,
he ordered that Paul be taken into the
barracks. 35When Paul reached the steps,
the violence of the mob was so great he
had to be carried by the soldiers. 36The
crowd that followed kept shouting, "Away
with him!"

Paul Speaks to the Crowd

37As the soldiers were about to take
Paul into the barracks, he asked the commander, "May I say something to you?"

"Do you speak Greek?" he replied.
38"Aren't you the Egyptian who started a
revolt and led four thousand terrorists out
into the desert some time ago?"

39Paul answered, "I am a Jew, from Tarsus in Cilicia, a citizen of no ordinary city.
Please let me speak to the people."

40Having received the commander's
permission, Paul stood on the steps and
motioned to the crowd. When they were
all silent, he said to them in Aramaic[a]:

22

1"Brothers and fathers, listen now
to my defense."

2When they heard him speak to them in
Aramaic, they became very quiet.

Then Paul said: 3"I am a Jew, born in
Tarsus of Cilicia, but brought up in this
city. Under Gamaliel I was thoroughly
trained in the law of our fathers and was
just as zealous for God as any of you are
today. 4I persecuted the followers of this
Way to their death, arresting both men
and women and throwing them into prison, 5as also the high priest and all the
Council can testify. I even obtained letters from them to their brothers in
Damascus, and went there to bring these
people as prisoners to Jerusalem to be
punished.

6"About noon as I came near Damascus, suddenly a bright light from heaven
flashed around me. 7I fell to the ground
and heard a voice say to me, 'Saul! Saul!
Why do you persecute me?'

8" 'Who are you, Lord?' I asked.

" 'I am Jesus of Nazareth, whom you
are persecuting,' he replied. 9My companions saw the light, but they did not understand the voice of him who was speaking
to me.

10" 'What shall I do, Lord?' I asked.

" 'Get up,' the Lord said, 'and go into
Damascus. There you will be told all that
you have been assigned to do.' 11My companions led me by the hand into Damascus, because the brilliance of the light
had blinded me.

12"A man named Ananias came to see
me. He was a devout observer of the law
and highly respected by all the Jews living
there. 13He stood beside me and said,

[a]40 Or possibly *Hebrew*; also in 22:2

'Brother Saul, receive your sight!' And at
that very moment I was able to see him.
14"Then he said: 'The God of our fathers has chosen you to know his will and
to see the Righteous One and to hear
words from his mouth. 15You will be his
witness to all men of what you have seen
and heard. 16And now what are you waiting for? Get up, be baptized and wash
your sins away, calling on his name.'
17"When I returned to Jerusalem and
was praying at the temple, I fell into a
trance 18and saw the Lord speaking.
'Quick!' he said to me. 'Leave Jerusalem
immediately, because they will not accept your testimony about me.'
19" 'Lord,' I replied, 'these men know
that I went from one synagogue to another to imprison and beat those who believe
in you. 20And when the blood of your mar-
tyr[a] Stephen was shed, I stood there giving my approval and guarding the clothes
of those who were killing him.'
21"Then the Lord said to me, 'Go; I will
send you far away to the Gentiles.' "

Paul the Roman Citizen

22The crowd listened to Paul until he
said this. Then they raised their voices
and shouted, "Rid the earth of him! He's
not fit to live!"
23As they were shouting and throwing
off their cloaks and flinging dust into the
air, 24the commander ordered Paul to be
taken into the barracks. He directed that
he be flogged and questioned in order to
find out why the people were shouting at
him like this. 25As they stretched him out
to flog him, Paul said to the centurion
standing there, "Is it legal for you to flog
a Roman citizen who hasn't even been
found guilty?"
26When the centurion heard this, he
went to the commander and reported it.
"What are you going to do?" he asked.
"This man is a Roman citizen."
27The commander went to Paul and
asked, "Tell me, are you a Roman citizen?"
"Yes, I am," he answered.
28Then the commander said, "I had to
pay a big price for my citizenship."
"But I was born a citizen," Paul replied.
29Those who were about to question
him withdrew immediately. The commander himself was alarmed when he realized that he had put Paul, a Roman citizen, in chains.

Before the Sanhedrin

30The next day, since the commander
wanted to find out exactly why Paul was
being accused by the Jews, he released
him and ordered the chief priests and all
the Sanhedrin to assemble. Then he
brought Paul and had him stand before
them.

23 Paul looked straight at the Sanhedrin and said, "My brothers, I have
fulfilled my duty to God in all good conscience to this day." 2At this the high
priest Ananias ordered those standing
near Paul to strike him on the mouth.
3Then Paul said to him, "God will strike
you, you whitewashed wall! You sit there
to judge me according to the law, yet you
yourself violate the law by commanding
that I be struck!"
4Those who were standing near Paul
said, "You dare to insult God's high
priest?"
5Paul replied, "Brothers, I did not realize that he was the high priest; for it is
written: 'Do not speak evil about the ruler
of your people.'[b]"
6Then Paul, knowing that some of
them were Sadducees and the others
Pharisees, called out in the Sanhedrin,
"My brothers, I am a Pharisee, the son of
a Pharisee. I stand on trial because of my
hope in the resurrection of the dead."
7When he said this, a dispute broke out
between the Pharisees and the Sadducees, and the assembly was divided.
8(The Sadducees say that there is no
resurrection, and that there are neither
angels nor spirits, but the Pharisees acknowledge them all.)
9There was a great uproar, and some of
the teachers of the law who were Pharisees stood up and argued vigorously. "We
find nothing wrong with this man," they
said. "What if a spirit or an angel has
spoken to him?" 10The dispute became so
violent that the commander was afraid
Paul would be torn to pieces by them. He
ordered the troops to go down and take
him away from them by force and bring
him into the barracks.
11The following night the Lord stood
near Paul and said, "Take courage! As you
have testified about me in Jerusalem, so
you must also testify in Rome."

The Plot to Kill Paul

12The next morning the Jews formed a

[a]20 Or *witness* [b]5 Exodus 22:28

conspiracy and bound themselves with an oath not to eat or drink until they had killed Paul. 13More than forty men were involved in this plot. 14They went to the chief priests and elders and said, "We have taken a solemn oath not to eat anything until we have killed Paul. 15Now then, you and the Sanhedrin petition the commander to bring him before you on the pretext of wanting more accurate information about his case. We are ready to kill him before he gets here."

16But when the son of Paul's sister heard of this plot, he went into the barracks and told Paul.

17Then Paul called one of the centurions and said, "Take this young man to the commander; he has something to tell him." 18So he took him to the commander.

The centurion said, "Paul, the prisoner, sent for me and asked me to bring this young man to you because he has something to tell you."

19The commander took the young man by the hand, drew him aside and asked, "What is it you want to tell me?"

20He said: "The Jews have agreed to ask you to bring Paul before the Sanhedrin tomorrow on the pretext of wanting more accurate information about him. 21Don't give in to them, because more than forty of them are waiting in ambush for him. They have taken an oath not to eat or drink until they have killed him. They are ready now, waiting for your consent to their request."

22The commander dismissed the young man and cautioned him, "Don't tell anyone that you have reported this to me."

Paul Transferred to Caesarea

23Then he called two of his centurions and ordered them, "Get ready a detachment of two hundred soldiers, seventy horsemen and two hundred spearmen[a] to go to Caesarea at nine tonight. 24Provide mounts for Paul so that he may be taken safely to Governor Felix."

25He wrote a letter as follows:

26Claudius Lysias,

To His Excellency, Governor Felix:

Greetings.

27This man was seized by the Jews and they were about to kill him, but I came with my troops and rescued him, for I had learned that he is a Roman citizen. 28I wanted to know why they were accusing him, so I brought him to their Sanhedrin. 29I found that the accusation had to do with questions about their law, but there was no charge against him that deserved death or imprisonment. 30When I was informed of a plot to be carried out against the man, I sent him to you at once. I also ordered his accusers to present to you their case against him.

31So the soldiers, carrying out their orders, took Paul with them during the night and brought him as far as Antipatris. 32The next day they let the cavalry go on with him, while they returned to the barracks. 33When the cavalry arrived in Caesarea, they delivered the letter to the governor and handed Paul over to him. 34The governor read the letter and asked what province he was from. Learning that he was from Cilicia, 35he said, "I will hear your case when your accusers get here." Then he ordered that Paul be kept under guard in Herod's palace.

The Trial Before Felix

24 Five days later the high priest Ananias went down to Caesarea with some of the elders and a lawyer named Tertullus, and they brought their charges against Paul before the governor. 2When Paul was called in, Tertullus presented his case before Felix: "We have enjoyed a long period of peace under you, and your foresight has brought about reforms in this nation. 3Everywhere and in every way, most excellent Felix, we acknowledge this with profound gratitude. 4But in order not to weary you further, I would request that you be kind enough to hear us briefly.

5"We have found this man to be a troublemaker, stirring up riots among the Jews all over the world. He is a ringleader of the Nazarene sect 6and even tried to desecrate the temple; so we seized him. 8By[b] examining him yourself you will be able to learn the truth about all these charges we are bringing against him."

[a]*23* The meaning of the Greek for this word is uncertain. [b]*6-8* Some manuscripts *him and wanted to judge him according to our law. 7But the commander, Lysias, came and with the use of much force snatched him from our hands 8and ordered his accusers to come before you. By*

9The Jews joined in the accusation, as-
serting that these things were true.
10When the governor motioned for him
to speak, Paul replied: "I know that for a
number of years you have been a judge
over this nation; so I gladly make my defense. 11You can easily verify that no more
than twelve days ago I went up to Jerusalem to worship. 12My accusers did not
find me arguing with anyone at the temple, or stirring up a crowd in the synagogues or anywhere else in the city. 13And
they cannot prove to you the charges they
are now making against me. 14However, I
admit that I worship the God of our fathers as a follower of the Way, which they
call a sect. I believe everything that
agrees with the Law and that is written in
the Prophets, 15and I have the same hope
in God as these men, that there will be a
resurrection of both the righteous and the
wicked. 16So I strive always to keep my
conscience clear before God and man.
17"After an absence of several years, I
came to Jerusalem to bring my people
gifts for the poor and to present offerings.
18I was ceremonially clean when they
found me in the temple courts doing this.
There was no crowd with me, nor was I
involved in any disturbance. 19But there
are some Jews from the province of Asia,
who ought to be here before you and
bring charges if they have anything
against me. 20Or these who are here
should state what crime they found in me
when I stood before the Sanhedrin—
21unless it was this one thing I shouted as
I stood in their presence: 'It is concerning
the resurrection of the dead that I am on
trial before you today.' "
22Then Felix, who was well acquainted
with the Way, adjourned the proceedings.
"When Lysias the commander comes," he
said, "I will decide your case." 23He ordered the centurion to keep Paul under
guard but to give him some freedom and
permit his friends to take care of his
needs.
24Several days later Felix came with his
wife Drusilla, who was a Jewess. He sent
for Paul and listened to him as he spoke
about faith in Christ Jesus. 25As Paul dis-
coursed on righteousness, self-control
and the judgment to come, Felix was
afraid and said, "That's enough for now!
You may leave. When I find it convenient,
I will send for you." 26At the same time he
was hoping that Paul would offer him a
bribe, so he sent for him frequently and
talked with him.
27When two years had passed, Felix
was succeeded by Porcius Festus, but because Felix wanted to grant a favor to the
Jews, he left Paul in prison.

The Trial Before Festus

25 Three days after arriving in the
province, Festus went up from Caesarea to Jerusalem, 2where the chief
priests and Jewish leaders appeared
before him and presented the charges
against Paul. 3They urgently requested
Festus, as a favor to them, to have Paul
transferred to Jerusalem, for they were
preparing an ambush to kill him along the
way. 4Festus answered, "Paul is being
held at Caesarea, and I myself am going
there soon. 5Let some of your leaders
come with me and press charges against
the man there, if he has done anything
wrong."
6After spending eight or ten days with
them, he went down to Caesarea, and the
next day he convened the court and ordered that Paul be brought before him.
7When Paul appeared, the Jews who had
come down from Jerusalem stood around
him, bringing many serious charges
against him, which they could not prove.
8Then Paul made his defense: "I have
done nothing wrong against the law of the
Jews or against the temple or against
Caesar."
9Festus, wishing to do the Jews a favor,
said to Paul, "Are you willing to go up to
Jerusalem and stand trial before me there
on these charges?"
10Paul answered: "I am now standing
before Caesar's court, where I ought to be
tried. I have not done any wrong to the
Jews, as you yourself know very well. 11If,
however, I am guilty of doing anything deserving death, I do not refuse to die. But
if the charges brought against me by
these Jews are not true, no one has the
right to hand me over to them. I appeal to
Caesar!"
12After Festus had conferred with his
council, he declared: "You have appealed
to Caesar. To Caesar you will go!"

Festus Consults King Agrippa

13A few days later King Agrippa and
Bernice arrived at Caesarea to pay their
respects to Festus. 14Since they were
spending many days there, Festus discussed Paul's case with the king. He said:
"There is a man here whom Felix left as
a prisoner. 15When I went to Jerusalem,
the chief priests and elders of the Jews

brought charges against him and asked
that he be condemned.

16“I told them that it is not the Roman
custom to hand over any man before he
has faced his accusers and has had an opportunity to defend himself against their
charges. 17When they came here with me,
I did not delay the case, but convened the
court the next day and ordered the man
to be brought in. 18When his accusers got
up to speak, they did not charge him with
any of the crimes I had expected. 19In-
stead, they had some points of dispute
with him about their own religion and
about a dead man named Jesus who Paul
claimed was alive. 20I was at a loss how to
investigate such matters; so I asked if he
would be willing to go to Jerusalem and
stand trial there on these charges.
21When Paul made his appeal to be held
over for the Emperor's decision, I ordered
him held until I could send him to Caesar.”

22Then Agrippa said to Festus, “I would
like to hear this man myself.”

He replied, “Tomorrow you will hear
him.”

Paul Before Agrippa

23The next day Agrippa and Bernice
came with great pomp and entered the
audience room with the high ranking officers and the leading men of the city.
At the command of Festus, Paul was
brought in. 24Festus said: “King Agrippa,
and all who are present with us, you see
this man! The whole Jewish community
has petitioned me about him in Jerusalem and here in Caesarea, shouting that
he ought not to live any longer. 25I found
he had done nothing deserving of death,
but because he made his appeal to the
Emperor I decided to send him to Rome.
26But I have nothing definite to write to
His Majesty about him. Therefore I have
brought him before all of you, and especially before you, King Agrippa, so that as
a result of this investigation I may have
something to write. 27For I think it is unreasonable to send on a prisoner without
specifying the charges against him.”

26 Then Agrippa said to Paul, “You
have permission to speak for yourself.”

So Paul motioned with his hand and
began his defense: 2“King Agrippa, I consider myself fortunate to stand before you
today as I make my defense against all
the accusations of the Jews, 3and especially so because you are well acquainted
with all the Jewish customs and controversies. Therefore, I beg you to listen to
me patiently.

4“The Jews all know the way I have
lived ever since I was a child, from the
beginning of my life in my own country,
and also in Jerusalem. 5They have known
me for a long time and can testify, if they
are willing, that according to the strictest
sect of our religion, I lived as a Pharisee.
6And now it is because of my hope in
what God has promised our fathers that I
am on trial today. 7This is the promise our
twelve tribes are hoping to see fulfilled as
they earnestly serve God day and night. O
king, it is because of this hope that the
Jews are accusing me. 8Why should any of
you consider it incredible that God raises
the dead?

9“I too was convinced that I ought to do
all that was possible to oppose the name
of Jesus of Nazareth. 10And that is just
what I did in Jerusalem. On the authority
of the chief priests I put many of the
saints in prison, and when they were put
to death, I cast my vote against them.
11Many a time I went from one synagogue
to another to have them punished, and I
tried to force them to blaspheme. In my
obsession against them, I even went to
foreign cities to persecute them.

12“On one of these journeys I was going
to Damascus with the authority and commission of the chief priests. 13About
noon, O king, as I was on the road, I saw
a light from heaven, brighter than the
sun, blazing around me and my companions. 14We all fell to the ground, and I
heard a voice saying to me in Aramaic,[a]
‘Saul, Saul, why do you persecute me? It
is hard for you to kick against the goads.’

15“Then I asked, ‘Who are you, Lord?’

“ ‘I am Jesus, whom you are persecuting,’ the Lord replied. 16‘Now get up and
stand on your feet. I have appeared to you
to appoint you as a servant and as a witness of what you have seen of me and
what I will show you. 17I will rescue you
from your own people and from the Gentiles. I am sending you to them 18to open
their eyes and turn them from darkness to
light, and from the power of Satan to God,
so that they may receive forgiveness of
sins and a place among those who are
sanctified by faith in me.’

19“So then, King Agrippa, I was not

[a]14 Or *Hebrew*

disobedient to the vision from heaven.
20First to those in Damascus, then to
those in Jerusalem and in all Judea, and
to the Gentiles also, I preached that they
should repent and turn to God and prove
their repentance by their deeds. 21That is
why the Jews seized me in the temple
courts and tried to kill me. 22But I have
had God's help to this very day, and so I
stand here and testify to small and great
alike. I am saying nothing beyond what
the prophets and Moses said would happen— 23that the Christ[a] would suffer
and, as the first to rise from the dead,
would proclaim light to his own people
and to the Gentiles."

24At this point Festus interrupted
Paul's defense. "You are out of your
mind, Paul!" he shouted. "Your great
learning is driving you insane."

25"I am not insane, most excellent Festus," Paul replied. "What I am saying is
true and reasonable. 26The king is familiar with these things, and I can speak
freely to him. I am convinced that none of
this has escaped his notice, because it
was not done in a corner. 27King Agrippa,
do you believe the prophets? I know you
do."

28Then Agrippa said to Paul, "Do you
think that in such a short time you can
persuade me to be a Christian?"

29Paul replied, "Short time or long—I
pray God that not only you but all who are
listening to me today may become what I
am, except for these chains."

30The king rose, and with him the governor and Bernice and those sitting with
them. 31They left the room, and while
talking with one another, they said, "This
man is not doing anything that deserves
death or imprisonment."

32Agrippa said to Festus, "This man
could have been set free if he had not
appealed to Caesar."

Paul Sails for Rome

27 When it was decided that we
would sail for Italy, Paul and some
other prisoners were handed over to a
centurion named Julius, who belonged to
the Imperial Regiment. 2We boarded a
ship from Adramyttium about to sail for
ports along the coast of the province of
Asia, and we put out to sea. Aristarchus,
a Macedonian from Thessalonica, was
with us.

3The next day we landed at Sidon; and
Julius, in kindness to Paul, allowed him
to go to his friends so they might provide
for his needs. 4From there we put out to
sea again and passed to the lee of Cyprus
because the winds were against us.
5When we had sailed across the open sea
off the coast of Cilicia and Pamphylia, we
landed at Myra in Lycia. 6There the centurion found an Alexandrian ship sailing
for Italy and put us on board. 7We made
slow headway for many days and had difficulty arriving off Cnidus. When the wind
did not allow us to hold our course, we
sailed to the lee of Crete, opposite Sal-
mone. 8We moved along the coast with
difficulty and came to a place called Fair
Havens, near the town of Lasea.

9Much time had been lost, and sailing
had already become dangerous because
by now it was after the Fast.[b] So Paul
warned them, 10"Men, I can see that our
voyage is going to be disastrous and bring
great loss to ship and cargo, and to our
own lives also." 11But the centurion, instead of listening to what Paul said, followed the advice of the pilot and of the
owner of the ship. 12Since the harbor was
unsuitable to winter in, the majority decided that we should sail on, hoping to
reach Phoenix and winter there. This was
a harbor in Crete, facing both southwest
and northwest.

The Storm

13When a gentle south wind began to
blow, they thought they had obtained
what they wanted; so they weighed anchor and sailed along the shore of Crete.
14Before very long, a wind of hurricane
force, called the "northeaster," swept
down from the island. 15The ship was
caught by the storm and could not head
into the wind; so we gave way to it and
were driven along. 16As we passed to the
lee of a small island called Cauda, we
were hardly able to make the lifeboat secure. 17When the men had hoisted it
aboard, they passed ropes under the ship
itself to hold it together. Fearing that
they would run aground on the sandbars
of Syrtis, they lowered the sea anchor and
let the ship be driven along. 18We took
such a violent battering from the storm
that the next day they began to throw the
cargo overboard. 19On the third day, they
threw the ship's tackle overboard with
their own hands. 20When neither sun nor
stars appeared for many days and the

[a]23 Or *Messiah*   [b]9 That is, the Day of Atonement (Yom Kippur)

storm continued raging, we finally gave up all hope of being saved.

21After the men had gone a long time without food, Paul stood up before them and said: "Men, you should have taken my advice not to sail from Crete; then you would have spared yourselves this damage and loss. 22But now I urge you to keep up your courage, because not one of you will be lost; only the ship will be destroyed. 23Last night an angel of the God whose I am and whom I serve stood beside me 24and said, 'Do not be afraid, Paul. You must stand trial before Caesar; and God has graciously given you the lives of all who sail with you.' 25So keep up your courage, men, for I have faith in God that it will happen just as he told me. 26Nevertheless, we must run aground on some island."

The Shipwreck

27On the fourteenth night we were still being driven across the Adriatic[a] Sea, when about midnight the sailors sensed they were approaching land. 28They took soundings and found that the water was a hundred and twenty feet[b] deep. A short time later they took soundings again and found it was ninety feet[c] deep. 29Fearing that we would be dashed against the rocks, they dropped four anchors from the stern and prayed for daylight. 30In an attempt to escape from the ship, the sailors let the lifeboat down into the sea, pretending they were going to lower some anchors from the bow. 31Then Paul said to the centurion and the soldiers, "Unless these men stay with the ship, you cannot be saved." 32So the soldiers cut the ropes that held the lifeboat and let it fall away.

33Just before dawn Paul urged them all to eat. "For the last fourteen days," he said, "you have been in constant suspense and have gone without food—you haven't eaten anything. 34Now I urge you to take some food. You need it to survive. Not one of you will lose a single hair from his head." 35After he said this, he took some bread and gave thanks to God in front of them all. Then he broke it and began to eat. 36They were all encouraged and ate some food themselves. 37Altogether there were 276 of us on board. 38When they had eaten as much as they wanted, they lightened the ship by throwing the grain into the sea.

39When daylight came, they did not recognize the land, but they saw a bay with a sandy beach, where they decided to run the ship aground if they could. 40Cutting loose the anchors, they left them in the sea and at the same time untied the ropes that held the rudders. Then they hoisted the foresail to the wind and made for the beach. 41But the ship struck a sandbar and ran aground. The bow stuck fast and would not move, and the stern was broken to pieces by the pounding of the surf.

42The soldiers planned to kill the prisoners to prevent any of them from swimming away and escaping. 43But the centurion wanted to spare Paul's life and kept them from carrying out their plan. He ordered those who could swim to jump overboard first and get to land. 44The rest were to get there on planks or on pieces of the ship. In this way everyone reached land in safety.

Ashore on Malta

28 Once safely on shore, we found out that the island was called Malta. 2The islanders showed us unusual kindness. They built a fire and welcomed us all because it was raining and cold. 3Paul gathered a pile of brushwood and, as he put it on the fire, a viper, driven out by the heat, fastened itself on his hand. 4When the islanders saw the snake hanging from his hand, they said to each other, "This man must be a murderer; for though he escaped from the sea, Justice has not allowed him to live." 5But Paul shook the snake off into the fire and suffered no ill effects. 6The people expected him to swell up or suddenly fall dead, but after waiting a long time and seeing nothing unusual happen to him, they changed their minds and said he was a god.

7There was an estate nearby that belonged to Publius, the chief official of the island. He welcomed us to his home and for three days entertained us hospitably. 8His father was sick in bed, suffering from fever and dysentery. Paul went in to see him and, after prayer, placed his hands on him and healed him. 9When this had happened, the rest of the sick on the island came and were cured. 10They honored us in many ways and when we were ready to sail, they furnished us with the supplies we needed.

[a]*27* In ancient times the name referred to an area extending well south of Italy. [b]*28* Greek *twenty orguias* (about 37 meters) [c]*28* Greek *fifteen orguias* (about 27 meters)

Arrival at Rome

11After three months we put out to sea in a ship that had wintered in the island. It was an Alexandrian ship with the figurehead of the twin gods Castor and Pollux. 12We put in at Syracuse and stayed there three days. 13From there we set sail and arrived at Rhegium. The next day the south wind came up, and on the following day we reached Puteoli. 14There we found some brothers who invited us to spend a week with them. And so we came to Rome. 15The brothers there had heard that we were coming, and they traveled as far as the Forum of Appius and the Three Taverns to meet us. At the sight of these men Paul thanked God and was encouraged. 16When we got to Rome, Paul was allowed to live by himself, with a soldier to guard him.

Paul Preaches at Rome Under Guard

17Three days later he called together the leaders of the Jews. When they had assembled, Paul said to them: "My brothers, although I have done nothing against our people or against the customs of our ancestors, I was arrested in Jerusalem and handed over to the Romans. 18They examined me and wanted to release me, because I was not guilty of any crime deserving death. 19But when the Jews objected, I was compelled to appeal to Caesar—not that I had any charge to bring against my own people. 20For this reason I have asked to see you and talk with you. It is because of the hope of Israel that I am bound with this chain."

21They replied, "We have not received any letters from Judea concerning you, and none of the brothers who have come from there has reported or said anything bad about you. 22But we want to hear what your views are, for we know that people everywhere are talking against this sect."

23They arranged to meet Paul on a certain day, and came in even larger numbers to the place where he was staying. From morning till evening he explained and declared to them the kingdom of God and tried to convince them about Jesus from the Law of Moses and from the Prophets. 24Some were convinced by what he said, but others would not believe. 25They disagreed among themselves and began to leave after Paul had made this final statement: "The Holy Spirit spoke the truth to your forefathers when he said through Isaiah the prophet:

26" 'Go to this people and say,
"You will be ever hearing but never
understanding;
you will be ever seeing but never
perceiving."
27For this people's heart has become
calloused;
they hardly hear with their ears,
and they have closed their eyes.
Otherwise they might see with their
eyes,
hear with their ears,
understand with their hearts
and turn, and I would heal them.'[a]

28"Therefore I want you to know that God's salvation has been sent to the Gentiles, and they will listen!"[b]

30For two whole years Paul stayed there in his own rented house and welcomed all who came to see him. 31Boldly and without hindrance he preached the kingdom of God and taught about the Lord Jesus Christ.

[a]*27* Isaiah 6:9,10 [b]*28* Some manuscripts *listen!" 29After he said this, the Jews left, arguing vigorously among themselves.*

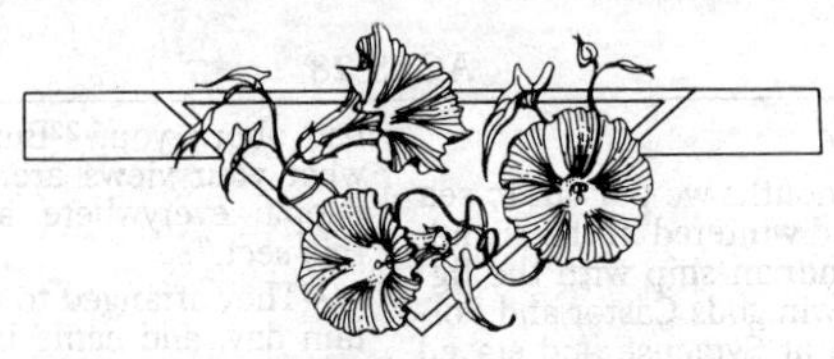

PAUL, planning a mission trip to Spain (Romans 15:23–29), writes this letter to introduce himself to the church at Rome. In it he summarizes what he has been preaching about sin, Christ, and the way of salvation. Everything you need to know about God's great plan for redemption lies in these sixteen chapters. As you read the book, think about how much God loves you in sending his Son Jesus and how you can say thank you to him by the life you live.

ROMANS

1 Paul, a servant of Christ Jesus, called
to be an apostle and set apart for the
gospel of God— 2the gospel he promised
beforehand through his prophets in the
Holy Scriptures 3regarding his Son, who
as to his human nature was a descendant
of David, 4and who through the Spirit[a] of
holiness was declared with power to be
the Son of God[b] by his resurrection from
the dead: Jesus Christ our Lord. 5Through
him and for his name's sake, we received
grace and apostleship to call people from
among all the Gentiles to the obedience
that comes from faith. 6And you also are
among those who are called to belong to
Jesus Christ.

7To all in Rome who are loved by God
and called to be saints:

Grace and peace to you from God our Father and from the Lord Jesus Christ.

Paul's Longing to Visit Rome

8First, I thank my God through Jesus
Christ for all of you, because your faith is
being reported all over the world. 9God,
whom I serve with my whole heart in
preaching the gospel of his Son, is my witness how constantly I remember you 10in
my prayers at all times; and I pray that

[a]4 Or *who as to his spirit* [b]4 Or *was appointed to be the Son of God with power*

now at last by God's will the way may be opened for me to come to you.

[11]I long to see you so that I may impart to you some spiritual gift to make you strong— [12]that is, that you and I may be mutually encouraged by each other's faith. [13]I do not want you to be unaware, brothers, that I planned many times to come to you (but have been prevented from doing so until now) in order that I might have a harvest among you, just as I have had among the other Gentiles.

[14]I am obligated both to Greeks and non-Greeks, both to the wise and the foolish. [15]That is why I am so eager to preach the gospel also to you who are at Rome.

[16]I am not ashamed of the gospel, because it is the power of God for the salvation of everyone who believes: first for the Jew, then for the Gentile. [17]For in the gospel a righteousness from God is revealed, a righteousness that is by faith from first to last,[a] just as it is written: "The righteous will live by faith."[b]

God's Wrath Against Mankind

[18]The wrath of God is being revealed from heaven against all the godlessness and wickedness of men who suppress the truth by their wickedness, [19]since what may be known about God is plain to them, because God has made it plain to them. [20]For since the creation of the world God's invisible qualities—his eternal power and divine nature—have been clearly seen, being understood from what has been made, so that men are without excuse.

[21]For although they knew God, they neither glorified him as God nor gave thanks to him, but their thinking became futile and their foolish hearts were darkened. [22]Although they claimed to be wise, they became fools [23]and exchanged the glory of the immortal God for images made to look like mortal man and birds and animals and reptiles.

[24]Therefore God gave them over in the sinful desires of their hearts to sexual impurity for the degrading of their bodies with one another. [25]They exchanged the truth of God for a lie, and worshiped and served created things rather than the Creator—who is forever praised. Amen.

[26]Because of this, God gave them over to shameful lusts. Even their women exchanged natural relations for unnatural ones. [27]In the same way the men also abandoned natural relations with women and were inflamed with lust for one another. Men committed indecent acts with other men, and received in themselves the due penalty for their perversion.

[28]Furthermore, since they did not think it worthwhile to retain the knowledge of God, he gave them over to a depraved mind, to do what ought not to be done. [29]They have become filled with every kind of wickedness, evil, greed and depravity. They are full of envy, murder, strife, deceit and malice. They are gossips, [30]slanderers, God-haters, insolent, arrogant and boastful; they invent ways of doing evil; they disobey their parents; [31]they are senseless, faithless, heartless, ruthless. [32]Although they know God's righteous decree that those who do such things deserve death, they not only continue to do these very things but also approve of those who practice them.

God's Righteous Judgment

2 You, therefore, have no excuse, you who pass judgment on someone else, for at whatever point you judge the other, you are condemning yourself, because you who pass judgment do the same things. [2]Now we know that God's judgment against those who do such things is based on truth. [3]So when you, a mere man, pass judgment on them and yet do the same things, do you think you will escape God's judgment? [4]Or do you show contempt for the riches of his kindness, tolerance and patience, not realizing that God's kindness leads you toward repentance?

[5]But because of your stubbornness and your unrepentant heart, you are storing up wrath against yourself for the day of God's wrath, when his righteous judgment will be revealed. [6]God "will give to each person according to what he has done."[c] [7]To those who by persistence in doing good seek glory, honor and immortality, he will give eternal life. [8]But for those who are self-seeking and who reject the truth and follow evil, there will be wrath and anger. [9]There will be trouble and distress for every human being who does evil: first for the Jew, then for the Gentile; [10]but glory, honor and peace for

[a]*17* Or *is from faith to faith* [b]*17* Hab. 2:4 [c]*6* Psalm 62:12; Prov. 24:12

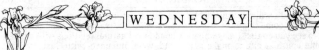

VERSE FOR THE DAY:
Romans 1:25

AUTHOR:
Carol L. Baldwin

PASSAGE FOR THE DAY:
Romans 1:18–25

From the Created to the Creator

WHICH one of us hasn't looked on a newborn baby with amazement and wondered at the exquisite delicacy of each limb, facial feature, fingernail or eyelash? Especially if that baby is our own, there is always the temptation to think this child is the perfect example of human conception—in spite of the fact that he or she may have no hair, be bright red or be shaped like a little potato!

Even the psalmist agrees that every baby has been "fearfully and wonderfully made" (Psalm 139:14).

From the first moment of awe when we gaze at our newborn children, and then during the hours, days and years that go into caring for them, it is tempting for us to allow these children to become the center of our lives—almost to become objects of our *worship*.

How can we keep ourselves from revolving our whole lives around these precious gifts from the Lord?

The answer is to look up from the intricacy and delicacy of these *creations* to see the one behind the magnificent way they have been knit together—their *Creator*.

Isn't this a part of Paul's warning to us in Romans 1:25? We must avoid the sin of the unbeliever, who sees God's eternal power and divine nature in all of creation, but neither glorifies him nor gives thanks to him (Romans 1:20–21). Unlike unbelievers, we Christians have been given by God new hearts and minds, enabling us to look at the product and praise the Master Craftsman.

It is our responsibility and joy to look at those babies and delight in their perfectly formed tiny hands and feet—and then worship the one who created those parts with infinite wisdom, care and direction.

Additional Scripture Readings:
Psalm 104:24–31; Acts 17:24–27

Go to page 207 for your next devotional reading.

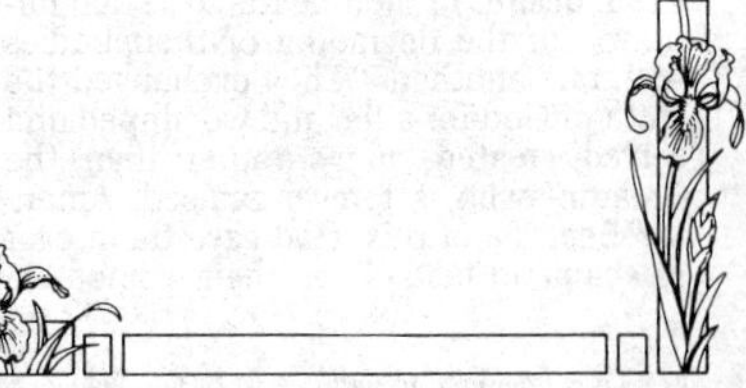

everyone who does good: first for the Jew,
then for the Gentile. 11For God does not
show favoritism.
12All who sin apart from the law will
also perish apart from the law, and all
who sin under the law will be judged by
the law. 13For it is not those who hear the
law who are righteous in God's sight, but
it is those who obey the law who will be
declared righteous. 14(Indeed, when Gentiles, who do not have the law, do by nature things required by the law, they are
a law for themselves, even though they do
not have the law, 15since they show that
the requirements of the law are written
on their hearts, their consciences also
bearing witness, and their thoughts now
accusing, now even defending them.)
16This will take place on the day when
God will judge men's secrets through
Jesus Christ, as my gospel declares.

The Jews and the Law

17Now you, if you call yourself a Jew; if
you rely on the law and brag about your
relationship to God; 18if you know his will
and approve of what is superior because
you are instructed by the law; 19if you are
convinced that you are a guide for the
blind, a light for those who are in the
dark, 20an instructor of the foolish, a
teacher of infants, because you have in
the law the embodiment of knowledge
and truth— 21you, then, who teach others, do you not teach yourself? You who
preach against stealing, do you steal?
22You who say that people should not
commit adultery, do you commit adultery? You who abhor idols, do you rob
temples? 23You who brag about the law,
do you dishonor God by breaking the law?
24As it is written: "God's name is blasphemed among the Gentiles because of
you."[a]
25Circumcision has value if you observe
the law, but if you break the law, you have
become as though you had not been circumcised. 26If those who are not circumcised keep the law's requirements, will
they not be regarded as though they were
circumcised? 27The one who is not circumcised physically and yet obeys the
law will condemn you who, even though
you have the[b] written code and circumcision, are a lawbreaker.
28A man is not a Jew if he is only one
outwardly, nor is circumcision merely
outward and physical. 29No, a man is a
Jew if he is one inwardly; and circumcision is circumcision of the heart, by the
Spirit, not by the written code. Such a
man's praise is not from men, but from
God.

God's Faithfulness

3 What advantage, then, is there in being a Jew, or what value is there in
circumcision? 2Much in every way! First
of all, they have been entrusted with the
very words of God.
3What if some did not have faith? Will
their lack of faith nullify God's faithfulness? 4Not at all! Let God be true, and
every man a liar. As it is written:

"So that you may be proved right
when you speak
and prevail when you judge."[c]

5But if our unrighteousness brings out
God's righteousness more clearly, what
shall we say? That God is unjust in bringing his wrath on us? (I am using a human
argument.) 6Certainly not! If that were so,
how could God judge the world? 7Some-
one might argue, "If my falsehood en-
hances God's truthfulness and so increases his glory, why am I still condemned as a sinner?" 8Why not say—as
we are being slanderously reported as
saying and as some claim that we say—
"Let us do evil that good may result"?
Their condemnation is deserved.

No One Is Righteous

9What shall we conclude then? Are we
any better[d]? Not at all! We have already
made the charge that Jews and Gentiles
alike are all under sin. 10As it is written:

"There is no one righteous, not even
one;
11 there is no one who understands,
no one who seeks God.
12All have turned away,
they have together become
worthless;
there is no one who does good,
not even one."[e]
13"Their throats are open graves;
their tongues practice deceit."[f]
"The poison of vipers is on their
lips."[g]
14 "Their mouths are full of cursing
and bitterness."[h]

[a]*24* Isaiah 52:5; Ezek. 36:22 [b]*27* Or *who, by means of a* [c]*4* Psalm 51:4 [d]*9* Or *worse*
[e]*12* Psalms 14:1-3; 53:1-3; Eccles. 7:20 [f]*13* Psalm 5:9 [g]*13* Psalm 140:3 [h]*14* Psalm 10:7

15"Their feet are swift to shed blood;
16 ruin and misery mark their ways,
17and the way of peace they do not
know."[a]
18 "There is no fear of God before
their eyes."[b]

19Now we know that whatever the law
says, it says to those who are under the
law, so that every mouth may be silenced
and the whole world held accountable to
God. 20Therefore no one will be declared
righteous in his sight by observing the
law; rather, through the law we become
conscious of sin.

Righteousness Through Faith

21But now a righteousness from God,
apart from law, has been made known, to
which the Law and the Prophets testify.
22This righteousness from God comes
through faith in Jesus Christ to all who
believe. There is no difference, 23for all
have sinned and fall short of the glory of
God, 24and are justified freely by his grace
through the redemption that came by
Christ Jesus. 25God presented him as a
sacrifice of atonement,[c] through faith in
his blood. He did this to demonstrate his
justice, because in his forbearance he had
left the sins committed beforehand unpunished— 26he did it to demonstrate his
justice at the present time, so as to be
just and the one who justifies those who
have faith in Jesus.

27Where, then, is boasting? It is excluded. On what principle? On that of observing the law? No, but on that of faith. 28For
we maintain that a man is justified by
faith apart from observing the law. 29Is
God the God of Jews only? Is he not the
God of Gentiles too? Yes, of Gentiles too,
30since there is only one God, who will
justify the circumcised by faith and the
uncircumcised through that same faith.
31Do we, then, nullify the law by this
faith? Not at all! Rather, we uphold the
law.

Abraham Justified by Faith

4 What then shall we say that Abraham,
our forefather, discovered in this matter? 2If, in fact, Abraham was justified by
works, he had something to boast about
—but not before God. 3What does the
Scripture say? "Abraham believed God,
and it was credited to him as righteousness."[d]

4Now when a man works, his wages are
not credited to him as a gift, but as an
obligation. 5However, to the man who
does not work but trusts God who justifies the wicked, his faith is credited as
righteousness. 6David says the same thing
when he speaks of the blessedness of the
man to whom God credits righteousness
apart from works:

7"Blessed are they
whose transgressions are forgiven,
whose sins are covered.
8Blessed is the man
whose sin the Lord will never count
against him."[e]

9Is this blessedness only for the circumcised, or also for the uncircumcised?
We have been saying that Abraham's faith
was credited to him as righteousness.
10Under what circumstances was it credited? Was it after he was circumcised, or
before? It was not after, but before! 11And
he received the sign of circumcision, a
seal of the righteousness that he had by
faith while he was still uncircumcised. So
then, he is the father of all who believe
but have not been circumcised, in order
that righteousness might be credited to
them. 12And he is also the father of the
circumcised who not only are circumcised but who also walk in the footsteps
of the faith that our father Abraham had
before he was circumcised.

13It was not through law that Abraham
and his offspring received the promise
that he would be heir of the world, but
through the righteousness that comes by
faith. 14For if those who live by law are
heirs, faith has no value and the promise
is worthless, 15because law brings wrath.
And where there is no law there is no
transgression.

16Therefore, the promise comes by
faith, so that it may be by grace and may
be guaranteed to all Abraham's offspring
—not only to those who are of the law but
also to those who are of the faith of
Abraham. He is the father of us all. 17As
it is written: "I have made you a father of
many nations."[f] He is our father in the
sight of God, in whom he believed—the
God who gives life to the dead and calls

[a]*17* Isaiah 59:7,8 [b]*18* Psalm 36:1 [c]*25* Or *as the one who would turn aside his wrath, taking away sin* [d]*3* Gen. 15:6; also in verse 22 [e]*8* Psalm 32:1,2 [f]*17* Gen. 17:5

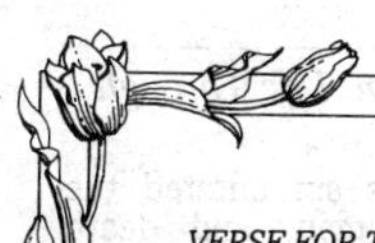

THURSDAY

VERSE FOR THE DAY: *Romans 3:22*

AUTHOR: *Gladys M. Hunt*

PASSAGE FOR THE DAY: *Romans 3:9–27*

Changed to Fit the Standard

THESE verses tell it like it is. No one is good enough for God. You can't pile up Brownie points and hope they make you acceptable in his sight. The only people who think they can make it on their own are people who have cut God down to their size. The problem is that God is *who he is* and he is perfect holiness. That's the bad news and it's the good news.

How can people like you or me be made right with God? Where do we get the righteousness we need? The good news is that God's kind of righteousness has been made available to us (Romans 3:21) as a free gift (Romans 3:24). It's for anyone who has faith in Jesus Christ (Romans 3:22), which simply means you don't get the gift unless you take it.

God can't pretend sin doesn't exist. He doesn't look at us and make excuses for us. He had to do something about sin to break its power over us. So he sent Jesus and we have been rescued—redeemed—by him (Romans 3:24). Jesus died as a sacrifice to pay sin's penalty (Romans 3:25), and to those who believe and receive his offer, he does a wonderful thing: he justifies us (Romans 3:24).

If you need to be justified, it means something is wrong. You don't match the standard. In justifying us, God takes care of our sin—and then does something even greater—he gives us the righteousness of Jesus Christ. It's like receiving new clothes that fit us and are appropriate for going into the presence of the king. What do we lack? Righteousness. What does Jesus give us? His righteousness. He doesn't change his standard in order to include us. He changes us to fit the standard.

We must take a good look at ourselves. Do we deserve this? No, it is God's grace (Romans 3:24) that brings about this marvelous change in our lives. How should a person respond to such a gift? Receive it thankfully. Remember who you are and whose clothes you are wearing. Remember how you came to belong to Jesus Christ. Share the Good News.

Additional Scripture Readings:
Matthew 22:8–13; Titus 3:3–7

Go to page 209 for your next devotional reading.

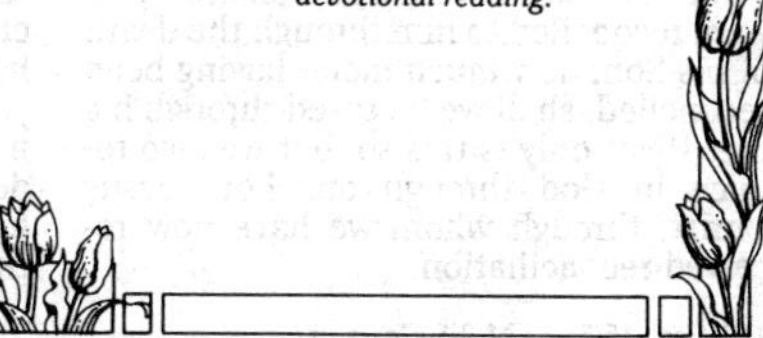

things that are not as though they were. [18]Against all hope, Abraham in hope believed and so became the father of many nations, just as it had been said to him, "So shall your offspring be."[a] [19]Without weakening in his faith, he faced the fact that his body was as good as dead—since he was about a hundred years old—and that Sarah's womb was also dead. [20]Yet he did not waver through unbelief regarding the promise of God, but was strengthened in his faith and gave glory to God, [21]being fully persuaded that God had power to do what he had promised. [22]This is why "it was credited to him as righteousness." [23]The words "it was credited to him" were written not for him alone, [24]but also for us, to whom God will credit righteousness—for us who believe in him who raised Jesus our Lord from the dead. [25]He was delivered over to death for our sins and was raised to life for our justification.

Peace and Joy

5 Therefore, since we have been justified through faith, we[b] have peace with God through our Lord Jesus Christ, [2]through whom we have gained access by faith into this grace in which we now stand. And we[b] rejoice in the hope of the glory of God. [3]Not only so, but we[b] also rejoice in our sufferings, because we know that suffering produces perseverance; [4]perseverance, character; and character, hope. [5]And hope does not disappoint us, because God has poured out his love into our hearts by the Holy Spirit, whom he has given us.

[6]You see, at just the right time, when we were still powerless, Christ died for the ungodly. [7]Very rarely will anyone die for a righteous man, though for a good man someone might possibly dare to die. [8]But God demonstrates his own love for us in this: While we were still sinners, Christ died for us.

[9]Since we have now been justified by his blood, how much more shall we be saved from God's wrath through him! [10]For if, when we were God's enemies, we were reconciled to him through the death of his Son, how much more, having been reconciled, shall we be saved through his life! [11]Not only is this so, but we also rejoice in God through our Lord Jesus Christ, through whom we have now received reconciliation.

Death Through Adam, Life Through Christ

[12]Therefore, just as sin entered the world through one man, and death through sin, and in this way death came to all men, because all sinned— [13]for before the law was given, sin was in the world. But sin is not taken into account when there is no law. [14]Nevertheless, death reigned from the time of Adam to the time of Moses, even over those who did not sin by breaking a command, as did Adam, who was a pattern of the one to come.

[15]But the gift is not like the trespass. For if the many died by the trespass of the one man, how much more did God's grace and the gift that came by the grace of the one man, Jesus Christ, overflow to the many! [16]Again, the gift of God is not like the result of the one man's sin: The judgment followed one sin and brought condemnation, but the gift followed many trespasses and brought justification. [17]For if, by the trespass of the one man, death reigned through that one man, how much more will those who receive God's abundant provision of grace and of the gift of righteousness reign in life through the one man, Jesus Christ.

[18]Consequently, just as the result of one trespass was condemnation for all men, so also the result of one act of righteousness was justification that brings life for all men. [19]For just as through the disobedience of the one man the many were made sinners, so also through the obedience of the one man the many will be made righteous.

[20]The law was added so that the trespass might increase. But where sin increased, grace increased all the more, [21]so that, just as sin reigned in death, so also grace might reign through righteousness to bring eternal life through Jesus Christ our Lord.

Dead to Sin, Alive in Christ

6 What shall we say, then? Shall we go on sinning so that grace may increase? [2]By no means! We died to sin; how can we live in it any longer? [3]Or don't you know that all of us who were baptized into Christ Jesus were baptized into his death? [4]We were therefore buried with him through baptism into death in order that, just as Christ was raised from the

[a]*18* Gen. 15:5 [b]*1,2,3* Or *let us*

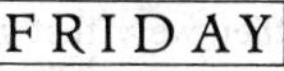

FRIDAY

VERSE FOR THE DAY:	*AUTHOR:*	*PASSAGE FOR THE DAY:*
Romans 5:1	*Gladys M. Hunt*	*Romans 5:1–5*

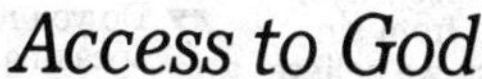

Access to God

BECOMING a Christian has enormous consequences. Relationships are changed; we are given privileges; we look at life differently; our resources are inexhaustible. How do we receive all of this? Paul makes it clear: *through our Lord Jesus Christ* (Romans 5:1).

Our relationships are changed: we have peace *with* God (Romans 5:1). When we are at odds with God, inner peace eludes us. Becoming a Christian necessitates being made right with God, and what a difference it makes! *Peace with God* is enough to sing about.

We are given privileges: we have access by faith into God's very presence (Romans 5:2). Once we knew only hostility; now we are invited into the King's presence. Once we were outside; now we are welcome inside. Access. What are you doing with the privilege of coming into God's presence?

We look at life differently: we can be joyful even when facing the hard things that come into our lives (Romans 5:3). We know life isn't purposeless. God is taking the stuff of our lives and making something good out of it. We are on our way somewhere. God wants to get us ready for heaven. Our joy is real because we know we will one day share the glory of God.

Our resources are inexhaustible: God keeps pouring his love into our hearts (Romans 5:5). He not only makes us feel very loved, but he is so generous in his supply that we have an overflow of love for other people. He gives us the Holy Spirit, who not only transforms our thinking, but makes God's love real to us.

Our trouble begins when we forget these great realities and concentrate on our inadequacies, our fears, and all the other manifestations of our smallness. The proof of God's love is that Jesus Christ died for us. We are no longer shivering outside in the cold with no credentials to come before the King. Jesus has invited us into his very presence and has given us all we need and more besides. This passage in Romans 5 is a renewed invitation to take advantage of your privileges as a daughter of the King.

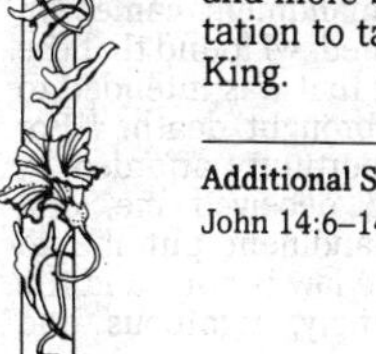

Additional Scripture Readings:
John 14:6–14; Hebrews 4:14–16

Go to page 211 for your next devotional reading.

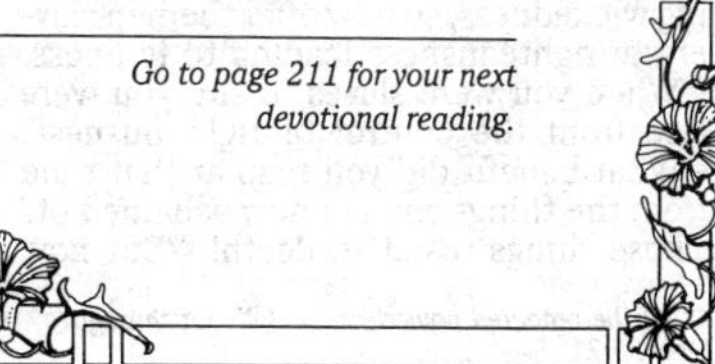

dead through the glory of the Father, we
too may live a new life.
[5]If we have been united with him like
this in his death, we will certainly also be
united with him in his resurrection. [6]For
we know that our old self was crucified
with him so that the body of sin might be
done away with,[a] that we should no longer be slaves to sin— [7]because anyone
who has died has been freed from sin.
[8]Now if we died with Christ, we believe
that we will also live with him. [9]For we
know that since Christ was raised from
the dead, he cannot die again; death no
longer has mastery over him. [10]The death
he died, he died to sin once for all; but
the life he lives, he lives to God.
[11]In the same way, count yourselves
dead to sin but alive to God in Christ
Jesus. [12]Therefore do not let sin reign in
your mortal body so that you obey its evil
desires. [13]Do not offer the parts of your
body to sin, as instruments of wickedness, but rather offer yourselves to God,
as those who have been brought from
death to life; and offer the parts of your
body to him as instruments of righteousness. [14]For sin shall not be your master,
because you are not under law, but under
grace.

Slaves to Righteousness

[15]What then? Shall we sin because we
are not under law but under grace? By no
means! [16]Don't you know that when you
offer yourselves to someone to obey him
as slaves, you are slaves to the one whom
you obey—whether you are slaves to sin,
which leads to death, or to obedience,
which leads to righteousness? [17]But
thanks be to God that, though you used
to be slaves to sin, you wholeheartedly
obeyed the form of teaching to which you
were entrusted. [18]You have been set free
from sin and have become slaves to righteousness.
[19]I put this in human terms because
you are weak in your natural selves. Just
as you used to offer the parts of your body
in slavery to impurity and to ever-increasing wickedness, so now offer them in slavery to righteousness leading to holiness.
[20]When you were slaves to sin, you were
free from the control of righteousness.
[21]What benefit did you reap at that time
from the things you are now ashamed of?
Those things result in death! [22]But now
that you have been set free from sin and
have become slaves to God, the benefit
you reap leads to holiness, and the result
is eternal life. [23]For the wages of sin is
death, but the gift of God is eternal life
in[b] Christ Jesus our Lord.

An Illustration From Marriage

7 Do you not know, brothers—for I am
speaking to men who know the law—
that the law has authority over a man only
as long as he lives? [2]For example, by law
a married woman is bound to her husband as long as he is alive, but if her husband dies, she is released from the law of
marriage. [3]So then, if she marries another
man while her husband is still alive, she
is called an adulteress. But if her husband
dies, she is released from that law and is
not an adulteress, even though she marries another man.
[4]So, my brothers, you also died to the
law through the body of Christ, that you
might belong to another, to him who was
raised from the dead, in order that we
might bear fruit to God. [5]For when we
were controlled by the sinful nature,[c] the
sinful passions aroused by the law were at
work in our bodies, so that we bore fruit
for death. [6]But now, by dying to what
once bound us, we have been released
from the law so that we serve in the new
way of the Spirit, and not in the old way
of the written code.

Struggling With Sin

[7]What shall we say, then? Is the law
sin? Certainly not! Indeed I would not
have known what sin was except through
the law. For I would not have known what
coveting really was if the law had not
said, "Do not covet."[d] [8]But sin, seizing
the opportunity afforded by the commandment, produced in me every kind of
covetous desire. For apart from law, sin is
dead. [9]Once I was alive apart from law;
but when the commandment came, sin
sprang to life and I died. [10]I found that the
very commandment that was intended to
bring life actually brought death. [11]For
sin, seizing the opportunity afforded by
the commandment, deceived me, and
through the commandment put me to
death. [12]So then, the law is holy, and the
commandment is holy, righteous and
good.

[a]6 Or *be rendered powerless* [b]23 Or *through* [c]5 Or *the flesh*; also in verse 25 [d]7 Exodus 20:17; Deut. 5:21

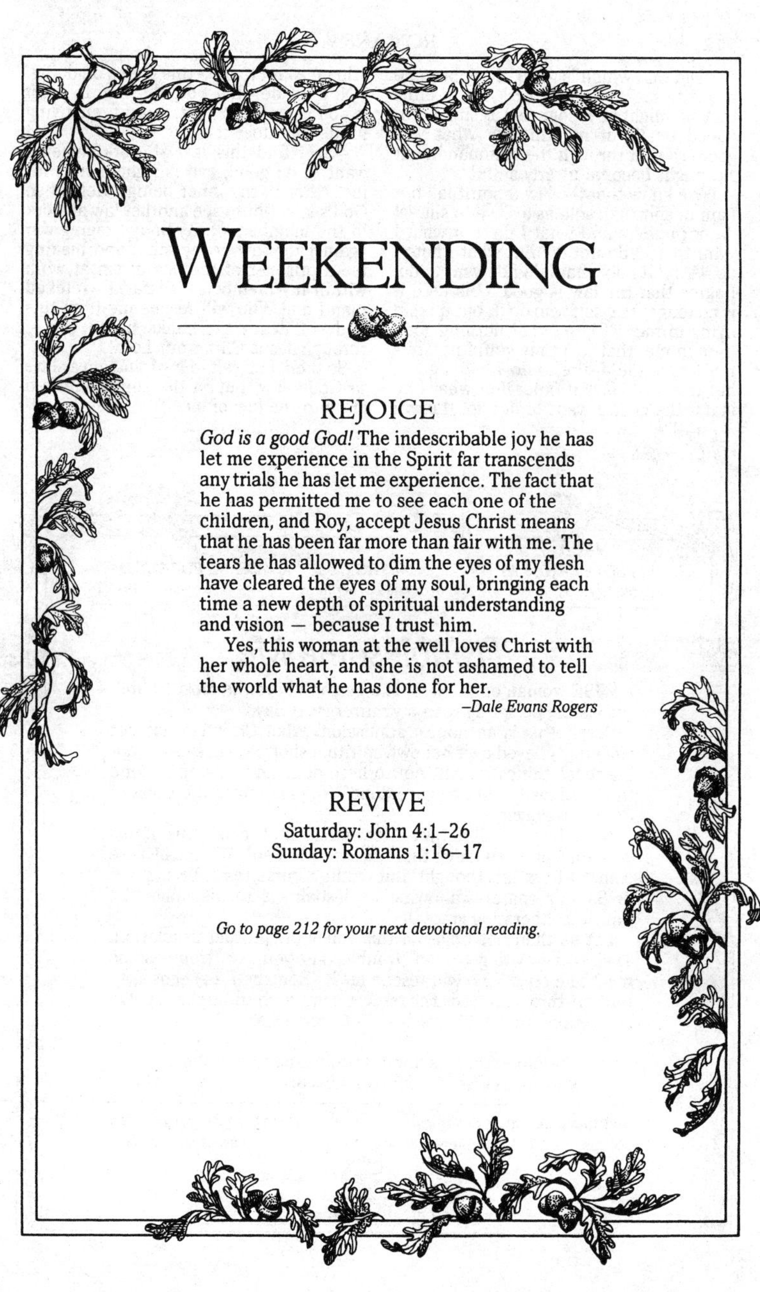

WEEKENDING

REJOICE

God is a good God! The indescribable joy he has let me experience in the Spirit far transcends any trials he has let me experience. The fact that he has permitted me to see each one of the children, and Roy, accept Jesus Christ means that he has been far more than fair with me. The tears he has allowed to dim the eyes of my flesh have cleared the eyes of my soul, bringing each time a new depth of spiritual understanding and vision — because I trust him.

Yes, this woman at the well loves Christ with her whole heart, and she is not ashamed to tell the world what he has done for her.

–Dale Evans Rogers

REVIVE

Saturday: John 4:1–26
Sunday: Romans 1:16–17

Go to page 212 for your next devotional reading.

[13]Did that which is good, then, become
death to me? By no means! But in order
that sin might be recognized as sin, it produced death in me through what was
good, so that through the commandment
sin might become utterly sinful.
[14]We know that the law is spiritual; but
I am unspiritual, sold as a slave to sin. [15]I
do not understand what I do. For what I
want to do I do not do, but what I hate I
do. [16]And if I do what I do not want to do,
I agree that the law is good. [17]As it is, it
is no longer I myself who do it, but it is sin
living in me. [18]I know that nothing good
lives in me, that is, in my sinful nature.[a]
For I have the desire to do what is good,
but I cannot carry it out. [19]For what I do
is not the good I want to do; no, the evil
I do not want to do—this I keep on doing.
[20]Now if I do what I do not want to do, it
is no longer I who do it, but it is sin living
in me that does it.
[21]So I find this law at work: When I
want to do good, evil is right there with
me. [22]For in my inner being I delight in
God's law; [23]but I see another law at work
in the members of my body, waging war
against the law of my mind and making
me a prisoner of the law of sin at work
within my members. [24]What a wretched
man I am! Who will rescue me from this
body of death? [25]Thanks be to God—
through Jesus Christ our Lord!

So then, I myself in my mind am a slave to God's law, but in the sinful nature a slave to the law of sin.

[a]18 Or *my flesh*

MONDAY

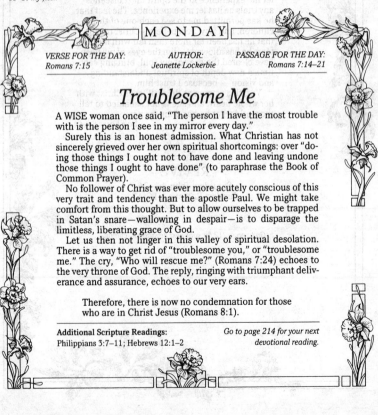

VERSE FOR THE DAY: Romans 7:15 | *AUTHOR:* Jeanette Lockerbie | *PASSAGE FOR THE DAY:* Romans 7:14–21

Troublesome Me

A WISE woman once said, "The person I have the most trouble with is the person I see in my mirror every day."

Surely this is an honest admission. What Christian has not sincerely grieved over her own spiritual shortcomings: over "doing those things I ought not to have done and leaving undone those things I ought to have done" (to paraphrase the Book of Common Prayer).

No follower of Christ was ever more acutely conscious of this very trait and tendency than the apostle Paul. We might take comfort from this thought. But to allow ourselves to be trapped in Satan's snare—wallowing in despair—is to disparage the limitless, liberating grace of God.

Let us then not linger in this valley of spiritual desolation. There is a way to get rid of "troublesome you," or "troublesome me." The cry, "Who will rescue me?" (Romans 7:24) echoes to the very throne of God. The reply, ringing with triumphant deliverance and assurance, echoes to our very ears.

> Therefore, there is now no condemnation for those who are in Christ Jesus (Romans 8:1).

Additional Scripture Readings:
Philippians 3:7–11; Hebrews 12:1–2

Go to page 214 for your next devotional reading.

Life Through the Spirit

8 Therefore, there is now no condemnation for those who are in Christ
Jesus,[a] 2because through Christ Jesus
the law of the Spirit of life set me free
from the law of sin and death. 3For what
the law was powerless to do in that it was
weakened by the sinful nature,[b] God did
by sending his own Son in the likeness of
sinful man to be a sin offering.[c] And so
he condemned sin in sinful man,[d] 4in order that the righteous requirements of
the law might be fully met in us, who do
not live according to the sinful nature but
according to the Spirit.

5Those who live according to the sinful
nature have their minds set on what that
nature desires; but those who live in accordance with the Spirit have their minds
set on what the Spirit desires. 6The mind
of sinful man[e] is death, but the mind
controlled by the Spirit is life and peace;
7the sinful mind[f] is hostile to God. It
does not submit to God's law, nor can it
do so. 8Those controlled by the sinful nature cannot please God.

9You, however, are controlled not by
the sinful nature but by the Spirit, if the
Spirit of God lives in you. And if anyone
does not have the Spirit of Christ, he does
not belong to Christ. 10But if Christ is in
you, your body is dead because of sin, yet
your spirit is alive because of righteousness. 11And if the Spirit of him who raised
Jesus from the dead is living in you, he
who raised Christ from the dead will also
give life to your mortal bodies through his
Spirit, who lives in you.

12Therefore, brothers, we have an obligation—but it is not to the sinful nature,
to live according to it. 13For if you live
according to the sinful nature, you will
die; but if by the Spirit you put to death
the misdeeds of the body, you will live,
14because those who are led by the Spirit
of God are sons of God. 15For you did not
receive a spirit that makes you a slave
again to fear, but you received the Spirit
of sonship.[g] And by him we cry, *"Abba,*[h]
Father." 16The Spirit himself testifies
with our spirit that we are God's children.
17Now if we are children, then we are
heirs—heirs of God and co-heirs with
Christ, if indeed we share in his sufferings
in order that we may also share in his
glory.

Future Glory

18I consider that our present sufferings
are not worth comparing with the glory
that will be revealed in us. 19The creation
waits in eager expectation for the sons of
God to be revealed. 20For the creation was
subjected to frustration, not by its own
choice, but by the will of the one who
subjected it, in hope 21that[i] the creation
itself will be liberated from its bondage to
decay and brought into the glorious freedom of the children of God.

22We know that the whole creation has
been groaning as in the pains of childbirth right up to the present time. 23Not
only so, but we ourselves, who have the
firstfruits of the Spirit, groan inwardly as
we wait eagerly for our adoption as sons,
the redemption of our bodies. 24For in
this hope we were saved. But hope that is
seen is no hope at all. Who hopes for
what he already has? 25But if we hope
for what we do not yet have, we wait for
it patiently.

26In the same way, the Spirit helps us in
our weakness. We do not know what we
ought to pray for, but the Spirit himself
intercedes for us with groans that words
cannot express. 27And he who searches
our hearts knows the mind of the Spirit,
because the Spirit intercedes for the
saints in accordance with God's will.

More Than Conquerors

28And we know that in all things God
works for the good of those who love
him,[j] who[k] have been called according
to his purpose. 29For those God foreknew
he also predestined to be conformed to
the likeness of his Son, that he might be
the firstborn among many brothers. 30And
those he predestined, he also called;
those he called, he also justified; those he
justified, he also glorified.

31What, then, shall we say in response
to this? If God is for us, who can be
against us? 32He who did not spare his
own Son, but gave him up for us all—how
will he not also, along with him, graciously give us all things? 33Who will bring any

[a]*1* Some later manuscripts *Jesus, who do not live according to the sinful nature but according to the Spirit,* [b]*3* Or *the flesh*; also in verses 4, 5, 8, 9, 12 and 13 [c]*3* Or *man, for sin* [d]*3* Or *in the flesh* [e]*6* Or *mind set on the flesh* [f]*7* Or *the mind set on the flesh* [g]*15* Or *adoption* [h]*15* Aramaic for *Father* [i]*20,21* Or *subjected it in hope.* [21]*For* [j]*28* Some manuscripts *And we know that all things work together for good to those who love God* [k]*28* Or *works together with those who love him to bring about what is good—with those who*

TUESDAY

VERSE FOR THE DAY:
Romans 8:26–27

AUTHOR:
Sue Richards

PASSAGE FOR THE DAY:
Romans 8:18–27

When It Hurts So Much . . .

THERE are times in the lives of all God's children when we are called on to suffer. We read in Romans 5:3–4 that "suffering produces perseverance; perseverance, character; and character, hope." For me suffering has also produced times of physical and emotional weakness. After the death of my first child, as I lay near death myself, I tried to pray, but I was in shock and heavily medicated. No words would come into my mind or to my lips. I wish I had known Romans 8:26–27 then. Yet, although I could not speak, I felt in close communication with the Lord. I just didn't understand how this was possible.

While believers are sustained in their suffering by hope, we also are sustained in our weakness in the most special way of all:

> The Spirit helps us in our weakness. We do not know what we ought to pray for, but the Spirit himself intercedes for us with groans that words cannot express. And he who searches our hearts knows the mind of the Spirit, because the Spirit intercedes for the saints in accordance with God's will (Romans 8:26–27).

God himself, who dwells within us in the person of the Holy Spirit, intercedes for us in our weakness. Not with flowery or powerful words, but with groans that words cannot express. How empowering in our weakest moments, when we don't know how to express our own overwhelming needs, to cling to the words of God.

"The Spirit himself intercedes for us with groans that words cannot express." And all of this intercession on our behalf is done "in accordance with God's will" for us personally. When Christ gave us the Holy Spirit, he left us much more than an inner spiritual discernment. Our triune God lives within and intercedes for each of us when we are in our weakest moments.

Abba, Father, your love and concern for me when I am at my most vulnerable times in life is beyond my understanding. I thank you for the gracious gift of your Holy Spirit. Amen.

Additional Scripture Readings:
John 14:26–27; Ephesians 6:17–18

Go to page 216 for your next devotional reading.

charge against those whom God has chosen? It is God who justifies. 34 Who is he that condemns? Christ Jesus, who died—more than that, who was raised to life—is at the right hand of God and is also interceding for us. 35 Who shall separate us from the love of Christ? Shall trouble or hardship or persecution or famine or nakedness or danger or sword? 36 As it is written:

"For your sake we face death all day
  long;
 we are considered as sheep to be
  slaughtered."[a]

37 No, in all these things we are more than conquerors through him who loved us. 38 For I am convinced that neither death nor life, neither angels nor demons,[b] neither the present nor the future, nor any powers, 39 neither height nor depth, nor anything else in all creation, will be able to separate us from the love of God that is in Christ Jesus our Lord.

God's Sovereign Choice

9 I speak the truth in Christ—I am not lying, my conscience confirms it in the Holy Spirit— 2 I have great sorrow and unceasing anguish in my heart. 3 For I could wish that I myself were cursed and cut off from Christ for the sake of my brothers, those of my own race, 4 the people of Israel. Theirs is the adoption as sons; theirs the divine glory, the covenants, the receiving of the law, the temple worship and the promises. 5 Theirs are the patriarchs, and from them is traced the human ancestry of Christ, who is God over all, forever praised![c] Amen.

6 It is not as though God's word had failed. For not all who are descended from Israel are Israel. 7 Nor because they are his descendants are they all Abraham's children. On the contrary, "It is through Isaac that your offspring will be reckoned."[d] 8 In other words, it is not the natural children who are God's children, but it is the children of the promise who are regarded as Abraham's offspring. 9 For this was how the promise was stated: "At the appointed time I will return, and Sarah will have a son."[e]

10 Not only that, but Rebekah's children had one and the same father, our father Isaac. 11 Yet, before the twins were born or had done anything good or bad—in order that God's purpose in election might stand: 12 not by works but by him who calls—she was told, "The older will serve the younger."[f] 13 Just as it is written: "Jacob I loved, but Esau I hated."[g]

14 What then shall we say? Is God unjust? Not at all! 15 For he says to Moses,

"I will have mercy on whom I have
  mercy,
 and I will have compassion on
  whom I have compassion."[h]

16 It does not, therefore, depend on man's desire or effort, but on God's mercy. 17 For the Scripture says to Pharaoh: "I raised you up for this very purpose, that I might display my power in you and that my name might be proclaimed in all the earth."[i] 18 Therefore God has mercy on whom he wants to have mercy, and he hardens whom he wants to harden.

19 One of you will say to me: "Then why does God still blame us? For who resists his will?" 20 But who are you, O man, to talk back to God? "Shall what is formed say to him who formed it, 'Why did you make me like this?' "[j] 21 Does not the potter have the right to make out of the same lump of clay some pottery for noble purposes and some for common use?

22 What if God, choosing to show his wrath and make his power known, bore with great patience the objects of his wrath—prepared for destruction? 23 What if he did this to make the riches of his glory known to the objects of his mercy, whom he prepared in advance for glory— 24 even us, whom he also called, not only from the Jews but also from the Gentiles? 25 As he says in Hosea:

"I will call them 'my people' who are
  not my people;
 and I will call her 'my loved one'
  who is not my loved one,"[k]

26 and,

"It will happen that in the very place
  where it was said to them,
 'You are not my people,'
 they will be called 'sons of the living
  God.' "[l]

27 Isaiah cries out concerning Israel:

[a] *36* Psalm 44:22 [b] *38* Or *nor heavenly rulers* [c] *5* Or *Christ, who is over all. God be forever praised!* Or *Christ. God who is over all be forever praised!* [d] *7* Gen. 21:12 [e] *9* Gen. 18:10,14 [f] *12* Gen. 25:23 [g] *13* Mal. 1:2,3 [h] *15* Exodus 33:19 [i] *17* Exodus 9:16 [j] *20* Isaiah 29:16; 45:9 [k] *25* Hosea 2:23 [l] *26* Hosea 1:10

"Though the number of the Israelites
be like the sand by the sea,
only the remnant will be saved.
28For the Lord will carry out
his sentence on earth with speed
and finality."[a]

29It is just as Isaiah said previously:

"Unless the Lord Almighty
had left us descendants,
we would have become like Sodom,
we would have been like
Gomorrah."[b]

Israel's Unbelief

30What then shall we say? That the
Gentiles, who did not pursue righteousness, have obtained it, a righteousness
that is by faith; 31but Israel, who pursued
a law of righteousness, has not attained

[a]*28* Isaiah 10:22,23 [b]*29* Isaiah 1:9

WEDNESDAY

VERSE FOR THE DAY: *Romans 8:28* | *AUTHOR:* *ann kiemel anderson* | *PASSAGE FOR THE DAY:* *Romans 8:28–39*

all things . . .

ROMANS 8:28 is engraved in my wedding band. it was the theme at my house as a child. my father, a preacher, clung to these words because they were a PROMISE from a Sovereign God with a PERFECT track record.

"in ALL things God works for the good" (caps mine). the rejection in one's childhood. alcoholic parents. the birth of a handicapped child. a husband leaving home for another woman. illness. no matter what life may have in store . . . absolutely ANYTHING . . . will turn into blessing if we love God.

i was 35 and will 38 when we married. both for the first time. we decided to try for a baby our first year. but i found i had a tendency to miscarry. to work with singleminded concentration to get pregnant and then be disappointed over and over. without romans 8:28 becoming my best friend, i would have been sucked under. i had been taught to UTTERLY trust God's Word. this verse had been stamped across my forehead and my heart.

it means God never takes away except to give us back something better. it means we must be brave enough and determined enough to wait . . . because it often takes God time to turn a painful situation to good. it means we can embrace our pain and not resent it because a blessing is coming!

today will and i stand in awe over four little boys . . . age four and under . . . God gave us through adoption. and we would be so shallow and careless with our love had we not traveled that black, seemingly hopeless, journey.

i love you. i run this glorious, hard race beside you. because of Jesus, everything . . . anything . . . will work for good as you love God.

Additional Scripture Readings:
Proverbs 19:21; Isaiah 55:8–11

Go to page 219 for your next devotional reading.

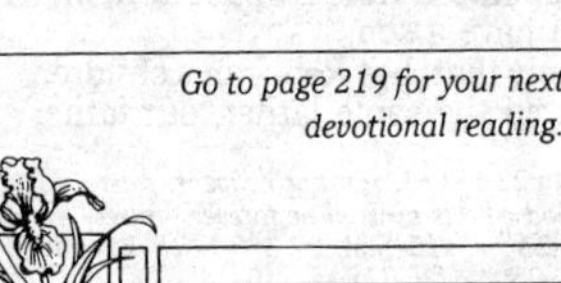

it. 32Why not? Because they pursued it
not by faith but as if it were by works.
They stumbled over the "stumbling
stone." 33As it is written:

"See, I lay in Zion a stone that causes
men to stumble
and a rock that makes them fall,
and the one who trusts in him will
never be put to shame."[a]

10 Brothers, my heart's desire and
prayer to God for the Israelites is
that they may be saved. 2For I can testify
about them that they are zealous for God,
but their zeal is not based on knowledge.
3Since they did not know the righteousness that comes from God and sought to
establish their own, they did not submit
to God's righteousness. 4Christ is the end
of the law so that there may be righteousness for everyone who believes.

5Moses describes in this way the righteousness that is by the law: "The man
who does these things will live by
them."[b] 6But the righteousness that is by
faith says: "Do not say in your heart, 'Who
will ascend into heaven?'[c]" (that is, to
bring Christ down) 7"or 'Who will descend into the deep?'[d]" (that is, to bring
Christ up from the dead). 8But what does
it say? "The word is near you; it is in your
mouth and in your heart,"[e] that is, the
word of faith we are proclaiming: 9That if
you confess with your mouth, "Jesus is
Lord," and believe in your heart that God
raised him from the dead, you will be
saved. 10For it is with your heart that you
believe and are justified, and it is with
your mouth that you confess and are
saved. 11As the Scripture says, "Anyone
who trusts in him will never be put to
shame."[f] 12For there is no difference between Jew and Gentile—the same Lord is
Lord of all and richly blesses all who call
on him, 13for, "Everyone who calls on the
name of the Lord will be saved."[g]

14How, then, can they call on the one
they have not believed in? And how can
they believe in the one of whom they have
not heard? And how can they hear without someone preaching to them? 15And
how can they preach unless they are sent?
As it is written, "How beautiful are the
feet of those who bring good news!"[h]

16But not all the Israelites accepted the
good news. For Isaiah says, "Lord, who
has believed our message?"[i] 17Conse-
quently, faith comes from hearing the
message, and the message is heard
through the word of Christ. 18But I ask:
Did they not hear? Of course they did:

"Their voice has gone out into all the
earth,
their words to the ends of the
world."[j]

19Again I ask: Did Israel not understand?
First, Moses says,

"I will make you envious by those
who are not a nation;
I will make you angry by a nation
that has no understanding."[k]

20And Isaiah boldly says,

"I was found by those who did not
seek me;
I revealed myself to those who did
not ask for me."[l]

21But concerning Israel he says,

"All day long I have held out my
hands
to a disobedient and obstinate
people."[m]

The Remnant of Israel

11 I ask then: Did God reject his people? By no means! I am an Israelite
myself, a descendant of Abraham, from
the tribe of Benjamin. 2God did not reject
his people, whom he foreknew. Don't you
know what the Scripture says in the passage about Elijah—how he appealed to
God against Israel: 3"Lord, they have
killed your prophets and torn down your
altars; I am the only one left, and they are
trying to kill me"[n]? 4And what was God's
answer to him? "I have reserved for myself seven thousand who have not bowed
the knee to Baal."[o] 5So too, at the present time there is a remnant chosen by
grace. 6And if by grace, then it is no longer by works; if it were, grace would no
longer be grace.[p]

7What then? What Israel sought so earnestly it did not obtain, but the elect did.
The others were hardened, 8as it is written:

[a] *33* Isaiah 8:14; 28:16 [b] *5* Lev. 18:5 [c] *6* Deut. 30:12 [d] *7* Deut. 30:13 [e] *8* Deut. 30:14
[f] *11* Isaiah 28:16 [g] *13* Joel 2:32 [h] *15* Isaiah 52:7 [i] *16* Isaiah 53:1 [j] *18* Psalm 19:4
[k] *19* Deut. 32:21 [l] *20* Isaiah 65:1 [m] *21* Isaiah 65:2 [n] *3* 1 Kings 19:10,14 [o] *4* 1 Kings 19:18
[p] *6* Some manuscripts *by grace. But if by works, then it is no longer grace; if it were, work would no longer be work.*

"God gave them a spirit of stupor,
eyes so that they could not see
and ears so that they could not hear,
to this very day."[a]

9And David says:

"May their table become a snare and a trap,
a stumbling block and a retribution for them.
10May their eyes be darkened so they cannot see,
and their backs be bent forever."[b]

Ingrafted Branches

11Again I ask: Did they stumble so as to fall beyond recovery? Not at all! Rather, because of their transgression, salvation has come to the Gentiles to make Israel envious. 12But if their transgression means riches for the world, and their loss means riches for the Gentiles, how much greater riches will their fullness bring!

13I am talking to you Gentiles. Inasmuch as I am the apostle to the Gentiles, I make much of my ministry 14in the hope that I may somehow arouse my own people to envy and save some of them. 15For if their rejection is the reconciliation of the world, what will their acceptance be but life from the dead? 16If the part of the dough offered as firstfruits is holy, then the whole batch is holy; if the root is holy, so are the branches.

17If some of the branches have been broken off, and you, though a wild olive shoot, have been grafted in among the others and now share in the nourishing sap from the olive root, 18do not boast over those branches. If you do, consider this: You do not support the root, but the root supports you. 19You will say then, "Branches were broken off so that I could be grafted in." 20Granted. But they were broken off because of unbelief, and you stand by faith. Do not be arrogant, but be afraid. 21For if God did not spare the natural branches, he will not spare you either.

22Consider therefore the kindness and sternness of God: sternness to those who fell, but kindness to you, provided that you continue in his kindness. Otherwise, you also will be cut off. 23And if they do not persist in unbelief, they will be grafted in, for God is able to graft them in again. 24After all, if you were cut out of an olive tree that is wild by nature, and contrary to nature were grafted into a cultivated olive tree, how much more readily will these, the natural branches, be grafted into their own olive tree!

All Israel Will Be Saved

25I do not want you to be ignorant of this mystery, brothers, so that you may not be conceited: Israel has experienced a hardening in part until the full number of the Gentiles has come in. 26And so all Israel will be saved, as it is written:

"The deliverer will come from Zion;
he will turn godlessness away from Jacob.
27And this is[c] my covenant with them
when I take away their sins."[d]

28As far as the gospel is concerned, they are enemies on your account; but as far as election is concerned, they are loved on account of the patriarchs, 29for God's gifts and his call are irrevocable. 30Just as you who were at one time disobedient to God have now received mercy as a result of their disobedience, 31so they too have now become disobedient in order that they too may now[e] receive mercy as a result of God's mercy to you. 32For God has bound all men over to disobedience so that he may have mercy on them all.

Doxology

33Oh, the depth of the riches of the
wisdom and[f] knowledge of God!
How unsearchable his judgments,
and his paths beyond tracing out!
34"Who has known the mind of the Lord?
Or who has been his counselor?"[g]
35"Who has ever given to God,
that God should repay him?"[h]
36For from him and through him and to him are all things.
To him be the glory forever! Amen.

Living Sacrifices

12 Therefore, I urge you, brothers, in view of God's mercy, to offer your bodies as living sacrifices, holy and pleasing to God—this is your spiritual[i] act of worship. 2Do not conform any longer to

[a]8 Deut. 29:4; Isaiah 29:10 [b]10 Psalm 69:22,23 [c]27 Or *will be* [d]27 Isaiah 59:20,21; 27:9; Jer. 31:33,34 [e]31 Some manuscripts do not have *now.* [f]33 Or *riches and the wisdom and the* [g]34 Isaiah 40:13 [h]35 Job 41:11 [i]1 Or *reasonable*

THURSDAY

VERSE FOR THE DAY: Romans 12:1–2 | *AUTHOR:* Marie Chapian | *PASSAGE FOR THE DAY:* Romans 12:1–8

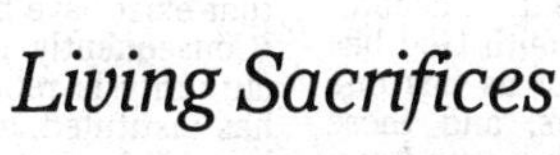

Living Sacrifices

IT is a challenge to live our lives as sacrifices to God. When we do, we aren't the masters of our bodies and minds—God is. All that we do or think must conform to the Word of God. Such a high calling is impossible without the Holy Spirit's guidance and help. We cannot make spiritual progress without the Holy Spirit, and that is why in Romans 12:1 the Lord tells us to offer our bodies to him as living sacrifices. If we try to grow and change spiritually without the supernatural empowering of the Holy Spirit, we are conforming to the pattern of the world. The Lord tells us to avoid this by becoming transformed by the renewing of our minds (Romans 12:1–2).

As a sacrificial act of worship, God expects us to be holy and pleasing to him. When I was sharing Romans 12 with a group of young people, one fifteen-year-old girl asked, "Does that mean that everything I do every day—at school, at home, in sports, in art and with friends—all these should be an act of worship to God?"

Another student replied, "How can I stay on my knees that long?"

We chuckled, knowing that we worship not only on our knees but also as we live our lives. Our everyday lives are important to God, important enough that he sent his Son to die on the cross so that Jesus could live in us through each day—including the ordinary ones.

We can now say: "I'm going to school to worship God." "I'm going to paint a picture to worship God." "I'm going to clean the kitchen to worship God." "I'm going to my job to worship God," as well as "I'm going to church to worship God."

When we conform to the world's patterns and methods, we do not please God, no matter how good we feel about ourselves or how much other people approve of us. But we do please God when our minds are renewed. Then we are able to test and approve God's perfect will (Romans 12:2).

Additional Scripture Readings:
Ephesians 4:22–24; 1 Peter 1:13–16

Go to page 221 for your next devotional reading.

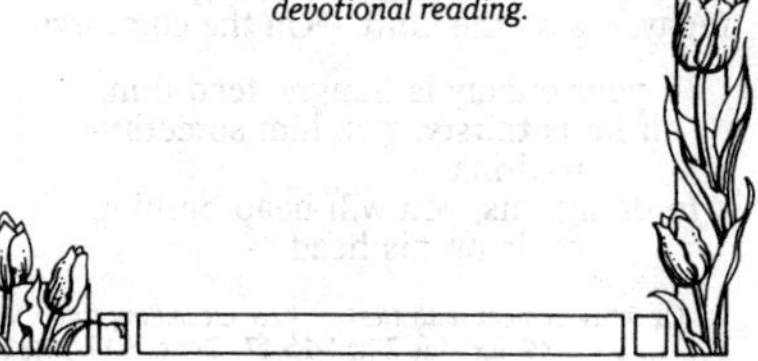

the pattern of this world, but be transformed by the renewing of your mind. Then you will be able to test and approve what God's will is—his good, pleasing and perfect will.

3For by the grace given me I say to every one of you: Do not think of yourself more highly than you ought, but rather think of yourself with sober judgment, in accordance with the measure of faith God has given you. 4Just as each of us has one body with many members, and these members do not all have the same function, 5so in Christ we who are many form one body, and each member belongs to all the others. 6We have different gifts, according to the grace given us. If a man's gift is prophesying, let him use it in proportion to his[a] faith. 7If it is serving, let him serve; if it is teaching, let him teach; 8if it is encouraging, let him encourage; if it is contributing to the needs of others, let him give generously; if it is leadership, let him govern diligently; if it is showing mercy, let him do it cheerfully.

Love

9Love must be sincere. Hate what is evil; cling to what is good. 10Be devoted to one another in brotherly love. Honor one another above yourselves. 11Never be lacking in zeal, but keep your spiritual fervor, serving the Lord. 12Be joyful in hope, patient in affliction, faithful in prayer. 13Share with God's people who are in need. Practice hospitality.

14Bless those who persecute you; bless and do not curse. 15Rejoice with those who rejoice; mourn with those who mourn. 16Live in harmony with one another. Do not be proud, but be willing to associate with people of low position.[b] Do not be conceited.

17Do not repay anyone evil for evil. Be careful to do what is right in the eyes of everybody. 18If it is possible, as far as it depends on you, live at peace with everyone. 19Do not take revenge, my friends, but leave room for God's wrath, for it is written: "It is mine to avenge; I will repay,"[c] says the Lord. 20On the contrary:

"If your enemy is hungry, feed him;
if he is thirsty, give him something
to drink.
In doing this, you will heap burning
coals on his head."[d]

21Do not be overcome by evil, but overcome evil with good.

Submission to the Authorities

13 Everyone must submit himself to the governing authorities, for there is no authority except that which God has established. The authorities that exist have been established by God. 2Consequently, he who rebels against the authority is rebelling against what God has instituted, and those who do so will bring judgment on themselves. 3For rulers hold no terror for those who do right, but for those who do wrong. Do you want to be free from fear of the one in authority? Then do what is right and he will commend you. 4For he is God's servant to do you good. But if you do wrong, be afraid, for he does not bear the sword for nothing. He is God's servant, an agent of wrath to bring punishment on the wrongdoer. 5Therefore, it is necessary to submit to the authorities, not only because of possible punishment but also because of conscience.

6This is also why you pay taxes, for the authorities are God's servants, who give their full time to governing. 7Give everyone what you owe him: If you owe taxes, pay taxes; if revenue, then revenue; if respect, then respect; if honor, then honor.

Love, for the Day Is Near

8Let no debt remain outstanding, except the continuing debt to love one another, for he who loves his fellowman has fulfilled the law. 9The commandments, "Do not commit adultery," "Do not murder," "Do not steal," "Do not covet,"[e] and whatever other commandment there may be, are summed up in this one rule: "Love your neighbor as yourself."[f] 10Love does no harm to its neighbor. Therefore love is the fulfillment of the law.

11And do this, understanding the present time. The hour has come for you to wake up from your slumber, because our salvation is nearer now than when we first believed. 12The night is nearly over; the day is almost here. So let us put aside the deeds of darkness and put on the armor of light. 13Let us behave decently, as in the daytime, not in orgies and drunkenness, not in sexual immorality and debauchery, not in dissension and jealousy. 14Rather,

[a]6 Or *in agreement with the* [b]16 Or *willing to do menial work* [c]19 Deut. 32:35 [d]20 Prov. 25:21,22 [e]9 Exodus 20:13-15,17; Deut. 5:17-19,21 [f]9 Lev. 19:18

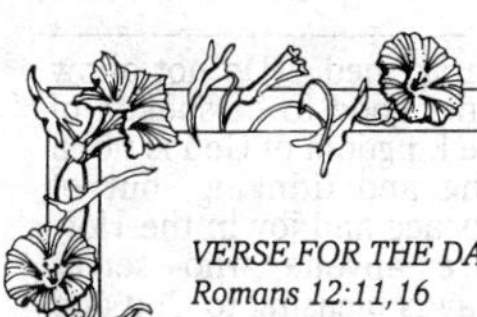

FRIDAY

VERSE FOR THE DAY:	*AUTHOR:*	*PASSAGE FOR THE DAY:*
Romans 12:11,16	*Gigi Graham Tchividjian*	*Romans 12:9–21*

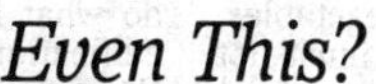

Even This?

THOUGH early morning is not my best time of day, after a couple of cups of coffee, I managed to fix breakfast, wash the dishes, and usher six children out the door to school before heading for the laundry room.

I stopped abruptly at the door and stood gazing in disbelief at the mountain of dirty clothes. Hadn't I just washed three loads yesterday? Sudden tears of frustration stung my eyes. I quickly brushed them away, a bit ashamed of myself, and put the first load in the washer.

Then I continued to tidy up, picking up the morning newspaper and various cups and glasses left from snacks the night before. Soon I found myself in my son's bathroom, scrubbing the tub. Once again the tears insisted on imposing themselves against my will. This time they found little resistance. I was frustrated and discouraged, and my self-esteem was about as low as it could get.

It was still morning, but I was tired—tired of the same mess day after day—of washing clothes that only yesterday I had folded and returned to their proper places; of doing the dishes, only to get them out a short time later to reset the table. I was sick of spending hours cooking a meal that was consumed in minutes.

Sitting in the middle of the bathroom floor, sponge and cleanser in hand and tears streaming down my cheeks, I found myself fussing, crying and praying all at the same time.

God in his loving-kindness came to meet me: "I tell you the truth, whatever you did for one of the least of these brothers of mine, you did for me" (Matthew 25:40).

"Lord, even this?" I asked.

"Especially this," he replied. "Who else is going to do it for me? In all these small ways, you are serving me."

Lovingly reassured and encouraged, I dried my tears and continued to scrub the tub.

Additional Scripture Readings:
Matthew 11:28–30; Philippians 2:1–8

Go to page 223 for your next devotional reading.

clothe yourselves with the Lord Jesus Christ, and do not think about how to gratify the desires of the sinful nature.[a]

The Weak and the Strong

14 Accept him whose faith is weak, without passing judgment on disputable matters. 2One man's faith allows him to eat everything, but another man, whose faith is weak, eats only vegetables. 3The man who eats everything must not look down on him who does not, and the man who does not eat everything must not condemn the man who does, for God has accepted him. 4Who are you to judge someone else's servant? To his own master he stands or falls. And he will stand, for the Lord is able to make him stand.

5One man considers one day more sacred than another; another man considers every day alike. Each one should be fully convinced in his own mind. 6He who regards one day as special, does so to the Lord. He who eats meat, eats to the Lord, for he gives thanks to God; and he who abstains, does so to the Lord and gives thanks to God. 7For none of us lives to himself alone and none of us dies to himself alone. 8If we live, we live to the Lord; and if we die, we die to the Lord. So, whether we live or die, we belong to the Lord.

9For this very reason, Christ died and returned to life so that he might be the Lord of both the dead and the living. 10You, then, why do you judge your brother? Or why do you look down on your brother? For we will all stand before God's judgment seat. 11It is written:

" 'As surely as I live,' says the Lord,
'every knee will bow before me;
every tongue will confess to
God.' "[b]

12So then, each of us will give an account of himself to God.

13Therefore let us stop passing judgment on one another. Instead, make up your mind not to put any stumbling block or obstacle in your brother's way. 14As one who is in the Lord Jesus, I am fully convinced that no food[c] is unclean in itself. But if anyone regards something as unclean, then for him it is unclean. 15If your brother is distressed because of what you eat, you are no longer acting in love. Do not by your eating destroy your brother for whom Christ died. 16Do not allow what you consider good to be spoken of as evil. 17For the kingdom of God is not a matter of eating and drinking, but of righteousness, peace and joy in the Holy Spirit, 18because anyone who serves Christ in this way is pleasing to God and approved by men.

19Let us therefore make every effort to do what leads to peace and to mutual edification. 20Do not destroy the work of God for the sake of food. All food is clean, but it is wrong for a man to eat anything that causes someone else to stumble. 21It is better not to eat meat or drink wine or to do anything else that will cause your brother to fall.

22So whatever you believe about these things keep between yourself and God. Blessed is the man who does not condemn himself by what he approves. 23But the man who has doubts is condemned if he eats, because his eating is not from faith; and everything that does not come from faith is sin.

15 We who are strong ought to bear with the failings of the weak and not to please ourselves. 2Each of us should please his neighbor for his good, to build him up. 3For even Christ did not please himself but, as it is written: "The insults of those who insult you have fallen on me."[d] 4For everything that was written in the past was written to teach us, so that through endurance and the encouragement of the Scriptures we might have hope.

5May the God who gives endurance and encouragement give you a spirit of unity among yourselves as you follow Christ Jesus, 6so that with one heart and mouth you may glorify the God and Father of our Lord Jesus Christ.

7Accept one another, then, just as Christ accepted you, in order to bring praise to God. 8For I tell you that Christ has become a servant of the Jews[e] on behalf of God's truth, to confirm the promises made to the patriarchs 9so that the Gentiles may glorify God for his mercy, as it is written:

"Therefore I will praise you among
the Gentiles;
I will sing hymns to your name."[f]

10Again, it says,

[a]14 Or *the flesh* [b]11 Isaiah 45:23 [c]14 Or *that nothing* [d]3 Psalm 69:9 [e]8 Greek *circumcision* [f]9 2 Samuel 22:50; Psalm 18:49

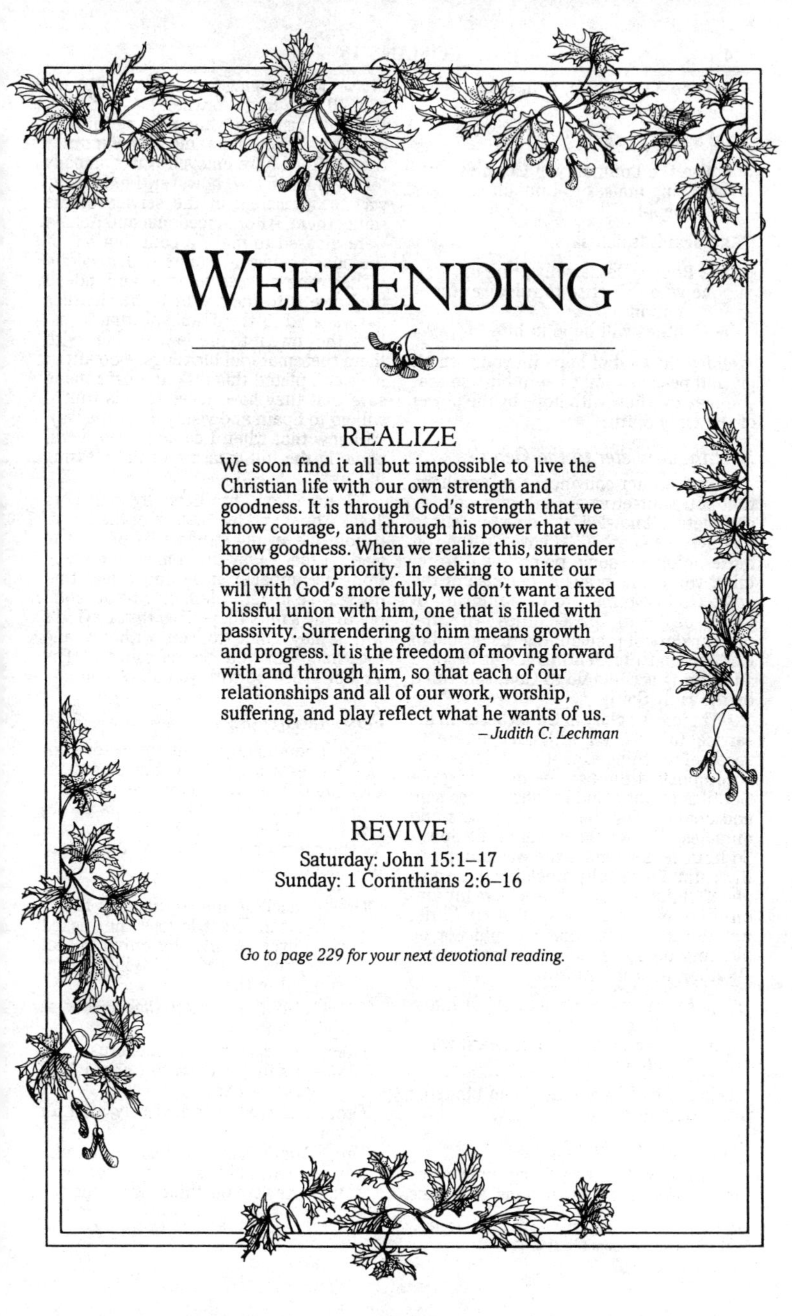

WEEKENDING

REALIZE

We soon find it all but impossible to live the Christian life with our own strength and goodness. It is through God's strength that we know courage, and through his power that we know goodness. When we realize this, surrender becomes our priority. In seeking to unite our will with God's more fully, we don't want a fixed blissful union with him, one that is filled with passivity. Surrendering to him means growth and progress. It is the freedom of moving forward with and through him, so that each of our relationships and all of our work, worship, suffering, and play reflect what he wants of us.

– Judith C. Lechman

REVIVE

Saturday: John 15:1–17
Sunday: 1 Corinthians 2:6–16

Go to page 229 for your next devotional reading.

"Rejoice, O Gentiles, with his
people."[a]

11And again,

"Praise the Lord, all you Gentiles,
and sing praises to him, all you
peoples."[b]

12And again, Isaiah says,

"The Root of Jesse will spring up,
one who will arise to rule over the
nations;
the Gentiles will hope in him."[c]

13May the God of hope fill you with all
joy and peace as you trust in him, so that
you may overflow with hope by the power
of the Holy Spirit.

Paul the Minister to the Gentiles

14I myself am convinced, my brothers,
that you yourselves are full of goodness,
complete in knowledge and competent to
instruct one another. 15I have written you
quite boldly on some points, as if to remind you of them again, because of the
grace God gave me 16to be a minister of
Christ Jesus to the Gentiles with the
priestly duty of proclaiming the gospel of
God, so that the Gentiles might become
an offering acceptable to God, sanctified
by the Holy Spirit.
17Therefore I glory in Christ Jesus in my
service to God. 18I will not venture to
speak of anything except what Christ has
accomplished through me in leading the
Gentiles to obey God by what I have said
and done— 19by the power of signs and
miracles, through the power of the Spirit.
So from Jerusalem all the way around to
Illyricum, I have fully proclaimed the gospel of Christ. 20It has always been my ambition to preach the gospel where Christ
was not known, so that I would not be
building on someone else's foundation.
21Rather, as it is written:

"Those who were not told about him
will see,
and those who have not heard will
understand."[d]

22This is why I have often been hindered
from coming to you.

Paul's Plan to Visit Rome

23But now that there is no more place
for me to work in these regions, and since
I have been longing for many years to see
you, 24I plan to do so when I go to Spain.
I hope to visit you while passing through
and to have you assist me on my journey
there, after I have enjoyed your company
for a while. 25Now, however, I am on my
way to Jerusalem in the service of the
saints there. 26For Macedonia and Achaia
were pleased to make a contribution for
the poor among the saints in Jerusalem.
27They were pleased to do it, and indeed
they owe it to them. For if the Gentiles
have shared in the Jews' spiritual blessings, they owe it to the Jews to share with
them their material blessings. 28So after I
have completed this task and have made
sure that they have received this fruit, I
will go to Spain and visit you on the way.
29I know that when I come to you, I will
come in the full measure of the blessing
of Christ.
30I urge you, brothers, by our Lord
Jesus Christ and by the love of the Spirit,
to join me in my struggle by praying to
God for me. 31Pray that I may be rescued
from the unbelievers in Judea and that
my service in Jerusalem may be acceptable to the saints there, 32so that by God's
will I may come to you with joy and
together with you be refreshed. 33The
God of peace be with you all. Amen.

Personal Greetings

16 I commend to you our sister Pho-
ebe, a servant[e] of the church in
Cenchrea. 2I ask you to receive her in the
Lord in a way worthy of the saints and to
give her any help she may need from you,
for she has been a great help to many people, including me.

3Greet Priscilla[f] and Aquila, my fellow
workers in Christ Jesus. 4They risked
their lives for me. Not only I but all
the churches of the Gentiles are
grateful to them.
5Greet also the church that meets at
their house.
Greet my dear friend Epenetus, who
was the first convert to Christ in the
province of Asia.
6Greet Mary, who worked very hard for
you.
7Greet Andronicus and Junias, my relatives who have been in prison with
me. They are outstanding among the

a10 Deut. 32:43 *b11* Psalm 117:1 *c12* Isaiah 11:10 *d21* Isaiah 52:15 *e1* Or *deaconess*
f3 Greek *Prisca*, a variant of *Priscilla*

apostles, and they were in Christ
before I was.
8Greet Ampliatus, whom I love in the
Lord.
9Greet Urbanus, our fellow worker in
Christ, and my dear friend Stachys.
10Greet Apelles, tested and approved in
Christ.
Greet those who belong to the
household of Aristobulus.
11Greet Herodion, my relative.
Greet those in the household of Narcis-
sus who are in the Lord.
12Greet Tryphena and Tryphosa, those
women who work hard in the Lord.
Greet my dear friend Persis, another
woman who has worked very hard in
the Lord.
13Greet Rufus, chosen in the Lord, and
his mother, who has been a mother
to me, too.
14Greet Asyncritus, Phlegon, Hermes, Pa-
trobas, Hermas and the brothers
with them.
15Greet Philologus, Julia, Nereus and his
sister, and Olympas and all the
saints with them.
16Greet one another with a holy kiss.
All the churches of Christ send greetings.

17I urge you, brothers, to watch out for
those who cause divisions and put obstacles in your way that are contrary to the
teaching you have learned. Keep away
from them. 18For such people are not
serving our Lord Christ, but their own ap-
petites. By smooth talk and flattery they
deceive the minds of naive people. 19Ev-
eryone has heard about your obedience,
so I am full of joy over you; but I want you
to be wise about what is good, and innocent about what is evil.

20The God of peace will soon crush Satan under your feet.

The grace of our Lord Jesus be with
you.

21Timothy, my fellow worker, sends his
greetings to you, as do Lucius, Jason and
Sosipater, my relatives.

22I, Tertius, who wrote down this letter,
greet you in the Lord.

23Gaius, whose hospitality I and the
whole church here enjoy, sends you his
greetings.

Erastus, who is the city's director of
public works, and our brother Quartus
send you their greetings.[a]

25Now to him who is able to establish
you by my gospel and the proclamation of
Jesus Christ, according to the revelation
of the mystery hidden for long ages past,
26but now revealed and made known
through the prophetic writings by the
command of the eternal God, so that all
nations might believe and obey him—
27to the only wise God be glory forever
through Jesus Christ! Amen.

[a]23 Some manuscripts *their greetings.* 24*May the grace of our Lord Jesus Christ be with all of you. Amen.*

PAUL, while staying in Ephesus (Acts 19), writes this letter to the church he started in Corinth (Acts 18:1–17). He addresses various problems he has heard about and answers questions they have asked of him in a letter (see 1 Corinthians 7:1). He places a high priority on being obedient to Christ and on striving for unity, humility and love in the church. As you read this book, make a decision to seek the Lord's will in everything you do and to work hard to be humble, to love others, and to become one in spirit with your fellow believers.

1 CORINTHIANS

1 Paul, called to be an apostle of Christ
Jesus by the will of God, and our
brother Sosthenes,

2To the church of God in Corinth, to
those sanctified in Christ Jesus and
called to be holy, together with all those
everywhere who call on the name of our
Lord Jesus Christ—their Lord and ours:

3Grace and peace to you from God our
Father and the Lord Jesus Christ.

Thanksgiving

4I always thank God for you because of
his grace given you in Christ Jesus. 5For
in him you have been enriched in every
way—in all your speaking and in all your
knowledge— 6because our testimony
about Christ was confirmed in you.
7Therefore you do not lack any spiritual
gift as you eagerly wait for our Lord Jesus
Christ to be revealed. 8He will keep you
strong to the end, so that you will be
blameless on the day of our Lord Jesus

Christ. 9God, who has called you into fellowship with his Son Jesus Christ our Lord, is faithful.

Divisions in the Church

10I appeal to you, brothers, in the name of our Lord Jesus Christ, that all of you agree with one another so that there may be no divisions among you and that you may be perfectly united in mind and thought. 11My brothers, some from Chloe's household have informed me that there are quarrels among you. 12What I mean is this: One of you says, "I follow Paul"; another, "I follow Apollos"; another, "I follow Cephas[a]"; still another, "I follow Christ."

13Is Christ divided? Was Paul crucified for you? Were you baptized into[b] the name of Paul? 14I am thankful that I did not baptize any of you except Crispus and Gaius, 15so no one can say that you were baptized into my name. 16(Yes, I also baptized the household of Stephanas; beyond that, I don't remember if I baptized anyone else.) 17For Christ did not send me to baptize, but to preach the gospel—not with words of human wisdom, lest the cross of Christ be emptied of its power.

Christ the Wisdom and Power of God

18For the message of the cross is foolishness to those who are perishing, but to us who are being saved it is the power of God. 19For it is written:

"I will destroy the wisdom of the
wise;
the intelligence of the intelligent I
will frustrate."[c]

20Where is the wise man? Where is the scholar? Where is the philosopher of this age? Has not God made foolish the wisdom of the world? 21For since in the wisdom of God the world through its wisdom did not know him, God was pleased through the foolishness of what was preached to save those who believe. 22Jews demand miraculous signs and Greeks look for wisdom, 23but we preach Christ crucified: a stumbling block to Jews and foolishness to Gentiles, 24but to those whom God has called, both Jews and Greeks, Christ the power of God and the wisdom of God. 25For the foolishness of God is wiser than man's wisdom, and the weakness of God is stronger than man's strength.

26Brothers, think of what you were when you were called. Not many of you were wise by human standards; not many were influential; not many were of noble birth. 27But God chose the foolish things of the world to shame the wise; God chose the weak things of the world to shame the strong. 28He chose the lowly things of this world and the despised things—and the things that are not—to nullify the things that are, 29so that no one may boast before him. 30It is because of him that you are in Christ Jesus, who has become for us wisdom from God—that is, our righteousness, holiness and redemption. 31Therefore, as it is written: "Let him who boasts boast in the Lord."[d]

2 When I came to you, brothers, I did not come with eloquence or superior wisdom as I proclaimed to you the testimony about God.[e] 2For I resolved to know nothing while I was with you except Jesus Christ and him crucified. 3I came to you in weakness and fear, and with much trembling. 4My message and my preaching were not with wise and persuasive words, but with a demonstration of the Spirit's power, 5so that your faith might not rest on men's wisdom, but on God's power.

Wisdom From the Spirit

6We do, however, speak a message of wisdom among the mature, but not the wisdom of this age or of the rulers of this age, who are coming to nothing. 7No, we speak of God's secret wisdom, a wisdom that has been hidden and that God destined for our glory before time began. 8None of the rulers of this age understood it, for if they had, they would not have crucified the Lord of glory. 9However, as it is written:

"No eye has seen,
no ear has heard,
no mind has conceived
what God has prepared for those
who love him"[f]—

10but God has revealed it to us by his Spirit.

The Spirit searches all things, even the deep things of God. 11For who among men knows the thoughts of a man except the man's spirit within him? In the same

[a] *12* That is, Peter [b] *13* Or *in*; also in verse 15 [c] *19* Isaiah 29:14 [d] *31* Jer. 9:24 [e] *1* Some manuscripts *as I proclaimed to you God's mystery* [f] *9* Isaiah 64:4

way no one knows the thoughts of God except the Spirit of God. 12We have not received the spirit of the world but the Spirit who is from God, that we may understand what God has freely given us. 13This is what we speak, not in words taught us by human wisdom but in words taught by the Spirit, expressing spiritual truths in spiritual words.[a] 14The man without the Spirit does not accept the things that come from the Spirit of God, for they are foolishness to him, and he cannot understand them, because they are spiritually discerned. 15The spiritual man makes judgments about all things, but he himself is not subject to any man's judgment:

16"For who has known the mind of the
  Lord
 that he may instruct him?"[b]

But we have the mind of Christ.

On Divisions in the Church

3 Brothers, I could not address you as spiritual but as worldly—mere infants in Christ. 2I gave you milk, not solid food, for you were not yet ready for it. Indeed, you are still not ready. 3You are still worldly. For since there is jealousy and quarreling among you, are you not worldly? Are you not acting like mere men? 4For when one says, "I follow Paul," and another, "I follow Apollos," are you not mere men?

5What, after all, is Apollos? And what is Paul? Only servants, through whom you came to believe—as the Lord has assigned to each his task. 6I planted the seed, Apollos watered it, but God made it grow. 7So neither he who plants nor he who waters is anything, but only God, who makes things grow. 8The man who plants and the man who waters have one purpose, and each will be rewarded according to his own labor. 9For we are God's fellow workers; you are God's field, God's building.

10By the grace God has given me, I laid a foundation as an expert builder, and someone else is building on it. But each one should be careful how he builds. 11For no one can lay any foundation other than the one already laid, which is Jesus Christ. 12If any man builds on this foundation using gold, silver, costly stones, wood, hay or straw, 13his work will be shown for what it is, because the Day will bring it to light. It will be revealed with fire, and the fire will test the quality of each man's work. 14If what he has built survives, he will receive his reward. 15If it is burned up, he will suffer loss; he himself will be saved, but only as one escaping through the flames.

16Don't you know that you yourselves are God's temple and that God's Spirit lives in you? 17If anyone destroys God's temple, God will destroy him; for God's temple is sacred, and you are that temple.

18Do not deceive yourselves. If any one of you thinks he is wise by the standards of this age, he should become a "fool" so that he may become wise. 19For the wisdom of this world is foolishness in God's sight. As it is written: "He catches the wise in their craftiness"[c]; 20and again, "The Lord knows that the thoughts of the wise are futile."[d] 21So then, no more boasting about men! All things are yours, 22whether Paul or Apollos or Cephas[e] or the world or life or death or the present or the future—all are yours, 23and you are of Christ, and Christ is of God.

Apostles of Christ

4 So then, men ought to regard us as servants of Christ and as those entrusted with the secret things of God. 2Now it is required that those who have been given a trust must prove faithful. 3I care very little if I am judged by you or by any human court; indeed, I do not even judge myself. 4My conscience is clear, but that does not make me innocent. It is the Lord who judges me. 5Therefore judge nothing before the appointed time; wait till the Lord comes. He will bring to light what is hidden in darkness and will expose the motives of men's hearts. At that time each will receive his praise from God.

6Now, brothers, I have applied these things to myself and Apollos for your benefit, so that you may learn from us the meaning of the saying, "Do not go beyond what is written." Then you will not take pride in one man over against another. 7For who makes you different from anyone else? What do you have that you did not receive? And if you did receive it, why do you boast as though you did not?

8Already you have all you want! Already you have become rich! You have become

[a]*13* Or *Spirit, interpreting spiritual truths to spiritual men* [b]*16* Isaiah 40:13 [c]*19* Job 5:13
[d]*20* Psalm 94:11 [e]*22* That is, Peter

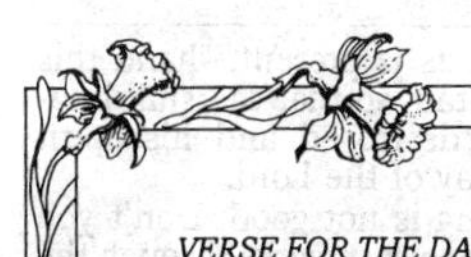

MONDAY

VERSE FOR THE DAY: *1 Corinthians 2:12* | *AUTHOR:* *June Hunt* | *PASSAGE FOR THE DAY:* *1 Corinthians 2:11–16*

The Holy Spirit

THE blackout took my neighborhood by surprise. Suddenly in total darkness, I inched my way to the bedside table and fumbled for the flashlight. What frustration . . . it didn't work. How useless—a flashlight that didn't function.

Just as useless is the person unable to function according to God's divine plan. Why? Because God originally designed the human spirit to contain the Holy Spirit. In the garden, Adam and Eve had perfect oneness with God. The Holy Spirit lived in their human spirits and enlightened every aspect of their lives. Once they pronounced their "declaration of independence" from God, however, sin came in and the Spirit went out. The pair were like a flashlight without batteries; with no power on the inside, there was no light on the outside. They spiraled downward into spiritual darkness.

Yet God did not give up on all those who were to be born into that same darkness. "The lamp of the LORD searches the spirit of a man" (Proverbs 20:27). God desired to reunite the Holy Spirit with the human spirit so that they could again be one.

When you feel the frustration of wandering in the dark, know that the Lord has already provided the perfect guide for your life. For "when he, the Spirit of truth, comes, he will guide you into all truth" (John 16:13). Your own personal Counselor, Conscience, Convictor and Comforter fills your soul—your mind, will and emotions—with perfect truth. He teaches your mind, directs your will and guides your emotions. As a result, those who are joined to the Spirit better understand spiritual things (1 Corinthians 2:14).

Like the flashlight, you were designed to shine; but you can never shine with your own power. The Holy Spirit provides the power to produce the light. And once you shine as you were intended to shine, you will never be useless!

Additional Scripture Readings:
Ephesians 5:8–14; 2 Timothy 1:8–14

Go to page 231 for your next devotional reading.

kings—and that without us! How I wish
that you really had become kings so that
we might be kings with you! 9For it seems
to me that God has put us apostles on
display at the end of the procession, like
men condemned to die in the arena. We
have been made a spectacle to the whole
universe, to angels as well as to men.
10We are fools for Christ, but you are so
wise in Christ! We are weak, but you are
strong! You are honored, we are dishon-
ored! 11To this very hour we go hungry
and thirsty, we are in rags, we are brutally
treated, we are homeless. 12We work hard
with our own hands. When we are cursed,
we bless; when we are persecuted, we endure it; 13when we are slandered, we answer kindly. Up to this moment we have
become the scum of the earth, the refuse
of the world.

14I am not writing this to shame you,
but to warn you, as my dear children.
15Even though you have ten thousand
guardians in Christ, you do not have
many fathers, for in Christ Jesus I became
your father through the gospel. 16There-
fore I urge you to imitate me. 17For this
reason I am sending to you Timothy, my
son whom I love, who is faithful in the
Lord. He will remind you of my way of life
in Christ Jesus, which agrees with what I
teach everywhere in every church.

18Some of you have become arrogant,
as if I were not coming to you. 19But I will
come to you very soon, if the Lord is willing, and then I will find out not only how
these arrogant people are talking, but
what power they have. 20For the kingdom
of God is not a matter of talk but of power. 21What do you prefer? Shall I come to
you with a whip, or in love and with a
gentle spirit?

Expel the Immoral Brother!

5 It is actually reported that there is
sexual immorality among you, and of
a kind that does not occur even among
pagans: A man has his father's wife. 2And
you are proud! Shouldn't you rather have
been filled with grief and have put out of
your fellowship the man who did this?
3Even though I am not physically present,
I am with you in spirit. And I have already
passed judgment on the one who did this,
just as if I were present. 4When you are
assembled in the name of our Lord Jesus
and I am with you in spirit, and the power
of our Lord Jesus is present, 5hand this
man over to Satan, so that the sinful nature[a] may be destroyed and his spirit
saved on the day of the Lord.

6Your boasting is not good. Don't you
know that a little yeast works through the
whole batch of dough? 7Get rid of the old
yeast that you may be a new batch without yeast—as you really are. For Christ,
our Passover lamb, has been sacrificed.
8Therefore let us keep the Festival, not
with the old yeast, the yeast of malice and
wickedness, but with bread without
yeast, the bread of sincerity and truth.

9I have written you in my letter not to
associate with sexually immoral people—
10not at all meaning the people of this
world who are immoral, or the greedy and
swindlers, or idolaters. In that case you
would have to leave this world. 11But now
I am writing you that you must not associate with anyone who calls himself a
brother but is sexually immoral or greedy,
an idolater or a slanderer, a drunkard or
a swindler. With such a man do not even
eat.

12What business is it of mine to judge
those outside the church? Are you not to
judge those inside? 13God will judge
those outside. "Expel the wicked man
from among you."[b]

Lawsuits Among Believers

6 If any of you has a dispute with
another, dare he take it before the
ungodly for judgment instead of before
the saints? 2Do you not know that the
saints will judge the world? And if you are
to judge the world, are you not competent
to judge trivial cases? 3Do you not know
that we will judge angels? How much
more the things of this life! 4Therefore, if
you have disputes about such matters,
appoint as judges even men of little account in the church![c] 5I say this to shame
you. Is it possible that there is nobody
among you wise enough to judge a dispute between believers? 6But instead,
one brother goes to law against another—
and this in front of unbelievers!

7The very fact that you have lawsuits
among you means you have been completely defeated already. Why not rather
be wronged? Why not rather be cheated?
8Instead, you yourselves cheat and do
wrong, and you do this to your brothers.
9Do you not know that the wicked will

[a]5 Or *that his body*; or *that the flesh* [b]13 Deut. 17:7; 19:19; 21:21; 22:21,24; 24:7 [c]4 Or *matters, do you appoint as judges men of little account in the church?*

VERSE FOR THE DAY:
1 Corinthians 4:21

AUTHOR:
Rebecca Manley Pippert

PASSAGE FOR THE DAY:
1 Corinthians 4:14–21

With Love and Gentleness

WHEN I first came to Portland, Oregon, I met a student on one of the campuses where I worked. He was brilliant and looked like he was always pondering the esoteric. His hair was always mussy, and in the entire time I knew him, I never once saw him wear a pair of shoes. Rain, sleet or snow, Bill was always barefoot. While he was attending college he had become a Christian. At this time a well-dressed, middle-class church across the street from the campus wanted to develop more of a ministry to the students. They were not sure how to go about it, but they tried to make them feel welcome. One day Bill decided to worship there. He walked into this church, wearing his blue jeans, tee shirt and of course no shoes. People looked a bit uncomfortable, but no one said anything. So Bill began walking down the aisle looking for a seat. The church was quite crowded that Sunday, so as he got down to the front pew and realized that there were no seats, he just squatted on the carpet—perfectly acceptable behavior at a college fellowship, but perhaps unnerving for a church.

Suddenly an elderly man began walking down the aisle toward the boy. Was he going to scold Bill? My friends who saw him approaching said they thought, "You can't blame him. He'd never guess Bill is a Christian. And his world is too distant from Bill's to understand. You can't blame him for what he's going to do."

As the man kept walking slowly down the aisle, the church became utterly silent, all eyes were focused on him, you could not hear anyone breathe. When the man reached Bill, with some difficulty he lowered himself and sat down next to him on the carpet. He and Bill worshiped together on the floor that Sunday. I was told there was not a dry eye in the congregation.

The irony is that probably the only one who failed to see how great the giving had been that Sunday was Bill. But grace is always that way. It gives without the receiver realizing how great the gift really is. As this man walked alongside his brother and loved him with all that he had received from Christ's love, so must we.

Additional Scripture Readings:
1 Samuel 16:7; James 2:1–5

Go to page 232 for your next devotional reading.

not inherit the kingdom of God? Do not
be deceived: Neither the sexually immoral nor idolaters nor adulterers nor male
prostitutes nor homosexual offenders
[10]nor thieves nor the greedy nor drunkards nor slanderers nor swindlers will inherit the kingdom of God. [11]And that is
what some of you were. But you were
washed, you were sanctified, you were
justified in the name of the Lord Jesus
Christ and by the Spirit of our God.

Sexual Immorality

[12]"Everything is permissible for me"—
but not everything is beneficial. "Everything is permissible for me"—but I will
not be mastered by anything. [13]"Food for
the stomach and the stomach for food"—
but God will destroy them both. The body
is not meant for sexual immorality, but
for the Lord, and the Lord for the body.
[14]By his power God raised the Lord from
the dead, and he will raise us also. [15]Do
you not know that your bodies are members of Christ himself? Shall I then take
the members of Christ and unite them
with a prostitute? Never! [16]Do you not
know that he who unites himself with a
prostitute is one with her in body? For
it is said, "The two will become one

WEDNESDAY

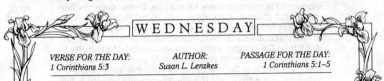

VERSE FOR THE DAY: *1 Corinthians 5:3* | *AUTHOR:* *Susan L. Lenzkes* | *PASSAGE FOR THE DAY:* *1 Corinthians 5:1–5*

Saying Good-by

ONE of the most heartrending moments of life comes when close friends say good-by, knowing that many miles will separate them from their countless shared experiences. Distance takes on the menacing look of an enemy when it dares to stand between such friends!

Soon they will find themselves building protective shields around the ache of separation. They will feel themselves both courting and resisting the urge to clip those threads that bind their hearts in love. And they will argue repeatedly with a voice that warns, "Don't build new friendships—life has a demolition crew around every corner!"

But discovery lies ahead. Real friendship is resilient. The very cords that make it strong—commitment, creativity, caring and sharing—are elastic, and friends can remain committed and even more creative in their long-distance sharing.

Now cards and letters—stackable memories to be relived over a cup of coffee—will communicate love in indelible ink. Now calls—where the value of every word, enhanced by the coming bill—will set precious priorities and release sentiment from the soul. Anticipated visits will be far richer for their infrequency. Thoughts and feelings long saved and protected will be unlocked and shared.

Best of all, a discovery will be made that hearts in harmony can just as easily carry a tune long-distance.

Additional Scripture Readings:
1 Samuel 20:41–42; Philippians 2:25–30

Go to page 236 for your next devotional reading.

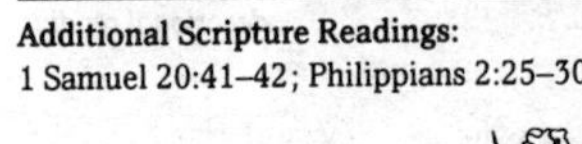

flesh."[a] 17But he who unites himself with
the Lord is one with him in spirit.

18Flee from sexual immorality. All other sins a man commits are outside his
body, but he who sins sexually sins
against his own body. 19Do you not know
that your body is a temple of the Holy
Spirit, who is in you, whom you have received from God? You are not your own;
20you were bought at a price. Therefore
honor God with your body.

Marriage

7 Now for the matters you wrote about:
It is good for a man not to marry.[b]
2But since there is so much immorality,
each man should have his own wife, and
each woman her own husband. 3The husband should fulfill his marital duty to his
wife, and likewise the wife to her husband. 4The wife's body does not belong to
her alone but also to her husband. In the
same way, the husband's body does not
belong to him alone but also to his wife.
5Do not deprive each other except by
mutual consent and for a time, so that
you may devote yourselves to prayer.
Then come together again so that Satan
will not tempt you because of your lack of
self-control. 6I say this as a concession,
not as a command. 7I wish that all men
were as I am. But each man has his own
gift from God; one has this gift, another
has that.

8Now to the unmarried and the widows
I say: It is good for them to stay unmarried, as I am. 9But if they cannot control
themselves, they should marry, for it is
better to marry than to burn with passion.

10To the married I give this command
(not I, but the Lord): A wife must not
separate from her husband. 11But if she
does, she must remain unmarried or else
be reconciled to her husband. And a husband must not divorce his wife.

12To the rest I say this (I, not the Lord):
If any brother has a wife who is not a believer and she is willing to live with him,
he must not divorce her. 13And if a woman has a husband who is not a believer
and he is willing to live with her, she must
not divorce him. 14For the unbelieving
husband has been sanctified through his
wife, and the unbelieving wife has been
sanctified through her believing husband.
Otherwise your children would be unclean, but as it is, they are holy.

15But if the unbeliever leaves, let him
do so. A believing man or woman is not
bound in such circumstances; God has
called us to live in peace. 16How do you
know, wife, whether you will save your
husband? Or, how do you know, husband,
whether you will save your wife?

17Nevertheless, each one should retain
the place in life that the Lord assigned to
him and to which God has called him.
This is the rule I lay down in all the churches. 18Was a man already circumcised
when he was called? He should not
become uncircumcised. Was a man uncircumcised when he was called? He should
not be circumcised. 19Circumcision is
nothing and uncircumcision is nothing.
Keeping God's commands is what counts.
20Each one should remain in the situation which he was in when God called
him. 21Were you a slave when you were
called? Don't let it trouble you—although if you can gain your freedom, do
so. 22For he who was a slave when he was
called by the Lord is the Lord's freedman;
similarly, he who was a free man when he
was called is Christ's slave. 23You were
bought at a price; do not become slaves of
men. 24Brothers, each man, as responsible to God, should remain in the situation
God called him to.

25Now about virgins: I have no command from the Lord, but I give a judgment as one who by the Lord's mercy is
trustworthy. 26Because of the present crisis, I think that it is good for you to remain as you are. 27Are you married? Do
not seek a divorce. Are you unmarried?
Do not look for a wife. 28But if you do
marry, you have not sinned; and if a virgin
marries, she has not sinned. But those
who marry will face many troubles in this
life, and I want to spare you this.

29What I mean, brothers, is that the
time is short. From now on those who
have wives should live as if they had
none; 30those who mourn, as if they did
not; those who are happy, as if they were
not; those who buy something, as if it
were not theirs to keep; 31those who use
the things of the world, as if not en-
grossed in them. For this world in its present form is passing away.

32I would like you to be free from concern. An unmarried man is concerned
about the Lord's affairs—how he can
please the Lord. 33But a married man is
concerned about the affairs of this world
—how he can please his wife— 34and his

[a]*16* Gen. 2:24 [b]*1* Or *"It is good for a man not to have sexual relations with a woman."*

interests are divided. An unmarried woman or virgin is concerned about the Lord's
affairs: Her aim is to be devoted to the
Lord in both body and spirit. But a married woman is concerned about the affairs of this world—how she can please
her husband. 35I am saying this for your
own good, not to restrict you, but that you
may live in a right way in undivided devotion to the Lord.

36If anyone thinks he is acting improp-
erly toward the virgin he is engaged to,
and if she is getting along in years and he
feels he ought to marry, he should do as
he wants. He is not sinning. They should
get married. 37But the man who has settled the matter in his own mind, who is
under no compulsion but has control over
his own will, and who has made up his
mind not to marry the virgin—this man
also does the right thing. 38So then, he
who marries the virgin does right, but he
who does not marry her does even better.[a]

39A woman is bound to her husband as
long as he lives. But if her husband dies,
she is free to marry anyone she wishes,
but he must belong to the Lord. 40In my
judgment, she is happier if she stays as
she is—and I think that I too have the
Spirit of God.

Food Sacrificed to Idols

8 Now about food sacrificed to idols:
We know that we all possess knowledge.[b] Knowledge puffs up, but love
builds up. 2The man who thinks he knows
something does not yet know as he ought
to know. 3But the man who loves God is
known by God.

4So then, about eating food sacrificed
to idols: We know that an idol is nothing
at all in the world and that there is no
God but one. 5For even if there are so-
called gods, whether in heaven or on
earth (as indeed there are many "gods"
and many "lords"), 6yet for us there is but
one God, the Father, from whom all
things came and for whom we live; and
there is but one Lord, Jesus Christ,
through whom all things came and
through whom we live.

7But not everyone knows this. Some
people are still so accustomed to idols
that when they eat such food they think
of it as having been sacrificed to an idol,
and since their conscience is weak, it is
defiled. 8But food does not bring us near
to God; we are no worse if we do not eat,
and no better if we do.

9Be careful, however, that the exercise
of your freedom does not become a stumbling block to the weak. 10For if anyone
with a weak conscience sees you who
have this knowledge eating in an idol's
temple, won't he be emboldened to eat
what has been sacrificed to idols? 11So
this weak brother, for whom Christ died,
is destroyed by your knowledge. 12When
you sin against your brothers in this way
and wound their weak conscience, you
sin against Christ. 13Therefore, if what I
eat causes my brother to fall into sin, I
will never eat meat again, so that I will
not cause him to fall.

The Rights of an Apostle

9 Am I not free? Am I not an apostle?
Have I not seen Jesus our Lord? Are
you not the result of my work in the Lord?
2Even though I may not be an apostle to
others, surely I am to you! For you are the
seal of my apostleship in the Lord.

3This is my defense to those who sit in
judgment on me. 4Don't we have the right
to food and drink? 5Don't we have the
right to take a believing wife along with
us, as do the other apostles and the
Lord's brothers and Cephas[c]? 6Or is it
only I and Barnabas who must work for a
living?

7Who serves as a soldier at his own expense? Who plants a vineyard and does
not eat of its grapes? Who tends a flock
and does not drink of the milk? 8Do I say
this merely from a human point of view?
Doesn't the Law say the same thing? 9For
it is written in the Law of Moses: "Do not
muzzle an ox while it is treading out the
grain."[d] Is it about oxen that God is concerned? 10Surely he says this for us, doesn't he? Yes, this was written for us, because when the plowman plows and the
thresher threshes, they ought to do so in
the hope of sharing in the harvest. 11If we
have sown spiritual seed among you, is it

[a]*36-38* Or *36If anyone thinks he is not treating his daughter properly, and if she is getting along in years, and he feels she ought to marry, he should do as he wants. He is not sinning. He should let her get married. 37But the man who has settled the matter in his own mind, who is under no compulsion but has control over his own will, and who has made up his mind to keep the virgin unmarried—this man also does the right thing. 38So then, he who gives his virgin in marriage does right, but he who does not give her in marriage does even better.*

[b]*1* Or *"We all possess knowledge,"* as you say

[c]*5* That is, Peter

[d]*9* Deut. 25:4

too much if we reap a material harvest from you? 12If others have this right of support from you, shouldn't we have it all the more?

But we did not use this right. On the contrary, we put up with anything rather than hinder the gospel of Christ. 13Don't you know that those who work in the temple get their food from the temple, and those who serve at the altar share in what is offered on the altar? 14In the same way, the Lord has commanded that those who preach the gospel should receive their living from the gospel.

15But I have not used any of these rights. And I am not writing this in the hope that you will do such things for me. I would rather die than have anyone deprive me of this boast. 16Yet when I preach the gospel, I cannot boast, for I am compelled to preach. Woe to me if I do not preach the gospel! 17If I preach voluntarily, I have a reward; if not voluntarily, I am simply discharging the trust committed to me. 18What then is my reward? Just this: that in preaching the gospel I may offer it free of charge, and so not make use of my rights in preaching it.

19Though I am free and belong to no man, I make myself a slave to everyone, to win as many as possible. 20To the Jews I became like a Jew, to win the Jews. To those under the law I became like one under the law (though I myself am not under the law), so as to win those under the law. 21To those not having the law I became like one not having the law (though I am not free from God's law but am under Christ's law), so as to win those not having the law. 22To the weak I became weak, to win the weak. I have become all things to all men so that by all possible means I might save some. 23I do all this for the sake of the gospel, that I may share in its blessings.

24Do you not know that in a race all the runners run, but only one gets the prize? Run in such a way as to get the prize. 25Everyone who competes in the games goes into strict training. They do it to get a crown that will not last; but we do it to get a crown that will last forever. 26Therefore I do not run like a man running aimlessly; I do not fight like a man beating the air. 27No, I beat my body and make it my slave so that after I have preached to others, I myself will not be disqualified for the prize.

Warnings From Israel's History

10 For I do not want you to be ignorant of the fact, brothers, that our forefathers were all under the cloud and that they all passed through the sea. 2They were all baptized into Moses in the cloud and in the sea. 3They all ate the same spiritual food 4and drank the same spiritual drink; for they drank from the spiritual rock that accompanied them, and that rock was Christ. 5Nevertheless, God was not pleased with most of them; their bodies were scattered over the desert.

6Now these things occurred as examples[a] to keep us from setting our hearts on evil things as they did. 7Do not be idolaters, as some of them were; as it is written: "The people sat down to eat and drink and got up to indulge in pagan revelry."[b] 8We should not commit sexual immorality, as some of them did—and in one day twenty-three thousand of them died. 9We should not test the Lord, as some of them did—and were killed by snakes. 10And do not grumble, as some of them did—and were killed by the destroying angel.

11These things happened to them as examples and were written down as warnings for us, on whom the fulfillment of the ages has come. 12So, if you think you are standing firm, be careful that you don't fall! 13No temptation has seized you except what is common to man. And God is faithful; he will not let you be tempted beyond what you can bear. But when you are tempted, he will also provide a way out so that you can stand up under it.

Idol Feasts and the Lord's Supper

14Therefore, my dear friends, flee from idolatry. 15I speak to sensible people; judge for yourselves what I say. 16Is not the cup of thanksgiving for which we give thanks a participation in the blood of Christ? And is not the bread that we break a participation in the body of Christ? 17Because there is one loaf, we, who are many, are one body, for we all partake of the one loaf.

18Consider the people of Israel: Do not those who eat the sacrifices participate in the altar? 19Do I mean then that a sacrifice offered to an idol is anything, or that an idol is anything? 20No, but the sacrifices of pagans are offered to demons, not

[a]6 Or *types*; also in verse 11 [b]7 Exodus 32:6

THURSDAY

VERSE FOR THE DAY:	AUTHOR:	PASSAGE FOR THE DAY:
1 Corinthians 10:13	*June Hunt*	*1 Corinthians 10:1–13*

God Gives Me Strength

FOR thousands of years a popular club has been offering memberships throughout the world. It's a prolific club. It's the "I Can't" club.

Under the bylaws, club members are required to make "I can't" statements with conviction: "I can't help but hate after what he's done to me." "I can't quit this sin." "I can't forgive again!" Because of the fervor of these statements, it sounds as if each is an unchangeable, universal law.

Everyone is subject to one law of science, the law of gravity—the force that pulls every object to the center of the earth. In a similar way, members of the "I Can't" club are prisoners to the downward pull of defeat—they are not only ground-bound, but sin-bound.

Do you feel bound to a specific sin? Does quitting the "I Can't" club seem impossible? The Father refuses to let "can't" be the universal password of his children. At your salvation he gave you the Spirit of God so that you would have the *strength* of God. He made it possible for you to overcome any sin. How? By replacing one law with another:

> The law of the Spirit of life set me free from the law of sin and death (Romans 8:2).

Let's think about the law of gravity again. Can you imagine a 190-ton mass of metal rising against gravity's pull? Impossible? It can't be done! Oh, yes it can . . . by using a "higher law." When you, in faith, give yourself over to the principle of aerodynamics, you can enter an airplane with full confidence that it will fly you from one city to another. You are no longer ground-bound.

Similarly, when you, in faith, give yourself over to the Spirit's control, the "I can't" statements will no longer bind you. When God fills your spirit with his Spirit and infuses you with his strength, you are no longer captive to any temptation. Every *can't* becomes a *can.*

Additional Scripture Readings:
2 Corinthians 12:7–10; 1 Peter 5:6–11

Go to page 238 for your next devotional reading.

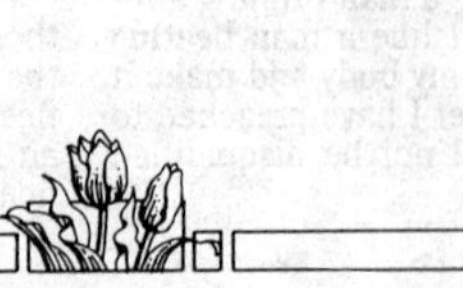

to God, and I do not want you to be participants with demons. 21You cannot
drink the cup of the Lord and the cup of
demons too; you cannot have a part in
both the Lord's table and the table of demons. 22Are we trying to arouse the Lord's
jealousy? Are we stronger than he?

The Believer's Freedom

23"Everything is permissible"—but not
everything is beneficial. "Everything is
permissible"—but not everything is con-
structive. 24Nobody should seek his own
good, but the good of others.
25Eat anything sold in the meat market
without raising questions of conscience,
26for, "The earth is the Lord's, and everything in it."[a]
27If some unbeliever invites you to a
meal and you want to go, eat whatever is
put before you without raising questions
of conscience. 28But if anyone says to
you, "This has been offered in sacrifice,"
then do not eat it, both for the sake of the
man who told you and for conscience'
sake[b]— 29the other man's conscience, I
mean, not yours. For why should my freedom be judged by another's conscience?
30If I take part in the meal with thankfulness, why am I denounced because of
something I thank God for?
31So whether you eat or drink or whatever you do, do it all for the glory of
God. 32Do not cause anyone to stumble,
whether Jews, Greeks or the church of
God— 33even as I try to please everybody
in every way. For I am not seeking my own
good but the good of many, so that they
11 may be saved. 1Follow my example, as I follow the example of
Christ.

Propriety in Worship

2I praise you for remembering me in everything and for holding to the teachings,[c] just as I passed them on to you.
3Now I want you to realize that the
head of every man is Christ, and the head
of the woman is man, and the head of
Christ is God. 4Every man who prays or
prophesies with his head covered dishonors his head. 5And every woman who
prays or prophesies with her head uncovered dishonors her head—it is just as
though her head were shaved. 6If a woman does not cover her head, she should
have her hair cut off; and if it is a disgrace
for a woman to have her hair cut or
shaved off, she should cover her head. 7A
man ought not to cover his head,[d] since
he is the image and glory of God; but the
woman is the glory of man. 8For man did
not come from woman, but woman from
man; 9neither was man created for woman, but woman for man. 10For this reason,
and because of the angels, the woman
ought to have a sign of authority on her
head.
11In the Lord, however, woman is not
independent of man, nor is man independent of woman. 12For as woman
came from man, so also man is born of
woman. But everything comes from God.
13Judge for yourselves: Is it proper for a
woman to pray to God with her head uncovered? 14Does not the very nature of
things teach you that if a man has long
hair, it is a disgrace to him, 15but that if
a woman has long hair, it is her glory? For
long hair is given to her as a covering. 16If
anyone wants to be contentious about
this, we have no other practice—nor do
the churches of God.

The Lord's Supper

17In the following directives I have no
praise for you, for your meetings do more
harm than good. 18In the first place, I hear
that when you come together as a church,
there are divisions among you, and to
some extent I believe it. 19No doubt there
have to be differences among you to
show which of you have God's approval.
20When you come together, it is not the
Lord's Supper you eat, 21for as you eat,
each of you goes ahead without waiting
for anybody else. One remains hungry,
another gets drunk. 22Don't you have
homes to eat and drink in? Or do you despise the church of God and humiliate
those who have nothing? What shall I say
to you? Shall I praise you for this? Certainly not!
23For I received from the Lord what I
also passed on to you: The Lord Jesus, on

[a]26 Psalm 24:1 [b]28 Some manuscripts *conscience' sake, for "the earth is the Lord's and everything in it"* [c]2 Or *traditions* [d]4-7 Or *4Every man who prays or prophesies with long hair dishonors his 5Head. And every woman who prays or prophesies with no covering ⌊of hair⌋ on her head dishonors her head—she is just like one of the "shorn women." 6If a woman has no covering, let her be for now with short hair, but since it is a disgrace for a woman to have her hair shorn or shaved, she should grow it again. 7A man ought not to have long hair*

FRIDAY

VERSE FOR THE DAY:
1 Corinthians 11:2

AUTHOR:
Alma Barkman

PASSAGE FOR THE DAY:
1 Corinthians 11:2–16

Pass It On

BACK in the days of our courtship, friend Hubby suggested I get the recipe for Jam Gem cookies from his mother. I duly inquired as to the ingredients, mixed up a batch and proudly served them to him the next time he came to call.

"They are quite good," he remarked as he reached for seconds.

"Quite good" was not good enough. I tried again. And again. I could never solicit the kind of praise I hoped to hear.

It wasn't until long after we were married that he very sheepishly divulged the reason for his reserved comments. "Those cookies have to be a certain shape to taste best."

"And what shape is that, pray tell?"

"Oval and about so big."

I went on a wild goose chase the likes of which uncovered every conceivable cookie cutter ever invented, but not one was "oval and about so big."

Months later I decided to confide in his mother. "Do you know," I whispered, "that your son insists that a genuine Jam Gem cookie has to be oval and about so big?"

She chuckled. "I suppose that's because I always made them that shape. Would you like my cookie cutter?"

I literally pounced on the offer. Wiping her hands on her apron, she pulled open a drawer and produced the elusive cookie cutter. It was the lid of a talcum powder can.

I have it still. Most people would consider it just another piece of junk, but my teenage daughter already has claimed it as an heirloom.

I suppose every family has little traditions that are handed down from one generation to the next. The family of God is no exception. Those spiritual values that have shaped our lives are cherished and retained for the benefit of our children. Sometimes, like Grandma's cookie cutter, they are temporarily forgotten, tossed aside in the clutter of daily living.

But eventually a growing emptiness creates a hunger for the Christian principles that once guided us, the fellowship that church involvement provided us, the family devotions that once united us. I believe the Holy Spirit uses our childhood memories to whet our appetite for the things of God. As we obediently search out his will and obey it, we in turn are establishing a Christian tradition for our children.

Additional Scripture Readings:
Psalm 78:4–7; 2 Timothy 3:14–15

Go to page 240 for your next devotional reading.

the night he was betrayed, took bread, [24]and when he had given thanks, he broke it and said, "This is my body, which is for you; do this in remembrance of me." [25]In the same way, after supper he took the cup, saying, "This cup is the new covenant in my blood; do this, whenever you drink it, in remembrance of me." [26]For whenever you eat this bread and drink this cup, you proclaim the Lord's death until he comes.

[27]Therefore, whoever eats the bread or drinks the cup of the Lord in an unworthy manner will be guilty of sinning against the body and blood of the Lord. [28]A man ought to examine himself before he eats of the bread and drinks of the cup. [29]For anyone who eats and drinks without recognizing the body of the Lord eats and drinks judgment on himself. [30]That is why many among you are weak and sick, and a number of you have fallen asleep. [31]But if we judged ourselves, we would not come under judgment. [32]When we are judged by the Lord, we are being disciplined so that we will not be condemned with the world.

[33]So then, my brothers, when you come together to eat, wait for each other. [34]If anyone is hungry, he should eat at home, so that when you meet together it may not result in judgment.

And when I come I will give further directions.

Spiritual Gifts

12 Now about spiritual gifts, brothers, I do not want you to be ignorant. [2]You know that when you were pagans, somehow or other you were influenced and led astray to mute idols. [3]Therefore I tell you that no one who is speaking by the Spirit of God says, "Jesus be cursed," and no one can say, "Jesus is Lord," except by the Holy Spirit.

[4]There are different kinds of gifts, but the same Spirit. [5]There are different kinds of service, but the same Lord. [6]There are different kinds of working, but the same God works all of them in all men.

[7]Now to each one the manifestation of the Spirit is given for the common good. [8]To one there is given through the Spirit the message of wisdom, to another the message of knowledge by means of the same Spirit, [9]to another faith by the same Spirit, to another gifts of healing by that one Spirit, [10]to another miraculous powers, to another prophecy, to another distinguishing between spirits, to another speaking in different kinds of tongues,[a] and to still another the interpretation of tongues.[a] [11]All these are the work of one and the same Spirit, and he gives them to each one, just as he determines.

One Body, Many Parts

[12]The body is a unit, though it is made up of many parts; and though all its parts are many, they form one body. So it is with Christ. [13]For we were all baptized by[b] one Spirit into one body—whether Jews or Greeks, slave or free—and we were all given the one Spirit to drink.

[14]Now the body is not made up of one part but of many. [15]If the foot should say, "Because I am not a hand, I do not belong to the body," it would not for that reason cease to be part of the body. [16]And if the ear should say, "Because I am not an eye, I do not belong to the body," it would not for that reason cease to be part of the body. [17]If the whole body were an eye, where would the sense of hearing be? If the whole body were an ear, where would the sense of smell be? [18]But in fact God has arranged the parts in the body, every one of them, just as he wanted them to be. [19]If they were all one part, where would the body be? [20]As it is, there are many parts, but one body.

[21]The eye cannot say to the hand, "I don't need you!" And the head cannot say to the feet, "I don't need you!" [22]On the contrary, those parts of the body that seem to be weaker are indispensable, [23]and the parts that we think are less honorable we treat with special honor. And the parts that are unpresentable are treated with special modesty, [24]while our presentable parts need no special treatment. But God has combined the members of the body and has given greater honor to the parts that lacked it, [25]so that there should be no division in the body, but that its parts should have equal concern for each other. [26]If one part suffers, every part suffers with it; if one part is honored, every part rejoices with it.

[27]Now you are the body of Christ, and each one of you is a part of it. [28]And in the church God has appointed first of all apostles, second prophets, third teachers,

[a]*10* Or *languages*; also in verse 28 [b]*13* Or *with*; or *in*

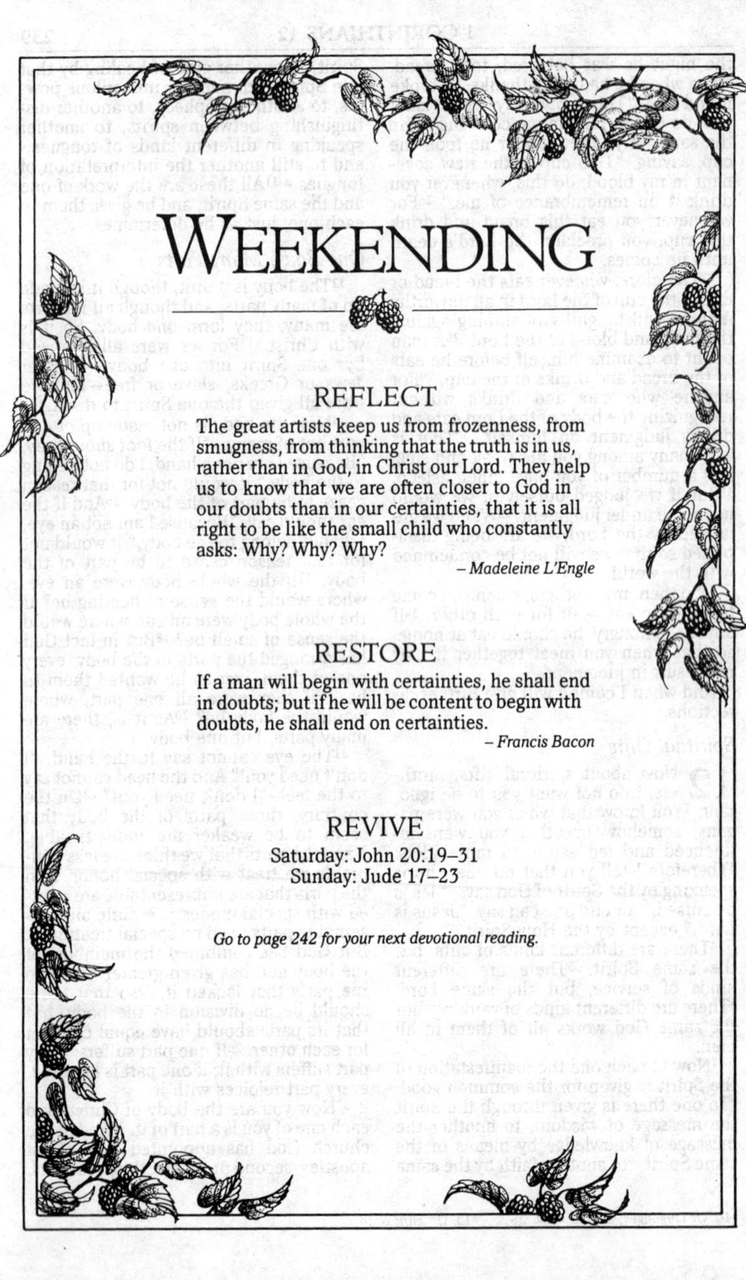

WEEKENDING

REFLECT

The great artists keep us from frozenness, from smugness, from thinking that the truth is in us, rather than in God, in Christ our Lord. They help us to know that we are often closer to God in our doubts than in our certainties, that it is all right to be like the small child who constantly asks: Why? Why? Why?

– Madeleine L'Engle

RESTORE

If a man will begin with certainties, he shall end in doubts; but if he will be content to begin with doubts, he shall end on certainties.

– Francis Bacon

REVIVE

Saturday: John 20:19–31
Sunday: Jude 17–23

Go to page 242 for your next devotional reading.

then workers of miracles, also those having gifts of healing, those able to help others, those with gifts of administration, and those speaking in different kinds of tongues. 29Are all apostles? Are all prophets? Are all teachers? Do all work miracles? 30Do all have gifts of healing? Do all speak in tongues[a]? Do all interpret? 31But eagerly desire[b] the greater gifts.

Love

And now I will show you the most excellent way.

13 If I speak in the tongues[c] of men and of angels, but have not love, I am only a resounding gong or a clanging cymbal. 2If I have the gift of prophecy and can fathom all mysteries and all knowledge, and if I have a faith that can move mountains, but have not love, I am nothing. 3If I give all I possess to the poor and surrender my body to the flames,[d] but have not love, I gain nothing.

4Love is patient, love is kind. It does not envy, it does not boast, it is not proud. 5It is not rude, it is not self-seeking, it is not easily angered, it keeps no record of wrongs. 6Love does not delight in evil but rejoices with the truth. 7It always protects, always trusts, always hopes, always perseveres.

8Love never fails. But where there are prophecies, they will cease; where there are tongues, they will be stilled; where there is knowledge, it will pass away. 9For we know in part and we prophesy in part, 10but when perfection comes, the imperfect disappears. 11When I was a child, I talked like a child, I thought like a child, I reasoned like a child. When I became a man, I put childish ways behind me. 12Now we see but a poor reflection as in a mirror; then we shall see face to face. Now I know in part; then I shall know fully, even as I am fully known.

13And now these three remain: faith, hope and love. But the greatest of these is love.

Gifts of Prophecy and Tongues

14 Follow the way of love and eagerly desire spiritual gifts, especially the gift of prophecy. 2For anyone who speaks in a tongue[e] does not speak to men but to God. Indeed, no one understands him; he utters mysteries with his spirit.[f] 3But everyone who prophesies speaks to men for their strengthening, encouragement and comfort. 4He who speaks in a tongue edifies himself, but he who prophesies edifies the church. 5I would like every one of you to speak in tongues,[g] but I would rather have you prophesy. He who prophesies is greater than one who speaks in tongues,[g] unless he interprets, so that the church may be edified.

6Now, brothers, if I come to you and speak in tongues, what good will I be to you, unless I bring you some revelation or knowledge or prophecy or word of instruction? 7Even in the case of lifeless things that make sounds, such as the flute or harp, how will anyone know what tune is being played unless there is a distinction in the notes? 8Again, if the trumpet does not sound a clear call, who will get ready for battle? 9So it is with you. Unless you speak intelligible words with your tongue, how will anyone know what you are saying? You will just be speaking into the air. 10Undoubtedly there are all sorts of languages in the world, yet none of them is without meaning. 11If then I do not grasp the meaning of what someone is saying, I am a foreigner to the speaker, and he is a foreigner to me. 12So it is with you. Since you are eager to have spiritual gifts, try to excel in gifts that build up the church.

13For this reason anyone who speaks in a tongue should pray that he may interpret what he says. 14For if I pray in a tongue, my spirit prays, but my mind is unfruitful. 15So what shall I do? I will pray with my spirit, but I will also pray with my mind; I will sing with my spirit, but I will also sing with my mind. 16If you are praising God with your spirit, how can one who finds himself among those who do not understand[h] say "Amen" to your thanksgiving, since he does not know what you are saying? 17You may be giving thanks well enough, but the other man is not edified.

18I thank God that I speak in tongues more than all of you. 19But in the church

[a]30 Or *other languages* [b]31 Or *But you are eagerly desiring* [c]1 Or *languages* [d]3 Some early manuscripts *body that I may boast* [e]2 Or *another language*; also in verses 4, 13, 14, 19, 26 and 27 [f]2 Or *by the Spirit* [g]5 Or *other languages*; also in verses 6, 18, 22, 23 and 39 [h]16 Or *among the inquirers*

I would rather speak five intelligible
words to instruct others than ten thousand words in a tongue.
20Brothers, stop thinking like children.
In regard to evil be infants, but in your
thinking be adults. 21In the Law it is written:

"Through men of strange tongues
and through the lips of foreigners
I will speak to this people,
but even then they will not listen
to me,"[a]
says the Lord.

22Tongues, then, are a sign, not for believers but for unbelievers; prophecy,
however, is for believers, not for unbelievers. 23So if the whole church comes
together and everyone speaks in tongues,
and some who do not understand[b] or
some unbelievers come in, will they not
say that you are out of your mind? 24But
if an unbeliever or someone who does not
understand[c] comes in while everybody is
prophesying, he will be convinced by all
that he is a sinner and will be judged by
all, 25and the secrets of his heart will be
laid bare. So he will fall down and worship God, exclaiming, "God is really
among you!"

Orderly Worship

26What then shall we say, brothers?
When you come together, everyone has a
hymn, or a word of instruction, a revelation, a tongue or an interpretation. All of
these must be done for the strengthening
of the church. 27If anyone speaks in a

[a]21 Isaiah 28:11,12 [b]23 Or *some inquirers* [c]24 Or *or some inquirer*

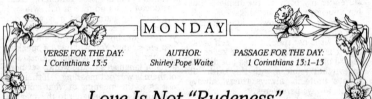

MONDAY

VERSE FOR THE DAY: 1 *Corinthians 13:5*

AUTHOR: *Shirley Pope Waite*

PASSAGE FOR THE DAY: *1 Corinthians 13:1–13*

Love Is Not "Rudeness"

WE have a Japanese "daughter," whom we first met when we hosted her and a classmate during a student exchange program. Later we were able to visit Sayuri and her family in Kamakura, Japan.

Our guidebook had told us that the Japanese are a very correct, proper people and offense is easily taken. So we were a little surprised when the family said good-by with such emotion. Sayuri shed tears and pointed to her watch, which she kept set at Walla Walla time.

Our surprise continued when we received the next letter from Sayuri. She ended with these words, "Can I write 'love'! Is it rudeness? But, I love you."

Yes, Sayuri, you may write love any time you want. Love is never rudeness. In fact 1 Corinthians 13 states, "Love . . . is not rude." Love transcends all cultures, races, nationalities and social status.

We love you too, dear Sayuri, our Japanese "daughter"!

Additional Scripture Readings:
John 13:34–35; 1 John 4:19–21

Go to page 243 for your next devotional reading.

tongue, two—or at the most three—should speak, one at a time, and someone must interpret. [28]If there is no interpreter, the speaker should keep quiet in the church and speak to himself and God.

[29]Two or three prophets should speak, and the others should weigh carefully what is said. [30]And if a revelation comes to someone who is sitting down, the first speaker should stop. [31]For you can all prophesy in turn so that everyone may be instructed and encouraged. [32]The spirits of prophets are subject to the control of prophets. [33]For God is not a God of disorder but of peace.

As in all the congregations of the saints, [34]women should remain silent in the churches. They are not allowed to speak, but must be in submission, as the Law says. [35]If they want to inquire about something, they should ask their own husbands at home; for it is disgraceful for a woman to speak in the church.

[36]Did the word of God originate with you? Or are you the only people it has reached? [37]If anybody thinks he is a prophet or spiritually gifted, let him acknowledge that what I am writing to you is the Lord's command. [38]If he ignores this, he himself will be ignored.[a]

[39]Therefore, my brothers, be eager to prophesy, and do not forbid speaking in tongues. [40]But everything should be done in a fitting and orderly way.

[a]38 Some manuscripts *If he is ignorant of this, let him be ignorant*

TUESDAY

VERSE FOR THE DAY: *1 Corinthians 14:7–8*

AUTHOR: *Delores Taylor*

PASSAGE FOR THE DAY: *1 Corinthians 14:6–12*

Sounds of Distinction

PAUL says that it is better to speak five words that people can understand than to speak volumes that they cannot comprehend. What good is a flute, harp or trumpet unless they play the notes written on the score? But when each player plays the notes written for her instrument, the result is beautiful harmony.

Paul adds that if the trumpet does not give a clear sound, men will not know to prepare for battle. How interesting that Paul mentions both types of instruments. The flute and harp are soft, melodic instruments. Some people are like that—so gentle, kind, comforting and calming. But there is also a need in God's musical ensemble for a trumpeter to warn us of his approach.

When the "notes" are sounding clear, the unbeliever who comes into our Christian gatherings will be convicted of his sin, and his heart will be laid open to the Word of God. Another lost one will have joined God's family.

May he help us to live according to the notes in the "Book."

Additional Scripture Readings:
Judges 7:17–22; Ezekiel 33:1–9

Go to page 248 for your next devotional reading.

The Resurrection of Christ

15 Now, brothers, I want to remind you of the gospel I preached to you, which you received and on which you have taken your stand. 2By this gospel you are saved, if you hold firmly to the word I preached to you. Otherwise, you have believed in vain.

3For what I received I passed on to you as of first importance[a]: that Christ died for our sins according to the Scriptures, 4that he was buried, that he was raised on the third day according to the Scriptures, 5and that he appeared to Peter,[b] and then to the Twelve. 6After that, he appeared to more than five hundred of the brothers at the same time, most of whom are still living, though some have fallen asleep. 7Then he appeared to James, then to all the apostles, 8and last of all he appeared to me also, as to one abnormally born.

9For I am the least of the apostles and do not even deserve to be called an apostle, because I persecuted the church of God. 10But by the grace of God I am what I am, and his grace to me was not without effect. No, I worked harder than all of them—yet not I, but the grace of God that was with me. 11Whether, then, it was I or they, this is what we preach, and this is what you believed.

The Resurrection of the Dead

12But if it is preached that Christ has been raised from the dead, how can some of you say that there is no resurrection of the dead? 13If there is no resurrection of the dead, then not even Christ has been raised. 14And if Christ has not been raised, our preaching is useless and so is your faith. 15More than that, we are then found to be false witnesses about God, for we have testified about God that he raised Christ from the dead. But he did not raise him if in fact the dead are not raised. 16For if the dead are not raised, then Christ has not been raised either. 17And if Christ has not been raised, your faith is futile; you are still in your sins. 18Then those also who have fallen asleep in Christ are lost. 19If only for this life we have hope in Christ, we are to be pitied more than all men.

20But Christ has indeed been raised from the dead, the firstfruits of those who have fallen asleep. 21For since death came through a man, the resurrection of the dead comes also through a man. 22For as in Adam all die, so in Christ all will be made alive. 23But each in his own turn: Christ, the firstfruits; then, when he comes, those who belong to him. 24Then the end will come, when he hands over the kingdom to God the Father after he has destroyed all dominion, authority and power. 25For he must reign until he has put all his enemies under his feet. 26The last enemy to be destroyed is death. 27For he "has put everything under his feet."[c] Now when it says that "everything" has been put under him, it is clear that this does not include God himself, who put everything under Christ. 28When he has done this, then the Son himself will be made subject to him who put everything under him, so that God may be all in all.

29Now if there is no resurrection, what will those do who are baptized for the dead? If the dead are not raised at all, why are people baptized for them? 30And as for us, why do we endanger ourselves every hour? 31I die every day—I mean that, brothers—just as surely as I glory over you in Christ Jesus our Lord. 32If I fought wild beasts in Ephesus for merely human reasons, what have I gained? If the dead are not raised,

"Let us eat and drink,
for tomorrow we die."[d]

33Do not be misled: "Bad company corrupts good character." 34Come back to your senses as you ought, and stop sinning; for there are some who are ignorant of God—I say this to your shame.

The Resurrection Body

35But someone may ask, "How are the dead raised? With what kind of body will they come?" 36How foolish! What you sow does not come to life unless it dies. 37When you sow, you do not plant the body that will be, but just a seed, perhaps of wheat or of something else. 38But God gives it a body as he has determined, and to each kind of seed he gives its own body. 39All flesh is not the same: Men have one kind of flesh, animals have another, birds another and fish another. 40There are also heavenly bodies and

[a]3 Or *you at the first* [b]5 Greek *Cephas* [c]27 Psalm 8:6 [d]32 Isaiah 22:13

there are earthly bodies; but the splendor of the heavenly bodies is one kind, and the splendor of the earthly bodies is another. 41The sun has one kind of splendor, the moon another and the stars another; and star differs from star in splendor.

42So will it be with the resurrection of the dead. The body that is sown is perishable, it is raised imperishable; 43it is sown in dishonor, it is raised in glory; it is sown in weakness, it is raised in power; 44it is sown a natural body, it is raised a spiritual body.

If there is a natural body, there is also a spiritual body. 45So it is written: "The first man Adam became a living being"[a]; the last Adam, a life-giving spirit. 46The spiritual did not come first, but the natural, and after that the spiritual. 47The first man was of the dust of the earth, the second man from heaven. 48As was the earthly man, so are those who are of the earth; and as is the man from heaven, so also are those who are of heaven. 49And just as we have borne the likeness of the earthly man, so shall we[b] bear the likeness of the man from heaven.

50I declare to you, brothers, that flesh and blood cannot inherit the kingdom of God, nor does the perishable inherit the imperishable. 51Listen, I tell you a mystery: We will not all sleep, but we will all be changed— 52in a flash, in the twinkling of an eye, at the last trumpet. For the trumpet will sound, the dead will be raised imperishable, and we will be changed. 53For the perishable must clothe itself with the imperishable, and the mortal with immortality. 54When the perishable has been clothed with the imperishable, and the mortal with immortality, then the saying that is written will come true: "Death has been swallowed up in victory."[c]

55"Where, O death, is your victory?
Where, O death, is your sting?"[d]

56The sting of death is sin, and the power of sin is the law. 57But thanks be to God! He gives us the victory through our Lord Jesus Christ.

58Therefore, my dear brothers, stand firm. Let nothing move you. Always give yourselves fully to the work of the Lord, because you know that your labor in the Lord is not in vain.

The Collection for God's People

16 Now about the collection for God's people: Do what I told the Galatian churches to do. 2On the first day of every week, each one of you should set aside a sum of money in keeping with his income, saving it up, so that when I come no collections will have to be made. 3Then, when I arrive, I will give letters of introduction to the men you approve and send them with your gift to Jerusalem. 4If it seems advisable for me to go also, they will accompany me.

Personal Requests

5After I go through Macedonia, I will come to you—for I will be going through Macedonia. 6Perhaps I will stay with you awhile, or even spend the winter, so that you can help me on my journey, wherever I go. 7I do not want to see you now and make only a passing visit; I hope to spend some time with you, if the Lord permits. 8But I will stay on at Ephesus until Pentecost, 9because a great door for effective work has opened to me, and there are many who oppose me.

10If Timothy comes, see to it that he has nothing to fear while he is with you, for he is carrying on the work of the Lord, just as I am. 11No one, then, should refuse to accept him. Send him on his way in peace so that he may return to me. I am expecting him along with the brothers.

12Now about our brother Apollos: I strongly urged him to go to you with the brothers. He was quite unwilling to go now, but he will go when he has the opportunity.

13Be on your guard; stand firm in the faith; be men of courage; be strong. 14Do everything in love.

15You know that the household of Stephanas were the first converts in Achaia, and they have devoted themselves to the service of the saints. I urge you, brothers, 16to submit to such as these and to everyone who joins in the work, and labors at it. 17I was glad when Stephanas, Fortunatus and Achaicus arrived, because they have supplied what was lacking from you. 18For they refreshed my spirit and yours also. Such men deserve recognition.

[a]*45* Gen. 2:7 [b]*49* Some early manuscripts *so let us* [c]*54* Isaiah 25:8 [d]*55* Hosea 13:14

Final Greetings

[19]The churches in the province of Asia
send you greetings. Aquila and Priscilla[a]
greet you warmly in the Lord, and so does
the church that meets at their house.
[20]All the brothers here send you greetings. Greet one another with a holy
kiss.

[21]I, Paul, write this greeting in my own
hand.
[22]If anyone does not love the Lord—a
curse be on him. Come, O Lord[b]!
[23]The grace of the Lord Jesus be with
you.
[24]My love to all of you in Christ Jesus.
Amen.[c]

[a]*19* Greek *Prisca*, a variant of *Priscilla* [b]*22* In Aramaic the expression *Come, O Lord* is *Marana tha.*
[c]*24* Some manuscripts do not have *Amen*.

PAUL writes this second letter to the church in Corinth from Macedonia (Acts 20:1; 2 Corinthians 7:5), while on his way to Corinth (2 Corinthians 13:1). As the most personal of all his letters, he expresses both how exciting and how painful his life as a missionary has been. He also finds it necessary to defend himself against those who are criticizing him. As you read this letter, think about how exciting it can be to serve the Lord, but realize too that being a Christian can sometimes lead to pain and suffering.

2 CORINTHIANS

1 Paul, an apostle of Christ Jesus by the will of God, and Timothy our brother,

To the church of God in Corinth, together with all the saints throughout Achaia:

2Grace and peace to you from God our Father and the Lord Jesus Christ.

The God of All Comfort

3Praise be to the God and Father of our Lord Jesus Christ, the Father of compassion and the God of all comfort, 4who
comforts us in all our troubles, so that we can comfort those in any trouble with the comfort we ourselves have received from
God. 5For just as the sufferings of Christ flow over into our lives, so also through
Christ our comfort overflows. 6If we are distressed, it is for your comfort and salvation; if we are comforted, it is for your comfort, which produces in you patient endurance of the same sufferings we suffer.
7And our hope for you is firm, because we know that just as you share in our sufferings, so also you share in our comfort.

[8]We do not want you to be uninformed,
brothers, about the hardships we suffered
in the province of Asia. We were under
great pressure, far beyond our ability to
endure, so that we despaired even of life.
[9]Indeed, in our hearts we felt the sentence of death. But this happened that we
might not rely on ourselves but on God,
who raises the dead. [10]He has delivered
us from such a deadly peril, and he will
deliver us. On him we have set our hope
that he will continue to deliver us, [11]as
you help us by your prayers. Then many
will give thanks on our[a] behalf for the
gracious favor granted us in answer to the
prayers of many.

Paul's Change of Plans

[12]Now this is our boast: Our conscience
testifies that we have conducted ourselves in the world, and especially in our
relations with you, in the holiness and
sincerity that are from God. We have done
so not according to worldly wisdom but
according to God's grace. [13]For we do not
write you anything you cannot read or understand. And I hope that, [14]as you have
understood us in part, you will come to
understand fully that you can boast of us
just as we will boast of you in the day of
the Lord Jesus.
[15]Because I was confident of this, I
planned to visit you first so that you

[a]11 Many manuscripts *your*

WEDNESDAY

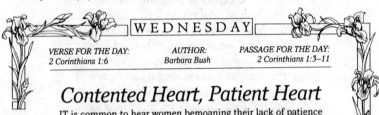

VERSE FOR THE DAY: 2 Corinthians 1:6 — *AUTHOR:* Barbara Bush — *PASSAGE FOR THE DAY:* 2 Corinthians 1:3–11

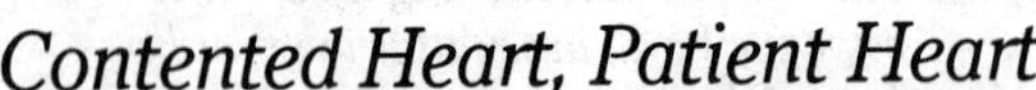

Contented Heart, Patient Heart

IT is common to hear women bemoaning their lack of patience as if it were the most difficult gift to pry from God's hand. In fact impatience stems almost solely from our exaggerated notions of what is due us. If we could but lower our estimation of the importance of *our* time, *our* plans and *our* feelings, we would find ourselves almost automatically more patient.

If we are impatient about the same things that anger God—repeated sin, inattention to his Word, social injustice—we cannot really be called impatient (as long as our opinions are expressed in love). Neither can we expect a woman to remain totally unperturbed if someone smashes into her new car. Certainly "learning patience" is not an acceptable reason for failure to discipline a rebellious child. Patience is not the same thing as resignation or the cynical attitude that always expects the worst possible outcome.

Patience is a more positive trait. It is the ability to bear affliction, delay and interruption with calmness, perseverance and confidence in the goodness of God (Colossians 1:11–12). It is inward peace as well as outward control. It is the submission of our schedules, our viewpoints, our dreams to the greater plan of God, with the conviction that he has a good reason for every delay he allows to come our way.

Additional Scripture Readings:
Romans 2:1–8; Colossians 1:10–12

Go to page 250 for your next devotional reading.

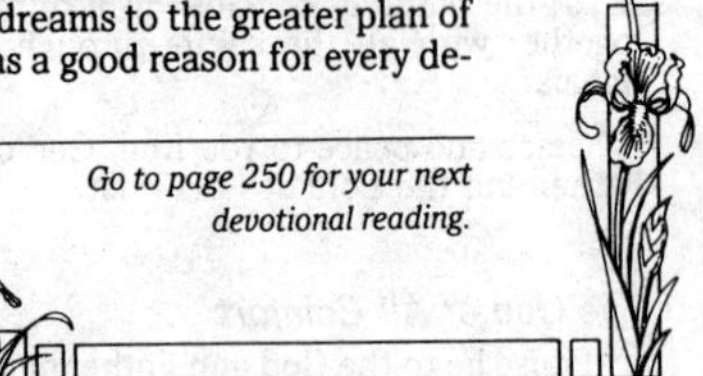

might benefit twice. 16I planned to visit you on my way to Macedonia and to come back to you from Macedonia, and then to have you send me on my way to Judea. 17When I planned this, did I do it lightly? Or do I make my plans in a worldly manner so that in the same breath I say, "Yes, yes" and "No, no"?

18But as surely as God is faithful, our message to you is not "Yes" and "No." 19For the Son of God, Jesus Christ, who was preached among you by me and Silas[a] and Timothy, was not "Yes" and "No," but in him it has always been "Yes." 20For no matter how many promises God has made, they are "Yes" in Christ. And so through him the "Amen" is spoken by us to the glory of God. 21Now it is God who makes both us and you stand firm in Christ. He anointed us, 22set his seal of ownership on us, and put his Spirit in our hearts as a deposit, guaranteeing what is to come.

23I call God as my witness that it was in order to spare you that I did not return to Corinth. 24Not that we lord it over your faith, but we work with you for your joy, because it is by faith you stand firm.

2 1So I made up my mind that I would not make another painful visit to you. 2For if I grieve you, who is left to make me glad but you whom I have grieved? 3I wrote as I did so that when I came I should not be distressed by those who ought to make me rejoice. I had confidence in all of you, that you would all share my joy. 4For I wrote you out of great distress and anguish of heart and with many tears, not to grieve you but to let you know the depth of my love for you.

Forgiveness for the Sinner

5If anyone has caused grief, he has not so much grieved me as he has grieved all of you, to some extent—not to put it too severely. 6The punishment inflicted on him by the majority is sufficient for him. 7Now instead, you ought to forgive and comfort him, so that he will not be overwhelmed by excessive sorrow. 8I urge you, therefore, to reaffirm your love for him. 9The reason I wrote you was to see if you would stand the test and be obedient in everything. 10If you forgive anyone, I also forgive him. And what I have forgiven—if there was anything to forgive—I have forgiven in the sight of Christ for your sake, 11in order that Satan might not outwit us. For we are not unaware of his schemes.

Ministers of the New Covenant

12Now when I went to Troas to preach the gospel of Christ and found that the Lord had opened a door for me, 13I still had no peace of mind, because I did not find my brother Titus there. So I said good-by to them and went on to Macedonia.

14But thanks be to God, who always leads us in triumphal procession in Christ and through us spreads everywhere the fragrance of the knowledge of him. 15For we are to God the aroma of Christ among those who are being saved and those who are perishing. 16To the one we are the smell of death; to the other, the fragrance of life. And who is equal to such a task? 17Unlike so many, we do not peddle the word of God for profit. On the contrary, in Christ we speak before God with sincerity, like men sent from God.

3 Are we beginning to commend ourselves again? Or do we need, like some people, letters of recommendation to you or from you? 2You yourselves are our letter, written on our hearts, known and read by everybody. 3You show that you are a letter from Christ, the result of our ministry, written not with ink but with the Spirit of the living God, not on tablets of stone but on tablets of human hearts.

4Such confidence as this is ours through Christ before God. 5Not that we are competent in ourselves to claim anything for ourselves, but our competence comes from God. 6He has made us competent as ministers of a new covenant—not of the letter but of the Spirit; for the letter kills, but the Spirit gives life.

The Glory of the New Covenant

7Now if the ministry that brought death, which was engraved in letters on stone, came with glory, so that the Israelites could not look steadily at the face of Moses because of its glory, fading though it was, 8will not the ministry of the Spirit be even more glorious? 9If the ministry that condemns men is glorious, how much more glorious is the ministry that brings righteousness! 10For what was glorious has no glory now in comparison with the surpassing glory. 11And if what

[a]19 Greek *Silvanus*, a variant of *Silas*

THURSDAY

VERSE FOR THE DAY:
2 Corinthians 3:3

AUTHOR:
Beth Donigan Seversen

PASSAGE FOR THE DAY:
2 Corinthians 3:3–5

A Lost Letter

The Screwtape Letters, by C. S. Lewis, is a fictitious diary of scolding letters from a mature demon (Screwtape) to his young nephew (Wormwood). It is Wormwood's job to keep a recent convert to Christianity from being productive for Christ (the Enemy). Screwtape's letters point out where Wormwood has failed or missed an opportunity. I have often mused that there must be a missing appendix to these letters somewhere that reads like this . . .

My dear Wormwood,

The following instructions shall help you proceed in handicapping your convert's effectiveness in the Enemy's kingdom. One of our great allies at present is her perception of herself. It is your task, therefore, to feed her poor self-esteem. Already she wastes time primping in front of the mirror and worrying about her looks.

You must continue to encourage her to compare herself with so-called "spiritual giants" whom she admires. This will eventually immobilize her. When she feels inadequate she will no longer attempt anything for the Enemy's kingdom because of her fear of failure. Her warped self-image will lead to unhealthy relationships and hinder her ability to love others. The more often she tells herself that she is a bad person—that she's not competent—the more easily she will feel threatened by others. This will turn others off to the Enemy and his loathsome Christianity.

Ultimately, her relationship with the Enemy himself will be adversely affected. Since she is not satisfied with how the Enemy has created her, her intimacy with him will be destroyed and she will find it difficult to trust the Enemy, pray to him or read that detestable Book.

Finally, emphasize her weaknesses so repeatedly that she begins to believe that she is unimportant to the Enemy. This will push her to compulsive striving to please him through her own accomplishments. Her works will no longer be motivated by faith, but by a dislike for herself. Confuse her so that she never feels forgiven. If you successfully convince her that the Enemy is never pleased with her, she will grow weary and give up altogether. But, more of this in my next letter.

Your affectionate uncle,
Screwtape

Additional Scripture Readings:
Jeremiah 17:7–8; Galatians 6:2–10

Go to page 252 for your next devotional reading.

was fading away came with glory, how much greater is the glory of that which lasts!

12Therefore, since we have such a hope, we are very bold. 13We are not like Moses, who would put a veil over his face to keep the Israelites from gazing at it while the radiance was fading away. 14But their minds were made dull, for to this day the same veil remains when the old covenant is read. It has not been removed, because only in Christ is it taken away. 15Even to this day when Moses is read, a veil covers their hearts. 16But whenever anyone turns to the Lord, the veil is taken away. 17Now the Lord is the Spirit, and where the Spirit of the Lord is, there is freedom. 18And we, who with unveiled faces all reflect[a] the Lord's glory, are being transformed into his likeness with ever-increasing glory, which comes from the Lord, who is the Spirit.

Treasures in Jars of Clay

4 Therefore, since through God's mercy we have this ministry, we do not lose heart. 2Rather, we have renounced secret and shameful ways; we do not use deception, nor do we distort the word of God. On the contrary, by setting forth the truth plainly we commend ourselves to every man's conscience in the sight of God. 3And even if our gospel is veiled, it is veiled to those who are perishing. 4The god of this age has blinded the minds of unbelievers, so that they cannot see the light of the gospel of the glory of Christ, who is the image of God. 5For we do not preach ourselves, but Jesus Christ as Lord, and ourselves as your servants for Jesus' sake. 6For God, who said, "Let light shine out of darkness,"[b] made his light shine in our hearts to give us the light of the knowledge of the glory of God in the face of Christ.

7But we have this treasure in jars of clay to show that this all-surpassing power is from God and not from us. 8We are hard pressed on every side, but not crushed; perplexed, but not in despair; 9persecuted, but not abandoned; struck down, but not destroyed. 10We always carry around in our body the death of Jesus, so that the life of Jesus may also be revealed in our body. 11For we who are alive are always being given over to death for Jesus' sake, so that his life may be revealed in our mortal body. 12So then, death is at work in us, but life is at work in you.

13It is written: "I believed; therefore I have spoken."[c] With that same spirit of faith we also believe and therefore speak, 14because we know that the one who raised the Lord Jesus from the dead will also raise us with Jesus and present us with you in his presence. 15All this is for your benefit, so that the grace that is reaching more and more people may cause thanksgiving to overflow to the glory of God.

16Therefore we do not lose heart. Though outwardly we are wasting away, yet inwardly we are being renewed day by day. 17For our light and momentary troubles are achieving for us an eternal glory that far outweighs them all. 18So we fix our eyes not on what is seen, but on what is unseen. For what is seen is temporary, but what is unseen is eternal.

Our Heavenly Dwelling

5 Now we know that if the earthly tent we live in is destroyed, we have a building from God, an eternal house in heaven, not built by human hands. 2Meanwhile we groan, longing to be clothed with our heavenly dwelling, 3because when we are clothed, we will not be found naked. 4For while we are in this tent, we groan and are burdened, because we do not wish to be unclothed but to be clothed with our heavenly dwelling, so that what is mortal may be swallowed up by life. 5Now it is God who has made us for this very purpose and has given us the Spirit as a deposit, guaranteeing what is to come.

6Therefore we are always confident and know that as long as we are at home in the body we are away from the Lord. 7We live by faith, not by sight. 8We are confident, I say, and would prefer to be away from the body and at home with the Lord. 9So we make it our goal to please him, whether we are at home in the body or away from it. 10For we must all appear before the judgment seat of Christ, that each one may receive what is due him for the things done while in the body, whether good or bad.

The Ministry of Reconciliation

11Since, then, we know what it is to fear the Lord, we try to persuade men. What we are is plain to God, and I hope it is also

[a]18 Or *contemplate* [b]6 Gen. 1:3 [c]13 Psalm 116:10

FRIDAY

VERSE FOR THE DAY: *2 Corinthians 4:16*

AUTHOR: *Karen Burton Mains*

PASSAGE FOR THE DAY: *2 Corinthians 4:1–18*

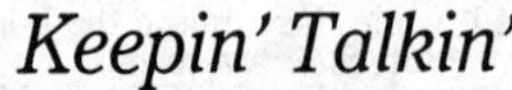

Keepin' Talkin'

FOR years, February days when I was housebound with small children were the hardest times of all. I longed for the sun to shine two days in a row. I yearned for spring, knowing all too well that madding March with its melted layers of accreted winter's filth barred my isolated heart from the rioting green blooms of April. It was during these shadowy days, dragging with plodding prisoner's feet, that I learned how important it is to "keepin' talkin' " (a phrase coined by my son David when he was two) with God.

A major part of the mature Christian journey is learning how to handle those times when the heavens are locked, when our lives are weighted with the winter garments of despair, pain, worry and loss. We try desperately to convince ourselves that we don't serve a God who has absented himself from the listening post, who has hung up a "Shop's Closed" sign and taken off to vacation somewhere in the balmy south.

The Psalms are a prayer journal, an ongoing record of one man's conversations with God. Many of these poem-songs are about times when David hit a roadblock to intimate dialogue with God:

O LORD, how many are my foes!
How many rise up against me!
Many are saying of me,
"God will not deliver him" (Psalm 3:1).

Give ear to my words, O LORD,
consider my sighing.
Listen to my cry for help,
my King and my God (Psalm 5:1–2).

O LORD, do not rebuke me in your anger
or discipline me in your wrath.
Be merciful to me, LORD, for I am faint;
O LORD, heal me, for my bones are in agony
(Psalm 6:1–2).

David's words reiterate the old truth I began to learn while sitting at the dining table, tutored by my own small child: When your soul feels like a gray February day, and all seems to be rain, fog and chill drizzle, the overcast can be lifted if you will learn to just "keepin' talkin' " with God.

Additional Scripture Readings:
1 Samuel 1:9–18; 1 Kings 19:3–18

Go to page 254 for your next devotional reading.

plain to your conscience. 12We are not
trying to commend ourselves to you
again, but are giving you an opportunity
to take pride in us, so that you can answer
those who take pride in what is seen rather than in what is in the heart. 13If we are
out of our mind, it is for the sake of God;
if we are in our right mind, it is for you.
14For Christ's love compels us, because
we are convinced that one died for all,
and therefore all died. 15And he died for
all, that those who live should no longer
live for themselves but for him who died
for them and was raised again.

16So from now on we regard no one
from a worldly point of view. Though we
once regarded Christ in this way, we do so
no longer. 17Therefore, if anyone is in
Christ, he is a new creation; the old
has gone, the new has come! 18All this is
from God, who reconciled us to himself
through Christ and gave us the ministry of
reconciliation: 19that God was reconciling
the world to himself in Christ, not counting men's sins against them. And he has
committed to us the message of reconciliation. 20We are therefore Christ's am-
bassadors, as though God were making
his appeal through us. We implore you on
Christ's behalf: Be reconciled to God.
21God made him who had no sin to be
sin[a] for us, so that in him we might
become the righteousness of God.

6 As God's fellow workers we urge you
not to receive God's grace in vain.
2For he says,

"In the time of my favor I heard you,
and in the day of salvation I helped
you."[b]

I tell you, now is the time of God's favor,
now is the day of salvation.

Paul's Hardships

3We put no stumbling block in anyone's path, so that our ministry will not
be discredited. 4Rather, as servants of
God we commend ourselves in every way:
in great endurance; in troubles, hardships
and distresses; 5in beatings, imprison-
ments and riots; in hard work, sleepless
nights and hunger; 6in purity, understanding, patience and kindness; in the
Holy Spirit and in sincere love; 7in truthful speech and in the power of God; with
weapons of righteousness in the right
hand and in the left; 8through glory and
dishonor, bad report and good report;
genuine, yet regarded as impostors;
9known, yet regarded as unknown; dying,
and yet we live on; beaten, and yet not
killed; 10sorrowful, yet always rejoicing;
poor, yet making many rich; having nothing, and yet possessing everything.

11We have spoken freely to you, Corinthians, and opened wide our hearts to
you. 12We are not withholding our affection from you, but you are withholding
yours from us. 13As a fair exchange—I
speak as to my children—open wide your
hearts also.

Do Not Be Yoked With Unbelievers

14Do not be yoked together with unbelievers. For what do righteousness and
wickedness have in common? Or what
fellowship can light have with darkness?
15What harmony is there between Christ
and Belial[c]? What does a believer have
in common with an unbeliever? 16What
agreement is there between the temple of
God and idols? For we are the temple of
the living God. As God has said: "I will
live with them and walk among them, and
I will be their God, and they will be my
people."[d]

17"Therefore come out from them
and be separate,
says the Lord.
Touch no unclean thing,
and I will receive you."[e]
18"I will be a Father to you,
and you will be my sons and
daughters,
says the Lord Almighty."[f]

7 Since we have these promises, dear
friends, let us purify ourselves from
everything that contaminates body and
spirit, perfecting holiness out of reverence for God.

Paul's Joy

2Make room for us in your hearts. We
have wronged no one, we have corrupted
no one, we have exploited no one. 3I do
not say this to condemn you; I have said
before that you have such a place in our
hearts that we would live or die with you.
4I have great confidence in you; I take
great pride in you. I am greatly encouraged; in all our troubles my joy
knows no bounds.
5For when we came into Macedonia,

[a]21 Or *be a sin offering* [b]2 Isaiah 49:8 [c]15 Greek *Beliar*, a variant of *Belial* [d]16 Lev. 26:12; Jer. 32:38; Ezek. 37:27 [e]17 Isaiah 52:11; Ezek. 20:34,41 [f]18 2 Samuel 7:14; 7:8

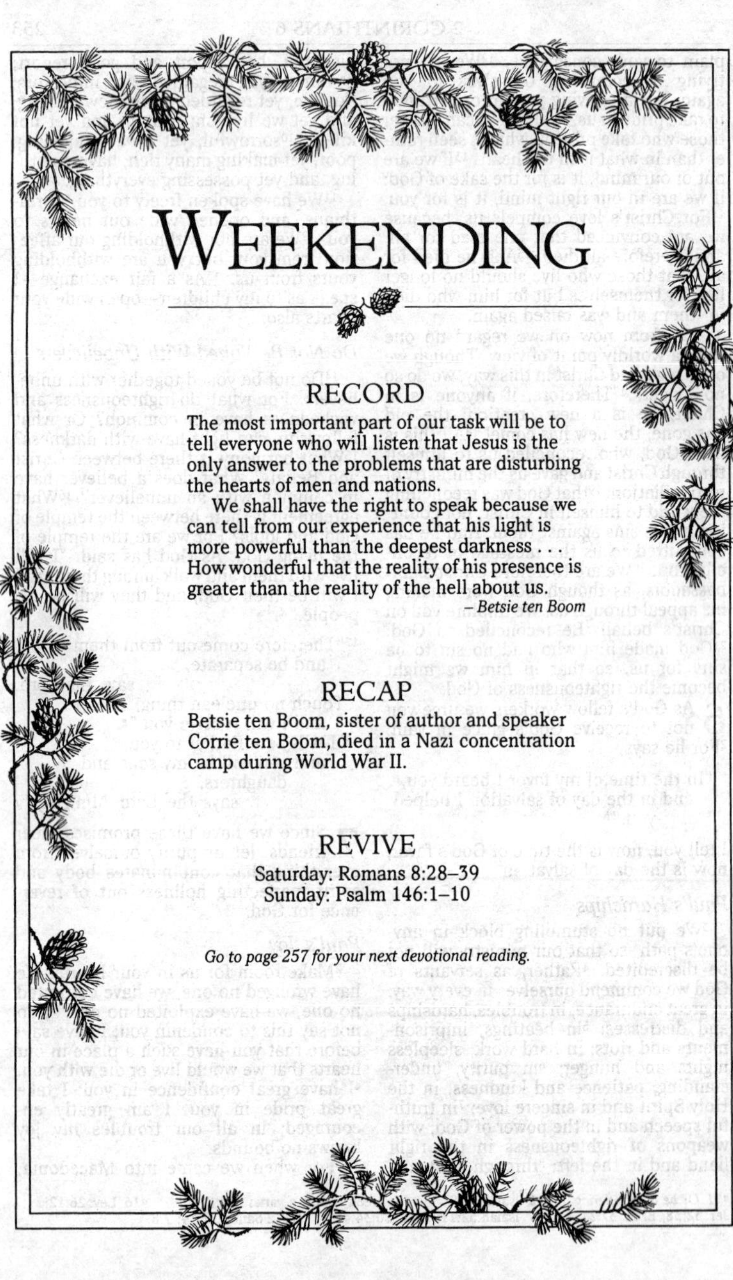

WEEKENDING

RECORD

The most important part of our task will be to tell everyone who will listen that Jesus is the only answer to the problems that are disturbing the hearts of men and nations.

We shall have the right to speak because we can tell from our experience that his light is more powerful than the deepest darkness . . . How wonderful that the reality of his presence is greater than the reality of the hell about us.

– Betsie ten Boom

RECAP

Betsie ten Boom, sister of author and speaker Corrie ten Boom, died in a Nazi concentration camp during World War II.

REVIVE

Saturday: Romans 8:28–39
Sunday: Psalm 146:1–10

Go to page 257 for your next devotional reading.

this body of ours had no rest, but we were harassed at every turn—conflicts on the outside, fears within. 6But God, who comforts the downcast, comforted us by the coming of Titus, 7and not only by his coming but also by the comfort you had given him. He told us about your longing for me, your deep sorrow, your ardent concern for me, so that my joy was greater than ever.

8Even if I caused you sorrow by my letter, I do not regret it. Though I did regret it—I see that my letter hurt you, but only for a little while— 9yet now I am happy, not because you were made sorry, but because your sorrow led you to repentance. For you became sorrowful as God intended and so were not harmed in any way by us. 10Godly sorrow brings repentance that leads to salvation and leaves no regret, but worldly sorrow brings death. 11See what this godly sorrow has produced in you: what earnestness, what eagerness to clear yourselves, what indignation, what alarm, what longing, what concern, what readiness to see justice done. At every point you have proved yourselves to be innocent in this matter. 12So even though I wrote to you, it was not on account of the one who did the wrong or of the injured party, but rather that before God you could see for yourselves how devoted to us you are. 13By all this we are encouraged.

In addition to our own encouragement, we were especially delighted to see how happy Titus was, because his spirit has been refreshed by all of you. 14I had boasted to him about you, and you have not embarrassed me. But just as everything we said to you was true, so our boasting about you to Titus has proved to be true as well. 15And his affection for you is all the greater when he remembers that you were all obedient, receiving him with fear and trembling. 16I am glad I can have complete confidence in you.

Generosity Encouraged

8 And now, brothers, we want you to know about the grace that God has given the Macedonian churches. 2Out of the most severe trial, their overflowing joy and their extreme poverty welled up in rich generosity. 3For I testify that they gave as much as they were able, and even beyond their ability. Entirely on their own, 4they urgently pleaded with us for the privilege of sharing in this service to the saints. 5And they did not do as we expected, but they gave themselves first to the Lord and then to us in keeping with God's will. 6So we urged Titus, since he had earlier made a beginning, to bring also to completion this act of grace on your part. 7But just as you excel in everything—in faith, in speech, in knowledge, in complete earnestness and in your love for us[a]—see that you also excel in this grace of giving.

8I am not commanding you, but I want to test the sincerity of your love by comparing it with the earnestness of others. 9For you know the grace of our Lord Jesus Christ, that though he was rich, yet for your sakes he became poor, so that you through his poverty might become rich.

10And here is my advice about what is best for you in this matter: Last year you were the first not only to give but also to have the desire to do so. 11Now finish the work, so that your eager willingness to do it may be matched by your completion of it, according to your means. 12For if the willingness is there, the gift is acceptable according to what one has, not according to what he does not have.

13Our desire is not that others might be relieved while you are hard pressed, but that there might be equality. 14At the present time your plenty will supply what they need, so that in turn their plenty will supply what you need. Then there will be equality, 15as it is written: "He who gathered much did not have too much, and he who gathered little did not have too little."[b]

Titus Sent to Corinth

16I thank God, who put into the heart of Titus the same concern I have for you. 17For Titus not only welcomed our appeal, but he is coming to you with much enthusiasm and on his own initiative. 18And we are sending along with him the brother who is praised by all the churches for his service to the gospel. 19What is more, he was chosen by the churches to accompany us as we carry the offering, which we administer in order to honor the Lord himself and to show our eagerness to help. 20We want to avoid any criticism of the way we administer this liberal gift. 21For we are taking pains to do what is right, not only in the eyes of the Lord but also in the eyes of men.

[a]7 Some manuscripts *in our love for you* [b]15 Exodus 16:18

22In addition, we are sending with them
our brother who has often proved to us in
many ways that he is zealous, and now
even more so because of his great confidence in you. 23As for Titus, he is my partner and fellow worker among you; as for
our brothers, they are representatives of
the churches and an honor to Christ.
24Therefore show these men the proof of
your love and the reason for our pride in
you, so that the churches can see it.

9 There is no need for me to write to
you about this service to the saints.
2For I know your eagerness to help, and I
have been boasting about it to the Macedonians, telling them that since last year
you in Achaia were ready to give; and your
enthusiasm has stirred most of them to
action. 3But I am sending the brothers in
order that our boasting about you in this
matter should not prove hollow, but that
you may be ready, as I said you would be.
4For if any Macedonians come with me
and find you unprepared, we—not to say
anything about you—would be ashamed
of having been so confident. 5So I thought
it necessary to urge the brothers to visit
you in advance and finish the arrange-
ments for the generous gift you had promised. Then it will be ready as a generous
gift, not as one grudgingly given.

Sowing Generously

6Remember this: Whoever sows sparingly will also reap sparingly, and whoever sows generously will also reap generously. 7Each man should give what he has
decided in his heart to give, not reluctantly or under compulsion, for God loves a
cheerful giver. 8And God is able to make
all grace abound to you, so that in all
things at all times, having all that you
need, you will abound in every good work.
9As it is written:

> "He has scattered abroad his gifts to
> the poor;
> his righteousness endures forever."[a]

10Now he who supplies seed to the sower
and bread for food will also supply and
increase your store of seed and will en-
large the harvest of your righteousness.
11You will be made rich in every way so
that you can be generous on every occasion, and through us your generosity will
result in thanksgiving to God.

12This service that you perform is not
only supplying the needs of God's people
but is also overflowing in many expressions of thanks to God. 13Because of the
service by which you have proved yourselves, men will praise God for the obedience that accompanies your confession
of the gospel of Christ, and for your
generosity in sharing with them and with
everyone else. 14And in their prayers for
you their hearts will go out to you, because of the surpassing grace God has giv-
en you. 15Thanks be to God for his indescribable gift!

Paul's Defense of His Ministry

10 By the meekness and gentleness of
Christ, I appeal to you—I, Paul,
who am "timid" when face to face with
you, but "bold" when away! 2I beg you
that when I come I may not have to be as
bold as I expect to be toward some people
who think that we live by the standards of
this world. 3For though we live in the
world, we do not wage war as the world
does. 4The weapons we fight with are not
the weapons of the world. On the contrary, they have divine power to demolish
strongholds. 5We demolish arguments
and every pretension that sets itself up
against the knowledge of God, and we
take captive every thought to make it
obedient to Christ. 6And we will be ready
to punish every act of disobedience, once
your obedience is complete.

7You are looking only on the surface of
things.[b] If anyone is confident that he belongs to Christ, he should consider again
that we belong to Christ just as much as
he. 8For even if I boast somewhat freely
about the authority the Lord gave us for
building you up rather than pulling you
down, I will not be ashamed of it. 9I do
not want to seem to be trying to frighten
you with my letters. 10For some say, "His
letters are weighty and forceful, but in
person he is unimpressive and his speaking amounts to nothing." 11Such people
should realize that what we are in our letters when we are absent, we will be in our
actions when we are present.

12We do not dare to classify or compare
ourselves with some who commend
themselves. When they measure themselves by themselves and compare themselves with themselves, they are not wise.
13We, however, will not boast beyond

[a]9 Psalm 112:9 [b]7 Or *Look at the obvious facts*

proper limits, but will confine our boasting to the field God has assigned to us, a
field that reaches even to you. 14We are
not going too far in our boasting, as would
be the case if we had not come to you, for
we did get as far as you with the gospel of
Christ. 15Neither do we go beyond our
limits by boasting of work done by others.[a] Our hope is that, as your faith continues to grow, our area of activity among
you will greatly expand, 16so that we can
preach the gospel in the regions beyond
you. For we do not want to boast about
work already done in another man's territory. 17But, "Let him who boasts boast in
the Lord."[b] 18For it is not the one who
commends himself who is approved, but
the one whom the Lord commends.

[a]13-15 Or 13*We, however, will not boast about things that cannot be measured, but we will boast according to the standard of measurement that the God of measure has assigned us—a measurement that relates even to you.* 14 . . . . 15*Neither do we boast about things that cannot be measured in regard to the work done by others.* [b]17 Jer. 9:24

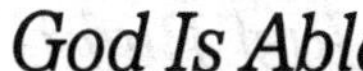

MONDAY

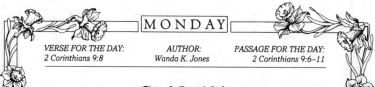

VERSE FOR THE DAY:	*AUTHOR:*	*PASSAGE FOR THE DAY:*
2 Corinthians 9:8	*Wanda K. Jones*	*2 Corinthians 9:6–11*

God Is Able

I NEEDED assurance from God that he would be with me when I was about to graduate from college, get married six weeks later and then leave with my minister husband to work in Harlem, New York. He gave me that assurance in 2 Corinthians 9:8.

The Lord proved to me over and over that his grace and favor are plentiful. He gave me wisdom and love as I sought to help young people handle the problems of daily living in the midst of poverty. As a result, many found that God is able to help them "abound in every good work." I found that God was able to give our family strength and courage during the time my husband was caught in a coup d'etat just as his evangelistic meetings had ended in Ghana. And God was able to bring my husband back to us.

I found that God was able to quiet fear when I visited one of my retarded students who was very ill in the hospital. She was apprehensive because she was not able to be at home or at school with the rest of her friends. But I prayed with her and said softly when I left, "Mary, don't be afraid. Jesus is in this very room. He is able to keep you from being afraid. He is here even though you can't see him." With that assurance of God's ability to care for her, Mary quietly smiled.

Perhaps as you read the "all's" of God in 2 Corinthians 9:8, you might think of some circumstances in your life that seem insurmountable. It's true that sometimes simple, everyday things can loom so large that you feel caught up in a maze with no exit.

In times like these, remember: God is able!

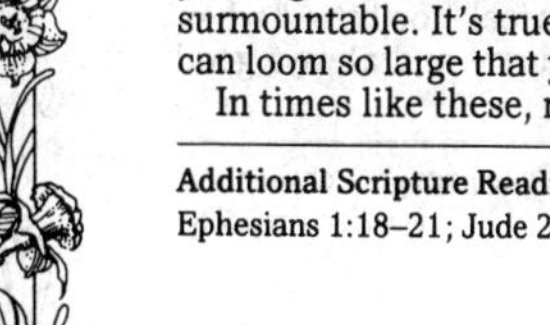

Additional Scripture Readings:
Ephesians 1:18–21; Jude 20–25

Go to page 258 for your next devotional reading.

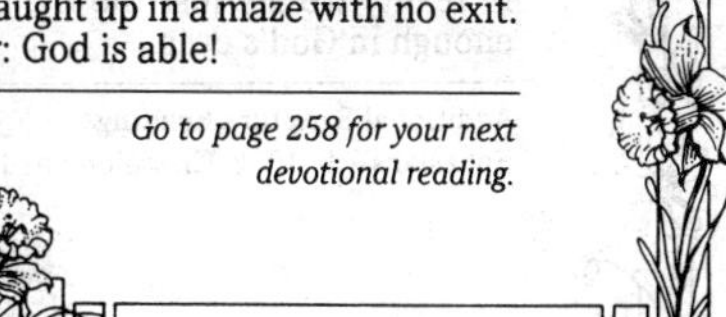

Paul and the False Apostles

11 I hope you will put up with a little
of my foolishness; but you are already doing that. 2I am jealous for you
with a godly jealousy. I promised you to
one husband, to Christ, so that I might
present you as a pure virgin to him. 3But
I am afraid that just as Eve was deceived
by the serpent's cunning, your minds may
somehow be led astray from your sincere
and pure devotion to Christ. 4For if someone comes to you and preaches a Jesus
other than the Jesus we preached, or if
you receive a different spirit from the one
you received, or a different gospel from
the one you accepted, you put up with it
easily enough. 5But I do not think I am in
the least inferior to those "super-apostles." 6I may not be a trained speaker, but
I do have knowledge. We have made this
perfectly clear to you in every way.
7Was it a sin for me to lower myself in
order to elevate you by preaching the gospel of God to you free of charge? 8I robbed
other churches by receiving support from
them so as to serve you. 9And when I was
with you and needed something, I was

TUESDAY

VERSE FOR THE DAY:	*AUTHOR:*	*PASSAGE FOR THE DAY:*
2 Corinthians 10:14	*Linda Ching Sledge*	*2 Corinthians 10:12–18*

Just Right!

"HEY, it fits good!" said five-year-old Geoffrey from inside the floppy tent of his older brother's sweatshirt.

When he heard me laugh, Geoffrey poked his head out like a turtle and said, "I'm NOT too little!" Then he stormed upstairs and slammed his door.

Later, I peeked in to find both boys sprawled on the bed.

"You're big enough," Tim was saying. "Bigger than the babies next door. You're just right for five years old."

I was struck by Tim's answer: You're just right . . . . For the last year, I had tried to model myself after a woman I admired: a well-known Christian churchwoman, mother and wife. How did she integrate God so effortlessly into her busy life? With a simple phrase, she turned ordinary events into unforgettable celebrations of God's love. I, on the other hand, was always scrambling to pull together a church school lesson a half hour before church.

It took me some time to see it, but gradually it dawned on me that growing spiritually is not climbing to perfection; it's doing what you do with genuine devotion. Looking back, I hadn't even come close to emulating the woman I admired. I wasn't her size! Nevertheless I had grown in simple and essential areas: reading the Bible regularly, enjoying teaching at church, praying often and walking closer to him.

Sometimes the desire to grow makes us feel "too little," when in reality we are just the right size for now—and always good enough in God's eyes.

Additional Scripture Readings:
Ephesians 2:8–10; 2 Thessalonians 1:3–4

Go to page 260 for your next devotional reading.

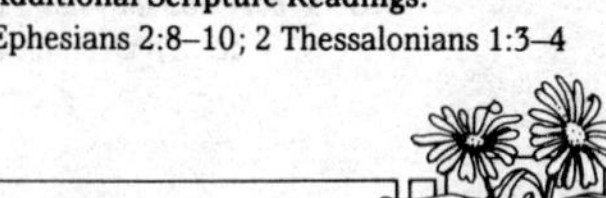

not a burden to anyone, for the brothers who came from Macedonia supplied what I needed. I have kept myself from being a burden to you in any way, and will continue to do so. 10As surely as the truth of Christ is in me, nobody in the regions of Achaia will stop this boasting of mine. 11Why? Because I do not love you? God knows I do! 12And I will keep on doing what I am doing in order to cut the ground from under those who want an opportunity to be considered equal with us in the things they boast about.

13For such men are false apostles, deceitful workmen, masquerading as apostles of Christ. 14And no wonder, for Satan himself masquerades as an angel of light. 15It is not surprising, then, if his servants masquerade as servants of righteousness. Their end will be what their actions deserve.

Paul Boasts About His Sufferings

16I repeat: Let no one take me for a fool. But if you do, then receive me just as you would a fool, so that I may do a little boasting. 17In this self-confident boasting I am not talking as the Lord would, but as a fool. 18Since many are boasting in the way the world does, I too will boast. 19You gladly put up with fools since you are so wise! 20In fact, you even put up with anyone who enslaves you or exploits you or takes advantage of you or pushes himself forward or slaps you in the face. 21To my shame I admit that we were too weak for that!

What anyone else dares to boast about —I am speaking as a fool—I also dare to boast about. 22Are they Hebrews? So am I. Are they Israelites? So am I. Are they Abraham's descendants? So am I. 23Are they servants of Christ? (I am out of my mind to talk like this.) I am more. I have worked much harder, been in prison more frequently, been flogged more severely, and been exposed to death again and again. 24Five times I received from the Jews the forty lashes minus one. 25Three times I was beaten with rods, once I was stoned, three times I was shipwrecked, I spent a night and a day in the open sea, 26I have been constantly on the move. I have been in danger from rivers, in danger from bandits, in danger from my own countrymen, in danger from Gentiles; in danger in the city, in danger in the country, in danger at sea; and in danger from false brothers. 27I have labored and toiled and have often gone without sleep; I have known hunger and thirst and have often gone without food; I have been cold and naked. 28Besides everything else, I face daily the pressure of my concern for all the churches. 29Who is weak, and I do not feel weak? Who is led into sin, and I do not inwardly burn?

30If I must boast, I will boast of the things that show my weakness. 31The God and Father of the Lord Jesus, who is to be praised forever, knows that I am not lying. 32In Damascus the governor under King Aretas had the city of the Damascenes guarded in order to arrest me. 33But I was lowered in a basket from a window in the wall and slipped through his hands.

Paul's Vision and His Thorn

12 I must go on boasting. Although there is nothing to be gained, I will go on to visions and revelations from the Lord. 2I know a man in Christ who fourteen years ago was caught up to the third heaven. Whether it was in the body or out of the body I do not know—God knows. 3And I know that this man—whether in the body or apart from the body I do not know, but God knows— 4was caught up to paradise. He heard inexpressible things, things that man is not permitted to tell. 5I will boast about a man like that, but I will not boast about myself, except about my weaknesses. 6Even if I should choose to boast, I would not be a fool, because I would be speaking the truth. But I refrain, so no one will think more of me than is warranted by what I do or say.

7To keep me from becoming conceited because of these surpassingly great revelations, there was given me a thorn in my flesh, a messenger of Satan, to torment me. 8Three times I pleaded with the Lord to take it away from me. 9But he said to me, "My grace is sufficient for you, for my power is made perfect in weakness." Therefore I will boast all the more gladly about my weaknesses, so that Christ's power may rest on me. 10That is why, for Christ's sake, I delight in weaknesses, in insults, in hardships, in persecutions, in difficulties. For when I am weak, then I am strong.

Paul's Concern for the Corinthians

11I have made a fool of myself, but you drove me to it. I ought to have been commended by you, for I am not in the least inferior to the "super-apostles," even though I am nothing. 12The things that mark an apostle—signs, wonders and

WEDNESDAY

VERSE FOR THE DAY:
2 Corinthians 12:9

AUTHOR:
Marie Chapian

PASSAGE FOR THE DAY:
2 Corinthians 12:1–10

His Power Made Perfect

WHILE in Europe researching my book *Of Whom the World Was Not Worthy* (Bethany House, 1979), I traveled through Yugoslavia from Slovenia to Macedonia. I interviewed factory workers, peasants, gypsies, doctors and laborers, as well as former Communist party officials. I wanted to know how Christians sustained their faith through the devastation of two world wars. I heard story after story of courage in the face of seemingly insurmountable obstacles.

I talked to those who had been imprisoned and whose future seemed hopeless; people who had been sick and wasted physically; frail women who fought in the Partisan army against the Fascists with only sticks for weapons; people who were starving, who ate scraps out of garbage cans. These were brave people—weak, defenseless people—but those for whom the grace of the Lord was sufficient. In their weakness, his power was made perfect.

I looked at my own life and asked myself if my weaknesses were an opportunity for God's power to be made perfect in me. Did I really accept his grace as sufficient in every situation? The apostle Paul suffered a thorn in the flesh that he begged the Lord to remove. The Lord responded not by removing the agonizing source of pain but by giving the apostle the strength to bear it (2 Corinthians 12:7–9). This is how God often works. He does not spare us from suffering but enables us to conquer it.

I've seen shy people become great leaders, and I've seen physically ill people become charged with spiritual energy and touch other lives with the power of the gospel of Christ. I've seen suffering people become shining examples of strength and power. And through this I've learned that nothing can break or destroy us when we allow our weaknesses to make us strong.

There is sublime joy in holy boasting of the power of God in a life that is totally dependent on him. There is sublime peace in accepting the sufficiency of God's grace by allowing him to be strong in us where we are weak.

Additional Scripture Readings:
Romans 8:26–27; 1 Corinthians 1:25–31

Go to page 263 for your next devotional reading.

miracles—were done among you with
great perseverance. 13How were you inferior to the other churches, except that
I was never a burden to you? Forgive me
this wrong!

14Now I am ready to visit you for the
third time, and I will not be a burden to
you, because what I want is not your possessions but you. After all, children
should not have to save up for their parents, but parents for their children. 15So I
will very gladly spend for you everything I
have and expend myself as well. If I love
you more, will you love me less? 16Be that
as it may, I have not been a burden to you.
Yet, crafty fellow that I am, I caught you
by trickery! 17Did I exploit you through
any of the men I sent you? 18I urged Titus
to go to you and I sent our brother with
him. Titus did not exploit you, did he?
Did we not act in the same spirit and follow the same course?

19Have you been thinking all along that
we have been defending ourselves to you?
We have been speaking in the sight of
God as those in Christ; and everything we
do, dear friends, is for your strengthening.
20For I am afraid that when I come I may
not find you as I want you to be, and you
may not find me as you want me to be. I
fear that there may be quarreling, jealousy, outbursts of anger, factions, slander, gossip, arrogance and disorder. 21I
am afraid that when I come again my God
will humble me before you, and I will be
grieved over many who have sinned earlier and have not repented of the impurity, sexual sin and debauchery in which
they have indulged.

Final Warnings

13 This will be my third visit to you.
"Every matter must be established
by the testimony of two or three witnesses."[a] 2I already gave you a warning
when I was with you the second time. I
now repeat it while absent: On my return
I will not spare those who sinned earlier
or any of the others, 3since you are demanding proof that Christ is speaking
through me. He is not weak in dealing
with you, but is powerful among you. 4For
to be sure, he was crucified in weakness,
yet he lives by God's power. Likewise, we
are weak in him, yet by God's power we
will live with him to serve you.

5Examine yourselves to see whether
you are in the faith; test yourselves. Do
you not realize that Christ Jesus is in you
—unless, of course, you fail the test?
6And I trust that you will discover that we
have not failed the test. 7Now we pray to
God that you will not do anything wrong.
Not that people will see that we have
stood the test but that you will do what is
right even though we may seem to have
failed. 8For we cannot do anything
against the truth, but only for the truth.
9We are glad whenever we are weak but
you are strong; and our prayer is for your
perfection. 10This is why I write these
things when I am absent, that when I
come I may not have to be harsh in my
use of authority—the authority the Lord
gave me for building you up, not for tearing you down.

Final Greetings

11Finally, brothers, good-by. Aim for
perfection, listen to my appeal, be of one
mind, live in peace. And the God of love
and peace will be with you.

12Greet one another with a holy kiss.
13All the saints send their greetings.

14May the grace of the Lord Jesus
Christ, and the love of God, and the fellowship of the Holy Spirit be with you all.

[a]*1* Deut. 19:15

PAUL writes this letter to the churches he founded in Galatia (Acts 13:13–14:28), warning them against certain false teachers. He reminds them of the simple message of salvation by faith alone, which he and other church leaders teach, and concludes with advice on how to live a Spirit-filled life. As you read this book, be sure that you are saved by a personal faith in Jesus, and ask God's Spirit to help you walk in Christian love and peace.

GALATIANS

1 Paul, an apostle—sent not from men
nor by man, but by Jesus Christ and
God the Father, who raised him from
the dead— 2and all the brothers with
me,

To the churches in Galatia:

3Grace and peace to you from God our
Father and the Lord Jesus Christ, 4who
gave himself for our sins to rescue us from
the present evil age, according to the will
of our God and Father, 5to whom be glory
for ever and ever. Amen.

No Other Gospel

6I am astonished that you are so quickly deserting the one who called you by the
grace of Christ and are turning to a different gospel— 7which is really no gospel at
all. Evidently some people are throwing
you into confusion and are trying to pervert the gospel of Christ. 8But even if we
or an angel from heaven should preach a
gospel other than the one we preached to
you, let him be eternally condemned! 9As
we have already said, so now I say again:
If anybody is preaching to you a gospel
other than what you accepted, let him be
eternally condemned!

10Am I now trying to win the approval
of men, or of God? Or am I trying to
please men? If I were still trying to please
men, I would not be a servant of Christ.

Paul Called by God

11I want you to know, brothers, that the
gospel I preached is not something that
man made up. 12I did not receive it from
any man, nor was I taught it; rather, I received it by revelation from Jesus Christ.
13For you have heard of my previous
way of life in Judaism, how intensely I
persecuted the church of God and tried to
destroy it. 14I was advancing in Judaism
beyond many Jews of my own age and
was extremely zealous for the traditions
of my fathers. 15But when God, who set
me apart from birth[a] and called me by his
grace, was pleased 16to reveal his Son in
me so that I might preach him among the
Gentiles, I did not consult any man, 17nor
did I go up to Jerusalem to see those who
were apostles before I was, but I went immediately into Arabia and later returned
to Damascus.
18Then after three years, I went up to
Jerusalem to get acquainted with Peter[b]

[a]15 Or *from my mother's womb* [b]18 Greek *Cephas*

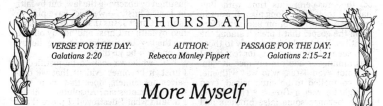

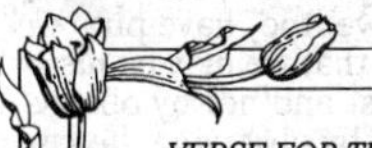

THURSDAY

VERSE FOR THE DAY: *Galatians 2:20*

AUTHOR: *Rebecca Manley Pippert*

PASSAGE FOR THE DAY: *Galatians 2:15–21*

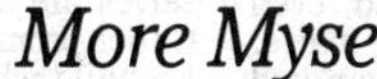

More Myself

CHRISTIANITY isn't a narcotic that dulls you into obedience. It involves battle—it's excruciating to give up control. But that is why we must not feel despair if we are struggling. To struggle does not mean we are incorrigible. It means we are *alive*!

A disciple says, "I hear you, Lord. It's the nuttiest thing I ever heard of. It's risky. I'll look like a fool, but I'll do it. Because my life is no longer committed to doing my thing but your thing." Heaven will not be filled with innocent people, running around saying, "Oh, was there another way? I guess I never noticed." Rather they will say, "You bet there were other options that begged to control me. By God's grace and my struggle, Jesus is my Lord."

Is Jesus' desire to be the Lord of our lives some little fetish of his? Why is it so important to him? Why should we want him to have control of our lives? Besides the fact that he deserves it because of who he is, he knows he is the only one in the universe who can control us without destroying us. No one will ever love you like Jesus. No one will ever know you better, care more for your wholeness. The last breath Jesus breathed on this planet was for you. Jesus will meet you wherever you are and he will help you. He is not intimidated by past failures, broken promises or wounds. He will make sense out of your brokenness. But he can only begin to be the Lord of your life today, not next Monday or next month, but now.

And the great and joyful paradox is that while he totally transforms us he makes us more ourselves than ever before.

Additional Scripture Readings:
Luke 9:23–25; Philippians 3:20–21

Go to page 265 for your next devotional reading.

and stayed with him fifteen days. [19]I saw none of the other apostles—only James, the Lord's brother. [20]I assure you before God that what I am writing you is no lie. [21]Later I went to Syria and Cilicia. [22]I was personally unknown to the churches of Judea that are in Christ. [23]They only heard the report: "The man who formerly persecuted us is now preaching the faith he once tried to destroy." [24]And they praised God because of me.

Paul Accepted by the Apostles

2 Fourteen years later I went up again to Jerusalem, this time with Barnabas. I took Titus along also. [2]I went in response to a revelation and set before them the gospel that I preach among the Gentiles. But I did this privately to those who seemed to be leaders, for fear that I was running or had run my race in vain. [3]Yet not even Titus, who was with me, was compelled to be circumcised, even though he was a Greek. [4]⌞This matter arose⌟ because some false brothers had infiltrated our ranks to spy on the freedom we have in Christ Jesus and to make us slaves. [5]We did not give in to them for a moment, so that the truth of the gospel might remain with you.

[6]As for those who seemed to be important—whatever they were makes no difference to me; God does not judge by external appearance—those men added nothing to my message. [7]On the contrary, they saw that I had been entrusted with the task of preaching the gospel to the Gentiles,[a] just as Peter had been to the Jews.[b] [8]For God, who was at work in the ministry of Peter as an apostle to the Jews, was also at work in my ministry as an apostle to the Gentiles. [9]James, Peter[c] and John, those reputed to be pillars, gave me and Barnabas the right hand of fellowship when they recognized the grace given to me. They agreed that we should go to the Gentiles, and they to the Jews. [10]All they asked was that we should continue to remember the poor, the very thing I was eager to do.

Paul Opposes Peter

[11]When Peter came to Antioch, I opposed him to his face, because he was clearly in the wrong. [12]Before certain men came from James, he used to eat with the Gentiles. But when they arrived, he began to draw back and separate himself from the Gentiles because he was afraid of those who belonged to the circumcision group. [13]The other Jews joined him in his hypocrisy, so that by their hypocrisy even Barnabas was led astray.

[14]When I saw that they were not acting in line with the truth of the gospel, I said to Peter in front of them all, "You are a Jew, yet you live like a Gentile and not like a Jew. How is it, then, that you force Gentiles to follow Jewish customs?

[15]"We who are Jews by birth and not 'Gentile sinners' [16]know that a man is not justified by observing the law, but by faith in Jesus Christ. So we, too, have put our faith in Christ Jesus that we may be justified by faith in Christ and not by observing the law, because by observing the law no one will be justified.

[17]"If, while we seek to be justified in Christ, it becomes evident that we ourselves are sinners, does that mean that Christ promotes sin? Absolutely not! [18]If I rebuild what I destroyed, I prove that I am a lawbreaker. [19]For through the law I died to the law so that I might live for God. [20]I have been crucified with Christ and I no longer live, but Christ lives in me. The life I live in the body, I live by faith in the Son of God, who loved me and gave himself for me. [21]I do not set aside the grace of God, for if righteousness could be gained through the law, Christ died for nothing!"[d]

Faith or Observance of the Law

3 You foolish Galatians! Who has bewitched you? Before your very eyes Jesus Christ was clearly portrayed as crucified. [2]I would like to learn just one thing from you: Did you receive the Spirit by observing the law, or by believing what you heard? [3]Are you so foolish? After beginning with the Spirit, are you now trying to attain your goal by human effort? [4]Have you suffered so much for nothing—if it really was for nothing? [5]Does God give you his Spirit and work miracles among you because you observe the law, or because you believe what you heard?

[6]Consider Abraham: "He believed God, and it was credited to him as righteousness."[e] [7]Understand, then, that those who believe are children of Abraham. [8]The Scripture foresaw that God would justify the Gentiles by faith, and an-

[a]7 Greek *uncircumcised* [b]7 Greek *circumcised*; also in verses 8 and 9 [c]9 Greek *Cephas*; also in verses 11 and 14 [d]21 Some interpreters end the quotation after verse 14. [e]6 Gen. 15:6

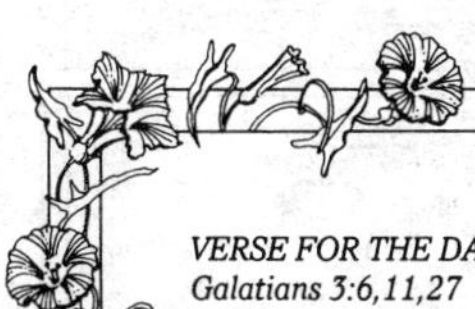

FRIDAY

VERSE FOR THE DAY: *Galatians 3:6,11,27* | *AUTHOR:* *June Hunt* | *PASSAGE FOR THE DAY:* *Galatians 3:1–29*

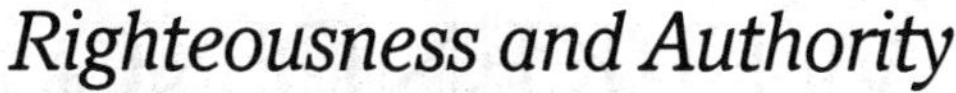

Righteousness and Authority

YOU'RE at the beach . . . you're famished . . . you find a restaurant . . . you rush in . . . you spot a sign:

No Shirt
No Shoes
No Service

This message is clear. To be accepted, you must be clothed according to the restaurant's standard.

God also has a standard. But he makes it possible for you to be acceptable to him at all times when he gives you "righteousness as [your] clothing" (Job 29:14). The word *righteous,* in its simplest form, means "right" and "just." The word also means "acquitted, vindicated." Your faith in Christ enables God to regard you as righteous. He doesn't see your sin any longer, but he sees you as clothed with the righteousness of Christ. As such you are acceptable and properly dressed to "come and dine."

If you have struggled with feeling too unworthy to be called "the righteousness of God" (2 Corinthians 5:21), realize that this "clothing" you are given is like a uniform that, because it represents righteousness, also carries authority.

Have you ever seen a gigantic eighteen-wheel semitrailer truck groaning to a stop just because a police officer walks in front of the traffic and holds up his or her hand? What gives this person the right to command such respect? Certainly not parentage, social status, education, personality or even church affiliation. The officer stands confidently in front of this awesome "king of the road" because of the *right clothing*—the uniform has undeniable authority.

At the moment of conversion you were issued a righteous uniform. The Lord not only covered your past but also gave you authority over your future. With the "breastplate of righteousness" (Ephesians 6:14), God gave you power over sin.

As a child of God, you have the righteousness of God. You have the power that backs the badge.

Additional Scripture Readings:
Isaiah 61:10; Revelation 3:4–5

Go to page 266 for your next devotional reading.

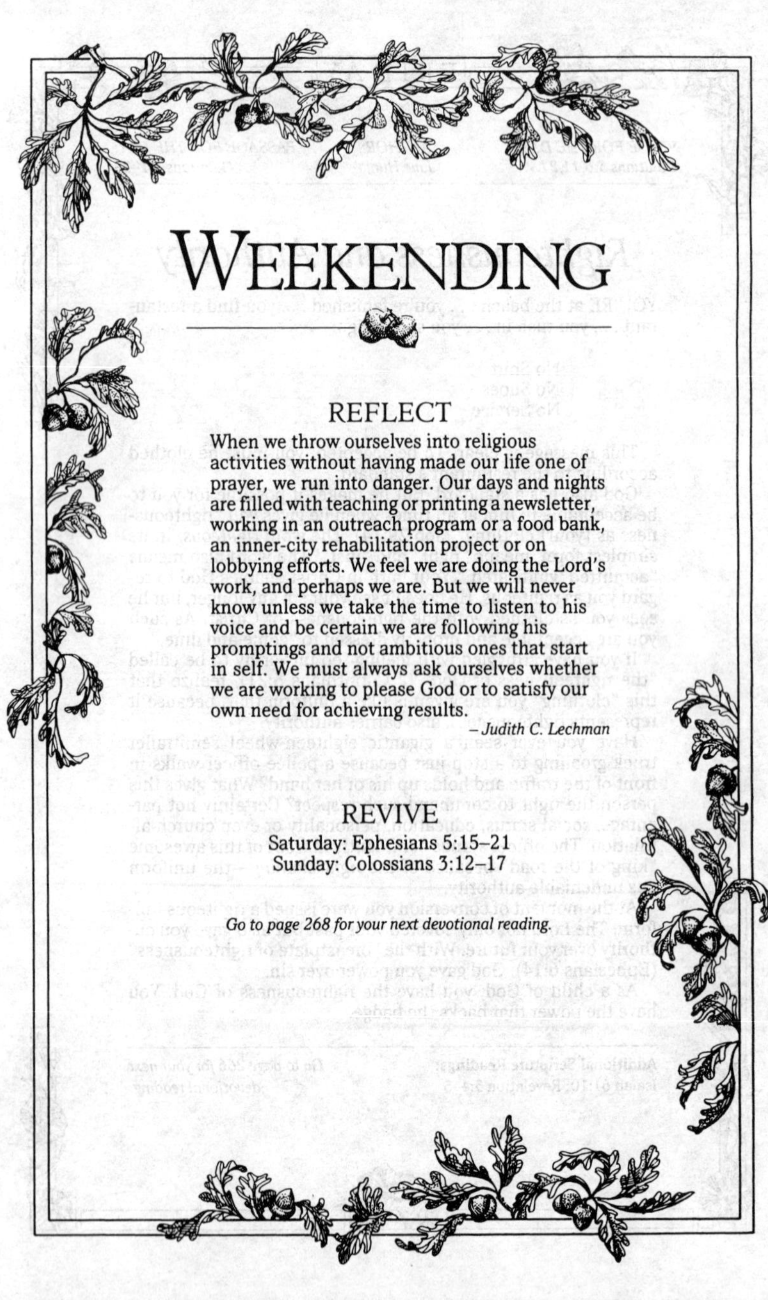

WEEKENDING

REFLECT

When we throw ourselves into religious activities without having made our life one of prayer, we run into danger. Our days and nights are filled with teaching or printing a newsletter, working in an outreach program or a food bank, an inner-city rehabilitation project or on lobbying efforts. We feel we are doing the Lord's work, and perhaps we are. But we will never know unless we take the time to listen to his voice and be certain we are following his promptings and not ambitious ones that start in self. We must always ask ourselves whether we are working to please God or to satisfy our own need for achieving results.

– Judith C. Lechman

REVIVE

Saturday: Ephesians 5:15–21
Sunday: Colossians 3:12–17

Go to page 268 for your next devotional reading.

nounced the gospel in advance to Abraham: "All nations will be blessed through you."[a] 9So those who have faith are blessed along with Abraham, the man of faith.

10All who rely on observing the law are under a curse, for it is written: "Cursed is everyone who does not continue to do everything written in the Book of the Law."[b] 11Clearly no one is justified before God by the law, because, "The righteous will live by faith."[c] 12The law is not based on faith; on the contrary, "The man who does these things will live by them."[d] 13Christ redeemed us from the curse of the law by becoming a curse for us, for it is written: "Cursed is everyone who is hung on a tree."[e] 14He redeemed us in order that the blessing given to Abraham might come to the Gentiles through Christ Jesus, so that by faith we might receive the promise of the Spirit.

The Law and the Promise

15Brothers, let me take an example from everyday life. Just as no one can set aside or add to a human covenant that has been duly established, so it is in this case. 16The promises were spoken to Abraham and to his seed. The Scripture does not say "and to seeds," meaning many people, but "and to your seed,"[f] meaning one person, who is Christ. 17What I mean is this: The law, introduced 430 years later, does not set aside the covenant previously established by God and thus do away with the promise. 18For if the inheritance depends on the law, then it no longer depends on a promise; but God in his grace gave it to Abraham through a promise.

19What, then, was the purpose of the law? It was added because of transgressions until the Seed to whom the promise referred had come. The law was put into effect through angels by a mediator. 20A mediator, however, does not represent just one party; but God is one.

21Is the law, therefore, opposed to the promises of God? Absolutely not! For if a law had been given that could impart life, then righteousness would certainly have come by the law. 22But the Scripture declares that the whole world is a prisoner of sin, so that what was promised, being given through faith in Jesus Christ, might be given to those who believe.

23Before this faith came, we were held prisoners by the law, locked up until faith should be revealed. 24So the law was put in charge to lead us to Christ[g] that we might be justified by faith. 25Now that faith has come, we are no longer under the supervision of the law.

Sons of God

26You are all sons of God through faith in Christ Jesus, 27for all of you who were baptized into Christ have clothed yourselves with Christ. 28There is neither Jew nor Greek, slave nor free, male nor female, for you are all one in Christ Jesus. 29If you belong to Christ, then you are Abraham's seed, and heirs according to the promise.

4 What I am saying is that as long as the heir is a child, he is no different from a slave, although he owns the whole estate. 2He is subject to guardians and trustees until the time set by his father. 3So also, when we were children, we were in slavery under the basic principles of the world. 4But when the time had fully come, God sent his Son, born of a woman, born under law, 5to redeem those under law, that we might receive the full rights of sons. 6Because you are sons, God sent the Spirit of his Son into our hearts, the Spirit who calls out, *"Abba,*[h] Father." 7So you are no longer a slave, but a son; and since you are a son, God has made you also an heir.

Paul's Concern for the Galatians

8Formerly, when you did not know God, you were slaves to those who by nature are not gods. 9But now that you know God—or rather are known by God—how is it that you are turning back to those weak and miserable principles? Do you wish to be enslaved by them all over again? 10You are observing special days and months and seasons and years! 11I fear for you, that somehow I have wasted my efforts on you.

12I plead with you, brothers, become like me, for I became like you. You have done me no wrong. 13As you know, it was because of an illness that I first preached the gospel to you. 14Even though my illness was a trial to you, you did not treat me with contempt or scorn. Instead, you welcomed me as if I were an angel of God, as if I were Christ Jesus himself. 15What

[a] *8* Gen. 12:3; 18:18; 22:18 [b] *10* Deut. 27:26 [c] *11* Hab. 2:4 [d] *12* Lev. 18:5 [e] *13* Deut. 21:23
[f] *16* Gen. 12:7; 13:15; 24:7 [g] *24* Or *charge until Christ came* [h] *6* Aramaic for *Father*

MONDAY

VERSE FOR THE DAY:	*AUTHOR:*	*PASSAGE FOR THE DAY:*
Galatians 5:13	*Kathy Narramore* *Alice Hill*	*Galatians 5:13–15*

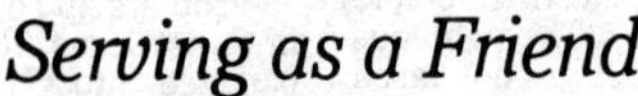

Serving as a Friend

AS friends we need to be two people discovering Christ together, standing at eye level equally in need of the Lord's redemption and grace, seeing each other as both gifted and needy. This Biblical perspective of each other creates a safe emotional climate in which we "serve one another" (Galatians 5:13) and "submit to one another" (Ephesians 5:21).

Serving each other is another way of expressing God's love. It means freely undertaking any task or commitment necessary or helpful to another's spiritual, emotional or physical welfare. It may even be menial such as Jesus offered when he bathed the sore and dirty feet of his followers, or it may be offering empathy, bearing a burden, comforting. But however we do serve in his spirit, we make his love tangible.

We also make his love real to each other as we submit to each other. We are to be adaptable to each other in working out decisions, solutions to problems, and in accepting instruction. Keep in mind that this is quite different from obedience, which is something that can be demanded or coerced. Submission in this Biblical sense must be freely and voluntarily given. It is self-imposed out of humility and desire to serve. The motives to be submissive can only be healthy when the choice is coming from a strong sense of worth and identity in Christ. Then it will not be submission out of fear and a slavish desire to please. It will reflect that characteristic of Christ so contrary to human nature, "Who, being in very nature God, did not consider equality with God something to be grasped, but made himself nothing, taking the very nature of a servant, being made in human likeness" (Philippians 2:6–7).

You may not encounter any of the barriers we have faced as friends, but you can be sure Satan will put some roadblocks in the path of godly friendships. He would love to have you limp along as a Christian lone ranger or as a person with many nice acquaintances but no one who really knows you well.

Additional Scripture Readings:
Ephesians 4:22–32; Philippians 2:1–4

Go to page 270 for your next devotional reading.

has happened to all your joy? I can testify that, if you could have done so, you would have torn out your eyes and given them to me. [16]Have I now become your enemy by telling you the truth?

[17]Those people are zealous to win you over, but for no good. What they want is to alienate you ⌊from us⌋, so that you may be zealous for them. [18]It is fine to be zealous, provided the purpose is good, and to be so always and not just when I am with you. [19]My dear children, for whom I am again in the pains of childbirth until Christ is formed in you, [20]how I wish I could be with you now and change my tone, because I am perplexed about you!

Hagar and Sarah

[21]Tell me, you who want to be under the law, are you not aware of what the law says? [22]For it is written that Abraham had two sons, one by the slave woman and the other by the free woman. [23]His son by the slave woman was born in the ordinary way; but his son by the free woman was born as the result of a promise.

[24]These things may be taken figuratively, for the women represent two covenants. One covenant is from Mount Sinai and bears children who are to be slaves: This is Hagar. [25]Now Hagar stands for Mount Sinai in Arabia and corresponds to the present city of Jerusalem, because she is in slavery with her children. [26]But the Jerusalem that is above is free, and she is our mother. [27]For it is written:

"Be glad, O barren woman,
  who bears no children;
break forth and cry aloud,
  you who have no labor pains;
because more are the children of the
    desolate woman
  than of her who has a husband."[a]

[28]Now you, brothers, like Isaac, are children of promise. [29]At that time the son born in the ordinary way persecuted the son born by the power of the Spirit. It is the same now. [30]But what does the Scripture say? "Get rid of the slave woman and her son, for the slave woman's son will never share in the inheritance with the free woman's son."[b] [31]Therefore, brothers, we are not children of the slave woman, but of the free woman.

Freedom in Christ

5 It is for freedom that Christ has set us free. Stand firm, then, and do not let yourselves be burdened again by a yoke of slavery.

[2]Mark my words! I, Paul, tell you that if you let yourselves be circumcised, Christ will be of no value to you at all. [3]Again I declare to every man who lets himself be circumcised that he is obligated to obey the whole law. [4]You who are trying to be justified by law have been alienated from Christ; you have fallen away from grace. [5]But by faith we eagerly await through the Spirit the righteousness for which we hope. [6]For in Christ Jesus neither circumcision nor uncircumcision has any value. The only thing that counts is faith expressing itself through love.

[7]You were running a good race. Who cut in on you and kept you from obeying the truth? [8]That kind of persuasion does not come from the one who calls you. [9]"A little yeast works through the whole batch of dough." [10]I am confident in the Lord that you will take no other view. The one who is throwing you into confusion will pay the penalty, whoever he may be. [11]Brothers, if I am still preaching circumcision, why am I still being persecuted? In that case the offense of the cross has been abolished. [12]As for those agitators, I wish they would go the whole way and emasculate themselves!

[13]You, my brothers, were called to be free. But do not use your freedom to indulge the sinful nature[c]; rather, serve one another in love. [14]The entire law is summed up in a single command: "Love your neighbor as yourself."[d] [15]If you keep on biting and devouring each other, watch out or you will be destroyed by each other.

Life by the Spirit

[16]So I say, live by the Spirit, and you will not gratify the desires of the sinful nature. [17]For the sinful nature desires what is contrary to the Spirit, and the Spirit what is contrary to the sinful nature. They are in conflict with each other, so that you do not do what you want. [18]But if you are led by the Spirit, you are not under law.

[19]The acts of the sinful nature are obvious: sexual immorality, impurity and debauchery; [20]idolatry and witchcraft; ha-

[a] *27* Isaiah 54:1 [b] *30* Gen. 21:10 [c] *13* Or *the flesh*; also in verses 16, 17, 19 and 24 [d] *14* Lev. 19:18

tred, discord, jealousy, fits of rage, selfish
ambition, dissensions, factions 21and
envy; drunkenness, orgies, and the like. I
warn you, as I did before, that those who
live like this will not inherit the kingdom
of God.

22But the fruit of the Spirit is love, joy,
peace, patience, kindness, goodness,
faithfulness, 23gentleness and self-control. Against such things there is no law.
24Those who belong to Christ Jesus have
crucified the sinful nature with its pas-

TUESDAY

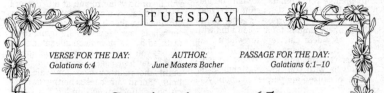

VERSE FOR THE DAY: *Galatians 6:4* | *AUTHOR:* *June Masters Bacher* | *PASSAGE FOR THE DAY:* *Galatians 6:1–10*

Starting Anew at 65

MY mother's friend had a thing about birthdays. She overcame it at 65.

It rained on Jo's birthday. "That figures," she said. "Gray month. Gray hair. Gray mood." She inspected herself from all angles looking for a bigger bulge or a new liver spot. Always bad, this one was the worst of all—a time (she said) when husbands became interesting "older men" and wives became dull "elderly women."

"Wanting to punish myself," she remembers, "I looked in my scrapbook at the list of advantages of being 21. A glorious day!"

She could vote, date, marry, seek a career, choose her own clothes, travel, live where she wished, read what she chose, forget school routine for a time and *enjoy her freedom!* So?

"That one did it," Jo admitted. "When had I ever been as free as *now?* " And that was when the dear lady began her list of advantages of turning 65.

Ah yes, she could draw Social Security, ride the city bus free, visit city parks without paying for admission, take adult ed courses free, collect Medicare, serve as the sage whose ideas were considered wise and whose services were valuable. There was nothing, in fact, in the first list Jo was unable to do or had not done already. There were countless things she could do now but not then. "Why, I'm a liberated woman!" she cried in discovery.

To think and pray about: It is good to pause and count our blessings at every birthday. They pile up with the years. God is changeless. He has work for us here and each milestone shows that he chose to have us remain to give him a hand. Resolve this year to enjoy your new freedom. Ask God how you can make it count.

Additional Scripture Readings:
Genesis 12:1–4; Hebrews 6:9–12

Go to page 273 for your next devotional reading.

sions and desires. 25Since we live by the Spirit, let us keep in step with the Spirit. 26Let us not become conceited, provoking and envying each other.

Doing Good to All

6 Brothers, if someone is caught in a sin, you who are spiritual should restore him gently. But watch yourself, or you also may be tempted. 2Carry each other's burdens, and in this way you will fulfill the law of Christ. 3If anyone thinks he is something when he is nothing, he deceives himself. 4Each one should test his own actions. Then he can take pride in himself, without comparing himself to somebody else, 5for each one should carry his own load.

6Anyone who receives instruction in the word must share all good things with his instructor.

7Do not be deceived: God cannot be mocked. A man reaps what he sows. 8The one who sows to please his sinful nature, from that nature[a] will reap destruction; the one who sows to please the Spirit, from the Spirit will reap eternal life. 9Let us not become weary in doing good, for at the proper time we will reap a harvest if we do not give up. 10Therefore, as we have opportunity, let us do good to all people, especially to those who belong to the family of believers.

Not Circumcision but a New Creation

11See what large letters I use as I write to you with my own hand!

12Those who want to make a good impression outwardly are trying to compel you to be circumcised. The only reason they do this is to avoid being persecuted for the cross of Christ. 13Not even those who are circumcised obey the law, yet they want you to be circumcised that they may boast about your flesh. 14May I never boast except in the cross of our Lord Jesus Christ, through which[b] the world has been crucified to me, and I to the world. 15Neither circumcision nor uncircumcision means anything; what counts is a new creation. 16Peace and mercy to all who follow this rule, even to the Israel of God.

17Finally, let no one cause me trouble, for I bear on my body the marks of Jesus.

18The grace of our Lord Jesus Christ be with your spirit, brothers. Amen.

[a]*8* Or *his flesh, from the flesh* [b]*14* Or *whom*

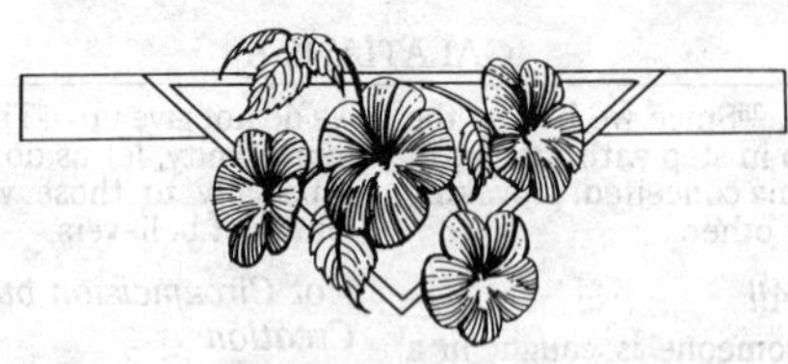

PAUL writes this letter from prison (Ephesians 4:1; probably in Rome, see Acts 28:30–31) to the church he started in Ephesus (Acts 19). In the first half he explains God's great plan to redeem the world through Christ, showing what this means for individual Christians and for the whole church. In the second half he gives practical advice on how to live the Christian life. As you read this book, first examine yourself to be sure that you are saved. Then move on to fight against Satan and show your love to your family, your church and your community.

EPHESIANS

1 Paul, an apostle of Christ Jesus by the
will of God,

To the saints in Ephesus,[a] the faithful[b] in Christ Jesus:

2Grace and peace to you from God our
Father and the Lord Jesus Christ.

Spiritual Blessings in Christ

3Praise be to the God and Father of our
Lord Jesus Christ, who has blessed us in
the heavenly realms with every spiritual
blessing in Christ. 4For he chose us in
him before the creation of the world to be
holy and blameless in his sight. In love
5he[c] predestined us to be adopted as his
sons through Jesus Christ, in accordance
with his pleasure and will— 6to the praise
of his glorious grace, which he has freely
given us in the One he loves. 7In him we

[a]1 Some early manuscripts do not have *in Ephesus.*
[b]1 Or *believers who are*
[c]4,5 Or *sight in love.* 5*He*

WEDNESDAY

VERSE FOR THE DAY:
Ephesians 1:17–23

AUTHOR:
Debby Boone

PASSAGE FOR THE DAY:
Ephesians 1:3–23

Resurrection Power

JAMES talks about the prayer of a righteous man being "powerful and effective" (James 5:16). I think Paul's prayer for the people of Ephesus here in Ephesians 1:17–23 is a model for one of the most essential and important prayers we could ever pray for ourselves or one another. This prayer has taken hold of my heart so firmly that I have committed it to memory (quite a feat in itself) and pray it for family members, friends who are struggling, and for the body of Christ in general. Frequently, I pray it aloud over the people at my concerts.

Of course, there are other ways one should pray for people's needs, but this one prayer seems to cover the most basic and fundamental needs of every believer. It addresses our core desire that God will enlighten our hearts with the truth about himself and the hope to which he has called each of us.

The way we see God—the positive or negative way we view him as a father and provider—will shape the way we live our lives as believers in a dark and weary world. All of us, to some extent, no matter how long or fervently we have walked with the Lord, have shades and colorations of falseness about what God is like or how we are to relate to him. Only as he reveals himself in truth can we be set free to walk with an understanding of the hope of the riches of the inheritance he has set before us.

The question that naturally evolves from this is: "Yes, that would be great, but can God really do that for me? I am so weak." That's exactly why Paul spends the rest of Ephesians 1 talking about the greatness of God's power and the strength of his might . . . the same power he used when he raised Jesus from the dead. That's the power that God has committed to use while working in my life. Resurrection power! And the areas of my life that I feel are barren . . . useless . . . dead . . . burnt-out . . . those are the areas that he will fill with nothing less than himself so that I too can be "the fullness of him who fills everything in every way" (Ephesians 1:23). Hallelujah!

Additional Scripture Readings:
Romans 6:8–14; 1 Corinthians 15:56–58

Go to page 275 for your next devotional reading.

have redemption through his blood, the forgiveness of sins, in accordance with the riches of God's grace [8]that he lavished on us with all wisdom and understanding. [9]And he[a] made known to us the mystery of his will according to his good pleasure, which he purposed in Christ, [10]to be put into effect when the times will have reached their fulfillment—to bring all things in heaven and on earth together under one head, even Christ.

[11]In him we were also chosen,[b] having been predestined according to the plan of him who works out everything in conformity with the purpose of his will, [12]in order that we, who were the first to hope in Christ, might be for the praise of his glory. [13]And you also were included in Christ when you heard the word of truth, the gospel of your salvation. Having believed, you were marked in him with a seal, the promised Holy Spirit, [14]who is a deposit guaranteeing our inheritance until the redemption of those who are God's possession—to the praise of his glory.

Thanksgiving and Prayer

[15]For this reason, ever since I heard about your faith in the Lord Jesus and your love for all the saints, [16]I have not stopped giving thanks for you, remembering you in my prayers. [17]I keep asking that the God of our Lord Jesus Christ, the glorious Father, may give you the Spirit[c] of wisdom and revelation, so that you may know him better. [18]I pray also that the eyes of your heart may be enlightened in order that you may know the hope to which he has called you, the riches of his glorious inheritance in the saints, [19]and his incomparably great power for us who believe. That power is like the working of his mighty strength, [20]which he exerted in Christ when he raised him from the dead and seated him at his right hand in the heavenly realms, [21]far above all rule and authority, power and dominion, and every title that can be given, not only in the present age but also in the one to come. [22]And God placed all things under his feet and appointed him to be head over everything for the church, [23]which is his body, the fullness of him who fills everything in every way.

Made Alive in Christ

2 As for you, you were dead in your transgressions and sins, [2]in which you used to live when you followed the ways of this world and of the ruler of the kingdom of the air, the spirit who is now at work in those who are disobedient. [3]All of us also lived among them at one time, gratifying the cravings of our sinful nature[d] and following its desires and thoughts. Like the rest, we were by nature objects of wrath. [4]But because of his great love for us, God, who is rich in mercy, [5]made us alive with Christ even when we were dead in transgressions—it is by grace you have been saved. [6]And God raised us up with Christ and seated us with him in the heavenly realms in Christ Jesus, [7]in order that in the coming ages he might show the incomparable riches of his grace, expressed in his kindness to us in Christ Jesus. [8]For it is by grace you have been saved, through faith—and this not from yourselves, it is the gift of God—[9]not by works, so that no one can boast. [10]For we are God's workmanship, created in Christ Jesus to do good works, which God prepared in advance for us to do.

One in Christ

[11]Therefore, remember that formerly you who are Gentiles by birth and called "uncircumcised" by those who call themselves "the circumcision" (that done in the body by the hands of men)—[12]remember that at that time you were separate from Christ, excluded from citizenship in Israel and foreigners to the covenants of the promise, without hope and without God in the world. [13]But now in Christ Jesus you who once were far away have been brought near through the blood of Christ.

[14]For he himself is our peace, who has made the two one and has destroyed the barrier, the dividing wall of hostility, [15]by abolishing in his flesh the law with its commandments and regulations. His purpose was to create in himself one new man out of the two, thus making peace, [16]and in this one body to reconcile both of them to God through the cross, by which he put to death their hostility. [17]He came and preached peace to you who were far away and peace to those who were near. [18]For through him we both

[a]8,9 Or *us. With all wisdom and understanding,* [9]*he* [b]11 Or *were made heirs* [c]17 Or *a spirit*
[d]3 Or *our flesh*

have access to the Father by one Spirit.
19Consequently, you are no longer foreigners and aliens, but fellow citizens
with God's people and members of God's
household, 20built on the foundation of
the apostles and prophets, with Christ
Jesus himself as the chief cornerstone.
21In him the whole building is joined
together and rises to become a holy temple in the Lord. 22And in him you too are
being built together to become a dwelling
in which God lives by his Spirit.

Paul the Preacher to the Gentiles

3 For this reason I, Paul, the prisoner of
Christ Jesus for the sake of you Gentiles—
2Surely you have heard about the administration of God's grace that was giv-
en to me for you, 3that is, the mystery
made known to me by revelation, as I
have already written briefly. 4In reading
this, then, you will be able to understand
my insight into the mystery of Christ,
5which was not made known to men in

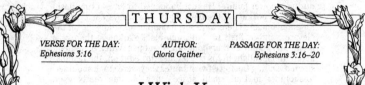

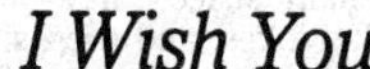

THURSDAY

VERSE FOR THE DAY:
Ephesians 3:16

AUTHOR:
Gloria Gaither

PASSAGE FOR THE DAY:
Ephesians 3:16–20

I Wish You

IT was Suzanne's college graduation party. Family friends and relatives, schoolmates and former teachers all sipped punch and ate raspberry cake under the willow trees beside the gazebo at the creek. She had played there as a child, fishing for catfish and catching turtles and garter snakes. Memories raced across the green hillside and peeped out from behind the apple tree in the orchard.

I listened as our friends wished her success as a writer, fame as a lyricist, fortune in her chosen work, and honor in grad school. What would we wish her, Bill and I later asked ourselves, as we sat in the yard swing apart from the others. It wouldn't be wealth, we decided, or notability. And success would be hard to define. What we would wish her would be some sunshine and some rain. We would wish her growth . . . and vision . . . and the ability to feel what those who are hurt or left out or lonely feel.

As we had done very often before, we found ourselves drawn that night to the passage of Scripture that had been read probably more often in our home than any other, for it stated very well what we wished then for Suzanne and for all our children as they faced life's shifts and changes . . . "that out of his glorious riches he may strengthen you with power through his Spirit in your inner being, so that Christ may dwell in your hearts through faith. And I pray that you, being rooted and established in love, may have power, together with all the saints, to grasp how wide and long and high and deep is the love of Christ, and to know this love that surpasses knowledge—that you may be filled to the measure of all the fullness of God" (Ephesians 3:16–19).

Additional Scripture Readings:
Philippians 1:9–11; Colossians 2:2–7

Go to page 276 for your next devotional reading.

FRIDAY

VERSE FOR THE DAY:
Ephesians 5:8

AUTHOR:
Luci Swindoll

PASSAGE FOR THE DAY:
Ephesians 5:8–10

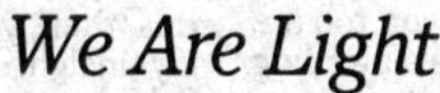

We Are Light

A FRIEND of mine was caught in an elevator in New York City during a power failure. He just happened to have a tiny flashlight in his pocket . . . the type of guy who always was prepared for emergencies. There were seven people, all strangers, on the elevator; and at first, in that pitch-black darkness, there was momentary panic as everybody talked at once. When he remembered the flashlight in his pocket and turned it on, the fear dissipated. During the forty-five minutes they were stuck shoulder-to-shoulder in that small space, they became pretty good friends, laughing, telling jokes, and even singing. The way he presented the story to me, it sounded more fun than fearsome.

Ephesians 5:8 says we are that flashlight. Note, it doesn't say we are like light, it says we *are* light. Just as the flashlight draws power from its batteries, we draw power from the Son of God. As light, we dissipate fear, bring relief and lift spirits. We don't even have to be big to be effective. We just have to be "on."

The last two lines of T.S. Eliot's poem, "The Rock," read:

> And we thank Thee that the darkness reminds us
> of light.
> O Light Invisible, we give Thee Thanks for Thy
> great glory!

As we grope in darkness, what do we want most? Light! We want direction, illumination. Darkness reminds us of our oppressive, burdensome need. It "feels" heavy even though it's intangible. Only light, which also is intangible, pushes that feeling away. It provides relief.

Today, let's pursue that which is good, right and truthful by shining through darkened circumstances. Don't keep the switch off or hold back as though our batteries have run down. Our source is the glorious "Light Invisible." Being switched on pleases the Lord. Stay on. Stay bright.

Additional Scripture Readings:
Proverbs 4:18–19; Matthew 6:14–16

Go to page 278 for your next devotional reading.

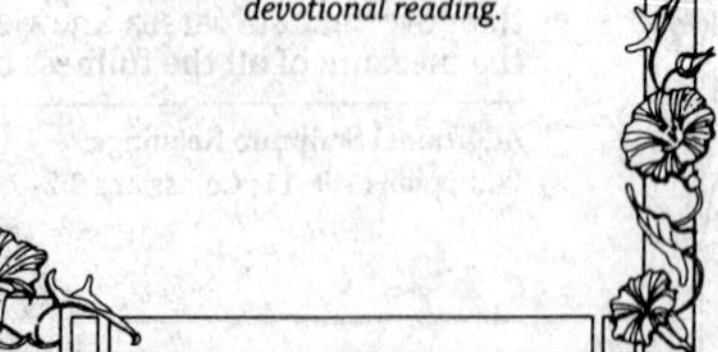

other generations as it has now been revealed by the Spirit to God's holy apostles and prophets. 6This mystery is that through the gospel the Gentiles are heirs together with Israel, members together of one body, and sharers together in the promise in Christ Jesus.

7I became a servant of this gospel by the gift of God's grace given me through the working of his power. 8Although I am less than the least of all God's people, this grace was given me: to preach to the Gentiles the unsearchable riches of Christ, 9and to make plain to everyone the administration of this mystery, which for ages past was kept hidden in God, who created all things. 10His intent was that now, through the church, the manifold wisdom of God should be made known to the rulers and authorities in the heavenly realms, 11according to his eternal purpose which he accomplished in Christ Jesus our Lord. 12In him and through faith in him we may approach God with freedom and confidence. 13I ask you, therefore, not to be discouraged because of my sufferings for you, which are your glory.

A Prayer for the Ephesians

14For this reason I kneel before the Father, 15from whom his whole family[a] in heaven and on earth derives its name. 16I pray that out of his glorious riches he may strengthen you with power through his Spirit in your inner being, 17so that Christ may dwell in your hearts through faith. And I pray that you, being rooted and established in love, 18may have power, together with all the saints, to grasp how wide and long and high and deep is the love of Christ, 19and to know this love that surpasses knowledge—that you may be filled to the measure of all the fullness of God.

20Now to him who is able to do immeasurably more than all we ask or imagine, according to his power that is at work within us, 21to him be glory in the church and in Christ Jesus throughout all generations, for ever and ever! Amen.

Unity in the Body of Christ

4 As a prisoner for the Lord, then, I urge you to live a life worthy of the calling you have received. 2Be completely humble and gentle; be patient, bearing with one another in love. 3Make every effort to keep the unity of the Spirit through the bond of peace. 4There is one body and one Spirit— just as you were called to one hope when you were called— 5one Lord, one faith, one baptism; 6one God and Father of all, who is over all and through all and in all.

7But to each one of us grace has been given as Christ apportioned it. 8This is why it[b] says:

> "When he ascended on high,
> he led captives in his train
> and gave gifts to men."[c]

9(What does "he ascended" mean except that he also descended to the lower, earthly regions[d]? 10He who descended is the very one who ascended higher than all the heavens, in order to fill the whole universe.) 11It was he who gave some to be apostles, some to be prophets, some to be evangelists, and some to be pastors and teachers, 12to prepare God's people for works of service, so that the body of Christ may be built up 13until we all reach unity in the faith and in the knowledge of the Son of God and become mature, attaining to the whole measure of the fullness of Christ.

14Then we will no longer be infants, tossed back and forth by the waves, and blown here and there by every wind of teaching and by the cunning and craftiness of men in their deceitful scheming. 15Instead, speaking the truth in love, we will in all things grow up into him who is the Head, that is, Christ. 16From him the whole body, joined and held together by every supporting ligament, grows and builds itself up in love, as each part does its work.

Living as Children of Light

17So I tell you this, and insist on it in the Lord, that you must no longer live as the Gentiles do, in the futility of their thinking. 18They are darkened in their understanding and separated from the life of God because of the ignorance that is in them due to the hardening of their hearts. 19Having lost all sensitivity, they have given themselves over to sensuality so as to indulge in every kind of impurity, with a continual lust for more.

20You, however, did not come to know Christ that way. 21Surely you heard of him and were taught in him in accordance with the truth that is in Jesus. 22You were taught, with regard to your former way of

[a] 15 Or *whom all fatherhood* [b] 8 Or *God* [c] 8 Psalm 68:18 [d] 9 Or *the depths of the earth*

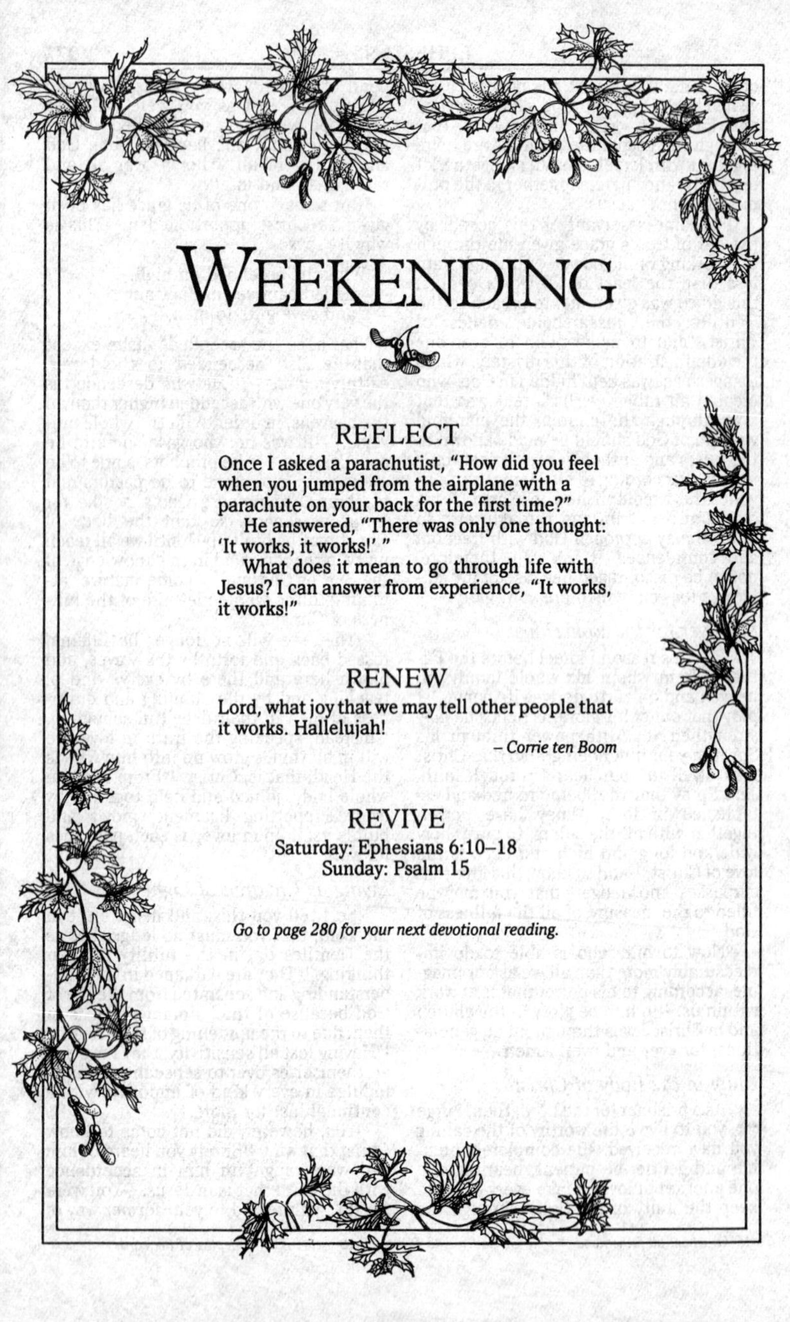

WEEKENDING

REFLECT

Once I asked a parachutist, "How did you feel when you jumped from the airplane with a parachute on your back for the first time?"

He answered, "There was only one thought: 'It works, it works!' "

What does it mean to go through life with Jesus? I can answer from experience, "It works, it works!"

RENEW

Lord, what joy that we may tell other people that it works. Hallelujah!

– Corrie ten Boom

REVIVE

Saturday: Ephesians 6:10–18
Sunday: Psalm 15

Go to page 280 for your next devotional reading.

life, to put off your old self, which is being
corrupted by its deceitful desires; 23to be
made new in the attitude of your minds;
24and to put on the new self, created to be
like God in true righteousness and holiness.

25Therefore each of you must put off
falsehood and speak truthfully to his
neighbor, for we are all members of one
body. 26"In your anger do not sin"[a]: Do
not let the sun go down while you are still
angry, 27and do not give the devil a foothold. 28He who has been stealing must
steal no longer, but must work, doing
something useful with his own hands,
that he may have something to share with
those in need.

29Do not let any unwholesome talk
come out of your mouths, but only what
is helpful for building others up according to their needs, that it may benefit
those who listen. 30And do not grieve the
Holy Spirit of God, with whom you were
sealed for the day of redemption. 31Get
rid of all bitterness, rage and anger,
brawling and slander, along with every
form of malice. 32Be kind and compassionate to one another, forgiving each
other, just as in Christ God forgave you.

5 Be imitators of God, therefore, as
dearly loved children 2and live a life
of love, just as Christ loved us and gave
himself up for us as a fragrant offering
and sacrifice to God.

3But among you there must not be even
a hint of sexual immorality, or of any kind
of impurity, or of greed, because these are
improper for God's holy people. 4Nor
should there be obscenity, foolish talk or
coarse joking, which are out of place, but
rather thanksgiving. 5For of this you can
be sure: No immoral, impure or greedy
person—such a man is an idolater—has
any inheritance in the kingdom of Christ
and of God.[b] 6Let no one deceive you
with empty words, for because of such
things God's wrath comes on those who
are disobedient. 7Therefore do not be
partners with them.

8For you were once darkness, but now
you are light in the Lord. Live as children
of light 9(for the fruit of the light consists
in all goodness, righteousness and truth)
10and find out what pleases the Lord.
11Have nothing to do with the fruitless
deeds of darkness, but rather expose
them. 12For it is shameful even to mention what the disobedient do in secret.
13But everything exposed by the light becomes visible, 14for it is light that makes
everything visible. This is why it is said:

"Wake up, O sleeper,
rise from the dead,
and Christ will shine on you."

15Be very careful, then, how you live—
not as unwise but as wise, 16making the
most of every opportunity, because the
days are evil. 17Therefore do not be foolish, but understand what the Lord's will
is. 18Do not get drunk on wine, which
leads to debauchery. Instead, be filled
with the Spirit. 19Speak to one another
with psalms, hymns and spiritual songs.
Sing and make music in your heart to the
Lord, 20always giving thanks to God the
Father for everything, in the name of our
Lord Jesus Christ.

21Submit to one another out of reverence for Christ.

Wives and Husbands

22Wives, submit to your husbands as to
the Lord. 23For the husband is the head of
the wife as Christ is the head of the
church, his body, of which he is the Savior. 24Now as the church submits to
Christ, so also wives should submit to
their husbands in everything.

25Husbands, love your wives, just as
Christ loved the church and gave himself
up for her 26to make her holy, cleansing[c]
her by the washing with water through
the word, 27and to present her to himself
as a radiant church, without stain or wrinkle or any other blemish, but holy and
blameless. 28In this same way, husbands
ought to love their wives as their own bodies. He who loves his wife loves himself.
29After all, no one ever hated his own
body, but he feeds and cares for it, just as
Christ does the church— 30for we are
members of his body. 31"For this reason a
man will leave his father and mother and
be united to his wife, and the two will
become one flesh."[d] 32This is a profound
mystery—but I am talking about Christ
and the church. 33However, each one of
you also must love his wife as he loves
himself, and the wife must respect her
husband.

Children and Parents

6 Children, obey your parents in the
Lord, for this is right. 2"Honor your
father and mother"—which is the first

[a]*26* Psalm 4:4 [b]*5* Or *kingdom of the Christ and God* [c]*26* Or *having cleansed* [d]*31* Gen. 2:24

MONDAY

VERSE FOR THE DAY:
Ephesians 6:13

AUTHOR:
Beverly LaHaye

PASSAGE FOR THE DAY:
Ephesians 6:10–18

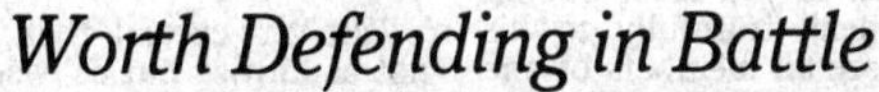

Worth Defending in Battle

WHEN you read Ephesians 6:10–18, you begin to realize that these verses prepare us for warfare. One of those battles is to fight against those things that keep us from having strong marriages and families. The last half of chapter five discusses husband-wife relationships within marriage. The first half of chapter six teaches children to obey, and then discusses the responsibilities of the father. Then verse ten says, "Finally, be strong in the Lord. . . ." These instructions help us clearly see that there *is* a way to keep marriages and families strong.

In this time when the divorce rate has skyrocketed, marriages *can* be strong in the Lord. Even now when family life is rapidly deteriorating, families *can* be strong.

The promises of Ephesians are an encouragement to young couples who wonder if they should marry in light of the high divorce rate. Other couples question if they should have children because the world is such an evil place in which to raise them. Ephesians 6:11 and 13 encourage us to know that we can stand against the schemes of the devil and that we can withstand in the evil day by taking the whole armor of God as our defense—the armor made up of truth, righteousness, the gospel of peace, faith, salvation, and the sword of the Spirit. A lasting marriage is of great value, but you have to be prepared for warfare to preserve it. The same is true with the family. It will be necessary to stand against the schemes of the devil to keep a family strong.

These verses have been a source of great strength to us in raising our family. There were times when all would have been lost were it not for the wisdom and strength we derived from the Word of God.

My husband and I have been teaching Family Life Seminars for many years. Most of the books we have written are based on some phase of family life. We have come across almost every problem possible in marriage and family relationships, and we still believe that it is possible to have a strong family life and marriage relationship if the Word of God is used as the armor to withstand every trial. We must use the Word of God as our basis for sorting out right from wrong, the basis for making decisions or resolving conflicts.

Marriage and the family are institutions founded by God. They are considered his highest priority for individuals next to personal salvation. They are worth defending in battle.

Additional Scripture Readings:
Malachi 2:13–16; Matthew 19:3–14

Go to page 283 for your next devotional reading.

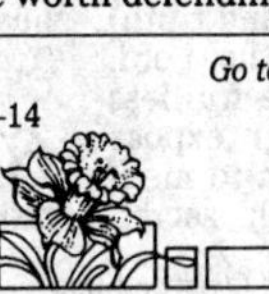

commandment with a promise— 3"that it
may go well with you and that you may
enjoy long life on the earth."[a]
4Fathers, do not exasperate your children; instead, bring them up in the training and instruction of the Lord.

Slaves and Masters

5Slaves, obey your earthly masters with
respect and fear, and with sincerity of
heart, just as you would obey Christ.
6Obey them not only to win their favor
when their eye is on you, but like slaves
of Christ, doing the will of God from your
heart. 7Serve wholeheartedly, as if you
were serving the Lord, not men, 8because
you know that the Lord will reward everyone for whatever good he does, whether
he is slave or free.
9And masters, treat your slaves in the
same way. Do not threaten them, since
you know that he who is both their Master and yours is in heaven, and there is no
favoritism with him.

The Armor of God

10Finally, be strong in the Lord and in
his mighty power. 11Put on the full armor
of God so that you can take your stand
against the devil's schemes. 12For our
struggle is not against flesh and blood,
but against the rulers, against the authorities, against the powers of this dark
world and against the spiritual forces of
evil in the heavenly realms. 13Therefore
put on the full armor of God, so that when
the day of evil comes, you may be able to
stand your ground, and after you have
done everything, to stand. 14Stand firm
then, with the belt of truth buckled
around your waist, with the breastplate of
righteousness in place, 15and with your
feet fitted with the readiness that comes
from the gospel of peace. 16In addition to
all this, take up the shield of faith, with
which you can extinguish all the flaming
arrows of the evil one. 17Take the helmet
of salvation and the sword of the Spirit,
which is the word of God. 18And pray in
the Spirit on all occasions with all kinds
of prayers and requests. With this in
mind, be alert and always keep on praying
for all the saints.
19Pray also for me, that whenever I
open my mouth, words may be given me
so that I will fearlessly make known the
mystery of the gospel, 20for which I am an
ambassador in chains. Pray that I may declare it fearlessly, as I should.

Final Greetings

21Tychicus, the dear brother and faithful servant in the Lord, will tell you everything, so that you also may know how I
am and what I am doing. 22I am sending
him to you for this very purpose, that you
may know how we are, and that he may
encourage you.
23Peace to the brothers, and love with
faith from God the Father and the Lord
Jesus Christ. 24Grace to all who love our
Lord Jesus Christ with an undying love.

[a]3 Deut. 5:16

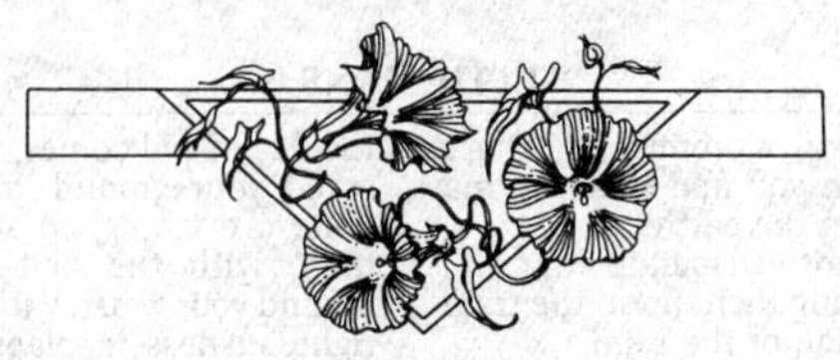

PAUL writes this letter to the church he started in Philippi (Acts 16:11–40). Even though he is in prison, he feels happy when he thinks of what Christ means to him and of what the Philippians are doing for him. He gives some very practical advice on how to live the Christian life. As you read this book, remember always to rejoice in the Lord and to be content, whatever the circumstances.

PHILIPPIANS

1 Paul and Timothy, servants of Christ Jesus,

To all the saints in Christ Jesus at Philippi, together with the overseers[a] and deacons:

2Grace and peace to you from God our Father and the Lord Jesus Christ.

Thanksgiving and Prayer

3I thank my God every time I remember
you. 4In all my prayers for all of you, I
always pray with joy 5because of your
partnership in the gospel from the first
day until now, 6being confident of this,
that he who began a good work in you will
carry it on to completion until the day of
Christ Jesus.

7It is right for me to feel this way about
all of you, since I have you in my heart; for
whether I am in chains or defending and
confirming the gospel, all of you share in
God's grace with me. 8God can testify
how I long for all of you with the affection
of Christ Jesus.

9And this is my prayer: that your love
may abound more and more in knowledge
and depth of insight, 10so that you may be
able to discern what is best and may be
pure and blameless until the day of
Christ, 11filled with the fruit of righteousness that comes through Jesus Christ—to
the glory and praise of God.

[a]1 Traditionally *bishops*

TUESDAY

VERSE FOR THE DAY: *Philippians 2:5*

AUTHOR: *Gigi Graham Tchividjian*

PASSAGE FOR THE DAY: *Philippians 2:1–5*

The Problem

I STOOD in the upstairs hallway, looking down over the bannister and waiting for the younger children to come in for their baths. My oldest daughter, taking a piano lesson, was in the living room directly below, and the repetitive melody she was playing echoed through my mind.

Suddenly the little ones bounded through the door. They bounced up to their rooms, cheeks flushed and eyes bright from their play.

I noticed, however, that one of my young sons was trudging slowly up the stairs, his head bowed, grubby hands covering his small, dirt-streaked face. When he reached the top, I asked him what was wrong.

"Aw, nothing," he replied.

"Then why are you holding your face in your hands?" I persisted.

"Oh, I was just praying."

Quite curious now, I asked what he was praying about.

"I can't tell you," he insisted, "because if I do, you'll be mad."

After much persuasion I convinced him that he could confide in me and that, whatever he told me, I would not get mad. So he explained that he was praying about a problem he had with his mind.

"A problem with your mind?" I asked, now more curious than ever, wondering what kind of problem a child of six could have with his mind. "What kind of problem?"

"Well," he said, "You see, every time I pass by the living room, I see my piano teacher, and my tongue sticks out."

Needless to say, it was hard to keep a straight face, but I took his problem seriously and assured him that God could, indeed, help him with it.

Later, on my knees beside the bathtub as I bathed this little fellow, I thought how I still struggle with the problem of controlling my mind and my tongue. That afternoon as I knelt to scrub that sturdy little body, the tub became my altar; the bathroom, my temple. I bowed my head, covered my face, and acknowledged that I, like my son, had a problem with my mind and tongue. I asked the Lord to forgive me and to give me more and more the mind and heart and attitude of Christ.

Additional Scripture Readings:
Psalm 39:1–2; James 1:26; 3:3–8

Go to page 285 for your next devotional reading.

Paul's Chains Advance the Gospel

12Now I want you to know, brothers,
that what has happened to me has really
served to advance the gospel. 13As a result, it has become clear throughout the
whole palace guard[a] and to everyone else
that I am in chains for Christ. 14Because
of my chains, most of the brothers in the
Lord have been encouraged to speak the
word of God more courageously and fearlessly.

15It is true that some preach Christ out
of envy and rivalry, but others out of
goodwill. 16The latter do so in love, knowing that I am put here for the defense of
the gospel. 17The former preach Christ
out of selfish ambition, not sincerely,
supposing that they can stir up trouble for
me while I am in chains.[b] 18But what
does it matter? The important thing is
that in every way, whether from false motives or true, Christ is preached. And because of this I rejoice.

Yes, and I will continue to rejoice, 19for
I know that through your prayers and the
help given by the Spirit of Jesus Christ,
what has happened to me will turn out for
my deliverance.[c] 20I eagerly expect and
hope that I will in no way be ashamed,
but will have sufficient courage so that
now as always Christ will be exalted in my
body, whether by life or by death. 21For to
me, to live is Christ and to die is gain. 22If
I am to go on living in the body, this will
mean fruitful labor for me. Yet what shall
I choose? I do not know! 23I am torn between the two: I desire to depart and be
with Christ, which is better by far; 24but it
is more necessary for you that I remain in
the body. 25Convinced of this, I know that
I will remain, and I will continue with all
of you for your progress and joy in the
faith, 26so that through my being with you
again your joy in Christ Jesus will overflow on account of me.

27Whatever happens, conduct yourselves in a manner worthy of the gospel of
Christ. Then, whether I come and see you
or only hear about you in my absence, I
will know that you stand firm in one spirit, contending as one man for the faith of
the gospel 28without being frightened in
any way by those who oppose you. This is
a sign to them that they will be destroyed,
but that you will be saved—and that by
God. 29For it has been granted to you on
behalf of Christ not only to believe on
him, but also to suffer for him, 30since
you are going through the same struggle
you saw I had, and now hear that I still
have.

Imitating Christ's Humility

2 If you have any encouragement from
being united with Christ, if any comfort from his love, if any fellowship with
the Spirit, if any tenderness and compassion, 2then make my joy complete by being like-minded, having the same love,
being one in spirit and purpose. 3Do nothing out of selfish ambition or vain con-
ceit, but in humility consider others better than yourselves. 4Each of you should
look not only to your own interests, but
also to the interests of others.

5Your attitude should be the same as
that of Christ Jesus:

6Who, being in very nature[d] God,
  did not consider equality with God
    something to be grasped,
7but made himself nothing,
  taking the very nature[e] of a
    servant,
  being made in human likeness.
8And being found in appearance as a
    man,
  he humbled himself
  and became obedient to death—
    even death on a cross!
9Therefore God exalted him to the
    highest place
  and gave him the name that is
    above every name,
10that at the name of Jesus every knee
    should bow,
  in heaven and on earth and under
    the earth,
11and every tongue confess that Jesus
    Christ is Lord,
  to the glory of God the Father.

Shining as Stars

12Therefore, my dear friends, as you
have always obeyed—not only in my presence, but now much more in my absence
—continue to work out your salvation
with fear and trembling, 13for it is God
who works in you to will and to act according to his good purpose.

14Do everything without complaining
or arguing, 15so that you may become
blameless and pure, children of God
without fault in a crooked and depraved

[a]*13* Or *whole palace* [b]*16,17* Some late manuscripts have verses 16 and 17 in reverse order.
[c]*19* Or *salvation* [d]*6* Or *in the form of* [e]*7* Or *the form*

VERSE FOR THE DAY: *Philippians 3:13* | *AUTHOR:* *Anne Ortlund* | *PASSAGE FOR THE DAY:* *Philippians 3:12–14*

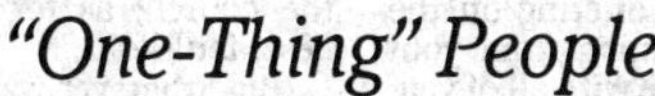

"One-Thing" People

"NOT that I've already arrived!" says the apostle Paul as he begins these comments. Well, whew! That makes us all identify with him!

Then we'd better pay attention to the rest of what he says—that even with all his imperfections and weaknesses Paul has in mind only *one thing*:

> Forgetting what is behind and straining toward what is ahead, I press on toward the goal to win the prize for which God has called me heavenward in Christ Jesus (Philippians 3:13–14).

"Forgetting what is behind"! We're little amateur psychologists these days, trying to remember all our pasts—bringing up why our mothers did this and our fathers did that—to explain all our idiosyncrasies and quirks.

The Bible doesn't so deal with us. It pronounces us sinners and then says to *get on with it,* to look up and forward! All the great people of faith in Hebrews 11 *looked forward* (Hebrews 11:10,14–16,20–22,26,39–40). So did Jesus: he endured the cross "for the joy set before him" (Hebrews 12:2).

Then, with Paul, we must strain toward what's ahead and fix our attention on that: all God's promises, all our inheritance, and the goal, the prize—Jesus himself!

"*One thing* I do," says Paul. It's "one-thing" believers who shed the clutter and baggage and *get there.* They "eliminate and concentrate," and they *make it.*

Take David, for instance:

> *One thing* I ask of the LORD,
> this is what I seek:
> that I may dwell in the house of the LORD
> all the days of my life,
> to gaze upon the beauty of the LORD
> and to seek him in his temple (Psalm 27:4,
> italics mine).

Or take Mary. She sat at the feet of Jesus. And he said to her bustling sister Martha, "Only *one thing* is needed. Mary has chosen what is better, and it will not be take away from her" (Luke 10:42, italics mine).

Be a "one-thing" Christian! Focus! Concentrate! Press on —and up!

Additional Scripture Readings:
Colossians 3:1–2; Hebrews 12:1–2

Go to page 287 for your next devotional reading.

generation, in which you shine like stars in the universe [16]as you hold out[a] the word of life—in order that I may boast on the day of Christ that I did not run or labor for nothing. [17]But even if I am being poured out like a drink offering on the sacrifice and service coming from your faith, I am glad and rejoice with all of you. [18]So you too should be glad and rejoice with me.

Timothy and Epaphroditus

[19]I hope in the Lord Jesus to send Timothy to you soon, that I also may be cheered when I receive news about you. [20]I have no one else like him, who takes a genuine interest in your welfare. [21]For everyone looks out for his own interests, not those of Jesus Christ. [22]But you know that Timothy has proved himself, because as a son with his father he has served with me in the work of the gospel. [23]I hope, therefore, to send him as soon as I see how things go with me. [24]And I am confident in the Lord that I myself will come soon.

[25]But I think it is necessary to send back to you Epaphroditus, my brother, fellow worker and fellow soldier, who is also your messenger, whom you sent to take care of my needs. [26]For he longs for all of you and is distressed because you heard he was ill. [27]Indeed he was ill, and almost died. But God had mercy on him, and not on him only but also on me, to spare me sorrow upon sorrow. [28]Therefore I am all the more eager to send him, so that when you see him again you may be glad and I may have less anxiety. [29]Welcome him in the Lord with great joy, and honor men like him, [30]because he almost died for the work of Christ, risking his life to make up for the help you could not give me.

No Confidence in the Flesh

3 Finally, my brothers, rejoice in the Lord! It is no trouble for me to write the same things to you again, and it is a safeguard for you.

[2]Watch out for those dogs, those men who do evil, those mutilators of the flesh. [3]For it is we who are the circumcision, we who worship by the Spirit of God, who glory in Christ Jesus, and who put no confidence in the flesh— [4]though I myself have reasons for such confidence.

If anyone else thinks he has reasons to put confidence in the flesh, I have more: [5]circumcised on the eighth day, of the people of Israel, of the tribe of Benjamin, a Hebrew of Hebrews; in regard to the law, a Pharisee; [6]as for zeal, persecuting the church; as for legalistic righteousness, faultless.

[7]But whatever was to my profit I now consider loss for the sake of Christ. [8]What is more, I consider everything a loss compared to the surpassing greatness of knowing Christ Jesus my Lord, for whose sake I have lost all things. I consider them rubbish, that I may gain Christ [9]and be found in him, not having a righteousness of my own that comes from the law, but that which is through faith in Christ—the righteousness that comes from God and is by faith. [10]I want to know Christ and the power of his resurrection and the fellowship of sharing in his sufferings, becoming like him in his death, [11]and so, somehow, to attain to the resurrection from the dead.

Pressing on Toward the Goal

[12]Not that I have already obtained all this, or have already been made perfect, but I press on to take hold of that for which Christ Jesus took hold of me. [13]Brothers, I do not consider myself yet to have taken hold of it. But one thing I do: Forgetting what is behind and straining toward what is ahead, [14]I press on toward the goal to win the prize for which God has called me heavenward in Christ Jesus.

[15]All of us who are mature should take such a view of things. And if on some point you think differently, that too God will make clear to you. [16]Only let us live up to what we have already attained.

[17]Join with others in following my example, brothers, and take note of those who live according to the pattern we gave you. [18]For, as I have often told you before and now say again even with tears, many live as enemies of the cross of Christ. [19]Their destiny is destruction, their god is their stomach, and their glory is in their shame. Their mind is on earthly things. [20]But our citizenship is in heaven. And we eagerly await a Savior from there, the Lord Jesus Christ, [21]who, by the power that enables him to bring everything under his control, will transform our lowly bodies so that they will be like his glorious body.

[a]16 Or *hold on to*

VERSE FOR THE DAY: *Philippians 4:6* | *AUTHOR:* *Hope MacDonald* | *PASSAGE FOR THE DAY:* *Philippians 4:4–9*

The Lord Is Near

THIS passage was very significant to me today. My life seemed filled with worries and anxieties. It was the kind of day when I just wanted to pull the covers back over my head and forget everything. Have you ever felt that way?

While reading these verses, I was reminded of the profound truth that prayer isn't something I *had* to do, rather, prayer is something I *get* to do. I *get* to bring to God every worry and concern that is on my heart today. In fact, I discovered when worry and anxiety knock on the door of life, if the door is opened by prayer, no one is there! God's cure for worry is always the same—prayer—not pulling the covers back over my head. His way is always action. That action begins with making everything known to him.

Why do we get to pray this way? Because "the Lord is near" (Philippians 4:5). This is the key to this entire magnificent passage. Because he is near, we need not be anxious for anything. Because he is near, we have peace within. A deep, abiding peace that passes all understanding. Because the Lord is near, a wellspring of joy fills every part of our lives. And because the Lord is near, our hearts and minds are renewed and restored in Christ Jesus. With this restoration we become, once again, fresh, vibrant and alive Christians.

Then we can understand the importance of taking our eyes off ourselves and thinking instead about whatever is true and noble, right, pure, admirable and lovely. We can see clearly again that a great deal that surrounds us is excellent and praiseworthy (Philippians 4:8). This doesn't come naturally to us, does it? But then, God never called us to a natural lifestyle.

This is the encouragement and comfort I received this morning as I set out to face another day under the care and direction of the Holy Spirit.

"Thank you, Jesus, for your power in every part of my life today—renewing me physically, mentally and spiritually."

Additional Scripture Readings:
Psalm 73:23–26; 2 Corinthians 4:16–18

Go to page 290 for your next devotional reading.

4 Therefore, my brothers, you whom I love and long for, my joy and crown, that is how you should stand firm in the Lord, dear friends!

Exhortations

2 I plead with Euodia and I plead with Syntyche to agree with each other in the Lord. 3 Yes, and I ask you, loyal yokefellow,[a] help these women who have contended at my side in the cause of the gospel, along with Clement and the rest of my fellow workers, whose names are in the book of life.

4 Rejoice in the Lord always. I will say it again: Rejoice! 5 Let your gentleness be evident to all. The Lord is near. 6 Do not be anxious about anything, but in everything, by prayer and petition, with thanksgiving, present your requests to God. 7 And the peace of God, which transcends all understanding, will guard your hearts and your minds in Christ Jesus.

8 Finally, brothers, whatever is true, whatever is noble, whatever is right, whatever is pure, whatever is lovely, whatever is admirable—if anything is excellent or praiseworthy—think about such things. 9 Whatever you have learned or received or heard from me, or seen in me—put it into practice. And the God of peace will be with you.

Thanks for Their Gifts

10 I rejoice greatly in the Lord that at last you have renewed your concern for me. Indeed, you have been concerned, but you had no opportunity to show it. 11 I am not saying this because I am in need, for I have learned to be content whatever the circumstances. 12 I know what it is to be in need, and I know what it is to have plenty. I have learned the secret of being content in any and every situation, whether well fed or hungry, whether living in plenty or in want. 13 I can do everything through him who gives me strength.

14 Yet it was good of you to share in my troubles. 15 Moreover, as you Philippians know, in the early days of your acquaintance with the gospel, when I set out from Macedonia, not one church shared with me in the matter of giving and receiving, except you only; 16 for even when I was in Thessalonica, you sent me aid again and again when I was in need. 17 Not that I am looking for a gift, but I am looking for what may be credited to your account. 18 I have received full payment and even more; I am amply supplied, now that I have received from Epaphroditus the gifts you sent. They are a fragrant offering, an acceptable sacrifice, pleasing to God. 19 And my God will meet all your needs according to his glorious riches in Christ Jesus.

20 To our God and Father be glory for ever and ever. Amen.

Final Greetings

21 Greet all the saints in Christ Jesus. The brothers who are with me send greetings. 22 All the saints send you greetings, especially those who belong to Caesar's household.

23 The grace of the Lord Jesus Christ be with your spirit. Amen.[b]

[a] 3 Or *loyal Syzygus* [b] 23 Some manuscripts do not have *Amen*.

PAUL writes this letter to the church in Colosse at about the same time as he writes Ephesians. False teachers are deceiving some of those to whom he writes (Colossians 2:4). Therefore, Paul stresses the power and glory of Christ and instructs his readers on how to live as Christians. As you read this book, put your faith in this glorious Savior who died for you, and promise him that you will show Christian love and compassion to others.

COLOSSIANS

1 Paul, an apostle of Christ Jesus
by the will of God, and Timothy our
brother,

2To the holy and faithful[a] brothers in
Christ at Colosse:

Grace and peace to you from God our
Father.[b]

Thanksgiving and Prayer

3We always thank God, the Father of
our Lord Jesus Christ, when we pray for
you, 4because we have heard of your faith
in Christ Jesus and of the love you have
for all the saints— 5the faith and love that
spring from the hope that is stored up for
you in heaven and that you have already
heard about in the word of truth, the gospel 6that has come to you. All over the
world this gospel is bearing fruit and
growing, just as it has been doing among
you since the day you heard it and understood God's grace in all its truth. 7You
learned it from Epaphras, our dear fellow
servant, who is a faithful minister of
Christ on our[c] behalf, 8and who also told
us of your love in the Spirit.

9For this reason, since the day we
heard about you, we have not stopped
praying for you and asking God to fill you
with the knowledge of his will through

a2 Or *believing* b2 Some manuscripts *Father and the Lord Jesus Christ* c7 Some manuscripts *your*

all spiritual wisdom and understanding.
[10]And we pray this in order that you may
live a life worthy of the Lord and may
please him in every way: bearing fruit in
every good work, growing in the knowledge of God, [11]being strengthened with
all power according to his glorious might
so that you may have great endurance and
patience, and joyfully [12]giving thanks to
the Father, who has qualified you[a] to
share in the inheritance of the saints in
the kingdom of light. [13]For he has rescued us from the dominion of darkness
and brought us into the kingdom of the
Son he loves, [14]in whom we have redemption,[b] the forgiveness of sins.

The Supremacy of Christ

[15]He is the image of the invisible God,
the firstborn over all creation. [16]For by

[a]12 Some manuscripts *us* [b]14 A few late manuscripts *redemption through his blood*

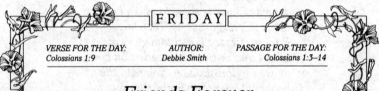

FRIDAY

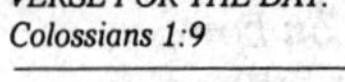

VERSE FOR THE DAY: *Colossians 1:9*

AUTHOR: *Debbie Smith*

PASSAGE FOR THE DAY: *Colossians 1:3–14*

Friends Forever

TIME has a way of defining true friends. I have discovered that passing years and growing distance are ineffective obstacles to the mutual love between my friends and me. Perhaps it is because of our common walk with the Lord that we can just pick up where we left off whenever we are together. And these are the dear ones I will spend eternity loving!

Of course, prayer is an important part of continuing that bond. Colossians 1:3–14 is an eloquent description of a Christian's prayer for her friends. Even though Paul had not even visited the Christians at Colosse (Colossians 1:7), his love for them through Christ was strong and ardent.

One Sunday afternoon soon after our wedding, Michael and I were getting ready for the weekly Bible study that would meet in our living room that night. It would be the final study led by Bill Jackson before he moved away. On a sudden whim, we decided to write a song for Bill. Michael went to take a shower; I sat down with the Bible and a pen. In less than an hour Michael had found a melody on the piano for the lyrics to "friends." We were happy to have something special for Bill, though it never occurred to us that anyone else would find this simple song meaningful.

God had different plans! He has used "Friends" for graduations, funerals, weddings and gatherings of all kinds. Michael and I continue to be blessed by letters from people who identify with this song and find comfort in its message. Both the Colossians passage and the song are a call to prayer for those we love—and a reminder that God's love unites people as friends forever!

Additional Scripture Readings:
Ephesians 3:14–19; Philemon 4–7

Go to page 291 for your next devotional reading.

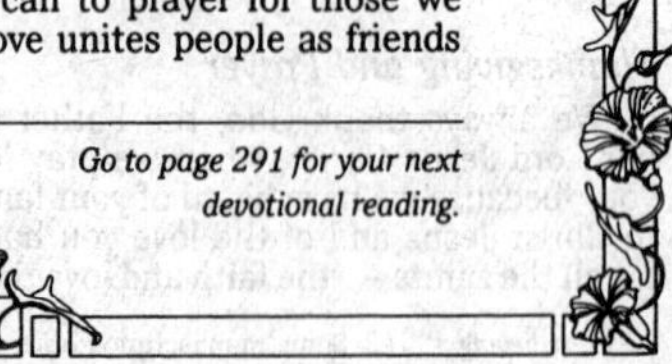

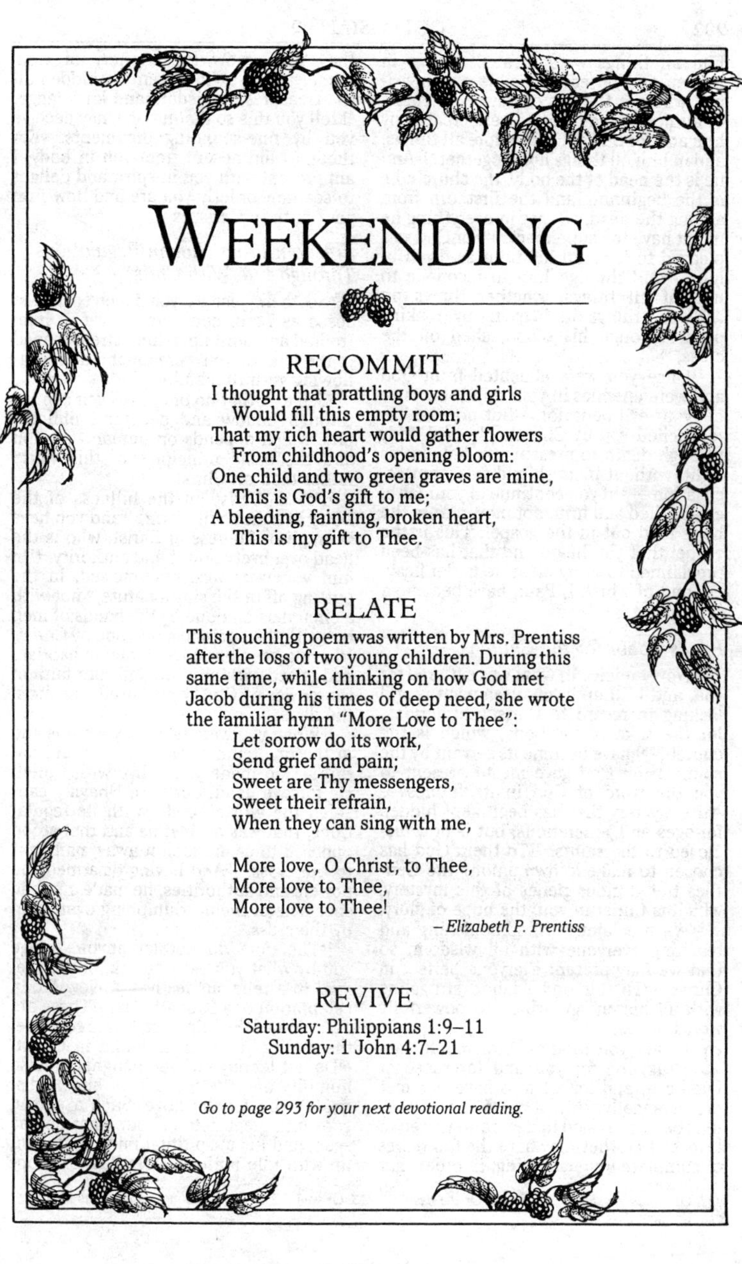

WEEKENDING

RECOMMIT

I thought that prattling boys and girls
   Would fill this empty room;
That my rich heart would gather flowers
   From childhood's opening bloom:
One child and two green graves are mine,
   This is God's gift to me;
A bleeding, fainting, broken heart,
   This is my gift to Thee.

RELATE

This touching poem was written by Mrs. Prentiss after the loss of two young children. During this same time, while thinking on how God met Jacob during his times of deep need, she wrote the familiar hymn "More Love to Thee":

Let sorrow do its work,
Send grief and pain;
Sweet are Thy messengers,
Sweet their refrain,
When they can sing with me,

More love, O Christ, to Thee,
More love to Thee,
More love to Thee!

– Elizabeth P. Prentiss

REVIVE

Saturday: Philippians 1:9–11
Sunday: 1 John 4:7–21

Go to page 293 for your next devotional reading.

him all things were created: things in
heaven and on earth, visible and invisible, whether thrones or powers or rulers
or authorities; all things were created by
him and for him. 17He is before all things,
and in him all things hold together. 18And
he is the head of the body, the church; he
is the beginning and the firstborn from
among the dead, so that in everything he
might have the supremacy. 19For God was
pleased to have all his fullness dwell in
him, 20and through him to reconcile to
himself all things, whether things on
earth or things in heaven, by making
peace through his blood, shed on the
cross.

21Once you were alienated from God
and were enemies in your minds because
of[a] your evil behavior. 22But now he has
reconciled you by Christ's physical body
through death to present you holy in his
sight, without blemish and free from accusation — 23if you continue in your faith,
established and firm, not moved from the
hope held out in the gospel. This is the
gospel that you heard and that has been
proclaimed to every creature under heav-
en, and of which I, Paul, have become a
servant.

Paul's Labor for the Church

24Now I rejoice in what was suffered for
you, and I fill up in my flesh what is still
lacking in regard to Christ's afflictions,
for the sake of his body, which is the
church. 25I have become its servant by the
commission God gave me to present to
you the word of God in its fullness—
26the mystery that has been kept hidden
for ages and generations, but is now disclosed to the saints. 27To them God has
chosen to make known among the Gentiles the glorious riches of this mystery,
which is Christ in you, the hope of glory.

28We proclaim him, admonishing and
teaching everyone with all wisdom, so
that we may present everyone perfect in
Christ. 29To this end I labor, struggling
with all his energy, which so powerfully
works in me.

2 I want you to know how much I am
struggling for you and for those at
Laodicea, and for all who have not met
me personally. 2My purpose is that they
may be encouraged in heart and united in
love, so that they may have the full riches
of complete understanding, in order that
they may know the mystery of God,
namely, Christ, 3in whom are hidden all
the treasures of wisdom and knowledge.
4I tell you this so that no one may deceive
you by fine-sounding arguments. 5For
though I am absent from you in body, I
am present with you in spirit and delight
to see how orderly you are and how firm
your faith in Christ is.

Freedom From Human Regulations Through Life With Christ

6So then, just as you received Christ
Jesus as Lord, continue to live in him,
7rooted and built up in him, strengthened
in the faith as you were taught, and overflowing with thankfulness.

8See to it that no one takes you captive
through hollow and deceptive philosophy, which depends on human tradition
and the basic principles of this world
rather than on Christ.

9For in Christ all the fullness of the
Deity lives in bodily form, 10and you have
been given fullness in Christ, who is the
head over every power and authority. 11In
him you were also circumcised, in the
putting off of the sinful nature,[b] not with
a circumcision done by the hands of men
but with the circumcision done by Christ,
12having been buried with him in baptism
and raised with him through your faith in
the power of God, who raised him from
the dead.

13When you were dead in your sins and
in the uncircumcision of your sinful nature,[c] God made you[d] alive with Christ.
He forgave us all our sins, 14having canceled the written code, with its regulations, that was against us and that stood
opposed to us; he took it away, nailing it
to the cross. 15And having disarmed the
powers and authorities, he made a public
spectacle of them, triumphing over them
by the cross.[e]

16Therefore do not let anyone judge
you by what you eat or drink, or with regard to a religious festival, a New Moon
celebration or a Sabbath day. 17These are
a shadow of the things that were to come;
the reality, however, is found in Christ.
18Do not let anyone who delights in false
humility and the worship of angels dis-
qualify you for the prize. Such a person
goes into great detail about what he has
seen, and his unspiritual mind puffs him
up with idle notions. 19He has lost con-

[a]21 Or *minds, as shown by* [b]11 Or *the flesh* [c]13 Or *your flesh* [d]13 Some manuscripts *us*
[e]15 Or *them in him*

MONDAY

VERSE FOR THE DAY: *Colossians 2:10* | *AUTHOR:* *Marie Chapian* | *PASSAGE FOR THE DAY:* *Colossians 2:6–12*

Fullness in Christ

EVERY time somebody asks me what my astrological sign is, I tell them, "Jesus is my sign. I'm a Christian." Often the person will continue, "Yes, but what month were you born in?" Still I persist, "I'm a Christian. I'm born again."

For centuries people have believed that their destiny is controlled by the month of their birth. They are slaves to the stars. Thank goodness that for those who believe in Jesus Christ there is freedom from such bondage.

Colossians 2:10 tells us we are complete in Christ—not in anything else. He is the head over every power in the universe. We need never be threatened by the forces of darkness that may surround us. Christ reigns above those forces. The stars can't control our destinies—Jesus created the stars! He is our authority.

It is a wonderful thing to be made whole and full. This means we can stop searching for identity and self-worth in the elemental and base philosophies of the world. Our future is sure in Christ because no longer are we incomplete creatures, helpless in the face of an unseen destiny.

Nonetheless, we must guard against seductive philosophies and false religions, just as we must look inward at our own personal, unbridled needs. I have counseled countless people who are insecure, fearful, moody, and desperately dependent on the approval of other people. These things can imprison us just as miserably as the deceptive philosophy of astrology.

Jesus Christ is the head over every power and authority, and he is more powerful than sorrow, gloom, fear, insecurity and the need for approval. It is important that we tell ourselves daily, "I find my personhood in the Lord Jesus and not in other people, not in success, relationships, ideal circumstances or the stars." Then tell the Lord triumphantly, "Thank you for giving me fullness in you."

Additional Scripture Readings:
Isaiah 47:8–15; Ephesians 6:11–18

Go to page 295 for your next devotional reading.

nection with the Head, from whom the whole body, supported and held together by its ligaments and sinews, grows as God causes it to grow.

[20]Since you died with Christ to the basic principles of this world, why, as though you still belonged to it, do you submit to its rules: [21]"Do not handle! Do not taste! Do not touch!"? [22]These are all destined to perish with use, because they are based on human commands and teachings. [23]Such regulations indeed have an appearance of wisdom, with their self-imposed worship, their false humility and their harsh treatment of the body, but they lack any value in restraining sensual indulgence.

Rules for Holy Living

3 Since, then, you have been raised with Christ, set your hearts on things above, where Christ is seated at the right hand of God. [2]Set your minds on things above, not on earthly things. [3]For you died, and your life is now hidden with Christ in God. [4]When Christ, who is your[a] life, appears, then you also will appear with him in glory.

[5]Put to death, therefore, whatever belongs to your earthly nature: sexual immorality, impurity, lust, evil desires and greed, which is idolatry. [6]Because of these, the wrath of God is coming.[b] [7]You used to walk in these ways, in the life you once lived. [8]But now you must rid yourselves of all such things as these: anger, rage, malice, slander, and filthy language from your lips. [9]Do not lie to each other, since you have taken off your old self with its practices [10]and have put on the new self, which is being renewed in knowledge in the image of its Creator. [11]Here there is no Greek or Jew, circumcised or uncircumcised, barbarian, Scythian, slave or free, but Christ is all, and is in all.

[12]Therefore, as God's chosen people, holy and dearly loved, clothe yourselves with compassion, kindness, humility, gentleness and patience. [13]Bear with each other and forgive whatever grievances you may have against one another. Forgive as the Lord forgave you. [14]And over all these virtues put on love, which binds them all together in perfect unity.

[15]Let the peace of Christ rule in your hearts, since as members of one body you were called to peace. And be thankful. [16]Let the word of Christ dwell in you richly as you teach and admonish one another with all wisdom, and as you sing psalms, hymns and spiritual songs with gratitude in your hearts to God. [17]And whatever you do, whether in word or deed, do it all in the name of the Lord Jesus, giving thanks to God the Father through him.

Rules for Christian Households

[18]Wives, submit to your husbands, as is fitting in the Lord.

[19]Husbands, love your wives and do not be harsh with them.

[20]Children, obey your parents in everything, for this pleases the Lord.

[21]Fathers, do not embitter your children, or they will become discouraged.

[22]Slaves, obey your earthly masters in everything; and do it, not only when their eye is on you and to win their favor, but with sincerity of heart and reverence for the Lord. [23]Whatever you do, work at it with all your heart, as working for the Lord, not for men, [24]since you know that you will receive an inheritance from the Lord as a reward. It is the Lord Christ you are serving. [25]Anyone who does wrong will be repaid for his wrong, and there is no favoritism.

4 Masters, provide your slaves with what is right and fair, because you know that you also have a Master in heaven.

Further Instructions

[2]Devote yourselves to prayer, being watchful and thankful. [3]And pray for us, too, that God may open a door for our message, so that we may proclaim the mystery of Christ, for which I am in chains. [4]Pray that I may proclaim it clearly, as I should. [5]Be wise in the way you act toward outsiders; make the most of every opportunity. [6]Let your conversation be always full of grace, seasoned with salt, so that you may know how to answer everyone.

Final Greetings

[7]Tychicus will tell you all the news about me. He is a dear brother, a faithful minister and fellow servant in the Lord. [8]I am sending him to you for the express purpose that you may know about our[c] circumstances and that he may encour-

a4 Some manuscripts *our* *b6* Some early manuscripts *coming on those who are disobedient*
c8 Some manuscripts *that he may know about your*

TUESDAY

VERSE FOR THE DAY: *Colossians 3:15–17*

AUTHOR: *Martha Manikas-Foster*

PASSAGE FOR THE DAY: *Colossians 3:1–17*

The Peace of Christ

IT was a working holiday for my husband. It turned into two weeks of baby-tending isolation for me. The chill of the northern Michigan spring was too much for my three-month-old daughter. So we spent much of our time in the small bedroom of a cottage bordering Lake Huron.

I was held captive. I was trapped only a few feet from my favorite piece of wilderness. I had spent times very close to God here, skiing among these trees and walking within range of the sound of the waves. But that was before.

This visit, I resigned myself to spending two weeks in closed quarters, and I unpacked the pens and editing supplies from my briefcase. I determined not to yearn for the birch trees, the sandy cove and the bay outside my window.

Several days into our stay, Connie's nap extended beyond its usual, frustratingly short fifteen-minute duration. I seized the opportunity and, grabbing the portable baby monitor, dashed out the door. I wanted to appreciate God's spellbinding creation. But my electronic tether kept me close to the cabin.

With the zeal of an eager girl scout, I began cutting tall grass and reed from along the bay and laying the bundles on a picnic table in the sun. I watched the sea gulls, sang favorite hymns, and from the pile on the table began to weave the still-damp materials into something of a basket. It wasn't much of a basket, but my efforts were sincere and my spirit exuberant.

I was at peace. It shouldn't have surprised me that enjoying God as revealed through his creation would bring peace. But it did. And once peaceful, it was easier to see my circumstances as opportunities to worship God through all I did. Thus, when my daughter woke up and called me to return, I went with renewed compassion and patience.

Since that time, when I have felt confined or frustrated, I have reached again to touch a part of God's creation. God's character is revealed, in part, through his excellent work in the details—his attention to the minuscule fibers of each tulip, each pine needle, each crab apple blossom. It is only by focusing on the One whose creation surrounds us and brings us peace that we can do "all in the name of the Lord Jesus, giving thanks to God the Father through him" (Colossians 3:17).

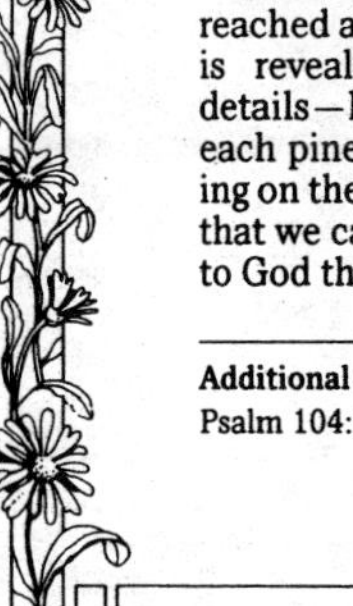

Additional Scripture Readings:
Psalm 104:24–34; Isaiah 55:12–13

Go to page 299 for your next devotional reading.

age your hearts. 9He is coming with Onesimus, our faithful and dear brother, who is one of you. They will tell you everything that is happening here.

10My fellow prisoner Aristarchus sends you his greetings, as does Mark, the cousin of Barnabas. (You have received instructions about him; if he comes to you, welcome him.) 11Jesus, who is called Justus, also sends greetings. These are the only Jews among my fellow workers for the kingdom of God, and they have proved a comfort to me. 12Epaphras, who is one of you and a servant of Christ Jesus, sends greetings. He is always wrestling in prayer for you, that you may stand firm in all the will of God, mature and fully assured. 13I vouch for him that he is working hard for you and for those at Laodicea and Hierapolis. 14Our dear friend Luke, the doctor, and Demas send greetings. 15Give my greetings to the brothers at Laodicea, and to Nympha and the church in her house.

16After this letter has been read to you, see that it is also read in the church of the Laodiceans and that you in turn read the letter from Laodicea.

17Tell Archippus: "See to it that you complete the work you have received in the Lord."

18I, Paul, write this greeting in my own hand. Remember my chains. Grace be with you.

PAUL writes this letter to the church he began in Thessalonica (Acts 17:1–9), shortly after leaving them and being unable to return (1 Thessalonians 2:17–18). He is excited about their Christian faith, reminds them of his intense love for them, and answers questions about what death means for a Christian. As you read this book, find comfort as a believer that when you die you will still be under God's care and will "be with the Lord forever" (1 Thessalonians 4:17).

1 THESSALONIANS

1 Paul, Silas[a] and Timothy,

To the church of the Thessalonians in God the Father and the Lord Jesus Christ:

Grace and peace to you.[b]

Thanksgiving for the Thessalonians' Faith

2We always thank God for all of you,
mentioning you in our prayers. 3We continually remember before our God and
Father your work produced by faith, your
labor prompted by love, and your endurance inspired by hope in our Lord Jesus Christ.

4For we know, brothers loved by God,
that he has chosen you, 5because our gos-
pel came to you not simply with words, but also with power, with the Holy Spirit and with deep conviction. You know how
we lived among you for your sake. 6You
became imitators of us and of the Lord; in spite of severe suffering, you welcomed the message with the joy given by the
Holy Spirit. 7And so you became a model
to all the believers in Macedonia and

[a]1 Greek *Silvanus,* a variant of *Silas* [b]1 Some early manuscripts *you from God our Father and the Lord Jesus Christ*

Achaia. 8The Lord's message rang out from you not only in Macedonia and Achaia—your faith in God has become known everywhere. Therefore we do not need to say anything about it, 9for they themselves report what kind of reception you gave us. They tell how you turned to God from idols to serve the living and true God, 10and to wait for his Son from heaven, whom he raised from the dead—Jesus, who rescues us from the coming wrath.

Paul's Ministry in Thessalonica

2 You know, brothers, that our visit to you was not a failure. 2We had previously suffered and been insulted in Philippi, as you know, but with the help of our God we dared to tell you his gospel in spite of strong opposition. 3For the appeal we make does not spring from error or impure motives, nor are we trying to trick you. 4On the contrary, we speak as men approved by God to be entrusted with the gospel. We are not trying to please men but God, who tests our hearts. 5You know we never used flattery, nor did we put on a mask to cover up greed—God is our witness. 6We were not looking for praise from men, not from you or anyone else.

As apostles of Christ we could have been a burden to you, 7but we were gentle among you, like a mother caring for her little children. 8We loved you so much that we were delighted to share with you not only the gospel of God but our lives as well, because you had become so dear to us. 9Surely you remember, brothers, our toil and hardship; we worked night and day in order not to be a burden to anyone while we preached the gospel of God to you.

10You are witnesses, and so is God, of how holy, righteous and blameless we were among you who believed. 11For you know that we dealt with each of you as a father deals with his own children, 12encouraging, comforting and urging you to live lives worthy of God, who calls you into his kingdom and glory.

13And we also thank God continually because, when you received the word of God, which you heard from us, you accepted it not as the word of men, but as it actually is, the word of God, which is at work in you who believe. 14For you, brothers, became imitators of God's churches in Judea, which are in Christ Jesus: You suffered from your own countrymen the same things those churches suffered from the Jews, 15who killed the Lord Jesus and the prophets and also drove us out. They displease God and are hostile to all men 16in their effort to keep us from speaking to the Gentiles so that they may be saved. In this way they always heap up their sins to the limit. The wrath of God has come upon them at last.[a]

Paul's Longing to See the Thessalonians

17But, brothers, when we were torn away from you for a short time (in person, not in thought), out of our intense longing we made every effort to see you. 18For we wanted to come to you—certainly I, Paul, did, again and again—but Satan stopped us. 19For what is our hope, our joy, or the crown in which we will glory in the presence of our Lord Jesus when he comes? Is it not you? 20Indeed, you are our glory and joy.

3 So when we could stand it no longer, we thought it best to be left by ourselves in Athens. 2We sent Timothy, who is our brother and God's fellow worker[b] in spreading the gospel of Christ, to strengthen and encourage you in your faith, 3so that no one would be unsettled by these trials. You know quite well that we were destined for them. 4In fact, when we were with you, we kept telling you that we would be persecuted. And it turned out that way, as you well know. 5For this reason, when I could stand it no longer, I sent to find out about your faith. I was afraid that in some way the tempter might have tempted you and our efforts might have been useless.

Timothy's Encouraging Report

6But Timothy has just now come to us from you and has brought good news about your faith and love. He has told us that you always have pleasant memories of us and that you long to see us, just as we also long to see you. 7Therefore, brothers, in all our distress and persecution we were encouraged about you because of your faith. 8For now we really live, since you are standing firm in the Lord. 9How can we thank God enough for you in return for all the joy we have in the

[a]16 Or *them fully*   [b]2 Some manuscripts *brother and fellow worker*; other manuscripts *brother and God's servant*

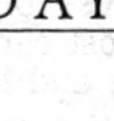

WEDNESDAY

VERSE FOR THE DAY:	*AUTHOR:*	*PASSAGE FOR THE DAY:*
1 Thessalonians 4:14	*Martha Manikas-Foster*	*1 Thessalonians 4:13–15*

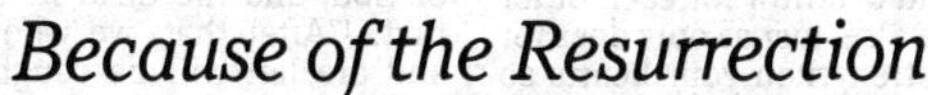

Because of the Resurrection

WHEN I was in high school, a Campus Life leader commented that before our group graduated, quite likely one of our classmates would die. Death is that near, he said. Even young people die.

His prediction was wrong. None of my high school classmates died. But a few years later, on one day, in the instant it takes for a car and truck to collide, six college classmates died.

These weren't anonymous men and women; I knew each of them. When they died I was hundreds of miles away taking classes at another university. After the phone call, I was overwhelmed by my powerlessness. Alone, I had no one to share my grief, to hold me when I sobbed. To grieve for one would have been torture enough. Grieving for six tore me apart.

Loving sets us up for sorrow, that's true. But it also encourages us to hope. Although I didn't understand it immediately, I grew to realize that the affection I had for these classmates had grown from a foundation of common faith. On such a foundation my hope began to flourish. What we had most in common was the very thing that assured me of their well-being. Because of the resurrection, the horror of death melted away. I would see them again because:

> We believe that Jesus died and rose again and so we believe that God will bring with Jesus those who have fallen asleep in him. According to the Lord's own word, we tell you that we who are still alive, who are left till the coming of the Lord, will certainly not precede those who have fallen asleep. . . . And so we will be with the Lord forever. Therefore encourage each other with these words (1 Thessalonians 4:14–15,17–18).

I can't help but grow sad when I look at some of the photographs in my college yearbooks. But I have hope because I know that "death has been swallowed up in victory" (1 Corinthians 15:54). Jesus Christ is the victor! He "has destroyed death and has brought life and immortality to light through the gospel" (2 Timothy 1:10).

Additional Scripture Readings:
John 11:21–27; 1 Corinthians 15:20–23

Go to page 301 for your next devotional reading.

presence of our God because of you? 10Night and day we pray most earnestly that we may see you again and supply what is lacking in your faith.

11Now may our God and Father himself and our Lord Jesus clear the way for us to come to you. 12May the Lord make your love increase and overflow for each other and for everyone else, just as ours does for you. 13May he strengthen your hearts so that you will be blameless and holy in the presence of our God and Father when our Lord Jesus comes with all his holy ones.

Living to Please God

4 Finally, brothers, we instructed you how to live in order to please God, as in fact you are living. Now we ask you and urge you in the Lord Jesus to do this more and more. 2For you know what instructions we gave you by the authority of the Lord Jesus.

3It is God's will that you should be sanctified: that you should avoid sexual immorality; 4that each of you should learn to control his own body[a] in a way that is holy and honorable, 5not in passionate lust like the heathen, who do not know God; 6and that in this matter no one should wrong his brother or take advantage of him. The Lord will punish men for all such sins, as we have already told you and warned you. 7For God did not call us to be impure, but to live a holy life. 8Therefore, he who rejects this instruction does not reject man but God, who gives you his Holy Spirit.

9Now about brotherly love we do not need to write to you, for you yourselves have been taught by God to love each other. 10And in fact, you do love all the brothers throughout Macedonia. Yet we urge you, brothers, to do so more and more.

11Make it your ambition to lead a quiet life, to mind your own business and to work with your hands, just as we told you, 12so that your daily life may win the respect of outsiders and so that you will not be dependent on anybody.

The Coming of the Lord

13Brothers, we do not want you to be ignorant about those who fall asleep, or to grieve like the rest of men, who have no hope. 14We believe that Jesus died and rose again and so we believe that God will bring with Jesus those who have fallen asleep in him. 15According to the Lord's own word, we tell you that we who are still alive, who are left till the coming of the Lord, will certainly not precede those who have fallen asleep. 16For the Lord himself will come down from heaven, with a loud command, with the voice of the archangel and with the trumpet call of God, and the dead in Christ will rise first. 17After that, we who are still alive and are left will be caught up together with them in the clouds to meet the Lord in the air. And so we will be with the Lord forever. 18Therefore encourage each other with these words.

5 Now, brothers, about times and dates we do not need to write to you, 2for you know very well that the day of the Lord will come like a thief in the night. 3While people are saying, "Peace and safety," destruction will come on them suddenly, as labor pains on a pregnant woman, and they will not escape.

4But you, brothers, are not in darkness so that this day should surprise you like a thief. 5You are all sons of the light and sons of the day. We do not belong to the night or to the darkness. 6So then, let us not be like others, who are asleep, but let us be alert and self-controlled. 7For those who sleep, sleep at night, and those who get drunk, get drunk at night. 8But since we belong to the day, let us be self-controlled, putting on faith and love as a breastplate, and the hope of salvation as a helmet. 9For God did not appoint us to suffer wrath but to receive salvation through our Lord Jesus Christ. 10He died for us so that, whether we are awake or asleep, we may live together with him. 11Therefore encourage one another and build each other up, just as in fact you are doing.

Final Instructions

12Now we ask you, brothers, to respect those who work hard among you, who are over you in the Lord and who admonish you. 13Hold them in the highest regard in love because of their work. Live in peace with each other. 14And we urge you, brothers, warn those who are idle, encourage the timid, help the weak, be patient with everyone. 15Make sure that nobody pays back wrong for wrong, but always try to be kind to each other and to everyone else.

16Be joyful always; 17pray continually; 18give thanks in all circumstances, for

[a]4 Or *learn to live with his own wife*; or *learn to acquire a wife*

THURSDAY

VERSE FOR THE DAY:	AUTHOR:	PASSAGE FOR THE DAY:
1 Thessalonians 5:18	Carol L. Baldwin	1 Thessalonians 5:16–22

Thanksgiving for All Things

"LORD, how can I thank you when I am single and want to be married?"

"Dear God, how can I ever be happy in this dead-end job?"

"God, how can I thank you for broken plumbing in our bathroom when we don't have the money to make repairs?"

How can we have thankful, contented hearts when the circumstances in our lives are not what we had planned and when they lie outside our control or our power to change?

Let's look at our alternatives. If we are not thankful, we become bitter and angry with God: he is not providing what we "rightfully" deserve. If we are not content, we become rebellious and complaining: after all, he gives our friends everything they pray for—why does he refuse us?

Underlying these complaints and questions lie two errors in our thinking: that God is not trustworthy and that he does not desire our good. When we compare these conclusions with Scripture, we discover how wrong we are! God's Word instructs us that God is sovereignly in control, providing for and working out *all* the circumstances in the lives of those who love him and whom he has called (Romans 8:28; 1 Corinthians 10:13a; Philippians 4:6–7). He is intimately involved with us; he works out his purposes through the events in our lives so that we may be conformed to the image of his Son.

We have further reason to praise him. The same God who formed the world in six days knows every hair on our heads. The same God who chose a people for himself before we were born sent his Son to die on the cross to redeem us from our sins.

God's love for his people is not determined by the circumstances in our lives. His love is steadfast. Our marital status, career or finances might fluctuate or totally break apart. In spite of that, however, we can and must give him thanks for his love toward us. We must serve him with unhesitating hearts.

Additional Scripture Readings:
Philippians 1:12–19; Colossians 2:6–7

Go to page 305 for your next devotional reading.

this is God's will for you in Christ Jesus.
19Do not put out the Spirit's fire; 20do
not treat prophecies with contempt.
21Test everything. Hold on to the good.
22Avoid every kind of evil.
23May God himself, the God of peace,
sanctify you through and through. May
your whole spirit, soul and body be kept
blameless at the coming of our Lord
Jesus Christ. 24The one who calls you is
faithful and he will do it.

25Brothers, pray for us. 26Greet all the
brothers with a holy kiss. 27I charge you
before the Lord to have this letter read to
all the brothers.
28The grace of our Lord Jesus Christ be
with you.

PAUL writes this letter shortly after 1 Thessalonians to clarify some things that the church failed to understand in his first letter. He tells them that the antichrist is coming, but they must continue with their regular schedules until Jesus returns. As you read this book, remember that God wants you to look forward to Christ's return as well as to continue doing your daily work.

2 THESSALONIANS

1 Paul, Silas[a] and Timothy,
To the church of the Thessalonians in
God our Father and the Lord Jesus Christ:
2Grace and peace to you from God the
Father and the Lord Jesus Christ.

Thanksgiving and Prayer

3We ought always to thank God for you,
brothers, and rightly so, because your
faith is growing more and more, and the
love every one of you has for each other is
increasing. 4Therefore, among God's
churches we boast about your perseverance and faith in all the persecutions and
trials you are enduring.
5All this is evidence that God's judgment is right, and as a result you will be
counted worthy of the kingdom of God,
for which you are suffering. 6God is just:
He will pay back trouble to those who
trouble you 7and give relief to you who are
troubled, and to us as well. This will happen when the Lord Jesus is revealed from
heaven in blazing fire with his powerful
angels. 8He will punish those who do not
know God and do not obey the gospel of
our Lord Jesus. 9They will be punished
with everlasting destruction and shut out
from the presence of the Lord and from
the majesty of his power 10on the day he
comes to be glorified in his holy people
and to be marveled at among all those
who have believed. This includes you, because you believed our testimony to you.
11With this in mind, we constantly pray
for you, that our God may count you
worthy of his calling, and that by his pow-

[a] *1* Greek *Silvanus*, a variant of *Silas*

er he may fulfill every good purpose of yours and every act prompted by your faith. 12We pray this so that the name of our Lord Jesus may be glorified in you, and you in him, according to the grace of our God and the Lord Jesus Christ.[a]

The Man of Lawlessness

2 Concerning the coming of our Lord Jesus Christ and our being gathered to him, we ask you, brothers, 2not to become easily unsettled or alarmed by some prophecy, report or letter supposed to have come from us, saying that the day of the Lord has already come. 3Don't let anyone deceive you in any way, for ⌞that day will not come⌟ until the rebellion occurs and the man of lawlessness[b] is revealed, the man doomed to destruction. 4He will oppose and will exalt himself over everything that is called God or is worshiped, so that he sets himself up in God's temple, proclaiming himself to be God.

5Don't you remember that when I was with you I used to tell you these things? 6And now you know what is holding him back, so that he may be revealed at the proper time. 7For the secret power of lawlessness is already at work; but the one who now holds it back will continue to do so till he is taken out of the way. 8And then the lawless one will be revealed, whom the Lord Jesus will overthrow with the breath of his mouth and destroy by the splendor of his coming. 9The coming of the lawless one will be in accordance with the work of Satan displayed in all kinds of counterfeit miracles, signs and wonders, 10and in every sort of evil that deceives those who are perishing. They perish because they refused to love the truth and so be saved. 11For this reason God sends them a powerful delusion so that they will believe the lie 12and so that all will be condemned who have not believed the truth but have delighted in wickedness.

Stand Firm

13But we ought always to thank God for you, brothers loved by the Lord, because from the beginning God chose you[c] to be saved through the sanctifying work of the Spirit and through belief in the truth. 14He called you to this through our gospel, that you might share in the glory of our Lord Jesus Christ. 15So then, brothers, stand firm and hold to the teachings[d] we passed on to you, whether by word of mouth or by letter.

16May our Lord Jesus Christ himself and God our Father, who loved us and by his grace gave us eternal encouragement and good hope, 17encourage your hearts and strengthen you in every good deed and word.

Request for Prayer

3 Finally, brothers, pray for us that the message of the Lord may spread rapidly and be honored, just as it was with you. 2And pray that we may be delivered from wicked and evil men, for not everyone has faith. 3But the Lord is faithful, and he will strengthen and protect you from the evil one. 4We have confidence in the Lord that you are doing and will continue to do the things we command. 5May the Lord direct your hearts into God's love and Christ's perseverance.

Warning Against Idleness

6In the name of the Lord Jesus Christ, we command you, brothers, to keep away from every brother who is idle and does not live according to the teaching[e] you received from us. 7For you yourselves know how you ought to follow our example. We were not idle when we were with you, 8nor did we eat anyone's food without paying for it. On the contrary, we worked night and day, laboring and toiling so that we would not be a burden to any of you. 9We did this, not because we do not have the right to such help, but in order to make ourselves a model for you to follow. 10For even when we were with you, we gave you this rule: "If a man will not work, he shall not eat."

11We hear that some among you are idle. They are not busy; they are busybodies. 12Such people we command and urge in the Lord Jesus Christ to settle down and earn the bread they eat. 13And as for you, brothers, never tire of doing what is right.

14If anyone does not obey our instruction in this letter, take special note of him. Do not associate with him, in order

[a] *12* Or *God and Lord, Jesus Christ* [b] *3* Some manuscripts *sin* [c] *13* Some manuscripts *because God chose you as his firstfruits* [d] *15* Or *traditions* [e] *6* Or *tradition*

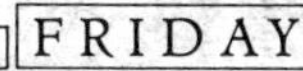

FRIDAY

VERSE FOR THE DAY:
2 Thessalonians 3:5,16

AUTHOR:
Gien Karssen

PASSAGE FOR THE DAY:
2 Thessalonians 3:1–18

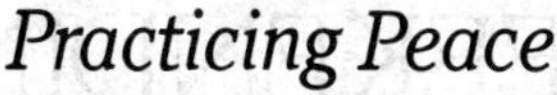

Practicing Peace

EACH of Paul's letters begins with a greeting of peace. Some, like this one to the Christians in the Greek city of Thessalonica, end the same way. These words were full of meaning. Paul was reminding the Thessalonians that the Lord, the author of peace, would give his peace always, in every way and under all circumstances. The Thessalonians needed this encouragement badly. They were people who suffered from oppression and persecution, who were confronted with the problem of immorality, who were full of sorrow because of loved ones who had died, who lived among difficult and pagan people, and who were confronted by false religious teachers and people with warped minds.

Paul's words referred back to the reality of the night in which Christ was born. The Lord who gives peace, because he himself is peace, was born to command peace. It is the same peace of which the Lord later would say to his disciples, "Peace I leave with you; my peace I give you" (John 14:27). "I have told you these things, so that in me you may have peace. In this world you will have trouble. But take heart! I have overcome the world" (John 16:33).

The Thessalonians claimed this peace, and proved it to be applicable and sufficient in their varied situations. This peace lifted them above their problems. In spite of pressure and adversity, their faith grew so that they became examples to others.

Even today we can draw comfort from the experiences of those who have gone before us. We can try to follow their good example, learn not to lose heart, and nurture hope.

Circumstances in the eighties are far from rosy. The world finds itself in chaos. Many a family is in a crisis. The church is often at a loss for the right answers. Small wonder that our hearts lack peace and are full of uncertainty. But in spite of this we can experience the Lord's peace continually, and in every way.

Peace must be practical and practiced! We best begin each new day with God, reading his Word and praying. Then we can think back to this quiet time throughout the day to claim his peace when unrest and discord are knocking at our door. We must remind ourselves that no situation we find ourselves in is beyond the range of God's interest in us.

Additional Scripture Readings:
Isaiah 26:3–4; James 3:17–18

Go to page 306 for your next devotional reading.

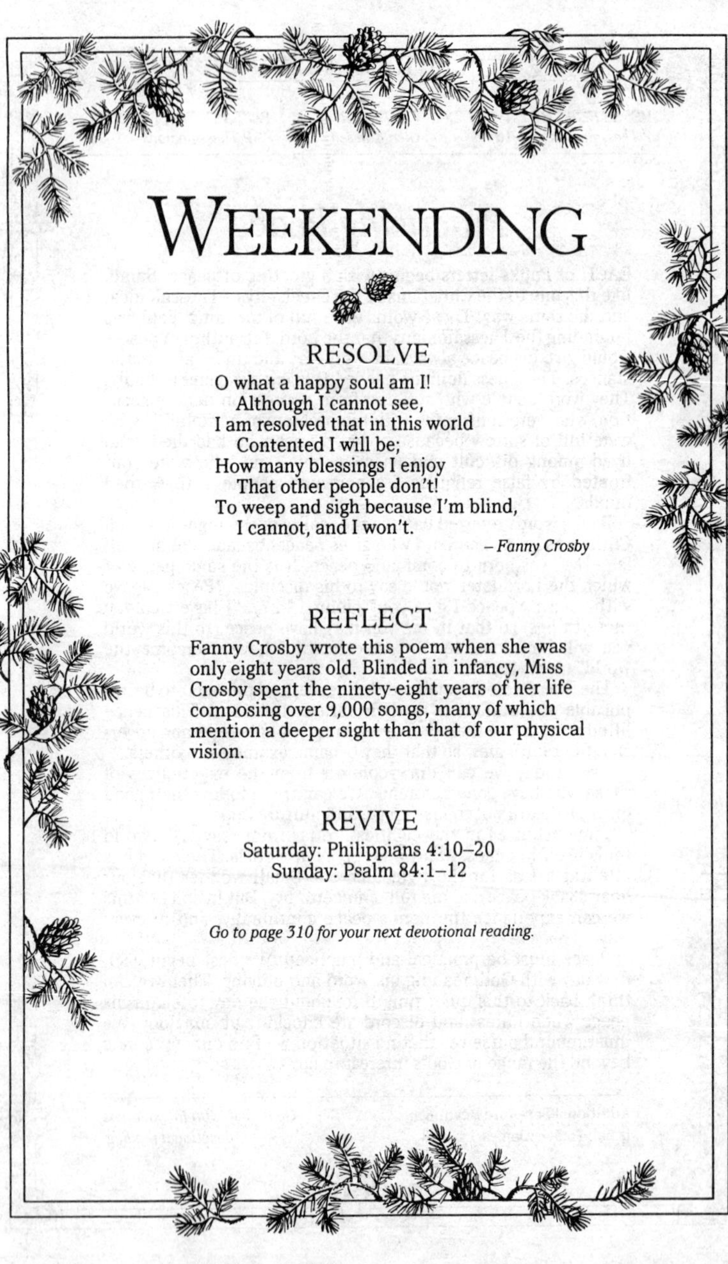

WEEKENDING

RESOLVE

O what a happy soul am I!
Although I cannot see,
I am resolved that in this world
Contented I will be;
How many blessings I enjoy
That other people don't!
To weep and sigh because I'm blind,
I cannot, and I won't.

– Fanny Crosby

REFLECT

Fanny Crosby wrote this poem when she was only eight years old. Blinded in infancy, Miss Crosby spent the ninety-eight years of her life composing over 9,000 songs, many of which mention a deeper sight than that of our physical vision.

REVIVE

Saturday: Philippians 4:10–20
Sunday: Psalm 84:1–12

Go to page 310 for your next devotional reading.

that he may feel ashamed. 15Yet do not
regard him as an enemy, but warn him as
a brother.

Final Greetings

16Now may the Lord of peace himself
give you peace at all times and in every
way. The Lord be with all of you.

17I, Paul, write this greeting in my own
hand, which is the distinguishing mark in
all my letters. This is how I write.

18The grace of our Lord Jesus Christ be
with you all.

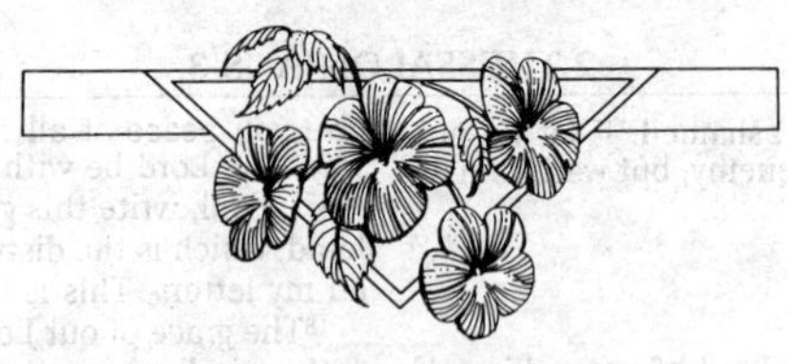

PAUL writes this letter to young Timothy, who is serving as a pastor in Ephesus. He instructs him how to organize and run the church and how to deal with false teachers and refute what they say. As you read this book, promise God that you will not stray from true faith.

1 TIMOTHY

1 Paul, an apostle of Christ Jesus by the command of God our Savior and of Christ Jesus our hope,

2To Timothy my true son in the faith:

Grace, mercy and peace from God the Father and Christ Jesus our Lord.

Warning Against False Teachers of the Law

3As I urged you when I went into Macedonia, stay there in Ephesus so that you
may command certain men not to teach
false doctrines any longer 4nor to devote themselves to myths and endless
genealogies. These promote controversies rather than God's work—which is by
faith. 5The goal of this command is love,
which comes from a pure heart and a
good conscience and a sincere faith.
6Some have wandered away from these
and turned to meaningless talk. 7They
want to be teachers of the law, but they
do not know what they are talking about
or what they so confidently affirm.

8We know that the law is good if one
uses it properly. 9We also know that law[a]
is made not for the righteous but for lawbreakers and rebels, the ungodly and sinful, the unholy and irreligious; for those
who kill their fathers or mothers, for murderers, 10for adulterers and perverts, for
slave traders and liars and perjurers—and
for whatever else is contrary to the sound
doctrine 11that conforms to the glorious
gospel of the blessed God, which he entrusted to me.

The Lord's Grace to Paul

12I thank Christ Jesus our Lord, who
has given me strength, that he considered
me faithful, appointing me to his service.
13Even though I was once a blasphemer
and a persecutor and a violent man, I was

[a]9 Or *that the law*

shown mercy because I acted in ignorance and unbelief. 14The grace of our
Lord was poured out on me abundantly,
along with the faith and love that are in
Christ Jesus.
15Here is a trustworthy saying that deserves full acceptance: Christ Jesus came
into the world to save sinners—of whom
I am the worst. 16But for that very reason
I was shown mercy so that in me, the
worst of sinners, Christ Jesus might display his unlimited patience as an example for those who would believe on
him and receive eternal life. 17Now to the
King eternal, immortal, invisible, the only
God, be honor and glory for ever and ever.
Amen.
18Timothy, my son, I give you this instruction in keeping with the prophecies
once made about you, so that by following them you may fight the good fight,
19holding on to faith and a good conscience. Some have rejected these and so
have shipwrecked their faith. 20Among
them are Hymenaeus and Alexander,
whom I have handed over to Satan to be
taught not to blaspheme.

Instructions on Worship

2 I urge, then, first of all, that requests,
prayers, intercession and thanksgiving be made for everyone— 2for kings and
all those in authority, that we may live
peaceful and quiet lives in all godliness
and holiness. 3This is good, and pleases
God our Savior, 4who wants all men to be
saved and to come to a knowledge of the
truth. 5For there is one God and one
mediator between God and men, the man
Christ Jesus, 6who gave himself as a ransom for all men—the testimony given in
its proper time. 7And for this purpose I
was appointed a herald and an apostle—I
am telling the truth, I am not lying—and
a teacher of the true faith to the Gentiles.
8I want men everywhere to lift up holy
hands in prayer, without anger or disputing.
9I also want women to dress modestly,
with decency and propriety, not with
braided hair or gold or pearls or expensive
clothes, 10but with good deeds, appropriate for women who profess to worship
God.
11A woman should learn in quietness
and full submission. 12I do not permit a
woman to teach or to have authority over
a man; she must be silent. 13For Adam
was formed first, then Eve. 14And Adam
was not the one deceived; it was the woman who was deceived and became a sinner. 15But women[a] will be saved[b]
through childbearing—if they continue
in faith, love and holiness with propriety.

Overseers and Deacons

3 Here is a trustworthy saying: If anyone sets his heart on being an overseer,[c] he desires a noble task. 2Now the
overseer must be above reproach, the
husband of but one wife, temperate, self-
controlled, respectable, hospitable, able
to teach, 3not given to drunkenness, not
violent but gentle, not quarrelsome, not a
lover of money. 4He must manage his own
family well and see that his children obey
him with proper respect. 5(If anyone does
not know how to manage his own family,
how can he take care of God's church?)
6He must not be a recent convert, or he
may become conceited and fall under the
same judgment as the devil. 7He must
also have a good reputation with outsiders, so that he will not fall into disgrace
and into the devil's trap.
8Deacons, likewise, are to be men
worthy of respect, sincere, not indulging
in much wine, and not pursuing dishonest gain. 9They must keep hold of the
deep truths of the faith with a clear conscience. 10They must first be tested; and
then if there is nothing against them, let
them serve as deacons.
11In the same way, their wives[d] are to
be women worthy of respect, not malicious talkers but temperate and trustworthy in everything.
12A deacon must be the husband of but
one wife and must manage his children
and his household well. 13Those who
have served well gain an excellent standing and great assurance in their faith in
Christ Jesus.
14Although I hope to come to you soon,
I am writing you these instructions so
that, 15if I am delayed, you will know how
people ought to conduct themselves in
God's household, which is the church of
the living God, the pillar and foundation
of the truth. 16Beyond all question, the
mystery of godliness is great:

He[e] appeared in a body,[f]
was vindicated by the Spirit,

[a] *15* Greek *she* [b] *15* Or *restored* [c] *1* Traditionally *bishop*; also in verse 2 [d] *11* Or *way, deaconesses* [e] *16* Some manuscripts *God* [f] *16* Or *in the flesh*

was seen by angels,
was preached among the nations,
was believed on in the world,
was taken up in glory.

Instructions to Timothy

4 The Spirit clearly says that in later
times some will abandon the faith
and follow deceiving spirits and things
taught by demons. 2Such teachings come
through hypocritical liars, whose consciences have been seared as with a hot
iron. 3They forbid people to marry and order them to abstain from certain foods,
which God created to be received with
thanksgiving by those who believe and
who know the truth. 4For everything God
created is good, and nothing is to be rejected if it is received with thanksgiving,
5because it is consecrated by the word of
God and prayer.
6If you point these things out to the
brothers, you will be a good minister of
Christ Jesus, brought up in the truths of
the faith and of the good teaching that
you have followed. 7Have nothing to do
with godless myths and old wives' tales;
rather, train yourself to be godly. 8For
physical training is of some value, but
godliness has value for all things, holding
promise for both the present life and the
life to come.
9This is a trustworthy saying that deserves full acceptance 10(and for this we
labor and strive), that we have put our
hope in the living God, who is the Savior
of all men, and especially of those who
believe.
11Command and teach these things.
12Don't let anyone look down on you because you are young, but set an example
for the believers in speech, in life, in love,
in faith and in purity. 13Until I come,
devote yourself to the public reading of

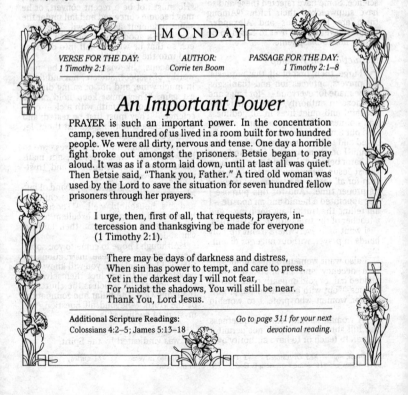

MONDAY

VERSE FOR THE DAY:	*AUTHOR:*	*PASSAGE FOR THE DAY:*
1 Timothy 2:1	*Corrie ten Boom*	*1 Timothy 2:1–8*

An Important Power

PRAYER is such an important power. In the concentration camp, seven hundred of us lived in a room built for two hundred people. We were all dirty, nervous and tense. One day a horrible fight broke out amongst the prisoners. Betsie began to pray aloud. It was as if a storm laid down, until at last all was quiet. Then Betsie said, "Thank you, Father." A tired old woman was used by the Lord to save the situation for seven hundred fellow prisoners through her prayers.

I urge, then, first of all, that requests, prayers, intercession and thanksgiving be made for everyone (1 Timothy 2:1).

There may be days of darkness and distress,
When sin has power to tempt, and care to press.
Yet in the darkest day I will not fear,
For 'midst the shadows, You will still be near.
Thank You, Lord Jesus.

Additional Scripture Readings:
Colossians 4:2–5; James 5:13–18

Go to page 311 for your next devotional reading.

Scripture, to preaching and to teaching.
14Do not neglect your gift, which was given you through a prophetic message when the body of elders laid their hands on you.

15Be diligent in these matters; give yourself wholly to them, so that everyone may see your progress.
16Watch your life and doctrine closely. Persevere in them, because if you do, you will save both yourself and your hearers.

Advice About Widows, Elders and Slaves

5 Do not rebuke an older man harshly, but exhort him as if he were your father. Treat younger men as brothers,
2older women as mothers, and younger women as sisters, with absolute purity.

3Give proper recognition to those widows who are really in need.
4But if a widow has children or grandchildren, these should learn first of all to put their religion into practice by caring for their own family and so repaying their parents and grandparents, for this is pleasing to God.
5The widow who is really in need and left all alone puts her hope in God and continues night and day to pray and to ask God for help.
6But the widow who lives for pleasure is dead even while she lives.
7Give the people these instructions, too, so that no one may be open to blame.
8If anyone does not provide for his relatives, and especially for his immediate family, he has denied the faith and is worse than an unbeliever.

9No widow may be put on the list of widows unless she is over sixty, has been faithful to her husband,[a]
10and is well known for her good deeds, such as bringing up children, showing hospitality, washing the feet of the saints, helping those in trouble and devoting herself to all kinds of good deeds.

11As for younger widows, do not put

[a]9 *Or has had but one husband*

TUESDAY

VERSE FOR THE DAY:	*AUTHOR:*	*PASSAGE FOR THE DAY:*
1 Timothy 4:16	*Florence Littauer*	*1 Timothy 4:9–16*

Cramming for Finals

A NINETY-six-year-old lady was a faithful attendant at my women's club Bible studies. She came with her lessons prepared and knew all the answers. One day a tactless member asked her, "Why do you work so hard on these lessons when you're so old and it doesn't matter?"

Little Bess Elkins looked up and said confidently, "I'm cramming for my finals."

It's never too late to get ready for our finals. Narrow is the way which leads to life and few there be that find it. It takes so little to be above average, but it does take a desire to learn and it does take preparation so when the great target appears we'll be able to hit the bull's-eye.

Additional Scripture Readings:
Psalm 119:33–37; Philippians 3:12–14

Go to page 313 for your next devotional reading.

them on such a list. For when their sensual desires overcome their dedication to Christ, they want to marry. [12]Thus they bring judgment on themselves, because they have broken their first pledge. [13]Besides, they get into the habit of being idle and going about from house to house. And not only do they become idlers, but also gossips and busybodies, saying things they ought not to. [14]So I counsel younger widows to marry, to have children, to manage their homes and to give the enemy no opportunity for slander. [15]Some have in fact already turned away to follow Satan.

[16]If any woman who is a believer has widows in her family, she should help them and not let the church be burdened with them, so that the church can help those widows who are really in need.

[17]The elders who direct the affairs of the church well are worthy of double honor, especially those whose work is preaching and teaching. [18]For the Scripture says, "Do not muzzle the ox while it is treading out the grain,"[a] and "The worker deserves his wages."[b] [19]Do not entertain an accusation against an elder unless it is brought by two or three witnesses. [20]Those who sin are to be rebuked publicly, so that the others may take warning.

[21]I charge you, in the sight of God and Christ Jesus and the elect angels, to keep these instructions without partiality, and to do nothing out of favoritism.

[22]Do not be hasty in the laying on of hands, and do not share in the sins of others. Keep yourself pure.

[23]Stop drinking only water, and use a little wine because of your stomach and your frequent illnesses.

[24]The sins of some men are obvious, reaching the place of judgment ahead of them; the sins of others trail behind them. [25]In the same way, good deeds are obvious, and even those that are not cannot be hidden.

6 All who are under the yoke of slavery should consider their masters worthy of full respect, so that God's name and our teaching may not be slandered. [2]Those who have believing masters are not to show less respect for them because they are brothers. Instead, they are to serve them even better, because those who benefit from their service are believers, and dear to them. These are the things you are to teach and urge on them.

Love of Money

[3]If anyone teaches false doctrines and does not agree to the sound instruction of our Lord Jesus Christ and to godly teaching, [4]he is conceited and understands nothing. He has an unhealthy interest in controversies and quarrels about words that result in envy, strife, malicious talk, evil suspicions [5]and constant friction between men of corrupt mind, who have been robbed of the truth and who think that godliness is a means to financial gain.

[6]But godliness with contentment is great gain. [7]For we brought nothing into the world, and we can take nothing out of it. [8]But if we have food and clothing, we will be content with that. [9]People who want to get rich fall into temptation and a trap and into many foolish and harmful desires that plunge men into ruin and destruction. [10]For the love of money is a root of all kinds of evil. Some people, eager for money, have wandered from the faith and pierced themselves with many griefs.

Paul's Charge to Timothy

[11]But you, man of God, flee from all this, and pursue righteousness, godliness, faith, love, endurance and gentleness. [12]Fight the good fight of the faith. Take hold of the eternal life to which you were called when you made your good confession in the presence of many witnesses. [13]In the sight of God, who gives life to everything, and of Christ Jesus, who while testifying before Pontius Pilate made the good confession, I charge you [14]to keep this command without spot or blame until the appearing of our Lord Jesus Christ, [15]which God will bring about in his own time—God, the blessed and only Ruler, the King of kings and Lord of lords, [16]who alone is immortal and who lives in unapproachable light, whom no one has seen or can see. To him be honor and might forever. Amen.

[17]Command those who are rich in this present world not to be arrogant nor to put their hope in wealth, which is so uncertain, but to put their hope in God, who richly provides us with everything for our enjoyment. [18]Command them to do good, to be rich in good deeds, and to be gen-

[a]*18* Deut. 25:4 [b]*18* Luke 10:7

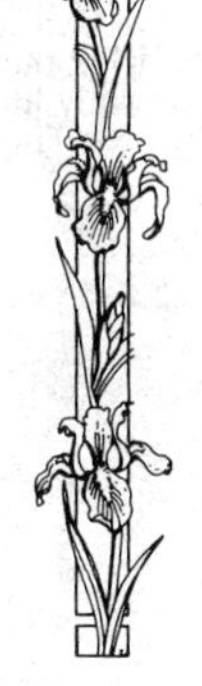

VERSE FOR THE DAY: *1 Timothy 6:9–10*

AUTHOR: *Martha Manikas-Foster*

PASSAGE FOR THE DAY: *1 Timothy 6:1–21*

True Success

I RECLINED on my hospital bed with my two-day-old daughter cuddled on my chest. As she slept I caressed her tiny fingers and wondered how she would use them as she grew up. Would they tap formulas and technical data into a now unimagined computer? Would they intricately stitch wounded human tissue? Or perhaps sculpt or paint using vibrant textures and colors? Although I randomly pictured professions at which she might excel, I focused my prayers then as I focus them now, not on *what* she might be, but on *who* she could be.

I know that one day, probably before she puts away her dolls and crayons, she'll learn that some people measure excellence and success solely by "the bottom line"—the money they take home. Some "put their hope in wealth" (1 Timothy 6:17) and build their lives to accommodate its pursuit.

I trust that by that time we'll have taught her to value many things above money. Scripture teaches not that riches themselves are evil but that the value we place on them can lead to our undoing.

> People who want to get rich fall into temptation and a trap and into many foolish and harmful desires that plunge men into ruin and destruction (1 Timothy 6:9).

On the other hand, "godliness with contentment is great gain" (1 Timothy 6:6). The apostle Paul's charge to young Timothy in 1 Timothy 6:11–16 is to flee from the pursuit of riches and instead pursue godliness. Paul further instructs Timothy to:

> Command those who are rich . . . to put their hope in God . . . . Command them to do good, to be rich in good deeds, and to be generous and willing to share (1 Timothy 6:17–18).

When Connie reaches elementary school and her teachers ask her what she wants to be when she grows up, I expect that she will list "teacher," "firefighter," and perhaps "doctor" among her choices. But my prayer will continue to be that no matter what profession she chooses, at the core she will truly succeed by being a righteous and godly woman, full of "faith, love, endurance and gentleness" (1 Timothy 6:11).

Additional Scripture Readings:
Proverbs 22:1–2; Mark 10:17–25

Go to page 316 for your next devotional reading.

erous and willing to share. [19]In this way
they will lay up treasure for themselves as
a firm foundation for the coming age, so
that they may take hold of the life that is
truly life.
[20]Timothy, guard what has been entrusted to your care. Turn away from godless chatter and the opposing ideas of
what is falsely called knowledge, [21]which
some have professed and in so doing have
wandered from the faith.

Grace be with you.

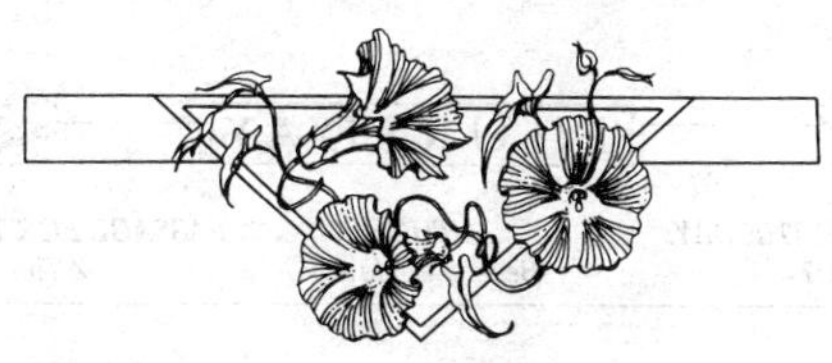

THIS second letter to Timothy is written by Paul shortly before Paul dies (2 Timothy 4:6–8). Times are difficult, both morally and spiritually, and Paul wants to encourage Timothy to persevere in his Christian faith and life. As you read this book, be sure to find your daily strength in Jesus Christ and in God's inspired word.

2 TIMOTHY

1 Paul, an apostle of Christ Jesus by the
will of God, according to the promise
of life that is in Christ Jesus,

2To Timothy, my dear son:

Grace, mercy and peace from God the
Father and Christ Jesus our Lord.

Encouragement to Be Faithful

3I thank God, whom I serve, as my forefathers did, with a clear conscience, as
night and day I constantly remember you
in my prayers. 4Recalling your tears, I
long to see you, so that I may be filled
with joy. 5I have been reminded of your
sincere faith, which first lived in your
grandmother Lois and in your mother Eu-
nice and, I am persuaded, now lives in
you also. 6For this reason I remind you to
fan into flame the gift of God, which is in
you through the laying on of my hands.
7For God did not give us a spirit of timidi-
ty, but a spirit of power, of love and of
self-discipline.
8So do not be ashamed to testify about
our Lord, or ashamed of me his prisoner.
But join with me in suffering for the gospel, by the power of God, 9who has saved
us and called us to a holy life—not because of anything we have done but because of his own purpose and grace. This
grace was given us in Christ Jesus before
the beginning of time, 10but it has now
been revealed through the appearing of
our Savior, Christ Jesus, who has destroyed death and has brought life and
immortality to light through the gospel.
11And of this gospel I was appointed a herald and an apostle and a teacher. 12That
is why I am suffering as I am. Yet I am not
ashamed, because I know whom I have
believed, and am convinced that he is
able to guard what I have entrusted to
him for that day.

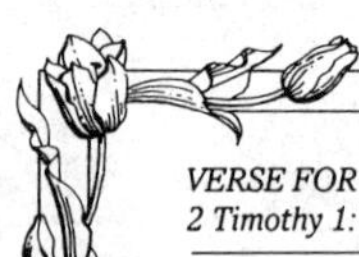

VERSE FOR THE DAY:
2 Timothy 1:7

AUTHOR:
Beverly LaHaye

PASSAGE FOR THE DAY:
2 Timothy 1:3–7

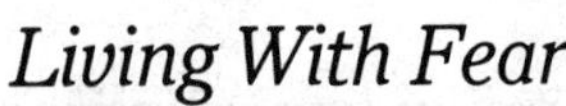

Living With Fear

WHEN I was a young minister's wife and new mother, I suffered from a serious case of low self-image and overcautiousness. Perhaps, more accurately, I could have been called fearful and anxious. It was very difficult for me to speak to a group of more than seven or eight ladies. When asked to speak, I would often hide behind my husband's ministerial cloak and say that he was the speaker and I was his "helpmeet." Mainly because I was fearful that I would make a mistake and not be accepted by my listeners, I would refuse an invitation to speak to adults. I was only comfortable working with children in church school and in the music department of our church.

In my heart I admired those who were poised in public and could speak articulately, and often I longed to be able to do so myself. But the more I thought about it, the greater my fear. This anxiety affected other areas of my life as well. I knew that sooner or later I would have to face this fear head-on.

After seventeen years as a minister's wife I came to realize that I did not have to continue like this. Living with fear was a choice I was making.

While attending a church school conference at beautiful Forest Home Christian Camp in California, God used Dr. Henry Brandt, a Christian psychologist, to minister his truth to me. Dr. Brandt used 2 Timothy 1:7 as his text; and that day, for the first time, I began to realize that my fears and anxieties were self-imposed. God's choice for me was to have power, love and self-discipline. God did not give me a spirit of fear! My poor self-image, my anxieties, my fears were all my own doing and my sin because I lacked faith to receive the power, love and self-discipline that God really wanted me to have.

As God began to help me with my fearfulness, my own self-image began to improve. Over a period of weeks, and then months, it began to be obvious that God was changing me.

Now, many years later, I can say "Thank you, Lord" for what he has done in me. I would not want to go back to the former Beverly for anything in the world—and the greatest thing is that God is not finished with me yet!

Additional Scripture Readings:
Psalm 34:4–10; Jeremiah 1:4–8

Go to page 317 for your next devotional reading.

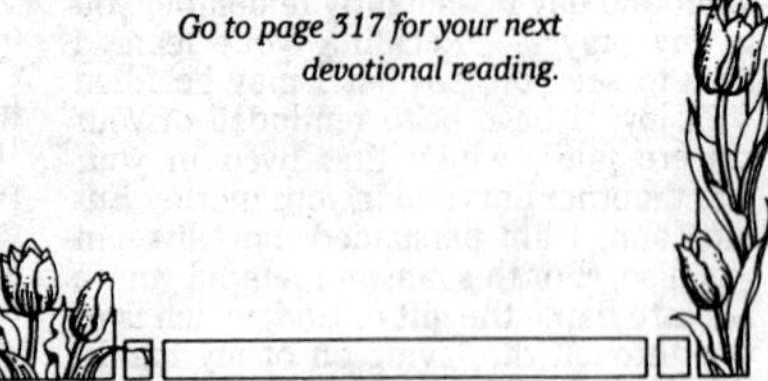

[13]What you heard from me, keep as the
pattern of sound teaching, with faith and
love in Christ Jesus. [14]Guard the good
deposit that was entrusted to you—guard
it with the help of the Holy Spirit who
lives in us.
[15]You know that everyone in the province of Asia has deserted me, including
Phygelus and Hermogenes.
[16]May the Lord show mercy to the
household of Onesiphorus, because he
often refreshed me and was not ashamed
of my chains. [17]On the contrary, when he
was in Rome, he searched hard for me
until he found me. [18]May the Lord grant
that he will find mercy from the Lord on
that day! You know very well in how many
ways he helped me in Ephesus.
2 You then, my son, be strong in the
grace that is in Christ Jesus. [2]And the
things you have heard me say in the presence of many witnesses entrust to reliable men who will also be qualified to
teach others. [3]Endure hardship with us
like a good soldier of Christ Jesus. [4]No
one serving as a soldier gets involved in
civilian affairs—he wants to please his
commanding officer. [5]Similarly, if anyone
competes as an athlete, he does not receive the victor's crown unless he competes according to the rules. [6]The hard-
working farmer should be the first to receive a share of the crops. [7]Reflect on
what I am saying, for the Lord will give
you insight into all this.
[8]Remember Jesus Christ, raised from
the dead, descended from David. This is
my gospel, [9]for which I am suffering even
to the point of being chained like a criminal. But God's word is not chained.
[10]Therefore I endure everything for the
sake of the elect, that they too may obtain
the salvation that is in Christ Jesus, with
eternal glory.

FRIDAY

VERSE FOR THE DAY:
2 Timothy 2:1

AUTHOR:
Doris Haase

PASSAGE FOR THE DAY:
2 Timothy 2:1–13

Be Strong in God's Grace

AFTER a long and terrifying captivity, Iranian hostage Gary Lee was home. It was a Sunday morning in February 1981, and I joined with others in his father's church to welcome him. Celebration filled the air as joyful voices sang "Amazing Grace." From my seat I noticed the bearded young man smile and shake his head as though in wonder at the miracle of his safe return.

Months earlier, however, he had experienced another miracle. Shortly after his capture he was allowed to have a Bible and one day he read Isaiah 43:5: "Do not be afraid, for I am with you; I will bring your children from the east and gather you from the west."

"When I read those words," he told his father later, "I felt God was making me a promise. Somehow I knew I would reach home safely. The whole experience became a lot easier after that."

How much lighter trials become when we realize God's grace is twofold. It is not only the happy ending. It is also the peace we can feel during a painful journey, when we trust in God—all the way.

Additional Scripture Readings:
Acts 6:8; 7:55–60; Romans 5:1–5

Go to page 319 for your next devotional reading.

11 Here is a trustworthy saying:

If we died with him,
  we will also live with him;
12 if we endure,
  we will also reign with him.
If we disown him,
  he will also disown us;
13 if we are faithless,
  he will remain faithful,
  for he cannot disown himself.

A Workman Approved by God

14 Keep reminding them of these things. Warn them before God against quarreling about words; it is of no value, and only ruins those who listen. 15 Do your best to present yourself to God as one approved, a workman who does not need to be ashamed and who correctly handles the word of truth. 16 Avoid godless chatter, because those who indulge in it will become more and more ungodly. 17 Their teaching will spread like gangrene. Among them are Hymenaeus and Philetus, 18 who have wandered away from the truth. They say that the resurrection has already taken place, and they destroy the faith of some. 19 Nevertheless, God's solid foundation stands firm, sealed with this inscription: "The Lord knows those who are his,"[a] and, "Everyone who confesses the name of the Lord must turn away from wickedness."

20 In a large house there are articles not only of gold and silver, but also of wood and clay; some are for noble purposes and some for ignoble. 21 If a man cleanses himself from the latter, he will be an instrument for noble purposes, made holy, useful to the Master and prepared to do any good work.

22 Flee the evil desires of youth, and pursue righteousness, faith, love and peace, along with those who call on the Lord out of a pure heart. 23 Don't have anything to do with foolish and stupid arguments, because you know they produce quarrels. 24 And the Lord's servant must not quarrel; instead, he must be kind to everyone, able to teach, not resentful. 25 Those who oppose him he must gently instruct, in the hope that God will grant them repentance leading them to a knowledge of the truth, 26 and that they will come to their senses and escape from the trap of the devil, who has taken them captive to do his will.

Godlessness in the Last Days

3 But mark this: There will be terrible times in the last days. 2 People will be lovers of themselves, lovers of money, boastful, proud, abusive, disobedient to their parents, ungrateful, unholy, 3 without love, unforgiving, slanderous, without self-control, brutal, not lovers of the good, 4 treacherous, rash, conceited, lovers of pleasure rather than lovers of God — 5 having a form of godliness but denying its power. Have nothing to do with them.

6 They are the kind who worm their way into homes and gain control over weak-willed women, who are loaded down with sins and are swayed by all kinds of evil desires, 7 always learning but never able to acknowledge the truth. 8 Just as Jannes and Jambres opposed Moses, so also these men oppose the truth—men of depraved minds, who, as far as the faith is concerned, are rejected. 9 But they will not get very far because, as in the case of those men, their folly will be clear to everyone.

Paul's Charge to Timothy

10 You, however, know all about my teaching, my way of life, my purpose, faith, patience, love, endurance, 11 persecutions, sufferings—what kinds of things happened to me in Antioch, Iconium and Lystra, the persecutions I endured. Yet the Lord rescued me from all of them. 12 In fact, everyone who wants to live a godly life in Christ Jesus will be persecuted, 13 while evil men and impostors will go from bad to worse, deceiving and being deceived. 14 But as for you, continue in what you have learned and have become convinced of, because you know those from whom you learned it, 15 and how from infancy you have known the holy Scriptures, which are able to make you wise for salvation through faith in Christ Jesus. 16 All Scripture is God-breathed and is useful for teaching, rebuking, correcting and training in righteousness, 17 so that the man of God may be thoroughly equipped for every good work.

4 In the presence of God and of Christ Jesus, who will judge the living and the dead, and in view of his appearing and his kingdom, I give you this charge: 2 Preach the Word; be prepared in season

[a] *19* Num. 16:5 (see Septuagint)

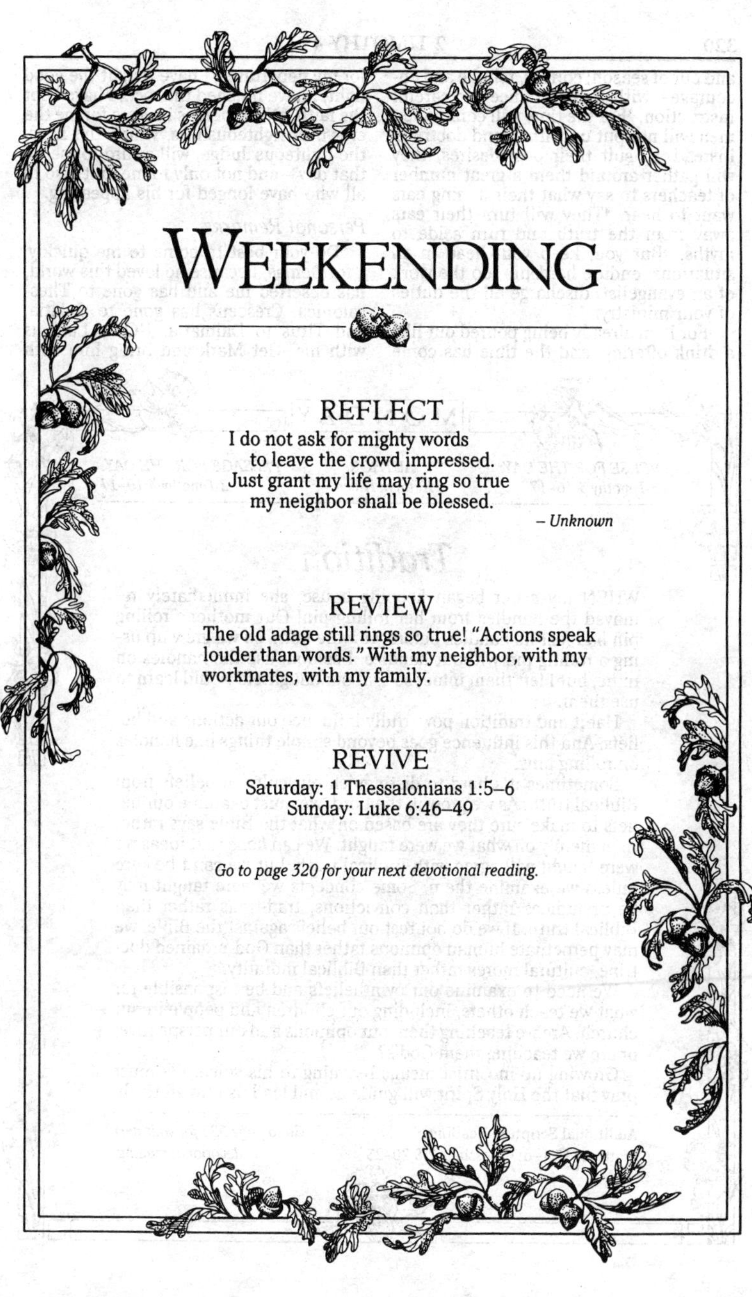

WEEKENDING

REFLECT

I do not ask for mighty words
to leave the crowd impressed.
Just grant my life may ring so true
my neighbor shall be blessed.

– Unknown

REVIEW

The old adage still rings so true! "Actions speak louder than words." With my neighbor, with my workmates, with my family.

REVIVE

Saturday: 1 Thessalonians 1:5–6
Sunday: Luke 6:46–49

Go to page 320 for your next devotional reading.

and out of season; correct, rebuke and encourage—with great patience and careful
instruction. 3For the time will come when
men will not put up with sound doctrine.
Instead, to suit their own desires, they
will gather around them a great number
of teachers to say what their itching ears
want to hear. 4They will turn their ears
away from the truth and turn aside to
myths. 5But you, keep your head in all
situations, endure hardship, do the work
of an evangelist, discharge all the duties
of your ministry.
6For I am already being poured out like
a drink offering, and the time has come
for my departure. 7I have fought the good
fight, I have finished the race, I have kept
the faith. 8Now there is in store for me the
crown of righteousness, which the Lord,
the righteous Judge, will award to me on
that day—and not only to me, but also to
all who have longed for his appearing.

Personal Remarks

9Do your best to come to me quickly,
10for Demas, because he loved this world,
has deserted me and has gone to Thessalonica. Crescens has gone to Galatia,
and Titus to Dalmatia. 11Only Luke is
with me. Get Mark and bring him with

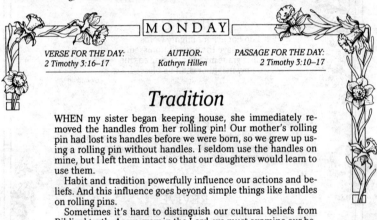

MONDAY

VERSE FOR THE DAY: *2 Timothy 3:16–17*

AUTHOR: *Kathryn Hillen*

PASSAGE FOR THE DAY: *2 Timothy 3:10–17*

Tradition

WHEN my sister began keeping house, she immediately removed the handles from her rolling pin! Our mother's rolling pin had lost its handles before we were born, so we grew up using a rolling pin without handles. I seldom use the handles on mine, but I left them intact so that our daughters would learn to use them.

Habit and tradition powerfully influence our actions and beliefs. And this influence goes beyond simple things like handles on rolling pins.

Sometimes it's hard to distinguish our cultural beliefs from Biblical truth. As we grow in the Lord, we must examine our beliefs to make sure they are based on what the Bible says rather than merely on what we were taught. We can *hope* that ideas we were taught will agree with Biblical truth, but we can't be sure unless we examine them. Some concepts we were taught may be prejudices rather than convictions, traditions rather than Biblical truth. If we do not test our beliefs against the Bible, we may perpetuate human opinions rather than God-ordained doctrine, cultural mores rather than Biblical morality.

We need to examine our own beliefs and be responsible for what we teach others, including our children and people in our church. Are we teaching them our opinions and our perspective, or are we teaching them God's?

Growing up in Christ means listening to his voice. We must pray that the Holy Spirit will guide us and lead us into all truth.

Additional Scripture Readings:
Matthew 15:1–6; Colossians 2:8,20–23

Go to page 323 for your next devotional reading.

you, because he is helpful to me in my
ministry. 12 I sent Tychicus to Ephesus.
13 When you come, bring the cloak that I
left with Carpus at Troas, and my scrolls,
especially the parchments.
14 Alexander the metalworker did me a
great deal of harm. The Lord will repay
him for what he has done. 15 You too
should be on your guard against him, because he strongly opposed our message.
16 At my first defense, no one came to
my support, but everyone deserted me.
May it not be held against them. 17 But the
Lord stood at my side and gave me
strength, so that through me the message
might be fully proclaimed and all the
Gentiles might hear it. And I was delivered from the lion's mouth. 18 The Lord
will rescue me from every evil attack and
will bring me safely to his heavenly kingdom. To him be glory for ever and ever.
Amen.

Final Greetings

19 Greet Priscilla[a] and Aquila and the
household of Onesiphorus. 20 Erastus
stayed in Corinth, and I left Trophimus
sick in Miletus. 21 Do your best to get here
before winter. Eubulus greets you, and so
do Pudens, Linus, Claudia and all the
brothers.
22 The Lord be with your spirit. Grace be
with you.

[a] 19 Greek *Prisca*, a variant of *Priscilla*

PAUL writes to Titus, a pastor serving in Crete, to advise him both on what to teach the churches and on how to organize them, especially with false teachers around. As you read this book, note God's concern for proper order in the church and for true teaching about Christ.

TITUS

1 Paul, a servant of God and an apostle
of Jesus Christ for the faith of God's
elect and the knowledge of the truth that
leads to godliness— 2a faith and knowledge resting on the hope of eternal life,
which God, who does not lie, promised
before the beginning of time, 3and at his
appointed season he brought his word to
light through the preaching entrusted to
me by the command of God our Savior,

4To Titus, my true son in our common
faith:

Grace and peace from God the Father
and Christ Jesus our Savior.

Titus' Task on Crete

5The reason I left you in Crete was that
you might straighten out what was left
unfinished and appoint[a] elders in every
town, as I directed you. 6An elder must be
blameless, the husband of but one wife, a
man whose children believe and are not
open to the charge of being wild and
disobedient. 7Since an overseer[b] is entrusted with God's work, he must be
blameless—not overbearing, not quick-
tempered, not given to drunkenness, not
violent, not pursuing dishonest gain.
8Rather he must be hospitable, one who
loves what is good, who is self-controlled,
upright, holy and disciplined. 9He must
hold firmly to the trustworthy message as
it has been taught, so that he can encourage others by sound doctrine and refute
those who oppose it.

10For there are many rebellious people,
mere talkers and deceivers, especially
those of the circumcision group. 11They
must be silenced, because they are ruin-
ing whole households by teaching things
they ought not to teach—and that for the
sake of dishonest gain. 12Even one of
their own prophets has said, "Cretans

[a]5 Or *ordain* [b]7 Traditionally *bishop*

are always liars, evil brutes, lazy gluttons." 13This testimony is true. Therefore,
rebuke them sharply, so that they will be
sound in the faith 14and will pay no attention to Jewish myths or to the commands
of those who reject the truth. 15To the
pure, all things are pure, but to those who
are corrupted and do not believe, nothing
is pure. In fact, both their minds and consciences are corrupted. 16They claim to
know God, but by their actions they deny
him. They are detestable, disobedient
and unfit for doing anything good.

What Must Be Taught to Various Groups

2 You must teach what is in accord
with sound doctrine. 2Teach the older
men to be temperate, worthy of respect,
self-controlled, and sound in faith, in love
and in endurance.

3Likewise, teach the older women to be
reverent in the way they live, not to be
slanderers or addicted to much wine, but
to teach what is good. 4Then they can
train the younger women to love their
husbands and children, 5to be self-controlled and pure, to be busy at home, to
be kind, and to be subject to their husbands, so that no one will malign the
word of God.

6Similarly, encourage the young men to
be self-controlled. 7In everything set
them an example by doing what is good.
In your teaching show integrity, serious-
ness 8and soundness of speech that cannot be condemned, so that those who oppose you may be ashamed because they
have nothing bad to say about us.

9Teach slaves to be subject to their
masters in everything, to try to please
them, not to talk back to them, 10and not

TUESDAY

VERSE FOR THE DAY: *Titus 1:13*

AUTHOR: *Doris Haase*

PASSAGE FOR THE DAY: *Titus 1:5–16*

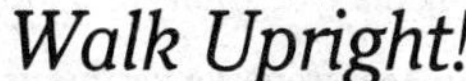

Walk Upright!

ONCE upon a time, in the early days of our country, a weary traveler arrived at the banks of the Mississippi. There was no bridge. It was winter and the water was covered by a layer of ice. Was it strong enough to hold his weight, he wondered? Still, he had to get across before nightfall, and so, terrified, he crept slowly on hands and knees across the frozen surface, certain he would never live to see the other side.

Suddenly he heard the clop, clop of a horse-drawn wagon. As it rattled past, he could hear the driver singing merrily. Unlike himself, the man, obviously familiar with these conditions, had no doubt at all that their glacial road was strong.

I sympathize with that traveler, for I too, am a creeper. I know God has promised no harm will befall me (Psalm 91:10) and that I should cast my cares upon him and he will sustain me (Psalm 55:22). So why do I so often forget that God is one who keeps his promises? He really can bear the weight of my every problem.

Today I resolve to follow the example of that long-ago wagoner. I will believe, walk upright and sing!

Additional Scripture Readings:
Deuteronomy 10:12–22; Psalm 23:4

Go to page 324 for your next devotional reading.

to steal from them, but to show that they
can be fully trusted, so that in every way
they will make the teaching about God
our Savior attractive.
11For the grace of God that brings salvation has appeared to all men. 12It
teaches us to say "No" to ungodliness
and worldly passions, and to live self-
controlled, upright and godly lives in this
present age, 13while we wait for the

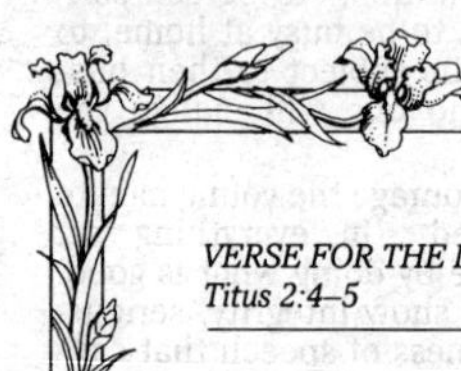

WEDNESDAY

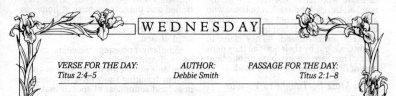

VERSE FOR THE DAY: *Titus 2:4–5*

AUTHOR: *Debbie Smith*

PASSAGE FOR THE DAY: *Titus 2:1–8*

Pleasing to God and Family

MY older son at preschool and the baby downstairs with the sitter, I settled into bed with my three-year-old daughter for a delicious afternoon nap. We giggled quietly, nose-to-nose, covers up to our chins. It was a precious mother-daughter moment that required no words . . . until Whitney spoke up.

"I like this kind of mommy!"

At times like these, I feel like I must be doing something right. Of course, the other side of the coin is obvious: sometimes I am *not* the "kind of mommy" she likes—or deserves!

That thought reminds me that loving children (and husbands) is a learning process. Titus 2:4 confirms that young mothers should be trained by the older women to love their husbands and children.

Interestingly, two Greek words for love are used in the original text. The word for love for husbands connotes nurturing as a friend: "fond of man." The word used here for love for children means maternal love: literally, "fond of one's children."

I am grateful that God addresses on the practical level the daily grind of living as women. Here he makes it clear that he expects holiness in our lives, whatever our ages. The older women are to be exemplary in speech and conduct so that "they can train the younger women" to be the same. Titus 2:5 sets the agenda for young mothers: learn to love family, learn self-control, tend to the home, and be kind and submissive to one's husband.

Running a home, Titus 2:5 implies, requires being a servant. And "if anyone serves, he should do it with the strength God provides, so that in all things God may be praised through Jesus Christ" (1 Peter 4:11).

Such a mommy is pleasing to the Lord . . . and to her children!

Additional Scripture Readings:
Proverbs 31:26–30; 1 Thessalonians 2:7–12

Go to page 327 for your next devotional reading.

blessed hope—the glorious appearing of
our great God and Savior, Jesus Christ,
14who gave himself for us to redeem us
from all wickedness and to purify for
himself a people that are his very own,
eager to do what is good.

15These, then, are the things you
should teach. Encourage and rebuke with
all authority. Do not let anyone despise
you.

Doing What Is Good

3 Remind the people to be subject to
rulers and authorities, to be obedient, to be ready to do whatever is good,
2to slander no one, to be peaceable and
considerate, and to show true humility
toward all men.

3At one time we too were foolish,
disobedient, deceived and enslaved by all
kinds of passions and pleasures. We lived
in malice and envy, being hated and hating one another. 4But when the kindness
and love of God our Savior appeared, 5he
saved us, not because of righteous things
we had done, but because of his mercy.
He saved us through the washing of
rebirth and renewal by the Holy Spirit,
6whom he poured out on us generously
through Jesus Christ our Savior, 7so that,
having been justified by his grace, we
might become heirs having the hope of
eternal life. 8This is a trustworthy saying.
And I want you to stress these things, so
that those who have trusted in God may
be careful to devote themselves to doing
what is good. These things are excellent
and profitable for everyone.

9But avoid foolish controversies and
genealogies and arguments and quarrels
about the law, because these are unprof-
itable and useless. 10Warn a divisive person once, and then warn him a second
time. After that, have nothing to do with
him. 11You may be sure that such a man
is warped and sinful; he is self-con-
demned.

Final Remarks

12As soon as I send Artemas or Tychicus to you, do your best to come to me
at Nicopolis, because I have decided to
winter there. 13Do everything you can to
help Zenas the lawyer and Apollos on
their way and see that they have everything they need. 14Our people must learn
to devote themselves to doing what is
good, in order that they may provide for
daily necessities and not live unproductive lives.

15Everyone with me sends you greetings. Greet those who love us in the faith.

Grace be with you all.

PAUL writes this brief letter to ask Philemon, a Christian brother living (probably) in Colosse, to forgive and take back Onesimus, a runaway slave who has become a Christian and is helping Paul in prison. As you read this book, be willing to forgive others, no matter what they do to you.

PHILEMON

[1]Paul, a prisoner of Christ Jesus, and
Timothy our brother,

To Philemon our dear friend and fellow
worker, [2]to Apphia our sister, to Archippus our fellow soldier and to the church
that meets in your home:

[3]Grace to you and peace from God our
Father and the Lord Jesus Christ.

Thanksgiving and Prayer

[4]I always thank my God as I remember
you in my prayers, [5]because I hear about
your faith in the Lord Jesus and your love
for all the saints. [6]I pray that you may be
active in sharing your faith, so that you
will have a full understanding of every
good thing we have in Christ. [7]Your love
has given me great joy and encouragement, because you, brother, have refreshed the hearts of the saints.

Paul's Plea for Onesimus

[8]Therefore, although in Christ I could
be bold and order you to do what you
ought to do, [9]yet I appeal to you on the
basis of love. I then, as Paul—an old man
and now also a prisoner of Christ Jesus—
[10]I appeal to you for my son Onesimus,[a]
who became my son while I was in
chains. [11]Formerly he was useless to you,
but now he has become useful both to
you and to me.
[12]I am sending him—who is my very
heart—back to you. [13]I would have liked
to keep him with me so that he could take
your place in helping me while I am in
chains for the gospel. [14]But I did not want
to do anything without your consent, so
that any favor you do will be spontaneous
and not forced. [15]Perhaps the reason he
was separated from you for a little while
was that you might have him back for

[a]10 *Onesimus* means *useful.*

good— 16no longer as a slave, but better
than a slave, as a dear brother. He is very
dear to me but even dearer to you, both as
a man and as a brother in the Lord.
17So if you consider me a partner, welcome him as you would welcome me. 18If
he has done you any wrong or owes you
anything, charge it to me. 19I, Paul, am
writing this with my own hand. I will pay
it back—not to mention that you owe me
your very self. 20I do wish, brother, that I
may have some benefit from you in the
Lord; refresh my heart in Christ. 21Confi-
dent of your obedience, I write to you,
knowing that you will do even more than
I ask.
22And one thing more: Prepare a guest
room for me, because I hope to be restored to you in answer to your prayers.

23Epaphras, my fellow prisoner in
Christ Jesus, sends you greetings. 24And
so do Mark, Aristarchus, Demas and
Luke, my fellow workers.
25The grace of the Lord Jesus Christ be
with your spirit.

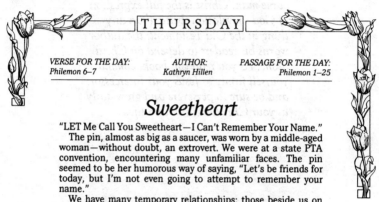

THURSDAY

VERSE FOR THE DAY: *Philemon 6–7* | *AUTHOR:* *Kathryn Hillen* | *PASSAGE FOR THE DAY:* *Philemon 1–25*

Sweetheart

"LET Me Call You Sweetheart—I Can't Remember Your Name."

The pin, almost as big as a saucer, was worn by a middle-aged woman—without doubt, an extrovert. We were at a state PTA convention, encountering many unfamiliar faces. The pin seemed to be her humorous way of saying, "Let's be friends for today, but I'm not even going to attempt to remember your name."

We have many temporary relationships: those beside us on the plane or in the laundromat, the people who camp next to us at a resort, and the neighbors who move in and out with such rapidity. It's up to us to decide if these contacts will be meaningless or significant.

Ask God, "What would you like to say to this person through me?" You may be surprised. He may ask you to speak words of appreciation and encouragement, to witness about Christ, or only to be friendly. When we look a person in the eye and ask about their lives, we show that they are valuable. And even if we never do learn the person's name, we have been a channel through which God can reach him or her. That is both exciting and humbling.

Additional Scripture Readings:
2 Corinthians 5:18–20; Colossians 4:2–6

Go to page 329 for your next devotional reading.

THE author of this letter encourages Christians who are being persecuted for their faith by pointing them to the greatness of the Son of God who became man. Christ is the full expression of God's revelation, better than anything in the Old Testament; the author warns his readers to depend on Christ alone. As you read this book, commit yourself firmly to Jesus your Intercessor, and be sure to persevere and grow daily in your Christian faith and life.

HEBREWS

The Son Superior to Angels

1 In the past God spoke to our forefathers through the prophets at many
times and in various ways, 2but in these
last days he has spoken to us by his Son,
whom he appointed heir of all things, and
through whom he made the universe.
3The Son is the radiance of God's glory
and the exact representation of his being,
sustaining all things by his powerful
word. After he had provided purification
for sins, he sat down at the right hand of
the Majesty in heaven. 4So he became as
much superior to the angels as the name
he has inherited is superior to theirs.
5For to which of the angels did God
ever say,

"You are my Son;
today I have become your Father[a]"[b]?

Or again,

"I will be his Father,
and he will be my Son"[c]?

6And again, when God brings his firstborn
into the world, he says,

[a]5 Or *have begotten you* [b]5 Psalm 2:7 [c]5 2 Samuel 7:14; 1 Chron. 17:13

"Let all God's angels worship him."[a]
7In speaking of the angels he says,

"He makes his angels winds,
his servants flames of fire."[b]

8But about the Son he says,

"Your throne, O God, will last for ever
and ever,
and righteousness will be the
scepter of your kingdom.
9You have loved righteousness and
hated wickedness;
therefore God, your God, has set
you above your companions
by anointing you with the oil of
joy."[c]

10He also says,

"In the beginning, O Lord, you laid
the foundations of the earth,
and the heavens are the work of
your hands.
11They will perish, but you remain;
they will all wear out like a
garment.
12You will roll them up like a robe;
like a garment they will be
changed.

[a]6 Deut. 32:43 (see Dead Sea Scrolls and Septuagint) [b]7 Psalm 104:4 [c]9 Psalm 45:6,7

FRIDAY

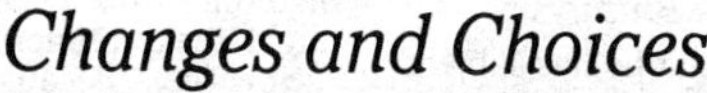

VERSE FOR THE DAY:
Hebrews 1:12

AUTHOR:
Janet C. Jones

PASSAGE FOR THE DAY:
Hebrews 1:1–14

Changes and Choices

RECENTLY my life has been filled with changes and choices. I guess that can be said of all of our lives. Would it not be good if we could choose a period of our lives that was enjoyable and let time stand still? But we cannot. Ecclesiastes 3:11 and 14 tell us, "he has made everything beautiful in its time," and "everything God does will endure forever."

If our childhood was a happy time, we did not want it to end. Everything was new, fresh and meaningful. We wanted our teen years to be over soon so we could be adults. In young adulthood, there were many changes and choices: college, marriage, the birth of children or the choice of a job. In middle age and even in our "golden years," there are still changes and choices.

My parents are in their golden years. Both of them have had severe physical problems. Because of this, I have had to make many choices and to endure a lot of changes. But Christ was and is precious, and his Word has been very real. When it became necessary to consider retirement housing for my mother and father, it was a difficult adjustment for all of us. But each day, as I went to God's Word, he had something just for me. For example, "Now go, lead the people to the place I spoke of, and my angel will go before you" (Exodus 32:34).

Yes, life is filled with changes and choices, but the right choice is Jesus Christ. He will take you through all the changes.

Additional Scripture Readings:
Luke 10:38–42; Hebrews 11:24–26

Go to page 331 for your next devotional reading.

But you remain the same,
and your years will never end."[a]

13 To which of the angels did God ever say,

"Sit at my right hand
until I make your enemies
a footstool for your feet"[b]?

14 Are not all angels ministering spirits
sent to serve those who will inherit salvation?

Warning to Pay Attention

2 We must pay more careful attention,
therefore, to what we have heard, so
that we do not drift away. 2 For if the message spoken by angels was binding, and
every violation and disobedience received
its just punishment, 3 how shall we escape
if we ignore such a great salvation? This
salvation, which was first announced by
the Lord, was confirmed to us by those
who heard him. 4 God also testified to it
by signs, wonders and various miracles,
and gifts of the Holy Spirit distributed according to his will.

Jesus Made Like His Brothers

5 It is not to angels that he has subjected the world to come, about which we are
speaking. 6 But there is a place where
someone has testified:

"What is man that you are mindful of
him,
the son of man that you care for
him?
7 You made him a little[c] lower than
the angels;
you crowned him with glory and
honor
8 and put everything under his
feet."[d]

In putting everything under him, God left
nothing that is not subject to him. Yet at
present we do not see everything subject
to him. 9 But we see Jesus, who was made
a little lower than the angels, now
crowned with glory and honor because he
suffered death, so that by the grace of
God he might taste death for everyone.

10 In bringing many sons to glory, it was
fitting that God, for whom and through
whom everything exists, should make the
author of their salvation perfect through
suffering. 11 Both the one who makes men
holy and those who are made holy are of
the same family. So Jesus is not ashamed
to call them brothers. 12 He says,

"I will declare your name to my
brothers;
in the presence of the congregation
I will sing your praises."[e]

13 And again,

"I will put my trust in him."[f]

And again he says,

"Here am I, and the children God has
given me."[g]

14 Since the children have flesh and
blood, he too shared in their humanity so
that by his death he might destroy him
who holds the power of death—that is,
the devil— 15 and free those who all their
lives were held in slavery by their fear of
death. 16 For surely it is not angels he
helps, but Abraham's descendants. 17 For
this reason he had to be made like his
brothers in every way, in order that he
might become a merciful and faithful
high priest in service to God, and that he
might make atonement for[h] the sins of
the people. 18 Because he himself suffered
when he was tempted, he is able to help
those who are being tempted.

Jesus Greater Than Moses

3 Therefore, holy brothers, who share
in the heavenly calling, fix your
thoughts on Jesus, the apostle and high
priest whom we confess. 2 He was faithful
to the one who appointed him, just as
Moses was faithful in all God's house.
3 Jesus has been found worthy of greater
honor than Moses, just as the builder of
a house has greater honor than the house
itself. 4 For every house is built by someone, but God is the builder of everything.
5 Moses was faithful as a servant in all
God's house, testifying to what would be
said in the future. 6 But Christ is faithful
as a son over God's house. And we are his
house, if we hold on to our courage and
the hope of which we boast.

Warning Against Unbelief

7 So, as the Holy Spirit says:

"Today, if you hear his voice,
8 do not harden your hearts

[a] *12* Psalm 102:25-27 [b] *13* Psalm 110:1 [c] *7* Or *him for a little while*; also in verse 9
[d] *8* Psalm 8:4-6 [e] *12* Psalm 22:22 [f] *13* Isaiah 8:17 [g] *13* Isaiah 8:18 [h] *17* Or *and that he might turn aside God's wrath, taking away*

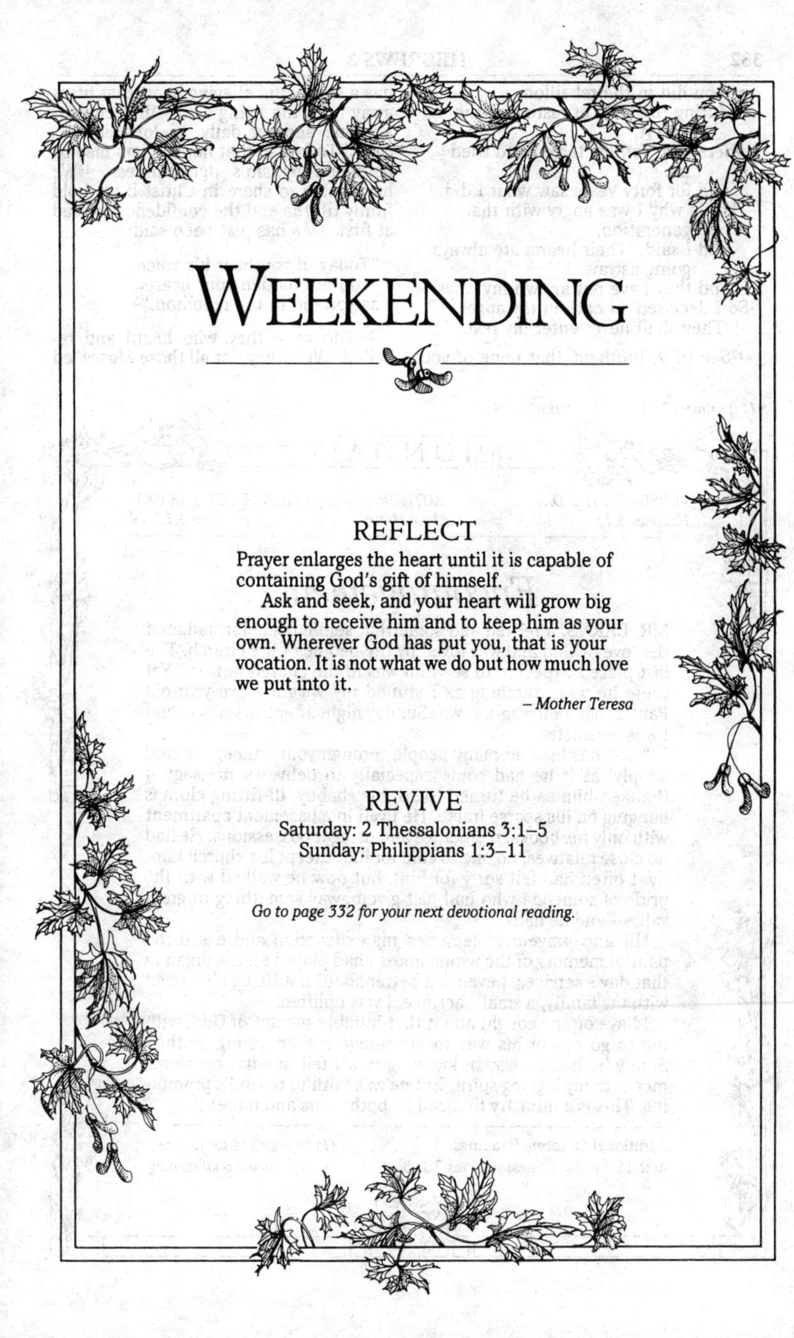

WEEKENDING

REFLECT

Prayer enlarges the heart until it is capable of containing God's gift of himself.

Ask and seek, and your heart will grow big enough to receive him and to keep him as your own. Wherever God has put you, that is your vocation. It is not what we do but how much love we put into it.

– Mother Teresa

REVIVE

Saturday: 2 Thessalonians 3:1–5
Sunday: Philippians 1:3–11

Go to page 332 for your next devotional reading.

as you did in the rebellion,
during the time of testing in the desert,
9where your fathers tested and tried me
and for forty years saw what I did.
10That is why I was angry with that generation,
and I said, 'Their hearts are always going astray,
and they have not known my ways.'
11So I declared on oath in my anger,
'They shall never enter my rest.' "[a]

12See to it, brothers, that none of you
has a sinful, unbelieving heart that turns
away from the living God. 13But encourage one another daily, as long as it is
called Today, so that none of you may be
hardened by sin's deceitfulness. 14We
have come to share in Christ if we hold
firmly till the end the confidence we had
at first. 15As has just been said:

"Today, if you hear his voice,
do not harden your hearts
as you did in the rebellion."[b]

16Who were they who heard and rebelled? Were they not all those Moses led

[a]*11* Psalm 95:7-11 [b]*15* Psalm 95:7,8

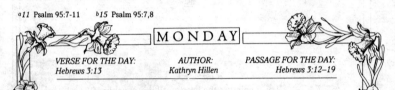

MONDAY

VERSE FOR THE DAY: *Hebrews 3:13*
AUTHOR: *Kathryn Hillen*
PASSAGE FOR THE DAY: *Hebrews 3:12–19*

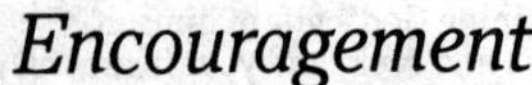

Encouragement

MR. BARNS, a retired and somewhat senile bachelor, radiated the love of God and was loved by the people of the church. The last place I expected to see him was in the church nursery. Yet there he was, watching as I stuffed my wiggling two-year-old Paul into his snowsuit. It was Sunday night after the service, and I was exhausted.

"God has blessed many people through your hands," he said simply, as if he had come especially to deliver a message. I thanked him as he turned to go, his shabby, ill-fitting clothes hanging on his sparse frame. He lived in a basement apartment with only his books, mementos and meager possessions. He had no close relatives, no one to care for him except his church family. I often had felt sorry for him, but now he walked with the pride of someone who had just given away something of great value—and he had.

His encouragement lessened my exhaustion and eased the painful memory of the wrong notes I had played on the organ in that day's services. I even felt better about not being able to sit with my family, a small sacrifice. I was uplifted.

I have often thought about that humble servant of God, willing to go out of his way to encourage a tired young mother. Surely he had no way of knowing how I felt or what his words meant to my lagging spirit. But he was faithful to God's prompting. This is a ministry that can be both yours and mine.

Additional Scripture Readings:
Acts 15:30–34; 1 Thessalonians 3:1–8

Go to page 334 for your next devotional reading.

out of Egypt? 17And with whom was he angry for forty years? Was it not with those who sinned, whose bodies fell in the desert? 18And to whom did God swear that they would never enter his rest if not to those who disobeyed[a]? 19So we see that they were not able to enter, because of their unbelief.

A Sabbath-Rest for the People of God

4 Therefore, since the promise of entering his rest still stands, let us be careful that none of you be found to have fallen short of it. 2For we also have had the gospel preached to us, just as they did; but the message they heard was of no value to them, because those who heard did not combine it with faith.[b] 3Now we who have believed enter that rest, just as God has said,

> "So I declared on oath in my anger,
> 'They shall never enter my rest.' "[c]

And yet his work has been finished since the creation of the world. 4For somewhere he has spoken about the seventh day in these words: "And on the seventh day God rested from all his work."[d] 5And again in the passage above he says, "They shall never enter my rest."

6It still remains that some will enter that rest, and those who formerly had the gospel preached to them did not go in, because of their disobedience. 7Therefore God again set a certain day, calling it Today, when a long time later he spoke through David, as was said before:

> "Today, if you hear his voice,
> do not harden your hearts."[e]

8For if Joshua had given them rest, God would not have spoken later about another day. 9There remains, then, a Sabbath-rest for the people of God; 10for anyone who enters God's rest also rests from his own work, just as God did from his. 11Let us, therefore, make every effort to enter that rest, so that no one will fall by following their example of disobedience.

12For the word of God is living and active. Sharper than any double-edged sword, it penetrates even to dividing soul and spirit, joints and marrow; it judges the thoughts and attitudes of the heart. 13Nothing in all creation is hidden from God's sight. Everything is uncovered and laid bare before the eyes of him to whom we must give account.

Jesus the Great High Priest

14Therefore, since we have a great high priest who has gone through the heavens,[f] Jesus the Son of God, let us hold firmly to the faith we profess. 15For we do not have a high priest who is unable to sympathize with our weaknesses, but we have one who has been tempted in every way, just as we are—yet was without sin. 16Let us then approach the throne of grace with confidence, so that we may receive mercy and find grace to help us in our time of need.

5 Every high priest is selected from among men and is appointed to represent them in matters related to God, to offer gifts and sacrifices for sins. 2He is able to deal gently with those who are ignorant and are going astray, since he himself is subject to weakness. 3This is why he has to offer sacrifices for his own sins, as well as for the sins of the people.

4No one takes this honor upon himself; he must be called by God, just as Aaron was. 5So Christ also did not take upon himself the glory of becoming a high priest. But God said to him,

> "You are my Son;
> today I have become your
> Father.[g]"[h]

6And he says in another place,

> "You are a priest forever,
> in the order of Melchizedek."[i]

7During the days of Jesus' life on earth, he offered up prayers and petitions with loud cries and tears to the one who could save him from death, and he was heard because of his reverent submission. 8Although he was a son, he learned obedience from what he suffered 9and, once made perfect, he became the source of eternal salvation for all who obey him 10and was designated by God to be high priest in the order of Melchizedek.

Warning Against Falling Away

11We have much to say about this, but it is hard to explain because you are slow to learn. 12In fact, though by this time you ought to be teachers, you need someone

[a] 18 Or *disbelieved* [b] 2 Many manuscripts *because they did not share in the faith of those who obeyed*
[c] 3 Psalm 95:11; also in verse 5 [d] 4 Gen. 2:2 [e] 7 Psalm 95:7,8 [f] 14 Or *gone into heaven*
[g] 5 Or *have begotten you* [h] 5 Psalm 2:7 [i] 6 Psalm 110:4

TUESDAY

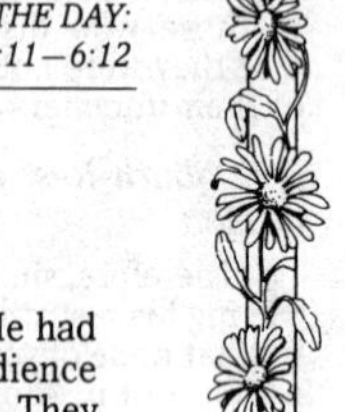

VERSE FOR THE DAY: *Hebrews 5:14*

AUTHOR: *Barbara Bush*

PASSAGE FOR THE DAY: *Hebrews 5:11–6:12*

The Wise Are Mature

THE writer of the letter to the Hebrews was frustrated. He had many wonderful truths he wanted to impart, but his audience did not want to expend much energy on spiritual growth. They had been Christians for some time, but they knew little more than when they first believed.

Those who feed on and digest the meat of God's Word attain maturity in their Christian lives. They gain the wisdom in speech and action that is the mark of the mature. If we are not mature, the reason is obvious: we have not been workmen but idlers in Bible study. We have not made constant use of the Scriptures to distinguish good from evil. We are still dependent on others for our knowledge, as children are, in danger of being misguided by those who sound knowledgeable but may be as ignorant as we.

This is why there are so few wise people. Those who get all their knowledge of God's Word from an hour or two on Sunday will never have a personal grasp of its content. Paul said that if we want to be wise, if we want to "correctly handle the word of truth," we must be workmen (2 Timothy 2:15). We must do the job ourselves instead of expecting a pastor or teacher to do it all for us. We must read the Bible. We must digest it, meditate on it, memorize it, understand it.

God does not want us to remain spiritually immature. He wants us to:

> . . . become mature, attaining to the whole measure of the fullness of Christ. Then we will no longer be infants, tossed back and forth by the waves, and blown here and there by every wind of teaching and by the cunning and craftiness of men in their deceitful scheming. Instead, speaking the truth in love, we will in all things grow up (Ephesians 4:13–15).

Additional Scripture Readings:
Luke 8:14–15; James 1:2–4

Go to page 335 for your next devotional reading.

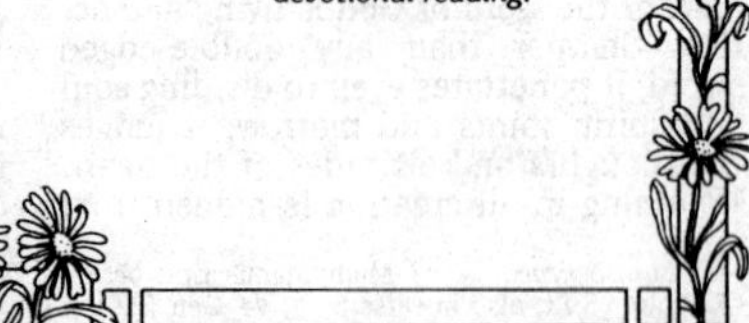

to teach you the elementary truths of
God's word all over again. You need milk,
not solid food! 13Anyone who lives on
milk, being still an infant, is not acquainted with the teaching about righteousness. 14But solid food is for the mature, who by constant use have trained
themselves to distinguish good from evil.

6 Therefore let us leave the elementary
teachings about Christ and go on to
maturity, not laying again the foundation
of repentance from acts that lead to
death,[a] and of faith in God, 2instruction
about baptisms, the laying on of hands,
the resurrection of the dead, and eternal
judgment. 3And God permitting, we will
do so.

4It is impossible for those who have
once been enlightened, who have tasted
the heavenly gift, who have shared in the
Holy Spirit, 5who have tasted the goodness of the word of God and the powers of

[a]1 Or *from useless rituals*

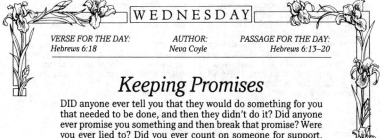

WEDNESDAY

VERSE FOR THE DAY: *Hebrews 6:18*

AUTHOR: *Neva Coyle*

PASSAGE FOR THE DAY: *Hebrews 6:13–20*

Keeping Promises

DID anyone ever tell you that they would do something for you that needed to be done, and then they didn't do it? Did anyone ever promise you something and then break that promise? Were you ever lied to? Did you ever count on someone for support, and then just when you needed it you found that your friend was not in a position to give that support? Did you ever read a brochure about a vacation spot, and when you got there found that the modern cabin in the photograph was the only one at the place and it was occupied? If any of these situations ring a bell with you, then you know what it is like to be disillusioned or deceived.

Deception—what a disabling, evil element. Falsehood, misrepresentation, fabrication, dishonesty, fraud—all synonymous with deception. I have used these words to illustrate what God is not. We tend to be skeptical because of past experiences. We want everything proven to us before we believe. Why? Because we may have believed something once too often, and been deceived one time too many. We are more acquainted with lies than truth.

God knows that we are more apt to be skeptical than believing. Yet we remain gullible and vulnerable. He knows that even with the intense conditioning most of us have had, we want to believe. We need to believe. We are immensely relieved when we find an honest friend whom we can trust. God can be to us that friend. Listen to his words to us from Hebrews 6:18: "It is impossible for God to lie." Think about it—impossible. When God makes a promise, you can count on him to keep it!

Additional Scripture Readings:
Psalm 103:17–18; Isaiah 40:6–8

Go to page 338 for your next devotional reading.

the coming age, 6if they fall away, to be brought back to repentance, because[a] to their loss they are crucifying the Son of God all over again and subjecting him to public disgrace.

7Land that drinks in the rain often falling on it and that produces a crop useful to those for whom it is farmed receives the blessing of God. 8But land that produces thorns and thistles is worthless and is in danger of being cursed. In the end it will be burned.

9Even though we speak like this, dear friends, we are confident of better things in your case—things that accompany salvation. 10God is not unjust; he will not forget your work and the love you have shown him as you have helped his people and continue to help them. 11We want each of you to show this same diligence to the very end, in order to make your hope sure. 12We do not want you to become lazy, but to imitate those who through faith and patience inherit what has been promised.

The Certainty of God's Promise

13When God made his promise to Abraham, since there was no one greater for him to swear by, he swore by himself, 14saying, "I will surely bless you and give you many descendants."[b] 15And so after waiting patiently, Abraham received what was promised.

16Men swear by someone greater than themselves, and the oath confirms what is said and puts an end to all argument. 17Because God wanted to make the unchanging nature of his purpose very clear to the heirs of what was promised, he confirmed it with an oath. 18God did this so that, by two unchangeable things in which it is impossible for God to lie, we who have fled to take hold of the hope offered to us may be greatly encouraged. 19We have this hope as an anchor for the soul, firm and secure. It enters the inner sanctuary behind the curtain, 20where Jesus, who went before us, has entered on our behalf. He has become a high priest forever, in the order of Melchizedek.

Melchizedek the Priest

7 This Melchizedek was king of Salem and priest of God Most High. He met Abraham returning from the defeat of the kings and blessed him, 2and Abraham gave him a tenth of everything. First, his name means "king of righteousness"; then also, "king of Salem" means "king of peace." 3Without father or mother, without genealogy, without beginning of days or end of life, like the Son of God he remains a priest forever.

4Just think how great he was: Even the patriarch Abraham gave him a tenth of the plunder! 5Now the law requires the descendants of Levi who become priests to collect a tenth from the people—that is, their brothers—even though their brothers are descended from Abraham. 6This man, however, did not trace his descent from Levi, yet he collected a tenth from Abraham and blessed him who had the promises. 7And without doubt the lesser person is blessed by the greater. 8In the one case, the tenth is collected by men who die; but in the other case, by him who is declared to be living. 9One might even say that Levi, who collects the tenth, paid the tenth through Abraham, 10because when Melchizedek met Abraham, Levi was still in the body of his ancestor.

Jesus Like Melchizedek

11If perfection could have been attained through the Levitical priesthood (for on the basis of it the law was given to the people), why was there still need for another priest to come—one in the order of Melchizedek, not in the order of Aaron? 12For when there is a change of the priesthood, there must also be a change of the law. 13He of whom these things are said belonged to a different tribe, and no one from that tribe has ever served at the altar. 14For it is clear that our Lord descended from Judah, and in regard to that tribe Moses said nothing about priests. 15And what we have said is even more clear if another priest like Melchizedek appears, 16one who has become a priest not on the basis of a regulation as to his ancestry but on the basis of the power of an indestructible life. 17For it is declared:

"You are a priest forever,
 in the order of Melchizedek."[c]

18The former regulation is set aside because it was weak and useless 19(for the law made nothing perfect), and a better hope is introduced, by which we draw near to God.

20And it was not without an oath! Oth-

[a]6 Or *repentance while* [b]14 Gen. 22:17 [c]17 Psalm 110:4

ers became priests without any oath,
21but he became a priest with an oath
when God said to him:

"The Lord has sworn
and will not change his mind:
'You are a priest forever.' "[a]

22Because of this oath, Jesus has become
the guarantee of a better covenant.
23Now there have been many of those
priests, since death prevented them from
continuing in office; 24but because Jesus
lives forever, he has a permanent priesthood. 25Therefore he is able to save completely[b] those who come to God through
him, because he always lives to intercede
for them.
26Such a high priest meets our need—
one who is holy, blameless, pure, set
apart from sinners, exalted above the
heavens. 27Unlike the other high priests,
he does not need to offer sacrifices day
after day, first for his own sins, and then
for the sins of the people. He sacrificed
for their sins once for all when he offered
himself. 28For the law appoints as high
priests men who are weak; but the oath,
which came after the law, appointed the
Son, who has been made perfect forever.

The High Priest of a New Covenant

8 The point of what we are saying is
this: We do have such a high priest,
who sat down at the right hand of the
throne of the Majesty in heaven, 2and
who serves in the sanctuary, the true
tabernacle set up by the Lord, not by
man.
3Every high priest is appointed to offer
both gifts and sacrifices, and so it was
necessary for this one also to have something to offer. 4If he were on earth, he
would not be a priest, for there are already men who offer the gifts prescribed
by the law. 5They serve at a sanctuary that
is a copy and shadow of what is in heaven.
This is why Moses was warned when he
was about to build the tabernacle: "See to
it that you make everything according to
the pattern shown you on the mountain."[c] 6But the ministry Jesus has received is as superior to theirs as the covenant of which he is mediator is superior
to the old one, and it is founded on better
promises.
7For if there had been nothing wrong
with that first covenant, no place would
have been sought for another. 8But God
found fault with the people and said[d]:

"The time is coming, declares the
Lord,
when I will make a new covenant
with the house of Israel
and with the house of Judah.
9It will not be like the covenant
I made with their forefathers
when I took them by the hand
to lead them out of Egypt,
because they did not remain faithful
to my covenant,
and I turned away from them,
declares the Lord.
10This is the covenant I will make with
the house of Israel
after that time, declares the Lord.
I will put my laws in their minds
and write them on their hearts.
I will be their God,
and they will be my people.
11No longer will a man teach his
neighbor,
or a man his brother, saying, 'Know
the Lord,'
because they will all know me,
from the least of them to the
greatest.
12For I will forgive their wickedness
and will remember their sins no
more."[e]

13By calling this covenant "new," he
has made the first one obsolete; and what
is obsolete and aging will soon disappear.

Worship in the Earthly Tabernacle

9 Now the first covenant had regulations for worship and also an earthly
sanctuary. 2A tabernacle was set up. In its
first room were the lampstand, the table
and the consecrated bread; this was
called the Holy Place. 3Behind the second
curtain was a room called the Most Holy
Place, 4which had the golden altar of incense and the gold-covered ark of the
covenant. This ark contained the gold jar
of manna, Aaron's staff that had budded,
and the stone tablets of the covenant.
5Above the ark were the cherubim of the
Glory, overshadowing the atonement cover.[f] But we cannot discuss these things
in detail now.
6When everything had been arranged
like this, the priests entered regularly

[a] *21* Psalm 110:4 [b] *25* Or *forever* [c] *5* Exodus 25:40 [d] *8* Some manuscripts may be translated *fault and said to the people.* [e] *12* Jer. 31:31-34 [f] *5* Traditionally *the mercy seat*

into the outer room to carry on their ministry. 7But only the high priest entered the
inner room, and that only once a year,
and never without blood, which he offered for himself and for the sins the people had committed in ignorance. 8The
Holy Spirit was showing by this that the
way into the Most Holy Place had not yet
been disclosed as long as the first tabernacle was still standing. 9This is an illustration for the present time, indicating
that the gifts and sacrifices being offered
were not able to clear the conscience of
the worshiper. 10They are only a matter of
food and drink and various ceremonial
washings—external regulations applying
until the time of the new order.

The Blood of Christ

11When Christ came as high priest of
the good things that are already here,[a] he
went through the greater and more perfect tabernacle that is not man-made,
that is to say, not a part of this creation.
12He did not enter by means of the blood
of goats and calves; but he entered the
Most Holy Place once for all by his own
blood, having obtained eternal redemption. 13The blood of goats and bulls and

[a]11 Some early manuscripts *are to come*

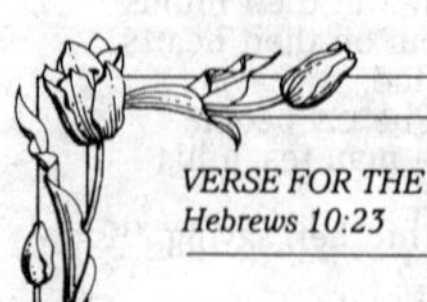

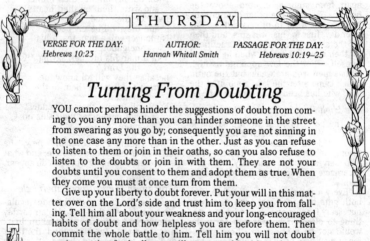

THURSDAY

VERSE FOR THE DAY: *Hebrews 10:23*

AUTHOR: *Hannah Whitall Smith*

PASSAGE FOR THE DAY: *Hebrews 10:19–25*

Turning From Doubting

YOU cannot perhaps hinder the suggestions of doubt from coming to you any more than you can hinder someone in the street from swearing as you go by; consequently you are not sinning in the one case any more than in the other. Just as you can refuse to listen to them or join in their oaths, so can you also refuse to listen to the doubts or join in with them. They are not your doubts until you consent to them and adopt them as true. When they come you must at once turn from them.

Give up your liberty to doubt forever. Put your will in this matter over on the Lord's side and trust him to keep you from falling. Tell him all about your weakness and your long-encouraged habits of doubt and how helpless you are before them. Then commit the whole battle to him. Tell him you will not doubt again, putting forth all your will power on his side and against his enemy and yours. Then "keep your eyes on Jesus" (Hebrews 12:2), looking away from yourself and away from your doubts, holding fast the profession of your faith without wavering, because "he who promised is faithful" (Hebrews 10:23). Rely on his faithfulness, not on your own. You have committed the keeping of your soul to him as the faithful Creator, and you must never again admit the possibility of his being unfaithful.

Cultivate a continuous habit of believing, and sooner or later all of your doubts will vanish in the glory of the absolute faithfulness of God.

Additional Scripture Readings:
Luke 1:11–20; John 20:26–29

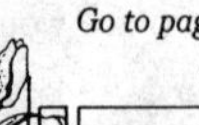

Go to page 340 for your next devotional reading.

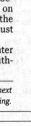

the ashes of a heifer sprinkled on those
who are ceremonially unclean sanctify
them so that they are outwardly clean.
14How much more, then, will the blood of
Christ, who through the eternal Spirit offered himself unblemished to God,
cleanse our consciences from acts that
lead to death,[a] so that we may serve the
living God!

15For this reason Christ is the mediator
of a new covenant, that those who are
called may receive the promised eternal
inheritance—now that he has died as a
ransom to set them free from the sins
committed under the first covenant.

16In the case of a will,[b] it is necessary
to prove the death of the one who made
it, 17because a will is in force only when
somebody has died; it never takes effect
while the one who made it is living. 18This
is why even the first covenant was not put
into effect without blood. 19When Moses
had proclaimed every commandment of
the law to all the people, he took the
blood of calves, together with water, scarlet wool and branches of hyssop, and
sprinkled the scroll and all the people.
20He said, "This is the blood of the covenant, which God has commanded you to
keep."[c] 21In the same way, he sprinkled
with the blood both the tabernacle and
everything used in its ceremonies. 22In
fact, the law requires that nearly everything be cleansed with blood, and without the shedding of blood there is no forgiveness.

23It was necessary, then, for the copies
of the heavenly things to be purified with
these sacrifices, but the heavenly things
themselves with better sacrifices than
these. 24For Christ did not enter a man-
made sanctuary that was only a copy of
the true one; he entered heaven itself,
now to appear for us in God's presence.
25Nor did he enter heaven to offer himself
again and again, the way the high priest
enters the Most Holy Place every year
with blood that is not his own. 26Then
Christ would have had to suffer many
times since the creation of the world. But
now he has appeared once for all at the
end of the ages to do away with sin by the
sacrifice of himself. 27Just as man is destined to die once, and after that to face
judgment, 28so Christ was sacrificed once
to take away the sins of many people; and
he will appear a second time, not to bear
sin, but to bring salvation to those who
are waiting for him.

Christ's Sacrifice Once for All

10 The law is only a shadow of the
good things that are coming—not
the realities themselves. For this reason it
can never, by the same sacrifices repeated endlessly year after year, make perfect
those who draw near to worship. 2If it
could, would they not have stopped being
offered? For the worshipers would have
been cleansed once for all, and would no
longer have felt guilty for their sins. 3But
those sacrifices are an annual reminder of
sins, 4because it is impossible for the
blood of bulls and goats to take away sins.

5Therefore, when Christ came into the
world, he said:

"Sacrifice and offering you did not
desire,
but a body you prepared for me;
6with burnt offerings and sin offerings
you were not pleased.
7Then I said, 'Here I am—it is written
about me in the scroll—
I have come to do your will,
O God.' "[d]

8First he said, "Sacrifices and offerings,
burnt offerings and sin offerings you did
not desire, nor were you pleased with
them" (although the law required them to
be made). 9Then he said, "Here I am, I
have come to do your will." He sets aside
the first to establish the second. 10And
by that will, we have been made holy
through the sacrifice of the body of Jesus
Christ once for all.

11Day after day every priest stands and
performs his religious duties; again and
again he offers the same sacrifices, which
can never take away sins. 12But when this
priest had offered for all time one sacrifice for sins, he sat down at the right hand
of God. 13Since that time he waits for his
enemies to be made his footstool, 14be-
cause by one sacrifice he has made perfect forever those who are being made
holy.

15The Holy Spirit also testifies to us
about this. First he says:

16"This is the covenant I will make with
them
after that time, says the Lord.
I will put my laws in their hearts,

[a]14 Or *from useless rituals* [b]16 Same Greek word as *covenant*; also in verse 17 [c]20 Exodus 24:8
[d]7 Psalm 40:6-8 (see Septuagint)

FRIDAY

VERSE FOR THE DAY:
Hebrews 11:39–40

AUTHOR:
Luci Swindoll

PASSAGE FOR THE DAY:
Hebrews 11:23–29,39–40

Moses' Choice—Your Choice

THIS inspiring chapter of Hebrews has been called the Faith Hall of Fame. These noted saints pleased God and were commended by him because, in faith, they trusted God for what they hoped for, even though they could not see the goal at the time.

The most amazing person in this whole bunch is Moses, because of a choice he made. And what did he choose? "He chose to be mistreated along with the people of God." Why would he do that? At that time, Egypt was the loftiest society of the day—rich in beauty, education, art, trade, culture—and the Hebrew people were, by comparison, nothing more than a dung heap on the outskirts of town. Moses, even though he had been reared from babyhood by the daughter of Pharaoh, chose the dung heap. Unbelievable! Instead of staying where things were nice and clean, prestigious and comfortable, he chose mistreatment. I find that thought-provoking.

Would I choose mistreatment? I wonder if I'd have that strength of character. Loving the nicer things in life, I'd have to reach down into that part of me where my values lie. What would it take to make me choose what's best rather than what's easiest? Such a decision would have to come from a sense of direction—from my faith.

By faith, Moses chose wisely and looked at the disgrace and mistreatment as a temporary burden, with his ultimate reward of greater value than what society had to offer. Faith willfully chooses even disgrace or mistreatment because it sees, through an act of trust, the eventual reward that comes from him who is invisible.

You have the same opportunity to choose either a reward that stops here or one that lies ahead in a place that cannot be seen. You have a chance to choose for your sake or for the sake of Christ. It boils down to that. How will you choose? Remember Moses.

Additional Scripture Readings:
Esther 4:6–16; Daniel 3:13–18

Go to page 342 for your next devotional reading.

and I will write them on their
minds."[a]

17Then he adds:

"Their sins and lawless acts
I will remember no more."[b]

18And where these have been forgiven,
there is no longer any sacrifice for sin.

A Call to Persevere

19Therefore, brothers, since we have
confidence to enter the Most Holy Place
by the blood of Jesus, 20by a new and living way opened for us through the curtain, that is, his body, 21and since we have
a great priest over the house of God, 22let
us draw near to God with a sincere heart
in full assurance of faith, having our
hearts sprinkled to cleanse us from a guilty conscience and having our bodies
washed with pure water. 23Let us hold un-
swervingly to the hope we profess, for he
who promised is faithful. 24And let us
consider how we may spur one another on
toward love and good deeds. 25Let us not
give up meeting together, as some are in
the habit of doing, but let us encourage
one another—and all the more as you see
the Day approaching.

26If we deliberately keep on sinning after we have received the knowledge of the
truth, no sacrifice for sins is left, 27but
only a fearful expectation of judgment
and of raging fire that will consume the
enemies of God. 28Anyone who rejected
the law of Moses died without mercy on
the testimony of two or three witnesses.
29How much more severely do you think
a man deserves to be punished who has
trampled the Son of God under foot, who
has treated as an unholy thing the blood
of the covenant that sanctified him, and
who has insulted the Spirit of grace? 30For
we know him who said, "It is mine to
avenge; I will repay,"[c] and again, "The
Lord will judge his people."[d] 31It is a
dreadful thing to fall into the hands of the
living God.

32Remember those earlier days after
you had received the light, when you
stood your ground in a great contest in
the face of suffering. 33Sometimes you
were publicly exposed to insult and persecution; at other times you stood side by
side with those who were so treated.
34You sympathized with those in prison
and joyfully accepted the confiscation of
your property, because you knew that you
yourselves had better and lasting possessions.

35So do not throw away your confidence; it will be richly rewarded. 36You
need to persevere so that when you have
done the will of God, you will receive
what he has promised. 37For in just a very
little while,

"He who is coming will come and will
not delay.
38 But my righteous one[e] will live by
faith.
And if he shrinks back,
I will not be pleased with him."[f]

39But we are not of those who shrink back
and are destroyed, but of those who believe and are saved.

By Faith

11 Now faith is being sure of what we
hope for and certain of what we do
not see. 2This is what the ancients were
commended for.

3By faith we understand that the universe was formed at God's command, so
that what is seen was not made out of
what was visible.

4By faith Abel offered God a better sacrifice than Cain did. By faith he was commended as a righteous man, when God
spoke well of his offerings. And by faith
he still speaks, even though he is dead.

5By faith Enoch was taken from this
life, so that he did not experience death;
he could not be found, because God had
taken him away. For before he was taken,
he was commended as one who pleased
God. 6And without faith it is impossible
to please God, because anyone who
comes to him must believe that he exists
and that he rewards those who earnestly
seek him.

7By faith Noah, when warned about
things not yet seen, in holy fear built an
ark to save his family. By his faith he condemned the world and became heir of the
righteousness that comes by faith.

8By faith Abraham, when called to go to
a place he would later receive as his inheritance, obeyed and went, even though
he did not know where he was going. 9By
faith he made his home in the promised
land like a stranger in a foreign country;
he lived in tents, as did Isaac and Jacob,

[a] *16* Jer. 31:33 [b] *17* Jer. 31:34 [c] *30* Deut. 32:35 [d] *30* Deut. 32:36; Psalm 135:14 [e] *38* One early manuscript *But the righteous* [f] *38* Hab. 2:3,4

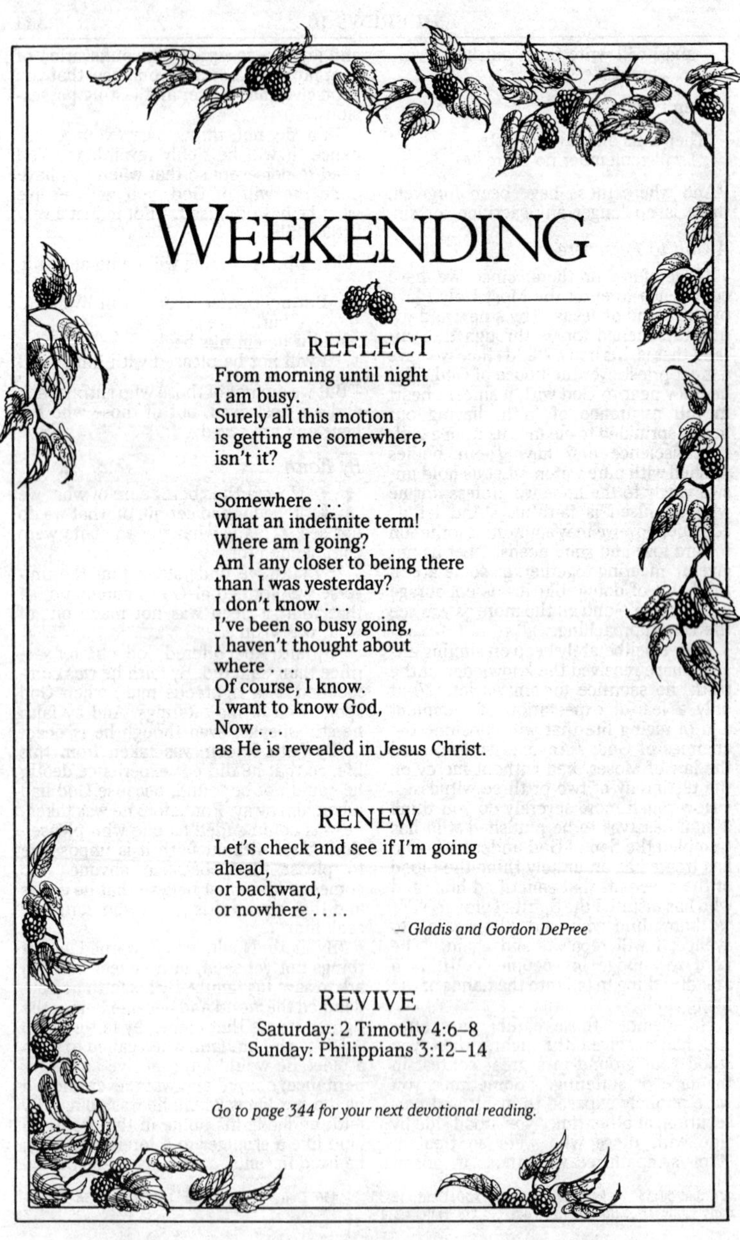

WEEKENDING

REFLECT

From morning until night
I am busy.
Surely all this motion
is getting me somewhere,
isn't it?

Somewhere . . .
What an indefinite term!
Where am I going?
Am I any closer to being there
than I was yesterday?
I don't know . . .
I've been so busy going,
I haven't thought about
where . . .
Of course, I know.
I want to know God,
Now . . .
as He is revealed in Jesus Christ.

RENEW

Let's check and see if I'm going
ahead,
or backward,
or nowhere . . . .

– *Gladis and Gordon DePree*

REVIVE

Saturday: 2 Timothy 4:6–8
Sunday: Philippians 3:12–14

Go to page 344 for your next devotional reading.

who were heirs with him of the same promise. 10For he was looking forward to the
city with foundations, whose architect
and builder is God.
11By faith Abraham, even though he
was past age—and Sarah herself was barren—was enabled to become a father because he[a] considered him faithful who
had made the promise. 12And so from this
one man, and he as good as dead, came
descendants as numerous as the stars in
the sky and as countless as the sand on
the seashore.
13All these people were still living by
faith when they died. They did not receive
the things promised; they only saw them
and welcomed them from a distance. And
they admitted that they were aliens and
strangers on earth. 14People who say such
things show that they are looking for a
country of their own. 15If they had been
thinking of the country they had left, they
would have had opportunity to return.
16Instead, they were longing for a better
country—a heavenly one. Therefore God
is not ashamed to be called their God, for
he has prepared a city for them.
17By faith Abraham, when God tested
him, offered Isaac as a sacrifice. He who
had received the promises was about to
sacrifice his one and only son, 18even
though God had said to him, "It is
through Isaac that your offspring[b] will be
reckoned."[c] 19Abraham reasoned that
God could raise the dead, and figuratively
speaking, he did receive Isaac back from
death.
20By faith Isaac blessed Jacob and Esau
in regard to their future.
21By faith Jacob, when he was dying,
blessed each of Joseph's sons, and worshiped as he leaned on the top of his staff.
22By faith Joseph, when his end was
near, spoke about the exodus of the Israelites from Egypt and gave instructions
about his bones.
23By faith Moses' parents hid him for
three months after he was born, because
they saw he was no ordinary child, and
they were not afraid of the king's edict.
24By faith Moses, when he had grown
up, refused to be known as the son of
Pharaoh's daughter. 25He chose to be
mistreated along with the people of God
rather than to enjoy the pleasures of sin
for a short time. 26He regarded disgrace
for the sake of Christ as of greater value
than the treasures of Egypt, because he
was looking ahead to his reward. 27By
faith he left Egypt, not fearing the king's
anger; he persevered because he saw him
who is invisible. 28By faith he kept the
Passover and the sprinkling of blood, so
that the destroyer of the firstborn would
not touch the firstborn of Israel.
29By faith the people passed through
the Red Sea[d] as on dry land; but when
the Egyptians tried to do so, they were
drowned.
30By faith the walls of Jericho fell, after
the people had marched around them for
seven days.
31By faith the prostitute Rahab, because she welcomed the spies, was not
killed with those who were disobedient.[e]
32And what more shall I say? I do not
have time to tell about Gideon, Barak,
Samson, Jephthah, David, Samuel and
the prophets, 33who through faith con-
quered kingdoms, administered justice,
and gained what was promised; who shut
the mouths of lions, 34quenched the fury
of the flames, and escaped the edge of the
sword; whose weakness was turned to
strength; and who became powerful in
battle and routed foreign armies. 35Wom-
en received back their dead, raised to life
again. Others were tortured and refused
to be released, so that they might gain a
better resurrection. 36Some faced jeers
and flogging, while still others were
chained and put in prison. 37They were
stoned[f]; they were sawed in two; they
were put to death by the sword. They
went about in sheepskins and goatskins,
destitute, persecuted and mistreated—
38the world was not worthy of them. They
wandered in deserts and mountains, and
in caves and holes in the ground.
39These were all commended for their
faith, yet none of them received what had
been promised. 40God had planned something better for us so that only together
with us would they be made perfect.

God Disciplines His Sons

12 Therefore, since we are surrounded by such a great cloud of witnesses, let us throw off everything that
hinders and the sin that so easily entan-
gles, and let us run with perseverance the

[a] *11* Or *By faith even Sarah, who was past age, was enabled to bear children because she* [b] *18* Greek *seed* [c] *18* Gen. 21:12 [d] *29* That is, Sea of Reeds [e] *31* Or *unbelieving* [f] *37* Some early manuscripts *stoned; they were put to the test;*

race marked out for us. 2Let us fix our
eyes on Jesus, the author and perfecter of
our faith, who for the joy set before him
endured the cross, scorning its shame,
and sat down at the right hand of the
throne of God. 3Consider him who endured such opposition from sinful men,
so that you will not grow weary and lose
heart.
4In your struggle against sin, you have
not yet resisted to the point of shedding
your blood. 5And you have forgotten that
word of encouragement that addresses
you as sons:

"My son, do not make light of the
Lord's discipline,
and do not lose heart when he
rebukes you,
6because the Lord disciplines those he
loves,
and he punishes everyone he
accepts as a son."[a]

7Endure hardship as discipline; God is

[a]6 Prov. 3:11,12

MONDAY

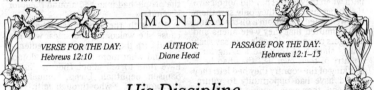

VERSE FOR THE DAY: *Hebrews 12:10*

AUTHOR: *Diane Head*

PASSAGE FOR THE DAY: *Hebrews 12:1–13*

His Discipline

MOST of us have had at least one week when everything seemed to go wrong. The kids knocked down the apple display at the market; the plumbing decided it was time to back up; the furnace died; the car had a flat (with the entire Brownie troop inside); and the stomach flu toppled the whole household.

These events don't always come in groups, but even one at a time they can be mildly irritating and sometimes downright exasperating.

Then there are the more serious events that enter our lives—seemingly without reason. The ones that slice at our very roots: perhaps a lost job or maybe a transfer to another city. Maybe it's the extended illness of a family member or a life-threatening accident or not enough money to go around.

Do you ever wonder about the calamities that meet us head-on in everyday life? Do you ever ask as I do, "Why me, Lord?" Are daily catastrophes just happenstance or is there a reason behind them?

God disciplines us for our good, that we may share in his holiness" (Hebrews 12:10). What a difference it makes in the atmosphere of our homes if we face those calamities with an attitude of joy. Not a fake, pasted-on joy—but a joy that comes from knowing that he is bringing us closer to a sharing in his holiness—through discipline.

So the next time those rough winds sweep through our homes—let's rejoice! It won't be long until we can lift our hearts and laugh in his sunshine . . . in his holiness.

Additional Scripture Readings:
Deuteronomy 8:1–5; Proverbs 3:11–12

Go to page 346 for your next devotional reading.

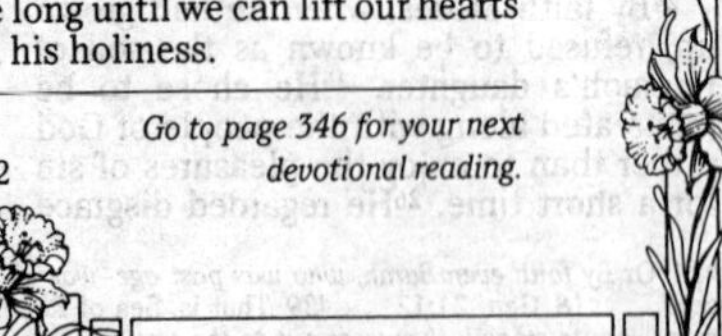

treating you as sons. For what son is not
disciplined by his father? 8If you are not
disciplined (and everyone undergoes discipline), then you are illegitimate children and not true sons. 9Moreover, we
have all had human fathers who disciplined us and we respected them for it.
How much more should we submit to the
Father of our spirits and live! 10Our fathers disciplined us for a little while as
they thought best; but God disciplines us
for our good, that we may share in his
holiness. 11No discipline seems pleasant
at the time, but painful. Later on, however, it produces a harvest of righteousness
and peace for those who have been
trained by it.

12Therefore, strengthen your feeble
arms and weak knees. 13"Make level
paths for your feet,"[a] so that the lame
may not be disabled, but rather healed.

Warning Against Refusing God

14Make every effort to live in peace with
all men and to be holy; without holiness
no one will see the Lord. 15See to it that
no one misses the grace of God and that
no bitter root grows up to cause trouble
and defile many. 16See that no one is sexually immoral, or is godless like Esau,
who for a single meal sold his inheritance
rights as the oldest son. 17Afterward, as
you know, when he wanted to inherit this
blessing, he was rejected. He could bring
about no change of mind, though he
sought the blessing with tears.

18You have not come to a mountain
that can be touched and that is burning
with fire; to darkness, gloom and storm;
19to a trumpet blast or to such a voice
speaking words that those who heard it
begged that no further word be spoken to
them, 20because they could not bear what
was commanded: "If even an animal
touches the mountain, it must be
stoned."[b] 21The sight was so terrifying
that Moses said, "I am trembling with
fear."[c]

22But you have come to Mount Zion, to
the heavenly Jerusalem, the city of the
living God. You have come to thousands
upon thousands of angels in joyful assembly, 23to the church of the firstborn,
whose names are written in heaven. You
have come to God, the judge of all men,
to the spirits of righteous men made perfect, 24to Jesus the mediator of a new
covenant, and to the sprinkled blood that
speaks a better word than the blood of
Abel.

25See to it that you do not refuse him
who speaks. If they did not escape when
they refused him who warned them on
earth, how much less will we, if we turn
away from him who warns us from heav-
en? 26At that time his voice shook the
earth, but now he has promised, "Once
more I will shake not only the earth but
also the heavens."[d] 27The words "once
more" indicate the removing of what can
be shaken—that is, created things—so
that what cannot be shaken may remain.

28Therefore, since we are receiving a
kingdom that cannot be shaken, let us be
thankful, and so worship God acceptably
with reverence and awe, 29for our "God is
a consuming fire."[e]

Concluding Exhortations

13 Keep on loving each other as
brothers. 2Do not forget to entertain strangers, for by so doing some people have entertained angels without
knowing it. 3Remember those in prison as
if you were their fellow prisoners, and
those who are mistreated as if you yourselves were suffering.

4Marriage should be honored by all,
and the marriage bed kept pure, for God
will judge the adulterer and all the sexually immoral. 5Keep your lives free from
the love of money and be content with
what you have, because God has said,

"Never will I leave you;
never will I forsake you."[f]

6So we say with confidence,

"The Lord is my helper; I will not be
afraid.
What can man do to me?"[g]

7Remember your leaders, who spoke
the word of God to you. Consider the outcome of their way of life and imitate their
faith. 8Jesus Christ is the same yesterday
and today and forever.

9Do not be carried away by all kinds of
strange teachings. It is good for our hearts
to be strengthened by grace, not by
ceremonial foods, which are of no value
to those who eat them. 10We have an altar
from which those who minister at the
tabernacle have no right to eat.

11The high priest carries the blood of

[a]*13* Prov. 4:26 [b]*20* Exodus 19:12,13 [c]*21* Deut. 9:19 [d]*26* Haggai 2:6 [e]*29* Deut. 4:24
[f]*5* Deut. 31:6 [g]*6* Psalm 118:6,7

TUESDAY

VERSE FOR THE DAY:	*AUTHOR:*	*PASSAGE FOR THE DAY:*
Hebrews 13:5	*Sue Richards*	*Hebrews 13:1–6*

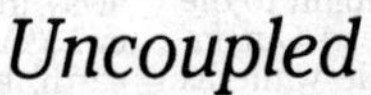

Uncoupled

MY husband of eight years left me at the beginning of my fourth month of pregnancy. I have never felt more rejected, vulnerable or unloved. I was nauseated, tired, and constantly trying to explain to my two-year-old son that Daddy wasn't coming back home because he didn't love Mommy anymore.

Michigan's howling winter winds, which seemed to seep through even brick walls, only added to my depression as I hauled groceries and toddler up three flights of stairs. We had just moved to Michigan from Virginia, and this was supposed to be our temporary apartment while our house in Virginia was being sold.

No house, no job, no husband, no church. Just an active little boy asking heartbreaking questions, a stomach that gagged at the thought of food, and an empty bed with sheets as cold as the February winds.

Yet, somewhere, there was something else too. It was deep inside my heart. It didn't feel overpowering or dramatic, but it gave me courage to get up each morning and make it through the day.

I knew that God loved me. I wish I could say I laughed in the face of all adversity, but I didn't. I sobbed into my pillow at night, then lay awake unable to breathe through my nose, wondering what would happen to me and my two babies.

I did more than wonder, though. I prayed. I prayed when I did my grocery shopping, when I bathed little Matthew, and when I strained over my ever-protruding belly to trim my toenails.

How reassuring it was for me in those lonely times to read God's words:

> Never will I leave you;
> never will I forsake you.

I held on to those words when I felt totally abandoned, totally alone. In those times, when I was willing to reach out to God and his reassuring words, he faithfully held me up.

Thank you, Lord, for granting me strength to live through the difficult times. And thank you for holding me up, especially in my most vulnerable moments.

Additional Scripture Readings:
Isaiah 40:11; 2 Corinthians 4:7–9

Go to page 349 for your next devotional reading.

animals into the Most Holy Place as a sin
offering, but the bodies are burned outside the camp. 12And so Jesus also suffered outside the city gate to make the
people holy through his own blood. 13Let
us, then, go to him outside the camp,
bearing the disgrace he bore. 14For here
we do not have an enduring city, but
we are looking for the city that is to
come.

15Through Jesus, therefore, let us continually offer to God a sacrifice of praise
—the fruit of lips that confess his name.
16And do not forget to do good and to
share with others, for with such sacrifices
God is pleased.

17Obey your leaders and submit to their
authority. They keep watch over you as
men who must give an account. Obey
them so that their work will be a joy, not
a burden, for that would be of no advantage to you.

18Pray for us. We are sure that we have
a clear conscience and desire to live hon-
orably in every way. 19I particularly urge
you to pray so that I may be restored to
you soon.

20May the God of peace, who through
the blood of the eternal covenant brought
back from the dead our Lord Jesus, that
great Shepherd of the sheep, 21equip you
with everything good for doing his will,
and may he work in us what is pleasing to
him, through Jesus Christ, to whom be
glory for ever and ever. Amen.

22Brothers, I urge you to bear with my
word of exhortation, for I have written
you only a short letter.

23I want you to know that our brother
Timothy has been released. If he arrives
soon, I will come with him to see you.

24Greet all your leaders and all God's
people. Those from Italy send you their
greetings.

25Grace be with you all.

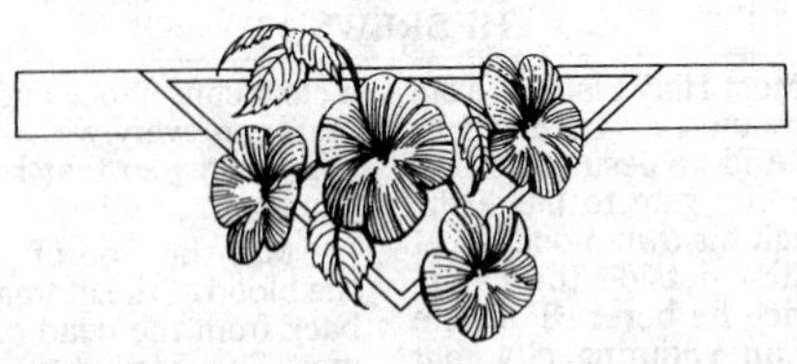

JAMES (a brother of Jesus) writes this letter to urge Christians to express their faith in daily living. He reminds them of what Jesus said, especially in the Sermon on the Mount (Matthew 5–7). As you read this book, ask yourself whether others can see by what you do and say that you believe in Jesus.

JAMES

1 James, a servant of God and of the
Lord Jesus Christ,

To the twelve tribes scattered among
the nations:

Greetings.

Trials and Temptations

2Consider it pure joy, my brothers,
whenever you face trials of many kinds,
3because you know that the testing of
your faith develops perseverance. 4Perse-
verance must finish its work so that you
may be mature and complete, not lacking
anything. 5If any of you lacks wisdom, he
should ask God, who gives generously to
all without finding fault, and it will be
given to him. 6But when he asks, he must
believe and not doubt, because he who
doubts is like a wave of the sea, blown
and tossed by the wind. 7That man should
not think he will receive anything from
the Lord; 8he is a double-minded man,
unstable in all he does.

9The brother in humble circumstances
ought to take pride in his high position.
10But the one who is rich should take
pride in his low position, because he will
pass away like a wild flower. 11For the sun
rises with scorching heat and withers the
plant; its blossom falls and its beauty is
destroyed. In the same way, the rich man
will fade away even while he goes about
his business.

12Blessed is the man who perseveres
under trial, because when he has stood
the test, he will receive the crown of life
that God has promised to those who love
him.

13When tempted, no one should say,
"God is tempting me." For God cannot be
tempted by evil, nor does he tempt anyone; 14but each one is tempted when, by
his own evil desire, he is dragged away
and enticed. 15Then, after desire has con-

ceived, it gives birth to sin; and sin, when
it is full-grown, gives birth to death.
16Don't be deceived, my dear brothers.
17Every good and perfect gift is from
above, coming down from the Father of
the heavenly lights, who does not change
like shifting shadows. 18He chose to give
us birth through the word of truth, that
we might be a kind of firstfruits of all he
created.

Listening and Doing

19My dear brothers, take note of this:
Everyone should be quick to listen, slow
to speak and slow to become angry, 20for
man's anger does not bring about the
righteous life that God desires. 21There-
fore, get rid of all moral filth and the evil
that is so prevalent and humbly accept
the word planted in you, which can save
you.
22Do not merely listen to the word, and
so deceive yourselves. Do what it says.
23Anyone who listens to the word but
does not do what it says is like a man who
looks at his face in a mirror 24and, after
looking at himself, goes away and immediately forgets what he looks like.
25But the man who looks intently into the
perfect law that gives freedom, and continues to do this, not forgetting what
he has heard, but doing it—he will be
blessed in what he does.
26If anyone considers himself religious
and yet does not keep a tight rein on his
tongue, he deceives himself and his religion is worthless. 27Religion that God our
Father accepts as pure and faultless is
this: to look after orphans and widows in
their distress and to keep oneself from
being polluted by the world.

Favoritism Forbidden

2 My brothers, as believers in our glorious Lord Jesus Christ, don't show
favoritism. 2Suppose a man comes into
your meeting wearing a gold ring and fine
clothes, and a poor man in shabby
clothes also comes in. 3If you show special attention to the man wearing fine

VERSE FOR THE DAY: *James 1:12*

AUTHOR: *Ruth Bell Graham*

PASSAGE FOR THE DAY: *James 1:12–15*

Temptations and Trials

TEMPTATION and testing (or a trial) are two sides of the same coin.

Satan uses an occasion or a person to tempt us to fall; God uses the same to try us and make us stronger. This we learn in Matthew 4:1 and the book of Job.

Additional Scripture Readings:
Job 2:3–8; 1 Peter 1:6–9

Go to page 351 for your next devotional reading.

clothes and say, "Here's a good seat for you," but say to the poor man, "You stand there" or "Sit on the floor by my feet," 4have you not discriminated among yourselves and become judges with evil thoughts?

5Listen, my dear brothers: Has not God chosen those who are poor in the eyes of the world to be rich in faith and to inherit the kingdom he promised those who love him? 6But you have insulted the poor. Is it not the rich who are exploiting you? Are they not the ones who are dragging you into court? 7Are they not the ones who are slandering the noble name of him to whom you belong?

8If you really keep the royal law found in Scripture, "Love your neighbor as yourself,"[a] you are doing right. 9But if you show favoritism, you sin and are convicted by the law as lawbreakers. 10For whoever keeps the whole law and yet stumbles at just one point is guilty of breaking all of it. 11For he who said, "Do not commit adultery,"[b] also said, "Do not murder."[c] If you do not commit adultery but do commit murder, you have become a lawbreaker.

12Speak and act as those who are going to be judged by the law that gives freedom, 13because judgment without mercy will be shown to anyone who has not been merciful. Mercy triumphs over judgment!

Faith and Deeds

14What good is it, my brothers, if a man claims to have faith but has no deeds? Can such faith save him? 15Suppose a brother or sister is without clothes and daily food. 16If one of you says to him, "Go, I wish you well; keep warm and well fed," but does nothing about his physical needs, what good is it? 17In the same way, faith by itself, if it is not accompanied by action, is dead.

18But someone will say, "You have faith; I have deeds."

Show me your faith without deeds, and I will show you my faith by what I do. 19You believe that there is one God. Good! Even the demons believe that—and shudder.

20You foolish man, do you want evidence that faith without deeds is useless[d]? 21Was not our ancestor Abraham considered righteous for what he did when he offered his son Isaac on the altar? 22You see that his faith and his actions were working together, and his faith was made complete by what he did. 23And the scripture was fulfilled that says, "Abraham believed God, and it was credited to him as righteousness,"[e] and he was called God's friend. 24You see that a person is justified by what he does and not by faith alone.

25In the same way, was not even Rahab the prostitute considered righteous for what she did when she gave lodging to the spies and sent them off in a different direction? 26As the body without the spirit is dead, so faith without deeds is dead.

Taming the Tongue

3 Not many of you should presume to be teachers, my brothers, because you know that we who teach will be judged more strictly. 2We all stumble in many ways. If anyone is never at fault in what he says, he is a perfect man, able to keep his whole body in check.

3When we put bits into the mouths of horses to make them obey us, we can turn the whole animal. 4Or take ships as an example. Although they are so large and are driven by strong winds, they are steered by a very small rudder wherever the pilot wants to go. 5Likewise the tongue is a small part of the body, but it makes great boasts. Consider what a great forest is set on fire by a small spark. 6The tongue also is a fire, a world of evil among the parts of the body. It corrupts the whole person, sets the whole course of his life on fire, and is itself set on fire by hell.

7All kinds of animals, birds, reptiles and creatures of the sea are being tamed and have been tamed by man, 8but no man can tame the tongue. It is a restless evil, full of deadly poison.

9With the tongue we praise our Lord and Father, and with it we curse men, who have been made in God's likeness. 10Out of the same mouth come praise and cursing. My brothers, this should not be. 11Can both fresh water and salt[f] water flow from the same spring? 12My brothers, can a fig tree bear olives, or a grapevine bear figs? Neither can a salt spring produce fresh water.

[a] *8* Lev. 19:18 [b] *11* Exodus 20:14; Deut. 5:18 [c] *11* Exodus 20:13; Deut. 5:17 [d] *20* Some early manuscripts *dead* [e] *23* Gen. 15:6 [f] *11* Greek *bitter* (see also verse 14)

THURSDAY

VERSE FOR THE DAY: *James 3:13*

AUTHOR: *Luci Swindoll*

PASSAGE FOR THE DAY: *James 3:13–18*

Real Wisdom

ONCE I asked my brother Chuck if he'd rather have wisdom or youth, presupposing the two don't reside in the same person at the same time. Without hesitation he answered, "Oh, wisdom, Sis, hands down. That way I don't keep doing the same dumb things I did as a kid." Then, with a twinkle in his eye, he added, "Of course, I'd really prefer having wisdom in a young body."

Sara Teasdale informs me, in her excellent poem "Wisdom," that when I calmly look life in the eye, having grown wise from beating and flapping against its imperfections, learning to compromise, and accepting the fact that everyone and everything has its shortcomings:

> Life will have given me the truth
> And taken in exchange, my youth.

Inadvertently, one is given up for the other.

There are two kinds of wisdom, the apostle James says: worldly wisdom that is contaminated, ambitious and envious; and heavenly wisdom that is pure, content, merciful and submissive. So to be spiritually wise, a person must exhibit understanding, acceptance and peace.

James also says that the one who is understanding and wise will show it by his "good life." It's taken me over fifty years to learn that the good life is *not* attaining a college degree, succeeding in one's career, owning an expensive car, having money in the bank or vacationing in Hawaii. While that stuff is wonderful and sweet to my worldly tastes, it's not the good life.

The good life is peace—knowing that I was considerate instead of crabby, that I stood by faithfully when all the chips were down for the other guy, that I sacrificially gave to a worthy cause, that I showed impartiality when I really wanted my preference, that I was real in the midst of phonies, that I was forgiving, that I had the courage to defer reward for something better down the road.

Why couldn't I have learned this when I still had a young body?

Additional Scripture Readings:
Proverbs 4:5–7; 1 Corinthians 2:6–13

Go to page 353 for your next devotional reading.

Two Kinds of Wisdom

13Who is wise and understanding among you? Let him show it by his good life, by deeds done in the humility that comes from wisdom. 14But if you harbor bitter envy and selfish ambition in your hearts, do not boast about it or deny the truth. 15Such "wisdom" does not come down from heaven but is earthly, unspiritual, of the devil. 16For where you have envy and selfish ambition, there you find disorder and every evil practice.

17But the wisdom that comes from heaven is first of all pure; then peace-loving, considerate, submissive, full of mercy and good fruit, impartial and sincere. 18Peacemakers who sow in peace raise a harvest of righteousness.

Submit Yourselves to God

4 What causes fights and quarrels among you? Don't they come from your desires that battle within you? 2You want something but don't get it. You kill and covet, but you cannot have what you want. You quarrel and fight. You do not have, because you do not ask God. 3When you ask, you do not receive, because you ask with wrong motives, that you may spend what you get on your pleasures.

4You adulterous people, don't you know that friendship with the world is hatred toward God? Anyone who chooses to be a friend of the world becomes an enemy of God. 5Or do you think Scripture says without reason that the spirit he caused to live in us envies intensely?[a] 6But he gives us more grace. That is why Scripture says:

"God opposes the proud
  but gives grace to the humble."[b]

7Submit yourselves, then, to God. Resist the devil, and he will flee from you. 8Come near to God and he will come near to you. Wash your hands, you sinners, and purify your hearts, you double-minded. 9Grieve, mourn and wail. Change your laughter to mourning and your joy to gloom. 10Humble yourselves before the Lord, and he will lift you up.

11Brothers, do not slander one another. Anyone who speaks against his brother or judges him speaks against the law and judges it. When you judge the law, you are not keeping it, but sitting in judgment on it. 12There is only one Lawgiver and Judge, the one who is able to save and destroy. But you—who are you to judge your neighbor?

Boasting About Tomorrow

13Now listen, you who say, "Today or tomorrow we will go to this or that city, spend a year there, carry on business and make money." 14Why, you do not even know what will happen tomorrow. What is your life? You are a mist that appears for a little while and then vanishes. 15Instead, you ought to say, "If it is the Lord's will, we will live and do this or that." 16As it is, you boast and brag. All such boasting is evil. 17Anyone, then, who knows the good he ought to do and doesn't do it, sins.

Warning to Rich Oppressors

5 Now listen, you rich people, weep and wail because of the misery that is coming upon you. 2Your wealth has rotted, and moths have eaten your clothes. 3Your gold and silver are corroded. Their corrosion will testify against you and eat your flesh like fire. You have hoarded wealth in the last days. 4Look! The wages you failed to pay the workmen who mowed your fields are crying out against you. The cries of the harvesters have reached the ears of the Lord Almighty. 5You have lived on earth in luxury and self-indulgence. You have fattened yourselves in the day of slaughter.[c] 6You have condemned and murdered innocent men, who were not opposing you.

Patience in Suffering

7Be patient, then, brothers, until the Lord's coming. See how the farmer waits for the land to yield its valuable crop and how patient he is for the autumn and spring rains. 8You too, be patient and stand firm, because the Lord's coming is near. 9Don't grumble against each other, brothers, or you will be judged. The Judge is standing at the door!

10Brothers, as an example of patience in the face of suffering, take the prophets who spoke in the name of the Lord. 11As you know, we consider blessed those who have persevered. You have heard of Job's perseverance and have seen what the Lord finally brought about. The Lord is full of compassion and mercy.

[a]5 Or *that God jealously longs for the spirit that he made to live in us*; or *that the Spirit he caused to live in us longs jealously* [b]6 Prov. 3:34 [c]5 Or *yourselves as in a day of feasting*

[12]Above all, my brothers, do not swear
—not by heaven or by earth or by anything else. Let your "Yes" be yes, and your
"No," no, or you will be condemned.

The Prayer of Faith

[13]Is any one of you in trouble? He
should pray. Is anyone happy? Let him
sing songs of praise. [14]Is any one of you
sick? He should call the elders of the
church to pray over him and anoint him
with oil in the name of the Lord. [15]And
the prayer offered in faith will make the
sick person well; the Lord will raise him
up. If he has sinned, he will be forgiven.
[16]Therefore confess your sins to each other and pray for each other so that you may
be healed. The prayer of a righteous man
is powerful and effective.

[17]Elijah was a man just like us. He
prayed earnestly that it would not rain,

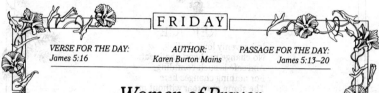

FRIDAY

VERSE FOR THE DAY: *James 5:16*

AUTHOR: *Karen Burton Mains*

PASSAGE FOR THE DAY: *James 5:13–20*

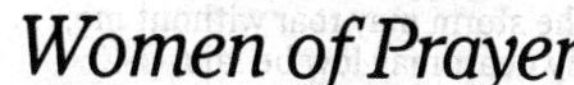

Women of Prayer

IN one year, Christianity lost three holy women of faith, Agnes Sanford, Corrie ten Boom and Catherine Marshall—as well as countless others whose names are unknown but who nevertheless did the work of God in this world. These are the women who knew what it meant to experience the presence of the unseen, who spent hours on their knees, who wept over the wounds of the world. For them, prayer was a second language. Who will take their place?

Frankly, there are very few candidates from our generation of women—those of us who have lavished hours in front of the television set, in the shopping plazas, in self-indulgence, in not developing a disciplined spiritual life.

Unless—unless, we begin to grow up spiritually. Unless we become convinced that we are the generation of Christian adults ultimately responsible for the spiritual condition of our nation. We must understand that there are increasingly few in that generation ahead of us left to pray over this world. We are coming of age. But are we coming to terms with our lack of spiritual depth and ability?

It is we who must learn the meaning of forbearing.

It is we who must develop the disciplines of spiritual perseverance, not shrinking back from growth but doing the will of God, having faith and keeping our souls.

It is we who must become women of faith and prayer and obedience and service.

It is we who must set a spiritual standard for the next generation.

It is time for us all to grow up.

Additional Scripture Readings:
Ephesians 6:18–20; Colossians 4:12–13

Go to page 354 for your next devotional reading.

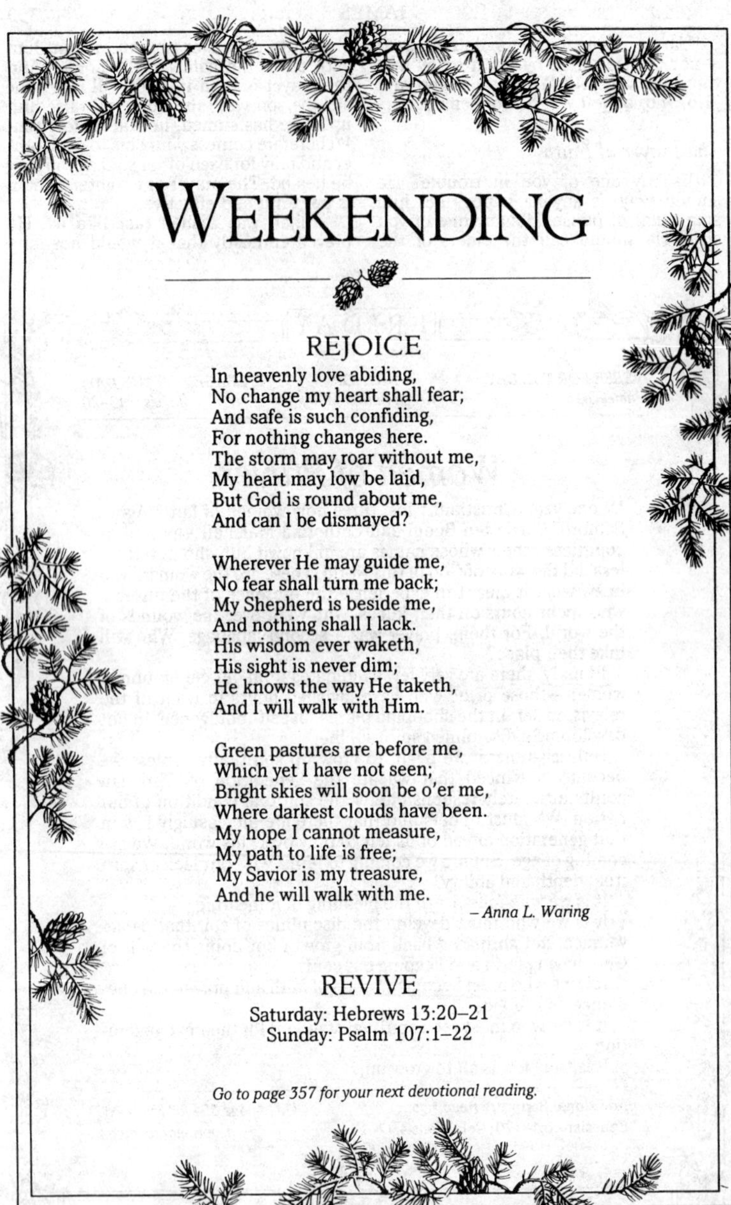

WEEKENDING

REJOICE

In heavenly love abiding,
No change my heart shall fear;
And safe is such confiding,
For nothing changes here.
The storm may roar without me,
My heart may low be laid,
But God is round about me,
And can I be dismayed?

Wherever He may guide me,
No fear shall turn me back;
My Shepherd is beside me,
And nothing shall I lack.
His wisdom ever waketh,
His sight is never dim;
He knows the way He taketh,
And I will walk with Him.

Green pastures are before me,
Which yet I have not seen;
Bright skies will soon be o'er me,
Where darkest clouds have been.
My hope I cannot measure,
My path to life is free;
My Savior is my treasure,
And he will walk with me.

– Anna L. Waring

REVIVE

Saturday: Hebrews 13:20–21
Sunday: Psalm 107:1–22

Go to page 357 for your next devotional reading.

and it did not rain on the land for three
and a half years. 18Again he prayed, and
the heavens gave rain, and the earth produced its crops.

19My brothers, if one of you should
wander from the truth and someone
should bring him back, 20remember this:
Whoever turns a sinner from the error of
his way will save him from death and cover over a multitude of sins.

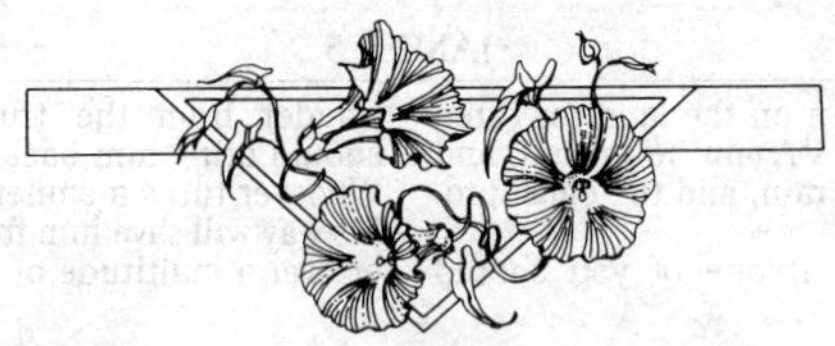

PETER writes this letter to a group of Christians suffering for their faith, reminding them of how much Jesus suffered. He inspires them with hope for the future and shows them how to grow in their faith. As you read this book, decide to do your best to live a holy life as you look forward to the return of Jesus and to the reward he promises to give his followers.

1 PETER

1 Peter, an apostle of Jesus Christ,
To God's elect, strangers in the
world, scattered throughout Pontus,
Galatia, Cappadocia, Asia and Bithynia,
2who have been chosen according to
the foreknowledge of God the Father,
through the sanctifying work of the Spirit,
for obedience to Jesus Christ and sprinkling by his blood:

Grace and peace be yours in abundance.

Praise to God for a Living Hope

3Praise be to the God and Father of our
Lord Jesus Christ! In his great mercy he
has given us new birth into a living hope
through the resurrection of Jesus Christ
from the dead, 4and into an inheritance
that can never perish, spoil or fade—kept
in heaven for you, 5who through faith are
shielded by God's power until the coming
of the salvation that is ready to be revealed in the last time. 6In this you greatly rejoice, though now for a little while
you may have had to suffer grief in all
kinds of trials. 7These have come so that
your faith—of greater worth than gold,
which perishes even though refined by
fire—may be proved genuine and may result in praise, glory and honor when Jesus
Christ is revealed. 8Though you have not
seen him, you love him; and even though
you do not see him now, you believe in
him and are filled with an inexpressible
and glorious joy, 9for you are receiving the
goal of your faith, the salvation of your
souls.

10Concerning this salvation, the prophets, who spoke of the grace that was to

come to you, searched intently and with
the greatest care, [11]trying to find out the
time and circumstances to which the
Spirit of Christ in them was pointing
when he predicted the sufferings of Christ
and the glories that would follow. [12]It was
revealed to them that they were not serving themselves but you, when they spoke
of the things that have now been told you
by those who have preached the gospel to
you by the Holy Spirit sent from heav-
en. Even angels long to look into these
things.

Be Holy

[13]Therefore, prepare your minds for action; be self-controlled; set your hope fully on the grace to be given you when Jesus
Christ is revealed. [14]As obedient children,
do not conform to the evil desires you had
when you lived in ignorance. [15]But just as
he who called you is holy, so be holy in all

MONDAY

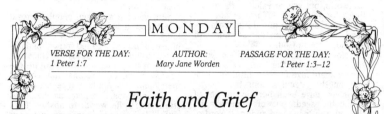

VERSE FOR THE DAY: *1 Peter 1:7* | *AUTHOR:* *Mary Jane Worden* | *PASSAGE FOR THE DAY:* *1 Peter 1:3–12*

Faith and Grief

IN the early years of my marriage I had, providentially, read many books about loss and grief, always reminding God that I was willing to help others through their crisis times. But in my prayers I also shared the desire to be spared this anguish in my own life.

For whatever reason, God chose not to spare me this deep pain. After the death of my husband Jim, in those agonizing early days, I knew enough about God's character to be able to say, "Someday I will be able to look back and say even out of this God has brought good." I can't imagine what good or how that could possibly be true; it goes contrary to everything I feel right now. But I choose to believe the truth of what I've been taught all these years about God's character. Someday it will be true.

Four years later, I can see good that God has done in our lives. Had I been given the choice, I would never have chosen this. But I am grateful for the growth that I see in all of us, although I would have wished it to come in another way. What we have learned in these four years about ourselves, about our world, about God is of great value. I feel confident that Jim would like the persons we are becoming.

The Scriptures teach that God will use suffering to build character and to purify our faith (see Romans 5 and 1 Peter 1). I can't presume to know all that he is doing in our lives; that he has allowed us to see a small part of it, I'm grateful.

Those strong words in Isaiah 61:1–3 ring true for me. Change. Growth. Healing. Beauty for ashes. Gladness for mourning. Praise out of despair. But the last phrase is all-important: that it might be to his glory, "for the display of his splendor."

Additional Scripture Readings:
Isaiah 61:1–3; Romans 5:3–5

Go to page 359 for your next devotional reading.

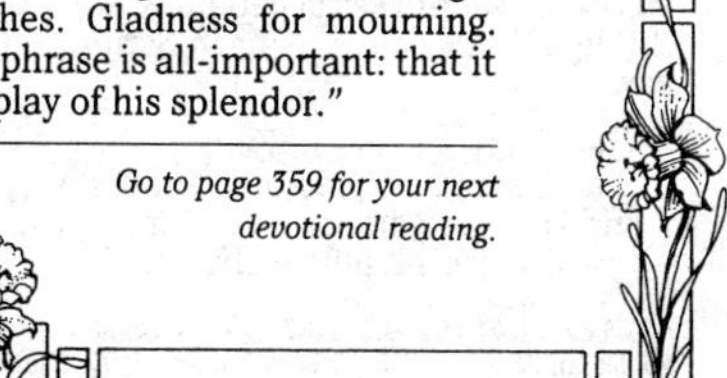

you do; 16for it is written: "Be holy, because I am holy."[a]

17Since you call on a Father who judges each man's work impartially, live your lives as strangers here in reverent fear. 18For you know that it was not with perishable things such as silver or gold that you were redeemed from the empty way of life handed down to you from your forefathers, 19but with the precious blood of Christ, a lamb without blemish or defect. 20He was chosen before the creation of the world, but was revealed in these last times for your sake. 21Through him you believe in God, who raised him from the dead and glorified him, and so your faith and hope are in God.

22Now that you have purified yourselves by obeying the truth so that you have sincere love for your brothers, love one another deeply, from the heart.[b] 23For you have been born again, not of perishable seed, but of imperishable, through the living and enduring word of God. 24For,

> "All men are like grass,
> and all their glory is like the
> flowers of the field;
> the grass withers and the flowers fall,
> 25 but the word of the Lord stands
> forever."[c]

And this is the word that was preached to you.

2 Therefore, rid yourselves of all malice and all deceit, hypocrisy, envy, and slander of every kind. 2Like newborn babies, crave pure spiritual milk, so that by it you may grow up in your salvation, 3now that you have tasted that the Lord is good.

The Living Stone and a Chosen People

4As you come to him, the living Stone—rejected by men but chosen by God and precious to him— 5you also, like living stones, are being built into a spiritual house to be a holy priesthood, offering spiritual sacrifices acceptable to God through Jesus Christ. 6For in Scripture it says:

> "See, I lay a stone in Zion,
> a chosen and precious cornerstone,
> and the one who trusts in him
> will never be put to shame."[d]

7Now to you who believe, this stone is precious. But to those who do not believe,

> "The stone the builders rejected
> has become the capstone,[e]"[f]

8and,

> "A stone that causes men to stumble
> and a rock that makes them fall."[g]

They stumble because they disobey the message—which is also what they were destined for.

9But you are a chosen people, a royal priesthood, a holy nation, a people belonging to God, that you may declare the praises of him who called you out of darkness into his wonderful light. 10Once you were not a people, but now you are the people of God; once you had not received mercy, but now you have received mercy.

11Dear friends, I urge you, as aliens and strangers in the world, to abstain from sinful desires, which war against your soul. 12Live such good lives among the pagans that, though they accuse you of doing wrong, they may see your good deeds and glorify God on the day he visits us.

Submission to Rulers and Masters

13Submit yourselves for the Lord's sake to every authority instituted among men: whether to the king, as the supreme authority, 14or to governors, who are sent by him to punish those who do wrong and to commend those who do right. 15For it is God's will that by doing good you should silence the ignorant talk of foolish men. 16Live as free men, but do not use your freedom as a cover-up for evil; live as servants of God. 17Show proper respect to everyone: Love the brotherhood of believers, fear God, honor the king.

18Slaves, submit yourselves to your masters with all respect, not only to those who are good and considerate, but also to those who are harsh. 19For it is commendable if a man bears up under the pain of unjust suffering because he is conscious of God. 20But how is it to your credit if you receive a beating for doing wrong and endure it? But if you suffer for doing good and you endure it, this is commendable before God. 21To this you were called, because Christ suffered for you, leaving you an example, that you should follow in his steps.

[a] *16* Lev. 11:44,45; 19:2; 20:7 [b] *22* Some early manuscripts *from a pure heart* [c] *25* Isaiah 40:6-8
[d] *6* Isaiah 28:16 [e] *7* Or *cornerstone* [f] *7* Psalm 118:22 [g] *8* Isaiah 8:14

TUESDAY

VERSE FOR THE DAY:
1 Peter 1:16

AUTHOR:
June Hunt

PASSAGE FOR THE DAY:
1 Peter 1:13–25

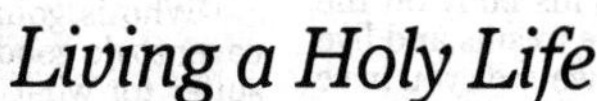

Living a Holy Life

HAVE you had difficulty with this Scripture verse: "Be holy, because I am holy" (Leviticus 11:44; 1 Peter 1:16)? Since most people think being holy is synonymous with being sinless, who could possibly be holy? It's unattainable . . . unimaginable!

A friend once said to me, "I know *holy* means 'set apart,' but I don't want to be set apart. That sounds like being in quarantine for having a constant case of measles!" Some people *do* think of a holy person as one who lives a monkish existence, praying twenty-three hours a day in order to avoid sin. Holiness, however, does not bring isolation but integration. With Christ in you, his character becomes a part of you so that his nature may be expressed through you. In other words, Christlikeness will come out of you *naturally.*

When I was little, my Uncle Jimmy walked me through his watermelon patch in Idabel, Oklahoma. Holding a tiny black seed he said, "These big melons grew from seeds just like this one." That seemed impossible to me! Yet eighty miles from Idabel is Hope, Arkansas, the town where something more "impossible" became reality. Young Jason Bright gave his watermelon seed proper care and the right environment to grow. The result? A world-record 260-pound watermelon! Watermelon seeds simply do what comes naturally to them—they grow. Their seeds are set apart by God for that purpose.

When you are set apart by God, holiness becomes natural. The Father is the gardener; Christ is the seed. With Christ in you, you will grow to be like him. It is explained in 1 John 3:9:

> No one who is born of God will continue to sin, because God's seed remains in him.

It is natural for the Lord not to sin. Therefore, with God's seed in you, it becomes increasingly natural for you not to sin. What seems impossible becomes possible. You will not become instantly sinless, but you will sin less and less and less.

God calls you holy. With his presence inside you, he will produce the impossible through you. Why settle for anything less?

Additional Scripture Readings:
Colossians 3:12–17; Hebrews 12:10–14

Go to page 361 for your next devotional reading.

22"He committed no sin,
and no deceit was found in his mouth."[a]

23When they hurled their insults at him, he did not retaliate; when he suffered, he made no threats. Instead, he entrusted himself to him who judges justly. 24He himself bore our sins in his body on the tree, so that we might die to sins and live for righteousness; by his wounds you have been healed. 25For you were like sheep going astray, but now you have returned to the Shepherd and Overseer of your souls.

Wives and Husbands

3 Wives, in the same way be submissive to your husbands so that, if any of them do not believe the word, they may be won over without words by the behavior of their wives, 2when they see the purity and reverence of your lives. 3Your beauty should not come from outward adornment, such as braided hair and the wearing of gold jewelry and fine clothes. 4Instead, it should be that of your inner self, the unfading beauty of a gentle and quiet spirit, which is of great worth in God's sight. 5For this is the way the holy women of the past who put their hope in God used to make themselves beautiful. They were submissive to their own husbands, 6like Sarah, who obeyed Abraham and called him her master. You are her daughters if you do what is right and do not give way to fear.

7Husbands, in the same way be considerate as you live with your wives, and treat them with respect as the weaker partner and as heirs with you of the gracious gift of life, so that nothing will hinder your prayers.

Suffering for Doing Good

8Finally, all of you, live in harmony with one another; be sympathetic, love as brothers, be compassionate and humble. 9Do not repay evil with evil or insult with insult, but with blessing, because to this you were called so that you may inherit a blessing. 10For,

"Whoever would love life
and see good days
must keep his tongue from evil
and his lips from deceitful speech.
11He must turn from evil and do good;
he must seek peace and pursue it.
12For the eyes of the Lord are on the righteous
and his ears are attentive to their prayer,
but the face of the Lord is against those who do evil."[b]

13Who is going to harm you if you are eager to do good? 14But even if you should suffer for what is right, you are blessed. "Do not fear what they fear[c]; do not be frightened."[d] 15But in your hearts set apart Christ as Lord. Always be prepared to give an answer to everyone who asks you to give the reason for the hope that you have. But do this with gentleness and respect, 16keeping a clear conscience, so that those who speak maliciously against your good behavior in Christ may be ashamed of their slander. 17It is better, if it is God's will, to suffer for doing good than for doing evil. 18For Christ died for sins once for all, the righteous for the unrighteous, to bring you to God. He was put to death in the body but made alive by the Spirit, 19through whom[e] also he went and preached to the spirits in prison 20who disobeyed long ago when God waited patiently in the days of Noah while the ark was being built. In it only a few people, eight in all, were saved through water, 21and this water symbolizes baptism that now saves you also—not the removal of dirt from the body but the pledge[f] of a good conscience toward God. It saves you by the resurrection of Jesus Christ, 22who has gone into heaven and is at God's right hand—with angels, authorities and powers in submission to him.

Living for God

4 Therefore, since Christ suffered in his body, arm yourselves also with the same attitude, because he who has suffered in his body is done with sin. 2As a result, he does not live the rest of his earthly life for evil human desires, but rather for the will of God. 3For you have spent enough time in the past doing what pagans choose to do—living in debauchery, lust, drunkenness, orgies, carousing and detestable idolatry. 4They think it strange that you do not plunge with them into the same flood of dissipation, and they heap abuse on you. 5But they will have to give account to him who is ready

[a] *22* Isaiah 53:9 [b] *12* Psalm 34:12-16 [c] *14* Or *not fear their threats* [d] *14* Isaiah 8:12
[e] *18,19* Or *alive in the spirit, 19through which* [f] *21* Or *response*

VERSE FOR THE DAY:
1 Peter 3:1

AUTHOR:
Beverly LaHaye

PASSAGE FOR THE DAY:
1 Peter 3:1–6

So They May Be Won Over

DURING the span of wonderful years of ministry God has given my husband and me, it has been our joy to have helped many couples during times of marital difficulty. Sometimes they were helped by reading one of our books relating to their problem, but often help came through a personal counseling meeting.

One such meeting took place several years ago when a lovely Christian woman came to us with a troubled, broken heart. She was married to a man who had professed Jesus Christ years before but who had turned away from those beliefs. Her story revealed that he was conducting himself in a manner that was disobedient to God's Word, making her miserable also.

The natural reaction for many wives caught in these circumstances is to lash back and to shut her husband out of her life. This woman quickly learned that if she took matters into her own hands there would not be much need for communication. Her heart resisted his role as head of the home.

In her attempt to separate herself from her husband—even though they remained living together—she decided to join an evening Bible study just to get out of the house.

God began to work in her heart and impress upon her that she was disobeying him by the way she lived and conducted herself. She learned through study of the Word that submission to and love for her husband was an outgrowth of spiritual development and a close relationship with the Lord.

As this woman sat before us one evening, pouring out her heart to the Lord, she longed for a close relationship with both God and her husband. We read 1 Peter 3:1–6 to her and challenged her to obey the principles taught there.

Not every wife's story ends on such a happy note, but this lovely woman found that God could change her conduct and give her a gentle and quiet spirit. As a result, her husband changed and began to walk in obedience to God.

Additional Scripture Readings:
Ephesians 5:22–33; Titus 2:3–5

Go to page 362 for your next devotional reading.

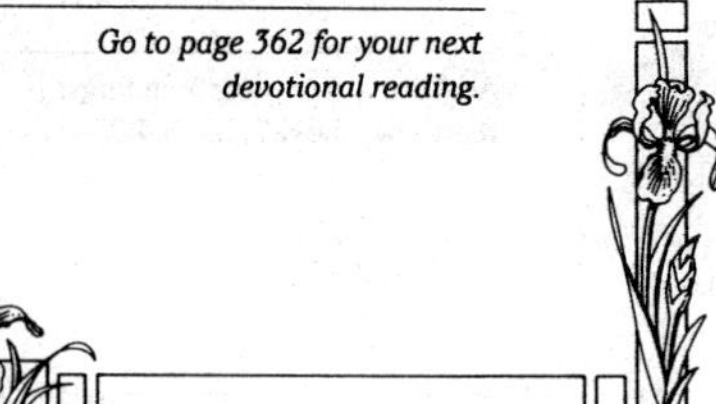

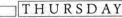

VERSE FOR THE DAY:	*AUTHOR:*	*PASSAGE FOR THE DAY:*
1 Peter 5:10	*Beth Donigan Seversen*	*1 Peter 5:1–11*

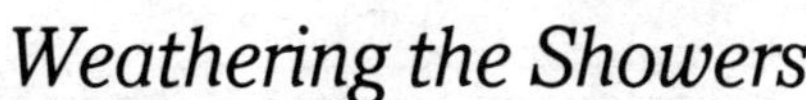

Weathering the Showers

THE *Water Garden*, by Claude Monet, is one of my favorite paintings. You will find the original in an impressionist museum, de l'Orangerie, in Paris. It is painted in the round and hangs in a circular room. When you stand in the center of the room you are completely engulfed in a luxuriant water garden!

My print, hanging over the desk in my office, is only a small representation of the delightful, full-scale original. If you study the painting, one of the surprises you will find is that the major part of the canvas is covered in dark shades of black, blue and green. These rather drab colors stand in stark contrast to the delicate pastels. Actually, they serve to highlight the beautiful florals, which appear rich and striking upon the deep, dark waters. At first glance, your eyes are drawn to the colorful petals; then you realize that Monet painted the dark tones to enhance the lighter.

Monet's painting has much to remind me about the water garden of my life, and of its Artist. First, it encourages me that there is a purpose and design to my life, and that perhaps, at times, I focus too exclusively on the darker portions of my painting.

It also reminds me that my Lord, the Artist of my life, has intentionally allowed the blue, green, and, yes, sometimes even the gray and black hues to be brushed on my canvas for a reason. God uses these shadows to make my life richer. Often, when I look back on difficulties, such as my father's death, times when I have been misunderstood by friends or my expectations have been dashed, I can see, now, his handiwork creating a brilliance of color and beauty from pain and suffering. The Artist uses a multitude of techniques in our lives to help us become the people he created us to be.

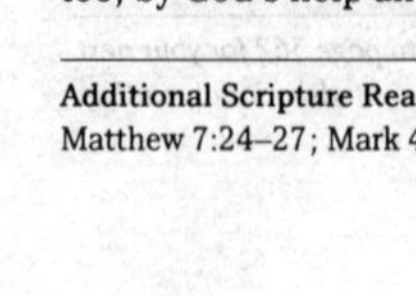

Finally, I am reminded that just like the water lilies in Monet's masterpiece, God keeps the leaves and petals afloat through the muck, wind and rain that are part of the storms of life. Water gardens survive April showers and worse, and I will too, by God's help and grace.

Additional Scripture Readings:
Matthew 7:24–27; Mark 4:35–41

Go to page 365 for your next devotional reading.

to judge the living and the dead. 6For this is the reason the gospel was preached even to those who are now dead, so that they might be judged according to men in regard to the body, but live according to God in regard to the spirit.

7The end of all things is near. Therefore be clear minded and self-controlled so that you can pray. 8Above all, love each other deeply, because love covers over a multitude of sins. 9Offer hospitality to one another without grumbling. 10Each one should use whatever gift he has received to serve others, faithfully administering God's grace in its various forms. 11If anyone speaks, he should do it as one speaking the very words of God. If anyone serves, he should do it with the strength God provides, so that in all things God may be praised through Jesus Christ. To him be the glory and the power for ever and ever. Amen.

Suffering for Being a Christian

12Dear friends, do not be surprised at the painful trial you are suffering, as though something strange were happening to you. 13But rejoice that you participate in the sufferings of Christ, so that you may be overjoyed when his glory is revealed. 14If you are insulted because of the name of Christ, you are blessed, for the Spirit of glory and of God rests on you. 15If you suffer, it should not be as a murderer or thief or any other kind of criminal, or even as a meddler. 16However, if you suffer as a Christian, do not be ashamed, but praise God that you bear that name. 17For it is time for judgment to begin with the family of God; and if it begins with us, what will the outcome be for those who do not obey the gospel of God? 18And,

"If it is hard for the righteous to be saved,
what will become of the ungodly
and the sinner?"[a]

19So then, those who suffer according to God's will should commit themselves to their faithful Creator and continue to do good.

To Elders and Young Men

5 To the elders among you, I appeal as a fellow elder, a witness of Christ's sufferings and one who also will share in the glory to be revealed: 2Be shepherds of God's flock that is under your care, serving as overseers—not because you must, but because you are willing, as God wants you to be; not greedy for money, but eager to serve; 3not lording it over those entrusted to you, but being examples to the flock. 4And when the Chief Shepherd appears, you will receive the crown of glory that will never fade away.

5Young men, in the same way be submissive to those who are older. All of you, clothe yourselves with humility toward one another, because,

"God opposes the proud
but gives grace to the humble."[b]

6Humble yourselves, therefore, under God's mighty hand, that he may lift you up in due time. 7Cast all your anxiety on him because he cares for you.

8Be self-controlled and alert. Your enemy the devil prowls around like a roaring lion looking for someone to devour. 9Resist him, standing firm in the faith, because you know that your brothers throughout the world are undergoing the same kind of sufferings.

10And the God of all grace, who called you to his eternal glory in Christ, after you have suffered a little while, will himself restore you and make you strong, firm and steadfast. 11To him be the power for ever and ever. Amen.

Final Greetings

12With the help of Silas,[c] whom I regard as a faithful brother, I have written to you briefly, encouraging you and testifying that this is the true grace of God. Stand fast in it.

13She who is in Babylon, chosen together with you, sends you her greetings, and so does my son Mark. 14Greet one another with a kiss of love.

Peace to all of you who are in Christ.

[a]*18* Prov. 11:31 [b]*5* Prov. 3:34 [c]*12* Greek *Silvanus*, a variant of *Silas*

PETER writes a second letter because false teachers are troubling the church and disturbing the faith of some by their heresy, immorality and greed. He wants Christians to grow in the knowledge of the truth of God's Word. As you read this book, remember that God will eventually win the battle against false teaching, and promise the Lord that you will study to increase your knowledge of the Bible.

2 PETER

1 Simon Peter, a servant and apostle of Jesus Christ,

To those who through the righteousness of our God and Savior Jesus Christ have received a faith as precious as ours:

2Grace and peace be yours in abundance through the knowledge of God and of Jesus our Lord.

Making One's Calling and Election Sure

3His divine power has given us everything we need for life and godliness
through our knowledge of him who called
us by his own glory and goodness.
4Through these he has given us his very
great and precious promises, so that
through them you may participate in the
divine nature and escape the corruption
in the world caused by evil desires.

5For this very reason, make every effort
to add to your faith goodness; and to
goodness, knowledge; 6and to knowledge,
self-control; and to self-control, perseverance; and to perseverance, godliness;
7and to godliness, brotherly kindness;
and to brotherly kindness, love. 8For if
you possess these qualities in increasing
measure, they will keep you from being
ineffective and unproductive in your
knowledge of our Lord Jesus Christ. 9But
if anyone does not have them, he is nearsighted and blind, and has forgotten that
he has been cleansed from his past
sins.

10Therefore, my brothers, be all the
more eager to make your calling and elec-

tion sure. For if you do these things, you
will never fall, 11and you will receive a
rich welcome into the eternal kingdom of
our Lord and Savior Jesus Christ.

Prophecy of Scripture

12So I will always remind you of these
things, even though you know them and
are firmly established in the truth you
now have. 13I think it is right to refresh
your memory as long as I live in the tent
of this body, 14because I know that I will
soon put it aside, as our Lord Jesus Christ
has made clear to me. 15And I will make
every effort to see that after my departure
you will always be able to remember
these things.
16We did not follow cleverly invented
stories when we told you about the power
and coming of our Lord Jesus Christ, but
we were eyewitnesses of his majesty.
17For he received honor and glory from
God the Father when the voice came to
him from the Majestic Glory, saying,
"This is my Son, whom I love; with him I

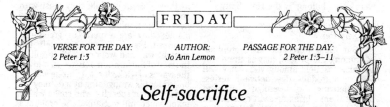

FRIDAY

VERSE FOR THE DAY: 2 Peter 1:3 | *AUTHOR:* Jo Ann Lemon | *PASSAGE FOR THE DAY:* 2 Peter 1:3–11

Self-sacrifice

THERE were once two porcupines who lived in Alaska. Desiring to get warm, they drew close to each other. As they did, they needled one another. It hurt so much that they pulled apart. But when they did, they got cold again, so they drew close once more, and hurt each other as before. Their predicament—they were either cold or hurting.

All too often this is the situation even in Christian homes. Personality differences are like the quills of the porcupines. They can get tangled and cause hurt. We must work at our relationships so that we will demonstrate the Christlike qualities of love, compassion, self-sacrifice and a forgiving spirit. The motto for our homes should be: "Be completely humble and gentle; be patient, bearing with one another in love" (Ephesians 4:2).

Love demonstrates itself in action. Have we done something today to demonstrate our love for our families? Love takes pleasure in its object. Jesus' example of love and compassion teaches us that it is possible for these qualities to be part of our Christian homes.

Self-sacrifice is against our human nature, yet it should be part of our "new nature." If each of us had an attitude of self-sacrifice, what a change would come about in the atmosphere of our homes. Self-sacrifice is total unselfishness.

Loving unselfishly does not mean making the least of ourselves but making the most of someone else. We view the other person through the eyes of Jesus.

This thought can transform relationships in our homes, especially with our unsaved loved ones!

Additional Scripture Readings:
Romans 12:9–13; 1 John 3:11–18

Go to page 367 for your next devotional reading.

am well pleased."[a] 18We ourselves heard this voice that came from heaven when we were with him on the sacred mountain.

19And we have the word of the prophets made more certain, and you will do well to pay attention to it, as to a light shining in a dark place, until the day dawns and the morning star rises in your hearts. 20Above all, you must understand that no prophecy of Scripture came about by the prophet's own interpretation. 21For prophecy never had its origin in the will of man, but men spoke from God as they were carried along by the Holy Spirit.

False Teachers and Their Destruction

2 But there were also false prophets among the people, just as there will be false teachers among you. They will secretly introduce destructive heresies, even denying the sovereign Lord who bought them—bringing swift destruction on themselves. 2Many will follow their shameful ways and will bring the way of truth into disrepute. 3In their greed these teachers will exploit you with stories they have made up. Their condemnation has long been hanging over them, and their destruction has not been sleeping.

4For if God did not spare angels when they sinned, but sent them to hell,[b] putting them into gloomy dungeons[c] to be held for judgment; 5if he did not spare the ancient world when he brought the flood on its ungodly people, but protected Noah, a preacher of righteousness, and seven others; 6if he condemned the cities of Sodom and Gomorrah by burning them to ashes, and made them an example of what is going to happen to the ungodly; 7and if he rescued Lot, a righteous man, who was distressed by the filthy lives of lawless men 8(for that righteous man, living among them day after day, was tormented in his righteous soul by the lawless deeds he saw and heard)— 9if this is so, then the Lord knows how to rescue godly men from trials and to hold the unrighteous for the day of judgment, while continuing their punishment.[d] 10This is especially true of those who follow the corrupt desire of the sinful nature[e] and despise authority.

Bold and arrogant, these men are not afraid to slander celestial beings; 11yet even angels, although they are stronger and more powerful, do not bring slanderous accusations against such beings in the presence of the Lord. 12But these men blaspheme in matters they do not understand. They are like brute beasts, creatures of instinct, born only to be caught and destroyed, and like beasts they too will perish.

13They will be paid back with harm for the harm they have done. Their idea of pleasure is to carouse in broad daylight. They are blots and blemishes, reveling in their pleasures while they feast with you.[f] 14With eyes full of adultery, they never stop sinning; they seduce the unstable; they are experts in greed—an accursed brood! 15They have left the straight way and wandered off to follow the way of Balaam son of Beor, who loved the wages of wickedness. 16But he was rebuked for his wrongdoing by a donkey—a beast without speech—who spoke with a man's voice and restrained the prophet's madness.

17These men are springs without water and mists driven by a storm. Blackest darkness is reserved for them. 18For they mouth empty, boastful words and, by appealing to the lustful desires of sinful human nature, they entice people who are just escaping from those who live in error. 19They promise them freedom, while they themselves are slaves of depravity—for a man is a slave to whatever has mastered him. 20If they have escaped the corruption of the world by knowing our Lord and Savior Jesus Christ and are again entangled in it and overcome, they are worse off at the end than they were at the beginning. 21It would have been better for them not to have known the way of righteousness, than to have known it and then to turn their backs on the sacred command that was passed on to them. 22Of them the proverbs are true: "A dog returns to its vomit,"[g] and, "A sow that is washed goes back to her wallowing in the mud."

The Day of the Lord

3 Dear friends, this is now my second letter to you. I have written both of them as reminders to stimulate you to wholesome thinking. 2I want you to recall the words spoken in the past by the holy

[a]17 Matt. 17:5; Mark 9:7; Luke 9:35 [b]4 Greek *Tartarus* [c]4 Some manuscripts *into chains of darkness* [d]9 Or *unrighteous for punishment until the day of judgment* [e]10 Or *the flesh* [f]13 Some manuscripts *in their love feasts* [g]22 Prov. 26:11

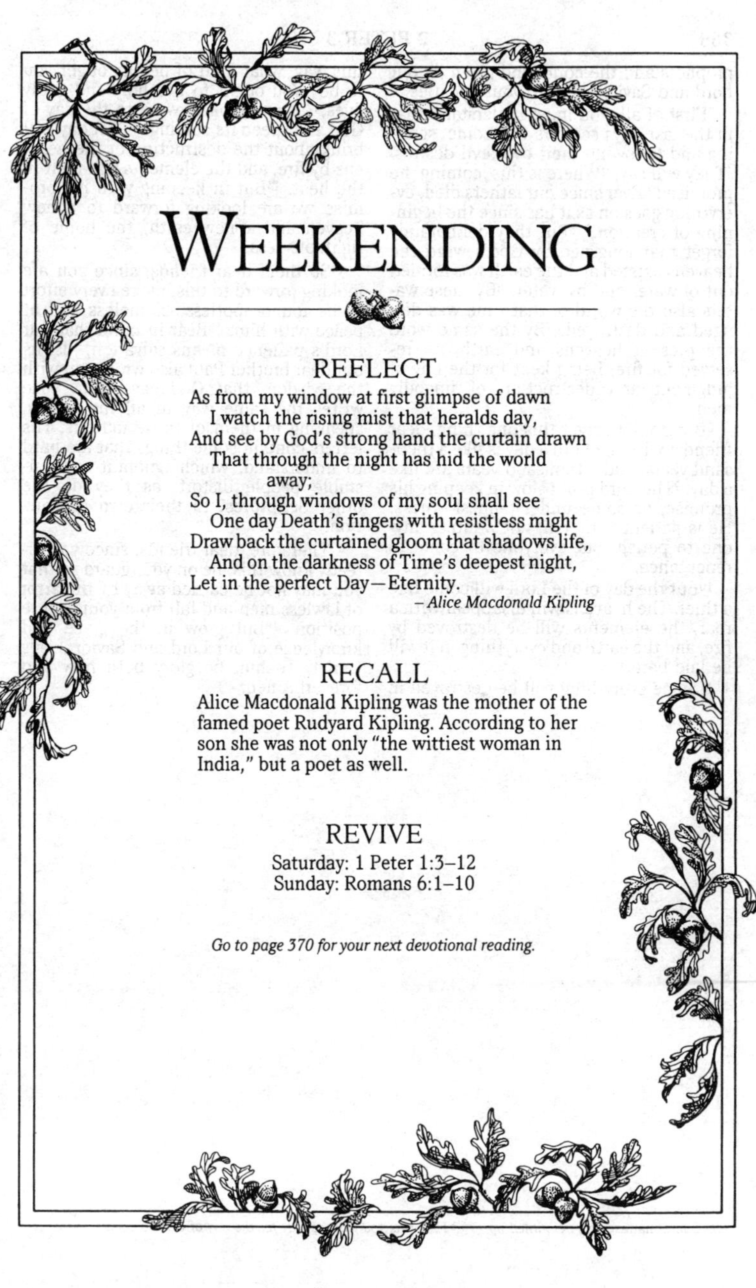

WEEKENDING

REFLECT

As from my window at first glimpse of dawn
I watch the rising mist that heralds day,
And see by God's strong hand the curtain drawn
That through the night has hid the world
away;
So I, through windows of my soul shall see
One day Death's fingers with resistless might
Draw back the curtained gloom that shadows life,
And on the darkness of Time's deepest night,
Let in the perfect Day—Eternity.

—Alice Macdonald Kipling

RECALL

Alice Macdonald Kipling was the mother of the famed poet Rudyard Kipling. According to her son she was not only "the wittiest woman in India," but a poet as well.

REVIVE

Saturday: 1 Peter 1:3–12
Sunday: Romans 6:1–10

Go to page 370 for your next devotional reading.

prophets and the command given by our
Lord and Savior through your apostles.

3First of all, you must understand that
in the last days scoffers will come, scoff-
ing and following their own evil desires.
4They will say, "Where is this 'coming' he
promised? Ever since our fathers died, everything goes on as it has since the beginning of creation." 5But they deliberately
forget that long ago by God's word the
heavens existed and the earth was formed
out of water and by water. 6By these waters also the world of that time was del-
uged and destroyed. 7By the same word
the present heavens and earth are reserved for fire, being kept for the day of
judgment and destruction of ungodly
men.

8But do not forget this one thing, dear
friends: With the Lord a day is like a thousand years, and a thousand years are like
a day. 9The Lord is not slow in keeping his
promise, as some understand slowness.
He is patient with you, not wanting anyone to perish, but everyone to come to
repentance.

10But the day of the Lord will come like
a thief. The heavens will disappear with a
roar; the elements will be destroyed by
fire, and the earth and everything in it will
be laid bare.[a]

11Since everything will be destroyed in
this way, what kind of people ought you
to be? You ought to live holy and godly
lives 12as you look forward to the day of
God and speed its coming.[b] That day will
bring about the destruction of the heavens by fire, and the elements will melt in
the heat. 13But in keeping with his promise we are looking forward to a new
heaven and a new earth, the home of
righteousness.

14So then, dear friends, since you are
looking forward to this, make every effort
to be found spotless, blameless and at
peace with him. 15Bear in mind that our
Lord's patience means salvation, just as
our dear brother Paul also wrote you with
the wisdom that God gave him. 16He
writes the same way in all his letters,
speaking in them of these matters. His
letters contain some things that are hard
to understand, which ignorant and unstable people distort, as they do the
other Scriptures, to their own destruction.

17Therefore, dear friends, since you already know this, be on your guard so that
you may not be carried away by the error
of lawless men and fall from your secure
position. 18But grow in the grace and
knowledge of our Lord and Savior Jesus
Christ. To him be glory both now and
forever! Amen.

[a] *10* Some manuscripts *be burned up* [b] *12* Or *as you wait eagerly for the day of God to come*

JOHN writes this first letter to emphasize some of the same themes as his Gospel (such as "walking in the light," "knowing the truth," and "loving one another"). He does so because antichrists are promoting false views of the Son of God. As you read this book, realize how much God wants you to fight sin, to love others and to believe in the true Jesus for eternal life.

1 JOHN

The Word of Life

1 That which was from the beginning,
which we have heard, which we have
seen with our eyes, which we have looked
at and our hands have touched—this we
proclaim concerning the Word of life.
2The life appeared; we have seen it and
testify to it, and we proclaim to you the
eternal life, which was with the Father
and has appeared to us. 3We proclaim to
you what we have seen and heard, so that
you also may have fellowship with us.
And our fellowship is with the Father and
with his Son, Jesus Christ. 4We write this
to make our[a] joy complete.

Walking in the Light

5This is the message we have heard
from him and declare to you: God is light;
in him there is no darkness at all. 6If we
claim to have fellowship with him yet
walk in the darkness, we lie and do not
live by the truth. 7But if we walk in the
light, as he is in the light, we have fellowship
with one another, and the blood of
Jesus, his Son, purifies us from all[b] sin.

8If we claim to be without sin, we deceive
ourselves and the truth is not in us.
9If we confess our sins, he is faithful and
just and will forgive us our sins and purify
us from all unrighteousness. 10If we claim
we have not sinned, we make him out to
be a liar and his word has no place in our
lives.

2 My dear children, I write this to you
so that you will not sin. But if anybody
does sin, we have one who speaks to

[a]4 Some manuscripts *your* [b]7 Or *every*

MONDAY

VERSE FOR THE DAY:
1 John 1:3–4

AUTHOR:
Rosemary Jensen

PASSAGE FOR THE DAY:
1 John 1:1–10

Telling Brings Fellowship

IN 1 John 1:3–4 we see John eager to tell his friends and associates what he knows of Jesus—what he has "seen and heard." It seems that he could hardly wait to tell them, because by telling them what he knew of Jesus he would promote fellowship with his friends. True fellowship was what John wanted, and it is what we want too. Fellowship is not just camaraderie; it is what two or more people experience when they have the same goals and desires, when they think alike and communicate in such a way as to actually enter into the other's experience.

John wanted this kind of communication with his friends. It was as if he was saying to them, "Let me tell you what I have seen and heard of Jesus Christ *so that* we may have the same mind about him, the same desire to know him better, the same experience of him." Then he goes on to say that we will have this fellowship because we have fellowship with the same Father and the same Son, Jesus Christ. We fellowship with God (the Father and the Son), and he brings us into fellowship with each other. He is the basis for our fellowship because together we share his life.

Are you eager to declare to your family and friends what you have "seen and heard" of Jesus Christ so that you may enter into true fellowship with them? Telling them about Jesus (and also listening to them tell you!) is the most fulfilling experience you can have with other human beings. Exchanging the knowledge of Jesus Christ with others will bring you greater joy than you can imagine. At least that's what John says in 1 John 1:4: "We write this to make our [and your] joy complete." *Telling brings fellowship and fellowship brings joy.*

Talking with others about Jesus is always risky. They may label you a fanatic. You may risk turning them off. But it is worth the risk, because it will bring that complete joy you desperately desire.

Additional Scripture Readings:
Galatians 2:8–9; 3 John 3–4

Go to page 373 for your next devotional reading.

the Father in our defense—Jesus Christ,
the Righteous One. 2He is the atoning
sacrifice for our sins, and not only for ours
but also for[a] the sins of the whole world.
3We know that we have come to know
him if we obey his commands. 4The man
who says, "I know him," but does not do
what he commands is a liar, and the truth
is not in him. 5But if anyone obeys his
word, God's love[b] is truly made complete
in him. This is how we know we are in
him: 6Whoever claims to live in him must
walk as Jesus did.
7Dear friends, I am not writing you a
new command but an old one, which you
have had since the beginning. This old
command is the message you have heard.
8Yet I am writing you a new command; its
truth is seen in him and you, because the
darkness is passing and the true light is
already shining.
9Anyone who claims to be in the light
but hates his brother is still in the darkness. 10Whoever loves his brother lives in
the light, and there is nothing in him[c] to
make him stumble. 11But whoever hates
his brother is in the darkness and walks
around in the darkness; he does not know
where he is going, because the darkness
has blinded him.

12I write to you, dear children,
because your sins have been
forgiven on account of his
name.
13I write to you, fathers,
because you have known him who
is from the beginning.
I write to you, young men,
because you have overcome the evil
one.
I write to you, dear children,
because you have known the
Father.
14I write to you, fathers,
because you have known him who
is from the beginning.
I write to you, young men,
because you are strong,
and the word of God lives in you,
and you have overcome the evil
one.

Do Not Love the World

15Do not love the world or anything in
the world. If anyone loves the world, the
love of the Father is not in him. 16For everything in the world—the cravings of
sinful man, the lust of his eyes and the
boasting of what he has and does—comes
not from the Father but from the world.
17The world and its desires pass away, but
the man who does the will of God lives
forever.

Warning Against Antichrists

18Dear children, this is the last hour;
and as you have heard that the antichrist
is coming, even now many antichrists
have come. This is how we know it is the
last hour. 19They went out from us, but
they did not really belong to us. For if
they had belonged to us, they would have
remained with us; but their going showed
that none of them belonged to us.
20But you have an anointing from the
Holy One, and all of you know the truth.[d]
21I do not write to you because you do not
know the truth, but because you do know
it and because no lie comes from the
truth. 22Who is the liar? It is the man who
denies that Jesus is the Christ. Such a
man is the antichrist—he denies the Father and the Son. 23No one who denies
the Son has the Father; whoever acknowledges the Son has the Father also.
24See that what you have heard from
the beginning remains in you. If it does,
you also will remain in the Son and in the
Father. 25And this is what he promised
us—even eternal life.
26I am writing these things to you about
those who are trying to lead you astray.
27As for you, the anointing you received
from him remains in you, and you do not
need anyone to teach you. But as his
anointing teaches you about all things
and as that anointing is real, not counterfeit—just as it has taught you, remain in
him.

Children of God

28And now, dear children, continue in
him, so that when he appears we may be
confident and unashamed before him at
his coming.
29If you know that he is righteous, you
know that everyone who does what is
right has been born of him.

3 How great is the love the Father has
lavished on us, that we should be
called children of God! And that is what
we are! The reason the world does not
know us is that it did not know him. 2Dear

[a]2 Or *He is the one who turns aside God's wrath, taking away our sins, and not only ours but also*
[b]5 Or *word, love for God* [c]10 Or *it* [d]20 Some manuscripts *and you know all things*

friends, now we are children of God, and
what we will be has not yet been made
known. But we know that when he appears,[a] we shall be like him, for we shall
see him as he is. 3Everyone who has this
hope in him purifies himself, just as he is
pure.

4Everyone who sins breaks the law; in
fact, sin is lawlessness. 5But you know
that he appeared so that he might take
away our sins. And in him is no sin. 6No
one who lives in him keeps on sinning.
No one who continues to sin has either
seen him or known him.

7Dear children, do not let anyone lead
you astray. He who does what is right is
righteous, just as he is righteous. 8He who
does what is sinful is of the devil, because
the devil has been sinning from the beginning. The reason the Son of God appeared was to destroy the devil's work.
9No one who is born of God will continue
to sin, because God's seed remains in
him; he cannot go on sinning, because he
has been born of God. 10This is how we
know who the children of God are and
who the children of the devil are: Anyone
who does not do what is right is not a
child of God; nor is anyone who does not
love his brother.

Love One Another

11This is the message you heard from
the beginning: We should love one another. 12Do not be like Cain, who belonged to
the evil one and murdered his brother.
And why did he murder him? Because his
own actions were evil and his brother's
were righteous. 13Do not be surprised, my
brothers, if the world hates you. 14We
know that we have passed from death to
life, because we love our brothers. Anyone who does not love remains in death.
15Anyone who hates his brother is a murderer, and you know that no murderer has
eternal life in him.

16This is how we know what love is:
Jesus Christ laid down his life for us. And
we ought to lay down our lives for our
brothers. 17If anyone has material possessions and sees his brother in need but has
no pity on him, how can the love of God
be in him? 18Dear children, let us not love
with words or tongue but with actions
and in truth. 19This then is how we know
that we belong to the truth, and how we
set our hearts at rest in his presence
20whenever our hearts condemn us. For
God is greater than our hearts, and he
knows everything.

21Dear friends, if our hearts do not condemn us, we have confidence before God
22and receive from him anything we ask,
because we obey his commands and do
what pleases him. 23And this is his command: to believe in the name of his Son,
Jesus Christ, and to love one another as
he commanded us. 24Those who obey his
commands live in him, and he in them.
And this is how we know that he lives in
us: We know it by the Spirit he gave us.

Test the Spirits

4 Dear friends, do not believe every
spirit, but test the spirits to see
whether they are from God, because
many false prophets have gone out into
the world. 2This is how you can recognize
the Spirit of God: Every spirit that acknowledges that Jesus Christ has come in
the flesh is from God, 3but every spirit
that does not acknowledge Jesus is not
from God. This is the spirit of the antichrist, which you have heard is coming and
even now is already in the world.

4You, dear children, are from God and
have overcome them, because the one
who is in you is greater than the one who
is in the world. 5They are from the world
and therefore speak from the viewpoint of
the world, and the world listens to them.
6We are from God, and whoever knows
God listens to us; but whoever is not from
God does not listen to us. This is how we
recognize the Spirit[b] of truth and the
spirit of falsehood.

God's Love and Ours

7Dear friends, let us love one another,
for love comes from God. Everyone who
loves has been born of God and knows
God. 8Whoever does not love does not
know God, because God is love. 9This is
how God showed his love among us: He
sent his one and only Son[c] into the world
that we might live through him. 10This is
love: not that we loved God, but that he
loved us and sent his Son as an atoning
sacrifice for[d] our sins. 11Dear friends,
since God so loved us, we also ought to
love one another. 12No one has ever seen
God; but if we love one another, God lives
in us and his love is made complete in us.
13We know that we live in him and he

[a]2 Or *when it is made known* [b]6 Or *spirit* [c]9 Or *his only begotten Son* [d]10 Or *as the one who would turn aside his wrath, taking away*

TUESDAY

VERSE FOR THE DAY: *1 John 5:4*

AUTHOR: *Luci Swindoll*

PASSAGE FOR THE DAY: *1 John 5:1–12*

Real Power

THIS verse, 1 John 5:4, has been a favorite of mine for years; but only lately have I come to realize that the verse is not so much about faith as it is about power. It's not an obvious power like that displayed by bulldozing through a riverbed in a GMC truck or by the ability to lift weights. It's a quiet power, like that inherent in a seed, which causes a plant to pop out of the ground and burst into flower, or in the meaningful words that fly across the airwaves altering convictions and changing hearts for all eternity.

Power. Have you ever been so mad at a person that you wanted to walk out and never talk to her again, but decided instead to hang in there, communicate, and make it right? Or, have you felt tremendously inadequate for an assigned task, found a Scripture of encouragement, and come out a winner? Have you invested love and concern into a person who was basically unlovable and witnessed a transformation in her behavior—primarily because of your sensitivity and acceptance? That's the kind of power I'm talking about.

This verse says that we, the children of God, actually can overcome the world by faithfully believing that we have God's power to effect change. Doesn't that make you want to try it in every area of your life? It does me!

I want to quit worrying about money. I want to lose weight. I want to be a kinder, more gentle person. I want to be supportive, not envious. I want to sing more and gripe less. I want to look for the positive, not dwell on the negative. I want to reach out to those who need me, not wait for them to come to me. I want to relax and laugh. I want to live fully.

Shall I go on? You make your own list, remembering that by faith you've already overcome the world. Claim that. When God commissions, he empowers. That power is absolutely yours, by faith. Take it and head out. The victories are just beginning.

Additional Scripture Readings:
Romans 8:31–39; 1 Corinthians 15:57–58

Go to page 376 for your next devotional reading.

in us, because he has given us of his Spirit. 14And we have seen and testify that the Father has sent his Son to be the Savior of the world. 15If anyone acknowledges that Jesus is the Son of God, God lives in him and he in God. 16And so we know and rely on the love God has for us.

God is love. Whoever lives in love lives in God, and God in him. 17In this way, love is made complete among us so that we will have confidence on the day of judgment, because in this world we are like him. 18There is no fear in love. But perfect love drives out fear, because fear has to do with punishment. The one who fears is not made perfect in love.

19We love because he first loved us. 20If anyone says, "I love God," yet hates his brother, he is a liar. For anyone who does not love his brother, whom he has seen, cannot love God, whom he has not seen. 21And he has given us this command: Whoever loves God must also love his brother.

Faith in the Son of God

5 Everyone who believes that Jesus is the Christ is born of God, and everyone who loves the father loves his child as well. 2This is how we know that we love the children of God: by loving God and carrying out his commands. 3This is love for God: to obey his commands. And his commands are not burdensome, 4for everyone born of God overcomes the world. This is the victory that has overcome the world, even our faith. 5Who is it that overcomes the world? Only he who believes that Jesus is the Son of God.

6This is the one who came by water and blood—Jesus Christ. He did not come by water only, but by water and blood. And it is the Spirit who testifies, because the Spirit is the truth. 7For there are three that testify: 8the[a] Spirit, the water and the blood; and the three are in agreement. 9We accept man's testimony, but God's testimony is greater because it is the testimony of God, which he has given about his Son. 10Anyone who believes in the Son of God has this testimony in his heart. Anyone who does not believe God has made him out to be a liar, because he has not believed the testimony God has given about his Son. 11And this is the testimony: God has given us eternal life, and this life is in his Son. 12He who has the Son has life; he who does not have the Son of God does not have life.

Concluding Remarks

13I write these things to you who believe in the name of the Son of God so that you may know that you have eternal life. 14This is the confidence we have in approaching God: that if we ask anything according to his will, he hears us. 15And if we know that he hears us—whatever we ask—we know that we have what we asked of him.

16If anyone sees his brother commit a sin that does not lead to death, he should pray and God will give him life. I refer to those whose sin does not lead to death. There is a sin that leads to death. I am not saying that he should pray about that. 17All wrongdoing is sin, and there is sin that does not lead to death.

18We know that anyone born of God does not continue to sin; the one who was born of God keeps him safe, and the evil one cannot harm him. 19We know that we are children of God, and that the whole world is under the control of the evil one. 20We know also that the Son of God has come and has given us understanding, so that we may know him who is true. And we are in him who is true—even in his Son Jesus Christ. He is the true God and eternal life.

21Dear children, keep yourselves from idols.

[a]7,8 Late manuscripts of the Vulgate *testify in heaven: the Father, the Word and the Holy Spirit, and these three are one. 8And there are three that testify on earth: the* (not found in any Greek manuscript before the sixteenth century)

JOHN writes this second letter to warn the church to stand firm against false teachers and to keep loving other Christians. As you read this book, learn how to stand up for your Lord whenever you encounter false teachers.

2 JOHN

1The elder,

To the chosen lady and her children, whom I love in the truth—and not I only, but also all who know the truth— 2because of the truth, which lives in us and will be with us forever:

3Grace, mercy and peace from God the Father and from Jesus Christ, the Father's Son, will be with us in truth and love.

4It has given me great joy to find some of your children walking in the truth, just as the Father commanded us. 5And now, dear lady, I am not writing you a new command but one we have had from the beginning. I ask that we love one another. 6And this is love: that we walk in obedience to his commands. As you have heard from the beginning, his command is that you walk in love.

7Many deceivers, who do not acknowledge Jesus Christ as coming in the flesh, have gone out into the world. Any such person is the deceiver and the antichrist. 8Watch out that you do not lose what you have worked for, but that you may be rewarded fully. 9Anyone who runs ahead and does not continue in the teaching of Christ does not have God; whoever continues in the teaching has both the Father and the Son. 10If anyone comes to you and does not bring this teaching, do not take him into your house or welcome him. 11Anyone who welcomes him shares in his wicked work.

12I have much to write to you, but I do not want to use paper and ink. Instead, I hope to visit you and talk with you face to face, so that our joy may be complete.

13The children of your chosen sister send their greetings.

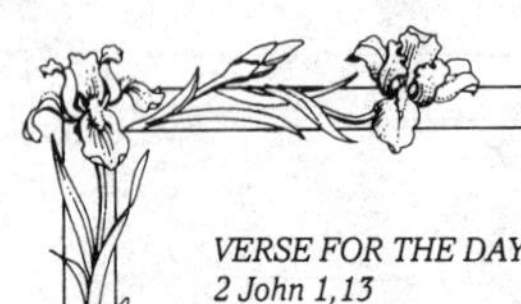

WEDNESDAY

VERSE FOR THE DAY:
2 John 1,13

AUTHOR:
Ruth A. Tucker

PASSAGE FOR THE DAY:
2 John 1–13

Chosen Ladies

WHO was this "chosen lady" who merited a letter from the apostle John? Where was she from? What was her role in the ministry? How did she come to faith in Christ? How often we wish the Bible offered more details about individuals and events, and in this letter we are left to wonder about an unnamed, unidentified woman and her "chosen sister." Scholars have speculated that these two women were leaders of house churches and that the children mentioned were their spiritual children. As such they may have had an important role in the foundational growth of the early church.

In one sense, it is their lack of identity that allows them to better represent the countless "chosen ladies" from around the world who have faithfully served the Lord through the centuries—women whose names have been lost in the annals of history.

I often wonder where I would be today were it not for two "chosen ladies." Miss Salthammer and Miss Cowan moved to my rural community in northern Wisconsin several years before I was born, and out of their sacrificial church-planting ministry came the Green Grove Alliance Church.

When I was growing up in that little country church, the two women had long since packed their bags and moved on to plant other churches. I know of them through prayer requests offered on their behalf and through their occasional return visits to teach vacation Bible school. As kids, we sometimes laughed at the way they dressed, and we told jokes about how they were paid with a load of potatoes or turnips instead of money. I later learned that when Miss Cowan died she was buried in a pauper's grave.

They were very ordinary women whose span of years has ended and whose names will soon be forgotten. But their ministry lives on through the generations of their spiritual children. They were chosen ladies.

Additional Scripture Readings:
Galatians 6:7–10; Revelation 14:12–13

Go to page 378 for your next devotional reading.

JOHN writes this third letter to commend a church leader for his hospitality and to warn against another one who is unfriendly and even cruel. As you read this book, think how you can act as a friend toward other Christians.

3 JOHN

1The elder,

To my dear friend Gaius, whom I love in the truth.

2Dear friend, I pray that you may enjoy
good health and that all may go well with
you, even as your soul is getting along
well. 3It gave me great joy to have some
brothers come and tell about your faithfulness to the truth and how you continue
to walk in the truth. 4I have no greater joy
than to hear that my children are walking
in the truth.

5Dear friend, you are faithful in what
you are doing for the brothers, even
though they are strangers to you. 6They
have told the church about your love. You
will do well to send them on their way in
a manner worthy of God. 7It was for the
sake of the Name that they went out, receiving no help from the pagans. 8We
ought therefore to show hospitality to
such men so that we may work together
for the truth.

9I wrote to the church, but Diotrephes,
who loves to be first, will have nothing to
do with us. 10So if I come, I will call attention to what he is doing, gossiping maliciously about us. Not satisfied with that,
he refuses to welcome the brothers. He
also stops those who want to do so and
puts them out of the church.

11Dear friend, do not imitate what is
evil but what is good. Anyone who does
what is good is from God. Anyone who
does what is evil has not seen God.
12Demetrius is well spoken of by everyone
—and even by the truth itself. We also
speak well of him, and you know that our
testimony is true.

13I have much to write you, but I do not
want to do so with pen and ink. 14I hope
to see you soon, and we will talk face to
face.

Peace to you. The friends here send their greetings. Greet the friends there by name.

VERSE FOR THE DAY:
3 John 4

AUTHOR:
Susan L. Lenzkes

PASSAGE FOR THE DAY:
3 John 1–14

My Boy

I LOOK at the shiny-shaggy hair
and round, blue-gray eyes;
the small pink tongue struggling
impatiently against tiny white teeth
to form a word,
to convey an exciting new-born thought;
the broad little boy hand
covered with dirt, reaching
to touch my cheek;
and suddenly I realize
the astounding responsibilities
that are mine before that hand
expands to a man's hand.
O God,
hold my son's hand while he crosses
the danger-filled street to manhood.

This was to be my stay-at-home-and-get-a-few-things-done day. That would be just fine, except for one thing: I have a toddler who wants to help.

I finish the washing, and he struggles the piles of clean clothes toward their dresser drawers. I suppose a hundred years from now I won't care that they started the trip neatly folded.

I sweep the floor, and he insists on helping me by emptying the dustpan. In the overall scheme of things, I suppose the fact that he dumped the dirt back onto the floor is relatively unimportant.

I begin mixing ingredients for yeast rolls, and he insists on adding the flour. If I look at the situation optimistically, unbleached white is a good color on me.

I do know he's really trying, Lord. And I know he needs practice to learn. But it would truly be so much easier to simply do it myself.

I watch, filled with apprehension, as he teeters toward me, chubby hands cupping fragile eggs, and I'm suddenly aware that you, God, have entrusted me with the fragile life of this child. Guide me as I help my little helper become your man.

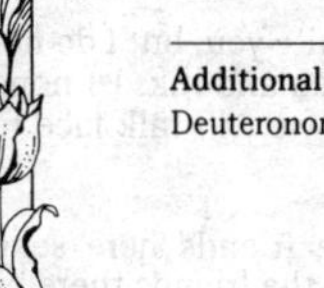

Additional Scripture Readings:
Deuteronomy 6:6–7; Luke 17:1–2

Go to page 380 for your next devotional reading.

JUDE (a brother of Jesus and James) writes this short letter to warn Christians against false teachers in the church and to urge them to strengthen their faith and love. As you read this book, begin to grow in faith and love by depending on the Father, Son, and Holy Spirit.

JUDE

1Jude, a servant of Jesus Christ and a brother of James,

To those who have been called, who are loved by God the Father and kept by[a] Jesus Christ:

2Mercy, peace and love be yours in abundance.

The Sin and Doom of Godless Men

3Dear friends, although I was very eager to write to you about the salvation we share, I felt I had to write and urge you to contend for the faith that was once for all entrusted to the saints. 4For certain men whose condemnation was written about[b] long ago have secretly slipped in among you. They are godless men, who change the grace of our God into a license for immorality and deny Jesus Christ our only Sovereign and Lord.

5Though you already know all this, I want to remind you that the Lord[c] delivered his people out of Egypt, but later destroyed those who did not believe. 6And the angels who did not keep their positions of authority but abandoned their own home—these he has kept in darkness, bound with everlasting chains for judgment on the great Day. 7In a similar way, Sodom and Gomorrah and the surrounding towns gave themselves up to sexual immorality and perversion. They serve as an example of those who suffer the punishment of eternal fire.

8In the very same way, these dreamers pollute their own bodies, reject authority and slander celestial beings. 9But even the archangel Michael, when he was disputing with the devil about the body of Moses, did not dare to bring a slanderous accusation against him, but said, "The

[a]1 Or *for;* or *in Jesus* [b]4 Or *men who were marked out for condemnation* [c]5 Some early manuscripts

Lord rebuke you!" 10Yet these men speak
abusively against whatever they do not
understand; and what things they do understand by instinct, like unreasoning animals—these are the very things that destroy them.
11Woe to them! They have taken the
way of Cain; they have rushed for profit
into Balaam's error; they have been destroyed in Korah's rebellion.
12These men are blemishes at your love
feasts, eating with you without the slight-
est qualm—shepherds who feed only
themselves. They are clouds without rain,
blown along by the wind; autumn trees,
without fruit and uprooted—twice dead.
13They are wild waves of the sea, foaming
up their shame; wandering stars, for
whom blackest darkness has been reserved forever.
14Enoch, the seventh from Adam, prophesied about these men: "See, the Lord
is coming with thousands upon thousands of his holy ones 15to judge everyone, and to convict all the ungodly of all
the ungodly acts they have done in the
ungodly way, and of all the harsh words
ungodly sinners have spoken against
him." 16These men are grumblers and
faultfinders; they follow their own evil de-

FRIDAY

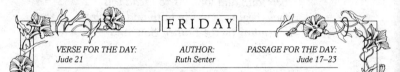

VERSE FOR THE DAY: *Jude 21*

AUTHOR: *Ruth Senter*

PASSAGE FOR THE DAY: *Jude 17–23*

Obstacles and Opportunities

THE story is told of an old Scottish fisherman who was having afternoon tea with some friends in a little tearoom by the sea. As he was describing some of his fishing exploits of the day, his hand accidentally knocked over his cup of tea. An ugly, brown tea stain appeared on the freshly whitewashed wall beside him.

"Never mind about the stain," said a friend as he rose from his chair and drew from his pocket a brown crayon. There emerged from that ugly, brown tea stain a magnificent stag with antlers spread and back arched. The friend of the fisherman was one of England's most famous painters.

Life is full of ugly tea stains that splash against whitewashed walls. Reality often seems to be more obstacle than opportunity, more pain than pleasure, more chaos than calm, more hurt than happiness, more tension than tenderness. But if I interpret Romans 8:28 correctly, I must believe that as God's woman, God is using everything in my life to make me more like himself.

Together, he and I can take the tea stains in my life and make something out of them. We can take the chaos and be calm, take the tensions and be tender, take the hurts and be content, take the obstacles and build opportunities. That is what God offers me from life.

And when God says that's what he can do for me, only my unbelief keeps me from experiencing it. If the Christian life is worth living, then God is worth believing. And if I believe God, there is no end to the possibilities.

Additional Scripture Readings:
Acts 4:28–30; Philippians 1:19–21

Go to page 381 for your next devotional reading.

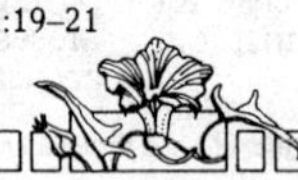

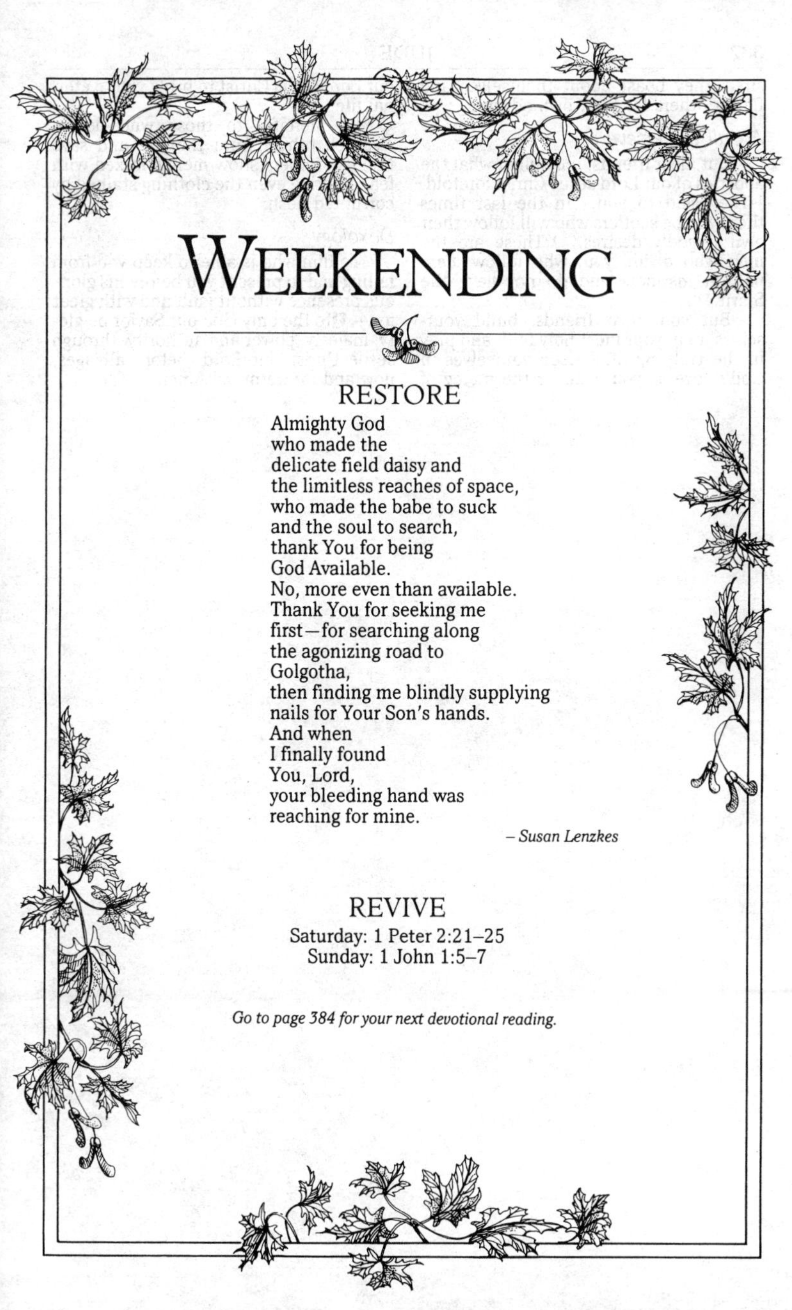

WEEKENDING

RESTORE

Almighty God
who made the
delicate field daisy and
the limitless reaches of space,
who made the babe to suck
and the soul to search,
thank You for being
God Available.
No, more even than available.
Thank You for seeking me
first—for searching along
the agonizing road to
Golgotha,
then finding me blindly supplying
nails for Your Son's hands.
And when
I finally found
You, Lord,
your bleeding hand was
reaching for mine.

– Susan Lenzkes

REVIVE

Saturday: 1 Peter 2:21–25
Sunday: 1 John 1:5–7

Go to page 384 for your next devotional reading.

sires; they boast about themselves and
flatter others for their own advantage.

A Call to Persevere

[17]But, dear friends, remember what the
apostles of our Lord Jesus Christ foretold.
[18]They said to you, "In the last times
there will be scoffers who will follow their
own ungodly desires." [19]These are the
men who divide you, who follow mere
natural instincts and do not have the
Spirit.

[20]But you, dear friends, build yourselves up in your most holy faith and pray
in the Holy Spirit. [21]Keep yourselves in
God's love as you wait for the mercy of
our Lord Jesus Christ to bring you to eternal life.

[22]Be merciful to those who doubt;
[23]snatch others from the fire and save
them; to others show mercy, mixed with
fear—hating even the clothing stained by
corrupted flesh.

Doxology

[24]To him who is able to keep you from
falling and to present you before his glorious presence without fault and with great
joy— [25]to the only God our Savior be glory, majesty, power and authority, through
Jesus Christ our Lord, before all ages,
now and forevermore! Amen.

JOHN, banished to the island of Patmos, writes what Christ reveals to him in order to comfort Christians suffering for their faith. Through visions of God in control of both the present and the future, he offers them hope, assuring them that in the end Christ will achieve victory over Satan, who is doomed to eternal punishment. As you read this book, rejoice in the awesome power of Christ, and remember that regardless of what happens now or in the future, nothing can ever separate you from his love.

REVELATION

Prologue

1 The revelation of Jesus Christ, which
God gave him to show his servants
what must soon take place. He made it
known by sending his angel to his servant
John, 2who testifies to everything he saw
—that is, the word of God and the testimony of Jesus Christ. 3Blessed is the
one who reads the words of this prophecy,
and blessed are those who hear it and
take to heart what is written in it, because
the time is near.

Greetings and Doxology

4John,

To the seven churches in the province of Asia:

Grace and peace to you from him who
is, and who was, and who is to come, and
from the seven spirits[a] before his throne,
5and from Jesus Christ, who is the faithful
witness, the firstborn from the dead, and
the ruler of the kings of the earth.

[a]4 Or *the sevenfold Spirit*

To him who loves us and has freed us
from our sins by his blood, 6and has made
us to be a kingdom and priests to serve
his God and Father—to him be glory and
power for ever and ever! Amen.

7Look, he is coming with the clouds,
and every eye will see him,
even those who pierced him;
and all the peoples of the earth will
mourn because of him.
So shall it be! Amen.

8"I am the Alpha and the Omega," says
the Lord God, "who is, and who was, and
who is to come, the Almighty."

One Like a Son of Man

9I, John, your brother and companion
in the suffering and kingdom and patient
endurance that are ours in Jesus, was on
the island of Patmos because of the word
of God and the testimony of Jesus. 10On
the Lord's Day I was in the spirit, and I
heard behind me a loud voice like a trumpet, 11which said: "Write on a scroll what
you see and send it to the seven churches:

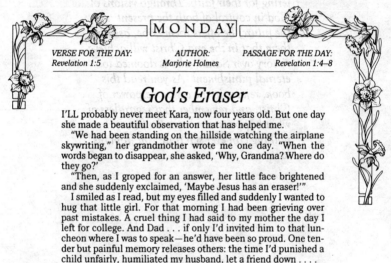

MONDAY

VERSE FOR THE DAY: *Revelation 1:5* — *AUTHOR:* *Marjorie Holmes* — *PASSAGE FOR THE DAY:* *Revelation 1:4–8*

God's Eraser

I'LL probably never meet Kara, now four years old. But one day she made a beautiful observation that has helped me.

"We had been standing on the hillside watching the airplane skywriting," her grandmother wrote me one day. "When the words began to disappear, she asked, 'Why, Grandma? Where do they go?'

"Then, as I groped for an answer, her little face brightened and she suddenly exclaimed, 'Maybe Jesus has an eraser!'"

I smiled as I read, but my eyes filled and suddenly I wanted to hug that little girl. For that morning I had been grieving over past mistakes. A cruel thing I had said to my mother the day I left for college. And Dad . . . if only I'd invited him to that luncheon where I was to speak—he'd have been so proud. One tender but painful memory releases others: the time I'd punished a child unfairly, humiliated my husband, let a friend down . . . .

No matter how much we mature as people, grow as Christians, try desperately to compensate, memories of our own failures rise up to haunt us, and sting—how they sting. For me, it's not the unkindnesses of others that hurt so much or last so long, it's the burden of my own. Yes, I ask God to forgive me, and try to believe that I am forgiven. But the memory won't go away. And if I can't forgive myself, how can God?

Then a little girl, in her innocence and wisdom, makes me realize: Like that writing on the sky that simply disappears, Jesus has wiped away all things I so bitterly regret. Jesus does have an eraser.

Additional Scripture Readings:
Psalm 103:11–12; Micah 7:18–19

Go to page 388 for your next devotional reading.

to Ephesus, Smyrna, Pergamum, Thyatira, Sardis, Philadelphia and Laodicea."
12I turned around to see the voice that
was speaking to me. And when I turned I
saw seven golden lampstands, 13and
among the lampstands was someone
"like a son of man,"[a] dressed in a robe
reaching down to his feet and with a gold-
en sash around his chest. 14His head and
hair were white like wool, as white as
snow, and his eyes were like blazing fire.
15His feet were like bronze glowing in a
furnace, and his voice was like the sound
of rushing waters. 16In his right hand he
held seven stars, and out of his mouth
came a sharp double-edged sword. His
face was like the sun shining in all its
brilliance.
17When I saw him, I fell at his feet as
though dead. Then he placed his right
hand on me and said: "Do not be afraid.
I am the First and the Last. 18I am the
Living One; I was dead, and behold I am
alive for ever and ever! And I hold the keys
of death and Hades.
19"Write, therefore, what you have
seen, what is now and what will take
place later. 20The mystery of the seven
stars that you saw in my right hand and of
the seven golden lampstands is this: The
seven stars are the angels[b] of the seven
churches, and the seven lampstands are
the seven churches.

To the Church in Ephesus

2 "To the angel[c] of the church in
Ephesus write:

These are the words of him who
holds the seven stars in his right
hand and walks among the seven
golden lampstands: 2I know your
deeds, your hard work and your
perseverance. I know that you cannot tolerate wicked men, that you
have tested those who claim to be
apostles but are not, and have found
them false. 3You have persevered and
have endured hardships for my
name, and have not grown weary.
4Yet I hold this against you: You
have forsaken your first love.
5Remember the height from which
you have fallen! Repent and do the
things you did at first. If you do not
repent, I will come to you and
remove your lampstand from its
place. 6But you have this in your favor: You hate the practices of the
Nicolaitans, which I also hate.
7He who has an ear, let him hear
what the Spirit says to the churches.
To him who overcomes, I will give
the right to eat from the tree of life,
which is in the paradise of God.

To the Church in Smyrna

8"To the angel of the church in Smyrna
write:

These are the words of him who is
the First and the Last, who died and
came to life again. 9I know your afflictions and your poverty—yet you
are rich! I know the slander of those
who say they are Jews and are not,
but are a synagogue of Satan. 10Do
not be afraid of what you are about to
suffer. I tell you, the devil will put
some of you in prison to test you, and
you will suffer persecution for ten
days. Be faithful, even to the point of
death, and I will give you the crown
of life.
11He who has an ear, let him hear
what the Spirit says to the churches.
He who overcomes will not be hurt at
all by the second death.

To the Church in Pergamum

12"To the angel of the church in Pergamum write:

These are the words of him who
has the sharp, double-edged sword.
13I know where you live—where Satan has his throne. Yet you remain
true to my name. You did not re-
nounce your faith in me, even in the
days of Antipas, my faithful witness,
who was put to death in your city—
where Satan lives.
14Nevertheless, I have a few things
against you: You have people there
who hold to the teaching of Balaam,
who taught Balak to entice the Israelites to sin by eating food sacrificed
to idols and by committing sexual
immorality. 15Likewise you also have
those who hold to the teaching of
the Nicolaitans. 16Repent therefore!
Otherwise, I will soon come to you
and will fight against them with the
sword of my mouth.
17He who has an ear, let him hear
what the Spirit says to the churches.
To him who overcomes, I will give

[a] *13* Daniel 7:13 [b] *20* Or *messengers* [c] *1* Or *messenger;* also in verses 8, 12 and 18

some of the hidden manna. I will
also give him a white stone with a
new name written on it, known only
to him who receives it.

To the Church in Thyatira

18"To the angel of the church in Thyatira
write:

These are the words of the Son of
God, whose eyes are like blazing fire
and whose feet are like burnished
bronze. 19I know your deeds, your
love and faith, your service and
perseverance, and that you are now
doing more than you did at first.
20Nevertheless, I have this against
you: You tolerate that woman Jeze-
bel, who calls herself a prophetess.
By her teaching she misleads my servants into sexual immorality and the
eating of food sacrificed to idols. 21I
have given her time to repent of her
immorality, but she is unwilling. 22So
I will cast her on a bed of suffering,
and I will make those who commit
adultery with her suffer intensely,
unless they repent of her ways. 23I
will strike her children dead. Then
all the churches will know that I am
he who searches hearts and minds,
and I will repay each of you according to your deeds. 24Now I say to the
rest of you in Thyatira, to you who do
not hold to her teaching and have
not learned Satan's so-called deep
secrets (I will not impose any other
burden on you): 25Only hold on to
what you have until I come.
26To him who overcomes and does
my will to the end, I will give authority over the nations—

27'He will rule them with an iron
scepter;
he will dash them to pieces
like pottery'[a]—

just as I have received authority from
my Father. 28I will also give him the
morning star. 29He who has an ear,
let him hear what the Spirit says to
the churches.

To the Church in Sardis

3 "To the angel[b] of the church in Sardis write:

These are the words of him who
holds the seven spirits[c] of God and
the seven stars. I know your deeds;
you have a reputation of being
alive, but you are dead. 2Wake up!
Strengthen what remains and is
about to die, for I have not found
your deeds complete in the sight of
my God. 3Remember, therefore,
what you have received and heard;
obey it, and repent. But if you do not
wake up, I will come like a thief, and
you will not know at what time I will
come to you.
4Yet you have a few people in Sardis who have not soiled their clothes.
They will walk with me, dressed
in white, for they are worthy. 5He
who overcomes will, like them, be
dressed in white. I will never blot out
his name from the book of life, but
will acknowledge his name before
my Father and his angels. 6He who
has an ear, let him hear what the
Spirit says to the churches.

To the Church in Philadelphia

7"To the angel of the church in Philadelphia write:

These are the words of him who is
holy and true, who holds the key of
David. What he opens no one can
shut, and what he shuts no one can
open. 8I know your deeds. See, I have
placed before you an open door that
no one can shut. I know that you
have little strength, yet you have
kept my word and have not denied
my name. 9I will make those who are
of the synagogue of Satan, who claim
to be Jews though they are not, but
are liars—I will make them come
and fall down at your feet and acknowledge that I have loved you.
10Since you have kept my command
to endure patiently, I will also keep
you from the hour of trial that is going to come upon the whole world to
test those who live on the earth.
11I am coming soon. Hold on to
what you have, so that no one will
take your crown. 12Him who overcomes I will make a pillar in the temple of my God. Never again will he
leave it. I will write on him the name
of my God and the name of the city
of my God, the new Jerusalem,
which is coming down out of heaven
from my God; and I will also write on

[a]27 Psalm 2:9 [b]1 Or *messenger*; also in verses 7 and 14 [c]1 Or *the sevenfold Spirit*

him my new name. 13He who has an ear, let him hear what the Spirit says to the churches.

To the Church in Laodicea

14"To the angel of the church in Laodicea write:

These are the words of the Amen, the faithful and true witness, the ruler of God's creation. 15I know your deeds, that you are neither cold nor hot. I wish you were either one or the other! 16So, because you are lukewarm—neither hot nor cold—I am about to spit you out of my mouth. 17You say, 'I am rich; I have acquired wealth and do not need a thing.' But you do not realize that you are wretched, pitiful, poor, blind and naked. 18I counsel you to buy from me gold refined in the fire, so you can become rich; and white clothes to wear, so you can cover your shameful nakedness; and salve to put on your eyes, so you can see.

19Those whom I love I rebuke and discipline. So be earnest, and repent. 20Here I am! I stand at the door and knock. If anyone hears my voice and opens the door, I will come in and eat with him, and he with me.

21To him who overcomes, I will give the right to sit with me on my throne, just as I overcame and sat down with my Father on his throne. 22He who has an ear, let him hear what the Spirit says to the churches."

The Throne in Heaven

4 After this I looked, and there before me was a door standing open in heaven. And the voice I had first heard speaking to me like a trumpet said, "Come up here, and I will show you what must take place after this." 2At once I was in the Spirit, and there before me was a throne in heaven with someone sitting on it. 3And the one who sat there had the appearance of jasper and carnelian. A rainbow, resembling an emerald, encircled the throne. 4Surrounding the throne were twenty-four other thrones, and seated on them were twenty-four elders. They were dressed in white and had crowns of gold on their heads. 5From the throne came flashes of lightning, rumblings and peals of thunder. Before the throne, seven lamps were blazing. These are the seven spirits[a] of God. 6Also before the throne there was what looked like a sea of glass, clear as crystal.

In the center, around the throne, were four living creatures, and they were covered with eyes, in front and in back. 7The first living creature was like a lion, the second was like an ox, the third had a face like a man, the fourth was like a flying eagle. 8Each of the four living creatures had six wings and was covered with eyes all around, even under his wings. Day and night they never stop saying:

"Holy, holy, holy
is the Lord God Almighty,
who was, and is, and is to come."

9Whenever the living creatures give glory, honor and thanks to him who sits on the throne and who lives for ever and ever, 10the twenty-four elders fall down before him who sits on the throne, and worship him who lives for ever and ever. They lay their crowns before the throne and say:

11"You are worthy, our Lord and God,
to receive glory and honor and power,
for you created all things,
and by your will they were created
and have their being."

The Scroll and the Lamb

5 Then I saw in the right hand of him who sat on the throne a scroll with writing on both sides and sealed with seven seals. 2And I saw a mighty angel proclaiming in a loud voice, "Who is worthy to break the seals and open the scroll?" 3But no one in heaven or on earth or under the earth could open the scroll or even look inside it. 4I wept and wept because no one was found who was worthy to open the scroll or look inside. 5Then one of the elders said to me, "Do not weep! See, the Lion of the tribe of Judah, the Root of David, has triumphed. He is able to open the scroll and its seven seals."

6Then I saw a Lamb, looking as if it had been slain, standing in the center of the throne, encircled by the four living creatures and the elders. He had seven horns and seven eyes, which are the seven spirits[a] of God sent out into all the earth. 7He

[a]5,6 Or *the sevenfold Spirit*

TUESDAY

VERSE FOR THE DAY: *Revelation 3:15–16*

AUTHOR: *Catherine Marshall*

PASSAGE FOR THE DAY: *Revelation 3:14–22*

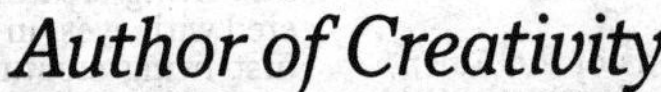

Author of Creativity

I AM troubled about a quality of blandness in our nation today, a lack of creativity. It's apparent in our leaders. Most gear their lives to television ratings, are afraid to take stands on issues. Movies and stage plays focus on sex and violence, with little originality. Sex so dominates advertising and the arts that it has become commonplace, almost boring.

Jesus lashed out at the spiritless quality in the people of his time:

> I know your deeds, that you are neither cold nor hot. I wish you were either one or the other! So, because you are lukewarm—neither hot nor cold—I am about to spit you out of my mouth (Revelation 3:15–16).

One of our new neighbors is no longer trapped in a bland way of life. Yet for the first twelve years of her marriage, Cynthia felt she was losing her identity in an endless procession of social events and chauffeuring of children.

In a search for answers, Cynthia set aside an hour each day for meditation. As she did this over a period of weeks there came to her the realization that she was being met in this quiet hour, at her point of need, by something more than her own thoughts and her own psyche, by Someone who loved her and who insisted that his love must be passed on to her family and her friends.

"I realized one day that my church had little more meaning for me than did our country club," Cynthia said. "I called our pastor and asked if there was a Bible study."

That's what brought Cynthia and her husband to our house, where eight couples were already meeting twice a month to find ways to relate the Bible to some everyday problems we were all facing. Out of this experience has come a new level of shared concerns for us all and the exciting discovery of answers sought out together.

As I ponder Cynthia's story, I've concluded that we don't have to settle for blandness in life; God, who is the Author of creativity, is ready to make a dull life adventuresome the moment we allow his Holy Spirit to go to work inside us.

Additional Scripture Readings:
1 Thessalonians 5:16–23; 1 Peter 1:3–6

Go to page 391 for your next devotional reading.

came and took the scroll from the right
hand of him who sat on the throne. 8And
when he had taken it, the four living creatures and the twenty-four elders fell down
before the Lamb. Each one had a harp
and they were holding golden bowls full
of incense, which are the prayers of the
saints. 9And they sang a new song:

"You are worthy to take the scroll
  and to open its seals,
because you were slain,
  and with your blood you purchased
    men for God
  from every tribe and language and
    people and nation.
10You have made them to be a kingdom
    and priests to serve our God,
  and they will reign on the earth."

11Then I looked and heard the voice of
many angels, numbering thousands upon
thousands, and ten thousand times ten
thousand. They encircled the throne and
the living creatures and the elders. 12In a
loud voice they sang:

"Worthy is the Lamb, who was slain,
to receive power and wealth and
    wisdom and strength
and honor and glory and praise!"

13Then I heard every creature in heaven
and on earth and under the earth and on
the sea, and all that is in them, singing:

"To him who sits on the throne and
    to the Lamb
be praise and honor and glory and
    power,
    for ever and ever!"

14The four living creatures said, "Amen,"
and the elders fell down and worshiped.

The Seals

6 I watched as the Lamb opened the
first of the seven seals. Then I heard
one of the four living creatures say in a
voice like thunder, "Come!" 2I looked,
and there before me was a white horse! Its
rider held a bow, and he was given a
crown, and he rode out as a conqueror
bent on conquest.

3When the Lamb opened the second
seal, I heard the second living creature
say, "Come!" 4Then another horse came
out, a fiery red one. Its rider was given
power to take peace from the earth and to
make men slay each other. To him was
given a large sword.

5When the Lamb opened the third seal,
I heard the third living creature say,
"Come!" I looked, and there before me
was a black horse! Its rider was holding a
pair of scales in his hand. 6Then I heard
what sounded like a voice among the four
living creatures, saying, "A quart[a] of
wheat for a day's wages,[b] and three
quarts of barley for a day's wages,[b] and
do not damage the oil and the wine!"

7When the Lamb opened the fourth
seal, I heard the voice of the fourth living
creature say, "Come!" 8I looked, and
there before me was a pale horse! Its rider
was named Death, and Hades was following close behind him. They were given
power over a fourth of the earth to kill by
sword, famine and plague, and by the
wild beasts of the earth.

9When he opened the fifth seal, I saw
under the altar the souls of those who had
been slain because of the word of God
and the testimony they had maintained.
10They called out in a loud voice, "How
long, Sovereign Lord, holy and true, until
you judge the inhabitants of the earth and
avenge our blood?" 11Then each of them
was given a white robe, and they were
told to wait a little longer, until the number of their fellow servants and brothers
who were to be killed as they had been
was completed.

12I watched as he opened the sixth seal.
There was a great earthquake. The sun
turned black like sackcloth made of goat
hair, the whole moon turned blood red,
13and the stars in the sky fell to earth, as
late figs drop from a fig tree when shaken
by a strong wind. 14The sky receded like
a scroll, rolling up, and every mountain
and island was removed from its place.

15Then the kings of the earth, the
princes, the generals, the rich, the
mighty, and every slave and every free
man hid in caves and among the rocks of
the mountains. 16They called to the
mountains and the rocks, "Fall on us and
hide us from the face of him who sits on
the throne and from the wrath of the
Lamb! 17For the great day of their wrath
has come, and who can stand?"

144,000 Sealed

7 After this I saw four angels standing
at the four corners of the earth, hold-

[a]6 Greek *a choinix* (probably about a liter) [b]6 Greek *a denarius*

ing back the four winds of the earth to
prevent any wind from blowing on the
land or on the sea or on any tree. 2Then
I saw another angel coming up from the
east, having the seal of the living God. He
called out in a loud voice to the four angels who had been given power to harm
the land and the sea: 3"Do not harm the
land or the sea or the trees until we put
a seal on the foreheads of the servants of
our God." 4Then I heard the number of
those who were sealed: 144,000 from all
the tribes of Israel.

5From the tribe of Judah 12,000 were
sealed,
from the tribe of Reuben 12,000,
from the tribe of Gad 12,000,
6from the tribe of Asher 12,000,
from the tribe of Naphtali 12,000,
from the tribe of Manasseh 12,000,
7from the tribe of Simeon 12,000,
from the tribe of Levi 12,000,
from the tribe of Issachar 12,000,
8from the tribe of Zebulun 12,000,
from the tribe of Joseph 12,000,
from the tribe of Benjamin 12,000.

The Great Multitude in White Robes

9After this I looked and there before me
was a great multitude that no one could
count, from every nation, tribe, people
and language, standing before the throne
and in front of the Lamb. They were wearing white robes and were holding palm
branches in their hands. 10And they cried
out in a loud voice:

"Salvation belongs to our God,
who sits on the throne,
and to the Lamb."

11All the angels were standing around the
throne and around the elders and the four
living creatures. They fell down on their
faces before the throne and worshiped
God, 12saying:

"Amen!
Praise and glory
and wisdom and thanks and honor
and power and strength
be to our God for ever and ever.
Amen!"

13Then one of the elders asked me,
"These in white robes—who are they, and
where did they come from?"
14I answered, "Sir, you know."
And he said, "These are they who have
come out of the great tribulation; they
have washed their robes and made them
white in the blood of the Lamb. 15There-
fore,

"they are before the throne of God
and serve him day and night in his
temple;
and he who sits on the throne will
spread his tent over them.
16Never again will they hunger;
never again will they thirst.
The sun will not beat upon them,
nor any scorching heat.
17For the Lamb at the center of the
throne will be their shepherd;
he will lead them to springs of
living water.
And God will wipe away every tear
from their eyes."

The Seventh Seal and the Golden Censer

8 When he opened the seventh seal,
there was silence in heaven for about
half an hour.
2And I saw the seven angels who stand
before God, and to them were given seven
trumpets.
3Another angel, who had a golden cens-
er, came and stood at the altar. He was
given much incense to offer, with the
prayers of all the saints, on the golden
altar before the throne. 4The smoke of the
incense, together with the prayers of the
saints, went up before God from the angel's hand. 5Then the angel took the cens-
er, filled it with fire from the altar, and
hurled it on the earth; and there came
peals of thunder, rumblings, flashes of
lightning and an earthquake.

The Trumpets

6Then the seven angels who had the
seven trumpets prepared to sound them.
7The first angel sounded his trumpet,
and there came hail and fire mixed with
blood, and it was hurled down upon the
earth. A third of the earth was burned up,
a third of the trees were burned up, and
all the green grass was burned up.
8The second angel sounded his trumpet, and something like a huge mountain,
all ablaze, was thrown into the sea. A
third of the sea turned into blood, 9a third
of the living creatures in the sea died, and
a third of the ships were destroyed.
10The third angel sounded his trumpet,
and a great star, blazing like a torch, fell
from the sky on a third of the rivers and
on the springs of water— 11the name of

the star is Wormwood.[a] A third of the waters turned bitter, and many people died
from the waters that had become bitter.
12The fourth angel sounded his trumpet, and a third of the sun was struck, a
third of the moon, and a third of the stars,
so that a third of them turned dark. A
third of the day was without light, and
also a third of the night.
13As I watched, I heard an eagle that
was flying in midair call out in a loud
voice: "Woe! Woe! Woe to the inhabitants
of the earth, because of the trumpet
blasts about to be sounded by the other
three angels!"

9 The fifth angel sounded his trumpet,
and I saw a star that had fallen from
the sky to the earth. The star was given
the key to the shaft of the Abyss. 2When
he opened the Abyss, smoke rose from it

[a]11 That is, Bitterness

WEDNESDAY

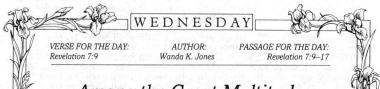

VERSE FOR THE DAY: *Revelation 7:9* | *AUTHOR:* *Wanda K. Jones* | *PASSAGE FOR THE DAY:* *Revelation 7:9–17*

Among the Great Multitude

ONE of the rewards of reading the Bible in its entirety is to see that our walk with Christ ends in joy and victory! Through the eyes of the apostle John in Revelation 7, we see a God-given picture of the joyful culmination of our journey here on earth.

Over the years, as I have listened to the sermons of godly men and women and as I have sat under professors who expounded the Word of God, it was with joy and expectancy that I visualized the great multitude that will eventually gather to worship the Lord. The throng will be so great that no one will be able to count its members. People "from every nation, tribe, people and language, standing before the throne and in front of the Lamb" (Revelation 7:9). Each time I visualized this glorious band of the redeemed, I thought, "Oh, how wonderful! I'm going to be among them!" I still feel that way. What a triumphant future for every believer!

Revelation 7 tells us that we will be rewarded by serving and loving the Lord. We have many opportunities to serve. In this land, and in many other countries, people are hungry and thirsty, homeless and with no one who really cares about them. Others may be well cared for physically and financially, but they carry many burdens both day and night.

Are you included among those who carry many burdens? Or are you numbered in the throng of believers? Will the final chapter of your life close in defeat or victory? If you have not asked Jesus to take your burden of sin, ask him to "wipe away every tear" (Revelation 7:17) from your eyes, to cleanse you in his blood. Then one day you will be a member of that great multitude that no one can number!

Additional Scripture Readings:
Matthew 24:10–14; Hebrews 10:35–39

Go to page 396 for your next devotional reading.

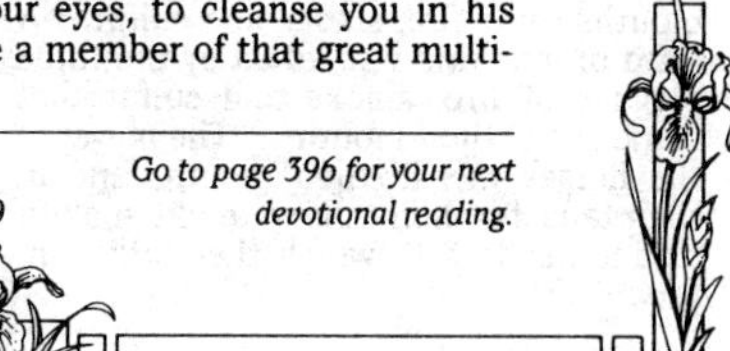

like the smoke from a gigantic furnace. The sun and sky were darkened by the smoke from the Abyss. 3And out of the smoke locusts came down upon the earth and were given power like that of scorpions of the earth. 4They were told not to harm the grass of the earth or any plant or tree, but only those people who did not have the seal of God on their foreheads. 5They were not given power to kill them, but only to torture them for five months. And the agony they suffered was like that of the sting of a scorpion when it strikes a man. 6During those days men will seek death, but will not find it; they will long to die, but death will elude them.

7The locusts looked like horses prepared for battle. On their heads they wore something like crowns of gold, and their faces resembled human faces. 8Their hair was like women's hair, and their teeth were like lions' teeth. 9They had breastplates like breastplates of iron, and the sound of their wings was like the thundering of many horses and chariots rushing into battle. 10They had tails and stings like scorpions, and in their tails they had power to torment people for five months. 11They had as king over them the angel of the Abyss, whose name in Hebrew is Abaddon, and in Greek, Apollyon.[a]

12The first woe is past; two other woes are yet to come.

13The sixth angel sounded his trumpet, and I heard a voice coming from the horns[b] of the golden altar that is before God. 14It said to the sixth angel who had the trumpet, "Release the four angels who are bound at the great river Euphrates." 15And the four angels who had been kept ready for this very hour and day and month and year were released to kill a third of mankind. 16The number of the mounted troops was two hundred million. I heard their number.

17The horses and riders I saw in my vision looked like this: Their breastplates were fiery red, dark blue, and yellow as sulfur. The heads of the horses resembled the heads of lions, and out of their mouths came fire, smoke and sulfur. 18A third of mankind was killed by the three plagues of fire, smoke and sulfur that came out of their mouths. 19The power of the horses was in their mouths and in their tails; for their tails were like snakes, having heads with which they inflict injury.

20The rest of mankind that were not killed by these plagues still did not repent of the work of their hands; they did not stop worshiping demons, and idols of gold, silver, bronze, stone and wood—idols that cannot see or hear or walk. 21Nor did they repent of their murders, their magic arts, their sexual immorality or their thefts.

The Angel and the Little Scroll

10 Then I saw another mighty angel coming down from heaven. He was robed in a cloud, with a rainbow above his head; his face was like the sun, and his legs were like fiery pillars. 2He was holding a little scroll, which lay open in his hand. He planted his right foot on the sea and his left foot on the land, 3and he gave a loud shout like the roar of a lion. When he shouted, the voices of the seven thunders spoke. 4And when the seven thunders spoke, I was about to write; but I heard a voice from heaven say, "Seal up what the seven thunders have said and do not write it down."

5Then the angel I had seen standing on the sea and on the land raised his right hand to heaven. 6And he swore by him who lives for ever and ever, who created the heavens and all that is in them, the earth and all that is in it, and the sea and all that is in it, and said, "There will be no more delay! 7But in the days when the seventh angel is about to sound his trumpet, the mystery of God will be accomplished, just as he announced to his servants the prophets."

8Then the voice that I had heard from heaven spoke to me once more: "Go, take the scroll that lies open in the hand of the angel who is standing on the sea and on the land."

9So I went to the angel and asked him to give me the little scroll. He said to me, "Take it and eat it. It will turn your stomach sour, but in your mouth it will be as sweet as honey." 10I took the little scroll from the angel's hand and ate it. It tasted as sweet as honey in my mouth, but when I had eaten it, my stomach turned sour. 11Then I was told, "You must prophesy again about many peoples, nations, languages and kings."

The Two Witnesses

11 I was given a reed like a measuring rod and was told, "Go and meas-

[a]11 *Abaddon* and *Apollyon* mean *Destroyer.* [b]13 That is, projections

ure the temple of God and the altar, and count the worshipers there. 2But exclude the outer court; do not measure it, because it has been given to the Gentiles. They will trample on the holy city for 42 months. 3And I will give power to my two witnesses, and they will prophesy for 1,260 days, clothed in sackcloth." 4These are the two olive trees and the two lampstands that stand before the Lord of the earth. 5If anyone tries to harm them, fire comes from their mouths and devours their enemies. This is how anyone who wants to harm them must die. 6These men have power to shut up the sky so that it will not rain during the time they are prophesying; and they have power to turn the waters into blood and to strike the earth with every kind of plague as often as they want.

7Now when they have finished their testimony, the beast that comes up from the Abyss will attack them, and overpower and kill them. 8Their bodies will lie in the street of the great city, which is figuratively called Sodom and Egypt, where also their Lord was crucified. 9For three and a half days men from every people, tribe, language and nation will gaze on their bodies and refuse them burial. 10The inhabitants of the earth will gloat over them and will celebrate by sending each other gifts, because these two prophets had tormented those who live on the earth.

11But after the three and a half days a breath of life from God entered them, and they stood on their feet, and terror struck those who saw them. 12Then they heard a loud voice from heaven saying to them, "Come up here." And they went up to heaven in a cloud, while their enemies looked on.

13At that very hour there was a severe earthquake and a tenth of the city collapsed. Seven thousand people were killed in the earthquake, and the survivors were terrified and gave glory to the God of heaven.

14The second woe has passed; the third woe is coming soon.

The Seventh Trumpet

15The seventh angel sounded his trumpet, and there were loud voices in heaven, which said:

"The kingdom of the world has
become the kingdom of our
Lord and of his Christ,
and he will reign for ever and ever."

16And the twenty-four elders, who were seated on their thrones before God, fell on their faces and worshiped God, 17saying:

"We give thanks to you, Lord God
Almighty,
the One who is and who was,
because you have taken your great
power
and have begun to reign.
18The nations were angry;
and your wrath has come.
The time has come for judging the
dead,
and for rewarding your servants the
prophets
and your saints and those who
reverence your name,
both small and great—
and for destroying those who destroy
the earth."

19Then God's temple in heaven was opened, and within his temple was seen the ark of his covenant. And there came flashes of lightning, rumblings, peals of thunder, an earthquake and a great hailstorm.

The Woman and the Dragon

12 A great and wondrous sign appeared in heaven: a woman clothed with the sun, with the moon under her feet and a crown of twelve stars on her head. 2She was pregnant and cried out in pain as she was about to give birth. 3Then another sign appeared in heaven: an enormous red dragon with seven heads and ten horns and seven crowns on his heads. 4His tail swept a third of the stars out of the sky and flung them to the earth. The dragon stood in front of the woman who was about to give birth, so that he might devour her child the moment it was born. 5She gave birth to a son, a male child, who will rule all the nations with an iron scepter. And her child was snatched up to God and to his throne. 6The woman fled into the desert to a place prepared for her by God, where she might be taken care of for 1,260 days.

7And there was war in heaven. Michael and his angels fought against the dragon, and the dragon and his angels fought back. 8But he was not strong enough, and they lost their place in heaven. 9The great dragon was hurled down—that ancient serpent called the devil, or Satan, who

leads the whole world astray. He was
hurled to the earth, and his angels with
him.
10 Then I heard a loud voice in heaven
say:

"Now have come the salvation and
the power and the kingdom of
our God,
and the authority of his Christ.
For the accuser of our brothers,
who accuses them before our God
day and night,
has been hurled down.
11 They overcame him
by the blood of the Lamb
and by the word of their testimony;
they did not love their lives so much
as to shrink from death.
12 Therefore rejoice, you heavens
and you who dwell in them!
But woe to the earth and the sea,
because the devil has gone down to
you!
He is filled with fury,
because he knows that his time is
short."

13 When the dragon saw that he had
been hurled to the earth, he pursued the
woman who had given birth to the male
child. 14 The woman was given the two
wings of a great eagle, so that she might
fly to the place prepared for her in the
desert, where she would be taken care of
for a time, times and half a time, out of
the serpent's reach. 15 Then from his
mouth the serpent spewed water like a
river, to overtake the woman and sweep
her away with the torrent. 16 But the earth
helped the woman by opening its mouth
and swallowing the river that the dragon
had spewed out of his mouth. 17 Then the
dragon was enraged at the woman and
went off to make war against the rest of
her offspring—those who obey God's
commandments and hold to the testimo-
13 ny of Jesus. 1 And the dragon[a]
stood on the shore of the sea.

The Beast out of the Sea

And I saw a beast coming out of the
sea. He had ten horns and seven heads,
with ten crowns on his horns, and on each
head a blasphemous name. 2 The beast I
saw resembled a leopard, but had feet
like those of a bear and a mouth like that
of a lion. The dragon gave the beast his
power and his throne and great authority.
3 One of the heads of the beast seemed to
have had a fatal wound, but the fatal
wound had been healed. The whole world
was astonished and followed the beast.
4 Men worshiped the dragon because he
had given authority to the beast, and they
also worshiped the beast and asked,
"Who is like the beast? Who can make
war against him?"
5 The beast was given a mouth to utter
proud words and blasphemies and to exercise his authority for forty-two months.
6 He opened his mouth to blaspheme God,
and to slander his name and his dwelling
place and those who live in heaven. 7 He
was given power to make war against the
saints and to conquer them. And he was
given authority over every tribe, people,
language and nation. 8 All inhabitants of
the earth will worship the beast—all
whose names have not been written in
the book of life belonging to the Lamb
that was slain from the creation of the
world.[b]
9 He who has an ear, let him hear.

10 If anyone is to go into captivity,
into captivity he will go.
If anyone is to be killed[c] with the
sword,
with the sword he will be killed.

This calls for patient endurance and
faithfulness on the part of the saints.

The Beast out of the Earth

11 Then I saw another beast, coming out
of the earth. He had two horns like a
lamb, but he spoke like a dragon. 12 He
exercised all the authority of the first
beast on his behalf, and made the earth
and its inhabitants worship the first
beast, whose fatal wound had been
healed. 13 And he performed great and
miraculous signs, even causing fire to
come down from heaven to earth in full
view of men. 14 Because of the signs he
was given power to do on behalf of the
first beast, he deceived the inhabitants of
the earth. He ordered them to set up an
image in honor of the beast who was
wounded by the sword and yet lived. 15 He
was given power to give breath to the image of the first beast, so that it could
speak and cause all who refused to worship the image to be killed. 16 He also
forced everyone, small and great, rich and

[a] 1 Some late manuscripts *And I* [b] 8 Or *written from the creation of the world in the book of life belonging to the Lamb that was slain* [c] 10 Some manuscripts *anyone kills*

poor, free and slave, to receive a mark on his right hand or on his forehead, [17]so that no one could buy or sell unless he had the mark, which is the name of the beast or the number of his name.

[18]This calls for wisdom. If anyone has insight, let him calculate the number of the beast, for it is man's number. His number is 666.

The Lamb and the 144,000

14 Then I looked, and there before me was the Lamb, standing on Mount Zion, and with him 144,000 who had his name and his Father's name written on their foreheads. [2]And I heard a sound from heaven like the roar of rushing waters and like a loud peal of thunder. The sound I heard was like that of harpists playing their harps. [3]And they sang a new song before the throne and before the four living creatures and the elders. No one could learn the song except the 144,000 who had been redeemed from the earth. [4]These are those who did not defile themselves with women, for they kept themselves pure. They follow the Lamb wherever he goes. They were purchased from among men and offered as firstfruits to God and the Lamb. [5]No lie was found in their mouths; they are blameless.

The Three Angels

[6]Then I saw another angel flying in midair, and he had the eternal gospel to proclaim to those who live on the earth—to every nation, tribe, language and people. [7]He said in a loud voice, "Fear God and give him glory, because the hour of his judgment has come. Worship him who made the heavens, the earth, the sea and the springs of water."

[8]A second angel followed and said, "Fallen! Fallen is Babylon the Great, which made all the nations drink the maddening wine of her adulteries."

[9]A third angel followed them and said in a loud voice: "If anyone worships the beast and his image and receives his mark on the forehead or on the hand, [10]he, too, will drink of the wine of God's fury, which has been poured full strength into the cup of his wrath. He will be tormented with burning sulfur in the presence of the holy angels and of the Lamb. [11]And the smoke of their torment rises for ever and ever. There is no rest day or night for those who worship the beast and his image, or for anyone who receives the mark of his name." [12]This calls for patient endurance on the part of the saints who obey God's commandments and remain faithful to Jesus.

[13]Then I heard a voice from heaven say, "Write: Blessed are the dead who die in the Lord from now on."

"Yes," says the Spirit, "they will rest from their labor, for their deeds will follow them."

The Harvest of the Earth

[14]I looked, and there before me was a white cloud, and seated on the cloud was one "like a son of man"[a] with a crown of gold on his head and a sharp sickle in his hand. [15]Then another angel came out of the temple and called in a loud voice to him who was sitting on the cloud, "Take your sickle and reap, because the time to reap has come, for the harvest of the earth is ripe." [16]So he who was seated on the cloud swung his sickle over the earth, and the earth was harvested.

[17]Another angel came out of the temple in heaven, and he too had a sharp sickle. [18]Still another angel, who had charge of the fire, came from the altar and called in a loud voice to him who had the sharp sickle, "Take your sharp sickle and gather the clusters of grapes from the earth's vine, because its grapes are ripe." [19]The angel swung his sickle on the earth, gathered its grapes and threw them into the great winepress of God's wrath. [20]They were trampled in the winepress outside the city, and blood flowed out of the press, rising as high as the horses' bridles for a distance of 1,600 stadia.[b]

Seven Angels With Seven Plagues

15 I saw in heaven another great and marvelous sign: seven angels with the seven last plagues—last, because with them God's wrath is completed. [2]And I saw what looked like a sea of glass mixed with fire and, standing beside the sea, those who had been victorious over the beast and his image and over the number of his name. They held harps given them by God [3]and sang the song of Moses the servant of God and the song of the Lamb:

"Great and marvelous are your deeds,
Lord God Almighty.

[a] *14* Daniel 7:13 [b] *20* That is, about 180 miles (about 300 kilometers)

Just and true are your ways,
King of the ages.
4Who will not fear you, O Lord,
and bring glory to your name?
For you alone are holy.
All nations will come
and worship before you,
for your righteous acts have been
revealed."

5After this I looked and in heaven the
temple, that is, the tabernacle of the Testimony, was opened. 6Out of the temple
came the seven angels with the seven
plagues. They were dressed in clean,
shining linen and wore golden sashes
around their chests. 7Then one of the four
living creatures gave to the seven angels
seven golden bowls filled with the wrath
of God, who lives for ever and ever. 8And
the temple was filled with smoke from
the glory of God and from his power, and
no one could enter the temple until the
seven plagues of the seven angels were
completed.

The Seven Bowls of God's Wrath

16 Then I heard a loud voice from the
temple saying to the seven angels,

THURSDAY

VERSE FOR THE DAY: *Revelation 14:13*

AUTHOR: *Gien Karssen*

PASSAGE FOR THE DAY: *Revelation 14:6–13*

Rest and Reward

THE Bible leaves no doubt that there is life after death. Humanity is created for eternity. The earthly life is but an overture, a prelude of the reality to come. Blessed—happy, to be envied—are the dead "who die in the Lord." They are people who during their earthly life believed in Jesus Christ as their Savior and Lord. When they exchange the temporal for the eternal, their work is done forever. They finally have rest. All the troubles and tensions of their earthly existence are behind them. They have arrived at their eternal destination. They are HOME!

The Scriptures paint a frightening alternative for people who do not seek God during their lifetime: "And the smoke of their torment rises for ever and ever. There is no rest day or night" (Revelation 14:11).

What a contrast!

The dead who die in the Lord not only enjoy eternally the absence of unrest, pain and sorrow, but they also are rewarded: "Their deeds will follow them."

Human beings are free to live their lives according to their own choices. But they have to keep in mind that there will be a future settling of accounts. All will—justly—be rewarded according to their deeds. The measuring staff will be administered according to their attitude toward the Lord Jesus Christ.

True rest awaits only those who during their life on earth took God seriously. Without him there is no real rest, in the present or in the future.

Additional Scripture Readings:
Matthew 25:31–46; Luke 16:19–26

Go to page 402 for your next devotional reading.

"Go, pour out the seven bowls of God's
wrath on the earth."
2The first angel went and poured out
his bowl on the land, and ugly and painful
sores broke out on the people who had
the mark of the beast and worshiped his
image.
3The second angel poured out his bowl
on the sea, and it turned into blood like
that of a dead man, and every living thing
in the sea died.
4The third angel poured out his bowl on
the rivers and springs of water, and they
became blood. 5Then I heard the angel in
charge of the waters say:

"You are just in these judgments,
you who are and who were, the
Holy One,
because you have so judged;
6for they have shed the blood of your
saints and prophets,
and you have given them blood to
drink as they deserve."

7And I heard the altar respond:

"Yes, Lord God Almighty,
true and just are your judgments."

8The fourth angel poured out his bowl
on the sun, and the sun was given power
to scorch people with fire. 9They were
seared by the intense heat and they
cursed the name of God, who had control
over these plagues, but they refused to
repent and glorify him.
10The fifth angel poured out his bowl
on the throne of the beast, and his kingdom was plunged into darkness. Men
gnawed their tongues in agony 11and
cursed the God of heaven because of their
pains and their sores, but they refused to
repent of what they had done.
12The sixth angel poured out his bowl
on the great river Euphrates, and its water
was dried up to prepare the way for the
kings from the East. 13Then I saw three
evil[a] spirits that looked like frogs; they
came out of the mouth of the dragon, out
of the mouth of the beast and out of the
mouth of the false prophet. 14They are
spirits of demons performing miraculous
signs, and they go out to the kings of the
whole world, to gather them for the battle
on the great day of God Almighty.
15"Behold, I come like a thief! Blessed
is he who stays awake and keeps his
clothes with him, so that he may not go
naked and be shamefully exposed."
16Then they gathered the kings together to the place that in Hebrew is called
Armageddon.
17The seventh angel poured out his
bowl into the air, and out of the temple
came a loud voice from the throne, saying, "It is done!" 18Then there came
flashes of lightning, rumblings, peals of
thunder and a severe earthquake. No
earthquake like it has ever occurred since
man has been on earth, so tremendous
was the quake. 19The great city split into
three parts, and the cities of the nations
collapsed. God remembered Babylon the
Great and gave her the cup filled with the
wine of the fury of his wrath. 20Every island fled away and the mountains could
not be found. 21From the sky huge hailstones of about a hundred pounds each
fell upon men. And they cursed God on
account of the plague of hail, because the
plague was so terrible.

The Woman on the Beast

17 One of the seven angels who had
the seven bowls came and said to
me, "Come, I will show you the punishment of the great prostitute, who sits on
many waters. 2With her the kings of the
earth committed adultery and the inhabitants of the earth were intoxicated with
the wine of her adulteries."
3Then the angel carried me away in the
Spirit into a desert. There I saw a woman
sitting on a scarlet beast that was covered
with blasphemous names and had seven
heads and ten horns. 4The woman was
dressed in purple and scarlet, and was
glittering with gold, precious stones and
pearls. She held a golden cup in her hand,
filled with abominable things and the
filth of her adulteries. 5This title was written on her forehead:

MYSTERY
BABYLON THE GREAT
THE MOTHER OF PROSTITUTES
AND OF THE ABOMINATIONS OF THE EARTH.

6I saw that the woman was drunk with the
blood of the saints, the blood of those
who bore testimony to Jesus.
When I saw her, I was greatly astonished. 7Then the angel said to me: "Why
are you astonished? I will explain to you
the mystery of the woman and of the
beast she rides, which has the seven
heads and ten horns. 8The beast, which
you saw, once was, now is not, and will

[a]*13* Greek *unclean*

come up out of the Abyss and go to his
destruction. The inhabitants of the earth
whose names have not been written in
the book of life from the creation of the
world will be astonished when they see
the beast, because he once was, now is
not, and yet will come.

9"This calls for a mind with wisdom.
The seven heads are seven hills on which
the woman sits. 10They are also seven
kings. Five have fallen, one is, the other
has not yet come; but when he does
come, he must remain for a little while.
11The beast who once was, and now is
not, is an eighth king. He belongs to the
seven and is going to his destruction.

12"The ten horns you saw are ten kings
who have not yet received a kingdom, but
who for one hour will receive authority as
kings along with the beast. 13They have
one purpose and will give their power and
authority to the beast. 14They will make
war against the Lamb, but the Lamb will
overcome them because he is Lord of
lords and King of kings—and with him
will be his called, chosen and faithful followers."

15Then the angel said to me, "The waters you saw, where the prostitute sits,
are peoples, multitudes, nations and languages. 16The beast and the ten horns you
saw will hate the prostitute. They will
bring her to ruin and leave her naked;
they will eat her flesh and burn her with
fire. 17For God has put it into their hearts
to accomplish his purpose by agreeing to
give the beast their power to rule, until
God's words are fulfilled. 18The woman
you saw is the great city that rules over
the kings of the earth."

The Fall of Babylon

18 After this I saw another angel coming down from heaven. He had
great authority, and the earth was illuminated by his splendor. 2With a
mighty voice he shouted:

"Fallen! Fallen is Babylon the Great!
She has become a home for
demons
and a haunt for every evil[a] spirit,
a haunt for every unclean and
detestable bird.
3For all the nations have drunk
the maddening wine of her
adulteries.
The kings of the earth committed
adultery with her,
and the merchants of the earth
grew rich from her excessive
luxuries."

4Then I heard another voice from heav-
en say:

"Come out of her, my people,
so that you will not share in her
sins,
so that you will not receive any of
her plagues;
5for her sins are piled up to heaven,
and God has remembered her
crimes.
6Give back to her as she has given;
pay her back double for what she
has done.
Mix her a double portion from her
own cup.
7Give her as much torture and grief
as the glory and luxury she gave
herself.
In her heart she boasts,
'I sit as queen; I am not a widow,
and I will never mourn.'
8Therefore in one day her plagues will
overtake her:
death, mourning and famine.
She will be consumed by fire,
for mighty is the Lord God who
judges her.

9"When the kings of the earth who
committed adultery with her and shared
her luxury see the smoke of her burning,
they will weep and mourn over her. 10Ter-
rified at her torment, they will stand far
off and cry:

" 'Woe! Woe, O great city,
O Babylon, city of power!
In one hour your doom has come!'

11"The merchants of the earth will
weep and mourn over her because no one
buys their cargoes any more— 12cargoes
of gold, silver, precious stones and pearls;
fine linen, purple, silk and scarlet cloth;
every sort of citron wood, and articles of
every kind made of ivory, costly wood,
bronze, iron and marble; 13cargoes of cinnamon and spice, of incense, myrrh and
frankincense, of wine and olive oil, of fine
flour and wheat; cattle and sheep; horses
and carriages; and bodies and souls of
men.

14"They will say, 'The fruit you longed

[a]2 Greek *unclean*

for is gone from you. All your riches and
splendor have vanished, never to be
recovered.' [15]The merchants who sold
these things and gained their wealth from
her will stand far off, terrified at her torment. They will weep and mourn [16]and
cry out:

" 'Woe! Woe, O great city,
dressed in fine linen, purple and scarlet,
and glittering with gold, precious stones and pearls!
[17]In one hour such great wealth has been brought to ruin!'

"Every sea captain, and all who travel
by ship, the sailors, and all who earn their
living from the sea, will stand far off.
[18]When they see the smoke of her burning, they will exclaim, 'Was there ever a
city like this great city?' [19]They will throw
dust on their heads, and with weeping
and mourning cry out:

" 'Woe! Woe, O great city,
where all who had ships on the sea
became rich through her wealth!
In one hour she has been brought to ruin!
[20]Rejoice over her, O heaven!
Rejoice, saints and apostles and prophets!
God has judged her for the way she treated you.' "

[21]Then a mighty angel picked up a
boulder the size of a large millstone and
threw it into the sea, and said:

"With such violence
the great city of Babylon will be thrown down,
never to be found again.
[22]The music of harpists and musicians,
flute players and trumpeters,
will never be heard in you again.
No workman of any trade
will ever be found in you again.
The sound of a millstone
will never be heard in you again.
[23]The light of a lamp
will never shine in you again.
The voice of bridegroom and bride
will never be heard in you again.
Your merchants were the world's great men.
By your magic spell all the nations
were led astray.
[24]In her was found the blood of
prophets and of the saints,
and of all who have been killed on the earth."

Hallelujah!

19 After this I heard what sounded
like the roar of a great multitude in
heaven shouting:

"Hallelujah!
Salvation and glory and power belong to our God,
[2] for true and just are his judgments.
He has condemned the great prostitute
who corrupted the earth by her adulteries.
He has avenged on her the blood of his servants."

[3]And again they shouted:

"Hallelujah!
The smoke from her goes up for ever and ever."

[4]The twenty-four elders and the four
living creatures fell down and worshiped
God, who was seated on the throne. And
they cried:

"Amen, Hallelujah!"

[5]Then a voice came from the throne,
saying:

"Praise our God,
all you his servants,
you who fear him,
both small and great!"

[6]Then I heard what sounded like a
great multitude, like the roar of rushing
waters and like loud peals of thunder,
shouting:

"Hallelujah!
For our Lord God Almighty reigns.
[7]Let us rejoice and be glad
and give him glory!
For the wedding of the Lamb has come,
and his bride has made herself ready.
[8]Fine linen, bright and clean,
was given her to wear."
(Fine linen stands for the righteous acts
of the saints.)

[9]Then the angel said to me, "Write:
'Blessed are those who are invited to the
wedding supper of the Lamb!' " And he
added, "These are the true words of God."
[10]At this I fell at his feet to worship
him. But he said to me, "Do not do it! I

am a fellow servant with you and with
your brothers who hold to the testimony
of Jesus. Worship God! For the testimony
of Jesus is the spirit of prophecy."

The Rider on the White Horse

11I saw heaven standing open and there
before me was a white horse, whose rider
is called Faithful and True. With justice
he judges and makes war. 12His eyes are
like blazing fire, and on his head are
many crowns. He has a name written on
him that no one knows but he himself.
13He is dressed in a robe dipped in blood,
and his name is the Word of God. 14The
armies of heaven were following him, riding on white horses and dressed in fine
linen, white and clean. 15Out of his
mouth comes a sharp sword with which
to strike down the nations. "He will rule
them with an iron scepter."[a] He treads
the winepress of the fury of the wrath of
God Almighty. 16On his robe and on his
thigh he has this name written:

KING OF KINGS AND LORD OF LORDS.

17And I saw an angel standing in the
sun, who cried in a loud voice to all the
birds flying in midair, "Come, gather
together for the great supper of God, 18so
that you may eat the flesh of kings, generals, and mighty men, of horses and their
riders, and the flesh of all people, free
and slave, small and great."
19Then I saw the beast and the kings of
the earth and their armies gathered
together to make war against the rider on
the horse and his army. 20But the beast
was captured, and with him the false prophet who had performed the miraculous
signs on his behalf. With these signs he
had deluded those who had received the
mark of the beast and worshiped his image. The two of them were thrown alive
into the fiery lake of burning sulfur. 21The
rest of them were killed with the sword
that came out of the mouth of the rider
on the horse, and all the birds gorged
themselves on their flesh.

The Thousand Years

20 And I saw an angel coming down
out of heaven, having the key to
the Abyss and holding in his hand a great
chain. 2He seized the dragon, that ancient serpent, who is the devil, or Satan,
and bound him for a thousand years. 3He
threw him into the Abyss, and locked and
sealed it over him, to keep him from deceiving the nations anymore until the
thousand years were ended. After that, he
must be set free for a short time.
4I saw thrones on which were seated
those who had been given authority to
judge. And I saw the souls of those who
had been beheaded because of their testimony for Jesus and because of the word
of God. They had not worshiped the beast
or his image and had not received his
mark on their foreheads or their hands.
They came to life and reigned with Christ
a thousand years. 5(The rest of the dead
did not come to life until the thousand
years were ended.) This is the first resurrection. 6Blessed and holy are those who
have part in the first resurrection. The second death has no power over them, but
they will be priests of God and of Christ
and will reign with him for a thousand
years.

Satan's Doom

7When the thousand years are over, Satan will be released from his prison 8and
will go out to deceive the nations in the
four corners of the earth—Gog and
Magog—to gather them for battle. In
number they are like the sand on the seashore. 9They marched across the breadth
of the earth and surrounded the camp of
God's people, the city he loves. But fire
came down from heaven and devoured
them. 10And the devil, who deceived
them, was thrown into the lake of burning
sulfur, where the beast and the false
prophet had been thrown. They will be
tormented day and night for ever and
ever.

The Dead Are Judged

11Then I saw a great white throne and
him who was seated on it. Earth and sky
fled from his presence, and there was no
place for them. 12And I saw the dead,
great and small, standing before the
throne, and books were opened. Another
book was opened, which is the book of
life. The dead were judged according to
what they had done as recorded in the
books. 13The sea gave up the dead that
were in it, and death and Hades gave up
the dead that were in them, and each person was judged according to what he had
done. 14Then death and Hades were
thrown into the lake of fire. The lake of
fire is the second death. 15If anyone's

a15 Psalm 2:9

name was not found written in the book
of life, he was thrown into the lake of fire.

The New Jerusalem

21 Then I saw a new heaven and a
new earth, for the first heaven and
the first earth had passed away, and there
was no longer any sea. 2I saw the Holy
City, the new Jerusalem, coming down
out of heaven from God, prepared as a
bride beautifully dressed for her husband.
3And I heard a loud voice from the throne
saying, "Now the dwelling of God is with
men, and he will live with them. They will
be his people, and God himself will be
with them and be their God. 4He will wipe
every tear from their eyes. There will be
no more death or mourning or crying or
pain, for the old order of things has
passed away."

5He who was seated on the throne said,
"I am making everything new!" Then he
said, "Write this down, for these words
are trustworthy and true."

6He said to me: "It is done. I am the
Alpha and the Omega, the Beginning and
the End. To him who is thirsty I will give
to drink without cost from the spring of
the water of life. 7He who overcomes will
inherit all this, and I will be his God and
he will be my son. 8But the cowardly, the
unbelieving, the vile, the murderers, the
sexually immoral, those who practice magic arts, the idolaters and all liars—their
place will be in the fiery lake of burning
sulfur. This is the second death."

9One of the seven angels who had the
seven bowls full of the seven last plagues
came and said to me, "Come, I will show
you the bride, the wife of the Lamb."
10And he carried me away in the Spirit to
a mountain great and high, and showed
me the Holy City, Jerusalem, coming
down out of heaven from God. 11It shone
with the glory of God, and its brilliance
was like that of a very precious jewel, like
a jasper, clear as crystal. 12It had a great,
high wall with twelve gates, and with
twelve angels at the gates. On the gates
were written the names of the twelve
tribes of Israel. 13There were three gates
on the east, three on the north, three on
the south and three on the west. 14The
wall of the city had twelve foundations,
and on them were the names of the
twelve apostles of the Lamb.

15The angel who talked with me had a
measuring rod of gold to measure the
city, its gates and its walls. 16The city was
laid out like a square, as long as it was
wide. He measured the city with the rod
and found it to be 12,000 stadia[a] in
length, and as wide and high as it is long.
17He measured its wall and it was 144 cubits[b] thick,[c] by man's measurement,
which the angel was using. 18The wall was
made of jasper, and the city of pure gold,
as pure as glass. 19The foundations of the
city walls were decorated with every kind
of precious stone. The first foundation
was jasper, the second sapphire, the
third chalcedony, the fourth emerald,
20the fifth sardonyx, the sixth carnelian, the seventh chrysolite, the eighth
beryl, the ninth topaz, the tenth chrys-
oprase, the eleventh jacinth, and the
twelfth amethyst.[d] 21The twelve gates
were twelve pearls, each gate made of
a single pearl. The great street of the
city was of pure gold, like transparent
glass.

22I did not see a temple in the city, because the Lord God Almighty and the
Lamb are its temple. 23The city does not
need the sun or the moon to shine on it,
for the glory of God gives it light, and the
Lamb is its lamp. 24The nations will walk
by its light, and the kings of the earth will
bring their splendor into it. 25On no day
will its gates ever be shut, for there will be
no night there. 26The glory and honor of
the nations will be brought into it.
27Nothing impure will ever enter it, nor
will anyone who does what is shameful or
deceitful, but only those whose names
are written in the Lamb's book of life.

The River of Life

22 Then the angel showed me the river of the water of life, as clear as
crystal, flowing from the throne of God
and of the Lamb 2down the middle of the
great street of the city. On each side of
the river stood the tree of life, bearing
twelve crops of fruit, yielding its fruit every month. And the leaves of the tree are
for the healing of the nations. 3No longer
will there be any curse. The throne of God
and of the Lamb will be in the city, and
his servants will serve him. 4They will see
his face, and his name will be on their
foreheads. 5There will be no more night.
They will not need the light of a lamp or
the light of the sun, for the Lord God will

[a]*16* That is, about 1,400 miles (about 2,200 kilometers) [b]*17* That is, about 200 feet (about 65 meters) [c]*17* Or *high* [d]*20* The precise identification of some of these precious stones is uncertain.

give them light. And they will reign for
ever and ever.
6The angel said to me, "These words
are trustworthy and true. The Lord, the
God of the spirits of the prophets, sent his
angel to show his servants the things that
must soon take place."

Jesus Is Coming

7"Behold, I am coming soon! Blessed is
he who keeps the words of the prophecy
in this book."

8I, John, am the one who heard and saw
these things. And when I had heard and
seen them, I fell down to worship at the
feet of the angel who had been showing
them to me. 9But he said to me, "Do not
do it! I am a fellow servant with you and
with your brothers the prophets and of all
who keep the words of this book. Worship
God!"
10Then he told me, "Do not seal up the
words of the prophecy of this book, because the time is near. 11Let him who
does wrong continue to do wrong; let him
who is vile continue to be vile; let him
who does right continue to do right; and
let him who is holy continue to be holy."

12"Behold, I am coming soon! My reward is with me, and I will give to everyone according to what he has done. 13I am
the Alpha and the Omega, the First and
the Last, the Beginning and the End.

FRIDAY

VERSE FOR THE DAY: *Revelation 22:16* — *AUTHOR:* *Marilyn Morgan Helleberg* — *PASSAGE FOR THE DAY:* *Revelation 22:7–16*

Morning Star

"I AM . . . the bright Morning Star" (Revelation 22:16).

These words of the risen Christ correspond with a statement once made by a nineteen-year-old youth named Abe Lincoln: "I never behold the stars that I do not feel that I am looking into the face of God."

Stars! What is it about them that so kindles our sense of wonder? Scientists tell us that, when we look up at the night sky, we are seeing light that left some of those faraway stars thousands of light years ago. Tonight, if the sky is clear, you and I might actually see light rays that left some distant star on the night Jesus was born! That makes me aware that our lives touch eternity.

I need the stars. I need them because of my craving for beauty and my longing for perfection in this less-than-beautiful, imperfect world. I need them because I often buy security at the cost of my sense of enchantment, and the price is much too high. I need them to deepen my experience of awe and wonder, to remind me of the kingdom and the power and the glory of God and of his creation.

If the sky is clear tonight, let's step outside and look at the stars. Perhaps, like Abe Lincoln, we'll sense that we're looking into the face of God.

Additional Scripture Readings:
Psalm 19:1–6; Isaiah 40:25–26

Go to page 403 for your next devotional reading.

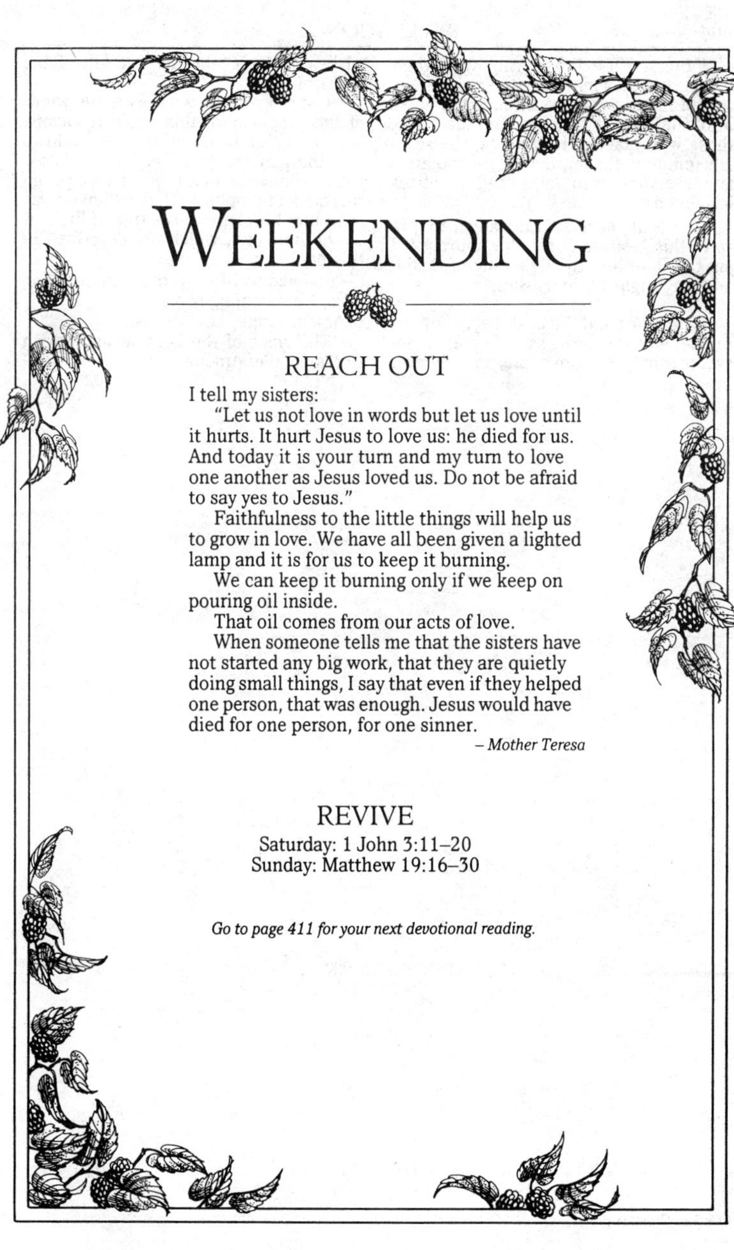

WEEKENDING

REACH OUT

I tell my sisters:

"Let us not love in words but let us love until it hurts. It hurt Jesus to love us: he died for us. And today it is your turn and my turn to love one another as Jesus loved us. Do not be afraid to say yes to Jesus."

Faithfulness to the little things will help us to grow in love. We have all been given a lighted lamp and it is for us to keep it burning.

We can keep it burning only if we keep on pouring oil inside.

That oil comes from our acts of love.

When someone tells me that the sisters have not started any big work, that they are quietly doing small things, I say that even if they helped one person, that was enough. Jesus would have died for one person, for one sinner.

– Mother Teresa

REVIVE

Saturday: 1 John 3:11–20
Sunday: Matthew 19:16–30

Go to page 411 for your next devotional reading.

14"Blessed are those who wash their
robes, that they may have the right to the
tree of life and may go through the gates
into the city. 15Outside are the dogs,
those who practice magic arts, the sexually immoral, the murderers, the idolaters
and everyone who loves and practices
falsehood.

16"I, Jesus, have sent my angel to give
you[a] this testimony for the churches. I
am the Root and the Offspring of David,
and the bright Morning Star."

17The Spirit and the bride say, "Come!"
And let him who hears say, "Come!" Whoever is thirsty, let him come; and whoever
wishes, let him take the free gift of the
water of life.

18I warn everyone who hears the words
of the prophecy of this book: If anyone
adds anything to them, God will add to
him the plagues described in this book.
19And if anyone takes words away from
this book of prophecy, God will take away
from him his share in the tree of life and
in the holy city, which are described in
this book.

20He who testifies to these things says,
"Yes, I am coming soon."

Amen. Come, Lord Jesus.

21The grace of the Lord Jesus be with
God's people. Amen.

[a]*16* The Greek is plural.

PSALMS
PROVERBS

DAVID, the shepherd boy and Israel's greatest king, writes most of the psalms. Together these 150 songs form the greatest collection of prayers ever written. A wide range of human emotion is expressed—joy, excitement, compassion, love, anger, grief, depression. As you read this book, remember that no matter what you are feeling, God wants to hear about it in your prayers to him. He promises to listen to all your concerns and to answer them for Jesus' sake.

PSALMS

BOOK I

Psalms 1–41

Psalm 1

1Blessed is the man
who does not walk in the counsel of the wicked
or stand in the way of sinners
or sit in the seat of mockers.
2But his delight is in the law of the LORD,
and on his law he meditates day and night.
3He is like a tree planted by streams of water,
which yields its fruit in season
and whose leaf does not wither.
Whatever he does prospers.

4Not so the wicked!
They are like chaff
that the wind blows away.
5Therefore the wicked will not stand in the judgment,
nor sinners in the assembly of the righteous.

6For the LORD watches over the way of the righteous,

but the way of the wicked will
perish.

Psalm 2

1Why do the nations conspire[a]
and the peoples plot in vain?
2The kings of the earth take their
stand
and the rulers gather together
against the LORD
and against his Anointed One.[b]
3"Let us break their chains," they say,
"and throw off their fetters."

4The One enthroned in heaven laughs;
the Lord scoffs at them.
5Then he rebukes them in his anger
and terrifies them in his wrath,
saying,
6"I have installed my King[c]
on Zion, my holy hill."

7I will proclaim the decree of the LORD:

He said to me, "You are my Son[d];
today I have become your Father.[e]
8Ask of me,
and I will make the nations your
inheritance,
the ends of the earth your
possession.
9You will rule them with an iron
scepter[f];
you will dash them to pieces like
pottery."

10Therefore, you kings, be wise;
be warned, you rulers of the earth.
11Serve the LORD with fear
and rejoice with trembling.
12Kiss the Son, lest he be angry
and you be destroyed in your way,
for his wrath can flare up in a
moment.
Blessed are all who take refuge in
him.

Psalm 3

A psalm of David. When he fled from
his son Absalom.

1O LORD, how many are my foes!
How many rise up against me!
2Many are saying of me,
"God will not deliver him." *Selah*[g]

3But you are a shield around me,
O LORD;
you bestow glory on me and lift[h]
up my head.
4To the LORD I cry aloud,
and he answers me from his holy
hill. *Selah*

5I lie down and sleep;
I wake again, because the LORD
sustains me.
6I will not fear the tens of thousands
drawn up against me on every side.

7Arise, O LORD!
Deliver me, O my God!
Strike all my enemies on the jaw;
break the teeth of the wicked.

8From the LORD comes deliverance.
May your blessing be on your
people. *Selah*

Psalm 4

For the director of music. With stringed
instruments. A psalm of David.

1Answer me when I call to you,
O my righteous God.
Give me relief from my distress;
be merciful to me and hear my
prayer.

2How long, O men, will you turn my
glory into shame[i]?
How long will you love delusions
and seek false gods[j]? *Selah*
3Know that the LORD has set apart the
godly for himself;
the LORD will hear when I call to
him.

4In your anger do not sin;
when you are on your beds,
search your hearts and be silent.
Selah
5Offer right sacrifices
and trust in the LORD.

6Many are asking, "Who can show us
any good?"
Let the light of your face shine
upon us, O LORD.
7You have filled my heart with greater
joy
than when their grain and new wine
abound.
8I will lie down and sleep in peace,

[a]1 Hebrew; Septuagint *rage* [b]2 Or *anointed one* [c]6 Or *king* [d]7 Or *son*; also in verse 12
[e]7 Or *have begotten you* [f]9 Or *will break them with a rod of iron* [g]2 A word of uncertain meaning, occurring frequently in the Psalms; possibly a musical term [h]3 Or *LORD, / my Glorious One, who lifts*
[i]2 Or *you dishonor my Glorious One* [j]2 Or *seek lies*

for you alone, O LORD,
make me dwell in safety.

Psalm 5

For the director of music. For flutes.
A psalm of David.

1Give ear to my words, O LORD,
consider my sighing.
2Listen to my cry for help,
my King and my God,
for to you I pray.
3In the morning, O LORD, you hear my voice;
in the morning I lay my requests before you
and wait in expectation.

4You are not a God who takes pleasure in evil;
with you the wicked cannot dwell.
5The arrogant cannot stand in your presence;
you hate all who do wrong.
6You destroy those who tell lies;
bloodthirsty and deceitful men
the LORD abhors.

7But I, by your great mercy,
will come into your house;
in reverence will I bow down
toward your holy temple.
8Lead me, O LORD, in your righteousness
because of my enemies—
make straight your way before me.

9Not a word from their mouth can be trusted;
their heart is filled with destruction.
Their throat is an open grave;
with their tongue they speak deceit.
10Declare them guilty, O God!
Let their intrigues be their downfall.
Banish them for their many sins,
for they have rebelled against you.

11But let all who take refuge in you be glad;
let them ever sing for joy.
Spread your protection over them,
that those who love your name may rejoice in you.
12For surely, O LORD, you bless the righteous;
you surround them with your favor
as with a shield.

Psalm 6

For the director of music. With stringed instruments. According to *sheminith.*[a]
A psalm of David.

1O LORD, do not rebuke me in your anger
or discipline me in your wrath.
2Be merciful to me, LORD, for I am faint;
O LORD, heal me, for my bones are in agony.
3My soul is in anguish.
How long, O LORD, how long?

4Turn, O LORD, and deliver me;
save me because of your unfailing love.
5No one remembers you when he is dead.
Who praises you from the grave[b]?

6I am worn out from groaning;
all night long I flood my bed with weeping
and drench my couch with tears.
7My eyes grow weak with sorrow;
they fail because of all my foes.

8Away from me, all you who do evil,
for the LORD has heard my weeping.
9The LORD has heard my cry for mercy;
the LORD accepts my prayer.
10All my enemies will be ashamed and dismayed;
they will turn back in sudden disgrace.

Psalm 7

A *shiggaion*[c] of David, which he sang to the LORD concerning Cush, a Benjamite.

1O LORD my God, I take refuge in you;
save and deliver me from all who pursue me,
2or they will tear me like a lion
and rip me to pieces with no one to rescue me.

3O LORD my God, if I have done this
and there is guilt on my hands—
4if I have done evil to him who is at peace with me
or without cause have robbed my foe—
5then let my enemy pursue and overtake me;
let him trample my life to the ground

[a]Title: Probably a musical term [b]5 Hebrew *Sheol* [c]Title: Probably a literary or musical term

and make me sleep in the dust.
Selah

6Arise, O LORD, in your anger;
rise up against the rage of my enemies.
Awake, my God; decree justice.
7Let the assembled peoples gather around you.
Rule over them from on high;
8 let the LORD judge the peoples.
Judge me, O LORD, according to my righteousness,
according to my integrity, O Most High.
9O righteous God,
who searches minds and hearts,
bring to an end the violence of the wicked
and make the righteous secure.

10My shield[a] is God Most High,
who saves the upright in heart.
11God is a righteous judge,
a God who expresses his wrath every day.
12If he does not relent,
he[b] will sharpen his sword;
he will bend and string his bow.
13He has prepared his deadly weapons;
he makes ready his flaming arrows.

14He who is pregnant with evil
and conceives trouble gives birth to disillusionment.
15He who digs a hole and scoops it out
falls into the pit he has made.
16The trouble he causes recoils on himself;
his violence comes down on his own head.

17I will give thanks to the LORD because of his righteousness
and will sing praise to the name of the LORD Most High.

Psalm 8

For the director of music. According to *gittith*.[c] A psalm of David.

1O LORD, our Lord,
how majestic is your name in all the earth!

You have set your glory
above the heavens.
2From the lips of children and infants
you have ordained praise[d]
because of your enemies,
to silence the foe and the avenger.

3When I consider your heavens,
the work of your fingers,
the moon and the stars,
which you have set in place,
4what is man that you are mindful of him,
the son of man that you care for him?
5You made him a little lower than the heavenly beings[e]
and crowned him with glory and honor.

6You made him ruler over the works of your hands;
you put everything under his feet:
7all flocks and herds,
and the beasts of the field,
8the birds of the air,
and the fish of the sea,
all that swim the paths of the seas.

9O LORD, our Lord,
how majestic is your name in all the earth!

Psalm 9[f]

For the director of music. To the tune of, "The Death of the Son." A psalm of David.

1I will praise you, O LORD, with all my heart;
I will tell of all your wonders.
2I will be glad and rejoice in you;
I will sing praise to your name,
O Most High.

3My enemies turn back;
they stumble and perish before you.
4For you have upheld my right and my cause;
you have sat on your throne,
judging righteously.
5You have rebuked the nations and destroyed the wicked;
you have blotted out their name for ever and ever.
6Endless ruin has overtaken the enemy,

[a]10 Or *sovereign* [b]12 Or *If a man does not repent, / God* [c]Title: Probably a musical term [d]2 Or *strength* [e]5 Or *than God* [f]Psalms 9 and 10 may have been originally a single acrostic poem, the stanzas of which begin with the successive letters of the Hebrew alphabet. In the Septuagint they constitute one psalm.

MONDAY

VERSE FOR THE DAY: *Psalm 8:1* | *AUTHOR:* *Debbie Smith* | *PASSAGE FOR THE DAY:* *Psalm 8:1–9*

How Majestic Is Your Name

MICHAEL and I fell in love and into marriage almost before we knew what happened! We both considered ourselves rational, logical twenty-three-year-olds; but within three weeks of laying eyes on each other, we were engaged. Five months later, after many hours of prayer and counsel, we made our life commitment—to get to know each other!

Part of getting acquainted included writing songs together. God had planned that in advance, because it had never crossed my mind that I would marry a musician, much less write songs with him! Early in our marriage, we spent some of our favorite moments in the evenings at the piano, a kerosene lamp flickering and the Bible opened to the Psalms.

One evening we turned to Psalm 8. What an expression of joy from a man who understood the majesty of creation . . . and that God had entrusted man to rule over it! Furthermore, the psalmist David affirms our worth in this psalm. No room for poor self-image here!

Michael began searching for a tune to the Scriptural line:

O LORD, our Lord,
how majestic is your name in all the earth!
(Psalm 8:1).

Fingers busy on the keyboard, he stopped, midmelody. Turning to me, he pointed to a large, framed poster hanging in our den. It lists all the names of Jesus found in the Bible. Reading down the list, my husband chose a few that fit the tune, and the song "How Majestic Is Your Name" was born!

O Lord our Lord, how majestic is your name
in all the earth.
O Lord our Lord, how majestic is your name
in all the earth.
O Lord, we praise your name.
O Lord, we magnify your name . . .
Prince of Peace, Mighty God, O Lord God
Almighty!*

Michael and I discovered that not only did our musical collaboration bring us closer together, it also brought us closer to our majestic God.

Additional Scripture Readings:
Ephesians 5:19–20; Philippians 2:9–11

Go to page 414 for your next devotional reading.

you have uprooted their cities;
even the memory of them has
perished.

7The LORD reigns forever;
he has established his throne for
judgment.
8He will judge the world in
righteousness;
he will govern the peoples with
justice.
9The LORD is a refuge for the
oppressed,
a stronghold in times of trouble.
10Those who know your name will trust
in you,
for you, LORD, have never forsaken
those who seek you.

11Sing praises to the LORD, enthroned in
Zion;
proclaim among the nations what
he has done.
12For he who avenges blood remembers;
he does not ignore the cry of the
afflicted.

13O LORD, see how my enemies
persecute me!
Have mercy and lift me up from the
gates of death,
14that I may declare your praises
in the gates of the Daughter of
Zion
and there rejoice in your salvation.
15The nations have fallen into the pit
they have dug;
their feet are caught in the net they
have hidden.
16The LORD is known by his justice;
the wicked are ensnared by the
work of their hands. *Higgaion.*[a]
Selah
17The wicked return to the grave,[b]
all the nations that forget
God.
18But the needy will not always be
forgotten,
nor the hope of the afflicted ever
perish.

19Arise, O LORD, let not man triumph;
let the nations be judged in your
presence.
20Strike them with terror, O LORD;
let the nations know they are but
men. *Selah*

Psalm 10[c]

1Why, O LORD, do you stand far off?
Why do you hide yourself in times
of trouble?

2In his arrogance the wicked man
hunts down the weak,
who are caught in the schemes he
devises.
3He boasts of the cravings of his heart;
he blesses the greedy and reviles
the LORD.
4In his pride the wicked does not seek
him;
in all his thoughts there is no room
for God.
5His ways are always prosperous;
he is haughty and your laws are far
from him;
he sneers at all his enemies.
6He says to himself, "Nothing will
shake me;
I'll always be happy and never have
trouble."
7His mouth is full of curses and lies
and threats;
trouble and evil are under his
tongue.
8He lies in wait near the villages;
from ambush he murders the
innocent,
watching in secret for his victims.
9He lies in wait like a lion in cover;
he lies in wait to catch the
helpless;
he catches the helpless and drags
them off in his net.
10His victims are crushed, they
collapse;
they fall under his strength.
11He says to himself, "God has
forgotten;
he covers his face and never sees."

12Arise, LORD! Lift up your hand, O God.
Do not forget the helpless.
13Why does the wicked man revile
God?
Why does he say to himself,
"He won't call me to account"?
14But you, O God, do see trouble and
grief;
you consider it to take it in hand.
The victim commits himself to you;
you are the helper of the fatherless.

[a]*16* Or *Meditation*; possibly a musical notation [b]*17* Hebrew *Sheol* [c]Psalms 9 and 10 may have been originally a single acrostic poem, the stanzas of which begin with the successive letters of the Hebrew alphabet. In the Septuagint they constitute one psalm.

15Break the arm of the wicked and evil man;
call him to account for his wickedness
that would not be found out.

16The LORD is King for ever and ever;
the nations will perish from his land.
17You hear, O LORD, the desire of the afflicted;
you encourage them, and you listen to their cry,
18defending the fatherless and the oppressed,
in order that man, who is of the earth, may terrify no more.

Psalm 11

For the director of music. Of David.

1In the LORD I take refuge.
How then can you say to me:
"Flee like a bird to your mountain.
2For look, the wicked bend their bows;
they set their arrows against the strings
to shoot from the shadows
at the upright in heart.
3When the foundations are being destroyed,
what can the righteous do[a]?"

4The LORD is in his holy temple;
the LORD is on his heavenly throne.
He observes the sons of men;
his eyes examine them.
5The LORD examines the righteous,
but the wicked[b] and those who love violence
his soul hates.
6On the wicked he will rain
fiery coals and burning sulfur;
a scorching wind will be their lot.

7For the LORD is righteous,
he loves justice;
upright men will see his face.

Psalm 12

For the director of music. According to *sheminith.*[c] A psalm of David.

1Help, LORD, for the godly are no more;
the faithful have vanished from among men.
2Everyone lies to his neighbor;
their flattering lips speak with deception.
3May the LORD cut off all flattering lips
and every boastful tongue
4that says, "We will triumph with our tongues;
we own our lips[d]—who is our master?"

5"Because of the oppression of the weak
and the groaning of the needy,
I will now arise," says the LORD.
"I will protect them from those who malign them."
6And the words of the LORD are flawless,
like silver refined in a furnace of clay,
purified seven times.

7O LORD, you will keep us safe
and protect us from such people forever.
8The wicked freely strut about
when what is vile is honored among men.

Psalm 13

For the director of music. A psalm of David.

1How long, O LORD? Will you forget me forever?
How long will you hide your face from me?
2How long must I wrestle with my thoughts
and every day have sorrow in my heart?
How long will my enemy triumph over me?

3Look on me and answer, O LORD my God.
Give light to my eyes, or I will sleep in death;
4my enemy will say, "I have overcome him,"
and my foes will rejoice when I fall.

5But I trust in your unfailing love;
my heart rejoices in your salvation.
6I will sing to the LORD,
for he has been good to me.

[a]3 Or *what is the Righteous One doing* [b]5 Or *The LORD, the Righteous One, examines the wicked, /* [c]Title: Probably a musical term [d]4 Or */ our lips are our plowshares*

Psalm 14

For the director of music. Of David.

1The fool[a] says in his heart,
"There is no God."
They are corrupt, their deeds are vile;
there is no one who does good.

2The LORD looks down from heaven
on the sons of men
to see if there are any who
understand,
any who seek God.
3All have turned aside,
they have together become corrupt;
there is no one who does good,
not even one.

4Will evildoers never learn—
those who devour my people as
men eat bread
and who do not call on the LORD?
5There they are, overwhelmed with
dread,
for God is present in the company
of the righteous.
6You evildoers frustrate the plans of
the poor,
but the LORD is their refuge.

7Oh, that salvation for Israel would
come out of Zion!
When the LORD restores the
fortunes of his people,
let Jacob rejoice and Israel be glad!

Psalm 15

A psalm of David.

1LORD, who may dwell in your
sanctuary?
Who may live on your holy hill?

2He whose walk is blameless
and who does what is righteous,
who speaks the truth from his heart
3 and has no slander on his tongue,
who does his neighbor no wrong

a1 The Hebrew words rendered *fool* in Psalms denote one who is morally deficient.

TUESDAY

VERSE FOR THE DAY: *Psalm 14:1*

AUTHOR: *Ruth Bell Graham*

PASSAGE FOR THE DAY: *Psalm 14:1–7*

The Fools

"THE fool says in his heart, 'There is no God.'" This designation goes for those who doubt God's sovereignty as well as those who deny Him. Either He is sovereign, or He is not God. Therefore, when we become so preoccupied with and dismayed by circumstances and certain people that we doubt God's ability to handle things in His own way, and in His own time, then we, too, are fools.

Additional Scripture Readings:
1 Kings 19:1–18; Luke 24:17–25

Go to page 419 for your next devotional reading.

and casts no slur on his fellowman,
4who despises a vile man
but honors those who fear the LORD,
who keeps his oath
even when it hurts,
5who lends his money without usury
and does not accept a bribe against the innocent.

He who does these things
will never be shaken.

Psalm 16

A *miktam*[a] of David.

1Keep me safe, O God,
for in you I take refuge.

2I said to the LORD, "You are my Lord;
apart from you I have no good thing."
3As for the saints who are in the land,
they are the glorious ones in whom is all my delight.[b]
4The sorrows of those will increase
who run after other gods.
I will not pour out their libations of blood
or take up their names on my lips.

5LORD, you have assigned me my portion and my cup;
you have made my lot secure.
6The boundary lines have fallen for me
in pleasant places;
surely I have a delightful inheritance.

7I will praise the LORD, who counsels me;
even at night my heart instructs me.
8I have set the LORD always before me.
Because he is at my right hand,
I will not be shaken.

9Therefore my heart is glad and my tongue rejoices;
my body also will rest secure,
10because you will not abandon me to the grave,[c]
nor will you let your Holy One[d] see decay.
11You have made[e] known to me the path of life;
you will fill me with joy in your presence,
with eternal pleasures at your right hand.

Psalm 17

A prayer of David.

1Hear, O LORD, my righteous plea;
listen to my cry.
Give ear to my prayer—
it does not rise from deceitful lips.
2May my vindication come from you;
may your eyes see what is right.

3Though you probe my heart and examine me at night,
though you test me, you will find nothing;
I have resolved that my mouth will not sin.
4As for the deeds of men—
by the word of your lips
I have kept myself
from the ways of the violent.
5My steps have held to your paths;
my feet have not slipped.

6I call on you, O God, for you will answer me;
give ear to me and hear my prayer.
7Show the wonder of your great love,
you who save by your right hand
those who take refuge in you from their foes.
8Keep me as the apple of your eye;
hide me in the shadow of your wings
9from the wicked who assail me,
from my mortal enemies who surround me.

10They close up their callous hearts,
and their mouths speak with arrogance.
11They have tracked me down, they now surround me,
with eyes alert, to throw me to the ground.
12They are like a lion hungry for prey,
like a great lion crouching in cover.

13Rise up, O LORD, confront them, bring them down;
rescue me from the wicked by your sword.
14O LORD, by your hand save me from such men,

[a]Title: Probably a literary or musical term [b]3 Or *As for the pagan priests who are in the land / and the nobles in whom all delight, I said:* [c]10 Hebrew *Sheol* [d]10 Or *your faithful one* [e]11 Or *You will make*

from men of this world whose
reward is in this life.

You still the hunger of those you
cherish;
their sons have plenty,
and they store up wealth for their
children.
15And I—in righteousness I will see
your face;
when I awake, I will be satisfied
with seeing your likeness.

Psalm 18

For the director of music. Of David the servant of the LORD. He sang to the LORD the words of this song when the LORD delivered him from the hand of all his enemies and from the hand of Saul. He said:

1I love you, O LORD, my strength.

2The LORD is my rock, my fortress and
my deliverer;
my God is my rock, in whom I take
refuge.
He is my shield and the horn[a] of
my salvation, my stronghold.
3I call to the LORD, who is worthy of
praise,
and I am saved from my enemies.

4The cords of death entangled me;
the torrents of destruction
overwhelmed me.
5The cords of the grave[b] coiled around
me;
the snares of death confronted me.
6In my distress I called to the LORD;
I cried to my God for help.
From his temple he heard my voice;
my cry came before him, into his
ears.

7The earth trembled and quaked,
and the foundations of the
mountains shook;
they trembled because he was
angry.
8Smoke rose from his nostrils;
consuming fire came from his
mouth,
burning coals blazed out of it.
9He parted the heavens and came
down;
dark clouds were under his feet.
10He mounted the cherubim and flew;
he soared on the wings of the wind.
11He made darkness his covering, his
canopy around him—
the dark rain clouds of the sky.
12Out of the brightness of his presence
clouds advanced,
with hailstones and bolts of
lightning.
13The LORD thundered from heaven;
the voice of the Most High
resounded.[c]
14He shot his arrows and scattered ⌊the
enemies⌋,
great bolts of lightning and routed
them.
15The valleys of the sea were exposed
and the foundations of the earth
laid bare
at your rebuke, O LORD,
at the blast of breath from your
nostrils.

16He reached down from on high and
took hold of me;
he drew me out of deep waters.
17He rescued me from my powerful
enemy,
from my foes, who were too strong
for me.
18They confronted me in the day of my
disaster,
but the LORD was my support.
19He brought me out into a spacious
place;
he rescued me because he
delighted in me.

20The LORD has dealt with me according
to my righteousness;
according to the cleanness of my
hands he has rewarded me.
21For I have kept the ways of the LORD;
I have not done evil by turning
from my God.
22All his laws are before me;
I have not turned away from his
decrees.
23I have been blameless before him
and have kept myself from sin.
24The LORD has rewarded me according
to my righteousness,
according to the cleanness of my
hands in his sight.

25To the faithful you show yourself
faithful,
to the blameless you show yourself
blameless,

[a]2 *Horn* here symbolizes strength. [b]5 Hebrew *Sheol* [c]13 Some Hebrew manuscripts and Septuagint (see also 2 Samuel 22:14); most Hebrew manuscripts *resounded, / amid hailstones and bolts of lightning*

26to the pure you show yourself pure,
but to the crooked you show
yourself shrewd.
27You save the humble
but bring low those whose eyes are
haughty.
28You, O LORD, keep my lamp burning;
my God turns my darkness into
light.
29With your help I can advance against
a troop[a];
with my God I can scale a wall.

30As for God, his way is perfect;
the word of the LORD is flawless.
He is a shield
for all who take refuge in him.
31For who is God besides the LORD?
And who is the Rock except our
God?
32It is God who arms me with strength
and makes my way perfect.
33He makes my feet like the feet of a
deer;
he enables me to stand on the
heights.
34He trains my hands for battle;
my arms can bend a bow of bronze.
35You give me your shield of victory,
and your right hand sustains me;
you stoop down to make me great.
36You broaden the path beneath me,
so that my ankles do not turn.

37I pursued my enemies and overtook
them;
I did not turn back till they were
destroyed.
38I crushed them so that they could not
rise;
they fell beneath my feet.
39You armed me with strength for
battle;
you made my adversaries bow at my
feet.
40You made my enemies turn their
backs in flight,
and I destroyed my foes.
41They cried for help, but there was no
one to save them—
to the LORD, but he did not answer.
42I beat them as fine as dust borne on
the wind;
I poured them out like mud in the
streets.

43You have delivered me from the
attacks of the people;
you have made me the head of
nations;
people I did not know are subject
to me.
44As soon as they hear me, they obey
me;
foreigners cringe before me.
45They all lose heart;
they come trembling from their
strongholds.

46The LORD lives! Praise be to my Rock!
Exalted be God my Savior!
47He is the God who avenges me,
who subdues nations under me,
48 who saves me from my enemies.
You exalted me above my foes;
from violent men you rescued me.
49Therefore I will praise you among the
nations, O LORD;
I will sing praises to your name.
50He gives his king great victories;
he shows unfailing kindness to his
anointed,
to David and his descendants
forever.

Psalm 19

For the director of music. A psalm
of David.

1The heavens declare the glory of God;
the skies proclaim the work of his
hands.
2Day after day they pour forth speech;
night after night they display
knowledge.
3There is no speech or language
where their voice is not heard.[b]
4Their voice[c] goes out into all the
earth,
their words to the ends of the
world.
In the heavens he has pitched a tent
for the sun,
5 which is like a bridegroom coming
forth from his pavilion,
like a champion rejoicing to run his
course.
6It rises at one end of the heavens
and makes its circuit to the other;
nothing is hidden from its heat.

7The law of the LORD is perfect,
reviving the soul.
The statutes of the LORD are
trustworthy,

[a]29 *Or can run through a barricade* [b]3 *Or They have no speech, there are no words; / no sound is heard from them* [c]4 Septuagint, Jerome and Syriac; Hebrew *line*

making wise the simple.
8The precepts of the LORD are right,
giving joy to the heart.
The commands of the LORD are radiant,
giving light to the eyes.
9The fear of the LORD is pure,
enduring forever.
The ordinances of the LORD are sure
and altogether righteous.
10They are more precious than gold,
than much pure gold;
they are sweeter than honey,
than honey from the comb.
11By them is your servant warned;
in keeping them there is great reward.

12Who can discern his errors?
Forgive my hidden faults.
13Keep your servant also from willful sins;
may they not rule over me.
Then will I be blameless,
innocent of great transgression.

14May the words of my mouth and the meditation of my heart
be pleasing in your sight,
O LORD, my Rock and my Redeemer.

Psalm 20

For the director of music. A psalm of David.

1May the LORD answer you when you are in distress;
may the name of the God of Jacob protect you.
2May he send you help from the sanctuary
and grant you support from Zion.
3May he remember all your sacrifices
and accept your burnt offerings. *Selah*
4May he give you the desire of your heart
and make all your plans succeed.
5We will shout for joy when you are victorious
and will lift up our banners in the name of our God.
May the LORD grant all your requests.

6Now I know that the LORD saves his anointed;
he answers him from his holy heaven
with the saving power of his right hand.
7Some trust in chariots and some in horses,
but we trust in the name of the LORD our God.
8They are brought to their knees and fall,
but we rise up and stand firm.

9O LORD, save the king!
Answer[a] us when we call!

Psalm 21

For the director of music. A psalm of David.

1O LORD, the king rejoices in your strength.
How great is his joy in the victories you give!
2You have granted him the desire of his heart
and have not withheld the request of his lips. *Selah*
3You welcomed him with rich blessings
and placed a crown of pure gold on his head.
4He asked you for life, and you gave it to him—
length of days, for ever and ever.
5Through the victories you gave, his glory is great;
you have bestowed on him splendor and majesty.
6Surely you have granted him eternal blessings
and made him glad with the joy of your presence.
7For the king trusts in the LORD;
through the unfailing love of the Most High
he will not be shaken.

8Your hand will lay hold on all your enemies;
your right hand will seize your foes.
9At the time of your appearing
you will make them like a fiery furnace.
In his wrath the LORD will swallow them up,
and his fire will consume them.
10You will destroy their descendants from the earth,
their posterity from mankind.
11Though they plot evil against you

[a]9 Or *save! / O King, answer*

WEDNESDAY

VERSE FOR THE DAY:
Psalm 19:1

AUTHOR:
Gloria Gaither

PASSAGE FOR THE DAY:
Psalm 19:1–14

I Declare

IT was the sun pouring through the kitchen window at 7:00 A.M., for the first time after the long winter, that made me turn to Psalm 19 instead of the chapter in Colossians we had been reading that week to the kids at the breakfast table. I was reading it for the kids, right? So they would focus on the glorious, first sunny morning of early spring.

But as I read, I became overwhelmed with the way this fellow-poet had reached from the circumstances of his life into mine.

The psalm opened with the familiar verse:

> The heavens declare the glory of God;
> the skies proclaim the work of his hands.

The psalmist then moves on to list the all-encompassing, beautiful declarations of God's law. These declarations so powerfully bring into focus what life should be about, so speak to our human frailties, so heal our broken dreams, so reassure our lost confidences, so pinpoint our areas of weakness, that the psalmist literally falls to his knees in repentance.

His error and hidden faults, his smallness and willful sins are all exposed. And more than that, he begins to ask himself, "If we are supposed to be the most articulate of all God's creatures, what are our lives saying? What are we making as the declaration of our days?"

Shamed by the articulate heavens, we hear our own voices praying aloud with the psalmist in repentance and supplication:

> May the words of my mouth and the meditation
> of my heart
> be pleasing in your sight,
> O LORD, my Rock and my Redeemer
> (Psalm 19:14).

The children were very silent as I, overwhelmed by what I had read, sobbed through these final words of the psalm. Then together we prayed, "Jesus, this day let our actions and attitudes be in sync with all creation. May we articulate praise with the moments we are given today. Amen."

(As a result of this experience, Gloria wrote: "Praise You; I Will Praise You," "Anthem," "What Are the Words?" "I'd Say 'I Love You' in a Thousand Ways," and "Hallelu—Hallelujah!")

Additional Scripture Readings:
Proverbs 4:23–27; Matthew 5:14–16

Go to page 421 for your next devotional reading.

and devise wicked schemes, they
cannot succeed;
12for you will make them turn their
backs
when you aim at them with drawn
bow.

13Be exalted, O LORD, in your strength;
we will sing and praise your might.

Psalm 22

For the director of music. To the tune of, "The Doe of the Morning." A psalm of David.

1My God, my God, why have you
forsaken me?
Why are you so far from saving me,
so far from the words of my
groaning?
2O my God, I cry out by day, but you
do not answer,
by night, and am not silent.

3Yet you are enthroned as the Holy
One;
you are the praise of Israel.[a]
4In you our fathers put their trust;
they trusted and you delivered
them.
5They cried to you and were saved;
in you they trusted and were not
disappointed.

6But I am a worm and not a man,
scorned by men and despised by
the people.
7All who see me mock me;
they hurl insults, shaking their
heads:
8"He trusts in the LORD;
let the LORD rescue him.
Let him deliver him,
since he delights in him."

9Yet you brought me out of the womb;
you made me trust in you
even at my mother's breast.
10From birth I was cast upon you;
from my mother's womb you have
been my God.
11Do not be far from me,
for trouble is near
and there is no one to help.

12Many bulls surround me;
strong bulls of Bashan encircle me.
13Roaring lions tearing their prey
open their mouths wide against me.
14I am poured out like water,
and all my bones are out of joint.
My heart has turned to wax;
it has melted away within me.
15My strength is dried up like a
potsherd,
and my tongue sticks to the roof of
my mouth;
you lay me[b] in the dust of death.
16Dogs have surrounded me;
a band of evil men has encircled
me,
they have pierced[c] my hands and
my feet.
17I can count all my bones;
people stare and gloat over me.
18They divide my garments among them
and cast lots for my clothing.

19But you, O LORD, be not far off;
O my Strength, come quickly to
help me.
20Deliver my life from the sword,
my precious life from the power of
the dogs.
21Rescue me from the mouth of the
lions;
save[d] me from the horns of the
wild oxen.

22I will declare your name to my
brothers;
in the congregation I will praise
you.
23You who fear the LORD, praise him!
All you descendants of Jacob,
honor him!
Revere him, all you descendants of
Israel!
24For he has not despised or disdained
the suffering of the afflicted one;
he has not hidden his face from him
but has listened to his cry for help.

25From you comes the theme of my
praise in the great assembly;
before those who fear you[e] will I
fulfill my vows.
26The poor will eat and be satisfied;
they who seek the LORD will praise
him—
may your hearts live forever!
27All the ends of the earth
will remember and turn to the
LORD,
and all the families of the nations
will bow down before him,

[a]3 Or *Yet you are holy, / enthroned on the praises of Israel* [b]15 Or */ I am laid* [c]16 Some Hebrew manuscripts, Septuagint and Syriac; most Hebrew manuscripts */ like the lion,* [d]21 Or */ you have heard* [e]25 Hebrew *him*

THURSDAY

VERSE FOR THE DAY: *Psalm 22:11* | *AUTHOR:* *Susan L. Lenzkes* | *PASSAGE FOR THE DAY:* *Psalm 22:1–24*

Teen Trouble

SOME days should never be recorded, repeated or remembered.

Take today, for instance. After a morning of upheaval with my daughter, she confided in me that she was in the absolute pits of a mood (she could have saved the trouble of making the announcement). Then she needed my complete attention for the next hour to gripe about everything and anything that has ever touched her nineteen-year-old world. She said she didn't know what's the matter with her lately, and I have a permanent crease across my tongue from resisting the urge to tell her!

She finally left for work, and my number-one son must have thought I'd be lonely for disaster, so he proceeded to erupt. He became incensed over some infraction to his personal sense of justice and shoved a bike at his brother.

After tending to the offended, I tried to deal with the offender and got a verbal volley that could knock any mother off her Nikes. An impartial jury surely would have labeled it "mother abuse" and given him a few years in solitary.

So in the middle of this—I mean in the very middle of this scene, not knowing whether to laugh or to cry because this five-foot-ten-inch kid is exhibiting every characteristic of the "terrible twos" in outsized triplicate—a man called and asked if he had reached the Lenzkes' residence . . . the Susan L. Lenzkes' residence.

It seems he had discovered my book *When the Handwriting on the Wall Is in Brown Crayon* in, of all places, a doctor's waiting room, and he and his wife were so taken by it that they had headed straight for a bookstore and bought one.

At the bookstore they found out where I live. Then they found my phone number in the directory and called to tell me what a blessing my life was to them! (The Lord's timing is most humbling!)

But, I know that our Lord is faithful. He promised we could pick up snakes with our bare hands and drink deadly poison, and live with teenagers (well, that last addition seems to fit nicely here) and not be hurt at all!

Additional Scripture Readings:
Mark 16:14–18; Philippians 2:1–4

Go to page 426 for your next devotional reading.

[28]for dominion belongs to the LORD
and he rules over the nations.

[29]All the rich of the earth will feast and worship;
all who go down to the dust will kneel before him—
those who cannot keep themselves alive.
[30]Posterity will serve him;
future generations will be told about the Lord.
[31]They will proclaim his righteousness
to a people yet unborn—
for he has done it.

Psalm 23

A psalm of David.

[1]The LORD is my shepherd, I shall not be in want.
[2] He makes me lie down in green pastures,
he leads me beside quiet waters,
[3] he restores my soul.
He guides me in paths of righteousness
for his name's sake.
[4]Even though I walk
through the valley of the shadow of death,[a]
I will fear no evil,
for you are with me;
your rod and your staff,
they comfort me.

[5]You prepare a table before me
in the presence of my enemies.
You anoint my head with oil;
my cup overflows.
[6]Surely goodness and love will follow me
all the days of my life,
and I will dwell in the house of the LORD
forever.

Psalm 24

Of David. A psalm.

[1]The earth is the LORD's, and everything in it,
the world, and all who live in it;
[2]for he founded it upon the seas
and established it upon the waters.

[3]Who may ascend the hill of the LORD?
Who may stand in his holy place?
[4]He who has clean hands and a pure heart,
who does not lift up his soul to an idol
or swear by what is false.[b]
[5]He will receive blessing from the LORD
and vindication from God his Savior.
[6]Such is the generation of those who seek him,
who seek your face, O God of Jacob.[c] *Selah*

[7]Lift up your heads, O you gates;
be lifted up, you ancient doors,
that the King of glory may come in.
[8]Who is this King of glory?
The LORD strong and mighty,
the LORD mighty in battle.
[9]Lift up your heads, O you gates;
lift them up, you ancient doors,
that the King of glory may come in.
[10]Who is he, this King of glory?
The LORD Almighty—
he is the King of glory. *Selah*

Psalm 25[d]

Of David.

[1]To you, O LORD, I lift up my soul;
[2] in you I trust, O my God.
Do not let me be put to shame,
nor let my enemies triumph over me.
[3]No one whose hope is in you
will ever be put to shame,
but they will be put to shame
who are treacherous without excuse.

[4]Show me your ways, O LORD,
teach me your paths;
[5]guide me in your truth and teach me,
for you are God my Savior,
and my hope is in you all day long.
[6]Remember, O LORD, your great mercy and love,
for they are from of old.
[7]Remember not the sins of my youth
and my rebellious ways;
according to your love remember me,
for you are good, O LORD.

[8]Good and upright is the LORD;

[a]4 Or *through the darkest valley* [b]4 Or *swear falsely* [c]6 Two Hebrew manuscripts and Syriac (see also Septuagint); most Hebrew manuscripts *face, Jacob* [d]This psalm is an acrostic poem, the verses of which begin with the successive letters of the Hebrew alphabet.

therefore he instructs sinners in his
ways.
9He guides the humble in what is right
and teaches them his way.
10All the ways of the LORD are loving
and faithful
for those who keep the demands of
his covenant.
11For the sake of your name, O LORD,
forgive my iniquity, though it is
great.
12Who, then, is the man that fears the
LORD?
He will instruct him in the way
chosen for him.
13He will spend his days in prosperity,
and his descendants will inherit the
land.
14The LORD confides in those who fear
him;
he makes his covenant known to
them.
15My eyes are ever on the LORD,
for only he will release my feet
from the snare.

16Turn to me and be gracious to me,
for I am lonely and afflicted.
17The troubles of my heart have
multiplied;
free me from my anguish.
18Look upon my affliction and my
distress
and take away all my sins.
19See how my enemies have increased
and how fiercely they hate me!
20Guard my life and rescue me;
let me not be put to shame,
for I take refuge in you.
21May integrity and uprightness protect
me,
because my hope is in you.

22Redeem Israel, O God,
from all their troubles!

Psalm 26

Of David.

1Vindicate me, O LORD,
for I have led a blameless life;
I have trusted in the LORD
without wavering.
2Test me, O LORD, and try me,
examine my heart and my mind;
3for your love is ever before me,
and I walk continually in your
truth.
4I do not sit with deceitful men,
nor do I consort with hypocrites;
5I abhor the assembly of evildoers
and refuse to sit with the wicked.
6I wash my hands in innocence,
and go about your altar, O LORD,
7proclaiming aloud your praise
and telling of all your wonderful
deeds.
8I love the house where you live,
O LORD,
the place where your glory dwells.

9Do not take away my soul along with
sinners,
my life with bloodthirsty men,
10in whose hands are wicked schemes,
whose right hands are full of bribes.
11But I lead a blameless life;
redeem me and be merciful to me.

12My feet stand on level ground;
in the great assembly I will praise
the LORD.

Psalm 27

Of David.

1The LORD is my light and my
salvation—
whom shall I fear?
The LORD is the stronghold of my
life—
of whom shall I be afraid?
2When evil men advance against me
to devour my flesh,[a]
when my enemies and my foes attack
me,
they will stumble and fall.
3Though an army besiege me,
my heart will not fear;
though war break out against me,
even then will I be confident.

4One thing I ask of the LORD,
this is what I seek:
that I may dwell in the house of the
LORD
all the days of my life,
to gaze upon the beauty of the LORD
and to seek him in his temple.
5For in the day of trouble
he will keep me safe in his
dwelling;
he will hide me in the shelter of his
tabernacle
and set me high upon a rock.
6Then my head will be exalted

[a]2 Or *to slander me*

above the enemies who surround
me;
at his tabernacle will I sacrifice with
shouts of joy;
I will sing and make music to the
LORD.

7Hear my voice when I call, O LORD;
be merciful to me and answer me.
8My heart says of you, "Seek his[a]
face!"
Your face, LORD, I will seek.
9Do not hide your face from me,
do not turn your servant away in
anger;
you have been my helper.
Do not reject me or forsake me,
O God my Savior.
10Though my father and mother forsake
me,
the LORD will receive me.
11Teach me your way, O LORD;
lead me in a straight path
because of my oppressors.
12Do not turn me over to the desire of
my foes,
for false witnesses rise up against
me,
breathing out violence.

13I am still confident of this:
I will see the goodness of the LORD
in the land of the living.
14Wait for the LORD;
be strong and take heart
and wait for the LORD.

Psalm 28

Of David.

1To you I call, O LORD my Rock;
do not turn a deaf ear to me.
For if you remain silent,
I will be like those who have gone
down to the pit.
2Hear my cry for mercy
as I call to you for help,
as I lift up my hands
toward your Most Holy Place.

3Do not drag me away with the
wicked,
with those who do evil,
who speak cordially with their
neighbors
but harbor malice in their hearts.
4Repay them for their deeds
and for their evil work;
repay them for what their hands have
done
and bring back upon them what
they deserve.
5Since they show no regard for the
works of the LORD
and what his hands have done,
he will tear them down
and never build them up again.

6Praise be to the LORD,
for he has heard my cry for mercy.
7The LORD is my strength and my
shield;
my heart trusts in him, and I am
helped.
My heart leaps for joy
and I will give thanks to him in
song.

8The LORD is the strength of his
people,
a fortress of salvation for his
anointed one.
9Save your people and bless your
inheritance;
be their shepherd and carry them
forever.

Psalm 29

A psalm of David.

1Ascribe to the LORD, O mighty ones,
ascribe to the LORD glory and
strength.
2Ascribe to the LORD the glory due his
name;
worship the LORD in the splendor of
his[b] holiness.

3The voice of the LORD is over the
waters;
the God of glory thunders,
the LORD thunders over the mighty
waters.
4The voice of the LORD is powerful;
the voice of the LORD is majestic.
5The voice of the LORD breaks the
cedars;
the LORD breaks in pieces the
cedars of Lebanon.
6He makes Lebanon skip like a calf,
Sirion[c] like a young wild ox.
7The voice of the LORD strikes
with flashes of lightning.
8The voice of the LORD shakes the
desert;

[a]8 Or *To you, O my heart, he has said, "Seek my* [b]2 Or *LORD with the splendor of* [c]6 That is, Mount Hermon

the LORD shakes the Desert of Kadesh.
9The voice of the LORD twists the oaks[a]
and strips the forests bare.
And in his temple all cry, "Glory!"

10The LORD sits[b] enthroned over the flood;
the LORD is enthroned as King forever.
11The LORD gives strength to his people;
the LORD blesses his people with peace.

Psalm 30

A psalm. A song. For the dedication of the temple.[c] Of David.

1I will exalt you, O LORD,
for you lifted me out of the depths
and did not let my enemies gloat over me.
2O LORD my God, I called to you for help
and you healed me.
3O LORD, you brought me up from the grave[d];
you spared me from going down into the pit.

4Sing to the LORD, you saints of his;
praise his holy name.
5For his anger lasts only a moment,
but his favor lasts a lifetime;
weeping may remain for a night,
but rejoicing comes in the morning.

6When I felt secure, I said,
"I will never be shaken."
7O LORD, when you favored me,
you made my mountain[e] stand firm;
but when you hid your face,
I was dismayed.

8To you, O LORD, I called;
to the Lord I cried for mercy:
9"What gain is there in my destruction,[f]
in my going down into the pit?
Will the dust praise you?
Will it proclaim your faithfulness?
10Hear, O LORD, and be merciful to me;
O LORD, be my help."

11You turned my wailing into dancing;
you removed my sackcloth and clothed me with joy,
12that my heart may sing to you and not be silent.
O LORD my God, I will give you thanks forever.

Psalm 31

For the director of music. A psalm of David.

1In you, O LORD, I have taken refuge;
let me never be put to shame;
deliver me in your righteousness.
2Turn your ear to me,
come quickly to my rescue;
be my rock of refuge,
a strong fortress to save me.
3Since you are my rock and my fortress,
for the sake of your name lead and guide me.
4Free me from the trap that is set for me,
for you are my refuge.
5Into your hands I commit my spirit;
redeem me, O LORD, the God of truth.

6I hate those who cling to worthless idols;
I trust in the LORD.
7I will be glad and rejoice in your love,
for you saw my affliction
and knew the anguish of my soul.
8You have not handed me over to the enemy
but have set my feet in a spacious place.

9Be merciful to me, O LORD, for I am in distress;
my eyes grow weak with sorrow,
my soul and my body with grief.
10My life is consumed by anguish
and my years by groaning;
my strength fails because of my affliction,[g]
and my bones grow weak.
11Because of all my enemies,
I am the utter contempt of my neighbors;
I am a dread to my friends—
those who see me on the street flee from me.
12I am forgotten by them as though I were dead;
I have become like broken pottery.

[a]9 Or *LORD makes the deer give birth* [b]10 Or *sat* [c]Title: Or *palace* [d]3 Hebrew *Sheol* [e]7 Or *hill country* [f]9 Or *there if I am silenced* [g]10 Or *guilt*

13For I hear the slander of many;
there is terror on every side;
they conspire against me
and plot to take my life.

14But I trust in you, O LORD;
I say, "You are my God."
15My times are in your hands;
deliver me from my enemies
and from those who pursue me.
16Let your face shine on your servant;
save me in your unfailing love.
17Let me not be put to shame, O LORD,
for I have cried out to you;
but let the wicked be put to shame
and lie silent in the grave.[a]
18Let their lying lips be silenced,
for with pride and contempt

[a]17 Hebrew *Sheol*

FRIDAY

VERSE FOR THE DAY: *Psalm 30:5*

AUTHOR: *Mary Jane Worden*

PASSAGE FOR THE DAY: *Psalm 30:1–12*

Night Weeping

AS I walked past the kitchen bulletin board I glanced, as usual, at our family picture. I was surprised by the sudden intense pain, the almost doubling-over kind from those first days of grief, after my husband Jim's death. Somehow there aren't enough words (in my vocabulary at least) to describe the great varieties of pain. Today it was the stomach-turning kind, producing that urge to bolt, to run or somehow try to squirm away from the source of pain. Impossible—like trying to crawl out from under the labor contractions of childbirth. Agonizing, but necessary I guess, and (sometimes to my disappointment) survivable. Just there, and unavoidable, at least for this moment. Do I need to learn to work with it, sort of "riding" it rather than fighting it, as they taught us in childbirth classes? Sometimes the evil behind death peers through, and it seems such a horror. It makes me wish I were a screamer. Instead the silent tears slip down my cheeks. Tonight the pain and sadness are specific and profound, not just the vague weeping of fatigue.

As I read back in my journals I find myself almost relieved to see the variety of feelings. One big component of the pain is fear—a fear that this experience of pain may not be momentary but might settle down on me as a permanent condition, an incurable disease, an overwhelming and unmoving cloud cover. This time it's got me and it may never let me go. I need to keep reminding myself, in the midst of the pain, that I can acknowledge it and give in to it because it isn't a life sentence.

Weeping may remain for a night,
but rejoicing comes in the morning
(Psalm 30:5).

Additional Scripture Readings:
Matthew 5:4; Revelation 21:3–4

Go to page 428 for your next devotional reading.

they speak arrogantly against the
righteous.

19How great is your goodness,
which you have stored up for those
who fear you,
which you bestow in the sight of men
on those who take refuge in you.
20In the shelter of your presence you
hide them
from the intrigues of men;
in your dwelling you keep them safe
from accusing tongues.

21Praise be to the LORD,
for he showed his wonderful love to
me
when I was in a besieged city.
22In my alarm I said,
"I am cut off from your sight!"
Yet you heard my cry for mercy
when I called to you for help.

23Love the LORD, all his saints!
The LORD preserves the faithful,
but the proud he pays back in full.
24Be strong and take heart,
all you who hope in the LORD.

Psalm 32

Of David. A *maskil.*[a]

1Blessed is he
whose transgressions are forgiven,
whose sins are covered.
2Blessed is the man
whose sin the LORD does not count
against him
and in whose spirit is no deceit.

3When I kept silent,
my bones wasted away
through my groaning all day long.
4For day and night
your hand was heavy upon me;
my strength was sapped
as in the heat of summer. *Selah*
5Then I acknowledged my sin to you
and did not cover up my iniquity.
I said, "I will confess
my transgressions to the LORD"—
and you forgave
the guilt of my sin. *Selah*

6Therefore let everyone who is godly
pray to you
while you may be found;
surely when the mighty waters rise,
they will not reach him.
7You are my hiding place;
you will protect me from trouble
and surround me with songs of
deliverance. *Selah*

8I will instruct you and teach you in
the way you should go;
I will counsel you and watch over
you.
9Do not be like the horse or the mule,
which have no understanding
but must be controlled by bit and
bridle
or they will not come to you.
10Many are the woes of the wicked,
but the LORD's unfailing love
surrounds the man who trusts in
him.

11Rejoice in the LORD and be glad, you
righteous;
sing, all you who are upright in
heart!

Psalm 33

1Sing joyfully to the LORD, you
righteous;
it is fitting for the upright to praise
him.
2Praise the LORD with the harp;
make music to him on the
ten-stringed lyre.
3Sing to him a new song;
play skillfully, and shout for joy.

4For the word of the LORD is right and
true;
he is faithful in all he does.
5The LORD loves righteousness and
justice;
the earth is full of his unfailing
love.

6By the word of the LORD were the
heavens made,
their starry host by the breath of
his mouth.
7He gathers the waters of the sea into
jars[b];
he puts the deep into storehouses.
8Let all the earth fear the LORD;
let all the people of the world
revere him.
9For he spoke, and it came to be;
he commanded, and it stood firm.
10The LORD foils the plans of the
nations;
he thwarts the purposes of the
peoples.

[a]Title: Probably a literary or musical term [b]7 Or *sea as into a heap*

WEEKENDING

RELATE

In the late 1800's Mrs. Louisa M.R. Stead watched as her husband died while trying to save a drowning boy. This familiar hymn was written as a response to her struggle with the "why?" questions she asked God during that difficult time.

RESPOND

'Tis so sweet to trust in Jesus,
Just to take Him at His word,
Just to rest upon His promise,
Just to know, "Thus saith the Lord."

I'm so glad I learned to trust Thee,
Precious Jesus, Savior, Friend;
And I know that Thou art with me,
Wilt be with me to the end.

Jesus, Jesus, how I trust Him!
How I've proved Him o'er and o'er!
Jesus, Jesus, precious Jesus!
O for grace to trust Him more!

– Louisa M.R. Stead

REVIVE

Saturday: Psalm 125:1–5
Sunday: John 14:1–4

Go to page 430 for your next devotional reading.

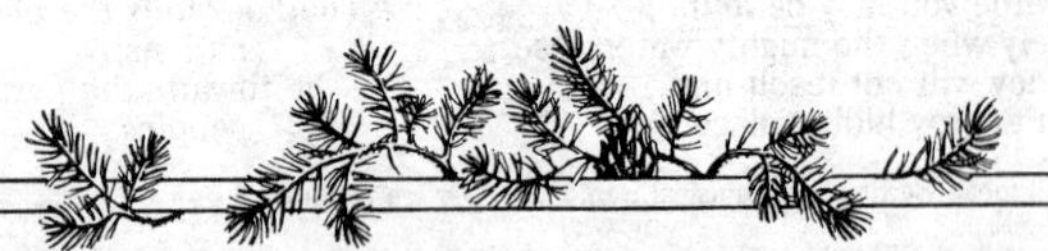

[11]But the plans of the LORD stand firm
forever,
the purposes of his heart through
all generations.

[12]Blessed is the nation whose God is
the LORD,
the people he chose for his
inheritance.
[13]From heaven the LORD looks down
and sees all mankind;
[14]from his dwelling place he watches
all who live on earth—
[15]he who forms the hearts of all,
who considers everything they do.
[16]No king is saved by the size of his
army;
no warrior escapes by his great
strength.
[17]A horse is a vain hope for deliverance;
despite all its great strength it
cannot save.
[18]But the eyes of the LORD are on those
who fear him,
on those whose hope is in his
unfailing love,
[19]to deliver them from death
and keep them alive in famine.

[20]We wait in hope for the LORD;
he is our help and our shield.
[21]In him our hearts rejoice,
for we trust in his holy name.
[22]May your unfailing love rest upon us,
O LORD,
even as we put our hope in you.

Psalm 34[a]

Of David. When he pretended to be insane before Abimelech, who drove him away, and he left.

[1]I will extol the LORD at all times;
his praise will always be on my lips.
[2]My soul will boast in the LORD;
let the afflicted hear and rejoice.
[3]Glorify the LORD with me;
let us exalt his name together.

[4]I sought the LORD, and he answered
me;
he delivered me from all my fears.
[5]Those who look to him are radiant;
their faces are never covered with
shame.
[6]This poor man called, and the LORD
heard him;
he saved him out of all his
troubles.
[7]The angel of the LORD encamps
around those who fear him,
and he delivers them.

[8]Taste and see that the LORD is good;
blessed is the man who takes
refuge in him.
[9]Fear the LORD, you his saints,
for those who fear him lack
nothing.
[10]The lions may grow weak and hungry,
but those who seek the LORD lack
no good thing.

[11]Come, my children, listen to me;
I will teach you the fear of the
LORD.
[12]Whoever of you loves life
and desires to see many good days,
[13]keep your tongue from evil
and your lips from speaking lies.
[14]Turn from evil and do good;
seek peace and pursue it.

[15]The eyes of the LORD are on the
righteous
and his ears are attentive to their
cry;
[16]the face of the LORD is against those
who do evil,
to cut off the memory of them from
the earth.

[17]The righteous cry out, and the LORD
hears them;
he delivers them from all their
troubles.
[18]The LORD is close to the
brokenhearted
and saves those who are crushed in
spirit.

[19]A righteous man may have many
troubles,
but the LORD delivers him from
them all;
[20]he protects all his bones,
not one of them will be broken.

[21]Evil will slay the wicked;
the foes of the righteous will be
condemned.
[22]The LORD redeems his servants;
no one will be condemned who
takes refuge in him.

[a]This psalm is an acrostic poem, the verses of which begin with the successive letters of the Hebrew alphabet.

Psalm 35

Of David.

[1]Contend, O LORD, with those who
contend with me;
fight against those who fight
against me.
[2]Take up shield and buckler;
arise and come to my aid.
[3]Brandish spear and javelin[a]
against those who pursue me.
Say to my soul,
"I am your salvation."

[4]May those who seek my life
be disgraced and put to shame;
may those who plot my ruin

[a]3 Or *and block the way*

MONDAY

VERSE FOR THE DAY: *Psalm 34:6*

AUTHOR: *Wanda K. Jones*

PASSAGE FOR THE DAY: *Psalm 34:1–22*

The Lord Hears

PSALM 34 has been a source of strength and encouragement ever since I drank from the "living waters" of eternal salvation in Jesus Christ. Praising, glorifying and honoring the Lord as David did has proven to be a great blessing even in extremely difficult circumstances.

As a young Christian in college I was often on my knees asking the Lord to help with college fees and even incidentals—stockings, underwear, notebook paper and a warm scarf. The wonderful thing was that when I sought him in prayer, he answered!

The main building on our college campus was perched on a hill overlooking the Hudson River. The setting was beautiful. Maneuvering was more difficult. It was easy going when we walked down into the town but coming back was the struggle. Groups of students often stopped along the way to rest.

I learned and quoted Psalm 34 on those walks up the hillside. I had no problem with verse 6:

> This poor man called, and the LORD heard him;
> he saved him out of all his troubles.

I knew then, as I know now, that anyone—man, woman, young, old, rich, poor, black or white—can call on the Lord, and he will answer and meet the need.

If you have been going through a difficult period in your life, if you have been crushed by some unkind deed, or if you have lost a loved one and are feeling the pangs of loneliness, remember: the psalmist said that "the LORD is close to the brokenhearted" (Psalm 34:18).

Why not take refuge in him?

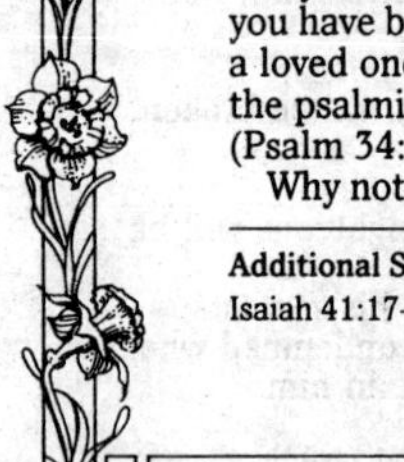

Additional Scripture Readings:
Isaiah 41:17–20; 2 Thessalonians 2:11–12

Go to page 433 for your next devotional reading.

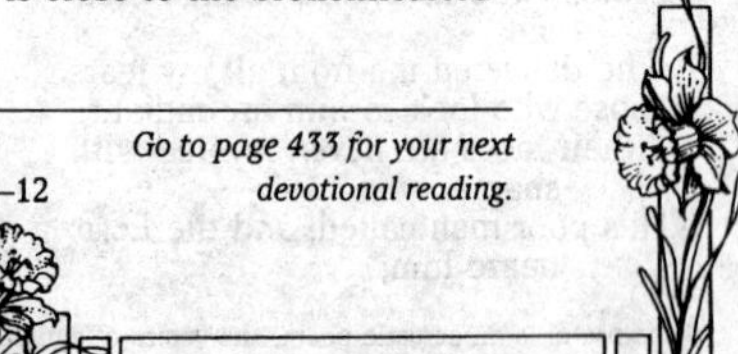

be turned back in dismay.
5May they be like chaff before the wind,
with the angel of the LORD driving them away;
6may their path be dark and slippery,
with the angel of the LORD pursuing them.
7Since they hid their net for me without cause
and without cause dug a pit for me,
8may ruin overtake them by surprise—
may the net they hid entangle them,
may they fall into the pit, to their ruin.
9Then my soul will rejoice in the LORD
and delight in his salvation.
10My whole being will exclaim,
"Who is like you, O LORD?
You rescue the poor from those too strong for them,
the poor and needy from those who rob them."

11Ruthless witnesses come forward;
they question me on things I know nothing about.
12They repay me evil for good
and leave my soul forlorn.
13Yet when they were ill, I put on sackcloth
and humbled myself with fasting.
When my prayers returned to me unanswered,
14 I went about mourning
as though for my friend or brother.
I bowed my head in grief
as though weeping for my mother.
15But when I stumbled, they gathered in glee;
attackers gathered against me when I was unaware.
They slandered me without ceasing.
16Like the ungodly they maliciously mocked[a];
they gnashed their teeth at me.
17O Lord, how long will you look on?
Rescue my life from their ravages,
my precious life from these lions.
18I will give you thanks in the great assembly;
among throngs of people I will praise you.

19Let not those gloat over me
who are my enemies without cause;
let not those who hate me without reason
maliciously wink the eye.
20They do not speak peaceably,
but devise false accusations
against those who live quietly in the land.
21They gape at me and say, "Aha! Aha!
With our own eyes we have seen it."

22O LORD, you have seen this; be not silent.
Do not be far from me, O Lord.
23Awake, and rise to my defense!
Contend for me, my God and Lord.
24Vindicate me in your righteousness,
O LORD my God;
do not let them gloat over me.
25Do not let them think, "Aha, just what we wanted!"
or say, "We have swallowed him up."

26May all who gloat over my distress
be put to shame and confusion;
may all who exalt themselves over me
be clothed with shame and disgrace.
27May those who delight in my vindication
shout for joy and gladness;
may they always say, "The LORD be exalted,
who delights in the well-being of his servant."
28My tongue will speak of your righteousness
and of your praises all day long.

Psalm 36

For the director of music. Of David the servant of the LORD.

1An oracle is within my heart
concerning the sinfulness of the wicked:[b]
There is no fear of God
before his eyes.
2For in his own eyes he flatters himself
too much to detect or hate his sin.
3The words of his mouth are wicked and deceitful;
he has ceased to be wise and to do good.
4Even on his bed he plots evil;

[a]16 Septuagint; Hebrew may mean *ungodly circle of mockers.* [b]1 Or *heart: / Sin proceeds from the wicked.*

he commits himself to a sinful
course
and does not reject what is wrong.

[5]Your love, O LORD, reaches to the
heavens,
your faithfulness to the skies.
[6]Your righteousness is like the mighty
mountains,
your justice like the great deep.
O LORD, you preserve both man and
beast.
[7] How priceless is your unfailing love!
Both high and low among men
find[a] refuge in the shadow of your
wings.
[8]They feast on the abundance of your
house;
you give them drink from your river
of delights.
[9]For with you is the fountain of life;
in your light we see light.

[10]Continue your love to those who
know you,
your righteousness to the upright in
heart.
[11]May the foot of the proud not come
against me,
nor the hand of the wicked drive
me away.
[12]See how the evildoers lie fallen—
thrown down, not able to rise!

Psalm 37[b]

Of David.

[1]Do not fret because of evil men
or be envious of those who do
wrong;
[2]for like the grass they will soon
wither,
like green plants they will soon die
away.

[3]Trust in the LORD and do good;
dwell in the land and enjoy safe
pasture.
[4]Delight yourself in the LORD
and he will give you the desires of
your heart.

[5]Commit your way to the LORD;
trust in him and he will do this:
[6]He will make your righteousness
shine like the dawn,
the justice of your cause like the
noonday sun.

[7]Be still before the LORD and wait
patiently for him;
do not fret when men succeed in
their ways,
when they carry out their wicked
schemes.

[8]Refrain from anger and turn from
wrath;
do not fret—it leads only to evil.
[9]For evil men will be cut off,
but those who hope in the LORD
will inherit the land.

[10]A little while, and the wicked will be
no more;
though you look for them, they will
not be found.
[11]But the meek will inherit the land
and enjoy great peace.

[12]The wicked plot against the righteous
and gnash their teeth at them;
[13]but the Lord laughs at the wicked,
for he knows their day is coming.

[14]The wicked draw the sword
and bend the bow
to bring down the poor and needy,
to slay those whose ways are
upright.
[15]But their swords will pierce their own
hearts,
and their bows will be broken.

[16]Better the little that the righteous
have
than the wealth of many wicked;
[17]for the power of the wicked will be
broken,
but the LORD upholds the righteous.

[18]The days of the blameless are known
to the LORD,
and their inheritance will endure
forever.
[19]In times of disaster they will not
wither;
in days of famine they will enjoy
plenty.

[20]But the wicked will perish:
The LORD's enemies will be like the
beauty of the fields,
they will vanish—vanish like
smoke.

[21]The wicked borrow and do not repay,
but the righteous give generously;
[22]those the LORD blesses will inherit the
land,

[a]7 Or *love, O God! / Men find*; or *love! / Both heavenly beings and men / find* [b]This psalm is an acrostic poem, the stanzas of which begin with the successive letters of the Hebrew alphabet.

TUESDAY

VERSE FOR THE DAY: *Psalm 37:5*

AUTHOR: *Ruth Bell Graham*

PASSAGE FOR THE DAY: *Psalm 37:1–7*

Commit to God

THE Amplified Bible pictures us committing our load to God by rolling it onto Him. It is helpful to note that we can roll something that is too heavy to carry or to cast.

What are we to commit—to trust—to God?

Ourselves. Psalm 22:8:

> He trusts in the LORD;
> let the LORD rescue him.
> Let him deliver him, since he delights in him.

Our Burden. Psalm 55:22:

> Cast your cares on the LORD
> and he will sustain you;
> he will never let the righteous fall.

Our Souls. 1 Peter 4:19:

So then, those who suffer according to God's will should commit themselves to their faithful Creator and continue to do good.

Our Way. Psalm 37:5:

> Commit your way to the LORD;
> trust in him.

Our Cause. 1 Peter 2:23:

When they hurled their insults at him, he did not retaliate; when he suffered, he made no threats. Instead, he entrusted himself to him who judges justly.

Our Works. Proverbs 16:3:

> Commit to the LORD whatever you do,
> and your plans will succeed.

Additional Scripture Readings:
1 Samuel 7:2–4; Acts 14:23–26

Go to page 434 for your next devotional reading.

but those he curses will be cut
off.

23If the LORD delights in a man's
way,
he makes his steps firm;
24though he stumble, he will not fall,
for the LORD upholds him with his
hand.

25I was young and now I am old,
yet I have never seen the righteous
forsaken
or their children begging bread.
26They are always generous and lend
freely;
their children will be blessed.

27Turn from evil and do good;
then you will dwell in the land
forever.
28For the LORD loves the just
and will not forsake his faithful
ones.

They will be protected forever,
but the offspring of the wicked will
be cut off;
29the righteous will inherit the land
and dwell in it forever.

30The mouth of the righteous man
utters wisdom,
and his tongue speaks what is just.
31The law of his God is in his heart;
his feet do not slip.

32The wicked lie in wait for the
righteous,
seeking their very lives;
33but the LORD will not leave them in
their power
or let them be condemned when
brought to trial.

34Wait for the LORD
and keep his way.
He will exalt you to inherit the land;
when the wicked are cut off, you
will see it.

35I have seen a wicked and ruthless
man
flourishing like a green tree in its
native soil,

WEDNESDAY

VERSE FOR THE DAY: *Psalm 37:12–13*

AUTHOR: *Ruth Bell Graham*

PASSAGE FOR THE DAY: *Psalm 37:10–17*

Don't Fret

WHEN "the wicked plot . . . the LORD laughs" (also see Psalm 2:4).

When he prospers, don't fret (Psalm 39:6–7).
When he persecutes:

Rejoice and be glad (Matthew 5:12).
Love your enemies (Matthew 5:44).
Bless them (Romans 12:14).
Do good to them (Luke 6:27).
Pray for them (Matthew 5:44).

Additional Scripture Readings:
Genesis 50:15–20; Psalm 73:2,21–24

Go to page 440 for your next devotional reading.

36but he soon passed away and was no more;
though I looked for him, he could not be found.

37Consider the blameless, observe the upright;
there is a future[a] for the man of peace.
38But all sinners will be destroyed;
the future[b] of the wicked will be cut off.

39The salvation of the righteous comes from the LORD;
he is their stronghold in time of trouble.
40The LORD helps them and delivers them;
he delivers them from the wicked and saves them,
because they take refuge in him.

Psalm 38

A psalm of David. A petition.

1O LORD, do not rebuke me in your anger
or discipline me in your wrath.
2For your arrows have pierced me,
and your hand has come down upon me.
3Because of your wrath there is no health in my body;
my bones have no soundness because of my sin.
4My guilt has overwhelmed me
like a burden too heavy to bear.

5My wounds fester and are loathsome
because of my sinful folly.
6I am bowed down and brought very low;
all day long I go about mourning.
7My back is filled with searing pain;
there is no health in my body.
8I am feeble and utterly crushed;
I groan in anguish of heart.

9All my longings lie open before you, O Lord;
my sighing is not hidden from you.
10My heart pounds, my strength fails me;
even the light has gone from my eyes.
11My friends and companions avoid me because of my wounds;
my neighbors stay far away.
12Those who seek my life set their traps,
those who would harm me talk of my ruin;
all day long they plot deception.

13I am like a deaf man, who cannot hear,
like a mute, who cannot open his mouth;
14I have become like a man who does not hear,
whose mouth can offer no reply.
15I wait for you, O LORD;
you will answer, O Lord my God.
16For I said, "Do not let them gloat
or exalt themselves over me when my foot slips."

17For I am about to fall,
and my pain is ever with me.
18I confess my iniquity;
I am troubled by my sin.
19Many are those who are my vigorous enemies;
those who hate me without reason are numerous.
20Those who repay my good with evil
slander me when I pursue what is good.

21O LORD, do not forsake me;
be not far from me, O my God.
22Come quickly to help me,
O Lord my Savior.

Psalm 39

For the director of music. For Jeduthun. A psalm of David.

1I said, "I will watch my ways
and keep my tongue from sin;
I will put a muzzle on my mouth
as long as the wicked are in my presence."
2But when I was silent and still,
not even saying anything good,
my anguish increased.
3My heart grew hot within me,
and as I meditated, the fire burned;
then I spoke with my tongue:

4"Show me, O LORD, my life's end
and the number of my days;
let me know how fleeting is my life.
5You have made my days a mere handbreadth;
the span of my years is as nothing before you.

[a]37 Or *there will be posterity* [b]38 Or *posterity*

Each man's life is but a breath.
Selah
6Man is a mere phantom as he goes to and fro:
He bustles about, but only in vain;
he heaps up wealth, not knowing who will get it.

7"But now, Lord, what do I look for?
My hope is in you.
8Save me from all my transgressions;
do not make me the scorn of fools.
9I was silent; I would not open my mouth,
for you are the one who has done this.
10Remove your scourge from me;
I am overcome by the blow of your hand.
11You rebuke and discipline men for their sin;
you consume their wealth like a moth—
each man is but a breath. *Selah*

12"Hear my prayer, O LORD,
listen to my cry for help;
be not deaf to my weeping.
For I dwell with you as an alien,
a stranger, as all my fathers were.
13Look away from me, that I may rejoice again
before I depart and am no more."

Psalm 40

For the director of music. Of David.
A psalm.

1I waited patiently for the LORD;
he turned to me and heard my cry.
2He lifted me out of the slimy pit,
out of the mud and mire;
he set my feet on a rock
and gave me a firm place to stand.
3He put a new song in my mouth,
a hymn of praise to our God.
Many will see and fear
and put their trust in the LORD.

4Blessed is the man
who makes the LORD his trust,
who does not look to the proud,
to those who turn aside to false gods.[a]
5Many, O LORD my God,
are the wonders you have done.
The things you planned for us
no one can recount to you;
were I to speak and tell of them,
they would be too many to declare.

6Sacrifice and offering you did not desire,
but my ears you have pierced[b,c];
burnt offerings and sin offerings
you did not require.
7Then I said, "Here I am, I have come—
it is written about me in the scroll.[d]
8I desire to do your will, O my God;
your law is within my heart."

9I proclaim righteousness in the great assembly;
I do not seal my lips,
as you know, O LORD.
10I do not hide your righteousness in my heart;
I speak of your faithfulness and salvation.
I do not conceal your love and your truth
from the great assembly.

11Do not withhold your mercy from me, O LORD;
may your love and your truth
always protect me.
12For troubles without number
surround me;
my sins have overtaken me, and I cannot see.
They are more than the hairs of my head,
and my heart fails within me.

13Be pleased, O LORD, to save me;
O LORD, come quickly to help me.
14May all who seek to take my life
be put to shame and confusion;
may all who desire my ruin
be turned back in disgrace.
15May those who say to me, "Aha! Aha!"
be appalled at their own shame.
16But may all who seek you
rejoice and be glad in you;
may those who love your salvation
always say,
"The LORD be exalted!"

17Yet I am poor and needy;
may the Lord think of me.
You are my help and my deliverer;
O my God, do not delay.

[a]4 Or *to falsehood* [b]6 Hebrew; Septuagint *but a body you have prepared for me* (see also Symmachus and Theodotion) [c]6 Or *opened* [d]7 Or *come / with the scroll written for me*

Psalm 41

For the director of music. A psalm of David.

1Blessed is he who has regard for the weak;
the LORD delivers him in times of trouble.
2The LORD will protect him and preserve his life;
he will bless him in the land
and not surrender him to the desire of his foes.
3The LORD will sustain him on his sickbed
and restore him from his bed of illness.

4I said, "O LORD, have mercy on me;
heal me, for I have sinned against you."
5My enemies say of me in malice,
"When will he die and his name perish?"
6Whenever one comes to see me,
he speaks falsely, while his heart gathers slander;
then he goes out and spreads it abroad.

7All my enemies whisper together against me;
they imagine the worst for me, saying,
8"A vile disease has beset him;
he will never get up from the place where he lies."
9Even my close friend, whom I trusted,
he who shared my bread,
has lifted up his heel against me.

10But you, O LORD, have mercy on me;
raise me up, that I may repay them.
11I know that you are pleased with me,
for my enemy does not triumph over me.
12In my integrity you uphold me
and set me in your presence forever.

13Praise be to the LORD, the God of Israel,
from everlasting to everlasting.
Amen and Amen.

BOOK II

Psalms 42–72

Psalm 42[a]

For the director of music. A *maskil*[b] of the Sons of Korah.

1As the deer pants for streams of water,
so my soul pants for you, O God.
2My soul thirsts for God, for the living God.
When can I go and meet with God?
3My tears have been my food
day and night,
while men say to me all day long,
"Where is your God?"
4These things I remember
as I pour out my soul:
how I used to go with the multitude,
leading the procession to the house of God,
with shouts of joy and thanksgiving
among the festive throng.

5Why are you downcast, O my soul?
Why so disturbed within me?
Put your hope in God,
for I will yet praise him,
my Savior and 6my God.

My[c] soul is downcast within me;
therefore I will remember you
from the land of the Jordan,
the heights of Hermon—from Mount Mizar.
7Deep calls to deep
in the roar of your waterfalls;
all your waves and breakers
have swept over me.

8By day the LORD directs his love,
at night his song is with me—
a prayer to the God of my life.

9I say to God my Rock,
"Why have you forgotten me?
Why must I go about mourning,
oppressed by the enemy?"
10My bones suffer mortal agony
as my foes taunt me,
saying to me all day long,
"Where is your God?"

11Why are you downcast, O my soul?
Why so disturbed within me?
Put your hope in God,

[a]In many Hebrew manuscripts Psalms 42 and 43 constitute one psalm. [b]Title: Probably a literary or musical term [c]5,6 A few Hebrew manuscripts, Septuagint and Syriac; most Hebrew manuscripts *praise him for his saving help. / 6O my God, my*

for I will yet praise him,
my Savior and my God.

Psalm 43[a]

1Vindicate me, O God,
and plead my cause against an ungodly nation;
rescue me from deceitful and wicked men.
2You are God my stronghold.
Why have you rejected me?
Why must I go about mourning,
oppressed by the enemy?
3Send forth your light and your truth,
let them guide me;
let them bring me to your holy mountain,
to the place where you dwell.
4Then will I go to the altar of God,
to God, my joy and my delight.
I will praise you with the harp,
O God, my God.

5Why are you downcast, O my soul?
Why so disturbed within me?
Put your hope in God,
for I will yet praise him,
my Savior and my God.

Psalm 44

For the director of music. Of the Sons of Korah. A *maskil.*[b]

1We have heard with our ears, O God;
our fathers have told us
what you did in their days,
in days long ago.
2With your hand you drove out the nations
and planted our fathers;
you crushed the peoples
and made our fathers flourish.
3It was not by their sword that they won the land,
nor did their arm bring them victory;
it was your right hand, your arm,
and the light of your face, for you loved them.

4You are my King and my God,
who decrees[c] victories for Jacob.
5Through you we push back our enemies;
through your name we trample our foes.
6I do not trust in my bow,
my sword does not bring me victory;
7but you give us victory over our enemies,
you put our adversaries to shame.
8In God we make our boast all day long,
and we will praise your name forever. *Selah*

9But now you have rejected and humbled us;
you no longer go out with our armies.
10You made us retreat before the enemy,
and our adversaries have plundered us.
11You gave us up to be devoured like sheep
and have scattered us among the nations.
12You sold your people for a pittance,
gaining nothing from their sale.

13You have made us a reproach to our neighbors,
the scorn and derision of those around us.
14You have made us a byword among the nations;
the peoples shake their heads at us.
15My disgrace is before me all day long,
and my face is covered with shame
16at the taunts of those who reproach and revile me,
because of the enemy, who is bent on revenge.

17All this happened to us,
though we had not forgotten you
or been false to your covenant.
18Our hearts had not turned back;
our feet had not strayed from your path.
19But you crushed us and made us a haunt for jackals
and covered us over with deep darkness.

20If we had forgotten the name of our God
or spread out our hands to a foreign god,
21would not God have discovered it,
since he knows the secrets of the heart?
22Yet for your sake we face death all day long;

[a]In many Hebrew manuscripts Psalms 42 and 43 constitute one psalm. [b]Title: Probably a literary or musical term [c]4 Septuagint, Aquila and Syriac; Hebrew *King, O God; / command*

we are considered as sheep to be
slaughtered.

23Awake, O Lord! Why do you sleep?
Rouse yourself! Do not reject us
forever.
24Why do you hide your face
and forget our misery and
oppression?

25We are brought down to the dust;
our bodies cling to the ground.
26Rise up and help us;
redeem us because of your
unfailing love.

Psalm 45

For the director of music. To ⌞the tune of,⌟ "Lilies." Of the Sons of Korah. A *maskil.*[a] A wedding song.

1My heart is stirred by a noble theme
as I recite my verses for the king;
my tongue is the pen of a skillful
writer.

2You are the most excellent of men
and your lips have been anointed
with grace,
since God has blessed you forever.
3Gird your sword upon your side,
O mighty one;
clothe yourself with splendor and
majesty.
4In your majesty ride forth victoriously
in behalf of truth, humility and
righteousness;
let your right hand display awesome
deeds.
5Let your sharp arrows pierce the
hearts of the king's enemies;
let the nations fall beneath your
feet.
6Your throne, O God, will last for ever
and ever;
a scepter of justice will be the
scepter of your kingdom.
7You love righteousness and hate
wickedness;
therefore God, your God, has set
you above your companions
by anointing you with the oil of joy.
8All your robes are fragrant with myrrh
and aloes and cassia;
from palaces adorned with ivory
the music of the strings makes you
glad.
9Daughters of kings are among your
honored women;
at your right hand is the royal bride
in gold of Ophir.

10Listen, O daughter, consider and give
ear:
Forget your people and your
father's house.
11The king is enthralled by your beauty;
honor him, for he is your lord.
12The Daughter of Tyre will come with
a gift,[b]
men of wealth will seek your favor.

13All glorious is the princess within ⌞her
chamber⌟;
her gown is interwoven with gold.
14In embroidered garments she is led to
the king;
her virgin companions follow her
and are brought to you.
15They are led in with joy and gladness;
they enter the palace of the king.

16Your sons will take the place of your
fathers;
you will make them princes
throughout the land.
17I will perpetuate your memory
through all generations;
therefore the nations will praise you
for ever and ever.

Psalm 46

For the director of music. Of the Sons of Korah. According to *alamoth.*[c] A song.

1God is our refuge and strength,
an ever-present help in trouble.
2Therefore we will not fear, though the
earth give way
and the mountains fall into the
heart of the sea,
3though its waters roar and foam
and the mountains quake with their
surging. *Selah*

4There is a river whose streams make
glad the city of God,
the holy place where the Most High
dwells.
5God is within her, she will not fall;
God will help her at break of day.
6Nations are in uproar, kingdoms fall;
he lifts his voice, the earth melts.

7The LORD Almighty is with us;

[a]Title: Probably a literary or musical term [b]12 Or *A Tyrian robe is among the gifts* [c]Title: Probably a musical term

the God of Jacob is our fortress.
Selah

8Come and see the works of the LORD,
the desolations he has brought on the earth.
9He makes wars cease to the ends of the earth;
he breaks the bow and shatters the spear,
he burns the shields[a] with fire.
10"Be still, and know that I am God;
I will be exalted among the nations,
I will be exalted in the earth."

11The LORD Almighty is with us;
the God of Jacob is our fortress.
Selah

[a]9 Or *chariots*

Psalm 47

For the director of music. Of the Sons of Korah. A psalm.

1Clap your hands, all you nations;
shout to God with cries of joy.
2How awesome is the LORD Most High,
the great King over all the earth!
3He subdued nations under us,
peoples under our feet.
4He chose our inheritance for us,
the pride of Jacob, whom he loved.
Selah

5God has ascended amid shouts of joy,
the LORD amid the sounding of trumpets.

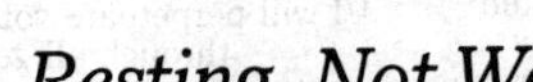

THURSDAY

VERSE FOR THE DAY: *Psalm 46:10*

AUTHOR: *Hannah Whitall Smith*

PASSAGE FOR THE DAY: *Psalm 46:1–11*

Resting, Not Worrying

AMONG the peaks of the Sierra Nevada mountains, not far from the busy whirl of San Francisco, lies Lake Tahoe. It is twenty-three miles long, ten miles wide, and so deep that a line dropped nineteen hundred feet does not touch bottom; and it lies five thousand feet above the neighboring ocean. Storms come and go in waters that are lower down the mountains, but this lake is so still and clear that the eye can penetrate, it is said, a hundred feet into its depths. Around its mild verdant sides are the mountains, ever crowned with snow. The sky above is as calm as the motionless water. Nature loses scarcely anything of its clear outline as it is reflected there. Here the soul may learn something of what rest is, as day after day one opens one's heart to let the sweet influence of nature's sabbath enter and reign. This is but a faint type of what we may find in Christ.

In the pressure of the greatest responsibilities, in the worry of the smallest cares, in the perplexities of life's moments of crisis, we may have the Lake Tahoe rest in the security of God's will. Learn to live in this rest. In the calmness of spirit it will give, your soul will reflect, as in a mirror, the beauty of the Lord; and the tumult of men's lives will be calmed in your presence, as your tumults have been calmed in his presence.

Additional Scripture Readings:
Psalm 131:1–3; Philippians 4:4–7

Go to page 444 for your next devotional reading.

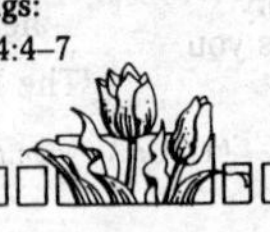

6Sing praises to God, sing praises;
sing praises to our King, sing praises.
7For God is the King of all the earth;
sing to him a psalm[a] of praise.
8God reigns over the nations;
God is seated on his holy throne.
9The nobles of the nations assemble
as the people of the God of Abraham,
for the kings[b] of the earth belong to God;
he is greatly exalted.

Psalm 48

A song. A psalm of the Sons of Korah.

1Great is the LORD, and most worthy of praise,
in the city of our God, his holy mountain.
2It is beautiful in its loftiness,
the joy of the whole earth.
Like the utmost heights of Zaphon[c]
is Mount Zion,
the[d] city of the Great King.
3God is in her citadels;
he has shown himself to be her fortress.

4When the kings joined forces,
when they advanced together,
5they saw ⌞her,⌟ and were astounded;
they fled in terror.
6Trembling seized them there,
pain like that of a woman in labor.
7You destroyed them like ships of Tarshish
shattered by an east wind.

8As we have heard,
so have we seen
in the city of the LORD Almighty,
in the city of our God:
God makes her secure forever.
Selah

9Within your temple, O God,
we meditate on your unfailing love.
10Like your name, O God,
your praise reaches to the ends of the earth;
your right hand is filled with righteousness.
11Mount Zion rejoices,
the villages of Judah are glad
because of your judgments.

12Walk about Zion, go around her,
count her towers,
13consider well her ramparts,
view her citadels,
that you may tell of them to the next generation.
14For this God is our God for ever and ever;
he will be our guide even to the end.

Psalm 49

For the director of music. Of the Sons of Korah. A psalm.

1Hear this, all you peoples;
listen, all who live in this world,
2both low and high,
rich and poor alike:
3My mouth will speak words of wisdom;
the utterance from my heart will give understanding.
4I will turn my ear to a proverb;
with the harp I will expound my riddle:

5Why should I fear when evil days come,
when wicked deceivers surround me—
6those who trust in their wealth
and boast of their great riches?
7No man can redeem the life of another
or give to God a ransom for him—
8the ransom for a life is costly,
no payment is ever enough—
9that he should live on forever
and not see decay.

10For all can see that wise men die;
the foolish and the senseless alike perish
and leave their wealth to others.
11Their tombs will remain their houses[e] forever,
their dwellings for endless generations,
though they had[f] named lands after themselves.

12But man, despite his riches, does not endure;
he is[g] like the beasts that perish.

[a]7 Or *a maskil* (probably a literary or musical term) [b]9 Or *shields* [c]2 *Zaphon* can refer to a sacred mountain or the direction north. [d]2 Or *earth, / Mount Zion, on the northern side / of the* [e]11 Septuagint and Syriac; Hebrew *In their thoughts their houses will remain* [f]11 Or */ for they have* [g]12 Hebrew; Septuagint and Syriac read verse 12 the same as verse 20.

13This is the fate of those who trust in
themselves,
and of their followers, who approve
their sayings. *Selah*
14Like sheep they are destined for the
grave,[a]
and death will feed on them.
The upright will rule over them in the
morning;
their forms will decay in the
grave,[a]
far from their princely mansions.
15But God will redeem my life[b] from
the grave;
he will surely take me to himself.
Selah

16Do not be overawed when a man
grows rich,
when the splendor of his house
increases;
17for he will take nothing with him
when he dies,
his splendor will not descend with
him.
18Though while he lived he counted
himself blessed—
and men praise you when you
prosper—
19he will join the generation of his
fathers,
who will never see the light ⌊of life⌋.

20A man who has riches without
understanding
is like the beasts that perish.

Psalm 50

A psalm of Asaph.

1The Mighty One, God, the LORD,
speaks and summons the earth
from the rising of the sun to the
place where it sets.
2From Zion, perfect in beauty,
God shines forth.
3Our God comes and will not be silent;
a fire devours before him,
and around him a tempest rages.
4He summons the heavens above,
and the earth, that he may judge
his people:
5"Gather to me my consecrated ones,
who made a covenant with me by
sacrifice."
6And the heavens proclaim his
righteousness,
for God himself is judge. *Selah*

7"Hear, O my people, and I will speak,
O Israel, and I will testify against
you:
I am God, your God.
8I do not rebuke you for your sacrifices
or your burnt offerings, which are
ever before me.
9I have no need of a bull from your
stall
or of goats from your pens,
10for every animal of the forest is mine,
and the cattle on a thousand hills.
11I know every bird in the mountains,
and the creatures of the field are
mine.
12If I were hungry I would not tell
you,
for the world is mine, and all that
is in it.
13Do I eat the flesh of bulls
or drink the blood of goats?
14Sacrifice thank offerings to God,
fulfill your vows to the Most High,
15and call upon me in the day of
trouble;
I will deliver you, and you will
honor me."

16But to the wicked, God says:

"What right have you to recite my
laws
or take my covenant on your
lips?
17You hate my instruction
and cast my words behind you.
18When you see a thief, you join with
him;
you throw in your lot with
adulterers.
19You use your mouth for evil
and harness your tongue to deceit.
20You speak continually against your
brother
and slander your own mother's
son.
21These things you have done and I
kept silent;
you thought I was altogether[c] like
you.
But I will rebuke you
and accuse you to your face.

22"Consider this, you who forget God,
or I will tear you to pieces, with
none to rescue:
23He who sacrifices thank offerings
honors me,
and he prepares the way

[a]14 Hebrew *Sheol*; also in verse 15 [b]15 Or *soul* [c]21 Or *thought the 'I AM' was*

so that I may show him[a] the
salvation of God."

Psalm 51

For the director of music. A psalm of David. When the prophet Nathan came to him after David had committed adultery with Bathsheba.

1Have mercy on me, O God,
according to your unfailing love;
according to your great compassion
blot out my transgressions.
2Wash away all my iniquity
and cleanse me from my sin.

3For I know my transgressions,
and my sin is always before me.
4Against you, you only, have I sinned
and done what is evil in your sight,
so that you are proved right when you
speak
and justified when you judge.
5Surely I was sinful at birth,
sinful from the time my mother
conceived me.
6Surely you desire truth in the inner
parts[b];
you teach[c] me wisdom in the
inmost place.

7Cleanse me with hyssop, and I will be
clean;
wash me, and I will be whiter than
snow.
8Let me hear joy and gladness;
let the bones you have crushed
rejoice.
9Hide your face from my sins
and blot out all my iniquity.

10Create in me a pure heart, O God,
and renew a steadfast spirit within
me.
11Do not cast me from your presence
or take your Holy Spirit from me.
12Restore to me the joy of your
salvation
and grant me a willing spirit, to
sustain me.

13Then I will teach transgressors your
ways,
and sinners will turn back to you.
14Save me from bloodguilt, O God,
the God who saves me,
and my tongue will sing of your
righteousness.
15O Lord, open my lips,
and my mouth will declare your
praise.
16You do not delight in sacrifice, or I
would bring it;
you do not take pleasure in burnt
offerings.
17The sacrifices of God are[d] a broken
spirit;
a broken and contrite heart,
O God, you will not despise.

18In your good pleasure make Zion
prosper;
build up the walls of Jerusalem.
19Then there will be righteous
sacrifices,
whole burnt offerings to delight
you;
then bulls will be offered on your
altar.

Psalm 52

For the director of music. A *maskil*[e] of David. When Doeg the Edomite had gone to Saul and told him: "David has gone to the house of Ahimelech."

1Why do you boast of evil, you mighty
man?
Why do you boast all day long,
you who are a disgrace in the eyes
of God?
2Your tongue plots destruction;
it is like a sharpened razor,
you who practice deceit.
3You love evil rather than good,
falsehood rather than speaking the
truth. *Selah*
4You love every harmful word,
O you deceitful tongue!

5Surely God will bring you down to
everlasting ruin:
He will snatch you up and tear you
from your tent;
he will uproot you from the land of
the living. *Selah*
6The righteous will see and fear;
they will laugh at him, saying,
7"Here now is the man
who did not make God his
stronghold
but trusted in his great wealth
and grew strong by destroying
others!"

[a]23 Or *and to him who considers his way / I will show* [b]6 The meaning of the Hebrew for this phrase is uncertain. [c]6 Or *you desired . . . ; / you taught* [d]17 Or *My sacrifice, O God, is* [e]Title: Probably a literary or musical term

FRIDAY

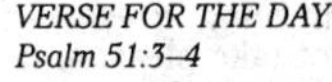

VERSE FOR THE DAY: *Psalm 51:3–4*

AUTHOR: *Gini Andrews*

PASSAGE FOR THE DAY: *Psalm 51:1–19*

Losing the Way

FROM top to bottom, our society is success oriented, however one may define that in terms of one's own goals. Christians are not immune; "Everything comes out okay for Christians," "The King's kids are always winners" are misleading slogans to live by. We develop unrealistic expectations of the Christian life and of ourselves; and then when our wings get broken, we think failure ends our usefulness.

For those of us who know too well the salt taste of failure, it helps to remember that even the great ones of the faith failed, yet God continued to use them, often in a deeper way *after* their fall.

Some of David's greatest psalms came after his greatest mistakes. God called him "a man after his own heart" (1 Samuel 13:14). Abraham lied, perhaps to save his skin, yet he is the towering example of faith for three major religions and is called "God's friend" (James 2:23).

It is those who have plumbed the depths of failure to whom God invariably gives the call to shepherd others. This is not a call given only to the gifted, the highly trained, or the polished as such. Without a bitter experience of their own inadequacy and poverty, they are quite unfitted to bear the burden of spiritual ministry. It takes a person who has discovered something of the measure of his own weakness to be patient with the foibles of others.

Too often we live in a quid-pro-quo relationship with God: "I've been faithful to you, I've worked hard, so please give me this or that." Or, "I've failed again; I can't expect any blessing." We forget that the whole of our life is grace.

Too many sincere Christians, facing their failures, berate themselves unmercifully and keep asking God for forgiveness. Each of us should memorize, hang on the mirror, and make forever our own the ringing truth: "There is now no [repeat *no*] condemnation for those who are in Christ Jesus" (Romans 8:1).

Not only does he not condemn us; he even brings blessings from the ashes of our failures.

Additional Scripture Readings:
John 18:15–27; 21:15–17; Acts 9:1–6,15–16

Go to page 447 for your next devotional reading.

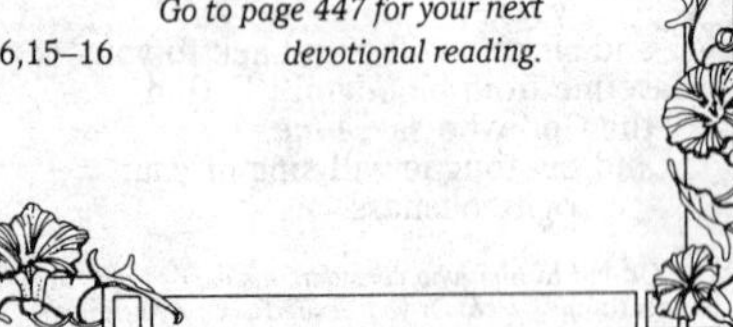

8But I am like an olive tree
flourishing in the house of God;
I trust in God's unfailing love
for ever and ever.
9I will praise you forever for what you have done;
in your name I will hope, for your name is good.
I will praise you in the presence of your saints.

Psalm 53

For the director of music. According to *mahalath.*[a] A *maskil*[b] of David.

1The fool says in his heart,
"There is no God."
They are corrupt, and their ways are vile;
there is no one who does good.

2God looks down from heaven
on the sons of men
to see if there are any who understand,
any who seek God.
3Everyone has turned away,
they have together become corrupt;
there is no one who does good,
not even one.

4Will the evildoers never learn—
those who devour my people as men eat bread
and who do not call on God?
5There they were, overwhelmed with dread,
where there was nothing to dread.
God scattered the bones of those who attacked you;
you put them to shame, for God despised them.

6Oh, that salvation for Israel would come out of Zion!
When God restores the fortunes of his people,
let Jacob rejoice and Israel be glad!

Psalm 54

For the director of music. With stringed instruments. A *maskil*[b] of David. When the Ziphites had gone to Saul and said, "Is not David hiding among us?"

1Save me, O God, by your name;
vindicate me by your might.
2Hear my prayer, O God;
listen to the words of my mouth.

3Strangers are attacking me;
ruthless men seek my life—
men without regard for God. *Selah*

4Surely God is my help;
the Lord is the one who sustains me.

5Let evil recoil on those who slander me;
in your faithfulness destroy them.

6I will sacrifice a freewill offering to you;
I will praise your name, O LORD,
for it is good.
7For he has delivered me from all my troubles,
and my eyes have looked in triumph on my foes.

Psalm 55

For the director of music. With stringed instruments. A *maskil*[b] of David.

1Listen to my prayer, O God,
do not ignore my plea;
2 hear me and answer me.
My thoughts trouble me and I am distraught
3 at the voice of the enemy,
at the stares of the wicked;
for they bring down suffering upon me
and revile me in their anger.

4My heart is in anguish within me;
the terrors of death assail me.
5Fear and trembling have beset me;
horror has overwhelmed me.
6I said, "Oh, that I had the wings of a dove!
I would fly away and be at rest—
7I would flee far away
and stay in the desert; *Selah*
8I would hurry to my place of shelter,
far from the tempest and storm."

9Confuse the wicked, O Lord,
confound their speech,
for I see violence and strife in the city.
10Day and night they prowl about on its walls;
malice and abuse are within it.

[a]Title: Probably a musical term [b]Title: Probably a literary or musical term

11Destructive forces are at work in the city;
threats and lies never leave its streets.

12If an enemy were insulting me,
I could endure it;
if a foe were raising himself against me,
I could hide from him.
13But it is you, a man like myself,
my companion, my close friend,
14with whom I once enjoyed sweet fellowship
as we walked with the throng at the house of God.

15Let death take my enemies by surprise;
let them go down alive to the grave,[a]
for evil finds lodging among them.

16But I call to God,
and the LORD saves me.
17Evening, morning and noon
I cry out in distress,
and he hears my voice.
18He ransoms me unharmed
from the battle waged against me,
even though many oppose me.
19God, who is enthroned forever,
will hear them and afflict them—
Selah
men who never change their ways
and have no fear of God.

20My companion attacks his friends;
he violates his covenant.
21His speech is smooth as butter,
yet war is in his heart;
his words are more soothing than oil,
yet they are drawn swords.

22Cast your cares on the LORD
and he will sustain you;
he will never let the righteous fall.
23But you, O God, will bring down the wicked
into the pit of corruption;
bloodthirsty and deceitful men
will not live out half their days.

But as for me, I trust in you.

Psalm 56

For the director of music. To ˻the tune of,˼ "A Dove on Distant Oaks." Of David. A *miktam*.[b] When the Philistines had seized him in Gath.

1Be merciful to me, O God, for men hotly pursue me;
all day long they press their attack.
2My slanderers pursue me all day long;
many are attacking me in their pride.

3When I am afraid,
I will trust in you.
4In God, whose word I praise,
in God I trust; I will not be afraid.
What can mortal man do to me?

5All day long they twist my words;
they are always plotting to harm me.
6They conspire, they lurk,
they watch my steps,
eager to take my life.

7On no account let them escape;
in your anger, O God, bring down the nations.
8Record my lament;
list my tears on your scroll[c]—
are they not in your record?

9Then my enemies will turn back
when I call for help.
By this I will know that God is for me.
10In God, whose word I praise,
in the LORD, whose word I praise—
11in God I trust; I will not be afraid.
What can man do to me?

12I am under vows to you, O God;
I will present my thank offerings to you.
13For you have delivered me[d] from death
and my feet from stumbling,
that I may walk before God
in the light of life.[e]

Psalm 57

For the director of music. ˻To the tune of,˼ "Do Not Destroy." Of David. A *miktam*.[b] When he had fled from Saul into the cave.

1Have mercy on me, O God, have mercy on me,

[a]*15* Hebrew *Sheol* [b]Title: Probably a literary or musical term [c]*8* Or *I put my tears in your wineskin* [d]*13* Or *my soul* [e]*13* Or *the land of the living*

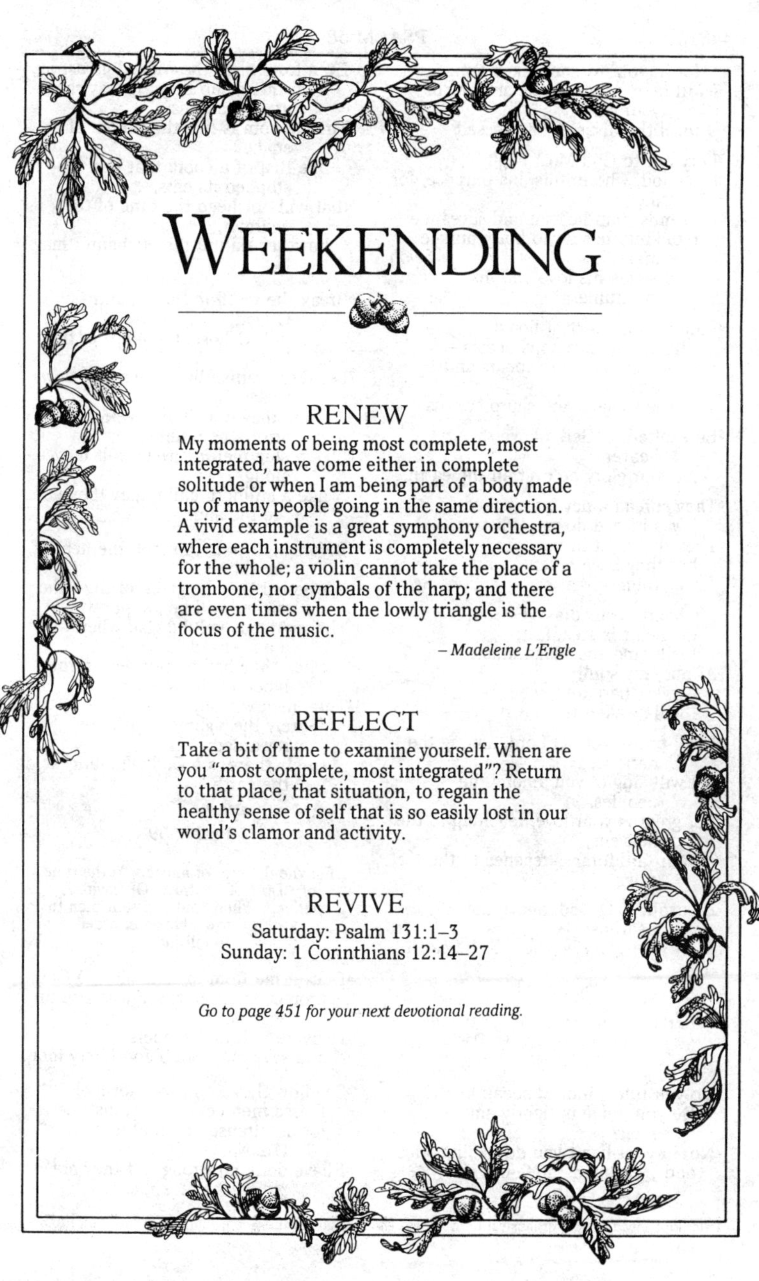

WEEKENDING

RENEW

My moments of being most complete, most integrated, have come either in complete solitude or when I am being part of a body made up of many people going in the same direction. A vivid example is a great symphony orchestra, where each instrument is completely necessary for the whole; a violin cannot take the place of a trombone, nor cymbals of the harp; and there are even times when the lowly triangle is the focus of the music.

– Madeleine L'Engle

REFLECT

Take a bit of time to examine yourself. When are you "most complete, most integrated"? Return to that place, that situation, to regain the healthy sense of self that is so easily lost in our world's clamor and activity.

REVIVE

Saturday: Psalm 131:1–3
Sunday: 1 Corinthians 12:14–27

Go to page 451 for your next devotional reading.

for in you my soul takes refuge.
I will take refuge in the shadow of your wings
until the disaster has passed.

2I cry out to God Most High,
to God, who fulfills ˌhis purposeˌ for me.
3He sends from heaven and saves me,
rebuking those who hotly pursue me; *Selah*
God sends his love and his faithfulness.

4I am in the midst of lions;
I lie among ravenous beasts—
men whose teeth are spears and arrows,
whose tongues are sharp swords.

5Be exalted, O God, above the heavens;
let your glory be over all the earth.

6They spread a net for my feet—
I was bowed down in distress.
They dug a pit in my path—
but they have fallen into it themselves. *Selah*

7My heart is steadfast, O God,
my heart is steadfast;
I will sing and make music.
8Awake, my soul!
Awake, harp and lyre!
I will awaken the dawn.

9I will praise you, O Lord, among the nations;
I will sing of you among the peoples.
10For great is your love, reaching to the heavens;
your faithfulness reaches to the skies.

11Be exalted, O God, above the heavens;
let your glory be over all the earth.

Psalm 58

For the director of music. ˌTo the tune of,ˌ "Do Not Destroy." Of David. A *miktam.*[a]

1Do you rulers indeed speak justly?
Do you judge uprightly among men?
2No, in your heart you devise injustice,
and your hands mete out violence on the earth.
3Even from birth the wicked go astray;
from the womb they are wayward and speak lies.
4Their venom is like the venom of a snake,
like that of a cobra that has stopped its ears,
5that will not heed the tune of the charmer,
however skillful the enchanter may be.

6Break the teeth in their mouths, O God;
tear out, O LORD, the fangs of the lions!
7Let them vanish like water that flows away;
when they draw the bow, let their arrows be blunted.
8Like a slug melting away as it moves along,
like a stillborn child, may they not see the sun.

9Before your pots can feel ˌthe heat ofˌ the thorns—
whether they be green or dry—the wicked will be swept away.[b]
10The righteous will be glad when they are avenged,
when they bathe their feet in the blood of the wicked.
11Then men will say,
"Surely the righteous still are rewarded;
surely there is a God who judges the earth."

Psalm 59

For the director of music. ˌTo the tune of,ˌ "Do Not Destroy." Of David. A *miktam.*[a] When Saul had sent men to watch David's house in order to kill him.

1Deliver me from my enemies, O God;
protect me from those who rise up against me.
2Deliver me from evildoers
and save me from bloodthirsty men.

3See how they lie in wait for me!
Fierce men conspire against me
for no offense or sin of mine,
O LORD.
4I have done no wrong, yet they are ready to attack me.

[a]Title: Probably a literary or musical term [b]9 The meaning of the Hebrew for this verse is uncertain.

Arise to help me; look on my
plight!
5O LORD God Almighty, the God of
Israel,
rouse yourself to punish all the
nations;
show no mercy to wicked traitors.
Selah

6They return at evening,
snarling like dogs,
and prowl about the city.
7See what they spew from their
mouths—
they spew out swords from their
lips,
and they say, "Who can hear us?"
8But you, O LORD, laugh at them;
you scoff at all those nations.

9O my Strength, I watch for you;
you, O God, are my fortress, 10my
loving God.

God will go before me
and will let me gloat over those
who slander me.
11But do not kill them, O Lord our
shield,[a]
or my people will forget.
In your might make them wander
about,
and bring them down.
12For the sins of their mouths,
for the words of their lips,
let them be caught in their pride.
For the curses and lies they utter,
13 consume them in wrath,
consume them till they are no
more.
Then it will be known to the ends of
the earth
that God rules over Jacob. *Selah*

14They return at evening,
snarling like dogs,
and prowl about the city.
15They wander about for food
and howl if not satisfied.
16But I will sing of your strength,
in the morning I will sing of your
love;
for you are my fortress,
my refuge in times of trouble.

17O my Strength, I sing praise to you;
you, O God, are my fortress, my
loving God.

Psalm 60

For the director of music. To the tune of, "The Lily of the Covenant." A *miktam*[b] of David. For teaching. When he fought Aram Naharaim[c] and Aram Zobah,[d] and when Joab returned and struck down twelve thousand Edomites in the Valley of Salt.

1You have rejected us, O God, and
burst forth upon us;
you have been angry—now restore
us!
2You have shaken the land and torn it
open;
mend its fractures, for it is
quaking.
3You have shown your people
desperate times;
you have given us wine that makes
us stagger.

4But for those who fear you, you have
raised a banner
to be unfurled against the bow.
Selah

5Save us and help us with your right
hand,
that those you love may be
delivered.
6God has spoken from his sanctuary:
"In triumph I will parcel out
Shechem
and measure off the Valley of
Succoth.
7Gilead is mine, and Manasseh is
mine;
Ephraim is my helmet,
Judah my scepter.
8Moab is my washbasin,
upon Edom I toss my sandal;
over Philistia I shout in
triumph."

9Who will bring me to the fortified
city?
Who will lead me to Edom?
10Is it not you, O God, you who have
rejected us
and no longer go out with our
armies?
11Give us aid against the enemy,
for the help of man is worthless.
12With God we will gain the
victory,
and he will trample down our
enemies.

[a]11 Or *sovereign* [b]Title: Probably a literary or musical term [c]Title: That is, Arameans of Northwest Mesopotamia [d]Title: That is, Arameans of central Syria

Psalm 61

For the director of music. With stringed instruments. Of David.

1Hear my cry, O God;
listen to my prayer.
2From the ends of the earth I call to you,
I call as my heart grows faint;
lead me to the rock that is higher than I.
3For you have been my refuge,
a strong tower against the foe.

4I long to dwell in your tent forever
and take refuge in the shelter of your wings. *Selah*
5For you have heard my vows, O God;
you have given me the heritage of those who fear your name.

6Increase the days of the king's life,
his years for many generations.
7May he be enthroned in God's presence forever;
appoint your love and faithfulness to protect him.

8Then will I ever sing praise to your name
and fulfill my vows day after day.

Psalm 62

For the director of music. For Jeduthun. A psalm of David.

1My soul finds rest in God alone;
my salvation comes from him.
2He alone is my rock and my salvation;
he is my fortress, I will never be shaken.

3How long will you assault a man?
Would all of you throw him down—
this leaning wall, this tottering fence?
4They fully intend to topple him
from his lofty place;
they take delight in lies.
With their mouths they bless,
but in their hearts they curse. *Selah*

5Find rest, O my soul, in God alone;
my hope comes from him.
6He alone is my rock and my salvation;
he is my fortress, I will not be shaken.
7My salvation and my honor depend on God[a];
he is my mighty rock, my refuge.
8Trust in him at all times, O people;
pour out your hearts to him,
for God is our refuge. *Selah*

9Lowborn men are but a breath,
the highborn are but a lie;
if weighed on a balance, they are nothing;
together they are only a breath.
10Do not trust in extortion
or take pride in stolen goods;
though your riches increase,
do not set your heart on them.

11One thing God has spoken,
two things have I heard:
that you, O God, are strong,
12 and that you, O Lord, are loving.
Surely you will reward each person
according to what he has done.

Psalm 63

A psalm of David. When he was in the Desert of Judah.

1O God, you are my God,
earnestly I seek you;
my soul thirsts for you,
my body longs for you,
in a dry and weary land
where there is no water.

2I have seen you in the sanctuary
and beheld your power and your glory.
3Because your love is better than life,
my lips will glorify you.
4I will praise you as long as I live,
and in your name I will lift up my hands.
5My soul will be satisfied as with the richest of foods;
with singing lips my mouth will praise you.

6On my bed I remember you;
I think of you through the watches of the night.
7Because you are my help,
I sing in the shadow of your wings.
8My soul clings to you;
your right hand upholds me.

9They who seek my life will be destroyed;
they will go down to the depths of the earth.
10They will be given over to the sword
and become food for jackals.

[a]7 Or / *God Most High is my salvation and my honor*

VERSE FOR THE DAY:
Psalm 63:1

AUTHOR:
Rosalind Rinker

PASSAGE FOR THE DAY:
Psalm 63:1–11

A Spring of Living Water

O GOD, you are my God,
earnestly I seek you;
my soul thirsts for you . . .
in a dry and weary land
where there is no water (Psalm 63:1).

The book of Psalms is a book of prayer that embraces every experience possible to human beings. As we read Psalm 63, we see that David was a fugitive in the desert of Judah. He was greatly distressed. He thirsted after God.

We can identify with David's great thirst, but that may be where the parallel ends. Unlike David, who fought on the side of God, often our enemies are the result of our personal failures.

The thirst that we have in common with David is worth looking into. We thirst for different things at different times: recognition, friends, a life-mate, a home, children, a home church, an education, a job and money, and gifts to serve our Lord (wisdom, insight, courage). But most of all we thirst to love and be loved.

In John 4, Jesus used earthly water to introduce living water, which alone can quench our thirsty hearts, no matter who we are. When Jesus asked for a drink from the Samaritan woman, he did so even though the request broke all Jewish religious, racial, and sexual laws. These laws and customs, however, were not as important to Jesus as his desire to offer the woman living water.

Today the invitation still stands: "Everyone who drinks this water will be thirsty again, but whoever drinks the water I give him will never thirst. Indeed, the water I give him will become in him a spring of water welling up to eternal life" (John 4:13–14).

Psalm 63 joyfully proclaims the blessings David received when he cried out to God; they can be yours also: to see the glory of God, to know God's love is better than life, to praise him with singing lips, to meditate on him when sleepless, and to stay close to him because his right hand upholds you.

We serve a risen Savior who has given us his Holy Spirit (John 7:37–39) as "living water," which becomes like an artesian well within us. He invites us: If anyone thirsts, let her ask, "for everyone who asks receives" (Matthew 7:7–9).

Additional Scripture Readings:
Isaiah 55:1–3; Matthew 5:6

Go to page 457 for your next devotional reading.

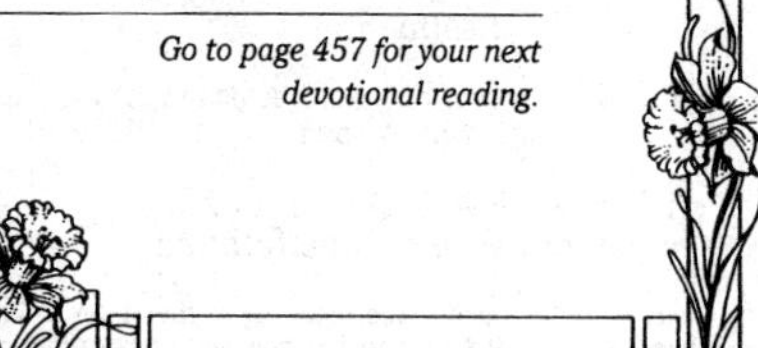

11But the king will rejoice in God;
all who swear by God's name will praise him,
while the mouths of liars will be silenced.

Psalm 64

For the director of music. A psalm of David.

1Hear me, O God, as I voice my complaint;
protect my life from the threat of the enemy.
2Hide me from the conspiracy of the wicked,
from that noisy crowd of evildoers.

3They sharpen their tongues like swords
and aim their words like deadly arrows.
4They shoot from ambush at the innocent man;
they shoot at him suddenly, without fear.

5They encourage each other in evil plans,
they talk about hiding their snares;
they say, "Who will see them[a]?"
6They plot injustice and say,
"We have devised a perfect plan!"
Surely the mind and heart of man are cunning.

7But God will shoot them with arrows;
suddenly they will be struck down.
8He will turn their own tongues against them
and bring them to ruin;
all who see them will shake their heads in scorn.

9All mankind will fear;
they will proclaim the works of God
and ponder what he has done.
10Let the righteous rejoice in the LORD
and take refuge in him;
let all the upright in heart praise him!

Psalm 65

For the director of music. A psalm of David. A song.

1Praise awaits[b] you, O God, in Zion;
to you our vows will be fulfilled.
2O you who hear prayer,
to you all men will come.
3When we were overwhelmed by sins,
you forgave[c] our transgressions.
4Blessed are those you choose
and bring near to live in your courts!
We are filled with the good things of your house,
of your holy temple.

5You answer us with awesome deeds of righteousness,
O God our Savior,
the hope of all the ends of the earth
and of the farthest seas,
6who formed the mountains by your power,
having armed yourself with strength,
7who stilled the roaring of the seas,
the roaring of their waves,
and the turmoil of the nations.
8Those living far away fear your wonders;
where morning dawns and evening fades
you call forth songs of joy.

9You care for the land and water it;
you enrich it abundantly.
The streams of God are filled with water
to provide the people with grain,
for so you have ordained it.[d]
10You drench its furrows
and level its ridges;
you soften it with showers
and bless its crops.
11You crown the year with your bounty,
and your carts overflow with abundance.
12The grasslands of the desert overflow;
the hills are clothed with gladness.
13The meadows are covered with flocks
and the valleys are mantled with grain;
they shout for joy and sing.

Psalm 66

For the director of music. A song. A psalm.

1Shout with joy to God, all the earth!
2 Sing the glory of his name;
make his praise glorious!

[a]5 Or *us* [b]1 Or *befits*; the meaning of the Hebrew for this word is uncertain. [c]3 Or *made atonement for* [d]9 Or *for that is how you prepare the land*

3Say to God, "How awesome are your
deeds!
So great is your power
that your enemies cringe before
you.
4All the earth bows down to you;
they sing praise to you,
they sing praise to your name."
Selah

5Come and see what God has done,
how awesome his works in man's
behalf!
6He turned the sea into dry land,
they passed through the waters on
foot—
come, let us rejoice in him.
7He rules forever by his power,
his eyes watch the nations—
let not the rebellious rise up
against him. *Selah*

8Praise our God, O peoples,
let the sound of his praise be
heard;
9he has preserved our lives
and kept our feet from slipping.
10For you, O God, tested us;
you refined us like silver.
11You brought us into prison
and laid burdens on our backs.
12You let men ride over our heads;
we went through fire and water,
but you brought us to a place of
abundance.

13I will come to your temple with burnt
offerings
and fulfill my vows to you—
14vows my lips promised and my mouth
spoke
when I was in trouble.
15I will sacrifice fat animals to you
and an offering of rams;
I will offer bulls and goats. *Selah*

16Come and listen, all you who fear
God;
let me tell you what he has done
for me.
17I cried out to him with my mouth;
his praise was on my tongue.
18If I had cherished sin in my heart,
the Lord would not have listened;
19but God has surely listened
and heard my voice in prayer.
20Praise be to God,
who has not rejected my prayer
or withheld his love from me!

Psalm 67

For the director of music. With stringed instruments. A psalm. A song.

1May God be gracious to us and bless
us
and make his face shine upon us,
Selah
2that your ways may be known on
earth,
your salvation among all nations.

3May the peoples praise you, O God;
may all the peoples praise you.
4May the nations be glad and sing for
joy,
for you rule the peoples justly
and guide the nations of the earth.
Selah
5May the peoples praise you, O God;
may all the peoples praise you.

6Then the land will yield its harvest,
and God, our God, will bless us.
7God will bless us,
and all the ends of the earth will
fear him.

Psalm 68

For the director of music. Of David. A psalm. A song.

1May God arise, may his enemies be
scattered;
may his foes flee before him.
2As smoke is blown away by the wind,
may you blow them away;
as wax melts before the fire,
may the wicked perish before God.
3But may the righteous be glad
and rejoice before God;
may they be happy and joyful.

4Sing to God, sing praise to his name,
extol him who rides on the
clouds[a]—
his name is the LORD—
and rejoice before him.
5A father to the fatherless, a defender
of widows,
is God in his holy dwelling.
6God sets the lonely in families,[b]
he leads forth the prisoners with
singing;
but the rebellious live in a
sun-scorched land.

7When you went out before your
people, O God,

[a]4 Or *I prepare the way for him who rides through the deserts* [b]6 Or *the desolate in a homeland*

when you marched through the
wasteland, *Selah*
8the earth shook,
the heavens poured down rain,
before God, the One of Sinai,
before God, the God of Israel.
9You gave abundant showers, O God;
you refreshed your weary
inheritance.
10Your people settled in it,
and from your bounty, O God, you
provided for the poor.

11The Lord announced the word,
and great was the company of those
who proclaimed it:
12"Kings and armies flee in haste;
in the camps men divide the
plunder.
13Even while you sleep among the
campfires,[a]
the wings of ⌞my⌟ dove are sheathed
with silver,
its feathers with shining gold."
14When the Almighty[b] scattered the
kings in the land,
it was like snow fallen on Zalmon.

15The mountains of Bashan are
majestic mountains;
rugged are the mountains of Bashan.
16Why gaze in envy, O rugged
mountains,
at the mountain where God chooses
to reign,
where the LORD himself will dwell
forever?
17The chariots of God are tens of
thousands
and thousands of thousands;
the Lord ⌞has come⌟ from Sinai into
his sanctuary.
18When you ascended on high,
you led captives in your train;
you received gifts from men,
even from[c] the rebellious—
that you,[d] O LORD God, might dwell
there.

19Praise be to the Lord, to God our
Savior,
who daily bears our burdens. *Selah*
20Our God is a God who saves;
from the Sovereign LORD comes
escape from death.
21Surely God will crush the heads of his
enemies,
the hairy crowns of those who go
on in their sins.
22The Lord says, "I will bring them
from Bashan;
I will bring them from the depths of
the sea,
23that you may plunge your feet in the
blood of your foes,
while the tongues of your dogs have
their share."

24Your procession has come into view,
O God,
the procession of my God and King
into the sanctuary.
25In front are the singers, after them
the musicians;
with them are the maidens playing
tambourines.
26Praise God in the great congregation;
praise the LORD in the assembly of
Israel.
27There is the little tribe of Benjamin,
leading them,
there the great throng of Judah's
princes,
and there the princes of Zebulun
and of Naphtali.

28Summon your power, O God[e];
show us your strength, O God, as
you have done before.
29Because of your temple at Jerusalem
kings will bring you gifts.
30Rebuke the beast among the reeds,
the herd of bulls among the calves
of the nations.
Humbled, may it bring bars of silver.
Scatter the nations who delight in
war.
31Envoys will come from Egypt;
Cush[f] will submit herself to God.

32Sing to God, O kingdoms of the earth,
sing praise to the Lord, *Selah*
33to him who rides the ancient skies
above,
who thunders with mighty voice.
34Proclaim the power of God,
whose majesty is over Israel,
whose power is in the skies.
35You are awesome, O God, in your
sanctuary;
the God of Israel gives power and
strength to his people.
Praise be to God!

[a]*13* Or *saddlebags* [b]*14* Hebrew *Shaddai* [c]*18* Or *gifts for men, / even* [d]*18* Or *they* [e]*28* Many Hebrew manuscripts, Septuagint and Syriac; most Hebrew manuscripts *Your God has summoned power for you* [f]*31* That is, the upper Nile region

Psalm 69

For the director of music. To ˛the tune of˛ "Lilies." Of David.

1Save me, O God,
for the waters have come up to my neck.
2I sink in the miry depths,
where there is no foothold.
I have come into the deep waters;
the floods engulf me.
3I am worn out calling for help;
my throat is parched.
My eyes fail,
looking for my God.
4Those who hate me without reason
outnumber the hairs of my head;
many are my enemies without cause,
those who seek to destroy me.
I am forced to restore
what I did not steal.

5You know my folly, O God;
my guilt is not hidden from you.

6May those who hope in you
not be disgraced because of me,
O Lord, the LORD Almighty;
may those who seek you
not be put to shame because of me,
O God of Israel.
7For I endure scorn for your sake,
and shame covers my face.
8I am a stranger to my brothers,
an alien to my own mother's sons;
9for zeal for your house consumes me,
and the insults of those who insult you fall on me.
10When I weep and fast,
I must endure scorn;
11when I put on sackcloth,
people make sport of me.
12Those who sit at the gate mock me,
and I am the song of the drunkards.

13But I pray to you, O LORD,
in the time of your favor;
in your great love, O God,
answer me with your sure salvation.
14Rescue me from the mire,
do not let me sink;
deliver me from those who hate me,
from the deep waters.
15Do not let the floodwaters engulf me
or the depths swallow me up
or the pit close its mouth over me.

16Answer me, O LORD, out of the goodness of your love;
in your great mercy turn to me.
17Do not hide your face from your servant;
answer me quickly, for I am in trouble.
18Come near and rescue me;
redeem me because of my foes.

19You know how I am scorned,
disgraced and shamed;
all my enemies are before you.
20Scorn has broken my heart
and has left me helpless;
I looked for sympathy, but there was none,
for comforters, but I found none.
21They put gall in my food
and gave me vinegar for my thirst.

22May the table set before them become a snare;
may it become retribution and[a] a trap.
23May their eyes be darkened so they cannot see,
and their backs be bent forever.
24Pour out your wrath on them;
let your fierce anger overtake them.
25May their place be deserted;
let there be no one to dwell in their tents.
26For they persecute those you wound
and talk about the pain of those you hurt.
27Charge them with crime upon crime;
do not let them share in your salvation.
28May they be blotted out of the book of life
and not be listed with the righteous.

29I am in pain and distress;
may your salvation, O God, protect me.

30I will praise God's name in song
and glorify him with thanksgiving.
31This will please the LORD more than an ox,
more than a bull with its horns and hoofs.
32The poor will see and be glad—
you who seek God, may your hearts live!
33The LORD hears the needy
and does not despise his captive people.

[a]22 Or *snare / and their fellowship become*

34Let heaven and earth praise him,
the seas and all that move in them,
35for God will save Zion
and rebuild the cities of Judah.
Then people will settle there and possess it;
36 the children of his servants will inherit it,
and those who love his name will dwell there.

Psalm 70

For the director of music. Of David. A petition.

1Hasten, O God, to save me;
O LORD, come quickly to help me.
2May those who seek my life
be put to shame and confusion;
may all who desire my ruin
be turned back in disgrace.
3May those who say to me, "Aha! Aha!"
turn back because of their shame.
4But may all who seek you
rejoice and be glad in you;
may those who love your salvation always say,
"Let God be exalted!"

5Yet I am poor and needy;
come quickly to me, O God.
You are my help and my deliverer;
O LORD, do not delay.

Psalm 71

1In you, O LORD, I have taken refuge;
let me never be put to shame.
2Rescue me and deliver me in your righteousness;
turn your ear to me and save me.
3Be my rock of refuge,
to which I can always go;
give the command to save me,
for you are my rock and my fortress.
4Deliver me, O my God, from the hand of the wicked,
from the grasp of evil and cruel men.

5For you have been my hope,
O Sovereign LORD,
my confidence since my youth.
6From birth I have relied on you;
you brought me forth from my mother's womb.
I will ever praise you.
7I have become like a portent to many,
but you are my strong refuge.
8My mouth is filled with your praise,
declaring your splendor all day long.

9Do not cast me away when I am old;
do not forsake me when my strength is gone.
10For my enemies speak against me;
those who wait to kill me conspire together.
11They say, "God has forsaken him;
pursue him and seize him,
for no one will rescue him."
12Be not far from me, O God;
come quickly, O my God, to help me.
13May my accusers perish in shame;
may those who want to harm me
be covered with scorn and disgrace.

14But as for me, I will always have hope;
I will praise you more and more.
15My mouth will tell of your righteousness,
of your salvation all day long,
though I know not its measure.
16I will come and proclaim your mighty acts, O Sovereign LORD;
I will proclaim your righteousness, yours alone.
17Since my youth, O God, you have taught me,
and to this day I declare your marvelous deeds.
18Even when I am old and gray,
do not forsake me, O God,
till I declare your power to the next generation,
your might to all who are to come.

19Your righteousness reaches to the skies, O God,
you who have done great things.
Who, O God, is like you?
20Though you have made me see troubles, many and bitter,
you will restore my life again;
from the depths of the earth
you will again bring me up.
21You will increase my honor
and comfort me once again.

22I will praise you with the harp
for your faithfulness, O my God;
I will sing praise to you with the lyre,
O Holy One of Israel.
23My lips will shout for joy
when I sing praise to you—
I, whom you have redeemed.

TUESDAY

VERSE FOR THE DAY: *Psalm 71:3* | *AUTHOR:* *Gloria Gaither* | *PASSAGE FOR THE DAY:* *Psalm 71:1–24*

The Cleft

SO that is what a "cleft of the rock" looks like! I thought of the Fanny Crosby hymn "He Hideth My Soul" as I looked at this place "overshadowed" by a desert mountain, which is nothing more than a "towering" rock. I've heard all these words and phrases in hymns and ancient poetry. Yet, having grown up in Michigan, I more easily related to "the ageless billows roll," or having sins buried in "the depths" never to be remembered again. I could easily visualize the Master warning the man "who puts his hand to the plow and looks back " (Luke 9:62). Or Jesus taking in his hand a mustard seed, planting it in the moist black soil, then pointing to a matured plant so big "that the birds of the air come and perch in its branches" (Matthew 13:32).

I could relate to "shifting sand," for I've seen the "waves" of the sand dunes, or the "shelter from the storm," for I've been caught in the fury of a Midwestern thunderstorm. I've experienced the eye of a tornado, the area that is peaceful and quiet while the circle around it rages and destroys.

But clefts. I'd never really thought much of hiding in the cleft of a rock. Yet, here above me is exactly that: a "cleft of the rock." All around this indentation made eons ago are rugged surfaces exposed constantly to the fury and heat of the desert climate. Yet, inside this cleft the rock is its original pink color, unspoiled and protected. I realize that if the "storm in fury beat around me" I'd want to be in the solid rock, halfway up the mountain, hiding in the fortress made by nature itself, in the cleft of the rock. Perhaps it was about such a place that Fanny Crosby wrote:

A wonderful Savior is Jesus My Lord,
  A wonderful Savior to me;
He hideth my soul in the cleft of the rock,
  Where rivers of pleasure I see.

He hideth my soul in the cleft of the rock
  That shadows a dry, thirsty land;
He hideth my life in the depths of His love,
  And covers me there with His hand,
  And covers me there with His hand.

Additional Scripture Readings:
Exodus 33:18–23; Colossians 3:1–3

Go to page 467 for your next devotional reading.

[24]My tongue will tell of your righteous acts
all day long,
for those who wanted to harm me
have been put to shame and confusion.

Psalm 72

Of Solomon.

[1]Endow the king with your justice, O God,
the royal son with your righteousness.
[2]He will[a] judge your people in righteousness,
your afflicted ones with justice.
[3]The mountains will bring prosperity to the people,
the hills the fruit of righteousness.
[4]He will defend the afflicted among the people
and save the children of the needy;
he will crush the oppressor.

[5]He will endure[b] as long as the sun,
as long as the moon, through all generations.
[6]He will be like rain falling on a mown field,
like showers watering the earth.
[7]In his days the righteous will flourish;
prosperity will abound till the moon is no more.

[8]He will rule from sea to sea
and from the River[c] to the ends of the earth.[d]
[9]The desert tribes will bow before him
and his enemies will lick the dust.
[10]The kings of Tarshish and of distant shores
will bring tribute to him;
the kings of Sheba and Seba
will present him gifts.
[11]All kings will bow down to him
and all nations will serve him.

[12]For he will deliver the needy who cry out,
the afflicted who have no one to help.
[13]He will take pity on the weak and the needy
and save the needy from death.
[14]He will rescue them from oppression and violence,
for precious is their blood in his sight.

[15]Long may he live!
May gold from Sheba be given him.
May people ever pray for him
and bless him all day long.
[16]Let grain abound throughout the land;
on the tops of the hills may it sway.
Let its fruit flourish like Lebanon;
let it thrive like the grass of the field.
[17]May his name endure forever;
may it continue as long as the sun.

All nations will be blessed through him,
and they will call him blessed.

[18]Praise be to the LORD God, the God of Israel,
who alone does marvelous deeds.
[19]Praise be to his glorious name forever;
may the whole earth be filled with his glory.
Amen and Amen.

[20]This concludes the prayers of David son of Jesse.

BOOK III

Psalms 73–89

Psalm 73

A psalm of Asaph.

[1]Surely God is good to Israel,
to those who are pure in heart.

[2]But as for me, my feet had almost slipped;
I had nearly lost my foothold.
[3]For I envied the arrogant
when I saw the prosperity of the wicked.

[4]They have no struggles;
their bodies are healthy and strong.[e]
[5]They are free from the burdens common to man;
they are not plagued by human ills.
[6]Therefore pride is their necklace;
they clothe themselves with violence.

[a]*2* Or *May he*; similarly in verses 3-11 and 17 [b]*5* Septuagint; Hebrew *You will be feared* [c]*8* That is, the Euphrates [d]*8* Or *the end of the land* [e]*4* With a different word division of the Hebrew; Masoretic Text *struggles at their death; / their bodies are healthy*

7From their callous hearts comes
iniquity[a];
the evil conceits of their minds
know no limits.
8They scoff, and speak with malice;
in their arrogance they threaten
oppression.
9Their mouths lay claim to heaven,
and their tongues take possession
of the earth.
10Therefore their people turn to them
and drink up waters in
abundance.[b]
11They say, "How can God know?
Does the Most High have
knowledge?"

12This is what the wicked are like—
always carefree, they increase in
wealth.

13Surely in vain have I kept my heart
pure;
in vain have I washed my hands in
innocence.
14All day long I have been plagued;
I have been punished every
morning.

15If I had said, "I will speak thus,"
I would have betrayed your
children.
16When I tried to understand all this,
it was oppressive to me
17till I entered the sanctuary of God;
then I understood their final
destiny.

18Surely you place them on slippery
ground;
you cast them down to ruin.
19How suddenly are they destroyed,
completely swept away by terrors!
20As a dream when one awakes,
so when you arise, O Lord,
you will despise them as fantasies.

21When my heart was grieved
and my spirit embittered,
22I was senseless and ignorant;
I was a brute beast before you.

23Yet I am always with you;
you hold me by my right hand.
24You guide me with your counsel,
and afterward you will take me into
glory.
25Whom have I in heaven but you?
And earth has nothing I desire
besides you.
26My flesh and my heart may fail,
but God is the strength of my heart
and my portion forever.

27Those who are far from you will
perish;
you destroy all who are unfaithful
to you.
28But as for me, it is good to be near
God.
I have made the Sovereign LORD my
refuge;
I will tell of all your deeds.

Psalm 74

A *maskil*[c] of Asaph.

1Why have you rejected us forever,
O God?
Why does your anger smolder
against the sheep of your
pasture?
2Remember the people you purchased
of old,
the tribe of your inheritance, whom
you redeemed—
Mount Zion, where you dwelt.
3Turn your steps toward these
everlasting ruins,
all this destruction the enemy has
brought on the sanctuary.

4Your foes roared in the place where
you met with us;
they set up their standards as signs.
5They behaved like men wielding axes
to cut through a thicket of trees.
6They smashed all the carved paneling
with their axes and hatchets.
7They burned your sanctuary to the
ground;
they defiled the dwelling place of
your Name.
8They said in their hearts, "We will
crush them completely!"
They burned every place where God
was worshiped in the land.
9We are given no miraculous signs;
no prophets are left,
and none of us knows how long
this will be.

10How long will the enemy mock you,
O God?
Will the foe revile your name
forever?
11Why do you hold back your hand,
your right hand?

[a]7 Syriac (see also Septuagint); Hebrew *Their eyes bulge with fat* [b]10 The meaning of the Hebrew for this verse is uncertain. [c]Title: Probably a literary or musical term

Take it from the folds of your
garment and destroy them!

12But you, O God, are my king from of
old;
you bring salvation upon the earth.
13It was you who split open the sea by
your power;
you broke the heads of the monster
in the waters.
14It was you who crushed the heads of
Leviathan
and gave him as food to the
creatures of the desert.
15It was you who opened up springs
and streams;
you dried up the ever flowing rivers.
16The day is yours, and yours also the
night;
you established the sun and moon.
17It was you who set all the boundaries
of the earth;
you made both summer and winter.

18Remember how the enemy has
mocked you, O LORD,
how foolish people have reviled
your name.
19Do not hand over the life of your dove
to wild beasts;
do not forget the lives of your
afflicted people forever.
20Have regard for your covenant,
because haunts of violence fill the
dark places of the land.
21Do not let the oppressed retreat in
disgrace;
may the poor and needy praise your
name.
22Rise up, O God, and defend your
cause;
remember how fools mock you all
day long.
23Do not ignore the clamor of your
adversaries,
the uproar of your enemies, which
rises continually.

Psalm 75

For the director of music. To the tune of, "Do Not Destroy." A psalm of Asaph. A song.

1We give thanks to you, O God,
we give thanks, for your Name is
near;
men tell of your wonderful deeds.

2You say, "I choose the appointed
time;
it is I who judge uprightly.
3When the earth and all its people
quake,
it is I who hold its pillars firm.
Selah

4To the arrogant I say, 'Boast no
more,'
and to the wicked, 'Do not lift up
your horns.
5Do not lift your horns against heaven;
do not speak with outstretched
neck.' "

6No one from the east or the west
or from the desert can exalt a man.
7But it is God who judges:
He brings one down, he exalts
another.
8In the hand of the LORD is a cup
full of foaming wine mixed with
spices;
he pours it out, and all the wicked of
the earth
drink it down to its very dregs.

9As for me, I will declare this forever;
I will sing praise to the God of
Jacob.
10I will cut off the horns of all the
wicked,
but the horns of the righteous will
be lifted up.

Psalm 76

For the director of music. With stringed instruments. A psalm of Asaph. A song.

1In Judah God is known;
his name is great in Israel.
2His tent is in Salem,
his dwelling place in Zion.
3There he broke the flashing arrows,
the shields and the swords, the
weapons of war. *Selah*

4You are resplendent with light,
more majestic than mountains rich
with game.
5Valiant men lie plundered,
they sleep their last sleep;
not one of the warriors
can lift his hands.
6At your rebuke, O God of Jacob,
both horse and chariot lie still.
7You alone are to be feared.
Who can stand before you when
you are angry?
8From heaven you pronounced
judgment,

and the land feared and was
quiet—
9when you, O God, rose up to judge,
to save all the afflicted of the land.
Selah
10Surely your wrath against men brings
you praise,
and the survivors of your wrath are
restrained.[a]
11Make vows to the LORD your God and
fulfill them;
let all the neighboring lands
bring gifts to the One to be feared.
12He breaks the spirit of rulers;
he is feared by the kings of the
earth.

Psalm 77

For the director of music. For Jeduthun.
Of Asaph. A psalm.

1I cried out to God for help;
I cried out to God to hear me.
2When I was in distress, I sought the
Lord;
at night I stretched out untiring
hands
and my soul refused to be
comforted.

3I remembered you, O God, and I
groaned;
I mused, and my spirit grew faint.
Selah
4You kept my eyes from closing;
I was too troubled to speak.
5I thought about the former days,
the years of long ago;
6I remembered my songs in the night.
My heart mused and my spirit
inquired:

7"Will the Lord reject forever?
Will he never show his favor again?
8Has his unfailing love vanished
forever?
Has his promise failed for all time?
9Has God forgotten to be merciful?
Has he in anger withheld his
compassion?" *Selah*

10Then I thought, "To this I will appeal:
the years of the right hand of the
Most High."
11I will remember the deeds of the
LORD;
yes, I will remember your miracles
of long ago.
12I will meditate on all your works
and consider all your mighty deeds.

13Your ways, O God, are holy.
What god is so great as our God?
14You are the God who performs
miracles;
you display your power among the
peoples.
15With your mighty arm you redeemed
your people,
the descendants of Jacob and
Joseph. *Selah*

16The waters saw you, O God,
the waters saw you and writhed;
the very depths were convulsed.
17The clouds poured down water,
the skies resounded with thunder;
your arrows flashed back and forth.
18Your thunder was heard in the
whirlwind,
your lightning lit up the world;
the earth trembled and quaked.
19Your path led through the sea,
your way through the mighty
waters,
though your footprints were not
seen.

20You led your people like a flock
by the hand of Moses and Aaron.

Psalm 78

A *maskil*[b] of Asaph.

1O my people, hear my teaching;
listen to the words of my mouth.
2I will open my mouth in parables,
I will utter hidden things, things
from of old—
3what we have heard and known,
what our fathers have told us.
4We will not hide them from their
children;
we will tell the next generation
the praiseworthy deeds of the LORD,
his power, and the wonders he has
done.
5He decreed statutes for Jacob
and established the law in Israel,
which he commanded our forefathers
to teach their children,
6so the next generation would know
them,
even the children yet to be born,

[a]*10* Or *Surely the wrath of men brings you praise, / and with the remainder of wrath you arm yourself*
[b]Title: Probably a literary or musical term

and they in turn would tell their
children.
7Then they would put their trust in
God
and would not forget his deeds
but would keep his commands.
8They would not be like their
forefathers—
a stubborn and rebellious
generation,
whose hearts were not loyal to God,
whose spirits were not faithful to
him.
9The men of Ephraim, though armed
with bows,
turned back on the day of battle;
10they did not keep God's covenant
and refused to live by his law.
11They forgot what he had done,
the wonders he had shown them.
12He did miracles in the sight of their
fathers
in the land of Egypt, in the region
of Zoan.
13He divided the sea and led them
through;
he made the water stand firm like a
wall.
14He guided them with the cloud by
day
and with light from the fire all
night.
15He split the rocks in the desert
and gave them water as abundant
as the seas;
16he brought streams out of a rocky
crag
and made water flow down like
rivers.

17But they continued to sin against
him,
rebelling in the desert against the
Most High.
18They willfully put God to the test
by demanding the food they craved.
19They spoke against God, saying,
"Can God spread a table in the
desert?
20When he struck the rock, water
gushed out,
and streams flowed abundantly.
But can he also give us food?
Can he supply meat for his
people?"
21When the LORD heard them, he was
very angry;
his fire broke out against Jacob,
and his wrath rose against Israel,
22for they did not believe in God
or trust in his deliverance.
23Yet he gave a command to the skies
above
and opened the doors of the
heavens;
24he rained down manna for the people
to eat,
he gave them the grain of heaven.
25Men ate the bread of angels;
he sent them all the food they
could eat.
26He let loose the east wind from the
heavens
and led forth the south wind by his
power.
27He rained meat down on them like
dust,
flying birds like sand on the
seashore.
28He made them come down inside
their camp,
all around their tents.
29They ate till they had more than
enough,
for he had given them what they
craved.
30But before they turned from the food
they craved,
even while it was still in their
mouths,
31God's anger rose against them;
he put to death the sturdiest
among them,
cutting down the young men of
Israel.

32In spite of all this, they kept on
sinning;
in spite of his wonders, they did
not believe.
33So he ended their days in futility
and their years in terror.
34Whenever God slew them, they would
seek him;
they eagerly turned to him again.
35They remembered that God was their
Rock,
that God Most High was their
Redeemer.
36But then they would flatter him with
their mouths,
lying to him with their tongues;
37their hearts were not loyal to him,
they were not faithful to his
covenant.
38Yet he was merciful;
he forgave their iniquities
and did not destroy them.
Time after time he restrained his
anger

and did not stir up his full wrath.
39He remembered that they were but flesh,
a passing breeze that does not return.

40How often they rebelled against him in the desert
and grieved him in the wasteland!
41Again and again they put God to the test;
they vexed the Holy One of Israel.
42They did not remember his power—
the day he redeemed them from the oppressor,
43the day he displayed his miraculous signs in Egypt,
his wonders in the region of Zoan.
44He turned their rivers to blood;
they could not drink from their streams.
45He sent swarms of flies that devoured them,
and frogs that devastated them.
46He gave their crops to the grasshopper,
their produce to the locust.
47He destroyed their vines with hail
and their sycamore-figs with sleet.
48He gave over their cattle to the hail,
their livestock to bolts of lightning.
49He unleashed against them his hot anger,
his wrath, indignation and hostility—
a band of destroying angels.
50He prepared a path for his anger;
he did not spare them from death
but gave them over to the plague.
51He struck down all the firstborn of Egypt,
the firstfruits of manhood in the tents of Ham.
52But he brought his people out like a flock;
he led them like sheep through the desert.
53He guided them safely, so they were unafraid;
but the sea engulfed their enemies.
54Thus he brought them to the border of his holy land,
to the hill country his right hand had taken.
55He drove out nations before them
and allotted their lands to them as an inheritance;
he settled the tribes of Israel in their homes.

56But they put God to the test
and rebelled against the Most High;
they did not keep his statutes.
57Like their fathers they were disloyal and faithless,
as unreliable as a faulty bow.
58They angered him with their high places;
they aroused his jealousy with their idols.
59When God heard them, he was very angry;
he rejected Israel completely.
60He abandoned the tabernacle of Shiloh,
the tent he had set up among men.
61He sent ⌊the ark of⌋ his might into captivity,
his splendor into the hands of the enemy.
62He gave his people over to the sword;
he was very angry with his inheritance.
63Fire consumed their young men,
and their maidens had no wedding songs;
64their priests were put to the sword,
and their widows could not weep.

65Then the Lord awoke as from sleep,
as a man wakes from the stupor of wine.
66He beat back his enemies;
he put them to everlasting shame.
67Then he rejected the tents of Joseph,
he did not choose the tribe of Ephraim;
68but he chose the tribe of Judah,
Mount Zion, which he loved.
69He built his sanctuary like the heights,
like the earth that he established forever.
70He chose David his servant
and took him from the sheep pens;
71from tending the sheep he brought him
to be the shepherd of his people Jacob,
of Israel his inheritance.
72And David shepherded them with integrity of heart;
with skillful hands he led them.

Psalm 79

A psalm of Asaph.

1O God, the nations have invaded your inheritance;
they have defiled your holy temple,

they have reduced Jerusalem to
rubble.
2They have given the dead bodies of
your servants
as food to the birds of the air,
the flesh of your saints to the
beasts of the earth.
3They have poured out blood like
water
all around Jerusalem,
and there is no one to bury the
dead.
4We are objects of reproach to our
neighbors,
of scorn and derision to those
around us.

5How long, O LORD? Will you be angry
forever?
How long will your jealousy burn
like fire?
6Pour out your wrath on the
nations
that do not acknowledge you,
on the kingdoms
that do not call on your name;
7for they have devoured Jacob
and destroyed his homeland.
8Do not hold against us the sins of the
fathers;
may your mercy come quickly to
meet us,
for we are in desperate need.

9Help us, O God our Savior,
for the glory of your name;
deliver us and forgive our sins
for your name's sake.
10Why should the nations say,
"Where is their God?"
Before our eyes, make known among
the nations
that you avenge the outpoured
blood of your servants.
11May the groans of the prisoners come
before you;
by the strength of your arm
preserve those condemned to
die.

12Pay back into the laps of our
neighbors seven times
the reproach they have hurled at
you, O Lord.
13Then we your people, the sheep of
your pasture,
will praise you forever;
from generation to generation
we will recount your praise.

Psalm 80

For the director of music. To the tune
of "The Lilies of the Covenant."
Of Asaph. A psalm.

1Hear us, O Shepherd of Israel,
you who lead Joseph like a flock;
you who sit enthroned between the
cherubim, shine forth
2 before Ephraim, Benjamin and
Manasseh.
Awaken your might;
come and save us.

3Restore us, O God;
make your face shine upon us,
that we may be saved.

4O LORD God Almighty,
how long will your anger smolder
against the prayers of your people?
5You have fed them with the bread of
tears;
you have made them drink tears by
the bowlful.
6You have made us a source of
contention to our neighbors,
and our enemies mock us.

7Restore us, O God Almighty;
make your face shine upon us,
that we may be saved.

8You brought a vine out of Egypt;
you drove out the nations and
planted it.
9You cleared the ground for it,
and it took root and filled the land.
10The mountains were covered with its
shade,
the mighty cedars with its
branches.
11It sent out its boughs to the Sea,[a]
its shoots as far as the River.[b]

12Why have you broken down its walls
so that all who pass by pick its
grapes?
13Boars from the forest ravage it
and the creatures of the field feed
on it.
14Return to us, O God Almighty!
Look down from heaven and see!
Watch over this vine,
15 the root your right hand has
planted,
the son[c] you have raised up for
yourself.

[a]*11* Probably the Mediterranean [b]*11* That is, the Euphrates [c]*15* Or *branch*

16Your vine is cut down, it is burned
with fire;
at your rebuke your people perish.
17Let your hand rest on the man at
your right hand,
the son of man you have raised up
for yourself.
18Then we will not turn away from you;
revive us, and we will call on your
name.

19Restore us, O LORD God Almighty;
make your face shine upon us,
that we may be saved.

Psalm 81

For the director of music. According to *gittith.*[a] Of Asaph.

1Sing for joy to God our strength;
shout aloud to the God of Jacob!
2Begin the music, strike the
tambourine,
play the melodious harp and lyre.

3Sound the ram's horn at the New
Moon,
and when the moon is full, on the
day of our Feast;
4this is a decree for Israel,
an ordinance of the God of Jacob.
5He established it as a statute for
Joseph
when he went out against Egypt,
where we heard a language we did
not understand.[b]

6He says, "I removed the burden from
their shoulders;
their hands were set free from the
basket.
7In your distress you called and I
rescued you,
I answered you out of a
thundercloud;
I tested you at the waters of
Meribah. *Selah*

8"Hear, O my people, and I will warn
you—
if you would but listen to me,
O Israel!
9You shall have no foreign god among
you;
you shall not bow down to an alien
god.
10I am the LORD your God,
who brought you up out of Egypt.
Open wide your mouth and I will
fill it.

11"But my people would not listen to
me;
Israel would not submit to me.
12So I gave them over to their stubborn
hearts
to follow their own devices.

13"If my people would but listen to me,
if Israel would follow my ways,
14how quickly would I subdue their
enemies
and turn my hand against their
foes!
15Those who hate the LORD would
cringe before him,
and their punishment would last
forever.
16But you would be fed with the finest
of wheat;
with honey from the rock I would
satisfy you."

Psalm 82

A psalm of Asaph.

1God presides in the great assembly;
he gives judgment among the
"gods":

2"How long will you[c] defend the
unjust
and show partiality to the wicked?
Selah
3Defend the cause of the weak and
fatherless;
maintain the rights of the poor and
oppressed.
4Rescue the weak and needy;
deliver them from the hand of the
wicked.

5"They know nothing, they understand
nothing.
They walk about in darkness;
all the foundations of the earth are
shaken.

6"I said, 'You are "gods";
you are all sons of the Most High.'
7But you will die like mere men;
you will fall like every other ruler."

8Rise up, O God, judge the earth,
for all the nations are your
inheritance.

[a]Title: Probably a musical term [b]5 Or / *and we heard a voice we had not known* [c]2 The Hebrew is plural.

Psalm 83

A song. A psalm of Asaph.

1O God, do not keep silent;
be not quiet, O God, be not still.
2See how your enemies are astir,
how your foes rear their heads.
3With cunning they conspire against your people;
they plot against those you cherish.
4"Come," they say, "let us destroy them as a nation,
that the name of Israel be remembered no more."

5With one mind they plot together;
they form an alliance against you—
6the tents of Edom and the Ishmaelites,
of Moab and the Hagrites,
7Gebal,[a] Ammon and Amalek,
Philistia, with the people of Tyre.
8Even Assyria has joined them
to lend strength to the descendants of Lot. *Selah*

9Do to them as you did to Midian,
as you did to Sisera and Jabin at the river Kishon,
10who perished at Endor
and became like refuse on the ground.
11Make their nobles like Oreb and Zeeb,
all their princes like Zebah and Zalmunna,
12who said, "Let us take possession
of the pasturelands of God."

13Make them like tumbleweed, O my God,
like chaff before the wind.
14As fire consumes the forest
or a flame sets the mountains ablaze,
15so pursue them with your tempest
and terrify them with your storm.
16Cover their faces with shame
so that men will seek your name, O LORD.

17May they ever be ashamed and dismayed;
may they perish in disgrace.
18Let them know that you, whose name is the LORD—
that you alone are the Most High
over all the earth.

Psalm 84

For the director of music. According to *gittith.*[b] Of the Sons of Korah. A psalm.

1How lovely is your dwelling place,
O LORD Almighty!
2My soul yearns, even faints,
for the courts of the LORD;
my heart and my flesh cry out
for the living God.
3Even the sparrow has found a home,
and the swallow a nest for herself,
where she may have her young—
a place near your altar,
O LORD Almighty, my King and my God.
4Blessed are those who dwell in your house;
they are ever praising you. *Selah*
5Blessed are those whose strength is in you,
who have set their hearts on pilgrimage.
6As they pass through the Valley of Baca,
they make it a place of springs;
the autumn rains also cover it with pools.[c]
7They go from strength to strength,
till each appears before God in Zion.

8Hear my prayer, O LORD God Almighty;
listen to me, O God of Jacob. *Selah*
9Look upon our shield,[d] O God;
look with favor on your anointed one.

10Better is one day in your courts
than a thousand elsewhere;
I would rather be a doorkeeper in the house of my God
than dwell in the tents of the wicked.
11For the LORD God is a sun and shield;
the LORD bestows favor and honor;
no good thing does he withhold
from those whose walk is blameless.

12O LORD Almighty,
blessed is the man who trusts in you.

[a] 7 That is, Byblos [b] Title: Probably a musical term [c] 6 Or *blessings* [d] 9 Or *sovereign*

WEDNESDAY

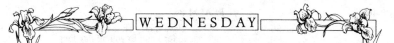

VERSE FOR THE DAY: *Psalm 84:3* | *AUTHOR:* *Debby Boone* | *PASSAGE FOR THE DAY:* *Psalm 84:1–12*

I Will Meet All Their Needs

I READ Psalm 84:3 one morning while on an airplane flying across the country, after I'd left my family for a few days to sing in different churches. As I read the verse, I knew that the Lord wanted to use this Scripture to teach me something about raising children. I took out my journal to record some thoughts about this "nest" where I could lay down my own young: 1. A nest is a place of security, rest and provision. 2. It is a place to lay my children on God's altar daily. 3. It will take a sacrifice of time to seek knowledge and wisdom for my young.

I closed my journal, feeling a sense of accomplishment and great motivation to begin building the perfect nest for my four children.

The next morning I was on another plane headed for one more concert when I read the psalm again. This time the second verse jumped out at me:

> My soul yearns, even faints,
> for the courts of the LORD;
> my heart and my flesh cry out
> for the living God.

I was overwhelmed by this expression of great love and desire to be with the Lord. Yet it did not match the uneasy feeling in my own heart. My feeling of impending failure. The feeling that, sure, I can make a great list of how to raise my kids, but can I live up to it? Instead of seeking God's presence, I wanted to hide from him and avoid facing my own discouragement and his disappointment.

Then I felt the Lord speak gently to my heart: "Debby, this nest is not made up of *your* sacrifices. It is made up of *mine.* I have made every sacrifice necessary to provide a place for your family to dwell. There I will meet all their needs. Come to my courts and be reminded of my love for you and all that that love has made available to you."

Joseph Scriven's hymn "What a Friend We Have in Jesus" came to my heart as the plane started to descend. I now knew that I could trust. Not in the nest I could build, but in the Lord's altar.

Additional Scripture Readings:
Psalm 23:5–6; John 14:1–4

Go to page 473 for your next devotional reading.

Psalm 85

For the director of music. Of the Sons of Korah. A psalm.

1You showed favor to your land,
O LORD;
you restored the fortunes of Jacob.
2You forgave the iniquity of your
people
and covered all their sins. *Selah*
3You set aside all your wrath
and turned from your fierce anger.

4Restore us again, O God our Savior,
and put away your displeasure
toward us.
5Will you be angry with us forever?
Will you prolong your anger through
all generations?
6Will you not revive us again,
that your people may rejoice in
you?
7Show us your unfailing love, O LORD,
and grant us your salvation.

8I will listen to what God the LORD will
say;
he promises peace to his people,
his saints—
but let them not return to folly.
9Surely his salvation is near those who
fear him,
that his glory may dwell in our
land.

10Love and faithfulness meet together;
righteousness and peace kiss each
other.
11Faithfulness springs forth from the
earth,
and righteousness looks down from
heaven.
12The LORD will indeed give what is
good,
and our land will yield its harvest.
13Righteousness goes before him
and prepares the way for his steps.

Psalm 86

A prayer of David.

1Hear, O LORD, and answer me,
for I am poor and needy.
2Guard my life, for I am devoted to
you.
You are my God; save your servant
who trusts in you.
3Have mercy on me, O Lord,
for I call to you all day long.
4Bring joy to your servant,
for to you, O Lord,
I lift up my soul.

5You are forgiving and good, O Lord,
abounding in love to all who call to
you.
6Hear my prayer, O LORD;
listen to my cry for mercy.
7In the day of my trouble I will call to
you,
for you will answer me.

8Among the gods there is none like
you, O Lord;
no deeds can compare with
yours.
9All the nations you have made
will come and worship before you,
O Lord;
they will bring glory to your
name.
10For you are great and do marvelous
deeds;
you alone are God.

11Teach me your way, O LORD,
and I will walk in your truth;
give me an undivided heart,
that I may fear your name.
12I will praise you, O Lord my God,
with all my heart;
I will glorify your name forever.
13For great is your love toward me;
you have delivered me from the
depths of the grave.[a]

14The arrogant are attacking me,
O God;
a band of ruthless men seeks my
life—
men without regard for you.
15But you, O Lord, are a compassionate
and gracious God,
slow to anger, abounding in love
and faithfulness.
16Turn to me and have mercy on
me;
grant your strength to your
servant
and save the son of your
maidservant.[b]
17Give me a sign of your goodness,
that my enemies may see it and be
put to shame,
for you, O LORD, have helped me
and comforted me.

[a]*13* Hebrew *Sheol* [b]*16* Or *save your faithful son*

Psalm 87

Of the Sons of Korah. A psalm. A song.

1He has set his foundation on the holy
mountain;
2 the LORD loves the gates of Zion
more than all the dwellings of
Jacob.
3Glorious things are said of you,
O city of God: *Selah*
4"I will record Rahab[a] and Babylon
among those who acknowledge
me—
Philistia too, and Tyre, along with
Cush[b]—
and will say, 'This[c] one was born
in Zion.' "

5Indeed, of Zion it will be said,
"This one and that one were born
in her,
and the Most High himself will
establish her."
6The LORD will write in the register of
the peoples:
"This one was born in Zion." *Selah*
7As they make music they will sing,
"All my fountains are in you."

Psalm 88

A song. A psalm of the Sons of Korah. For the director of music. According to *mahalath leannoth.* [d] A *maskil*[e] of Heman the Ezrahite.

1O LORD, the God who saves me,
day and night I cry out before you.
2May my prayer come before you;
turn your ear to my cry.

3For my soul is full of trouble
and my life draws near the grave.[f]
4I am counted among those who go
down to the pit;
I am like a man without strength.
5I am set apart with the dead,
like the slain who lie in the grave,
whom you remember no more,
who are cut off from your care.

6You have put me in the lowest pit,
in the darkest depths.
7Your wrath lies heavily upon me;
you have overwhelmed me with all
your waves. *Selah*
8You have taken from me my closest
friends
and have made me repulsive to
them.
I am confined and cannot escape;
9 my eyes are dim with grief.

I call to you, O LORD, every day;
I spread out my hands to you.
10Do you show your wonders to the
dead?
Do those who are dead rise up and
praise you? *Selah*
11Is your love declared in the grave,
your faithfulness in Destruction[g]?
12Are your wonders known in the place
of darkness,
or your righteous deeds in the land
of oblivion?

13But I cry to you for help, O LORD;
in the morning my prayer comes
before you.
14Why, O LORD, do you reject me
and hide your face from me?

15From my youth I have been afflicted
and close to death;
I have suffered your terrors and am
in despair.
16Your wrath has swept over me;
your terrors have destroyed me.
17All day long they surround me like a
flood;
they have completely engulfed me.
18You have taken my companions and
loved ones from me;
the darkness is my closest friend.

Psalm 89

A *maskil*[e] of Ethan the Ezrahite.

1I will sing of the LORD's great love
forever;
with my mouth I will make your
faithfulness known through all
generations.
2I will declare that your love stands
firm forever,
that you established your
faithfulness in heaven itself.
3You said, "I have made a covenant
with my chosen one,
I have sworn to David my servant,
4'I will establish your line forever

[a]4 A poetic name for Egypt [b]4 That is, the upper Nile region [c]4 Or *"O Rahab and Babylon, / Philistia, Tyre and Cush, / I will record concerning those who acknowledge me: / 'This* [d]Title: Possibly a tune, "The Suffering of Affliction" [e]Title: Probably a literary or musical term [f]3 Hebrew *Sheol* [g]11 Hebrew *Abaddon*

and make your throne firm through
all generations.' " *Selah*

5The heavens praise your wonders,
O LORD,
your faithfulness too, in the
assembly of the holy ones.
6For who in the skies above can
compare with the LORD?
Who is like the LORD among the
heavenly beings?
7In the council of the holy ones God is
greatly feared;
he is more awesome than all who
surround him.
8O LORD God Almighty, who is like
you?
You are mighty, O LORD, and your
faithfulness surrounds you.

9You rule over the surging sea;
when its waves mount up, you still
them.
10You crushed Rahab like one of the
slain;
with your strong arm you scattered
your enemies.
11The heavens are yours, and yours also
the earth;
you founded the world and all that
is in it.
12You created the north and the south;
Tabor and Hermon sing for joy at
your name.
13Your arm is endued with power;
your hand is strong, your right hand
exalted.

14Righteousness and justice are the
foundation of your throne;
love and faithfulness go before you.
15Blessed are those who have learned to
acclaim you,
who walk in the light of your
presence, O LORD.
16They rejoice in your name all day
long;
they exult in your righteousness.
17For you are their glory and strength,
and by your favor you exalt our
horn.[a]
18Indeed, our shield[b] belongs to the
LORD,
our king to the Holy One of Israel.

19Once you spoke in a vision,
to your faithful people you said:
"I have bestowed strength on a
warrior;
I have exalted a young man from
among the people.
20I have found David my servant;
with my sacred oil I have anointed
him.
21My hand will sustain him;
surely my arm will strengthen him.
22No enemy will subject him to tribute;
no wicked man will oppress him.
23I will crush his foes before him
and strike down his adversaries.
24My faithful love will be with him,
and through my name his horn[c]
will be exalted.
25I will set his hand over the sea,
his right hand over the rivers.
26He will call out to me, 'You are my
Father,
my God, the Rock my Savior.'
27I will also appoint him my firstborn,
the most exalted of the kings of the
earth.
28I will maintain my love to him
forever,
and my covenant with him will
never fail.
29I will establish his line forever,
his throne as long as the heavens
endure.

30"If his sons forsake my law
and do not follow my statutes,
31if they violate my decrees
and fail to keep my commands,
32I will punish their sin with the rod,
their iniquity with flogging;
33but I will not take my love from him,
nor will I ever betray my
faithfulness.
34I will not violate my covenant
or alter what my lips have uttered.
35Once for all, I have sworn by my
holiness—
and I will not lie to David—
36that his line will continue forever
and his throne endure before me
like the sun;
37it will be established forever like the
moon,
the faithful witness in the sky."
Selah

38But you have rejected, you have
spurned,
you have been very angry with your
anointed one.
39You have renounced the covenant
with your servant

[a]*17 Horn* here symbolizes strong one. [b]*18* Or *sovereign* [c]*24 Horn* here symbolizes strength.

and have defiled his crown in the
dust.
40You have broken through all his walls
and reduced his strongholds to
ruins.
41All who pass by have plundered him;
he has become the scorn of his
neighbors.
42You have exalted the right hand of his
foes;
you have made all his enemies
rejoice.
43You have turned back the edge of his
sword
and have not supported him in
battle.
44You have put an end to his splendor
and cast his throne to the ground.
45You have cut short the days of his
youth;
you have covered him with a
mantle of shame. *Selah*

46How long, O LORD? Will you hide
yourself forever?
How long will your wrath burn like
fire?
47Remember how fleeting is my life.
For what futility you have created
all men!
48What man can live and not see death,
or save himself from the power of
the grave[a]? *Selah*
49O Lord, where is your former great
love,
which in your faithfulness you
swore to David?
50Remember, Lord, how your servant
has[b] been mocked,
how I bear in my heart the taunts
of all the nations,
51the taunts with which your enemies
have mocked, O LORD,
with which they have mocked every
step of your anointed one.

52Praise be to the LORD forever!
Amen and Amen.

BOOK IV

Psalms 90–106

Psalm 90

A prayer of Moses the man of God.

1Lord, you have been our dwelling
place
throughout all generations.
2Before the mountains were born
or you brought forth the earth and
the world,
from everlasting to everlasting you
are God.

3You turn men back to dust,
saying, "Return to dust, O sons of
men."
4For a thousand years in your sight
are like a day that has just gone by,
or like a watch in the night.
5You sweep men away in the sleep of
death;
they are like the new grass of the
morning—
6though in the morning it springs up
new,
by evening it is dry and withered.

7We are consumed by your anger
and terrified by your indignation.
8You have set our iniquities before
you,
our secret sins in the light of your
presence.
9All our days pass away under your
wrath;
we finish our years with a moan.
10The length of our days is seventy
years—
or eighty, if we have the strength;
yet their span[c] is but trouble and
sorrow,
for they quickly pass, and we fly
away.

11Who knows the power of your anger?
For your wrath is as great as the
fear that is due you.
12Teach us to number our days aright,
that we may gain a heart of
wisdom.

13Relent, O LORD! How long will it be?
Have compassion on your servants.
14Satisfy us in the morning with your
unfailing love,
that we may sing for joy and be
glad all our days.
15Make us glad for as many days as you
have afflicted us,
for as many years as we have seen
trouble.
16May your deeds be shown to your
servants,
your splendor to their children.

[a]48 Hebrew *Sheol* [b]50 Or *your servants have* [c]10 Or *yet the best of them*

[17]May the favor[a] of the Lord our God
rest upon us;
establish the work of our hands for
us—
yes, establish the work of our
hands.

Psalm 91

[1]He who dwells in the shelter of the
Most High
will rest in the shadow of the
Almighty.[b]
[2]I will say[c] of the LORD, "He is my
refuge and my fortress,
my God, in whom I trust."

[3]Surely he will save you from the
fowler's snare
and from the deadly pestilence.
[4]He will cover you with his feathers,
and under his wings you will find
refuge;
his faithfulness will be your shield
and rampart.
[5]You will not fear the terror of night,
nor the arrow that flies by day,
[6]nor the pestilence that stalks in the
darkness,
nor the plague that destroys at
midday.
[7]A thousand may fall at your side,
ten thousand at your right hand,
but it will not come near you.
[8]You will only observe with your eyes
and see the punishment of the
wicked.

[9]If you make the Most High your
dwelling—
even the LORD, who is my refuge—
[10]then no harm will befall you,
no disaster will come near your
tent.
[11]For he will command his angels
concerning you
to guard you in all your ways;
[12]they will lift you up in their hands,
so that you will not strike your foot
against a stone.
[13]You will tread upon the lion and the
cobra;
you will trample the great lion and
the serpent.

[14]"Because he loves me," says the LORD,
"I will rescue him;
I will protect him, for he
acknowledges my name.
[15]He will call upon me, and I will
answer him;
I will be with him in trouble,
I will deliver him and honor him.
[16]With long life will I satisfy him
and show him my salvation."

Psalm 92

A psalm. A song. For the Sabbath day.

[1]It is good to praise the LORD
and make music to your name,
O Most High,
[2]to proclaim your love in the morning
and your faithfulness at night,
[3]to the music of the ten-stringed lyre
and the melody of the harp.

[4]For you make me glad by your deeds,
O LORD;
I sing for joy at the works of your
hands.
[5]How great are your works, O LORD,
how profound your thoughts!
[6]The senseless man does not know,
fools do not understand,
[7]that though the wicked spring up like
grass
and all evildoers flourish,
they will be forever destroyed.

[8]But you, O LORD, are exalted forever.

[9]For surely your enemies, O LORD,
surely your enemies will perish;
all evildoers will be scattered.
[10]You have exalted my horn[d] like that
of a wild ox;
fine oils have been poured upon
me.
[11]My eyes have seen the defeat of my
adversaries;
my ears have heard the rout of my
wicked foes.

[12]The righteous will flourish like a palm
tree,
they will grow like a cedar of
Lebanon;
[13]planted in the house of the LORD,
they will flourish in the courts of
our God.
[14]They will still bear fruit in old age,
they will stay fresh and green,
[15]proclaiming, "The LORD is upright;
he is my Rock, and there is no
wickedness in him."

[a]*17* Or *beauty* [b]*1* Hebrew *Shaddai* [c]*2* Or *He says* [d]*10* *Horn* here symbolizes strength.

THURSDAY

VERSE FOR THE DAY:
Psalm 91:2

AUTHOR:
Hope MacDonald

PASSAGE FOR THE DAY:
Psalm 91:1–16

Our Dwelling Place

THE other night I took care of my grandchildren. Six-year-old Shane woke up crying. He had been dreaming of goblins and other childhood terrors. After he quieted down, he showed me the well-worn Bible his grandfather had given him. Shane always keeps it under his pillow. As I left the room, he said, "You know, Grandma, when you sleep with your Bible, it's almost like sleeping with Jesus!" And he lay down like a little lamb and went to sleep. He was resting in the shadow of the Almighty. Later I found myself asking, "Is this where I'm resting today?"

Try reading Psalm 91 every day for the next month. Your life will be changed, as mine was, because this is a triumphant song of faith. In it we learn that God is our dwelling place. It's under his wings that we find refuge, even in the midst of the universal evil that surrounds us.

We all face dangers and heartaches in life because we live in a lost and fallen world. But in the midst of these difficulties we can be absolutely confident that we are not left alone to deal with them. God's faithfulness is our constant shield. We are covered by the shadow of the Almighty! Oh, the security that is ours in God's promise that he will be with us in trouble (Psalm 91:15)!

These unchanging promises are for those who choose, by an act of their will, to put themselves under the care and protection of the living God. These promises are for those who dwell within the shelter of the Most High, who make their home with Jesus.

Why is this a psalm of irrepressible beauty? Because in it we are given a fresh glimpse into all that is ours through Jesus Christ our Lord. We come away from this psalm with an overwhelming sense of awe and wonder at God's continual provision for us.

Additional Scripture Readings:
Psalm 121:1–8; Lamentations 3:19–26

Go to page 479 for your next devotional reading.

Psalm 93

1The LORD reigns, he is robed in
majesty;
the LORD is robed in majesty
and is armed with strength.
The world is firmly established;
it cannot be moved.
2Your throne was established long
ago;
you are from all eternity.

3The seas have lifted up, O LORD,
the seas have lifted up their voice;
the seas have lifted up their
pounding waves.
4Mightier than the thunder of the great
waters,
mightier than the breakers of the
sea—
the LORD on high is mighty.

5Your statutes stand firm;
holiness adorns your house
for endless days, O LORD.

Psalm 94

1O LORD, the God who avenges,
O God who avenges, shine forth.
2Rise up, O Judge of the earth;
pay back to the proud what they
deserve.
3How long will the wicked, O LORD,
how long will the wicked be
jubilant?

4They pour out arrogant words;
all the evildoers are full of boasting.
5They crush your people, O LORD;
they oppress your inheritance.
6They slay the widow and the alien;
they murder the fatherless.
7They say, "The LORD does not see;
the God of Jacob pays no heed."

8Take heed, you senseless ones among
the people;
you fools, when will you become
wise?
9Does he who implanted the ear not
hear?
Does he who formed the eye not
see?
10Does he who disciplines nations not
punish?
Does he who teaches man lack
knowledge?
11The LORD knows the thoughts of man;
he knows that they are futile.

12Blessed is the man you discipline,
O LORD,
the man you teach from your law;
13you grant him relief from days of
trouble,
till a pit is dug for the wicked.
14For the LORD will not reject his
people;
he will never forsake his
inheritance.
15Judgment will again be founded on
righteousness,
and all the upright in heart will
follow it.

16Who will rise up for me against the
wicked?
Who will take a stand for me
against evildoers?
17Unless the LORD had given me help,
I would soon have dwelt in the
silence of death.
18When I said, "My foot is slipping,"
your love, O LORD, supported me.
19When anxiety was great within me,
your consolation brought joy to my
soul.

20Can a corrupt throne be allied with
you—
one that brings on misery by its
decrees?
21They band together against the
righteous
and condemn the innocent to
death.
22But the LORD has become my fortress,
and my God the rock in whom I
take refuge.
23He will repay them for their sins
and destroy them for their
wickedness;
the LORD our God will destroy them.

Psalm 95

1Come, let us sing for joy to the LORD;
let us shout aloud to the Rock of
our salvation.
2Let us come before him with
thanksgiving
and extol him with music and song.

3For the LORD is the great God,
the great King above all gods.
4In his hand are the depths of the
earth,
and the mountain peaks belong to
him.
5The sea is his, for he made it,
and his hands formed the dry land.

6Come, let us bow down in worship,

let us kneel before the LORD our Maker;
[7]for he is our God
and we are the people of his pasture,
the flock under his care.

Today, if you hear his voice,
8 do not harden your hearts as you did at Meribah,[a]
as you did that day at Massah[b] in the desert,
[9]where your fathers tested and tried me,
though they had seen what I did.
[10]For forty years I was angry with that generation;
I said, "They are a people whose hearts go astray,
and they have not known my ways."
[11]So I declared on oath in my anger,
"They shall never enter my rest."

Psalm 96

[1]Sing to the LORD a new song;
sing to the LORD, all the earth.
[2]Sing to the LORD, praise his name;
proclaim his salvation day after day.
[3]Declare his glory among the nations,
his marvelous deeds among all peoples.

[4]For great is the LORD and most worthy of praise;
he is to be feared above all gods.
[5]For all the gods of the nations are idols,
but the LORD made the heavens.
[6]Splendor and majesty are before him;
strength and glory are in his sanctuary.

[7]Ascribe to the LORD, O families of nations,
ascribe to the LORD glory and strength.
[8]Ascribe to the LORD the glory due his name;
bring an offering and come into his courts.
[9]Worship the LORD in the splendor of his[c] holiness;
tremble before him, all the earth.

[10]Say among the nations, "The LORD reigns."
The world is firmly established, it cannot be moved;
he will judge the peoples with equity.
[11]Let the heavens rejoice, let the earth be glad;
let the sea resound, and all that is in it;
12 let the fields be jubilant, and everything in them.
Then all the trees of the forest will sing for joy;
13 they will sing before the LORD, for he comes,
he comes to judge the earth.
He will judge the world in righteousness
and the peoples in his truth.

Psalm 97

[1]The LORD reigns, let the earth be glad;
let the distant shores rejoice.

[2]Clouds and thick darkness surround him;
righteousness and justice are the foundation of his throne.
[3]Fire goes before him
and consumes his foes on every side.
[4]His lightning lights up the world;
the earth sees and trembles.
[5]The mountains melt like wax before the LORD,
before the Lord of all the earth.
[6]The heavens proclaim his righteousness,
and all the peoples see his glory.

[7]All who worship images are put to shame,
those who boast in idols—
worship him, all you gods!

[8]Zion hears and rejoices
and the villages of Judah are glad
because of your judgments, O LORD.
[9]For you, O LORD, are the Most High over all the earth;
you are exalted far above all gods.

[10]Let those who love the LORD hate evil,
for he guards the lives of his faithful ones
and delivers them from the hand of the wicked.
[11]Light is shed upon the righteous
and joy on the upright in heart.
[12]Rejoice in the LORD, you who are righteous,
and praise his holy name.

[a]8 *Meribah* means *quarreling.* [b]8 *Massah* means *testing.* [c]9 Or *LORD with the splendor of*

Psalm 98

A psalm.

1Sing to the LORD a new song,
for he has done marvelous things;
his right hand and his holy arm
have worked salvation for him.
2The LORD has made his salvation known
and revealed his righteousness to the nations.
3He has remembered his love
and his faithfulness to the house of Israel;
all the ends of the earth have seen
the salvation of our God.

4Shout for joy to the LORD, all the earth,
burst into jubilant song with music;
5make music to the LORD with the harp,
with the harp and the sound of singing,
6with trumpets and the blast of the ram's horn—
shout for joy before the LORD, the King.

7Let the sea resound, and everything in it,
the world, and all who live in it.
8Let the rivers clap their hands,
let the mountains sing together for joy;
9let them sing before the LORD,
for he comes to judge the earth.
He will judge the world in righteousness
and the peoples with equity.

Psalm 99

1The LORD reigns,
let the nations tremble;
he sits enthroned between the cherubim,
let the earth shake.
2Great is the LORD in Zion;
he is exalted over all the nations.
3Let them praise your great and awesome name—
he is holy.

4The King is mighty, he loves justice—
you have established equity;
in Jacob you have done
what is just and right.
5Exalt the LORD our God
and worship at his footstool;
he is holy.

6Moses and Aaron were among his priests,
Samuel was among those who called on his name;
they called on the LORD
and he answered them.
7He spoke to them from the pillar of cloud;
they kept his statutes and the decrees he gave them.

8O LORD our God,
you answered them;
you were to Israel[a] a forgiving God,
though you punished their misdeeds.[b]
9Exalt the LORD our God
and worship at his holy mountain,
for the LORD our God is holy.

Psalm 100

A psalm. For giving thanks.

1Shout for joy to the LORD, all the earth.
2 Worship the LORD with gladness;
come before him with joyful songs.
3Know that the LORD is God.
It is he who made us, and we are his[c];
we are his people, the sheep of his pasture.

4Enter his gates with thanksgiving
and his courts with praise;
give thanks to him and praise his name.
5For the LORD is good and his love endures forever;
his faithfulness continues through all generations.

Psalm 101

Of David. A psalm.

1I will sing of your love and justice;
to you, O LORD, I will sing praise.
2I will be careful to lead a blameless life—
when will you come to me?

I will walk in my house
with blameless heart.
3I will set before my eyes
no vile thing.

[a]8 Hebrew *them* [b]8 Or *l an avenger of the wrongs done to them* [c]3 Or *and not we ourselves*

The deeds of faithless men I hate;
they will not cling to me.
4Men of perverse heart shall be far from me;
I will have nothing to do with evil.

5Whoever slanders his neighbor in secret,
him will I put to silence;
whoever has haughty eyes and a proud heart,
him will I not endure.

6My eyes will be on the faithful in the land,
that they may dwell with me;
he whose walk is blameless
will minister to me.

7No one who practices deceit
will dwell in my house;
no one who speaks falsely
will stand in my presence.

8Every morning I will put to silence
all the wicked in the land;
I will cut off every evildoer
from the city of the LORD.

Psalm 102

A prayer of an afflicted man. When he is faint and pours out his lament before the LORD.

1Hear my prayer, O LORD;
let my cry for help come to you.
2Do not hide your face from me
when I am in distress.
Turn your ear to me;
when I call, answer me quickly.

3For my days vanish like smoke;
my bones burn like glowing embers.
4My heart is blighted and withered like grass;
I forget to eat my food.
5Because of my loud groaning
I am reduced to skin and bones.
6I am like a desert owl,
like an owl among the ruins.
7I lie awake; I have become
like a bird alone on a roof.
8All day long my enemies taunt me;
those who rail against me use my name as a curse.
9For I eat ashes as my food
and mingle my drink with tears
10because of your great wrath,
for you have taken me up and thrown me aside.
11My days are like the evening shadow;
I wither away like grass.

12But you, O LORD, sit enthroned forever;
your renown endures through all generations.
13You will arise and have compassion on Zion,
for it is time to show favor to her;
the appointed time has come.
14For her stones are dear to your servants;
her very dust moves them to pity.
15The nations will fear the name of the LORD,
all the kings of the earth will revere your glory.
16For the LORD will rebuild Zion
and appear in his glory.
17He will respond to the prayer of the destitute;
he will not despise their plea.

18Let this be written for a future generation,
that a people not yet created may praise the LORD:
19"The LORD looked down from his sanctuary on high,
from heaven he viewed the earth,
20to hear the groans of the prisoners
and release those condemned to death."
21So the name of the LORD will be declared in Zion
and his praise in Jerusalem
22when the peoples and the kingdoms
assemble to worship the LORD.

23In the course of my life[a] he broke my strength;
he cut short my days.
24So I said:
"Do not take me away, O my God,
in the midst of my days;
your years go on through all generations.
25In the beginning you laid the foundations of the earth,
and the heavens are the work of your hands.
26They will perish, but you remain;
they will all wear out like a garment.
Like clothing you will change them
and they will be discarded.
27But you remain the same,
and your years will never end.

[a]23 Or *By his power*

28The children of your servants will live
in your presence;
their descendants will be
established before you."

Psalm 103

Of David.

1Praise the LORD, O my soul;
all my inmost being, praise his holy
name.
2Praise the LORD, O my soul,
and forget not all his benefits—
3who forgives all your sins
and heals all your diseases,
4who redeems your life from the pit
and crowns you with love and
compassion,
5who satisfies your desires with good
things
so that your youth is renewed like
the eagle's.

6The LORD works righteousness
and justice for all the oppressed.

7He made known his ways to Moses,
his deeds to the people of Israel:
8The LORD is compassionate and
gracious,
slow to anger, abounding in love.
9He will not always accuse,
nor will he harbor his anger forever;
10he does not treat us as our sins
deserve
or repay us according to our
iniquities.
11For as high as the heavens are above
the earth,
so great is his love for those who
fear him;
12as far as the east is from the west,
so far has he removed our
transgressions from us.
13As a father has compassion on his
children,
so the LORD has compassion on
those who fear him;
14for he knows how we are formed,
he remembers that we are dust.
15As for man, his days are like grass,
he flourishes like a flower of the
field;
16the wind blows over it and it is gone,
and its place remembers it no
more.
17But from everlasting to everlasting
the LORD's love is with those who
fear him,
and his righteousness with their
children's children—
18with those who keep his covenant
and remember to obey his precepts.

19The LORD has established his throne
in heaven,
and his kingdom rules over all.

20Praise the LORD, you his angels,
you mighty ones who do his
bidding,
who obey his word.
21Praise the LORD, all his heavenly
hosts,
you his servants who do his will.
22Praise the LORD, all his works
everywhere in his dominion.

Praise the LORD, O my soul.

Psalm 104

1Praise the LORD, O my soul.

O LORD my God, you are very great;
you are clothed with splendor and
majesty.
2He wraps himself in light as with a
garment;
he stretches out the heavens like a
tent
3 and lays the beams of his upper
chambers on their waters.
He makes the clouds his chariot
and rides on the wings of the wind.
4He makes winds his messengers,[a]
flames of fire his servants.

5He set the earth on its foundations;
it can never be moved.
6You covered it with the deep as with
a garment;
the waters stood above the
mountains.
7But at your rebuke the waters fled,
at the sound of your thunder they
took to flight;
8they flowed over the mountains,
they went down into the valleys,
to the place you assigned for them.
9You set a boundary they cannot cross;
never again will they cover the
earth.

10He makes springs pour water into the
ravines;
it flows between the mountains.

[a]4 Or *angels*

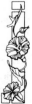

FRIDAY

VERSE FOR THE DAY: *Psalm 103:3*

AUTHOR: *Janice Kempe*

PASSAGE FOR THE DAY: *Psalm 103:1–22*

Time With Daddy

KEVIN and I walked Krista to kindergarten today. Her school is up and over a large hill and through a woods, so we noticed each flower and green leaf that told us spring was near and listened to the birds that had returned after a long, cold winter.

After the good-by kisses Kevin and I began our walk back up and over the big hill. He was fascinated by the selection of rocks and sticks and immediately began gathering a collection. Our progress was slow because we had to stop every few steps to retrieve dropped treasures. The capacity of his two hands just wasn't enough to accommodate the desires of his curious little mind! He had no more time for noticing birds and flowers. With grim determination, he tended to the safe passage of his wonderful new collection.

I couldn't understand why each stone was so special, nor why he needed so many sticks, but he guarded them with great care and knew instantly if he had dropped one.

Upon reaching our front door, Kevin and I were both exhausted!

He struggled up the front steps through the front door. But suddenly he let go of his precious treasures, and they fell to the front hall floor. His determined scowl melted into a wide grin. He ran off as if the things he had struggled to bring home had lost their value. Kevin had seen something far more important, and immediately his focus had changed to a new center of attention—Daddy!

I long to keep in mind that picture of my little boy dropping his burdensome treasures to run to his father. I too get burdened down by my treasures. My house, my belongings, my responsibilities, and all the things I've spent so much time and energy acquiring seem to take me over sometimes. I find myself attending to their care with an overwhelming single-mindedness. Sometimes I need to see God and do more than just acknowledge his presence. I need to drop everything else and run to him. I need to forsake the housework, the shopping, and the thousand other things that occupy my time, and go to him for a time of togetherness.

Additional Scripture Readings:
Luke 10:38–42; John 21:4–7

Go to page 484 for your next devotional reading.

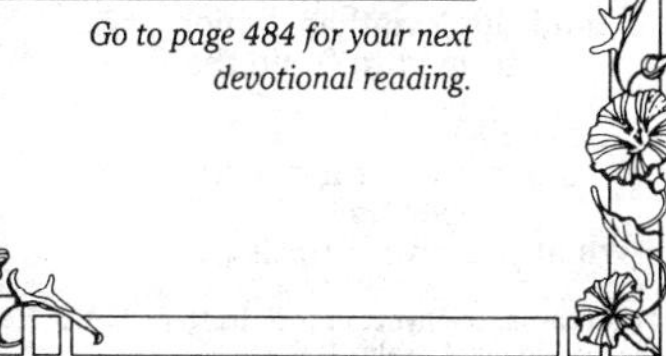

[11]They give water to all the beasts of
the field;
the wild donkeys quench their
thirst.
[12]The birds of the air nest by the
waters;
they sing among the branches.
[13]He waters the mountains from his
upper chambers;
the earth is satisfied by the fruit of
his work.
[14]He makes grass grow for the cattle,
and plants for man to cultivate—
bringing forth food from the earth:
[15]wine that gladdens the heart of man,
oil to make his face shine,
and bread that sustains his heart.
[16]The trees of the LORD are well
watered,
the cedars of Lebanon that he
planted.
[17]There the birds make their nests;
the stork has its home in the pine
trees.
[18]The high mountains belong to the
wild goats;
the crags are a refuge for the
coneys.[a]

[19]The moon marks off the seasons,
and the sun knows when to go
down.
[20]You bring darkness, it becomes night,
and all the beasts of the forest
prowl.
[21]The lions roar for their prey
and seek their food from God.
[22]The sun rises, and they steal away;
they return and lie down in their
dens.
[23]Then man goes out to his work,
to his labor until evening.

[24]How many are your works, O LORD!
In wisdom you made them all;
the earth is full of your creatures.
[25]There is the sea, vast and spacious,
teeming with creatures beyond
number—
living things both large and small.
[26]There the ships go to and fro,
and the leviathan, which you
formed to frolic there.

[27]These all look to you
to give them their food at the
proper time.
[28]When you give it to them,
they gather it up;
when you open your hand,
they are satisfied with good things.
[29]When you hide your face,
they are terrified;
when you take away their breath,
they die and return to the dust.
[30]When you send your Spirit,
they are created,
and you renew the face of the
earth.

[31]May the glory of the LORD endure
forever;
may the LORD rejoice in his works—
[32]he who looks at the earth, and it
trembles,
who touches the mountains, and
they smoke.

[33]I will sing to the LORD all my life;
I will sing praise to my God as long
as I live.
[34]May my meditation be pleasing to
him,
as I rejoice in the LORD.
[35]But may sinners vanish from the earth
and the wicked be no more.

Praise the LORD, O my soul.

Praise the LORD.[b]

Psalm 105

[1]Give thanks to the LORD, call on his
name;
make known among the nations
what he has done.
[2]Sing to him, sing praise to him;
tell of all his wonderful acts.
[3]Glory in his holy name;
let the hearts of those who seek the
LORD rejoice.
[4]Look to the LORD and his strength;
seek his face always.

[5]Remember the wonders he has done,
his miracles, and the judgments he
pronounced,
[6]O descendants of Abraham his
servant,
O sons of Jacob, his chosen ones.
[7]He is the LORD our God;
his judgments are in all the earth.

[8]He remembers his covenant forever,
the word he commanded, for a
thousand generations,
[9]the covenant he made with Abraham,

[a]18 That is, the hyrax or rock badger

[b]35 Hebrew *Hallelu Yah*; in the Septuagint this line stands at the beginning of Psalm 105.

the oath he swore to Isaac.
10He confirmed it to Jacob as a decree,
to Israel as an everlasting covenant:
11"To you I will give the land of Canaan
as the portion you will inherit."

12When they were but few in number,
few indeed, and strangers in it,
13they wandered from nation to nation,
from one kingdom to another.
14He allowed no one to oppress them;
for their sake he rebuked kings:
15"Do not touch my anointed ones;
do my prophets no harm."

16He called down famine on the land
and destroyed all their supplies of food;
17and he sent a man before them—
Joseph, sold as a slave.
18They bruised his feet with shackles,
his neck was put in irons,
19till what he foretold came to pass,
till the word of the LORD proved him true.
20The king sent and released him,
the ruler of peoples set him free.
21He made him master of his household,
ruler over all he possessed,
22to instruct his princes as he pleased
and teach his elders wisdom.

23Then Israel entered Egypt;
Jacob lived as an alien in the land of Ham.
24The LORD made his people very fruitful;
he made them too numerous for their foes,
25whose hearts he turned to hate his people,
to conspire against his servants.
26He sent Moses his servant,
and Aaron, whom he had chosen.
27They performed his miraculous signs among them,
his wonders in the land of Ham.
28He sent darkness and made the land dark—
for had they not rebelled against his words?
29He turned their waters into blood,
causing their fish to die.
30Their land teemed with frogs,
which went up into the bedrooms of their rulers.
31He spoke, and there came swarms of flies,
and gnats throughout their country.
32He turned their rain into hail,
with lightning throughout their land;
33he struck down their vines and fig trees
and shattered the trees of their country.
34He spoke, and the locusts came,
grasshoppers without number;
35they ate up every green thing in their land,
ate up the produce of their soil.
36Then he struck down all the firstborn in their land,
the firstfruits of all their manhood.
37He brought out Israel, laden with silver and gold,
and from among their tribes no one faltered.
38Egypt was glad when they left,
because dread of Israel had fallen on them.
39He spread out a cloud as a covering,
and a fire to give light at night.
40They asked, and he brought them quail
and satisfied them with the bread of heaven.
41He opened the rock, and water gushed out;
like a river it flowed in the desert.

42For he remembered his holy promise
given to his servant Abraham.
43He brought out his people with rejoicing,
his chosen ones with shouts of joy;
44he gave them the lands of the nations,
and they fell heir to what others had toiled for—
45that they might keep his precepts
and observe his laws.

Praise the LORD.[a]

Psalm 106

1Praise the LORD.[b]

Give thanks to the LORD, for he is good;
his love endures forever.
2Who can proclaim the mighty acts of the LORD
or fully declare his praise?
3Blessed are they who maintain justice,

[a]45 Hebrew *Hallelu Yah* [b]1 Hebrew *Hallelu Yah*; also in verse 48

who constantly do what is right.
4Remember me, O LORD, when you show favor to your people,
come to my aid when you save them,
5that I may enjoy the prosperity of your chosen ones,
that I may share in the joy of your nation
and join your inheritance in giving praise.

6We have sinned, even as our fathers did;
we have done wrong and acted wickedly.
7When our fathers were in Egypt,
they gave no thought to your miracles;
they did not remember your many kindnesses,
and they rebelled by the sea, the Red Sea.[a]
8Yet he saved them for his name's sake,
to make his mighty power known.
9He rebuked the Red Sea, and it dried up;
he led them through the depths as through a desert.
10He saved them from the hand of the foe;
from the hand of the enemy he redeemed them.
11The waters covered their adversaries;
not one of them survived.
12Then they believed his promises
and sang his praise.

13But they soon forgot what he had done
and did not wait for his counsel.
14In the desert they gave in to their craving;
in the wasteland they put God to the test.
15So he gave them what they asked for,
but sent a wasting disease upon them.

16In the camp they grew envious of Moses
and of Aaron, who was consecrated to the LORD.
17The earth opened up and swallowed Dathan;
it buried the company of Abiram.
18Fire blazed among their followers;
a flame consumed the wicked.
19At Horeb they made a calf
and worshiped an idol cast from metal.
20They exchanged their Glory
for an image of a bull, which eats grass.
21They forgot the God who saved them,
who had done great things in Egypt,
22miracles in the land of Ham
and awesome deeds by the Red Sea.
23So he said he would destroy them—
had not Moses, his chosen one,
stood in the breach before him
to keep his wrath from destroying them.

24Then they despised the pleasant land;
they did not believe his promise.
25They grumbled in their tents
and did not obey the LORD.
26So he swore to them with uplifted hand
that he would make them fall in the desert,
27make their descendants fall among the nations
and scatter them throughout the lands.

28They yoked themselves to the Baal of Peor
and ate sacrifices offered to lifeless gods;
29they provoked the LORD to anger by their wicked deeds,
and a plague broke out among them.
30But Phinehas stood up and intervened,
and the plague was checked.
31This was credited to him as righteousness
for endless generations to come.

32By the waters of Meribah they angered the LORD,
and trouble came to Moses because of them;
33for they rebelled against the Spirit of God,
and rash words came from Moses' lips.[b]

34They did not destroy the peoples
as the LORD had commanded them,

[a]7 Hebrew *Yam Suph*; that is, Sea of Reeds; also in verses 9 and 22 [b]33 Or *against his spirit, / and rash words came from his lips*

[35]but they mingled with the nations
and adopted their customs.
[36]They worshiped their idols,
which became a snare to them.
[37]They sacrificed their sons
and their daughters to demons.
[38]They shed innocent blood,
the blood of their sons and daughters,
whom they sacrificed to the idols of Canaan,
and the land was desecrated by their blood.
[39]They defiled themselves by what they did;
by their deeds they prostituted themselves.

[40]Therefore the LORD was angry with his people
and abhorred his inheritance.
[41]He handed them over to the nations,
and their foes ruled over them.
[42]Their enemies oppressed them
and subjected them to their power.
[43]Many times he delivered them,
but they were bent on rebellion
and they wasted away in their sin.

[44]But he took note of their distress
when he heard their cry;
[45]for their sake he remembered his covenant
and out of his great love he relented.
[46]He caused them to be pitied
by all who held them captive.

[47]Save us, O LORD our God,
and gather us from the nations,
that we may give thanks to your holy name
and glory in your praise.

[48]Praise be to the LORD, the God of Israel,
from everlasting to everlasting.
Let all the people say, "Amen!"

Praise the LORD.

BOOK V

Psalms 107–150

Psalm 107

[1]Give thanks to the LORD, for he is good;
his love endures forever.
[2]Let the redeemed of the LORD say this—
those he redeemed from the hand of the foe,
[3]those he gathered from the lands,
from east and west, from north and south.[a]

[4]Some wandered in desert wastelands,
finding no way to a city where they could settle.
[5]They were hungry and thirsty,
and their lives ebbed away.
[6]Then they cried out to the LORD in their trouble,
and he delivered them from their distress.
[7]He led them by a straight way
to a city where they could settle.
[8]Let them give thanks to the LORD for his unfailing love
and his wonderful deeds for men,
[9]for he satisfies the thirsty
and fills the hungry with good things.

[10]Some sat in darkness and the deepest gloom,
prisoners suffering in iron chains,
[11]for they had rebelled against the words of God
and despised the counsel of the Most High.
[12]So he subjected them to bitter labor;
they stumbled, and there was no one to help.
[13]Then they cried to the LORD in their trouble,
and he saved them from their distress.
[14]He brought them out of darkness and the deepest gloom
and broke away their chains.
[15]Let them give thanks to the LORD for his unfailing love
and his wonderful deeds for men,
[16]for he breaks down gates of bronze
and cuts through bars of iron.

[17]Some became fools through their rebellious ways
and suffered affliction because of their iniquities.
[18]They loathed all food
and drew near the gates of death.
[19]Then they cried to the LORD in their trouble,
and he saved them from their distress.

[a]3 Hebrew *north and the sea*

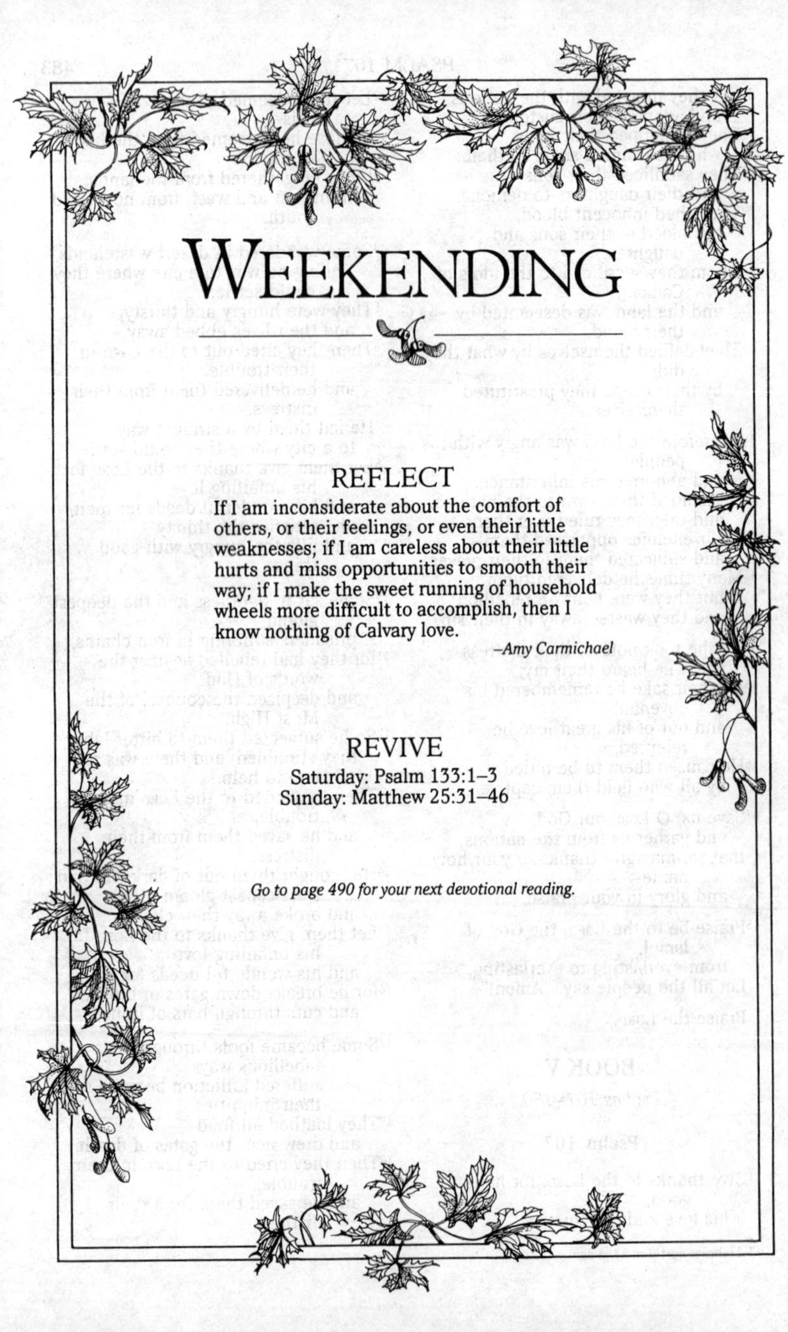

WEEKENDING

REFLECT

If I am inconsiderate about the comfort of others, or their feelings, or even their little weaknesses; if I am careless about their little hurts and miss opportunities to smooth their way; if I make the sweet running of household wheels more difficult to accomplish, then I know nothing of Calvary love.

—Amy Carmichael

REVIVE

Saturday: Psalm 133:1–3
Sunday: Matthew 25:31–46

Go to page 490 for your next devotional reading.

20He sent forth his word and healed
them;
he rescued them from the grave.
21Let them give thanks to the LORD for
his unfailing love
and his wonderful deeds for men.
22Let them sacrifice thank offerings
and tell of his works with songs of
joy.

23Others went out on the sea in ships;
they were merchants on the mighty
waters.
24They saw the works of the LORD,
his wonderful deeds in the deep.
25For he spoke and stirred up a tempest
that lifted high the waves.
26They mounted up to the heavens and
went down to the depths;
in their peril their courage melted
away.
27They reeled and staggered like
drunken men;
they were at their wits' end.
28Then they cried out to the LORD in
their trouble,
and he brought them out of their
distress.
29He stilled the storm to a whisper;
the waves of the sea were hushed.
30They were glad when it grew calm,
and he guided them to their desired
haven.
31Let them give thanks to the LORD for
his unfailing love
and his wonderful deeds for men.
32Let them exalt him in the assembly
of the people
and praise him in the council of
the elders.

33He turned rivers into a desert,
flowing springs into thirsty ground,
34and fruitful land into a salt waste,
because of the wickedness of those
who lived there.
35He turned the desert into pools of
water
and the parched ground into
flowing springs;
36there he brought the hungry to live,
and they founded a city where they
could settle.
37They sowed fields and planted
vineyards
that yielded a fruitful harvest;
38he blessed them, and their numbers
greatly increased,
and he did not let their herds
diminish.

39Then their numbers decreased, and
they were humbled
by oppression, calamity and sorrow;
40he who pours contempt on nobles
made them wander in a trackless
waste.
41But he lifted the needy out of their
affliction
and increased their families like
flocks.
42The upright see and rejoice,
but all the wicked shut their
mouths.

43Whoever is wise, let him heed these
things
and consider the great love of the
LORD.

Psalm 108

A song. A psalm of David.

1My heart is steadfast, O God;
I will sing and make music with all
my soul.
2Awake, harp and lyre!
I will awaken the dawn.
3I will praise you, O LORD, among the
nations;
I will sing of you among the
peoples.
4For great is your love, higher than the
heavens;
your faithfulness reaches to the
skies.
5Be exalted, O God, above the
heavens,
and let your glory be over all the
earth.

6Save us and help us with your right
hand,
that those you love may be
delivered.
7God has spoken from his sanctuary:
"In triumph I will parcel out
Shechem
and measure off the Valley of
Succoth.
8Gilead is mine, Manasseh is mine;
Ephraim is my helmet,
Judah my scepter.
9Moab is my washbasin,
upon Edom I toss my sandal;
over Philistia I shout in triumph."

10Who will bring me to the fortified
city?
Who will lead me to Edom?

[11]Is it not you, O God, you who have rejected us
and no longer go out with our armies?
[12]Give us aid against the enemy,
for the help of man is worthless.
[13]With God we will gain the victory,
and he will trample down our enemies.

Psalm 109

For the director of music. Of David. A psalm.

[1]O God, whom I praise,
do not remain silent,
[2]for wicked and deceitful men
have opened their mouths against me;
they have spoken against me with lying tongues.
[3]With words of hatred they surround me;
they attack me without cause.
[4]In return for my friendship they accuse me,
but I am a man of prayer.
[5]They repay me evil for good,
and hatred for my friendship.

[6]Appoint[a] an evil man[b] to oppose him;
let an accuser[c] stand at his right hand.
[7]When he is tried, let him be found guilty,
and may his prayers condemn him.
[8]May his days be few;
may another take his place of leadership.
[9]May his children be fatherless
and his wife a widow.
[10]May his children be wandering beggars;
may they be driven[d] from their ruined homes.
[11]May a creditor seize all he has;
may strangers plunder the fruits of his labor.
[12]May no one extend kindness to him
or take pity on his fatherless children.
[13]May his descendants be cut off,
their names blotted out from the next generation.
[14]May the iniquity of his fathers be remembered before the LORD;
may the sin of his mother never be blotted out.
[15]May their sins always remain before the LORD,
that he may cut off the memory of them from the earth.

[16]For he never thought of doing a kindness,
but hounded to death the poor
and the needy and the brokenhearted.
[17]He loved to pronounce a curse—
may it[e] come on him;
he found no pleasure in blessing—
may it be[f] far from him.
[18]He wore cursing as his garment;
it entered into his body like water,
into his bones like oil.
[19]May it be like a cloak wrapped about him,
like a belt tied forever around him.
[20]May this be the LORD's payment to my accusers,
to those who speak evil of me.

[21]But you, O Sovereign LORD,
deal well with me for your name's sake;
out of the goodness of your love,
deliver me.
[22]For I am poor and needy,
and my heart is wounded within me.
[23]I fade away like an evening shadow;
I am shaken off like a locust.
[24]My knees give way from fasting;
my body is thin and gaunt.
[25]I am an object of scorn to my accusers;
when they see me, they shake their heads.

[26]Help me, O LORD my God;
save me in accordance with your love.
[27]Let them know that it is your hand,
that you, O LORD, have done it.
[28]They may curse, but you will bless;
when they attack they will be put to shame,
but your servant will rejoice.
[29]My accusers will be clothed with disgrace
and wrapped in shame as in a cloak.

[30]With my mouth I will greatly extol the LORD;

a6 Or *They say:, "Appoint* (with quotation marks at the end of verse 19) b6 Or *the Evil One* c6 Or *let Satan* d10 Septuagint; Hebrew *sought* e17 Or *curse, / and it has* f17 Or *blessing, / and it is*

in the great throng I will praise
him.
31For he stands at the right hand of the
needy one,
to save his life from those who
condemn him.

Psalm 110

Of David. A psalm.

1The LORD says to my Lord:
"Sit at my right hand
until I make your enemies
a footstool for your feet."

2The LORD will extend your mighty
scepter from Zion;
you will rule in the midst of your
enemies.
3Your troops will be willing
on your day of battle.
Arrayed in holy majesty,
from the womb of the dawn
you will receive the dew of your
youth.[a]

4The LORD has sworn
and will not change his mind:
"You are a priest forever,
in the order of Melchizedek."

5The Lord is at your right hand;
he will crush kings on the day of
his wrath.
6He will judge the nations, heaping up
the dead
and crushing the rulers of the
whole earth.
7He will drink from a brook beside the
way[b];
therefore he will lift up his head.

Psalm 111[c]

1Praise the LORD.[d]

I will extol the LORD with all my heart
in the council of the upright and in
the assembly.

2Great are the works of the LORD;
they are pondered by all who
delight in them.
3Glorious and majestic are his deeds,
and his righteousness endures
forever.
4He has caused his wonders to be
remembered;
the LORD is gracious and
compassionate.
5He provides food for those who fear
him;
he remembers his covenant forever.
6He has shown his people the power of
his works,
giving them the lands of other
nations.
7The works of his hands are faithful
and just;
all his precepts are trustworthy.
8They are steadfast for ever and ever,
done in faithfulness and
uprightness.
9He provided redemption for his
people;
he ordained his covenant forever—
holy and awesome is his name.

10The fear of the LORD is the beginning
of wisdom;
all who follow his precepts have
good understanding.
To him belongs eternal praise.

Psalm 112[c]

1Praise the LORD.[d]

Blessed is the man who fears the
LORD,
who finds great delight in his
commands.

2His children will be mighty in the
land;
the generation of the upright will
be blessed.
3Wealth and riches are in his house,
and his righteousness endures
forever.
4Even in darkness light dawns for the
upright,
for the gracious and compassionate
and righteous man.[e]
5Good will come to him who is
generous and lends freely,
who conducts his affairs with
justice.
6Surely he will never be shaken;
a righteous man will be
remembered forever.
7He will have no fear of bad news;

[a]3 Or / *your young men will come to you like the dew* [b]7 Or / *The One who grants succession will set him in authority* [c]This psalm is an acrostic poem, the lines of which begin with the successive letters of the Hebrew alphabet. [d]1 Hebrew *Hallelu Yah* [e]4 Or / *for ⌞the LORD⌟ is gracious and compassionate and righteous*

his heart is steadfast, trusting in
the LORD.
8His heart is secure, he will have no
fear;
in the end he will look in triumph
on his foes.
9He has scattered abroad his gifts to
the poor,
his righteousness endures forever;
his horn[a] will be lifted high in
honor.

10The wicked man will see and be
vexed,
he will gnash his teeth and waste
away;
the longings of the wicked will
come to nothing.

Psalm 113

1Praise the LORD.[b]

Praise, O servants of the LORD,
praise the name of the LORD.
2Let the name of the LORD be praised,
both now and forevermore.
3From the rising of the sun to the
place where it sets,
the name of the LORD is to be
praised.

4The LORD is exalted over all the
nations,
his glory above the heavens.
5Who is like the LORD our God,
the One who sits enthroned on
high,
6who stoops down to look
on the heavens and the earth?

7He raises the poor from the dust
and lifts the needy from the ash
heap;
8he seats them with princes,
with the princes of their people.
9He settles the barren woman in her
home
as a happy mother of children.

Praise the LORD.

Psalm 114

1When Israel came out of Egypt,
the house of Jacob from a people
of foreign tongue,
2Judah became God's sanctuary,
Israel his dominion.

3The sea looked and fled,
the Jordan turned back;
4the mountains skipped like rams,
the hills like lambs.

5Why was it, O sea, that you fled,
O Jordan, that you turned back,
6you mountains, that you skipped like
rams,
you hills, like lambs?

7Tremble, O earth, at the presence of
the Lord,
at the presence of the God of
Jacob,
8who turned the rock into a pool,
the hard rock into springs of water.

Psalm 115

1Not to us, O LORD, not to us
but to your name be the glory,
because of your love and
faithfulness.

2Why do the nations say,
"Where is their God?"
3Our God is in heaven;
he does whatever pleases him.
4But their idols are silver and gold,
made by the hands of men.
5They have mouths, but cannot speak,
eyes, but they cannot see;
6they have ears, but cannot hear,
noses, but they cannot smell;
7they have hands, but cannot feel,
feet, but they cannot walk;
nor can they utter a sound with
their throats.
8Those who make them will be like
them,
and so will all who trust in them.

9O house of Israel, trust in the LORD—
he is their help and shield.
10O house of Aaron, trust in the LORD—
he is their help and shield.
11You who fear him, trust in the LORD—
he is their help and shield.

12The LORD remembers us and will bless
us:
He will bless the house of Israel,
he will bless the house of Aaron,
13he will bless those who fear the
LORD—
small and great alike.

14May the LORD make you increase,
both you and your children.
15May you be blessed by the LORD,
the Maker of heaven and earth.

[a]9 *Horn* here symbolizes dignity. [b]1 Hebrew *Hallelu Yah*; also in verse 9

16The highest heavens belong to the
LORD,
but the earth he has given to man.
17It is not the dead who praise the
LORD,
those who go down to silence;
18it is we who extol the LORD,
both now and forevermore.

Praise the LORD.[a]

Psalm 116

1I love the LORD, for he heard my
voice;
he heard my cry for mercy.
2Because he turned his ear to me,
I will call on him as long as I live.

3The cords of death entangled me,
the anguish of the grave[b] came
upon me;
I was overcome by trouble and
sorrow.
4Then I called on the name of the
LORD:
"O LORD, save me!"

5The LORD is gracious and righteous;
our God is full of compassion.
6The LORD protects the simplehearted;
when I was in great need, he saved
me.

7Be at rest once more, O my soul,
for the LORD has been good to you.

8For you, O LORD, have delivered my
soul from death,
my eyes from tears,
my feet from stumbling,
9that I may walk before the LORD
in the land of the living.
10I believed; therefore[c] I said,
"I am greatly afflicted."
11And in my dismay I said,
"All men are liars."

12How can I repay the LORD
for all his goodness to me?
13I will lift up the cup of salvation
and call on the name of the LORD.
14I will fulfill my vows to the LORD
in the presence of all his people.

15Precious in the sight of the LORD
is the death of his saints.
16O LORD, truly I am your servant;
I am your servant, the son of your
maidservant[d];
you have freed me from my chains.

17I will sacrifice a thank offering to you
and call on the name of the LORD.
18I will fulfill my vows to the LORD
in the presence of all his people,
19in the courts of the house of the
LORD—
in your midst, O Jerusalem.

Praise the LORD.[a]

Psalm 117

1Praise the LORD, all you nations;
extol him, all you peoples.
2For great is his love toward us,
and the faithfulness of the LORD
endures forever.

Praise the LORD.[a]

Psalm 118

1Give thanks to the LORD, for he is
good;
his love endures forever.

2Let Israel say:
"His love endures forever."
3Let the house of Aaron say:
"His love endures forever."
4Let those who fear the LORD say:
"His love endures forever."

5In my anguish I cried to the LORD,
and he answered by setting me free.
6The LORD is with me; I will not be
afraid.
What can man do to me?
7The LORD is with me; he is my helper.
I will look in triumph on my
enemies.

8It is better to take refuge in the LORD
than to trust in man.
9It is better to take refuge in the LORD
than to trust in princes.

10All the nations surrounded me,
but in the name of the LORD I cut
them off.
11They surrounded me on every side,
but in the name of the LORD I cut
them off.
12They swarmed around me like bees,
but they died out as quickly as
burning thorns;
in the name of the LORD I cut them
off.

13I was pushed back and about to fall,
but the LORD helped me.

[a]*18,19,2* Hebrew *Hallelu Yah* [b]*3* Hebrew *Sheol* [c]*10* Or *believed even when* [d]*16* Or *servant, your faithful son*

MONDAY

VERSE FOR THE DAY: *Psalm 116:3*

AUTHOR: *Carol L. Baldwin*

PASSAGE FOR THE DAY: *Psalm 116:1–19*

Comfort in Bereavement

"I FEEL like I could cry forever. I miss him so much that I actually hurt inside. Will my life ever be the same?"

Have you felt the deep sorrow of the mourning widow? If you have lost a child, parent, close relative or friend, perhaps you have also felt comfortless. Is there anyone who can minister to you when you feel overwhelmed with grief?

The psalmist shows that he identifies with the pain of the bereaved:

> The cords of death entangled me,
> the anguish of the grave came upon me;
> I was overcome by trouble and sorrow
> (Psalm 116:3).

Enveloped by emptiness, loneliness and stress, who does the psalmist turn to?

> I called on the name of the LORD:
> "O LORD, save me!' (Psalm 116:4).

He turns to the only one who will dry all of our tears (Isaiah 25:8); the one who carries all of our sorrows (Isaiah 53:4); the man acquainted with grief (Isaiah 53:3).

Likewise, we must turn to God and his Word for comfort in our times of sorrow. Without denying our pain, Scripture gives us a proper perspective, something we can easily lose in times of emotional trauma and crisis.

God's Word gives hope when we feel utterly alone and hopeless. We can take comfort in knowing that God does not allow a trial in our lives that is too great for us to bear (1 Corinthians 10:13). We can also be assured that death does not conquer those who die in Christ (1 Corinthians 15:22,53-56).

God is in charge of all things. Even the terrible destruction and the traumatic aftermath of death for those who mourn are under his lordship. God's Word and Spirit can comfort our grieving hearts so that we will be able to say with the psalmist:

> I may walk before the LORD
> in the land of the living . . .
> I am [his] servant. . . .
> Praise the LORD (Psalm 116:9,16,19).

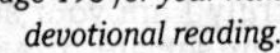

Additional Scripture Readings:
2 Corinthians 1:3–4; 1 Thessalonians 4:13–18

Go to page 498 for your next devotional reading.

14The LORD is my strength and my song;
he has become my salvation.

15Shouts of joy and victory
resound in the tents of the righteous:
"The LORD's right hand has done mighty things!
16 The LORD's right hand is lifted high;
the LORD's right hand has done mighty things!"

17I will not die but live,
and will proclaim what the LORD has done.
18The LORD has chastened me severely,
but he has not given me over to death.

19Open for me the gates of righteousness;
I will enter and give thanks to the LORD.
20This is the gate of the LORD
through which the righteous may enter.
21I will give you thanks, for you answered me;
you have become my salvation.

22The stone the builders rejected
has become the capstone;
23the LORD has done this,
and it is marvelous in our eyes.
24This is the day the LORD has made;
let us rejoice and be glad in it.

25O LORD, save us;
O LORD, grant us success.
26Blessed is he who comes in the name of the LORD.
From the house of the LORD we bless you.[a]
27The LORD is God,
and he has made his light shine upon us.
With boughs in hand, join in the festal procession
up[b] to the horns of the altar.

28You are my God, and I will give you thanks;
you are my God, and I will exalt you.

29Give thanks to the LORD, for he is good;
his love endures forever.

Psalm 119[c]

א Aleph

1Blessed are they whose ways are blameless,
who walk according to the law of the LORD.
2Blessed are they who keep his statutes
and seek him with all their heart.
3They do nothing wrong;
they walk in his ways.
4You have laid down precepts
that are to be fully obeyed.
5Oh, that my ways were steadfast
in obeying your decrees!
6Then I would not be put to shame
when I consider all your commands.
7I will praise you with an upright heart
as I learn your righteous laws.
8I will obey your decrees;
do not utterly forsake me.

ב Beth

9How can a young man keep his way pure?
By living according to your word.
10I seek you with all my heart;
do not let me stray from your commands.
11I have hidden your word in my heart
that I might not sin against you.
12Praise be to you, O LORD;
teach me your decrees.
13With my lips I recount
all the laws that come from your mouth.
14I rejoice in following your statutes
as one rejoices in great riches.
15I meditate on your precepts
and consider your ways.
16I delight in your decrees;
I will not neglect your word.

ג Gimel

17Do good to your servant, and I will live;
I will obey your word.
18Open my eyes that I may see
wonderful things in your law.
19I am a stranger on earth;
do not hide your commands from me.
20My soul is consumed with longing
for your laws at all times.

[a]26 The Hebrew is plural. [b]27 Or *Bind the festal sacrifice with ropes / and take it* [c]This psalm is an acrostic poem; the verses of each stanza begin with the same letter of the Hebrew alphabet.

21You rebuke the arrogant, who are cursed
and who stray from your commands.
22Remove from me scorn and contempt,
for I keep your statutes.
23Though rulers sit together and slander me,
your servant will meditate on your decrees.
24Your statutes are my delight;
they are my counselors.

ד Daleth

25I am laid low in the dust;
preserve my life according to your word.
26I recounted my ways and you answered me;
teach me your decrees.
27Let me understand the teaching of your precepts;
then I will meditate on your wonders.
28My soul is weary with sorrow;
strengthen me according to your word.
29Keep me from deceitful ways;
be gracious to me through your law.
30I have chosen the way of truth;
I have set my heart on your laws.
31I hold fast to your statutes, O LORD;
do not let me be put to shame.
32I run in the path of your commands,
for you have set my heart free.

ה He

33Teach me, O LORD, to follow your decrees;
then I will keep them to the end.
34Give me understanding, and I will keep your law
and obey it with all my heart.
35Direct me in the path of your commands,
for there I find delight.
36Turn my heart toward your statutes
and not toward selfish gain.
37Turn my eyes away from worthless things;
preserve my life according to your word.[a]
38Fulfill your promise to your servant,
so that you may be feared.
39Take away the disgrace I dread,
for your laws are good.
40How I long for your precepts!
Preserve my life in your righteousness.

ו Waw

41May your unfailing love come to me, O LORD,
your salvation according to your promise;
42then I will answer the one who taunts me,
for I trust in your word.
43Do not snatch the word of truth from my mouth,
for I have put my hope in your laws.
44I will always obey your law,
for ever and ever.
45I will walk about in freedom,
for I have sought out your precepts.
46I will speak of your statutes before kings
and will not be put to shame,
47for I delight in your commands
because I love them.
48I lift up my hands to[b] your commands, which I love,
and I meditate on your decrees.

ז Zayin

49Remember your word to your servant,
for you have given me hope.
50My comfort in my suffering is this:
Your promise preserves my life.
51The arrogant mock me without restraint,
but I do not turn from your law.
52I remember your ancient laws, O LORD,
and I find comfort in them.
53Indignation grips me because of the wicked,
who have forsaken your law.
54Your decrees are the theme of my song
wherever I lodge.
55In the night I remember your name, O LORD,
and I will keep your law.
56This has been my practice:
I obey your precepts.

ח Heth

57You are my portion, O LORD;
I have promised to obey your words.
58I have sought your face with all my heart;

[a]37 Two manuscripts of the Masoretic Text and Dead Sea Scrolls; most manuscripts of the Masoretic Text *life in your way* [b]48 Or *for*

be gracious to me according to your promise.
[59]I have considered my ways
and have turned my steps to your statutes.
[60]I will hasten and not delay
to obey your commands.
[61]Though the wicked bind me with ropes,
I will not forget your law.
[62]At midnight I rise to give you thanks
for your righteous laws.
[63]I am a friend to all who fear you,
to all who follow your precepts.
[64]The earth is filled with your love, O LORD;
teach me your decrees.

ט Teth

[65]Do good to your servant
according to your word, O LORD.
[66]Teach me knowledge and good judgment,
for I believe in your commands.
[67]Before I was afflicted I went astray,
but now I obey your word.
[68]You are good, and what you do is good;
teach me your decrees.
[69]Though the arrogant have smeared me with lies,
I keep your precepts with all my heart.
[70]Their hearts are callous and unfeeling,
but I delight in your law.
[71]It was good for me to be afflicted
so that I might learn your decrees.
[72]The law from your mouth is more precious to me
than thousands of pieces of silver and gold.

י Yodh

[73]Your hands made me and formed me;
give me understanding to learn your commands.
[74]May those who fear you rejoice when they see me,
for I have put my hope in your word.
[75]I know, O LORD, that your laws are righteous,
and in faithfulness you have afflicted me.
[76]May your unfailing love be my comfort,
according to your promise to your servant.
[77]Let your compassion come to me that I may live,
for your law is my delight.
[78]May the arrogant be put to shame for wronging me without cause;
but I will meditate on your precepts.
[79]May those who fear you turn to me,
those who understand your statutes.
[80]May my heart be blameless toward your decrees,
that I may not be put to shame.

כ Kaph

[81]My soul faints with longing for your salvation,
but I have put my hope in your word.
[82]My eyes fail, looking for your promise;
I say, "When will you comfort me?"
[83]Though I am like a wineskin in the smoke,
I do not forget your decrees.
[84]How long must your servant wait?
When will you punish my persecutors?
[85]The arrogant dig pitfalls for me,
contrary to your law.
[86]All your commands are trustworthy;
help me, for men persecute me without cause.
[87]They almost wiped me from the earth,
but I have not forsaken your precepts.
[88]Preserve my life according to your love,
and I will obey the statutes of your mouth.

ל Lamedh

[89]Your word, O LORD, is eternal;
it stands firm in the heavens.
[90]Your faithfulness continues through all generations;
you established the earth, and it endures.
[91]Your laws endure to this day,
for all things serve you.
[92]If your law had not been my delight,
I would have perished in my affliction.
[93]I will never forget your precepts,
for by them you have preserved my life.
[94]Save me, for I am yours;
I have sought out your precepts.
[95]The wicked are waiting to destroy me,
but I will ponder your statutes.
[96]To all perfection I see a limit;

but your commands are boundless.

מ Mem

97Oh, how I love your law!
I meditate on it all day long.
98Your commands make me wiser than my enemies,
for they are ever with me.
99I have more insight than all my teachers,
for I meditate on your statutes.
100I have more understanding than the elders,
for I obey your precepts.
101I have kept my feet from every evil path
so that I might obey your word.
102I have not departed from your laws,
for you yourself have taught me.
103How sweet are your words to my taste,
sweeter than honey to my mouth!
104I gain understanding from your precepts;
therefore I hate every wrong path.

נ Nun

105Your word is a lamp to my feet
and a light for my path.
106I have taken an oath and confirmed it,
that I will follow your righteous laws.
107I have suffered much;
preserve my life, O LORD, according to your word.
108Accept, O LORD, the willing praise of my mouth,
and teach me your laws.
109Though I constantly take my life in my hands,
I will not forget your law.
110The wicked have set a snare for me,
but I have not strayed from your precepts.
111Your statutes are my heritage forever;
they are the joy of my heart.
112My heart is set on keeping your decrees
to the very end.

ס Samekh

113I hate double-minded men,
but I love your law.
114You are my refuge and my shield;
I have put my hope in your word.
115Away from me, you evildoers,
that I may keep the commands of my God!
116Sustain me according to your promise, and I will live;
do not let my hopes be dashed.
117Uphold me, and I will be delivered;
I will always have regard for your decrees.
118You reject all who stray from your decrees,
for their deceitfulness is in vain.
119All the wicked of the earth you discard like dross;
therefore I love your statutes.
120My flesh trembles in fear of you;
I stand in awe of your laws.

ע Ayin

121I have done what is righteous and just;
do not leave me to my oppressors.
122Ensure your servant's well-being;
let not the arrogant oppress me.
123My eyes fail, looking for your salvation,
looking for your righteous promise.
124Deal with your servant according to your love
and teach me your decrees.
125I am your servant; give me discernment
that I may understand your statutes.
126It is time for you to act, O LORD;
your law is being broken.
127Because I love your commands
more than gold, more than pure gold,
128and because I consider all your precepts right,
I hate every wrong path.

פ Pe

129Your statutes are wonderful;
therefore I obey them.
130The unfolding of your words gives light;
it gives understanding to the simple.
131I open my mouth and pant,
longing for your commands.
132Turn to me and have mercy on me,
as you always do to those who love your name.
133Direct my footsteps according to your word;
let no sin rule over me.
134Redeem me from the oppression of men,
that I may obey your precepts.
135Make your face shine upon your servant

and teach me your decrees.
136Streams of tears flow from my eyes,
for your law is not obeyed.

צ Tsadhe

137Righteous are you, O LORD,
and your laws are right.
138The statutes you have laid down are righteous;
they are fully trustworthy.
139My zeal wears me out,
for my enemies ignore your words.
140Your promises have been thoroughly tested,
and your servant loves them.
141Though I am lowly and despised,
I do not forget your precepts.
142Your righteousness is everlasting
and your law is true.
143Trouble and distress have come upon me,
but your commands are my delight.
144Your statutes are forever right;
give me understanding that I may live.

ק Qoph

145I call with all my heart; answer me, O LORD,
and I will obey your decrees.
146I call out to you; save me
and I will keep your statutes.
147I rise before dawn and cry for help;
I have put my hope in your word.
148My eyes stay open through the watches of the night,
that I may meditate on your promises.
149Hear my voice in accordance with your love;
preserve my life, O LORD, according to your laws.
150Those who devise wicked schemes are near,
but they are far from your law.
151Yet you are near, O LORD,
and all your commands are true.
152Long ago I learned from your statutes
that you established them to last forever.

ר Resh

153Look upon my suffering and deliver me,
for I have not forgotten your law.
154Defend my cause and redeem me;
preserve my life according to your promise.
155Salvation is far from the wicked,
for they do not seek out your decrees.
156Your compassion is great, O LORD;
preserve my life according to your laws.
157Many are the foes who persecute me,
but I have not turned from your statutes.
158I look on the faithless with loathing,
for they do not obey your word.
159See how I love your precepts;
preserve my life, O LORD, according to your love.
160All your words are true;
all your righteous laws are eternal.

ש Sin and Shin

161Rulers persecute me without cause,
but my heart trembles at your word.
162I rejoice in your promise
like one who finds great spoil.
163I hate and abhor falsehood
but I love your law.
164Seven times a day I praise you
for your righteous laws.
165Great peace have they who love your law,
and nothing can make them stumble.
166I wait for your salvation, O LORD,
and I follow your commands.
167I obey your statutes,
for I love them greatly.
168I obey your precepts and your statutes,
for all my ways are known to you.

ת Taw

169May my cry come before you, O LORD;
give me understanding according to your word.
170May my supplication come before you;
deliver me according to your promise.
171May my lips overflow with praise,
for you teach me your decrees.
172May my tongue sing of your word,
for all your commands are righteous.
173May your hand be ready to help me,
for I have chosen your precepts.
174I long for your salvation, O LORD,
and your law is my delight.
175Let me live that I may praise you,
and may your laws sustain me.
176I have strayed like a lost sheep.
Seek your servant,

for I have not forgotten your
commands.

Psalm 120

A song of ascents.

1I call on the LORD in my distress,
and he answers me.
2Save me, O LORD, from lying lips
and from deceitful tongues.

3What will he do to you,
and what more besides, O deceitful
tongue?
4He will punish you with a warrior's
sharp arrows,
with burning coals of the broom
tree.

5Woe to me that I dwell in Meshech,
that I live among the tents of
Kedar!
6Too long have I lived
among those who hate peace.
7I am a man of peace;
but when I speak, they are for war.

Psalm 121

A song of ascents.

1I lift up my eyes to the hills—
where does my help come from?
2My help comes from the LORD,
the Maker of heaven and earth.

3He will not let your foot slip—
he who watches over you will not
slumber;
4indeed, he who watches over Israel
will neither slumber nor sleep.

5The LORD watches over you—
the LORD is your shade at your right
hand;
6the sun will not harm you by day,
nor the moon by night.

7The LORD will keep you from all
harm—
he will watch over your life;
8the LORD will watch over your coming
and going
both now and forevermore.

Psalm 122

A song of ascents. Of David.

1I rejoiced with those who said to me,
"Let us go to the house of the
LORD."
2Our feet are standing
in your gates, O Jerusalem.

3Jerusalem is built like a city
that is closely compacted together.
4That is where the tribes go up,
the tribes of the LORD,
to praise the name of the LORD
according to the statute given to
Israel.
5There the thrones for judgment stand,
the thrones of the house of David.

6Pray for the peace of Jerusalem:
"May those who love you be secure.
7May there be peace within your walls
and security within your citadels."
8For the sake of my brothers and
friends,
I will say, "Peace be within you."
9For the sake of the house of the LORD
our God,
I will seek your prosperity.

Psalm 123

A song of ascents.

1I lift up my eyes to you,
to you whose throne is in heaven.
2As the eyes of slaves look to the hand
of their master,
as the eyes of a maid look to the
hand of her mistress,
so our eyes look to the LORD our God,
till he shows us his mercy.

3Have mercy on us, O LORD, have
mercy on us,
for we have endured much
contempt.
4We have endured much ridicule from
the proud,
much contempt from the arrogant.

Psalm 124

A song of ascents. Of David.

1If the LORD had not been on our
side—
let Israel say—
2if the LORD had not been on our side
when men attacked us,
3when their anger flared against us,
they would have swallowed us alive;
4the flood would have engulfed us,
the torrent would have swept over
us,
5the raging waters
would have swept us away.

6Praise be to the LORD,
who has not let us be torn by their teeth.
7We have escaped like a bird
out of the fowler's snare;
the snare has been broken,
and we have escaped.
8Our help is in the name of the LORD,
the Maker of heaven and earth.

Psalm 125

A song of ascents.

1Those who trust in the LORD are like Mount Zion,
which cannot be shaken but endures forever.
2As the mountains surround Jerusalem,
so the LORD surrounds his people
both now and forevermore.

3The scepter of the wicked will not remain
over the land allotted to the righteous,
for then the righteous might use
their hands to do evil.

4Do good, O LORD, to those who are good,
to those who are upright in heart.
5But those who turn to crooked ways
the LORD will banish with the evildoers.

Peace be upon Israel.

Psalm 126

A song of ascents.

1When the LORD brought back the captives to[a] Zion,
we were like men who dreamed.[b]
2Our mouths were filled with laughter,
our tongues with songs of joy.
Then it was said among the nations,
"The LORD has done great things for them."
3The LORD has done great things for us,
and we are filled with joy.

4Restore our fortunes,[c] O LORD,
like streams in the Negev.
5Those who sow in tears
will reap with songs of joy.
6He who goes out weeping,
carrying seed to sow,
will return with songs of joy,
carrying sheaves with him.

Psalm 127

A song of ascents. Of Solomon.

1Unless the LORD builds the house,
its builders labor in vain.
Unless the LORD watches over the city,
the watchmen stand guard in vain.
2In vain you rise early
and stay up late,
toiling for food to eat—
for he grants sleep to[d] those he loves.

3Sons are a heritage from the LORD,
children a reward from him.
4Like arrows in the hands of a warrior
are sons born in one's youth.
5Blessed is the man
whose quiver is full of them.
They will not be put to shame
when they contend with their enemies in the gate.

Psalm 128

A song of ascents.

1Blessed are all who fear the LORD,
who walk in his ways.
2You will eat the fruit of your labor;
blessings and prosperity will be yours.
3Your wife will be like a fruitful vine
within your house;
your sons will be like olive shoots
around your table.
4Thus is the man blessed
who fears the LORD.

5May the LORD bless you from Zion
all the days of your life;
may you see the prosperity of Jerusalem,
6 and may you live to see your children's children.

Peace be upon Israel.

Psalm 129

A song of ascents.

1They have greatly oppressed me from my youth—
let Israel say—

[a]1 Or *LORD restored the fortunes of* [b]1 Or *men restored to health* [c]4 Or *Bring back our captives*
[d]2 Or *eat— / for while they sleep he provides for*

TUESDAY

VERSE FOR THE DAY:	*AUTHOR:*	*PASSAGE FOR THE DAY:*
Psalm 126:5	*Ruth A. Tucker*	*Psalm 126:1–6*

Sowing in Tears

SO often it is assumed that someone who is going through difficult times is incapable of effectively ministering to someone else. Indeed, as we are counseling those who are depressed and struggling with personal problems, it never seems to occur to us to encourage them to reach out to minister to others rather than focus exclusively on themselves. How insightful the psalmist was in writing:

> He who goes out weeping,
> carrying seed to sow,
> will return with songs of joy,
> carrying sheaves with him (Psalm 126:6).

It was during a very stressful period in my own life a few years ago that I was thrust suddenly into a care-giving situation. I had promised a friend that I would be a "daughter" to her mother while she and her husband fulfilled a two-year mission commitment in Africa. I might have had second thoughts about my new role had I realized that the day after my friend would leave, her mother would enter the hospital where her condition would utterly bewilder the doctors until she died several weeks later.

I was in no condition to minister to someone else—so I thought. But as I began making those daily hospital visits to Clara, I discovered that instead of adding to my stress, my time with her was rejuvenating. As I identified with her needs, my own problems paled into insignificance. And as I served her and focused on her well-being, I felt better about myself. Clara certainly was not passive in the care-giving process. She responded to my love and gave back to me far more than I gave her. She helped me make it through a very tough time in my life, and I will always have the sweet memories of being close to her during her final days, when I went out weeping and returned with songs of joy.

Additional Scripture Readings:
Isaiah 61:1–3; 2 Timothy 1:6–12

Go to page 500 for your next devotional reading.

[2]they have greatly oppressed me from
my youth,
but they have not gained the victory
over me.
[3]Plowmen have plowed my back
and made their furrows long.
[4]But the LORD is righteous;
he has cut me free from the cords
of the wicked.

[5]May all who hate Zion
be turned back in shame.
[6]May they be like grass on the roof,
which withers before it can grow;
[7]with it the reaper cannot fill his
hands,
nor the one who gathers fill his
arms.
[8]May those who pass by not say,
"The blessing of the LORD be upon
you;
we bless you in the name of the
LORD."

Psalm 130

A song of ascents.

[1]Out of the depths I cry to you,
O LORD;
[2] O Lord, hear my voice.
Let your ears be attentive
to my cry for mercy.

[3]If you, O LORD, kept a record of sins,
O Lord, who could stand?
[4]But with you there is forgiveness;
therefore you are feared.

[5]I wait for the LORD, my soul waits,
and in his word I put my hope.
[6]My soul waits for the Lord
more than watchmen wait for the
morning,
more than watchmen wait for the
morning.

[7]O Israel, put your hope in the LORD,
for with the LORD is unfailing love
and with him is full redemption.
[8]He himself will redeem Israel
from all their sins.

Psalm 131

A song of ascents. Of David.

[1]My heart is not proud, O LORD,
my eyes are not haughty;
I do not concern myself with great
matters
or things too wonderful for me.
[2]But I have stilled and quieted my
soul;
like a weaned child with its mother,
like a weaned child is my soul
within me.

[3]O Israel, put your hope in the LORD
both now and forevermore.

Psalm 132

A song of ascents.

[1]O LORD, remember David
and all the hardships he endured.

[2]He swore an oath to the LORD
and made a vow to the Mighty One
of Jacob:
[3]"I will not enter my house
or go to my bed—
[4]I will allow no sleep to my eyes,
no slumber to my eyelids,
[5]till I find a place for the LORD,
a dwelling for the Mighty One of
Jacob."

[6]We heard it in Ephrathah,
we came upon it in the fields of
Jaar[a]:[b]
[7]"Let us go to his dwelling place;
let us worship at his footstool—
[8]arise, O LORD, and come to your
resting place,
you and the ark of your might.
[9]May your priests be clothed with
righteousness;
may your saints sing for joy."

[10]For the sake of David your servant,
do not reject your anointed one.

[11]The LORD swore an oath to David,
a sure oath that he will not revoke:
"One of your own descendants
I will place on your throne—
[12]if your sons keep my covenant
and the statutes I teach them,
then their sons will sit
on your throne for ever and ever."

[13]For the LORD has chosen Zion,
he has desired it for his dwelling:
[14]"This is my resting place for ever and
ever;
here I will sit enthroned, for I have
desired it—

[a]6 That is, Kiriath Jearim [b]6 Or *heard of it in Ephrathah, / we found it in the fields of Jaar.* (And no quotes around verses 7-9)

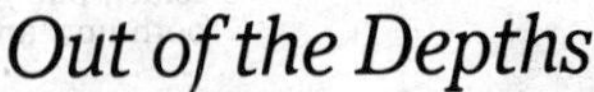

WEDNESDAY

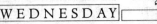

VERSE FOR THE DAY:
Psalm 130:1–2

AUTHOR:
Janice Kempe

PASSAGE FOR THE DAY:
Psalm 130:1–8

Out of the Depths

I'LL bet I've washed that dish a million times! My kitchen sink seems like a hole that I keep falling into and can't escape from. I wonder how many spoons and forks I've washed in the last ten years? And the laundry basket. It's perpetually full! I'll bet I could go to the dryer any time, day or night, and find at least ten ragged towels, six wrinkled shirts, and twenty-three socks, five of which have no mate. Who cares?

> Out of the depths I cry to you, O LORD;
> O LORD, hear my voice.
> Let your ears be attentive
> to my cry for mercy (Psalm 130:1–2)

Am I in the depths? Is this utter despair? I don't think so, but it is definitely uncomfortable. I'm having the blahs.

"Out of my blahs I cry to you, O Lord. Lord, hear my voice; Let your ears be attentive to my cry for mercy" (Kempe 1983).

That's my translation! Sometimes I have trouble relating to the trials and tragedies that drove God's people of the Old Testament to cry to him for deliverance. They make my own trial seem unimportant in comparison. But today I think God is telling me to stop comparing and to realize that the depressions and setbacks I experience are just as important to him as the conflicts and moral dilemmas faced by people in Bible times. They were his children, and he heard their voices and led them out of the depths. I also am his child, and he hears my voice and will lead me out of my depths. God is as eager to hear my pleas as he was to hear theirs.

My Lord cares! He cares when I feel like a failure. He cares when I feel as if all my education and training have led me to nothing but a sinkful of dishes. I think he smiles when I mop up spilled milk at each meal. I think he smiles when he hears a resounding "Yuck" in response to a new recipe I tried. He smiles and gives me gentle words of encouragement.

Additional Scripture Readings:
Numbers 11:10–23; Hebrews 4:14–16

Go to page 504 for your next devotional reading.

15I will bless her with abundant
provisions;
her poor will I satisfy with food.
16I will clothe her priests with
salvation,
and her saints will ever sing for joy.

17"Here I will make a horn[a] grow for
David
and set up a lamp for my anointed
one.
18I will clothe his enemies with shame,
but the crown on his head will be
resplendent."

Psalm 133

A song of ascents. Of David.

1How good and pleasant it is
when brothers live together in
unity!
2It is like precious oil poured on the
head,
running down on the beard,
running down on Aaron's beard,
down upon the collar of his robes.
3It is as if the dew of Hermon
were falling on Mount Zion.
For there the LORD bestows his
blessing,
even life forevermore.

Psalm 134

A song of ascents.

1Praise the LORD, all you servants of
the LORD
who minister by night in the house
of the LORD.
2Lift up your hands in the sanctuary
and praise the LORD.

3May the LORD, the Maker of heaven
and earth,
bless you from Zion.

Psalm 135

1Praise the LORD.[b]

Praise the name of the LORD;
praise him, you servants of the
LORD,
2you who minister in the house of the
LORD,
in the courts of the house of our
God.

3Praise the LORD, for the LORD is good;
sing praise to his name, for that is
pleasant.
4For the LORD has chosen Jacob to be
his own,
Israel to be his treasured
possession.

5I know that the LORD is great,
that our Lord is greater than all
gods.
6The LORD does whatever pleases him,
in the heavens and on the earth,
in the seas and all their depths.
7He makes clouds rise from the ends
of the earth;
he sends lightning with the rain
and brings out the wind from his
storehouses.

8He struck down the firstborn of
Egypt,
the firstborn of men and animals.
9He sent his signs and wonders into
your midst, O Egypt,
against Pharaoh and all his
servants.
10He struck down many nations
and killed mighty kings—
11Sihon king of the Amorites,
Og king of Bashan
and all the kings of Canaan—
12and he gave their land as an
inheritance,
an inheritance to his people Israel.

13Your name, O LORD, endures forever,
your renown, O LORD, through all
generations.
14For the LORD will vindicate his people
and have compassion on his
servants.

15The idols of the nations are silver and
gold,
made by the hands of men.
16They have mouths, but cannot speak,
eyes, but they cannot see;
17they have ears, but cannot hear,
nor is there breath in their mouths.
18Those who make them will be like
them,
and so will all who trust in them.

19O house of Israel, praise the LORD;
O house of Aaron, praise the LORD;
20O house of Levi, praise the LORD;
you who fear him, praise the LORD.
21Praise be to the LORD from Zion,
to him who dwells in Jerusalem.

Praise the LORD.

[a]17 *Horn* here symbolizes strong one, that is, king.

[b]1 Hebrew *Hallelu Yah*; also in verses 3 and 21

Psalm 136

1Give thanks to the LORD, for he is
good.
His love endures forever.
2Give thanks to the God of gods.
His love endures forever.
3Give thanks to the Lord of lords:
His love endures forever.

4to him who alone does great wonders,
His love endures forever.
5who by his understanding made the
heavens,
His love endures forever.
6who spread out the earth upon the
waters,
His love endures forever.
7who made the great lights—
His love endures forever.
8the sun to govern the day,
His love endures forever.
9the moon and stars to govern the
night;
His love endures forever.

10to him who struck down the firstborn
of Egypt
His love endures forever.
11and brought Israel out from among
them
His love endures forever.
12with a mighty hand and outstretched
arm;
His love endures forever.

13to him who divided the Red Sea[a]
asunder
His love endures forever.
14and brought Israel through the midst
of it,
His love endures forever.
15but swept Pharaoh and his army into
the Red Sea;
His love endures forever.

16to him who led his people through
the desert,
His love endures forever.
17who struck down great kings,
His love endures forever.
18and killed mighty kings—
His love endures forever.
19Sihon king of the Amorites
His love endures forever.
20and Og king of Bashan—
His love endures forever.
21and gave their land as an inheritance,
His love endures forever.
22an inheritance to his servant Israel;
His love endures forever.

23to the One who remembered us in
our low estate
His love endures forever.
24and freed us from our enemies,
His love endures forever.
25and who gives food to every creature.
His love endures forever.

26Give thanks to the God of heaven.
His love endures forever.

Psalm 137

1By the rivers of Babylon we sat and
wept
when we remembered Zion.
2There on the poplars
we hung our harps,
3for there our captors asked us for
songs,
our tormentors demanded songs of
joy;
they said, "Sing us one of the songs
of Zion!"

4How can we sing the songs of the
LORD
while in a foreign land?
5If I forget you, O Jerusalem,
may my right hand forget ⌊its skill⌋.
6May my tongue cling to the roof of
my mouth
if I do not remember you,
if I do not consider Jerusalem
my highest joy.

7Remember, O LORD, what the
Edomites did
on the day Jerusalem fell.
"Tear it down," they cried,
"tear it down to its foundations!"
8O Daughter of Babylon, doomed to
destruction,
happy is he who repays you
for what you have done to us—
9he who seizes your infants
and dashes them against the rocks.

Psalm 138

Of David.

1I will praise you, O LORD, with all my
heart;
before the "gods" I will sing your
praise.

[a]13 Hebrew *Yam Suph*; that is, Sea of Reeds; also in verse 15

[2]I will bow down toward your holy temple
and will praise your name
for your love and your faithfulness,
for you have exalted above all things
your name and your word.
[3]When I called, you answered me;
you made me bold and stouthearted.

[4]May all the kings of the earth praise you, O LORD,
when they hear the words of your mouth.
[5]May they sing of the ways of the LORD,
for the glory of the LORD is great.

[6]Though the LORD is on high, he looks upon the lowly,
but the proud he knows from afar.
[7]Though I walk in the midst of trouble,
you preserve my life;
you stretch out your hand against the anger of my foes,
with your right hand you save me.
[8]The LORD will fulfill ⌊his purpose⌋ for me;
your love, O LORD, endures forever—
do not abandon the works of your hands.

Psalm 139

For the director of music. Of David. A psalm.

[1]O LORD, you have searched me
and you know me.
[2]You know when I sit and when I rise;
you perceive my thoughts from afar.
[3]You discern my going out and my lying down;
you are familiar with all my ways.
[4]Before a word is on my tongue
you know it completely, O LORD.

[5]You hem me in—behind and before;
you have laid your hand upon me.
[6]Such knowledge is too wonderful for me,
too lofty for me to attain.

[7]Where can I go from your Spirit?
Where can I flee from your presence?
[8]If I go up to the heavens, you are there;
if I make my bed in the depths,[a]
you are there.
[9]If I rise on the wings of the dawn,
if I settle on the far side of the sea,
[10]even there your hand will guide me,
your right hand will hold me fast.

[11]If I say, "Surely the darkness will hide me
and the light become night around me,"
[12]even the darkness will not be dark to you;
the night will shine like the day,
for darkness is as light to you.

[13]For you created my inmost being;
you knit me together in my mother's womb.
[14]I praise you because I am fearfully and wonderfully made;
your works are wonderful,
I know that full well.
[15]My frame was not hidden from you
when I was made in the secret place.
When I was woven together in the depths of the earth,
[16]your eyes saw my unformed body.
All the days ordained for me
were written in your book
before one of them came to be.

[17]How precious to[b] me are your thoughts, O God!
How vast is the sum of them!
[18]Were I to count them,
they would outnumber the grains of sand.
When I awake,
I am still with you.

[19]If only you would slay the wicked, O God!
Away from me, you bloodthirsty men!
[20]They speak of you with evil intent;
your adversaries misuse your name.
[21]Do I not hate those who hate you, O LORD,
and abhor those who rise up against you?
[22]I have nothing but hatred for them;
I count them my enemies.

[23]Search me, O God, and know my heart;
test me and know my anxious thoughts.

[a]8 Hebrew *Sheol* [b]17 Or *concerning*

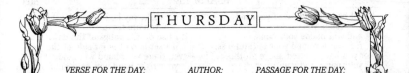

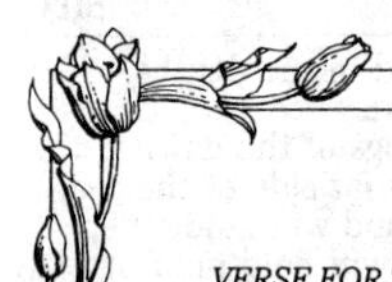

THURSDAY

VERSE FOR THE DAY:
Psalm 139:1

AUTHOR:
Hope MacDonald

PASSAGE FOR THE DAY:
Psalm 139:1–24

God's Active Presence

"OH! If only I could take this big tummy and set it on a chair for just one hour," sighed my eight-month-pregnant daughter. But we both knew that she couldn't. That little life went with her wherever she went, day or night.

I thought about that as I read this psalm today. I believe it is one of the most personal passages in all of Scripture. It is a psalm about God's continual, active presence with me wherever I go, day or night.

Christ in me means that God knows everything about me. He knows when I sit down and when I stand up (Psalm 139:2). He knows my name (Isaiah 43:1). He knows how many hairs I have on my head (Luke 12:7)! He knows my words completely, even before they are spoken (Psalm 139:4)! In fact, he saw me when I was being formed in my mother's womb. He was there, knitting me together (Psalm 139:13–16)! Indeed, such knowledge is too wonderful, too lofty for any of us to fully comprehend (Psalm 139:6).

Not only do we learn about God's eternal presence *with* us every moment, but we also get a tiny glimpse into the absolute holiness of God and his unconditional love for us. We are reminded that God knows and understands us better than anyone else ever will. His love for us is everlasting and personal. St. Augustine said, "God loves each one of us as though there were only one of us to love." What a treasure this truth is. Because of it, we can live in the certainty that his grace is sufficient for us today, regardless of our circumstances.

Just as my daughter could not set aside that little life she was carrying, not even for an hour, neither can we, who have received Jesus as Savior, ever be without him. We are bonded together in love. His Spirit is at work within us, making us more like Jesus with each passing day. We are each an everlasting child of God.

Additional Scripture Readings:
Jeremiah 1:4–8; Ephesians 1:17–21

Go to page 507 for your next devotional reading.

24See if there is any offensive way in me,
and lead me in the way everlasting.

Psalm 140

For the director of music. A psalm of David.

1Rescue me, O LORD, from evil men;
protect me from men of violence,
2who devise evil plans in their hearts
and stir up war every day.
3They make their tongues as sharp as a serpent's;
the poison of vipers is on their lips. *Selah*

4Keep me, O LORD, from the hands of the wicked;
protect me from men of violence
who plan to trip my feet.
5Proud men have hidden a snare for me;
they have spread out the cords of their net
and have set traps for me along my path. *Selah*

6O LORD, I say to you, "You are my God."
Hear, O LORD, my cry for mercy.
7O Sovereign LORD, my strong deliverer,
who shields my head in the day of battle—
8do not grant the wicked their desires, O LORD;
do not let their plans succeed,
or they will become proud. *Selah*

9Let the heads of those who surround me
be covered with the trouble their lips have caused.
10Let burning coals fall upon them;
may they be thrown into the fire,
into miry pits, never to rise.
11Let slanderers not be established in the land;
may disaster hunt down men of violence.

12I know that the LORD secures justice for the poor
and upholds the cause of the needy.
13Surely the righteous will praise your name
and the upright will live before you.

Psalm 141

A psalm of David.

1O LORD, I call to you; come quickly to me.
Hear my voice when I call to you.
2May my prayer be set before you like incense;
may the lifting up of my hands be like the evening sacrifice.

3Set a guard over my mouth, O LORD;
keep watch over the door of my lips.
4Let not my heart be drawn to what is evil,
to take part in wicked deeds
with men who are evildoers;
let me not eat of their delicacies.

5Let a righteous man[a] strike me—it is a kindness;
let him rebuke me—it is oil on my head.
My head will not refuse it.

Yet my prayer is ever against the deeds of evildoers;
6 their rulers will be thrown down from the cliffs,
and the wicked will learn that my words were well spoken.
7They will say, "As one plows and breaks up the earth,
so our bones have been scattered at the mouth of the grave.[b]"

8But my eyes are fixed on you, O Sovereign LORD;
in you I take refuge—do not give me over to death.
9Keep me from the snares they have laid for me,
from the traps set by evildoers.
10Let the wicked fall into their own nets,
while I pass by in safety.

Psalm 142

A *maskil*[c] of David. When he was in the cave. A prayer.

1I cry aloud to the LORD;
I lift up my voice to the LORD for mercy.
2I pour out my complaint before him;
before him I tell my trouble.

3When my spirit grows faint within me,

[a]5 Or *Let the Righteous One* [b]7 Hebrew *Sheol* [c]Title: Probably a literary or musical term

it is you who know my way.
In the path where I walk
men have hidden a snare for me.
4Look to my right and see;
no one is concerned for me.
I have no refuge;
no one cares for my life.

5I cry to you, O LORD;
I say, "You are my refuge,
my portion in the land of the living."
6Listen to my cry,
for I am in desperate need;
rescue me from those who pursue me,
for they are too strong for me.
7Set me free from my prison,
that I may praise your name.

Then the righteous will gather about me
because of your goodness to me.

Psalm 143

A psalm of David.

1O LORD, hear my prayer,
listen to my cry for mercy;
in your faithfulness and righteousness
come to my relief.
2Do not bring your servant into judgment,
for no one living is righteous before you.
3The enemy pursues me,
he crushes me to the ground;
he makes me dwell in darkness
like those long dead.
4So my spirit grows faint within me;
my heart within me is dismayed.

5I remember the days of long ago;
I meditate on all your works
and consider what your hands have done.
6I spread out my hands to you;
my soul thirsts for you like a parched land. *Selah*

7Answer me quickly, O LORD;
my spirit fails.
Do not hide your face from me
or I will be like those who go down to the pit.
8Let the morning bring me word of your unfailing love,
for I have put my trust in you.
Show me the way I should go,
for to you I lift up my soul.
9Rescue me from my enemies, O LORD,
for I hide myself in you.
10Teach me to do your will,
for you are my God;
may your good Spirit
lead me on level ground.

11For your name's sake, O LORD,
preserve my life;
in your righteousness, bring me out of trouble.
12In your unfailing love, silence my enemies;
destroy all my foes,
for I am your servant.

Psalm 144

Of David.

1Praise be to the LORD my Rock,
who trains my hands for war,
my fingers for battle.
2He is my loving God and my fortress,
my stronghold and my deliverer,
my shield, in whom I take refuge,
who subdues peoples[a] under me.

3O LORD, what is man that you care for him,
the son of man that you think of him?
4Man is like a breath;
his days are like a fleeting shadow.

5Part your heavens, O LORD, and come down;
touch the mountains, so that they smoke.
6Send forth lightning and scatter ⌞the enemies⌟;
shoot your arrows and rout them.
7Reach down your hand from on high;
deliver me and rescue me
from the mighty waters,
from the hands of foreigners
8whose mouths are full of lies,
whose right hands are deceitful.

9I will sing a new song to you, O God;
on the ten-stringed lyre I will make music to you,
10to the One who gives victory to kings,
who delivers his servant David from the deadly sword.

11Deliver me and rescue me
from the hands of foreigners
whose mouths are full of lies,

a2 Many manuscripts of the Masoretic Text, Dead Sea Scrolls, Aquila, Jerome and Syriac; most manuscripts of the Masoretic Text *subdues my people*

FRIDAY

VERSE FOR THE DAY:
Psalm 145:18

AUTHOR:
Debbie Smith

PASSAGE FOR THE DAY:
Psalm 145:1–21

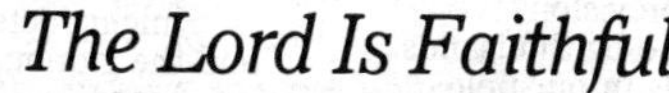

The Lord Is Faithful

"CAROL has gone into labor. She's at the hospital now . . . but they think the baby is dead!"

How could Carol, a friend who had suffered through three miscarriages, be asked to endure this tragedy? I hung up the phone, only to pick it up again to dial friends and family with a plea for prayer. God in his power could save that child!

The afternoon stretched on, and I remember praying almost constantly. "The LORD is near to all who call on him" (Psalm 145:18). I felt his presence, knowing that Carol and Bill surely felt it too.

Responding to a nudge to go to the hospital, I left the children with a sitter and set out on the thirty-minute drive, both desiring to "be there" for my friends and dreading what I might have to face.

By the time I reached the hospital the baby had been born, dead. Our pastor emerged from the room, assuring those of us waiting outside that Carol and Bill were taking their loss well, resting on faith. I wept with my friends, then listened as they spoke of the faith and comfort that God was providing. They recognized that God was in control, and they insisted that the prayers of believers had eased the pain. His peace was on their faces and in their words.

I left, numbed by the ordeal, yet strangely consoled. Driving home, I thanked my "gracious and compassionate" Lord (Psalm 145:8) for guiding my steps to that hospital room. The experience seemed an answer to many prayers for courage—for myself. For years I had struggled to believe that "the LORD watches over all who love him" (Psalm 145:20)—that he would be enough in any crisis I might have to face. My doubts were put to rest in five minutes inside that room.

The song Michael and I had written years before became vibrant again for me:

> Great is the Lord, he is holy and just;
> By his power we trust in his love.*

Yes. God is sufficient.

Additional Scripture Readings:
1 Corinthians 1:4–9; 1 Peter 1:3–9

Go to page 509 for your next devotional reading.

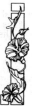

whose right hands are deceitful.

12Then our sons in their youth
will be like well-nurtured plants,
and our daughters will be like pillars
carved to adorn a palace.
13Our barns will be filled
with every kind of provision.
Our sheep will increase by thousands,
by tens of thousands in our fields;
14 our oxen will draw heavy loads.[a]
There will be no breaching of walls,
no going into captivity,
no cry of distress in our streets.

15Blessed are the people of whom this
is true;
blessed are the people whose God
is the LORD.

Psalm 145[b]

A psalm of praise. Of David.

1I will exalt you, my God the King;
I will praise your name for ever and
ever.
2Every day I will praise you
and extol your name for ever and
ever.

3Great is the LORD and most worthy of
praise;
his greatness no one can fathom.
4One generation will commend your
works to another;
they will tell of your mighty acts.
5They will speak of the glorious
splendor of your majesty,
and I will meditate on your
wonderful works.[c]
6They will tell of the power of your
awesome works,
and I will proclaim your great
deeds.
7They will celebrate your abundant
goodness
and joyfully sing of your
righteousness.

8The LORD is gracious and
compassionate,
slow to anger and rich in love.
9The LORD is good to all;
he has compassion on all he has
made.

10All you have made will praise you,
O LORD;
your saints will extol you.
11They will tell of the glory of your
kingdom
and speak of your might,
12so that all men may know of your
mighty acts
and the glorious splendor of your
kingdom.
13Your kingdom is an everlasting
kingdom,
and your dominion endures through
all generations.

The LORD is faithful to all his
promises
and loving toward all he has
made.[d]
14The LORD upholds all those who fall
and lifts up all who are bowed
down.
15The eyes of all look to you,
and you give them their food at the
proper time.
16You open your hand
and satisfy the desires of every
living thing.

17The LORD is righteous in all his ways
and loving toward all he has made.
18The LORD is near to all who call on
him,
to all who call on him in truth.
19He fulfills the desires of those who
fear him;
he hears their cry and saves them.
20The LORD watches over all who love
him,
but all the wicked he will destroy.

21My mouth will speak in praise of the
LORD.
Let every creature praise his holy
name
for ever and ever.

Psalm 146

1Praise the LORD.[e]

Praise the LORD, O my soul.
2 I will praise the LORD all my life;
I will sing praise to my God as long
as I live.

[a]14 Or *our chieftains will be firmly established* [b]This psalm is an acrostic poem, the verses of which (including verse 13b) begin with the successive letters of the Hebrew alphabet. [c]5 Dead Sea Scrolls and Syriac (see also Septuagint); Masoretic Text *On the glorious splendor of your majesty / and on your wonderful works I will meditate* [d]13 One manuscript of the Masoretic Text, Dead Sea Scrolls and Syriac (see also Septuagint); most manuscripts of the Masoretic Text do not have the last two lines of verse 13. [e]1 Hebrew *Hallelu Yah*; also in verse 10

WEEKENDING

REJOICE

Each day, upon my daily round,
I find myself on holy ground—
The morning-glories on my fence
Inspire quiet reverence.
Just one small, tender seedling grew,
And now, this miracle in blue.
A robin in the apple tree
Sings out his glad doxology.
I hear the pure, unsullied joy
Of laughter from a little boy;
I bow before the firm belief
And faith of one who lives with grief;
I watch a jet plane skim the skies
And marvel at man's enterprise;
I look upon a field of wheat
And thank God for the bread we eat;
I watch the benedictive rain
On low-bowed heads of flower and grain.
A friend drops in, a neighbor calls,
The lamps are lit, night gently falls;
Contentment settles with the sun
In labors of the day well done.
So many little altars there,
So many simple calls to prayer,
So many reasons for thanksgiving—
The sacraments of daily living.

– Helen Lowrie Marshall

REVIVE

Saturday: Psalm 135:1–21
Sunday: Exodus 3:1–22

Go to page 511 for your next devotional reading.

3 Do not put your trust in princes,
in mortal men, who cannot save.
4 When their spirit departs, they return to the ground;
on that very day their plans come to nothing.

5 Blessed is he whose help is the God of Jacob,
whose hope is in the LORD his God,
6 the Maker of heaven and earth,
the sea, and everything in them—
the LORD, who remains faithful forever.
7 He upholds the cause of the oppressed
and gives food to the hungry.
The LORD sets prisoners free,
8 the LORD gives sight to the blind,
the LORD lifts up those who are bowed down,
the LORD loves the righteous.
9 The LORD watches over the alien
and sustains the fatherless and the widow,
but he frustrates the ways of the wicked.

10 The LORD reigns forever,
your God, O Zion, for all generations.

Praise the LORD.

Psalm 147

1 Praise the LORD.[a]

How good it is to sing praises to our God,
how pleasant and fitting to praise him!

2 The LORD builds up Jerusalem;
he gathers the exiles of Israel.
3 He heals the brokenhearted
and binds up their wounds.

4 He determines the number of the stars
and calls them each by name.
5 Great is our Lord and mighty in power;
his understanding has no limit.
6 The LORD sustains the humble
but casts the wicked to the ground.

7 Sing to the LORD with thanksgiving;
make music to our God on the harp.
8 He covers the sky with clouds;
he supplies the earth with rain
and makes grass grow on the hills.
9 He provides food for the cattle
and for the young ravens when they call.

10 His pleasure is not in the strength of the horse,
nor his delight in the legs of a man;
11 the LORD delights in those who fear him,
who put their hope in his unfailing love.

12 Extol the LORD, O Jerusalem;
praise your God, O Zion,
13 for he strengthens the bars of your gates
and blesses your people within you.
14 He grants peace to your borders
and satisfies you with the finest of wheat.

15 He sends his command to the earth;
his word runs swiftly.
16 He spreads the snow like wool
and scatters the frost like ashes.
17 He hurls down his hail like pebbles.
Who can withstand his icy blast?
18 He sends his word and melts them;
he stirs up his breezes, and the waters flow.

19 He has revealed his word to Jacob,
his laws and decrees to Israel.
20 He has done this for no other nation;
they do not know his laws.

Praise the LORD.

Psalm 148

1 Praise the LORD.[b]

Praise the LORD from the heavens,
praise him in the heights above.
2 Praise him, all his angels,
praise him, all his heavenly hosts.
3 Praise him, sun and moon,
praise him, all you shining stars.
4 Praise him, you highest heavens
and you waters above the skies.
5 Let them praise the name of the LORD,
for he commanded and they were created.
6 He set them in place for ever and ever;
he gave a decree that will never pass away.

[a] 1 Hebrew *Hallelu Yah*; also in verse 20 [b] 1 Hebrew *Hallelu Yah*; also in verse 14

MONDAY

VERSE FOR THE DAY: Psalm 147:10 | *AUTHOR:* Debbie Smith | *PASSAGE FOR THE DAY:* Psalm 147:7–11

Delight Only in Him

I AM convinced that there is no insignificant verse in the Bible. Surely the Holy Spirit has used them all to convict, correct, encourage and edify. When I recall a very difficult time in my life, I also remember how he showed me an important, though unlikely, verse in his Word:

> His pleasure is not in the strength of the horse,
> *nor his delight in the legs of a man* (Psalm 147:10, italics mine).

I was struggling with anorexia nervosa when that verse jumped out of the page and hit my heart. I had been obsessed with the size of legs, arms, waist—with *everything* about my physical appearance. Here, God tells me that the condition of my heart is important to him, much more important than the condition of my body. David goes on to say:

> The LORD delights in those who fear him,
> who put their hope in his unfailing love
> (Psalm 147:11).

I realized that I had feared the opinions of others; I had feared that I would not measure up. I had placed my hope, not in God's unconditional love, but in controlling my weight.

What began in the eighth grade as a week-long diet with a friend became seven years of starvation for me. For some deep psychological, emotional and spiritual reasons, I kept losing weight. By my senior year of high school, I was five feet, three inches tall and all of seventy-nine pounds.

When I sank below eighty pounds, my internal battle intensified. I was a Christian, desiring to serve God, yet enslaved to food. I was miserable. Night after night I sobbed into my pillow, pleading that God would make me normal.

He answered those prayers slowly and gently. First, he showed me my sin and forgave me. He gave me caring friends to talk to, reassurance from his Word, and a wonderful husband. Michael loves *me*, not my dress size!

And, as confirmation that my healing is complete, God has given us three beautiful children—our three miracles, we call them, since I was told I would never be able to bear children as a result of my anorexia.

Now I desire only to fear God and put my hope in his love . . . and through his strength, I will delight only in him!

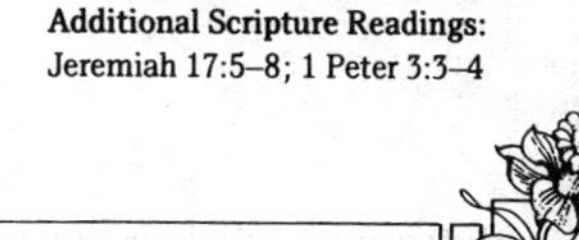

Additional Scripture Readings:
Jeremiah 17:5–8; 1 Peter 3:3–4

Go to page 516 for your next devotional reading.

7Praise the LORD from the earth,
you great sea creatures and all ocean depths,
8lightning and hail, snow and clouds,
stormy winds that do his bidding,
9you mountains and all hills,
fruit trees and all cedars,
10wild animals and all cattle,
small creatures and flying birds,
11kings of the earth and all nations,
you princes and all rulers on earth,
12young men and maidens,
old men and children.

13Let them praise the name of the LORD,
for his name alone is exalted;
his splendor is above the earth and the heavens.
14He has raised up for his people a horn,[a]
the praise of all his saints,
of Israel, the people close to his heart.

Praise the LORD.

Psalm 149

1Praise the LORD.[b]

Sing to the LORD a new song,
his praise in the assembly of the saints.

2Let Israel rejoice in their Maker;
let the people of Zion be glad in their King.
3Let them praise his name with dancing
and make music to him with tambourine and harp.
4For the LORD takes delight in his people;
he crowns the humble with salvation.
5Let the saints rejoice in this honor
and sing for joy on their beds.

6May the praise of God be in their mouths
and a double-edged sword in their hands,
7to inflict vengeance on the nations
and punishment on the peoples,
8to bind their kings with fetters,
their nobles with shackles of iron,
9to carry out the sentence written against them.
This is the glory of all his saints.

Praise the LORD.

Psalm 150

1Praise the LORD.[c]

Praise God in his sanctuary;
praise him in his mighty heavens.
2Praise him for his acts of power;
praise him for his surpassing greatness.
3Praise him with the sounding of the trumpet,
praise him with the harp and lyre,
4praise him with tambourine and dancing,
praise him with the strings and flute,
5praise him with the clash of cymbals,
praise him with resounding cymbals.

6Let everything that has breath praise the LORD.

Praise the LORD.

[a]14 *Horn* here symbolizes strong one, that is, king.
[b]1 Hebrew *Hallelu Yah*; also in verse 9
[c]1 Hebrew *Hallelu Yah*; also in verse 6

SOLOMON "spoke three thousand proverbs" (1 Kings 4:32), many of which are collected in this book. These wise sayings describe patterns that operate in everyday life, offering us advice on how to conduct ourselves in various situations. Solomon's fundamental instruction is to fear and trust the Lord. As you read this book, remember that God has something to say about every aspect of your life; seek his wisdom in the decisions you must make each day.

PROVERBS

Prologue: Purpose and Theme

1 The proverbs of Solomon son of David, king of Israel:

2for attaining wisdom and discipline;
for understanding words of insight;
3for acquiring a disciplined and prudent life,
doing what is right and just and fair;
4for giving prudence to the simple,
knowledge and discretion to the young—
5let the wise listen and add to their learning,
and let the discerning get guidance—
6for understanding proverbs and parables,
the sayings and riddles of the wise.

7The fear of the LORD is the beginning of knowledge,
but fools[a] despise wisdom and discipline.

[a]7 The Hebrew words rendered *fool* in Proverbs, and often elsewhere in the Old Testament, denote one who is morally deficient.

Exhortations to Embrace Wisdom

Warning Against Enticement

8Listen, my son, to your father's
instruction
and do not forsake your mother's
teaching.
9They will be a garland to grace your
head
and a chain to adorn your neck.

10My son, if sinners entice you,
do not give in to them.
11If they say, "Come along with us;
let's lie in wait for someone's
blood,
let's waylay some harmless soul;
12let's swallow them alive, like the
grave,[a]
and whole, like those who go down
to the pit;
13we will get all sorts of valuable things
and fill our houses with plunder;
14throw in your lot with us,
and we will share a common
purse"—
15my son, do not go along with them,
do not set foot on their paths;
16for their feet rush into sin,
they are swift to shed blood.
17How useless to spread a net
in full view of all the birds!
18These men lie in wait for their own
blood;
they waylay only themselves!
19Such is the end of all who go after
ill-gotten gain;
it takes away the lives of those who
get it.

Warning Against Rejecting Wisdom

20Wisdom calls aloud in the street,
she raises her voice in the public
squares;
21at the head of the noisy streets[b] she
cries out,
in the gateways of the city she
makes her speech:

22"How long will you simple ones[c] love
your simple ways?
How long will mockers delight in
mockery
and fools hate knowledge?
23If you had responded to my rebuke,
I would have poured out my heart
to you
and made my thoughts known to
you.
24But since you rejected me when I
called
and no one gave heed when I
stretched out my hand,
25since you ignored all my advice
and would not accept my rebuke,
26I in turn will laugh at your disaster;
I will mock when calamity
overtakes you—
27when calamity overtakes you like a
storm,
when disaster sweeps over you like
a whirlwind,
when distress and trouble
overwhelm you.

28"Then they will call to me but I will
not answer;
they will look for me but will not
find me.
29Since they hated knowledge
and did not choose to fear the
LORD,
30since they would not accept my
advice
and spurned my rebuke,
31they will eat the fruit of their ways
and be filled with the fruit of their
schemes.
32For the waywardness of the simple
will kill them,
and the complacency of fools will
destroy them;
33but whoever listens to me will live in
safety
and be at ease, without fear of
harm."

Moral Benefits of Wisdom

2 My son, if you accept my words
and store up my commands within
you,
2turning your ear to wisdom
and applying your heart to
understanding,
3and if you call out for insight
and cry aloud for understanding,
4and if you look for it as for silver
and search for it as for hidden
treasure,
5then you will understand the fear of
the LORD
and find the knowledge of God.
6For the LORD gives wisdom,

[a]12 Hebrew *Sheol* [b]21 Hebrew; Septuagint / *on the tops of the walls* [c]22 The Hebrew word rendered *simple* in Proverbs generally denotes one without moral direction and inclined to evil.

and from his mouth come
knowledge and understanding.
7He holds victory in store for the
upright,
he is a shield to those whose walk
is blameless,
8for he guards the course of the just
and protects the way of his faithful
ones.

9Then you will understand what is
right and just
and fair—every good path.
10For wisdom will enter your heart,
and knowledge will be pleasant to
your soul.
11Discretion will protect you,
and understanding will guard you.

12Wisdom will save you from the ways
of wicked men,
from men whose words are
perverse,
13who leave the straight paths
to walk in dark ways,
14who delight in doing wrong
and rejoice in the perverseness of
evil,
15whose paths are crooked
and who are devious in their ways.

16It will save you also from the
adulteress,
from the wayward wife with her
seductive words,
17who has left the partner of her youth
and ignored the covenant she made
before God.[a]
18For her house leads down to death
and her paths to the spirits of the
dead.
19None who go to her return
or attain the paths of life.

20Thus you will walk in the ways of
good men
and keep to the paths of the
righteous.
21For the upright will live in the land,
and the blameless will remain in it;
22but the wicked will be cut off from
the land,
and the unfaithful will be torn from
it.

Further Benefits of Wisdom

3 My son, do not forget my teaching,
but keep my commands in your
heart,
2for they will prolong your life many
years
and bring you prosperity.

3Let love and faithfulness never leave
you;
bind them around your neck,
write them on the tablet of your
heart.
4Then you will win favor and a good
name
in the sight of God and man.

5Trust in the LORD with all your heart
and lean not on your own
understanding;
6in all your ways acknowledge him,
and he will make your paths
straight.[b]

7Do not be wise in your own eyes;
fear the LORD and shun evil.
8This will bring health to your body
and nourishment to your bones.

9Honor the LORD with your wealth,
with the firstfruits of all your crops;
10then your barns will be filled to
overflowing,
and your vats will brim over with
new wine.

11My son, do not despise the LORD's
discipline
and do not resent his rebuke,
12because the LORD disciplines those he
loves,
as a father[c] the son he delights in.

13Blessed is the man who finds wisdom,
the man who gains understanding,
14for she is more profitable than silver
and yields better returns than gold.
15She is more precious than rubies;
nothing you desire can compare
with her.
16Long life is in her right hand;
in her left hand are riches and
honor.
17Her ways are pleasant ways,
and all her paths are peace.
18She is a tree of life to those who
embrace her;
those who lay hold of her will be
blessed.

19By wisdom the LORD laid the earth's
foundations,
by understanding he set the
heavens in place;

[a]17 Or *covenant of her God* [b]6 Or *will direct your paths* [c]12 Hebrew; Septuagint / *and he punishes*

TUESDAY

VERSE FOR THE DAY:	*AUTHOR:*	*PASSAGE FOR THE DAY:*
Proverbs 3:5–6	*ann kiemel anderson*	*Proverbs 3:1–8*

trust

THIS is another verse with a command: "TRUST . . . LEAN NOT on your own understanding"; and a promise: "he WILL make your paths straight" (caps mine).

trust is such a lovely word in a world thoroughly self-indulged and complicated. it is quiet. simple. it represents freedom. rest. letting go.

a favorite, old hymn my father would often sing was, "tis so sweet to trust in Jesus, just to take him at his word . . . just to REST upon his promise. . . . " most of us are too busy and noisy to hear the "still, small voice." to identify it. to trust in its power above our human strivings.

friends of ours, who had been down the battered road of infertility, longed for another baby. a perfect situation came about. a young birth mother who felt the only answer for her baby was adoption.

a precious baby girl was born. i loved the birth mother and knew that this was a very painful decision. the adoptive couple came from another city to meet the birth mother and to take their new baby home. it was thanksgiving week. relatives had flown in for a family celebration. the birth mother signed the papers, releasing the baby from the hospital. but in the courtroom, days later, she broke down. she just couldn't give up her baby. she drove hundreds of miles on thanksgiving day to take back her baby.

the couple's celebration turned to heartbreak. immediately, they began to trust. not to figure it all out, or judge the birth mother. they waited quietly. in a year, twin girls were born and theirs was the chosen family. they lost one, and God gave them back two.

there are very many unknowns in life. a husband's job. our children's struggles. a tentative move. critical talk behind our backs. a search for our own identity. bills to pay. aged parents to look after.

let go completely. trust. live with it all in an open hand before God. Jesus promises he WILL work it all out. i do believe for you, always . . . a new sunrise.

Additional Scripture Readings:
Isaiah 26:3–14; Romans 15:13

Go to page 525 for your next devotional reading.

[20]by his knowledge the deeps were divided,
and the clouds let drop the dew.
[21]My son, preserve sound judgment and discernment,
do not let them out of your sight;
[22]they will be life for you,
an ornament to grace your neck.
[23]Then you will go on your way in safety,
and your foot will not stumble;
[24]when you lie down, you will not be afraid;
when you lie down, your sleep will be sweet.
[25]Have no fear of sudden disaster
or of the ruin that overtakes the wicked,
[26]for the LORD will be your confidence
and will keep your foot from being snared.

[27]Do not withhold good from those who deserve it,
when it is in your power to act.
[28]Do not say to your neighbor,
"Come back later; I'll give it tomorrow"—
when you now have it with you.
[29]Do not plot harm against your neighbor,
who lives trustfully near you.
[30]Do not accuse a man for no reason—
when he has done you no harm.
[31]Do not envy a violent man
or choose any of his ways,
[32]for the LORD detests a perverse man
but takes the upright into his confidence.

[33]The LORD's curse is on the house of the wicked,
but he blesses the home of the righteous.
[34]He mocks proud mockers
but gives grace to the humble.
[35]The wise inherit honor,
but fools he holds up to shame.

Wisdom Is Supreme

4 Listen, my sons, to a father's instruction;
pay attention and gain understanding.
[2]I give you sound learning,
so do not forsake my teaching.
[3]When I was a boy in my father's house,
still tender, and an only child of my mother,
[4]he taught me and said,
"Lay hold of my words with all your heart;
keep my commands and you will live.
[5]Get wisdom, get understanding;
do not forget my words or swerve from them.
[6]Do not forsake wisdom, and she will protect you;
love her, and she will watch over you.
[7]Wisdom is supreme; therefore get wisdom.
Though it cost all you have,[a] get understanding.
[8]Esteem her, and she will exalt you;
embrace her, and she will honor you.
[9]She will set a garland of grace on your head
and present you with a crown of splendor."

[10]Listen, my son, accept what I say,
and the years of your life will be many.
[11]I guide you in the way of wisdom
and lead you along straight paths.
[12]When you walk, your steps will not be hampered;
when you run, you will not stumble.
[13]Hold on to instruction, do not let it go;
guard it well, for it is your life.
[14]Do not set foot on the path of the wicked
or walk in the way of evil men.
[15]Avoid it, do not travel on it;
turn from it and go on your way.
[16]For they cannot sleep till they do evil;
they are robbed of slumber till they make someone fall.
[17]They eat the bread of wickedness
and drink the wine of violence.

[18]The path of the righteous is like the first gleam of dawn,
shining ever brighter till the full light of day.
[19]But the way of the wicked is like deep darkness;
they do not know what makes them stumble.

[a]7 Or *Whatever else you get*

[20]My son, pay attention to what I say;
listen closely to my words.
[21]Do not let them out of your sight,
keep them within your heart;
[22]for they are life to those who find them
and health to a man's whole body.
[23]Above all else, guard your heart,
for it is the wellspring of life.
[24]Put away perversity from your mouth;
keep corrupt talk far from your lips.
[25]Let your eyes look straight ahead,
fix your gaze directly before you.
[26]Make level[a] paths for your feet
and take only ways that are firm.
[27]Do not swerve to the right or the left;
keep your foot from evil.

Warning Against Adultery

5 My son, pay attention to my wisdom,
listen well to my words of insight,
[2]that you may maintain discretion
and your lips may preserve knowledge.
[3]For the lips of an adulteress drip honey,
and her speech is smoother than oil;
[4]but in the end she is bitter as gall,
sharp as a double-edged sword.
[5]Her feet go down to death;
her steps lead straight to the grave.[b]
[6]She gives no thought to the way of life;
her paths are crooked, but she knows it not.

[7]Now then, my sons, listen to me;
do not turn aside from what I say.
[8]Keep to a path far from her,
do not go near the door of her house,
[9]lest you give your best strength to others
and your years to one who is cruel,
[10]lest strangers feast on your wealth
and your toil enrich another man's house.
[11]At the end of your life you will groan,
when your flesh and body are spent.
[12]You will say, "How I hated discipline!
How my heart spurned correction!
[13]I would not obey my teachers
or listen to my instructors.
[14]I have come to the brink of utter ruin
in the midst of the whole assembly."
[15]Drink water from your own cistern,
running water from your own well.
[16]Should your springs overflow in the streets,
your streams of water in the public squares?
[17]Let them be yours alone,
never to be shared with strangers.
[18]May your fountain be blessed,
and may you rejoice in the wife of your youth.
[19]A loving doe, a graceful deer—
may her breasts satisfy you always,
may you ever be captivated by her love.
[20]Why be captivated, my son, by an adulteress?
Why embrace the bosom of another man's wife?

[21]For a man's ways are in full view of the LORD,
and he examines all his paths.
[22]The evil deeds of a wicked man ensnare him;
the cords of his sin hold him fast.
[23]He will die for lack of discipline,
led astray by his own great folly.

Warnings Against Folly

6 My son, if you have put up security for your neighbor,
if you have struck hands in pledge for another,
[2]if you have been trapped by what you said,
ensnared by the words of your mouth,
[3]then do this, my son, to free yourself,
since you have fallen into your neighbor's hands:
Go and humble yourself;
press your plea with your neighbor!
[4]Allow no sleep to your eyes,
no slumber to your eyelids.
[5]Free yourself, like a gazelle from the hand of the hunter,
like a bird from the snare of the fowler.

[6]Go to the ant, you sluggard;
consider its ways and be wise!
[7]It has no commander,
no overseer or ruler,
[8]yet it stores its provisions in summer
and gathers its food at harvest.

[a]*26* Or *Consider the* [b]*5* Hebrew *Sheol*

9How long will you lie there, you
sluggard?
When will you get up from your
sleep?
10A little sleep, a little slumber,
a little folding of the hands to
rest—
11and poverty will come on you like a
bandit
and scarcity like an armed man.[a]

12A scoundrel and villain,
who goes about with a corrupt
mouth,
13 who winks with his eye,
signals with his feet
and motions with his fingers,
14 who plots evil with deceit in his
heart—
he always stirs up dissension.
15Therefore disaster will overtake him
in an instant;
he will suddenly be
destroyed—without remedy.

16There are six things the LORD hates,
seven that are detestable to him:
17 haughty eyes,
a lying tongue,
hands that shed innocent blood,
18 a heart that devises wicked
schemes,
feet that are quick to rush into
evil,
19 a false witness who pours out lies
and a man who stirs up
dissension among brothers.

Warning Against Adultery

20My son, keep your father's commands
and do not forsake your mother's
teaching.
21Bind them upon your heart forever;
fasten them around your neck.
22When you walk, they will guide you;
when you sleep, they will watch
over you;
when you awake, they will speak to
you.
23For these commands are a lamp,
this teaching is a light,
and the corrections of discipline
are the way to life,
24keeping you from the immoral
woman,
from the smooth tongue of the
wayward wife.
25Do not lust in your heart after her
beauty
or let her captivate you with her
eyes,
26for the prostitute reduces you to a
loaf of bread,
and the adulteress preys upon your
very life.
27Can a man scoop fire into his lap
without his clothes being burned?
28Can a man walk on hot coals
without his feet being scorched?
29So is he who sleeps with another
man's wife;
no one who touches her will go
unpunished.

30Men do not despise a thief if he
steals
to satisfy his hunger when he is
starving.
31Yet if he is caught, he must pay
sevenfold,
though it costs him all the wealth
of his house.
32But a man who commits adultery
lacks judgment;
whoever does so destroys himself.
33Blows and disgrace are his lot,
and his shame will never be wiped
away;
34for jealousy arouses a husband's fury,
and he will show no mercy when he
takes revenge.
35He will not accept any compensation;
he will refuse the bribe, however
great it is.

Warning Against the Adulteress

7 My son, keep my words
and store up my commands within
you.
2Keep my commands and you will live;
guard my teachings as the apple of
your eye.
3Bind them on your fingers;
write them on the tablet of your
heart.
4Say to wisdom, "You are my sister,"
and call understanding your
kinsman;
5they will keep you from the
adulteress,
from the wayward wife with her
seductive words.

6At the window of my house
I looked out through the lattice.
7I saw among the simple,
I noticed among the young men,
a youth who lacked judgment.

[a]11 Or *like a vagrant / and scarcity like a beggar*

[8]He was going down the street near
her corner,
walking along in the direction of
her house
[9]at twilight, as the day was fading,
as the dark of night set in.

[10]Then out came a woman to meet
him,
dressed like a prostitute and with
crafty intent.
[11](She is loud and defiant,
her feet never stay at home;
[12]now in the street, now in the squares,
at every corner she lurks.)
[13]She took hold of him and kissed him
and with a brazen face she said:

[14]"I have fellowship offerings[a] at home;
today I fulfilled my vows.
[15]So I came out to meet you;
I looked for you and have found
you!
[16]I have covered my bed
with colored linens from Egypt.
[17]I have perfumed my bed
with myrrh, aloes and cinnamon.
[18]Come, let's drink deep of love till
morning;
let's enjoy ourselves with love!
[19]My husband is not at home;
he has gone on a long journey.
[20]He took his purse filled with money
and will not be home till full
moon."

[21]With persuasive words she led him
astray;
she seduced him with her smooth
talk.
[22]All at once he followed her
like an ox going to the slaughter,
like a deer[b] stepping into a noose[c]
[23] till an arrow pierces his liver,
like a bird darting into a snare,
little knowing it will cost him his
life.

[24]Now then, my sons, listen to me;
pay attention to what I say.
[25]Do not let your heart turn to her ways
or stray into her paths.
[26]Many are the victims she has brought
down;
her slain are a mighty throng.
[27]Her house is a highway to the grave,[d]
leading down to the chambers of
death.

Wisdom's Call

8 Does not wisdom call out?
Does not understanding raise her
voice?
[2]On the heights along the way,
where the paths meet, she takes
her stand;
[3]beside the gates leading into the city,
at the entrances, she cries aloud:
[4]"To you, O men, I call out;
I raise my voice to all mankind.
[5]You who are simple, gain prudence;
you who are foolish, gain
understanding.
[6]Listen, for I have worthy things to
say;
I open my lips to speak what is
right.
[7]My mouth speaks what is true,
for my lips detest wickedness.
[8]All the words of my mouth are just;
none of them is crooked or
perverse.
[9]To the discerning all of them are
right;
they are faultless to those who have
knowledge.
[10]Choose my instruction instead of
silver,
knowledge rather than choice gold,
[11]for wisdom is more precious than
rubies,
and nothing you desire can
compare with her.

[12]"I, wisdom, dwell together with
prudence;
I possess knowledge and discretion.
[13]To fear the LORD is to hate evil;
I hate pride and arrogance,
evil behavior and perverse speech.
[14]Counsel and sound judgment are
mine;
I have understanding and power.
[15]By me kings reign
and rulers make laws that are just;
[16]by me princes govern,
and all nobles who rule on earth.[e]
[17]I love those who love me,
and those who seek me find me.
[18]With me are riches and honor,
enduring wealth and prosperity.
[19]My fruit is better than fine gold;
what I yield surpasses choice silver.
[20]I walk in the way of righteousness,
along the paths of justice,

[a]14 Traditionally *peace offerings* [b]22 Syriac (see also Septuagint); Hebrew *fool* [c]22 The meaning of the Hebrew for this line is uncertain. [d]27 Hebrew *Sheol* [e]16 Many Hebrew manuscripts and Septuagint; most Hebrew manuscripts *and nobles—all righteous rulers*

[21]bestowing wealth on those who love me
and making their treasuries full.

[22]"The LORD brought me forth as the first of his works,[a,b]
before his deeds of old;
[23]I was appointed[c] from eternity,
from the beginning, before the world began.
[24]When there were no oceans, I was given birth,
when there were no springs abounding with water;
[25]before the mountains were settled in place,
before the hills, I was given birth,
[26]before he made the earth or its fields
or any of the dust of the world.
[27]I was there when he set the heavens in place,
when he marked out the horizon on the face of the deep,
[28]when he established the clouds above
and fixed securely the fountains of the deep,
[29]when he gave the sea its boundary
so the waters would not overstep his command,
and when he marked out the foundations of the earth.
[30] Then I was the craftsman at his side.
I was filled with delight day after day,
rejoicing always in his presence,
[31]rejoicing in his whole world
and delighting in mankind.

[32]"Now then, my sons, listen to me;
blessed are those who keep my ways.
[33]Listen to my instruction and be wise;
do not ignore it.
[34]Blessed is the man who listens to me,
watching daily at my doors,
waiting at my doorway.
[35]For whoever finds me finds life
and receives favor from the LORD.
[36]But whoever fails to find me harms himself;
all who hate me love death."

Invitations of Wisdom and of Folly

9 Wisdom has built her house;
she has hewn out its seven pillars.
[2]She has prepared her meat and mixed her wine;
she has also set her table.
[3]She has sent out her maids, and she calls
from the highest point of the city.
[4]"Let all who are simple come in here!"
she says to those who lack judgment.
[5]"Come, eat my food
and drink the wine I have mixed.
[6]Leave your simple ways and you will live;
walk in the way of understanding.

[7]"Whoever corrects a mocker invites insult;
whoever rebukes a wicked man incurs abuse.
[8]Do not rebuke a mocker or he will hate you;
rebuke a wise man and he will love you.
[9]Instruct a wise man and he will be wiser still;
teach a righteous man and he will add to his learning.

[10]"The fear of the LORD is the beginning of wisdom,
and knowledge of the Holy One is understanding.
[11]For through me your days will be many,
and years will be added to your life.
[12]If you are wise, your wisdom will reward you;
if you are a mocker, you alone will suffer."

[13]The woman Folly is loud;
she is undisciplined and without knowledge.
[14]She sits at the door of her house,
on a seat at the highest point of the city,
[15]calling out to those who pass by,
who go straight on their way.
[16]"Let all who are simple come in here!"
she says to those who lack judgment.
[17]"Stolen water is sweet;
food eaten in secret is delicious!"
[18]But little do they know that the dead are there,
that her guests are in the depths of the grave.[d]

[a]22 Or *way*; or *dominion* [b]22 Or *The LORD possessed me at the beginning of his work*; or *The LORD brought me forth at the beginning of his work* [c]23 Or *fashioned* [d]18 Hebrew *Sheol*

Proverbs of Solomon

10 The proverbs of Solomon:
A wise son brings joy to his father,
but a foolish son grief to his mother.

2Ill-gotten treasures are of no value,
but righteousness delivers from death.

3The LORD does not let the righteous go hungry
but he thwarts the craving of the wicked.

4Lazy hands make a man poor,
but diligent hands bring wealth.

5He who gathers crops in summer is a wise son,
but he who sleeps during harvest is a disgraceful son.

6Blessings crown the head of the righteous,
but violence overwhelms the mouth of the wicked.[a]

7The memory of the righteous will be a blessing,
but the name of the wicked will rot.

8The wise in heart accept commands,
but a chattering fool comes to ruin.

9The man of integrity walks securely,
but he who takes crooked paths will be found out.

10He who winks maliciously causes grief,
and a chattering fool comes to ruin.

11The mouth of the righteous is a fountain of life,
but violence overwhelms the mouth of the wicked.

12Hatred stirs up dissension,
but love covers over all wrongs.

13Wisdom is found on the lips of the discerning,
but a rod is for the back of him who lacks judgment.

14Wise men store up knowledge,
but the mouth of a fool invites ruin.

15The wealth of the rich is their fortified city,
but poverty is the ruin of the poor.

16The wages of the righteous bring them life,
but the income of the wicked brings them punishment.

17He who heeds discipline shows the way to life,
but whoever ignores correction leads others astray.

18He who conceals his hatred has lying lips,
and whoever spreads slander is a fool.

19When words are many, sin is not absent,
but he who holds his tongue is wise.

20The tongue of the righteous is choice silver,
but the heart of the wicked is of little value.

21The lips of the righteous nourish many,
but fools die for lack of judgment.

22The blessing of the LORD brings wealth,
and he adds no trouble to it.

23A fool finds pleasure in evil conduct,
but a man of understanding delights in wisdom.

24What the wicked dreads will overtake him;
what the righteous desire will be granted.

25When the storm has swept by, the wicked are gone,
but the righteous stand firm forever.

26As vinegar to the teeth and smoke to the eyes,
so is a sluggard to those who send him.

27The fear of the LORD adds length to life,
but the years of the wicked are cut short.

28The prospect of the righteous is joy,
but the hopes of the wicked come to nothing.

29The way of the LORD is a refuge for the righteous,

[a]6 Or *but the mouth of the wicked conceals violence*; also in verse 11

but it is the ruin of those who do
evil.

30The righteous will never be uprooted,
but the wicked will not remain in
the land.

31The mouth of the righteous brings
forth wisdom,
but a perverse tongue will be cut
out.

32The lips of the righteous know what
is fitting,
but the mouth of the wicked only
what is perverse.

11 The LORD abhors dishonest
scales,
but accurate weights are his
delight.

2When pride comes, then comes
disgrace,
but with humility comes wisdom.

3The integrity of the upright guides
them,
but the unfaithful are destroyed by
their duplicity.

4Wealth is worthless in the day of
wrath,
but righteousness delivers from
death.

5The righteousness of the blameless
makes a straight way for them,
but the wicked are brought down
by their own wickedness.

6The righteousness of the upright
delivers them,
but the unfaithful are trapped by
evil desires.

7When a wicked man dies, his hope
perishes;
all he expected from his power
comes to nothing.

8The righteous man is rescued from
trouble,
and it comes on the wicked
instead.

9With his mouth the godless destroys
his neighbor,
but through knowledge the
righteous escape.

10When the righteous prosper, the city
rejoices;
when the wicked perish, there are
shouts of joy.

11Through the blessing of the upright a
city is exalted,
but by the mouth of the wicked it
is destroyed.

12A man who lacks judgment derides
his neighbor,
but a man of understanding holds
his tongue.

13A gossip betrays a confidence,
but a trustworthy man keeps a
secret.

14For lack of guidance a nation falls,
but many advisers make victory
sure.

15He who puts up security for another
will surely suffer,
but whoever refuses to strike hands
in pledge is safe.

16A kindhearted woman gains respect,
but ruthless men gain only wealth.

17A kind man benefits himself,
but a cruel man brings trouble on
himself.

18The wicked man earns deceptive
wages,
but he who sows righteousness
reaps a sure reward.

19The truly righteous man attains life,
but he who pursues evil goes to his
death.

20The LORD detests men of perverse
heart
but he delights in those whose
ways are blameless.

21Be sure of this: The wicked will not
go unpunished,
but those who are righteous will go
free.

22Like a gold ring in a pig's snout
is a beautiful woman who shows no
discretion.

23The desire of the righteous ends only
in good,
but the hope of the wicked only in
wrath.

24One man gives freely, yet gains even
more;
another withholds unduly, but
comes to poverty.

25A generous man will prosper;
he who refreshes others will himself
be refreshed.

26People curse the man who hoards grain,
but blessing crowns him who is willing to sell.

27He who seeks good finds goodwill,
but evil comes to him who searches for it.

28Whoever trusts in his riches will fall,
but the righteous will thrive like a green leaf.

29He who brings trouble on his family will inherit only wind,
and the fool will be servant to the wise.

30The fruit of the righteous is a tree of life,
and he who wins souls is wise.

31If the righteous receive their due on earth,
how much more the ungodly and the sinner!

12 Whoever loves discipline loves knowledge,
but he who hates correction is stupid.

2A good man obtains favor from the LORD,
but the LORD condemns a crafty man.

3A man cannot be established through wickedness,
but the righteous cannot be uprooted.

4A wife of noble character is her husband's crown,
but a disgraceful wife is like decay in his bones.

5The plans of the righteous are just,
but the advice of the wicked is deceitful.

6The words of the wicked lie in wait for blood,
but the speech of the upright rescues them.

7Wicked men are overthrown and are no more,
but the house of the righteous stands firm.

8A man is praised according to his wisdom,
but men with warped minds are despised.

9Better to be a nobody and yet have a servant
than pretend to be somebody and have no food.

10A righteous man cares for the needs of his animal,
but the kindest acts of the wicked are cruel.

11He who works his land will have abundant food,
but he who chases fantasies lacks judgment.

12The wicked desire the plunder of evil men,
but the root of the righteous flourishes.

13An evil man is trapped by his sinful talk,
but a righteous man escapes trouble.

14From the fruit of his lips a man is filled with good things
as surely as the work of his hands rewards him.

15The way of a fool seems right to him,
but a wise man listens to advice.

16A fool shows his annoyance at once,
but a prudent man overlooks an insult.

17A truthful witness gives honest testimony,
but a false witness tells lies.

18Reckless words pierce like a sword,
but the tongue of the wise brings healing.

19Truthful lips endure forever,
but a lying tongue lasts only a moment.

20There is deceit in the hearts of those who plot evil,
but joy for those who promote peace.

21No harm befalls the righteous,
but the wicked have their fill of trouble.

22The LORD detests lying lips,
but he delights in men who are truthful.

23A prudent man keeps his knowledge to himself,
but the heart of fools blurts out folly.

[24]Diligent hands will rule,
but laziness ends in slave labor.

[25]An anxious heart weighs a man down,
but a kind word cheers him up.

[26]A righteous man is cautious in friendship,[a]
but the way of the wicked leads them astray.

[27]The lazy man does not roast[b] his game,
but the diligent man prizes his possessions.

[28]In the way of righteousness there is life;
along that path is immortality.

13 A wise son heeds his father's instruction,
but a mocker does not listen to rebuke.

[2]From the fruit of his lips a man enjoys good things,
but the unfaithful have a craving for violence.

[3]He who guards his lips guards his life,
but he who speaks rashly will come to ruin.

[4]The sluggard craves and gets nothing,
but the desires of the diligent are fully satisfied.

[5]The righteous hate what is false,
but the wicked bring shame and disgrace.

[6]Righteousness guards the man of integrity,

[a]26 Or *man is a guide to his neighbor* [b]27 The meaning of the Hebrew for this word is uncertain.

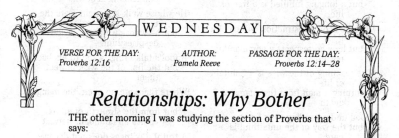

WEDNESDAY

VERSE FOR THE DAY:
Proverbs 12:16

AUTHOR:
Pamela Reeve

PASSAGE FOR THE DAY:
Proverbs 12:14–28

Relationships: Why Bother

THE other morning I was studying the section of Proverbs that says:

A fool shows his annoyance at once,
but a prudent man overlooks an insult
(Proverbs 12:16).

I said to the Lord, "You know, that's great, that's tremendous! That's where I want to be, Lord. That's for me today." Within two hours after I arrived at my office, I did not ignore what I saw as an insult. I showed my annoyance immediately!

All of the good spiritual input that we receive and enjoy is put to the test as we relate to other people. My real growth that morning did not take place as I was reading the Bible verse and thinking, "Isn't that marvelous?" The real growth came from blowing it and realizing I had really blown it. "Lord, forgive me. Wrong way. No good. Bring me another test and help me respond properly." That is growth.

Additional Scripture Readings:
James 1:22–25; 1 John 2:1–6

Go to page 527 for your next devotional reading.

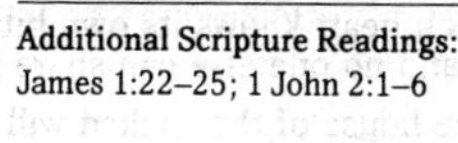

but wickedness overthrows the
sinner.

7One man pretends to be rich, yet has
nothing;
another pretends to be poor, yet
has great wealth.

8A man's riches may ransom his life,
but a poor man hears no threat.

9The light of the righteous shines
brightly,
but the lamp of the wicked is
snuffed out.

10Pride only breeds quarrels,
but wisdom is found in those who
take advice.

11Dishonest money dwindles away,
but he who gathers money little by
little makes it grow.

12Hope deferred makes the heart sick,
but a longing fulfilled is a tree of
life.

13He who scorns instruction will pay for
it,
but he who respects a command is
rewarded.

14The teaching of the wise is a fountain
of life,
turning a man from the snares of
death.

15Good understanding wins favor,
but the way of the unfaithful is
hard.[a]

16Every prudent man acts out of
knowledge,
but a fool exposes his folly.

17A wicked messenger falls into trouble,
but a trustworthy envoy brings
healing.

18He who ignores discipline comes to
poverty and shame,
but whoever heeds correction is
honored.

19A longing fulfilled is sweet to the
soul,
but fools detest turning from evil.

20He who walks with the wise grows
wise,
but a companion of fools suffers
harm.

21Misfortune pursues the sinner,
but prosperity is the reward of the
righteous.

22A good man leaves an inheritance for
his children's children,
but a sinner's wealth is stored up
for the righteous.

23A poor man's field may produce
abundant food,
but injustice sweeps it away.

24He who spares the rod hates his son,
but he who loves him is careful to
discipline him.

25The righteous eat to their hearts'
content,
but the stomach of the wicked goes
hungry.

14 The wise woman builds her
house,
but with her own hands the foolish
one tears hers down.

2He whose walk is upright fears the
LORD,
but he whose ways are devious
despises him.

3A fool's talk brings a rod to his back,
but the lips of the wise protect
them.

4Where there are no oxen, the manger
is empty,
but from the strength of an ox
comes an abundant harvest.

5A truthful witness does not deceive,
but a false witness pours out lies.

6The mocker seeks wisdom and finds
none,
but knowledge comes easily to the
discerning.

7Stay away from a foolish man,
for you will not find knowledge on
his lips.

8The wisdom of the prudent is to give
thought to their ways,
but the folly of fools is deception.

9Fools mock at making amends for sin,
but goodwill is found among the
upright.

10Each heart knows its own bitterness,
and no one else can share its joy.

11The house of the wicked will be
destroyed,

[a]15 Or *unfaithful does not endure*

THURSDAY

VERSE FOR THE DAY: *Proverbs 13:3* | *AUTHOR:* *Susan L. Lenzkes* | *PASSAGE FOR THE DAY:* *Proverbs 13:1–5*

That's a Mouthful!

DON'T look now, Lord!
I don't want You
to see me
standing here with
my big foot
crammed in my mouth.

Don't worry, child.
If I didn't love you
just as much with your
foot in your mouth,
I'd hardly ever get a
chance to love you.

Mothers are often forced to utter things other people wouldn't even think. One day I actually heard myself yelling in my hands-on-hips tone of voice, "All right! Who put the fire truck in the toilet?"

A lot of motherly queries seem to be preceded by the weary word, "Who put the . . . ," and end with a scramble of objects so strange they could be a mad Parker Brothers' game of chance.

Over the years, anyone who happened to be in the wrong place at the right time could have heard me asking who put: the cereal behind the couch? (the ants found it first); the pine cones in my purse? (I discovered them during church); the lemon pudding mix in the wading pool? (it was gelling in the corners); the toothpaste on the wall? (it looked like a fluoridated Picasso); the toy dish in the oven? (the flames were leaping out the vent).

Actually, parents should be taught not to ask questions, because either no one did it, or the other guy did it. And if you ever do manage to pin the culprit, you tend to ask why. "*Why* did you put the rock in the refrigerator?" And then you get an answer: "Because I wanted a cold rock."

It's obvious that parenthood requires carloads of patience. And I could feel reasonably righteous about boisterously losing that patience when the going gets rough, if it weren't for the fact that God has to lavish so much of it on me.

Occasionally, after I've lost my temper at the children, I've heard my heavenly Father patiently asking, "Who put the foot in the mouth?"

Additional Scripture Readings:
Ephesians 5:29; James 1:19–21

Go to page 529 for your next devotional reading.

but the tent of the upright will flourish.

12There is a way that seems right to a man,
but in the end it leads to death.

13Even in laughter the heart may ache,
and joy may end in grief.

14The faithless will be fully repaid for their ways,
and the good man rewarded for his.

15A simple man believes anything,
but a prudent man gives thought to his steps.

16A wise man fears the LORD and shuns evil,
but a fool is hotheaded and reckless.

17A quick-tempered man does foolish things,
and a crafty man is hated.

18The simple inherit folly,
but the prudent are crowned with knowledge.

19Evil men will bow down in the presence of the good,
and the wicked at the gates of the righteous.

20The poor are shunned even by their neighbors,
but the rich have many friends.

21He who despises his neighbor sins,
but blessed is he who is kind to the needy.

22Do not those who plot evil go astray?
But those who plan what is good find[a] love and faithfulness.

23All hard work brings a profit,
but mere talk leads only to poverty.

24The wealth of the wise is their crown,
but the folly of fools yields folly.

25A truthful witness saves lives,
but a false witness is deceitful.

26He who fears the LORD has a secure fortress,
and for his children it will be a refuge.

27The fear of the LORD is a fountain of life,
turning a man from the snares of death.

28A large population is a king's glory,
but without subjects a prince is ruined.

29A patient man has great understanding,
but a quick-tempered man displays folly.

30A heart at peace gives life to the body,
but envy rots the bones.

31He who oppresses the poor shows contempt for their Maker,
but whoever is kind to the needy honors God.

32When calamity comes, the wicked are brought down,
but even in death the righteous have a refuge.

33Wisdom reposes in the heart of the discerning
and even among fools she lets herself be known.[b]

34Righteousness exalts a nation,
but sin is a disgrace to any people.

35A king delights in a wise servant,
but a shameful servant incurs his wrath.

15 A gentle answer turns away wrath,
but a harsh word stirs up anger.

2The tongue of the wise commends knowledge,
but the mouth of the fool gushes folly.

3The eyes of the LORD are everywhere,
keeping watch on the wicked and the good.

4The tongue that brings healing is a tree of life,
but a deceitful tongue crushes the spirit.

5A fool spurns his father's discipline,
but whoever heeds correction shows prudence.

6The house of the righteous contains great treasure,
but the income of the wicked brings them trouble.

7The lips of the wise spread knowledge;

[a]22 Or *show* [b]33 Hebrew; Septuagint and Syriac / *but in the heart of fools she is not known*

not so the hearts of fools.

8The LORD detests the sacrifice of the
wicked,
but the prayer of the upright
pleases him.

9The LORD detests the way of the
wicked
but he loves those who pursue
righteousness.

10Stern discipline awaits him who
leaves the path;
he who hates correction will die.

11Death and Destruction[a] lie open
before the LORD—
how much more the hearts of men!

12A mocker resents correction;
he will not consult the wise.

13A happy heart makes the face
cheerful,
but heartache crushes the spirit.

14The discerning heart seeks
knowledge,
but the mouth of a fool feeds on
folly.

15All the days of the oppressed are
wretched,
but the cheerful heart has a
continual feast.

16Better a little with the fear of the
LORD

[a] 11 Hebrew *Sheol and Abaddon*

FRIDAY

VERSE FOR THE DAY:
Proverbs 15:13,15,30

AUTHOR:
Marjorie Holmes

PASSAGE FOR THE DAY:
Proverbs 15:13–33

It's Been a Good Day

IT'S been a good day, Lord. Yes, a very good day.

I didn't realize it while it was happening. There were many frustrations. I was very discouraged when the letter I was praying for didn't come. Then the telephone rang, bringing good news.

When a child was carried home from the playground hurt and we rushed him to the hospital, you knew my awful fears. But to learn that it wasn't really serious brought a sense of heightened joy. (Sheer relief can generate sheer bliss.)

So now the child is asleep, with the bandage slipped rather comically from his head. My husband stands in the yard, leaning on his rake as he visits with a neighbor.

Other children come spilling across the yard. The sun is a golden glory behind the trees. I can smell the pot roast mingling with the tangy fragrance of burning leaves.

I look back on this day with its usual ups and downs. Its moments of anguish, its moments of gratefulness and joy. And now that it's ending, an aching awareness fills me. I realize that it's been a good day, Lord. A very good day.

For it's been filled with life. The life you have given me to cope with, and to contribute to. And I wouldn't want to have missed it, not a single moment of it.

Thank you, God, for this good day.

Additional Scripture Readings:
Psalm 118:24; Matthew 6:33–34

Go to page 532 for your next devotional reading.

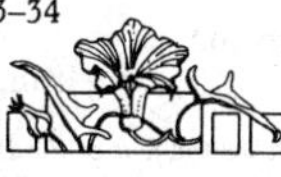

than great wealth with turmoil.

17Better a meal of vegetables where
there is love
than a fattened calf with hatred.

18A hot-tempered man stirs up
dissension,
but a patient man calms a quarrel.

19The way of the sluggard is blocked
with thorns,
but the path of the upright is a
highway.

20A wise son brings joy to his father,
but a foolish man despises his
mother.

21Folly delights a man who lacks
judgment,
but a man of understanding keeps a
straight course.

22Plans fail for lack of counsel,
but with many advisers they
succeed.

23A man finds joy in giving an apt
reply—
and how good is a timely word!

24The path of life leads upward for the
wise
to keep him from going down to
the grave.[a]

25The LORD tears down the proud man's
house
but he keeps the widow's
boundaries intact.

26The LORD detests the thoughts of the
wicked,
but those of the pure are pleasing
to him.

27A greedy man brings trouble to his
family,
but he who hates bribes will live.

28The heart of the righteous weighs its
answers,
but the mouth of the wicked
gushes evil.

29The LORD is far from the wicked
but he hears the prayer of the
righteous.

30A cheerful look brings joy to the
heart,
and good news gives health to the
bones.

31He who listens to a life-giving rebuke
will be at home among the wise.

32He who ignores discipline despises
himself,
but whoever heeds correction gains
understanding.

33The fear of the LORD teaches a man
wisdom,[b]
and humility comes before honor.

16 To man belong the plans of the
heart,
but from the LORD comes the reply
of the tongue.

2All a man's ways seem innocent to
him,
but motives are weighed by the
LORD.

3Commit to the LORD whatever you do,
and your plans will succeed.

4The LORD works out everything for his
own ends—
even the wicked for a day of
disaster.

5The LORD detests all the proud of
heart.
Be sure of this: They will not go
unpunished.

6Through love and faithfulness sin is
atoned for;
through the fear of the LORD a man
avoids evil.

7When a man's ways are pleasing to
the LORD,
he makes even his enemies live at
peace with him.

8Better a little with righteousness
than much gain with injustice.

9In his heart a man plans his course,
but the LORD determines his steps.

10The lips of a king speak as an oracle,
and his mouth should not betray
justice.

11Honest scales and balances are from
the LORD;
all the weights in the bag are of his
making.

12Kings detest wrongdoing,
for a throne is established through
righteousness.

13Kings take pleasure in honest lips;

[a]24 Hebrew *Sheol* [b]33 Or *Wisdom teaches the fear of the LORD*

they value a man who speaks the
truth.

14A king's wrath is a messenger of
death,
but a wise man will appease it.

15When a king's face brightens, it
means life;
his favor is like a rain cloud in
spring.

16How much better to get wisdom than
gold,
to choose understanding rather
than silver!

17The highway of the upright avoids
evil;
he who guards his way guards his
life.

18Pride goes before destruction,
a haughty spirit before a fall.

19Better to be lowly in spirit and among
the oppressed
than to share plunder with the
proud.

20Whoever gives heed to instruction
prospers,
and blessed is he who trusts in the
LORD.

21The wise in heart are called
discerning,
and pleasant words promote
instruction.[a]

22Understanding is a fountain of life to
those who have it,
but folly brings punishment to
fools.

23A wise man's heart guides his mouth,
and his lips promote instruction.[b]

24Pleasant words are a honeycomb,
sweet to the soul and healing to
the bones.

25There is a way that seems right to a
man,
but in the end it leads to death.

26The laborer's appetite works for him;
his hunger drives him on.

27A scoundrel plots evil,
and his speech is like a scorching
fire.

28A perverse man stirs up dissension,
and a gossip separates close
friends.

29A violent man entices his neighbor
and leads him down a path that is
not good.

30He who winks with his eye is plotting
perversity;
he who purses his lips is bent on
evil.

31Gray hair is a crown of splendor;
it is attained by a righteous life.

32Better a patient man than a warrior,
a man who controls his temper
than one who takes a city.

33The lot is cast into the lap,
but its every decision is from the
LORD.

17 Better a dry crust with peace and
quiet
than a house full of feasting,[c] with
strife.

2A wise servant will rule over a
disgraceful son,
and will share the inheritance as
one of the brothers.

3The crucible for silver and the furnace
for gold,
but the LORD tests the heart.

4A wicked man listens to evil lips;
a liar pays attention to a malicious
tongue.

5He who mocks the poor shows
contempt for their Maker;
whoever gloats over disaster will
not go unpunished.

6Children's children are a crown to the
aged,
and parents are the pride of their
children.

7Arrogant[d] lips are unsuited to a
fool—
how much worse lying lips to a
ruler!

8A bribe is a charm to the one who
gives it;
wherever he turns, he succeeds.

9He who covers over an offense
promotes love,
but whoever repeats the matter
separates close friends.

[a]21 Or *words make a man persuasive* [b]23 Or *mouth / and makes his lips persuasive* [c]1 Hebrew *sacrifices* [d]7 Or *Eloquent*

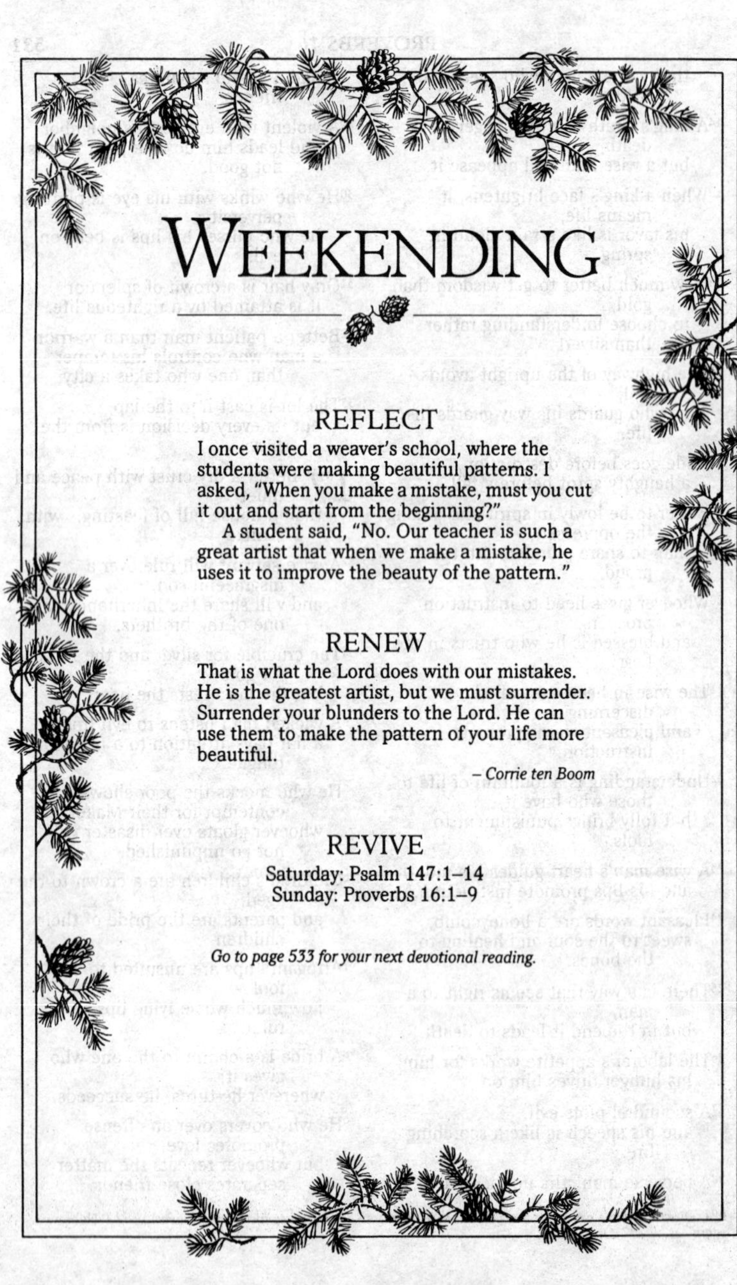

WEEKENDING

REFLECT

I once visited a weaver's school, where the students were making beautiful patterns. I asked, "When you make a mistake, must you cut it out and start from the beginning?"

A student said, "No. Our teacher is such a great artist that when we make a mistake, he uses it to improve the beauty of the pattern."

RENEW

That is what the Lord does with our mistakes. He is the greatest artist, but we must surrender. Surrender your blunders to the Lord. He can use them to make the pattern of your life more beautiful.

– Corrie ten Boom

REVIVE

Saturday: Psalm 147:1–14
Sunday: Proverbs 16:1–9

Go to page 533 for your next devotional reading.

[10]A rebuke impresses a man of discernment
more than a hundred lashes a fool.

[11]An evil man is bent only on rebellion;
a merciless official will be sent against him.

[12]Better to meet a bear robbed of her cubs
than a fool in his folly.

[13]If a man pays back evil for good,
evil will never leave his house.

[14]Starting a quarrel is like breaching a dam;
so drop the matter before a dispute breaks out.

[15]Acquitting the guilty and condemning the innocent—
the LORD detests them both.

[16]Of what use is money in the hand of a fool,
since he has no desire to get wisdom?

[17]A friend loves at all times,
and a brother is born for adversity.

[18]A man lacking in judgment strikes hands in pledge
and puts up security for his neighbor.

[19]He who loves a quarrel loves sin;
he who builds a high gate invites destruction.

[20]A man of perverse heart does not prosper;
he whose tongue is deceitful falls into trouble.

[21]To have a fool for a son brings grief;
there is no joy for the father of a fool.

[22]A cheerful heart is good medicine,
but a crushed spirit dries up the bones.

MONDAY

VERSE FOR THE DAY: *Proverbs 17:17* | *AUTHOR:* *Susan L. Lenzkes* | *PASSAGE FOR THE DAY:* *Proverbs 17:14–22*

A Friend in Need

FRIENDSHIP gives license to show up at the door of need without asking, "When would you like me to come?" or "What would you like me to do?" Nor does friendship call out, "Just let me know if you need anything."

Practiced friendship whispers, "I'll be there" and promptly steps through the door with sensitivity, respect, and understanding.

But what about honoring the right to invite? Those who wait for parchment invitations wait long, for need rarely throws a party—rarely even has a voice.

Yet need has its own needs. It needs protection from strangers tromping in with work boots and good intentions. And it needs relief from acquaintances wearing the spiked heels of advice and pat answers.

Need waits with longing for the familiar entrance of dear ones who pad barefoot through the soul on ordinary days.

Additional Scripture Readings:
Ruth 1:11–18; Mark 2:1–5

Go to page 536 for your next devotional reading.

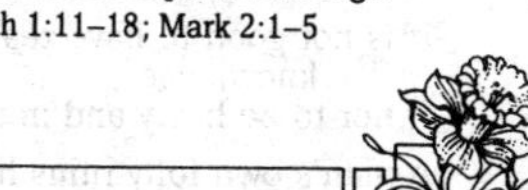

23 A wicked man accepts a bribe in secret
to pervert the course of justice.

24 A discerning man keeps wisdom in view,
but a fool's eyes wander to the ends of the earth.

25 A foolish son brings grief to his father
and bitterness to the one who bore him.

26 It is not good to punish an innocent man,
or to flog officials for their integrity.

27 A man of knowledge uses words with restraint,
and a man of understanding is even-tempered.

28 Even a fool is thought wise if he keeps silent,
and discerning if he holds his tongue.

18 An unfriendly man pursues selfish ends;
he defies all sound judgment.

2 A fool finds no pleasure in understanding
but delights in airing his own opinions.

3 When wickedness comes, so does contempt,
and with shame comes disgrace.

4 The words of a man's mouth are deep waters,
but the fountain of wisdom is a bubbling brook.

5 It is not good to be partial to the wicked
or to deprive the innocent of justice.

6 A fool's lips bring him strife,
and his mouth invites a beating.

7 A fool's mouth is his undoing,
and his lips are a snare to his soul.

8 The words of a gossip are like choice morsels;
they go down to a man's inmost parts.

9 One who is slack in his work
is brother to one who destroys.

10 The name of the LORD is a strong tower;
the righteous run to it and are safe.

11 The wealth of the rich is their fortified city;
they imagine it an unscalable wall.

12 Before his downfall a man's heart is proud,
but humility comes before honor.

13 He who answers before listening—
that is his folly and his shame.

14 A man's spirit sustains him in sickness,
but a crushed spirit who can bear?

15 The heart of the discerning acquires knowledge;
the ears of the wise seek it out.

16 A gift opens the way for the giver
and ushers him into the presence of the great.

17 The first to present his case seems right,
till another comes forward and questions him.

18 Casting the lot settles disputes
and keeps strong opponents apart.

19 An offended brother is more unyielding than a fortified city,
and disputes are like the barred gates of a citadel.

20 From the fruit of his mouth a man's stomach is filled;
with the harvest from his lips he is satisfied.

21 The tongue has the power of life and death,
and those who love it will eat its fruit.

22 He who finds a wife finds what is good
and receives favor from the LORD.

23 A poor man pleads for mercy,
but a rich man answers harshly.

24 A man of many companions may come to ruin,
but there is a friend who sticks closer than a brother.

19 Better a poor man whose walk is blameless
than a fool whose lips are perverse.

2 It is not good to have zeal without knowledge,
nor to be hasty and miss the way.

3 A man's own folly ruins his life,
yet his heart rages against the LORD.

4Wealth brings many friends,
but a poor man's friend deserts him.

5A false witness will not go unpunished,
and he who pours out lies will not go free.

6Many curry favor with a ruler,
and everyone is the friend of a man who gives gifts.

7A poor man is shunned by all his relatives—
how much more do his friends avoid him!
Though he pursues them with pleading,
they are nowhere to be found.[a]

8He who gets wisdom loves his own soul;
he who cherishes understanding prospers.

9A false witness will not go unpunished,
and he who pours out lies will perish.

10It is not fitting for a fool to live in luxury—
how much worse for a slave to rule over princes!

11A man's wisdom gives him patience;
it is to his glory to overlook an offense.

12A king's rage is like the roar of a lion,
but his favor is like dew on the grass.

13A foolish son is his father's ruin,
and a quarrelsome wife is like a constant dripping.

14Houses and wealth are inherited from parents,
but a prudent wife is from the LORD.

15Laziness brings on deep sleep,
and the shiftless man goes hungry.

16He who obeys instructions guards his life,
but he who is contemptuous of his ways will die.

17He who is kind to the poor lends to the LORD,
and he will reward him for what he has done.

18Discipline your son, for in that there is hope;
do not be a willing party to his death.

19A hot-tempered man must pay the penalty;
if you rescue him, you will have to do it again.

20Listen to advice and accept instruction,
and in the end you will be wise.

21Many are the plans in a man's heart,
but it is the LORD's purpose that prevails.

22What a man desires is unfailing love[b];
better to be poor than a liar.

23The fear of the LORD leads to life:
Then one rests content, untouched by trouble.

24The sluggard buries his hand in the dish;
he will not even bring it back to his mouth!

25Flog a mocker, and the simple will learn prudence;
rebuke a discerning man, and he will gain knowledge.

26He who robs his father and drives out his mother
is a son who brings shame and disgrace.

27Stop listening to instruction, my son,
and you will stray from the words of knowledge.

28A corrupt witness mocks at justice,
and the mouth of the wicked gulps down evil.

29Penalties are prepared for mockers,
and beatings for the backs of fools.

20 Wine is a mocker and beer a brawler;
whoever is led astray by them is not wise.

2A king's wrath is like the roar of a lion;
he who angers him forfeits his life.

3It is to a man's honor to avoid strife,
but every fool is quick to quarrel.

[a]7 The meaning of the Hebrew for this sentence is uncertain. [b]22 Or *A man's greed is his shame*

4A sluggard does not plow in season;
so at harvest time he looks but
finds nothing.

5The purposes of a man's heart are
deep waters,
but a man of understanding draws
them out.

6Many a man claims to have unfailing
love,
but a faithful man who can
find?

7The righteous man leads a blameless
life;
blessed are his children after him.

8When a king sits on his throne to
judge,
he winnows out all evil with his
eyes.

TUESDAY

VERSE FOR THE DAY: *Proverbs 19:21*
AUTHOR: *Marlene Obie*
PASSAGE FOR THE DAY: *Proverbs 19:21–29*

I Got It!

I CAN'T believe I got the job, Lord.

Well, I can too believe it. What's the matter with my faith anyway? No matter how often you answer my prayers, I always do a double take when I get the answer.

I asked for your guidance about whether or not to go to work and where I should work. Thank you for showing me your will.

Now I'm really in trouble. My wardrobe is straight out of the frumpville collection. Except for my combination interview-banquet-church outfit, I honestly have nothing decent to wear. I know my closet is crammed with material that resembles clothing. However half of these pieces have some permanent spot on them. And the other half doesn't match. Help me to figure something out, Lord. I can't afford to buy anything new right now. I'll have to make do.

I have a few days to try to organize our family schedules and duties, but I'm afraid my faith is weak here, too. If I couldn't get it together in the last twenty years, can I reasonably assume I'll do it in the next two days? Some people say that working outside the home forces you to be more organized. I hope that's true.

My feelings are jumbled. I'm glad I got the job and feel both confident and nervous about my competence. I wonder what my bosses and co-workers will really be like. Will they accept me? Will the job be exciting and challenging? Can I handle juggling a career with being a wife and mother?

Lord, keep me from these needless questions and worries. I know you led me to this job, and I know that you'll walk with me. Because I know this is your plan, I can face anything—even a new job.

Additional Scripture Readings:
Matthew 7:7–11; 1 John 5:14–15

Go to page 541 for your next devotional reading.

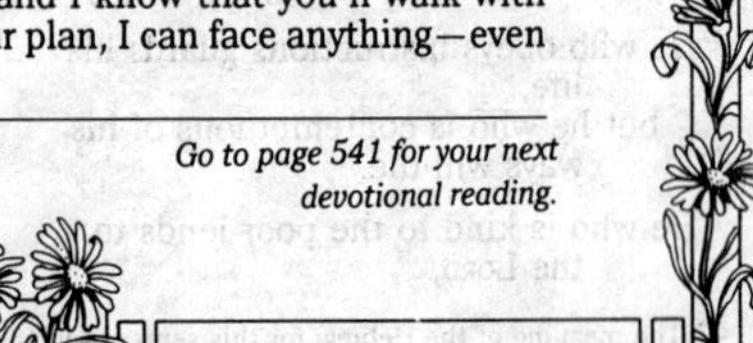

9Who can say, "I have kept my heart
pure;
I am clean and without sin"?

10Differing weights and differing
measures—
the LORD detests them both.

11Even a child is known by his actions,
by whether his conduct is pure and
right.

12Ears that hear and eyes that see—
the LORD has made them both.

13Do not love sleep or you will grow
poor;
stay awake and you will have food
to spare.

14"It's no good, it's no good!" says the
buyer;
then off he goes and boasts about
his purchase.

15Gold there is, and rubies in
abundance,
but lips that speak knowledge are a
rare jewel.

16Take the garment of one who puts up
security for a stranger;
hold it in pledge if he does it for a
wayward woman.

17Food gained by fraud tastes sweet to
a man,
but he ends up with a mouth full of
gravel.

18Make plans by seeking advice;
if you wage war, obtain guidance.

19A gossip betrays a confidence;
so avoid a man who talks too
much.

20If a man curses his father or mother,
his lamp will be snuffed out in
pitch darkness.

21An inheritance quickly gained at the
beginning
will not be blessed at the end.

22Do not say, "I'll pay you back for this
wrong!"
Wait for the LORD, and he will
deliver you.

23The LORD detests differing weights,
and dishonest scales do not please
him.

24A man's steps are directed by the
LORD.
How then can anyone understand
his own way?

25It is a trap for a man to dedicate
something rashly
and only later to consider his vows.

26A wise king winnows out the wicked;
he drives the threshing wheel over
them.

27The lamp of the LORD searches the
spirit of a man[a];
it searches out his inmost being.

28Love and faithfulness keep a king
safe;
through love his throne is made
secure.

29The glory of young men is their
strength,
gray hair the splendor of the old.

30Blows and wounds cleanse away evil,
and beatings purge the inmost
being.

21 The king's heart is in the hand
of the LORD;
he directs it like a watercourse
wherever he pleases.

2All a man's ways seem right to him,
but the LORD weighs the heart.

3To do what is right and just
is more acceptable to the LORD than
sacrifice.

4Haughty eyes and a proud heart,
the lamp of the wicked, are sin!

5The plans of the diligent lead to
profit
as surely as haste leads to poverty.

6A fortune made by a lying tongue
is a fleeting vapor and a deadly
snare.[b]

7The violence of the wicked will drag
them away,
for they refuse to do what is right.

8The way of the guilty is devious,
but the conduct of the innocent is
upright.

9Better to live on a corner of the roof
than share a house with a
quarrelsome wife.

[a]27 Or *The spirit of man is the LORD's lamp* [b]6 Some Hebrew manuscripts, Septuagint and Vulgate; most Hebrew manuscripts *vapor for those who seek death*

10The wicked man craves evil;
his neighbor gets no mercy from him.

11When a mocker is punished, the simple gain wisdom;
when a wise man is instructed, he gets knowledge.

12The Righteous One[a] takes note of the house of the wicked
and brings the wicked to ruin.

13If a man shuts his ears to the cry of the poor,
he too will cry out and not be answered.

14A gift given in secret soothes anger,
and a bribe concealed in the cloak pacifies great wrath.

15When justice is done, it brings joy to the righteous
but terror to evildoers.

16A man who strays from the path of understanding
comes to rest in the company of the dead.

17He who loves pleasure will become poor;
whoever loves wine and oil will never be rich.

18The wicked become a ransom for the righteous,
and the unfaithful for the upright.

19Better to live in a desert
than with a quarrelsome and ill-tempered wife.

20In the house of the wise are stores of choice food and oil,
but a foolish man devours all he has.

21He who pursues righteousness and love
finds life, prosperity[b] and honor.

22A wise man attacks the city of the mighty
and pulls down the stronghold in which they trust.

23He who guards his mouth and his tongue
keeps himself from calamity.

24The proud and arrogant man—"Mocker" is his name;
he behaves with overweening pride.

25The sluggard's craving will be the death of him,
because his hands refuse to work.

26All day long he craves for more,
but the righteous give without sparing.

27The sacrifice of the wicked is detestable—
how much more so when brought with evil intent!

28A false witness will perish,
and whoever listens to him will be destroyed forever.[c]

29A wicked man puts up a bold front,
but an upright man gives thought to his ways.

30There is no wisdom, no insight, no plan
that can succeed against the LORD.

31The horse is made ready for the day of battle,
but victory rests with the LORD.

22

A good name is more desirable than great riches;
to be esteemed is better than silver or gold.

2Rich and poor have this in common:
The LORD is the Maker of them all.

3A prudent man sees danger and takes refuge,
but the simple keep going and suffer for it.

4Humility and the fear of the LORD
bring wealth and honor and life.

5In the paths of the wicked lie thorns and snares,
but he who guards his soul stays far from them.

6Train[d] a child in the way he should go,
and when he is old he will not turn from it.

7The rich rule over the poor,
and the borrower is servant to the lender.

8He who sows wickedness reaps trouble,
and the rod of his fury will be destroyed.

[a] 12 Or *The righteous man* [b] 21 Or *righteousness* [c] 28 Or */ but the words of an obedient man will live on* [d] 6 Or *Start*

[9]A generous man will himself be
blessed,
for he shares his food with the
poor.

[10]Drive out the mocker, and out goes
strife;
quarrels and insults are ended.

[11]He who loves a pure heart and whose
speech is gracious
will have the king for his friend.

[12]The eyes of the LORD keep watch over
knowledge,
but he frustrates the words of the
unfaithful.

[13]The sluggard says, "There is a lion
outside!"
or, "I will be murdered in the
streets!"

[14]The mouth of an adulteress is a deep
pit;
he who is under the LORD's wrath
will fall into it.

[15]Folly is bound up in the heart of a
child,
but the rod of discipline will drive
it far from him.

[16]He who oppresses the poor to
increase his wealth
and he who gives gifts to the
rich—both come to poverty.

Sayings of the Wise

[17]Pay attention and listen to the
sayings of the wise;
apply your heart to what I teach,
[18]for it is pleasing when you keep them
in your heart
and have all of them ready on your
lips.
[19]So that your trust may be in the LORD,
I teach you today, even you.
[20]Have I not written thirty[a] sayings for
you,
sayings of counsel and knowledge,
[21]teaching you true and reliable words,
so that you can give sound answers
to him who sent you?

[22]Do not exploit the poor because they
are poor
and do not crush the needy in
court,
[23]for the LORD will take up their case
and will plunder those who plunder
them.

[24]Do not make friends with a
hot-tempered man,
do not associate with one easily
angered,
[25]or you may learn his ways
and get yourself ensnared.

[26]Do not be a man who strikes hands in
pledge
or puts up security for debts;
[27]if you lack the means to pay,
your very bed will be snatched from
under you.

[28]Do not move an ancient boundary
stone
set up by your forefathers.

[29]Do you see a man skilled in his work?
He will serve before kings;
he will not serve before obscure
men.

23

When you sit to dine with a
ruler,
note well what[b] is before you,
[2]and put a knife to your throat
if you are given to gluttony.
[3]Do not crave his delicacies,
for that food is deceptive.

[4]Do not wear yourself out to get rich;
have the wisdom to show restraint.
[5]Cast but a glance at riches, and they
are gone,
for they will surely sprout wings
and fly off to the sky like an eagle.

[6]Do not eat the food of a stingy man,
do not crave his delicacies;
[7]for he is the kind of man
who is always thinking about the
cost.[c]
"Eat and drink," he says to you,
but his heart is not with you.
[8]You will vomit up the little you have
eaten
and will have wasted your
compliments.

[9]Do not speak to a fool,
for he will scorn the wisdom of
your words.

[10]Do not move an ancient boundary
stone
or encroach on the fields of the
fatherless,

[a]20 Or *not formerly written*; or *not written excellent* [b]1 Or *who* [c]7 Or *for as he thinks within himself, / so he is*; or *for as he puts on a feast, / so he is*

11for their Defender is strong;
he will take up their case against you.

12Apply your heart to instruction
and your ears to words of knowledge.

13Do not withhold discipline from a child;
if you punish him with the rod, he will not die.
14Punish him with the rod
and save his soul from death.[a]

15My son, if your heart is wise,
then my heart will be glad;
16my inmost being will rejoice
when your lips speak what is right.

17Do not let your heart envy sinners,
but always be zealous for the fear of the LORD.
18There is surely a future hope for you,
and your hope will not be cut off.

19Listen, my son, and be wise,
and keep your heart on the right path.
20Do not join those who drink too much wine
or gorge themselves on meat,
21for drunkards and gluttons become poor,
and drowsiness clothes them in rags.

22Listen to your father, who gave you life,
and do not despise your mother when she is old.
23Buy the truth and do not sell it;
get wisdom, discipline and understanding.
24The father of a righteous man has great joy;
he who has a wise son delights in him.
25May your father and mother be glad;
may she who gave you birth rejoice!

26My son, give me your heart
and let your eyes keep to my ways,
27for a prostitute is a deep pit
and a wayward wife is a narrow well.
28Like a bandit she lies in wait,
and multiplies the unfaithful among men.

29Who has woe? Who has sorrow?
Who has strife? Who has complaints?
Who has needless bruises? Who has bloodshot eyes?
30Those who linger over wine,
who go to sample bowls of mixed wine.
31Do not gaze at wine when it is red,
when it sparkles in the cup,
when it goes down smoothly!
32In the end it bites like a snake
and poisons like a viper.
33Your eyes will see strange sights
and your mind imagine confusing things.
34You will be like one sleeping on the high seas,
lying on top of the rigging.
35"They hit me," you will say, "but I'm not hurt!
They beat me, but I don't feel it!
When will I wake up
so I can find another drink?"

24 Do not envy wicked men,
do not desire their company;
2for their hearts plot violence,
and their lips talk about making trouble.

3By wisdom a house is built,
and through understanding it is established;
4through knowledge its rooms are filled
with rare and beautiful treasures.

5A wise man has great power,
and a man of knowledge increases strength;
6for waging war you need guidance,
and for victory many advisers.

7Wisdom is too high for a fool;
in the assembly at the gate he has nothing to say.

8He who plots evil
will be known as a schemer.
9The schemes of folly are sin,
and men detest a mocker.

10If you falter in times of trouble,
how small is your strength!

11Rescue those being led away to death;
hold back those staggering toward slaughter.
12If you say, "But we knew nothing about this,"

[a]*14* Hebrew *Sheol*

does not he who weighs the heart
perceive it?
Does not he who guards your life
know it?
Will he not repay each person
according to what he has done?

13Eat honey, my son, for it is good;
honey from the comb is sweet to
your taste.
14Know also that wisdom is sweet to
your soul;
if you find it, there is a future hope
for you,
and your hope will not be cut off.

15Do not lie in wait like an outlaw
against a righteous man's
house,
do not raid his dwelling place;
16for though a righteous man falls seven
times, he rises again,
but the wicked are brought down
by calamity.

WEDNESDAY

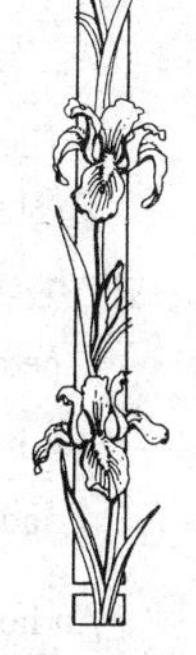

VERSE FOR THE DAY: *Proverbs 23:25*
AUTHOR: *Shirley Dobson*
PASSAGE FOR THE DAY: *Proverbs 23:17–25*

Sunshine of My Life

THE gift was not one that you would expect to receive from an eight-year-old boy. He had bought me a lovely desk set. The ostrich-feathered white pen looked like an old fashioned quill that Ben Franklin might have used to sign the Declaration of Independence. The stand was padded in matching white, with a spray of pink flowers delicately painted around the edges. I was so touched that my eyes brimmed with tears as I hugged and thanked my son for such an extravagant gift. It has been five years since that day and the pen still sits on the nightstand near my bed as a reminder of Ryan's spontaneous gift of love.

There are times in our lives when the cost of parenting seems staggeringly high! No matter how you look at it, children are emotionally exhausting, time-consuming, sometimes frustrating, and always maddeningly complex. In fact, their developmental years are governed entirely by "Murphy's Law." For example, if they drop a slice of bread on the carpet, it will inevitably land buttered side down. And when they catch the flu, they never vomit in the bathroom. They turn up their noses at their oatmeal and gag at the sight of their eggs, but enthusiastically drink the dog's water and float their rubber duckies in the toilet. I'm sure you could add to this list of childhood "Murphyisms."

But in moments when you are touched by the soul of a child, as I was through Ryan's act of love, you suddenly realize the eternal significance of these precious years. Then, no other task on earth seems quite as important or meaningful as raising and training and guiding him through his developmental experiences.

Additional Scripture Readings:
2 Kings 4:1–7; Luke 2:51–52

Go to page 549 for your next devotional reading.

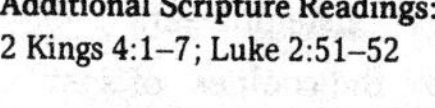

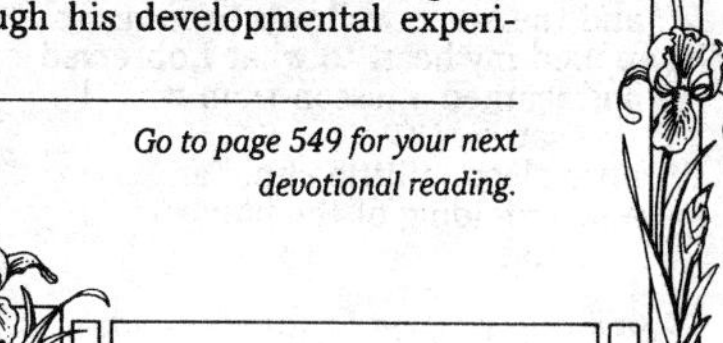

[17]Do not gloat when your enemy falls;
when he stumbles, do not let your heart rejoice,
[18]or the LORD will see and disapprove
and turn his wrath away from him.

[19]Do not fret because of evil men
or be envious of the wicked,
[20]for the evil man has no future hope,
and the lamp of the wicked will be snuffed out.

[21]Fear the LORD and the king, my son,
and do not join with the rebellious,
[22]for those two will send sudden destruction upon them,
and who knows what calamities they can bring?

Further Sayings of the Wise

[23]These also are sayings of the wise:

To show partiality in judging is not good:
[24]Whoever says to the guilty, "You are innocent"—
peoples will curse him and nations denounce him.
[25]But it will go well with those who convict the guilty,
and rich blessing will come upon them.

[26]An honest answer
is like a kiss on the lips.

[27]Finish your outdoor work
and get your fields ready;
after that, build your house.

[28]Do not testify against your neighbor without cause,
or use your lips to deceive.
[29]Do not say, "I'll do to him as he has done to me;
I'll pay that man back for what he did."

[30]I went past the field of the sluggard,
past the vineyard of the man who lacks judgment;
[31]thorns had come up everywhere,
the ground was covered with weeds,
and the stone wall was in ruins.
[32]I applied my heart to what I observed
and learned a lesson from what I saw:
[33]A little sleep, a little slumber,
a little folding of the hands to rest—
[34]and poverty will come on you like a bandit
and scarcity like an armed man.[a]

More Proverbs of Solomon

25 These are more proverbs of Solomon, copied by the men of Hezekiah king of Judah:

[2]It is the glory of God to conceal a matter;
to search out a matter is the glory of kings.

[3]As the heavens are high and the earth is deep,
so the hearts of kings are unsearchable.

[4]Remove the dross from the silver,
and out comes material for[b] the silversmith;
[5]remove the wicked from the king's presence,
and his throne will be established through righteousness.

[6]Do not exalt yourself in the king's presence,
and do not claim a place among great men;
[7]it is better for him to say to you, "Come up here,"
than for him to humiliate you before a nobleman.

What you have seen with your eyes
[8] do not bring[c] hastily to court,
for what will you do in the end
if your neighbor puts you to shame?

[9]If you argue your case with a neighbor,
do not betray another man's confidence,
[10]or he who hears it may shame you
and you will never lose your bad reputation.

[11]A word aptly spoken
is like apples of gold in settings of silver.

[12]Like an earring of gold or an ornament of fine gold
is a wise man's rebuke to a listening ear.

[13]Like the coolness of snow at harvest time

[a]34 Or *like a vagrant / and scarcity like a beggar* [b]4 Or *comes a vessel from* [c]7,8 Or *nobleman / on whom you had set your eyes. / [8]Do not go*

is a trustworthy messenger to those
who send him;
he refreshes the spirit of his
masters.
14Like clouds and wind without rain
is a man who boasts of gifts he
does not give.

15Through patience a ruler can be
persuaded,
and a gentle tongue can break a
bone.

16If you find honey, eat just enough—
too much of it, and you will vomit.
17Seldom set foot in your neighbor's
house—
too much of you, and he will hate
you.

18Like a club or a sword or a sharp
arrow
is the man who gives false
testimony against his neighbor.

19Like a bad tooth or a lame foot
is reliance on the unfaithful in
times of trouble.

20Like one who takes away a garment
on a cold day,
or like vinegar poured on soda,
is one who sings songs to a heavy
heart.

21If your enemy is hungry, give him
food to eat;
if he is thirsty, give him water to
drink.
22In doing this, you will heap burning
coals on his head,
and the LORD will reward you.

23As a north wind brings rain,
so a sly tongue brings angry looks.

24Better to live on a corner of the roof
than share a house with a
quarrelsome wife.

25Like cold water to a weary soul
is good news from a distant land.

26Like a muddied spring or a polluted
well
is a righteous man who gives way to
the wicked.

27It is not good to eat too much honey,
nor is it honorable to seek one's
own honor.

28Like a city whose walls are broken
down
is a man who lacks self-control.

26 Like snow in summer or rain in
harvest,
honor is not fitting for a fool.

2Like a fluttering sparrow or a darting
swallow,
an undeserved curse does not come
to rest.

3A whip for the horse, a halter for the
donkey,
and a rod for the backs of fools!

4Do not answer a fool according to his
folly,
or you will be like him yourself.

5Answer a fool according to his folly,
or he will be wise in his own eyes.

6Like cutting off one's feet or drinking
violence
is the sending of a message by the
hand of a fool.

7Like a lame man's legs that hang
limp
is a proverb in the mouth of a fool.
8Like tying a stone in a sling
is the giving of honor to a fool.

9Like a thornbush in a drunkard's
hand
is a proverb in the mouth of a fool.

10Like an archer who wounds at
random
is he who hires a fool or any
passer-by.

11As a dog returns to its vomit,
so a fool repeats his folly.

12Do you see a man wise in his own
eyes?
There is more hope for a fool than
for him.

13The sluggard says, "There is a lion in
the road,
a fierce lion roaming the streets!"

14As a door turns on its hinges,
so a sluggard turns on his bed.

15The sluggard buries his hand in the
dish;
he is too lazy to bring it back to his
mouth.

16The sluggard is wiser in his own eyes
than seven men who answer
discreetly.

17Like one who seizes a dog by the ears
is a passer-by who meddles in a
quarrel not his own.

[18]Like a madman shooting
firebrands or deadly arrows
[19]is a man who deceives his neighbor
and says, "I was only joking!"

[20]Without wood a fire goes out;
without gossip a quarrel dies down.

[21]As charcoal to embers and as wood to fire,
so is a quarrelsome man for kindling strife.

[22]The words of a gossip are like choice morsels;
they go down to a man's inmost parts.

[23]Like a coating of glaze[a] over earthenware
are fervent lips with an evil heart.

[24]A malicious man disguises himself with his lips,
but in his heart he harbors deceit.
[25]Though his speech is charming, do not believe him,
for seven abominations fill his heart.
[26]His malice may be concealed by deception,
but his wickedness will be exposed in the assembly.

[27]If a man digs a pit, he will fall into it;
if a man rolls a stone, it will roll back on him.

[28]A lying tongue hates those it hurts,
and a flattering mouth works ruin.

27 Do not boast about tomorrow,
for you do not know what a day may bring forth.

[2]Let another praise you, and not your own mouth;
someone else, and not your own lips.

[3]Stone is heavy and sand a burden,
but provocation by a fool is heavier than both.

[4]Anger is cruel and fury overwhelming,
but who can stand before jealousy?

[5]Better is open rebuke
than hidden love.

[6]Wounds from a friend can be trusted,
but an enemy multiplies kisses.

[7]He who is full loathes honey,
but to the hungry even what is bitter tastes sweet.

[8]Like a bird that strays from its nest
is a man who strays from his home.

[9]Perfume and incense bring joy to the heart,
and the pleasantness of one's friend springs from his earnest counsel.

[10]Do not forsake your friend and the friend of your father,
and do not go to your brother's house when disaster strikes you—
better a neighbor nearby than a brother far away.

[11]Be wise, my son, and bring joy to my heart;
then I can answer anyone who treats me with contempt.

[12]The prudent see danger and take refuge,
but the simple keep going and suffer for it.

[13]Take the garment of one who puts up security for a stranger;
hold it in pledge if he does it for a wayward woman.

[14]If a man loudly blesses his neighbor early in the morning,
it will be taken as a curse.

[15]A quarrelsome wife is like
a constant dripping on a rainy day;
[16]restraining her is like restraining the wind
or grasping oil with the hand.

[17]As iron sharpens iron,
so one man sharpens another.

[18]He who tends a fig tree will eat its fruit,
and he who looks after his master will be honored.

[19]As water reflects a face,
so a man's heart reflects the man.

[20]Death and Destruction[b] are never satisfied,
and neither are the eyes of man.

[21]The crucible for silver and the furnace for gold,

[a]23 With a different word division of the Hebrew; Masoretic Text *of silver dross* [b]20 Hebrew *Sheol and Abaddon*

but man is tested by the praise he
receives.

22Though you grind a fool in a mortar,
grinding him like grain with a
pestle,
you will not remove his folly from
him.

23Be sure you know the condition of
your flocks,
give careful attention to your herds;
24for riches do not endure forever,
and a crown is not secure for all
generations.
25When the hay is removed and new
growth appears
and the grass from the hills is
gathered in,
26the lambs will provide you with
clothing,
and the goats with the price of a
field.
27You will have plenty of goats' milk
to feed you and your family
and to nourish your servant girls.

28 The wicked man flees though no
one pursues,
but the righteous are as bold as a
lion.

2When a country is rebellious, it has
many rulers,
but a man of understanding and
knowledge maintains order.

3A ruler[a] who oppresses the poor
is like a driving rain that leaves no
crops.

4Those who forsake the law praise the
wicked,
but those who keep the law resist
them.

5Evil men do not understand justice,
but those who seek the LORD
understand it fully.

6Better a poor man whose walk is
blameless
than a rich man whose ways are
perverse.

7He who keeps the law is a discerning
son,
but a companion of gluttons
disgraces his father.

8He who increases his wealth by
exorbitant interest
amasses it for another, who will be
kind to the poor.

9If anyone turns a deaf ear to the law,
even his prayers are detestable.

10He who leads the upright along an
evil path
will fall into his own trap,
but the blameless will receive a
good inheritance.

11A rich man may be wise in his own
eyes,
but a poor man who has
discernment sees through him.

12When the righteous triumph, there is
great elation;
but when the wicked rise to power,
men go into hiding.

13He who conceals his sins does not
prosper,
but whoever confesses and
renounces them finds mercy.

14Blessed is the man who always fears
the LORD,
but he who hardens his heart falls
into trouble.

15Like a roaring lion or a charging bear
is a wicked man ruling over a
helpless people.

16A tyrannical ruler lacks judgment,
but he who hates ill-gotten gain
will enjoy a long life.

17A man tormented by the guilt of
murder
will be a fugitive till death;
let no one support him.

18He whose walk is blameless is kept
safe,
but he whose ways are perverse will
suddenly fall.

19He who works his land will have
abundant food,
but the one who chases fantasies
will have his fill of poverty.

20A faithful man will be richly blessed,
but one eager to get rich will not
go unpunished.

21To show partiality is not good—
yet a man will do wrong for a piece
of bread.

22A stingy man is eager to get rich

[a]3 Or *A poor man*

and is unaware that poverty awaits
him.

23He who rebukes a man will in the
end gain more favor
than he who has a flattering
tongue.

24He who robs his father or mother
and says, "It's not wrong"—
he is partner to him who destroys.

25A greedy man stirs up dissension,
but he who trusts in the LORD will
prosper.

26He who trusts in himself is a fool,
but he who walks in wisdom is kept
safe.

27He who gives to the poor will lack
nothing,
but he who closes his eyes to them
receives many curses.

28When the wicked rise to power,
people go into hiding;
but when the wicked perish, the
righteous thrive.

29 A man who remains stiff-necked
after many rebukes
will suddenly be
destroyed—without remedy.

2When the righteous thrive, the people
rejoice;
when the wicked rule, the people
groan.

3A man who loves wisdom brings joy
to his father,
but a companion of prostitutes
squanders his wealth.

4By justice a king gives a country
stability,
but one who is greedy for bribes
tears it down.

5Whoever flatters his neighbor
is spreading a net for his feet.

6An evil man is snared by his own sin,
but a righteous one can sing and be
glad.

7The righteous care about justice for
the poor,
but the wicked have no such
concern.

8Mockers stir up a city,
but wise men turn away anger.

9If a wise man goes to court with a
fool,
the fool rages and scoffs, and there
is no peace.

10Bloodthirsty men hate a man of
integrity
and seek to kill the upright.

11A fool gives full vent to his anger,
but a wise man keeps himself
under control.

12If a ruler listens to lies,
all his officials become wicked.

13The poor man and the oppressor have
this in common:
The LORD gives sight to the eyes of
both.

14If a king judges the poor with
fairness,
his throne will always be secure.

15The rod of correction imparts wisdom,
but a child left to himself disgraces
his mother.

16When the wicked thrive, so does sin,
but the righteous will see their
downfall.

17Discipline your son, and he will give
you peace;
he will bring delight to your soul.

18Where there is no revelation, the
people cast off restraint;
but blessed is he who keeps the
law.

19A servant cannot be corrected by
mere words;
though he understands, he will not
respond.

20Do you see a man who speaks in
haste?
There is more hope for a fool than
for him.

21If a man pampers his servant from
youth,
he will bring grief[a] in the end.

22An angry man stirs up dissension,
and a hot-tempered one commits
many sins.

23A man's pride brings him low,
but a man of lowly spirit gains
honor.

[a]*21* The meaning of the Hebrew for this word is uncertain.

[24]The accomplice of a thief is his own
enemy;
he is put under oath and dare not
testify.

[25]Fear of man will prove to be a snare,
but whoever trusts in the LORD is
kept safe.

[26]Many seek an audience with a ruler,
but it is from the LORD that man
gets justice.

[27]The righteous detest the dishonest;
the wicked detest the upright.

Sayings of Agur

30 The sayings of Agur son of Jakeh—an oracle[a]:

This man declared to Ithiel,
to Ithiel and to Ucal:[b]

[2]"I am the most ignorant of men;
I do not have a man's
understanding.
[3]I have not learned wisdom,
nor have I knowledge of the Holy
One.
[4]Who has gone up to heaven and come
down?
Who has gathered up the wind in
the hollow of his hands?
Who has wrapped up the waters in his
cloak?
Who has established all the ends of
the earth?
What is his name, and the name of
his son?
Tell me if you know!

[5]"Every word of God is flawless;
he is a shield to those who take
refuge in him.
[6]Do not add to his words,
or he will rebuke you and prove you
a liar.

[7]"Two things I ask of you, O LORD;
do not refuse me before I die:
[8]Keep falsehood and lies far from me;
give me neither poverty nor riches,
but give me only my daily bread.
[9]Otherwise, I may have too much and
disown you
and say, 'Who is the LORD?'
Or I may become poor and steal,
and so dishonor the name of my
God.

[10]"Do not slander a servant to his
master,
or he will curse you, and you will
pay for it.

[11]"There are those who curse their
fathers
and do not bless their mothers;
[12]those who are pure in their own eyes
and yet are not cleansed of their
filth;
[13]those whose eyes are ever so haughty,
whose glances are so disdainful;
[14]those whose teeth are swords
and whose jaws are set with knives
to devour the poor from the earth,
the needy from among mankind.

[15]"The leech has two daughters.
'Give! Give!' they cry.

"There are three things that are never
satisfied,
four that never say, 'Enough!':
[16]the grave,[c] the barren womb,
land, which is never satisfied with
water,
and fire, which never says,
'Enough!'

[17]"The eye that mocks a father,
that scorns obedience to a mother,
will be pecked out by the ravens of
the valley,
will be eaten by the vultures.

[18]"There are three things that are too
amazing for me,
four that I do not understand:
[19]the way of an eagle in the sky,
the way of a snake on a rock,
the way of a ship on the high seas,
and the way of a man with a
maiden.

[20]"This is the way of an adulteress:
She eats and wipes her mouth
and says, 'I've done nothing wrong.'

[21]"Under three things the earth
trembles,
under four it cannot bear up:
[22]a servant who becomes king,
a fool who is full of food,
[23]an unloved woman who is married,
and a maidservant who displaces
her mistress.

[24]"Four things on earth are small,
yet they are extremely wise:
[25]Ants are creatures of little strength,

[a]1 Or *Jakeh of Massa* [b]1 Masoretic Text; with a different word division of the Hebrew *declared, "I am weary, O God; / I am weary, O God, and faint.* [c]16 Hebrew *Sheol*

yet they store up their food in the
summer;
26coneys[a] are creatures of little power,
yet they make their home in the
crags;
27locusts have no king,
yet they advance together in ranks;
28a lizard can be caught with the hand,
yet it is found in kings' palaces.

29"There are three things that are
stately in their stride,
four that move with stately bearing:
30a lion, mighty among beasts,
who retreats before nothing;
31a strutting rooster, a he-goat,
and a king with his army around
him.[b]

32"If you have played the fool and
exalted yourself,
or if you have planned evil,
clap your hand over your mouth!
33For as churning the milk produces
butter,
and as twisting the nose produces
blood,
so stirring up anger produces
strife."

Sayings of King Lemuel

31 The sayings of King Lemuel—an oracle[c] his mother taught him:

2"O my son, O son of my womb,
O son of my vows,[d]
3do not spend your strength on
women,
your vigor on those who ruin kings.

4"It is not for kings, O Lemuel—
not for kings to drink wine,
not for rulers to crave beer,
5lest they drink and forget what the
law decrees,
and deprive all the oppressed of
their rights.
6Give beer to those who are perishing,
wine to those who are in anguish;
7let them drink and forget their
poverty
and remember their misery no
more.

8"Speak up for those who cannot
speak for themselves,
for the rights of all who are
destitute.
9Speak up and judge fairly;
defend the rights of the poor and
needy."

Epilogue: The Wife of Noble Character

10[e]A wife of noble character who can
find?
She is worth far more than rubies.
11Her husband has full confidence in
her
and lacks nothing of value.
12She brings him good, not harm,
all the days of her life.
13She selects wool and flax
and works with eager hands.
14She is like the merchant ships,
bringing her food from afar.
15She gets up while it is still dark;
she provides food for her family
and portions for her servant girls.
16She considers a field and buys it;
out of her earnings she plants a
vineyard.
17She sets about her work vigorously;
her arms are strong for her tasks.
18She sees that her trading is profitable,
and her lamp does not go out at
night.
19In her hand she holds the distaff
and grasps the spindle with her
fingers.
20She opens her arms to the poor
and extends her hands to the
needy.
21When it snows, she has no fear for
her household;
for all of them are clothed in
scarlet.
22She makes coverings for her bed;
she is clothed in fine linen and
purple.
23Her husband is respected at the city
gate,
where he takes his seat among the
elders of the land.
24She makes linen garments and sells
them,
and supplies the merchants with
sashes.
25She is clothed with strength and
dignity;
she can laugh at the days to
come.
26She speaks with wisdom,

[a]*26* That is, the hyrax or rock badger [b]*31* Or *king secure against revolt* [c]*1* Or *of Lemuel king of Massa, which* [d]*2* Or */ the answer to my prayers* [e]*10* Verses 10-31 are an acrostic, each verse beginning with a successive letter of the Hebrew alphabet.

THURSDAY

VERSE FOR THE DAY:
Proverbs 31:30–31

AUTHOR:
Dorothy Patterson

PASSAGE FOR THE DAY:
Proverbs 31:10–31

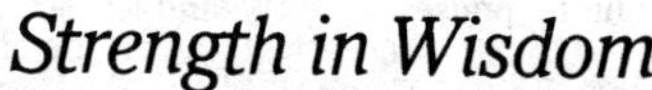

Strength in Wisdom

THE Sabbath service in the Jewish home unashamedly reveals the high position of women in Israel from Biblical times until the present. Sabbath is primarily a home-centered, family celebration, which makes it only natural that the mother of the home receive the honor of welcoming the Sabbath by lighting of the candles. Traditionally, the husband recites what is without doubt the most eloquent tribute to a godly woman that has ever been penned.*

Proverbs 31:10–31 presents the divine challenge for womanhood—diligent homemaker, valuable helper, nurturing mother, upright and God-fearing woman. The "wife of noble character" receives a reward for faithfulness because she is not dependent on the temporary, superficial, deceptive façade of "charm," which is a mere outward varnish easily scarred and marred by people and circumstances, and "beauty," which can depart like an unfaithful friend to make room for wrinkles and blemishes. Rather she crowns an enduring, satisfying fear of the Lord with a reverent and obedient spirit that makes her worthy of praise and honor from her family and the Creator himself (Proverbs 31:30).

Homemaking is unique in combining the most menial jobs with the most meaningful tasks: it is a challenge to accommodate others without losing one's own identity: it is a demanding pursuit, but the fringe benefits are terrific!

William Booth, the founder of the Salvation Army, gave this glowing tribute of his wife Catherine at the time of her death:

> To me she has been made of God, never-failing sympathy, reliable wisdom, and unvarnished truth—in short, all that is noble and good; and consequently a tower of strength, a mine of wealth, and an everflowing fountain of comfort and joy.†

With "undistracted devotion to the Lord" Catherine Booth was a woman to be praised because she feared the Lord.

Additional Scripture Readings:
Genesis 2:18–24; Luke 1:39–49

Go to page 550 for your next devotional reading.

*Hyman E. Goldin, *The Jewish Woman and Her Home*, New York: Hebrew Publishing Company, 1941, pp. 124-131.
†. T. Stead, *Catherine Booth,* Oakville, Canada: Triumph Press, pp. 119, 120-121.

and faithful instruction is on her
tongue.
27She watches over the affairs of her
household
and does not eat the bread of
idleness.
28Her children arise and call her
blessed;
her husband also, and he praises
her:
29"Many women do noble things,
but you surpass them all."
30Charm is deceptive, and beauty is
fleeting;
but a woman who fears the LORD is
to be praised.
31Give her the reward she has
earned,
and let her works bring her praise
at the city gate.

FRIDAY

VERSE FOR THE DAY: *Proverbs 31:31*

AUTHOR: *Marlene Obie*

PASSAGE FOR THE DAY: *Proverbs 31:25–31*

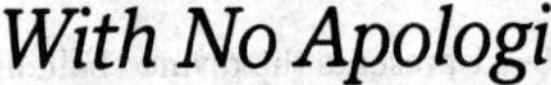

With No Apologies

SHOULD I apologize for liking my career, Lord?

I've had inklings that I'm expected to dislike working. Some women pity me because my house and yard resemble a junk shop and I can't attend the neighborhood coffees and luncheons. They shake their heads at my time-clock schedule. They think I couldn't possibly enjoy such an existence.

Sure, I have days when everything goes wrong and I question whether this is a calling or a sentence in a forced labor camp. However, when the boss is grumpy, customers are unreasonable and auditors are looking over my shoulder, I remember comparable days when I worked solely at home. Those days were not without disasters, interruptions and stresses.

Thank you for showing me the joys of each of the different businesses I've worked in. I especially appreciate the way I'm treated by my peers. (My family would be surprised to know that I'm respected at the office.) Requests for my assistance are made politely and are addressed to my given name. I feel like a member of a team and not a quarterback without anyone to pass to.

No, I won't apologize for liking my careers. I feel my work as a wife, a mother, a homemaker, a writer, and a secretary are all important.

Lord, thank you for giving me gifts to use in these various capacities. What I have I must use, and no matter what anyone else thinks, I won't apologize. I like who I am and what I do at least ninety percent of the time.

Additional Scripture Readings:
Judges 4:4–10; 1 Thessalonians 4:11–12

Go to page 5 for your next devotional reading.

INDEXES
READING PLANS

WEIGHTS & MEASURES

The figures of the table are calculated on the basis of a shekel equaling 11.5 grams, a cubit equaling 18 inches and an ephah equaling 22 liters. The quart referred to is either a dry quart (slightly larger than a liter) or a liquid quart (slightly smaller than a liter), whichever is applicable. The ton referred to in the footnotes is the American ton of 2,000 pounds.

This table is based upon the best available information, but it is not intended to be mathematically precise; like the measurement equivalents in the footnotes, it merely gives approximate amounts and distances. Weights and measures differed somewhat at various times and places in the ancient world. There is uncertainty particularly about the ephah and the bath; further discoveries may give more light on these units of capacity.

	BIBLICAL UNIT		APPROXIMATE AMERICAN EQUIVALENT	APPROXIMATE METRIC EQUIVALENT
WEIGHTS	talent	*(60 minas)*	75 pounds	34 kilograms
	mina	*(50 shekels)*	1 1/4 pounds	0.6 kilogram
	shekel	*(2 bekas)*	2/5 ounce	11.5 grams
	pim	*(2/3 shekel)*	1/3 ounce	7.6 grams
	beka	*(10 gerahs)*	1/5 ounce	5.5 grams
	gerah		1/50 ounce	0.6 gram
LENGTH	cubit		18 inches	0.5 meter
	span		9 inches	23 centimeters
	handbreadth		3 inches	8 centimeters
CAPACITY	cor [homer]	*(10 ephahs)*	6 bushels	220 liters
Dry Measure	lethek	*(5 ephahs)*	3 bushels	110 liters
	ephah	*(10 omers)*	3/5 bushel	22 liters
	seah	*(1/3 ephah)*	7 quarts	7.3 liters
	omer	*(1/10 ephah)*	2 quarts	2 liters
	cab	*(1/18 ephah)*	1 quart	1 liter
Liquid Measure	bath	*(1 ephah)*	6 gallons	22 liters
	hin	*(1/6 bath)*	4 quarts	4 liters
	log	*(1/72 bath)*	1/3 quart	0.3 liter

ACKNOWLEDGMENTS INDEX

Page 5: Taken from WOMEN IN GOD'S PRESENCE compiled by Delores Taylor. Copyright © 1988 by Christian Publications, Camphill, PA. Used by permission.

Page 8: By Beth Donigan Seversen. Copyright © 1990 by The Zondervan Corporation.

Page 12: Reprinted with permission from Daily Guideposts 1987. Copyright © 1986 by Guideposts Associates, Inc., Carmel, NY 10512.

Page 14: By Jill Briscoe. Copyright © 1990 by The Zondervan Corporation.

Page 16: Taken from COME TO THE WATERS by Diane Head. Copyright © 1985 by Diane Head. Published by Zondervan Publishing House. Used by permission.

Page 20: Taken from SITTING BY MY LAUGHING FIRE by Ruth Bell Graham. Copyright © 1977 by Ruth Bell Graham. Published by Word, Inc., Irving, TX. Used by permission.

Page 24: Taken from A CLOSER WALK by Catherine Marshall. Copyright © 1986 by Calen, Inc. Published by Chosen Books, Fleming H. Revell Company. Used by permission.

Page 26: By Rosalind Rinker. Copyright © 1990 by The Zondervan Corporation.

Page 35: By Hope MacDonald. Copyright © 1990 by The Zondervan Corporation.

Page 37: By Sue Richards. Copyright © 1990 by The Zondervan Corporation.

Page 39: By Carol L. Baldwin. Copyright © 1990 by The Zondervan Corporation.

Page 41: Taken from EXPERIENCE GOD'S FORGIVENESS by Luis Palau. Copyright © 1984 by Multnomah Press. Used by permission.

Page 43: Taken from LISTENING TO GOD by Janice Kempe. Copyright © 1985 by The Zondervan Corporation. Used by permission.

Page 47: By Jill Briscoe. Copyright © 1990 by The Zondervan Corporation.

Page 52: By Wanda K. Jones. Copyright © 1990 by The Zondervan Corporation.

Page 55: From the book ON ASKING GOD WHY by Elisabeth Elliot. Copyright © (1898) by Fleming H. Revell. Used by permission of Fleming H. Revell Company.

Page 60: From the book PASSION AND PURITY by Elisabeth Elliot. Copyright © (1984) by Fleming H. Revell. Used by permission of Fleming H. Revell Company.

Page 62: By Rosalind Rinker. Copyright © 1990 by The Zondervan Corporation.

Page 64: By Ruth A. Tucker. Copyright © 1990 by The Zondervan Corporation.

Page 66: By Hope MacDonald. Copyright © 1990 by The Zondervan Corporation.

Page 72: By Anne Ortlund. Copyright © 1968 by Anne Ortlund. Used by permission.

Page 76: By Anne Ortlund. Copyright © 1982 by Anne Ortlund. Used by permission.

Page 78: Excerpt from GIVE US THIS DAY OUR DAILY BREAD by Colleen Townsend Evans, copyright © (1981) by Colleen Townsend Evans and Laura Hobe. Used by permission of Doubleday, a division of Bantam, Doubleday, Dell Publishing Group, Inc.

Page 81: By Rosemary Jensen. Copyright © 1990 by The Zondervan Corporation.

Page 85: Taken from A VIOLENT GRACE by Gini Andrews. Copyright © 1986 by Gini Andrews. Used by permission of Zondervan Publishing House.

Page 93: Taken from RISE AND SHINE by Alma Barkman. Copyright © 1987. Moody Bible Institute of Chicago. Moody Press. Used by permission.

Page 95: By Jill Briscoe. Copyright © 1990 by The Zondervan Corporation.

Page 97: Taken from THE QUIET HEART by June Masters Bacher. Copyright © 1988 by Harvest House Publishers, Eugene, OR 97402. Used by permission.

Page 100: Taken from STARTLED BY SILENCE by Ruth Senter. Copyright © 1987 by Ruth Senter. Used by permission of Zondervan Publishing House.

Page 102: By Jill Briscoe. Copyright © 1990 by The Zondervan Corporation.

Page 104: By Joni Eareckson Tada. Copyright © 1990 by The Zondervan Corporation.

Page 106: By Rosalind Rinker. Copyright © 1990 by The Zondervan Corporation.

Page 110: From the book EACH NEW DAY by Corrie ten Boom. Copyright © 1977 by Corrie ten Boom. Used by permission of Fleming H. Revell Company.

Page 113: By Jill Briscoe. Copyright © 1990 by The Zondervan Corporation.

Page 115: Copyright © 1987, CRC Publications, a Ministry of the Christian Reformed Church. Reprinted from *The Banner* (April 6, 1987) with permission.

Page 117: From the book WITH MY WHOLE HEART by Karen Burton Mains. Copyright © 1987 by Multnomah Press. Published by Multnomah Press, Portland, Oregon 97266. Used by permission.

Page 119: Taken from A WOMAN'S CHOICE by Eugenia Price. Copyright © 1962 by Eugenia Price. Published by Zondervan Bible Publishers. Used by permission.

Page 124: By Rosemary Jensen. Copyright © 1990 by The Zondervan Corporation.

Page 127: Taken from MEMORIES by Kathryn Hillen. Copyright © 1987 by Kathryn Hillen. Used by permission of Zondervan Publishing House.

Page 129: By Jill Briscoe. Copyright © 1990 by The Zondervan Corporation.

Page 131: Taken from Luke 1:46–50.

Page 132: Taken from BE STILL AND KNOW by Millie Stamm. Copyright © 1978 by Millie Stamm. Used by permission of Zondervan Publishing House.

Page 135: By Rosalind Rinker. Copyright © 1990 by The Zondervan Corporation.

Page 145: By Gloria Gaither. Copyright © 1990 by Gloria Gaither.

Page 147: By Carol L. Baldwin. Copyright © 1990 by The Zondervan Corporation.

Page 148: Taken from KINDRED SPIRITS by Kathy Narramore and Alice Hill. Copyright © 1985 by The Zondervan Corporation. Used by permission.

Page 149: Copyright © 1987, CRC Publications, a Ministry of the Christian Reformed Church. Reprinted from *The Banner* (May 18, 1987) with permission.

Page 151: By Sue Richards. Copyright © 1990 by The Zondervan Corporation.

Page 153: By Anne Ortlund. Copyright © 1990 by The Zondervan Corporation.

Page 157: By Ruth A.Tucker. Copyright © 1990 by The Zondervan Corporation.

Page 161: Taken from OUT OF THE SALTSHAKER AND INTO THE WORLD by Rebecca Manley Pippert. Copyright © 1979 by InterVarsity Christian Fellowship of the USA. Used by permission of InterVarsity Press, P.O. Box 1400, Downers Grove, IL 60515.

Page 165: Reprinted with permission from Daily Guideposts 1987. Copyright © 1986 by Guideposts Associates, Inc., Carmel, NY 10512.

Page 167: Taken from MY LIFE FOR THE POOR by Mother Teresa of Calcutta. Copyright © 1985 by Jose Gonzalez-Balado and Janet N. Playfoot. Published by Harper & Row, Publishers, Inc. Used by permission.

Page 169: By June Gunden. Copyright © 1990 by The Zondervan Corporation.

Page 174: By Jean Syswerda. Copyright © 1990 by The Zondervan Corporation.

Page 177: Taken from A MOMENT A DAY, compiled by Mary Beckwith and Kathi Mills. Copyright © 1988 by Mary Beckwith and Kathi Mills. Published by Regal Books, Ventura, CA 93006. Used by permission.

Page 182: Taken from THE QUIET HEART by June Masters Bacher. Copyright © 1988 by Harvest House Publishers, Eugene, OR 97402. Used by permission.

Page 185: Taken from QUIET MOMENTS by June Masters Bacher. Copyright © 1979 by Harvest House Publishers, Eugene, OR 97402. Used by permission.

Page 186: Taken from IT'S MY TURN by Ruth Bell Graham. Copyright © 1989 by Ruth Bell Graham. Published by Fleming H. Revell Company. Used by permission.

Page 188: Taken from A MOMENT A DAY, compiled by Mary Beckwith and Kathi Mills. Copyright © 1988 by Mary Beckwith and Kathi Mills. Published by Regal Books, Ventura, CA 93006. Used by permission.

Page 193: Reprinted with permission from Daily Guideposts 1987. Copyright © 1986 by Guideposts Associates, Inc., Carmel, NY 10512.

Page 204: By Carol L. Baldwin. Copyright © 1990 by The Zondervan Corporation.

Page 207: By Gladys M. Hunt. Copyright © 1990 by The Zondervan Corporation.

Page 209: By Gladys M. Hunt. Copyright © 1990 by The Zondervan Corporation.

Page 211: Taken from THE WOMAN AT THE WELL by Dale Evans Rogers. Copyright © (1970) Fleming H. Revell. Used by permission of Fleming H. Revell.

Page 212: From SALT IN MY KITCHEN by Jeannette Lockerbie. Copyright © 1967. Moody Bible Institute of Chicago. Moody Press. Used by permission.

Page 214: By Sue Richards. Copyright © 1990 by The Zondervan Corporation.

Page 216: By Ann Kiemel Anderson. Copyright © 1990 by The Zondervan Corporation.

Page 219: By Marie Chapian. Copyright © 1990 by The Zondervan Corporation.

Page 221: Taken from SINCERELY by Gigi Graham Tchividjian. Copyright © 1984 by The Zondervan Corporation. Used by permission.

Page 223: Taken from THE SPIRITUALITY OF GENTLENESS: GROWING TOWARD CHRISTIAN WHOLENESS by Judith C. Lechman. Copyright © 1987 by Judith C. Lechman. Published by Harper & Row Publishers, Inc. Used by permission.

Page 229: By June Hunt. Copyright © 1990 by June Hunt.

Page 231: Taken from OUT OF THE SALTSHAKER AND INTO THE WORLD by Rebecca Manley Pippert. Copyright © 1979 by InterVarsity Christian Fellowship of the USA. Used by permission of InterVarsity Press, P.O. Box 1400, Downers Grove, IL 60515.

Page 232: Taken from A SILVER PEN FOR CLOUDY DAYS by Susan L. Lenzkes. Copyright © 1987 by Susan L. Lenzkes. Used by permission of Zondervan Publishing House.

Page 236: By June Hunt. Copyright © 1990 by June Hunt.

Page 238: Taken from RISE AND SHINE by Alma Barkman. Copyright © 1987. Moody Bible Institute of Chicago. Moody Press. Used by permission.

Page 240: Reprinted from WALKING ON WATER: REFLECTIONS ON FAITH AND ART by Madeleine L'Engle. Copyright © 1980 by Crosswicks. Used by permission of Harold Shaw Publishers, Wheaton, IL 60189.

Page 242: Reprinted with permission from Daily Guideposts 1988. Copyright © 1987 by Guideposts Associates, Inc., Carmel, NY 10512.

Page 243: Taken from WOMEN IN GOD'S PRESENCE compiled by Delores Taylor. Copyright © 1988 by Christian Publications, Camphill, PA. Used by permission.

Page 248: Taken from HEART TROUBLE by Barbara Bush. Copyright © 1981 by the Zondervan Corporation. Used by permission.

Page 250: By Beth Donigan Seversen. Copyright © 1990 by The Zondervan Corporation.

Page 252: From the book WITH MY WHOLE HEART by Karen Burton Mains. Copyright © 1987 by Multnomah Press. Published by Multnomah Press, Portland, Oregon 97266. Used by permission.

Page 254: Taken from AMAZING LOVE by Corrie ten Boom. Copyright © 1953 Christian Literature Crusade, London. (Ft. Washington, PA: Christian Literature Crusade.) Used by permission.

Page 257: By Wanda K. Jones. Copyright © 1990 by The Zondervan Corporation.

Page 258: Reprinted with permission from Daily Guideposts 1987. Copyright © 1986 by Guideposts Associates, Inc., Carmel, NY 10512.

Page 260: By Marie Chapian. Copyright © 1990 by The Zondervan Corporation.

Page 263: Taken from OUT OF THE SALTSHAKER AND INTO THE WORLD by Rebecca Manley Pippert. Copyright © 1979 by InterVarsity Christian Fellowship of the USA. Used by permission of InterVarsity Press, P.O. Box 1400, Downers Grove, IL 60515.

Page 265: By June Hunt. Copyright © 1990 June Hunt.

Page 266: Taken from THE SPIRITUALITY OF GENTLENESS: GROWING TOWARD CHRISTIAN WHOLENESS by Judith C. Lechman. Copyright © 1987 by Judith C. Lechman. Published by Harper & Row Publishers, Inc. Used by permission.

Page 268: Taken from KINDRED SPIRITS by Kathy Narramore and Alice Hill. Copyright © 1985 by The Zondervan Corporation. Used by permission.

Page 270: Taken from THE QUIET HEART by June Masters Bacher. Copyright © 1988 by Harvest House Publishers, Eugene, OR 97402. Used by permission.

Page 273: By Debby Boone. Copyright © 1990 by Debby Boone.
Page 275: By Gloria Gaither. Copyright © 1990 by Gloria Gaither.
Page 276: By Luci Swindoll. Copyright © 1990 by The Zondervan Corporation.
Page 278: From the book EACH NEW DAY by Corrie ten Boom. Copyright © 1977 by Corrie ten Boom. Used by permission of Fleming H. Revell Company.
Page 280: By Beverly LaHaye. Copyright © 1990 by The Zondervan Corporation.
Page 283: Taken from SINCERELY by Gigi Graham Tchividijian. Copyright © 1984 by The Zondervan Corporation. Used by permission.
Page 285: By Anne Ortlund. Copyright © 1990 by The Zondervan Corporation.
Page 287: By Hope MacDonald. Copyright © 1990 by The Zondervan Corporation.
Page 290: By Debbie Smith. Copyright © 1990 by The Zondervan Corporation.
Page 291: Taken from 101 MORE HYMN STORIES by Kenneth W. Osbeck. Copyright © 1985 by KREGEL PUBLICATIONS, P.O. Box 2607, Grand Rapids, MI 49501. Used by permission.
Page 293: By Marie Chapian. Copyright © 1990 by The Zondervan Corporation.
Page 295: By Martha Manikas-Foster. Copyright © 1990 by Martha Manikas-Foster.
Page 299: By Martha Manikas-Foster. Copyright © 1990 by Martha Manikas-Foster.
Page 301: By Carol L. Baldwin. Copyright © 1990 by The Zondervan Corporation.
Page 305: Taken from BESIDE STILL WATERS by Gien Karssen. Copyright © 1985 by Gien Karssen. Used by permission of NavPress.
Page 310: From the book EACH NEW DAY by Corrie ten Boom. Copyright © 1977 by Corrie ten Boom. Used by permission of Fleming H. Revell Company.
Page 311: Taken from IT TAKES SO LITTLE TO BE ABOVE AVERAGE by Florence Littauer. Copyright © 1983 by Harvest House Publishers, Eugene, OR 97402. Used by permission.
Page 313: By Martha Manikas-Foster. Copyright © 1990 by Martha Manikas-Foster.
Page 316: By Beverly LaHaye. Copyright © 1990 by The Zondervan Corporation.
Page 317: Reprinted with permission from Daily Guideposts 1987. Copyright © 1986 by Guideposts Associates, Inc., Carmel, NY 10512.
Page 320: Taken from MEMORIES by Kathryn Hillen. Copyright © 1987 by Kathryn Hillen. Used by permission of Zondervan Publishing House.
Page 323: Reprinted with permission from Daily Guideposts 1987. Copyright © 1986 by Guideposts Associates, Inc., Carmel, NY 10512.
Page 324: By Debbie Smith. Copyright © 1990 by The Zondervan Corporation.
Page 327: Taken from MEMORIES by Kathryn Hillen. Copyright © 1987 by Kathryn Hillen. Used by permission of Zondervan Publishing House.
Page 329: Taken from WOMEN IN GOD'S PRESENCE compiled by Delores Taylor. Copyright © 1988 by Christian Publications, Camphill, PA. Used by permission.
Page 331: Taken from MY LIFE FOR THE POOR by Mother Teresa of Calcutta. Copyright © 1985 by Jose Gonzalez-Balado and Janet N. Playfoot. Published by Harper & Row, Publishers, Inc. Used by permission.
Page 332: Taken from MEMORIES by Kathryn Hillen. Copyright © 1987 by Kathryn Hillen. Used by permission of Zondervan Publishing House.
Page 334: Taken from HEART TROUBLE by Barbara Bush. Copyright © 1981 by the Zondervan Corporation. Used by permission.
Page 335: Reprinted by permission from DAILY THOUGHTS ON LIVING FREE by Neva Coyle. Published and copyrighted by Bethany House Publishers, Minneapolis, MN 55438.
Page 338: Taken from GOD IS ENOUGH by Hannah Whitall Smith. Published by Zondervan Publishing House.
Page 340: By Luci Swindoll. Copyright © 1990 by The Zondervan Corporation.
Page 342: Taken from A BLADE OF GRASS by Gladis and Gordon DePree. Copyright © 1967 by Gladis and Gordon DePree. Published by Zondervan Publishing House. Used by permission.
Page 344: Taken from COME TO THE WATERS by Diane Head. Copyright © 1985 by Diane Head. Published by Zondervan Publishing House. Used by permission.
Page 346: By Sue Richards. Copyright © 1990 by The Zondervan Corporation.
Page 349: By Ruth Bell Graham. Copyright © 1990 by Ruth Bell Graham.
Page 351: By Luci Swindoll. Copyright © 1990 by The Zondervan Corporation.
Page 353: From the book WITH MY WHOLE HEART by Karen Burton Mains. Copyright © 1987 by Multnomah Press. Published by Multnomah Press, Portland, Oregon 97266. Used by permission.
Page 357: Taken from EARLY WIDOW by Mary Jane Worden. Copyright © 1989 by Mary Jane Worden. Used by permission of InterVarsity Press, P.O. Box 1400, Downers Grove, IL 60515.
Page 359: By June Hunt. Copyright © 1990 by June Hunt.
Page 361: By Beverly LaHaye. Copyright © 1990 by The Zondervan Corporation.
Page 362: By Beth Donigan Seversen. Copyright © 1990 by The Zondervan Corporation.
Page 365: Taken from WOMEN IN GOD'S PRESENCE compiled by Delores Taylor. Copyright © 1988 by Christian Publications, Camphill, PA. Used by permission.
Page 370: By Rosemary Jensen. Copyright © 1990 by The Zondervan Corporation.
Page 373: By Luci Swindoll. Copyright © 1990 by The Zondervan Corporation.
Page 376: By Ruth A. Tucker. Copyright © 1990 by The Zondervan Corporation.
Page 378: Taken from WHEN THE HANDWRITING ON THE WALL IS IN BROWN CRAYON by Susan L. Lenzkes. Copyright © 1981 by Susan L. Lenzkes. Used by permission of Zondervan Publishing House.
Page 380: Taken from SO YOU'RE THE PASTOR'S WIFE by Ruth Senter. Copyright © 1990 by Victor Books. Used by permission.
Page 381: Taken from WHEN THE HANDWRITING ON THE WALL IS IN BROWN CRAYON by Susan L. Lenzkes. Copyright © 1981 by Susan L. Lenzkes. Used by permission of Zondervan Publishing House.
Page 384: Reprinted with permission from Daily Guideposts 1988. Copyright © 1987 by Guideposts Associates, Inc., Carmel, NY 10512.
Page 388: Taken from A CLOSER WALK by Catherine Marshall. Copyright © 1986 by Calen, Inc. Published by Chosen Books, Fleming H. Revell Company. Used by permission.
Page 391: By Wanda K. Jones. Copyright © 1990 by The Zondervan Corporation.

Page 396: Taken from BESIDE STILL WATERS by Gien Karssen. Copyright © 1985 by Gien Karssen. Used by permission of NavPress.

Page 402: Reprinted with permission from Daily Guideposts 1989. Copyright © 1988 by Guideposts Associates, Inc., Carmel, NY 10512.

Page 403: Taken from MY LIFE FOR THE POOR by Mother Teresa of Calcutta. Copyright © 1985 by Jose Gonzalez-Balado and Janet N. Playfoot. Published by Harper & Row, Publishers, Inc. Used by permission.

Page 411: By Debbie Smith. Copyright © 1990 by The Zondervan Corporation.

Page 414: By Ruth Bell Graham. Copyright © 1990 by Ruth Bell Graham.

Page 419: By Gloria Gaither. Copyright © 1990 by Gloria Gaither.

Page 421: Taken from A SILVER PEN FOR CLOUDY DAYS by Susan L. Lenzkes. Copyright © 1987 by Susan L. Lenzkes. Used by permission of Zondervan Publishing House.

Page 426: Taken from EARLY WIDOW by Mary Jane Worden. Copyright © 1989 by Mary Jane Worden. Used by permission of InterVarsity Press, P.O. Box 1400, Downers Grove, IL 60515.

Page 428: Taken from 101 MORE HYMN STORIES by Kenneth W. Osbeck. Copyright © 1985 by KREGEL PUBLICAIONS, P.O. Box 2607, Grand Rapids, MI 49501. Used by permission.

Page 430: By Wanda K. Jones. Copyright © 1990 by The Zondervan Corporation.

Page 433: By Ruth Bell Graham. Copyright © 1990 by Ruth Bell Graham.

Page 434: By Ruth Bell Graham. Copyright © 1990 by Ruth Bell Graham.

Page 440: Taken from GOD IS ENOUGH by Hannah Whitall Smith. Published by Zondervan Publishing House.

Page 444: Taken from A VIOLENT GRACE by Gini Andrews. Copyright © 1986 by Gini Andrews. Used by permission of Zondervan Publishing House.

Page 447: Taken from THE IRRATIONAL SEASON by Madeleine L'Engle. Copyright © 1977 by Crosswicks, Ltd. Published by Harper & Row Publishers, Inc. Used by permission.

Page 451: By Roslind Rinker. Copyright © 1990 by The Zondervan Corporation.

Page 457: By Gloria Gaither. Copyright © 1990 by Gloria Gaither.

Page 467: By Debby Boone. Copyright © 1990 by The Zondervan Corporation.

Page 473: By Hope MacDonald. Copyright © 1990 by The Zondervan Corporation.

Page 479: Taken from LISTENING TO GOD by Janice Kempe. Copyright © 1985 by The Zondervan Corporation. Used by permission.

Page 484: Taken from IF by Amy Carmichael. Copyright © 1980 by The Zondervan Corporation. Used by permission.

Page 490: By Carol L. Baldwin. Copyright © 1990 by The Zondervan Corporation.

Page 498: By Ruth A. Tucker. Copyright © 1990 by The Zondervan Corporation.

Page 500: Taken from LISTENING TO GOD by Janice Kempe. Copyright © 1985 by The Zondervan Corporation. Used by permission.

Page 504: By Hope MacDonald. Copyright © 1990 by The Zondervan Corporation.

Page 507: By Debbie Smith. Copyright © 1990 by The Zondervan Corporation.

Page 509: "Sacraments of Daily Living" taken from CLOSE TO THE HEART by Helen Lowrie Marshall. Copyright © 1958 by Helen Lowrie Marshall (renewed 1986). Used by permission.

Page 511: By Debbie Smith. Copyright © 1990 by The Zondervan Corporation.

Page 516: By Ann Kiemel Anderson. Copyright © 1990 by The Zondervan Corporation.

Page 525: From the booklet RELATIONSHIPS by Pamela Reeve. Copyright © 1982 by Multnomah Press. Published by Multnomah Press, Portland, Oregon 97266. Used by permission.

Page 527: Taken from WHEN THE HANDWRITING ON THE WALL IS IN BROWN CRAYON by Susan L. Lenzkes. Copyright © 1981 by Susan L. Lenzkes. Used by permission of Zondervan Publishing House.

Page 529: Excerpt from WHO AM I GOD? by Marjorie Holmes. Copyright © 1970, 1971 by Marjorie Holmes Mighell. Used by permission of Doubleday, a division of Bantam, Doubleday, Dell Publishing Group, Inc.

Page 532: From the book EACH NEW DAY by Corrie ten Boom. Copyright © 1977 by Corrie ten Boom. Used by permission of Fleming H. Revell Company.

Page 533: Taken from A SILVER PEN FOR CLOUDY DAYS by Susan L. Lenzkes. Copyright © 1987 by Susan L. Lenzkes. Used by permission of Zondervan Publishing House.

Page 536: Taken from WHAT COLOR IS MY COLLAR? by Marlene Obie. Copyright © 1985 by The Zondervan Corporation. Used by permission.

Page 541: Taken from LET'S MAKE A MEMORY by Gloria Gaither and Shirley Dobson. Copyright © 1983 by Gloria Gaither, Shirley Dobson, and James Dobson, Inc. Published by Word, Inc., Dallas, Texas. Used by permission.

Page 549: By Dorothy Patterson. Copyright © 1990 by The Zondervan Corporation.

Page 550: Taken from WHAT COLOR IS MY COLLAR? by Marlene Obie. Copyright © 1985 by The Zondervan Corporation. Used by permission.

Every effort has been made to give proper credit for each devotion used in this Women's Devotional Bible. If any error or inaccuracy is noted, please inform the publishers.

READING PLAN

God's Word is full of promises, encouragement and guidance for you. This reading plan gives you a simple structure for reading through the New Testament, Psalms and Proverbs in one year.

DATE	PASSAGE
January 1	Matthew 1 Proverbs 1:1–7
January 2	Matthew 2 Proverbs 1:8–19
January 3	Matthew 3 Proverbs 1:20–33
January 4	Matthew 4 Proverbs 2:1–11
January 5	Matthew 5 Proverbs 2:12–22
January 6	Matthew 6 Proverbs 3:1–4
January 7	Matthew 7 Proverbs 3:5–10
January 8	Matthew 8 Proverbs 3:11–18
January 9	Matthew 9 Proverbs 3:19–26
January 10	Matthew 10 Proverbs 3:27–35
January 11	Matthew 11 Proverbs 4:1–9
January 12	Matthew 12 Proverbs 4:10–19
January 13	Matthew 13:1–52 Proverbs 4:20–27
January 14	Matthew 13:53—14:36 Proverbs 5:1–6
January 15	Matthew 15 Proverbs 5:7–14
January 16	Matthew 16 Proverbs 5:15–23
January 17	Matthew 17 Proverbs 6:1–5
January 18	Matthew 18 Proverbs 6:6–11
January 19	Matthew 19:1—20:16 Proverbs 6:12–15
January 20	Matthew 20:17—21:17 Proverbs 6:16–19
January 21	Matthew 21:18–46 Proverbs 6:20–29
January 22	Matthew 22:1–40 Proverbs 6:30–35
January 23	Matthew 22:41—23:38 Proverbs 7:1–5
January 24	Matthew 24:1–44 Proverbs 7:6–23
January 25	Matthew 24:45—25:30 Proverbs 7:24–27
January 26	Matthew 25:31—26:16 Proverbs 8:1–11
January 27	Matthew 26:17–56 Proverbs 8:12–21
January 28	Matthew 26:57–75 Proverbs 8:22–36
January 29	Matthew 27:1–31 Proverbs 9:1–6
January 30	Matthew 27:32–66 Proverbs 9:7–12
January 31	Matthew 28 Proverbs 9:13–18
February 1	Mark 1:1–20 Proverbs 10:1–5
February 2	Mark 1:21–45 Proverbs 10:6–11
February 3	Mark 2 Proverbs 10:12–16
February 4	Mark 3:1–19 Proverbs 10:17–23
February 5	Mark 3:20–35 Proverbs 10:24–27
February 6	Mark 4:1–34 Proverbs 10:28–32
February 7	Mark 4:35—5:20 Proverbs 11:1–4
February 8	Mark 5:21–43 Proverbs 11:5–9
February 9	Mark 6:1–13 Proverbs 11:10–14
February 10	Mark 6:14–29 Proverbs 11:15–19
February 11	Mark 6:30–56 Proverbs 11:20–26
February 12	Mark 7:1–23 Proverbs 11:27–31
February 13	Mark 7:24–37 Proverbs 12:1–6
February 14	Mark 8:1–21 Proverbs 12:7–10
February 15	Mark 8:22—9:13 Proverbs 12:11–14

DATE	PASSAGE
February 16	Mark 9:14–50 Proverbs 12:15–22
February 17	Mark 10:1–31 Proverbs 12:23–28
February 18	Mark 10:32–52 Proverbs 13:1–6
February 19	Mark 11:1–19 Proverbs 13:7–12
February 20	Mark 11:20–12:12 Proverbs 13:13–18
February 21	Mark 12:13–44 Proverbs 13:19–25
February 22	Mark 13 Proverbs 14:1–4
February 23	Mark 14:1–26 Proverbs 14:5–9
February 24	Mark 14:27–52 Proverbs 14:10–18
February 25	Mark 14:53–72 Proverbs 14:19–24
February 26	Mark 15:1–20 Proverbs 14:25–30
February 27	Mark 15:21–47 Proverbs 14:31–35
February 28	Mark 16 Proverbs 15:1–4
March 1	Luke 1:1–38 Proverbs 15:5–10
March 2	Luke 1:39–56 Proverbs 15:11–19
March 3	Luke 1:57–80 Proverbs 15:20–24
March 4	Luke 2 Proverbs 15:25–29
March 5	Luke 3 Proverbs 15:30–33
March 6	Luke 4 Proverbs 16:1–5
March 7	Luke 5 Proverbs 16:6–9
March 8	Luke 6:1–16 Proverbs 16:10–15
March 9	Luke 6:17–49 Proverbs 16:16–19
March 10	Luke 7:1–35 Proverbs 16:20–24
March 11	Luke 7:36–50 Proverbs 16:25–28
March 12	Luke 8 Proverbs 16:29–33
March 13	Luke 9:1–36 Proverbs 17:1–5
March 14	Luke 9:37–62 Proverbs 17:6–10

DATE	PASSAGE
March 15	Luke 10 Proverbs 17:11–15
March 16	Luke 11 Proverbs 17:16–21
March 17	Luke 12 Proverbs 17:22–28
March 18	Luke 13 Proverbs 18:1–7
March 19	Luke 14 Proverbs 18:8–15
March 20	Luke 15 Proverbs 18:16–19
March 21	Luke 16 Proverbs 18:20–24
March 22	Luke 17 Proverbs 19:1–6
March 23	Luke 18 Proverbs 19:7–12
March 24	Luke 19 Proverbs 19:13–19
March 25	Luke 20 Proverbs 19:20–29
March 26	Luke 21:1–36 Proverbs 20:1–5
March 27	Luke 21:37–22:23 Proverbs 20:6–12
March 28	Luke 22:24–53 Proverbs 20:13–19
March 29	Luke 22:54–23:25 Proverbs 20:20–25
March 30	Luke 23:26–56 Proverbs 20:26–30
March 31	Luke 24 Proverbs 21:1–8
April 1	John 1:1–28 Proverbs 21:9–16
April 2	John 1:29–51 Proverbs 21:17–24
April 3	John 2 Proverbs 21:25–31
April 4	John 3 Proverbs 22:1–5
April 5	John 4:1–42 Proverbs 22:6–9
April 6	John 4:43–54 Proverbs 22:10–16
April 7	John 5 Proverbs 22:17–21
April 8	John 6:1–21 Proverbs 22:22–29
April 9	John 6:22–65 Proverbs 23:1–8
April 10	John 6:66–7:13 Proverbs 23:9–14

DATE	PASSAGE
April 11	John 7:14–44 Proverbs 23:15–21
April 12	John 7:45—8:11 Proverbs 23:22–28
April 13	John 8:12–30 Proverbs 23:29–35
April 14	John 8:31–59 Proverbs 24:1–7
April 15	John 9 Proverbs 24:8–12
April 16	John 10:1–21 Proverbs 24:13–22
April 17	John 10:22–42 Proverbs 24:23–29
April 18	John 11 Proverbs 24:30–34
April 19	John 12:1–36 Proverbs 25:1–5
April 20	John 12:37–50 Proverbs 25:6–12
April 21	John 13:1–30 Proverbs 25:13–20
April 22	John 13:31—14:31 Proverbs 25:21–28
April 23	John 15 Proverbs 26:1–10
April 24	John 16 Proverbs 26:11–16
April 25	John 17 Proverbs 26:17–22
April 26	John 18 Proverbs 26:23–28
April 27	John 19:1–27 Proverbs 27:1–7
April 28	John 19:28–42 Proverbs 27:8–11
April 29	John 20 Proverbs 27:12–18
April 30	John 21 Proverbs 27:19–27
May 1	Acts 1 Proverbs 28:1–5
May 2	Acts 2 Proverbs 28:6–10
May 3	Acts 3:1—4:4 Proverbs 28:11–14
May 4	Acts 4:5–37 Proverbs 28:15–22
May 5	Acts 5:1–11 Proverbs 28:23–28
May 6	Acts 5:12—6:7 Proverbs 29:1–6
May 7	Acts 6:8—8:1a Proverbs 29:7–11

DATE	PASSAGE
May 8	Acts 8:1b–40 Proverbs 29:12–16
May 9	Acts 9 Proverbs 29:17–21
May 10	Acts 10 Proverbs 29:22–27
May 11	Acts 11 Proverbs 30:1–4
May 12	Acts 12 Proverbs 30:5–9
May 13	Acts 13 Proverbs 30:10–14
May 14	Acts 14 Proverbs 30:15–17
May 15	Acts 15:1–21 Proverbs 30:18–23
May 16	Acts 15:22–41 Proverbs 30:24–28
May 17	Acts 16:1–15 Proverbs 30:29–33
May 18	Acts 16:16–40 Proverbs 31:1–9
May 19	Acts 17 Proverbs 31:10–31
May 20	Acts 18 Psalm 1
May 21	Acts 19:1–22 Psalm 2
May 22	Acts 19:23–41 Psalm 3
May 23	Acts 20 Psalm 4
May 24	Acts 21:1–36 Psalm 5
May 25	Acts 21:37—22:29 Psalm 6
May 26	Acts 22:30—23:35 Psalm 7:1–9
May 27	Acts 24 Psalm 7:10–17
May 28	Acts 25:1–22 Psalm 8
May 29	Acts 25:23—26:32 Psalm 9:1–10
May 30	Acts 27 Psalm 9:11–20
May 31	Acts 28 Psalm 10
June 1	Romans 1:1–17 Psalm 11
June 2	Romans 1:18–32 Psalm 12
June 3	Romans 2:1–16 Psalm 13

DATE	PASSAGE
June 4	Romans 2:17–29 Psalm 14
June 5	Romans 3:1–20 Psalm 15
June 6	Romans 3:21–31 Psalm 16
June 7	Romans 4:1–12 Psalm 17
June 8	Romans 4:13–25 Psalm 18:1–19
June 9	Romans 5:1–11 Psalm 18:20–29
June 10	Romans 5:12–21 Psalm 18:30–36
June 11	Romans 6:1–14 Psalm 18:37–50
June 12	Romans 6:15–23 Psalm 19
June 13	Romans 7:1–6 Psalm 20
June 14	Romans 7:7–25 Psalm 21
June 15	Romans 8:1–17 Psalm 22:1–11
June 16	Romans 8:18–39 Psalm 22:12–24
June 17	Romans 9:1–29 Psalm 22:25–31
June 18	Romans 9:30—10:21 Psalm 23
June 19	Romans 11:1–10 Psalm 24
June 20	Romans 11:11–24 Psalm 25:1–7
June 21	Romans 11:25–36 Psalm 25:8–15
June 22	Romans 12:1–8 Psalm 25:16–22
June 23	Romans 12:9–21 Psalm 26
June 24	Romans 13:1–7 Psalm 27
June 25	Romans 13:8–14 Psalm 28
June 26	Romans 14:1–12 Psalm 29
June 27	Romans 14:13–23 Psalm 30
June 28	Romans 15:1–13 Psalm 31:1–8
June 29	Romans 15:14–33 Psalm 31:9–18
June 30	Romans 16 Psalm 31:19–24

DATE	PASSAGE
July 1	1 Corinthians 1:1—2:5 Psalm 32
July 2	1 Corinthians 2:5–16 Psalm 33:1–11
July 3	1 Corinthians 3 Psalm 33:12–22
July 4	1 Corinthians 4 Psalm 34:1–10
July 5	1 Corinthians 5 Psalm 34:11–22
July 6	1 Corinthians 6 Psalm 35:1–18
July 7	1 Corinthians 7 Psalm 35:19–28
July 8	1 Corinthians 8 Psalm 36
July 9	1 Corinthians 9 Psalm 37:1–22
July 10	1 Corinthians 10:1—11:1 Psalm 37:23–40
July 11	1 Corinthians 11:2–34 Psalm 38
July 12	1 Corinthians 12:1–31a Psalm 39
July 13	1 Corinthians 12:31b—13:13 Psalm 40:1–10
July 14	1 Corinthians 14:1–25 Psalm 40:11–17
July 15	1 Corinthians 14:26–40 Psalm 41
July 16	1 Corinthians 15:1–34 Psalm 42
July 17	1 Corinthians 15:35–58 Psalm 43
July 18	1 Corinthians 16 Psalm 44:1–8
July 19	2 Corinthians 1:1—2:11 Psalm 44:9–26
July 20	2 Corinthians 2:12—3:18 Psalm 45
July 21	2 Corinthians 4 Psalm 46
July 22	2 Corinthians 5:1–10 Psalm 47
July 23	2 Corinthians 5:11—6:2 Psalm 48
July 24	2 Corinthians 6:3—7:1 Psalm 49:1–15
July 25	2 Corinthians 7:2–16 Psalm 49:16–20
July 26	2 Corinthians 8:1–15 Psalm 50
July 27	2 Corinthians 8:16—9:15 Psalm 51

DATE	PASSAGE
July 28	2 Corinthians 10 Psalm 52
July 29	2 Corinthians 11:1–15 Psalm 53
July 30	2 Corinthians 11:16–12:10 Psalm 54
July 31	2 Corinthians 12:11–13:14 Psalm 55
August 1	Galatians 1 Psalm 56
August 2	Galatians 2 Psalm 57
August 3	Galatians 3:1–14 Psalm 58
August 4	Galatians 3:15–25 Psalm 59:1–9
August 5	Galatians 3:26–4:20 Psalm 59:10–17
August 6	Galatians 4:21–5:15 Psalm 60
August 7	Galatians 5:16–26 Psalm 61
August 8	Galatians 6 Psalm 62
August 9	Ephesians 1:1–14 Psalm 63
August 10	Ephesians 1:15–23 Psalm 64
August 11	Ephesians 2:1–10 Psalm 65
August 12	Ephesians 2:11–22 Psalm 66:1–7
August 13	Ephesians 3 Psalm 66:8–20
August 14	Ephesians 4:1–16 Psalm 67
August 15	Ephesians 4:17–5:2 Psalm 68:1–18
August 16	Ephesians 5:3–20 Psalm 68:19–35
August 17	Ephesians 5:21–33 Psalm 69:1–18
August 18	Ephesians 6:1–9 Psalm 69:19–36
August 19	Ephesians 6:10–24 Psalm 70
August 20	Philippians 1 Psalm 71:1–18
August 21	Philippians 2:1–11 Psalm 71:19–24
August 22	Philippians 2:12–18 Psalm 72
August 23	Philippians 2:19–30 Psalm 73:1–20

DATE	PASSAGE
August 24	Philippians 3:1–14 Psalm 73:21–28
August 25	Philippians 3:15–4:9 Psalm 74:1–11
August 26	Philippians 4:10–23 Psalm 74:12–23
August 27	Colossians 1:1–14 Psalm 75
August 28	Colossians 1:15–2:5 Psalm 76
August 29	Colossians 2:6–23 Psalm 77
August 30	Colossians 3:1–4:1 Psalm 78:1–8
August 31	Colossians 4:2–18 Psalm 78:9–39
September 1	1 Thessalonians 1 Psalm 78:40–55
September 2	1 Thessalonians 2:1–16 Psalm 78:56–72
September 3	1 Thessalonians 2:17–3:13 Psalm 79
September 4	1 Thessalonians 4:1–12 Psalm 80
September 5	1 Thessalonians 4:13–18 Psalm 81
September 6	1 Thessalonians 5:1–11 Psalm 82
September 7	1 Thessalonians 5:12–28 Psalm 83
September 8	2 Thessalonians 1 Psalm 84
September 9	2 Thessalonians 2:1–12 Psalm 85
September 10	2 Thessalonians 2:13–3:5 Psalm 86
September 11	2 Thessalonians 3:6–18 Psalm 87
September 12	1 Timothy 1:1–11 Psalm 88
September 13	1 Timothy 1:12–20 Psalm 89:1–13
September 14	1 Timothy 2 Psalm 89:14–29
September 15	1 Timothy 3 Psalm 89:30–45
September 16	1 Timothy 4:1–10 Psalm 89:46–52
September 17	1 Timothy 4:11–5:8 Psalm 90
September 18	1 Timothy 5:9–6:2 Psalm 91
September 19	1 Timothy 6:3–10 Psalm 92

DATE	PASSAGE
September 20	1 Timothy 6:11–21 Psalm 93
September 21	2 Timothy 1:1–14 Psalm 94:1–15
September 22	2 Timothy 1:15—2:13 Psalm 94:16–23
September 23	2 Timothy 2:14–26 Psalm 95
September 24	2 Timothy 3:1–9 Psalm 96
September 25	2 Timothy 3:10—4:8 Psalm 97
September 26	2 Timothy 4:9–22 Psalm 98
September 27	Titus 1 Psalm 99
September 28	Titus 2 Psalm 100
September 29	Titus 3 Psalm 101
September 30	Philemon Psalm 102:1–17
October 1	Hebrews 1 Psalm 102:18–28
October 2	Hebrews 2:1–4 Psalm 103:1–18
October 3	Hebrews 2:5–18 Psalm 103:19–22
October 4	Hebrews 3:1–6 Psalm 104:1–23
October 5	Hebrews 3:7–19 Psalm 104:24–35
October 6	Hebrews 4:1–13 Psalm 105:1–22
October 7	Hebrews 4:14—5:10 Psalm 105:23–45
October 8	Hebrews 5:11—6:12 Psalm 106:1–5
October 9	Hebrews 6:13–20 Psalm 106:6–31
October 10	Hebrews 7:1–10 Psalm 106:32–48
October 11	Hebrews 7:11–28 Psalm 107:1–3
October 12	Hebrews 8 Psalm 107:4–9
October 13	Hebrews 9:1–10 Psalm 107:10–16
October 14	Hebrews 9:11–28 Psalm 107:17–22
October 15	Hebrews 10:1–18 Psalm 107:23–32
October 16	Hebrews 10:19–39 Psalm 107:33–43

DATE	PASSAGE
October 17	Hebrews 11:1–16 Psalm 108
October 18	Hebrews 11:17–40 Psalm 109:1–20
October 19	Hebrews 12:1–13 Psalm 109:21–31
October 20	Hebrews 12:14–29 Psalm 110
October 21	Hebrews 13 Psalm 111
October 22	James 1:1–18 Psalm 112
October 23	James 1:19–27 Psalm 113
October 24	James 2:1–13 Psalm 114
October 25	James 2:14–26 Psalm 115
October 26	James 3:1–12 Psalm 116:1–6
October 27	James 3:13—4:3 Psalm 116:7–14
October 28	James 4:4–12 Psalm 116:15–19
October 29	James 4:13—5:6 Psalm 117
October 30	James 5:7–12 Psalm 118:1–7
October 31	James 5:13–20 Psalm 118:8–14
November 1	1 Peter 1:1–12 Psalm 118:15–21
November 2	1 Peter 1:13—2:3 Psalm 118:22–29
November 3	1 Peter 2:4–12 Psalm 119:1–8
November 4	1 Peter 2:13–25 Psalm 119:9–16
November 5	1 Peter 3:1–7 Psalm 119:17–24
November 6	1 Peter 3:8–22 Psalm 119:25–32
November 7	1 Peter 4:1–11 Psalm 119:33–40
November 8	1 Peter 4:12–19 Psalm 119:41–48
November 9	1 Peter 5 Psalm 119:49–56
November 10	2 Peter 1:1–11 Psalm 119:57–64
November 11	2 Peter 1:12–21 Psalm 119:65–72
November 12	2 Peter 2:1–9 Psalm 119:73–80

DATE	PASSAGE
November 13	2 Peter 2:10–22 Psalm 119:81–88
November 14	2 Peter 3:1–9 Psalm 119:89–96
November 15	2 Peter 3:10–18 Psalm 119:97–104
November 16	1 John 1:1–4 Psalm 119:105–112
November 17	1 John 1:5—2:2 Psalm 119:113–120
November 18	1 John 2:3–11 Psalm 119:121–128
November 19	1 John 2:12–17 Psalm 119:129–136
November 20	1 John 2:18–27 Psalm 119:137–144
November 21	1 John 2:28—3:10 Psalm 119:145–152
November 22	1 John 3:11–24 Psalm 119:153–160
November 23	1 John 4:1–6 Psalm 119:161–168
November 24	1 John 4:7–21 Psalm 119:169–176
November 25	1 John 5:1–12 Psalm 120
November 26	1 John 5:13–21 Psalm 121
November 27	2 John Psalm 122
November 28	3 John Psalm 123
November 29	Jude 1–16 Psalm 124
November 30	Jude 17–25 Psalm 125
December 1	Revelation 1:1–8 Psalm 126
December 2	Revelation 1:9–20 Psalm 127
December 3	Revelation 2:1–11 Psalm 128
December 4	Revelation 2:12–29 Psalm 129
December 5	Revelation 3:1–6 Psalm 130
December 6	Revelation 3:7–13 Psalm 131

DATE	PASSAGE
December 7	Revelation 3:14–22 Psalm 132
December 8	Revelation 4 Psalm 133
December 9	Revelation 5 Psalm 134
December 10	Revelation 6 Psalm 135:1–12
December 11	Revelation 7 Psalm 135:13–21
December 12	Revelation 8 Psalm 136
December 13	Revelation 9 Psalm 137
December 14	Revelation 10 Psalm 138
December 15	Revelation 11:1–14 Psalm 139:1–16
December 16	Revelation 11:15–19 Psalm 139:17–24
December 17	Revelation 12:1—13:1a Psalm 140
December 18	Revelation 13:1b–10 Psalm 141
December 19	Revelation 13:11–18 Psalm 142
December 20	Revelation 14 Psalm 143
December 21	Revelation 15 Psalm 144
December 22	Revelation 16 Psalm 145:1–7
December 23	Revelation 17 Psalm 145:8–13a
December 24	Revelation 18 Psalm 145:13b–21
December 25	Revelation 19:1–10 Psalm 146
December 26	Revelation 19:11–21 Psalm 147:1–6
December 27	Revelation 20:1–6 Psalm 147:7–11
December 28	Revelation 20:7–15 Psalm 147:12–20
December 29	Revelation 21:1–8 Psalm 148
December 30	Revelation 21:9–27 Psalm 149
December 31	Revelation 22 Psalm 150

AUTHOR BIOGRAPHIES

Many gifted women contributed their insights to this Women's Devotional New Testament. This index gives you information about each author and tells you where her contributions can be found.

Ann Kiemel Anderson is the author of ten books, including *I'm Out to Change My World*, and *I Love the Word Impossible*. Formerly a school teacher, a youth director and a college dean of women, she now devotes her time primarily to being a wife and the mother of four young sons. *Devotions by this author can be found on pages 216, 516.*

Gini Andrews has written several best-selling books that reflect in a personal way her walk with God. As a single Christian woman she wrote *Your Half of the Apple*. In *A Violent Grace* she shares her failures and heartache after marriage. She also wrote *Sons of Freedom* and *Esther*. *Devotions by this author can be found on pages 35, 444.*

June Masters Bacher taught elementary school and English until her retirement several years ago. She has written several books, including *Quiet Moments for Women* and a series of pioneer romance novels. June and her husband George live in California. *Devotions by this author can be found on pages 97, 182, 185, 270.*

Carol L. Baldwin is a marriage, group and individual counselor and the author of the book *Friendship Counseling*. Much of the material in her devotional readings developed from the trauma of being widowed at age twenty-seven. She is now married again and lives with her husband and their four daughters. *Devotions by this author can be found on pages 39, 147, 204, 301, 490.*

Alma Barkman is the mother of four children, living in Manitoba. As a free-lance writer she is the author of numerous articles and several books. *Devotions by this author can be found on pages 93, 238.*

Mary Beckwith, an editor, enjoys traveling, teaching, organizing and correspondence. She has written and conducted a variety of workshops for women, young girls and writers. She lives in California with her husband Clint and their three children. *A devotion by this author can be found on page 177.*

Debby Boone is a popular recording artist, performer, actress and author. Debby's recording of the song "You Light Up My Life" won her the Grammy Award for the best new artist in 1977. She has since recorded ten albums and has won two additional Grammy Awards. She is the author of *Debby Boone—So Far*, and two children's books. She and her husband Gabriel have four children. *Devotions by this author can be found on pages 273, 467.*

Jill Briscoe is the coordinator of women's ministries at Elmbrook Church in Waukesha, Wisconsin and the director of "Telling the Truth" media ministries. She is the author of numerous books, including *There's a Snake in My Garden*, *Prime Rib and Apple*, and *Thank You for Being a Friend*. She and her husband Stuart have three children. *Devotions by this author can be found on pages 14, 47, 95, 102, 113, 129.*

Barbara Bush, a pastor's wife and mother of four children, has written several books including *Ask Adam* and *I Can't Stand Cindy, Lord*. She enjoys her writing as well as sewing, stitchery, music and travel. *Devotions by this author can be found on pages 248, 334.*

Amy Carmichael (1867–1951) worked for many years in South India, rescuing children who had been "married to the gods" in nearby temples. Her brilliant style has made the stories of these children and the ministry of Dohnavur Fellowship known around the world. *A devotion by this author can be found on page 484.*

Marie Chapian has written twenty-four books, including the *A Heart for God* devotional series, *Mothers and Daughters*, and *Am I the Only One Here With Faded Jeans?* for which she won a Campus Life Gold Medallion award in 1988. Marie studied at Moody Bible Institute, Metropolitan State University and the University of Minnesota (where she received her Ph.D.). She is the mother of two daughters. *Devotions by this author can be found on pages 219, 260, 293.*

Mrs. Charles E. Cowman and her husband served as pioneer missionaries in Japan and China from 1901 to 1917. Mr. Cowman's poor health forced them to return to the U.S., and Mrs. Cowman nursed him until his death six years later. Mrs. Cowman's devotional books, *Streams in the Desert*, have been popular for more than sixty years. *A devotion by this author can be found on page 58.*

Neva Coyle was educated in Minnesota and California, where she now lives with her husband and three children. As president and founder of Overeaters Victorious, she lectures and leads her "Free to Be Thin" seminars. *A devotion by this author can be found on page 335.*

Fanny Crosby (1820–1915) was blinded in infancy supposedly by the ministrations of a "quack" physician called in to look at her eye infection. The hymns she wrote in her lifetime, over 9,000, have influenced thousands throughout the years. *A devotion by this author can be found on page 306.*

Gladis and Gordon DePree are the authors of several books, including *A Blade of Grass* and *Faces of God*. Gladis also wrote *Festival*, a book about life on Hong Kong Island. The DePrees live and work in the Middle East. *Devotions by this author can be found on page 342.*

Shirley Dobson is an author, homemaker, wife, and mother of a daughter and a son. She has served as a Bible Study Fellowship leader and as director for her church's ministry to women. She and her husband Dr. James Dobson often have appeared together on radio and television. *Devotions by this author can be found on page 541.*

Elisabeth Elliot was a young missionary wife and mother when her husband and four other men were killed while attempting to reach the Auca Indians. She is the author of many books, including *Through Gates of Splendor, Shadow of the Almighty* and *These Strange Ashes. Devotions by this author can be found on pages 55, 60.*

Colleen Townsend Evans lives with her husband in the Washington, D.C., area where he pastors the National Presbyterian Church. They have four children. She is a best-selling author of many books, including *A Deeper Joy* and *Make Me Like You, Lord. Devotions by this author can be found on page 78.*

Gloria Gaither is a lyricist, teacher, speaker, wife and mother. With the Bill Gaither Trio, Gloria has recorded over forty albums and is the coauthor of close to five hundred songs. Her ten books include *We Have This Moment*, and *Hands Across the Seasons*. She has won many awards, including the 1986 Dove Award for songwriter of the year. She and her husband Bill have three children. *Devotions by this author can be found on pages 145, 275, 419, 457.*

Ruth Bell Graham is the daughter of missionaries to China, the wife of evangelist Billy Graham, the mother of five, a grandmother to eighteen, and now a great-grandmother as well. She is the author of *Our Christmas Story, It's My Turn, Legacy of a Pack Rat*, and a collection of poems titled *Sitting by My Laughing Fire. Devotions by this author can be found on pages 20, 186, 349, 414, 433, 434.*

June Gunden graduated from Goshen College with a degree in English. She taught that subject for several years on the junior high level. She now works as a free-lance Bible editor and proofreader. She and her husband Doug have two sons, Troy and Benjamin. *Devotions by this author can be found on page 169.*

Doris Haase lives in California where she is part of a support group that reaches out to troubled people. She tries daily to put into practice one of her favorite Biblical principles found in Psalm 39:1–2: "I will . . . keep my tongue from sin." *Devotions by this author can be found on pages 317, 323.*

Diane Head is a homemaker, free-lance writer and illustrator. She has written two books, *Come to the Waters* and *A Precious Bit of Forever*. In 1980 she was selected as an "Outstanding Young Woman of America" in recognition of her personal and professional accomplishments. She and her husband have two daughters. *Devotions by this author can be found on pages 16, 344.*

Marilyn Morgan Helleberg began a lifelong career in writing when her first-grade teacher set a poem to music and taught it to the class. She has filled thirty-five notebooks over the past fifteen years and looks at them as a chronicle of her life with God. *Devotions by this author can be found on page 402.*

Alice Hill attended Asbury College, where her friendship with Kathy Narramore began, culminating in their book *Kindred Spirits*. Alice has also written *Help!* She enjoys running and classical music. Alice and her husband Dick have two children. *Devotions by this author can be found on pages 148, 268.*

Kathryn Hillen retired several years ago from her profession as an executive secretary to pursue a degree in Biblical literature. She and her husband have four grown children. Her book credits include *There Came Unto Him . . . Women* and *Memories. Devotions by this author can be found on pages 127, 320, 327, 332.*

Phyllis Hobe, a full-time writer, now makes her home in the country, after living most of her life in the city. The dog and cat who live with her are finding the free and open country lifestyle as enjoyable as she does. *A devotion by this author can be found on page 12.*

Marjorie Holmes first gained national attention as an author for her book of prayers, *I've Got to Talk to Somebody, God*. She has also written seven novels. Now living in Pennsylvania with her husband George, their four children and their families gather at her lakefront home in Virginia every Christmas. *Devotions by this author can be found on pages 384, 529.*

Gladys Hunt is the author of fifteen books, including *Honey for a Child's Heart*, and *We Need Each Other: The Miracle of Relationships*. Because inductive Bible study is one of her principle interests, she is active in small group Bible studies and is the author of eight Fisherman Bible Study guides. She is an enthusiastic wife, mother and grandmother. *Devotions by this author can be found on pages 207, 209.*

June Hunt is a speaker, singer, author and the host of the award-winning national radio program "Hope for the Heart." Through three music albums and her devotional book *Seeing Yourself Through God's Eyes*, she is committed to unraveling the difficult "heart" issues of life with practical help and Biblical hope. *Devotions by this author can be found on pages 229, 236, 265, 359.*

Rosemary Jensen is the executive director of Bible Study Fellowship, with headquarters in San Antonio, Texas. Prior to taking the post in 1980 she served as a high school teacher, medical specialist, business woman and Bible teacher. Together with her husband, Dr. Robert T. Jensen, she served as a missionary to Tanzania, Africa, for nine years. Rosemary and her husband have three daughters and six grandchildren. *Devotions by this author can be found on pages 81, 124, 370.*

Janet C. Jones was born into a Christian family and graduated from Nyack College in 1953. That same year she married Rev. George Jones. They raised three children, have cared for five foster children, and now minister to and nurture other people's children. *A devotion by this author can be found on page 329.*

Wanda K. Jones is a popular teacher and seminar speaker and the coordinator of Christian Family Outreach, Inc. She and her husband Howard, the first black evangelist on the Billy Graham Crusade staff, have been married over forty-five years. They enjoy five children and six grandchildren. While serving as missionaries in Africa they preached, taught and became well-known personalities on radio station ELWA. *Devotions by this author can be found on pages 52, 257, 391, 430.*

Gien Karssen served on the Navigator's staff at The Hague in the Netherlands. She started the work of the Navigators in the Netherlands as well as Europe. Gien pursues a writing ministry and is the author of eight books. *Devotions by this author can be found on pages 305, 396.*

Janice Kempe is a writer and homemaker. She and her husband are parents of two sons and one daughter. Janice has taught elementary school and has written two books, *Listening to God* and *Growing Up Together. Devotions by this author can be found on pages 43, 479, 500.*

Sue Monk Kidd has written many articles for *Guideposts* magazine as well as one book *God's Joyful Surprise*. She and her husband Sandy have two teenagers, Bob and Ann. *Devotions by this author can be found on page 193.*

Alice Macdonald Kipling, who died in 1910, was the mother of famed poet Rudyard Kipling. *A devotion by this author can be found on page 367.*

Beverly LaHaye is the founder and president of Concerned Women for America and is an advocate, author and spokesperson on women's and family issues. She has written the books *The Restless Woman* and *Who But a Woman*, and she is the coauthor of *The Act of Marriage*. She and her husband have four children and eight grandchildren. *Devotions by this author can be found on pages 280, 316, 361.*

Elizabeth Larsen has written one novel and enjoys reading, needlepoint, cooking and writing. She and her husband Jerry have one son. *A devotion by this author can be found on page 188.*

Judith Lechman is a workshop leader and speaker. She has published over one hundred short stories as well as two books, *The World of Emily Howland* and *Yielding to Courage. Devotions by this author can be found on pages 223, 266.*

JoAnn Lemon and her husband Stan served as missionaries to Viet Nam from 1958–1972. In 1980 they returned overseas to serve in a church in Kowloon, Hong Kong for eight years. During these various ministries JoAnn was actively involved in women's ministries as well as music ministries. JoAnn and her husband have three children and four grandchildren. *A devotion by this author can be found on page 365.*

Madeleine L'Engle is a graduate of Smith College and Columbia University. She has been active in theater, as a teacher, lecturer and writer. Her books for children (and those who are children at heart) have won many awards. Probably the best known is *A Wrinkle in Time. Devotions by this author can be found on pages 240, 447.*

Susan L. Lenzkes lives and writes in California with her three children and her husband Herb. She is the author of *A Silver Pen for Cloudy Days* and *When the Writing on the Wall Is in Brown Crayon*. Susan enjoys singing in choirs and trios and ensembles, teaching Bible studies, and arranging flowers. *Devotions by this author can be found on pages 232, 378, 381, 421, 527, 533.*

Florence Littauer graduated with honors from the University of Massachusetts and is the founder of C.L.A.S.S. (Christian Leaders and Speakers Seminars). She has authored many books, including *Hope for Hurting People* and *After Every Wedding Comes a Marriage*. She makes frequent guest appearances on radio and television and has spoken to groups all over the world. *Devotions by this author can be found on page 311.*

Jeanette Lockerbie and her husband have retired in Florida. Before retiring she worked as an editor for *Psychology for Living*. As a free-lance writer she has published many books, including *Salt in My Kitchen* and *Time Out for Coffee*. *Devotions by this author can be found on page 212.*

Hope MacDonald has written articles for *Partnership, Today's Christian Woman* and *Faith at Work*, and is the author of *Discovering How to Pray, Discovering the Joy of Obedience* and *When Angels Appear*. Hope and her husband have been married forty-one years and have three children and six grandchildren. *Devotions by this author can be found on pages 35, 66, 287, 473, 504.*

Karen Burton Mains lives and ministers in the Chicago area, with her husband David co-hosting and speaking on The Chapel of the Air radio program. Karen wrote the best-selling book, *Open Heart, Open Home*. Her other book credits include *Karen, Karen, Making Sunday Special* and *The Fragile Curtain*. *Devotions by this author can be found on pages 117, 252, 353.*

Martha Manikas-Foster is a book editor and free-lance writer who studied at Houghton College and the University of Iowa. She worked as a newspaper reporter before entering book publishing in 1983. She has written articles for *Bookstore Journal* and *Paraplegia News*. She and her husband David have one daughter. *Devotions by this author can be found on pages 295, 299, 313.*

Catherine Marshall wrote many books before her death in 1983. They include: *A Man Called Peter, To Live Again,* and *Meeting God at Every Turn. Devotions by this author can be found on pages 24, 388.*

Helen Lowrie Marshall's (1904–1975) first book of poetry was printed and bound by hand in the home of her brother. She wrote many poems for use in Hallmark cards. A wife and mother of two sons, she was active in church and civic groups, and was in demand as a lecturer. *A devotion by this author can be found on page 509.*

Joan Rae Mills, married and the mother of two young children, is a free-lance writer and former English teacher. She enjoys restoring antiques, reading, writing and decorating. *Devotions by this author can be found on page 115.*

Kathy Narramore, a teacher and speaker, was born in Peking and lived her childhood years in several Chinese cities and the island of Taiwan. She graduated from Asbury College. Kathy and her husband Bruce live in California and are the parents of two children. *Devotions by this author can be found on pages 148, 268.*

Marlene Obie spends her time as a homemaker, free-lance writer, secretary, wife, and mother of three. She is the author of *What's a Mother to Do?* and *What Color Is My Collar?* Her articles have appeared in many Christian periodicals. *Devotions by this author can be found on pages 536, 550.*

Anne Ortlund is an award-winning musician and the author of seven books including *Building a Great Marriage*, and *Children Are Wet Cement*, which won the Christy Award as the best marriage-family book of 1982. She and her husband Ray are the coauthors of four additional books. Anne and Ray minister together through Renewal Ministries. They have four children. *Devotions by this author can be found on pages 72, 76, 153, 285.*

Luis Palau's story about Clara Barton, founder of the Red Cross, appears in his book *Experiencing God's Forgiveness*. He has written several other books on the Christian walk. *A devotion by this author can be found on page 41.*

Dorothy Patterson is a homemaker, author, conference speaker and adjunct professor of Christian Marriage and Family at the Criswell College in Dallas, Texas. She holds several degrees and is a member of the Council for Biblical Manhood and Womanhood, the Advisory Board of Concerned Women for America, and the Board of Directors for the Religious Roundtable Issue and Answers. She and her husband Dr. Paige Patterson have two children. *Devotions by this author can be found on page 549.*

Rebecca Manley Pippert, has spoken on four continents and written several books. They include *Out of the Saltshaker*, which has been translated into more than ten languages, *Hope Has Its Reasons* and *Pizza Parlor Evangelism*. She and her husband Wesley have two children. *Devotions by this author can be found on pages 161, 231, 263.*

Elizabeth Prentiss (1818–1878) early in life showed an ability for writing both prose and poetry. She taught school in Massachusetts and Virginia before marrying a minister in 1845. She wrote *Stepping Heavenward*, a popular book in her time. *A devotion by this author can be found on page 291.*

Eugenia Price is the author of twenty-two books, which have been translated into eleven languages. She holds the Georgia Distinguished Service Award and numerous fiction awards from the Dixie Council of Authors and the Georgia Writer's Association. Her manuscripts and letters make up a special collection at Boston University's Mugar Library. *Devotions by this author can be found on page 119.*

Pamela Reeve graduated from New York University with a degree in architecture. After several year's work in that field, she felt God's call to build people rather than things. That change, and further education, finally led her to a position as Dean of Women for Multnomah School of the Bible. She has now retired but continues to advise, teach part-time and speak at conferences and retreats. *A devotion by this author can be found on page 525.*

Sue Richards has lived in seven states as well as West Germany. She and her two children and husband Larry now live in Florida. Sue teaches eleventh-grade English and enjoys tennis and fishing. She has written one book, *Ministry to the Divorced*. *Devotions by this author can be found on pages 37, 151, 214, 346.*

Rosalind Rinker served for fourteen years as a missionary in China and then worked for twelve years with college students as a staff counselor with InterVarsity Christian Fellowship. She is active in a Mandarin-speaking Chinese church and teaches among Chinese churches in the Los Angeles area. For the past thirty years she has been a free-lance writer and speaker. Her fifteen books include *Prayer: Conversing With God*. *Devotions by this author can be found on pages 26, 62, 106, 135, 451.*

Dale Evans Rogers has traveled nationwide, appearing on radio and television as an actress, singer and speaker. She has written over a dozen books, including *Angel Unaware* and *Dearest Debbie*. She and her husband, Roy Rogers, live in California. *Devotions by this author can be found on page 211.*

Ruth Senter is a pastor's daughter and a pastor's wife, and therefore is uniquely capable of writing a book called *So You're the Pastor's Wife*. She has been involved in many aspects of book, periodical and curriculum publishing. She and her husband Mark have two children. *Devotions by this author can be found on pages 100, 380.*

Beth Donigan Seversen earned her master of divinity degree from Trinity Evangelical Divinity School and serves as the Associate pastor of Women's Ministries at Elmbrook Church, Waukesha, Wisconsin. She is also Jill Briscoe's writing assistant and in this capacity has written four inductive Bible studies. She and her husband have one daughter. *Devotions by this author can be found on pages 8, 250, 362.*

Linda Ching Sledge teaches at Westchester, New York, Community College. She lives there with her husband Gary and two sons. All the family enjoy trips to New York's Museum of Natural History to see the dinosaur exhibit. One of her hobbies is reading detective novels. *Devotions by this author can be found on pages 165, 258.*

Debbie Smith has written over one hundred songs with her husband, musician and recording artist Michael W. Smith. During her college years at Wheaton she spent six months in Haiti, where she helped establish a nutrition clinic. She now devotes most of her energies to her three children. *Devotions by this author can be found on pages 290, 324, 411, 507, 511.*

Hannah Whithall Smith (1832–1911) and her husband, Robert Pearsall Smith, were popular Bible conference leaders for many years. Personal tragedy led Mrs. Smith to write several books on suffering and obedience to the will of God, including *The Christian's Secret of a Happy Life* and *The God of All Comfort*. *Devotions by this author can be found on pages 338, 440.*

Millie Stamm has worked for many years directing Meditation Moments, a prayer ministry to Christian women. Her concern for Christian women in all walks of life has shown itself in her writing and speaking ministry. She has published two popular devotional books, *Meditation Moments* and *Be Still and Know*. *A devotion by this author can be found on page 132.*

Louisa Stead (1850–1917) heard the call of God to missionary service while still a child. After the death of her first husband, Mrs. Stead and her daughter served as missionaries in South Africa. While there Mrs. Stead married a South African native and worked on the mission field there until her death. *A devotion by this author can be found on page 428.*

Charlotte Stemple and her husband spent ten years as missionaries in Viet Nam in church planting and nursing ministries. The Stemples now live in the U.S. where Charlotte is involved in women's ministries. They have two sons. *A devotion by this author can be found on page 5.*

Luci Swindoll chose to retire early from her thirty-year career with the Mobil Oil Corporation to join Insight for Living, an international radio ministry where she is the vice president of public relations. Luci is a nationwide speaker and the author of seven books. *Devotions by this author can be found on pages 276, 340, 351, 373.*

Jean E. Syswerda, an editor with Zondervan Bible Publishers, keeps busy with her work, her family, with her church's ministry to teens, and with reading, gardening and decorating with antiques. She and her husband and three children enjoy country life in West Michigan. *A devotion by this author can be found on page 174.*

Joni Eareckson Tada is an internationally known mouth artist and author who developed her artistic talents after a diving accident in 1967 left her paralyzed below her shoulders. Her eleven books include her autobiography *Joni* and *Choices . . . Changes.* She works for the disabled as the founder and president of Joni and Friends. She also serves on the National Council for Disability, to which she was appointed by President Reagan in 1987. *A devotion by this author can be found on page 104.*

Delores Taylor, a singer and songwriter, has over fifty gospel songs to her credit. She graduated from Nyack College in Nyack, New York, and spent the next fifteen years touring and singing with the Alliance Trio. Delores and her husband Roy live in Virginia, where she now operates a dress shop and is president of her church's Women's Missionary Prayer Fellowship. *A devotion by this author can be found on page 243.*

Gigi Graham Tchividjian, daughter of Dr. Billy Graham, is first of all a wife and mother. She and her husband are the parents of seven children whose ages span twenty years. She is the author of *A Woman's Quest for Serenity* and *Sincerely, Gigi*. *Devotions by this author can be found on pages 221, 283.*

Rebecca Tempest works at present in a research laboratory at the University of Michigan in Ann Arbor, Michigan. She is a writer, mainly of poetry, and has had several of her poems published. *A devotion by this author can be found on page 149.*

Betsie ten Boom, the sister of writer and speaker Corrie ten Boom, died during World War II in a Nazi concentration camp. She and her sister ministered to many during the Nazi occupation of the Netherlands, hiding Jews in their home and providing encouragement to fellow prisoners in the camps. *A devotion by this author can be found on page 254.*

Corrie ten Boom, as a single Dutch woman, courageously hid Jews in her home during the Nazi occupation of World War II. She related her experiences in her most famous book *The Hiding Place*. After the war until her death she traveled and spoke, making people aware of the strength and contentment available in a close walk with God. *Devotions by this author can be found on pages 110, 278, 310, 532.*

Mother Theresa was born and raised in Albania. Her early religious training as a Sister of Loreto and her years of teaching in India were followed by the founding of her own order, the Sisters of Charity, to work with the poorest of the poor. Her work with the poor in India won her the Nobel Peace Prize. *Devotions by this author can be found on pages 167, 331, 403.*

Ruth A. Tucker earned her doctorate in history from Northern Illinois University and is a visiting professor at Trinity Evangelical Divinity School and a teacher at Moffat College of Bible in Kenya. She is the author of eight books and has won Gold Medallion Awards for *First Ladies of the Parish* (1989) and *From Jerusalem to Irian Jaya* (1984). She has one son. *Devotions by this author can be found on pages 64, 157, 376, 498.*

Shirley Pope Waite's writing career began back in high school when a teacher encouraged her to use those abilities. She has been a free-lance writer for many years and teaches courses on writing at a nearby college. She and husband Kyle raised six children. *A devotion by this author can be found on page 242.*

Anna L. Waring (1820–1910) was a Welsh poet. Several of her poems were set to music and became familiar and popular hymns. *A devotion by this author can be found on page 354.*

Mary Jane Worden and her husband Jim worked as staff members of Inter-Varsity Christian Fellowship until his death in a car accident in 1983. Out of those experiences came her book *Early Widow*. With her three children, Jane now lives and works in Nairobi, Kenya. *Devotions by this author can be found on pages 357, 426.*

SUBJECT INDEX

The subjects covered in the devotions are many and varied. This subject index will help you locate material on just about any topic or issue of interest, or about any problem confronting you.

NOTES

NOTES

NOTES

NOTES

In the eyes and hearts of those who continue to fall under its spell, the Loire Valley represents the very soul of *la douce France*, a place of enchantment in which anything seems possible. And it's easy to see why, for where else can you find such a dazzling selection of extraordinary places in quite such an appealing package? No wonder a large proportion of the region is now classified by UNESCO as a World Heritage Site. The signs are everywhere, from world renowned vineyards, whose origins lie in the vines planted by the Romans, to elegant Renaissance chateaux created by kings and noblemen as places of pleasure and diversion. Gardens, too, are often exquisitely landscaped, creating an earthly paradise in what has long been aptly referred to as the Garden of France. It's also a realm of mysticism and spirituality, of holy sites dating from the dawn of Christianity, spectacular Gothic cathedrals reaching skywards and where a medieval abbey still resonates to the haunting chant of centuries-old plainsong. And, ever present, flowing among gentle landscapes shaped through millennia by the extraordinary people who have settled here, is the hypnotic presence of France's longest river.

This guide traces the path of the river downstream from the esteemed vineyards of Sancerre on the eastern edge of the Loire Valley to the charismatic town of Amboise to the west. Highlights of the journey include the remarkable chateaux of Chambord, Chaumont, Cheverny, Chenonceau and Blois, as well as Briare's Port-Canal and the La Cave des Roches in Bourré. Whether you choose to enjoy the region by car, bicycle or hot air balloon, you'll find the ever-present river convincingly upstaged by the countless star attractions which lie along its banks.

Best time to vist the Loire Valley

In winter the weather is likely to be cold and either damp or frosty for long periods; the upside of which is the chance of crisp blue skies, off-season accommodation prices and far fewer crowds. Major sights remain open all year round and some chateaux host special Christmas events or candlelit tours.

Spring is usually mild with variable weather. Don't be suprised if you get some rain in March and April, but there's every chance of suprisingly warm, sunny days, too. Both the countryside and towns start to blossom, low season prices still apply and there's plenty of availability outside of the Easter holidays.

May and June are often characterized by plenty of sun but without excessive heat. Long hours of daylight allow you to pack a lot in, although the evenings can still be chilly in May. It's the ideal time to explore the countryside, take a woodland walk or make use of the Loire Valley's ever-expanding network of cycle paths. Sights are uncrowded, except during French May bank holiday periods (*jours feriés*) and during the Cheverny and Orléans jazz festivals.

Temperatures reach their highest in July and August, with late summer seing some unpredictable weather. Prolonged dry periods can be followed by thunderstoms, which are often spectacular but soon pass, leaving things noticeably cooler and fresher. The warm weather allows you to enjoy long relaxing evenings sitting outside and to take in one of the state-of-the-art son et lumière events at the chateaux of Chambord and Chenonceau. In addition, you'll find lots of extra events staged specifically for the French holidays. Bear in mind, though, that tourist sights will be at their most crowded and accommodation is more expensive and harder to find.

Autumn days can still be warm even though the evenings are drawing in. The countryside becomes more colourful as the leaves start to turn, including the famous vines. October is the perfect grape-picking time (the *vendange*) and sees a flurry of activity in the wine-producing villages. There are several festivals for harvests, food and wines and you can visit historic and other important sites not usually open to the public during the annual *Journées du Patrimoine* weekend, normally in mid-September.

Getting to the Loire Valley

Air

From UK and Ireland Nantes Atlantique airport receives **Ryanair** ⓘ *www.ryanair.com*, flights from Shannon, Dublin, Liverpool and East Midlands airports plus **Aer Arann** ⓘ *www.aerarann.com*, services from Cork. Ryanair also flies from Dublin and London Stansted to Tours Val de Loire airport. Alternatively, about an hour's drive south of Tours, Poitiers-Biard airport has seasonal flights from Edinburgh and London Stansted with Ryanair.

From North America There are currently no regular direct flights to the Loire Valley region from North America except a weekly flight between Nantes and Quebec during the summer with **CorsairFly** ⓘ *www.corsairfly.com*. **Continental** ⓘ *www.continental.com*, **British Airways** ⓘ *www.britishairways.com* and **Air France** ⓘ *www.airfrance.com*, all fly to Paris from New York. **Delta** ⓘ *www.delta.com*, flies to Paris from New York and Seattle, and **American Airlines** ⓘ *www.aa.com*, flies from Boston and Chicago, as well as New York. **Air Canada** ⓘ *www.aircanada.com*, flies direct to Paris from both Toronto and Vancouver. There are regular rail services from the **Gare TGV** at Roissy Charles de Gaulle airport to

Don't miss...

1 **Pont-Canal de Briare**, page 28.
2 **Musée des Beaux-Arts, Orléans**, page 37.
3 **Château Royal de Blois**, page 53.
4 **Domaine and Château de Chambord**, page 56.
5 **Château de Cheverny**, page 58.
6 **Festival International des Parcs et Jardins**, page 64.
7 **La Cave des Roches, Bourré**, page 65.
8 **Château de Chenonceau**, page 66.
9 **Château du Clos Lucé**, page 75.

Numbers relate to the map on page 4.

Tours (one hour 45 minutes) and Nantes (three hours). An alternative would be to fly with **Aer Lingus** ⓘ *www.aerlingus.com*, from New York to Dublin then direct to Nantes Atlantique via **Ryanair** ⓘ *www.ryanair.com*.

Airport information Nantes Atlantique ⓘ *T02 40 84 80 00, www.nantes.aeroport.fr*, is close to the Grand-Lieu Exit (51) on the western Nantes ring road. The shuttle bus between the city centre (south entrance of Nantes central railway station) and the airport is operated by the **Tan** ⓘ *T0810 444 444, www.tan.fr*, city transport network. It departs every 30 minutes Monday to Saturday 0530-2315, Sunday and bank holidays 0615-2315. Tickets cost €7.50 one way, or free if you have a valid **Pass Nantes** (see page 10). Taxis wait just outside the terminal building, with a dedicated area for disabled passengers to alight. Car-hire offices and parking are directly in front of the terminal building, and there is a fuel station at the entrance. Inside the terminal hall, you'll find a *bureau de change* and ATM, plus shops and a choice of places to eat.

Tours Val de Loire airport ⓘ *T02 47 49 37 00, www.tours.aeroport.fr*, is 10 minutes from Exit 20 on the A10 autoroute and just 20 minutes from the city centre. There's a shuttle bus to Tours city centre, which costs €5 one way. The buses leave from the airport 20 minutes after the arrival of flights and will take you to the **bus station** ⓘ *T02 47 05 30 49*, adjacent to the rail station in the heart of the city. Return shuttles to the airport depart from the bus station two hours before flight departure times. Val de Loire is a small airport with limited services, but you can get a snack in the restaurant, and there's a shop which opens when flights are due. The car-hire office is in the long-stay car park (only open when **Ryanair** flights are due).

Rail

Rail travel in France is quick and efficient, with high speed TGV (*Train à Grande Vitesse*) services between major cities and modern sprinter TER (*Train Expresse Régional*) services on regional lines. All seats on TGV services must be booked in advance, which can be done at a station or online (www.voyages-sncf.com). For local services, you can purchase your ticket online or at the station. Travellers from the UK to France have frequent **Eurostar** ⓘ *www.eurostar.com*, services from London to Paris, with onward connections direct to Orléans (one hour), Blois (1½ hours), Amboise (two hours), Tours (1¼ hours) and Angers (1½ hours). There are also regular connections from Lille to Tours and Angers. Fares from

London to the Loire Valley start at around £179 per person for a standard class return via either Paris or Lille.

Road

From London to Tours, in the heart of the Loire Valley, is around a 700-km journey, with a drive time of just under eight hours if you travel on autoroutes (in which case expect to pay around €40 in tolls). The National Centre for Traffic Information **Bison Futé** ⓘ *www.bison-fute.equipement.gouv.fr*, website offers drivers current information on all major routes in France including roadworks, accidents and hazardous weather conditions.

Eurotunnel ⓘ *www.eurotunnel.co.uk*, trains take just 35 minutes and have up to four crossings an hour at peak times. Fares cost from £47 per car for a short break or from £64 for a longer stay or single. The Eurotunnel has motorway access on both sides of the channel at Folkestone and Calais and with 30-minute check-ins, can be a fast and easy alternative to the ferry (see below).

Bus/coach **Eurolines** ⓘ *T+44(0)8717-818177, www.eurolines.co.uk*, coaches depart from London and Folkestone, and serve a number of destinations in France, including Tours and Angers. Standard tickets can be booked up until the day of travel. Adult return fares from London to Tours cost around £108, or £130 to Angers – youth and senior travellers get a small discount. Journeys are overnight, departing Friday afternoon from London and arriving the following morning. Return services to London from Tours and Angers depart on Sunday evenings.

Sea

The western ports of St Mâlo and Caen are the most convenient points of arrival to access the Loire Valley. **Brittany Ferries** ⓘ *www.brittanyferries.com*, has daily services from Portsmouth to St Mâlo (excluding Saturday from November) making an overnight crossing to France and a daytime crossing on the return journey; up to three crossings a day from Portsmouth to Caen (between 3¾ hours and seven hours), including convenient overnight journeys. St Mâlo is about 320 km from Tours (3¼ hours drive time) via Rennes and Le Mans. From Caen you can access the Loire Valley at Tours, 275 km (2½ hours) via Alençon and Le Mans. Daily services operated by **Condor Ferries** ⓘ *www.condorferries.co.uk*, leave from Poole (eight hours) for St Mâlo but scheduled stops in the Channel Islands can cause delays. **P&O Ferries** ⓘ *www.poferries.com*, **MyFerryLink** ⓘ *www.myferrylink.com*, and **LD Lines** ⓘ *www.ldlines.co.uk*, serve Calais from Dover (1½ hours). Calais is 520 km from Tours (five hours). Other routes to consider are Portsmouth to Le Havre and Newhaven to Dieppe with LD Lines. You can travel from Cork to Roscoff, 465 km from Tours (five hours), with Brittany Ferries.

Transport in the Loire Valley

Rail

Most local rail journeys within the Loire Valley are on **TER** trains ⓘ *www.ter-sncf.com*. Fast, comfortable and affordable, you don't need to make a reservation and bikes travel free (www.velo.sncf.com) although some restrictions apply during rush-hours. See the TER website for full rail timetables, service information and special offers.

It's possible to visit most of the major towns and some chateaux by train and there are regular services Monday to Saturday but not Sunday. Using Tours as an example, take the train east to Amboise (less than 20 minutes), to Onzain for the Domaine de Chaumont and the Festival Gardens (about 30 minutes), to Blois (about 40 minutes) or Orléans (about one hour 20 minutes). Fares largely depend on what time of day you travel; Tours–Blois, for instance, is around €20 for a return ticket outside of peak times. Travel west from Tours, and you can visit Savonnières, Langeais (10 minutes), Saumur (45 minutes), Angers (one hour 20 minutes) and Nantes (one hour 40 minutes). Azay-le-Rideau is about 25 minutes away on the Tours–Chinon line and costs €11 return. Check before you travel on this line if you have a bike, as some of these services are replaced by buses. Chenonceaux is about 25 minutes from Tours and costs €13 for a return ticket. For information about specific train stations see www.gares-en-mouvement.com.

Road

Car Speed limits on French roads are 130 kph (autoroutes), 110 kph (dual carriageways, urban autoroutes), 90 kph (single carriageways) and 50 kph (villages and towns) unless stated otherwise. When it's raining speed limits drop by 10 kph on motorways and dual-carriageways. *Péage* autoroutes are toll-roads. When driving in France it is compulsory to carry a warning triangle, breathalyser (*éthylotest* – available in supermarkets, etc.) and a reflective jacket – the latter must be in the car, not in the boot. The law is enforced by on-the-spot fines of between €90 and €135. For regulations and advice on driving in France visit www.theaa.com.

Unleaded (*sans plomb*) petrol (95 and 98 octane), diesel (sometimes labelled *gasoil* or *gazole*) and LPG are available. The SP95-E10 (unleaded 95 octane containing 10% ethanol) is now being sold throughout France. This fuel is not compatible with all vehicles, so check with the manufacturer before using it.

It's generally easy to find parking in smaller towns, often right in the centre (except on market days) and it is usually free. Blue-Zone parking is free, but you are required to display a blue parking disc, which can be obtained from supermarkets, tourist offices and some local shops. In larger towns and cities, street parking is often charged (*payant*) with ticket machines (*horodateurs*) nearby. Charges vary, so read information on the machine, particularly as parking is usually free at lunchtimes, and after 1830. Multi-storey car parks issue a ticket on entry, and charge by the hour. Expect to pay €2-3 per hour, depending on the location.

Roads in France are still relatively quiet, and relaxed touring on empty countryside roads is a pleasure. However, town centre traffic systems can be confusing – if in doubt just follow *Centre Ville* or *Office de Tourisme* signs and you'll reach the heart of any town.

Car hire Airports at Tours and Nantes and the main rail stations of Orléans, Tours, Angers and Nantes all have car-hire offices. It's best to reserve your vehicle before you travel, and to confirm that the office will be open when you'll be arriving – at Tours airport, for example, offices only open just before and just after Ryanair flights are due. For the best deals try **Holiday Autos** ⓘ *www.holidayautos.com*, a discount hire company which works with major rental businesses. Not all companies operate in the Loire Valley, but you'll find **National Citer** ⓘ *www.citer.fr*, **Europcar** ⓘ *www.europcar.com*, **Hertz** ⓘ *www.hertz.co.uk* and **Avis** ⓘ *www.avis.co.uk*, present in most large towns.

Requirements for hiring a car might vary, but you must possess a driving licence which is valid in France. If your normal licence is in a different language from the country in which you're renting the vehicle, you might also need an international driving licence.

Be aware that there is normally an insurance excess, which could find you paying a substantial amount for any damage, however minor. There are companies where you can purchase low-cost car-hire excess insurance for Europe or worldwide, either by the day or with an annual policy.

Bicycle The region has hundreds of kilometres of well-signed, dedicated cycle routes and long-distance trails, notably the **Loire à Vélo** ⓘ *www.cycling-loire.com*, the **Châteaux à Vélo network** ⓘ *www.chateauxavelo.com*, and part of the **Euro Vélo 6** ⓘ *www.eurovelo6.org*, that links the Atlantic with the Black Sea. There are bike-hire shops throughout the region and companies such as **Détours de Loire** ⓘ *T02 47 61 22 23, www.locationdevelos.com*, offer baggage-carrying services, and can suggest itineraries of varying length and difficulty. They work with local agents, allowing cyclists to pick up and drop off bikes where they choose. Hire costs start from around €14 for a day to €59 per week.

Bus The main tourist sites in the heart of the region are well-served by bus services. From Blois, for example, **TLC** ⓘ *T02 54 58 55 55, www.transports-du-loir-et-cher.com*, offers a 'Circuit Châteaux' from April to September costing around €6. From **Tours** ⓘ *www.filbleu.fr*, services to the Château de Chenonceau and Amboise operate all year, whereas Azay-le-Rideau and Villandry are best-served during school holidays. **Saumur** ⓘ *www.agglobus.fr*, has good, year-round services to outlying villages like Montsoreau and Montreuil-Bellay. Bus journeys generally cost between €1.15 and €1.40 for a single journey within one hour, so day tickets for around €4 may be better value if you are planning a day out.

When staying in one of the cities, check to see if the local tourist pass offers free travel – the **Pass Nantes**, for example, starts at €17 for 24 hours and includes entry to 30 sites, plus all public transport (including, usefully, the airport shuttle). For occasional journeys in Orléans, Angers and Nantes, trams are much more frequent than buses and are simple to use. For the best value buy a day/weekend ticket.

Key bus companies throughout the region are **Ulys** ⓘ *www.ulys-loiret.com*, **Fil Vert** ⓘ *www.tourainefilvert.com*, **Agglobus** ⓘ *www.agglobus.fr*, **COTRA** ⓘ *www.cotra.fr*, and **Tan** ⓘ *www.tan.fr*.

Where to stay in the Loire Valley

The region offers an enormous range of different places to stay. You can choose from historic chateaux, family-run hotels, charming *chambres d'hôtes* (B&Bs), unusual troglodytic dwellings, self-catering cottages and campsites amidst vineyards or on the banks of the Loire and its many tributaries. Whether you are looking for peace and quiet in idyllic countryside or a city-based break with plenty to see and lots of nightlife, the chances are that the area can provide it for you somewhere. A note of caution, though: if you don't like crowds, come outside the peak season. You'll sometimes feel as if you have the place to yourself – and you'll have a huge choice of accommodation.

Prices

Prices and quality are fairly standard throughout the region, although there's a high proportion of luxury accommodation (with higher than average prices). City centre hotels cost slightly more than elsewhere, although France has a huge number of cheap chain hotels placed strategically around the edge of cities, ensuring that budget rooms, too, are available. Most hotel bills will include an additional modest sum called a *taxe de sejour* – a tourist tax.

A double room in most hotels graded three-star and above cost from €110-150, though this can exceed €400 for the most luxurious rooms in outstanding hotels and chateaux. The Loire Valley also has a large number of small two-star hotels typically costing €60-80 for a double room. Single occupancy will cost a little more.

Hotel breakfasts are regarded as optional in France and are hardly ever included in the price. They cost anything from around €8 per person, substantially more in expensive hotels. Half-board options in hotels with restaurants can offer a considerable saving on dining bills.

Self-catering rural gîte accommodation first appeared in 1951. The National Federation of Gîtes de France now has over 56,000 properties to rent (including 'Charmance' B&Bs and 'Pre Vert' campsites). The average price for a gîte is around €400 per week in high season and €270 in low season. Gîtes are normally let for a minimum of one week during the summer months but at other times it's possible to rent them for a weekend or a few days. Other self-catering properties are available through property directories or by booking direct with private owners – always check what services are included in the price, as there may be extras like end-of-stay cleaning and electricity. Prices vary considerably according to the season, the highest being at Easter and during July and August.

The best value accommodation is often in B&B-style *chambres d'hôtes*, rooms in a family home or annexe that cost from around €50-100 per night for two people sharing. Rooms usually come with a private bathroom, and breakfast is generally included in the price.

There are good deals for short breaks outside the peak season – tourism websites are a good place to start looking. Tours, for example, offers rooms and entry to tourist sites at a 50% discount over 6 weekends in November and December through the annual Plus de Touraine scheme. It's a great opportunity to whisk your partner away at short notice and indulge in a luxury hotel at an affordable price. City tourist offices encourage low season travellers by offering attractive short-break packages; in Angers you can get a hotel room and a 24-hour City Pass (worth €14 each) through the central reservation service for as little as €50 per night, based on two people sharing.

Price codes

Where to stay

€€€€ over €200 | **€€€** €100-200
€€ €60-100 | **€** under €60

Price codes refer to the cost of a standard double room per night in high season.

Restaurants

€€€ over €30 | **€€** €20-30 | **€** under €20

Price codes refer to the cost of a two-course meal per person with a drink, including service and cover charge.

Booking

If you are visiting during peak periods, book your accommodation well in advance. Sought-after self-catering accommodation is often booked almost a year in advance, and the most charming chambres d'hôtes can disappoint those trying to book at short notice.

Prices quoted on hotel websites will depend on your arrival date and the levels of occupancy. You can often get a great deal if you are flexible on dates. If you book by phone, always make sure you get written confirmation. This Is especially true if you have requested a particular room or adapted accommodation. Let your accommodation provider know what time you'll be arriving – some hotels state they will let the room to someone else if you don't show up by a specified time, whereas in chambres d'hôtes you are usually expected to turn up *after* 1600-1700 on the first day of your stay.

Some hotels and B&Bs close during winter, normally November to March. Most gîtes are only booked for an average of 16 weeks annually and may close for most of the autumn and winter unless they can be adequately heated (expect to pay extra for this).

If you want a room with a view, overlooking the Loire or a chateau for instance, specify this when you book, confirming how much extra it will cost. It's also worth checking whether rooms are on a busy or noisy road. Review websites such as tripadvisor.com can be helpful in deciding whether a hotel is suitable. Don't assume that small hotels, chambres d'hôtes, gîte owners or campsites are able to accept payment by credit card – check this when booking.

Chateaux

Central to the Loire Valley's reputation as a premium tourist destination is its selection of luxury chateau-hotels and manor houses in superb settings. Expect antique furniture, stone staircases, tapestries and even a four-poster bed, plus high levels of comfort and modern facilities. Of course, they vary enormously, but depending on what sort of experience you want, you should be able to find something suitable. You can get away from it all in a small manor house offering B&B or do it in style in one of the larger chateaux with gastronomic restaurants, spa facilities, or even a golf course. Chateau-hotels can also provide an unforgettable venue for wedding celebrations, and you can even rent an entire chateau for a family holiday.

Hotels

Hotels are graded on a star system, with five stars being the highest grade possible in France. Most, though, are two-star and above but you'll find considerable variations, especially in three-star hotels, where the decor and furnishings can at worst be tired and dated, and at best offer high quality contemporary rooms with seductive en suite bathrooms, flat screen TVs and Wi-Fi as standard. Many now provide facilities to prepare hot drinks in the rooms.

If you are booking a hotel on the internet you'll generally be able to see pictures of the rooms. If you haven't booked in advance and just turn up looking for a room, you'll be shown what is available so you can choose. If this isn't offered you should ask – it's normal practice.

Chambres d'hôtes

Staying with local people is one of the nicest ways to really get to know your surroundings. Guestsare welcomed into the family home, which can be anything from a quite ordinary house to a troglodyte dwelling, farm or manor house, or even a chateau. Chambres d'hôtes can have up to five guest rooms and breakfast is included in the price. This is often served with home-made jams, fresh bread and pastries, local cheeses, dairy products and cold meats (*charcuterie*). If you really want to immerse yourself in the local culture, take advantage of the evening meals (*tables d'hôtes*) offered by some owners, usually for around €20 per person.

Self-catering/gîtes

There is an almost overwhelming choice of rural gîtes and other self-catering accommodation throughout the region. The Gîtes de France label ensures that certain standards and levels of comfort are met through their rating system, which awards between 1 and 5 *épis* (ears of corn) – one being the most basic. Other organizations such as Clévacances have a similar system. Expect accommodation to be self-contained, with some private outside space. It should be satisfactorily furnished and equipped for the requisite number of guests. Make sure that you confirm whether bed linen and towels are supplied and take your own beach towels for swimming, etc. The owner may not necessarily live on-site, so make sure you have a way of contacting them if there is a problem. Quite a few campsites have chalet-style cabins for those who like the camaraderie of camping but enjoy some home comforts. Alternatively, hire a boat and gently cruise the canals and rivers.

Food and drink in the Loire Valley

Here in the Garden of France fine food and wines are part of daily life, a simple pleasure for all to enjoy rather than a luxury reserved for the privileged few. Not that you can't dine in considerable style (and expense) if you so wish. After all, indulging your every desire is a local tradition which stretches back to the days when kings and nobles built their chateaux with just that in mind. But, to our mind, nothing surpasses the down-to-earth enjoyment of visiting a local market, preparing a picnic and savouring the results in the perfect spot, whether it be a shady riverbank, within sight of a noble landmark or even in a lively city square.

Practical information

You'll find a huge range of *auberges*, restaurants and hotels at every price, and gastronomic, level. Most larger towns have particular squares or streets dedicated to restaurants, where you will be able to browse and compare menus. Tourist offices can give you information about restaurants, particularly those specializing in local cuisine. Restaurants generally only serve lunch between 1200 and 1400. During the afternoon, unless you are in a city or at a major sight, it's hard to find anything more than a sandwich in a bar or *boulangerie*. Evening meals are served from around 1900, and many finish taking orders at around 2130 (even earlier in smaller places). Two courses plus a drink typically cost around €20-30 per person, and in most French restaurants a service charge is included (see Tipping, page 23). The menu reader on page 90 gives further explanations of the various French terms for foods and dishes mentioned here.

Entrées

You'll find sometimes *foie gras de canard* served with a fruit chutney, savoury tarts such as *Tourte Tourangelle aux rillons et Ste-Maure de Touraine*, assorted *fromages de chèvres*, fresh vegetables and salads. There is often a vegetable soup (*potage de légumes*), although vegetarians should be wary, as it is likely to incorporate a meat stock. The entrée is sometimes preceded by an appetizer called *amuse bouches*, examples of which could be *rillettes* or a few mouthfuls of an intensely flavoured seasonal soup. They are normally complimentary. Look for seasonal starters such as *asperge* or *primeurs* (new, young vegetables) in late spring, and come late summer, you'll find wild mushrooms, local tomatoes or dishes using varieties of pumpkin (*citrouille*, *potiron*, etc).

Plats

The main course is usually meat or fish accompanied by a wine-based sauce, and can be roasted, baked or sautéed. Surprisingly, main dishes rarely come with many vegetables – sometimes nothing other than *frites*, another potato side dish, pasta or rice. (The French, doubtless anxious to reach their 'five-a-day', will often start with a salad or eat one after the main course and before launching into the cheese board.)

It is more common now for restaurants to offer a vegetarian main course, but always check ingredients, as many French chefs regard *lardons* (diced bacon pieces), anchovies or tinned tuna as perfectly acceptable vegetarian fare. Always let restaurants or *tables d'hôtes* hosts know in advance if you have any particular dietary requirements.

Fish

The Loire is the main source of wild fish. They are caught by a handful of professional fishermen who brave the occasionally wild river in order to fill their nets. Carp, pike, trout and pike-perch (the ubiquitous *sandre*) are often served with *beurre blanc* – a delicious sauce made with butter, shallots, garlic and white wine. Small deep-fried fish served like whitebait are known as *la friture* and are excellent with a glass of crisp white wine. Fresh eel (*angouille*), simply grilled, is worth sampling in a riverside restaurant, or when cooked in red wine in a dish called *matelote*.

Meat

Prior to the 19th century, sheep were principally reared for wool, but farmers soon realized that *l'agneau de Touraine* lamb raised in the Maine-Touraine area produced a tender and sweet meat. Its quality is recognized by the coveted Label Rouge (see menu reader page 90). The *Géline de Touraine* chicken, another Label Rouge holder, was originally bred in the 19th century from a farmyard hen from Touraine and a Langshan from Asia. The resulting *Dame Noire* is so called because of its black feathers, and is highly prized for its tender meat. You will often see *coq au vin rouge* (chicken cooked in red wine), sometimes with a local twist such as *à l'angevin* (with onion and bacon). In Touraine, and particularly in Tours itself, pork dishes predominate but a French classic – *pièce de boeuf* – is given a local touch when served with a Ste-Maure de Touraine goat's cheese sauce. As you travel further upriver wild game, rabbit and veal appear regularly on the menu.

Cheese

Most good restaurants will have a selection of regional cheeses and will be able to assist you in making your choice. You can ask for several different types, perhaps starting with a delicately flavoured fresh goat's cheese and working up to a tasty (demi-sec) *Crottin de Chavignol* (try it with a Sancerre wine). The flavour and character of the cheese changes markedly according to its age. South of Tours the cylindrical *Ste-Maure de Touraine*, whose crust is coated in ash, has a straw running through the centre – look carefully and you'll find the maker's identification etched onto it. It partners very well with a Sauvignon de Touraine. Both the *Pouligny-St-Pierre* and the *Valançay* are shaped like a pyramid. Finally, the *Selles-sur-Cher* has a nutty flavour and a fine texture; its blue mould the result of at least 10 days maturation.

There are also two cow's milk cheeses to note. *Cendré d'Olivet* is made when the cows graze on the banks of the Loire in early spring, when the grass has most flavour. *Feuille de Dreux* is a soft-centred, mild cheese wrapped in a chestnut leaf, which adds to its flavour.

Dessert

French classics feature on every dessert menu. The most well-known native of the Loire Valley is the *tarte Tatin*, an upside-down apple tart. Apples and pears from the local orchards feature strongly, and cherries are a popular fruit for a *clafoutis*. Also look out for strawberries and melons; either is just as likely to appear as a starter or as a dessert. The French also adore rich and creamy chocolate desserts, so there is always a large choice of ice cream and sorbets. If all this sounds too sweet, try *fromage blanc* (sometimes called *faiselle*), an unsweetened dairy product a bit like a light fromage frais often served plain or with sugar, honey or a berry *coulis*.

Also striking is the infinite selection of cakes, biscuits and confectionery, either offered at the end of a meal or on sale in *pâtisseries* throughout the region. Tours has its *nougat de Tours* (in fact more of a cake), Angers tempts you with the *quernon d'ardoise* (a square of chocolate stuffed with nougat and resembling a roofing slate) and there are *cotignacs d'Orléans* made from a highly concentrated quince jelly and sold in tiny round boxes. And many, many more.

Wine

Despite being among the most northerly of France's vineyards, Loire Valley wines have real personality. They're versatile, too, with something for every taste and occasion. In the east lies the AOC growth area of **Sancerre** covering some 2457 ha, three-quarters of it planted with Sauvignon Blanc vines which produce the classy white wines for which the area is renowned. Much less well-known outside the region are the reds and rosés produced from local Pinot Noir plantings. But what ultimately separates the drinking qualities of one region's produce from another's is the complex combination of climate and *terroir* – the soil and underlying geology of the very land itself. Subtly different drinking qualities in the wines of individual communes – tiny areas like Bannay, Bué, Crézancy, Menetou-Ratel, Montigny and Verdigny, for instance – each have their aficionados.

You can discover some of the best red and white AOC Sancerre wines on the family estate of father and son Emmanuel and Jean-Paul Fleuriet **Cave de la Petite Fontaine** ⓘ *rue de la Petite Fontaine, Chaudoux, Verdigny, T02 48 79 40 49, www.scev-fleuriet.fr*, open throughout the year during variable working hours) who work the family's 12-ha vineyards. They also carry out the entire wine-making process in traditional stone vaulted cellars constructed by their ancestors in 1735.

Further west, both Anjou and Touraine also offer tremendous choice, and far more variety than is generally understood: a full-bodied Bourgueil, Chinon or Saumur are well able to counter those who still equate the region with crisp whites and gentle rosés. For an insight into more complex qualities, take a look at **Vouvray**, a few kilometres upstream from Tours. The appellation now comprises 1800 ha, with 300 estates in and around eight villages, and the *vendanges* (harvest) are typically among the latest in all France. Like both Muscadet and Sancerre, production is founded upon a single *cépage* or grape variety – Chenin Blanc, also known locally as Pineau d'Anjou, Pineau de la Loire or simply 'Chenin'.

An acknowledged master is the **Domaine Huet l'Echansonne** ⓘ *11/13 rue de la Croix-Buisée, Vouvray, T02 47 52 78 87, www.huet-echansonne.com, Mon-Sat 0900-1200 and 1400-1800, closed bank holidays, tastings by appointment*, founded in 1928 just above Vouvray on a family estate totalling 35 ha, and now with a total commitment to 'bio-dynamic' management. The estate's *mousseux* (sparkling) wines – whites only – are characterized by fruity sweetness balanced with fresh acidity. The results, whether *demi-sec* (medium dry) or *moelleux* (sweet) can be sublime.

Dramatically higher in their annual output are the Loire Valley's most westerly **Muscadet** AOC vineyards – Muscadet des Cotteaux de la Loire, Muscadet Côtes de Grandlieu and Muscadet de Sèvre-et-Maine – centred around Nantes. Uniting them is a single grape variety, the Melon de Bourgogne (known to Californians as Pinot Blanc). When the spectacularly harsh winter of 1709 decimated the Nantes wine industry, only the Melon de Bourgogne vines survived. It requires careful handling, to overcome a susceptibility to both mildew and botrytis, but in skilled hands magical things can happen and today endless rows cloak the shallow undulations of the Sèvre-et-Maine hills. For many years Muscadet, France's most exported wine, was seen merely as a light, refreshing and affordable 'dry white', best drunk young and, for the most part, informally. Now, though, 'new' Muscadets are being created, adding real fruitiness for modern wine drinkers. Some of the region's best AOC wines, both 'new' and classic, come from the **Château de Cléray-Savion en Eolie** ⓘ *Vallet, T02 40 36 22 55, www.sauvion.fr, Mon-Fri 0900-1200 and 1330-1630, visits preferably by appointment*, where Jean-Ernest Sauvion is one of the great emissaries for Muscadet de Sèvre-et-Maine. Some are designed to be drunk young, while the Château du Cléray Sauvion Cuvée de Garde, produced exclusively from old vines, has complex aromas and peppery, nutty undertones, combined with ageing potential up to (and beyond) 20 years.

Festivals in the Loire Valley

True to a nation whose climate favours outdoor life, the Loire Valley has a long tradition of mounting festivals and other events for the sheer enjoyment of it. It makes no difference whether you're resident or just visiting; everyone is welcome. Some are grand affairs attracting thousands celebrating, for example, regional food and fine wines. Others are more modest, convivial get-togethers with a charm of their own. Along the way you'll find enthusiastic gardeners opening their gates to all, local actors working together to re-enact important historical events, dancers and musicians taking to the stage before equally passionate audiences, and much more. Mixing like this offers much more than mere entertainment; you'll be rubbing shoulders with local people (and those from other nations) and gaining a real sense of being part of the area you're visiting. After all, the landscapes, architecture, food and drink with which you fell in love were all created by the skill, passion and spirit of the local people. And their traditions are alive and well, as you'll soon discover.

January

La Folle Journée, T08 92 70 52 05 (€0.34/mn), www.follejournee.fr. Nearly 300 short classical music concerts spanning 5 days at the end of Jan in Nantes.

February

La Fête des Vins d'Anjou, Chalonnes-sur-Loire, T06 60 34 36 26, www.chalonnes-sur-loire.fr. An annual event in the last weekend in Feb showcasing the wines of Anjou and Saumur, with wine-tasting classes, walks through the vineyards and more.

March

Printemps Musical de St-Cosme Symphonia, La Riche (5 mins from the centre of Tours), T02 47 32 07 11, www.lesmusicales.fr. A chamber music festival dedicated to the promotion of young musicians which takes place in the Priory of St-Cosme, last residence of the famous poet Pierre de Ronsard.

April

Festival International de Guitare de Vendôme, T02 54 89 44 00, www.vendomeguitarfest.com. The festival features all of the available genres of guitar music, from traditional to Celtic to mariachi to Argentinian tango. The event also includes the opportunity to take a masterclass with performers.

Fêtes de Jeanne d'Arc, T02 38 24 05 05 (tourist office), www.fetesjeannedarc.com. There's plenty to see and do in Orléans at the end of Apr and beginning of May, including a medieval festival and market, concerts, exhibitions, son et lumière at the cathedral and parades.

May

Le Printemps des Arts de Nantes, T02 40 20 69 70, www.printempsdesarts.fr. European baroque music festival with concerts throughout the spring and early summer at venues in Nantes and heritage sites in Pays de la Loire.

June

Chinon en Jazz, T02 47 38 67 62. Free music events at locations all round the town in early Jun.

Festival Aucard de Tours, T02 47 51 11 33, www.radiobeton.com. Rock festival held in early Jun in the parc de la Gloriette in Tours plus live music in the streets and bars around the city.

Festival du Sully et du Loiret, T02 38 25 43 43, www.festival-sully.com.Held at various venues in the Loiret, this international festival held in the 1st 2 weeks in Jun presents classical and choral music.

Foire aux Fromages et Gastronomie, Sainte-Maure-de-Touraine, T02 47 72 00 13, www.sainte-maure-de-touraine.fr. A celebration in the 1st weekend in Jun of regional foods, with the distinctive goat's cheese from Ste-Maure-de-Touraine taking pride of place. The streets of the town come alive with performances from wonderful French musicians and artists.

Les Courants, T02 47 30 43 05, www.lescourants.com. Amboise hosts a week (end Jun) of contemporary music combined with a strip cartoon (*bandes dessinnées* or BD) festival – a huge craze in France.

Rendez-vous aux jardins, www.rendezvousauxjardins.culture.fr. A national event in the 1st weekend in Jun when famous and not so well-known gardens are opened to the public. A detailed brochure on the parks and gardens in the Loire Valley in English can be downloaded from the Loire Valley Tourist Board website (www.visaloire.com).

July

Avoine Zone Blues, T02 47 98 11 15, www.avoine-zone-blues.com. The Touraine blues festival held annually at the beginning of Jul in Avoine, between Chinon and Saumur.

Garlic and Basil Festival, T02 47 21 60 00. Gastronomic sights and smells of summer in Tours at the end of Jul.

Nuits des Mille Feux (The Night of a Thousand Candles), T02 47 50 02 09, www.chateauvillandry.com. For 2 consecutive evenings in early Jul the gardens at Villandry are candlelit and animated by players and acrobats. The night ends with an extraordinary fireworks display – very different to traditional sound and light shows.

Tous sur le Pont, T02 54 58 84 56, www.toussurlepont.com. Annual music festival held over 5 days in mid-Jul with concerts staged in the courtyard of the Château Royal in Blois, free live music in the town centre, dancing and fireworks.

August

Blues in Chédigny y Musicas de Cuba, T02 47 92 51 43, www.blues-in-chedigny.com. International artists perform blues and Cuban music in the heart of this Touraine village (mid-month).

Les Grandes Tablées du Saumur Champigny, Reserve on T02 41 40 20 60 (tourist office). For 2 nights in early Aug, the centre of Saumur is filled with tables and 10,000 diners enjoy good food from the region and plenty of Saumur Champigny wine. Advance bookings for dining (€10 per person) are essential but you can buy a glass (€4) to taste wine on the night.

September

Festival de Loire, www.festivaldeloire.com. 5-day festival at the end of Sep on the quays in Orléans, with hundreds of traditional boats from the Loire and its tributaries, music and entertainment.

Festival Européen de Musique Renaissance, T02-47 57 00 73, www.vinci-closluce.com. Amboise hosts 3 days of Renaissance music around the third weekend of the month. Internationally renowned musicians grace the wonderful surroundings of Leonardo da Vinci's home at the Château du Clos Lucé.

Fête du Vélo, T02 54 79 95 63 (Blois tourist office). Join hundreds of others in a day of cycling in chateau country around Blois in early Sep. (There are shorter trails for families.) Competitions and surprises along the route.

Jazz en Touraine, T02 47 45 85 10 (tourist office), www.jazzentouraine.com. Even though it's called a jazz festival, you can expect various musical styles like salsa, electro, gypsy jazz and blues in this well-established late summer revelry. Official and fringe events are staged at Montlouis-sur-Loire and venues nearby during mid-Sep.

Journées du Patrimoine (European heritage days), www.journeesdupatrimoine.culture.fr. On the 3rd weekend in Sep, thousands of historic sites (from a modest pigeonnier to private chateaux) open their doors to the public.

La Fête de la Citrouille (Pumpkin Feast), T02 47 95 77 47, www.chateaudurivau.com. In mid-Sep, the remarkable gardens at the

Château du Rivau come alive with activities and performers celebrating the pumpkin and other unusual vegetables.

Les Journées du Potager, T02 47 50 02 09, www.chateauvillandry.com. On the last weekend of the month, Villandry gardeners share their knowledge in demonstrations, workshops and guided tours with special activities for children.

Tomato Festival, T02 47 45 16 31. Discover hundreds of varieties of tomatoes for sale at the Château de la Bourdaisière in mid-Sep.

October

Journées Gastronomiques de Sologne, T02 54 96 99 88, www.romorantin.fr/jgs/. In the last weekend in Oct, Romorantin-Lanthenay hosts producers and artisans from the region all competing for one of various prestigious trophies.

November

Euro Gusto, T02 47 64 24 38, www.eurogusto.org. European gathering of the international Slow Food movement that takes place every 2 years in Tours' Parc des Expositions. You can sample over 1000 wines, taste regional foods, take part in workshops or watch demonstrations.

December

Grand Marché Animé de Noël au Château de Brissac, T02 41 91 22 21, www.chateau-brissac.fr. The last weekend in Nov finds France's tallest chateau enlivened by a traditional Christmas market with all the trimmings, lots of stalls and of course Père Noël.

Marché aux Truffes & Produits de Terroir, T02 47 58 31 11. As the festive season approaches, visit the traditional truffle market at Marigny-Marmande. The markets take place on the Sat before and after Christmas, 2nd and 4th Sat in Jan, and 2nd Sat in Feb.

Noël au Château de La Ferté St-Aubin, T02 38 76 52 72, www.chateau-ferte-st-aubin.com. For 3 weekends before Christmas (and from 26-30 Dec) the chateau (about 20 km south of Orléans) is open 1400-1800 for a traditional Noël au Château.

Shopping in the Loire Valley

Gifts and souvenirs

There are the usual gift shops in all the chateaux and visitor attractions, which offer some interesting, high quality items alongside the mugs, T-shirts and keyrings. Both the **Château d'Azay-le-Rideau** and the **Château Royal d'Amboise** boutiques sell a good range of tapestries if you fancy introducing a medieval theme to your home. The Festival des Jardins at **Chaumont** sells a wide range of books on French gardens, garden design and wildlife, plus some lovely eco-friendly gifts. If you're feeling inspired after visiting the gardens at **Villandry**, there is a super little shop selling must-have garden accessories and plants. Rose lovers should visit **Doué-la-Fontaine**, a centre of European rose production near Saumur. Each year the growers put on a fabulous mid-July spectacle, but you can visit and buy plants at any time of year. Still on a scented theme, the Savonnerie Artisanale Martin de Candre at **Fontévraud** produces fine traditional soaps.

At the **Château de Cheverny**, the Orangerie has a collection of Gien tableware, full settings being beautifully displayed on tables around the shop – especially interesting if you can't visit the celebrated Faïencerie in **Gien**. Notable ceramicists in the region include Charles Hair, who works from his studio in **Thizay**, near Chinon, and whose work is displayed in the Musée Pincé in Angers and several galleries in Paris. He produces unique contemporary items and particularly beautiful Celadons. The village of **La Borne** near Henrichement has evolved into an artistic centre with a community of working potters selling their creations direct from individual studios. You can stroll around the village, visit the potters and discover their work.

For another lasting memory of your trip to the Loire Valley, there's an amazing range of wickerwork products for just about any use or decoration at the basketwork cooperative in **Villaines-les-Rochers**, near Azay-le-Rideau. The village is home to the largest number of basket workers in France. Artisan studios are dotted around the village and visitors can buy individual pieces direct from the makers.

It would be hard to resist buying some of the confectionery and chocolate produced by artisan *pâtissiers* and *chocolatiers* throughout the region. **Orléans** has a wonderful selection of food shops in and around the Châtelet indoor market, although you must see Les Musardises on rue République for its fine display of local specialities like the *cotignac d'Orléans*, a quince-based fruit confection. **Blois** is host to master chocolatier Max Vauché, who also has a large shop near Chambord in **Bracieux**, where visitors can watch chocolates being made. In **Angers**, visit rue des Lices, where you can find the famous *quernon d'Ardoise*, small chocolates stuffed with nougat and made to represent the slate roof tiles. You'll also be tempted by the delicious hand-made chocolates and macarons; beautifully wrapped, they make an ideal gift. In **Nantes**, look out for colourful sweets known as *berlingots* and *rigollettes*, produced from the sugar which helped bring wealth to this Atlantic port. Visit Débotté Gautier on rue de la Fosse – the interior is as stunning as the chocolates. Specialities include *le Muscadet Nantais*, a wonderful marriage of wine and chocolate which they recommend you simply allow to melt in your mouth. For something less sweet, the *sel de Guérande* salt goes down well with cooks and foodies.

Markets and local produce

Food is one of the main reasons that people love to visit France. Feast your eyes on the magnificent displays of fresh and regional produce on sale in the regular markets throughout the Loire Valley region and you'll soon realize why it's called the 'Garden of

France'. Best buys are seasonal fresh produce such as asparagus (in spring), cherries and strawberries (in early summer) and apples, pears and pumpkins (in the autumn). At the height of summer expect to find tasty local tomatoes, cucumbers and beetroot, with a range of different varieties to try. Visit **Chateau de la Bourdaisière** in Montlouis-sur-Loire which grows all the old varieties of tomato and holds an annual tomato festival in September. Similarly, the **Château de Rivau** has a pumpkin festival around the same time, where you'll discover pumpkins in all shapes, sizes and colours, plus other ancient vegetables.

Some apple and pear orchards sell direct to the public; others will take huge crates to market and sell them freshly harvested and very cheap. One apple variety to look out for is the Reine des Reinettes, said to be best for the famous *tarte Tatin*. A really interesting local product is the Poire- or Pomme-Tapée. Visit the artisan producers at **Rivarennes** (pears) or **Turquant** (apples) and discover the traditional method of preserving the fruit by slow drying and 'tapping' to verify removal of the moisture. The end product is deliciously sweet dried fruit which, when preserved in wine, can be added to sweet or savoury dishes (and is often seen on restaurant menus).

Autumn also brings wild mushrooms to market, although visit one of the troglodyte mushroom growers at any time and you can buy more unusual varieties of mushroom as well as the ubiquitous Champignon de Paris button mushroom sold in French supermarkets. Covered market halls like Châtelet in **Orléans**, Talensac in **Nantes** or Les Halles in **Tours** present the very best from the region's producers. If you are shopping for a picnic, look out for traditional *charcuterie* and pork products – Hardouin in **Vouvray** and **Tours** are particularly renowned. They also sell a huge range of preserved meats. Alternatively, try any of the five AOC *fromages de chèvres* (goat's cheeses) from the region, which you will find at any market.

For details of recommended wine producers see page 15; for information on wine tours, see respective listings sections.

Shopping hours

The French shopping week is generally Monday to Saturday. The restrictions on Sunday trading have been relaxed in Paris, Lille and Marseille, but elsewhere you'll only find *boulangeries*, some supermarkets and florists opening on Sunday mornings. The traditional two-hour closure between 1200 and 1400 is still observed, although in recent years larger supermarkets and many independent shops in towns have started to remain open. Some boulangeries open until 1300 for the lunchtime trade but may not re-open until 1500. If you need anything for a picnic buy it before midday. Many clothes shops and small traders are closed on Mondays.

Essentials A-Z

Customs and immigration

UK and EU citizens do not require a visa, but need a valid passport to enter France. You are required to carry some form of identification with you at all times in France. Travellers from outside the EU may need to obtain a standard tourist visa, valid for up to 90 days.

Disabled travellers

Tourism sites in France have improved facilities for disabled visitors over recent years with the installation of ramps, dedicated car parking and toilets with wheelchair-access. However, many historic buildings and town centres have uneven surfaces underfoot, lots of gravel and assorted street furniture, which can pose difficulties for wheelchair-users and blind or partially sighted visitors. The Ministry of Tourism has been working with the industry to develop the *Tourisme & Handicap* label, to communicate reliable, consistent and objective information regarding accessibility of tourist sites (see www.tourisme-handicaps.org for links to local tourism websites, plus details of attractions and accommodation with the Tourisme & Handicap label).

Electricity

France functions on a 230V mains supply. Plugs are the standard European 2-pin variety.

Emergencies

Ambulance T15; **Police** T17; **Fire Service** T18 (if calling from a landline). The European emergency number T112 can be dialled free from any phone, including mobiles and call boxes.

Health

EU citizens should obtain a **European Health Insurance Card** ⓘ *www.ehic.ie*, before travelling to France. This entitles you to emergency medical treatment on the same terms as French nationals. If you develop a minor ailment while on holiday, pharmacists can give medical advice and recommend treatment. Outside normal opening hours, the address of the nearest duty pharmacy (*pharmacie de garde*) is displayed in other pharmacy windows. The out-of-hours number for a local doctor (*médecin généraliste*) may also be listed.

In a serious emergency, go to the accident and emergency department (*urgences*) at the nearest *Centre Hospitalier* (numbers listed in the Essentials boxes in each chapter) or call an ambulance (SAMU) by dialling T15.

Insurance

Comprehensive travel and medical insurance are strongly recommended, as the **European Health Insurance Card** (EHIC) does not cover medical repatriation, ongoing medical treatment or treatment considered to be non-urgent.

Language

The French are a formal and very courteous society, and it is normal to greet everyone you meet. *Bonjour* (*Bonsoir* during the evening), followed by *Monsieur*, *Madame*, or for a young single woman, *Madamoiselle* (pronounced '*Mam'selle*') will start you off on the right foot. When meeting someone for the first time, people often shake hands. Even with people who you know, such as a waiter at your favourite restaurant, a greeting will start with a crisp handshake. A *bisou* (kiss on the cheek) is strictly for good friends and family. Always use the formal *vous* to say 'you' in French rather than the more intimate form *tu*, which is normally reserved for friends and family. It is best to let the French decide when they do it, then return the compliment.

Money

The French unit of currency is the euro. ATMs throughout France accept major credit and debit cards. Currency exchange is available in some banks, and at airports, train stations and bureaux de change. Most restaurants, shops, and tourist attractions accept major credit cards, although restaurants in smaller towns may only accept cash. Toll (*péage*) routes accept Visa, MasterCard and American Express cards but not Maestro or Visa Electron cards.

Police

There are 3 national police forces in France. The *Police nationale* operate mainly in urban areas and are distinguished by silver buttons on their uniforms. The *Gendarmerie nationale* are under the control of the Ministry of Defence, and wear blue uniforms with gold buttons. They deal with serious crime on a national level. The *Douane* is a civilian customs service. Only these 3 services have the power of arrest. All police in France are armed.

Post

You can buy stamps (*timbres*) in post offices or over the counter in tabacs. A stamp for a postcard will cost around €0.77. Many post offices now have self-service stamp machines with instructions in several languages, including English.

Safety

Away from very large cities, the crime rate in France is generally low. Think carefully, though, about where you park your car at night – and never leave valuables in your car, even briefly. In provincial towns and cities it is generally safe to walk where you please, although at night avoid wandering into unlit areas. Only carry small amounts of cash, and keep passport, credit cards and cash separate. Travelling on public transport in France is generally very safe. Never leave luggage unattended at bus or railway stations, and always be alert to risk, especially late at night. If you are a victim of theft, report the crime to the police (*Gendarmerie*) immediately, as you will need their report (*constat de vol*) to claim on your insurance.

Telephone

French telephone numbers consist of 10 digits, and always start with a zero. Area codes are incorporated into the number so the first 2 digits denote the region (02 in the Loire Valley), the second pair is the town, the third pair the district. To call France from abroad dial the international prefix 00 plus 33 (the country code) followed by the phone number required (drop the first 0). Search online for phone numbers using www.pagesblanches.fr (private numbers) or www.pagesjaunes.fr (business numbers). For France Télécom directory enquiries dial 118 712 (calls cost €1.46 per min) or visit www.118712.fr.

Time difference

France uses Central European Time, GMT+1.

Tipping

Most restaurants include service in their prices (*servis inclus* or *compris* is usually stated at the foot of the menu), so leaving extra for a tip is not necessary. Taxi drivers expect a small tip, usually 5-10% of the fare.

Loire Valley: Sancerre to Amboise

Contents

Footprint features

Sancerre to the Orléanais

Our journey begins in a hilly landscape described by Balzac as "a chain of small mountains" – an appropriately romantic setting for a love affair with the Loire to begin. Climb the steep ramparts of the town of Sancerre to see the surrounding contours draped with the productive vines which have made this ancient hilltop settlement and its wine-producing neighbours world-famous. In past times the little port of St-Thibault shipped the wines and unloaded timber for local barrel-makers. Today you can take to the water by cruising on the nearby Canal Latéral à la Loire – while you enjoy the landscapes you'll never be far from the river. In fact, you'll eventually pass high above it on the spectacular 19th-century Pont-Canal aqueduct at Briare, a perfect place to moor and meet other boating types or relax at a quayside restaurant.

The Loire, meanwhile, continues through gentle landscapes, passing chateau towns such as Gien and Sully-sur-Loire on its way towards Orléans. Joan of Arc's town has become a vibrant, elegant city and nearby are over 35,000 ha of ancient forests and lakes of the Fôret d'Orléans, where you might chance upon eagles, ospreys and, of course, deer and wild boar. Beyond Orléans lies historic Beaugency, whose 26-arch former toll-bridge across the Loire dates from the 14th century.

Sancerre and downstream to Châteauneuf → *For listings, see pages 44-50.*

While Sancerre attracts many visitors, drawn by the allure of some of the region's most prestigious wines, this is an otherwise quiet and often overlooked corner of the Loire Valley. But the river landscapes are perhaps at their most beautiful here and offer plenty of opportunities for relaxed picnicking, walking and birdwatching as the Loire flows past historic towns and villages towards Châteauneuf-sur-Loire. During your own journey find time to pause, too, at the great Benedictine abbey of Fleury in St-Benoît-sur-Loire, as travellers and pilgrims have done for a thousand years.

Getting around

Most people will choose the convenience of the car to get around this region; however, thanks to the *Loire à Vélo* cycle route and the network of canals, it is possible to visit the area at a slower pace. Gien is the largest town and is about halfway between Sancerre and Orléans. Bus services throughout the Loiret region are operated by Ulys. Lines 3 and 7 from Orléans serve this area as far as Châtillon-sur-Loire. There are regular trains to Gien, Briare and Tracy-sur-Loire (for Sancerre) from Paris Bercy (about 1½ hours' journey time).

Tourist information

Tourist information offices ⓘ *1 place de Gaulle, Briare, T02 38 31 24 51;* ⓘ *3 place Aristide Briand, Châteauneuf-sur-Loire, T02 38 58 44 79;* ⓘ *47 rue Franche, Châtillon-sur-Loire, T02 38 31 42 88;* ⓘ *place Jean Jaurés, Gien, T02 38 67 25 28;* ⓘ *44 rue Orléanaise, St Benoît-sur-Loire, T02 38 35 79 00;* ⓘ *Esplanade Porte César, Sancerre, T02 48 54 08 21;* ⓘ *place de Gaulle, Sully-sur-Loire, T02 38 36 23 703.*

Sancerre → *For listings, see pages 44-50.*

Sancerre looks and feels like a major centre of wine production. It smells like one too, during the annual *vendange* period, when freshly picked grapes are being crushed in and around this ancient hilltop town. Short of transporting it to Provence, the setting couldn't be better, with productive vineyards draped over the surrounding hills and valleys as far as the eye can see. The town's medieval layout converges on place du Befroi and the Notre-Dame, near which the **Maison des Sancerre** ⓘ *www.maison-des-sancerre.com, daily end Mar to mid-Nov*, a beautifully restored townhouse dating from the 14th century, offers lots of information and insight into local wine production. There are plenty of options for wine tastings (and purchases) in and around the town, whose visitor focus has shifted towards the Nouvelle Place, an agreeable spot for a cool drink or an evening meal. Explore the streets which rise behind the square and you'll find the **Tour des Fiefs**, an early 16th-century circular tower which now has a viewing platform perched on the summit offering definitive panoramas of the town and the surrounding landscapes.

Before leaving the Sancerre area it's worth sampling the local de Chavignol 's cheeses and visiting the nearby, slightly sleepy pleasure port of **St-Thibault St-Satur**, nestled between the Loire and its Lateral Canal.

Châtillon-sur-Loire → *For listings, see pages 44-50.*

Châtillon's spidery suspension bridges across the Lateral Canal and the Loire itself are much better known than the historic town, which therefore counts as something of a

Vendange

For more full-on exposure to wine production you can't do better than to head for nearby **Chavignol**, a normally peaceful village which erupts into frenzied activity during the annual *vendange*, typically around early to mid-October. In the hills above the village are footpaths leading into the very heart of the vineyards, where you can see the picking process first hand (an experience which will bring a new dimension to your subsequent wine enjoyment).

discovery. Its name comes from the 10th-12th-century *castellio* known locally as Château Gaillard, a few ruined sections of which survive high above the town. After parking near the tourist office (see page 27) in the town centre (which you'll probably have all to yourself around midday) follow rue des Prés then take rue Haute, which climbs to the most ancient part of the town. On either side are stone façades, one of which retains a four-storey, half-timbered *escalier* (an external spiral staircase) accessed by a further set of stone steps. A little further on you'll reach the surprisingly large **Eglise St-Maurice**, whose 19th-century neo-Gothic interior is beautifully proportioned. There's also some rich stained glass in the choir windows and an ornate Gothic altarpiece. Just beyond the church you'll find a footpath leading to the chateau ruins and a bird's-eye view of the valley. After returning to the lower town, turn left before the tourist office into rue Franche, where a tall bell tower denotes a former **Protestant Temple** (only the third to be built in France and dating from 1596) which alternated between destruction and rebuilding amid attacks on the fiercely Protestant town during the Wars of Religion.

As you leave Châtillon it's worth turning right off rue Martial Vuidet onto rue du Port, which has a bar/restaurant and leads to a small pleasure port on the canal. The port begins just above the gardens to your left and there's an upmarket restaurant, **La Fayette** (T02 38 38 18 63), on one of the barges moored at the quayside.

Briare → *For listings, see pages 44-50.*

Pont-Canal de Briare

ⓘ *Access via the Port de Commerce, Briare or St-Firmin-sur-Loire on the left bank of the Loire. Information from the Office de Tourisme, 1 place de Gaulle, Briare, T02 38 31 24 51, www.briare-le-canal.com, or the Musée des Deux Marines et du Pont-Canal, 58 bd Buyser, Briare, T02 38 31 28 27.*

The 17th-century Canal de Briare, one of France's oldest waterways, flows beside the *rive gauche* (left bank) of the river, while the Lateral Canal sits on the *rive droite* (right bank). Linking the two would have opened up the lucrative Parisian market to businesses below the Loire, but was always going to be technically challenging. The solution, achieved with the help of Gustave Eiffel's engineers, was the sensational Pont-Canal de Briare, a 663-m-long aqueduct whose 3000-tonne water channel of structural steel is carried on rugged stone piers. It took seven years to complete and opened in 1876, carrying barges and other waterway traffic across the Loire in belle époque style. It's still in use and is particularly appreciated by river cruisers, for whom Briare's Port de Plaisance (leisure port) has expanded its facilities in recent years. Alternatively, you can cross on foot, or see things differently from the leafy riverbank footpaths below.

What to see in…

…one day

Wake up in the cheerful riverside town of **Sully-sur-Loire**, visit the moated chateau then follow the river to **St-Benoît-sur-Loire** to see the sculpted tomb figure of **King Philippe I** in the magnificent medieval abbey of **Fleury**. Picnic on the riverbank then visit the fascinating **Musée de la Marine de Loire** in nearby **Châteauneuf-sur-Loire**. Pause at the old river port of **Combleux** before ending your day in style with a meal and a stroll around the historic heart of Orléans.

…a weekend or more

After an overnight stay in **Orléans** visit the vast **Cathédrale Ste-Croix**, right beside which you'll see the dazzling treasures of the city's **Musée des Beaux-Arts**. Then simply cross the road to the 16th-century Renaissance **Hôtel Groslot**, which once played host to the several kings of France. After lunch in the **old town**, head south to **La Ferté-St-Aubin's** time-warp chateau (with an *Orient Express* train in its grounds), before crossing the Loire on a 14th-century bridge to discover the medieval heart of **Beaugency**.

Musée de la Mosaïque et des Emaux

ⓘ *1 bd Loreau, T02 38 31 20 51, www.emauxdebriare.com. 1 Jun-30 Sep daily 1000-1830, 1 Oct-31 Oct and 21-30 Apr 1000-1200 and 1400-1800, 1 Nov-31 Dec and 30 Jan-20 Apr daily 1400-1800. €5.50.*

The story of how Briare became world-famous during the 19th and early 20th centuries for its buttons, beads, costume pearls and enamel-glazed mosaic tiles is recounted in this stylish collection, housed in the former factory building of the company which produced them. Period examples of Emaux de Briare's mainstream products are ultimately less inspiring, however, than the important collection of decorative mosaic panels spanning art nouveau and art deco periods, plus work by today's contemporary designers. Production of newly fashionable ceramic mosaic tiles continues and there's a small factory shop behind the museum building.

Gien → *For listings, see pages 44-50.*

Getting there

Buses to Gien stop at various locations in the town, place Leclerc is the most central stop. Trains arrive and depart from the **Gare SNCF** ⓘ *Place de la Gare, T08-36 35 35 35.*

Château de Gien and Musée de la Chasse et de la Nature

ⓘ *The Château de Gien is closed for work until winter 2013. Entry by rue du Château (parking in front of the church) or climb the Escalier des Degrés from the town, T02 38 67 69 69, www.loiret.com. Feb-Mar and Oct-Dec Wed-Sun 1400-1700, Apr-Jun and Sep Wed-Sun 1330-1800, Jul-Aug 1330-1800 daily, closed 25 Dec and Jan. €3, €1.50 (6-17s), €10 family (2 adults, 2 children).*

Cross Gien's 16th-century *dos d'âne* (donkey-back) stone bridge to admire classic views of the town rising from the right bank of the Loire. Notice how the red-brick Eglise Ste-Jeanne-d'Arc blends almost seamlessly into the main body of the chateau. Like the church, the chateau's oldest feature is a stone tower (the **Tour Charlemagne**, retained from a much earlier structure), although the remainder of the building is hardly youthful, its construction having started in the late 15th century. This places it among the very earliest of all the Loire Valley chateaux, comfortably pre-dating the wave of building which would elsewhere be fuelled by the Renaissance. Not that it remained untouched by the arrival of the new stylistic influences, however, notably in the romantic-looking wing rising from the opposite (eastern) end of the building. For a closer look recross the bridge to the town centre and climb the steps of l'Escalier des Degrés which ascend to the chateau from avenue du Maréchal Leclerc. Today it's hard to appreciate the scale of destruction which the site endured during the Second World War, as a long campaign of skillful and patient reconstruction has restored the building to its former glory. Note the intricate brickwork – diamond patterns for the Renaissance wing and individual motifs (including a crossbow) for the main body of the building. The site was long a meeting place for hunters, a theme developed in the museum within the chateau. The exhibits may fail to convert you to the pursuit and killing of assorted wildlife for pleasure, but they present a pretty definitive overview (with works by great animal painters) of a historically important activity which for centuries helped feed the people of the region.

Eglise Ste-Jeanne d'Arc

ⓘ *Rue du Château, information available from tourist office, T02 38 67 25 28.*

With its commanding position high above the town, there's no mistaking the heavily buttressed Gothic tower of the early 16th-century royal collegiate church of St-Etienne, damaged during the Revolution and effectively abandoned in 1828. The church's baroque successor was dedicated to St Pierre in 1832, but was virtually destroyed by the aerial bombardments in June 1940 which claimed much of the town. The tower's massive structure, however, enabled it to survive. The present neo-Romanesque church, completed in 1954 and dedicated to St Joan, was constructed in reinforced concrete, which was then entirely clad in red brickwork. The style is curious, to say the least, and becomes a lot more so when you enter the other-worldly interior. As your eyes acclimatize to the low light levels, notice the nave and side aisles divided by circular columns (drum piers) whose round-arched arcades sit on simple terracotta capitals depicting the life of the patron saint. These in turn support plain barrel vaults, of which the central arch, hanging 22 m above the 12-m-wide nave, represents an impressive architectural achievement. The pencil-like diamond-arched lancet windows, on the other hand, are neither Gothic nor Romanesque, but those of the nave do at least contain vibrant stained glass panels by master glassmaker Max Ingrand, who also worked nearby in Azay-le-Rideau, Blois, Chenonceau and Tours. The altar, hewn from solid Vosges marble – red, naturally – is decorated with further panels by Ingrand. Sadly the eastern Ste-Jeanne windows by François Bertrand were partly obscured following the bizarre decision in 1986 to install a giant organ (manufactured by Roethinger of Strasbourg) in front of them. The remaining interior decoration is mainly confined to tall Orléans ceramic figures of the Virgin and Saints adorning the piers, along with the *Stations of The Cross* in glazed ceramic panels by Jean Bertholle and manufactured in Gien.

Musée de la Faïencerie

ⓘ *78 place de la Victoire, T02 38 05 21 06, www.gien.com. Open 0900-1200 and 1400-1800. Closed 1 May, 1 and 11 Nov, 25 Dec, 1 Jan, Mon and Tue during Jan-Feb, Sun Nov-Mar. No studio visits Jul, Aug and Dec. The adjacent factory shop is closed Sun. Museum only €4, €2 (7-15s), €3 groups (minimum 20 people). Studios only €8 per person (groups only). Studios and museum €10 per person (groups only).*

France has something of a reputation for fine *faïence* (glazed earthenware, or majolica) and the Musée de la Faïencerie in Gien, and the company (which is also called Gien) ranks among the very finest and most highly prized of all producers. The business was established in 1821 by Englishman Thomas Hall, who was attracted to Gien because of its proximity to substantial deposits of the high quality clay and sand on which the manufacturing process depended. Better still, the local forests would provide timber to fire the kilns, while the finished goods could then be shipped direct from Gien's quays. He purchased a former convent dating from the 16th century and set about establishing his new factory. Using production techniques popularized in England, the company went on to develop a steadily broadening range of tableware and other domestic items. Much of Gien's success was due to the decision to base its designs on (and even convincingly replicate) the forms and decorative styles from other renowned centres of production including Rouen, Marseille and Delft, plus the Italian designs of Faenza, from which the French product takes its name. The whole story is recounted in the company's museum, which is housed in a former clay store cellar dating from the 16th century. The displays show examples of work from 180 years of production, including several large showpieces created for important exhibitions. There's also a faithful recreation of a 19th-century dining room, the table laid with colourful Gien faïencerietableware. Should you be tempted, there's a factory shop adjacent to the museum.

Downstream from Gien → *For listings, see pages 44-50.*

Château de Sully-sur-Loire

ⓘ *About 50 km southeast of Orléans, T02 38 36 36 86, www.loiret.com. Feb, Mar, Oct-Dec Tue-Sun 1000-1200 and 1400-1700, Apr-Sep Tue-Sun 1000-1800, Jul-Aug daily 1000-1800. Closed 25 Dec and Jan. €6, €3 (6-17s), €15 family (2 adults, 2 children), small supplement for guided visits. Try to visit on a Mon for one of Sully's lively markets.*

On a warm summer evening, when the sinking sun turns Sully's pale grey stones to fiery gold, the chateau appears to float on the mirror-like surface of its wide moat. Most of what you see was constructed before 1360, at which time the scene would have looked very different. The chateau originally stood right beside the Loire, defending Sully's important river crossing with a square keep flanked by massive rounded corner towers and equipped with crenelated sentry walks, plus numerous *meurtrier* for bows or crossbows. It was conceived by royal architect Raymond du Temple (creator of the Palais du Louvre) for Guy de la Trémoille, a close friend of Charles VII. The king, a frequent guest, received Joan of Arc at Sully in 1429 and 1430. To increase accommodation, the eastern Pétit Château wing was added around 1524, and in 1602 the chateau passed to Henri IV's treasurer Maximilien de Béthune, first Duc de Sully. After the river burst its banks in 1608 he made the improvements to flood defences which created the present moat-style canals, then set about establishing gardens and landscaped parkland. He also began the process of restyling, which would determine the chateau's present appearance, including lowering the towers and adding their distinctive slate roofs. More recent extensive restoration work included a 19th-century study and three 18th-century apartments, the Salle d'Honneur (in which the young Voltaire performed his plays with his friends), the royal bed chamber used by Louis XIV and the famous and extraordinary roof space, whose timbers resemble those of a vast, upturned boat.

Abbaye de Fleury

ⓘ *St-Benoît-sur-Loire, T02 38 35 72 43, www.abbaye-fleury.com. Visits are welcome between 0630 and 2200, guided visits are only given between Easter and All Saints (1 Nov). Daily Mass is held at 1200 (1100 on Sun) and is accompanied by Gregorian chant (duration about 1 hr). You can attend the service, or quietly observe and listen. Visits are discouraged until after services end.*

The unassuming village of St-Benoît-sur-Loire would pass largely unnoticed by the outside world but for the presence of its Benedictine abbey, founded in the seventh century near one of the wilder sections of the Loire. Around 673 a group of monks travelled to Italy, disinterred the remains of St Benoît (or Benedict) from the ruined abbey of Monte Casino and brought them here. As the resting place of the Patriarch of Western monasticism, Fleury immediately became a major place of pilgrimage, and eventually transformed its abbey into the immense structure we see today. The massive entry portal (named the Tour de Gauzlin after the abbot who conceived it) had its upper storey removed after the monks refused to accept an externally appointed abbot in 1527. The capitals of the supporting piers are a dazzling showcase for the skills of the 11th-century masons who carved them – one capital is inscribed UNBERTUS ME FECIT ('*Unbertus made me*'). Compare the work here with the bas-reliefs in the left-hand wall of the tower, the nearby Gothic portal of the main body of the church, and the countless other decorated capitals inside.

The subtly magnificent 12th-century nave is late Romanesque beneath a later Gothic rib vault. The choir, though, is pure 11th-century and the Sanctuary retains the Roman polychrome marble mosaic floor of the previous fifth/sixth-century abbey. Here you'll find the sculpted tomb figure of King Philippe I, close to a flight of steps descending to the dimly lit and rather melancholy crypt containing St-Benoît's remains. A much more uplifting experience is provided each day in the church above by the monks, whose Gregorian plainsong will haunt you long after your visit.

L'Oratoire de Germigny-des-Prés

ⓘ *Place du Bourg, Germigny-des-Prés (on D60 about 30 km southeast of Orléans), tourist office T02 38 58 27 97, www.tourisme-loire-foret.com. Oratory open to visitors Jun-Sep 0900-1900, Oct-May 0900-1700. Free. Guided visits €3, children €1.50, under 12s free.*

The area has no shortage of historic architecture, but this is in a league of its own. Over 1200 years ago (in AD 806) Théodulphe, Abbot of Fleury, Bishop of Orléans and a key advisor at the court of Charlemagne, built a Gallo-Roman villa complex here in what the Romans referred to as *Germanicus*, including a private chapel. A century or so later pillaging destroyed the remainder of the site, but the little stone oratory survived the flames to become one of the earliest religious structures in France. The nave was enlarged around the 15th century, and major renovation between 1867 and 1876 produced a deceptively youthful appearance inside, but look beyond the immaculate paintwork and almost surreal light fittings and you'll begin to notice details such as the horseshoe-shaped arches of the apse, which have more of the spirit of the Orient than of early France. Other important surviving features include a 12th-century reliquary decorated with Limoges enamels, a 14th-century carved figure of the Virgin and a beautiful Pietà from the same period. Lighting it all is a tall, airy lantern tower poised above the transept crossing arches. What makes this place really important, however, is the celebrated Ravenna School mosaic which was applied to the ceiling of the apse during the 11th century. Around 130,000 tiny squares of gilded glass and richly enamelled stones provide a startling vision of the Ark of The Covenant descending from heaven beneath the outstretched hands of God.

Probably unique in the world, the presence of the priceless image was concealed by layers of applied limewash, and only came to light when unsuspecting 19th-century restorers uncovered it. A coin-in-the-slot box illuminates things further and supplies a descriptive commentary in your preferred language.

Eglise St-Martial

ⓘ *Grand' Rue, Châteauneuf-sur-Loire.*

The assertive 50-m-high bell tower looks promising but, as you'll soon see, Châteauneuf's occasionally troubled history has left its mark on this once-noble church (which has also suffered more visibly than most at the hands of insensitive restorers). Completed in 1154 with a square lantern tower above the transept crossing, it survived more or less intact until the Wars of Religion, which left it in ruin. By 1627, however, the nave had been rebuilt and the present tower was added shortly afterwards. Blame the Revolution, and particularly the bombardments of June 1940, for the worst of what followed. Subsequent rebuilding ran out of steam some way short of replacing the full nave, which is now linked to the tower by a curious long, arched porch. But the church remains worth visiting, if only to see one treasure which has somehow survived – the magnificently over-the-top monument of Marquise Louis-Phélypeaux de la Vrillière, Secretary of State to Louis XIV and owner of the nearby chateau. Attributed to virtuoso Italian sculptor Guidi, who also worked at Versailles, the centrepiece of his spectacular creation is the Marquess gazing Heavenwards while an angel prepares to bear him aloft. Caryatid figures on either side in skeleton form add a macabre touch, and are replicas of those destroyed during 1940.

Musée de la Marine de Loire

ⓘ *Ecuries du Château, 1 place Aristide Briand, Châteauneuf-sur-Loire, T02 38 46 84 46, www.musees.regioncentre.fr. Apr-Oct Wed-Mon 1000-1800, Nov-Mar Wed-Mon 1400-1800. Closed 1 Jan, 1 May, 25 Dec. €3.50, €2 concessions. interesting and well-written English translation of exhibits and related information is available at reception.*

Little remains of the town's 'new chateau' and its grand estate (which once rivalled Versailles) apart from some modest but pleasantly landscaped gardens and the elegant former stables. Inside is the Loire Marine Museum filled with memorabilia recounting not only the long history of navigation on the river but also the town's related activities. You'll discover, for example, that the famous transporter bridges of great ports like Marseille, Rochefort, Nantes and even Newport, were designed and built here in Châteauneuf – the documentation is all there, along with an impressively detailed scale model. Everything is presented very stylishly in a beautifully restored historic setting, and the visit will give you real insight into many of the things you'll see during your visits along the Loire.

Musée Campanaire Bollée

ⓘ *56 Faubourg Bourgogne, St-Jean-de-Braye (a few kilometres east of Orléans centre on N152), T02 38 86 29 47, www.visaloire.com. All year, guided tours by arrangement. €3. To park, turn right by the Courtepaille restaurant.*

You'll barely notice the suburban village of St-Jean-de-Braye straggling anonymously along the road, much less a grimy old workshop set well back from it behind iron railings. But look a little closer and you'll see a modest Musée Campanaire sign pointing towards an unlikely looking alleyway. Follow it and you'll be rewarded with something extraordinary. Since 1715 eight generations of the Bollé family have been *maîtres-saintiers* (master bellmakers), at first travelling to cast their creations close to the sites where they were required but from 1838 based here in a cavernous foundry on the outskirts of Orléans. They've since produced 45,000 bells, and today the workshop (one of only three remaining bell foundries in France) is very much a working museum, which in a typical year still consumes around 30 tonnes of bronze. During a visit you'll learn about the whole process, including how each bell's tonal purity depends on precise mathematical calculation – and that, having established its personality, each bell is given a name. You might also see some of the bells being made to fulfil orders from throughout the world.

If, by the time you leave, you're ready for a stroll, turn right and right again to reach the towpath of the nearby river, a popular haunt for local fishermen. A little further upstream the Loire is joined by the Canal d'Orléans and the Canal de Briare in the charming old port of **Combleux**, whose iron swing bridge once permitted cattle to reach fertile grazing on the river banks. Today you can dine in some style at the elegant **Restaurant de la Marine** (see page 47) beside the old lock gates, while enjoying views of unspoilt landscapes designated as a nature reserve.

Orléans → *For listings, see pages 44-50.*

If Joan of Arc were to return today she wouldn't believe her eyes. But the city in whose destiny the Maid of Orléans played such a pivotal part continues to pursue its role as a dynamic centre of commerce and trade, and looks just as unstoppable as it proved to

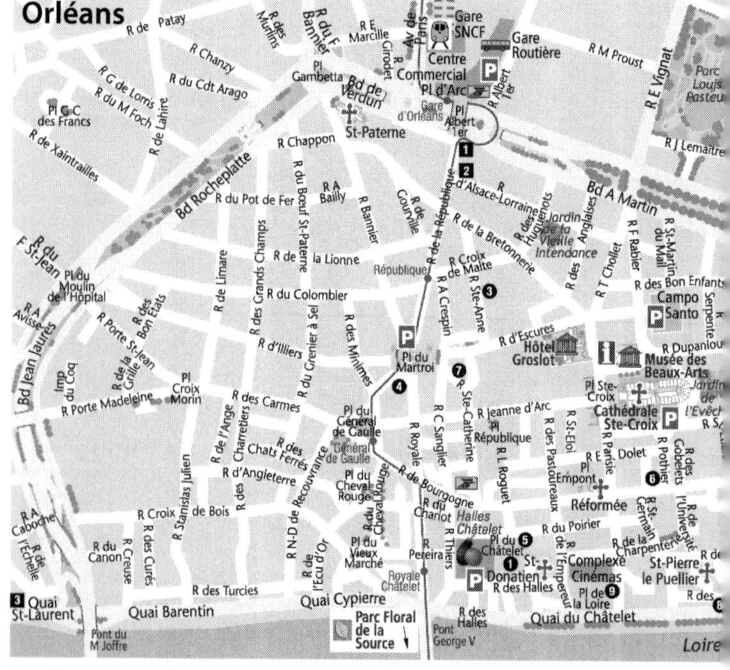

be back in 1429 – or in AD 451, when its inhabitants succeeded in fending off the army of Attila the Hun. The city's formidable defences may have long since vanished but their trace is still followed by the modern road system, within whose occasionally gridlocked embrace lies evidence of a long and eventful history. Dominating the skyline is the Cathédrale Ste-Croix, a huge and grandiose 18th- and 19th-century homage to the great Gothic cathedrals. Nearby is the Renaissance Hôtel Groslot, which accommodated François II, Charles IX, Henri III and Henri IV during state visits. Meanwhile, below wide boulevards and narrow streets lined with medieval half-timbered houses, lie old quays from which goods and travellers once departed for Nantes and the coast, a journey which could take six days or more. It's here, too, that the history and traditions of the river are celebrated in style during the annual **Festival de Loire**.

Getting there

The **Gare SNCF** ⓘ *avenue de Paris*, has a striking modern façade. It is served by TER regional trains, which include regular services to Paris and stops along the western Loire Valley. Visit www.gares-en-mouvement.com for all station information and services. There is a shuttle service between Orléans central station and Les Aubrais Orléans, 3 km north of the city, from which some train services depart. Ligne A tramway services also stop there. Buses arrive and depart from the **Gare Routière** ⓘ *behind the train station, in place d'Arc*. You can join the tram or catch a local bus to access other parts of the city from here.

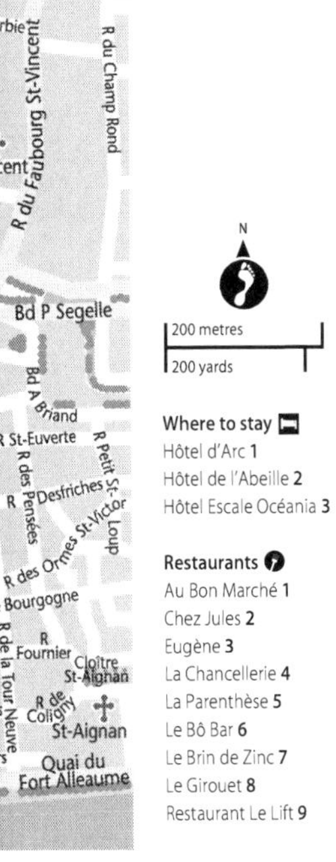

Getting around

It's cheaper and easier to park your car at the edge of the city in one of the designated P+R (Parcs Relais) sites and use the tramway to get around. Lines run north–south and east–west, see www.cleo.agglo-orleans.fr for details. The **TAO** ⓘ *www.reseau-tao.fr*, transport network has a useful website which shows clearly all bus, tramway routes and park and ride (P+R) around Orléans. The operator **Ulys** ⓘ *www.ulys-loiret.com*, serves towns throughout the Loiret.

Tourist information

Tourist offices ⓘ *111 rue du Maréchal Foch, Cléry-St-André, T02 38 45 94 33;* ⓘ *Moulin Massot 7 rue des Mauves, Meung-sur-Loire, T02 38 44 32 28;* ⓘ *2 place de l'Etape, Orléans, T02 38 24 05 05, www.tourisme-orleans.com.*

Old Orléans

The legendary spirit of old Orléans has been much diluted by events in its turbulent past, but what remains is scattered around a relatively compact area between the cathedral and the river. Tracking it down can take time, so you might prefer to follow

Plan-Vélo

Orléans is one of a growing number of French towns that has signed up to the Plan-Vélo bike-hire scheme (for details, including online subscription and an instruction video, visit agglo-veloplus.fr). In Orléans the system is called Vélo+ and provides 300 bikes at 32 stations, ready and waiting for anyone to use. To start using the service go to the tourist office (or the train station), provide some personal details and you'll be given a user card and a pin number. Subscriptions ('*abonnements*') work on a pay-as-you-go basis, either weekly (€3) or by the day (€1). Once you have your card you can go to the information post at any of the bike stations (you'll see eye-catching racks of cheerful bicycles positioned throughout the city centre), pass your card over a reader, enter your pin number and the number of the bike you wish to use. The bike (which can be adjusted to suit your height) is then released for use. When you've finished your journey, simply plug it back into a vacant slot at any other station. Your first 30 minutes of use are free of charge, so your subscription could be all you pay, and charges for longer periods are modest.

the 'Orléans & The Middle Ages' itinerary, one of nine themed walks created by the city's tourist office. The route takes you first to the grandiose and much-reconstructed **Eglise St-Aignan** begun in 1439 by Charles VII. Its complex crypt, a remarkable survivor from the previous 11th-century church, contains one of the earliest known Gallo-Roman carved capitals. Next comes the **Tour Blanche**, a 15th-century watchtower, followed by **rue des Tanneurs**, a medieval leather-tanning area whose by-products once discharged into the nearby Loire. In rue de la Tour is the Gothic residence of a wealthy merchant, indicated by a crest above the doorway, while a few steps away lies the 12th-century Romanesque **Eglise St-Pierre-le-Peullier**, now beautifully restored and used as an exhibition space. Notice the humorous carved corbel heads on the exterior of the apse. The route passes more half-timbered houses en-route for place des Halles, where a single forlorn tower survives (in rue du Lin) from the Châtelet or fortress which guarded the main river crossing. More medieval houses follow from time to time as the route returns to place Ste-Croix and the cathedral. The handsome **Maison Jeanne d'Arc** ⓘ *3 place de Gaulle, T02 38 68 32 63, www.jeannedarc.com.fr; Oct-Mar 1400-1800, Apr-Sep 1000-1800, closed Mon and bank holidays; entry €4, concessions €2, under 16s free*, is actually a total reconstruction (completed in 1965) of a medieval building destroyed during the Second World War. Inside you'll find a wealth of information relating to the Maid of Orléans, including a large model of the fortified town under attack by the English forces in 1429.

Other places of interest

In addition to the precious fragments of its illustrious history, Orléans has much to reward those with a more eclectic eye. A good starting-point is the **place du Martroi**, where an arresting bronze figure of Joan of Arc, on horseback with sword in hand, surveys the scene from a huge plinth of pink granite. Look closer and you'll find a bronze bas-relief depiction of her in the thick of the celebrated battle to defend Orléans. Across the square, on the corner of rue de la République, is the belle époque (with added Renaissance touches) **La Rotonde**. Opened in 1898, its once-grand café was for years the most fashionable meeting place in town. Further up rue de la République is an even more assertive period piece: the towering **Hôtel Moderne**, in full-blown, swirling art nouveau and designed by Louis Duthoit in 1902.

Bizarrely, the interior decoration installed by the present owners combines Louis XVI with *art deco*. You'll find further art nouveau façades at 46 rue Saint-Marc, 7 bis route d'Olivet and 10 quai Barentin. As for the surviving Renaissance architecture, among the best is the **Hôtel Euverte Hatte** ⓘ *11 rue de Tabour*, whose three Italianate façades were created around a courtyard in 1524 for a wealthy merchant. More in the French style, with red brick and pale stone, are the four elegant residences constructed opposite the gardens of the Hôtel Groslot (see below) in rue d'Escures. Intended from the outset for letting, they represent an early piece of property speculation on the part of Henri IV's chief military commander Pierre Fougueu Escures. Ultimately, though, it's grand vistas like the view towards the cathedral from rue Jeanne d'Arc which create the most enduring impressions of the city.

Musée des Beaux-Arts

ⓘ *Place Ste-Croix, T02 38 79 21 55, www.musees.regioncentre.fr. Tue-Sun 1000-1800. Closed 1 Jan, 1 and 8 May, 14 Jul, 1 and 11 Nov, 25 Dec. Audio guides in English available free. €3 entry fee also gives access to the History and Archaeological Museum of Orléans. Free entry 1st Sun every month. Visit on a Sun morning and you'll have the fabulous collections virtually to yourself – the nearby cathedral bells only heighten the sense of occasion.*

Spread across five floors of a light and elegant modern building designed by Christian Langlois, it's worth taking your time to immerse yourself in one of the finest art collections to be found outside Paris. The setting, beside the cathedral, is also near-perfect. Like Tours, Orléans' Fine Art Museum was founded on the spoils of the Revolution, and began displaying the substantial cache of possessions plundered from both church and aristocracy in 1797. Subsequent donations from wealthy traders, wine merchants and other art collectors added many Flemish and Dutch canvasses, while the State financed the acquisition of important Italian School works. The visit begins on the second floor, with 15th- to 18th-century Dutch, Flemish, Spanish, Italian and Scandinavian works. Here you'll find *Madonna and Child* Sienese School painter Matteo di Giovanni, plus *Holy Family* Correggio, from Parma. Other heavyweights include Brueghel, Tintoretto, Velázquez and van Dyck. The floor below counters with the full force of what 17th- and 18th-century France had to offer – particularly interesting are canvasses by Deruet and Fréminet from the lost Château de Richelieu. Eighteenth-century works include portraits by Tocque, Drouais and Perronneau, along with sculptures by Houdon and Pigalle. Descend to two mezzanine floors to see how things evolved during the 19th century. One of the most haunting images, *Scène d'Incendie* by Orléans' own Alexandre Antigna, is a graphic portrayal of a family attempting to flee from a fire raging in their home. Rather underwhelming in comparison, the museum's collection of 20th-century works is consigned to the basement.

Hôtel Groslot

ⓘ *3 place de l'Etape. Mon-Fri 0900-1200 and 1400-1800, Sun 1000-1200 and 1400-1800 (without interruption during summer). Closed Sat for marriage ceremonies. Free.*

This subtly magnificent creation was completed around 1552 by town bailiff Jacques Groslot. Its Renaissance style is reminiscent of the Château de Blois (see page 53), combining diamond-pattern black-and-pink brickwork with pale stone detailing. The effect is complemented by a pair of elegantly styled stone staircases, which unite at their mid-point before going their separate ways to first-floor level. Set between them is a bronze statue of Joan of Arc (calmly contemplating the bullet holes she acquired during the Second World War) by Princess Marie d'Orléans, daughter of Louis Philippe. In its heyday the roll-call of visitors included François II (who died here in his teens during a meeting of the French General Council in 1560), Catherine de' Medici, Charles IX, Henri III and Henri IV. Everything changed abruptly when the Revolution found the *hôtel particulier* (gentleman's mansion) a new role as the Hôtel de Ville (town hall). It then underwent major alterations, including the addition of two outer wings. Fortunately the architectural style was retained, leaving the underlying spirit largely intact. The city council eventually outgrew its surroundings and moved out, leaving the sumptuous interiors to stun unsuspecting visitors with a sizzling tour de force of 19th-century neo-Gothic splendour. Every surface is painted, papered, panelled or gilded, and the whole thing is set off with vast crystal chandeliers which would not look out of place in Versailles. Detail touches include a wooden chest given by Louis XI to the canons of St-Aignan, plus stirring bas-relief panels above the largest of the fireplaces. Their theme takes the exploits of Joan of Arc, who also appears in stained-glass form in the windows. Intriguingly, the city's Salle de Mariage is the very room in which Charles IX met his future mistress Marie Touchet in 1569.

Cathédrale Ste-Croix

ⓘ *Place Ste-Croix. Oct-Apr daily 0915-1200 and 1400-1800, May-Sep 0915-1800.*

The Cathedral of the Holy Cross is built on the site of a fourth-century basilica. Construction began with the choir in the early 12th century but over-hasty construction resulted in the nave collapsing in 1227. Work recommenced in 1288 and was completed with the patronage of Charles VII and Louis XI. In 1568 Protestants pillaged the cathedral, destabilising the crossing piers and causing the nave and transepts to collapse. The subsequent long campaign of rebuilding, with contributions from Henri III, Henri IV, Louis XIII, Louis XIV and Louis XV, was not completed until 1829. The styling of the later work has divided opinion ever since, Marcel Proust declaring it 'the ugliest church in France'. But ignore the slightly kitsch, Miss World-style crowns of the 113-m-high towers and look instead at the scene round at the eastern *chevet* (apse) and you might feel very differently. It's the same inside, particularly when the nave fills with multicoloured light from the wealth of stained glass. Many windows depict the life and trial of St Joan – look closely and you'll see that some of the characters have a distinctly 19th-century appearance. The geometric rose windows of the transepts look a little undersized, unlike the magnificent panelling of the choir, designed by Jules Hardouin-Mansart. The medallions above the 95 stalls were executed between 1680-1708 by Louis XIV's most skilled artists. Notice also the magnificent organ mounted above the western portals of the nave. It was built in 1631 for the Abbaye de Fleury in St-Benoît-sur-Loire (see page 32), where it remained until being sold during the Revolution. Construction work on the cathedral meant that it would not finally be transported down the Loire by boat, reassembled and installed in Orléans until 1821.

Around Orléans → *For listings, see pages 44-50.*

Château de La Ferté St-Aubin

ⓘ *About 20 km south of Orléans via the N20 (direction Vierzon), T02 38 61 55 45, www.chateau-ferte-st-aubin.com. The chateau reopens its doors to visitors on 30 Mar 2013 following extensive works – see website for dates, times and other details. €9, €6 (4-12s). Tickets valid for a whole day, allowing multiple admissions and time to explore the surrounding parkland. Allow at least 2 hrs for a visit with young children, picnics permitted. Special events include a large annual plant fair at the beginning of May and traditional Noël au Château before and after Christmas.*

Whatever your image of Loire Valley chateaux, this is something else – a classic Sologne estate with 350 years of history behind it, but which fell on such prolonged hard times that visiting it was for some years like opening a time capsule. An heroic rescue plan launched back in 1987 has gradually progressed to the point where the interior, which once looked and felt like having stumbled upon a long-abandoned family home, now feels loved and cherished once again. Visitors can explore virtually everything at their own pace, from comfortable family apartments to the below-stairs world of estate staff. The kitchens in particular retain all the evidence of their working past, putting firmly into perspective the manicured presentation of showpiece attractions elsewhere in the region. When you climb the stairs to explore the upper floors you'll be equally surprised to find perfect reconstructions of a village post office, an *épicerie* (grocer) and a school classroom. You can even enter the forest of roof timbers supporting the slate roof, hundreds of thousands of which have been replaced, thanks to visitor revenue.

Outside, the stables have also been lovingly restored (the horses' names appear above their respective stalls) while the former orangery now houses a vast collection of dolls and other childhood toys from chateau life. But what lies just across the moat in a forest clearing is even more unexpected: a recreated 1900s railway station, complete with stationmaster's office, waiting room and *bagagerie* (luggage room). The cherry on the top is a period train comprising 1920s and 1930s carriages from the legendary *Orient Express*, headed by a large steam locomotive dating from 1917. Broadening the family appeal still further, the visit now includes a selection of traditional family games plus mini-golf.

Basilique Notre-Dame de Cléry

ⓘ *15 km southwest of Orléans, entrance on rue du Cloître, Cléry-St-André, www.clery-saint-andre.com. Information from the tourist office, T02 38 45 94 33, o-tourismedeclery@wanadoo.fr.*
From a distance this vast church rises from the surrounding plains like a beached ocean liner. The cathedral-like scale becomes even more impressive as you draw closer, the symphony of 15th-century flamboyant Gothic contrasting with a *clocher* (bell tower) which is clearly much older. The vast building's presence here is due to a single item which survives inside – a beautifully carved wooden statue of the Virgin and Child, unearthed by a farm labourer's plough in 1280. Acquiring a reputation for miraculous powers, the statue was installed in a chapel, which soon proved inadequate for the number of pilgrims it attracted. In 1309 Philippe IV sanctioned construction of a much larger Gothic collegiate church, of which all but the tower perished at the time of the Siege of Orléans in 1429. The interior of the present church (declared a basilica by Pope Leon XIII in 1894) soars, the nave piers rising all the way to the 27-m-high rib-vaults in a seamless flight, with not a capital in sight – and with nothing between the arcades and the upper windows but smooth, tooled stone. Not surprisingly, you can't help but focus on the precious statue, which sits in a shrine-like setting behind the main altar at the far end of the church. Beside the northern aisle stands the tomb of Louis XI, who ordered the enlargement of the nave shortly before his death in 1483. The French monarchy's attachment to Cléry is expressed elsewhere in the choir windows, given by Charles III, and five doorways bearing the arms of Henri II. Notice also the extravagantly decorated chapels of the south aisle and the huge panels on the western wall recording a quite extraordinary succession of visitors throughout the centuries. If you're visiting the area in late July look out for son et lumière spectacles.

La Collégiale St-Liphard and Château de Meung-sur-Loire

ⓘ *Entrance to La Collégiale and the Château on place Martroi, Meung-sur-Loire (18 km west of Orléans), www.chateau-de-meung.com. Chateau Apr-May and Sep-11 Nov Tue-Sun 1400-1800, Jun-Aug Tue-Sun 1000-1800, Dec weekends 1400-1900. Closed 7 Jan-29 Mar. Chateau and park €8.50, €5.50 (6-15s and students).*

You could easily miss the charming small town of Meung-sur-Loire altogether, which might explain how it has managed to retain such a palpable sense of the past. In 1429 Meung witnessed a decisive battle during the Hundred Years' War, being freed from English occupation by forces led by Joan of Arc. It retained its defensive ramparts for centuries, and the main gatehouse survives at the northern end of rue Porte d'Amont (if you look carefully you'll notice that the tower's ancient clock dial displays 61 minutes). Retrace your steps through the heart of the town to place Martroi, a broad, sunny square with a restaurant terrace popular with lunchtime diners. Ahead is the substantial collegiate church dedicated to St-Liphard, who was buried in the monastery he founded here during the sixth century. Its 11th- to 13th-century replacement retains the spirit of an earlier style, and the main doorway and rounded transepts are essentially pure Romanesque. Inside it's light and airy, if rather over-restored, and the apse in particular is surprisingly plain. But odd details are interesting: the far left-hand corbel below the organ sprouts three carved heads, while the junction of the choir and the transept from which you entered features the head of an ox with an endearingly comical smile. On the wall of the transept is a large section of a medieval painting. As you leave turn left and you'll find the church tower base still mated to the circular bastion of a military chateau built during the early 12th century by bishop Manasses de Garlande. It was here in AD 861 that a treaty was signed by Robert le Fort and King Charles le Chauve, laying the foundations of the Capetian dynasty of Frankish kings. One of the bishop's successors constructed the present chateau, whose stern and satisfyingly crumbly rear façade overlooks the church. Head round to the main façade, though, and you'll be rewarded with a startlingly contradictory impression, the result of 14th- and 18th-century additions and embellishments which transformed the original 13th-century defensive structure into a vision of refined sophistication. In addition to witnessing the turmoil of the Hundred Years' War, the chateau would host François I, Charles VII and Louis XI, establishing a celebrity status which inspired bishop Jarente de la Bruyère to plan an extravagant scheme to create a showpiece to rival Versailles (a feat which Richelieu so nearly pulled off further west). Seized during the Revolution, the chateau escaped destruction but served instead as a prison before being purchased by one of the founders of the Banque de France. It remains in private hands, a fact which perhaps explains it having retained much of the endearing authenticity which makes it well worth visiting.

Beaugency → *For listings, see pages 44-50.*

For centuries this historic town on the north bank of the Loire offered the only crossing between Orléans and Blois. Its celebrated 26-arch former toll bridge dates from the 14th century, and once incorporated a chapel for pilgrims on the route to Compostela. Its melancholy cobbled quays tell of long-departed port activity, but Beaugency's real charm lies elsewhere, in the heart of the old town, which has escaped modern development and is a joy to explore on foot. Overlooking it all are the vast Tour de César, part of an 11th-century feudal chateau built to defend the town and its river crossing, and the handsome bell tower of a 16th-century church lost during the Revolution. Three times daily (0800, 1200 and 1900) its fine peal sounds the *Carillon de Vendôme* (see page 43).

Getting there and around

Beaugency **Gare SNCF** ⓘ *rue de la Gare, T02 38 44 50 28*, is served by train from Paris, via Orléans or Blois and Tours from the west. The Ulys bus services numbers 8 and 9 operate between Orléans Gare Routière and Beaugency and stop at various locations; the stop on rue Nationale is just above the old town. The historic centre of Beaugency is so compact that you'll have no problem exploring the town on foot.

Around the Old Town

The layout of the town – which is almost village-like in look and spirit – takes some working-out, but you'll soon discover that everything is neatly packed into the surprisingly small area defined by its original medieval defences. Almost every street has a story to tell, via a wealth of architectural survivors. One of the earliest is the **Maison des Templiers**, a 12th-century former Knights Templars' hall in rue du Puits de l'Ange, whose sober Romanesque decoration is in total contrast to the exuberantly sculpted Renaissance façade of the Hôtel de Ville (1526-1528) in rue du Change. You'll find medallion busts, bas-relief friezes, the salamander emblem of François I, the arms of Beaugency's own Dunois-Longueville family and more. Things became almost surreal with the addition of a pair of fanciful watch towers when the building was 'restored' during the 19th century. Inside, the first-floor Council Chamber conserves a series of magnificent 17th- and 18th-century embroidered panels from the Abbaye Notre-Dame, which ended up here (minus their borders) after being seized during the Revolution. Nearby, roughly parallel to the abbey, is the Château de Dunois, originally a fortress occupied by the Lords of Beaugency and much modified for more civilized living during the 15th century. In its heyday it entertained both Louis XI (after his Coronation at Reims in 1461) and Francis I (who spent 10 days here in October 1526 after being freed from captivity in Madrid). The guest list took a dive, though, after the building was confiscated during the Revolution and eventually ended up homing beggars and the insane. In 1928 it finally became a museum for arts and traditions of the Orléans region.

L'Abbatiale Notre-Dame

ⓘ *Rue de l'Abbaye. You are free to visit any time except during prayer.*

Chance upon it from rue du Pont and you'll be startled by the smoothly curving apse of a giant abbey looming over the former convent (now a hotel) huddled against it. Round in the more peaceful place St-Firmin, though, things look very different. The western façade looks pretty dull, apart from two Romanesque doorways, a line of corbels and a single *clocher* barely taller than the gable of the nave, but don't be put off, for inside it's huge, and has a real sense of medieval mystery. The rich (modern) stained-glass windows make it quite dark, but as your eyes acclimatize you'll notice signs of the serenity of Romanesque giving way to the dawning of the Gothic spirit; the nave arcade arches sit on simple drum-piers but are pointed, not rounded, and the side aisles have Angevin-style rib-vaults. Less immediately obvious is the fact that the nave ceiling is a dazzling piece of all-timber construction created in 1663-1665 to replace the original stone vaults lost during the Wars of Religion. The entire southern aisle was also painstakingly rebuilt after being destroyed by aerial bombardments in 1940. It's nevertheless still possible to picture the scene in 1103 when the Council of Beaugency heard Philippe I's plea to reconsider his excommunication for leaving his wife Berthe de Hollande in favour of Bertrade, Comtesse d'Anjou – or when in 1152 it forbade the marriage of Louis VII and Eleanor of Aquitaine (who were considered too closely related). In the square outside is a stirring bronze statue of Joan of Arc, erected in 1896, before the 50-m-high Clocher St-Firmin of 1530. This handsome bell-tower is all that remains of a Romanesque church dating from the 11th century and lost during the Revolution.

Château de Talcy

ⓘ *About 16 km east of Beaugency off the D15, T02 54 81 03 01, www.talcy.monuments-nationaux.fr. 2 May-4 Sep daily 0930-1200 and 1400-1800, 5 Sep-30 Apr daily 1000-1230 and 1400-1700. Closed Tue 1 Oct- 1 Mar, 25 Dec, 1 Jan and 1 May. €5.50, under 18s free.*

While other gracious chateaux have their origins in feudal military strongholds, Talcy was originally the manor-house of a nobleman. Its subtle reverse-transformation began in 1517 when the estate was acquired by Florentine banker Bernard Salviati, a financial supporter of Francis I during the Italian wars, and cousin of Catherine de' Medici. Around 1520 he added defensive features to the chateau (stopping short of the drawbridge which would have made things more secure) in an austere form of French Gothic, rather than the Italianate style which was proving fashionable elsewhere. The mood had obviously relaxed by the time his wife Isabelle enlarged the domestic accommodation between 1533 and 1543. On 21 April 1545 Talcy entered literary history when 21-year-old Pierre de Ronsard attended a party given by the Salviatis and fell in love with their daughter, who at the time was just 14. The result was the epic series of love poems entitled '*Les Amours de Cassandre*'.

In 1704 the estate passed to the Burgeats family, who added further refinements and created Renaissance gardens, today bounded by productive fruit orchards. Nearby are a 16th-century dovecote and a 17th-century barn, complete with a huge and venerable wine-press. For the majority of visitors, though, Talcy's greatest attraction is undoubtedly the chateau itself, whose interior layout and furniture have survived intact from the 18th century.

Vendôme → *For listings, see pages 44-50.*

ⓘ *31 km northwest of Blois.*

This attractive and atmospheric town sits below its ruined feudal chateau in a fork of the Loir, whose waterways then subdivide to create the sensation that you are moving among a series of islands. If your time is limited simply follow one of two discovery trails marked by brass studs in the town centre paving. This way you won't miss the 15th-century **Porte St-Georges**, sole survivor of the four gates which once controlled access to the town, or a handsome iron-framed covered market opened in 1896. The adjoining **place du Marché** was formerly the place du Pilori and until the 16th century witnessed public executions. More conventionally elegant is the **Hôtel de Ville**, built in French Classical style between 1639 and 1777 as the Collège des Oratoriens (among whose pupils was Honoré de Balzac) and which also later served as a royal military academy. Further echoes of the town's long military associations survive (but only just) in the former Benedictine abbey buildings which became the **Rochambeau Barracks**, home to an illustrious mounted cavalry regiment which would be decimated by the horrors of 1914. Perhaps most surprising of all, however, is the genuine charm which persists in the town centre, despite TGV rail services having placed Vendôme firmly in Parisian commuter territory. Rue du Change, for example, successfully blends modern prosperity with medieval-style half-timbering. Not all of the façades are as old as they appear, though, since this cost-effective construction style survived locally until the 18th and even 19th centuries.

Le Carillon de Vendôme

During the Hundred Years' War, the legacy of the Dauphin, the 11th of 12 children of Isabeau of Bavaria, and later King Charles VII, was limited to Bourges – where he installed his little court – and the small towns of Beaugency, Cléry-St-André and Vendôme. A 15th-century rhyme tells the tale of his much-reduced circumstances:

Mes amis que reste-t-il
à ce Dauphin si gentil?
Orléans, Beaugency,
Notre-Dame de Cléry,
Vendôme, Vendôme.

Les ennemis ont tout pris
Ne lui laissant par mépris
Qu'Orléans, Beaugency,
Notre-Dame de Cléry,
Vendôme, Vendôme!

The accompanying chimes sound hourly in Vendôme, and three times each day in Beaugency and Cléry-St-André. If you try singing along with these words, remember that the French usually extend the last syllable, as in: *Frère Jacques* (*Frèr-e Jacq-ues*).

Eglise de la Trinité

ⓘ *Rue de l'Abbaye. Daily. Free.*

The greatest of Vendôme's many historic assets is a cathedral-like abbey founded around 1032 and which later blossomed into one of the very finest examples of flamboyant Gothic in all France. Seen from the nearby place St-Martin, the vibrant western façade smoulders coyly and invitingly behind an early 12th-century *clocher* (bell-tower) soaring skywards. Between them lie the Benedictine abbey cloisters, which are worth visiting to appreciate part of an 11th- and 12th-century fresco lost for 600 years before being rediscovered in 1972. You'll find the characters in the *Miraculous Catch of Fishes* gazing with a conspiratorial glow from the wall of the *salle capitulaire* (chapter house) in the far left-hand corner of the square.

Enter the church by the western door to get the full impact of the medieval Gothic *tour-de-force* lies within – the side aisles alone rise higher than many lesser churches. Notice too the slender piers of the nave launching straight up to lightweight rib vaults suspended above tall windows and a skeletal glazed triforium stage. At the far end of the choir is a rounded apse (or *déambulatoire*) with five radiating chapels. In the centre, and most beautiful of all, is the Chapelle du St-Sacrament, where you'll find the stained-glass panel of Notre-Dame, a miraculous survivor created for the previous Romanesque abbey in 1125. And don't miss the choir stalls, whose 16th-century carved misericord panels depict characters including wine producers at their daily labours.

Sancerre to the Orléanais listings

For hotel and restaurant price codes and other relevant information, see pages 11-16.

Where to stay

Sancerre and downstream to Châteauneuf *p27*

€€€€-€€ Château de la Verrerie, Oizon (32 km southwest of Gien), T02 48 81 51 60, www.chateaudelaverrerie.com. Choose from 12 guest rooms, all cosy, charming and romantic, in this restored 15th-century chateau in the heart of the Sologne. Its early 16th-century Renaissance gallery overlooks a large lake surrounded by woodland. The **Maison d'Hélène** restaurant, created in the former farm, offers intimate dining and, for those who find the idea appealing, the chateau can arrange a day's hunting or stalking.

€€€ Le Domaine des Roches, 2 rue de la Plaine, Briare, T02 38 05 09 00, www.domainedesroches.fr. A 19th-century manor house set in its own park in the heart of Briare-le-Canal, with beautifully appointed rooms opening out onto gardens. There are also cottages to rent within the grounds, and a restaurant with a terrace.

€€€ Hôtel du Rivage, 1 quai de Nice, Gien, T02 38 37 79 00. The hotel enjoys a superb location overlooking the Loire and Gien's Vieux Pont, or the gardens to the rear. The rooms have private bathrooms, free Wi-Fi and are simply but adequately furnished, although the hotel's best feature is undoubtedly its setting. The town and the riverside restaurants are just a few mins' walk away.

€€€ Hôtel Le Panoramic, Rempart des Augustins, Sancerre, T02 48 54 22 44, www.panoramicotel.com. An aptly named hotel with sweeping views across the vineyards. Many rooms share the same panorama and are fully equipped to a high standard. The luxury suites are sumptuous, with separate lounge areas furnished in classic French style. Standard rooms are less charming, with plainer decor and contemporary furniture. Rooms on the town side are significantly cheaper. Free Wi-Fi.

€€ Hostellerie du Grand Sully, 10 bd du Champ de Foire, Sully-sur-Loire, T02 38 36 27 56, www.grandsully.com. A comfortable, quiet hotel with a range of accommodation. The cheapest rooms are comfortably furnished and have their own bathroom. Pay a little more for elegantly furnished bedrooms with antique furniture and lovely fabrics adorning the beds and windows. The hotel serves a really rather nice breakfast with plentiful fresh bread and pastries, delicious coffee and home-made jams in china pots. Private parking, free Wi-Fi and a/c. The hotel restaurant, offering a range of excellent regional menus from €28-52, is one for special occasions (open Tue-Fri).

€€ Hôtel du Parc, 5 place Aristide Briand, Châteauneuf-sur-Loire, T02 38 56 13 13, www.hotel-du-parc-45110-chateauneuf-sur-loire.com. Situated opposite the park and entrance to the Musée de la Marine de Loire, the hotel offers reliable and clean accommodation at an affordable price. The rooms are light and bright although very plain, but there is a/c and secure parking. Expect a basic buffet breakfast. Some rooms have wheelchair access. Free Wi-Fi.

€€ Hôtel-Restaurant Le Laurier, 29 rue du Commerce, St-Satur (a few kilometres north of Sancerre), T02 48 54 17 20, www.lelaurier18.com. Closed Sun eve and Mon, 20 Dec-10 Feb. Entering this ivy-clad former post-house is like stepping back in time, with many original features, low beams and a classic French dining room with crisp white table linen. The rooms are traditional, too, but brightly decorated and comfortable (don't be surprised to find a rather old-fashioned bathroom). Free Wi-Fi. Sancerre is just a few mins' drive away.

€€ Les Logis du Grillon, 100 Rempart des Dames, Sancerre, T02 36 42 00 21, www.chambres-hotes-sancerre.com. Offers bed and breakfast or gîtes full of period charm, with stone fireplaces and exposed beams. The guest rooms are individually styled and decorated in fresh colours and traditional French fabrics. Guests can expect high levels of comfort, a gourmet breakfast with regional produce and home-made jams, calm surroundings, a/c and free Wi-Fi.

Orléans *p34, map p34*

€€€ Château de Champvallins, 1079 rue de Champvallins, Sandillon (about 10 km southeast of Orléans), T02 38 41 16 53, www.chateaudechampvallins.com. This 18th-century chateau hotel the heart of the Sologne near Orléans is set in 10 ha of woodland and has an outdoor swimming pool. 5 spacious rooms all overlook the park and are luxuriously decorated with silk and antique furnishings in the purest French tradition.

€€€ Hôtel d'Arc, 37 rue de la République, T02 38 53 10 94, www.hoteldarc.fr. A fully-modernized hotel, located centrally behind a striking art nouveau-style façade. The rooms are light and spacious with neutral decor punctuated by additional, more individual splashes of colour, giving an overall sense of elegance and simplicity. All rooms have high levels of comfort and services, including free Wi-Fi, international TV channels and a mini-bar. The location is just 10 mins' walk from the heart of Orléans, tram services stop almost at the front door and the rail station is within a few mins' walk.

€€€ L'Orée des Chênes, 921 Route de Marcilly-en-Vilette, La Ferté-St-Aubin, T02 38 64 84 00, www.loreedeschenes.com. A charming hotel-restaurant surrounded by superb grounds with a lake in the heart of the Sologne. Decorated in neutral shades with classic French-style furniture, the bedrooms are restful and elegant. If possible, compare Classic and Superior room choices before you commit. Rooms available with disabled access. Free Wi-Fi. The excellent restaurant is highly recommended – but not for those on a tight budget.

€€€ Relais Louis XI, 2 rue St Pierre, Meung-sur-Loire, T02 38 44 27 71, www.lerelaislouisxi.com. Restaurant closed Sun eve and Mon. Strategically located by the river, this collection of ancient buildings around a courtyard was fortified by the British during the 100 Years' War. In 1429 Joan of Arc and her troops surrounded the place and destroyed the bridge between here and the road to Beaugency. Opened as a 'completely environmental' hotel in late 2008 it employs geothermal energy, organic cotton bed-linen and, of course, only organic wines and produce are served in the gourmet restaurant. The rooms are light and airy, with simple contemporary furnishings in varying styles and have views to the Loire River, with the exception of the Garden Room, which is suitable for disabled guests.

€€ Hôtel de l'Abeille, 64 rue Alsace Lorraine, T02 38 53 54 87, www.hoteldelabeille.com. A traditional French hotel with a certain charm – there's a small café-bar at the entrance, plus balconies decorated with greenery and flowers. The rooms are individually styled, decorated with patterned wallpaper and draped fabric in typical French country style but modern bathrooms and free Wi-Fi, plus 24-hr room service. The roof-terrace affords good views of the cathedral.

€€ Hôtel Escale Océania, 16 quai St-Laurent, T02 38 54 47 65, www.oceaniahotels.com/escale-oceania-orleans.php. On the quays, just a few mins' walk from the medieval quarter and the centre of Orléans, this quiet hotel has functional, bright and modern rooms with free Wi-Fi. Private parking is a big bonus in this part of the city.

€€ Hôtel Villa Marjane, 121 route de Sandillon,St-Jean-le-Blanc (2.5 km south of Orléans), T02 38 66 35 13, www.villamarjane.com. The villa sits in its own wooded grounds on a main road southeast of the centre of Orléans (5-min drive from the centre) and offers a restful ambiance with a warm and personal welcome. The rooms are slightly old-fashioned classic-French style but have modern bathrooms and represent good value for money. Free Wi-Fi.

€€ La Ferme des Foucault, Ménestreau-en-Villette (6 km east of La Ferté-St-Aubin), T02 38 76 94 41, www.ferme-des-foucault.com. This typical late 19th-century red-brick farmhouse in the heart of the Sologne has been fully restored by its French-American owners. The result is a beautiful haven with charming rooms, plenty of light and views to the surrounding forest. Guests enjoy a hearty breakfast and modern comforts including free Wi-Fi and a swimming pool.

Campsites

Parc des Alicourts, Pierrefitte-sur-Sauldre (30 km southeast of La Ferté-St-Aubin), T02 54 88 63 34, www.alicourtstreehouses.com. Nature-lovers might like to try living in their very own tree house, hidden away in a holiday resort in the heart of the Sologne. Choose between the 6-m-high cabin with its own staircase and bridge, or ladder tree-houses – not quite so vertigo-inducing.

Beaugency *p40*

€€€ Hostellerie de l'Ecu de Bretagne, Place du Martroi, T02 38 44 67 60, www.ecudebretagne.fr. A stone-built former coaching inn, the hotel encompasses the main building (which overlooks the square) and completely restored annexes. Rooms are beautifully and luxuriously furnished. Parking, heated swimming pool and free Wi-Fi available. The fine hotel restaurant serves traditional regional dishes.

€€€ Le Saint George, 14 rue Poterie, Vendôme, T02 54 67 42 10, www.hotel-saint-georges-vendome.com. Situated in a prominent position in the heart of the town, the hotel has modern, comfortable rooms, each with a useful kitchenette and some with a spa bath. The restaurant is decorated with South American artefacts and the menu features dishes from around the world accompanied by an equally international wine list. Hotel parking available and free Wi-Fi throughout.

€€ Hôtel de la Sologne, 6 place St-Firmin, T02 38 44 50 27, www.hoteldelasologne.com. A charming hotel on the prettiest square in town. Individually styled traditional rooms face onto the square or the inner courtyard, and are incredibly quiet, apart for the thrice-daily *Carillon de Vendôme* from the nearby clock-tower. Other attractions are a warm welcome and delicious breakfasts served in a cosy dining room or sunny terrace. Free Wi-Fi and secure area for bicycles.

€€ Hôtel le Relais des Templiers, 68 rue du Pont, T02 38 44 53 78, www.hotelrelaistempliers.com. Situated at the end of this pretty street, the hotel provides a warm welcome for tourists and offers good-value accommodation in basic but adequately furnished rooms. The public lounge downstairs offers a cosy corner, and there's free Wi-Fi and a computer available for guests. Secure area provided for bicycles.

Campsites

Val de Flux, T02 38 44 50 39, www.beaugency.fr. end Aug. A large, well-managed municipal site in a calm and shady position on the banks of the Loire, with views across the river to the town.

Restaurants

Sancerre and downstream to Châteauneuf *p27*

€€€ Côtes et Jardin, 8 rue Grand Sully, Sully-sur-Loire, T02 38 36 35 89, www.cotes-jardins.fr. 1200-1430 and 1900-2130. Closed Tue evening and Wed. Situated in Sully's main street, the restaurant is housed in a fine Renaissance building with a large and airy dining room. Choose from a sumptuous menu of classic French dishes and several seasonal daily specials.

€€ Auberge l'Écurie, 31 Nouvelle Place, Sancerre, T02 48 54, 16 50, www.auberge-ecurie.fr. Relaxed dining in what comes close in both style and ambiance to a British pub. Varied menu including grills, salads and Italian dishes served in generous portions.

There's also a tempting display of gâteaux and flans.

€€ Le Petit Saint Trop, 5 rue Tissier, Briare, T02 38 37 00 31, le-petit-saint-trop@wanadoo.fr. Closed Sun evening and Mon. Next to the bridge in the Port de Plaisance, this brasserie restaurant has built up a faithful local clientele with its refreshing menus and friendly service. Apart from standard brasserie fare, look out for more refined fish courses with fresh vegetables.

€€ Le Trevi, 5 rue Faubourg St-Germain, Sully-sur-Loire, T02 38 36 26 92. A friendly Italian restaurant and grill a short walk from the chateau, and where you'll receive a warm welcome and efficient service. Arrive promptly, before the dining room fills up with locals enjoying a convivial evening with friends.

€ L'Epicerie de la Borne, La Borne d'en Bas, Henrichemont (23 km west of Sancerre near Henrichement), T02 48 26 90 80. Restaurant mid-Jul to end Aug daily 1230-1430 and 1930-2200, rest of the year Tue-Sun 1230-1430 and 1930-2100 (closed Sun evening and Mon). Salon de Thés 1500-1900. Tucked away in this working potters' haven, enjoy a wholesome lunch or scrumptious cake in the leafy garden or rustic salon. Local fresh produce makes up the daily *menu surprise* or *plats du jour*, which include a vegetarian option. Reservations preferred.

Orléans *p34, map p34*

€€€ Chez Jules, 136 rue de Bourgogne, T02 38 54 30 80. Closed Mon lunch, Sat lunch and Sun, annual holidays mid-Jul. Chez Jules looks rustic and rather small but provides a warm welcome and generous servings of traditional dishes with a modern approach.

€€€ Eugène, 24 rue Ste Anne, T02 38 53 82 64, www.restauranteugene.fr. Mon-Fri evening, 1200-1400 and 1915-2115. Chef Alain Gérard is of Breton origin but draws inspiration from the south of France – which clearly makes his diners very happy indeed, since this is one of the most popular restaurants in the Loiret. Booking essential.

€€€ Le Girouet, 14 quai du Châtelet, T02 38 81 07 14, www. legirouet.com. Tue-Fri, Sat evening only. The interior of the Girouet is distinctly nautical, as befits its position on the river bank – the terrace has views directly over the Loire. The enticing menu changes twice weekly and reflects what is in season, much of it organic and river-fresh.

€€€ Les Toqués, 71 chemin du Halage, St-Jean-de-Braye, T02 38 86 50 20. Closed Sun and Mon. A fashionable address with a stylish terrace on the towpath just a short distance from the city centre. It brings a contemporary twist to traditional dishes using seasonal produce and has a divine choice of desserts.

€€€ Restaurant de la Marine, 12 l'Embouchure, Combleux (8 km east of Orléans), T02 38 55 12 69, www.restaurant-la-marine.com. Open daily. Situated in a picturesque village on the banks of the Loire, La Marine is delightful for summer dining outside under lime trees. The delicious menu is based upon classic French dishes, using regional produce.

€€€ Restaurant Le Lift, Place de la Loire, T02 38 53 63 48, www. restaurant-le-lift.com. Daily. With its contemporary interior design and elevated terrace overlooking the Loire, Le Lift is one of the more chic addresses in Orléans. The menu has unmistakable regional and seasonal origins but chef Philippe Bardau brings his own refreshing personality to the dishes. Booking advised.

€€ Au Bon Marché, 12 place du Châtelet, T02 38 53 04 35, www. aubonmarche-orleans.com. Daily 1200-1430 and 1900-2200. In the bustling heart of old Orléans, this is a restaurant, a *cave à vins* and an *épicerie*. Expect regional dishes using fresh produce, an excellent *plat du jour* around €8 plus a good selection of local wines.

€€ Le Brin de Zinc, 62 rue Ste-Catherine, T02 38 53 38 77, www.groupedegenne.com. Tucked away in a side street off place du Martroi, this is a lively brasserie restaurant with an extensive menu – on summer evenings the terrace is always packed with diners.

€€ La Parenthèse, 26 place du Châtelet, T02 38 62 07 50, www.restaurant-la-parenthese.com. Tue-Sat 1200-1330 and 1930-2130. An elegant restaurant in the heart of the old city, with a lovely little terrace in summer and a simply decorated dining room. Excellent service from friendly staff, and a refined, traditional menu.

Cafés and bars

Head for rue de Bourgogne, in the heart of the pedestrian area, for a seemingly endless selection of bars and restaurants. Look out for **Le Paxton's Head** or **L'Atelier** for a drink, or **Le Bô Bar** (see below) for an aperitif. Otherwise, make for the busy place du Martroi, where **Le Martroi** is worth a look for its art deco interior.

La Chancellerie, 27 place du Martroi, T02 38 53 57 54. Once a favoured rendezvous for Chopin and his lover, novelist George Sand, this splendid building houses a gastronomic brasserie. Its large new terrace is a great place to watch the world go by.

Le Bô Bar, 193 rue de Bourgogne, T02 38 53 83 18. Tue-Sun 1800-0100 (May-Oct 1800-0200). A wine bar and cocktail lounge with a warm and welcoming atmosphere. Occasional music throughout the year, and a permanent exhibition of paintings and photographs.

Beaugency *p40*

€€€ Le Petit Bateau, 54-56 rue du Pont, T02 38 44 56 38, lepetitbateau@wanadoo.fr. Closed all day Mon and Tue lunchtime. Traditional French menu served in a character dining room with exposed beams and fire-place. Evening menus between €28 and €45.

€€ Le Patio, 5 place du Petit Marché, T02 38 44 02 43. Tue-Sat 1200-1400 and 1900-2200, Jun-Sep closed all day Mon and Tue lunchtime. An Italian restaurant whose friendly chefs also serve at your table. Good value pizzas, along with some original pasta dishes such as: '*Spaghetti à la Mauricienne*' – featuring an improbable-sounding, but tasty, creamy sauce with curry spices.

Cafés and bars

Bar le Saint Martin, Place St-Martin, Vendôme, T02 54 77 23 63. Daily (closed Mon low season). This half-timbered building is a popular meeting place, and ideal for a light lunch on the large terrace. There's a good selection of bottled and draught beers, and you might catch one of the regular music nights.

Entertainment

Orléans *p34, map p34*

Cinema

Les Carmes, 7 rue des Carmes, T02 38 62 94 79, www.cinemalescarmes.com. Showing international films in original language and art house French films. €7.50.

Festivals

End Apr to early May Fêtes de Jeanne d'Arc, Orléans, T02 38 24 05 05 (tourist office), www.fetesjeannedarc.com. There's plenty to see and do, including a medieval festival and market, concerts, exhibitions, son et lumière around the cathedral plus parades. The city becomes crowded, so book your accommodation well in advance.

End May to mid-Jun International Music Festival, Sully-sur-Loire, T02 38 25 43 43 (Mon-Fri), www.festival-sully.com. Classical music festival with concerts staged at various venues throughout Le Loiret, such as the cathedral in Orléans or the collégiale at Meung-sur-Loire.

Mid- to late Jun Orléans Jazz Festival, T02 38 24 05 05 (tourist office), www.orleansjazz.fr. 2 weeks of music centred around the Place au Jazz Bourgogne, le Jardin de l'Evêché and the Campo Santo in the heart of Orléans. Internationally renowned names (which included Al Jarreau in 2012), jazz musicians of tomorrow and local jazz performers produce a packed programme of entertainment.

Late Sep Festival de Loire, Orléans, T02 38 24 05 05 (tourist office), www.festivaldeloire.

com. The riverside quays come alive with the sound of sea shanties and a visual feast of traditional and unusual river craft. Visitors can take short river trips and see all manner of crafts and regional produce on the stalls lining the quays. The weekend can get very crowded, but it's well worth joining the throng for the atmosphere and to see the fabulous fireworks reflected in the river.

What to do

Boats and cruises

Les Bateaux Touristiques de Briare, Port de Plaisance or Port de Commerce, Briare, T02 38 37 12 75, www.bateaux-touristiques.com. Enjoy a slower pace of life on the canal. Cruises on the Pont-Canal and the Canal de Briare run from Apr to Oct.

Les Passeurs de Loire, La Tuilerie, Sigloy, T06 74 54 36 61, www.passeursdeloire.fr. Memorable trips on the Loire between St-Benoît and Sigloy in traditional river boats. Introduction to the natural history of the river, opportunities for picnics and special dawn or dusk itineraries.

Canal boat hire

Charmes Nautiques, Port de Plaisance, Briare, T02 38 31 28 73, www.charmes-nautiques.com. Boat hire company based in Briare offering a choice of vessels, with plenty of helpful advice before you set off on your canal adventure.

Cycle hire and routes

Vélo+, Orléans self-service cycle hire system means you can hire from one station and leave it at another when you reach your destination. It costs as little as €1 for the day or €3 per week. 8 of the stations can take instant credit card subscriptions, otherwise you can subscribe online at www.agglo-veloplus.fr.

Détours de Loire, T02 47 61 22 23, www.locationdevelos.com. Has the following partners where you can hire or leave your bikes: **Hotel de la Sologne**, 6 Place St Firmin, Beaugency, T02 38 44 50 27, www.hoteldelasologne.com; **Hôtel Le Cerf**, 22 bd Buyser, Briare, T02 38 37 00 80, hotelducerf.com. Contact **Détours de Loire** for partners in Orléans. System operates May-Sep.

Loire à Vélo, cyclists following the *Loire à Vélo* can begin in Sancerre or enjoy a brief glimpse of the Loire at St-Thibault before following the route of the Canal Latéral. Much of the route between Sancerre, Briare and Orléans is on quiet roads though the final section is on a dedicated cycle path alongside the Loire into the heart of the city. Route maps and detailed descriptions are available in English on www.cycling-loire.com.

Gardens

Château de la Bussière, La Bussière (between Gien and Briare), T02 38 35 93 35, www.chateau-labussiere.com. Apr to mid-Nov Wed-Mon 1000-1200 and 1400-1800, Jul-Aug open daily all day. €7.50, €4 children. Originally a medieval fortress, this impressive residence in red brick typical of the region is noted for its fishpond and its remarkable vegetable and fruit gardens.

Le Jardin de Roquelin, Meung-sur-Loire (cross the bridge to the left bank and turn left), T06 70 95 37 70, www.lesjardinsderoquelin.com. Apr to mid-Jul and Sep to mid-Oct, 1000-1800 Wed-Mon. €5, under 18s free. Beautiful rose gardens in a superb setting, just metres from the Loire river. The nursery is open all year.

Parc Floral de la Source, about 7 km south of Orléans, T02 38 49 30 00, www.parc-floral-la-source.com. Access via the tramway Ligne A (about 20-min journey time), alighting at Université – Parc Floral. It's then just a short, level walk through the campus. Open all year except 25 Dec and 1 Jan; times vary according to season. €6, €4 children (6-16 years). See the source of the River Loiret and wander around this peaceful parkland setting enjoying the various collections including a rose garden and *potager* (kitchen garden) plus butterfly house, flamingos and, in autumn, a glorious display of dahlias.

Golf

This part of the Loire Valley is famous for its magnificent golf courses. They range from 18 to 27 holes, where amateurs and experienced players can test their skills in exceptional natural settings. For a list of courses in the area visit www.golf.tourismloiret.com.

Brittany Ferries Golf Breaks, T+44(0)871-244 1818 (Golf Desk), www.brittany-ferries.co.uk/golf. Book your ferry, hotel accommodation and pay your green fees with Brittany Ferries – choose from a selection of golf courses in the Loire Valley.

Road trips/scenic routes

Sancerre to Romorantin-Lanthenay, this scenic drive on the D22, via Crézancy-en-Sancerre, meanders through vines and ancient oak woodland towards Henrichement. Along the way you can stop in the pottery village of La Borne. Continue through Neuvy-sur-Barangeon towards Romorantin-Lanthenay on quiet roads amid forests and lakes. Visit the Musée de Sologne (see page 61) in Romorantin for an excellent introduction to this beautiful and mysterious region.

Wine

Maison des Sancerre, 3 rue du Méridien (next to the church), Sancerre, T02 48 54 11 35, www.maison-des-sancerre.com. 1 Apr-11 Nov, daily. Modern exhibitions help visitors understand the complexity of the soils and the surprising world of viticulture. The visit ends in a superb perfumed garden designed to highlight the aromas and flavours of the Sancerre wines. (See also page 15.)

Directory

Gien *p29*

ATMs You'll find ATMs in Gien town centre just north of the old bridge. **Hospital** 2 av Jean Villejean, Gien, T02 38 29 38 29, www.ch-gien.com. **Pharmacy** Pharmacie du Centre, quai Lenoir, Gien, T02 38 67 21 63. Other towns and large villages will all have at least 1 pharmacy. **Post office** Quai Lenoir, Gien, T02-38 29 54 80.

Orléans *p34, map p34*

ATMs Around place du Martroi and the main shopping street, rue de la République. **Hospital** Hôpital de La Source, 14 av de l'Hôpital, about 10 km from the centre, T02 38 51 44 44, deals with emergencies and is accessible via the Ligne A tram. **Pharmacies** Several on rue des Carmes and near the market hall in the Châtelet area of Orléans, also on rue de la République. **Post office** At the entrance to the place d'Arc shopping centre near the rail station and at 9 rue Ste-Catherine, near the market hall and the medieval quarter.

Blois and the Sologne

Beyond Orléans the Loire flows towards the town of Blois, where giant golden salamanders burst from the innocent-looking Maison de la Magie, and whose sumptuous Château Royal was once the favoured seat of the French monarchy. South of the river lies la Sologne, among whose vast hardwood forests, countless man-made lakes and open, undeveloped landscapes lie noble hunting estates such as Cheverny and the greatest of all the Loire Valley chateaux: Chambord. It's the perfect place to get away from it all, particularly for walkers, cyclists and lovers of wildlife. Dramatically less visited are the cheerful villages of local red-brick, smaller chateaux such as Le Moulin and the courses of rivers including the Seaudre and Beuvron which help drain this former marshland. You can learn how it was reclaimed and much more about this fascinating and little-known area at the Musée de la Sologne in Romorantin-Lanthenay, whose other museum (the Espace Matra) recounts the town's long involvement with motoring and motor sport. On the southern edge of the Sologne the River Cher is joined by the Canal du Berry at Selles-sur-Cher, where you can discover renowned locally produced goat's cheeses and visit the huge, and now beautifully restored, 900-year-old Romanesque abbey church of Notre-Dame-la-Blanche.

Arriving in Blois and the Sologne

Getting there

Blois Gare SNCF ⓘ *bd Daniel Dupuis, north of the town*, receives trains from the east including Beaugency (20 minutes), Meung-sur-Loire (30 minutes) and Orléans (45 minutes), as well as trains from the west including Tours (30 minutes), Saumur (one hour), Angers and Nantes. Most services will carry bikes free of charge. Radio taxis are available from place de la Gare, in front of the train station, T02 54 78 65, and offer 'Circuits Châteaux', as well as links with TGV stations and airports. Buses arrive at the **Gare Routière** ⓘ *2 place Victor Hugo, T02 54 78 15 66, www.tub-blois.fr*. Outside Blois roads are generally quiet, apart from peak periods around big attractions such as Chambord and Cheverny. Cyclists have miles of dedicated tracks in the Domaine de Chambord, and the *Loire à Vélo* routes are well signed.

Tourist information

Loir-et-Cher Tourism ⓘ *5 rue de la Voûte du Château, T02 54 57 00 41, www.chambordcountry.com;* ⓘ *23 place du Château, Blois, T02 54 90 41 41, www.bloispaysdechambord.com;* ⓘ *Bracieux, 10 Les Jardins du Moulin, T02 54 46 09 15;* ⓘ *Chambord, place St Louis, T02 54 33 39 16;* ⓘ *Chaumont-sur-Loire, 24 rue du Maréchal Leclerc, T02 54 20 91 73;* ⓘ *Cheverny-Cour-Cheverny, 12 rue du Chêne aux Dames, T02 54 79 95 63;* ⓘ *Montrichard, 1 rue du Pont, T02 54 32 05 10;* ⓘ *Romorantin-Lanthenay, place de la Paix, T02 54 76 43 89.*

Getting around

Blois is relatively small and has multi-storey car parks within easy walking distance of the main sights. A bus journey costs €2 for up to one hour. Pay the driver as you board the bus (try to have the correct change) or purchase *un carnet de dix voyages* (a book of 10 tickets, €18) from **POINT BUS** ⓘ *place Victor Hugo*, or from newsagents around the town. You can see all the routes on the website, with bus stops, timetables and where to buy your ticket books. **TLC buses** ⓘ *T02 54 58 55 54, www.transports-du-loir-et-cher.com*, offer a *'Circuit Châteaux'*, with services departing daily from Blois Gare SNCF (train station) from early April to September. There's a single tariff of €6. You'll also receive a discounted entry to the chateaux on production of your ticket. Purchase tickets at the tourist office or on the bus.

Blois → *For listings, see pages 68-72.*

The sumptuous Château Royal de Blois provides a timely reminder of the period when this expanding town on the north bank of the Loire enjoyed political influence second only to that of Paris. Much may have since changed, but you can still cross one of the broader stretches of the Loire via the graceful 18th-century Pont Jacques Gabriel and discover a medieval network of narrow streets hidden away behind the town's vibrant but less instantly lovable commercial heart. Among the ancient alleys and *degrés* (stone steps) things are much calmer, to the point where you almost feel as if you've stepped straight into an archive photograph. Powerful echoes of an even earlier spirit haunt both the Cathédrale St-Louis and the former abbey of St-Nicolas, each of which offers cool solace on a hot summer day. On the other hand, for instant immersion into modern-day Blois, grab a table beneath the plane trees and parasols of the elegant café terraces in place Louis XII, just below the Château Royal. On balmy summer evenings, or when the area resonates with the buzz and bustle of a Saturday street market, there's nowhere better to tap into the spirit of this atmospheric town.

Château Royal de Blois

ⓘ *Place du Château, T02 54 90 33 33, www.chateaudeblois.fr. Daily (except 25 Dec and 1 Jan) from 0900, closing times vary. €9.50, €7 concessions, €4 (6-17s). Ask at the desk or tourist office (near chateau entrance) about money-saving combined tickets. Daily guided tours are available at no extra charge, with scheduled tours in English. The 'Visite Insolite' (available on request) allows visitors to discover parts of the chateau normally closed to the public. A dramatized audioguide is available in 4 languages (€4/€3 additional charge) and lasts 1 hr. Son et lumière shows in summer: for details,* *see page 70.*

For all its obvious (and less obvious) restored features, the chateau still resonates with the proud spirit of the kings of France at the height of their power and influence, and presides over the town with a magisterial air. The northern façade of the François I wing looks vast, detached and Italianate, with long rows of ornate, *loggia* like galleries beneath a covered walkway. Climb to the Place du Château, though, and you come face to face with a more accessible, mostly flamboyant Gothic façade, whose sizzling stonework embellishes decorative red and black brickwork laid in a diamond pattern. Above the main entrance is an imposing niche figure (a 19th-century replica replacing the original destroyed during the French Revolution) of Louis XII mounted on horseback along with the royal porcupine emblem and the letters L (for Louis XII) and A (for Anne de Bretagne).

Self-guided visits begin with a climb to the **Salle des Etats Généraux** built in 1214 and beautifully restored during the 19th century. The vast hall is divided by a slender central arcade while neo-Gothic decoration covers virtually every surface, including the rich blue roof vaults adorned with almost 7000 golden fleurs-de-lys. Descend a flight of stairs at the end of the hall and you'll enter the **Musée Lapidaire**, a series of rooms filled with gargoyles, pinnacles, capitals and many other chunks of ornamental stonework (some of them plaster casts) replaced during restoration works. Climb a stairway from here and you reach the François I wing via the **Grande Salle**. Among the vibrant decoration, notice the two huge fireplaces decorated with gilded salamander emblems. Adjoining this room is a **guard room** displaying armour, swords, pikes and other weaponry. Also present is the porcupine emblem, along with another salamander over an ornate doorway leading to a **music room**. There's a welcome lightness here, more sumptuous floor-to-ceiling decoration and an interesting selection of objects including an early clavichord, *faïence* (glazed earthenware) violin and mandolin ornaments, plus a series of busts of French monarchs. Beyond is **Catherine de' Medici's study**, whose 237 intricate restored, original 16th-century panels conceal the secret compartments described by Alexandre Dumas in *La Reine Margot*.

On the second floor, accessed by the famous lavishly decorated *grand escalier* (spiral staircase), are the sumptuous **Royal Apartments**. In 1588 the King's Chamber was the scene of the assassination of the Duc de Guise on the orders of Henri III (who watched events unfold while concealed behind a large wall-hanging).

When you finally descend to the large central courtyard you'll see clearly how changing fashions inspired the various portions of the chateau, starting with the early 13th-century Salle d'Etats Généraux and flamboyant Gothic Louis XII wing of 1498-1501. Just 12 years or so later the radically different François I wing was begun, drawing inspiration from the Italian Renaissance. Last came the much more sober Gaston d'Orléans or Classical wing, begun in 1634 and designed by François Mansart. A casualty of Mansart's work was the Chapelle St-Calais, whose nave was among the sections demolished to make way for the new wing. Only the holiest part of the king's private chapel (in which Henri III attended a thanksgiving Mass immediately after dispatching the Duc de Guise) has survived. The tall, richly coloured 1950s windows are by master glass-maker Max Ingrand and substituted previous (19th-century) replacements lost during Second World War bombardments. Outside, the neo-Gothic western façade and portal, created by Félix Duban and Jules de la Morandière in 1870, restore some dignity to this wounded, but still beautiful survivor.

Maison de la Magie

ⓘ *1 place du Château, T02 54 90 33 33, www.maisondelamagie.fr. Early Apr to late Sep, late Oct to mid-Nov (school holidays), opening times vary. Last entry 30 mins before closing. €8, €6.50 concessions, €5 (6-17s). 30-min shows 3-4 times daily.*

It takes something pretty spectacular to instantly grab your full attention after the chateau visit, but an innocent-looking townhouse across the place du Château will do just that. Every hour the peace is shattered by dark, horror-movie sounds, shutters open of their own accord and six golden salamander heads emerge amid clouds of smoke, followed by claws and a forked tail. As the dragon-like creatures peer around at the startled onlookers in the square below, they begin to open and snap their jaws menacingly. A few minutes later, having made their point, they retreat, the shutters close and peace returns. It's quite a show, and provides a foretaste of the remarkable museum dedicated to magic, and in particular to local illusionist Jean-Eugène Robert-Houdin (who inspired young Erich Weiss to change his name to Harry Houdini). Inside you can expect a live magic show, automatons, memorabilia from both Houdin and Houdini, plus a gallery of optical illusions, the most spectacular of which is the Hallucinascope, a virtual-reality experience in which visitors wear special inverting glasses. The result is a sensation of walking on air through other worlds, across oceans, etc (the scenery responsible being in fact mounted high above them). Pure magic.

Cathédrale St-Louis

ⓘ *Place St-Louis, T02 54 78 17 90. Daily 0900-1800.*

Relatively few visitors climb the old stone steps which wind from the heart of the historic quarter behind quai St-Jean to Place St-Louis. Take this time-worn approach, though, and the cathedral suddenly towering above you looks a lot less underwhelming than from most other viewpoints. Blame the present jarring lack of unity on a troubled history stretching back to the 10th century, when a crypt was created to house relics of St-Solenne, an early Bishop of Chartres. Two successive, much larger structures followed, the second (built by order of François I) being virtually destroyed by a hurricane in 1678 and rebuilt in Gothic style. Bizarrely, though, the single tower was later topped off in French baroque.

Against all expectation, the interior is beautiful and a picture of Gothic harmony, despite a lack of transepts and the fact that only three of the huge stone slabs above the nave arcades ever received their planned bas-relief decoration. Second World War bombardments claimed the original stained glass but their worthy contemporary replacements by Dutch conceptual artist Jan Dibbets tint the entering sunlight, warming the pale stone interior. Real enough are the mystical qualities of the Carolingian crypt, which survives (complete with the bones of the Saint) below the floor of the nave. A world apart, it's in the eerie silence of early sacred places like this that you'll still tap into the spirit of the dawn of Christianity which transformed ordinary sites into important centres of pilgrimage – and which in turn would inspire the creation of vast medieval abbeys and cathedrals.

Eglise St-Nicolas

ⓘ *Rue St Laumer, T02 54 90 41 41. Daily 0900-1830.*

The three handsome, slated spires rising assertively between the Château Royal and the Loire belong to the 12th- and 13th-century Eglise St-Nicolas, originally the centrepiece of a Benedictine abbey destroyed by Huguenots and partly rebuilt during the 17th century. The startling effect of the tall, Chartres-influenced western façade is sustained by the soaring height of the interior, whose modest window areas make things much darker and more mysterious than the Cathédrale St-Louis. The narrow span of the vaults has the effect of making the nave look even taller, with things being taken a stage further by suspending a lantern tower above the mighty piers of the transept crossing. Above its low windows is a stone cupola symbolizing the waiting Heaven, a sensational effect which must have seemed even more so when this eastern portion was completed between 1138 and 1186. Smaller, less obvious details around the choir are also worth a closer look, particularly the outer chapels and the pier capitals, whose surprisingly irreverent imagery hints at a much earlier Romanesque spirit. The large axial or central chapel, on the other hand, is a 14th-century addition. Before leaving you'll find it well worth walking slowly around the exterior for an object lesson in how an early medieval Gothic building is constructed, and to see the whole thing still comfortably upstaging the surrounding rooftops.

Muséum d'Histoire Naturelle de Blois

ⓘ *Les Jacobins, 6 rue des Jacobins, T02 54 90 21 00. Open all year Tue-Sun 1400-1800 plus Fri mornings during school holidays. €3, €1.50 (concessions and 12-18s), free under 12s.*

The museum's permanent displays concentrate on the natural history, landscapes and geology of the Loire Valley, including the plains of the Beauce, the lakes heathland and forests of the Sologne, plus the river itself. Interactive and audiovisual displays bring it all to life in the setting of a former convent founded in 1273. The museum also hosts a programme of temporary exhibitions.

Château and Parc de Beauregard

ⓘ *Allée de Beauregard, Cellettes, 7 km south of Blois off the D956, T02 54 70 36 74, www.beauregard-loire.com. Apr-Sep daily, Oct-Feb weekends and weekday afternoons, times vary. Closed mid-Nov to mid-Feb. €12.50 for chateau and park, €9 park only, €5 (5-13s). Guided visits available at no extra charge.*

The chateau exudes Franco-Italian grace and beauty from every pore, with a setting to match, in landscaped parkland bounded by the dense Forêt de Russy, on the northern fringes of the Sologne. Beauregard has been occupied since the 15th century, serving as a hunting lodge for both Louis XII and François I before being acquired by Henri II's Secretary of State Jean du Thier in 1545. A man of culture (and patron of poet Pierre de Ronsard), his workplace, the exquisitely decorated Cabinet des Grelots, survives on the first floor of the building for which he was largely responsible. The outer wings, though, were added after 1617, when the estate passed to 72-year-old Paul Ardier, who also began the celebrated Gallerie des Illustres, whose walls would eventually display 327 portraits of key figures from European history. The work took three generations to complete and the floor has around 5500 Delft tiles emblazoned with military horsemen. The room remains the centrepiece of visits to the chateau, whose decor represents the creative input of a succession of aristocratic owners. Other surprises include a Dutch long-case clock dated 1711, the complete jawbone of a whale (also dating from the 18th century) and the original chateau kitchens, in use until 1968. In the park are the ruins of a

15th-century chapel inscribed with the shell emblem of St-Jacques de Compostelle and the cross of the Knights Templar.

Château de Ménars

ⓘ *Closed to visitors – riverside viewpoint signed from lay-by on D951 about 10 km east of Blois.*
If you intend driving between Blois and Orléans it's worth taking the slower, less-travelled road which hugs the *rive gauche*, or southern bank of the Loire – not least to get the definitive view of an important, privately owned chateau rarely accessible to visitors. The Château de Ménars was begun around 1645 by Royal Councillor Guillaume Charron and purchased in 1670 by the newly ennobled Madame de Pompadour. With the help of Court architect Ange-Jacques Gabriel (who conceived the Petite Trianon at Versailles and the Place de la Concorde in Paris) she enlarged the original building by adding symmetrical wings, updated the interior in a lighter, more fashionable style and laid out the parkland and formal parterregardens. Disliking the smell of cooking, had the kitchens removed from the house and installed in a separate new building linked to the dining room an underground passage. On her death in 1764 the estate passed to her brother, Abel-François Poisson de Vandières, who was by then Director General of Buildings to the king. On his instructions, architect Jacques-Germain Soufflot effectively doubled the size of the main building and covered the wings added by Gabriel with pitched slate roofs *à la Française*. So sensitive was the work that the chateau became one of the most perfect examples of surviving 18th-century French architecture. Add to this a definitive setting, amid substantial landscaped gardens with elevated, uninterrupted views across the river, and you'll have every reason to hope that one day the chateau will once again reveal some of its secrets to visitors. As it is, if you visit the village of Ménars a closer view of the chateau you'll be disappointed. There's the pleasant village bar-restaurant **Café de la Pompadour**, however, and if you follow the small sign to the Loire 'll find ample parking and space for a picnic overlooking the river, with access onto the cycle route along the bank.

Chambord → *For listings, see pages 68-72.*

In 1519 the young King François I resolved to create a definitive statement of absolute power. Almost five centuries later, from the moment its unmistakable outline rears up on a horizon bounded by dense forest you already know that the largest and most celebrated of all the Loire chateaux is not going to disappoint. When you eventually finish exploring the wonders which lie within, climb the celebrated double-helix staircase to the rooftop terraces, from whose privileged viewpoints you can admire the surrounding landscapes of ancient forest. So is this the ultimate hunting lodge or a decadent pleasure palace? You decide.

Domaine and Château de Chambord

ⓘ *T02 54 50 40 00, www.chambord.org. Daily except 1 Jan, and 25 Dec, opening hours vary (last entry 30 mins before closing). €9.50, €8 concessions, under 18s free with family. Purchase tickets at the central office or walk direct to the chateau entrance and pay there. The audio handset (€5, available in 10 languages, deposit of a passport required) provides an excellent commentary when and where you want it. Parking €3 per day for a car. Access to the chateau grounds and estate free. There's also a variety of restaurants and shops, an ATM, tourist information and toilets (payable) on site as well as cycle and boat hire facilities and carriage rides. For details of evening son et lumière shows, see page 70.*

The sheer scale of Chambord defies belief: 156 m long and 56 m high, with 426 rooms (containing 282 fireplaces) served by no fewer than 77 staircases. From a distance it appears almost weightless in the landscape, but draw closer and you can appreciate how the construction consumed 220,000 tonnes of pale *tuffeau* limestone from Bourré and worked on site by around 1800 masons and labourers. Surprisingly, however, the identity of the architect is a mystery, although it's tempting to ascribe at least some of its features to Leonardo da Vinci, who spent his last years nearby in Amboise as the king's guest. Despite its apparent complexity, Chambord was planned around a square *donjon* (keep) with four massive corner towers. However, being essentially symbolic, it had no need for outer defences, so the courtyard walls are little more than wings for the central building.

Today's visitors enter lofty doors on the far side, feeling suddenly dwarfed by the towering of the surroundings. Inside you're free to explore three floors whose layout is broadly similar, with rooms served by four central hallways converging upon an ingenious double-helix staircase. Notice the exquisitely carved decoration, including the salamander of François I. The ground floor reception rooms display hunting paintings and computer-generated presentations outlining the chateau's layout and construction.

The first-floor rooms have been furnished to replicate their appearance during key periods in the chateau's varied history. The **royal wing** houses the apartments of François I, a council chamber and a small oratory. Alongside is the **Queen's Apartment** occupied by the two wives of Louis XIV: Maria-Theresa of Spain and Françoise d'Aubigny. In the opposite wing is the chateau's largest room, a serene vaulted **chapel** completed by Jules Hardouin Mansart, architect of Versailles, while the central body of the building presents **state rooms** in their last-known decorative style. On this floor you can also visit the apartments of two of the chateau's 18th-century governors, exiled King of Poland Stanislaus Leszynski and Maréchal Maurice de Saxe, who had been handed Chambord for life by Louis XV in 1748 (and who died here just two years later). Further rooms are dedicated to Henri V, Comte de Chambord from 1821-1883, who spent just three days here. Perhaps the most remarkable of the related exhibits is a huge glass case containing the intended future French king's childhood toy collection – beautifully engineered scale models of contemporary weapons of warfare.

The second-floor rooms display huge tapestries and other historic hunting imagery, although at least as interesting are the vast, shallow-arched Italianate stone vaults of the hallways, with 400 sculpted salamander emblems, plus the royal 'F' and rope-work monogram. Above lie the roof terraces created to survey the estate and the point where the architecture finally lets rip. Gaze in awe at a forest of 365 chimneys, assorted towers and spires reaching skywards, then peer over the balustrades to the courtyard spread far below.

The surrounding 5440-ha hunting domain is enclosed by 32 km of impenetrable stone walls (enough to encircle the city of Paris) whose construction took 100 years. Around 1000 ha of the estate are freely accessible to walkers, riders, cyclists and wildlife watchers.

Château de Villesavin

ⓘ *8 km south of Chambord via Bracieux off the D52, T02 54 46 42 88, www.chateau-de-villesavin.com. Mar-May 1000-1230 and 1400-1900; Jun-Sep daily 1000-1900; Oct-15 Nov daily 1000-1230 and 1400-1800; 16 Nov-1 Mar open Thu. €8, €6.50 (10-16s), €4.50 (6-9s); guided visit, €6, €4.50 (10-16s) unaccompanied, both tariffs include Musée du Mariage and games.*

After the unbridled magnificence of Chambord, Villesavin (whose name derives from the Roman Villa Savini which once stood nearby) looks calmer and altogether more human. However, the two estates are much more closely linked than you'd imagine, since this chateau was built (between 1527 and 1537) by François I's Financial Secretary (and Seigneur de Villandry) Jean le Breton, who had been appointed to project-manage the king's great adventure. It's hardly surprising, then, that with both construction sites running concurrently, Chambord's teams of masons also worked here, or that the many shared visual references include the royal emblems adorning Villesavin's stone gables. Otherwise it's essentially a single-story country manor house, with dormer windows permitting attic space accommodation, and it remains privately owned. Guided tours visit a selection of 16th- and 18th-century interiors, and you can also include in this tour the *Musée du Mariage*, whose 1500 or so display items retrace traditions of marriage since 1840. Marginally more mainstream is a display of *hippomobiles* (horse-drawn carriages) and *voitures d'enfants* – early forerunners of prams and pushchairs. Transcending it all is Villesavin's serene chapel, which was visited by Catherine de' Medici in 1611. Its walls and vaults are adorned with late 16th-century frescoes (currently undergoing patient restoration) by the influential Modenese artist Nicolò dell' Abate, who also worked at the Château Royal de Fontainebleau. Don't miss seeing the estate's huge 16th-century dovecote – and look out too for some of the big, furry Baudet du Poitou donkeys which are bred on site.

Cheverny → *For listings, see pages 68-72.*

Here on the borders of Touraine and the Sologne you sense that you're in the very heart of chateau country. The undoubted star attraction is Cheverny, the definitive French country hunting estate, which is still occupied by descendants of the family which built it almost four centuries ago. As a result, the chateau's opulent apartments offer a rare glimpse of aristocratic French country living that you'll long remember. And there's insight into more down-to-earth country life nearby in a museum at the Château de Troussay, a 15th-century gentleman's residence, and one of the Loire Valley's smallest chateaux. Almost as close, and altogether more feudal looking, is the Château de Fougères-sur-Bièvre, whose assertive towers dominate the heart of an otherwise unassuming country village. Dramatically less visible, but well worth discovering, is the Château de Gué-Péan, tucked away in a clearing among gently undulating forests above the River Cher. Its owner, a talented architect responsible for styling the famous Futuroscope theme park further south near Poitiers, dedicates his spare time to patiently restoring this ancient family chateau.

Château de Cheverny

ⓘ *T02 54 79 96 29, www.chateau-cheverny.fr. Jan-Mar daily 0945-1700, Apr-Jun daily 0915-1815, Jul-Aug daily 0915-1845, Sep daily 0915-1815, Oct daily 0945-1730, Nov-Dec daily 0945-1700. Entry €8.70-17.90, concessions for under 7s, students, families, disabled visitors and groups. In peak season arrive early, beat the ticket queues and enjoy a cool leisurely visit before tour operator coach parties arrive.*

The efficiency of Cheverny's visitor management gives some idea of the numbers who since 1914 have been converging on this small village to see one of the largest privately owned chateaux in France. Beyond the gift shop and ticket sales point the vast and immaculately groomed lawns of this historic hunting estate unfold against a backdrop of dense forest. The chateau remains largely hidden by trees to your right, but walk on and it will gradually be revealed, looking surprisingly youthful despite the passage of almost four centuries. The unmistakable Louis XIII-style exterior in pale *tuffeau* stone quarried in Bourré was designed by Jacques Bougier, who also worked at Blois and Chambord. Classical details include dentil cornices, arched window lintels plus medallions sculpted with heads of Roman Emperors. Perfect symmetry and deeply incised horizontal banding holds everything together visually.

As you enter the interior you'll receive an informative brochure describing the main rooms to be visited at your own pace. To your right is a large dining room sizzling with decorative panels of scenes from Don Quixote, plus a huge gilded neo-Renaissance fireplace surmounted by a bust of Henri IV. Above is an appropriately intricately decorated beamed ceiling.

Climb the Louis XIII main staircase, clearly dated 1634, whose sculpted decoration includes several Green Man fertility symbol references – something of a recurring theme at Cheverny. On the first floor you'll discover beautifully preserved private apartments, beginning with a salon reserved for the presentation of newborn babies. Next come a nursery with a Napoléon III rocking-horse, a ladies' drawing room and a bridal chamber, complete with early en suite facilities. The family dining room is set with a specially commissioned *Autumn in Cheverny* dinner service and tablecloth, while in the small salon is a life-sized statue of Anne-Victor Hurault de Vibraye, whose descendants still own the estate.

A very different aspect of this elegant family home is revealed in the huge **Arms Room**, whose collection of polished armour includes a complete suit made for the four-year-old Duc de Bordeaux (who became Comte de Chambord). There's also 15th- to 17th-century weaponry, Henri IV's travelling chest and a still-vibrant 17th-century Gobelins tapestry. This room also preserves the meticulous decorative work of Jean Monier, who created the next room, the **King's Chamber**, designed to welcome the monarch and other distinguished guests. Its walls are hung with huge Paris-made tapestries, beneath a ceiling emblazoned with gilded panels decorated with romantic themes from Greek mythology. Their dazzling effect was no doubt appreciated by Henri IV, who occupied the royal bed (covered in 16th-century Persian embroidery) during a visit to the estate.

The visit continues on the ground floor, among hunting trophies, portraits, a large family tree plus a 17th-century Flemish tapestry in the vestibule. The **Grand Salon**, whose intricate pastel-toned panelling adorns even the ceiling, displays fine portraits of great historical significance (one is attributed to Titian) and a Louis XVI table is signed 'Stockel', cabinetmaker to Marie Antoinette. Beyond lies the **Galerie**, with canvases by François Clouet, portrait artist to François I, a Coronation portrait of Louis XVI and a document signed by George Washington. Completing the visit are a **library** with 2000 leather-bound works and a **salon** hung with giant 17th-century Flanders tapestries. Its Louis XV longcase clock remains in perfect working order.

Leave by the rear doors, crossing the stone bridge spanning a dry moat. Ahead, beyond the Apprentices' Garden created in 1996, lies a large 18th-century orangery. During the Second World War it housed many of France's greatest art treasures, including the *Mona Lisa*, but now contains an up market gift boutique.

Cheverny (minus its outer towers) will be familiar to Tintin aficionados as Moulinsart – Marlinspike Hall in English texts – an association celebrated in a colourful museum created between the exit gates and the estate's walled *potager* (vegetable garden). A spectacle in itself, the garden's aromatic qualities also help offset those wafting, not always pleasantly, from the nearby kennels of around 100 handsome hunting dogs. Late afternoon feeding times are frenzied affairs which you might decide to miss.

Château de Troussay

ⓘ *Route de Troussay, a short distance southwest of Cheverny, T02 54 44 29 07, www.chateaudetroussay.com. Apr-Jun and Sep daily 1030-1230 and 1400-1800, Jul-Aug daily 1000-1830, Oct 1030-1230 and 1400-1730. Closed Nov-Mar. Guided tour interior and exterior €7, €5.50, exterior only (exhibition, museum and henhouse) €5.50.*

One of the smallest of the Loire chateaux, Troussay is nevertheless a delight, with a nobility and grace of all proportion to its physical dimensions. The central body, constructed around 1450 for Robert de Bugy, *écuyer* (equerry) to François I, clearly took its design cues from great structures like Blois, Chambord and Cheverny, as you'll discover during a guided visit of six rooms of the privately owned chateau.

The original brick-and-stone Renaissance façade was extended two centuries or so later with wings framed by handsome circular towers topped with decorative *clochers*. Completing the effect is a broad courtyard a 500-year-old holly tree and sheltered on either side by long, low *dépendences* (farm-style outbuildings) now occupied by a museum giving worthwhile insight into bygone rural life in the surrounding Sologne region. The rear of the chateau bears Louis XII's porcupine emblem, the salamander of François I plus an *escalier* (staircase) tower added during the 19th century and decorated with playful corbel figures. Little remains of the original formal gardens apart from the tell-tale depression of a former lake, venerable cedars and sequoias, plus a still-productive *potager*. But the spirit survives, and the beautiful, secluded location completes this perfect antidote to the occasional sensory overload of its big-league neighbours.

Château de Fougères-sur-Bièvre

ⓘ *11 km southwest of Cheverny on the D52, T02 54 20 27 18, www.fougeres-sur-bievre.monuments-nationaux.fr. 8 May-10 Sep daily 0930-1230 and 1400-1830, 11 Sep-7 May Wed-Mon 1000-1230 and 1400-1700. Closed 1 Jan, 1 May, 1 and 11 Nov, 25 Dec. €5.50, €4 (18-25s), under 18s free. Guided visit by arrangement, otherwise self-guided visit with literature in 9 languages.*

The chateau has more of a dual personality than most. Its upper parts look the very epitome of the French country castle, with its massive towers, cannon, arrow-slits and sentry walk. However, instead of being isolated within a protective moat (which was filled in around the 17th century) it's now bounded on one side by a meadow and on the other by the grassy roadside verges of the slightly laid-back village. But the building can trace its history back to 1030, and was occupied during the Hundred Years' War by the English who, after their defeat in 1429, left it in ruins. In 1470 Louis XI's Chancellor Pierre de Refuge rebuilt the structure, adding the square *donjon* and most of the other defensive features we see today. The purely decorative Renaissance-inspired embellishments of 1510-1520 were the work of his grandson Jean de Villebresme, who also removed the upper crenelated battlements and added the present steeply pitched slate roofs. Sadly, the interiors were stripped when the site was acquired by Réné Lambot, who already owned the nearby Château de Boissay and who used Fougères from 1812 until 1901 for a milling enterprise. Happily, the chateau and its dignity have now been fully restored, and the self-guided visit offers a worthwhile insight into medieval military construction techniques. Undoubted highlights are the sentry walk and the forest of massive roof timbers.

Château du Gué-Péan

ⓘ *13 km east of Monthou-sur-Cher, about 23 km south of Cheverny, T02 54 71 37 10, www.guepean.com. 14 Jul-26 Aug 1030-1230 and 1400-1830. €6.50, €5 (9-12s, groups 20+, students), under 8s free.*

In contrast to the long-celebrated sites of the Loire Valley, Gué (pronounced 'gae')-Péan is that rarest of things: a romantic chateau in a peaceful clearing amid ancient hunting forests, so far largely undiscovered by the outside world. To visit you must cross the remains of a medieval drawbridge and tug a modest bell-pull beside a stone gateway. Soon the gate will open, welcoming you to an unimagined haven in largely Renaissance style. The self-guided visit begins in a vaulted family chapel and continues with a winding climb to the sentry walk around the highest of the medieval towers, whose walls wear the inscriptions of visitors from centuries past. Take a seat beneath the complex supporting timbers of the Imperial, bell-shaped roof and you can watch a well-produced video outlining the history and restoration of the estate, formerly the site of a Roman camp. From up here there's also a bird's-eye view of the courtyard and surrounding countryside.

From the 16th century onwards the chateau gradually evolved into a gracious country home, as you'll now discover during a tour (guided only) of several of the more historically important rooms. Highlights include a hunting trophy room, a ladies' salon, the king's bedroom (lest he should decide to drop in unexpectedly) and a music room used by Chopin, a rather more frequent visitor. Further history unfolds in the library housed in another tower, with letters signed by personalities including Napoléon, General de Gaulle and Marie Antoinette. There's also an early map-style illustration of the estate, whose stables are once again occupied, as part of a large equestrian centre.

Romorantin-Lanthenay → *For listings, see pages 68-72.*

The capital of the Sologne is inexorably linked to French history as the setting in which François d'Angoulême – who would later become King François I – spent his childhood, and also as the birthplace of his future wife, Claude de France. Her father Louis XII so loved the town that he commissioned Leonardo da Vinci to design a chateau here. Although the innovative building never materialized, the old town, beside the River Sauldre, is worth visiting, not least to see the excellent Musée de la Sologne, housed in three ancient water mill buildings. Nearby is the Espace Matra, a very different museum dedicated to the town's former motor manufacturing industry. Meanwhile, tucked away in a romantic forest clearing not far from the town is the fairy-tale castle you've been secretly searching for – the 16th-century Château du Moulin. A little further to the southwest lies Selles-sur-Cher, where you can picnic on the riverbanks before visiting the huge Romanesque abbey-church of Notre-Dame-la-Blanche, close to the spot on which Joan of Arc's 6000-strong army awaited the command of Charles VII in 1429.

Musée de Sologne

ⓘ *Moulin du Chapitre, T02 54 95 33 66, www.museedesologne.com. 2 Jan-31 Dec 1200 and 1400-1800, Sun and bank holidays 1400-1800. Closed Tue, 1 Jan, 1 May, 25 Dec. €5, €3.50 concessions. Ask for an English translation of the exhibition at the desk. Combined tickets available for this and the Matra museum €8, €5 concessions.*

Simply defining the Sologne region is far from straightforward, but this well-conceived museum gives a firm grounding in so many facets of its landscapes, history, culture, architecture and wildlife that you'll immediately begin to see things differently, and start piecing together something of the puzzle. The displays are housed in three former watermills, one of which (the Tour Jacquemart) dates from the 12th century. Contrasts between simple peasant farming and the privileged life in the great chateaux are particularly revealing, and everything is documented in a well-translated printed guide to accompany your visit.

Espace Automobiles Matra

ⓘ *17 rue des Capucins, T02 54 94 55 58, www.museematra.com (French only). Open daily 0900-1200 and 1400-1800, Sat-Sun and bank holidays 1000-1200 and 1400-1800. Closed*

1 Jan, 1 May, 25 Dec. €5, €3.50 concessions. Combined tickets for this and the Musée de Sologne €8. Exhibit information provided in English.

The Matra company's motor racing pedigree is celebrated in this extravagant collection of historic vehicles, displayed in an appropriately high-tech setting (in which Beaulieu cine cameras were once assembled). Each year there's an additional themed display. Meanwhile, the lower floor, displays some of the concept vehicles developed by the company's styling and engineering studios. Pride of place goes to variations (including a roadster) on the Espace, rejected by Peugeot before Renault turned it into a world-beater and took all the credit, and which for many years the company assembled in Romarantin.

Château du Moulin

ⓘ *Lassay-sur-Croisne (10 km west of Romorantin-Lanthenay), T02 54 83 83 51, www.chateau-moulin-fraise.com. 1 Apr-30 Sep daily 1000-1230 and 1400-1830. Guided tours of chateau, museum and garden at 30 mins past the hour from 1030. €9, €7 (12-18s), €4 (under 12s); €7 museum and gardens only.*

The 'pearl of the Sologne' sits in a romantic and secretive location deep within silent, broadleaf forest, where reflections of its tall, pale pink brick towers shimmer in the dark waters of a satisfyingly wide moat. The chateau was constructed between around 1492 by court architect Jacques de Persigny for nobleman Phillippe du Moulin, who, it is said, saved the life of Charles VIII at the Battle of Fornoue (Italy) in 1495. The initial visual effect today, though, is much more fairy-tale castle than feudal fortress, with only one of the four outer bastions retaining its full height, and virtually all the brickwork incorporating the same diamond-pattern decoration found at Blois. That said, the towers feature *meurtrier* openings for archers, outermost faces are curved to maximize their strength and those of the drawbridge gatehouse rise to an impressive height. Renaissance influences are obvious in the main residential building or *châtelet*, whose steeply pitched roof has dormer windows, alongside more typically Gothic touches such as crocketed gables and a small but sturdy chapel. The private chateau remains inhabited, but guided visits include a selection of rooms with period furnishings, looking much as they did after major but sensitive renovation works in 1901-1914. The estate is today home to the Conservatoire de la Fraise, the former chateau stables now housing a museum celebrating the history and culture of the far-from-humble strawberry, 40 or so varieties of which are grown in the adjoining gardens.

Eglise Abbatiale Notre-Dame-la-Blanche

ⓘ *Selles-sur-Cher (18 km southwest of Romorantin-Lanthenay).*

The pleasant town of Selles-sur-Cher takes its name from the *cella* (Latin for 'refuge') of Eusice, an early Christian hermit who arrived to set up home on a known flood-plain, which thereafter remained miraculously dry, whatever the state of the river. When he died around 540 he was buried in a simple vaulted chamber beneath the nave of the monastery which he had by then established. Around 1200-1215 the monastery, an important place of pilgrimage, was replaced by the huge abbey church of Notre-Dame-la-Blanche. Despite the hostile actions of the Revolution, which saw the abbey's prized possessions sold off, the tomb survives. You'll find it by descending a small flight of stone steps from the south aisle (a rather primitive wall-mounted timer activates fittingly atmospheric lighting). Surprisingly, the Romanesque church above has a slated timber roof, with Gothic rib vaults in the side aisles, whose interesting carved capitals include vine-leaf decoration. The exterior of the apse has a primitive early frieze thought to depict events in the life of the Saint.

In 1429 Selles witnessed a key event in French history unfolding after the liberation of Orléans, when Joan of Arc and the Duke of Alençon assembled an army of 6000 to await the command of Charles VII. At the time, the abbey and the village were protected by a feudal *donjon* sited on the riverbanks. It was replaced during the early 17th century by an elegant private chateau. There's talk of it becoming a hotel, but for now it remains a tantalising enigma gazing coyly across the river. The town has also given its name to a high quality local goat's cheese, which in 1975 was awarded AOC (*Appellation d'Origine Contrôlé*) status.

Domaine de Chaumont-sur-Loire → *For listings, see pages 68-72.*

The Château de Chaumont sits imperiously on a broad plateau high above the Loire. In 1560 Henri II's widow Catherine de' Medici acquired it in order to oust the king's mistress Diane de Poitiers (whom she had long despised) from Chenonceau and instead take up residence here. Today it's hard to see why she never did so, for the estate and its setting seem near faultless, particularly during the annual **Festival des Jardins** which have made Chaumont world-famous. When you've completed your tour of the chateau and the display gardens created for the festival by some of the best contemporary garden designers, head down to the banks of the River Cher to dine under the stars in Montrichard, or climb to the town's ruined fortress to enjoy an historic re-enactment performance recalling events in the town's history. In the nearby village of Bourré is another unmissable attraction – a traditional village sculpted deep underground in the same pale *tuffeau* stone that was quarried here for centuries to build the great chateaux of the Loire.

Château de Chaumont

ⓘ *T02 54 20 99 22, www.domaine-chaumont.fr. Daily from 1000, closing times vary (last entry 45 mins before closing). Closed 25 Dec and 1 Jan. Festival des Jardins runs from end Apr to mid-Oct. All-inclusive Domaine ticket including Festival des Jardins €15.50, €11 (12-18s), €5.50 (6-11s), under 6s free. Festival des Jardins and park €11, €7.50, €5, free. Chateau only €10, €6, €4, free. Village entrance involves a 10-min gentle uphill walk. Visitors with reduced mobility are advised to enter via the Plateau entrance, which offers adjacent level parking.*

At first glance the Château de Chaumont looks like a French castle should, with mighty towers and a commanding strategic placement high above the banks of the Loire. Make the gentle climb from the village for a closer look, though, and its *tourelles*, Italianate detailing and private chapel tell a very different story. Unlike its predecessor, built in AD 990 to defend nearby Blois, this is less a military fortress and more a showpiece country residence. Look inside and you'll discover a succession of rooms in neo-Gothic and Renaissance styles, replicating as closely as possible the fashionably romantic effect visualized by 19th-century architectural stylist Paul-Ernest Sanson for the estate's last private owners. In 1875 16-year-old Marie Say visited the chateau with her father and instantly fell in love with it. Naturally, the wealthy sugar company magnate purchased it for her. Marie subsequently married Amédée de Broglie and the couple began pouring a vast fortune into the radical transformation of both the chateau and its estate, along the way producing such fantastic creations as a guardroom complete with polished arms and armour, and a council chamber hung with 16th-century tapestries and floored with 17th-century *majolica* tiles shipped from a palazzo in Palermo. Then for good measure they restored the bedchambers of Catherine de' Medici and her personal astrologer Cosimo Ruggieri.

After these visual fireworks, the beautiful Flamboyant Gothic *grand escalier* back down to the ground floor provides a welcome interlude of serenity, and a curtain-raiser for the

Festival des Jardins

Chaumont is today renowned the world over for its summer-long International Garden Festival which has been hosted here since 1992 and which showcases the art of contemporary garden design. Landscape designers, horticulturalists and artists are invited to submit designs expressing imagination and resourcefulness for gardens of 210 sq m (average for a typical home garden) and within a set maximum budget. A jury selects the best designs, whose creators then bring them to life in 26 plots at Chaumont. Each season there's a new theme to be interpreted and the results vary from subtle to spectacular, attracting widespread press coverage. Visitors, too, keep returning in search of fresh inspiration for their own gardens. See listings, page 70, for details of the Festival des Jardins opening times and nocturnal visits.

long, Pugin-esque ground floor salon, whose monumental fireplace is emblazoned with a large painted porcupine. Louis XII's curious emblem reappears outside as a stone bas-relief overlooking what must have been a rather dark, enclosed central courtyard up until 1739, when the north wall was demolished. The result is a vast terrace bathed in sunlight and affording panoramic views across the river.

Don't leave without visiting the palatial *écuries* (stables) created by the Broglies for their beloved horses, and whose fully stocked tack-room is curiously atmospheric. Dominating the buildings is an immense bastion-like tower looking like a classic piece of English Arts and Crafts architecture. In fact it began life as the kiln of a pottery and glass works which stood on the site, and was spared demolition to serve as an indoor pony training school. Perhaps unsurprisingly, the family fortunes eventually declined, and in 1938 the estate passed into state ownership (now the Region Centre).

Chaumont offers something for just about everyone (including wheelchair-users) and its two restaurants are outstanding, offering inspired, wholesome menus in a choice of settings; dine in style in an elegant marquee or less formally beneath tall, mature lime trees. For smaller budgets there's also a sandwich bar. In its additional role as *Centre d'Arts et de Nature* the Domaine is adding an experimental farm-style *potager* (vegetable garden), hosts open-air film festivals inspired by nature (*Jardin d'Images*) and will be welcoming and encouraging fresh artistic talents. But the underlying spirit remains undiluted, as you'll discover during *Les Nocturnes* – evenings when the chateau is entirely candle-lit, or when the festival display gardens are transformed by thousands of coloured LED lights.

Montrichard

ⓘ *Museum and Donjon entrance on Grand Degré Ste Croix, T02 54 32 05 10, www.officetourisme-montrichard.com. Apr-Sep, times vary. Closed Mon. €5, €3 (7-12s).*

Seen from across the river Cher on a sunny day, the town of Montrichard (whose 't' is pronounced) looks perky and contented, as if refusing to be dominated by the blockhouse-like *donjon* of its forlorn, ruined chateau. Cross the ancient multi-arched bridge, continue past a time-warp saddler's workshop and you'll enter a square shaded by a huddle of billowing lime trees. A seat beneath one of the pastel parasols of of the various bar-restaurants is the perfect spot in which to relax with a cool drink and contemplate the medieval half-timbered façades just across the square. You can thank the sturdy *clocher* (church tower) rising behind the most colourful pair for having protected them when part of the chateau walls collapsed in 1753. The Eglise Ste-Croix itself (in which Jeanne de Valois married the future King Louis in 1476) fared less well, only its Romanesque façade being spared. Consequently, it's today less visited than the nearby museum of local archeological finds and the chateau ruins, from whose elevated site you can enjoy sweeping views of the river and surrounding landscapes. Each summer the site hosts ambitious medieval re-enactments, whose spectacle value is heightened at nightfall. Stop at the tourist office, in the 16th-century Maison de l'Ave Maria, for a town map with walking tour.

La Cave des Roches

ⓘ *Bourré (4 km east of Montrichard).* *See page 72 for opening times and other details.*

On the surface, Bourré (whose name means 'drunken' in French) looks like a typical riverside village, but for centuries it provided the beautiful, pale limestone known as *tuffeau* used in the construction of many of the great chateaux. In fact, everybody wanted it and the quarries, pushing deep underground, happily obliged, calling a halt only when hundreds of kilometres of galleries were beginning to cause real concerns for the safety of the village they had undermined. The site found a new lease of life, though, when dark conditions and consistently low temperatures of around 12°C proved ideal for large-scale mushroom production. You can see for yourself by taking a guided tour, although arguably more compelling is the chance to visit silent, long-abandoned galleries. Here, with upwards of 50 m of stone poised unnervingly above your head, you'll learn about the techniques and tough working conditions of the quarrymen, before moving on to *La Ville Souterraine* – billed as an underground town in stone. This unlikely creation is being systematically sculpted *in situ* by a dedicated young stonemason in his spare time, for the benefit of future generations. Tours are conducted in both French and English, which slows things down considerably, but your patience will be rewarded with the kind of insight which enables you to see things on the surface very differently. Less surprisingly, while you're here you can purchase mushrooms direct from the producer.

Château de Chenonceau

ⓘ *34 km southeast of Tours, T02 47 23 90 07, www.chenonceau.com. You can travel from Tours to Chenonceaux by train (25 mins). The train station is just 50 m from the entrance. Open daily though hours vary. €11, €8.50 (7-18s and students). Audio guide €4. Arrive early during peak periods to avoid overcrowding inside the chateau. However, if you're keen to see the gardens at their best, visit them in late afternoon, when the light softens. Romantic evening walks in the gardens accompanied by music, early evenings Jul and Aug. €5, under 7s free. Entry included in the Pass Châteaux (see page 74). If you take a river cruise from Chisseaux, you'll pass beaneath the arches of the chateau.*

However many pictures you've seen, nothing comes close to seeing for yourself this exquisite chateau reflected in the waters of the River Cher. Adding to the effect are not one but two extravagant Renaissance gardens conceived on the banks of the river by two powerful women. To the left, lawned *parterres* and swirling filigree plantings of santolina radiate from a central fountain in the immense garden of Henri II's mistress, Diane de Poitiers. In 1533 the king married Catherine de' Medici who, upon his sudden death in 1559, forced her rival to leave Chenonceau for Chaumont. Her own garden, on your right, is more intimate but just as elegant with its box topiary, standard roses and well over a thousand lavender plants laid out around a large fountain. The estate also preserves its 18th-century farm and the *potager* (kitchen garden) which supplied fresh vegetables for the chateau.

The chateau is reached via the two footbridges of a small island, where the lone **Tour des Marques** survives from the feudal chateau acquired by Thomas Bohier in 1513. Pressure of his duties as François I's Financial Receiver led him to leave project managing of its Renaissance replacement to his wife Catherine Briçonnet, who oversaw the creation of the beautiful turreted main building and its chapel (built on the site of a former mill). The costs eventually proved ruinous, however, and when Bohier died in 1535 his son was forced by accumulated debts to relinquish the chateau to the Crown. Eight years later Henri II gave Chenonceau to Diane de Poitiers, who carried out a series of embellishments, including the multi-arched bridge across the river, which her successor Catherine de' Medici transformed by adding the celebrated Italianate gallery visible today.

Self-guided visits are unaffected by prolonged restoration works on the exterior of the chateau and begin in the vaulted vestibule, whose curious offset rib vaults date from 1515. On your left is the **Salle des Gardes**, whose pale stone walls are hung with large tapestries beneath an intricately decorated beamed ceiling. A magnificent doorway leads to the Renaissance-Gothic chapel – notice the shell emblems where the piers meet the vault ribs, and the niches below them which doubtless once contained sculpted figures. Beyond the guardroom lies the bedchamber of **Diane de Poitiers**, complete with a huge, pure white fireplace now hung with a somewhat sinister looking portrait of Catherine de' Medici. The imagery adorning her adjoining study is more uplifting, and includes a vast wall-hanging featuring exotic birds in a sea of verdure. Now comes the 60-m-long gallery, cunningly designed with window openings positioned above the load-bearing arches of Diane de Poitiers' bridge, alternating with deep niches set above its sturdy piers. A small wall plaque records the many casualties treated here during the First World War, when the gallery served as a hospital.

After the palatially decorated bedroom occupied by **François I**, climb the visibly Italian-influenced stone staircase to a light hallway extending the full width of the building and dedicated to Catherine Briçonnet. The **Chambre des Cinq Reines**, on the other hand, honours Catherine de' Medici's two daughters and three daughters-in-law, and is followed by her own equally sumptuous bedroom. Beyond it the **Cabinet d'Estampes** displays interesting early engravings of Chenonceau beneath a richly painted Florentine ceiling. After the capacious bedchambers of **César de Vendôme** and **Gabrielle d'Estrées** (son and daughter-in-law of King Henry IV) who acquired Chenonceau in 1624, the visit continues on the second floor, where another beautifully decorated hallway (this time in 19th-century taste) contrasts with the movingly funereal bedchamber of **Louise de Lorraine**, to which she retreated after her husband Henri III's assassination in 1589. Descend to the ground floor to see a room occupied by **Louis XIV**. Note the stirring portraits and a huge fireplace emblazoned with gilded salamander and ermine emblems, before you plunge into the very different world of Chenonceau's vast kitchens.

After the visit you can recover on the café terrace of the nearby former stables, or dine in the elegant **Orangerie Restaurant**, tucked away beside the Jardin Vert behind them. Don't miss visiting the *potager* (kitchen gardens) and the preserved 18th-century estate farm.

Blois and the Sologne listings

For hotel and restaurant price codes and other relevant information, see pages 11-16.

Where to stay

Blois *p52*

€€€ Hotel Mercure, 28 quai St Jean, T02 54 56 66 66, www.mercure.com. Modern and spacious rooms in a riverside location a few steps from the town centre. Parking (payable), Wi-Fi, swimming pool and hotel restaurant make this hotel comfortable and convenient, if slightly lacking in charm.

€€€ Le Médicis, 2 allée François 1er, T02 54 43 94 04, www.le-medicis.com. Closed Jan. Well-known for its gastronomic restaurant, the hotel, about 1 km from the centre of town, has fully modernized, sound-proof and a/c bedrooms. Decorated in warm colours with cushions and throws, the accommodation, which includes family rooms and suites, has a welcoming, cosy feel throughout. Free parking and Wi-Fi.

€€ Anne de Bretagne, 31 av Jean Laigret, T02 54 78 05 38, www.hotelannedebretagne.com. Situated on a tree-lined square close to the chateau and a 5-min walk from Blois centre. The rooms are rather basically furnished, but refreshed with colourful wallpapers and fabrics. Some underground parking and a secure area for bicycles, free Wi-Fi. Rooms available with disabled access. The train station is within 150 m.

€€ Côté Loire, 2 place de la Grève, T02 54 78 07 86, www.coteloire.com. A small 16th-century former coaching inn in a quiet spot on the right bank of the Loire. The bedrooms are attractive, bright and airy. Those at the front have river views, while at the rear is a charming courtyard. There's also a secure place for bikes. Free Wi-Fi. Its popular restaurant (open Tue-Sat) serves different dishes every day, with ingredients fresh from the market.

€€ Hotel Le Monarque, 61 rue Porte Chartraine, T02 54 78 02 35, www.hotel-lemonarque.com. A welcoming hotel with cheerfully decorated rooms and a restaurant flooded with light. Situated at the top of the town, there's a pleasant walk down through pedestrianized shopping streets to the centre. Free Wi-Fi, limited car parking plus a secure area for bicycles.

Campsite

Camping Val de Blois, Base de Loisirs du Val de Blois, Vineuil (4 km from Blois centre, direction Chambord on D951), T02 54 78 82 05, www.campingvaldeblois.fr. End Apr-Oct. Spread around 40 ha of riverbank, this exceptional campsite has plenty of shady pitches and easy access to Blois and Chambord. A good base for cyclists.

Chambord *p56*

€€ Hotel and Restaurant Grand Saint-Michel, Place St-Louis, T02 54 20 31 31, www.saintmichel-chambord.com. The only hotel in Chambord, and where you'll virtually have the chateau and the grounds to yourself after the visitors have gone. Some rooms overlook the chateau. Ground-floor room available for disabled guests. Breakfast on the terrace with that fabulous view, weather permitting.

€€ Hôtel de la Bonnheure, 9 rue René Masson, Bracieux (between Cheverny and Chambord), T02 54 46 41 57, www.hoteldelabonnheur.com. You'll receive a warm welcome at this rural hotel with typical decorative brick features and cosy dining room with exposed beams. Situated in the heart of the village of Bracieux, it's set in its own charming gardens and has quiet rooms overlooking the grounds. Breakfast includes a speciality egg served in a small pot. Secure bike park and enclosed private parking.

€€ La Maison d'à Côte, 25 route de Chambord, Montlivault, T02 54 20 62 30, www.lamaisondacote.fr. Situated conveniently between Blois and Chambord, this hotel and restaurant extends a warm and friendly welcome to guests. The stylish and comfortable contemporary-chic rooms are for 1 or 2 people and all have a/c and free Wi-Fi. The restaurant serves fine cuisine from local produce prepared by Michelin-starred chef Ludovic Laurenty. Vegetarian dishes available.

€ Le Saint Florent, 14 rue de la Chabardière, Mont-Près-Chambord, T02 54 70 81 00, www.hotel-saint-florent.com. A friendly hotel a 10-min drive from the heart of Blois and close to the chateaux of Chambord and Cheverny. The rooms are comfortable and homely, with good bathrooms, although perhaps a little dated. Rear bedrooms are quieter. Free Wi-Fi on request. Evening meals can be taken in the restaurant (closed Mon) to the rear of the hotel.

Cheverny *p58*

€€ Domaine de la Rabouillère, Chemin de Marçon, Contres (21 km south of Blois), T02 54 79 05 14, www.larabouillere.com. Closed mid-Nov to mid-Mar. Set within a wooded estate with its own lake, this Sologne-style farmhouse offers delightful rooms in the main house, or a pretty cottage for families. All rooms are immaculately furnished, some have fine views over the parkland and there is a ground-floor suite with easy access. Free Wi-Fi.

€€ Domaine Le Clos Bigot, Le Clos Dussons, Chitenay (12 km south of Blois), T02 54 44 21 28, www.gites-cheverny.com. Peaceful accommodation in Sologne-style buildings set around a courtyard. There's a selection of lovely rooms including a suite on 2 floors in a former *pigeonnier*. Breakfast includes home-made jams and cakes – a good start for a day exploring some of the remarkable sites nearby.

€€ Les Chambres Vertes, Le Clos de la Chartrie, Cormeray (13 km south of Blois), T09 73 84 44 55, www.chambresvertes.net. An eco-friendly bed and breakfast, with spacious and simply furnished rooms, with one twin room specially adapted for disabled visitors. There is a bright and welcoming common room (with internet access) which leads onto the terrace and garden. Evening meals are served 4 days a week (€25.50 including wine, reservations required) and are made with organic, locally sourced ingredients. meals available on request.

Chaumont *p63*

€€€ Château de Chissay, 1-3 place Paul Boncour, Chissay-en-Touraine, T02 54 32 32 01, www.chateaudechissay.com. A beautiful chateau hotel in pale *tuffeau* stone not far from Montrichard and convenient for many magnificent sites. The rooms are all different, unusual and beautifully furnished. Everyone can enjoy the extensive grounds, outdoor pool and dine in style.

€ Le Clos du Verêt, 9 Route des Vallée, Bourré, T02 54 32 07 58, www.lestabourelles-leveret.com. In the troglodyte village of Bourré on the northern banks of the River Cher, the Domaine des Tabourelles wine estate offers very pleasant rooms in an 18th-century home which is full of character. Guests have their own entrance into a common area which includes a handy small kitchen. There is a family suite plus 2 doubles, 1 with a small terrace and another with views over the Cher valley.

Restaurants

Blois *p52*

€€€ Au Rendez-vous des Pêcheurs, 27 rue du Foix, T02 54 74 67 48, www.rendezvousdespecheurs.com. Daily except Sun and Mon lunch. Chef Christophe Cosme established this bistro-style dining room in 1999 and has become a star of local cuisine. He expresses the spirit of the Loire in his menus using seasonal vegetables and locally caught river fish such as *sandre* (pike-perch). Menus are from €35, although the *Menu Découverte* at €76 (per table only) best illustrates what modern Loire cuisine has to offer.

€€€ Le Bouchon Lyonnais, 25 rue des Violettes (just off place Louis XII towards rue

St Lubin), T02-54 74 12 87, www.aubouchon lyonnais.com. Tue-Sat. Immerse yourself in a huge and very traditional Lyonnais menu – not for the fainthearted. There's a set menu for €22, although many dishes have supplements (and wines are expensive).

€€€ Les Banquettes Rouges, 16 rue des Trois Marchands, T02 54 78 74 92, www.lesbanquettesrouges.com. Open Tue-Sat 1200-1330 and 1900-2130. Booking advisable. A mouth-watering culinary journey through French tradition presented in an inventive, contemporary style. *Bistrot*-style dining room with welcoming staff.

€€ Le Castelet, 40 rue St Lubin, T02 54 74 66 09, www.cuisine-traditionnelle-restaurant-gastronomique.castelet.fr. Closed Wed and Sun, otherwise open 1200-1345 and 1900-2145. Traditional menus served in a cosy, characterful dining room. Expect to find fresh, seasonal produce, with the opportunity to savour particular local *charcuterie* and river fish with an appropriate wine for between €16 and €32. There's also a vegetarian menu for around €20.

€€ Le Duc de Guise, 13-15 place Louis XII, T02 54 78 22 39. Apr-Aug daily, Sep-Mar closed Sun and Mon evenings. A popular Italian restaurant serving a good range of pizza and pasta dishes. Efficient and friendly service from the staff, regardless of how busy they are. The upper terrace and dining room are than those on the square.

Cafés and bars

Ben's Blues Bar, L'Orangerie, 41 rue St Lubin, www.bensbluesbar.com. Thu-Tue 1830-0200. Live blues and occasional gypsy, *manouche* style jazz at this small, atmospheric venue in the old quarter of Blois.

Le Clipper, 13-15 place Louis XII, T02 54 78 22 39. Daily 0900-0100, closed public holidays, 24-26 Dec and 31 Dec-2 Jan. Le Clipper bar has comfortable covered seating in the shade of the trees in the square. At night it's a popular meeting place and serves as the street-level dining area for the de Guise Italian restaurant.

Velvet Jazz Lounge, 15 bis rue Haute, T02 54 78 36 32, www.velvet-jazz-lounge.com. Tue-Sat 1700-0200. Situated at the foot of the Denis Papin steps; relax in the velvety interior and enjoy some smooth jazz sounds.

Romorantin-Lanthenay *p61*

€€€ Grand Hôtel du Lion d'Or, 69 rue Georges Clemenceau, T02 54 94 15 15, www.hotel-liondor.fr. Daily except Tue lunch, closed mid-Feb to end Mar. A Michelin-starred restaurant within a beautiful 16th-century Renaissance building, which is now an unashamedly luxurious hotel, in the centre of town. Chef Didier Clement is celebrated for his harmonious flavours, in dishes which are a feast for both the eye and the palate.

Festivals

Early Apr-30 Sep Château Royal de Blois Son-et-Lumière, T02 54 90 33 33, www.chateaudeblois.fr. Presentations every evening with exceptions for special events. English version every Wed. €7.50, €6 concessions, €4 (6-17s); combined ticket with chateau €14.50. Audience arrives 30 mins before the show, which starts at 2200 Apr, May, Sep and 2230 Jun-Aug. This 45-min performance, set to an original text and musical score, tells the story of the loves, tragedies and mysteries of the chateau.

End Apr to mid-Oct Festival des Jardins, Domaine de Chaumont-sur-Loire, T02 54 20 99 22, www.domaine-chaumont.fr. Daily end Apr-end Aug 1000-1900, Sep 1000-1830, 1 Oct to mid-Oct 1000-1800 (last entry 90 mins before closing). Illuminated visits 2200-2400 every evening (except Fri) Jul-Aug. €11, €7.50 concessions, €5 (6-11s), free under 6s and for disabled visitors and their helper companion.

Jun-Sep Chambord Son et Lumière, T02 54 50 40 00, www.chambord.org. Every evening at nightfall. €12, €10 concessions, combined ticket with chateau €17. Bookings at the central ticket office.

A nocturnal sound and light show (about 50 mins duration) projected onto the façade of the chateau.

Jul-Aug Des Lyres d'été, T02 54 58 84 56, www.bloischambord.com. Summer festival including over 200 events with concerts, street theatre, cinema, magic and circus performances. Starting with a firework display and open-air concert in mid-Jul, the festivities continue throughout the summer.

Last weekend in Oct Journées Gastronomiques de Sologne, Romorantin-Lanthenay, information from the tourist office, T02 54 76 43 89, www.romorantin.fr/jgs. €7 (1 day), €9 (2 days). Massive food and wine fair with a different theme each year, featuring a region or country, but pride of place goes to the enormous range and quality of Sologne and Loire Valley regional produce.

Shopping

Blois *p52*

Food and drink

Comtesse du Barry, 5 rue St-Martin (opposite the steps just off Place St Louis XII), T02 54 78 80 00, www.comtessedubarry.com. Mon 1430-1900, Tue-Sat 0930-1230 and 1430-1930. One of a chain of stores, but a good place to choose a small souvenir from a wide choice of fine foods and regional produce.

La Caf'Thé, 14 rue du Commerce, T02 54 74 50 65, www.lacafthe.fr. Tue–Sat 0830-1300 and 1400-1900. The smell of freshly roasted coffee and shelves full of colourful tea-caddies draw you into this fascinating emporium packed with everything you could desire for a small moment of caffeinated pleasure.

Le Théâtre du Pain, 26 rue Trois Marchands, T02 54 78 05 91. Fresh bread baked in the shop, all flavours of *macarons* and fantastic selection of sandwiches and tarts to take away. Ideal for a picnic lunch or sandwich.

Max Vauché, 50 rue du Commerce, T02 54 78 23 55, www.maxvauche-chocolatier.com. Tue-Fri 0930-1200 and 1400-1900, Sat 0900-1230 and 1400-1900. The beautiful window displays will stop you in your tracks. You can also go on a guided tour of the Max Vauché *chocolaterie* in Bracieux (see below), but if all you want to do is buy and enjoy it, come here.

What to do

Balloon flights

France Montgolfières, T03 80 97 38 61, www.franceballoons.com. Hot-air balloon flights from a choice of locations and offering various different packages.

Cycle routes and hire

Cyclists following the *Loire à Vélo* path (for full details, see page 36) have the option of 2 routes between Muides-sur-Loire and Blois by either passing through the forests around Chambord, or following the right bank of the Loire river (www.cycling-loire.com) to Blois. The route continues on the south bank to Candé-sur-Beuvron. If based in the Blois and Sologne area take advantage of 300 km of possible bike rides and themed circuits on the *Châteaux à Vélo* routes around Chambord, Blois and Cheverny (www.chateauxavelo.com). Below are 2 bike hire places in Blois, and there are other hire shops in Bracieux, Chambord and Cour-Cheverny.

Detours de Loire, 35 rue Charles Gille, Blois, T02 47 61 22 23, www.locationdevelos.com. Apr-Oct Mon-Fri (open weekends on request). Hire and repair of bikes, choice of self-guided itineraries, pick-up and drop-off service along the Loire. Prices start from €59 per adult per week.

Loire Vélo Nature, Hôtel Anne de Bretagne, 31 av Jean Laigret, Blois, T02 47 96 42 39, www.loirevelonature.com. Hire of bikes, baggage service, large number of pick-up and drop-off sites along the Loire. Prices start from €55 per adult per week.

Food and drink

Chocolaterie Max Vauché, 22 les Jardins du Moulin, Bracieux, T02 54 46 07 96, www.maxvauche-chocolatier.com. 1 Jul-31 Aug daily 1000-1230 and 1400-1900 (guided tours 1030, 1530 and 1630, 1430 in English), 1 Sep-30 Jun Tue-Sat 1000-1230 and 1400-1900 (guided tours 1030, 1530 and 1630), all year round Sun 1500-1830 (guided tours 1530 and 1630). €4. Disabled access. On entering the factory you will be given a sample to taste, before moving on to discover the world of chocolate-making from the raw cocoa to the final product. There's also a boutique.

La Cave des Roches, 40 route des Roches, Bourré, about 3 km from Montrichard signed left off the D176, T02 54 32 95 33, www.le-champignon.com. Cave Champignonnière or Carrière and the Ville Souterraine open daily mid-Mar to Sep with hourly guided tours Jul-Aug (website gives details of visiting times throughout the year). €6 or €10 duo visit, €5 children (7-14) or €7 duo visit. Visit a former *tuffeau* quarry and incredible underground town or the mushroom cellars where rare varieties of fungi are grown in the cool, subterranean atmosphere. Either of the guided tours takes about an hour and it's possible to do both on a combined ticket. There's a shop selling varieties of mushrooms and related speciality products, plus a restaurant with terrace open at lunchtimes (May-Sep) where you can savour simple mushroom-based dishes.

Guided tours

Boat Rides, Port de la Creusille, left bank, T02 54 56 09 24, www.bloischambord.co.uk. May-Oct, minimum €9, €6-50. 1 hr duration. Trips in a 'futreau' (traditional flat-bottomed barge) through the centre of historic Blois.

Horse-Drawn Carriage Rides, place du Château, Blois, T02 54 90 41 41 (tourist office), www.bloischambord.co.uk. Tours run Apr-Jun and Sep 1400-1800, Jul-Aug 1100-1900. €7, €4 (2-12s). Disabled access. Departing from the chateau entrance, for a 25-min circuit of the town (with commentary) in a covered horse-drawn carriage.

Wellbeing

Spa du Domaine des Thomeaux, 12 rue des Thomeaux, Mosnes (between Chaumont-sur-Loire and Amboise), T02 47 30 40 14, www.domainedesthomeaux.fr. The calm and relaxing Thomeaux spa, health and beauty centre offers hammam, sauna, indoor swimming pool, hydro-massage bath, body and facial treatments and body-sculpting massages from around the world. See website for details of wellbeing packages.

Wildlife

Zooparc de Beauval, St-Aignan, T02 54 75 74 26, www.zoobeauval.com. Open all year; mid-Mar to Oct 0900-1800; Nov to mid-Mar 0900-1600. €24, €18 children (3-10). The largest collection of its kind in France, with over 4000 animals in 22 ha, and considered to be in the top 15 zoos worldwide. See lions and tigers, the only pandas in France, primates, koala bears, a large tropical aquarium plus vast tropical glasshouses and botanical trail.

Amboise

Amboise gets its fair share of road traffic but its buzz and sheer charisma are irresistible; having long been a halt for pilgrims on the route to Santiago de Compostela, the town knows how to make visitors feel welcome. The chateau rises above the old town like a slumbering giant from the rocky promontory which in earliest times made it an obvious place for settlement. During the 11th century Comte d'Anjou Foulques Nerra (see page 83) built the first stone fortress here, but the effect today is more gracious than threatening, thanks to the chateau's transformation into a Renaissance-style royal pleasure palace during the reigns of Louis XII and François I. For maximum effect, see it from across the river at sunset, or simply take a seat at your preferred bar on place Michel Debre and admire the closer view – an option which adds a sense of drama, courtesy of the vast stone walls which rise almost sheer from the square to the chateau terraces. Projecting from them on a tall pillar of stone is an exquisite Gothic chapel in which Leonardo da Vinci lies buried. A few minutes' walk will bring you to his last home at Clos Lucé.

Arriving in Amboise

Getting there

Buses to Amboise run from Tours (45 minutes) on a regular service (except Sunday). The **Gare SNCF** ⓘ *bd Gambetta on the north bank*, has good connections with stations throughout the Loire Valley and you can travel direct from Paris in just over two hours.

Getting around

Amboise itself is small enough to visit on foot and it's a pleasure to wander through its narrow streets and stroll along the embankment. If using public transport, the train station is a short distance from the town on the north bank. Cyclists will find plenty of secure places to leave their bikes while visiting the town.

Tourist information

Tourist information office ⓘ *Quai du Général de Gaulle, T02 47 57 09 28, www.amboise-valdeloire.com.* A *Pass Châteaux* gives reductions on entry to a variety of attractions, eg a four-chateaux pass including Amboise, Clos Lucé, Chenonceau and Chambord for €38 (a saving of only €3 but it's valid for a year and you won't have to queue to get into the attractions). You can buy them from tourist offices or in advance online at www.amboise-valdeloire.com.

Places in Amboise → *For listings, see pages 76-78.*

Château Royal d'Amboise

ⓘ *Access on rue Victor Hugo, T08 20 20 50 50 (€0.09 per min), www.chateau-amboise.com. Daily from 0900 all year (except 25 Dec and 1 Jan), closing times vary, closed lunchtimes in winter. €10.20 (€14.20 with audio-guide), €8.50 (7-18s), under 7s free, €9 disabled plus accompanying person. Guided visits to the underground passages and towers (French only) must be booked in advance, €14.70, €11.50 children (7-18). Nocturnal events are held during the summer, information and bookings T02 47 57 14 47.*

Shallow steps set against the western ramparts take you through a dark archway to the visitor ticketing area. You'll emerge beside the inevitable gift shop, and climb to a grassy plateau, around which lie the remains of the original chateau buildings. The visit begins in the Gothic **Chapelle Saint-Hubert**, dedicated to the Patron Saint of hunting (hence the vivid scene carved above the doorway and copper antlers incorporated into the spire). The **Chapelle Royale** sits, like its predecessor created by Louis XI, on a vast pillar of stone clinging dramatically to the ramparts, and is breathtakingly beautiful inside; note the delicate snowflake-like central bosses adorning the complex vaulting. In the tiny south transept is the simple tomb of Leonardo da Vinci (see page 75).

Continue along the ramparts to the **Tour des Garçonnets** for panoramic views of the town and river. The large building nearby was begun by Charles VIII in French Gothic style and enlarged by Louis XII and François I, who added a new Italianate Renaissance wing. Inside is a primary guardroom displaying 16th-century armour and weaponry, followed by the **Promenoir des Gardes**, a vaulted open gallery overlooking the Loire, whose stonework bears traces of much later conflicts. Next comes the **Salle des Gardes Nobles**, protecting the royal apartments on the floor above. The room displays 16th-century armour plus an early mariner's chest. Creature comforts improve in the **Salle des Tambourineurs** (Drummers' Room), which contains a Renaissance table, a Charles VIII chest plus the throne of Cardinal Georges d'Amboise, who conducted the marriage of Charles VIII and Anne de Bretagne.

Floor tiles feature fleurs-de-lys, and a 16th-century Flemish tapestry depicts Alexander the Great. The architectural showpiece, though, is the **Salle du Conseil** (council chamber), whose pink brickwork complements stone features including ornate Renaissance fireplaces and lightweight rib-vaulting. The capitals of the slender piers depict hunting scenes plus grape-laden vines being filched by animals and birds.

Renaissance rooms begin with the **Salle de l'Echanson** (Cupbearer's Room) used for court banquets conducted around large Italian-style tables. Notice the large 17th-century Aubusson tapestries. Next is Henri II's bedchamber, with a suitably regal four-poster bed, a false-bottomed jewel chest and 16th- and 17th-century Belgian tapestries. The following **Antichambre de la Cordelière** a Renaissance fireplace bearing a royal crest above decorative ropework of the Ordre de St-Michel, founded at Amboise in 1469 by Louis XI. The mood changes in the apartments of King Philippe I, displaying fine family portraits amid the vibrant colours of the mid-19th century.

After leaving the apartments you can stand on the roof of the mighty **Tour des Minimes**, 40 m or so above the river. The tower's dark secret is revealed when you peer through the central iron grille or descend a staircase to discover a huge spiral ramp conceived by Charles VII's military engineers to permit cavalry and carriages to reach the chateau terraces. Another tower just like it was created on the opposite side of the plateau, providing a (relatively) safe descent. Between the two lie the Loire Valley's very first Renaissance garden (the Terrasse de Naples) and a contemporary Tuscan-style garden planted with cypresses, muscat vines and countless clipped-box spheres. Above is the **Porte des Lions** and a raised terrace overlooking defensive ditches created by the Romans.

Make your exit via the ticket area, or (for a more climactic experience) the spiral ramp of the dimly lit Tour des Minimes, accessible from the gift shop.

Château du Clos Lucé and Parc Léonardo da Vinci

ⓘ *2 rue du Clos Lucé, T02 47 57 00 73, www.vinci-closluce.com. Daily (except 25 Dec and 1 Jan) Jan 1000-1800, Feb-Jun 0900-1900, Jul-Aug 0900-2000, Sep-Oct 0900-1900, Nov-Dec 0900-1800. Chateau and park (mid-Mar to mid-Nov) €13.50, €11.20 concessions, €8.70 (7-18s), €37 family ticket (2 adults and up to 2 children). Chateau only (mid-Nov to 28 Feb) €11.20, €8.70 concession, €7.70 children, family ticket from €30, under 7s and disabled visitors free.*

A short walk from the heart of Amboise lies Clos Lucé, the 15th-century brick and limestone *manoir* (mansion) in which Leonardo da Vinci spent his final years as a guest of François I. The visit begins with a steep climb via a narrow spiral staircase to his **bedroom**, whose richly carved dark oak furnishings include a grand four-poster bed. Next come the **kitchen** in which his vegetarian meals were prepared, the **study** where he worked on refining his inventions, plus several Renaissance-style rooms hung with vast Aubusson tapestries. Numerous framed quotes from his writings give valuable insight into this remarkable man, who no doubt enjoyed gazing from the Italianate loggia connecting the upper rooms.

From here descend to the Gothic **chapel**, whose vaults feature frescoes by his companion and pupil Francesco di Melzi, then to the large **cellar rooms**. A museum in themselves, they contain scale models of his most important inventions, bilingual information panels plus the entrance to a mysterious tunnel believed to have once been connected to the Château d'Amboise.

Leonardo also apparently loved observing nature during walks around the beautiful private **parkland**, a pleasure which you can now share. You will also see giant canvasses depicting his works and full-size replicas of his inventions. A terrace overlooking the park has an exquisite formal Renaissance garden with shaded tables for relaxed *crêperie* dining.

La Pagode de Chanteloup

ⓘ 3 km south of Amboise direction D31 Bléré/Loches, T02 47 57 20 97, www.pagode-chanteloup.com. Open daily Apr to mid-Nov, Feb-Mar weekends and school holidays. Opening times vary. €8.90, €7.90 students, €6.90 (7-15s) and disabled, €28.20 family ticket (2 adults and up to 6 children), under 7s free. Last entry 1 hr before closing, guided visits by arrangement.

Glimpsed from the far end of a broad, tree-lined avenue, the pagoda's romantic coyness is irresistible. Give in to temptation and a few minutes later you'll discover that it sits beside a huge, semi-circular lake bounded by the slightly melancholy remains of once-grandiose landscaped parkland laid out in 1762. The pagoda was constructed in 1775, and while there are arguably more elegant structures, it's not short on period charm and rises (with a hint of a Pisa-esque lean) through seven storeys to an impressive 44 m, giving it real presence in the landscape. It also simply begs to be climbed, which you can do if you have a cool head for heights – you'll need it when you reach the topmost slender ironwork parapet. The views, though, are sensational, taking in the lake and 4000 ha of surrounding forest. On the way down you can compare what you've seen with a display of archive material, including the photographs of heroic restoration works carried out in 1909-1910 to save the pagoda from certain collapse.

If you'd like to know more, you'll find the small museum dedicated to the estate in a nearby gatehouse well worth visiting. Set beside the lake are a Chinese garden and a collection of traditional games, a good quality gift shop and a café with parasol-shaded tables.

Amboise listings

For hotel and restaurant price codes and other relevant information, see pages 11-16.

Where to stay

Amboise *p73*

€€€ Château des Arpentis, St-Règle (a few kilometres east of Amboise off the D31), T02 47 23 00 00, www.chateaudesarpentis.com. Located in a former *Seigneury*, Arpentis offers luxury chateau accommodation in the heart of peaceful landscaped parkland. All the rooms, decorated with murals and tapestries, are different. Those under the eaves are full of character, with exposed beams, and have the best views over the estate. Prices include breakfast.

€€€ Hôtel Restaurant l'Aubinière, 29 rue Jules Gautier, St-Ouen-les-Vignes (5 km north of Amboise), T02 47 30 15 29, www.aubiniere.com. Open all year. An absolutely lovely 3-star hotel with bright and spacious rooms furnished in a comfortable contemporary style. Guests can enjoy a luxury heated swimming pool, spa and wellbeing centre. Treat yourself to a meal in the excellent restaurant which serves refined, delicious French cuisine.

€€€ Le Fleuray, Fleuray (15 km northeast of Amboise; follow D952 east on north bank, turn onto the D74, direction Cangey), T02 47 56 09 25, www.lefleurayhotel.com. Positioned conveniently close to Amboise, Blois and Tours, this family-friendly country house hotel and restaurant has welcoming, beautifully appointed rooms. Each room has views over the gardens and the elegant restaurant also has a shaded garden terrace, where you can enjoy French cuisine with a contemporary twist (vegetarian menus also provided).

€€€ Le Manoir St Thomas, 1 Mail St-Thomas, T02 47 23 21 82, www.manoir-saint-thomas.com. Originally a 12th-century priory, this hotel and restaurant in the centre of Amboise has undergone many changes but still retains several historic architectural features. Some of the rooms include spacious suites with comfortable lounge seating and separate, stylish bathrooms.

€€€ Manoir du Parc, 8 av Léonard de Vinci, T02 47 30 13 96, www. manoirparc.com. Just a few mins' walk from the chateau and Clos Lucé, you can stay in a charming manor house, a luxurious treehouse or a suite with jacuzzi and hammam. All accommodation is beautifully furnished and well-equipped. There's a heated swimming pool in the enclosed gardens, plus free Wi-Fi and parking. The treehouses (for 2 people), each with private jacuzzi, cost about €1000 per week in peak season (breakfast, linen and housekeeping included).

€€ Art-Thé, 8 place Michel Debré, T02 47 30 54 00. *Chambres d'hôtes* and a *salon de thé* at the chateau entrance. Steep stairs take you to 2 double rooms and a family room, all simply furnished and surprisingly spacious. Rooms at the front have a view of the chateau. Breakfast is served in the salon, or on the terrace in fine weather.

€€ Villa Mary, 14 rue de la Concorde, T02 47 23 03 31, www. villa-mary.fr. This charming townhouse offers very comfortable accommodation in 4 bedrooms, all tastefully decorated in classic French *toile de jouy* style. Families of up to 6 people are easily accommodated in adjoining rooms. 2 of the rooms have views over the Loire. There's also a relaxing salon and a garden.

€ Le Blason, 11 place Richelieu, T02 47 23 22 41, www. leblason.fr. A hotel in the centre of Amboise with a charming half-timbered façade and quaint interior. The rooms are bright, well-furnished and have modern fittings, although the bathroom in our small double room was tiny. In summer ask for an a/c room on the top floor. There's secure parking for cars and bikes about 100 m from the hotel.

Campsites

Camping Municipal de L'Ile d'Or, 100 rue de l'Ile d'Or (on the island), T02 47 57 23 37 (Apr-Sep) or T02 47 23 47 18, www. campsite-amboise.com. Spread over 4 ha, there are 400 mostly shaded pitches (with or without electricity). The island enjoys fantastic views over the chateau, although midges could be a problem on summer evenings. Friendly welcome and activities provided for children in the summer. Internet access (payable) during office hours.

Restaurants

Amboise *p73*

€€€ L'Alliance, 14 rue Joyeuse, T02 47 30 52 13, www.restaurant-alliance.com. Apr to mid-Nov daily 1830-2130, Sun and bank holidays 1200-1330. Inspired by the market, the *terroir* and the seasons, the young proprietors have established a big reputation for their stylish cuisine. In summer, the shady terrace is a delight and the dining room bright and contemporary.

€€ Chez Bruno, 40 place Michel-Debré (opposite the chateau), T02 47 57 73 49, www.bistrotchezbruno.com. 1100-2230, closed Sun evening and Mon, also Tue in winter. Wine bar and bistro with an inviting display of local wines, which you can taste and buy. There are several tables on the pavement terrace, with views to the chateau opposite. Serves tasty *bistrot*-style regional dishes in its small restaurant.

€€ L'Amboiserie, 7 rue Victor Hugo, T02 47 30 50 40, www.lamboiserie.fr. At the foot of the chateau walls, and not far from Clos Lucé, L'Amboiserie offers a good variety of dishes or fixed-price menus, including grills, salads and a gourmet selection of crêpes. You can dine on the colourful terrace on sunny days.

€ Bigot, Place du Château, T02 47 57 04 46, www.bigot-amboise.com. Daily during the summer. *Salon de thé* serving delicious light meals all day. Choose from a large selection of salads, omelettes and savoury flans, but be sure to leave room for one of the irresistible cakes. The tea-room is delightful, or you can enjoy chateau views from a table outside.

€ La Scala Amboise, 6 quai Géneral de Gaulle, T02 47 23 09 93, www.lascala-amboise.fr. Open daily 1200-1400 and

1900-2200, Fri-Sat until 2300. Situated opposite the tourist office and the river bank, this Italian restaurant a movie theme provides a warm welcome and efficient service from friendly staff in its stylish dining room or vast terrace. Choose from pizzas, pastas, bruschettas and meat dishes, all at reasonable prices. (La Scala restaurants appear throughout the region, though not all have the same quality and service.)

Cafés and bars

Café des Arts, 32 rue Victor Hugo, T02 47 57 25 04, www.cafedesarts.net. Daily except Tue. Friendly bar between the chateau and Clos Lucé where you can pause a while and gaze up at the chateau walls. You might catch a musical *soirée* here, or simply be tempted by their generous snacks. They also offer basic accommodation for travellers on a budget.

Le Shaker, 3 quai Francois Tissard, L'Ile d'Or, T02 47 23 24 26. Daily 1800-0300 (-0400 at weekends), closed Mon in low season and throughout Jan. Cocktail bar with the definitive view of the chateau from its terrace – best just before sunset. Cross the bridge from the main town and descend the steps to the right. The barman is a world champion cocktail-maker, and has 140 for you to choose from.

What to do

Amboise *p73*

Balloon flights

Au Grès des Vents, T02 54 46 42 40, www.au-gre-des-vents.com. Departures from Cheverny with launch sites here and at Chambord, Blois, Fougères, Chaumont and Chenonceau.

BalloonRevolution, T02 47 23 99 63, www.balloonrevolution.com. Based in Amboise, the company offers a personalized service with individual, couple or group tickets.

Cycle routes and hire

There are 4 *Loire à Vélo* routes to follow in the Touraine area (leaflets are available in English from a tourist office or downloadable, French only, from the website www.loire-a-velo.fr). See full details for Loire à Vélo on page 36.

Food and drink

Chocolaterie Bigot, Place du Château, T02 47 57 04 46, www.bigot-amboise.com. Master chocolate makers since 1913, Maison Bigot give demonstrations and tastings on a visite gourmande by appointment only (Mar-Oct).

Spa and wellbeing

Domaine des Thomeaux Hôtel & Spa, 12 rue des Thomeaux, Mosnes (10 km east of Amboise), T08 25 37 00 00, www.domainedesthomeaux.fr. The Domaine is a great place to recharge your batteries with the focus on relaxation. A full day of luxury and pampering, alone or with a partner costs between €100 and €210.

Wine tours

Cheese & wine tour, T02 47 50 64 42, www.riverloire.com. A half-day package including a private tour through the famous wine caves at Rochecorbon followed by a tasting of the most important wines of the region accompanied by selected local cheeses. Every day from the Amboise area.

Directory

Amboise *p73*

ATMs Near the bridge on quai du Général de Gaulle and on rue Nationale. **Hospital** Centre Hospitalier Intercommunal, Amboise–Château-Renault, rue des Ursulines, T02 42 33 33. **Pharmacy** Pharmacie Centrale, 30 rue Nationale, T02 47 57 09 04. **Post office** 20 quai du Général de Gaulle, T02 47 30 65 00.

Background

Contents

Footprint features

History

A little knowledge of the key events and personalities in the turbulent and convoluted history of France will add a whole new dimension to your visits here in the Valley of Kings.

Prehistory

At the dawn of mankind, during the Middle Palaeolithic period (90,000-40,000 BC), much of the area of what now constitutes the Loire Valley would have been inhabited by Neanderthal hunter-gatherers, who led a nomadic existence and fashioned primitive stone hand tools. Their successor, 'modern' man, endured the Ice Age about 20,000 years ago, witnessed the disappearance of mammoth, reindeer and rhinoceros from the area, refined hunting techniques and began to settle, herd animals and sow crops. As cultivation became widespread, settlements grew and areas of forest began to be cleared. The presence of numerous menhirs, dolmens and other megalithic monuments dating from around 3500 BC indicates that the southern banks of the Loire were settled extensively by Neolithic man. The establishment of a regional identity came a significant stage closer during the first century BC with the arrival – probably from the Celtic lands – of what are generally referred to as the Gallic tribes. The Cenomani people, for example, developed into a highly organized society and traded in its own currency. They would also fight fiercely when threatened by outside forces, as the Barbarians, and even the Roman legions, discovered. Other tribes existing in this area at about the same time included the Namnetes around Nantes, the Andes (or Andecavi) from the Anjou area, the Pictones from northern Poitou, the Turones from Tours and the Bituriges and Carnutes around Orléans. Subjugating their combined resistance would prove to be a protracted and tiresome affair for the Romans.

Roman occupation – a modest local legacy

The Roman conquest of what they referred to as Gaul was eventually completed in AD 52, although not without a final indignant revolt the following year by Dumnacos, commander of the Andes. Then began a long period of occupation during which the familiar model of Roman refinement was systematically applied to this new territory. Not surprisingly, it wasn't long before centres of trade and authority were established – one of the first was the former Carnute stronghold of Cenabum, on which Orléans now stands. It was rebuilt from its post-battle ruined state and renamed Aurelianis, its surrounding territories becoming civitatis Aurelianorum. The process continued along the Loire (which they referred to as the Liger), the Turone settlement of what is now Tours becoming Caesarodunum and the present site of Angers developed as Juliomagus. With the establishment of trade and commerce, estates also appeared, centred around villas, thus promoting a period of stability and prosperity that lasted until the late third century – by which time it was deemed necessary to fortify much of what had been created. It was an early but ominous indicator of a changing world order; the occupation ended with an urgent return to a very different Rome during the late fifth century.

Today there's relatively little in the way of visible evidence of the Roman presence. But although you won't find the great, well preserved arenas of Provence, you are likely to stumble upon more modest traces of early construction when and where you least expect

Prehistoric remains

The Dolmen de Bagneux, near Saumur, is the largest in all France, with a length of 23 m by 5 m wide, while you'll find what is quite possibly the smallest tucked away in the Landes-le-Gaulois just north of Blois. To find some of the less obvious and wooded sites, you'll have to refer to detailed IGN maps and be prepared to walk, but a fine menhir is visible at the roadside (D751) north of Gennes.

them. The city of Tours,for example, preserves parts of the original fortified castrum walls, traces of a huge arena and private baths. A little further west near Luynes you'll find an arched section of a Gallo-Roman aqueduct, along with a curious brick-built tower from the second century at Cinq-Mars-la-Pile. Its purpose (possibly a burial monument) is now unknown, unlike the forlorn coursed limestone walls and trenches which are all that remain of Tasciaca, an early centre of pottery and ceramics production. You'll find it at Thésée-la-Romaine, south of Montrichard. Discoveries from these and nearby excavations are displayed in the village Musée Archéologique, and you can visit the site of a Gallo-Roman temple and thermal baths at nearby Pouillé.

Elsewhere you'll have occasional chance encounters with Roman artefacts in churches, either in the form of fonts and other stone objects (see Collégiale St-Ours in Loches) or in sections of early masonry incorporated in later rebuilding. Of course, for the most potent visual legacy of the Roman presence in the Loire Valley you need look no further than the great vineyards which drape the landscape like giant candlewick bedspreads, and which continue a tradition of viticulture dating back to the first vines transported here and planted in the Pays Nantais by the occupying forces of Rome.

The coming of Christianity

According to fifth-century St Gregory (Gregorius) of Tours, Pope Fabian's emissary Gatianus began preaching the gospel locally in AD 250, possibly from a hermit-like cave close to Vouvray. At first he was met with great hostility, but he persevered and during the course of 50 years of constant and dedicated toil he gathered many converts, some of whom he then dispatched to establish churches in other areas of France. He became first Evêque (Bishop) of Tours in AD 304 and the city's Cathédrale St-Gatien is still dedicated to him. On his death things entered a period of instability until the appointment of St-Martin (a former Roman officer who had converted to Christianity) as Bishop of Tours in AD 371. Two years later he founded the nearby abbey of Marmoutiers. He died in AD 397 and lies in the Basilique St-Martin.

The fifth century was a difficult period, with invasions by Visigoths (who took Tours in AD 476) and Huns, who attacked Orléans in AD 451, but were successfully resisted by forces led by Bishop (later St) Aignan. The invaders were finally routed, further south in Poitou, by Frankish King Clovis in AD 507. The following year Clovis, reformer of the Merovingian dynasty of Franks, celebrated his own coronation in the Basilica in Tours. The greatest documenter of this era was Gregory, sixth-century Bishop of Tours, who created his *Decem Libri Historiarum* (Ten Historic Chronicles), which later became known as *l'Historia Francorum* (A History of the Franks).

Another key event in western history took place between Tours and Poitiers in AD 732 when the Saracens were vanquished by the forces of Charles Martel in the Battle of

Poitiers – the prisoners were held in or around Véron, west of Chinon, and many later settled in the area. Martel's descendant Charlemagne (AD 768-814) unified the Carolingian dynasty, which endured until the 10th century.

Medieval era and the Renaissance

In AD 987 Hugues Capet (the first Capetian King) was elected ruler in the Cathédrale Ste-Croix d'Orléans (see page 38), heralding a period of relative stability for the Franks. However, bitter rivalries flared over Touraine, which was eyed covetously by the counts of both Anjou and Blois. The victor proved to be feared warrior Foulques III, count of Anjou, who was dubbed *'le Noir'* (the Black) and became known as Foulques Nerra. With his son Geoffroi Martel he then expanded his territories by seizing Maine and the Vendômois, and constructed a series of impressive fortresses, including the donjons of Langeais, Loches and Montrichard (see page 64). In 1110 one of his descendants, Geoffroi V d'Anjou, married Mathilde, daughter of Henry I of England, beginning a train of events which eventually saw his son Henri Plantagenêt becoming King Henry II of England after his marriage to Aliénore (Eleanor) d'Aquitaine in 1152. Her previous annulled marriage to Louis VII only added to the bitterness of the subsequent power struggle between the Capetian and Plantagenêt empires which ended with Henri accepting defeat (and dying shortly afterwards) at Chinon in 1189. He and Aliénor lie buried in the Abbaye de Fontevraud.

The last of the Capetian Kings, Charles I, died in 1328, leaving no male heir. Soon afterwards pretender to the throne Philippe de Valois was crowned Philippe VI of France. Already heir to Anjou, Maine and Valois, he had a fondness for the Loire Valley, and established a royal presence here which would last for two centuries. Philippe's thwarted rival for the French throne was Edward III of England, who began what was eventually to become known as the Hundred Years' War between the two nations in 1337. By 1369 Aquitaine had fallen under English rule, and in 1415 Henry V defeated the French armies in the Battle of Agincourt. Within five years Charles VI had reluctantly signed the Treaty of Troyes, disinheriting his son the Dauphin Charles, who escaped to the Loire, staying in the chateaux of both Chinon and Loches. However, in 1421 the English forces were routed at Baugé near Saumur, encouraging Charles to reclaim the French throne. The Loire soon became a battle zone, English troops famously laying siege to Orléans in 1428. Against all odds, and with Joan of Arc's encouragement and spiritual leadership, the French forces triumphed and the Dauphin became Charles VII. Joan, on the other hand, was tried for heresy and burnt at the stake in 1431 when she was just 19 years old. After driving the English from most of France, Charles settled into an easier life in Loches with his wife Marie d'Anjou and his mistress Agnès Sorel.

The Loire power base shifted to Tours, which assumed great prosperity after Louis XI came to power in 1461 and saw powerful families flexing their economic muscle by constructing showpiece townhouses and chateaux. The Court moved again to Gien (see page 29) when his successor, 13-year-old Charles VIII, inherited the throne. Six years later, he married Anne de Bretagne in the Château de Langeais, thereby uniting France and Brittany. He was also persuaded to re-launch Anjou's longstanding claim on Italy, his artillery proving victorious at the Battle of Naples in early 1495. Within months, though, his troops were in retreat and the campaign proved a costly mistake. The King had, however, developed an admiration for Italian architecture which blossomed into a passion (shared by his successor François I) and produced the Loire Valley's first Renaissance expressions at Amboise (see page 74) and Blois (see page 52). Soon the effect would inspire

The enduring legacy of Foulques Nerra

Throughout the Loire Valley you'll come across the name of Foulques (Foulque or Fulk) Nerra. This powerful Count of Anjou (AD 987-1040) proved himself both a formidable warrior in battle and a similarly unforgiving adversary in everyday life – it is said, for example, that after suspecting her of adultery he had his wife burnt alive. He also eyed Touraine covetously, as did his counterpart Eudes (or Odo) de Blois, whom he defeated at Pontlevoy (between Tours and Blois) in 1016. As his territories continued to expand he defended them by constructing a series of fortresses at strategic locations such as Langeais, Loches and Montrichard (see page 64). Of the many such structures he originally built only foundations and other less-visible portions now remain, underpinning later and more sophisticated reconstructions. At Langeais, however, you can still see a substantial part of the donjon he created around 990 (the earliest stone fortress in France), standing on a hill behind the present chateau. Nerra's aggressive qualities were obviously only part of a complex personality, for he undertook four pilgrimages to the Holy Lands in penance for his actions, and was also responsible for establishing the abbey of St-Nicolas d'Angers and another at Beaulieu-les-Loches, where he was buried.

Not that all his monuments are confined to early architecture. During a violent storm at sea during one of his voyages, Nerra prayed for deliverance to the Patron Saint of mariners. In gratitude for his prayers apparently having been answered, he created the Etang St-Nicolas, a large lake just to the east of Angers. Completed around 1000, the works yielded huge quantities of slate which were then used in the construction of the vast chateau of Angers.

Chambord (see page 56), Cheverny (see page 58) and many other chateaux which have come to define architectural splendours of the Loire Valley.

Revolution and beyond

Despite (or perhaps because of) the visible power and privilege of the monarchy and ruling classes, for the remainder of the population prosperity and equality for all remained a distant dream. In 1562 tensions between Catholics and Huguenot Protestants gave rise to the Wars of Religion, during which great symbolic monuments including the Cathédrale Ste-Croix d'Orléans (see page 38), the Basilique St-Martin de Tours and Blois' Benedictine Eglise St-Nicolas (see page 55) were decimated. (The Edict of Nantes, signed by Henri IV in 1598, offered tolerance to non-Catholic sects within France.) In the 18th-century Age of Enlightenment, powerful literary figures such as Rousseau and Voltaire reflected a shift in public mood, as spiralling debts and taxation sat uneasily beside barely concealed displays of decadence by those in positions of power. Things came to a head in 1789 with the convening of 'les Etats-Généraux' – a People's National Assembly, which proved to be a pivotal moment in France's history. The subsequent Révolution Française replaced the monarchy with a democratic republic (whose founding principles of *Liberté, Egalité et Fraternité* still adorn the façades of French official buildings), abolished feudalism and saw the break up and dispersal of vast Church-owned estates representing around 10% of mainland France. Many chateaux were stripped of their furnishings, the best of the spoils being stored and entered into the inventories which eventually formed the basis of fine-art museums like those of Tours and Orléans (see page 37). In some cases grand showpiece chateaux like those of Chanteloup (see page 76), Châteauneuf-sur-Loire (see page 33) and Richelieu, were so badly damaged that they were eventually deemed beyond economic repair and demolished.

The early 19th century saw la République replaced by the first Empire, ruled by Napoléon I, whose expansionist policies brought much of Western Europe under French control. After his defeat by allied forces of England, Austria, Prussia and Russia in 1814, power passed through various hands via Restoration, a second Revolution, two further Empires and Républiques. Through it all life continued much as it always had for most people, despite such memorable events as Napoléon III's Interior Minister Léon Gambetta landing in Tours after having fled Paris in a hot-air balloon. It was the arrival of the Industrial Revolution, however, with its effects on manufacturing, communications and trade, which finally shaped the society we see today.

Troubled times

First and Second World Wars and the post-war 20th century

The dawn of a new century found the whole of France in a celebratory mood, as the nation hosted the Olympic Games during the Exposition Universelle in Paris, which welcomed 50 million visitors between April and November 1900. Among the more enduring repercussions of this was the adoption elsewhere of the art nouveau style which caused such a stir in decorative displays at the show. The movement soon filtered down to the cities and towns of the Loire Valley, where you can still find examples of both the pure form and an interesting hybrid which fused elements of the new art with those of the belle époque. Orléans, for example, has large-scale architectural landmarks in each style – La Rotonde and the Hôtel Moderne (see page 36) – plus several art nouveau private home façades. The real gem, however, is the time-warp brasserie interior of La Cigale in Nantes, which is simply impossible to ignore. The confident (and perhaps naïve) exuberance expressed in the movement persisted until a troubled Europe fell under the dark shadow of the First World War, in which France soon found itself hopelessly entangled. Several chateaux were commandeered for military use, even the exquisite 16th-century Grande Galerie of Chenonceau being adapted to serve as a hospital to care for some of the huge numbers wounded on the battlefields further north. In 1917 a US command centre was established in Tours and American troops were spreading themselves along the Loire, after disembarking beyond Nantes at St-Nazaire. By the end of the conflict France had been decimated by an estimated 1.4 million military and civilian casualties.

A failure to resolve the underlying causes of the conflict made it inevitable that a period of considerable unrest would follow. As the people of the Loire shared the sombre mood of a nation in mourning and began repairing the ravages of battle, France suffered economic depression and became divided politically. It was thus poorly prepared for the outbreak in 1939 of the Second World War, the speed of the German advance forcing the Government to flee Paris and once again commandeer several chateaux in the Touraine before heading further south to Bordeaux. As Tours suffered aerial bombardments several bridges along the Loire were partially destroyed in an attempt to stem the flow of refugees fleeing across the river. An uneasy armistice signed in June 1939 divided the region in two, Chinon and the west falling under German occupation, while the remainder was controlled by the French Vichy regime, whose collaboration with Germany was agreed

United by the mother tongue

With such a startling diversity of architecture, climate, culture, landscape and geology, it's hardly surprising that France can sometimes look and feel more like a continent than a mere country. If making sense of it all can take a lifetime (a pleasurable prospect in itself) at least here in the Loire Valley you somehow sense that you're getting to the heart of things. For one thing, it's in and around Tours that you'll hear what is generally agreed to be the purest spoken French, uncoloured by the multitude of regional variations which at their most extreme can make things almost incomprehensible to outsiders. Yet for all its elegance, the definitive French of Touraine now has little to do with class; it's just the way things sound in everyday life here in the gentle, unchanging rural world of *la douce France*.

The common accent also unites a population whose individual identities are rooted in the pre-Revolutionary provinces of Anjou, Maine and Touraine, not to mention the Celtic former Duchy of Bretagne. You'll also hear the term *ligérien* ('Loire' is thought to be a corruption of 'Liger') used when referring to all manner of things from the region, including the people themselves.

by Hitler and Pétain in the station of Montoire-sur-Loire in October. The period which followed found countless agricultural workers shipped off to labour in Germany, while those who remained suffered the ignominy of their situation until allied troops reached the area in August 1944. However, the lead up to the liberation produced some of the worst conflict of the war, with riverside towns like Gien suffering devastation from both sides, and more river crossings being attacked.

The euphoria which accompanied the allied forces' liberation of France was followed by a prolonged period of post-war austerity, as the nation struggled to get back on its feet. A US aid scheme saw tractors and agricultural equipment shipped in, starting the process of modernisation which would make France a leader in farming efficiency. As mechanisation cut the need for such a vast labour force, the region's towns and cities began to attract those leaving the land, in turn fuelling their economic development. Later, new opportunities for university education also drew more young people to the cities, and revealed a lifestyle which many were reluctant to leave after their graduation.

Considerable controversy still surrounds the nuclear power plants (*centrales nucléaires*) that the government decided during the early 1960s to site at key points along the Loire, at Belleville, Chinon, Dampierre and St-Laurent. The main inducement, of course, was a ready source of water for cooling, but this was one of many factors in a less-than-glorious period of the river's management. After protracted wrangling, however, UNESCO was sufficiently reassured that the Loire had successfully recovered to grant its coveted World Heritage status to the valley in December 2000.

Clearly they're not the only ones who are reassured, judging by the resident population who seem content to remain in the land of their birth. Joining them in steadily increasing numbers are those who come to put down roots of their own. The process was kick-started during the late 1980s by the arrival in of the LGV (Ligne à Grande Vitesse) Atlantique which brought Tours-St-Pierre-des-Corps within a mere 70-minute train journey from Paris, and Vendôme closer still. Nantes followed, with similar benefits, both practical and economic. The region's present dynamism, coupled with an enviable international image as a tourism destination, have made the area a popular centre for conferences.

In terms of leisure tourism, the Loire Valley remains perhaps the most desirable of all locations in France, a country renowned as one of the world's most popular holiday destinations. Mindful of their still-powerful historical resonance, tourism marketing has revived the names of the old Provinces – welcome back Anjou, Brétagne, Poitou, l'Orléanais and Touraine. In addition to new construction, heavy (and continuing) investment has transformed traditional accommodation enjoyed by the majority of visitors, while private chateaux offer ever-higher levels of comfort and services for the most demanding guests.

Art and architecture

Romanesque

Today's visitors mainly come to see the Gothic and Renaissance architectural jewels which have made the Loire Valley world-famous, but the area also preserves some extraordinary examples of the Romanesque ecclesiastical buildings which generally pre-date them. Instantly identifiable for its use of round-arched windows, doors and stone vaults, this form of construction's reliance on the thick masonry of its walls for structural stability limited the ambitions of both architects and masons. As a result, windows and doorways tended to be small and to admit relatively little daylight compared to those of later Gothic buildings. Larger early structures were often roofed in timber, which was lighter than vaulted stone but inherently flammable. (As the highest features in the landscape, countless important buildings were destroyed by fire after lightning strikes.) Those which did employ stone were limited in size by the weight of the vaults forcing walls outwards, so side aisles were often added to help share the loading. So much for the theory. But for all their limitations, early Romanesque buildings often have a serene (and occasionally mysterious) beauty and their carved or painted decorative features make them truly fascinating.

Gothic

For all its beauty and eventual refinement, the Gothic Revolution in France began as a practical response to the structural and stylistic limitations of Romanesque. What changed everything was the arrival, after the Crusades, of the *ogival* (pointed) arch, whose dramatically improved load-bearing abilities allowed windows to be much larger (important, since stained-glass imagery communicated the messages of the Holy Scriptures to a largely illiterate population). In religious buildings the arrival of flying buttress (external arched props which resist the outward force of the heavy stone vaults inside) allowed walls to become lighter and to rise ever higher. In the 12th century the cathedral of St-Maurice d'Angers used huge Gothic arches and higher dome-like diagonal ribs to span the nave, in what became known as Angevin, or Plantagenet, vaulting. Later, intersecting arches of uniform height created the lightweight rib vaults seen to great effect in vast cathedrals like St-Gatien de Tours.

This new freedom of expression liberated the architects and masons to explore decorative embellishments for their creations. By the 14th century the potential was expanding dramatically as ecclesiastical construction projects like cathedrals and abbeys were joined by more decadent secular architecture – initially manor houses for wealthy traders and eventually the new chateaux. Military fortresses like Loches and Saumur underpinned their military muscle with Gothic influences, but it was in the Château Royal de Blois (see page 53) that things really took off, employing the full-blown Flamboyant French Gothic which marked the apogee of the great medieval cathedrals. Even Chambord (see page 56), the greatest of all the Loire chateaux, is essentially a Gothic building in Renaissance clothing.

Renaissance

Charles VIII's ill-fated invasion of Italy in 1494 had one positive outcome: it heightened awareness of Italian style in French high society. Some 20 years later, François I returned to France from a resounding victory at the Battle of Marignano (near Milan) and enjoyed a chance meeting with Leonardo da Vinci, his artistic sensibilities dazzled by the elegance of the Italian Renaissance. The young French king, at the height of the monarchy's wealth and power, sought to express his passion by transforming the previously severe Château d'Amboise (see page 74) into an elegant Renaissance palace for pleasure and luxury. Soon influential artistic figures like Celini, Rosso and Primaticcio were enticed to leave Italy but, while eminently capable of applying their talents to architectural styling, they were not trained in construction techniques. Unsurprisingly, the French master masons were unimpressed, but were persuaded to adapt the new designs into a workable, structurally sound format. The resulting fusion of French and Italian creativity established an architectural style which would come to define the Renaissance chateaux of the Loire Valley.

François eventually tired of life in Amboise and transferred his court to the new Renaissance wing which he had created in the Château de Blois (see page 53). As the French chateau's raison d'être shifted from fortress to fashionable pleasure retreat, so attention turned to the wealth of opportunities presented by beautiful and secluded locations (with hunting terrain) along the Loire. Classic early examples like Azay-le-Rideau, Chenonceau and Chambord inspired numerous others, as the spirit of the Renaissance fired the imaginations of those with the means to indulge their fantasies. Soon the defensive corner towers of medieval donjons evolved into decorative *tourelles* with slated spires, while previously unusable roof spaces were freed for habitation by the addition of dormer windows.

Trogolodyte

The construction of the architectural treasures of the Loire Valley consumed vast quantities of pale *tuffeau* and other forms of limestone, all of which had to be extracted from beneath the region's apparently undisturbed green and pleasant landscapes. Around all the great construction sites were quarries created by countless former peasant farmers who now spent their lives hand-cutting stone in near-darkness, as they worked their way ever further from daylight. The resourceful stone cutters then began to add walls, windows and doors to sections of the caves they had created, providing a secure refuge for themselves and their precious grain supplies during troubled times, and establishing a pattern of troglodytic architecture which is surprisingly widespread along the Loire Valley. In the past, it was not uncommon for whole communes to live this way: as recently as the 19th century around half of the population of the Saumur region, for example, was still living in 'troglo' homes. From the mid-20th century, though, a more prosperous society viewed the dwellings with mounting disenchantment, and many were abandoned during this period. More recently, however, they have been rediscovered by a new generation which values their low environmental impact, sense of tradition and potential for providing characterful tourist accommodation. Add modern heating and ventilation systems, and you see why the expression 'troglo' now carries a certain cachet in the Loire Valley.

Contents

Footnotes

Menu reader

General

Agriculture Biologique (AB) organically produced product
à la carte individually priced menu items.
Appellation d'Origine Contrôlée (AOC) label of regulated origin
biologique or *bio* organic
carte des vins wine list
déjeuner lunch
dîner dinner or supper
entrées starters
fait(e) maison home-made
hors d'oeuvre appetisers
Label Rouge often applied to poultry, label indicates premium quality and standards in production.
les plats main courses
menu/formule set menu
petit déjeuner breakfast
plat du jour dish of the day
plat principal main course

Drinks (*boissons*)

apéritif drink taken before dinner
bière a beer
café coffee (black espresso)/
grand crème a large white coffee
chocolat chaud hot chocolate
cidre cider
dégustation tasting
demi small beer (33cl)
demi-sec medium dry – or slightly sweet when referring to Champagne
digestif after-dinner drink, usually a liqueur or spirit
doux the sweetest Champagne or cider
eau gazeuse/pétillante sparkling/slightly sparkling mineral water
eau plate/minérale still/mineral water
grand(e) big, large
jus de fruit fruit juice
kir apéritif made with white wine and a fruit liqueur usually *cassis* (blackcurrant)
lait milk
noisette espresso with a dash of milk.
panaché beer/lemonade shandy
petit(e) small
pichet jug, used to serve water, wine or cider
pression a glass of draught beer
sec dry
thé tea, usually served with a slice of lemon (*au citron*) *une tisane/* infusion herbal tea, *tisane de menthe* (mint tea), *tisane de camomille* (camomile tea) and *tisane de tilleul* (lime blossom) are the most popular
verre a glass
vin rouge/blanc/rosé red/white/rosé wine

Fruit (*fruits*) and vegetables (*légumes*)

artichaut artichoke
asperge asparagus
cassis blackcurrants
céleri-rave celeriac, usually served grated in mayonnaise
champignons de paris button mushrooms
châtaignes chestnuts
choux cabbage
citron lemon
citrouille or *potiron* pumpkin

courge	marrow or squash
épinard	spinach
fenouil	fennel
fraises	strawberries
framboises	raspberries
gratin	Dauphinois potato slices layered with cream, garlic and butter and baked in the oven
haricots verts	green beans
lentilles vertes	green lentils
mesclun	a mixture of young salad leaves
mirabelles	small golden plums
myrtilles	blueberries
noix	walnuts
oseille	sorrel
pêches	peaches
petits pois	peas
poireaux	leeks
poires	pears
pomme de terre	potato (*primeurs* are new potatoes and *frites* are chips)
pommes	apples (Reinette d'Orléans and Reine des Reinettes are local varieties)
prunes	plums

Meat (*viande*) and poultry (*volaille*)

agneau	lamb
andouillette	soft sausage made from pig's small intestines
blanquette de veau	veal stew in white sauce with cream, vegetables and mushrooms
boeuf	beef
boudin blanc	smooth white sausage, made from various white meats
boudin noir	blood sausage or black pudding made with pig's blood, onions and spices
canard	duck
charcuterie	encompasses sausages, hams and cured or salted meats
chevreuil	venison, roe deer
confit	process used to preserve meat, usually duck, goose or pork
cuisse de grenouille	frog's leg
dinde	turkey
escalope	thin, boneless slice of meat
faux-filet	beef sirloin
foie gras	fattened goose or duck liver
fumé(e)	smoked
géline de Touraine or *la Dame Noire*	grain-fed chicken prized by restaurateurs
gigot d'agneau	leg of lamb
jambon	ham
lapin	rabbit
médaillon	small, round cut of meat or fish.
mouton	mutton
pâté au biquion	puff pastry filled with minced pork, veal and cheese
pavé	thickly cut steak
pintade	guinea-fowl
porc	pork
pot-au-feu du braconnier	a stew of rabbit and diced bacon, slow-cooked with vegetables and served with poached liver
poulet	chicken
rillettes	a coarse pork pâté
rillons	chunks of pork cooked in pork fat
ris de veau	sweetbreads
sanglier	wild boar
saucisse	small sausage
saucisson	salami, eaten cold
saucisson sec	air-dried salami

soupe Tourangelle	a vegetable soup (leek, new turnips and fresh peas) with salt pork
veau	veal

Fish (*poisson*) and seafood (*fruits de mer*)

aiglefin or *églefin*	haddock
alose	shad
anchois	anchovies
anguille	eel
brème	bream
brochet	pike
cabillaud	cod
coquillage	shellfish
colin	hake
crevettes	prawns
dorade	sea bream
friture de la Loire	small fish such as smelt and gudgeon deep-fried like whitebait
homard	lobster
huîtres	oysters
lotte	monkfish
loup de mer	sea bass
matelote	fish stew (often eel) cooked in red wine
moules	mussels
poissons de rivière	river fish
sandre	zander or pike-perch
saumon	salmon
thon	tuna
truite	trout

Desserts (*desserts*)

chantilly	whipped, sweetened cream
clafoutis	a fruit tart (usually cherries) covered in a custard-style filling, served hot or cold
compôte	stewed fruit, often as a purée
crème anglaise	thin custard normally served cold
fromage blanc	unsweetened dairy product with a refreshing flavour served on its own or with a fruit coulis
glace	ice cream
coupe glacée	cold dessert with ice cream, fruit or nuts, chocolate or chantilly
le parfum	flavour, when referring to ice cream or yoghurt
île flottante	soft meringue floating on custard, topped with caramel sauce
liègeois	chilled chocolate or coffee ice cream-based dessert topped with chantilly
nougat de Tours	a cake made with preserved fruits on a bed of Reine des Reinettes apples
pâtisserie	pastries, cakes and tarts (also the place where they are sold)
quernon d'ardoise	a crunchy nougatine square enrobed in chocolate
sabayon	creamy dessert made with beaten eggs, sugar and wine or liqueur
tarte Tatin	a celebrated upside-down apple tart

Other

assiette	plate (eg *assiette de charcuterie*)
beurre	butter
beurre blanc	buttery white wine sauce often served with fish
Bordelaise	red wine sauce served with steak

brioche	a soft, sweet bread made with eggs and butter
crêpe	large pancake served with various fillings as a dessert or snack
croque-monsieur	grilled ham and cheese sandwich
croissant	rich and flaky crescent-shaped roll usually served at breakfast
crudités	raw vegetables served sliced or diced with a dressing, as a starter or sandwich filling
en croûte	literally 'in crust'; food cooked in a pastry parcel
escargots	snails
forestière	generally sautéed with mushrooms
fouée or *fouace*	a flat bread, baked in a wood oven, often filled with rillettes, beans, mushrooms, bacon pieces or pâté
fromage	cheese
fromage de chèvre	goat's cheese
galette	savoury filled pancake made with buckwheat flour, served as a starter or main course
garniture	garnish, side dish
gaufre	waffle, usually served with chocolate sauce
oeuf	egg
pain	bread
pain au chocolat	similar to a croissant, but pillow-shaped and filled with chocolate
pâte	pastry or dough, not to be confused with pâtes, which is pasta or pâté, the meat terrine
riz	rice
salade verte	simple green salad with vinaigrette dressing
soupe/potag	soup
viennoiserie	baked items such as croissants and brioches

Index

Titles available in the Footprint *Focus* range

Latin America	UK RRP	US RRP
Bahia & Salvador	£7.99	$11.95
Brazilian Amazon	£7.99	$11.95
Brazilian Pantanal	£6.99	$9.95
Buenos Aires & Pampas	£7.99	$11.95
Cartagena & Caribbean Coast	£7.99	$11.95
Costa Rica	£8.99	$12.95
Cuzco, La Paz & Lake Titicaca	£8.99	$12.95
El Salvador	£5.99	$8.95
Guadalajara & Pacific Coast	£6.99	$9.95
Guatemala	£8.99	$12.95
Guyana, Guyane & Suriname	£5.99	$8.95
Havana	£6.99	$9.95
Honduras	£7.99	$11.95
Nicaragua	£7.99	$11.95
Northeast Argentina & Uruguay	£8.99	$12.95
Paraguay	£5.99	$8.95
Quito & Galápagos Islands	£7.99	$11.95
Recife & Northeast Brazil	£7.99	$11.95
Rio de Janeiro	£8.99	$12.95
São Paulo	£5.99	$8.95
Uruguay	£6.99	$9.95
Venezuela	£8.99	$12.95
Yucatán Peninsula	£6.99	$9.95

Asia	UK RRP	US RRP
Angkor Wat	£5.99	$8.95
Bali & Lombok	£8.99	$12.95
Chennai & Tamil Nadu	£8.99	$12.95
Chiang Mai & Northern Thailand	£7.99	$11.95
Goa	£6.99	$9.95
Gulf of Thailand	£8.99	$12.95
Hanoi & Northern Vietnam	£8.99	$12.95
Ho Chi Minh City & Mekong Delta	£7.99	$11.95
Java	£7.99	$11.95
Kerala	£7.99	$11.95
Kolkata & West Bengal	£5.99	$8.95
Mumbai & Gujarat	£8.99	$12.95

For the latest books, e-books and a wealth of travel information, visit us at: www.footprinttravelguides.com

footprinttravelguides.com

Africa & Middle East	UK RRP	US RRP
Beirut	£6.99	$9.95
Cairo & Nile Delta	£8.99	$12.95
Damascus	£5.99	$8.95
Durban & KwaZulu Natal	£8.99	$12.95
Fès & Northern Morocco	£8.99	$12.95
Jerusalem	£8.99	$12.95
Johannesburg & Kruger National Park	£7.99	$1
Kenya's Beaches	£8.99	$1
Kilimanjaro & Northern Tanzania	£8.99	$1
Luxor to Aswan	£8.99	$1
Nairobi & Rift Valley	£7.99	$1
Red Sea & Sinai	£7.99	$1
Zanzibar & Pemba	£7.99	$1

Europe	UK RRP	U
Bilbao & Basque Region	£6.99	$9
Brittany West Coast	£7.99	$1
Cádiz & Costa de la Luz	£6.99	$9
Granada & Sierra Nevada	£6.99	$9
Languedoc: Carcassonne to Montpellier	£7.99	$11.95
Málaga	£5.99	$8.95
Marseille & Western Provence	£7.99	$11.95
Orkney & Shetland Islands	£5.99	$8.95
Santander & Picos de Europa	£7.99	$11.95
Sardinia: Alghero & the North	£7.99	$11.95
Sardinia: Cagliari & the South	£7.99	$11.95
Seville	£5.99	$8.95
Sicily: Palermo & the Northwest	£7.99	$11.95
Sicily: Catania & the Southeast	£7.99	$11.95
Siena & Southern Tuscany	£7.99	$11.95
Sorrento, Capri & Amalfi Coast	£6.99	$9.95
Skye & Outer Hebrides	£6.99	$9.95
Verona & Lake Garda	£7.99	$11.95

North America	UK RRP	US RRP
Vancouver & Rockies	£8.99	$12.95

Australasia	UK RRP	US RRP
Brisbane & Queensland	£8.99	$12.95
Perth	£7.99	$11.95

Join us on facebook for the latest travel news, product releases, offers and amazing competitions: www.facebook.com/footprintbooks.